THE CROSSLINGUISTIC STUDY OF LANGUAGE ACQUISITION

Volume 1: The Data

THE CROSSLINGUISTIC STUDY OF LANGUAGE ACQUISITION

Volume 1: The Data

Edited by

DAN ISAAC SLOBIN
University of California, Berkeley

LAWRENCE ERLBAUM ASSOCIATES, PUBLISHERS
Hillsdale, New Jersey   London

Copyright © 1985 by Lawrence Erlbaum Associates, Inc.
All rights reserved. No part of this book may be reproduced in
any form, by photostat, microform, retrieval system, or any other
means, without the prior written permission of the publisher.

Lawrence Erlbaum Associates, Inc., Publishers
365 Broadway
Hillsdale, New Jersey 07642

Library of Congress Cataloging-in-Publication Data
Main entry under title:

The crosslinguistic study of language acquisition.

Includes bibliographies and indexes.
Contents: v. 1. The data — v. 2. Theoretical issues.
1. Language acquisition. I. Slobin, Dan Isaac
1939–
P118.C69   1985   401'.9   85-27411
ISBN 0-89859-367-0 (set)
Printed in the United States of America
10 9 8 7 6 5 4 3 2 1

Contents

Volume 1: THE DATA

Volume 2: Theoretical Issues

Format and Abbreviations
for Glosses*

All foreign language examples are given in Italics. (Small caps are used for emphasis and other usual functions of Italics.) In running text, English glosses and grammatical codes are given in single quotes, and optional free translations follow in parentheses, indicated by an equal sign and single quotes. Grammatical codes are always given in capital letters (see list, below). For example:

gel-me-di-n 'come-NEG-PAST-2SG' (= 'you didn't come').

In interlinear format, translation equivalents appear below each foreign element, and the free translation is placed below in single quotes:

gel   -me -di   -n
come NEG PAST 2SG

'you didn't come'

Hyphens in a gloss always correspond to hyphens in the foreign example. If one foreign element corresponds to more than one English element and/or grammatical code, the collection of meaning equivalents is joined by colons; e.g. *gel-medin* 'come-NEG:PAST:2SG', or even *gelmedin* 'come:NEG:PAST:2SG'.

---

*The abbreviations are adapted from a list used by Bernard Comrie (*The languages of the Soviet Union,* Cambridge University Press, 1981, p. xv). The format is based on useful suggestions offered by Christian Lehmann in "Guidelines for interlinear morphemic translations: A proposal for a standardization" (Institut für Sprachwissenschaft, Universität Köln, Arbeitspapier Nr. 37, 1980). The system presented here is offered as a proposal for standardization in child language studies.

If it is relevant to indicate the possibility of segmentation, equal signs can be used in place of colons. The preceding example consists of segmentable morphemes, and could also be glossed, for example, as *gel-medin* 'come-NEG+PAST+2SG'. Use of colons is neutral in regard to the possibility of segmentation, and in most instances either colons or hyphens are used. (The degree of precision of segmentation and glossing of an example, of course, depends on the role it plays in the exposition.)

If a grammatical code consists of two words or abbreviations they are joined by a period; e.g. DEF.ART means "definite article." Combining the principles for use of colons and periods, consider the gloss for the German definite article in its masculine singular accusative form: *den* 'DEF.ART:MASC:SG:ACC'.

LIST OF GRAMMATICAL CODES

1 First Person
2 Second Person
3 Third Person
ABESS Abessive ('without X')
ABL Ablative ('from X')
ABS Absolutive
ACC Accusative
ACT Active
ADESS Adessive ('toward X')
ADJ Adjective, Adjectival
ADV Adverb(ial)
AFFIRM Affirmative
AGR Agreement
AGENT Agent
ALLAT Allative ('to(wards) X')
AN Animate
AORIST Aorist
ART Article
ASP Aspect
AUG Augmentative
AUX Auxiliary
BEN Benefactive
CAUS Causative
CL Clitic
CMPLR Complementizer
COMIT Comitative ('(together) with X')
COMPAR Comparative
COMPL Completive
CONC Concessive
COND Conditional
CONJ Conjunction

CONN Connective
CONSEC Consecutive
CONT Continuous, Continuative
COP Copula
DAT Dative
DECL Declarative
DEF Definite
DEICT Deictic
DEM Demonstrative
DESID Desiderative
DIM Diminutive
DIREC Directional
DO Direct Object
DYN Dynamic (Nonstative)
ELAT Elative ('out of X')
EMPH Emphatic
ERG Ergative
ESS Essive ('as X')
EVID Evidential
EXCL Exclusive
EXIS Existential
FACT Factive
FEM Feminine
FIN Finite
FOC Focus
FUT Future
GEN Genitive
HAB Habitual
HON Honorific
HUM Human
ILL Illative ('into X')

IMP Imperative
INAN Inanimate
INCH Inchoative
INCL Inclusive
INDEF Indefinite
INESS Inessive ('in X')
INF Infinitive
INFER Inferential
INSTR Instrumental
INT Interrogative
INTENT Intentive
INTERJ Interjection
INTRANS Intransitive
IO Indirect Object
IPFV Imperfective
IRR Irrealis
ITER Iterative
LOC Locative
MASC Masculine
MOD Modal
N Noun
NEG Negative
NEUT Neuter
NEUTRAL Neutral
NOM Nominative
NOML Nominal
NONPAST Non-past
NONVIR Non-virile
NUM Numeral, Numeric
OBJ Object
OBLIG Obligatory
OPT Optative
PART Participle
PARTIT Partitive
PASS Passive
PAST Past
PAT Patient
PERF Perfect
PFV Perfective
PL Plural
POL Polite
POSS Possessive

POST Postposition
POT Potential
PP Past Participle
PRE Prefix
PREP Preposition
PRES Present
PRESUM Presumptive
PRO Pronoun
PROG Progressive
PROL Prolative ('along X')
PTL Particle
PURP Purposive
Q Question
QUANT Quantifier
QUOT Quotative
RECENT Recent
RECIP Reciprocal
REFL Reflexive
REL Relative
REM Remote
REPET Repetition
REPORT Reportative
RES Resultative
SG Singular
SIMUL Simultaneous
STAT Stative
SUBJ Subject
SUBJV Subjunctive
SUBL Sublative ('onto X')
SUFF Suffix
SUPER Superessive ('on X')
SUPERL Superlative
TEMP Temporal
TNS Tense
TOP Topic
TRANS Transitive
TRANSL Translative ('becoming X')
V Verb
VIR Virile
VN Verbal noun
VOC Vocative

THE CROSSLINGUISTIC STUDY OF LANGUAGE ACQUISITION

Volume 1: The Data

Volume 1   THE DATA

Introduction:
Why Study
Acquisition
Crosslinguistically?

Dan I. Slobin
University of California, Berkeley

Contents

> *Child language study can be more than the analysis of individual instances of language development, because it is possible to formulate laws of formation that are operative in every child language. This commonality is even international; therefore we will not need to limit our evidence solely to German children.*[1]
>
> —Clara and Wilhelm Stern, *Die Kindersprache* (1907)

---

[1] "Und dennoch kann die Kindersprachkunde mehr als die Analyse individueller Sprachentwicklungen sein; denn sie vermag Bildungsgesetze zu formulieren, die in jeder Kindersprache wirksam sind. Diese Gemeinsamkeit ist sogar international; wir werden unsere Belege daher nicht ausschließlich auf deutsche Kinder zu beschränken brauchen."

CROSSLINGUISTIC STUDY AS A METHOD IN
DEVELOPMENTAL PSYCHOLINGUISTICS

In 1907, when the Sterns published the first edition of their great diary study of German child language, they were able to point to a significant body of nineteenth century research on the acquisition of a number of European languages. They, and their contemporaries, were aware that there were clear crosslinguistic parallels in development, based on common principles of child psychology. The goals of investigators were directed beyond individual languages to the discovery of general principles. For example, the great Russian diarist, A. N. Gvozdev, publishing an article in 1928 under the title, "The significance of the study of child language for linguistics," noted that (1961, p. 9):

> The acquisition of the native language follows strict regularities and is characterized by the same features in different children. This supports the idea that native language acquisition is determined by general psychophysiological conditions which function uniformly in all people, thus leaving their mark on the strcuture of language.[2]

The emphasis was on the universal, rather than the particular. The value of data from various languages was the same as that of data from various children: to demonstrate commonalities. And with the rise of an insular American psychology, "language development" became a summary of the facts of the acquisition of English, taken as representative of general patterns. Thus Dorothea McCarthy could summarize a large body of systematic observational studies and conclude, in 1950, that such studies:

> have yielded considerable uniformity of results, and a fairly accurate description can now be given of linguistic development in the age range of two to five years (p. 165).

It is the burden of the present collection of studies to demonstrate that crosslinguistic study does more than reveal uniformities of development, because properties of individual languages influence the course of development. Beginning with Melissa Bowerman's study of the acquisition of Finnish in 1965 (Bowerman, 1973), followed by a series of crosslinguistic studies organized by John Gumperz, Susan Ervin-Tripp, and Dan Slobin at Berkeley (Slobin, 1967), it has become clear that different types of languages pose different types of acquisition problems.[3] One cannot study universals without exploring particulars

---

[2]"Usvoenie rodnogo jazyka po otnošeniju ko mnogim gruppam jazykovyx javlenij proxodit so strogoj zakonomernost'ju i xarakterizuetsja u raznyx detej odnimi i temi že čertami; i eto podtverždaet mysl' o tom, čto usvoenie rodnogo jazyka opredeljaetsja takimi obščimi psixofiziologičeskimi uslovijami, kotorye dejstvujut edinoobrazno u vsex ljudej i kotorye poetomu kladut svoj otpečatok i na strukturu jazyka."

[3]The following Berkeley dissertations on the acquisition of various native languages emerged

(Slobin, 1982). The world provides us with a marvelous set of "natural experiments," in which children with similar endowments master languages of varying forms. Gvozdev was right that psychophysiological commonalities "leave their mark on the structure of language," but that mark is on a more abstract level—the level of language universals. By combining attention to universals and particulars, we are beginning to discern a more differentiated picture of child language—one in which we can see why patterns of acquisition of specific properties VARY from language to language, while they are determined by common principles of a higher order. Such principles are summarized in my concluding chapter (Slobin, 1985). The task of this Introduction is to spell out the ways in which crosslinguistic study constitutes a METHOD for the discovery of general principles of acquisition.[4]

There are two major pacesetters to language development, involved with the poles of function and of form (Slobin, 1973): (1) on the functional level, development is paced by the growth of conceptual and communicative capacities, operating in conjunction with innate schemas of cognition; and (2) on the formal level, development is paced by the growth of perceptual and information-processing capacities, operating in conjunction with innate schemas of grammar. The course of acquisition of any particular linguistic form reflects an interaction of the child's abilities to decipher and cognize both structure and content. By examining the meanings of children's grammatical forms crosslinguistically, we can determine conceptual starting points for linguistic form; and by examining the forms of child grammar we can determine children's strategies for constructing morphosyntactic systems.

The crosslinguistic method can be used to reveal both developmental universals and language-specific developmental patterns in the interaction of form and content. Let us first examine evidence for the NULL HYPOTHESIS that language development is everywhere the same, and then turn to HYPOTHESES OF SPECIFIC LANGUAGE EFFECTS upon the course of development.

NULL HYPOTHESIS: DEVELOPMENTAL UNIVERSALS

The null hypothesis, as discussed earler, guided early work in child language development, and it still provides an important part of the picture. Wherever we

---

from *A field manual for cross-cultural study of the acquisition of communicative competence* (Slobin, 1967): Arabic (Badry, 1983), Black English (Mitchell-Kernan, 1969), Finnish (Argoff, 1976), Hungarian (MacWhinney, 1973), Japanese (Clancy, 1980), Luo (Blount, 1969), Mandarin (Erbaugh, 1982), Samoan (Kernan, 1969) Serbo-Croatian (Radulovic, 1975), Spanish (Eisenberg, 1982), Turkish (Aksu, 1978), Tzeltal (Stross, 1969).

[4]In this chapter, various pieces of data from the volume are presented as examples of the use of the crosslinguistic method. Many of the same facts are also discussed in my final chapter, "Crosslinguistic evidence for the Language-Making Capacity," where they are used to support the formulation of general "operating principles" for acquisition. (See volume 2.)

find similar patterns of development crosslinguistically, in function or in form, we see evidence for strong developmental universals which may operate across all settings. On the functional level, there is evidence for the primacy of conceptual development in providing the first meanings for grammatical forms and in pacing the course of development of certain forms. And on the formal level, there is evidence for general language acquisition strategies that take precedence over the constraints of particular linguistic forms in individual languages.

Conceptual Development and the Construction of Grammar

The acquisition studies of numerous languages reported in this volume reveal conceptual underpinnings of child grammar that could not be determined by study of any one language in isolation. This is because the crosslinguistic method allows us to track the course of acquisition of particular semantic notions across a range of differing surface expressions. Children acquire word-order patterns and morphological markers, such as case inflections, adpositions, and verbal inflections, before they master the full range of uses of these grammatical devices in the adult language. Across languages, common meanings are assigned to diverse forms. The point can be made by examining the following four propositions about the ways in which children use grammatical marking to express linguistically relevant notions.

1. *Conceptual Development Provides Starting Points for Grammatical Marking.*

One of the clearest examples of this proposition is offered by comparison of the notions expressed by children in their early marking of transitivity. In child speech in various languages early grammatical marking of agent-patient relations (accusative or ergative inflections, word-order patterns) focuses on basic causal events in which an agent carries out a physical and perceptible change of state in a patient by means of direct body contact or with an instrument under the agent's control (Slobin, 1981). Crosslinguistic comparison shows a striking UNDER-extension of both accusative and ergative inflections to such "highly transitive" (Hopper & Thompson, 1980) events. For example, Gvozdev (1949) noted that in his son's acquisition of Russian, the accusative inflection was apparently first limited to the direct objects of verbs involving manipulative physical action on things—such as 'give', 'carry', 'put', and 'throw', while uninflected nouns served as objects of verbs like 'see' and 'read'. Investigating the acquisition of Kaluli, an ergative language of New Guinea, Schieffelin (1985) found that the ergative inflection first appears only on the subjects of verbs such as 'give', 'grab', 'take', and 'hit', and that it tends to be omitted in sentences with verbs such as 'say', 'call-out', and 'see'. She has found in addition, that the ergative is used earlier, and with greater consistency, in utterances with past-tense verbs, as opposed to present or future; and that negated verbs tend to be accompanied by grammatically unmarked agents. In all of these instances an event has to be overtly manipulative and actually realized in order to receive ergative marking. Furthermore, in two quite different ergative languages, Kaluli and Quiche (Pye, 1979), children do not extend ergative markers to intransitive constructions, indicating that they are specifically grammaticizing only agents of highly transitive, manipulative activities. These examples suggest that such activities constitute a central semantic organizing point for grammatical marking—a starting point with a particular salient conceptual basis from the point of view of child development. Crosslinguistic study is necessary to discover and define such conceptual bases of grammatical marking.

2. Preferred Event Perspectives Provide Starting Points for Grammatical Marking.

We have noted that children focus on events that have been realized and actually completed. Taking a perspective on immediate results has consequences for the meanings underlying the first uses of forms used for marking tense, aspect, and voice crosslinguistically. For example, the first uses of past-tense, perfect, or perfective verb inflections seem to comment on an immediately completed event that results in a visible change of state or location of some object, with later development into a more general past tense. The past tense or perfect appears first on verbs like 'fall', 'drop', 'break', and 'spill' across a very wide range of languages and language types.

Focus on results often precludes or excludes focus on agency. There are examples in child speech in which a past-tense form is reinterpreted as a description of an affected object, such as attempts by Italian children to make the past participle of transitive verbs agree in number and gender with the direct object, though the participle does not agree with the object in the input language (Antinucci & Miller, 1976). In Hebrew (Berman, 1985), children appear to simplify the system of verb patterns into an opposition between a middle-voice "result" perspective and a transitive "agentive perspective." And in Turkish (Savasir & Gee, 1982) the first passive verb forms are used in situations in which a child, having failed to bring about a desired result, focuses on the object of manipulation with a negative, third-person passive. For example, a child tries to open a door, fails, and says the equivalent of 'it isn't being opened', thereby shifting attention from her own action to the resisting object. In instances such as these, children narrow the meaning of a particular grammatical marking—a verb participle, a derivational verb pattern, a passive marker—to express a conceptually salient perspective on events of a particular type.

3. Universal Conceptual Schemas can Override Input Language Patterns.

The aforementioned examples deal with children's narrowing of the semantic content of a grammatical category in the first phases of its acquisition, apparently making distinctions that are not grammatically marked in the input language. In other instances, children's definitions of grammatical categories may be too broad, in that they ignore or neutralize distinctions that are grammatically marked by mature speakers. The resulting mapping of form and content reflects basic conceptual organization which may well be universal. For example, early uses of grammatical markers of location, movement, and possession (case inflections, pre- and postpositions) focus simply on the relation of a figure to a ground, whether or not the figure is static or moving with respect to the ground, and whether or not the ground is a physical location or an animate being (possessor or recipient of the figure). For example, in languages which provide distinct case inflections for locative STATE (e.g., 'in', 'on') and locative GOAL ('into', 'onto'), a typical child error consists in confusion of the two forms, generally with the stative form used for both functions. Such errors are found in German (Mills, 1985) in regard to dative (static) and accusative (directional) casemarking on articles; in Slavic languages (Gvozdev, 1949; Radulovic, 1975; Smoczyńska, 1985) in regard to nominal suffixes of the accusative and other cases; and in Turkish (Aksu-Koc & Slobin, 1985) in regard to the locative and dative-directional suffixes on nouns and deictics. These patterns suggest a conceptual schema oriented simply to the figure-ground relation, with later development of

TABLE I.1
Order of Acquisition of Locative Expressions in Four Languages
and Percentage of Subjects Producing Each[a]

Scale Point	English		Italian		Serbo-Croatian		Turkish	
1	IN	90	IN	91	ON	88	IN	90
2	ON	83	ON	88	IN	84	ON	80
3	UNDER	81	UNDER	84	BESIDE	82	UNDER	79
4	BESIDE	74	BESIDE	77	UNDER	72	BESIDE	79
5	BETWEEN	49	BETWEEN	57	$BACK_f$	31	$BACK_f$	71
6	$FRONT_f$	30	$BACK_f$	42	BETWEEN	26	$FRONT_f$	53
7	$BACK_f$	21	$FRONT_f$	41	$FRONT_f$	19	BETWEEN	50
8	BACK	14	BACK	23	BACK	16	BACK	7
9	FRONT	3	FRONT	18	FRONT	12	FRONT	4
Gutman coefficient of reproducibility	0.93		0.89		0.86		0.91	
Number of subjects	86		74		90		70	

[a]Data come from an elicitation task carried out with subjects between the ages of 2;0 and 4;8. The subscript f on BACK and FRONT denotes location with regard to reference objects that have an inherent front-back orientation (e.g., cars, houses), while BACK and FRONT without the subscript denote non-oriented reference objects (e.g., plates, blocks). This table appears as Table 5 in Johnston and Slobin (1979, p. 537).

orientation to the means in which the relationship is temporally manifested (enduring versus coming-into-being).

In addition, we find that children are not particularly concerned to indicate grammatically whether the locative reference point is animate or inanimate. For example, in languages like Hungarian (MacWhinney, 1985), which distinguish an allative (directed movement) from a dative (beneficiary) case, children often use the dative for both meanings. Bowerman (1981) gives related examples from English, where the data consist of confusion of forms that mark a distinction that is not marked in some other languages: English-speaking children confuse *give* and *put,* as in languages that do not distinguish animate from inanimate goals, saying things like "put one to me" and "give some in here."

Similar inattention to animacy as a locative feature is seen in expressions of location and possession. Broadly conceived, possession is a locative state in which an object is located in relation to a person in an enduring or socially-sanctioned manner. In languages in which location and possession are marked by distinct means, we sometimes find that children use a single means of expression for both notions, as in German children's use of the locative preposition *zu* 'to' to indicate possession as well (Mills, 1985). Such examples indicate that a basic conceptual schema can override distinctions that are grammatically marked in the input language. In the instances noted above, a schema of object location is recruited to grammatical use of case inflections, adpositions, or verbs, overriding distinctions of static location versus direction, or distinctions of animate versus inanimate reference points for object location or object transfer.

4. *Conceptual Development Determines Order of Emergence of Grammatical Forms.*

Within a domain of form-function mapping, we typically find orders of emergence based on conceptual development. For example, when children begin to acquire locative expressions (pre- or postpositions, locative case inflections), they do not acquire the means for expressing all locative relations at once; rather, there is a common order of development across languages. Johnston and Slobin (1979) found similar sequences of development in English, Italian, Serbo-Croatian, and Turkish, as shown in Table I.1. The means of expression are different across these languages, involving prepositions (English, Italian), prepositions and case inflections (Serbo-Croatian), and postpositions and case inflections (Turkish). The absolute ages of acquisition of the various terms also differ between these languages. However, the common order of development of major conceptual categories is determined by children's ability to conceptualize spatial relations, moving from simple topological relations to more complex projective relations (Parisi & Antinucci, 1970). (Differences in order of development in the middle section of the table are due to language-specific effects, as discussed below. Tables such as these reveal both common orders of development on conceptual grounds and the influence of factors of linguistic complexity on particular points in the sequence.) Similarly, in regard to other conceptually-paced domains, various investigators have found common crosslinguistic orders of development of question words and connectives based on the meanings of these terms (e.g. Bloom et al., 1980; Clancy et al., 1976).

Data such as these support the claim "that there is a fairly atuonomous development of intentions to express various semantic notions" (Slobin, 1973, p. 183). In addition, on the level of linguistic STRUCTURE, the null hypothesis predicts instances in which general language acquisition strategies override FORMAL characteristics of the input language.

Formal Pattern Preferences and Grammar

Along with universal preferences for the semantic content of grammatical markers in early child speech, crosslinguistic study also reveals preferences for the placement of such markers and for the construction of morphological paradigms and word-order patterns of particular types. Some formal pattern preferences are tied to the underlying meanings of grammatical expressions, while others seem to be relatively content-free.

1. Concepts are Combined in Grammatical Morphemes According to Semantic Affinities

We have noted that children make use of a particular set of concepts as the semantic bases for early grammatical marking crosslinguistically. We can now make an additional observation about basic semantic categories—namely: they exist in a sort of SIMILARITY SPACE in which categories are arrayed according to certain NATURAL AFFINITIES of varying degree. We can begin to map out this similarity space by examining the acquisition of grammatical forms for which two or more semantic notions combine or interact in determining the choice of form. As an example, let us examine the ways in which verb forms can be conditioned by various semantic distinctions. In the Slavic languages, the verb has different forms for perfective and imperfective aspect. For example, in Polish one uses the verb *otworzyć* 'open' to refer to a single, completed act of opening, and the verb *otwierać* to refer to ongoing or repeated acts of opening. Children acquiring such languages have no difficulty in learning pairs of perfective and imperfective verbs, and even create their own neologisms for new perfective or imperfective forms before age 3 (Gvozdev, 1949; Smoczyńska, 1985). Notions of verbal aspect are not only highly accessible to the child, but they are also so close to the meaning of the verb itself that children quickly learn to combine verb meaning and verb aspect in a single form, easily learning separate forms for separate aspects. However, other notions are not so easily combinable with verb meaning. Wherever we encounter verbs which change their form on the basis of present versus past tense, or affirmative versus negative, or distinctions of person, we find that children prefer to use a single form of the verb for all tenses, or for both affirmative and negative, or for all persons. Tense, negation, and person are apparently not inherently part of verb meaning for children, as we find in early errors in Japanese, Slavic, and Romance languages. In Spanish (Clark, 1985), for example, children will use a single verb stem for all persons or tenses, even if the input language provides systematic stem variations for particular verbs. In Japanese (Clancy, 1985), where the form of negation is different for past and non-past tense verbs, we find children using a single negative form regardless of tense. Apparently children operate with built-in preferences for the combinability of notions in morphemes. In these examples—which could not be determined by the study of any individual language alone—it seems that children recognize that person does not change the meaning of the verb in the way that aspect does, and that notions like tense and negation affect the meaining of the entire clause, and not just the meaning of the verb.

2. Grammatical Morphemes are Positioned According to their Scope of Operation

These examples move us from the morphological to the syntactic level of early child grammar. Children are sensitive to the SCOPE or RANGE of operation of grammatical elements. For example, they seem to recognize that if an element operates on the meaning of the clause, it should, ideally, be placed outside of the clause, and should not alter the internal form of the clause. Negation provides a prime example of this principle. Wherever possible, children will move negative elements, leaving verb forms and word order intact. For example, in Turkish (Aksu-Koç & Slobin, 1985) and Japanese (Clancy, 1985), where negative particles are sometimes placed inside the verb, children tend to move these particles to the end of the clause, following the standard verb-final order of these languages. Similar examples could be offered from other languages in regard to the placement of negation as well as other forms that operate on clauses as a whole, such as markers of questions and conditional forms. For example, in both Polish (Smoczyńska, 1985) and Hungarian (MacWhinney, 1985) a conditional marker is placed immediately after the verb stem, preceding person-marking. However, children tend to reverse the order, marking person close to the verb stem and placing the conditional marker after markers of person and tense. All of these examples reflect a general language acquisition strategy to extrapose operators whose scope is the clause:

Japanese:
      *VERB+PAST+NEGATIVE
      (=VERB+NEGATIVE+PAST)

Turkish:
>   *VERB+TENSE+PERSON NEGATIVE
>   (=VERB+NEGATIVE+TENSE+PERSON)

Polish:
>   *VERB+PERSON+CONDITIONAL
>   (=VERB+CONDITIONAL+PERSON)

Hungarian:
>   *VERB+PERSON CONDITIONAL
>   (=VERB+CONDITIONAL+PERSON)

Again, invididual instances of such phenomena could be interpreted in terms of language-specific features, while the crosslinguistic commonality of such patterns, across differing morphosyntactic forms, suggests general formal pattern principles.

3. Grammatical Markers are Placed According to Principles of Semantic Relevance

The examples we have just considered also suggest another type of syntactic principle in regard to the placement of inflectional morphemes in relation to the words that they operate on. In these examples we note preferences to keep grammatical markers of aspect, tense, and person close to the verb, while keeping negation and conditionality peripheral. More generally, we can speak of the degree of "relevance" (Bybee, 1985) of the meaning of a grammatical marker to the meaning of the stem to which it is affixed. In Polish, for example, person-marking is attached to conditional particles and conditional connectives, but children avoid applying a verbal suffix to such non-verbal elements as conditionals and connectives, preferring to mark person and number on the verb. In Hungarian, the verb receives a suffix indicating the definiteness of the direct object, and children have great difficulty in acquiring this form. On the other hand, where definiteness is indicated by a marker on the nounphrase as in English and German definite and indefinite articles, or Bulgarian (Gheorgov, 1908) noun suffixes for definiteness, children have little difficulty in learning to mark these notions grammatically. Apparently the noun is a more "relevant" locus of definiteness than is the verb.

Findings such as these suggest that children follow a general principle, across an array of language-specific instances: Morphemes that go together semantically should be placed together syntactically. To briefly summarize, many of the crosslinguistic child language patterns we have examined suggest that children operate with a hierarchy of relevance of grammatical markers in relation to the part-of-speech they modify. For example, tense and person are more inherently part of the meaning of a verb than are negation and conditionality, which operate on the meaning of an entire clause. Accordingly, it is easier for children to learn to affix tense and person markers to the verb than to affix negation and conditional markers to the verb, and it is difficult for them to learn to affix verbal notions like tense and person to non-verbal elements. A hierarchy of relevance also affects the ease with which children can acquire stem changes of the verb. Whereas children can easily acquire stem changes for perfective and imperfective aspect, they find it difficult to vary the form of the verb for person or tense. This whole array of data suggests a hierarchy of relevance of semantic notions in relation to the verb, with aspect closest to the inherent meaning of the verb, tense and person more distant, and negation and modalities such as the conditional the most distant. Particular languages present pieces of this pattern; comparison across languages reveals the more general pattern.

4. Morphological Systems are Constructed According to Formal (Non-semantic) Criteria

Examples such as those summarized earlier show that children are engaged in mapping particular types of semantic categories onto lexical items and grammatical forms in specific and limited ways. Such examples show subtle interactions of semantic and non-semantic criteria in the construction of grammar. It is also evident, however, that many systematic aspects of early child grammar have no semantic bases at all. Children are equipped with capacities to construct morphological paradigms and syntactic rules. To use Annette Karmiloff-Smith's (1979) felicitous phrase, they approach language as a formal "problem-space" in its own right, in addition to the acquisition of a tool for communication and thought. Our crosslinguistic data show many attempts to work on the structures of language per se.

For example, it is evident that children work at constructing morphological paradigms—that is, principles for the systematic alteration of forms of particular morphemes. Much of the classical child language literature deals with children's attempts to regularize inflectional systems, reflecting universal patterns of systematicity, such as the familiar overregularization of the English past tense. Such examples show a preference for uniform marking of a grammatical category in all instances. There are also preferences to build PARADIGMS on the basis of systematic distinctions. For example, Spanish-speaking children (Clark, 1985) have little trouble in realizing that nouns are divided into two classes on the basis of their endings, although these endings generally have no semantic basis. They make use of this division in matching the forms of associated articles and nouns. In Spanish, nouns that take the indefinite article *un* and the definite article *el* generally end in *-o*, and nouns that take the articles *una* and *la* generally end in *-a*. Children adjust inconsistencies in the input language, saying things like **un papelo* instead of *un papel* and **la flora* instead of *la flor*. In this way they show their grasp of a purely formal characteristic of their language—namely, a binary division of nouns for grammatical purposes. Crosslinguistic comparison suggests that binary divisions may be high on a built-in hierarchy of formal criteria for choice of grammatical morphemes. For example, nouns in Hebrew (Berman, 1985) are pluralized by the addition of -*im* to masculine nouns and -*ot* to feminine nouns. At first, children use the single form -*im* to pluralize all nouns, indicating that the semantic notion of 'plural' is basic, taking precedence over formal, nonsemantic variation. However, at the next stage of development, Israeli children divide their nouns into two classes on an idiosyncratic basis. In the adult language, words that end in stressed -*a* and unstressed -*et* and -*at* generally take the feminine plural. Little children, however, arrive at a simpler binary split, adding the feminine -*ot* to all nouns that end in -*a*, whether or not the final vowel is stressed, retaining the masculine -*im* for all other nouns. This results in many errors in regard to the adult system, which has more complex means of distinguishing masculine and feminine nouns. But the children's solution shows a basic ability to deal with a formal basis for suffixing if it is based on a highly salient and binary division of words on a single criterion, such as the final sound of the word.

Sometimes children's regularizations even reflect patterns that are not modeled in the input language, suggesting quite general preferences. For example, Bowerman (1974) and others have noted tendencies to use the sentence frame alone to define the valence of the verb, without special lexical or inflectional marking of transitivity or causativity, as in familiar English examples such as "Kendall fall that toy" (= 'drop') and "I come it closer" (= 'bring/make come'). There are examples in the child language literature of such constructions in English, French, Portuguese, Polish, Hebrew, Hungarian, and Turkish. What is striking is the fact that children attempt such forms even in those languages in which the input does not model this possibility. As another example, consider children's preferences for analytic over synthetic expressions. Where the input language provides both options, the analytic forms are used early on, such as the French possessive *de moi* in place of the synthetic *mon/ma/mes*. Note that the child's option allows for separate expression of possession, person, and number, reflecting a general tendency towards one-to-one mapping. In instances where the language provides synthetic forms, children often invent their own analytic equivalents, such as the early use in Hebrew of a separate PREPOSITION + PRONOUN construction in place of adult fused forms (e.g. *al* + *ani* 'on + I' instead of *alay* 'on:me').

In sum, the acquisition literature is full of examples of children's attempts to simplify or restructure the input language along universal lines of child grammar formation, supporting the null hypothesis that language acquisition is everywhere the same, regardless of particularities of individual languages. However, language acquisition takes place in a web of universals and particulars, and much recent crosslinguistic work seeks to evaluate hypotheses of the effects of features of particular languages on the course of acquisition. While the longterm goal remains one of discovering general processes, the course of language acquisition is not everywhere the same in its details.

HYPOTHESES OF SPECIFIC LANGUAGE EFFECTS

1. Form-function Interaction Influences Rate or Sequence of Development

We have already noted that conceptual development plays a key role in providing starting points and developmental sequences of the meanings of grammatical forms. However, factors of accessibility of linguistic forms to the child also play a role in individual cases.

Locative Development.   Although the overall sequence of development of locative adpositions follows the scheme presented by Johnston and Slobin (1979) and others, relative linguistic difficulty can cause minor changes in developmental sequence. Consider Table I.1 once again. Earlier, we noted that the middle section of the table reflected crosslinguistic differences in the order of development of pre- or postpositions expressing the notions 'between' and 'front/back' with featured objects. The expected order of development on grounds of conceptual complexity is 'back' < 'front' < 'between' (Johnston & Slobin, 1979). This order matches the sequence of linguistic development in Turkish, where the terms do not differ in linguistic complexity: each locative expression is a single semantically transparent postposition. The English and Italian terms for 'back' and 'front' are sufficiently complex linguistically to retard the emergence of these terms in relation to terms for 'between', even though 'between' is a conceptually more advanced notion. In English we have two terms for 'back' rather than one, with the further complexity that one of the options is morphologically complex: *behind* and *in back of*. The Italian expression, *dietro a*, is also morphologically complex, and does not correspond to the word for the body part 'back'. Apparently formal factors such as these can exert a degree of influence on aspects of the emergence of linguistic forms. Johnston and Slobin conclude (1979, p. 541): "Wherever conceptual complexity fails to predict actual order of acquisition, we find some pocket of relative LINGUISTIC difficulty." Crosslinguistic comparisons of this sort help to define the sorts of linguistic difficulty that can interact with conceptual factors in pacing acquisition.

Tense/Aspect.   Although past-tense marking of non-punctual events is generally later than marking of punctual events, both types of past tense seem to be early in Slavic languages. For example, in Polish, where there is a clear morphological distinction between perfective and imperfective verb forms, there is evidence that very young children use past imperfectives to refer to anterior nonpunctual events, while using past perfectives to refer to completed punctual events (Smoczyńska, 1985; Weist et al., 1985). Here the presence of a clear linguistic distinction may accelerate children's ability to mark a tense/aspect contrast.

Pragmatic Functions.   In languages which provide clear grammatical marking of pragmatic functions it is possible to find evidence for children's early attention to functions that may not be clearly discernible in the development of other languages; and it is even possible that the existence of such marking draws children's attention to the relevant functions. For example, Clancy (1985) reports very early aquisition of perceptually salient, sentence-final particles in Japanese—appropriately used to express pragmatic functions not as clearly evident in other sorts of languages:

> *Yo* is used when the child is encountering resistance or lack of mutuality, and feels
> he can impose his information or will on the addressee; *ne* is used when the child is
> in rapport with the addressee, agreeing with him or expecting his confirmation or
> approval. The emotional content of *no* is less fixed than *yo* and *ne;* typically *no*
> seems to be fairly neutral in affect, occurring in the ordinary give and take of
> information shared in the speech context.

2. Particular Linguistic Forms are Relatively More Accessible, Holding Content Constant

About a decade ago (Slobin, 1973) I noted that postpositions and suffixes tend to be acquired earlier than prepositions and prefixes for the expression of particular locative notions and grammatical cases, suggesting that children pay special attention to the ends of words. Such comparisons can only be carried out crosslinguistically, since one must try to hold meaning and frequency of use constant. Thus, for example, the emergence of the first morphological marking of simple locatives like 'in' and 'on' is earlier in postpositional and inflectional languages like Hungarian and Turkish than in prepositional languages like English and Serbo-Croatian. Peters (1985) reports additional data on the salience of postposed over preposed grammatical markers. To cite another type of example, it appears that case inflections are acquired earlier than word-order regularities for the expression of comparable semantic relations such as agent-patient (Ammon & Slobin, 1979; Slobin, 1973, 1982; Slobin & Bever, 1982). Ammon and Slobin suggest that it is easier for children to attend to ''local cues'' on individual words than to process and store patterned configurations of words in clauses. Crosslinguistic comparison thus reveals general language acquisition strategies which have different effects on the course of acquisition of particular languages.

3. Separate Marking of Notions in Particular Languages Reveals a Conceptual Substratum

The early acquisition of pragmatic particles in Japanese reveals children's ability to attend to the relevant underlying distinctions. Similar evidence is provided wherever a particular language divides up a conceptual area in more detail than others. For example, Japanese has several distinct negative markers, and children show only certain types of confusions in acquiring these markers (Clancy, 1985). The directions of confusion reveal an underlying conceptual substratum which could not readily be seen in a language with less elaborate negative marking. The arrows in the following chart represent the directions of children's overextensions of the meaning of one form to include that of another:

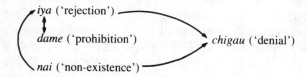

The early confusion of *iya* ('rejection') and *dame* ('prohibition') suggest "an undifferentiated semantic complex [of] rejecting, demanding, commanding, prohibiting, and insisting" (Clancy, 1985), along with independent status for *chigau* ('denial') and *nai* ('non-existence'). Note also that 'non-existence' and 'rejection' can be overextended to expressions of 'denial', while 'prohibition' is not extended to this function. What emerges is a more subtle map of a terrain that can be compared with languages that make fewer, more, or different distinctions.

4. Language-specific Co-occurrences Reveal Patterns of Conceptual Relevance

Earlier we noted ways in which combinability and placement of grammatical morphemes reveal general notions of semantic affinity and relevance. Co-occurrence patterns in particular languages can facilitate or impede acquisition. For example, noun suffixes expressing case notions are easily acquired (e.g., ergative, accusative, dative, and other case notions discussed above). But children have varying degrees of difficulty in acquiring conflations of casemarking with other semantic notions. Children easily learn to use different direct-object inflections for whole and partial objects, as in Russian (Gvozdev, 1949) and Finnish (Toivainen, 1980), but they have difficulty with distinctions of the accusative on the basis of animacy or natural gender, as in Russian and Polish (Smoczyńska, 1985). Children readily make the verb agree with the object of resultant activity, even if not allowed by the language, as in Italian (Antinucci & Miller, 1976); but agreement of the verb with the definiteness of the object is difficult, as in Hungarian (MacWhinney, 1985). It is easier for children to learn to change the form of the verb stem for aspect than for tense (Polish), and easier for tense than for person (Spanish, Portuguese). Detailed crosslinguistic comparison of this sort reveals universal patterns of conceptual relevance in semantic space, allowing for language-specific predictions of ease or difficulty of acquisition of particular conflations.

5. Crosslinguistic Differences in Degree of Coding an Area Reveal Linguistic Capacities

Finally, the crosslinguistic method is useful in instances where languages differ in the degree of elaboration of paradigms. For example, languages can be contrasted in terms of the dimensions that play a role in their verb paradigms. In our sample we have a range—from English, with minimal marking of person-number, through Portuguese, with extensive marking of person-number, to Hebrew, with extensive marking of person-number-gender. We need this full range in order to better understand the means available to children for constructing paradigms. Using data from a language like Portuguese, Bybee was able to discover generalization of person-marking across tenses and the use of 3SG as the base for generalizations within tenses (Bybee Hooper, 1979; Simões & Stoel-Gammon, 1979), while such patterns could simply not exist in a language like English. Hebrew developmental data were needed to show precocious acquisition of sex-marking of verbs in first and third persons, with difficulty in second person (Berman, 1985; Levy, 1983), since gender is not marked on the verb in most other languages in our sample. Similar comparisons could be made with respect to crosslinguistic differences in the degree of elaboration of other systems, such as casemarking, temporal and locative expressions, and gender and noun classifiers.

THE PLAN OF THE BOOK

By the late seventies, linguists and psycholinguists in many countries were convinced of the need for gathering data on the acquisition of different types of languages and using the crosslinguistic method for purposes such as those summarized above. It was clearly time to draw together available data as a resource for constructing more detailed and universally valid theoretical accounts of child language development. In November 1979 the authors of this volume were invited to prepare interpretive summaries of the course of acquisition of various languages. We were limited in our choice of languages on the basis of the richness of available data—but luckily a fair range of diversity is represented in our sample. The authors were asked to contribute to "a book in which findings on the acquisition of different types of languages will be examined in terms of their contribution to language acquisition theory generally." Thus the chapters are intended to be selective reviews, rather than exhaustive summaries of the acquisition of each language. Each author was asked to approach his or her partucular language "as a case study in a potential crosslinguistic typology of acquisitional problems," considering those data which "contribute to an issue of general theoretical concern in developmental psycholinguistics." With these ends in mind, a common framework was suggested, as reflected in the following outline and guiding questions (which we hope will be used for future acquisition summaries as well):

Introductory Materials

1. Brief grammatical sketch of the language or language group, presenting those linguistic facts which are relevant to the following developmental analysis.

2. Summary of basic sources of evidence, characterizing methods of gathering data, and listing key references. (Note that the sources of evidence vary widely, ranging from ethnographic and longitudinal study of several children in the early years, as in Kaluli, to longitudinal and experimental studies of many children across a large age range, as in English.)

3. Brief summary of the overall course of linguistic development in the language or language group. (The reader interested in obtaining a rapid crosslinguistic survey of the materials covered in the book is advised to read sections 1 and 3 of each chapter.)

Language Acquisition Data

Sections 4–6 present detailed summaries of the acquisition of linguistic forms, orienting to issues of ease and difficulty of acquisition of various systems of the language.

4. Typical errors: What sorts of errors typically occur? How can they be accounted for? What are the most general problems posed to the child in acquiring a language of this type?

5. Error-free acquisition: What systems are learned relatively free of error? How can this be accounted for? In what ways is a language of this sort well-suited to the child's language-acquisition capacities?

6. Timing of acquisition: What systems are acquired strikingly early or strikingly late in comparison with general crosslinguistic or English-based expectations? What constitutes linguistic complexity for the learner?

Data on the Setting of Language Acquisition

Sections 7–10 situate language acquisition in regard to issues of cognitive and social development, exploring interactions between linguistic form and conceptual representation, interpersonal communication, and individual patterns of acquisition.

7. Cognitive pacesetting of language development: What evidence is there for the influence of cognitive development on problems of acquiring linguistic forms? (This issue is the special topic of Johnston's chapter in Vol. 2.)

8. Linguistic pacesetting of cognitive development: What evidence is there for the role of language development in guiding or shaping the course of cognitive or conceptual development?

9. Input and adult-child interaction: In what ways do patterns of communication and social interaction influence the course of linguistic development?

10. Individual differences: What evidence is there for distinct patterns of acquisition within a language, based on individual characteristics of the type of learner? Are there data on individual differences that cast light on developmental processes?

Theoretical Conclusions

11. Reorganizations in development: At what points in development is there evidence for significant linguistic reorganization on the part of the child? What do reorganizations suggest about underlying processes of acquisition?

12. Theoretical implications: What general principles of language development are suggested by study of a language of this type? (The chapters, in Vol. 2, by Bowerman, MacWhinney, Peters, and Slobin seek general theoretical implications across the array of languages surveyed here.)

13. Suggestions for further study: What issues could be illuminated by further study of languages of this type, or in explicit compairson with other types of languages?

Preliminary versions of chapters on individual languages were studied in a seminar on crosslinguistic approaches to language acquisition at the 1980 Summer Linguistic Institute at the University of New Mexico, followed by a conference at Berkeley in November 1980, supported by the Sloan Foundation Program in Cognitive Science. Talmy Givón and Melissa Bowerman were invited to be discussants at that conference, examining the data from the perspectives of linguistics and developmental psycholinguistics. Judith Johnston explored the issue of cognitive prerequisites for language acquisition; and workshops were held on individual differences (Elena Lieven) and cultural determinants (Susan Ervin-Tripp). Some of the participants took part in an additional workshop in the summer of 1981 at the Max-Planck-Institut für Psycholinguistik in Nijmegen, The Netherlands (Aksu-Koç, Berman, Bowerman, Clark, Ervin-Tripp, Lieven, MacWhinney, Slobin, Smoczyńska). The National Science Foundation supported Slobin in systematic summary and interpretation of the body of crosslinguistic data (1980–83, Grant BNS 80-09340). Chapters were revised and re-written in 1982–83, with a fair degree of communication between authors. Although some writers have chosen alternative means of organization, all of the chapters address the basic issues in the above outline (to the extent that relevant data are available for the given language).

What emerged – and what we offer to our readers – is a compendium of detailed surveys of the acquisition of a number of different types of languages, drawn from a fair sampling of language groups: (1) INDO-EUROPEAN: (a) GERMANIC: English, German; (b) ROMANCE: French, Italian, Portuguese, Rumanian, Spanish; (c) SLAVIC: Polish; (2) SEMITIC: Hebrew; (3) FINNO-UGRIC: Hungarian; (4) URAL-ALTAIC: Turkish; (5) JAPANESE-RYUKYUAN: Japanese; (6)

TRANS-NEW GUINEA NON-AUSTRONESIAN: Kaluli; (7) POLYNESIAN: Samoan; (8) SIGN LANGUAGE: ASL.[5]

Given the states of the art in both developmental psycholinguistics and linguistics, our data are limited in particular ways. In almost all instances, we have data on production rather than comprehension—simply because it is easier to taperecord speech than to construct and evaluate measures of comprehension. Furthermore, much of the speech has been recorded in semi-controlled situations, or only in a small sample of situations in which speech naturally occurs. Ethnographic data, such as those of Schieffelin in New Guinea and Ochs in Samoa, show how much more can be learned from a detailed study of language-in-use; and experimental data, such as those reported by de Villiers and de Villers for English, how what can be learned from detailed and systematic probes of children's competence. The analyses are heavily weighted towards issues of the acquisition of morphology and word-order patterns—issues that can be dealt with fairly easily in terms of traditional grammar. Studies of English acquisition show what can be achieved by investigators who are equipped with more subtle and complex theoretical models of the language in question, but most of the languages of our collection have not yet been submitted to the sort of detailed syntactic study which would allow for acquisition data that would be relevant to issues of universal grammar. We are only beginning to glimpse the outlines of general syntactic theories that would lead to interesting crosslinguistic developmental questions.

We are also forced to rely heavily on error data, though all investigators raise caveats about the status of such data. What is of interest, of course, is not that the child was "wrong," but that the way in which he or she was wrong may illuminate some underlying attempt to structure language in a particular direction. Thus we are interested in the ways in which child speech regularly, frequently, and systematically deviates from the speech which the child hears. Error data thus must be evaluated in the light of the input, and often we lack sufficient input data to fully evaluate the source of children's "errors." The authors also pay close attention to the TIMING of development: early errors mean something different than late errors; errors occurring together at a point in development mean something different than isolated errors; errors that reorganize previous systems are different from errors at the onset of acquisition of a system; and so forth. Wherever possible, we also try to find elusive but highly significant "non-occurring errors"—that is, places in the grammar where our theories lead us to expect children to restructure the system, but where they quickly master adult

---

[5]The individual chapters, all appearing in this series, were written by the following authors: ENGLISH: Jill and Peter de Villiers, GERMAN: Anne E. Mills, ROMANCE LANGUAGES: Eve V. Clark, POLISH: Magdalena Smoczyńska, with assistance of Richard M. Weist, HEBREW: Ruth A. Berman, HUNGARIAN: Brian MacWhinney, TURKISH: Ayhan A. Aksu-Koç and Dan I. Slobin, JAPANESE: Patricia M. Clancy, KALULI: Bambi B. Schieffelin, SAMOAN: Elinor Ochs, ASL: Elissa L. Newport and Richard P. Meier.

forms without error. Error-free acquisition, and developmental sequences in acquisition, thus supplement inferences drawn from errors. This range of data provides quite a rich base for crosslinguistic theorizing. In the background, however, we must always be aware of the fact that we have not only studied a limited sample of languages, but also a very small number of children, and that considerable individual differences exist between children acquiring a given language.

The authors are well aware of the many limitations of their material, yet they are able to lay out broad patterns of acquisition of their particular languages, suggesting general developmental principles in relation to other languages. It is our hope that the ways in which we have presented our materials and our ideas will stimulate further crosslinguistic study along similar lines, contributing to a psychological and developmental explanation for the phenomenon already noted by Roger Bacon in the thirteenth century: "Grammar is substantially the same in all languages, even though it may vary accidentally" (Lyons, 1968, p. 15).

ACKNOWLEDGMENTS

It is a pleasant task to acknowledge the many friends and colleagues who contributed to the project published here. The first—and continuing—encouragement came from my friend and publisher, Larry Erlbaum, who stood by patiently and supportingly as so many writers tried to do so much, taking more more time than we had hoped. All of the authors were of immeasurable help to me and to each other, in meeting together, corresponding, evaluating and re-evaluating their own work and the work of the others. This was truly a collegial endeavor. Laurie Wagner kept the correspondence and the production and circulation of manuscripts alive; while working space, computer facilities, and financial aid were provided by the Institute of Human Learning and Department of Psychology of the University of California at Berkeley, the Max-Planck-Institut für Psycholinguistik in Nijmegen, and the Summer Linguistic Institute at the Department of Linguistics of the University of New Mexico in Albuquerque, with grant support from the National Science Foundation (Grant BNS 80-09340), the Sloan Foundation Program in Cognitive Science, and the Committee on Research of the University of California at Berkeley. My children, Heida and Shem, and my wife, Ayşegül, graciously accepted the many long hours and days when I was lost in my study and seemingly fused with my terminal. They will no doubt be pleased when "the book" comes to mean an object on a shelf once again.

—Dan Isaac Slobin
Berkeley

REFERENCES

Aksu, A. A. *Aspect and modality in the child's acquisition of the Turkish past tense.* Unpublished doctoral dissertation, University of California, Berkeley. 1978.

Aksu-Koç, A. A., & Slobin, D. I. The acquisition of Turkish. In D. I. Slobin (Ed.), *The crosslinguistic study of language acquisition* (Vol. 1). Hillsdale, NJ: Lawrence Erlbaum Associates, 1985.

Ammon, M. S., & Slobin, D. I. A cross-linguistic study of the processing of causative sentences. *Cognition*, 1979, *7*, 3–17.

Antinucci, F., & Miller, R. How children talk about what happened. *Journal of Child Language*, 1976, *3*, 167–189.

Argoff, H. D. *The acquisition of Finnish inflectional morphology*. Unpublished doctoral dissertation, University of California, Berkeley, 1976.

Badry, F. *Acquisition of lexical derivation rules in Moroccan Arabic: Implications for the development of Standard Arabic as a second language through literacy*. Unpublished doctoral dissertation, University of California, Berkeley, 1983.

Berman, R. The acquisition of Hebrew. In D. I. Slobin (Ed.), *The crosslinguistic study of language acquisition* (Vol. 1). Hillsdale, NJ: Lawrence Erlbaum Associates, 1985.

Bloom, L., Lahey, M., Hood, L., Lifter, K., & Fiess, K. Complex sentences: Acquisition of syntactic connections and the semantic relations they encode. *Journal of Child Language*, 1980, *7*, 235–261.

Blount, B. G. *Acquisition of language by Luo children*. Unpublished doctoral dissertation, University of California, Berkeley, 1969.

Bowerman, M. F. *Early syntactic development: A cross-linguistic study with special reference to Finnish*. Cambridge: Cambridge University Press, 1973.

Bowerman, M. Learning the structure of causative verbs: A study in the relationship of cognitive, semantic and syntactic development. *Papers and Reports on Child Language Development* (Department of Linguistics, Stanford University) 1974, *8*, 142–178.

Bowerman, M. Beyond communicative adequacy: From piecemeal knowledge to an integrated system in the child's acquisition of language. *Papers and Reports on Child Language Development* (Department of Linguistics, Stanford University), 1981, *20*, 1–24.

Bybee, J. L. *Morphology: A study of the relation between meaning and form*. Amsterdam: John Benjamins, 1985.

Clancy, P. M. *The acquisition of narrative discourse: A study in Japanese*. Unpublished doctoral dissertation, University of California, Berkeley, 1980.

Clancy, P. The acquisition of Japanese. In D. I. Slobin (Ed.), *The crosslinguistic study of language acquisition* (Vol. 1), Hillsdale, NJ: Lawrence Erlbaum Associates, 1985.

Clancy, P., Jacobsen, T., & Silva, M. The acquisition of conjunction: A cross-linguistic study. *Papers and Reports on Child Language Development* (Department of Linguistics, Stanford University), 1976, *12*, 71–80.

Clark, E. The acquisition of Romance, with special reference to French. In D. I. Slobin (Ed.), *The crosslinguistic study of language acquisition* (Vol. 1). Hillsdale, NJ: Lawrence Erlbaum Associates, 1985.

Eisenberg, A. R. *Language acquisition in cultural perspective: Talk in three Mexicano homes*. Unpublished doctoral dissertation, University of California, Berkeley, 1982.

Erbaugh, M. S. *Coming to order: Natural selection and the origin of syntax in the Mandarin speaking child*. Unpublished doctoral dissertation, University of California, Berkeley, 1982.

Gheorgov, I. A. *Ein Beitrag zur grammatischen Entwicklung der Kindersprache*. Leipzig: Engelmann, 1908. [Also in *Archiv für die gesamte Psychologie*, 1908, *11*, 242–432.]

Gvozdev, A. N. Značenie izučenija detskogo jazyka dlja jazykovedenija. *Rodnoj jazyk i literatura v trudovoj škole*, 1928, No. 3, 4, 5. [Reprinted in A. N. Gvozdev, *Voprosy izučenija detskoj reči;* Moscow: Izd-vo Akademii Pedagogičeskix Nauk RSFSR, 1961.]

Gvozdev, A. N. *Formirovanie u rebenka grammatičeskogo stroja russkogo jazyka*. Moscow: Izd-vo Akademii Pedagogičeskix Nauk RSFSR, 1949.

Hopper, P. J., & Thompson, S. Transitivity. *Language*, 1980, *56*, 251–299.

Johnston, J. R., & Slobin, D. I. The development of locative expressions in English, Italian, Serbo-Croatian and Turkish. *Journal of Child Language*, 1979, *6*, 529–545.

Karmiloff-Smith, A. *A functional approach to child language*. Cambridge: Cambridge University Press, 1979.

Kernan, K. T. *The acquisition of language by Samoan children*. Unpublished doctoral dissertation, University of California, Berkeley, 1969.

Levy, Y. It's frogs all the way down. *Cognition*, 1983, *15*, 75–93.

Lyons, J. *Introduction to theoretical linguistics.* Cambridge: Cambridge University Press, 1968.

MacWhinney, B. *How Hungarian children learn to speak.* Unpublished doctoral dissertation, University of California, Berkeley, 1973.

McCarthy, D. Language development. In W. S. Monroe (Ed.), *Encyclopedia of Educational Research.* American Educational Research Association, 1950. [Reprinted in A. Bar-Adon & W. F. Leopold (Eds.), *Child language: A book of readings.* Englewood Cliffs, NJ: Prentice-Hall, 1971.]

MacWhinney, B. Hungarian language acquisition as an exemplification of a general model of grammatical development. In D. I. Slobin (Ed.), *The crosslinguistic study of language acquisition* (Vol. 2). Hillsdale, NJ: Lawrence Erlbaum Associates, 1985.

Mills, A. E. The acquisition of German. In D. I. Slobin (Ed.), *The crosslinguistic study of language acquisition* (Vol. 1). Hillsdale, NJ: Lawrence Erlbaum Associates, 1985.

Mitchell-Kernan, C. *Language behavior in a black urban community.* Unpublished doctoral dissertation, University of California, Berkeley, 1969.

Parisi, D., & Antinucci, F. Lexical competence. In G. B. Flores d'Arcais & W. J. M. Levelt (Eds.), *Advances in psycholinguistics.* Amsterdam: North-Holland, 1970.

Peters, A. M. Language segmentation: Operating principles for the perception and analysis of language. In D. I. Slobin (Ed.), *The crosslinguistic study of language acquisition* (Vol. 2). Hillsdale, NJ: Lawrence Erlbaum Associates, 1985.

Pye, C. L. *The acquisition of grammatical morphemes in Quiche Mayan.* Unpublished doctoral dissertation, University of Pittsburgh, 1979.

Radulovic, L. *Acquisition of language: Studies of Dubrovnik children.* Unpublished doctoral dissertation, University of California, Berkeley, 1975.

Savasir, I., & Gee, J. The functional equivalents of the middle voice in child language. *Proceedings of the Berkeley Linguistic Society,* 1982.

Schieffelin, B. B. The acquisition of Kaluli. In D. I. Slobin (Ed.), *The crosslinguistic study of language acquisition* (Vol. 1). Hillsdale, NJ: Lawrence Erlbaum Associates, 1985.

Simões, M. C. P., & Stoel-Gammon, C. The acquisition of inflections in Portuguese: A study of the development of person markers on verbs. *Journal of Child Language,* 1979, *6,* 53–67.

Slobin, D. I. (Ed.) *A field manual for cross-cultural study of the acquisition of communicative competence.* Berkeley, CA: ASUC Bookstore, 1967.

Slobin, D. I. Cognitive prerequisites for the development of grammar. In C. A. Ferguson & D. I. Slobin (Eds.), *Studies of child language development.* New York: Holt, Rinehart & Winston, 1973.

Slobin, D. I. The origins of grammatical encoding of events. In W. Deutsch (Ed.), *The child's construction of grammar.* London: Academic Press, 1981.

Slobin, D. I. Universal and particular in the acquisition of language. In E. Wanner & L. R. Gleitman (Eds.), *Language acquisition: The state of the art.* Cambridge: Cambridge University Press, 1982.

Slobin, D. I. Crosslinguistic evidence for the language-making capacity. In D. I. Slobin (Ed.), *The crosslinguistic study of language acquisition* (Vol. 2). Hillsdale, NJ: Lawrence Erlbaum Associates, 1985.

Slobin, D. I., & Bever, T. G. Children use canonical sentence schemas: A crosslinguistic study of word order and inflections. *Cognition,* 1982, *12,* 229–265.

Smoczynska, M. The acquisition of Polish. In D. I. Slobin (Ed.), *The crosslinguistic study of language acquisition* (Vol. 1). Hillsdale, NJ: Lawrence Erlbaum Associates, 1985.

Stern, C., & Stern, W. *Die Kindersprache: Eine psychologische und sprachtheoretische Untersuchung.* Leipzig: Barth, 1907.

Stross, B. *Language acquisition by Tenejapa Tzeltal children.* Unpublished doctoral dissertation, University of California, Berkeley, 1969.

Toivainen, J. *Inflectional affixes used by Finnish-speaking children aged 1–3 years.* Helsinki: Suomalaisen Kirjallisuuden Seura, 1980.

Weist, R. M., Wysocka, H., Witkowska-Stadnik, K., Buczowska, E., & Konieczna, E. The defective tense hypothesis: On the emergence of tense and aspect in child Polish. *Journal of Child Language,* 1984, *11,* 347–374.

SPOKEN LANGUAGES

1 The Acquisition of English

Jill G. de Villiers
Peter A. de Villiers
Smith College

Contents

INTRODUCTION

1. Descriptive Sketch of English

The English language has attracted more attention than virtually any other, and has been described in extensive detail. The wealth of linguistic analysis presents the writer of a thumbnail sketch with something of a problem. It is difficult to present facts about English from an atheoretical perspective, especially some of its more complex aspects. We have selected to describe the major forms of sentence construction from the barest simple sentence to complementation, focusing upon the processes that have been most heavily researched in child language. In this selection process we owe a substantial debt to Brown's (1973) readable survey of English in the introduction to his book *A First Language*. The seven sections on English also constitute the major subheadings of the material

27

on child language to follow. We have chosen to focus not at all on phonology, derivational morphology, or word meanings. Each area is rich and fascinating in its own right, but syntax is of central importance in linguistics and as a defining quality of human language.

1.1.*Word Order*

The basic word order in English is SVO, and in contrast to some languages, word order is affected little by pragmatic factors. Stress is a preferred device for signaling changes in focus while preserving the SVO structure. However there are structural devices such as the passive which allow the logical object to be the focus, e.g.

> John was chased by a wasp.

and constructions such as the cleft and pseudocleft allow various constituents to be highlighted, e.g.

> What he wanted was a drink.
> or:
> It was Sally that John liked.

These constructions are rare even in adult speech, however.

Left or right dislocation of an NP is another device used for pragmatic purposes, but it is also relatively uncommon except in certain dialects, e.g.

> That man I would like to meet.
> or:
> She loves oranges, my mother.

Imperatives can also follow the verb with a subject specification after a slight pause, and hence violate the SVO order, e.g.

> Move over, son.
> or:
> Help me, Bill.

Articles invariably precede the noun, and most often other determiners and adjectives are in prenominal position. However they can be placed in predicate position with the copula *be,* e.g.

> The book is red.
> The house is ours.

when they constitute the comment rather than a specification. The relation of possession can be marked by an inflection on the possessor, in which case the order is possessor-'s + possessed, or by the preposition *of,* in which case the order is possessed-*of*-possessor. Similarly there is some freedom of order with locative expressions, one can say both:

> There is the book.
> The book is there.

with little change of meaning.

As far as language development goes, one could therefore expect the input to be heavily biased towards canonical SVO structures, though from the child's perspective there might appear to be variation in adjective and locative order.

1.2. *Noun and Verb Inflections*

Compared to other languages, English has a relatively impoverished morphology. In terms of noun markings, there exist inflections for plurality (one versus many) and possession. These are phonologically governed but have no semantic variations. Articles are usually required before common nouns. They mark the dimension definite/indefinite (*the* versus *a/an*) but are not affected by gender or other properties of the object, with the exception of the mass/count and proper/common noun distinctions. The rules governing these variations have not been completely worked out, sometimes to the exasperation of foreigners. For instance, mass nouns cannot take *a,* but can take the plural form *some,* even though they are not marked by a plural inflection. So one has:

> I would like some soup.
> or:
> I would like soup.

However if it is a definite referent, *the* is used:

> I like the soup.

The mass/count distinction is not easily identified with a semantic distinction between substance and thing, but is largely defined by its distributional privileges with articles and quantifiers. The proper/common noun distinction is semantically defined, but some proper nouns must take articles c.f. *the Eiffel Tower; the King Dome.* Finally, even the distinction definite/indefinite referent is enormously complex and dependent upon the listener's knowledge as well as the speaker's knowledge (Maratsos, 1975).

Verbs in the present tense require only one inflection,-*s,* for the third person singular. There are only a limited number of exceptions, e.g. *has* and *does.* The present progressive tense is used for ongoing actions, and has two required markings; the inflection *-ing* on the verb and the auxiliary *be* before it, e.g.

> He is going
> They are talking.

The form of *be* varies with person, number, and tense but not gender. The plural forms are not distinguished by person. The past progressive is the same form with the past tenses of *be*. There is no irregularity in the progressive form.

The past tense is the third major verb inflection, and exceptions are the rule for common verbs in English. The regular past tense *-ed* is phonologically conditioned by the final consonant of the root with the allomorphs /t/, /d/, and /ɪd/ but it is insensitive to number or person. However, irregular past tenses abound and take a variety of forms e.g.

> *fall-fell*
> *bring-brought*
> but   *sing-sang* and *string-strung, tell-told, stand-stood, eat-ate*

Virtually all of these must be learned by rote.

The perfect form of the verb, used to mark current relevance, consists of the modal *have* plus the past participle inflection on the verb, which can be either *-ed, -en,* or some irregular form, e.g.

> I have eaten lunch.
> I have spilled it.
> I have sung in a choir.

Have has one variant, the third person singular *has*. The past tense form *had* creates the past perfect form. There are virtually no verbs (but see *prove*) which are perfectly regular in English in taking present *-s*, past *-ed*, and perfect *-en* together.

Hence for an English language learner, person and number distinctions are rarely marked on verbs, but are needed nonetheless for the common verb *be*. Gender is irrelevant, and verbs do not incorporate other constituents such as pronominal objects, indirect objects, directions, or locations within their boundaries. However, several linguists have proposed that such elements as CAUSE are incorporated in some verbs without overt marking, c.f.

> The door opened.
> John opened (cause to open) the door.

(e.g. Jackendoff, 1972). An account of the morphological prefixes such as *re-, mis-, dis-* and so on would take us beyond the bounds of our present task.

Finally, verbs can be modified by an extensive modal auxiliary system in English, which uses preposed modals to indicate possibility/ability, e.g.

I can swim.

hypothetical, e.g.

I may go.

obligatory, e.g.

I must leave.

future tense, e.g.

I will leave.

conditional tense, e.g.

I would go if you came too.

The modal auxiliaries can combine with *be* and *have* to make more complex expressions, e.g.

I might have been eating supper when you called.

The phrase structure rule for expansion of the auxiliary component is complex, and can be written as:

Aux→tense (modal) (have) (be)

Some linguistic treatments control the affixes required following each component by coding them with that form and allowing a transformation called affix-hopping to move them to the appropriate verbal element, e.g.

Aux→tense (modal) (have + en) (be + ing)

(Akmajian & Henry, 1975).

As one final complexity: in cases where there is no auxiliary in the present form, a "dummy" form *do* appears in the corresponding emphatic, negative, or question form, e.g.

He likes me.
He does like me!

He doesn't like me.
Does he like me?

Obviously, the auxiliary component in English is rich and complex.

1.3. *Modalities of the Simple Sentence*

The declarative sentence form described above can be mapped onto other sentence modalities: yes-no questions, constituent (wh) questions, imperatives, negatives, and tag questions. The auxiliary component plays an essential role in these modalities.

In yes-no question forms, the distinctive feature is an inversion of the subject and the first auxiliary component following tense, e.g.

You can come.
Can you come?
She must have been doodling.
Must she have been doodling?

When tense is the only component, *do* is introduced, e.g.

He ate it.
Did he eat it?

This aux-inversion occurs also in wh- or constituent questions, such as

When can you come?
What did he eat?

However it does not occur in embedded wh-forms, e.g.

I asked you when you can come.
I told him where I must go.

but these do not have interrogative force. Wh-questions have the questioned constituent preposed to the front, though there is a less common variant in which it is not preposed, e.g.

You want to go where?

For negatives, generally the first auxiliary component after tense is marked with *n't,* or *not* is inserted after it, e.g.

You can't come.
She mustn't have been doodling.

Again, if tense is the only component, *do* is inserted:

He didn't eat it.

However unlike questions, there is some optionality about where in the auxiliary the negative element can go. It is permissible to say:

She must have not been doodling.
or:
He might have been not listening on purpose.

but the placement makes subtle differences in meaning that reflect the different scope of the negative element.

The imperative form in English has no subject or auxiliary on the surface, though reflexive forms such as

Wash yourself!

and tag questions, e.g.

Help me, won't you!

have suggested an "underlying" structure contains those elements (e.g. Jacobs & Rosenbaum, 1968).

Tag questions are complex in English and require a series of rules that are governed by the preceding declarative: pronominalization of the subject, truncation of the predicate to the first auxiliary, aux-subject inversion as in questions, and negation/affirmation, e.g.

John might be coming, mightn't he?
versus:
John shouldn't have gone, should he?

Simple variants such as "right?" "O.K?" or "Hey?" also exist in more informal speech.

1.4. *Dative and Passive*

Before turning attention to complex sentences, consider for a moment two other sentence forms in English that involve some variations in the canonical SVO order. The passive form has been widely discussed in linguistics and has served as a cornerstone of many transformational accounts (e.g. Chomsky, 1957). In the passive, the usual order of logical subject and object is reversed, and the logical subject (or agent) is marked with *by*. In addition, the form of the verb changes: the auxiliary *be* or *get* is required, and the past participle of the verb, e.g.

John got beaten by Bill in the race.

Controversy exists over whether the passive should derive by transformation from the active form or whether passive verbs should have their own listing in the lexicon with a redundancy rule mapping them to the active verbs (Bresnan, 1978), and the agent by-phrase generated in the base as a prepositional phrase. Regardless of the linguistic treatment, passive sentences stand as a major exception to the canonical sentence order.

Datives also involve a prepositional phrase, in this case marking the indirect object as distinct from the direct object:

Harry sent the book to his teacher.

The optional form of the dative omits the marking, and re-orders the direct and indirect object:

Harry sent his teacher the book.

Again, whether the two forms are transformationally related or should be treated as distinct lexical rules (Roeper et al., 1981) is a matter of dispute. The first form is normally considered basic, and the second version "transformed." The transformed version not only constitutes a violation of SVO order, but may be blocked for some verbs:

* Harry transmitted his teacher the message.

and with pronominal objects (in most English dialects):

* Harry sent his teacher it.

1.5. *Coordination*

Joining two propositions together with *and* is perhaps the simplest way to generate a complex sentence in English. Redundant elements of the two propositions need not be specified, so some linguistic treatments consider the phrasal coordination to be derived from the full sentential form by a deletion schema (Harries, 1973). The rules include deletion in a forward direction (null site in the right conjunct), e.g.

Birds like strawberries and (☐) hate cucumbers.

and in a backward direction (null site in the left conjunct), e.g.

Birds (☐) and children like strawberries.

The direction of deletion depends on the constituents that are redundant. Further details of English coordination are provided later.

1.6. *Relative Clauses*

Relative clauses are one of the major forms of sentence embedding in English, and may modify noun phrases playing any role in the basic sentence. The sentence can be embedded in a variety of places and the head noun may also play a wide variety of roles within the embedded sentence (the focus). Keenan and Comrie (1977) surveyed over 40 different languages and concluded that there exists a universal hierarchy of "accessibility" of noun phrases. For example, some languages allow the head noun to be the subject or the object of the embedded clause, but not other types of focus. The proposed hierarchy is: subject < direct object < indirect object < object of a preposition < possessive noun phrase < object of a comparative particle. English is very tolerant relative to other languages, even permitting the head noun to be the object of a comparative particle, e.g.

I met the kid that Paul is smarter than.

The complementizer with relative clauses may be a wh-word, or *that,* but it is commonly deleted:

I saw the man you met.
I know the reason you didn't go.

The head noun is not redundantly marked, though it was in seventeenth century English, e.g.

I saw the man which man you met.

The absence of clear marking of the embedded S might be expected to cause children some problems in acquisition, and it does cause adults processing difficulties in experimental tasks (Fodor, Bever, & Garrett, 1974). The configural properties of relative clauses in English will be described in more detail on page 112.

1.7. *Complements*

Embedded sentences of a variety of types occur as elaborations of the VP, and the system of sentential complements in English is extremely rich. For example, one can have *to* infinitives:

John likes to swim in rivers.
Jane promised Sally to come home.

or "bare" verbs, e.g.

Andrew saw Bill drop his coffee.

gerundive complements:

Carol likes Sam watching T.V.

and tensed clauses:

Mary knew Sally picked the rose.

The complementizer may be absent as in the above, or take the form *for* before a *to*-infinitive, e.g.

Harry likes for Sally to rub his back.

that before a tensed clause, or possessive *'s* marking the subject of a gerundive complement:

Alice enjoyed Bill's playing the national anthem.

To add to the complexity, different matrix verbs allow different forms of complementation, so that Bresnan (1978) has proposed that the possibilities must be lexically encoded. For instance, only perception verbs take the bare form of complement verb. One cannot have:

Andrew liked Bill drop his coffee.

The potential for error and overgeneralization would be everywhere in the English complement system if the rules were not coded with the particular verbs.

2. Sources of Evidence

Children learning English as a first language have been extensively studied in natural environments. Several studies have observed small groups of children longitudinally for a number of years (e.g. Bloom, 1970; Bowerman, 1974; Braine, 1963; Brown, 1973; Brown & Bellugi, 1964; Leonard, 1976; Limber, 1973; Miller & Ervin, 1964; Wells, 1979). The data come chiefly from American English, with some material from British and Australian English. The focus of most of the studies was on early stages of grammar. More complex grammar has been studied primarily using experimental tasks to test groups of preschool or gradeschool children. The data base on the acquisition of English is thus rich and varied, and is growing at a rapid rate.

3. Overall Course of Development

In the material that follows, the acquisition of English syntax is explored in the order that it was discussed for adult English, since that roughly parallels the course of development. We begin with the child at Stage I, when his utterances are still less than 2.0 morphemes long (Brown, 1973). The focus of interest there is the rules for ordering basic relations in a sentence, and the research on that question has been extensive.

The next accomplishment for the child is to begin adding the grammatical elements—articles, tenses, plurals, prepositions—that modulate the meaning of the content words. This process begins at the two word stage but is not completed for several years. There is considerable orderliness in the way these morphemes are added to the child's speech, and an account of it occupies the next section.

Addition of auxiliary verbs also begins at the two or three word stage, and the child begins to use auxiliary verbs to signal questions and negatives, using a limited set at first. Interest here lies in how the child's rules are being formulated, and what kinds of errors occur.

There is little or no evidence of transformed datives and passives in the speech of 3- and 4-year-olds, yet they are beginning to understand these deviations from the canonical word order in English, especially when semantic and contextual clues are available. The fourth section considers the literature on these forms in acquisition.

The acquisition of the rules for joining sentences together is the next focus of attention, since coordination of sentences seems to occur before sentence embeddings, although the full syntax and semantics of conjunction is not complete at age 4 years.

Relative clauses are discussed in the section following coordination. Though the rudiments of embedding may be found in the speech of 2-year-olds, most researchers agree that the child's knowledge of relative clauses is not complete until much later.

Finally, verb complements are discussed as another example of embedding. Again, the earliest complements are found in 2-year-olds, but it is many years before children understand the full grammar of the English complement system in all its complexity.

For each area of acquisition, we have attempted to answer a similar set of questions. These are:

1. What is the course of acquisition of the form? Is there a reliable order of acquisition of the construction?

2. How does the order of acquisition relate to the cognitive complexity of the form? Are there related cognitive achievements?

3. What are the typical errors made in acquisition of the construction?

4. Are there individual differences in order of acquisition, or in the kinds of errors made?

5. What is known about the information in the input concerning that form? Do input variations affect acquisition?

6. How does the semantics of the construction interact with the syntax in acquisition?

7. What is known about the pragmatics, or function, of the construction? Are pragmatic factors significant in its acquisition?

There were several instances in which we could find no data bearing on one or more of these questions, hence the sub-headings under each area vary to some extent. Also, the order of consideration of the questions is constrained by either the particular history of investigation of each form, or the way the story best unfolds. Nevertheless, we hope sufficient uniformity exists to allow the reader to pursue particular interests throughout.

THE DATA

4. Word Order and Basic Relations in Stage I

Although some investigators have claimed to find the roots of grammatical development in children's single-word utterances (e.g. Greenfield & Smith, 1976; Ingram, 1971), the use of clear syntactic devices in English begins with the earliest multi-word utterances. This first stage, defined by Brown as the period in which mean length of utterance (MLU) in morphemes grows from 1.0 to 2.0 (Brown, 1973; Brown & Bellugi, 1964), has drawn a great deal of attention. In part this stems from a natural interest in the beginning stages of the mastery of English grammar; in part it arises from the possibility of exploring the links between the emergence of grammar and cognitive development at the end of the sensorimotor period. Finally, children typically spend a few weeks in the stage of one- and two-word utterances, with longer utterances rare, so that researchers can collect fairly stable and sizeable samples of speech that promise a good chance of capturing crucial developments during this stage.

Historically there have been several shifts in emphasis in attempts to characterize language development during Stage I.

4.1. *Syntactic Approaches*

Accounts of Stage I speech during the early 1960s tried to give purely formal, context-free descriptions of the child's utterances, following the prevailing model in linguistics of writing grammars for the language that were independent of semantic or pragmatic considerations. Some descriptions were fairly general, such as Brown and Bellugi's (1964) characterization of Stage I speech as telegraphic—made up predominantly of content words (nouns, verbs, and adjectives), and omitting function words like prepositions, auxiliaries, and copulas (see also Brown & Fraser, 1963). Others described the phrase and clause structure of the child's early sentences in terms of traditional grammatical categories like nouns, verbs, determiners, and adjectives (or modifiers in general), and examined the elaboration and expansion of noun and verb phrases as the child developed (Brown & Bellugi, 1964; Menyuk, 1969; Miller & Ervin, 1964).

Most of these approaches imposed syntactic categories and phrase structure rules from the adult language onto the child's utterances, although Miller and Ervin (1964) distinguished between three classes of operator words (words like *this/that, a/the*) that frequently combined with nouns or verbs. These were categorized separately on the basis of a distributional analysis of the sentence positions in which they occurred and the lexical items with which they combined. At approximately the same period of time Braine (1963) performed distributional analyses of Stage I speech in an attempt to determine the child's own rules governing his initial word combinations. Noting that for several children early two-word utterances consisted of a few high frequency words that appeared in fixed positions combined with a much larger category of less frequent words that appeared in varying positions, Braine specified what he called a pivot grammar of early child language. The high frequency words were fixed pivots around which simple sentences were organized: some (P1) always appeared in initial position; others (P2) always followed the words with which they were combined. The less frequent open class words (O) could combine with either type of pivot word or with each other; pivot words could not occur alone or combined with each other.

It was soon apparent that there were problems with a pivot grammar as a complete account of the rules underlying Stage I speech. The grammar could not appeal to semantic considerations to restrict the productivity of the system, so it predicted combinations that did not occur and made little or no sense (e.g. *night-night see, get say,* and *more away*). In the early 1970s research began to appear (e.g., Bowerman, 1973) demonstrating that the two-word utterances of some children in early Stage I did not conform to the pivot and open pattern—words defined as pivots on the basis of frequency and rigidity of sentence position occurred alone and in combination with each other. But the strongest argument against pivot grammar was also an argument against any purely formal, context-free account of Stage I speech, namely that such analyses underrepresented the child's linguistic knowledge. Bloom (1970) presented several examples of structural homonyms—two-word utterances that would be given the same formal description in their surface forms, but which had clearly different meanings when considered in context. The best known of these is Allison's use of *Mommy sock,* said once while Allison's mother was putting Allison's sock on, and once when Allison found her mother's sock. If this difference in underlying meaning was to be reflected in the child's grammar, a different approach from a distributional analysis at the level of surface structure was needed. Bloom argued for an interpretive analysis (what Brown (1973) called a "rich" interpretation) of children's utterances based on what they said, the context in which they said it, and such other clues as the responses of the adult listeners. Nevertheless, Bloom did not abandon giving a formal syntactic description of the early sentences. She suggested that the meanings of the homonymous sentences be represented as distinct deep structures in a transformational grammar, much as surface ambiguous sentences in the adult grammar were disambiguated in deep structure (Chomsky, 1965). The same surface forms arose because elements from the deep structure were automatically deleted under cognitive processing limitations (by a deletion transformation) when the child produced the utterances. Bloom therefore continued to describe two- and three-word utterances in terms of abstract linguistic categories like subject, verb, and object, plus transformational rules that derived surface forms from underlying deep structures. Interpretive analysis was used to decide what the deep structure should be.

During the 1970s, although they were no longer the dominant approach to Stage I speech, formal syntactic analyses continued to be performed. Brown (1973) refined his earlier description of telegraphic speech by specifying that not all the morphemes classified linguistically as functors (Gleason, 1961; Hockett, 1958) were reliably missing in Stage I. Several phonological, syntactic, and semantic features of those morphemes seemed to determine the likelihood that the child would use them. Fairly frequent and perceptually salient (syllabic and occasionally stressed) functors that express basic semantic or grammatical relationships in sentences (e.g. pronouns or demonstratives) tend to be used productively quite early in Stage I, especially if they are not phonologically or grammatically conditioned by the linguistic contexts in which they appear. In contrast, inflections that merely modulate basic meanings and are usually unstressed, appear rarely, and if at all, in prefabricated routines that are not productive.

Several studies in the late 1960s had reported that predicate constructions seemed to emerge first in Stage I, with V+N sequences being the earliest and most frequent patterns (McNeill, 1970; Menyuk, 1969). Menyuk noted that the child herself was usually the presupposed subject of such sentences and proposed that the child could describe her own actions before she could comment on the actions of others. Sinclair (1976) similarly suggested that the distinction between child-as-agent and other-as-agent might only be acquired after the onset of two-word utterances. In more detailed longitudinal studies by Bloom (1970) and Ramer (1976), VERB + OBJECT sentences emerged before SUBJECT + VERB and SUBJECT + OBJECT for some of their children, but for other children all three forms seemed to emerge at the same time.

Garman (1979) (following Crystal, Fletcher, & Garman, 1976) described the clausal and phrasal structure of early multiword utterances in terms of noun and verb sequences plus other structural elements such as pronouns, adjectives, and prepositions, and more specific lexical items like *this/that, here/there,* and numbers. His analysis of the data from Braine's (1976) study yielded a syntactic profile for each child at different stages and revealed variations in clause and phrase structures across the children. For David, V + N predominated over N + V combinations in both samples 1 and 2; for Kendall, N + V combinations predominated in both samples; while for Jonathon, the two patterns were of roughly equal frequency. Earlier emergence and greater frequency of V + N sequences therefore does not appear to be a consistent pattern in Stage I speech. On the other hand, toward the end of Stage I when clause and phrase structures begin to "blend" together into longer sentences (Crystal et al., 1976), the object noun phrase seems to be elaborated before the subject NP (Garman, 1979; Limber, 1973, 1976). This could reflect the predominance of personal pronoun or proper name subjects in Stage I, which do not allow for expansion or elaboration (Limber, 1976).

Considerable disagreement remains over the extent to which the Stage I child should be credited with knowledge of syntactic categories that are formally defined. For example, Bowerman (1973,1974) and Braine (1976) questioned the appropriateness of analyzing Stage I sentences in terms of such abstract linguistic categories as subject and predicate, although they thought these may be appropriate in later stages. In opposition, Bloom (1970) and Bloom, Lightbown and Hood (1975) argued that such categories are needed to capture the structural properties of early sentences. Bowerman (1973) pointed out that the structural information that defines these abstract categories is absent from Stage I, and the characteristics of early two- and three-word utterances are more compatible with a description that is semantically based.

Some researchers have even questioned the attribution of such categories as noun, verb, and adjective to the child in Stage I. Maratsos (1979) proposes that the child begins by learning specific information about the sentence position and other syntactic properties of specific lexical items. Only after a considerable amount of information has been collected in this way does the child form more general categories on the basis of the distributional patterns shared by groups of lexical items. Macnamara (1977) and Bates and MacWhinney (1982) argue that initially the child defines nouns, verbs, and adjectives semantically, as things, actions, and properties. In sharp contrast to this, Bloom (1970) and Garman (1979) assume the appropriateness of these syntactic categories—if a lexical item used by the child would be a noun if so used by an adult, then it is classified as a noun. Valian (1984) tested for the presence of the categories determiner, adjective, noun, and noun phrase in the spontaneous speech of six children. The tests consisted of examining whether lexical items that *prima facie* fall into those categories were in fact used in appropriate distributional patterns that specify category membership for the linguist. Valian concluded that all of the children had syntactic knowledge of the four categories (with the possible exception of one child who showed borderline performance on adjectives), and that knowledge of the ways languages divide up such categories must be innate, so that not much syntactic evidence is needed for their formation. Unfortunately, the least developed of Valian's subjects had an MLU of nearly 3.0, so the appropriateness of using these categories to describe the syntactic knowledge of the child in Stage I remains in doubt. Indeed, it is possible that much of the distributional evidence necessary for testing for the presence of these categories is missing in Stage I. Valian points out that very few syntactic tests allow reliable attribution of the category VP, for example, and those that do are missing from early child speech.

Different approaches to the child's acquisition of linguistic categories like subject and object, or noun, verb, and adjective will be discussed in more detail later in the chapter.

4.2. *Semantic Approaches*

In her 1970 book, Bloom had added to her formal syntactic description of Stage I speech an analysis of the semantic relationships holding between elements of the sentence. She pointed out that syntactically similar negative sentences can convey very different meanings when seen in context. For example, one of the children in her study produced both *no dirty soap* and *no pocket;* the first while pushing away a bar of soap, the second after searching her mother's skirt in vain for a pocket. From the context, Bloom interpreted the first as a rejection of the object and the second as an expression of the nonexistence of the object. She also reported that the different meanings of the negative emerged at different points in the course of syntactic development—nonexistence first, then rejection, and finally denial of the truth of a preceding proposition. The child's acquisition of underlying semantic notions could therefore interact with syntactic learning in determining the course of language development.

Schlesinger (1971) went still further in proposing that all of the child's two- and three-word utterances derived directly from underlying semantic relationships (encoded in what he called intention-markers or I-markers). He believed that the child perceived the world in terms of agents, actions, objects, and locations and learned to map these categories directly onto the syntactic forms available in his language. Realization rules (in Stage I English, primarily word order rules) derived the surface forms of utterances from the underlying semantic I-marker. Thus while Bloom resolved the ambiguity of Allison's *Mommy sock* by postulating two different formal deep structures, Schlesinger derived these utterances from two different I-markers—AGENT + ACTION and MODIFIER + X (more specifically POSSESSOR + POSSESSED).

Applications of semantic-based rule systems to Stage I speech dominated research on Stage I during the 1970s. Some researchers took linguistic systems like those of Fillmore's (1968,1971) case grammar, Chafe's (1970) analysis of verb relations, or generative semantics (Lakoff, 1972; McCawley, 1968), and applied them to child language. Others attempted to derive the child's own semantic categories from an analysis of her speech in context together with assumptions about the cognitive and/or semantic distinctions available to her at this stage. Table 1.1 shows some of the more frequent semantic notions or relations applied to Stage I speech by different researchers.

There are apparent differences between the respective classifications, usually as one researcher divides into subcategories a semantic relation applied in more general form by another. Schlesinger (1971) has a single category of MODIFIER + X; Bloom et al. (1975) and Leonard (1976) subdivide that into RECURRENCE, ATTRIBUTION, and POSSESSION. Schlesinger and Leonard use a single locative category; Brown has two, one involving action and the other not; and Bloom et al. suggest three locative categories. In general, however, these researchers converged on roughly thé same set of semantic notions that described the communicated meaning of almost all of the early multiword sentences. Brown (1973), for example, reported that his limited set of eight predominant types accounted for some 70% of his subjects' two-word utterances. Furthermore, the same semantic notions captured the meanings of Stage I utterances across a wide range of languages (see Brown, 1973; Bowerman, 1973), leading Slobin (1970) to suggest that "the rate and order of development of semantic notions are fairly constant across languages, regardless of the formal means of expression employed." Another positive aspect of this approach was the continuity it stressed between language acquisition and cognitive development in general. If the child in Stage I has knowledge of abstract linguistic categories like subject and object that are defined by deep structure configurations, any theory of learning must incorporate a substantial language-specific innate mechanism (Fodor, Bever, & Garrett, 1974; McNeill, 1970). In contrast, the semantic notions so prevalent in Stage I speech reflected just those cognitive distinctions among agents, their actions, and the things acted upon, that developmentalists regarded to be the culmination of the sensorimotor period—the period that ends at about the same age as syntax begins (Ingram, 1975a; Piaget, 1963; Sinclair-de Zwart, 1971). (The issue of the relationship between cognitive development and the acquisition of semantic relations will be discussed in more detail in section 4.4.)

On the other hand, it was apparent to several researchers that application of semantic relations to children's speech was not without its problems. Noting that some theorists subdivided semantic categories that were generic to others, Brown (1973) wrote that:

TABLE 1.1
The More Frequent Semantic Notions or Relations
Applied to Stage I Speech by Different Researchers

Schlesinger (1971)	Brown (1973)[a]	Bloom et al (1975)	Leonard (1976)	Example
		Existence	Designated/object	
Introducer + X (Ostensive sentence)	Demonstrative + Entity		Nominative	This is a Teddy
		Notice[b]	Notice	Hi, Teddy
Negation + X		Negation[c]	Negation	No pocket
Modifier + Head		Recurrence	Recurrence	More juice
	Entity + Attribute[d]	Attribution	Attribution	Red car
	Possessor + Possessed	Possession	Possessor	Daddy pipe
Agent + Object	Agent + Object		Agent	Adam ball
Agent + Action	Agent + Action	Action	Action	Doggie bite
Action + Object	Action + Object			Push car
X + Locative	Action + Locative	Locative action	Place	Walk store
		Place of action		Swim pool
	Entity + Locative	Locative State		Cup table
		State	Experience	Like candy
			Experiencer	I need it
		Intention		Wanna swim
		Instrument	Instrument	key open
X + Dative		Dative		Give Mommy

[a]Brown also notes uses of instrumental (*Sweep broom*), benefactive (*For Daddy*), dative (*Give me book*), experiencer (*Adam see*), comitative (*Go Mommy*), conjunction (in the sense of sequential naming of two present objects) (*Kimmy Phil*), and classificatory (*Mommy lady*) semantic notions, but they were infrequent and only appeared in a few of the children in Stage I. Vocatives (Notice), questions and negatives were placed in Brown's category of "other" constructions, the first because he regarded them to be of little grammatical or semantic interest, the latter two modalities because most of their syntactic development took place in Stage III and they seem to be a rather different class of semantic relation than the others. As major modalities they can be superimposed on almost any of the other types of semantic relation.

[b]The category of notice for Leonard differed markedly from that of Bloom et al. For Leonard any vocative counted as an expression of notice, but for Bloom et al. a verb of attention (e.g. *see, hear,* or *look at*) had to appear in the utterance.

[c]Bloom (1970) subdivided negation into expressions of nonexistence, rejection and denial. In their 1978 book Bloom and Lahey distinguish between five categories of negation—nonexistence, disappearance, nonoccurrence, rejection, and denial.

[d]Brown does not use a separate category of recurrence. Utterances involving *more + N* were counted as a form of attribution.

This . . . makes clear that the relations or roles are abstract taxonomies applied to child utterances: That it is not known how finely the abstractions should be sliced and that no proof exists that the semantic levels hit on by any theorist, whether Bloom, Schlesinger, Fillmore or whomever, are psychologically functional. Nor is this a nonsense question. It is an empirical question awaiting a technique of investigation. (p. 177)

Bowerman (1976) outlines the myriad ways in which action verbs in a typical 2-year-old's vocabulary can be subdivided on semantic grounds—for example, into those that refer to actions that are momentary (*throw, hit*) versus those that continue for a period of time (*carry, fly*); those that result in a change of location (*put, throw*) versus those that result in a change in state (*break, open*); those that create something (*build, draw*) versus those that act on existing objects, and so on. An extreme case of fine distinctions made in semantic notions is found in Wells (1974), where attributive is subdivided into physical, quantity, class, evaluative, substance, and dispositional; experiences are further specified as physical, affective, cognitive (perceptual), cognitive (mental), and wanting; and locative becomes movement, directional, directional movement, target, and directional target. As Brown (1973) points out:

> Meanings of sentences may be described so generically as to make no distinctions (a sentence expresses a complete thought) or so specifically as to make as many distinctions as there are sentences or with any number of distinctions in between these extremes. The question is, which of the possible distinctions is, in fact, functional or "psychologically real." (p. 146)

Howe (1976) critically examined the approaches of Schlesinger (1971), Bloom (1973), and Brown (1973), and concluded that the evidence from Stage I supports the existence of only three broad semantic categories: action of concrete object, state of concrete object, and name of concrete object. She notes that not only do the above researchers differ in how they divide up some categories, but also in how they categorize specific utterances even when they agree on categories. This arises from two fundamental problems: there are few if any surface syntactic features that distinguish the specific semantic relations from each other in adult English; and when a particular syntactic rule like word order is used to interpret an utterance, the nonlinguistic context may not specify a single interpretation. *Daddy hat*, produced in a context in which the child's father is wearing a hat, could be intended to communicate either a possessive or a locative or a simple association between the two objects. Finally, Howe (1976; see also 1981) questions whether there is sufficient developmental evidence to attribute to the child an understanding of semantic roles like agenthood, possession, or attribute and all that they entail. While there is evidence from Piagetian tasks that the child at the onset of syntax may be able to distinguish actors from their actions and objects from things done to them, that is not sufficient to ascribe to the child knowledge of a general semantic role like agent or patient (see section 4.4 for further discussion of this issue).

These problems with a rich interpretation of children's utterances based primarily on the nonlinguistic context are not as worrisome if the researcher is trying to describe the emergence of the communication of different meanings by early single- or multiword utterances. Parents continually interpret the meaning of what their toddlers say (Cross, 1978; Nelson, 1973), and communication between them is usually quite effective. Indeed, as we shall see when we discuss the issue of the order of emergence of semantic notions, the kinds of things little children talk about and are able to communicate may change systematically with development. But if the researcher is trying to determine the child's linguistic knowledge in the form of what categories enter into his earliest syntactic rules, then the criteria for attribution of a category need to be stronger.

Schlesinger (1974) proposed two criteria for deciding the appropriate level at which to describe a child's utterances. Utterances that (1) enter the child's productive speech at about the same time, and (2) that share the same syntactic device, e.g. a particular word order, are reasonably classified together as having the same underlying semantic relation and entering into the same rule. Braine (1976) followed these criteria in a study of the Stage I language of eleven children learning either English, Finnish, Samoan, Hebrew, or Swedish, and concluded that, "the first productive structures are formulae of limited scope for realizing specific kinds of meaning. They define how a meaning is to be expressed by specifying where in the utterance the words expressing the meaning should be placed." According to Braine the categories upon which the ordering rules operate are semantic rather than syntactic, but they are narrower than categories like agent or action or possessor. An illustration of Braine's analysis is provided by Jonathan's use of two-word utterances using *big* and *little*. In the first sample of his speech Jonathan used *big* + X and *little* + X with the word for size consistently in initial position. This suggested to Braine that a word order rule like SIZE + X was operating. However, since utterances with other adjectives like *hot* + X and *old* + X appeared around the same time, Braine entertained the possibility that the rule operated on a more general category like property or attribute. In this case Braine argued that the more specific category was appropriate for the word order rule because Johathan also produced utterances with *wet* in a variable pattern *wet* + X or X + *wet,* as if the ordering rule did not yet apply to them. Braine found some ordering formulae that were fairly common across children, e.g. patterns that draw attention to things (*see* + X, *here/there* + X), or location (X + PREPOSITION + *here/there*), and patterns indicating possession (*my*/PROPER NAME + X). Others were less common and appeared in few children. VERB + OBJECT sentences were infrequent in Braine's subjects and were usually of variable word order or reflected ordering rules applying to either individual lexical items (e.g. *see* + X or *want* + X) or small sets of verbs with a common semantic context like *eat/bite/drink* ("oral consumption"). Surprisingly, Braine found that a broad AGENT + ACTION pattern seemed to be productive for many children.

Braine's study was thus considerably more cautious in attributing knowledge of semantic categories to children than were many earlier studies. A particular word order had to be used consistently above chance level, even if the adult language could potentially use both orderings in expressing a semantic relation e.g. *The dog is here* or *Here is the dog* to express the locative. The variety of lexical items used in a pattern was also important in determining the semantic categories attributed to the child. Bowerman's (1976) study of her own children, Christy and Eva, contained data that were even more valuable in establishing the appropriate categories entering into early rules. In addition to the earliest two-word utterances, Bowerman had a record of the one-word utterances preceding the onset of syntax as well as overlapping with it. Taped samples were recorded weekly and there were extensive daily entries, so the emergence of syntax could be traced in great detail. Bowerman could thus establish not only what two-word combinations occurred but also which did not but might have done because the lexical items appeared in single-word utterances at the same time. In this way she showed that Eva's initial combination rules seemed to be lexically-based, producing patterns like *want + X, more + X, no + X,* and *here + X* (while handing over an object). The pattern *more + X* did not spread rapidly to semantically similar words like *again, no more,* or *allgone;* in fact, these terms only started to combine with other words about a month after the appearance of *more + X* and then did so one at a time over a period of weeks. Rather mysteriously, Eva went rapidly from this system of lexical-item-based combination rules to a much more mature system that seemed to Bowerman to be best described by context-free syntactic categories like subject and object. Bowerman could find no evidence for an intermediate stage of rules based on broad semantic categories like agent or action.

Christy, on the other hand, seemed to begin with more broadly based semantic categories and proceeded with less discontinuity in development. For example, although she used many adjectives as one-word utterances and knew the names for the objects she seemed to be describing, Christy did not use MODIFIER + MODIFIED sequences until roughly two months after she produced her first two-word combination. Within a few days she then expressed many sentences like *That wet, Daddy hot,* and *Bottle allgone,* combining *that* or the name of an object with *hot, wet, allgone,* and *alldone,* with the modifier always in second position. At about the same time she began to produce predicate nominatives like *that airplane,* forms that share with predicate adjectives the copula construction in adult English, and may also be described as attributing something (a name) to an object (Bowerman, 1976). We discuss individual differences in the acquisition of English syntax in Stage I in more detail in section 4.7, but these examples from Braine and Bowerman suggest that many children begin with syntactic rules of more limited semantic scope than those rules have in the adult system. They also illustrate the kind of caution necessary in attempts to determine the child's syntactic knowledge in Stage I.

A different approach to children's knowledge of word order rules and semantic relations has examined their comprehension of sentences exemplifying a particular rule or relationship. Thus, de Villiers and de Villiers (1973a) investigated Stage I children's ability to act out reversible active sentences like *The boy pushed the girl* in which the only clue to the semantic roles of agent and object is the word order. Children with an MLU < 1.5 were unable to act out the sentences above chance level. Both Bowerman (1973) and de Villiers and de Villiers (1974) noted that children's agents in early agent-object and agent-action sentences were overwhelmingly animate nouns and pronouns, so their ordering rules at this stage could apply to a more restricted semantic category than agent. They would then understandably fail to comprehend sentences in which agenthood could not be identified with animacy. Only in late Stage I or Stage II did children succeed at this task. Several other studies established that children rely on event probabilities in interpreting agent-action-object sentences before they use word order information alone (Chapman & Miller, 1975; Strohner & Nelson, 1974).

Golinkoff and Markessini (1980) studied comprehension of three types of possessive relationships—alienable (*the mommy's ball*), intrinsic (*the mommy's face*), and reciprocal/reversible (*the mommy's baby*). For each of 24 possessive sentences that their mother produced, the child had to point out the possessed object in one of two pictures. Both sensible and anomalous (e.g. *the face's mommy*) possessives of each type were tested. All of the late Stage I (MLU > 1.5) children and three out of six of the early Stage I children were at or above 75% correct on picking out sensible intrinsic and alienable possessives when semantic probability constrained the interpretation. Reversible possessives, in which word order was the only cue, did not reach that criterion of accuracy until MLU was over 4.0 (Stage V). These results suggest that Stage I children have a basic understanding of the notion of what objects are likely to be possessions and possessors, but cannot use word order alone to comprehend a possessive relationship. Howe (1981) criticized Golinkoff and Markessini for assuming the chance probability of pointing to the correct referent was 25% when the pictures contained two possessors and two possessions. She points out that the crucial possessor—*mommy* in *the mommy's shoe*—only appeared in one picture even though the possessed object occurred in both. The child could thus reduce the chances of being wrong by simply picking the picture in which the possessor referent was shown. Nevertheless, even if chance is thereby reduced to 50%, consistent performance above 75% by the late Stage I children suggests understanding of the constrained possessives at this point.

In her own study in 1981, Howe investigated comprehension of the semantic roles of beneficiary and locative in a similar picture-cued comprehension procedure. The target referent appeared in both pictures but in different roles. For example, when asked, "Where is the hat on the boy?" the child had to choose between a picture of a girl putting a hat on a boy and a picture of a boy putting a hat on a girl. For "Where is the tea for the lady?" the choice pictures depicted a man giving tea to a woman versus a woman giving tea to a man. Stage I children could not pick out the appropriate picture representing a beneficiary or locative, even though control conditions revealed that they knew the lexical items and succeeded in the task when the object (hat or tea in the examples above) was varied rather than the beneficiary or locative. Late Stage II and Stage III children did show an understanding of these semantic roles.

In conclusion, recent studies of both production and comprehension question early Stage I children's use of broad semantic roles like agent and beneficiary and the syntactic means of expressing them in English. Early rules of production and strategies of comprehension are frequently based on more specific semantic categories or particular relationships between referents. We address the issue of the child's conceptual understanding of agent, action, location and so on, later in this section.

4.3. Order of Acquisition

In their longitudinal studies of the emergence of semantic notions Bloom et al. (1975) and Leonard (1976) both conclude that the notions are acquired in a consistent order in Stage I and Stage II. In sharp contrast, Braine (1976) observed no consistency across children in the order in which syntactic patterns to express semantic notions became productive. In fact, for two of his English-speaking subjects, Andrew and Kendall, there was no overlap in productive patterns in Stage I.

Several factors seem to determine whether or not a common order of acquisition is observed within and across studies. Aside from sample size and frequency of sampling, a major determinant is whether evidence for a consistent and productive syntactic rule is required before a semantic notion is attributed to the child. Braine required that consistent word order be used to mark a semantic notion, so a fairly substantial number of utterances of a given type were needed to establish productive control of the rule. Bloom et al. and Leonard relied more heavily on a rich interpretation of the utterances in context and allowed word order to vary. In Bloom's study the child was credited with productive mastery of a semantic notion when five utterances expressing that notion had been observed; for Leonard the first nonstereotypical multiword expression of a notion sufficed. These methodological differences clearly affect the reported orders of acquisition. For example, Bloom (1970), Ramer (1976), and Leonard (1976) all report either earlier expression of ACTION + OBJECT than AGENT + ACTION, or simultaneous emergence of these relations; Braine (1976) reports that AGENT + ACTION constructions were consistently productive before constructions expressing ACTION + OBJECT. For Braine that means that consistent positional formulae for agent + action preceded the formulae for AGENT + OBJECT. Leonard (1976) reanalyzed the data from the subjects on which Braine had longitudinal data, using his own criterion for attribution of a semantic notion to the child. The emergent order of acquisition of agent, action, and object categories as well as other semantic notions was then much more consistent with the other studies. Leonard therefore distinguishes between the child's ability to communicate a semantic notion in a multiword utterance and his mastery of a syntactic device to encode that notion.

Another factor influencing convergence on a common order of acquisition is the level of specificity of the proposed semantic notions. Braine's set of meanings expressed by early syntactic formulae are quite narrowly defined, and vary from child to child. Bloom et al. and Leonard applied a simple system of relativity broad semantic notions to all of their subjects, although there remain some differences in how these notions are defined in the two studies. Table 1.2 shows the overall order of acquisition for each of these two studies produced by averaging the ranked acquisition order of the notions across the children. There was substantial similarity in the ordering of notions among the children in each study. For Bloom et al.'s four subjects the concordance was greater than .8; for Leonard's eight subjects it was over .5 (p < .001 in each case).

Grouping the notions together into broader categories produces an order of acquisition that is very similar across these and other studies (e.g. Wells, 1974). Operations of reference that name an object or note its presence, absence, disap-

TABLE 1.2
Order of Acquisition
of Major Semantic Relations
in Early Multiword Utterances

Bloom et al. (1975)	*Leonard (1976)[a,b]*
Existence (Nomination)	Notice
Recurrence	Nomination
Negation	Action
Action	Place[c]
Locative Action	Agent
Attribution	Negation
Possession	Attribution
State	Possessor
Notice	Recurrence
Locative State	Experience/Experiencer[d]
Intention	Instrument
Instrument	
Dative	

[a]This ordering leaves out Leonard's category of designated/ object, which is so defined that it must appear when either notice or nomination occur. Any such referring expression must involve designation of an entity. Experience and experiencer are also conflated. Leonard scored them separately, but in fact any utterance containing reference to an experience also specified the experiencer e.g. *I need letter please. I wanna see that.*

[b]In cases in which a semantic notion did not occur in any sample from a child (they were only recorded up to an MLU of 2.3) it was ranked as the last to be acquired. Specification of an instrument only appeared in the sample of speech from two of

pearance, or recurrence are usually the first to appear, and they are closely followed by expressions encoding actions. Specification of the properties or static relationships of objects (attribution, possession, location) emerge next, then reference to experiences or internal states of the subject. Finally, constructions involving instruments or dative recipients of actions become productive very late if at all in Stage I.

As the categories are more narrowly defined, however, the agreement between studies begins to disappear. The major discrepancies between the orderings of the semantic notions in Table 1.2 involve the categories of notice, negation, and recurrence. The later acquisition of notice in Bloom et al.'s children is readily explained by differences in the definition of the category. Leonard accepted any vocative (e.g. *Hi, camel*) plus utterances like *Here box* and *Hey shoe* as an expression of notice; Bloom et al. required a verb of attention such as

---

TABLE 1.2 (continued)

the eight children in Leonard's study; expressions of recurrence were missing for two of the children.

^cLeonard's place category subsumes Bloom et al.'s notions of locative action, locative state, and place of action.

^dLeonard's experience and experiencer categories incorporate several of Bloom et al.'s categories—state utterances (those with verbs like *need* and *like*), notice utterances (those with verbs of attention like *see, hear,* and *look at*), and intention utterances (e.g. *I want go park*). Actually there are some ambiguities about Leonard's classification of experience/experiencer utterances. Consider the following three utterances:

See that (Lynn turns the cash register over, bends and looks.)

I see hat (Alec sees a toy barrel on the floor.)

I see in here (Morton hits the cash register drawer, which opens. Morton looks inside the cash register.)

Leonard classifies the first as notice, the second as AGENT + ACTION, and the third as EXPERIENCER + EXPERIENCE. Presumably the grounds for the difference in categorization have to do with the point in development at which these utterances were observed, but when one is attempting to determine the order of acquisition of the notions, that is a dangerous degree of flexibility to have. There may be grounds for classifying initial sentences with *want* and *see* separately, since several researchers (e.g. Wells, 1974; Braine, 1976) have found utterances with these verbs early in Stage I even though reference to other feelings and perceptions is late. But evidence of the limited semantic nature of such combinations and the availability or nonavailability of other words for experiences should be gathered to justify such a decision. Many of the initial instances of EXPERIENCER + EXPERIENCE in Leonard's data involved use of *I want X*.

see or *look at*. The relatively late acquisition of recurrence and negation in Leonard's subjects is not as easily accounted for, though it may be a sampling artifact. These notions were infrequent in the speech samples from Leonard's subjects (for two subjects expressions of recurrence were not observed at all in Stage I), and their rank orderings across the eight subjects were particularly variable. Frequent constructions would be more likely to appear in a sample and so be counted as acquired (see Bowerman, 1975). In Leonard's study the rank order correlation between the order of acquisition of the semantic notions and their frequency in the children's speech was greater than .90. The relative salience of the notions may also depend on the situation or may vary across children (see the discussion in section 4.8 of pragmatic factors that may affect the expression of semantic notions).

Examining more narrowly defined semantic relations in other studies reveals disagreement about order of acquisition. Bloom (1970) wrote that multiword negative sentences emerged in the order nonexistence, then rejection, and then denial; McNeill (1968) found denial before rejection in the child he studied; and Ramer (1976) observed great variability across her seven subjects in the order in which the negations were produced. Bloom et al. (1975) and Wells (1974) reported locative actions (A moves to B) before locative states (A is at B), but Braine (1976) found productive expressions of locative states before locative actions in some children and simultaneous emergence of these two notions in others. Finally, Wells (1974) reported that utterances concerned with the functions of people (*eat, play, sing, kiss*, etc.) are produced before utterances noting changes of state (*break, open, cut*, etc.). Braine (1976) found just the opposite.

All of this suggests that only when meanings are defined in general terms is there orderliness in the child's changing ability to communicate meanings that may be tied to his cognitive development. There is less orderliness in the mastery of specific syntactic rules to express those meanings. We will now turn to the issue of cognitive constraints on the expression of semantic relations in Stage I, and will return to consideration of individual differences in the acquisition of syntactic devices at a later point.

4.4. Cognitive Development and Semantic Relations

Three different issues have dominated discussions of the relationship between cognition and semantic or syntactic development in Stage I:

1. What are the prerequisite cognitive skills for the emergence of multiword utterances?
2. What is the relationship between the order of acquisition of semantic notions and the cognitive distinctions that may underlie them?
3. Do semantic categories like agent, action, and object that enter into early syntactic rules simply map onto existing cognitive categories of the same scope?

Several theorists have argued that the internalization of action schemas into the mental representations that are the culminating achievements of Piaget's sixth stage of sensorimotor development (at approximately 18-months-of-age) represent the necessary prerequisites for word combinations (see for example, Ingram, 1974,1978; McNeill, 1974; Moerk, 1975; Morehead & Morehead, 1974; Sinclair-de Zwart, 1971). The cognitive achievements postulated to occur at this stage include the concept of permanent objects that continue to exist independent of actions upon them, together with an understanding that whole categories of objects can be used for the same action and a variety of actions can be performed with one object. In addition the child comes to understand the causal relationship between objects that can initiate actions and changes in the objects that are acted upon. The argument that these achievements must underlie any ability to produce operations of reference, or utterances expressing semantic relations among agents, actions, or objects, is plausible on the basis of logic alone, but it has proven difficult to establish a clear synchrony between the cognitive and linguistic skills. Most of the earlier accounts of cognitive prerequisites for the acquisition of syntax supported the logical argument by appeals to correlations between the age norms for the mastery of the different Piagetian tasks and the emergence of two-word utterances. More recent empirical studies that tested the relationship between performance on Piagetian tasks and various measures of language acquisition in the same children have produced only equivocal support for such a strong correspondence between skills in the two domains. Some children appear to pass through Stage 6 of sensorimotor operations as much as 6 months before the onset of syntax; others produce two-word utterances before they succeed on Stage 6 cognitive tasks.

Sixty-five percent of the children in a study by Bates, Benigni, Bretherton, Camaioni, and Volterra (1977) passed the Stage 6 object permanence task around 13 months of age and many of them showed other Stage 6 behaviors like symbolic play, deferred imitation, or memory for absent objects, long before multiword utterances emerged in their speech. Bates (1976) therefore suggested that it is not the onset of mental representation, but increases in the span of the child's representational capacity, allowing him to represent and operate on groups of objects or events, which are crucial for the onset of syntax. This is similar to Bloom's (1973) notion that the relations among objects and events come to be represented in the late sensorimotor period. However, outside of informal behavioral observations like those of Piaget, it is not clear how to assess the achievement of this cognitive ability.

Ingram (1975a) and Corrigan (1976) both reported that most of the children in their longitudinal studies began to produce their first multiword utterances just after showing Stage 6 performance on object permanence tasks. But one child in each study produced multiword utterances before reaching Stage 6. Ingram noted that the maverick child in his study was the most imitative of the children and suggests that her early sentences may have been imitated routines and not syntactically productive.

Corrigan (1979) points out that much of the confusion in this area stems from different operational definitions of representation and object permanence. All measures of mental representation may not be equivalent, and there is no substantial synchrony in children's mastery of the tasks Piaget used to define stages of sensorimotor development—in fact, decalage is the rule rather than the exception (Fischer, 1980; Uzgiris, 1976). A close correspondence between cognitive and linguistic skills is therefore only likely to be found when the same skills are required and the task demands are similar in the two domains.

It does not follow from the fact that understanding of semantic notions may depend on cognitive abilities that they must emerge in child language in the same order as they are acquired nonlinguistically (Fodor, Bever, & Garrett, 1974). Nevertheless, a plausible account of the order of acquisition of general semantic categories can be given in terms of their cognitive difficulty, defined by the order of attainment in cognitive development (Leonard, 1976). Thus operations of reference like notice, nomination, and recurrence seem to require only the level of understanding of objects that is achieved in the third and fourth stages of the sensorimotor period (Brown, 1973), and they are the earliest semantic notions to appear. Specification of agents and objects, however, requires encoding and relations between objects and events, plus an understanding of causality in the sense that the child appreciates that other people as well as herself are potential sources of actions as well as recipients of actions. Similarly, semantic notions like attribution and possession seem to reflect the child's ability to represent the properties and relationships between objects independent of relevant action. These cognitive achievements emerge in Stages 5 and 6 of sensorimotor intelligence (Piaget, 1954). Finally, notions of experience and experiencer do not deal directly with overt activity but rather encode internal psychological state. Since the primary source of information in the sensorimotor period is overt action, these more abstract notions would be expected to emerge relatively late in Stage I (Leonard, 1976). The same assessment of cognitive difficulty based on nonlinguistic development cannot be used to account for the time lag between reference to agents and reference to instruments, however. Piaget (1954) suggests that the understanding of causality that underlies both of these notions emerges in Stage 5, when the child is observed to use objects as tools and also seems to appreciate the agency of other people.

Some writers have suggested that linguistic semantic categories map directly onto cognitive categories of the same scope formed in prelinguistic cognitive development (Sinclair-de Zwart, 1971). Early meanings are seen as representing a set of internalized sensorimotor schemata rather than as a set of linguistic deep structures (Bates, 1976). Others have distinguished more sharply between conceptual and linguistic knowledge. Thus, although Bloom (1973) stated that "children learn a language as a linguistic coding of developmentally prior conceptual representations of experience" (p. 16), she does not believe that cognitive categories develop "in a one-to-one correspondence with eventual linguistic categories" (p. 121). According to Bloom et al. (1975) the cognitive representations of the relationship among objects and events are more global, not distinguishing between the respective semantic roles of the elements, but rather representing the entire relationship. "Such differential semantic categories as agent, place, affected object, etc. are linguistic inductions that the child has made on the basis of his linguistic experience" (Bloom et al., 1975, p. 30). A similar point is made by Bowerman (1975) when she argues a child's general cognitive understanding of object permanence, causality, or actions as distinct from the objects acted upon, does not tell the child how finely or broadly to slice the semantic categories that rules of word combination might act upon.

Schlesinger (1974,1982) proposes that exposure to the way the language encodes various events and relationships interacts with the child's nonlinguistic experience in forming semantic categories. For example, "by hearing sentences in which all agents are treated the same way, the child acquires the agent concept with rules for realizing it in his speech" (1974, p. 45).

There is little empirical evidence to support either position, but recent developmental research has set out to show that infants possess general concepts of agent and recipient (Golinkoff, 1981). Golinkoff and co-workers investigated the habituation and recovery of visual fixation to films of agents engaging in actions on objects. For example, Golinkoff and Kerr (1978) showed films of a man (A) pushing another man (B) to 15- to 18-month-old infants who were not yet producing two-word utterances. The positions of the actors and the direction of the movement were continually changing, but A always pushed B. After several presentations visual fixation time to the film declined, then the agent and recipient roles were reversed—now B pushed A—and the recovery of fixation time was measured. Significant recovery was observed, and Golinkoff and Kerr interpret this as showing that the infants had perceived the change of actor and recipient. However, Schlesinger (1982) has rightly argued that this experiment only shows that the infant could discriminate between "A as pusher" and "A as pushed," not between categories as broad as agent and recipient. A subsequent experiment by Golinkoff (1981) is more promising because it varied the actions that A performed on B in the habituation series. In the dishabituation test, either A performed a new action on B (action change), or B performed the same new action on A (action change plus role reversal). Unfortunately, only the younger girls (16 months) and older boys (24 months) showed more recovery from habituation for the role reversal with an action change than to the action change alone. The other subjects dishabituated to both test films to the same degree. Differential recovery is needed to argue that the child can detect the additional role change. Clearly more research is warranted to investigate the kind of agent and action events that presyntactic infants can discriminate.

4.5. *Relation to Input*

There is considerable disagreement about the ways in which modifications in parental speech to children might facilitate early language acquisition. Studies that have correlated differences in mothers' speech to their children in Stage I with the children's rate of language development have come out with diametrically opposed results and conclusions. For example, Newport, Gleitman, and Gleitman (1977) studied the language of 15 mother-daughter dyads at two points 6 months apart. At the first sample the children fell into three age groups—12–15 months, 18–21 months, and 24–27 months. Partialling out age and the initial language competence of the child, Newport et al. correlated the types of constructions (e.g. declarative, imperative, yes/no questions, and wh-questions) in the parental speech at the time of the initial sample with measures of the child's language development over the 6 month period. They distinguished between "language general" (i.e. universal) aspects of the children's speech that included major structural variables like the number of verb or noun phrases per utterance, and "language specific" aspects such as use of auxiliaries or noun inflections. The obtained correlations suggested that variations in the input had only a limited effect on language specific aspects of the child's development—for example, frequent use of initial auxiliaries in yes/no questions was positively related to the later use of auxiliaries in the children (see p. 80 for a fuller discussion of this finding). There were no significant effects on more general structural aspects of the child's language acquisition. Newport et al. concluded that "whether mothers speak in long sentences or short ones, restricted or wide-ranging sentence types, complex sentences or simple ones—none of these plausible candidates for a teaching style have a discernible effect on the child's language growth during the six month interval we investigated" (p. 136).

In sharp contrast to this, Furrow, Nelson, and Benedict (1979) found that several aspects of mothers' speech reflecting the use of a simpler communicative style were positively correlated with productive language growth in their children. Seven first-born children (four boys and three girls) were recorded in verbal interaction with their mothers at 18 months and again at 27 months. At 18 months six of the children had no word-combinations in their speech (MLU = 1.0) and the seventh had very few (MLU < 1.4), so both the age and level of language production at the first sample of mothers' speech was controlled for. Several factors that added semantic or syntactic complexity to the mothers' speech when the children were 18 months old were negatively correlated with basic measures of the children's language production at 27 months. For example, a mother's use of more verbs, more pronouns relative to nouns, and more copulas and contracted forms correlated negatively with her child's MLU, verbs per utterance, and noun phrases per utterance nine months later. The major difference between these two studies lies in how they controlled for differences in the children's language abilities when the initial sample of parental speech was taken. Newport et al. partialled it out statistically; Furrow et al. recorded the sample when the children were at the same age and linguistic competence. Furrow et al. argue that the weakness of the statistical procedure is that it assumes that variations in the input are going to have similar effects regardless of the age and levels of language development over which the 6 months of growth are measured. Furthermore, Nelson (1982) points out that statistical adjustments for overall language competence in terms of utterance length may work unequally for different aspects of syntax. For example, in his subjects, axiliary use correlated only weakly with utterance length; noun phrase complexity correlated more strongly. Hence, adjustments for initial MLU may not control for level of syntactic ability in specific domains. Finally, Hardy-Brown (1983) points out that the likelihood of replicating a significant correlation is very low with small sample sizes like those in the above studies. Of 24 mother-child correlations in common between Newport et al. and Furrow et al. only one was significant in both studies—half of the others were in the same direction, but the remainder were in opposite directions. We must conclude that evidence for a strong relation between the parental input in Stage I and rate of syntactic development in the child's language production remains equivocal.

These studies primarily explored syntactic aspects of parent and child language, but others have looked more closely at semantic aspects. Wells (1974) suggested that children learn linguistic structure from hearing adults describe situations and events that they clearly understand in cognitive terms. For him an ideal situation for the child acquiring the linguistic encoding of semantic relations would be "a shared activity with an adult in which the adult gave linguistic expression to just those meanings in the situation which the child was capable of intending and to which he was at that particular moment paying attention" (p. 267). Several studies of mothers' linguistic interaction with their young children have commented on the extent to which mothers restrict themselves to talking about the here-and-now for the child (see Snow, 1977, 1979 for reviews).

In her study of 16 children aged 19 to 32 months, Cross (1977) noted that 72% of the maternal utterances encoded the child's or mother's ongoing activities or referred to present persons or objects. Furthermore, there was a close referential and semantic contingency between the child's utterances and the mother's utterances. Some 55% of the mothers' utterances referred back to topics in the children's speech, or incorporated them exactly. Overall, the less mature children in comprehension and production received a greater proportion of these semantically related utterances, suggesting that the parental speech was tailored or "fine-tuned" to the linguistic competence of the child. In a different analysis of the same data, Cross (1978) discovered that children receiving a greater number of semantically related utterances (expansions and semantic extensions of their own utterances) were likely to be linguistically accelerated in MLU relative to children of the same age who received fewer of them.

In a study of nine Dutch mothers, Snow (1977) found that 65 to 87% of their utterances to their toddlers could be described by Brown's (1973) eight prevalent semantic relations from Stage I speech. Van der Geest (1977) reported a still more dramatic case of fine-tuning of parental input to children's level of development. Van der Geest and co-workers scored the speech of eight Dutch mother-child pairs for reference to a range of underlying "semantic" notions (including tense, modals, locative, possession, and definite and indefinite reference) based on a rich interpretation of the utterances in context. In general, the frequency of the semantic notions peaked in the children's speech before they peaked in the parental input, but frequency of the syntactic realization of those notions peaked first in the mothers' speech. Van der Geest concludes that "in mother-child interaction the child somehow determines how complex the daily conversation with him may be in semantic cognitive terms, and the mother takes the opportunity to provide the child with the correct realization rules to cover the semantics of the conversation" (1977, p. 91).

Retherford, Schwartz and Chapman (1981) set out to test this claim of fine-tuning by the mother by examining the relative frequency of 15 semantic roles and five broader syntactic categories in the speech of six English speaking mothers and their toddlers at two points in development. The MLU's of the children varied from 1.0 to 1.95 (mean = 1.32) at the first sample, and from 1.38 to 2.92 (mean = 1.91) when the second sample was taken 3 to 6 months later. Mother and child utterances from a half-hour play session were coded for the expression of the following semantic roles, using a rich interpretation from context: action, agent, object, locative, demonstrative, recurrence, possessor, quantifier, experiencer, recipient, beneficiary, comitative, created object, instrument, and state. Also coded were five grammatically defined categories: one-term expressions of entity, multiterm expressions of entity, negation, attribute, and adverbial. Note that both one-word and multiword utterances were included in the scoring, and several of the "syntactic categories" were used as semantic notions by Bloom et al. (1975) and Leonard (1976). Cross-lagged panel correlations on the relative frequency of use of the semantic roles and syntactic categories were used to determine the probable direction of effect—did the mother tune in to the child or vice versa? The pattern of correlations suggested that the mothers were ahead of the children. The children's use of the categories from sample one to sample two changed to become more like the mothers' both in which semantic roles were present and in how frequently they were used. If a mother used a semantic role with relatively high frequency in sample one, the child was more likely to use it frequently in sample two: the reverse was not true. Overall, the mothers used a fairly wide range of semantic categories in both samples, and differences in frequency were quite stable. Brown's (1973) prevalent semantic relations accounted for around 70% of the multiterm utterances that were categorized. Retherford et al. argue against the fine-tuning hypothesis and suggest that the relative frequency of the different semantic roles in the mothers' speech, and presumably the children's speech as they became more similar to their mothers, is determined by pragmatic factors to do with the here-and-now topics of conversation and the redundancy of certain roles in dyadic interaction. The effects of pragmatic factors on the frequency of semantic relations is considered in section 4.8.

There are many differences between the studies of Van der Geest et al. and Retherford et al. that could account for the discrepancy in their results; not the least being the difference in languages studied, differences in the semantic notions scored and in the way the data were analyzed. Thus it is fairly well established that mothers' speech to young children is to a large degree limited to the objects and events of the ongoing interaction, tends to maintain the topic of conversation (especially to linguistically less developed children), and in that sense provides an input that could enhance learning of the way the language encodes different semantic relations. What remains unresolved is the extent to which particular simplifications in the input do or do not facilitate acquisition of those semantic and syntactic forms. Finally, the way in which such pragmatic factors as the topic of conversation and the desire to communicate effectively control the relative frequency of different semantic and syntactic features in mother-child conversations also needs further specification.

4.6. *Typical Errors*

The most obvious error in Stage I speech is the omission of elements that are obligatory in adult language, either entire constituents of the sentence or grammatical morphemes that modulate its meaning. The gradual acquisition of grammatical morphemes like articles, inflections, and prepositions is the topic of the next major section of the chapter. Here it will suffice to note Brown's (1973) characterization of the ",'telegraphic" look of early utterances. In English, as well as in German, Finnish, and Hebrew (Brown, 1973), the morphemes left out in Stage I are primarily those that have little phonetic substance (i.e. are non-syllabic and/or unstressed) and do not encode primary semantic relations. Slobin's (1973,1985) "operating principles" supplement Brown's characterization by specifying processing variables that contribute to the early or late emergence of grammatical morphemes in many different languages.

Several explanations have been proposed for the omission of major constituents like agent, action, or object. The least interesting case is when the child does not know the lexical item needed to express one of the semantic roles; however, many times the child possesses the requisite vocabulary but still deletes constituents. The question that arises in these cases is to what extent the missing element should be represented in the proposition underlying the child's utterance (whether that is conceived of as a semantic I-marker or an abstract syntactic deep structure). The question is posed most forcefully by replacement sequences— successive two- and three-word utterances in which all the elements of an agent-action-object sentence are expressed, but never all in a single utterance. For example, Bloom (1970) notes the sequence:

Lois read.
Read book.
Lois book.

This leads her to suggest that all the obligatory constituents are present in the deep structure of the sentence, but because of cognitive processing limitations the child often cannot express them all in one utterance. One or more constituents is automatically deleted in production. Several factors that plausibly increase information processing load seem to increase the likelihood that an element is deleted. The addition of negation is one such factor, and Bloom reports the following sequence from Kathryn:

> Me like coffee.
> Daddy like coffee.
> Lois no coffee.

Other factors are the use of two-part verbs like *turn on* and *take off*, the addition of modifiers to the object noun phrase (e.g. *Drive blue car*), or the use of words that the child has just acquired, especially new verbs or pronouns. Use of articles or verb inflections did not seem to make constituent omissions more likely.

Other theorists (e.g. Antinucci & Parisi, 1973; Greenfield & Smith, 1976; and Parisi, 1974) do not accept Bloom's notion of underlying syntactic deep structures and deletion transformations, but they too argue that the child intends to communicate an entire proposition. Thus, an elaborate semantic structure underlies both one- and two-word utterances, but it is not fully expressed because of cognitive limitations. Those elements that are semantically most informative are the ones produced, while elements that are more redundant in context are omitted. For example, when it is obvious that the child herself is the agent of an action on an object, the agent will frequently not be specified.

Brown (1973) offers a complementary explanation. He suggests that the Stage I child may consider all sentence constituents to be optional, not in the strictly syntactic sense that prepositional phrases or adverbial modifiers are optional elements in predicate noun phrases, but in the sense that elliptical utterances are allowed in discourse. He points out that parental speech models many non-sentence fragments that are usually well-formed constituents of sentences. For example, rules of ellipsis allow answers to Wh-questions to specify just the constituent being queried,

> What did the boy do?   Hit the dog.
> Who hit the dog?   The boy did.

Parents also often repeat a final constituent or some other element of a sentence to get the child to respond or to emphasize what is being communicated, e.g.

> Give me the red truck. The red truck.
> Give it to me. That truck.

In addition, imperatives in which the subject is understood (e.g. *Go to your room*) and truncated yes-no question forms like *Want your juice?* are quite frequent in the input to the child. Finally, Maratos (1984) notes that in declarative sentences in English it is acceptable to delete the object for some verbs but not others. Thus,

He ate something.——He ate.

but not,

He made something.——He made.

So the child must know which verbs must take objects and which need not.

Brown argues that the child may develop the impression that ellipsis is more freely allowed than it is, that a full sentence or any part of it can be produced in discourse. The child has to learn when more of the sentence must be expressed in order to communicate effectively, as well as when it is not optional to delete elements even though communication would not be impaired.

However, Maratsos points out that Brown's theory about the optionality of constituent elements must be supplemented by some specification of which elements are pragmatically more important to the child if it is to account for the pattern of deletions in Stage I speech. All constitutents are not deleted equally often; in particular, deletion of the verb is relatively rare. Of the children in Brown's (1973) sample, only Eve showed an equal frequency of agent-action, action-object, and agent-object utterances; agent-object utterances did not appear in either Adam or Sarah in Stage I. Bloom et al. (1975) also recorded agent-object sequences in only two of their four subjects. For some children agent-action predominate (e.g. Kendall (Bowerman, 1973) for others action-object strings are most frequent (e.g. Adam (Brown, 1973)). (Individual differences and pragmatic factors are discussed in more detail in later sections.)

Another error in Stage I speech that has been much discussed is the use of incorrect word order, primarily because of its apparent rarity. As we outlined on p. 28, English has a normal SVO (agent-action-object) order, and Brown (1973) remarks that "in all the samples of Stage I English listed in Table 9 (some 17 samples from 12 children) the violations of normal order order are triflingly few" (p. 189, emphasis added). Many researchers have therefore used word order as a cue to the intended semantic relations in a rich interpretation of early multiword utterances. Stage I children do seem to adopt fairly consistent word order to express most semantic relations, even when English does allow some variation in the ordering of semantic roles, for example in the case of possessor and possessed, or attribute and object (Braine, 1976). But it is questionable whether many of the variations in word order that do appear in early utterances should be considered as "errors" since English does allow alternative orders. It is rare that an appropriate English gloss cannot be derived for a child's two-word utterance, regardless of the ordering of the words. Nevertheless, some variation in the word order of early utterances has been reported, especially in the early stages of the emergence of a semantic relation. Braine (1976) referred to "groping patterns" of variable word order before the child fixed on a consistent ordering to express a semantic notion. Thus Gregory produced *Gregory fix it* and *Fix it Gregory; Fall down rabbit* and *Rabbit fall down*. And for many weeks Bowerman's daughter Eva observed consistent subject-verb and possessor-possessed ordering only when *I* was the subject and *my* was the possessor. Other possessives and agent-object relations occurred in variable order.

English-speaking children may differ from each other in the prevalence of variable word order in their speech. Ramer (1976) found that the three children in her study who acquired syntax more slowly made almost no errors in word order, but the four faster developing children used odd word order in 3 to 4% of their multiword utterances. She suggested that the faster developing children were more likely to experiment and take risks before they were sure of a rule (see p. 64 for further discussion of Ramer's study and her hypothesis about styles of syntax acquisition).

A third kind of error that shows up in early syntactic development involves inappropriate segmentation of the input so that functors are incorporated into the word that precedes them. Common examples are the presence of *-a* or *-s* in words like *this-a, have-a, get-a, that's* or *it's*. Sometimes the chunks are larger, adding a neutral pronoun like *it* to a verb; as in *get-it* or *have-it*. They reveal themselves as "prefabricated routines" (Brown, 1973) rather than productive uses when utterances like *This-a Bonnie pants, Have-a pants, Mommy get-it ladder, Have-it juice,* and *It's went* appear. R. Clark (1974) reports quite substantial segments of previous parental utterances being produced as unanalyzed wholes by a child. Many examples of rote-learned routines are discussed by MacWhinney (1982,1985).

4.7. Individual Differences

Many researchers have commented on the presence of semantically limited pivot patterns in the early multiword utterances of some children, but other children do not seem to produce as many of them. In accounting for this discrepancy, Bloom (1973) contrasts two approaches to the acquisition of syntax—a "pivotal" approach and a "categorical" approach. Most of the early two-word utterances of children who adopt the pivotal strategy use a small set of words that express a constant functional relationship to the words they combine with. Examples of these include *more* + *X* to express recurrence, *my* + *X* to encode possession, and *this* + *X* to draw attention to an object. Children who adopt a categorical strategy, on the other hand, produce sentences in which the grammatical or semantic relations between the words do not depend on the lexical items used. Thus a noun like *Mommy* may not only enter into an AGENT + ACTION relation but also be used as a possessor in a POSSESSOR + POSSESSED pattern. Bloom et al. (1975) expanded on Bloom's original observation by noting that Peter and Eric, children who initially followed the pivotal strategy, also used pronouns and other proforms in place of nouns to express semantic roles. Although they knew many of the names of the objects or people referred to, and used those words in single word utterances, in word combinations they tended to us *it, this one* or *that* for patients, *my* for possession, and *here* or *there* for location. They concluded that the grammar the two boys were learning "consisted of relations between different verb forms and a number of constant functional forms" (p. 19). When later semantic relations entered into their speech, they began with the same approach as they had for earlier relations, using proforms to combine with content words. In contrast, Gia and Kathryn followed the categorical strategy, and their early sentences contained far fewer pronouns. Semantic roles in their speech were filled by different nouns. Over a period of some months the two groups of children began to look more alike, until at an MLU of about 2.5 morphemes their expression of the major semantic relations was very similar. Bloom et al. proposed that "children can break into the adult linguistic code in one of (at least) two ways: with a system of formal markers, or with a system of rules for deriving grammatical categories" (p. 35).

Nelson (1975) also found that some children used few pronouns in their early constructions, while others used more of a balance of nouns and pronouns. She traced this to differences in their approach to the language in the one-word stage. Children whom she classified as "referential"—because names for objects predominated in their early vocabulary—used a much higher proportion of nouns than pronouns in early multiword utterances. "Expressive" children, so termed because their early vocabulary was made up primarily of verbs and social-expressive words like *hi, more, allgone,* used a more evenly balanced proportion of nouns and pronouns in word combinations. Unlike Bloom et al., Nelson did not observe children whose early constructions were marked by almost exclusive use of proforms in major semantic roles, possibly because she averaged pronoun usage across her groups of children and possibly because some of her speech samples were close to the MLU of 2.5 by which Bloom et al. reported the disappearance of differences in pronoun use (Bowerman, 1978).

Both of these studies tried to classify children into one of two major types of developmental pattern. Nelson clearly regarded them as points along a continuum, but Bloom et al. went so far as to suggest that the children "were learning two different systems of semantic-syntactic structure that were virtually mutually exclusive in the beginning" (p. 20). In a review of Bloom et al. (1975), Maratsos (1975) argues that by mid-Stage I there is evidence for no more than a preference for pronoun use rather than the exclusive use of one system over another. At MLU 1.69 Eric used pronouns for patients 32 times (e.g. *Get it*) and nouns 33 times (*Get ball*). By comparison Kathryn at MLU 1.89 used 81 nouns and 41 pronouns for patients. Maratsos concluded that when pronoun use was really dominant in Eric's and Peter's speech the relevant semantic relations were marginally productive. Bowerman's (1978) study of her own daughter Eva emphasizes the difficulty in characterizing different developmental strategies. Eva was classified as a "referential" speaker on the basis of her first 50 vocabulary items. However, like the "expressive" speakers in Nelson's study she used a pivotal strategy in her early two-word utterances, with many semantically limited formulae like *want + X*, *more + X*, and *here + X*, but she did not later depend on pronominal forms in fixed syntactic frames. At 18 months almost all VERB + OBJECT constructions used nouns as objects, with *it* only beginning to substitute for nouns around 20 months; but SUBJECT + VERB and possessive constructions used both nouns and pronouns as soon as they appeared at around 19 months. The exclusivity of Bloom et al.'s strategies is therefore questionable, though they may capture a dimension along which children differ.

Another possible dimension underlying individual differences was described by Ramer (1976). She followed seven children from when they began to combine words until 20% of their multiword utterances were subject-verb-complement constructions. The children were divided into slower learners (the three boys) and faster learners (the four girls) on the basis of how many months it took from the onset of word combinations until the 20% subject-verb-complement criterion was reached. The slower learners took from 6½ to 9 months, the faster learners took 1½ to 4½ months, so none of the children were particularly slow learners. The syntactic development of the two groups of children differed in several notable respects. Slower learners used many more dummy forms like *a + N*, reduplications of the same word, or combinations of meaningful words with empty forms for which no lexical meaning could be established. They also acquired VERB + COMPLEMENT constructions well before SUBJECT + VERB and SUBJECT + COMPLEMENT forms. For the faster learners all three of these grammatical relations seemed to be productive from the beginning. Finally, the faster learners were freer with their use of word order, with three to four percent of their utterances deviating from the expected English order. Deviations from expected word order almost never occurred in the slower learners. Ramer suggests that the variability in word order represents a greater predilection on the part of the faster learners to take risks with syntactic rules they had not yet completely mastered.

Though speculative, such a difference in cognitive (or personality?) style is an interesting notion. What is needed is more detailed (and longer) study of individual children in order to establish if such a tendency is found in a particular child's acquisition of several syntactic rules, or in other domains besides language acquisition. From a grand sample size of one we can report that our own son showed very systematic errors in several aspects of language acquisition— from overextensions in early word use, the creation of expected but unacceptable verb forms (*ham* from *hammer* and *hoove* from *hoover*, after the model of *mow* from *mower* and *run* from *runner*) and inappropriate causatives (*He fell me down*), to very persistent use of overregularized *-ed* past tenses.

Thus while individual children may differ in their reliance on pivot patterns for their initial two-word utterances, in the proportion of nouns and pronouns that they use, and in the variability of their word order, a great deal more work is needed to establish the existence or absence of consistent or coherent styles of language acquisition.

4.8. Pragmatics

Most of the research on the relationship between pragmatic factors and early language acquisition has concentrated on prelinguistic interaction and the emergence of words (e.g. Bruner, 1975,1977; Bates, 1976; Bates et al., 1977,1979). But some writers have noted effects of pragmatic considerations on the prevalence of different semantic notions in two-word utterances and on the ordering or differential stress of elements in those utterances. For example, the context in which the conversation takes place is going to influence the frequency of particular relations. The mother of Brown's subject Sarah spent a great deal of time naming or eliciting names for objects from her child. Sarah therefore shows relatively frequent use of forms expressing nomination (Brown, 1973). Lieven (1978) reports that one of her children seemed preoccupied with attracting her mother's attention, so notice, nomination, and recurrence were frequent semantic notions; the other child was much more concerned with exploring the environment and produced far more utterances encoding locative action or attribution. Children in constant interaction with siblings of a similar age are likely to dwell on possession (see Schaerlaekens (1973) for a study of Dutch triplets). Finally, even very rare semantic notions can be increased dramatically in frequency in an appropriate pragmatic context—for example, increases in reference to created objects where children are playing with play-dough (Retherford et al., 1981). However, while these observations suggest that the relative frequency of semantic notions in conversation varies with pragmatic constraints, they do not show that pragmatic factors affect the order of emergence of those notions in children's speech.

Bates and MacWhinney (1982) provide a detailed analysis of the relationship between the topic-comment function in language and grammatical devices like surface subject positioning, pronominalization, ellipsis, and prosodic stress. Selection of topics and comments depends on such factors as the givenness or newness of information (topics tend to be given information and comments provide new information, though the correlation is not exact), and the salience of different elements of the proposition. In spontaneous speech and elicited production (picture description) studies in which given and new information was manipulated, MacWhinney and Bates (1978) investigated the use of word order and other syntactic devices to mark topic and comment in Italian, Hungarian, and English-speaking children. Though Italian children began by placing comments ("new" information) in initial position, most English children at the corresponding stage of development seemed to place agents or actors (Brown, 1973) at the beginning of agent-action strings regardless of pragmatic role. The English children initially used contrastive stress to mark new information (Wieman, 1976), and ellipsis and pronominalization were used to indicate given information (MacWhinney & Bates, 1978)

Nelson (1978) has suggested that individual differences in children's initial orientation to the communicative functions of language may also have implications for the pragmatic uses of early two- and three-word utterances. She analyzed the first ten multiterm utterances recorded from two children, one of whom had been categorized as extremely referential (object oriented) and the other of whom was categorized as extremely expressive (a social, interpersonal orientation) on the basis of early vocabulary. In terms of Halliday's (1975) functional categories, the early constructions of the referential child were primarily available for mathetic (or ideational) functions of speech, those related to learning, knowing and informing. The expressive child's utterances were primarily pragmatic and interpersonal in function, regulating social interaction between the interlocutors. The expressive child also seemed to have a wider variety of semantic relations available for expression. Hence the communicative context in which the child's early language is acquired and possible cognitive or personality characteristics of the child and parents may also influence the pattern of acquisition.

5. Grammatical Morphemes

5.1. Brown's Fourteen Morphemes

In the period when MLU is between 2.0 and 2.5 (Brown's Stage II) another major syntactic development begins. Function words and inflections that do not seem to have independent meaning on their own but in Brown's felicitous phrase "modulate" the meaning of the utterance now begin to appear. These include a few prepositions, articles, plural and possessive inflections on nouns, inflections marking progressive, past, and third person present on the verb, and the occasional copula form of *be*. In Brown's (1973) words, "All these, like an intricate sort of ivy, begin to grow up between and upon the major construction blocks, the nouns and verbs, to which Stage I is largely limited" (p. 289). Brown points out that they only "sprout" in Stage II, however, and the acquisition of many of them is not complete by Stage V, when MLU exceeds 4.0 morphemes.

Brown chose to focus on 14 grammatical morphemes for which obligatory contexts could be identified, that is, contexts in which the morpheme would be obligatory for an adult speaking English. These were the present progressive inflection -*ing;* the third person singular, regular -*s* and irregular (e.g. *has*); past tense, both regular -*ed* and irregular (e.g. *went* or *fell*); the copula and auxiliary *be;* two noun inflections, the regular plural and possessive -*s;* and two prepositions, *in* and *on*. Most of these are quite frequent in adult English and appear in a variety of lexical or syntactic settings (the exceptions being the irregular forms of the past and third person present that must be learned by rote).

The obligatory contexts for each morpheme were identified on the basis of the linguistic context, both the child's utterance itself and the preceding or following adult utterances, or the non-linguistic context. Thus a linguistic obligatory context for the plural could be a sentence in which a plural quantifier was used, "two——" or "some——"; or one in which the number of the subject constrained the number of the predicate, "Those are——." A non-linguistic context that required a plural noun might consist of the child requesting items that normally occur in the plural, e.g. shoes, or referring to a set of identical objects, e.g. blocks. Occasionally it is impossible to tell which morpheme is missing, especially when the child uses unmarked verbs, but these cases were infrequent in Brown's longitudinal sample (1973) and de Villiers and de Villiers cross-sectional sample (1973b), and very few data had to be discarded. The use of obligatory contexts has obvious advantages over simply scoring the frequency or point of first (or fifth, or whatever number) use of a morpheme. Since the morpheme is required by the grammar, its presence or absence indicates what the child is able to say rather than what he chooses to say. Topic of conversation affects the frequency of contexts, but not the accuracy of supplying the morphemes. Brown took as his criterion for acquisition the presence of a morpheme in 90% of its obligatory contexts in three successive 2-hour-long speech samples from a child, the samples being collected approximately bi-weekly.

Two major findings emerged from Brown's longitudinal study of Adam, Eve, and Sarah. First, the morphemes were gradually acquired. Even in the same linguistic context they did not rapidly go from never being supplied to always being supplied. For some morphemes, the time from first appearance to 90% accuracy was as long as a year.

Second, although there was some individual variation in the chronological rate of acquisition of particular morphemes, the overall order of acquisition of the morphemes was remarkably similar across the three children.

5.2. *Order of Acquisition*

Brown ranked the morphemes in the order in which they reached the 90% criterion (the first of the three successive samples) for each child. Morphemes that had not reached 90% accuracy by Stage V for a particular child were ranked in terms of the accuracy with which they were supplied at that point. The rank order correlation between orders of acquisition for Adam and Sarah was +.88, between Adam and Eve +.86, and between Eve and Sarah +.87. The average rank-ordering is given in Table 1.3. A very similar order of acquisition was reported by de Villiers and de Villiers in their cross-sectional study of the same morphemes. Whether the morphemes were ranked according to the lowest MLU sample at which each of them first appeared in 90% or more obligatory contexts

TABLE 1.3
Rank Order Correlation
Between Orders of Acquisition

The 14 Grammatical Morphemes	Average Order of Acquisition from Brown (1973)	Order of Acquisition from de Villiers and de Villiers (1973b) (Method I)
Present Progressive	1	2
on	2.5	2
in	2.5	4
Plural	4	2
Past Irregular	5	5
Possessive	6	7
Uncontractible Copula	7	12
Articles	8	6
Past Regular	9	10.5
Third Person Regular	10	10.5
Third Person Irregular	11	8.5
Uncontractible Auxiliary	12	14
Contractible Copula	13	8.5
Contractible Auxiliary	14	13

(Method I), or in terms of the average accuracy of each morpheme across all of the children (Method II), the resulting ordering was highly correlated with Brown's mean ranking (Rho = + .84 with Method I and + .78 with Method II).

Brown explored several possible determinants of the order of acquisition. First, differences among the allomorphs of some inflections are found in elicited production studies with older children (e.g. Berko, 1958; Bryant & Anisfeld, 1969). One class of allomorph is governed by a simple phonological rule of voicing assimilation: the voiceless allomorph is attached to a stem with a voiceless terminal consonant (e.g. *bik-biks*) and the voiced allomorph is attached to a voiced terminal consonant (e.g. *wug-wugs*). Allomorphs following this rule are significantly easier for children on elicited production tasks than other allomorphs. A second class of stems ending in /l/, /m/, /n/, /r/, or any vowel, requires the voiced allomorph but Brown argues that the rule is not a phonological necessity since there are English words with voiceless terminal consonants following the same stems (e.g. *her-hers*, but see *hearse*). These allomorphs are in turn supplied more readily by children than the third class of stems, those ending in the same consonant as the inflection, or a closely similar one. This type of stem requires a vowel, /ɨ/, before the voiced allomorph (e.g. *gutch-gutches*). Brown did not score allomorphs of morphemes separately because of insufficient frequency in some cases and uncertain transcription in others. But phonological factors cannot be a major determinant of the ordering of the 14 morphemes as a group. The plural, possessive, third person present singular, and some forms of the contractible copula and auxiliary *be* share the same phonological form, but they are mastered at very different times.

Two different factors were highly correlated with the order of acquisition. Brown calculated the syntactic complexity of the morphemes (with the exception of the possessive) in terms of the number of transformations involved in their derivation in a representative transformational grammar of English (Jacobs & Rosenbaum, 1968). He also considered several authors' characterizations of the meanings of the morphemes and determined the number of unitary meanings involved in their correct use by the children. Rank order correlations between syntactic and semantic complexity and the orders of acquisition determined by Brown and de Villiers and de Villiers were over +.8. However, assessing complexity in terms of the sheer number of transformations or dimensions of meaning involved in a morpheme's use is a dubious procedure since it presumes that each transformation or meaning adds a constant amount of complexity. Brown therefore suggested that cumulative complexity be used as an index of grammatical or semantic difficulty. In this metric a construction involving rule X would be easier than one involving X + Y, which would in turn be simpler than one involving X + Y + Z. The predictions made by partially ordering the morphemes on the basis of cumulative syntactic and semantic complexity were confirmed in both studies.

The major discrepancy between the two studies was in the order of acquisition of the contractible and uncontractible forms of the copula and auxiliary. Brown found the uncontractible forms were better supplied than their contractible equivalents by all of these children. In our study we generally found the opposite, although only the copula forms could be compared within children since none of the subjects reached a sampling criterion of five or more contexts for both the contractible and uncontractible auxiliary. Kuczaj (1979) suggested that the difference could result from the relative frequency of yes/no questions versus wh-questions and declaratives in the samples from the two studies. In his own study Kuczaj found no reliable difference in order of acquisition of the two forms, but uncontractible forms of *be* were more consistently supplied in some linguistic contexts than in others.

5.3. *Cognitive Complexity*

Brown (1973) and de Villiers and de Villiers (1973) concluded that the relative contributions of syntactic and semantic complexity could not be teased apart, since the two variables made almost identical predictions. Using a more sophisiticated multiple regression procedure, Block and Kessell (1980) discovered that each of the variables accounted for a significant percentage of the variance in the order of acquisition of the morphemes when it was entered into the regression analysis first. However, adding the other variable did not add significantly to the variance accounted for. A commonality analysis revealed that most of the variance was common to both syntax and semantics, and each alone accounted for very little extra variance. They suggest that this is because a single factor under-lies both syntactic and semantic complexity, namely cognitive complexity. As Pinker (1981) has pointed out, however, the postulation of such a third underly-ing factor, while not forbidden by their analysis, is by no means implied by it either, especially since they give no good ancillary arguments as to how such a factor should be characterized. Indeed, they conclude that there are ''a number of ways to define the underlying construct implied by this reanalysis. In terms of Piagetian sensorimotor intelligence as developed by Bates (1976); in terms of communicative functions and speech acts as developed by Bruner (1975) and Dore (1975); in terms of cognitive and perceptual strategies as developed by Clark (1977); and so on'' (p. 188). But Block and Kessell give no indication of how the different morphemes could be characterized according to any of these approaches. Finally, we might add that an account in terms of cognitive com-plexity, as distinct from the semantic complexity described by Brown, might be expected to predict the order of emergence of obligatory contexts, i.e. reference to the notions underlying the morpheme, rather than the syntactic realization of these notions in English. Crosslinguistic studies of the acquisition of inflections and other grammatical morphemes are more likely to reveal the factors that determine an order of acquisition (see Johnston & Slobin (1979) for an analysis of the linguistic and conceptual factors that contribute to the order of acquisition of locative expressions in English, Italian, Serbo-Croatian and Turkish).

5.4. *Relation to Input*

Brown calculated the relative frequency of the 14 morphemes in the speech of the parents to their children immediately preceding Stage III. The rank orders of the frequencies were very similar across the three parental pairs, suggesting that this frequency profile was quite stable. However, when the average order of acquisition was correlated with their average order of frequency in the parental input, rho was calculated as +.26, a nonsignificant value. From this general analysis and more specific analyses of prepositional phrases and allomorphs of the contractible copula, Brown concludes that the frequency of the morphemes in the input to the child is not a significant determinant of the order of acquisition.

More recently, however, a couple of studies have claimed to find effects of input frequency on use of some of the morphemes. Newport et al. (1975) found that the children of parents who used frequent deictic expressions like ''That's a dog'' tended to produce more plural inflections per noun phrase. But they scored changes in the frequency of the inflections, not their presence and absence in obligatory contexts.

Moerk (1980) reanalyzed some of Brown's data. He criticized Brown's use of a single parental frequency profile taken some months or years before the chil-dren mastered many of the morphemes. He argued that the input frequencies for particular morphemes may change even within a single recording session and are bound to change over a period of months as the child matures. Furthermore, the effect of the input may depend on the child's cognitive and linguistic level. Therefore, Moerk selected out just those morphemes acquired during Stage II for Adam and Sarah and Stages II and III for Eve (because she went through the stages so quickly). These morphemes were acquired relatively soon after the parental sample was taken. He was left with the present progressive, *in, on,* and the plural for Adam; with the same four plus the possessive and past irregular for Sarah; and with those four plus the possessive and past regular for Eve. For each child he correlated the approximate age (in months) at which the morphemes reached the 90% criterion with the absolute frequency of those morphemes in their respective parents' speech. For all three children Moerk reported sizable negative correlations (Pearson's r) between input frequency and the age at which a morpheme was mastered. They varied from −.56 for Adam to −.76 for Eve. Although none of these correlations were significant with an N as small as four or six, Moerk was impressed by the size of the effects and the agreement across children. Sarah was slower than the other two children in acquiring the morphemes, and her parents also used them relatively less frequently in speech to her. Moerk found a substantial correlation between how impoverished Sarah's input was with respect to particular morphemes and how far she was behind the other two children (in months) in acquiring them. Finally, Moerk noted that the frequency with which Eve used particular prepositional phrases with *in* was related to their frequency in her parents' speech. He concluded that the relationship between input frequency and the acquisition of the grammatical morphemes is worth another look, and that Brown was wrong when he dismissed it as an insignificant variable.

Moerk's reanalysis of Brown's data has been strongly criticized by Pinker (1981). In our view Pinker's most effective arguments concern the selection of the morphemes that were correlated with parental frequency. In particular, Moerk leaves out the irregular past tense that was acquired by Sarah in Stage II – "Since it appears in many and widely differing forms" (p. 109) and presumably each form has to be learned by rote. But if it is included, the correlation between frequency and Sarah's order of acquisition drops from −.66 to −.48, and the percentage of variance accounted for decreases from 43% to 23%. Similarly, Moerk included two constructions acquired in Stage III by Eve on the grounds that she passed through the stages faster than the other children, but Pinker notes that if the correlation used only morphemes acquired in Stage II, the percentage of the variance accounted for drops from 57% to 9%. We think Moerk's reasons for including and excluding morphemes are plausible, but the extent to which the correlations change is alarming. Moerk also ends up with a rather strange subset of morphemes, two prepositions that are much more like lexical items, plus one or two noun and verb inflections. The primary reason why the overall correlation performed by Brown was nonsignificant was because the two most frequent morphemes, the articles and the contractible copula, were somewhat late acquired, the articles in the middle of the order and the copula towards the end.

These morphemes are always the most frequent in the parental input and do not change substantially in frequency between Stage II and Stage V, yet they did not enter into Moerk's correlations. There are also problems with Moerk's analysis of Sarah's comparative linguistic deprivation and her relative delay in acquiring those morphemes. Although Adam and Eve's inputs are the most similar in frequency, with several morphemes actually being more frequent in the input to Adam, Adam was much more like Sarah in his rate of acquisition of the morphemes than he was like Eve. He varied from 9 to 15 months behind Eve in mastering the morphemes, but only 4 to 6 months ahead of Sarah. If Sarah's slower development is tied to the input frequency, what do we make of Adam's delay relative to Eve? Finally, Moerk and Pinker differ on the significance of the data on the acquisition of *in* (see also Moerk's [1981] reply to Pinker). Moerk made much of the difference in frequency of the phrases *in a minute* and *in a while* in Eve's speech. Despite their semantic similarity, *in a minute* appeared frequently in both the input and Eve's speech; *in a while* was modeled by the parents only once in the early samples and on the few occasions on which Eve produced it, the *in* was missing. Pinker noted that frequent *in* phrases like *in a minute* may have been learned as idiomatic routines. Furthermore, 19 phrases with *in* were used correctly by Eve even though they never appeared in any sample of the input and were presumably rare.

However, there are other suggestive data on input frequency and the order of acquisition of a linguistic subset of Brown's morphemes. Moerk cites a study by Forner (1977) that found extremely high correlations between the order of acquisition of bound morphemes and their frequency in parental speech. Table 1.4 shows this pattern for the five bound noun and verb inflections. It also gives the rank order correlations relating each child's order of mastery of these morphemes with the ranked input frequency. The concordance (Kendall's W) between the children on order of acquisition is .89 (p < .01); between the parents on ranked frequency of use it is .82 (p < .025). Finally, the average ranked frequency of the morphemes in the input correlates almost perfectly with the average order of acquisition across the three children in Brown's study (Rho = +.90, p < .05), as well as with the acquisition order of these morphemes in de Villiers and de Villiers' (1973) cross-sectional study (Rho = +.975, p < .05).

It is interesting to note that Brown's measure of cumulative syntactic complexity makes no predictions about the order of acquisition of these forms (only four of them are represented in the Jacobs and Rosenbaum grammar). Cumulative semantic complexity only orders the third person regular, predicting that it should follow the plural and the past regular—the first of these predictions is supported, the second is not for Adam and Sarah. Moerk suggests that the bound morphemes add semantic information, but the auxiliary and copula forms of *be,* and the articles, for which input frequency seems to have no effect, add only minimal information. But this is questionable, especially for the articles. A far more likely explanation of the later acquisition of articles concerns their

TABLE 1.4
Pattern for the Five Bound Noun and Verb Inflections

Adam		Sarah		Eve	
Morphemes in Order of Acquisition	Parental Frequency	Morphemes in Order of Acquisition	Parental Frequency	Morphemes in Order of Acquisition	Parental Frequency
Present Progressive	65 (1)	Plural	57 (1)	Present Progressive	67 (1)
Plural	57 (2)	Present Progressive	28 (2)	{ Plural	33 (2)
Possessive	25 (4.5)	Possessive	16 (4)	{ Possessive	30 (3)
3rd person regular	25 (4.5)	3rd person regular	19 (3)	Past regular	7 (4.5)
Past regular	28 (3)	Past regular	9 (5)	3rd person regular	7 (4.5)
Rho = +.675 (n.s.)		Rho = +.90 (p < .05)		Rho = +.95 (p < .05)	

cognitive complexity since they require some appreciation of the knowledge of the listener (Maratsos, 1976). In short, Brown dismissed parental input as a major variable determining the acquisition of the grammatical morphemes, but for at least some classes of morphemes that seems to have been premature. (See also p. 74 for an inverse relationship between the input frequency of different irregular verbs and the likelihood that they will be regularized by preschoolers.)

5.5. Typical Errors

The prototypical error in the acquisition of English inflections is the over-regularization of plurals and past tenses. In each case, when the regular inflection begins to be mastered it is overgeneralized to irregular forms, resulting in errors like *foots, sheeps, goed,* and *eated* (Brown, 1973; Cazden, 1968; Ervin, 1964; Kuczaj, 1977; Slobin, 1971). In the case of the past tense, children usually begin by correctly using a few irregular forms like *fell* and *broke,* perhaps because these forms are frequent in the input and the child learns them by rote. At first they may not be fully analyzed in the sense of being syntactically related to their corresponding generic forms (Kuczaj, 1977). But as soon as the child begins to produce regular past tense endings, they apply that form more widely than they should, and irregular forms that were previously correctly produced may now be regularized (e.g. *falled* and *breaked*). Ervin (1964) and Slobin (1971) even report cases in which forms like *comed, buyed,* and *doed* appeared before any correct regular past tenses were produced. Two kinds of past-tense overgeneralization errors are observed: one in which the *-ed* ending is attached to the generic form of the irregular verb (e.g. *eat—eated*), and another in which it is added to the irregular past form of the verb (e.g. *went—wented*). Kuczaj (1977, 1978a) showed that there are age differences in the relative frequency of the two types of errors, with the double-marked past generally being more common and judged acceptable in older children (around 5 years old). He suggests that the difference reflects an increasing emphasis on syntactic regularity as the child gets older, so that the child will add the regular past marker even to verbs he has analyzed as expressing earlierness.

Slobin (1971,1973) made the strong prediction that overgeneralized past tenses for a time completely replace irregular pasts. This was derived from an operating principle stating that there is a universal preference not to mark a semantic category by a zero morpheme. However, Kuczaj (1977) reports that some children produce forms such as *goed, went,* and *wented* at the same point in development. And some children do not overgeneralize the *-ed* ending to all irregular verbs. Of the 14 children in Kuczaj's cross-sectional sample, eight never applied *-ed* to irregular verbs like *hit* and *cut* that have the same present and past form, even though they had many opportunities to do so. Thus overgeneralization does not seem to be an all-or-none process at any point in development.

Frequency of usage in the input to the child appears to be an important determinant of which irregular verbs will be overregularized. In an analysis of past-tense overregularization errors in several sets of spontaneous speech samples from preschool children, Bybee and Slobin (1982) found a significant negative rank order correlation $(-.67)$ between the number of times the adult caregivers used irregular verb forms and the number of times those forms were overregularized by the children. This finding is in keeping with the notion that the irregular forms must in large part be learned by rote from the input.

Finally, Slobin (1971) suggested that irregular verbs in which there is a systematic phonological change relating the generic to the past tense form (e.g. *lose—lost; make-made*) will be more resistant to overgeneralization since they are partially regular. Other irregular verbs that either make a dramatic change (e.g. *go—went*), change only the internal vowel (e.g. *bite—bit; fall—fell*), or make no change at all (e.g. *hurt—hurt; hit—hit*) will be much more susceptible to the addition of *-ed.* Kuczaj did find that overgeneralizations were most likely to occur with verbs making only a vowel change, but for many children verbs that do not change at all were least likely to be overgeneralized.

Recently, Bybee and Slobin (1982) have suggested that in addition to the rote-learning of irregular past-tense forms, young children form phonological generalizations or schemas about them. These are not strictly phonological rules that relate base to derived forms, but are somewhat looser statement about similarities between the phonological properties of past tenses that help in organizing and accessing the lexicon. An example of such a schema would be the statement that past-tense verbs typically end in [t] or [d]. In a sentence-completion task that elicited past-tense forms, Bybee and Slobin observed that preschoolers systematically failed to add the regular *-ed* suffix to verbs already ending in [t] or [d], even if they were regular verbs like *melt* or *pat.* The application of such a schema about past tense ending in [t] or [d] accounts for Kuczaj's (1977, 1978a) finding that verbs that do not change at all in the past tense are most resistant to overregularization, since those verbs end in [t] or [d]. Verbs making only a vowel change typically do not end in [t] or [d], so are much more likely to be overregularized. The preschoolers thus seem to be working with both a regular suffixation rule to form the past tense and a schema for the phonological properties of past forms. Similar observations were made by Berko (1958) for both plural and past-tense formations in her elicited production tasks. Preschoolers and first-grade children rarely added the plural suffix to nonsense syllable names ending in silibants, perhaps because these forms fit a schema about the phonological properties of plurals.

The child's problem in mastering the past tense seems to be in relating the present and past forms of an irregular verb to each other, and in learning that the irregular past is the only past tense form for that verb (Kuczaj, 1977,1981). Even when the child seems to understand that a verb like *went* is used only in the past, he may also produce *goed* as the past for *go,* and even *wented* as an overmarked past. The learning process is complicated by the fact that parents rarely correct ungrammatical past tenses so the child has to learn from the mismatch between his own production and the speech of the adults he hears, a still more difficult task as his peers are also overgeneralizing the regular past tense. Furthermore, the child has to learn the relation between irregular pasts and their generic forms in a rather piecemeal fashion, since there are few regularities, so overgeneralization errors with -*ed* only, disappear over a period of years.

5.6. *Relation to Semantics*

Two interesting interactions between semantics and the acquisition of morphemes have recently been proposed. Leonard (1976) scored the first emergence of the articles, copula and present progressive in utterances expressing different underlying semantic notions. The articles, which can appear in the widest range of semantic relations, were first provided in utterances reflecting Leonard's earlier emerging group of semantic notions (cf. Table 1.2). Similar findings (though with a much smaller number of observations) were noted for the copula and progressive. The copula tended to appear first in utterances expressing nomination, negation and recurrence, rather than in utterances expressing later-emerging semantic notions like attribution, location, or possessor. The present progressive emerged in utterances expressing agents and actions before it was supplied in EXPERIENCER + EXPERIENCE or instrumental semantic relations. These results are in keeping with the notion that there is less processing-load in earlier-acquired semantic relations, allowing the child to apply a new morphological rule. Unfortunately, Leonard recorded first emergence of the morphemes rather than percent supplied in obligatory contexts, so his findings are confounded by the much greater frequency of the earlier emerging semantic notions. It would be interesting to examine the types of semantic relations in which the morphemes were first reliably supplied.

Bloom, Lifter and Hafitz (1980) studied four verb inflections—present progressive, third person singular, and regular and irregular past tense—as they emerged in obligatory contexts in the speech of four children observed longitudinally. They found that the early usage of the inflections was dependent on the semantics of the verbs to which they were attached. The progressive -*ing* was correctly supplied most often with action verbs that have continuous duration and no clear result, e.g. *singing*. The past tense was used initially to inflect actions that are punctual and have a clear end result, e.g. *closed*. And the third person occurred most reliably with verbs indicating the placement of an object, e.g. *fits, sits* or *goes*. Since Bloom et al. scored accuracy in obligatory contexts, this result was independent of the sheer frequency of the morphemes or contexts—at the same time as a past tense was supplied for a verb like *eat* or *close*, it would be omitted in an obligatory context with a verb like *sing* or *walk*. Bloom et al. argue from this finding that the inflections mark aspect rather than tense when they first emerge. Progressive -*ing* marks imperfective action or duration of an activity; the past tense marks perfective or punctate action.

Bronckart and Sinclair (1973) made a similar, but even stronger claim about the present and past tense in French-speaking children. They had their subjects describe different events enacted in front of them. Long duration events with no clear conclusion tended to be described in the present. Shorter, perfective actions were described in the past tense. Bronckart and Sinclair conclude that the past encodes aspect rather than temporal earlierness until the child is 6 years old. However, Smith (1980) analyzed samples of spontaneous speech (the children from Brown, 1973 and Kuczaj, 1978b), and repeated Bronckart and Sinclair's experiment with English-speaking children. She found that even the youngest children (MLU 2.94, age 29 months) used the past tense for verbs with both perfective and imperfective aspect.

The children in the study of Bloom et al. (1980) were still far short of Brown's criterion for mastery of the morphemes. Even in the most advanced stage of development that was examined (MLU 2.5–3.0), the morphemes as a set were only supplied in an average of 54% of the obligatory contexts, and three of the four children had very little use of the regular past. Thus, the use of the past tense to mark perfective aspect may be a short-lived phenomenon. For example, at the time Kuczaj's son Abe was 31 months old (MLU 3.5), Smith (1980) found that between 25 and 40% of his use of the regular past was on imperfective verbs, even though he was not yet supplying the -*ed* inflection in 90% of obligatory contexts. Further research needs to explore how the inflections spread across verb types as the child approaches consistent use of morphemes.

At a later point in the acquisition of the regular past, when the child begins to overgeneralize the use of -*ed*, it seems to be applied across all verb types, and the child ignores some semantic distinctions that he clearly makes with respect to other inflections. Children acquiring American English do not generalize the use of the progressive -*ing* inflection from action or process verbs like *hit* or *break* to state verbs like *want, think,* and *know* (Brown, 1973; Kuczaj, 1981). In the input they receive -*ing* only occurs on action and process verbs. In their over-generalizations of -*ed* to irregular verbs, however, errors like *knowed, thinked,* and *seed* are as common as forms like *runned* or *breaked*. Nor is it the case that overgeneralizations of *-ed* begin with action verbs and then spread to state verbs (Maratsos, Kuczaj, Fox & Chalkley, 1979).

Thus, children observe semantic restrictions on inflection use at certain periods of time and for particular inflections, but at other times there appear to be no semantic limitations. The manner in which those semantic restrictions are loosened must still be specified.

6. Modalities of the Simple Sentence

6.1. Auxiliaries

Fletcher (1979) provides a useful discussion of the knowledge an English-speaking child must acquire of the auxiliary system. There are many forms of the auxiliary, they must appear in certain positions relative to one another, and there are restrictions on co-occurrence. Chomsky's phrase structure rule (1957) was:

Aux→Tense (modal) (have+en) (be+ing).

The three areas of meaning expressed in the verb phrase are time, aspect, and mood, though many of the forms are plurifunctional, e.g. past-tense forms can refer to unreal events, as in the conditional. Even for declaratives, then, the auxiliary system presents some complexity to the language learner, and data concerning that development will be reviewed before turning to the modalities of the simple sentence.

6.1.1. *Course of acquisition.*   Fletcher (1979) uses Leopold's diary data from Hildegard to describe the acquisition of the verb phrase. Her first auxiliaries were *won't* and *can't,* at the age of 2;0–2;2 years. She did not have the positive auxiliaries *will* or *can* in her speech at that time. About a month later, she acquired *will* in yes-no questions and responses to them, but never used the contracted form *'ll*. Klima and Bellugi (1966) report a similar phenomenon: although the mothers of their three subjects used the contracted form *'ll* almost always, the children used *will* (see also Kuczaj & Maratsos (1975)). Hildegard used *will* in sentences not dependent on a question within about one more month, at 2;4. She also acquired *I may* at that time. By 2;5, she was using the progressive form *be+ing* but it was "variable in use," and the details of that acquisition have already been discussed (Brown, 1973; see page 68). At 2;6, Hildegard used *will* to refer to future, along with the expression *going to*. Late acquisitions were the modals *should, would,* and *could,* and the perfect forms with *have* (see also Cromer, 1968). Hildegard seems to have been a rapid learner, but the overall course of her development concurs with other accounts.

Kuczaj and Maratsos (1975) used elicited imitation to explore one child's knowledge of the auxiliary system before he used it productively in spontaneous speech. Among other sentences, Abe was given declaratives to imitate that were either correct, or ungrammatical in one of two ways: the aux was misplaced, e.g.

The slow turtle wash did his dirty hands.

or a tensed verb followed the aux, e.g.

The monkey's mommy will yelled at the lion.

Abe's imitations showed a sensitivity to the rules of aux placement although his spontaneous speech showed no auxiliary use. For instance, he imitated 38/48 of grammatical declaratives correctly, failing primarily on sentences with unstressed positive *do*. With misplaced auxiliaries, he either deleted the aux or put it in the correct sentence position (but never with *do*). With tensed verbs, he either de-tensed the verb or deleted the aux, both of which would result in a grammatical sentence.

Before producing auxiliaries in spontaneous speech, Abe seemed to know that modal auxiliaries (except unstressed *do*) could occur before the main verb in declaratives, and that the main verb must not be tensed. At this point, Abe did not know how to imitate yes/no questions correctly. It is interesting that two months later, when he did show some ability to imitate aux in yes/no questions, he also began using auxiliaries in his spontaneous declaratives.

Elicited imitation may thus reveal knowledge that is not expressed in spontaneous speech, but it is not a technique that is equally informative with all children (Bloom, 1974). Comprehension studies of auxiliary use hold little promise, however, so the information base is not likely to become richer.

6.1.2. *Typical Errors.*   Errors in auxiliary use seem surprisingly rare. One would expect children not to know co-occurrence restrictions, and so produce:

He must will go.

Or, the affixes might not be properly attached to the preceding aux, so one should hear:

He have going.
or
He will eaten it.

Tense could be attached to the main verb rather than the first aux, so the child should produce:

He does ate it.

When double or triple auxs are produced, they could be scrambled:

He have been might going there.

These errors are not commonly observed, however. One that has been reported is overmarking, e.g.

I did broke it.
I did rode my bike.
Jenni did left with Daddy.

(all from Mayer, Erreich, & Valian, 1978). The researchers argue that the error results when the child copies the tense marker to its correct position following the main verb, but fails to delete it from its original position in the aux. A stranded tense marker normally triggers *do*-insertion, and so the child ends up with two tensed morphemes. The account rests on the assumption that the transformation of tense-hopping is composed of two "basic operations"—copying and deletion. Mayer et al. argue that the child misformulated the rule as consisting only of tense-copying, hence generating the errors. They make a similar claim about errors found in aux-inversions, to be discussed later under "questions." Maratsos and Kuczaj (1978) argue against the transformational account, pointing out that many other errors of this type should occur but do not. The overmarking error occurred in their subjects primarily with *do,* and only in cases with a main verb. One would expect to find mistakes such as:

He did could have it.

but no-one has reported them. Maratsos and Kuczaj contend that the error occurs because children have not worked out when *do*-support is necessary. They also report the overmarking in negative utterances such as:

It didn't broke.

and

It didn't disappeared.

yet these are not readily explained by the basic operations hypothesis. A further possibility that they raise is that the error is more likely with irregular past tenses, which may more closely resemble unmarked verbs or be misanalyzed as such by the child. Further data on overmarking errors are needed to decide among the alternative accounts, but the error does not seem to be a typical one, or to be as prevalent within the grammar of a child who does produce these errors, as one would expect from the basic operations hypothesis.

6.1.3.   *Relation to Input.*   The child's acquisition of the auxiliary system seems to be one development in which input variation makes a difference. Three different studies have found an impressive correlation between the mother's use of auxiliaries and the child's rate of development in auxiliaries per verb phrase. Newport et al. (1977) found that the number of yes/no questions asked of 15 1- and 2-year-olds by their mothers predicted the children's change in auxiliary use 6 months later. They argue that the salient initial position of the auxiliary draws the child's attention to the form. In the only convergence between the two studies, Furrow et al. (1979) also found a correlation of similar magnitude (+.85) between mother's overall use of yes/no questions to seven children of MLU 1.0, and the children's own auxiliary use at 2;3 years. Unfortunately the convergence is less evident upon closer inspection. In Furrow et al.'s study, the mother's use of initial auxiliaries in yes/no questions did not correlate significantly with aux development in the child. Use of "other" yes/no questions was the variable resulting in the high correlation, and the majority of these contained no auxiliary! Furrow et al. argue that a mother who uses both regular yes/no questions and these other forms that contain no auxiliary but have the same intonation, e.g.

You want to go home?

causes the child to correctly analyze the auxiliary when it is present. In both studies, however, a high use of imperatives was negatively correlated with auxiliary growth. Possibly, then, it is the optionality of the initial auxiliary, not its overall frequency, that enhances the child's understanding of the forms.

Nelson (1982) also found mothers who used verbs rich in auxiliaries to their 22-month-olds had children who advanced rapidly in auxiliary use from 22 to 27 months (r = +.52). Even more impressive was that the mother's initial use was not at all tied to the child's use at 22 months (r = −.03). Newport et al. (1977) however, found no significant relation between overall use of auxiliaries by the mother and children's rate of auxiliary development. Hence in finer detail, the studies are not in close agreement.

6.2. Negatives

6.2.1. *Course of Acquisition.*   Following detailed analysis of the negative sentences produced by Adam, Eve and Sarah, Bellugi (1967) described the stages of development of negative syntax. These stages, she argued, followed the stages in the linguistic derivation of a negative sentence (Klima, 1964). The grammar postulated an initial stage when the deep structure of a negative sentence consisted of a negative marker external to the sentence, and the earliest multiword utterances of children seemed to be simple propositions preceded or followed by *no* or *not*.

In the second derivational step, the negative marker was placed adjacent to the verb stem, and in the second stage of negative development (MLU 2.8 to 3.0) the three children used four negative elements internal to the sentence: *no, not, can't,* and *don't.* Since the positive auxiliaries *can* and *do* did not appear at this point, Bellugi argued that *can't* and *don't* were unanalyzed wholes.

Affixing the negative element to the appropriate auxiliary verb would be the third derivational stage, and the children next acquired a range of auxiliaries and their negative counterparts, between MLU 3.4 and 3.9. Most of the elementary syntax was then mastered, though it took many more months or even years to master the correct use of double negatives, and indefinites, such as *not-any* or *no-one.*

Maratsos and Kuczaj (1976) looked at one further aspect of negative auxiliaries: do young children perceive the contracted *n't* form as equivalent to *not*? They used an imitation task to elicit production of double and triple auxiliary sentences with various placements of *not* and *n't* in the models, e.g.

The dog would have not been barking.

Little consistency was observed across children, but individual children were quite consistent. For instance, two children consistently placed *not* before the verb and after all auxiliaries, yet the same children correctly imitated *n't* on the first auxiliary. Such observations suggest that children may believe the two forms have different privileges of occurrence, which is true in adult speech. Data from Kuczaj's own son Abe, similarly suggest that children may not relate AUX + *not* to AUX + *n't.* Abe followed his parents' practice in showing an overwhelming preference for *don't* over *do not,* and *can't* over *cannot.* However with the auxiliary *be,* though the parents again preferred the contracted form *isn't,* Abe at an early stage preferred the full form such as *is not.* Maratsos and Kuczaj propose that *not* is learned as an early negative for various constituents: adjectives, NPs, and progressive VPs, which all can take *be* before them. When the child learns to produce *be* in such sentences, the full negative marker *not* may be retained.

6.2.2. *Typical Errors.*   Much subsequent work on the development of negation has focused on Bellugi's first stage, in which the child produces negatives external to the sentence. McNeill (1970) surveyed data from a number of languages, and concluded that this was a first step not just in English, but universally. Other investigators have searched for an alternative account, or questioned the existence of such a stage. Bloom (1970) pointed out that the critical data came from sentences in which the subject is expressed, e.g.

No the sun shining.   (Adam)(= 'The sun's not shining.')
Not Fraser read it.   (Eve)(= "Fraser mustn't read it.")

If the subject is not expressed, then it is not clear that the subject has been "deleted" from the left or the right of the negative morpheme, e.g.

? not ? hold it.

In her own longitudinal study, Bloom (1970) identified a small number of sentences with subject expressed, but in every case the negative morpheme was anaphoric, i.e. referring back to an earlier utterance rather than negating the proposition to which it was attached, e.g.

No mommy do it. (meaning: 'No, let Mommy do it'.)

Wode (1977) proposed that anaphoric negatives of that sort might provide the false analogy for the child to produce nonanaphoric negatives external to the sentence. However his data from English are anecdotal, and the stages he describes for German are refuted by Park (1979).

We reanalyzed the early negatives of Adam, Eve, and Sarah, and agreed that very few critical examples existed in which the negative element was nonanaphoric, and the subject was expressed (de Villiers & de Villiers, 1979). Our motivation for the reanalysis derived from observation of our son, Nicholas, who produced plenty of examples of the critical sentences between 23 and 29 months. Clearly then, the initial-*no* negatives do not seem to constitute a universal first step, but individual children may adopt such a strategy. Before turning to an account of these individual differences, it may be useful to consider the range of meanings that are expressed via negative sentences.

6.2.3. *Relation to Semantics.*   Actually, in the case of negation it seems especially difficult to determine what falls in the domain of "semantics" and what constitutes "pragmatics." The negative meanings that have been described by McNeill (1968) and Bloom (1970), may also be classified as illocutionary forces, that is, the functions that the utterances serve. Bloom's major categories are:

1. nonexistence: where the child expects something but does not see it. For instance, a child might look at a place setting and say "no fork."
2. rejection: the child opposes some action, event or object that is either present, proposed or imminent. For instance, the child says "no brush!" to a mother approaching with a hairbrush.
3. denial: the child negates the truth of a proposition uttered by someone, e.g. "I am not a baby" in response to "You're a baby."

Pea (1979) adds others such as "self-prohibition" and "unfulfilled expectation," as do Bloom and Lahey (1978).

In terms of the interaction between syntactic development and the semantics of negation, Bloom (1970) found that sentences indicating nonexistence appeared before those expressing rejection, with denial last to appear in sentences. Furthermore, when auxiliaries began to appear, variation in auxiliary forms appeared in sentences expressing nonexistence before it occurred in sentences expressing rejection (Bloom & Lahey, 1978).

6.2.4. *Individual Differences.*   We have reported individual differences concerning the frequency with which various negative functions were expressed in sentences. For instance, Nicholas had a clear preference for the expression of rejection, by a stereotyped and primitive form, namely *no + S*. However, he produced rarer but well-formed expressions of denial during the same time period, with correctly placed negatives. Hence his initial-*no* sentences were reserved for a limited function. Eve showed a similar pattern: her initial-*no* sentences were primarily for rejection. In contrast Adam used *don't* for rejection: a form not used by Eve or Nicholas during the early period.

6.2.5. *Relation to Input.*   The source of individual differences in negative use can be traced to the input the children received. For example, Adam's mother used *don't* in her rejection negatives, and sentences with an initial *no* were predominantly used for denial. Adam's speech showed the same pattern. Eve's mother and Nicholas' parents used initial-*no* sentences for rejection, usually an initial emphatic *no*, followed by a polite negative, such as:

No, I don't think you should do that.

Very rarely did they use *don't* imperatives for rejection, paralleling the children's use. Eve, and especially Nicholas, seem to have learned the initial *no* as a convenient way to express rejection, but not denial. Interestingly, the patterns of anaphoric negation revealed a similar parallelism: Adam's mother used anaphoric negatives to deny an earlier statement, as did Adam; Eve's mother used anaphoric negatives to reject actions, as did Eve (de Villiers & de Villiers, 1979).

Maratsos and Kuczaj (1976) also reported close matching to the input use of *not* and *n't* by Abe, except in the case of the verb *be*. Finally, Pea (1979) traced idiosyncratic forms of his subjects to particular parental forms, e.g. *mustn't bite* used by one child in self-prohibition.

Maratsos and Kuczaj found double auxiliaries very rare in the input to Abe, and always with the contracted negative. As usual, it is difficult to imagine how children master the more complex aspects of syntax given the rarity of the crucial examples.

6.2.6. *Relation to Cognition.*   Pea (1979) analyzed the three major functions of negation—rejection, nonexistence and truth-functional (denial) negation—in terms of their cognitive complexity. According to Pea, rejection should be the simplest, since it expresses the child's emotional attitudes towards something present in the context, hence no internal representation is required. Nonexistence does require internal representation since the object is not present to the child's sense experience but expected given the context. Truth-functional negation needs internal representation of a proposition, hence it is even more cognitively complex. Bloom (1970) and Pea (1979) found single-word expressions of rejections to come in first, then nonexistence, with denial expressed last. However the evidence that this order is recapitulated as the first sentences emerge, is equivocal (see p. 83).

6.2.7. *Pragmatics.*   As mentioned earlier, the distinction between semantics and pragmatics is difficult to make for negation, but there are some phenomena that appear to fall clearly in the traditional concern of pragmatics. For instance, take the effect of contextual factors on denial. Adults find it relatively easy to process the affirmatives concerning an object, e.g. "This is an apple." They are slower, but still accurate, with a false affirmative, e.g. "This is a pear." The false negative "This is not an apple" takes a little longer, but the true negative "This is not a pear" is the most difficult of all. Hence there is a reliable interaction between truth/falsity and affirmation/negation, that has been found also in children (e.g. Kim, 1980). The phenomenon has been accounted for in a variety of ways, including a logical processing model by Clark and Chase (1972). Nevertheless, Wason (1972) has a convincing argument that the use of a negative requires a plausible context: there has to be some reason for someone to believe the opposite, or the felicity conditions are not met. In the above situation, the listener is shocked by the true negative, as were the preschool children in Kim's study: it might be true, but one wouldn't say it.

Naturalistic speech is a poor domain for investigating children's knowledge of felicity conditions for negation, but Antinucci and Volterra (1973) argue that early denials are in keeping with the constraint on plausibility. de Villiers and Tager-Flusberg (1975) adapted Wason's (1965) experimental task for use with young children, and provided evidence of enhanced production of true denials under conditions of plausibility, albeit in a very limited domain. Their subjects viewed arrays of seven objects, six of which were alike and the seventh was different. The children could much more easily complete the statement "This is not . . ." about the odd item, than about one of the identical items. Hence even for 2-year-olds, contextual factors influence the difficulty of negative sentences.

6.3. Questions

6.3.1. *Course of Acquisition.*   Questions in English involve three linguistic devices: rising intonation, inversion of the usual order of subject and auxiliary, and initial placement of the wh-word. Rising intonation seems to be the earliest device used by children, but there may be individual differences in this regard (for review, see de Villiers & de Villiers, 1978; Crystal, 1978).

Klima and Bellugi (1966) undertook the first systematic study of interrogative syntax in the speech of Adam, Eve and Sarah. At an average MLU of 1.75, the three children marked yes/no questions with rising intonation, but had no auxiliary verbs at that time. Wh-questions in this period consisted of routines such as:

What's that?
Where (NP) go?

and

What (NP) doing?

More complex questions were not comprehended. In the second period, when the children averaged 2.75 in MLU, they understood more wh-questions and more variants appeared in their own speech, suggesting that they understood that the wh-word stood in place of a specific sentence constituent. By the third period (MLU 3.5), auxiliary verbs were produced, and correctly placed in initial position in yes/no questions. However wh-questions retained the subject-aux order of declaratives. Hence the children produced correct forms such as:

Does the kitty stand up?

at the same time as errors on wh-questions, e.g.

Why kitty can't stand up?

The discrepancy was accounted for by a theory of transformational complexity: wh-questions involved a second transformation of wh-fronting, and it was theorized that the children had some limit on the number of transformations they could use in one sentence. Several subsequent studies have questioned the generality of this finding, and the debate will be discussed under "typical errors" below.

A second theoretical debate concerns the nature of the child's formulation of the category "auxiliary." That is, do children regard all auxiliaries as one general class, with equivalent privileges of occurrence? If so, one might expect the initial auxiliaries of yes/no questions to be as varied as the auxiliaries in declaratives, once the child has discovered how to form yes/no questions. If, however, the child has not discovered the general category, auxiliary placement in yes/no questions might be acquired in a piecemeal fashion. Unfortunately the data are not convincingly in favor of either alternative. Kuczaj and Maratsos (1983) collected longitudinal data on two children: Abe and his younger brother Ben, as well as cross-sectional samples from 14 other children. A variety of initial auxiliaries emerged simultaneously rather than piecemeal, but two auxiliaries—*haven't* and *couldn't*—were used several months in declaratives before appearing in yes/no questions. Furthermore, if children are using the declarative contexts of auxiliaries to predict which elements can occur in initial position in yes/no questions, Kuczaj and Maratsos argue that they should make certain errors, e.g. produce

Better you go?

if they say,

You better go.

No such overgeneralizations were observed. Children appear to have a representation of auxiliaries as a class, but it is one that fails to include certain members (e.g. *haven't, couldn't*) at the same time as it correctly excludes other words (e.g. *better*). However to be certain, it would be necessary to have evidence that the excluded forms did appear in questions but not in the correct place. Having established that the opportunity occurred, arguments about incomplete scope of the auxiliary rule would be on firmer ground.

A clearer example of piecemeal acquisition of a rule concerning auxiliaries was reported by Kuczaj and Brannick (1979). Using imitation and judgment tasks, they assessed young children's knowledge of the rule of auxiliary placement in different types of wh-questions. They discovered that the auxiliary placement rule was acquired at different points for different wh-questions, rather than being an across-the-board rule. Labov and Labov (1978) reported the same phenomenon: wh-words for their subject influenced the correct placement of the auxiliary in the order: *how, which, who, where, what, when,* and *why*. Unfortunately there is little consistency across studies in this ordering (Erreich, 1980). Erreich's subjects also had different rates of correct auxiliary placement, but in her study the order of difficulty was: most often correct with *which(one), who, what,* and *where*; less often correct with *how, why,* and *when*. Erreich also argues against Kuczaj and Brannick's view that the rule is a piecemeal one, despite these equivalent data. Instead, she believes the rule has been formulated in abstract terms, e.g. referring to the category of wh-words and auxiliaries, but the child has not yet learned the membership of the category. On either account, the child has some reason for caution, since the phrase *how come* is an exception to the general rule in that the auxiliary remains in declarative position:

How come you didn't go?

Kuczaj and Brannick nevertheless found some children in their tasks overgeneralized the inverted auxiliary to *how come* questions, but the prevalence of that error in spontaneous speech has not been established. If children do over-generalize to the exceptional case, the notion that they are piecing the rule (or category membership) together from positive evidence is not well supported.

The final issue about question acquisition that has attracted the attention of researchers concerns the development of the wh-forms themselves. Many studies have reported consistency in the order of wh-question emergence, among the first being Ervin-Tripp (1970) using a comprehension study. Wooten, Merkin, Hood, and Bloom (1979) described the sequence of spontaneous speech acquisition in seven subjects studied longitudinally. The earlier appearing forms were *what, where,* and *who,* but *why, how* and *when* were later to emerge. Wooten et al. point to a possible linguistic difference between the early and late forms. The early forms are wh-pronominals, that request information about major sentence constituents: noun phrases and prepositional phrases. In contrast, they argue, *why, how,* and *when* question the semantic relations in the sentence as a whole, they are wh-sententials that do not simply stand for a missing constituent. For this reason, the child might not be able to produce them until later. Wooten et al. found that when the wh-sententials did emerge, they appeared in more complex constructions than *what, where,* and *who.* The latter tended to occur with verb proforms of very general character, such as *do* or *go* or *be.* Although the distinction between wh-pronominals and wh-sententials has intuitive appeal, it runs counter to traditional accounts (e.g. Brown, 1973) that describe wh-questions all as replacing sentence constituents, and in particular the distinction between *where* and *when* is difficult to recognize since both could replace prepositional phrases:

Where did you go?　　To the shop.
When did you leave?　After dinner.

However it is clear that there is some interaction between the wh-words and sentence complexity that deserves further exploration.

Other researchers have analyzed the order in which wh-questions are understood. The structure of the questions and the transitivity of the verb are both influences on the comprehension of wh-questions (Cairns & Hsu, 1978; Tyack & Ingram, 1977), as well as the semantics of the verb (Winzemer, 1981). Hence the order of difficulty of wh-questions varies across studies of comprehension, but is still in keeping with the order of emergence in spontaneous speech. The relative contributions of cognitive complexity, structural variables and semantic factors in the verb, will be discussed further in the material to follow.

6.3.2. *Typical Errors.* Klima and Bellugi (1966) reported the existence of a stage during which children inverted auxiliaries in yes/no questions, but failed to invert in wh-questions. Three other studies have failed to identify such a stage. Hecht and Morse (1974) looked at inversion rates for the two types of questions in spontaneous speech samples from 12 children at the same age (30 months) but varying widely in linguistic development. No child had a higher rate of inversion for yes/no questions than for wh-questions. Ingram and Tyack (1979) analyzed samples of questions recorded by parents from 21 children aged between 2 and 4 years. Again, rates of inversion were equivalent at all stages of development. The most complete study of this phenomenon was performed by Erreich (1980). Eighteen subjects ranging in MLU from 2.66 to 4.26 provided spontaneous questions and questions elicited by the experimenter over a series of sessions. For ten of the children, the rate of inversion was equal for wh- and yes/no questions. Five other children presented an unexpected pattern: a higher rate of inversion in wh-questions than in yes/no questions!

Therefore, the hypothesis that children are more likely to invert the auxiliary in a yes/no question than in a wh-question, does not seem well-supported. Only one study, using elicited imitation, confirmed the original finding (Kuczaj & Maratsos, 1975) but only with a single child. Furthermore, the experimental task may have biased the child: half of the models for wh-questions contained uninverted auxiliaries, but none of the models for yes/no questions contained uninverted auxiliaries (see de Villiers, 1984).

Overmarking errors have also been reported in yes/no questions by Hurford (1975). His subject produced sentences such as:

Did you came home?
What's that is?

One explanation offered is that the first aux element has been copied to the initial position, but not deleted from its original declarative position. Once again, such errors have been held as evidence for the basic operations hypothesis (Valian et al., 1981). However Maratsos and Kuczaj (1978) did not find them to be frequent in their data, and favor a processing account of the error.

6.3.3. *Individual Differences.*   Evidently, individual variation is the rule in the development of interrogative syntax. The rate of inversion in yes/no versus wh-questions is different across individuals (Erreich, 1980; Tyack & Ingram, 1977). In addition the wh-words that have the most correct auxiliary placement vary across subjects (Labov & Labov, 1978; Erreich, 1980; Kuczaj & Brannick, 1979). Unfortunately no research has explored the reasons for these individual differences either in the input the children receive, or by exploring the functions of the forms, their relative frequency of use by individuals, and such factors as the productivity of the different questions with different verbs or subjects. All of these factors might be influences on the course of individual acquisition patterns in interrogative syntax, just as they are in other areas of grammar (e.g. negation, see p. 83).

6.3.4. *Relation to Cognition.*   The reason most often given for the order of emergence of the wh-forms is that they vary in cognitive complexity, since *why* and *how* questions encode more abstract ideas than questions such as *what* or *who* (Ervin-Tripp, 1970). Wooten et al. (1979) argue that cognitive complexity is but one variable in the order of emergence, and perhaps not so important as linguistic factors. For example, Lightbown (1978) demonstrated that second-language learners of English acquire wh-questions in the same order as first language learners, even though they are cognitively more advanced and have sufficient conceptual ability to ask the questions in their first language. Secondly, Wooten et al. point out that the conceptual notions held to cause difficulty, such as time and causality, were encoded in other linguistic devices such as connectives (Bloom et al., 1980) at an earlier point. It is therefore the linguistic complexity of the question forms, not just the concepts they encode, that delays their appearance in spontaneous speech.

Yet children may use questions spontaneously before they understand their meaning. Blank (1975) discusses the special nature of *why* questions, which encode a complex of abstract notions of natural laws, human motivation and logical reasoning that a young child could not possibly grasp. She provides anecdotes from the spontaneous speech of a young child, Dusty, who follows the common practice of asking a great many *why* questions, many of which have no sensible interpretation, e.g.

Adult   "That's the garage door."
Dusty   "Why the garage door?"

Blank argues that it is only by engaging in a great deal of discourse involving *why* questions and their answers, that the child can unravel the meanings that *why* encodes and begin to determine the circumstances under which the question becomes appropriate.

Given all of these convincing linguistic and cognitive complexity arguments for the piecemeal emergence of wh-questions, one result in the literature becomes especially anomalous. Genie, the child who received little linguistic or cognitive stimulation before her rescue at 13 years 7 months (Curtiss, 1977) appeared able to answer all wh-questions at the same point in time. However the fact that she never produced a syntactically marked question, and the discrepancy between her responses to "real-life" versus test questions, suggest that she may have been dependent upon contextual clues rather than a true understanding of the forms.

6.3.5. *Relation to Semantics.*   With respect to a particular scene, some questions seem more plausible than others. For instance, if a picture contains a girl eating an orange, the question

What is the girl eating?

sounds more reasonable than:

Where is the girl eating?

Winzemer (1981) suggests it is in the semantics of the verb that this plausibility resides. Her model proposes that verbs have certain implied constituents as components of their meaning, e.g. *eat* has an object as an expected constituent, but not a location. *Drive,* however, has a location as an expected constituent. If children know these properties of verbs, then questions that ask for expected constituents would be easier than questions that ask for an unexpected constituent. Her prediction was confirmed with preschool children, who often made the error of answering an unexpected question with the expected component. In a picture-cued comprehension test, verb choice could have a significant impact on question difficulty. In real life discourse however, there may be cues other than the verb semantics to the meaning of a question.

6.3.6. *Interaction with Pragmatics.*   The functions served by interrogative forms in English are numerous, and several writers have developed classification schemes for them. Holzman (1972) analyzed the functions of questions in the speech of Adam, Eve, and Sarah and their mothers, and found five broad categories:

1. requests for information
2. requests for behavior
3. "test" questions for which the speaker already knows the answer
4. interrogatives such as *what* to indicate a lack of understanding
5. other purposes, such as threats or suggestions, e.g. "What do you keep asking me for?"

Shatz (1979) identified 11 categories of interrogative function in parental speech, including challenge, calling attention to something, and a variety of conversational fillers. Despite the fine categorization, she found coder agreement to be around 80%.

In terms of children's use, Griffiths (1979) argues that the early-appearing functions are requests for actions and object, and calling attention. True requests for information may come in relatively late in the one- or two-word period. Holzman's results indicate that children with an MLU of 3.0 use many but not all of the major functions of the interrogative, including questions serving as requests for information, indicating a lack of understanding, and suggestions for behavior. Two of the children also used test questions, though Sarah did not. At this stage they did not use interrogative forms as requests for behavior or as negative evaluations of another person's behavior. Garvey (1975) found requests expressed indirectly as interrogatives in dyads of 4- and 5-year-old children. Furthermore, the forms reflected the variety found in adult discourse: they questioned

ability: Can you hold this?
desires: Do you want to catch me?
future actions: Will you get me one?
reasons: Why don't you hold it?

just as described for adult polite requests (e.g. Searle, 1975).

The mapping between form and function in questions is therefore particularly rich, and yet disappointingly little data exist on how individual children enter the system. The research to date has focused almost exclusively on form (e.g. Klima & Bellugi, 1966; Kuczaj & Maratsos, 1983) or on function (Holzman, 1972) in an individual's development. Do wh-question forms become immediately available for all functions, or are they tied to particular functions at the start? The limited data that have been reported suggest that at least the wh-words themselves originate in restricted interaction routines (Johnson, 1980) but little is known beyond the earlies stages.

6.3.7. *Relation to Input.*   Researchers have focused on parental speech to children to determine whether or not the input is especially revealing about the structure of questions, and arguments can be found for both positions. For instance, parents frequently omit the initial auxiliary of a yes/no question:

You want juice?

Newport et al. (1975) used this as an illustration of the problems that "motherese" presents to the language learner. As discussed earlier, Furrow et al. (1979) find a correlation between parental omission of initial auxiliary, and children's rate of auxiliary development, so they argue that the optionality draws attention to the auxiliary!

Snow (1972) found mothers made use of occasional questions—wh-forms in which the wh-word is not preposed but occupies the place of the missing constituent, e.g.

You're trying to find what?

These structures might reveal the role of the wh-word more clearly than the preposed question. Interestingly, children themselves do not seem to use occasional questions.

Shatz (1979) studied the questions that 17 mothers used with their young children during play sessions. Some of the children were linguistically advanced (three or four words per sentence), and others were less advanced (less than two words per sentence). Shatz's interest was in the stereotypicality of the questions with regard to the functions they served, to explore whether mothers used limited form-function pairings that might enhance the child's decoding of language. However the stereotypicality of the questions was defined on a group rather than an individual level: her objective was to discover form-function pairings that would facilitate understanding of language in general, not of a particular mother's speech. Shatz did find more stereotypical questions used by mothers of less linguistically advanced children, but even their speech revealed substantial variation in the forms for particular functions. Furthermore, there was only weak evidence that the children responded more successfully to characteristic pairings of form and function than to noncharacteristic pairings. The only statistically significant result was that of the mothers of less advanced children, those who tended to produce stereotyped "test" questions, had children who understood them readily. Presumably these questions developed as routines between particular mother and child pairs (see Snow, 1977). Data from Holzman (1972) confirm Shatz's claim that questions even to young children serve many distinct functions. Bellinger (1979), however, describes parents' increasing use of interrogative forms rather than imperative forms serving as directives as children increase in age, suggesting that parents may diversify the use of interrogative forms as their children mature.

Nevertheless, Shatz (1978b) has demonstrated that even 2-year-olds will respond appropriately to requests veiled as questions, such as "Can you shut the door?" Children do not seem to process the form as a question, then reason that it must have an indirect meaning (e.g. Clark & Lucy, 1975). Rather, Shatz proposed that they respond with action whenever they can, and often overgeneralize this strategy in responding with action to real questions such as:

Do you brush your teeth?

7. Dative and Passive

7.1. Parallel Concerns

There are parallel concerns for research on the dative and passive constructions in child speech, and before considering each type it might be helpful to point to those issues:

1. English-speaking children develop a heuristic of sentence interpretation based on the canonical sentence order of S-V-O found in English declaratives. In the dative and passive constructions, such a strategy could lead the child astray when there are no semantic clues to interpretation, e.g.

The boy gave the dog the duck.
The boy was kissed by the girl.

When do these strategies come into play?

2. Both the passive and the dative constructions have been argued to be lexical rules rather than syntactic rules, with the possibilities of transformations or alternative phrase structures coded directly with the verbs in the lexicon (Bresnan, 1978). There are restrictions for both constructions on the verbs that can occur in them, for instance, there is no passive equivalent of

> The bottle contained shampoo.
> cf * Shampoo was contained by the bottle.

and there is no transformed dative of

> The man announced the winner to the crowd.
> cf * The man announced the crowd the winner.

Hence, as Baker (1979) has argued, perhaps the child should be cautious about generalizing either the passive or the dative to verbs without positive evidence from the input that they can appear in those forms. How specific or general is the child's formulation of the dative and passive rules?

3. For both construction types, there are biases in the frequency of use in the language, possibly reflecting the *a priori* likelihood of agents being animate, and of recipients being animate. Hence the models that the child receives are not semantically neutral, but could be given an alternative, semantic description. These biased sentences can be readily interpreted by the child because they do not depend upon his knowing the syntax, only the likelihood of certain events in the world.

So for instance,

> John gave Mary the book.

has only one plausible reading, as does

> The car was driven by the girl.

Hence children's early understanding of these constructions may not be syntactically based. How prevalent and how lasting are these semantic biases?

7.2. Datives

7.2.1. *Order of Acquisition.* Roeper, Lapointe, Bing and Tavakolian (1981) and Osgood and Zehler (1981) confirmed earlier reports (e.g. Fraser, Bellugi & Brown, 1963) that the transformed dative, which violates the canonical SVO order, is more difficult for children to understand than the simple dative when no semantic supports are provided. Both studies found a prevalent error of acting out the S-V-IO-DO sentence as if it had a missing *to,* e.g. interpreting:

> The dog gave the cat the puppy.

as:

> The dog gave the cat to the puppy.

Osgood and Zehler argue that the canonical order is S-V-DO-IO in adult processing (Waryas & Stremel, 1974) and furthermore, IO-marking is more common than DO-marking in the world's languages. Verb incorporation of pronominal direct objects is also a common occurrence crosslinguistically, while virtually nonexistent for pronominal indirect objects (Sedlack, 1975).

In production, Osgood and Zehler found the basic form to be heavily preferred in their task, but the transformed version was beginning to be used by the 4- and 5-year-olds for describing selected event types. There are plenty of examples in the spontaneous speech of much younger children of transformed datives, e.g.

> Give me that.
> Show me the book.

but they may be frozen forms with particular pronominal indirect objects. The full analysis of the transformed dative may take considerably longer. It may also be important to look at a wider variety of verbs in experimental studies: both Roeper et al. and Osgood and Zehler used only the verb *give.*

7.2.2. *Relation to Input.*

No studies exist on the natural input children receive on the dative, but one study used a training technique to explicitly test the hypothesis that children should be cautious about generalizing the dative transformation in the absence of positive evidence. Wilson, Pinker, Zaenen and Lebeaux (1981) taught 4- and 5-year-olds new words for novel bitransitive actions (e.g. passing an object through a tube to a recipient). Subjects heard the word either in the basic or transformed dative construction, and they were subsequently tested on their ability to comprehend and produce both forms with the novel verb. Despite being taught the verb in the transformed version, these subjects showed virtually no production or understanding of that form. Instead, they heavily preferred the basic dative even for verbs not heard in that construction. The subjects in this age group may have had too little knowledge of the transformed dative to provide an adequate test population. Perhaps older subjects who are in control of both variants of the dative would provide a better test of the hypothesis of lexical specificity.

7.2.3. *Typical Errors.* In comprehension tests, the typical error made by young children is to rely on the canonical S-V-DO order, in the absence of semantic constraints, and hence to misinterpret the transformed dative as described earlier. For sentences with semantic constraints, children tend to rely on animacy as a clue to identify the recipient (see below under "semantics").

In production, Bowerman (1982) has reported errors made by her daughters that suggest overgeneralizations can occur in the dative, the type of error that Baker (1979) proposed would not be seen. For instance, she reports such utterances as:

She said me the answer.

occurring late in the preschool years. Errors of this sort violate the predictions made from a lexicalist position (Roeper et al., 1981) but we do not know how prevalent or long-lasting the overgeneralizations might be.

7.2.4. *Relation to Semantics.* The most thorough study to date of 3–5-year-old children's comprehension and production of both forms of the dative was conducted by Osgood and Zehler (1981). Previous research (e.g. Cromer, 1975; Fraser, Bellugi, & Brown, 1963) had suggested that the transformed dative was difficult and acquired late by children, but these investigators had carefully controlled the sentences to remove semantic clues. Osgood and Zehler employed sentences which varied semantically, including nonhuman agents/recipients and both inanimate and animate objects:

e.g. 1. Brother gives block to sister.
2. Mother gives puppy to father.
3. Dog gives ball to cat.
4. Tiger gives puppy to cat.

In addition, they had four levels of sentence complexity; e.g.

A. Mother gives the hat to the girl.
B. Father gives the hat and the book to the girl.
C. Mother gives the hat to the girl and mother gives the book to the boy.
D. Father gives the bird to the boy and then the boy gives the bird to the girl.

Osgood and Zehler argued that the semantics of the situation in (1) are prototypical transfers, and their subjects performed best in producing and comprehending datives describing such situations. Additionally, the children were best able to use the transformed dative for prototypical events. They reverted to the basic *to*-form when the semantics became less typical. Comprehension was predictably impaired for the transformed sentences with animate transfer objects, e.g.

The tiger gives the cat the puppy.

Osgood and Zehler (1981) argue that the prototypicality of the transfer events provided a support for the children's initial use of syntactic forms. "Only later does a syntactic ability that is independent of contextual support develop" (p. 381).

Roeper et al. (1981) studied older children (kindergarten, second and fourth grade) and found a similar dependence upon semantic cues in comprehension. They constructed questionnaires that counterbalanced animacy so that it could not provide a systematic cue to interpretation, but their second graders in particular relied on animacy as an indicator of the indirect objects. The kindergartners also relied on animacy in cases where the prototypical semantics was reversed, e.g.

The dog gave the spoon the cow.

hence misinterpreting those sentences more than the other varieties.

It is one thing to argue that children's comprehension of dative sentences is dependent upon the probabilities of events in the real world. Such dependence reflects a lack of understanding of the syntax, particularly of the "transformed" version. However Osgood and Zehler wish to go one step further, and to argue that children's syntactic analysis of the transformed dative is complete first for the typical events. Then, the children are able to produce transformed datives as long as the event they are describing is a typical transfer. There are two possible alternatives: one, that children's knowledge of the syntactic form is complete for different semantic domains at different times; two, that children's ability to produce/comprehend the syntactic form is subject to processing constraints, such that when semantic supports are lacking, their performance declines. These alternatives have not been well distinguished in the literature to date.

7.3. Passives

7.3.1. *Order of Acquisition.*   The course of acquisition of the passive construction is not entirely worked out, primarily because it is a rare construction in spontaneous speech even in adulthood. Truncated passives, with the agent unspecified, are much more frequent than full passives. Watt (1970) made the proposal that despite the linguistic treatment of truncated passives as deriving from full passives, in acquisition truncated passives should appear first. He argued that psychologically, truncated passives might be analogous to predicate adjectives, e.g.

He was kicked.

may be perceived as the same structure as:

He was sore.

Horgan (1978) presented evidence on the acquisition of the passive in the speech of 2- to 4-year-olds describing pictures, and argued that the truncated passive had a distinct course of acquisition from the full passive. Her evidence was that the truncated passives almost all had inanimate surface subjects, e.g.

The lamp was broken.

whereas the majority of the full passives had animate surface subjects, e.g.

The girl is chased by the boy.

Furthermore, the truncated passives had verbs such as *break* that were also used as statives; the full passives contained a wide variety of action verbs. So topics and verbs were distinct for truncated versus full passives.

The conclusion that truncated precede full passives in development is disputed by Maratsos and Abramovitch (1975) who studied comprehension of the two forms. To match the sentences on semantics, they tested comprehension of full passives with an unspecified agent, e.g.

The cow was pushed by someone.

Their preschool subjects performed equally well on truncated and full passives. It seems likely, however, that with a specified agent, children might show more errors because of the processing load. When the semantics are controlled, truncated and full passives seem to be perceived as equivalent structures. Maratsos and Abramovitch argue that truncated passives may appear earlier in samples of spontaneous speech because of their greater frequency than full passives in adult speech. They point out that for a rare construction like the full passive, the time of appearance in spontaneous samples should not be taken as the time of acquisition. Wells (1979) makes a similar point; in 18,000 utterances taken from 60 children aged 36–42 months, only 19 passive verbs were recorded. However, in elicited production also, truncated passives are more often produced than full passives (Baldie, 1976).

Knowledge of the form of the agentive *by*-phrase was also investigated by both Horgan (1978), and Maratsos and Abramovitch (1975). In Horgan's study of spontaneous speech, 75% of logical subjects were inanimate NPs for the 2- to 4-year-olds, but older children (5 to 13 years) used inanimate logical subjects less often (39.5%). It should be noted, however, that the populations were describing different picture sets.

Furthermore, individual differences were found among the 2- to 4-year-olds in the types of passives used. About half of the children used only reversible passives, such as

The cat was chased by the girl.

However most of these had the word order reversed, i.e. the picture was of the cat chasing the girl. The other children used only nonreversible passives, and then only with an instrument as the logical subject, e.g.

The lamp was broken by the ball.

No nonreversible passives with agents as logical subjects, e.g.

The lamp was broken by the girl.

appeared before 9 years. The possibility is raised by Horgan that individual children might develop the passive forms along different lines. It was only at age 11 that Horgan found the same children producing both reversible and nonreversible passives. However it is difficult to believe that this result reflects knowledge rather than encoding preferences, given the data on comprehension from preschoolers. Nevertheless the bias against having an inanimate NP chosen over an animate NP as the sentence topic seems to be a pervasive one (see also Baldie, 1976; de Villiers, 1980).

Horgan argued that the nonreversible passives might be produced by analogy to other constructions also found in the speech samples, in particular reflexives and sentences with *from*. Both constructions were used in a restricted way similar to the nonreversible passives e.g. the reflexives had inanimate nouns following *by*, as in

The ball bounced by itself.

The earliest uses of *from* were locative, or encoded non-agentive causation e.g.

Snowman is melting from the sun.

Hence for all these constructions only nonagentive causation was signaled, and the noun phrase following the preposition was inanimate. Horgan speculated that the child assumes that *by* signals nonagentive causation on analogy with the other constructions, and adds the *by*-phrase or *from*-phrase onto the truncated structure that she already uses to comment on the state of things.

Maratsos and Abramovitch (1975) add to the picture of children's syntactic knowledge of the full passive. They gave children sentences to act out that were anomalous in several ways, e.g. no *be* form:

The cat licked by the dog.

or no *by* preposition:

The cat is licked the dog.

and demonstrated that young children require both features to be present in order for the sentence to be treated as a passive. The failure when the preposition was absent also serves as a demonstration that the children were not processing the full passives simply by processing the truncated passive in the first portion. Evidently they know that a prepositional phrase should be part of the structure. Substitution of the preposition *of* for *by* resulted in the sentence being treated as a passive also, though children tended to imitate it as *from*, in keeping with Horgan's observation. However, the children did not regard a sentence with a fake preposition as a passive, e.g.

The girl was chased po the squirrel.

The subjects thus had a fairly well-defined knowledge of the permissible structure of the prepositional phrase found in the passive, and the closed class items that could appear therein.

In comprehension studies, questions about the productivity of the active-passive relation have only recently been asked. In attempts to control the semantic cues to comprehension, investigators have used reversible passive sentences, generally with two animate NP's. For both act-out and picture-cued comprehension, verbs that referred to a clear action were selected for the sentences. As a result, our knowledge of the generality of the active-passive relation was impoverished.

Maratsos et al. (1979) tested children's understanding of passive sentences with either action verbs or nonaction verbs. The latter included: *remember, forget, know, like, miss, see, hear,* and *watch.* To examine children's comprehension, they employed two different procedures with the same results. In one procedure, they told the child a sentence, e.g.

Donald was liked by Goofy.

and then asked ''Who did it?'' While recognizing the peculiarity of such a question about a nonaction, the authors argued that the question should have been equally peculiar for the equivalent active sentence, but their subjects generally answered it correctly in that case. The results revealed a clear interaction between sentence type (active versus passive) and verb type, with passive sentences containing action verbs being well understood by the 4- and 5-year-old subjects, but passives containing nonaction verbs not being understood. In a second task, the passive sentences were embedded in a story context in which answering a question e.g. ''Who really didn't like the other one?'' depended upon understanding a crucial sentence, e.g.

The cat was hated by the raccoon.

Again, the children understood the active sentences with nonaction verbs but not the corresponding passives.

Maratsos et al. argue that children of 4 and 5 years do not therefore have a full knowledge of the passive-active relation. They contend that this relationship provides one of the major reasons for positing the abstract concepts of logical subject and logical object in English, and children are not able to formulate the relation in such general terms. Rather, the learning of the passive proceeds piecemeal.

Using picture-cued comprehension, de Villiers, Phinney and Avery (1982) have confirmed that children fail to understand nonaction verb passives while they do understand both action verb passives and nonaction verb actives. However they also find that at an earlier developmental stage, the nonaction verbs are poorly understood in the active sentences. Maratsos et al. did not find this result, though they used older subjects. The significance of this finding is that the presence of nonaction verbs could increase processing load, which may not matter if the sentence is active, but might be sufficient to interfere with processing of the passive sentences by a child with only a fragile hold on the syntax. Hence it is not clear whether the results should be interpreted as piecemeal acquisition of knowledge, or as complete knowledge but a processing limitation. These alternatives are particularly difficult to distinguish in preschool children.

7.3.2. *Typical Errors.*   Bever (1970) studied the comprehension of semantically reversible and irreversible passive sentences by children between 2 and 5-years-of-age. Between 3½ and 4, with girls in advance of boys, the subjects performed at better than chance level with semantically reversible sentences. However the group of children who were slightly older showed a worse performance, systematically reversing the passive sentences with no semantic constraints, i.e. interpreting

The boy was kissed by the girl.

as:

The boy kissed the girl.

Bever suggested that these children were using a perceptual strategy by which any N-V-N sequence was treated as the active order agent-action-object. Maratsos (1975) replicated Bever's finding of a regression in performance at around 4 years, when subjects tend to reverse passives.

Strohner and Nelson (1974) failed to find evidence of an earlier stage when children perform above chance level on reversible passives. Their 2-year-olds performed at random on such sentences, their 3-year-olds tended to reverse them, using the noun-verb-noun strategy.

de Villiers and de Villiers (1973) attempted to relate the comprehension of reversible active and passive sentences to MLU rather than age. Their sample was younger, with a mean of only 26.8 months. With reversible passive sentences, the group of children in early Stage IV (MLU 3.0–3.50) showed the greatest tendency to choose the first noun as agent. Again, there was no evidence that the less advanced children were acting out passives correctly.

7.3.3. *Individual Differences.*   Bridges (1980) claimed that the grouping of children in previous studies was concealing individual response patterns to passive sentences. Her large-scale study was concerned with identifying individual response patterns to active and passive sentences in four variants of the comprehension task. In all the tasks, response patterns based on word order were infrequent (10% overall) compared to "situationally derived" strategies, for instance, where the child used the toy closest to his dominant hand to perform the action. Although Bridges' point is an important one, that "strategies" should be considered at an individual rather than at a group level, her study resulted in a rather low estimate of the prevalence of word-order strategies. Unfortunately she does not present data separated by sentence type, so active and passive sentences are considered together in the tables. The low incidence might be due to the more stringent criterion that one must apply in judging the existence of a strategy for an individual child. On the other hand, her tasks included sentences of a more homogeneous variety than other studies: the only verb studied was *push,* and all the nouns referred to toy vehicles. Possibly in this particular area, young children are responsive to more sources of contextual bias than in the usual testing situation where subjects may have little to rely on other than word order in the instructions. At present then, the prevalence of the word-order strategy is not clear.

7.3.4. *Relation to Input.*   On all estimates, the number of passives that children hear in the input is small. Brown (1973) found no full passives in the speech samples of 713 utterances from the parents of Adam, Eve and Sarah, but the children were in Stage I. Maratsos (1984) claims that passives containing action verbs are more frequent in parental speech than passives containing nonaction verbs. However, no direct study of passives in the natural input to children has been done.

Several training studies, however, have manipulated the conditions of modeling passive sentences and observed the effects on children's use of the form. Strohner and Nelson (1974) conducted an interesting training study with the passive using 100 4-year-old subjects divided into five treatment groups. Previous research (e.g. Turner & Rommetveit, 1967) had shown that if attention were drawn to the patient in an event, the possibility that a subject would employ the passive voice was increased. The function of the English passive is to highlight the patient by placing it in the salient sentence position. Strohner and

Nelson's subjects were pretested on passive comprehension, then four groups received training that consisted of presenting either a passive or an active sentence along with a picture. One passive and one active group had their attention drawn to the patient, e.g. "Look at this cat." For the other groups the actor was highlighted. The fifth group received no training. The hypothesis was that active sentences were a better match to the situation drawing attention to the actor; passive sentences were a better match when the patient was the focus of interest. After modeling 12 sentences with appropriate pictures, a comprehension posttest with novel sentences was given. The group that received passive sentences matched to an event with the patient highlighted, showed the greatest (and significant) improvement in comprehension of passives from pretest to posttest. No corresponding improvement occurred for the matched active group.

Apparently even this brief (12 sentence) exposure to passive sentences in appropriate felicity conditions was enough to decrease the 4-year-olds' dependence on an actor-action-patient strategy. Brown (1976) found a similar improvement after modeling passive sentences to children in appropriately motivated contexts in a story. Providing a suitable context for use of the passive voice by calling attention to the patient in a sentence can thus enhance children's decoding of the roles of the noun phrases in passive sentences. The standard comprehension test, in which passives are presented in inappropriate felicity conditions, may in fact underestimate what children know, and increase the likelihood of use of a processing strategy.

Two further training studies involving the passive have been concerned with the productivity of the passive rule. In opposition to the claims of Maratsos et al. (1979), Lebeaux and Pinker (1981) argued that the child's passive rule works as well for sensory predicates like *see* as it does for action predicates like *push*. Their study involved teaching a new verb to 4-year-old children, one that referred to a sensory predicate e.g. looking through a tube. They found their subjects able to use the new verb in passive sentences with no difficulty, even though they had only heard it in the active voice. Hence there was no restriction of the passive voice to action verbs, and also the subjects produced passives containing the new verb in the absence of positive evidence that it could occur in that construction. Of course, their subjects may have considered the new activity to be an action.

In the second study that examined productivity of the passive rule, de Villiers (1980) attempted to teach the passive to 3-year-old children who failed on a pretest of passive comprehension. The children heard modeled either "prototypical" passives involving an action verb and an animate patient, e.g.

The dog is being licked by the cat.

or "atypical" passives containing a nonaction verb and an inanimate patient, e.g.

The book is being read by the lion.

Passive sentences were modeled with pictures, and the child had to produce sentences about other interspersed pictures that included actions and nonactions, animate, and inanimate patients. The subjects produced few passives, but those that they did produce were "prototypical" regardless of the modeling they received. de Villiers argued that those events constituted the most appropriate conditions for use of the passive in a picture-cued task, and that the subjects came into the experiment with that bias from previous experience. However, a follow-up study (de Villiers, 1984) which elicited many more full passives failed to find an effect of differential training on the range of passive types produced by 3–and 4-year-old children.

7.3.5. *Relation to Semantics.*   Quite apart from the issue of semantic limitations on the passive rule discussed above, there is a question about the extent of children's reliance on semantic cues to comprehension. Bever (1970) reported that 2-year-olds performed at random on passive sentences even when semantic constraints were available to help them, e.g.

The dog was patted by the boy.

Bever argued that this contradicted the claim that young children rely on non-linguistic, contextual information in their decoding of language (e.g. Macnamara, 1972). In contrast, the 3-year-old subjects placed heavy reliance on the probability of the events in decoding passive sentences.

Contradicting this report, Strohner and Nelson (1974) systematically varied event probability in their stimulus sentences presented to 2- to 5-year-old children, and found even 2-year-olds relied on event probability. However Chapman (1978) argued that 2-year-olds may not know the differential likelihood of certain events, such as dogs chasing rats rather than vice-versa. Hence there may be an improvement in using event probabilities over the preschool years. By 6 years, however, children can generally use the syntactic form of the passive even when the event probability is very low, (Bever, 1970) as in

The policeman was eaten by the candy.

8. Coordination

8.1. Issues in Acquisition

Of all varieties of combining sentences together, coordination is the simplest. Yet there are rules governing coordination with *and* that involve a complex interplay of syntax, semantics and pragmatics. According to the standard transformational treatment (e.g. Harries, 1973), phrasal coordinations such as:

Bill and John loved apples.

are derived from the full sentential coordination in deep structure:

Bill loved apples and John loved apples.

If the redundant elements are deleted from the left conjunct, it is referred to as backward deletion; forward deletion occurs if the redundant elements are deleted from the right conjunct. In English, subject and verb redundancies are deleted in a forward direction, verb phrase and object redundancies are deleted in a backward direction, e.g.

forward deletion
    subject redundancy: John loved apples and <John> hated lemons.
    verb redundancy: John loved apples and Bill <loved> lemons.
    subject and verb redundancy: John loved apples and <John loved> lemons.

backward deletion
    verb phrase redundancy: John <loved apples> and Bill loved apples.
    object redundancy: John loved <apples> and Bill hated apples.

Backward deletion is less common in the world's languages, and is considered to be a more controversial process in English than is forward deletion (Harries, 1973).

More recent grammatical treatments (e.g. Lasnik, 1976) do not transformationally derive phrasal coordination from sentential forms, but talk of "gaps" in the surface structure of phrasal coordinations which the semantic interpretive rules fill in by mapping to the full form. Hence the relationship to the structural form is still considered essential to the phrasal form's interpretation. Other accounts (Dougherty, 1967), less favored in general, generate phrasal conjunctions as base phrase structures on the grounds that this is necessary for certain phrasal conjunctions, e.g.

John and Sally are a married couple.

for which there is no sentential counterpart. It is easier to write phrase structure rules to generate conjunctions of like constituents, however, than it is to include conjunction of nonconstituents e.g. (SV+SV)O or SVO+SO. In contrast, the deletion schema can deal with all structural varieties of phrasals.

It should be noted that in order for the sentential form to be reduced, the redundant noun phrases ought to be coreferential, so for example,

John patted his dog and Bill stroked his dog.

could not reduce to:

John patted and Bill stroked his dog.

Whether or not one should consider this a syntactic constraint or a pragmatic one, the child clearly must learn the conditions under which phrasal and sentential forms mean the same thing, and when the alternative forms are each appropriate. Finally, the semantic relationship between the two propositions in a conjunction can be very varied, even with the conjunction *and*.

For English language acquisition, the issues for coordination are:

1. What is the order of acquisition of the sentential versus phrasal forms, and of backward versus forward deleted forms?
2. Do children respect the conditions of use of phrasal versus sentential forms?
3. How does the semantics of the conjunction affect acquisition?

8.2. *Order of Acquisition*

Lust (1977; Lust & Mervis, 1980) has made a strong argument that in acquisition, sentential forms have primacy over phrasal forms. In elicited imitation, phrasal forms were more difficult for children than sentential forms matched in syllable length. Furthermore, children demonstrated that they understood the mapping by elaborating phrasals to sententials, and reducing sententials to phrasals when imitating. Lust argued in addition for the primacy of deletion in a forward direction in child speech, since forward phrasals were imitated more readily, and forward sententials more often reduced, than their backward counterparts. Lust and Mervis (1980) make a similar case based on spontaneous speech samples from a cross-sectional sample of young children.

Other researchers (Tager-Flusberg, de Villiers & Hakuta (1982); Bloom, Lahey, Lifter & Feiss (1980); and Ardery (1980) have disputed the fundamental finding of primacy of the sentential form. In data on comprehension, elicited imitation and elicited production tasks with preschool children, and in spontaneous speech analysis from the three subjects Brown (1973) studied longitudinally, Tager-Flusberg et al. found no clear evidence that phrasals on the whole are more difficult than sententials. Two particular phrasal forms, (SV+SV)O and SVO+SO, gave children inordinate trouble in the experimental tasks, and those are precisely the forms that could not easily be generated by phrase structure rules in the base. Hence Tager-Flusberg et al. argue that children's phrasal conjunctions are generated directly by phrase structure rules, but they leave open the possibility that later in childhood, children might learn a mapping rule between the sentential and phrasal forms.

All the researchers concur, however, in finding children's earliest phrasal coordinations to be forward deletions rather than backward deletions. Primarily this is because subject conjunctions are rare in child speech. When appropriate conditions were provided for subject conjunction in the elicited production task used by Tager-Flusberg et al., it was used 75% of the time compared to appropriate object conjunction which was used 95% of the time. The other opportunity for backward deletion involves the conjunction of the nonconstituents SV and SV, and such constructions are vanishingly rare even when opportunities are provided.

8.3. *Relation to Cognition*

Greenfield and Dent (1982) explored the influence of various aspects of the nonlinguistic context on children's use of conjunction reduction, using an older population of subjects (6 years and 10 years). The subjects had to describe an action sequence of putting differently colored beads in a cup for the benefit of a listener behind a screen who had to repeat the action. In one condition, the subjects described the action as it was occurring ("simultaneous"), in the second ("post") the subjects communicated after the action was completed. The utterances were scored as forward or backward deletions and for the constituent that was conjoined.

Their hypothesis was that certain features of the communication situation have salience and motivate the use of different syntactic structures. For instance, in the simultaneous condition, the subject might focus on the redundancy of the repeated action, and hence omit redundant mentions of the verb:

She put the red in the yellow and the blue in the green.

As a result, forward deletions should predominate, and they did. In fact, sometimes this resulted in nonstandard forms, such as:

She putting a red bead in the yellow and a green one a blue one.

where the locative phrase *in the yellow* has been forward deleted by mistake.

In contrast, when children were describing a completed action, the salience of the perceptual grouping supposedly came into play, resulting in more object conjunction and backward deletion of the locative phrase, e.g.

She put the blue red and green into the yellow one.

Interestingly, forward deletions still predominated.

Greenfield and Dent argue that the production process for phrasal coordinations could not plausibly derive them from the corresponding sentential forms. Instead, the referential situation is directly encoded into the surface structure of the sentence as it is produced. The salience of perceptual groupings, and the referential redundancy are responsible for the choice of linguistic expression.

The question of a production model for coordination is an interesting one, but the subjects in Greenfield and Dent's study were already competent in the requisite linguistic structures. Hakuta, de Villiers, and Tager-Flusberg (1982) propose a tentative model for younger children's production of coordinate structures, from the assumption that the process underlying phrasal coordination consists of conjunction of constituents and proceeds in a left-to-right fashion.

A second area where cognitive achievements are likely to be significant lies in the meaning relationships that hold between the connected propositions in a conjunction. Work on acquisition of these meanings by Bloom et al. (1980) is discussed later under Interaction with Semantics.

8.4. Relation to Input

Data on the types of coordination found in parental speech to children are scarce. Only one study examined the forms in the detail necessary, and then only for one mother-child pair (de Villiers, Tager-Flusberg & Hakuta, 1977). Nevertheless, the result was intriguing. In the same way as the researchers categorized Eve's coordinations for percentages of sentential versus phrasal, forward versus backward deletions, they also categorized her mother's coordinations. In plotting changes over time in the proportions of the different types, there was a striking resemblance between Eve and her mother. Forward phrasals heavily predominated, but the proportion dropped with time, and forward sententials increased. Backward phrasals similarly outnumbered the corresponding sentential forms. Finally, the number of coordinations in Eve's samples suddenly increased, and the mother's use of coordination increased in tandem. A trivial explanation would either be that Eve mimicked her mother's sentences, or her mother glossed Eve's, resulting in a parallel change. However the contents of their coordinated sentences were not closely matched: the parallelism existed at a more global level than individual sentences. Until further data of the same sort are analyzed, it is not clear whether Eve's mother was responding to changes in Eve, or leading the way. Whichever is true, these preliminary data suggest that the biases in children's spontaneous speech are closely mirrored in the input they receive.

A report from Bloom et al. (1980) provided some evidence on children's ability to connect their sentences to preceding input sentences from the adult in discourse. Their focus was on the meaning relationship encoded by the syntactic forms (see below) and their subjects proved more able to express complex meanings entirely in their own speech, rather than in conversational interchange with an adult. In contrast to the view that discourse provides the learning opportunities for linguistic expressions, Bloom et al. claim that the child learns the linguistic forms of the connective first in his own speech, and can only then extend them to encode meanings expressed in discourse between child and adult. However, an examination of how the adult connected her response to the child's statement, might display an increasing complexity as the child matured. These data are not presently available.

8.5. *Typical Errors and Individual Differences*

In imitation tasks, the typical "errors" that children make in coordinated sentences are elaborations of phrasal forms into sententials, and reductions of sentential forms into phrasals. However, these errors are not evenly distributed across sentence types: both Lust (1977) and Tager-Flusberg et al. (1982) reported an effect of direction of deletion, such that children do not reduce backward sententials, but more often reduce in a forward direction. Even the latter may not be too frequent: 8% overall for Lust's subjects, 4% for Tager-Flusberg et al.'s subjects. In the latter study, the majority of changes were made for sentences that had one redundant element deleted, but the potential for another deletion, e.g.

>   Susy bought a necklace and bought a bracelet.
> or: Stephen chased the balloon and hit the balloon.

Such linguistic structures sound particularly poorly motivated out of context, as in an imitation task.

In a comprehension task, Tager-Flusberg et al. found two particular structures attracted many errors, the SVO+SO form, and the SV+SVO sentence. For example, in response to:

> The zebra pushed and the zebra licked the alligator.

71% of the errors involved selecting another, unmentioned animal as the object of *push*. In response to:

> The sheep patted the kangaroo and the pig the giraffe.

children acted out the first NVN sequence correctly, then were at a loss to know what to do with the remaining creatures!

Errors in spontaneous speech have not been reported, except by Greenfield and Dent from older subjects. If children are working with a deletion schema, it is surprising that there are not more errors of deletion in the wrong direction, such as:

>   Mary went home and John.
> or: Likes apples and John lemons.

The paucity of errors favors the view that children are not producing phrasal coordinations by deleting elements from the sentential forms.

Individual differences are a factor in the spontaneous speech patterns reported here. For instance, in Tager-Flusberg et al.'s study of Brown's three subjects,

Eve had many more backward phrasals than Adam or Sarah. Bloom et al. (1980) found that for three of their subjects, sentential and phrasal forms emerged simultaneously, for the fourth, phrasals emerged earlier. Explanations for these variations will only emerge after more detailed study of the input and contexts of use to which individual children are exposed.

8.6. *Relation to Semantics*

Bloom et al. (1980) described the acquisition of connective forms, and the meaning relations between connected clauses. The data came from the spontaneous speech of four children studied longitudinally between 2 and 3 years. By using contextual information, the researchers noted the meanings encoded by the conjoined sentences, identifying them as one of eight varieties:

1. additive, e.g.

   Maybe you can carry that and I can carry this.

2. temporal, e.g.

   Jocelyn's going home and take her sweater off.

3. causal, e.g.

   She put a bandaid on her shoe and it maked her feel better.

4. adversative, e.g.

   'Cause I was tired but now I'm not tired.

5. object specification, e.g.

   It looks like a fishing thing and you fish with it.

6. epistemic, e.g.

   I think that that's where the baby will go.

7. notice, e.g.

   Watch what I'm doing.

8. other, e.g.

   Tell Iris that I wet my bed.

The latter three types were mostly expressed as complements, to be discussed later. The mean rank order of development was as above for the four children, with some variation in the order of epistemic relations.

The order of emergence of the connectives: *and, and-then, when, because, what, so, then, if, but* and *that*, was more variable across children. *And*, the first connective and the most frequent, was used with the most different meaning relations. It was used to encode conjunction with the different meaning relations in the order: additive, temporal, causal, and then adversative. The other connectives were less productive and tended to encode particular meaning relations. Finally, the syntactic structure used to encode these connected meanings was used first for coordination, then for relativization, and then for complementization.

Clearly then, the meaning relation between the connected propositions is a significant variable in the acquisition of conjunction in English, and the relationship of the orders described here to cognitive development is a rich topic for crosslinguistic investigation.

8.7. Pragmatics

As mentioned in the beginning of the section on coordination, certain conditions must obtain before a phrasal form can be used rather than sentential form. In particular, the redundant noun phrases must be identical in reference in order for one of them to be omitted. Tager-Flusberg et al. note that one difference between Lust and Mervis (1980) and their own study of spontaneous speech lies in the different way that sentential forms were treated. They argued that a true test of the primacy of sentential forms over phrasal forms requires counting only sentential forms with a potential for deletion that is not realized. Lust and Mervis argue that any linguistic redundancy will suffice; Tager-Flusberg et al. contend that the condition of semantic redundancy must also hold. As one example of dispute, take the sentence:

This is Daddy's and this is Mommy's.

where the referents of *this* are distinct. Tager-Flusberg et al. contend that there is no possibility for phrasal coordination in such a statement. In an elicited production task, they controlled the relevant referent variables that influence the likelihood of sentential versus phrasal forms, to see whether young children were sensitive to this dimension. For instance, two contrasting pictures contained:

A frog watching television and a turtle watching another television.

and:

A frog and a turtle watching the same television.

For all age groups from 3 to 6 years, the percentage of phrasal coordination was much higher for the second type of picture (73%) than for the first (13%). Furthermore, the children rarely made errors that involved deleting a linguistically, but not referentially, redundant item, but instead produced sentences such as:

A frog and a turtle watching television sets.

Referential context thus had an important effect in determining whether a sentential or phrasal form was produced, with sentential forms being used to mark the fact that linguistically identical NPs have different referents. This functional distinction between phrasal and sentential forms seems to operate early in child language.

9. Relative Clauses

Research on children's knowledge of sentence embeddings has been motivated by a number of concerns, not all of them from linguistic theory. For example, some have tried to determine when the first attempts at sentence embedding occur. Other researchers have tried to describe general processing strategies that preschool children might use with complex sentences. There has been no systematic work on the input children receive concerning relative clause constructions. Neither has there been much work on prerequisite cognitive achievements, except Greenfield et al. (1972) who argued for formal parallels in the nonlinguistic domain of embedding containers. Since this achievement occurs years before, it is not clear that it is related to the corresponding linguistic achievement. The following issues for English revolve primarily around acquisition stages and typical errors.

9.1. *Order of Acquisition*

How do relative clauses come into child speech? Hamburger and Crain (1982) argue that they appear in the early speech of 2 year olds, albeit in structurally impoverished form. For instance, they report sentences such as

This is my did it.
Look-a my made.

as representing the first sentence embeddings. Initially the child embeds a VP in a NP to restrict the referent set, then later learns to embed an S, still later includes the head noun, and eventually adds the complementizer. In keeping with these claims, Flynn and Lust (1980) found headless relatives, e.g.

Cookie monster hits what pushes Big Bird.

to be more successfully imitated than headed relatives, e.g.

Big Bird pushes the balloon which bumps Ernie.

in an elicited imitation task. They argue that the effect was not due to the semantic indeterminacy of the headless relative, since indeterminate heads such as

the thing which Mary's got

were difficult for their subjects to imitate. The children seemed better able to nominalize a sentence when no separate NP head was involved, and could embed that nominalization as a noun phrase. Only by 6½ years could children differentiate the head and complementizer in relative clauses, so Flynn and Lust claim that full structural knowledge of relative clause constructions does not come in until late in the preschool years.

These results are in keeping with other data demonstrating the paucity of relative clauses in children's free speech before the age of 6 years. In fact Ingram (1971) proposed that the first spontaneous relative clauses may be stereotyped forms such as "a girl called Cinderella," but Hamburger and Crain's data stand in contradiction to that claim. Others (Limber, 1973, Menyuk, 1971) have reported that the first relative clauses are elaborations of the object noun phrase rather than the subject noun phrase. However, that asymmetry could result from the fact that children's sentence subjects are generally pronouns (Limber, 1973) which do not require further specification. Tager-Flusberg (1982) used an elicited production task with preschool children, and demonstrated that when opportunities for object and subject relativization are equalized, children show no differential difficulty in producing subject relatives. In dative sentences, however, her subjects could only produce relatives on the last NP, the indirect object.

The data on comprehension of relative clauses partially support the argument that preschool children know little of the adult structure. However there are clearly different variables entering into these tasks, such that it is difficult to generalize results across performances. As one example, in Flynn and Lust's parallel study of the comprehension of free versus headed relatives, the children found determinate, headed relatives easier than headless or nondeterminate headed relatives. Hence the structure was not as important as the semantics for the comprehension task, the reverse of the imitation task.

Questions about the sensitivity of the comprehension measure to structural variables pervade research on relative clause constructions, leading one researcher (Maratsos, 1984) to discount that performance as providing useful data about syntactic knowledge. Maratsos argues that the strategies children adopt in experimental tasks mask their true knowledge of the construction under investigation. It is true that the experimental sentences are decidedly unnatural, since semantic clues are removed to study syntactic variables. Most investigators would agree with Goodluck and Tavakolian (1982), who take the position that children's competence can be obscured by performance variables. It is worthwhile to consider the rather long list of task variables together with the structural variables that influence comprehension.

The two major structural variables are embeddedness, namely the role of the complex NP in the sentence, and focus, or the role of the head noun within the complex NP. Table 1.5 indicates the possible combinations that can occur with only two roles: subject and object. The conventional labels for these types are the abbreviations listed in the table.

Many early investigators investigated only one structural variable, e.g. embeddedness, without controlling the second (for review, see de Villiers, Tager-Flusberg, Hakuta & Cohen, 1979). However even among those researchers who carefully controlled embeddedness and focus, there is disagreement about the relative difficulty of the four sentence types in Table 1.5, as well as the typical errors that are found.

Sheldon (1974) theorized that sentence types SS and OO would be more readily understood than SO and OS, since in the former the head noun has a parallel function in the complex NP and in the matrix sentence. In an act-out procedure with toy animals, preschool children found SS and OO easier than SO and OS.

Tavakolian (1981) investigated comprehension of the same four sentence types and argued against the parallel function claim. Instead, she argued that her subjects imposed a conjoined-clause analysis on the complex sentences, treating them as coordinates rather than embeddings. In particular, SS sentences were well understood, since a conjoined-clause analysis corresponds to the correct interpretation in this task. OS sentences were poorly understood, and in fact were responded to as if they were SS sentences. OO and SO sentences were intermediate in difficulty. Hence the order was: SS, OO, SO, and OS, though the latter three types were generally poorly understood.

TABLE 1.5
Types of Relative Clause

Role of Complex NP in Matrix Sentence (Embeddedness)	Role of Head Noun in Relative Clause (Focus)	Abbreviation	Example
subject	subject	SS	The cat that bit the dog chased the rat.
subject	object	SO	The cat that the dog bit chased the rat.
object	subject	OS	The cat bit the dog that chased the rat.
object	object	OO	The cat bit the dog that the cat chased.

de Villiers et al. (1979) conducted a study rather similar to Sheldon's and Tavakolian's, using the same sentence types and act-out procedure, with a larger sample of subjects. Their data present a different order of difficulty, primarily in that OS was no more difficult than SS. The order for their subjects was: OS=SS, OO, SO. The error data supported neither parallel function nor a conjoined-clause analysis, but was best accomodated by a set of processing heuristics, such as the N-V-N strategy, that children might adopt in such a task. Again, the percentages of correct responses were all quite low.

9.2. *Typical Errors*

As just described, there are several proposals concerning the typical errors that children make in understanding sentences with relative clauses. Sheldon (1974) contended that children were prone to maintain the same role of a noun phrase in both the relative clause and the matrix sentence. Legum (1975) suggested this may not have a structural basis, but may instead be an artifact of the act-out procedure, in which the child uses a "bird-in-the-hand" strategy to perform two actions with the same toy. However, such errors were relatively rare in the studies by Tavakolian (1981) and de Villiers et al. (1979).

Errors of interpreting the relative clause as a conjoined clause are frequent in Tavakolian's study, resulting in very poor performance on OS sentences. de Villiers et al. found that to be the most prevalent error on OS sentences, but correct responses outnumbered those errors. In general, they found children were more likely to ignore the syntactic marker *that* than to interpret it as *and*.

The discrepancies among the studies might stem in part from the averaging procedures: age is probably not the most revealing basis for grouping the subjects. None of the studies found significant interactions between age and performance on the various sentence types. Perhaps correlating the child's performance to some other linguistic measure would reveal whether particular strategies or hypotheses are more prevalent at different stages of development.

Two further studies have explored the variables that influence the conjoined-clause interpretation of OS sentences. Goodluck and Tavakolian (1982) investigated the influence of the animacy of the object, and the transitivity of the verb in the subordinate clause, in an act-out procedure. Goodluck (1978) had earlier observed that OS relatives with no animate object in the subordinate clause were well comprehended, e.g.

The cow kisses the horse that jumps over the fence.

For the subjects tested by Goodluck and Tavakolian, sentences with inanimate objects proved easier than sentences with animate objects, and intransitives were easier than transitives. The most common error was the subject coreference error predicted by the conjoined clause analysis. Thus they speculated that a processing load in the standard comprehension test could mask children's competence in relative clause comprehension. It is fairly obvious that restricting possible interpretations of NP roles would result in improved performance. Their second experiment was designed to show the inadequacy of a processing strategies account of OS relatives and VP complements e.g.

The dog tells the horse to knock over the table.

and argued that their evidence demonstrates that even 4-year-olds analyze relative clauses as constituents of the NP node. In particular the authors argue that children's interpretations are governed by the principle of c-command, a structural condition. The node A on a phrase structure tree is said to "c-command" a second node B, if the first branching node that dominates A also dominates B, and neither A nor B dominates the other. The c-command condition, held to be universal, states that a lexical NP must c-command an empty node with which it is co-indexed. Upon hearing either a relative clause sentence or a complement sentence, the child must find a coreferent NP for the empty NP in the subordinate clause. Goodluck and Tavakolian argued that if one assumes that their subjects' choice of coreferent NP was governed by the principle of c-command, then their responses on the tasks reveal adult-like structures for the relative clause construction. As will be discussed later under complements, the assumption of the c-command condition also constrains the authors to the position that children's temporal complements are mis-analyzed as VP constituents rather than being attached to the S-node as in adult grammar. It is not clear from the present evidence that the assumption is warranted.

Solan and Roeper (1978) also argue strongly that preschool children's comprehension of relative clauses is constrained by structural principles, not just by processing strategies. Again exploring OS sentences only, they compared the likelihood of a subject coreference error in the two sentence types:

The cat put the cow that kicked the dog in the barn.

versus

The cat pushed the cow that kicked the dog in the barn.

Notice that the first sentence containing the verb *put,* requires specification of three NP roles: the subject, object, and object of the preposition. Hence in that sentence, the PP is clearly attached to the verb phrase node. Their subjects were pretested on sentences with *put,* and preselected to know that subcategorization requirement. However, then the relative clause *that kicked the dog* could not be attached to the subject NP without creating crossed branches in the phrase structure tree (see Fig. 1.1). If children were sensitive to this no-tangle constraint on phrase structure rules, they should not make a subject coreference error for the *put* sentence. In fact, the children made no such errors, but failed to act out the relative clause at all. Conjoined clause responses were frequent for the sentence

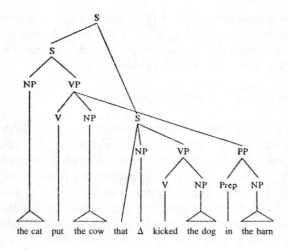

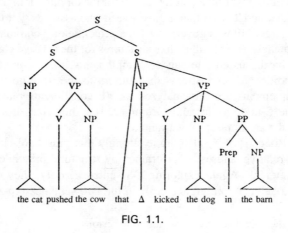

FIG. 1.1.

containing *pushed,* in which the PP can attach to the S-node too (see Fig. 1.1). Solan and Roeper claim that the experiment demonstrates that the typical error depends on structural considerations, rather than being a processing strategy of no structural import. It could be argued, however, that their subjects simply ignored the relative clause while searching for the final NP argument for *put,* that is, albeit ad hoc, a processing account of the phenomenon.

9.3. *Pragmatics*

The above experiments all suffer from one major weakness, according to Hamburger and Crain (1982). In the toy manipulation paradigm it is customary to supply only one instance of each animal mentioned in the sentence, and to ignore the order in which the child acts out the clauses. The sentences then become nonrestrictive relative clauses, akin to simple conjunction. The real function of the relative clauses, in contrast, is to disambiguate the NP referent by giving it further specification. Hamburger and Crain argue that violation of these felicity conditions for relative clause use might be an additional factor in preschool children's failure to understand them. These authors contend also that the use of the present tense is unnatural also, so they use the past tense, like Solan and Roeper (1978), Sheldon (1974), and de Villiers et al. (1979).

Unfortunately the only sentences considered by Hamburger and Crain were OS relatives, on the rationale that this type "presented the most difficulty for children in all the previous studies" (p. 264). In addition, the order of mention in an OS sentence is opposite to the conceptual order, and they wanted to see whether under improved felicity conditions, children would act out the subordinate clause first. In fact 3-year-olds in their study used an order-of-mention strategy, but their 5-year-olds acted out the relative clause first. Subject coreference errors were not frequent. Although a major conclusion of the study is that the appropriate felicity conditions resulted in improved performance by their 5-year-olds, their data reveal that 55% of the "correct" responses made by 5-year-olds involved acting out only the main clause of the OS relative. Hamburger and Crain counted this as correct, on the argument that the presupposition encoded by the relative clause could be assumed to have occurred already, so only the assertion needed to be acted out. If other researchers had counted matrix clause responses as correct, their subjects would look equally proficient. There is thus no guarantee that improved felicity conditions are as beneficial as one might suppose.

9.4. Summary

In sum, a large number of structural and task variables interact in determining children's performance on relative clause constructions. Some children make subject coreference errors as if they treated the relative clause structure as a flat, coordinate structure rather than an embedding. However this type of response is not universal (de Villiers et al., 1979, Hamburger & Crain, 1982) and appears more prevalent under a variety of processing overloads or pragmatic infelicities. Researchers are in substantial disagreement about the extent of children's structural knowledge in the preschool years, with Goodluck and Tavakolian, Solan and Roeper taking the position that children's knowledge of relatives is well developed, obedient to various structural constraints (c-command, no-tangle constraint) but masked by performance factors. Others (Flynn & Lust, 1980; de Villiers et al., 1979) stress the incompleteness of children's structural knowledge before age 6 or so, and Hamburger and Crain emphasize the piecemeal, stepwise character of relative acquisition in early childhood. The time is ripe for a detailed longitudinal study of a number of children, tested on a range of tasks at frequent intervals, to elucidate the paths children can take to an adult knowledge of this form of sentence embedding.

10. Verb Complements

Recently, increased interest has developed in how children deal with complex sentences. Much of the work in this area is motivated by considerations of learnability within current linguistic theory, for example, deriving tests of children's knowledge of putative universal constraints (e.g. Tavakolian, 1981; Phinney, 1981; Otsu, 1981). A number of investigators have used various kinds of complements as an avenue of exploration, and some of those studies are reviewed here. Primarily because of the motivation for the research, but also because of its recency, there has been virtually no work on the nature of the input, on related cognitive achievements, on individual differences, on semantic constraints or on the pragmatics of the forms. Attention has instead been directed towards the course of acquisition, questions of reorganization in the grammar, and typical errors made at different ages.

10.1. *Course of Acquisition*

Apart from the work on relative clauses, research has concentrated on the development of infinitival complements, with only a little on gerundive complements and embedded tensed clauses.

Bloom, Tackeff and Lahey (1982) studied the development of *to* in predicate complement constructions in four children studied longitudinally, whose spontaneous speech comprised the data base. All of the utterances containing sequences of V-*to*-V were considered, e.g.

I'm going to see Mommy.

The purpose of the study was to examine the distributional regularities of *to*: if it were being learned as a marker of the infinitive, then the regularities in distribution should occur with the complement verbs. However, *to* instead occurred regularly with particular matrix verbs, and in no pattern with the complement verbs.

Initially, the antecedent verbs were a small set that appeared to function as modal verbs, e.g.

I want open it.
I gonna get it.

The *to* was either absent, or marked with a schwa. Later, nonmodal matrix verbs e.g. *try, like,* entered the children's speech, and these usually had *to* after them. Only then did the modal verbs begin to be used with *to* rather than schwa. In contrast, the complement verbs did not seem to be conditioning use of *to* at all. That is, the presence of *to* was not affected by the following verb but by the verb preceding it. For instance, *like to* might be established as a frame, but *to eat* would not be. Furthermore, the sequence V-*to*-V was only very rarely interrupted by an intervening NP (only 4% of contexts) and even then the forms were highly constrained, e.g.

Want you to V.

Bloom et al. point out that this course of acquisition calls into question the traditional account of infinitives in which *to* is the marker of that form. Instead, it is in keeping with Bresnan's (1978) analysis in which verbs are subcategorized to take an infinitival complement, since the children seemed to learn the basic structure VERB + *to*. Hafitz, Gartner and Bloom (1980) report similar findings on other forms of verb complements following the verbs *see, look, know, think, say* and *tell*, in which the complementizers (e.g. *wh*) were acquired specific to individual verbs and only later generalized.

Two other studies suggest that children's knowledge of verb subcategorization for complements is not complete until much later. Phinney (1981) studied the emergence of the distinction between verbs such as *wish*, which block subject extraction from the infinitival complement, and verbs such as *want* which allow it. Compare the possible subjects of *kick* in:

Who did the bear wish to kick?
versus: Who did the bear want to kick?

In the second sentence there is the possibility that the bear wants someone else to do the kicking. Phinney found that 6-year-olds had not yet made a distinction between the verb types though older children were beginning to differentiate them. Goodluck and Roeper (1978) tested children's knowledge of a distinction between perception and nonperception verbs, namely that in the sentence

John saw Bill sitting on the beach.

the subject of *sitting* is ambiguous, but in

John hit Bill sitting on the beach.

there is no ambiquity. Five-year-olds had not acquired this distinction, even though it is one based on semantics. It should be pointed out that some adult native speakers have doubts about the existence of the distinction.

Admittedly these distinctions among verb types are more subtle than the information about which verb takes which form of complement. Children may encode the latter in the lexicon, but they clearly make generalizations across matrix verbs in their rules for interpreting complement subjects. It is to an account of those generalizations that we now turn.

10.2. *Typical Errors*

Most of the other research on verb complements has addressed the issue of interpreting the "null" subject of the complement, beginning with the experiment by Chomsky (1969). She asked children questions involving the matrix verbs *ask*, *tell*, and *promise*. A common tendency among children between 5- and 9-years-of-age, was to interpret the subject of the complement verb as coreferential with the object of the matrix verb, hence making an error on the exceptional verb *promise*. Compare:

> Bill told Bert to mow the lawn.
> Bill promised Bert to mow the lawn.

The children would believe that Bert mowed the lawn in both sentences. Furthermore, they had most difficulty with the verb *ask*, which is inconsistent in assignment of reference: compare e.g.

> Bill asked to go.
> Bill asked Bert to go.
> Bill asked Bert where to throw the ball.

Chomsky interpreted her findings in terms of a minimal distance principle, or MDP (Rosenbaum, 1967) such that children take the nearest noun to be the subject of the complement verb.

In later work Maratsos (1974) challenged Chomsky's account by using passive versions of the same sentences in which the MDP could not account for the results. Even in sentences such as:

> Bill was promised by Bert to mow the lawn.

his subjects believed *Bill*, the logical object but not the nearest NP, to be the subject of *mow*.

Goodluck (1981) argued that the available data on children's interpretation of complement sentences can be understood if it is assumed that children understand the constraint known as c-command. The c-command constraint described earlier specifies how NPs are to be co-indexed in a phrase structure, hence it is a constraint on the interpretation of anaphora (Solan, 1981) and null subjects of complements and relative clauses (Goodluck & Tavakolian, 1982). In particular it specifies that the subject of the complement can only be coreferential with the object of the matrix sentences if the complement is attached to the VP, not the S-node. So, for instance, Bill can be co-indexed with the empty subject node of *mow* in:

> John told Bill to mow the lawn.

since the infinitival complement is part of the VP (see Fig. 1.2). But in the sentence:

John hit Bill after mowing the lawn.

the participial complement is attached to the S-node in adult grammar, so *John* must be its subject, not *Bill*. Verbs like *promise* constitute an exceptional case.

The second ramification of the c-command condition is that the object of a prepositional phrase cannot be coreferential with the subject of the complement, e.g. in

John was asked before Bill to mow the lawn.

Bill could not be the subject of *mow*. If passive by-phrases are base-generated prepositional phrases (Bresnan, 1978), then interpretation of *Bill* as mower would also be blocked in:

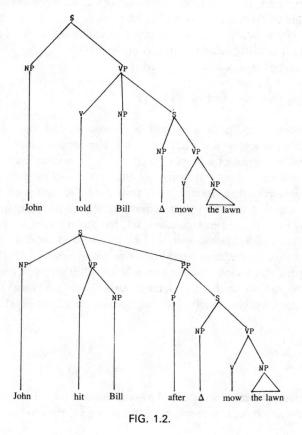

FIG. 1.2.

John was asked by Bill to mow the lawn.

hence accounting for Marastos' results.

Goodluck explored 4-, 5- and 6-year-old children's interpretation of participial complements such as:

The boy hits the girl after jumping over the fence.

as well as sentences with prepositional phrases, and passive matrix sentences. Unfortunately, in apparent violation of c-command, children tended to interpret *the girl* as the subject of *jumping* in the above sentence. Goodluck believes the independent evidence for c-command conditions in children's grammar (Solan, 1978 on anaphora) is so compelling that she prefers to argue that children's phrase structure for that sentence is not the same as adults'. That is, rather than contend that children are violating c-command, she claims that they have misanalysed that participial complement as a constituent of the VP rather than the S node. Of course then, their interpretation does not violate c-command. However given the weight of evidence in favor of children's phrase structures being flatter than adults', with a strong tendency to attach constituents to the S-node (Tavakolian, 1981) it is difficult to accept this argument.

When the complements were preposed, e.g.

After jumping the fence, the boy hits the girl.

children persisted in interpreting *the girl* as the subject of *jump,* again demonstrating the inadequacy of the MDP account. The second consequence of c-command, that the object of a prepositional phrase should not be the subject of the complement, was not entirely borne out either. Some of the younger subjects allowed that interpretation, though such responses declined with age. Goodluck's position is that the appropriate phrase structures for participial complements are only beginning to emerge at age six, but that position is a consequence of assuming that children are constrained by c-command conditions. Evidence independent of that assumption would be more convincing.

It does appear that young children prefer to interpret the object of the matrix sentence as the subject of the complement verb. Their individual spontaneous complements are all subject-controlled, but have no surface object (Bloom et al., 1982) e.g.

I want to go home.
I need to have that.

Perhaps children restrict subject control to sentences with no direct object on the surface. If a direct object is present, even if it is not adjacent to the complement verb, it tends to be interpreted as the complement's subject. Even in 'in order to' sentences such as:

Daisy hits Pluto to put on the watch.

Goodluck found a sizeable proportion of object control interpretations. What is missing at present is a careful analysis of individual, rather than group, response patterns, to check on the consistency of individuals in their interpretations across different sentences.

At present then, children's errors in interpreting complement subjects have several competing explanations, but Goodluck's account in terms of c-command is potentially more integrative than the MDP or Maratsos' (1974) account in terms of semantic relations.

10.3. *Nonoccurring Error*

In one last study using complement constructions as a vehicle for exploring children's knowledge of constraints, Phinney (1981) looked at embedded tensed clauses, such as the sentence:

The boy believed the girl swam in the pond.

A constraint operates against extracting subjects from tensed complements when a complementizer e.g. *that* is present but extracting objects is not blocked (Bresnan, 1972). The test compared children's responses to sentences such as:

1a. Who did the lion know swam in the pond?
1b. Who did the horse know that ate the hay?

which have a gap in the subject position of the embedded clause. In 1a, however, the wh-pronoun refers to the subject of the embedded verb. In 1b, the wh-prounoun must refer to the object of the matrix verb *know,* and the clause at the end is an extraposed relative. There is no difference, though, between the corresponding questions concerning the object, regardless of the presence of *that*:

2a. Who did the bear see the cow kicked?
2b. Who did the dog notice that the rooster kissed?

The sentences in the test were all well motivated by short cartoon stories which offered several alternatives for the referent of *who,* and allowed the researcher to determine how the subjects were interpreting the sentence. For example, they might process only the simple sentence

Who did the bear see?

and give one answer. Or, they could process it as a sentential complement, and give a different answer. A third alternative indicated that they had processed it as an extraposed relative clause. The hypothesis was that 1b could not be given a sentential complement reading as this would violate the constraint on extraction. Indeed, the proportion of sentential readings was very low compared to the other three sentences. Young children tended to process it as a simple sentence; only by grade two did a significant number (60%) of subjects respond to it as a relative clause, the adult reading.

These results suggest that children do know the specific constraint blocking the sentential reading of the critical sentnece. Phinney argues that this is not explicable in terms a more general constraint against extraction, since 1a, 2a, and 2b were well understood. The claim that children are in possession of the appropriate constraint (not easily derivable from input evidence) is an impressive one that deserves further exploration. For present purposes, it is clear that the full grammar of complementation including extraposed relatives, is not completed until at least grade two.

CONCLUSION

If we liken the research on the acquisition of English to a gigantic jigsaw puzzle, how near is it to completion? Armies of graduate students are joining pieces together in the vast middle terrain, where no clear benchmarks exist. Their mentors, meanwhile, have joined the easy edge pieces, but have come up with a bewildering array of competing frames. Particular areas of the puzzle, like Stage I speech, promise to hold the key and have thus attracted an undue amount of attention. Unfortunately the workers do not seem agreed upon which side of the pieces represent the puzzle. Some prefer to work with the cardboard side where false clues are minimized; others use the picture side and cut the pieces to suit their own needs. In other areas (later grammar?) the pieces have not all been found, but the researchers have painted the surface beneath the puzzle to create the illusion of completion.

In a task as large and multifaceted, each researcher must find a set of guiding principles, or theoretical questions, to make sense of the whole enterprise and to which new findings can be assimilated. We present here our own personal view of the field, not as a theoretical stance but as a framework of questions to which we continually seek answers.

Coloring the entire enterprise is the issue of nativism and empiricism. Chomsky is responsible for the modern revival of this ancient debate, and his views find representation in all the areas we have discussed. For example, if children have an innate propensity to select structure dependent rules, they might be prepared from the start to encounter abstract linguistic categories such as subject or NP, and to ignore the meaning of the terms in search of syntactic regularities. The child should entertain a limited set of hypotheses about grammars, constrained by innate knowledge of the forms that rules can take, and the input should provide no especial assistance in this regard over and above "exposure to the language." Certain errors predictable on any theory of "generalization" or "analogy" should never appear, and for all significant purposes, children could be regarded as linguistic replicas of one another.

On the other hand, if the child is equipped with very little in the way of linguistic hypotheses, induction of the rules from the input language must receive support from nonlinguistic achievements. Since a prelinguistic child has some skills in interpreting the world and engaging in social interaction, perhaps he can use this knowledge to help crack the linguistic code. Such a learner would be searching the input for convenient ways to express the meanings he already knows, and an account of his acquisitions will be derived from a description of the input and his nonlinguistic concepts. In this search the child may go through several early rule systems, revising them as the data base, the child's cognitive ability, and communicative needs grow. Of course, individual children will be exposed to different inputs, use language for different purposes, and hence variation will be the norm.

This is the way the boundaries have been drawn, but not all researchers are restricted by them. One doesn't have to be a nativist to be intrigued by nonoccurring errors, or be a learning theorist to be interested in the input. Nonetheless, the theoretical positions have influenced the way research has proceeded over the last ten or fifteen years, and provide the background to our discussion of the remaining questions.

The first very general question concerns the independence of semantics and syntax in an account of language acquisition. Do syntactic categories have a semantic basis in early childhood? Does the child exploit meaning in his search for early rules? Many different theorists have been attracted to the notion that children beginning to learn the language will formulate rules on the basis of the semantics of the terms involved, rather than abstract categories. In Stage I, the special attraction is that such rules would capitalize on the cognitive achievements of the sensorimotor period, the termination of which coincides with the onset of language. However problems remain with semantic descriptions of early speech. One is empirical: some children do not seem to go through a stage that can be described in general semantic terms; like Bowerman's Eva, who went from word-specific formulae to apparently adult-like, nonsemantic rules. The second is methodological: any particular utterance can be given an infinite number of semantic descriptions: what are the constraints in writing semantically based grammars? The third is theoretical: if we agree that children begin with semantically based grammars, do we agree that they have to give them up at a later point? (see Gleitman & Wanner, 1982).

In later stages of development, the data suggesting children make use of semantically based rules are not terribly strong, and can be given alternative accounts in terms of processing or vocabulary limitations. For instance, the data on restrictions on the passive rule are equivocal at present (Maratsos et al., 1979; Lebeaux & Pinker, 1981). If children's formulation of the category "verb" for the purpose of marking with the past tense is initially semantic, it seems to be rapidly revised (Maratsos & Chalkley, 1980). Finally, there are even instances where the child could make use of a broad semantic distinction that does correlate with adult grammatical distinctions, but fails to notice it (Goodluck & Roeper, 1978). Theoretical considerations have led other researchers to consider the possibility not that the child formulates rules in semantic terms, but that she uses semantics as a "bootstrap" (Pinker, 1982) or "trigger" (Roeper, 1982) to the grammatical categories themselves.

A second issue relates to the first in its concern with general rule formulations. Do children seek very general rules, or do they acquire the rule in a piecemeal fashion, perhaps verb-by-verb? (Kuczaj, 1982). Maratsos (1984) argues that there is plenty of evidence that adult grammars require a great deal of term-specific information, so both mechanisms must be in operation throughout life. Roeper et al. (1981) argue that children ought to be cautious in extending rules in the absence of positive evidence (see also Baker, 1979).

Evidence from early Stage I supports the view that many children are learning specific formulae for making sentences containing particular terms (Braine, 1976). In inflectional morphology, the evidence is less clear cut: generalization across terms is prevalent, but the positive evidence is probably present in the input too. Learning of auxiliary placement in wh-questions seems to be a piecemeal acquisition (Kuczaj & Brannick, 1979). Children's formulation of the dative and passive rules may not await positive evidence on particular verbs (Lebeaux & Pinker, 1981; Wilson et al., 1981), though learning which complementizers can follow particular verbs may be verb-specific (Hafitz et al., 1980).

To address the question properly, we need to accumulate data on when overgeneralization occurs, and when undergeneralization of a rule is the typical pattern. Do different constructions or rules show different tendencies in this regard, or are methodological differences in the way they are studied responsible for the different results? A final important consideration is the possibility that individual children might be bold or cautious in rule generalization, and this style might be found throughout the language system. Researchers need to be sensitized to the possibility of undergeneralization in rule learning just as they were to the phenomenon of underextension in vocabulary acquisition (Anglin, 1977). Both domains have benefitted from the introduction of systematic tests of generalization to test the limits of the child's knowledge. In the area of complex syntax, clever tests of generalizations that should be limited by universal constraints are just beginning to be devised (Otsu, 1981; Phinney, 1981). When more of these data are available, it will be possible to evaluate the various theories that predict generalization of different sorts.

On some accounts, the child might have established abstract categories and thus if a syntactic construction is exemplified with a known member of the category, the rule should be formulated in general terms and apply to all members. A lexicalist perspective would predict more caution: just because one verb, for instance, permits that construction does not guarantee that other verbs will. Hence a child should be alert for lexical information or subcategorizations for the rule. A third possibility, hypothetical at present, is that syntactic categories contain degrees of membership based not on semantics, but on distributional properties, for example as proposed by Ross (1972) (see Table 1.6). The rows refer to verbs, ordered by the number of different rules (the columns) that they enter. The rules are ordered in terms of choosiness, that is, the variety of verbs that they permit. Note that once such a matrix of possibilities is learned, the verbs become differentially informative about new rule generalizations. If a new rule is learned with respect to V1, the child does not know whether it can be generalized like R1, or is choosy, like R4. However if a new rule is learned with respect to V4, the child can be certain that V1, V2, and V3 are also allowed. Thus asymmetries of generalization could be predicted depending upon the "typicality" of the input examples to the category (see de Villiers, 1979, and 1980). All of these theoretical possibilities await new data.

The equivalence of children's and adults' grammars is also a central question for language acquisition research. Gleitman and Wanner (1982) point out that if we accept that early grammars are semantically based rather than syntactically based, we then require a discontinuous theory of learning. They take it as given that adult grammar is not semantically based, though there is dispute about that too (e.g. Bates & MacWhinney, 1982; Schlesinger, 1982). As pointed out earlier, even if children's early grammars are semantically grounded, at least by age four or so their language presents evidence of abstract categories. However the acquisition of complex syntactic constructions continues well beyond the pre-

TABLE 1.6

		Choosiness	$\rightarrow$			
		R1	R2	R3	R4	R5
$\uparrow$	V1	+	+	+	+	?
Typicality	V2	+	+	+		?
	V3	+	+			?
	V4	+				?

(After Ross, 1972.)

school years, and children's grammars are still not equivalent to adults' for embedded structures at age six or seven (see pp. 114–124). Nonetheless, claims have been made that although the phrase structure may not be correct, children's rule formulations are obedient to universal constraints (c-command, no-tangle constraint, A-over-A principle) and hence not significantly deviant from adult grammars. However since many of these discoveries are quite new, and heavily dependent upon the methodology of comprehension tasks (see Maratsos, 1984), it will be some time before they are accepted as established facts about language development. The phenomena in this area would seem a particularly appropriate area for crosslinguistic investigation.

Finally, we must return to the problems of competence versus performance. In language acquisition, the competence/performance distinction is used by researchers of all persuasions to try and define what constitutes data and what constitutes noise. To take a couple of examples: the error *He did broke it* is regarded by one group of researchers (Mayer et al., 1978) as a significant piece of evidence that transformations are acquired in units of basic operations. To others, it is a mere slip, a random error of the speech mechanism. When the first subjects that children use in sentences turn out to refer primarily to animate agents, it is seen as evidence that their rules are based on such categories as agent and action rather than subject and verb (e.g. Bowerman, 1973). However, it could be argued that the restriction is a performance limitation: very young children don't make reference to more abstract subjects or have the vocabulary to do so, but their rule formation may not be semantically tied (Valian, 1984). Obviously, theoretical convictions determine when and how the "performance" criticism is raised, but the possibility of that criticism should keep researchers methodologically sophisticated and alert to alternative accounts of their favorite phenomena.

REFERENCES

Akmajian, A., & Henry, F. *Introduction to the principles of transformational syntax.* Cambridge, MA: MIT Press, 1975.

Anglin, J. M. *Word, object and conceptual development.* New York: Norton, 1977.

Antinucci, F., & Parisi, D. Early language acquisition: A model and some data. In C. A. Ferguson & D. I. Slobin (Eds.), *Studies of child language development.* New York: Holt, Rinehart & Winston, 1973.

Antinucci, F., & Volterra, V. Lo sviluppo della negazione nel linguaggio infantile: Un studio pragmatico. In *Studi per un modello del linquaggio: Quaderni della Ricerca Scientifica,* Rome, 1973.

Ardery, G. On coordination in child language. *Journal of Child Language,* 1980, *7,* 305–320.

Baker, C. L. Syntactic theory and the projection problem. *Linguistic Inquiry,* 1979, *10,* 533–583.

Baldie, B. J. The acquisition of the passive voice. *Journal of Child Language,* 1976, *3,* 331–348.

Bates, E. *Language and context.* New York: Academic Press, 1976.

Bates, E., Benigni, L., Bretherton, I., Camaioni, L., & Volterra, V. From gesture to first word: On cognitive and social prerequisites. In M. Lewis & L. Rosenblum (Eds.), *Interaction, conversation and the development of language.* New York: Wiley, 1977.

Bates, E., Benigni, L., Bretherton, I., Camaioni, L., & Volterra, V. *The emergence of symbols: Communication and cognition in infancy.* New York: Academic Press, 1979.

Bates, E., & MacWhinney, B. Functionalist approaches to grammar. In E. Wanner & L. R. Gleitman (Eds.), *Language acquisition: The state of the art.* New York: Cambridge University Press, 1982.

Bellinger, D. Changes in the explicitness of mother's directives as children age. *Journal of Child Language,* 1979, *6,* 443–458.

Bellugi, U. *The acquisition of negation.* Unpublished doctoral dissertation, Harvard University, 1967.

Berko, J. The child's learning of English morphology. *Word,* 1958, *14,* 150–177.

Bever, T. G. The cognitive basis for linguistic structure. In J. R. Hayes (Ed.), *Cognition and the development of language.* New York: Wiley, 1970.

Blank, M. Mastering the intangible through language. In D. Aaronson & R. W. Rieber (Eds.). *Developmental psycholinguistics and communication disorders. Annals of the New York Academy of Sciences,* 1975, *263,* 44–58.

Block, E. M., & Kessell, F. S. Determinants of the acquisition order of grammatical morphemes: A re-analysis and re-interpretation. *Journal of Child Language,* 1980, *7,* 181–188.

Bloom, L. M. *Language development: Form and function in emerging grammars.* Cambridge, MA: MIT Press, 1970.

Bloom, L. M. *One word at a time: The use of single word utterances before syntax.* The Hague: Mouton, 1973.

Bloom, L. M. Talking, understanding and thinking. In R. L. Schiefelbusch & L. L. Lloyd (Eds.), *Language perspectives: Acquisition, retardation and intervention.* Baltimore: University Park Press, 1974.

Bloom, L. M., & Lahey, M. *Language development and language disorders.* New York: Wiley, 1978.

Bloom, L. M., Lahey, M., Hood, L., Lifter, K., & Fiess, K. Complex sentences: Acquisition of syntactic connectives and the semantic relations they encode. *Journal of Child Language,* 1980, *7,* 235–261.

Bloom, L. M., Lifter, K., & Hafitz, J. Semantics of verbs and the development of verb inflections in child language. *Language,* 1980, *56,* 386–412.

Bloom, L. M., Lightbown, P., & Hood, L. Structure and variation in child language. *Monographs of the Society for Research in Child Development,* 1975, *40* (2), Serial No. 160.

Bloom, L. M., Takeff, J., & Lahey, M. *Learning to in complement constructions.* Unpublished manuscript, 1982.

Bowerman, M. F. Structural relationships in children's utterances: Syntactic or semantic? In T. E. Moore (Ed.), *Cognitive development and the acquisition of language.* New York: Academic Press, 1973.

Bowerman, M. F. Discussion summary—development of concepts underlying language. In R. L. Schiefelbusch & L. L. Lloyd (Eds.), *Language perspectives: Acquisition, retardation and intervention.* Baltimore, MD: University Park Press, 1974.

Bowerman, M. F. Commentary on "Structure and variation in child language" by L. Bloom, P. Lightbown, & L. Hood. *Monographs of the Society for Research in Child Development,* 1975, *40* (2), Serial No. 160.

Bowerman, M. F. Semantic factors in the acquisition of rules for word use and sentence construction. In D. Morehead & A. Morehead (Eds.), *Directions in normal and deficient child language.* Baltimore, MD: University Park Press, 1976.

Bowerman, M. F. Words and sentences: Uniformity, individual variation, and shifts over time in patterns of acquisition. In F. D. Minifie & L. L. Lloyd (Eds.), *Communicative and cognitive abilities: Early behavioral assessment.* Baltimore: University Park Press, 1978.

Bowerman, M. F. Reorganizational processes in lexical and syntactic development. In E. Wanner & L. R. Gleitman (Eds.), *Language acquisition: The state of the art.* New York: Cambridge University Press, 1982.

Braine, M. D. S. The ontogeny of English phrase structure: The first phase. *Language*, 1963, *39*, 1–13.

Braine, M. D. S. Children's first word combinations. *Monographs of the Society for Research in Child Development*, 1976, *41*(1): Serial No. 164.

Bresnan, J. *Theory of complementation in English syntax.* Unpublished doctoral dissertation, MIT, 1972.

Bresnan, J. A realistic transformational grammar. In M. Halle, J. Bresnan, & G. A. Miller (Eds.), *Linguistic theory and psychological reality.* Cambridge, MA: MIT Press, 1978.

Bridges, A. SVO comprehension strategies reconsidered: The evidence of individual patterns of response. *Journal of Child Language*, 1980, *7*, 89–104.

Bronckart, J., & Sinclair, H. Time, tense and aspect. *Cognition*, 1973, *2*, 107–130.

Brown, I. Role of referent concreteness in the acquisition of passive sentence comprehension through abstract modeling. *Journal of Experimental Child Psychology*, 1976, *22*, 185–199.

Brown, R. *A first language: The early stages.* Cambridge, MA: Harvard University Press, 1973.

Brown, R., & Bellugi, U. Three processes in the child's acquisition of syntax. *Harvard Educational Review*, 1964, *34*, 133–151.

Brown, R., & Fraser, C. The acquisition of syntax. In C. N. Cofer & B. Musgrave (Eds.), *Verbal behavior and learning: Problems and processes.* New York: McGraw-Hill, 1963.

Bruner, J. S. The ontogenesis of speech acts. *Journal of Child Language*, 1975, *2*, 1–19.

Bruner, J. S. Early social interaction and language acquisition. In H. R. Schaffer (Ed.), *Studies in mother-infant interaction.* London: Academic Press, 1977.

Bryant, B., & Anisfeld, M. Feedback versus no-feedback in testing children's knowledge of English pluralization rules. *Journal of Experimental Child Psychology*, 1969, *8*, 250–255.

Bybee, J. L., & Slobin, D. I. Rules and schemas in the development and use of the English past tense. *Language*, 1982, *58*, 265–289.

Cairns, H. S., & Hsu, J. R. Who, why, when and how: A developmental study. *Journal of Child Language*, 1978, *5*, 477–488.

Cazden, C. The acquisition of noun and verb inflections. *Child Development*, 1968, *39*, 433–448.

Chafe, W. L. *Meaning and the structure of language.* IL: University of Chicago Press, 1970.

Chapman, R. S. Comprehension strategies in children. In J. Kavanagh & W. Strange (Eds.), *Speech and language in the laboratory, school and clinic.* Cambridge, MA: MIT Press, 1978.

Chapman, R. S., & Miller, J. F. Word order in early two and three word utterances: Does production precede comprehension? *Journal of Speech and Hearing Research*, 1975, *18*, 355–371.

Chomsky, C. *The acquisition of syntax in children from 5 to 10.* Cambridge, MA: MIT Press, 1969.

Chomsky, N. *Syntactic structures.* The Hague: Mouton, 1957.

Chomsky, N. *Aspects of the theory of syntax.* Cambridge, MA: MIT Press, 1965.

Clark, E. Strategies and the mapping problem in first language acquisition. In J. Macnamara (Ed.), *Language learning and thought.* New York: Academic Press, 1977.

Clark, H. H., & Chase, W. G. On the process of comparing sentences against pictures. *Cognitive Psychology*, 1972, *3*, 472–517.

Clark, H., & Lucy, P. Understanding what is meant from what is said: A study in conversationally conveyed requests. *Journal of Verbal Learning and Verbal Behavior*, 1975, *14*, 56–72.

Clark, R. Performing without competence. *Journal of Child Language*, 1974, *1*, 1–10.

Corrigan, R. Relationship between object permanence and language development: How much and how strong? *Paper presented at the Eighth Annual Stanford Child Language Research Forum,* Stanford, 1976.

Corrigan, R. Cognitive correlates of language: Differential criteria yield differential results. *Child Development,* 1979, *50,* 617–631.

Cromer, R. F. *The development of temporal reference during the acquisition of language.* Unpublished doctoral dissertation, Harvard University, 1968.

Cromer, R. F. An experimental investigation of a putative linguistic universal: Marking and the indirect object. *Journal of Experimental Child Psychology* 1975, *20,* 3–80.

Cross, T. G. Mothers' speech adjustments: The contribution of selected child listener variables. In C. E. Snow & C. A. Ferguson (Eds.), *Talking to children: Language input and acquisition.* New York: Cambridge University Press, 1977.

Cross, T. G. Motherese: Its association with rate of syntactic acquisition in young children. In N. Waterson & C. E. Snow (Eds.), *The development of communication.* New York: Wiley, 1978.

Crystal, D. The analysis of intonation in young children. In D. Minifie & L. L. Lloyd (Eds.), *Communicative and cognitive abilities: Early behavioral assessment.* Baltimore, MD: University Park Press, 1978.

Crystal, D., Fletcher, P., & Garman, M. *The grammatical analysis of language disability.* New York: Elsevier, 1976.

Curtiss, S. *Genie: A psycholinguistic study of a modern-day wild child.* New York: Academic Press, 1977.

de Villiers, J. G. Prototypes in grammatical rule learning. *Paper presented at the Biennial meeting of the Society for Research in Child Development.* San Francisco, March, 1979.

de Villiers, J. G. The process of rule learning in child speech: A new look. In K. E. Nelson (Ed.), *Children's Language: Volume 2.* New York: Gardner Press, 1980.

de Villiers, J. G. Form and force interactions: The development of negatives and questions. In R. L. Schiefelbusch & J. Pickar (Eds.), *Communicative competence: Acquisition and intervention.* Baltimore, MD: University Park Press, 1984.

de Villiers, J. G. Learning the passive from models: Some contradictory data. *Paper presented at the 9th Annual Boston University Conference.*

de Villiers, J. G., & de Villiers, P. A. Development of the use of word order in comprehension. *Journal of Psycholinquistic Research,* 1973, *2,* 331–341. (a)

de Villiers, J. G., & de Villiers, P. A. A cross-sectional study of the acquisition of grammatical morphemes in child speech. *Journal of Psycholinguistic Research,* 1973, *2,* 267–278. (b)

de Villiers, J. G., & de Villiers, P. A. Competence and performance in child language: Are children really competent to judge? *Journal of Child Language,* 1974, *1,* 11–22.

de Villiers, J. G., & de Villiers, P. A. Semantics and syntax in the first two years: The output of form and function and the form and function of the input. In F. Minifie & L. L. Lloyd (Eds.), *Communicative and cognitive abilities: Early behavioral assessment.* Baltimore, MD: University Park Press, 1978.

de Villiers, J. G., Phinney, M., & Avery, A. Understanding passives with non-action verbs. *Paper presented at Eighth Annual Boston University Conference on Language Acquisition,* October, 1982.

de Villiers, J. G., & Tager-Flusberg, H. Some facts one simply cannot deny. *Journal of Child Language,* 1975, *2,* 279–286.

de Villiers, J. G., Tager-Flusberg, H. B., & Hakuta, K. Deciding among theories of the development of coordination in child speech. *Papers and Reports on Child Language Development,* (Department of Linguistics, Stanford University), 1977, *13,* 118–125.

de Villiers, J. G., Tager-Flusberg, H. B., Hakuta, K., & Cohen, M. Children's comprehension of relative clauses. *Journal of Psycholinguistic Research,* 1979, *8,* 499–518.

de Villiers, P. A., & de Villiers, J. G. Form and function in the development of sentence negation.

Papers and Reports on Child Language Development (Department of Linguistics, Stanford University), 1979, *17*, 56–64.

Dore, J. Holophrases, speech acts and language universals. *Journal of Child Language*, 1975, *2*, 21–40.

Dougherty, R. A. *Coordination conjunction.* Unpublished paper, MIT, 1967.

Erreich, A. *The acquisition of inversion in wh-questions: What evidence the child uses?* Unpublished doctoral dissertation, City University of New York, 1980.

Ervin, S. Imitation and structural change in children's language. In E. H. Lenneberg (Ed.), *New directions in the study of language.* Cambridge, MA: MIT Press, 1964.

Ervin-Tripp, S. Discourse agreement: How children answer questions. In J. R. Hayes (Ed.), *Cognition and the development of language,* New York: Wiley, 1970.

Fillmore, C. J. The case for case. In E. Bach & R. T. Harms (Eds.), *Universals in linguistic theory.* New York: Holt, Rinehart & Winston, 1968.

Fillmore, C. J. Some problems for case grammar. In R. J. O'Brien (Ed.), *Georgetown University Round Table on Language and Linguistics.* Washington, D.C.: Georgetown University Press, 1971.

Fischer, K. W. A theory of cognitive development: The control and construction of hierarchies of skills. *Psychological Review,* 1980, *87,* 477–531.

Fletcher, P. The development of the verb phrase. In P. Fletcher & M. Garman (Eds.), *Language Acquisition.* New York: Cambridge University Press, 1979.

Flynn, S., & Lust, B. Acquisition of relative clauses: Developmental changes in their heads. In W. Harbert & J. Hershenson (Eds.), *Cornell University Working Papers in Linguistics,* 1980, *1.*

Fodor, J. A., Bever, T., & Garrett, M. *The psychology of language.* New York: McGraw Hill, 1974.

Forner, M. The mother as LAD: Interaction between order and frequency of parental input and child production. *Paper presented at the Sixth Annual University of Minnesota Linguistics Symposium,* Minneapolis, 1977.

Fraser, C., Bellugi, U., & Brown, R. W. Control of grammar in imitation, comprehension and production. *Journal of Verbal Learning and Verbal Behavior,* 1963, *2,* 121–135.

Furrow, D., Nelson, K., & Benedict, H. Mothers' speech to children and syntactic development: Some simple relationships. *Journal of Child Language,* 1979, *6,* 423–442.

Garman, M. Early grammatical development. In P. Fletcher & M. Garman (Eds.), *Language acquisition.* New York: Cambridge University Press, 1979.

Garvey, C. Requests and responses in children's speech. *Journal of Child Language,* 1975, *2,* 41–63.

Gleason, H. A., Jr. *An introduction to descriptive linguistics.* Rev. ed. New York: Holt, Rinehart & Winston, 1961.

Gleitman, L. R., & Wanner, E. Language acquistion: The state of the state of the art. In E. Wanner & L. R. Gleitman, (Eds.), *Language acquisition: The state of the art.* New York: Cambridge University Press, 1982.

Golinkoff, R. M. The case for semantic relations: Evidence from the verbal and nonverbal domains. *Journal of Child Language,* 1981, *8,* 413–437.

Golinkoff, R. M., & Kerr, L. J. Infants' perceptions of semantically defined action role changes in filmed events. *Merrill Palmer Quarterly,* 1978, *24,* 53–61.

Golinkoff, R. M., & Markessini, J. ''Mommy sock'': The child's understanding of possession as expressed in two-noun phrases. *Journal of Child Language,* 1980, *7,* 119–136.

Goodluck, H. *Linguistic principles in children's grammar of complement interpretation.* Unpublished doctoral dissertation, University of Massachusetts, Amherst, 1978.

Goodluck, H. Children's grammar of complement-subject interpretation. In S. L. Tavakolian (Ed.), *Language acquisition and linguistic theory.* Cambridge, MA: MIT Press, 1981.

Goodluck, H., & Roeper, T. The acquisition of perception verb complements. In H. Goodluck & L.

Solan, (Eds.), *Papers in the structure and development of child language.* University of Massachusetts, *Occasional Papers in Linguistics,* vol. 4, 1978.

Goodluck, H., & Tavakolian, S. Competence and processing in children's grammar of relative clauses. *Cognition,* 1982, *11,* 1–27.

Greenfield, P. M., & Dent, C. H. Pragmatic factors in children's phrasal coordination. *Journal of Child Language,* 1982, *9,* 425–444.

Greenfield, P. M., Nelson, K., & Saltzman, E. The development of rulebound strategies for manipulating seriated cups: A parallel between action and grammar. *Cognitive Psychology,* 1972, *3,* 291–310.

Greenfield, P. M., & Smith, J. H. *The structure of communication in early language development.* New York: Academic Press, 1976.

Griffiths, P. Speech acts and early sentences. In P. Fletcher & M. Garman (Eds.), *Language acquisition.* New York: Cambridge University Press, 1979.

Hafitz, J., Gartner, B., & Bloom, L. Giving complements when you're two: The acquisition of complement structures in child language. *Paper presented at the Fifth Annual Boston University Conference on Language Development,* October, 1980.

Hakuta, K., de Villiers, J. G., & Tager-Flusberg, H. Sentence coordination in Japanese and English. *Journal of Child Language,* 1982, *9,* 193–207.

Halliday, M. A. K. Learning how to mean. In E. H. Lenneberg & E. Lenneberg (Eds.), *Foundations of language development: A multidisciplinary approach* (vol. 1). New York: Academic Press, 1975.

Hamburger, H., & Crain, S. Relative acquisition. In S. A. Kuczaj (Ed.), *Language development: Syntax and semantics.* New York: Lawrence Erlbaum Associates, 1982.

Hardy-Brown, K. Universals and individual differences: Disentangling two approaches to the study of language acquisition. *Developmental Psychology,* 1983, *19,* 610–624.

Harries, H. Coordination reduction. *Stanford University Working Papers on Language Universals,* 1973, *11,* 139–209.

Hecht, B. F., & Morse, R. *What the hell are dese?* Unpublished paper, Harvard University, 1974.

Hockett, C. F. *A course in modern linguistics.* London: Macmillan, 1958.

Holtman, M. The use of interrogative forms in the interaction of three mothers and their children. *Journal of Psycholinguistic Research,* 1972, *1,* 311–336.

Horgan, D. The development of the full passive. *Journal of Child Language,* 1978, *5,* 65–80.

Howe, C. J. The meanings of two-word utterances in the speech of young children. *Journal of Child Language,* 1976, *3,* 29–48.

Howe, C. J. Interpretive analysis and role semantics: A ten-year mésalliance? *Journal of Child Language,* 1981, *8,* 439–456.

Hurford, J. A child and the English question-formation rule. *Journal of Child Language,* 1975, *2,* 299–301.

Ingram, D. Transivity in child language. *Language,* 1971, *47,* 888–910.

Ingram, D. Stages in the development of one-word utterances. *Paper presented at the Sixth Annual Child Language Research Forum,* Stanford, 1974.

Ingram, D. Language development during the sensori-motor period. *Paper presented at the Third International Child Language Symposium,* London, 1975. (a)

Ingram, D. If and when transformations are acquired by children. In D. P. Dato (Ed.), *Developmental psycholinguistics: Theory and application.* Twenty-sixth Annual Georgetown University Roundtable. Washington, D.C.: Georgetown University Press, 1975. (b)

Ingram, D. Sensorimotor intelligence and language development. In A. Lock (Ed.), *Action, gesture and symbol: The emergence of language.* New York: Academic Press, 1978.

Ingram, D., & Tyack, D. Inversion of subject NP and auxiliary in children's questions. *Journal of Psycholinguistic Research,* 1979, *8,* 333–341.

Jackendoff, R. S. *Semantic interpretation in generative grammar.* Cambridge, MA: MIT Press, 1972.

Jacobs, R. A., & Rosenbaum, P. S. *English transformational grammar.* Waltham, MA: Blaisdell, 1968.

Johnson, C. The ontogenesis of question words in children's language. *Paper presented at the Fifth Annual Boston University Conference on Language Acquisition,* October, 1980.

Johnston, J. R., & Slobin, D. I. The development of locative expressions in English, Italian, Serbo-Croatian and Turkish. *Journal of Child Language,* 1979, *6,* 529–545.

Keenan, E. L., & Comrie, B. Noun phrase accessibility and universal grammar. *Linguistic Inquiry,* 1977, *8,* 63–99.

Kim, K. *Development of the concept of truth-functional negation.* Unpublished doctoral dissertation, Harvard University, 1980.

Klima, E. S. Negation in English. In J. Fodor & J. J. Katz (Eds.), *The structure of language: Readings in the philosophy of language.* Englewood Cliffs, NJ: Prentice-Hall, 1964.

Klima, E. S., & Bellugi, U. Syntactic regularities in the speech of children. In J. Lyons & R. J. Wales (Eds.), *Psycholinguistic papers.* Edinburgh: Edinburgh University Press, 1966.

Kuczaj, S. A., II The acquisition of regular and irregular past tense forms. *Journal of Verbal Learning and Verbal Behavior,* 1977, *16,* 589–600.

Kuczaj, S. A., II Children's judgments of grammatical and ungrammatical irregular past-tense verbs. *Child Development,* 1978, *49,* 319–326. (a)

Kuczaj, S. A., II Why do children fail to overgeneralize the progressive inflection? *Journal of Child Language,* 1978, *5,* 167–171. (b)

Kuczaj, S. A. II Influence of contractibility on the acquisition of be: Substantial, meager, or unknown? *Journal of Psycholinguistic Research,* 1979, *8,* 1–11.

Kuczaj, S. A., II More on children's initial failure to relate specific acquisitions. *Journal of Child Language,* 1981, *8,* 485–487.

Kuczaj, S. A., II On the nature of syntactic development. In S. A. Kuczaj II (Ed.), *Language development* (Vol. 1). *Syntax and semantics.* Hillsdale, NJ: Lawrence Erlbaum Associates, 1982.

Kuczaj, S. A., II, & Brannick, N. Children's use of the Wh question modal auxiliary placement rule. *Journal of Experimental Child Psychology,* 1979, *28,* 43–67.

Kuczaj, S. A., II, & Maratsos, M. P. What children can say before they will. *Merrill-Palmer Quarterly,* 1975, *21,* 89–111.

Kuczaj, S. A., II, & Maratos, M. P. The initial verbs of yes–no questions: A different kind of general grammatical category. *Developmental Psychology,* 1983, *19,* 440–444.

Labov, W., & Labov, T. Learning the syntax of questions. In R. N. Campbell & P. T. Smith (Eds.), *Recent advances in the psychology of language: Language development and mother-child interaction.* London: Plenum Press, 1978.

Lakoff, G. *Generative semantics.* New York: Holt, Rinehart & Winston, 1972.

Lasnik, H. Remarks on coreference. *Linguistic Analysis,* 1976, *2,* 1–22.

Lebeaux, D., & Pinker, S. The acquisition of the passive. *Paper presented at the Sixth Annual Boston University Conference on Language Development,* October, 1981.

Legum, S. Strategies in the acquisition of relative clauses. *Southwest Regional Laboratory Technical Note,* No. TN 2-75-10, 1975.

Leonard, L. B. *Meaning in child language.* New York: Grune & Stratton, 1976.

Leopold, W. F. *Speech development of a bilingual child: A linquist's record* (vol. 3). *Grammar and general problems in the first two years.* Evanston, IL: Northwestern University Press, 1949.

Lieven, E. Conversations between mother and young children: Individual differences and their possible implications for the study of language learning. In N. Waterson & C. E. Snow (Eds.), *The development of communication.* New York: Wiley, 1978.

Lightbown, P. Question form and question function in the speech of young French L2 learners. In M. Paradis (Ed.), *Aspects of bilingualism.* Columbia, SC: Hornbeam Press, 1978.

Limber, J. The genesis of complex sentences. In T. E. Moore (Ed.), *Cognitive development and the acquisition of language.* New York: Academic Press, 1973.

Limber, J. Unravelling competence, performance and pragmatics in the speech of young children. *Journal of Child Language,* 1976, *3,* 309–318.

Lust, B. Conjunction reduction in child language. *Journal of Child Language,* 1977, *4,* 257–288.

Lust, B., & Mervis, C. Development of coordination in the natural speech of young children. *Journal of Child Language,* 1980, *7,* 279–304.

Macnamara, J. Cognitive basis of language learning in infants. *Psychological Review,* 1972, *79,* 1–14.

Macnamara, J. From sign to language. In J. Macnamara (Ed.), *Language learning and thought.* New York: Academic Press, 1977.

MacWhinney, B. Levels of syntactic acquisition. In S. A. Kuczaj II (Ed.), *Language development: Syntax and semantics.* Hillsdale, NJ: Lawrence Erlbaum Associates, 1982.

MacWhinney, B. Hungarian language acquisition as an exemplification of a general model of grammatical development. In D. I. Slobin (Ed.). *The crosslinguistic study of language acquisition* (Vol. II). Hillsdale, NJ: Lawrence Erlbaum Associates, 1985.

MacWhinney, B., & Bates, E. Sentential devices for conveying giveness and newness: A cross-cultural developmental study. *Journal of Verbal Learning and Verbal Behavior,* 1978, *17,* 539–558.

Maratsos, M. P. How preschool children understand missing complement subjects. *Child Development,* 1974, *45,* 700–706.

Maratsos, M. P. Commentary on "Structure and variation in child language" by L. Bloom, P. Lightbown, and L. Hood. *Monographs of the Society for Research in Child Development,* 1975, *40*(2), No. 160.

Maratsos, M. P. *The use of definite and indefinite reference in young children.* New York: Cambridge University Press, 1976.

Maratsos, M. P. How to get from words to sentences. In D. Aaronson & R. Rieber (Eds.), *Perspectives in psycholinguistics.* Hillsdale, NJ: Lawrence Erlbaum Associates, 1979.

Maratsos, M. P. The acquisition of syntax. In J. Flavell & E. Markman, (Eds.), *Carmichael's handbook of child psychology,* 1984.

Maratsos, M. P., & Abramovitch, R. How childen understand full, truncated and anomalous passives. *Journal of Verbal Learning and Verbal Behavior,* 1975, *14,* 145–157.

Maratsos, M. P., & Chalkley, M. A. The internal language of children's syntax: The ontogenesis and representation of syntactic categories. In K. E. Nelson (Ed.), *Children's language* (Vol. 2). New York: Gardner Press, 1980.

Maratsos, M. P., & Kuczaj, S. A., II Preschool children's use of not and n't: Is not (isn't) n't. *In Papers and Reports on Child Language Development,* (Department of Linquistics, Stanford University), 1976.

Maratsos, M., & Kuczaj, S. II Against a transformationalist account: A simpler analysis of auxiliary overmarkings. *Journal of Child Language,* 1978, *5,* 337–346.

Maratsos, M. P., Kuczaj, S. A., II, Fox, D. M., & Chalkley, M. A. Some empirical studies in the acquisition of transformational relations. In W. Collins (Ed.), *Children's language and communication. The Minnesota Symposia on Child Psychology,* Vol. 12. Hillsdale, NJ: Lawrence Erlbaum Associates, 1979.

Mayer, J., Erreich, A., & Valian, V. Transformations, basic operations and language acquisition. *Cognition,* 1978, *6,* 1–13.

McCawley, J. The role of semantics in grammar. In E. Bach & R. Harms (Eds.), *Universals in linguistic theory.* New York: Holt, Rinehart & Winston, 1968.

McNeill, D. A question in semantic development: What does a child mean when he says "no"?. In E. Zale (Ed.), *Conference on language and language behavior.* New York: Appleton-Century-Crofts, 1968.

McNeill, D. *The acquisition of language*. New York: Harper and Row, 1970.

McNeill, D. Semiotic extension. *Paper presented at the Loyola Symposium on Cognition*. Chicago, 1974.

Menyuk, P. *Sentences children use*. Cambridge, MA: MIT Press, 1969.

Menyuk, P. *The acquisition and development of language*. Englewood Cliffs, NJ: Prentice-Hall, 1971.

Miller, W., & Ervin, S. The development of grammar in child language. In U. Bellugi, & R. Brown, (Eds.), The acquisition of language. *Monographs of the Society for Research in Child Development*, 1964, *29*, 9–34.

Moerk, E. L. Piaget's research as applied to the explanation of language development. *Merrill-Palmer Quarterly*, 1975, *21*, 151–170.

Moerk, E. L. Relationships between parental input frequencies and children's language acquisition: A reanalysis of Brown's data. *Journal of Child Language*, 1980, *7*, 105–118.

Moerk, E. L. To attend or not to attend to unwelcome reanalyses? A reply to Pinker. *Journal of Child Language*, 1981, *8*, 627–631.

Morehead, D. M., & Morehead, A. From signal to sign: A Piagetian view of thought and language during the first two years. In R. L. Schiefelbusch & L. L. Lloyd (Eds.), *Language perspectives: Acquisition, retardation, and intervention*. Baltimore, MD: University Park Press, 1974.

Nelson, K. Structure and strategy in learning to talk. *Monographs of the Society for Research in Child Development*, 1973, *38*.

Nelson, K. Individual differences in early semantic and syntax development. In D. Aaronson & R. W. Rieber (Eds.), *Developmental psycholinguistics and communication disorders. Annals of the New York Academy of Sciences*, 1975, *263*, 132–139.

Nelson, K. Early speech in its communicative context. In F. Minifie & L. L. Lloyd (Eds.), *Communicative and cognitive abilities: Early behavioral assessment*. Baltimore, MD: University Park Press, 1978.

Nelson, K. E. Experimental gambits in the service of language acquisition theory: From the Fiffin project to operation input swap. In S. A. Kuczaj, II (Ed.), *Language development* (Vol. 1). *Syntax and semantics*. Hillsdale, NJ: Lawrence Erlbaum Associates, 1982.

Newport, E. Motherese: The speech of mothers to young children. In N. Castellan, D. Pisoni, & G. Potts (Eds.), *Cognitive Theory*, (Vol. II). Hillsdale, NJ: Lawrence Erlbaum Associates, 1976.

Newport, E., Gleitman, L., & Gleitman, H. A study of mother's speech and child language acquisition. *Papers and Reports on Child Language Development*, (Department of Linguistics, Stanford University), 1975, *10*, 111–116.

Newport, E., Gleitman, L., & Gleitman, H. Mother, I'd rather do it myself: Some effects and non-effects of maternal speech style. In C. E. Snow & C. A. Ferguson (Eds.), *Talking to children*. Cambridge: Cambridge University Press, 1977.

Osgood, C. E., & Zehler, A. M. Acquisition of bitransitive sentences: Pre-linguistic determinants of language acquisition. *Journal of Child Language*, 1981, *8*, 367–383.

Otsu, Y. *Grammatical constraints and syntactic development in children: Toward a theory of syntactic development in children*. Unpublished doctoral dissertation, MIT, 1981.

Parisi, D. What is behind child utterances? *Journal of Child Language*, 1974, *1*, 97–105.

Park, T. Z. Some facts on negation: Wode's four-stage developmental theory of negation revisited. *Journal of Child Language*, 1979, *6*, 147–151.

Pea, R. D. The development of negation in early child language. In D. R. Olson (Ed.), *The social foundations of language and thought: Essays in honor of Jerome S. Bruner*. New York: W. W. Norton, 1979.

Phinney, M. *Syntactic constraints and the acquisition of embedded sentential complements*. Unpublished doctoral dissertation, University of Massachusetts, Amherst, 1981.

Piaget, J. *The construction of reality in the child*. New York: Basic Books, 1954.

Piaget, J. *The origins of intelligence in children.* New York: W. W. Norton, 1963.

Pinker, S. On the acquisition of grammatical morphemes. *Journal of Child Language,* 1981, *8,* 477–484.

Pinker, S. A theory of the acquisition of lexical-interpretive grammars. In J. Bresnan (Ed.), *The mental representation of grammatical relations.* Cambridge, MA: MIT Press, 1982.

Ramer, A. L. H. Syntactic styles in emerging language. *Journal of Child Language,* 1976, *3,* 49–62.

Retherford, K. S., Schwartz, B. C., & Chapman, R. S. Semantic roles and residual grammatical categories in mother and child speech: Who tunes in to whom? *Journal of Child Language,* 1981, *8,* 583–608.

Roeper, T. On the importance of syntax and the logical use of evidence in language acquisition. In S. A. Kuczaj, II (Ed.), *Language development* (vol. 1). *Syntax and semantics.* Hillsdale, NJ: Lawrence Erlbaum Associates, 1982.

Roeper, T., Lapointe, S., Bing, J., & Tavakolian, S. L. A lexical approach to language acquisition. In S. L. Tavakolian (Ed.), *Language acquisition and linguistic theory.* Cambridge, MA: MIT Press, 1981.

Rosenbaum, P. *The grammar of English predicate complement constructions.* Cambridge, MA: MIT Press, 1967.

Ross, J. R. Act. In D. Davidson & G. Harman (Eds.), *Semantics of natural languages.* Dordrecht, Holland: Reidel, 1972.

Schaerlaekens, A. M. *The two-word stage in child language development: A study based on evidence provided by Dutch-speaking triplets.* The Hague: Mouton, 1973.

Schlesinger, I. M. Production of utterances and language acquisition. In D. I. Slobin (Ed.), *The ontogenesis of grammar.* New York: Academic Press, 1971.

Schlesinger, I. M. Relational concepts underlying language. In R. L. Schiefelbusch & L. L. Lloyd (Eds.), *Language perspectives: Acquisition, retardation and intervention.* Baltimore, MD: University Park Press, 1974.

Schlesinger, I. M. *Steps to language: Toward a theory of native language acquistion.* Hillsdale, NJ: Lawrence Erlbaum Associates, 1982.

Searle, J. Indirect speech acts. In P. Cole & J. L. Morgan (Eds.), *Syntax and semantics* (Vol. 3). New York: Academic Press, 1975.

Sedlak, P. A. S. Direct/indirect object word order: A cross-linguistic analysis. *Working papers on Language Universals,* 1975, *18.* Language Universals Project, Stanford University.

Shatz, M. Children's comprehension of their mother's question-directives. *Journal of Child Language,* 1978, *5,* 39–46. (a)

Shatz, M. The development of communicative understanding: An early strategy for interpreting and responding to messages. *Cognitive Psychology,* 1978, *10,* 271–301. (b)

Shatz, M. How to do things by asking: Form-function pairings in mother's questions and their relation to children's responses. *Child Development,* 1979, *50,* 1093–1099.

Sheldon, A. The role of parallel function in the acquisition of relative clauses in English. *Journal of Verbal Learning and Verbal Behavior,* 1974, *13,* 272–281.

Sinclair-de Zwart, H. Sensorimotor action patterns as a condition for the acquisition of syntax. In R. Huxley & E. Ingram (Eds.), *Language acquisition: Models and methods.* New York: Academic Press, 1971.

Sinclair, H. The role of cognitive structures in language acquisition. In E. H. Lenneberg & E. Lenneberg (Eds.), *Foundations of language development.* New York: Academic Press, 1976.

Slobin, D. I. Universals of grammatical development in children. In G. B. Flores d'Arcais & W. J. M. Levelt (Eds.), *Advances in psycholinguistics.* Amsterdam: North-Holland, 1970.

Slobin, D. I. On the learning of morphological rules. In D. I. Slobin (Ed.), *The ontogenesis of grammar.* New York: Academic Press, 1971.

Slobin, D. I. Cognitive prerequisites for the development of grammar. In C. A. Ferguson & D. I. Slobin (Eds.), *Studies of child language development.* New York: Holt, Rinehart & Winston, 1973.

Slobin, D. I. Crosslinguistic evidence for the Language-Making Capacity. In D. I. Slobin (Ed.), *The crosslinguistic study of language acquisition* (Vol. II). Hillsdale, NJ: Lawrence Erlbaum Associates, 1985.

Smith, C. S. The acquisition of time talk: Relations between child and adult grammars. *Journal of Child Language,* 1980, *7,* 263–278.

Snow, C. E. Mother's speech to children learning language. *Child Development,* 1972, *43,* 549–565.

Snow, C. E. Mother's speech research: From input to interaction. In C. E. Snow & C. A. Ferguson (Eds.), *Talking to children.* Cambridge: Cambridge University Press, 1977.

Snow, C. E. Conversations with children. In P. Fletcher & M. Garman (Eds.), *Language acquisition.* New York: Cambridge University Press, 1979.

Solan, L. *Anaphora in child language.* Unpublished doctoral dissertation, University of Massachusetts, Amherst, 1978.

Solan, L. The acquisition of structural restrictions on anaphora. In S. L. Tavakolian (Ed.), *Language acquisition and linguistic theory.* Cambridge, MA: MIT Press, 1981.

Solan, L. & Roeper, T. Children's use of syntactic structure in interpreting relative clauses. In H. Goodluck & L. Solan (Eds.), *Papers in the structure and development of child language. University of Massachusetts Occasional Papers in Linguistics* (Vol. 4), 1978.

Strohner, H., & Nelson, K. E. The young child's development of sentence comprehension: The influence of event probability, non-verbal context, syntactic form and strategies. *Child Development,* 1974, *45,* 567–576.

Tager-Flusberg, H. The development of relative clauses in child speech. *Papers and Reports on Child Language Development* (Department of Linguistics, Stanford University), 1982, *21,* 104–111.

Tager-Flusberg, H., de Villiers, J. S., & Hakuta, K. The development of sentence coordination. In S. A. Kuczaj, II (Ed.), *Language development* (Vol. 1). *Syntax and semantics.* Hillsdale, NJ: Lawrence Erlbaum Associates, 1982.

Tavakolian, S. L. The conjoined-clause analysis of relative clauses. In S. L. Tavakolian (Ed.), *Language acquisition and linguistic theory.* Cambridge, MA: MIT Press, 1981.

Turner, E. A., & Rommetveit, R. Experimental manipulation of the production of active and passive voice in children. *Language and Speech,* 1967, *10,* 169–180.

Tyack, D., & Ingram, D. Children's production and comprehension of questions. *Journal of Child Language,* 1977, *4,* 211–224.

Uzgiris, I. Organization of sensorimotor intelligence. In M. Lewis (Ed.), *Origins of intelligence.* New York: Plenum, 1976.

Valian, V. Noun phrases in young children's speech. *Paper presented at the Ninth Annual Boston University Conference on Language Development,* October, 1984.

Valian, V., Winzemer, J., & Erreich, A. A "Little Linguist" model of syntax learning. In S. L. Tavakolian (Ed.), *Language acquisition and linguistic theory.* Cambridge, MA: MIT Press, 1981.

Van der Geest, T. Some interactional aspects of language acquisition. In C. E. Snow & C. A. Ferguson (Eds.), *Talking to children: Language input and acquisition.* New York: Cambridge University Press, 1977.

Waryas, C. L., & Stremel, K. On the preferred form of the double object construction. *Journal of Psycholinguistic Research,* 1974, *3,* 271–280.

Wason, P. C. The contexts of plausible denial. *Journal of Verbal Learning and Verbal Behavior,* 1964, *4,* 7–11.

Wason, P. C. In real life negatives are false. *Logique et Analyse,* 1972, *57–58,* 17–38.

Watt, W. C. On two hypotheses concerning psycholinguistics. In J. R. Hayes (Ed.), *Cognition and the development of language*. New York: Wiley, 1970.

Wells, G. Learning to code experience through language. *Journal of Child Language*, 1974, *1*, 243–269.

Wells, G. Variation in child language. In P. Fletcher & M. Garman (Eds.), *Language acquisition*. New York: Cambridge University Press, 1979.

Wieman, L. A. Stress patterns of early child language. *Journal of Child Language*, 1976, *3*, 283–286.

Wilson, R., Pinker, S., Zaenen, A., & Lebeaux, D. Productivity and the dative alternation. *Paper presented at the Sixth Annual Boston University Conference on Language Development*, October, 1981.

Winzemer, J. A. *A lexical-expectation model for children's comprehension of wh-questions*. Unpublished doctoral dissertation, City University of New York, 1981.

Wode, H. Four early stages in the development of L1 negation. *Journal of Child Language*, 1977, *4*, 87–102.

Wooten, J., Merkin, S., Hood, L., & Bloom, L. Wh-questions: Linguistic evidence to explain the sequence of acquisition. *Paper presented to Biennial meeting of the Society for Research in Child Development*. San Francisco, March, 1979.

2 The Acquisition of German

Anne E. Mills
Universität Tübingen

Contents

INTRODUCTION

1. Descriptive Sketch of German[1]

1.1. *Regional and Social Variation*

German is an Indo-European language and within that family belongs to the Germanic group. It is spoken over a large area and has many different dialects. The languages which are spoken in some areas, for example Austria, German Switzerland, and Italian Tirol, are variants of German which are, however, often

---

[1] I am indebted to David A. Reibel, Rudolf Thiem, Christine Meinecke, and Fritz Hermanns for their helpful suggestions in the writing of this paper, and especially to Gisa Neumann for her constructive typing of it.

considered as being quite separate from German. The dialects within Germany also show considerable variation in phonology, lexical items, etc., so that difficulties of mutual understanding can arise. Standard High German, which is consistent with the written form of the language, and described in compendious grammars such as Helbig and Buscha (1972) and Curme (1904), is in fact an abstraction. The German spoken in the Hannover area is usually considered to be closest to this standard form.

The dialect a child is exposed to in his surroundings is extremely important when considering acquisition data, since the dialect form may be at variance with the standard form. Where it is appropriate, this has been discussed in the evaluation of the data presented in this chapter; unfortunately, though, in most cases too little is known about the linguistic environment of the children investigated and the linguistic features of the local dialect. This is an important point to be carefully considered in the planning of all future observational and experimental research.

1.2. *Structural Features*

A brief summary of the main structural features of Standard High German will be presented. A necessary selection of the structures to be described has been made with respect to the acquisition data to be presented below.

1.2.1. *Word Order.*   Word order is variable but rule governed, especially with respect to the position of the verb (Bierwisch, 1973). Grammar books refer to a canonical word order of subject-verb-object from which they derive other word orders. Finite verb in second position is an obligatory rule in declarative sentences. The canonical status of this word order with regard to the position of the other elements, however, is not clearly reflected in an overwhelming frequency of this word order in written or spoken language. In main clauses, elements other than subject may occur in initial position associated with topicalization and given-new distinction but the verb is then obligatorily in second position followed by the subject. Sentences 1-4 are examples of word order variants of the same sentence: 'the man gave the woman a bunch of flowers yesterday'.

(1) *der*   *Mann*   *gab*   *der*
    DEF.ART: man   gave   DEF.ART:
    MASC:SG:NOM   FEM:SG:DAT

    Frau   *gestern*   *ein*   *-en*   *Blumenstrauß**
    woman   yesterday   INDEF.ART   MASC:SG:ACC   bouquet

---

*[The German letter *β* represents historical *sz*, pronounced in the same way as *ss* (and sometimes written as *ss* or *sz*). German nouns are capitalized as in standard orthography. Where child speech is quoted, the orthographic conventions of the individual authors have been adopted. Ed.]

(2) *einen Blumenstrauß gab der Mann gestern der Frau*

(3) *der Frau gab der Mann gestern einen Blumenstrauß*

(4) *gestern gab der Mann der Frau einen Blumenstrauß*

In subordinate clauses the finite verb is generally in clause final position. For example:

(5) *das*   *Kind,*   *das*   *im*
    DEF.ART: child   REL.PRO: in+DEF.ART:
    NEUT:SG:NOM   NEUT:SG:NOM   MASC:SG:DAT
    Garten   *spiel*   *-t*
    garden   play   3SG:PRES
    'the child who is playing in the garden'

After an auxiliary or modal verb the main verb is also in final position in main sentences. For example:

(6) *das*   *Mädchen*   *muß*   20   *Stunden*   *arbeit*   *-en*
    DEF.ART: girl   must: 20   hours   work   INF
    NEUT:SG:NOM   MOD
    'the girl must work 20 hours'

(7) *das*   *Mädchen*   *wird*   20   *Stunden*   *arbeit*   *-en*
    DEF.ART: girl   FUT.AUX   20   hours   work   INF
    NEUT:SG:NOM
    'the girl will work 20 hours'

(8) *das*   *Mädchen*   *hat*   20   *Stunden*
    DEF.ART: girl   PAST.AUX 20   hours
    NEUT:SG:NOM
    ge   *-arbeit*   *-et*
    PAST.PART.PREFIX   work   PAST.PART.SUFFIX
    'the girl has worked 20 hours'

1.2.2. Noun Phrase Morphology.   All nouns have a syntactic gender which determines the set of inflections used to mark case relations. There are three genders in the singular: masculine, feminine, and neuter. The plural paradigm is common to all genders. The case inflections are present in the definite and indefinite articles, demonstrative adjectives, and attributive adjectives. Tables 2.1 and 2.2 illustrate these paradigms. The noun itself is marked for case only in the genitive case of masculine and neuter singular nouns and in the dative plural. In some set phrases the dative is marked on masculine and neuter singular nouns. Otherwise the noun occurs in citation form (MacWhinney, 1985). Examples 9-11 illustrate this for the nouns *die Hunde* 'the dogs' and *das Haus* 'the house'.

(9) *Peter*   *gab*   *es*   *den*   *Hund* -e -n
    Peter gave it:ACC DEF.ART:DAT:PL dog   PL DAT:PL
    'Peter gave it to the dogs'

(10) *die*   *Tür* *des*   *Haus* -es
     DEF.ART: door DEF.ART: house GEN
     FEM:SG:NOM   NEUT:SG:GEN
     'the door of the house'

(11) *zu* *Haus* -e
     at   house DAT
     'at home'

Adjectives in attributive function have inflectional endings, as Table 2.2 indicates. These endings vary, however, according to the presence or absence of an article and according to the type of article. If the adjective is preceded by a definite article or demonstrative adjective in the noun phrase, the adjective takes what are called the "weak" endings. If the adjective has no preceding article, the endings are "strong." If the adjective is preceded by an indefinite article, the endings are "mixed." For example:

(12) *der*   *gut* -e   *Käse*   "weak"
     DEF.ART: good MASC: cheese
     MASC:SG:NOM   SG:NOM
     'the good cheese'

TABLE 2.1
Definite and Indefinite Article Declension

	Masculine		Neuter		Feminine		Plural
	Def.	*Indef.*	*Def.*	*Indef.*	*Def.*	*Indef.*	*Def.*
Nominative	der	ein	das	ein	die	eine	die
Accusative	den	einen	das	ein	die	eine	die
Genitive	des	eines	des	eines	der	einer	der
Dative	dem	einem	dem	einem	der	einer	den

TABLE 2.2

Declension of Adjective *Gross* 'Big': "Strong" When Not Preceded by Article, "Mixed" When Preceded by Indefinite Article, or Similar Form, "Weak" When Preceded by Definite Article

| | Singular | | | | | | | | | Plural | | |
| | MASC | | | FEM | | | NEUT | | | | | |
Case	strong	mixed	weak	strong	mixed	weak	strong	mixed	weak	strong	mixed	weak
NOM	grosser	grosser	grosse	grosse	grosse	grosse	grosses	grosses	grosse	grosse	grossen	grossen
ACC	grossen	grossen	grossen	grosse	grosse	grosse	grosses	grosses	grosse	grosse	grossen	grossen
GEN	grosses	grossen	grossen	grosser	grosser	grossen	grosses	grossen	grossen	grosser	grossen	grossen
DAT	grossem	grossen	grossen	grosser	grossen	grossen	grossem	grossen	grossen	grossen	grossen	grossen

145

(13) *ein*   *gut*   *-er*   *Käse*   "mixed"

      INDEF.ART: good MASC: cheese
      MASC:SG:NOM   SG:NOM

      'a good cheese'

(14) *gut*   *-er*   *Käse*   "strong"

      good   MASC:SG:NOM   cheese

      'good cheese'

As can be seen from Tables 2.1 and 2.2, there is a considerable multiplicity of form, even within one gender paradigm. This presents a considerable problem for the child. He must rely on word order rules and semantic and pragmatic information to interpret strings before he has mastered this system. This is true to some extent even when the system has been learned, since formal ambiguity exists in some cases. This system of inflections and word order rules is a complex area for language acquisition in German and is of major interest.

1.2.3. Prepositions.   Prepositions require the use of particular cases, predominantly accusative and dative. Some prepositions can amalgamate with a following masculine or neuter definite article in the dative case and a following neuter definite article in accusative case, for example, *von dem* can become *vom* 'from the', *in + das* can become *ins* 'into the'. The contracted form is obligatory in some set phrases. This is an additional complexity for the child in the case-marking system.

Some prepositions can be used with either dative or accusative case to convey a stative or directional meaning.

(15) *ich*   *gehe*   *in*   *das*   *Haus*

      I   go   in:DIRECT   DEF.ART:NEUT:SG:ACC   house

      'I go into the house'

(16) *ich*   *arbeite*   *in*   *dem*   *Haus*

      I   work   in:STAT   DEF.ART:NEUT:SG:DAT   house

      'I work in the house'

(17) *die*   *Ameise*   *kriecht*   *auf*   *den*   *Tisch*

      DEF.ART: ant   crawls   on:DIRECT   DEF.ART: table
      FEM:SG:NOM   MASC:SG:ACC

      'the ant crawls onto the table'

(18) *die*   *Ameise*   *kriecht*   *auf*   *dem*   *Tisch*

      DEF.ART: ant   crawls   on:STAT   DEF.ART: table
      FEM:SG:NOM   MASC:SG:DAT

      'the ant is crawling on the table'

In most contexts the verb determines whether the preposition is being used in the stative or directional sense, as examples 15 and 16 illustrate. In sentences where the verb can allow both senses, however, the case information becomes crucial. The child's comprehension of such sentences and production of all sentences with prepositions relies on his control of the inflectional system.

1.2.4. *Verb Morphology.*   Verb morphology is not particularly complex. Verb tenses are formed by on the whole postfixed inflections on the verb root, or by using auxiliaries, as examples 19–22 illustrate with the verb *zeigen* 'to show'.

(19) *ich   zeig   -e*
     I   show   1SG
     'I show'

(20) *ich   zeig   -t   -e*
     I   show   PAST   1SG
     'I showed'

(21) *ich   hab   -e   ge-   zeig   -t*
     I   AUX   1SG   PAST   show   PAST
     'I have shown'

(22) *ich   werd   -e   zeig   -en*
     I   AUX   1SG   show   INF
     'I will show'

Some verbs behave irregularly in the formation of tenses involving changes in the root forms as well as the inflections. One group, the "strong" verbs, change

TABLE 2.3
Verb Inflections
in the Present Tense
of *Singen* 'to Sing'

1SG	*ich sing- e*
2SG	*du sing- st*
3SG	er
	sie ⎬ *sing- t*
	es
1PL	*wir sing- en*
2PL	*ihr sing- t*
3PL	*sie sing- en*[1]

[1]The third person plural form is identical in the pronoun and verb form with the second person polite form singular and plural.

the root form in some tenses and have different inflections; another smaller "mixed" group change the root form but have the regular inflections. For example, the simple past tense form of *ich bring-e* 'I bring' is *ich brach-t-e* but the past tense of *ich zieh- e* 'I pull' is *ich zog*. These exceptions present the main source of difficulty.

Person is also marked on the verb by postfixed inflections, as Table 2.3 indicates. There is some mutiplicity of form in the inflections associated with different persons, first and third person plural are identical for example. It is obligatory to use a personal pronoun if no full noun is present.

Some verbs are made up of a stem and a verbal particle. Some of these verbal particles are like prepositions and separate from the verb stem in some constructions. In a declarative sentence, for example, the particle in such verbs will be in clause final position as sentence 23 illustrates with the verb *an-ziehen* 'to put on'.

(23) *er   zog   seine   Jacke   an*
     he   pulled   his   jacket   on
     'he put his jacket on'

In the past participle the verbal particle is placed in front of the past prefix *ge-* so that the past participle of *an-ziehen* is *an-ge-zogen*. Many verb stems form a number of different verbs in combination with different verbal particles, so the particle would seem to be contributing a major part to the meaning of the verb. There are 60 different verbs (Mater, 1967) with such particles in combination with the stem *ziehen* 'to pull'. For example:

ab-	*ziehen*	'pull down'
ein-	*ziehen*	'draw in'
über-	*ziehen*	'cover'
weg-	*ziehen*	'pull off'

1.2.5. *Questions.* Questions are of two types: yes-no questions and wh-questions. Yes-no questions can be formed by a rising intonation only or by subject-verb inversion.

(24) *Peter   kauft   Brötchen?*
     Peter   buys   rolls
     'is Peter buying rolls?'

(25) *kauft   Peter   Brötchen?*
     buys   Peter   rolls
     'is Peter buying rolls?'

Tag questions can be formed on declarative sentences by adding a word or phrase, as sentence 26 illustrates. The exact form varies according to dialect. There can be a variation in intonation to indicate different functions of the tag as in English (see Mills [1981] for fuller discussion).

(26) *Peter   kauft   Brötchen,   oder?*
    Peter   buys   rolls   or
    'Peter is buying rolls, isn't he?'

Wh-questions involve a fronting of the interrogative pronoun and subject-verb inversion.

(27) *wo   kauft   Peter   Brötchen?*
    LOC.INT   buys   Peter   rolls
    'where is Peter buying rolls?'

1.2.6. Negation.   Negation on the verb requires the placement of *nicht* 'not' after the finite verb in most instances. Where subject-verb inversion has occurred, *nicht* is placed after the subject. In subordinate clauses, where the finite verb is in clause-final position, *nicht* is placed before the verb. There is however considerable variation in these rules. Negation on the noun requires the use of *kein* 'no' as an article.

(28) *Johann   geht   nicht   ins   Kino*
    Johann   goes   not   into+the   cinema
    'Johann isn't going to the cinema'

(29) *wir   haben   keine   Milch*
    we   have   no   milk
    'we haven't any milk'

1.2.7. Passive.   The passive is formed much as in English, that is by using the auxiliary *werden,* the preposition *von* 'by' before the agent (with dative case), and the past participle of the verb. This last element is however positioned at the end of the sentence, following the general rule in all complex verb forms. Sentences 30 and 31 illustrate the active and passive forms.

(30) *der   Mann   öffne   -t   die   Tür*
    DEF.ART: man   open   3SG:PRES   DEF.ART: door
    MASC:SG:NOM   FEM:SG:ACC
    'the man opens the door'

(31) *die*   *Tür*   *wird*   *von*   *dem*
DEF.ART: door   PRES.AUX   by   DEF.ART:
FEM:SG:NOM   [PREP] MASC:SG:DAT

Mann   *ge-*   *öffne*   *-t*
man   PAST   open   PAST

'the door is opened by the man'

1.2.8. *Subordinate Clauses.*

Subordinate clauses also have the verb in clause final position, as mentioned above. Relative clauses branch principally to the right of the head noun. The relative pronoun, which is in most cases identical to the definite article, is placed in clause initial position next to the head noun. German also allows a left branching relative construction, which requires no relative pronoun. The verb has the form of an adjectival present or past participle. Sentences 32 and 33 illustrate these two types of relative clause. The latter type, however, is mainly restricted to formal written language.

(32) *der*   *Brief,* *den*   *der*   *Mann*
DEF.ART: letter   REL.PRO: DEF.ART: man
MASC:SG:NOM   MASC:SG:ACC MASC:SG:NOM

ge-   *schrieben*   *hat,*   *ist*   *unklar*
PAST   write:PAST   AUX   is   unclear

'the letter which the man wrote is unclear'

(33) *der*   *von*   *dem*   *Mann*
DEF.ART: by   DEF.ART: man
MASC:SG:NOM   [PREP] MASC:SG:DAT

ge-   *schrieben*   *-e*   *Brief* *ist*   *unklar*
PAST   write:PAST   MASC:SG:NOM   letter   is   unclear
                      [ADJ.SUFF]

'the letter written by the man is unclear'

Many verbs allow verbal complements which can be formed either with *daß* 'that' and a finite verb in clause final position (34) or with an infinitive construction (35). As in English, the subject of the infinitival complement is usually the object of the main clause except with a few verbs such as *versprechen* 'to promise' etc.

(34) *der*   *Beamte*   *empfiehlt,*   *daß*   *die*
DEF.ART: official recommends   that   DEF.ART:
MASC:SG:NOM   FEM:SG:NOM

Universität	*den*		*Antrag*
university	DEF.ART: MASC:SG:ACC		application

rechtzeitig	*stell*	*-t*
in:good:time	submit	3SG:PRES

'the official recommends that the university submit the application in good time'

(35)

der	*Beamte*	*empfiehlt*	*der*	*Universität,*
DEF.ART: MASC:SG:NOM	official	recommends	DEF.ART: FEM:SG:DAT	university

den	*Antrag*	*rechtzeitig*	*zu*	*stell*	*-en*
DEF.ART: MASC:SG:ACC	application	in:good:time	to	submit	INF

'the official recommends the university to submit the application in good time'

2. Sources of Data[2]

The richest sources of data are still the diary studies made at the end of the last and at the beginning of this century (Preyer, 1882; Lindner, 1898; Schädel, 1905; Scupin & Scupin, 1907, 1910; Stern & Stern, 1928; Leopold, 1949). These have all the limitations of diary studies in that only selected material is recorded, for example, and in that full contextual information is usually missing. Studies such as Preyer and Scupin and Scupin did not concentrate on language but recorded utterances where they reflected another developmental aspect of the child. Although this is a major disadvantage in any analysis of the material, Scupin and Scupin contains such a wealth of examples (from one child up to the age of 6 years) that many insights can be gained from the study. Stern and Stern recorded their two children up to the ages of 5 and 6 but in their summarizing and analysis of their material they concentrated on vocabulary and morphology and neglected syntax. None of the studies describe the dialect the child or children were exposed to, so that it is impossible to detect the influence this might have had on some forms. Despite these limitations, the data from the diary studies can usefully be pooled when no other more detailed work is available. Later work has often in fact shown that the observations have more general validity.

---

[2]It is not the purpose of this chapter to review all the work that has ever been done on child language in German. The aim is rather to discuss the data which are of interest when considering which general principles may be involved in language acquisition and which problems language-specific features pose in the acquisition process. Within that framework I hope that I have not made too many omissions. A. E. M. November, 1981.

Apart from these studies, little work has been done on spontaneous productions, especially from the point of view of syntax and morphology. Many of the studies (e.g. König, 1972; Rickheit, 1975) have been of a statistical nature comparing the quantitative use of specific constructions in the written and spoken language of older children. Such studies are not very useful for present purposes since they trace changes in use only in quantitative terms and contain practically no information about errors or conditions of use of a construction. Grimm (1973) gives more detail of use but the data are still predominantly numerical with little analysis of structure. Park (1970, 1971a, 1971b, 1974) collected data from three Swiss-German children aged 2–3 years and analyzed various aspects of acquisition, for example verb morphology, use of the auxiliary.[3] The data presented are often few, however, and the proposed analysis is not always clearly supported. Miller (1976) collected a considerable amount of data from three children aged 1–2 years and analyzed the types of semantic constructions occurring in the, predominantly two-word, utterances. His aim was to show the importance of semantic and pragmatic information in providing a description of such utterances. He does not therefore enter into a highly detailed discussion of his results in terms of the principles of acquisition but his data are a useful source of information. Few researchers, Stephany (1976), Wode (1971, 1977), Clancy et al. (1976), use data from spontaneous utterances of German children to make explicit comparison with data from other languages. This has been done in the areas of word order, negation and question formation, and complex sentences.

Experimental studies on German child language are however far more common than studies of spontaneous productions and are too numerous to mention here individually. These studies test imitation, comprehension, and production of many different structures in varying situations. The children tested are principally older than 3-years-of-age. Since there are few data from spontaneous utterances from children of this age, however, it is frequently difficult to construct a balanced picture of acquisition.

Very little information is available on the structural aspects of caretakers' speech to their children. The work that has been done by Mills (in prep.) and Oksaar (1977) is based on a small sample and needs to be verified by data from a larger sample.

Although there has been a steadily growing interest in child language over the last 10 years in Germany, there is still relatively little research done in this area, especially in the way of longitudinal studies. The growing interest in child language has also coincided with a main focus in German linguistics on pragmatics and semantics, with the result that more work has been done on these aspects of child language than on the acquisition of structures. Very little is known about

---

[3]Park (1981) has analyzed the data from these papers, especially from one child, more extensively in a recent publication. Unfortunately this was received too late to be discussed here in detail.

the acquisition of many constructions in German, so that crosslinguistic comparison can only be made in a few areas.

3. Overall Course of Development

3.1. One-word Stage

The child's first utterances typically are produced around 1;0. The type of semantic functions in the child's first productions follow the pattern found in English; that is, they are predominantly constative and volitional, involving one entity rather than two. They most commonly refer to an object, action, appearance/existence/demonstrative, negation, and position. Utterances referring to agent, benefactor, possession, and disappearance are less frequently encountered.

Nouns predominate as a grammatical class, being produced in the unmarked singular except for those nouns which are most commonly used in the plural, such as *Schuh-e* 'shoes'. The child's productions usually contain many onomatopoeic forms and nursery words, which is probably a function of the amount of baby talk in the input speech, for example *adda* 'go for a walk', *wau-wau* 'dog'. These forms and the child's production of standard forms are commonly reduplicative, for example *mi-mi* for the name *Melanie*. Consonant cluster reduction is also typical, for example **lafen* for *schlafen* 'to sleep'; this continues until roughly age 3;0.

Verbal particles are common, especially with the semantic function of location, for example *auf* 'up', *runter* 'down'. They also frequently stand for a full verb, for example *an* from *an-ziehen* 'to put on (clothing)'. These occur clause-finally in adult speech and are stressed, which probably explains their early acquisition. When the child produces full verbs, they usually have the *-en* ending like the infinitive. This is probably attributable to the frequent use in adult speech of modals and auxiliaries which send the main verb in infinitive form to the end of the clause, infinitival imperatives, and syntactic baby talk in which no modal or auxiliary is used but the main verb is final in infinitive form. The verbs in the child's speech which do not have this *-en* ending are usually part of a set formula such as *schmeck-t* from *es schmeckt* 'it tastes good'. This is the answer to the frequent question from the adult, when any food is given to the child, *schmeckt's?* 'does it taste good?'.

Modification is variable in the amount it occurs as a function. When adjectives are used, they are used in predicative form, that is without the inflectional endings which are necessary in attributive position, for example *heiß* 'hot'. Other frequent forms in this function are the adverbs *auch* 'too', *nochmal* 'again', *mehr* 'more'. The negative is expressed by the sentence external negator *nein* 'no'. Demonstrative function is usually expressed through the deictic terms *da* 'there' and *hier* 'here'.

Some two word sequences are used at this stage but these appear to be unanalyzed forms which are frequent in the input speech, for example *guck mal* 'just look!'.

3.2. *Two-word Stage*

The first functional relations expressed at this stage are demonstrative/appearance/existence, in agreement with the findings for English. Actions are more commonly referred to than states. Nouns are still predominantly used in the unmarked singular but some plurals are used—usually correctly, for example *Bücher* 'books'. These appear to be examples of rote learning, however, rather than a production by rule. Articles are rare at this stage and, when they do occur, they are often reduced in form: *de* for the definite article and *n* for the indefinite article. These reduced forms cannot mark case or gender, which is necessary in the full forms of the article. The use of this common form may be due to the child's lack of control of the inflectional system but these reduced forms also occur in adult fast speech.

Adjectives are used in attributive position, that is before the noun, and are usually inflected to agree with the noun in case and gender. Since no article precedes the adjective at this stage, strong endings are appropriate and there are recorded examples of this correct use in children's production. A common error is to overgeneralize the ending *-e,* however, which is the most frequent across nominative and accusative case in the strong and weak paradigms. When the strong endings are used, they are usually correct for gender, for example *groß-es Loch* 'big hole' from a child aged 1;10.

Word order at this stage is most frequently verb-final, when a verb is expressed. This is probably attributable to the frequency of the main verb in final position in the input speech, as discussed above. The verb is most frequently in the infinitive form, that is with the ending *-en.* When the agent is expressed before the verb, it becomes more common for the verb to have the third person singular ending *-t.* This indicates the development of the link between subject and verb. Past participles are produced at this stage, although it is frequently not clear that a reference is being made to past time. When these are produced, the past affixes, especially the prefix *ge-,* are frequently missing, for example **nommen* instead of *ge-nommen* 'taken'. The past participles are also in verb-final position as is correct in adult speech. Auxiliaries and modal verbs are very rare at this stage. Verb particles are common, as in the one-word stage, but although these frequently have the same forms as prepositions, prepositions themselves are rare.

In negation a development takes place during this stage. The first constructions have *nein* 'no' in initial position, for example *nein trinken* '(I'm) not drinking'. Later the negator changes to *nicht* 'not', which is then correctly placed after the verb in most cases. Intonation questions are produced at this stage, for example *Mutti kommen*? '(is) Mummy coming?'. Locative questions also start to appear, for example *wo Teddy*? 'where (is) teddy?'

3.3. *Three and More Words (to Age 4;0)*

3.3.1. *Noun Phrase.*   Articles start to be used more regularly, although they are still omitted on occasion. When used, they are usually correct for gender which is possibly due to sensitivity to morphophonological regularities, though this is not clear from the data. If an error is made, it is usually to overgeneralize the feminine definite article *die*, probably since it is the most frequent form in nominative and accusative case across the singular and plural paradigms. With the indefinite article, the feminine form *eine* is overgeneralized, probably because it is salient through being polysyllabic.

The marking of case in the nominative and accusative is only apparent in the masculine gender paradigm. The distinctive marking of nominative and accusative is sporadic before age 3;0; otherwise the nominative case form is used. This can probably be attributed to an attempt to regularize the paradigm since in the feminine, neuter, and plural paradigms there is no distinction.

Dative case appears around age 3;0 and is usually marked correctly except after prepositions. Genitive case does not appear marked on the article in any of the data reported. The possessive relation is indicated by the suffix -*s* added to the noun referring to the possessor, which is ordered before the thing possessed. This is correct in adult speech with proper names but children overgeneralize this to all nouns, for example **Eisenbahn-s Wohnung* 'railway's house'. Possession is also expressed by placing the possessor before the thing possessed and using a possessive pronoun, which occurs in some dialect forms. This double marking makes the possessive relationship very clear. A third way to mark possession is by a preposition; *von* 'of' is used but also the incorrect *zu* 'to'.

The pronouns *ich* 'I' and *du* 'you' appear around 2;6 and occasionally are used in case-marked forms. These uses appear to be formulaic rather than indicating a control of the inflected forms, for example *für dich* (ACC) 'for you' when giving someone something, *gib mir* (DAT) 'give me' when requesting something.

Adjective endings are fairly well established in the strong and weak paradigms and case endings by the age of 4;0. Prior to that, there is some evidence that children attempt to mark the same endings on all forms preceding the nouns, for example *mein-*er gut-er Papa* 'my good Daddy'. The comparative is also produced with overgeneralization of the root in irregular forms, for example *gut-er* from *gut* 'good' instead of *besser*.

Prepositions start to appear regularly, predominantly in locative use, around age 3;0. Accusative case is frequently overgeneralized after prepositions. This is probably due to the easy confusion of *n* (marking accusative) and *m* (marking dative) in the masculine gender paradigm. From experimental evidence the stative meaning appears to be learned before directional meaning with those prepositions which can have both meanings.

3.3.2. *Verb.*   Around age 3;0 considerable developments take place in the verb. The verb-final rule is not as prevalent as in the two-word stage, although some children use it even with longer sentences for a while. With the placing of the verb in second position after the first element in the sentence, the marking of person becomes common and is usually correct. Auxiliaries and modals begin to appear and usually are placed correctly in second position, with the main verb then in final position. Few errors occur with this word order. The prefix *ge-* on the past participle starts to be used but it is still frequently omitted. Future tense starts to be marked with the auxiliary *werden*.

Overgeneralization in parts of the verb which are irregular becomes common. In the past participle the regular "weak" form is overgeneralized to the irregular "strong" verbs to produce errors such as *ge-geh-t* instead of *ge-gang-en* from *geh-en* 'to go'. The irregular forms in the present tense are also regularized, for example *er *lauf-t* from *lauf-en* 'to run' instead of *er läuf-t*. The simple past tense starts to be used and here too the regular form is overgeneralized to the irregular forms, for example *sie *stehl-t-en* from *stehl-en* 'to steal' instead of *sie stahl-en*. In all these regularizations the child is using the present tense as the basis of the form, which indicates that he is able to establish what the present tense is in each case.

3.3.3. *Complex Structures.*   In questions, the subject-verb inversion neces-sary after a question word is acquired. More question words are used, first *was* 'what', later *wer* 'who', then *wie* 'how' and *warum* 'why'. Tag questions are learned around age 3;0, apparently earlier than in English. This is possibly due to the simpler structure of the German form.

The passive is sporadic in spontaneous use until age 4;0 and is only ever agentless. In comprehension, children of this age rely heavily on a word order strategy, that is that the noun in first position is interpreted as being agent.

Relative clauses are rare. When they are produced, the verb is correctly in final position but the relative pronoun is frequently omitted or a form is used which is unmarked for case and gender, for example *das Mädchen, wo in die Schule geht* 'the girl that goes to school'. This form *wo* 'where' occurs as the relative pronoun in some dialects, but the influence of dialect on the children's use is unclear. Around age 4;0 the children who have used the *wo* pronoun, begin using a double form with the standard relative pronoun and *wo,* for example *ein Heinzelmann, der *wo so machen kann* 'a Heinzelmann that can go like this'. Children apparently have difficulty with the relative pronoun since it is similar to the definite article and must be marked for gender and case. Until they have mastered these features, they omit the pronoun, select a simple form or use the simple together with the more complex form. In comprehension at age 4;0

children are still having difficulty perceiving the structure of a relative clause and grouping the elements which belong to it. They will frequently assume the first noun of the sentence to be agent in both the main and relative clause, even when the relative clause occurs at the end of the sentence.

3.3.4. *Analytic Ability.*   From the questions children ask about language and the lexical innovations they produce, they start to work hard at analyzing structures between the ages of 3;0 and 4;0. It becomes important that parts of a word contribute clearly to the semantic content of the whole. False analyses are also made. This fits together with the general tendency to overregularize the most transparent rules.

3.4. *Later Development (Age 4;0 Onwards)*

Constructions which were sporadic previously appear with greater frequency, for example the future tense, relative clauses, and the passive, although this is still predominantly agentless. In the comprehension of these last two structures under experimental conditions, semantic information is relied on much more for interpretation. Only after the age of 7;0 can structure alone be used to establish agent and object relations independently of semantic information. Children now seem to be able to group together the elements of the relative clause but have problems establishing case relations within the clause. Where there is no cue from semantic information, they rely on a word order strategy associating subject or agent with first position in the clause, as do adults in the interpretation of ambiguous relative clauses. Time prepositions become more common as well as the temporal interrogative pronoun *wann* 'when'.

Children are still having difficulties with all those parts of the language which are highly irregular, celebrated by Mark Twain in "The Awful German Language." Errors still occur in the use of nominative case for accusative case. Plural mistakes are common with overgeneralization of the most regular form -*en*. Nouns which take the zero plural allomorph are often marked for plural, indicating a tendency to mark all forms clearly. The comparative adjective is also commonly marked twice, for example *größ-er-*er,* possibly because the ending is identical to a case/gender inflection in the masculine paradigm. The possessive pronoun *sein* (for 3rd person masculine and neuter gender) is overgeneralized to all singular 3rd person singular nouns, whereas *ihr* (feminine and plural) is used for plural only. Again one form is preferred for one clear function. Although the morphological rules of noun compounding are complex and have many exceptions, children make few errors in this area. Apparently they learn through the high frequency of compounds, which forms are possible for each noun when it occurs as determinans.

Errors are still frequent in the past tense of irregular verbs. Children tend to overgeneralize the use of the auxiliary *haben* to those verbs which should have *sein,* since this use cannot be predicted by any clear rule. The mistakes with the simple past and past participle of irregular verbs seem now to be interrelated. The errors reported tend not to be overgeneralizations of the regular form but rather an error in selection of the change in the root, for example the past participle *ge-ging-t* takes the simple past form *ging* from the verb *geh-en* 'to go' as the changed root, instead of the correct *ge-gang-en*.

Although word order errors are rare, errors do occur in the ordering of verbal elements in a subordinate clause where there is more than one verbal element. The rules here are complex and are apparently learned later than age 6;0.

THE DATA

4. Typical Errors

4.1. Word Order

4.1.1. *Word Order in the Two-word Phase.*   Word order is an area in which there is a considerable amount of error. At the stage when two-word utterances predominate, many researchers have observed that the dominant word order involves the placement of the verb in final position (Preyer, 1882; Stern & Stern, 1928; Park, 1970; Grimm, 1973; Miller, 1976; Stephany, 1976). In the two children aged 1–2 years, recorded by Miller (1976), this verb-final rule accounted for 70% of the utterances involving a verb.

The following examples are taken from Miller's data and collected from one child, Meike. They reveal that nouns in many different functions occur in first position before a verb.

(36) Miller (1;7)   *mädi*   *lafen*
,   girl:AGENT   sleep
                     'the girl is sleeping'

(37) Miller (1;8)   *teddy*   *holen*
                     teddy:OBJ   fetch
                     'fetch teddy'

(38) Miller (1;10)   *hause*   *gehen*
                      home:LOC   go
                      'go home'

(39) Miller (1;10)   *meike*   *ab-*   *machen*
                      Meike:BENEFACTOR   off   take
                      'take (it) off Meike'

In two-word utterances it is not clear that the verb-final position is an error, since it is a rule of adult German that the verb must occur as second element in main clauses, whatever the first element may be. Since the verb also occurs in final position in three-word utterances at this stage, as the following examples show, it is clear that the child is using a verb-final rule. It is therefore correctly classified as an error.

(40) Miller (1;8)   *teddy*   *sofa*   *fahren*

                    teddy:AGENT   moped:OBJ   drive

                    'teddy drives the moped'

(41) Miller (1;10) *meike*   *fenster*   *gucken*

                    Meike:AGENT   window:LOC   look

                    'Meike is looking out of the window'

Word order is clearly not being used as a basic means of indicating semantic functions at this stage, as Stephany (1976) observed. It is not, for example, the predominance of agent function in the preceding noun which accounts for the data. Roeper (1973) provides an explanation for this rule linked to linguistic theory. He argues that German is an SOV language in its deep structure and that clauses with the elements in this order are easier to process. Firstly, however, in terms of this linguistic description, if accepted, it is not at all clear that German is an SOV language or that the question is even relevant (Bartsch & Vennemann, 1972). Secondly, it is not clear that this underlying word order should necessarily have any relevance for language acquisition. More important for language acquisition seems to be the word order which is perceived as basic to the language and from which other word orders seem to be derived by rule. For German, this canonical word order would be SVO. Roeper's explanation cannot be dismissed, however, since it does provide an account of the data, but it can only be accepted if many other theoretical assumptions are met.

It has also been suggested that the verb-final rule may be related to the language input (Roeper, 1972; Stephany, 1976; Miller, 1976). No full survey of caretakers' speech to children has yet been carried out for German but from my own data this suggestion seems to have some validity. In adult German, certain constructions involve positioning the main verb at the end of the clause. In subordinate clauses the verb occurs finally but such clauses are less rather than more frequent in adults' speech to children. With a modal or future auxiliary verb, the main verb is in infinitive form at the end of the clause, as sentences 6 and 7 above illustrate. The use of modals and auxiliaries is common in caretakers' speech related to the structure of the discourse. Characteristic of adult-child discourse is the large number of indirect commands, suggestions, etc.

which involve the use of modals and auxiliaries. Sentences 42–44 taken from my data illustrate such use.

(42) *möchtest*   *du*   *ein*   *Haus* *bau*   *-en?*
     want [MOD] you   INDEF.ART: house build INF
                        NEUT:SG:ACC
     'would you like to build a house?'

(43) *willst*   *du*   *pipi*   *mach*   *-en?*
     want [MOD] you   wee-wee do   INF
     'do you want to do a wee-wee?'

(44) *du*   *sollst*   *nicht* *wein* *-en*
     you   should   NEG   cry   INF
           [MOD]
     'you shouldn't cry'

An alternative imperative form also involves positioning the verb at the end of the clause. Sentences 45.a and 46 illustrate this in comparison with the standard 2nd person singular imperative form in 45.b and 47. This infinitive-like form is particularly common with negative commands.

(45.a) *nicht* *beiss* *–en!*
       NEG   bite   INF/IMP
       'don't bite!'

(45.b) *beiss* *-e*   *nicht*
       bite   2SG:IMP NEG
       'don't bite!'

(46) *jetzt* *auf-* *stehen!*
     now   up   stand
     'now stand up!'

(47) *steh* *-e*   *jetzt* *auf!*
     stand 2SG:IMP now   up
     'stand up now!'

A construction which occurs in regional dialects but which is not an accepted standard German form, involves the use of the verb *tun* 'do' as an auxiliary in a declarative sentence. Its use seems to involve no change in meaning, however, so that sentence 48 is to be considered as identical in meaning to sentence 49.

(48) *wir*   *tu*   *-n*   *hier*   *Bilder*   *mal*   *-en*
    we   AUX   1PL:PRES   here   pictures   paint   INF
    'we're painting pictures here'

(49) *wir*   *mal*   *-en*   *hier*   *Bilder*
    we   paint   1PL:PRES   here   pictures
    'we're painting pictures here'

The use of the auxiliary *tun* again sends the main verb to the end of the clause.

In my own research, samples of speech from three mothers have been analyzed. It was found that the number of constructions involving the main verb in final position was extremely high. All three mothers used the dialectal *tun*, although one mother was not a speaker of a dialect which allows this construction. Her use of this construction was limited to speech addressed to her child. It is therefore possible that this construction is a baby-talk feature, but this needs to be investigated further. All three mothers did produce syntactic baby-talk, however, in that they produced utterances with a verb final rule and with the verb in infinitive form, although no modal or auxiliary was used. Sentence 50 taken from my data illustrates this, in contrast to the standard form of 51.

(50) *Mama*   *Bonbon*   *ess*   *-en?*
    mummy   sweet   eat   INF
    'mummy eat the sweet?'

(51) *soll*   *ich*   *das*   *Bonbon*   *ess*   *-en?*
    should [MOD]   I   DEF.ART: sweet   eat   INF
                NEUT:SG:ACC
    'should I eat the sweet?'

The mothers varied in their use of such baby-talk. In one mother the number of such utterances was extremely high.

This verb-final rule in the children is captured therefore by the universal suggested by Slobin (1973, p. 197) "word order in child speech reflects the word order of the input language." Particular emphasis is necessary in the case of German on INPUT LANGUAGE. The Operating Principle related to this universal: "pay attention to the order of the words and morphemes" would also be supported in the case of German by the generalized operating principle: "pay attention to the ends of words and sentences." It would appear that the role of the latter principle must be contributory rather than providing a total explanation, since it would not explain, for example, English data.

It has been argued that the structure of the caretakers' discourse is an explanation, at least in part, for the high frequency of main verb in final position. This was related to the adults' use of command, suggestions, etc. It would be interesting to know whether the children also are producing a large number of commands, questions, etc. If this were the case, it is possible that the verb–final rule is linked to the absence of the use of auxiliaries and modals in the child's own speech.

4.1.2. *Word Order in Longer Sentences.*   German has complex word-order rules, as has already been discussed. Unfortunately, apart from the data presented above, little information is available about word-order rules at later stages and in other constructions.

The verb-final rule was still being applied with three-word utterances in Miller's data, which is an error in terms of adult word-order rules. The rule then appears to be quickly learned that the verb is in second position whatever element is placed first, although one child has been recorded in my own data using the verb-final rule in four- and five-word utterances. There is no clear evidence that the canonical SVO order predominates in simple sentences. An investigation of the relationship of input to the child's utterances needs to be carried out in this area on the lines of Bowerman (1973). Stern and Stern (1928) discuss word order in longer utterances to some extent. They attribute deviant word order on the one hand to "imitation" and on the other to "spontaneity." In the case of imitation, they claim, the child's order has been affected by the immediate input speech.

(52) Stern (ca. 2;6)

    ADULT: *wo-*   *mit*   *ha*   *-st*   *Du*   *ge-*   *pfiffen?*

                INT.PRO with AUX 2SG you PAST whistle:PAST

                'what did you whistle with?'

    CHILD: *4   *Mund*   *mit*

                    mouth with

                    'with (my) mouth'

The correct answer should be *mit dem Mund.* The principle of spontaneity is related to topicalization and old and new information, but without a greater amount of systematic data and a detailed linguistic account of adult speakers' usage in this respect, this principle cannot usefully be discussed further here.

4.1.3. *Word Order in Questions.*   Wode (1971) describes one systematic error in the acquisition of word order in questions. The use of a question word requires the inversion of subject and verb, as described earlier. One of the first

---

    [4]The children's utterances quoted here and throughout the chapter are often deviant in more than the particular part marked with an asterisk. For the purposes of simplicity, the asterisk is used to mark only the deviant usage which is immediately under discussion.

question words is the interrogative pronoun *wo* 'where', as in English. First of all Wode's two children used *wo* in initial position but with no verb. Later they produced well-formed questions using *wo,* that is with subject-verb inversion, but only with forms of the verb *sein* 'to be' as in sentence 53.

(53) *Mama,   wo   bist   du?*
     mummy   INT.PRO:LOC   be:2SG   you
     'mummy, where are you?'

No other verbs were recorded. Before producing well-formed questions with all verbs, one child had a long intermediate stage using the order: *wo* SUBJECT VERB. The other child had only a few utterances in this order. Unfortunately all the utterances quoted contain only three words so that it is impossible to decide whether the child is using a word-order rule appropriate to a main clause but with the question word in initial position or a verb-final rule. The addition of a fourth linguistic unit X would indicate which interpretation was correct. The first rule would produce:

wo S V X

and the second rule:

wo S X V

Wode suggests it is the latter, on the basis that this one child also had a lengthy stage of verb-final rule in noninterrogative utterances. When he comes to summarize the general features of development, he describes word-order rules in questions by saying: "Multiword I(ntonation) Q(uestions) at first do not reflect adult interrogative word order if it differs from the non-interrogative one" (Wode, 1971, p. 308). He does not however specify which word order is then preferred. In interrogative pronoun questions, the first rule could be captured by Slobin's (1973) Universal D1: "Structures requiring permutation of elements will appear first in nonpermuted form." If the child were using the second rule mentioned above, however, this would appear to be an overgeneralization of the child's own noninterrogative order, that is with a verb-final rule. Unfortunately Wode does not present an analysis of the acquisition of yes-no questions in German which involve inversion of subject and verb. Data on this area might suggest which explanation is correct. These rules all fit together with the acquisition of word order-rules in noninterrogative sentences, where any element X at the beginning of a sentence which is not subject causes an inversion of verb and subject. Unfortunately data are not available on this area as a whole. Wode does note, however, that his impression is that inversion first occurs with yes-no questions and that once the other interrogative pronouns appear, that is those acquired after *wo,* the inversion rule appears to have been fully learned.

4.1.4. *Word Order in Subordinate Clauses.*   There are few data on the acquisition of the verb-final rule in subordinate clauses. Stern and Stern (1928), for example, do not report any word order errors in subordinate clauses. In other diary studies the first utterances containing a subordinate clause have the verb already in clause-final position.

(54) Scupin (2;2)   *mal   sehen,   daß   fort   ist*
                     just   see:INF   that   away   is
                     'let's see that it has gone away'

(55) Preyer (2;8)   *weiß   nicht,   wo   es   ist*
                     know   NEG   INT.PRO:LOC   it   is
                     '(I) don't know where it is'

A well-known children's rhyme *Backe, backe Kuchen* places an infinitive after a modal in non-clause-final position in order to obtain a rhyme: *der muß haben/sieben Sachen.* At age 2;10 Scupins' child corrects this line to produce the grammatical utterance:

(56) Scupin (2;10)   *der   muß   sieben   Sachen   hab   -en*
                      he   must   seven   things   have   INF
                      [EMPH]   [MOD]
                      'he must have seven things'

The verb-final rule in subordinate clauses would seem to be well established at an early age and could be seen as a continuation of a general verb-final order dominant at the two-word stage.

It would be interesting to know how the acquisition of the verb-final rule in subordinate clauses relates to the acquisition of subject-verb inversion in declarative main clauses which do not begin with the subject. One could be seen as a greater permutation than the other by two lines of argumentation. Any rule which removes subject from initial position is more complex and acquired later than a rule which preserves it in initial position, that is subject/verb inversion is acquired later than verb-final rule. Or the reverse, any rule which moves an element a greater distance from its original position is more complex and acquired later than one which moves an element a shorter distance, that is the verb-final rule is acquired later than subject-verb inversion.

Park (1976), in an imitation experiment, tested the ability of 3-, 4- and 5-year-olds to imitate, amongst other things, subordinate clauses with verb-final rule which are grammatical strings (sentence 57). He also tested imitation of ungrammatical versions, that is with SVO order (sentence 58) and with subject-verb inversion order (sentence 59).

(57) die   Kinder   sind   froh,   weil   der   Vater
     the   children   are   happy   because   the   father
     ein   Auto   kauf   -t
     a   car   buy   3SG
     'the children are happy, because their father is buying a car'

(58) *Die Kinder sind froh, weil der Vater kauft ein Auto.

(59) *Die Kinder sind froh, weil kauft der Vater ein Auto.

He used the subordinating conjunctions *weil* 'because' and *warum* 'why'.

Imitation of ungrammatical utterances is a problematic test procedure but, nevertheless, it is significant that the majority of children in this age range correctly imitated the grammatical form with verb-final rule. The behavior with the ungrammatical clauses was different according to which subordinating conjunction was used. More children changed the ungrammatical clauses with *weil* than they did with *warum*, transforming them into the grammatical form using the verb-final rule. The verb-final rule thus seemed far better established with *weil* than with *warum*. Park suggests, and I think this is clearly correct, that the difference is attributable to the different status of the two conjunctions. *Weil* can only be used with verb-final rule, whereas *warum* can also be used as an interrogative pronoun where subject-verb inversion rules apply. Two children converted the subject-verb inversion sentences into the SVO form. Two children, however, used the subject-verb inversion rule in their imitations of the grammatical and the SVO-rule sentences; one child used this rule in his imitation of all forms.

These results, although they only test two conjunctions with a small sample of children (n=7), suggest that, although the hypothetical principles discussed earlier may be significant, an important factor is the status of the conjunction in the child's grammar. The two functions of the same word *warum* have to be distinguished. Park (1971b) has one example, from a spontaneous utterance, of a word-order error.

(60) weil   ha   -st   du   das   ge-   sag   -t
     because   AUX   2SG   you   DEM.PRO:ACC   PAST   say   PAST
     'because you said that'

The child is treating *weil* as if it were an X element occurring at the beginning of the sentence rather than as a subordinating conjunction. This one error might suggest that subject-verb inversion has been in this case learned before the verb-final rule, or that the subject-verb inversion rule may dominate at one stage when the verb-final rule is perceived as inappropriate in declarative main clauses. Far more data are needed from many children before any firm conclusions can be drawn.

Although there are generally few word-order errors reported in subordinate clauses, older children still make errors in subordinate clauses where two or three verbal elements have to be ordered. This is to be expected since, in this case, the rules of ordering in adult German are more complex than the simple verb-final rule. If a subordinate clause contains two verbal elements, for example a modal and infinitive or an auxiliary and participle, the finite verb is ordered after the other verbal element. If the clause contains three verbal elements, the finite verb is ordered before the other two.

(61) *weil   du   gestern   komm -en   konn -te   -st*
     because you   yesterday come INF   can   PAST   2SG
     'because you could come yesterday'

(62) *weil   du   gestern   hätte   -st   komm -en   können*
     because you   yesterday have:PAST   2SG   come INF   can:PAST
     'because you could have come yesterday'

The material of both Scupin and Scupin and Stern and Stern contains examples of mistakes in such clauses as late as four and five years. In subordinate clauses containing two verbal elements, the finite verb is sometimes placed before the other verbal element instead of after it.

(63) Scupin (2;5)
     *weil   ich   dir   den   Apfel
     because I   you:DAT   the:ACC   apple
     hab   (ge)geben
     AUX   give:PAST
     'because I have given you the apple'

(64) Scupin (4;6)
     *daß   man   nicht   runter darf   fall -en
     that [CONJ]   one   NEG   down   may   fall INF
     'that one may not fall down'

(65) Stern (5;1)
     *wenn   du   's   uns   nicht
     if   you:NOM   it:ACC   us:DAT   NEG

würde	*-st*	*geb*	*-en*
would	2SG	give	INF

'if you wouldn't give it to us'

In other clauses the finite verb is ordered soon after the subject.

(66) Scupin (4;7)

*wenn	du		mich	hätte	-st
if	you:NOM		me:ACC	have:COND	2SG

einen		*Pfennig*	*in*	*den*
INDEF.ART:ACC		penny	in	DEF.ART:ACC

Automaten	*steck*	*-en*	*lassen*
slot:machine	put	INF	allow:PAST

'if you had allowed me to put the penny in the slot machine'

(67) Stern (5;5)

*wenn	ihr		*würd*	*-et*	*immerfort*
if	you:PL:NOM		would	2PL	always

in	*Berlin*	*ge-*	*blieben*
in	Berlin	PAST	stay:PAST

'if you were always to stay in Berlin'

These errors occur mainly in conditional clauses where it is most common to have three verbal elements and therefore the more complex rule in adult speech. It would seem as though the child has associated a different ordering with this type of clause or possibly with all clauses containing more than one verbal element but has not yet learned all the details of the rule with regard to the restrictions on its application and the positioning of the finite verb. From the data, the children involved show awareness of the fact that the rule involves multiplicity of verbal elements in the context of subordinate clause and the moving of the finite element out of final position. This indicates a quite high level of analysis in the child.

4.2. Verb Morphology

4.2.1. *Compound Past Tense.* The verb morphology of the past tense is a fairly complex area and is the source of considerable error. Many errors occur in the formation of the compound past tense which requires the use of an auxiliary and the past participle which is derived from the verb root. To this root is added the prefix *ge-* (with a few exceptions) and the suffix *-t*. Irregular or "strong" verbs generally have the suffix -en added to the root which frequently has a different form, for example:

regular—*kauf -en*	'to buy'	*ge-*	*kauf*	*-t*
irregular—*geh -en*	'to go'	*ge-*	*gang*	*-en*
lauf -en	'to run'	*ge-*	*lauf*	*-en*
sing -en	'to sing'	*ge-*	*sung*	*-en*

The past participle is placed at the end of the clause.

There is some evidence that the past participle appears first, without the auxiliary and prefix *ge-*, at a relatively early age.

(68) Scupin (1;11)

    *Decke   putt   mach   -t

    ceiling   broken make PAST

    'the ceiling has been broken' (?)

The context is often unclear, however, so that it cannot be established with certainty that a reference is being made to past time. The auxiliary does not appear until around age 3;0 but then it is in frequent use. The prefix *ge-* on the past participle also appears around this time but seems to present some difficulty in that its acquisition lasts a good deal longer (Preyer, 1882; Park, 1971b). MacWhinney claims that this is attributable to the fact that the auxiliary and *ge-* are parts of a discontinuous morpheme and the auxiliary is the part which is "subject to the most easily controlled variation" (MacWhinney, 1978, p. 53). This property he claims to be an important factor in the acquisition of morphology. This may well be a contributory factor in the earlier acquisition of the auxiliary but the fact that the prefix *ge-* is an unstressed syllable also seems to be important. In other words beginning with this syllable, but not the past morpheme, pronuciation is reported where this syllable is omitted.

(69) Preyer (2;3)

    *fährlich instead of *gefährlich* 'dangerous'

(70) Grimm (1973)

    *rage instead of *Garage* 'garage'

Omission of unstressed syllables is reported in the acquisition of many languages and would seem to be the most likely explanation here.

The early forms of the past participle, which the child produces, if they can be clearly classified as such, are often correct in terms of any vowel changes in the strong verbs and the selection of the *-t* or *-en* suffix. Around age 3;0 however there is a frequent overgeneralization of the weak form of the past participle. All the diary studies report such overgeneralization. The root used most often is the root which appears in the infinitive. This root MacWhinney calls the "citation allomorph." For example:

(71) Scupin (2;8)   *ge- geh -t* from *geh-en* 'to go'
                    instead of *ge- gang -en*
                    ge- denk -t from *denk-en* 'to think'
                    instead of *ge- dach -t*

MacWhinney claims that it is a general principle in the acquisition of morphology that the citation allomorph be taken as a base for inflections. There are some examples however of the simple past form being taken as the root for the past participle:

(72) Scupin (5;0)   *ge- ging -t* from *(ich) ging* 'I went'
                    instead of *ge- gang -en*

Since these examples are mostly later, this suggests that the child has established that a different root is used in the past of the strong verbs but has not sorted out which root form belongs to which past tense form. Some of the strong verbs have the same root in the simple past as in the past participle, so that the child may be overgeneralizing this class.

Further evidence of the child attempting to regularize the past forms comes from Neugebauer's (1915) child who at one stage formed irregular past participles (without *ge-*) of verbs which are regular using the vowel /o/ or /ɔ/ in every case. For example:

(73) Neugebauer (2;2)

    um-kopp-en   from *um-kipp-en* 'to tip over'
                     instead of *um-ge-kipp-t*
    klob-en   from *kleb-en* 'to stick'
                     instead of *ge-kleb-t*

All the examples Neugebauer recorded were from verbs which contain the vowel /e/, /I/, or /ɛ/ in the infinitive. A possible hypothesis is that the child was attempting to regularize the past participle forms on the basis of the vowel in the stem, like the correct examples: *ge-nomm-en* from *nehm-en* 'to take', *ge-schwomm-en* from *schwimm-en* 'to swim'.

4.2.2. *Auxiliary in the Past Tense.*   In the compound past tense either the auxiliary *hab-en* 'to have' or *sein* 'to be' is used. The selection is determined by rule (Helbig & Buscha, 1972, p. 119). The verbs which take the auxiliary *sein* in the past tense are relatively few and most commonly are perfective or a dynamic verb which involves a change of location. For example:

(74) *der Patient ist ge-storben*   'the patient has died'

(75) *der Sportler ist ge-laufen*   'the sportsman has run'

A few verbs can use both auxiliaries and the difference usually reflects the transitive versus the intransitive use or the durative versus the perfective aspect. For example:

(77) *ich habe den Bus ge-fahren*   'I drove the bus'

(78) *ich bin zu schnell ge-fahren*   'I drove too quickly'

(79) *sie hat jede Woche ge-tanzt*   'she went dancing every week'

(80) *sie ist durch den Saal ge-tanzt* 'she danced across the room'

Stern and Stern observed that Hildegard always used the correct auxiliary at age 3;2. Park (1971a,b) observed no errors in the choice of the correct auxiliary in his data either and suggests the child is using the rule that *haben* is linked with transitive verbs and *sein* with intransitive verbs. A strict application of this rule would produce many errors but Park's data contain no such errors. Scupin and Scupin's observations, however, contain examples of auxiliary errors from age 2;10 until age 5;0. In every case the child selected *haben* rather than *sein* as would be expected on the basis of frequency of use. This is possibly an area where individual differences in the tendency to overgeneralize as opposed to learning by rote could explain the variation. On the other hand, Ramge (1973) reports frequent self-corrections in the auxiliary in 6-year-olds, so that it would seem rather to be an area of general uncertainty.

4.2.3. *Simple Past Tense.*   The formation of the simple past tense is an area which produces many errors, since the group of strong verbs take different endings from the weak verbs and often have a different root. For example:

regular—*kauf-en*	*ich kauf- te*	'I bought'
irregular—*geh-en*	*ich ging*	'I went'
lauf-en	*ich lief*	'I ran'
sing-en	*ich sang*	'I sang'

The simple past tense appears later than the compound past tense and so the reported errors occur correspondingly later. Only Scupin and Scupin report errors in this tense; other studies do not comment on its acquisition. Scupins' child overgeneralized the weak ending -te with strong verbs, sometimes using the root from the infinitive and sometimes making a change. For example:

(81) Scupin (4;4)   er *kam-te   from komm-en 'to come'
                                    instead of er kam

(82) Scupin (5;0)   er *gang-te   from geh-en 'to go'
                                    instead of er ging

(83) Scupin (5;5)   sie *stehl-ten from stehl-en 'to steal'
                                    instead of sie stahl-en

The same child produced also the form *ging-te (3;7) and *gang (4;10) for the simple past of gehen. There are two separate problems here for the child: which verbs take the -te endings and which verbs have a changed root and what is the form of that root. The overgeneralization of -te can be explained by its being the most frequent form but also by its being a clear marker of simple past.

There is one example of the same vowel being overgeneralized in the simple past. Scupins' child in a highly excited state (5;0) produced all the simple past forms of weak and strong verbs in a narrative so that they contained the vowel /a/. It is not clear how this can be explained, but the child is obviously working on the basis that the vowel is changed in the simple past but has not restricted the application of this rule reliably. The strong verbs are often those most frequently used. The notion of frequency must include here the number of different verbs and the amount of use of the verbs. More data are needed to determine whether vowel change is frequently used as a basis for overgeneralization.

4.2.4. *Present Tense.*   Not many errors are reported in the present tense. The few that are reported are in connection with the irregular forms, as might be expected. The irregular forms occur only in the singular of some "strong" and "mixed" verbs, and involve a change of stem and, in modal verbs, the omission of the inflections marking first and third person (compare Table 2.3). For example:

from lauf-en 'to run'	ich lauf-e	'I run'
	du läuf-st	'you run'
es/sie/er läuf-t		'it/she/he runs'
	wir lauf-en	'we run'
	ihr lauf-t	'you:PL run'
	sie lauf-en	'they run'
from woll-en 'to want'	ich will	'I want'
	du will-st	'you want'
es/sie/er will		'it/she/he wants'

> *wir woll-en* 'we want'
> *ihr woll-t* 'you:PL want'
> *sie woll-en* 'they want'

The verb *sein* 'to be' is irregular in every person.

Scupin and Scupin's child correctly produced the 3rd person plural of the verb *sein* at age 2;0 and in fact corrected himself when he erroneously produced the singular. Also at age 2;0 he regularized the 3rd person singular forms of irregular verbs.

(84) Scupin (2;0)　*hab-t　from *hab-en* 'to have'
　　　　　　　　　　instead of *ha-t*

(85) Scupin (2;0)　*lauf-t　from *lauf-en* 'to run'
　　　　　　　　　　instead of *läuf-t*

(86) Scupin (2;0)　*hal-t　from *halt-en* 'to hold'
　　　　　　　　　　instead of *häl-t*

Around age 3;0, however, he overgeneralized the irregular singular root to the 3rd person plural and added *-n*. For example:

(87) Scupin (2;11)　*kann'n　from *könn-en* 'to be able'
　　　　　　　　　　 instead of *könn-en*

(88) Scupin (3;0)　*is-n　from *sein* 'to be'
　　　　　　　　　　instead of *sind*

(89) Scupin (3;2)　*will'n　from *woll-en* 'to want'
　　　　　　　　　　instead of *woll-en*

These errors are only with modal verbs or *sein* 'to be'. It is significant that this overgeneralization occurs rather than the overgeneralization of the regular form. It is likely that frequency is part of the explanation of these errors, that is the form most frequent within the paradigm is taken as a basis for generalization. With the modals, however, frequency of use is probably significant in that the child uses singular more often than plural.

4.3. Noun Phrase Morphology

4.3.1. *Gender.*　Morphology in the noun phrase is a highly complex area and is one of the most frequent sources of error. Both case and gender must be marked, as has been discussed earlier, but they are marked by one form only, so that it is difficult to establish whether an error is due to the selection of wrong gender or wrong case or both. The system is also potentially very confusing (see

Table 2.1), since within a gender paradigm the same form can mark different cases, for example, for feminine and neuter nouns the nominative and accusative cases in articles are marked in the same way. The same forms occur across gender paradigms marking the same cases, for example the dative case in masculine and neuter nouns. Finally, identical forms occur marking different cases in different gender paradigms, for example the nominative of the definite article with masculine nouns *der* is identical to the dative of the definite article with feminine nouns.

Adjectives are used in attributive position before articles are in frequent use. When the adjective is used without a preceding article, the strong endings are appropriate (see Table 2.2), which distinctively mark gender—at least in nominative and accusative cases. These cases, as associated with subject and object function, predominate in early usage and the gender marking is frequently correct:

(90) Preyer (2;7)   *ganz   -es   Battalion*
whole   battalion:NEUT
'whole battalion'

(91) Scupin (2;2)   *groß   -er   Ball*
big   ball:MASC
'big ball'

(92) Scupin (2;2)   *so   klein   -es   Pappa   -le*
such   little   daddy   DIM:NEUT
'such a little daddy'

(93) Scupin (2;2)   *ganz   klein   -e   Großmama*
very   little   grandma:FEM
'very little grandma'

The ending *-e* is also overgeneralized but this need not necessarily be a gender mistake. This ending is amongst the most frequent within the paradigms and is probably overgeneralized for that reason (see later discussion). It is rare that the *-er* and *-es* endings are used with nouns of a different gender. Scupins have only one such example:

(94) Scupin (2;0)   *klein   *-es   Durst*
little   thirst:MASC
'little thirst'

Gender would appear to be established therefore at an early stage.

The first occurrences of the definite and indefinite articles appear to be as part of an amalgam with the nouns. These first forms are also frequently reduced. In the definite articles, the form *de* is reported by Preyer at age 2;6 (Preyer, 1882, p. 330) and by Stern and Stern in both their daughter and son at age 1;10 and 1;2 respectively (Stern & Stern, 1928, pp. 44, 86). This form can be seen as a reduction of the nominative forms *der* (MASC) und *die* (FEM) but is quite distinct from the neuter form *das*. In fact, no errors are reported of this form being produced with neuter forms. The indefinite article is commonly reduced to *n* or *e* which could apply to all genders. Stern and Stern report the insertion of this form on a large scale. Hilde (1;10) and Günther (2;4) also inserted it in inappropriate contexts, for example before adverbs, so that its status is unclear.

The correct choice of gender only becomes clear when the full form of the articles is produced. The three gender paradigms are distinct in the nominative case of the definite article, so that the use of the definite article provides the clearest evidence as to the correct selection of gender. The definite articles appear gradually from around age 2;0 onwards but it is common for the article to be missing in an utterance until age 2;6. When the definite article is produced in its full form, it is most frequently correct in gender. Again, at this age, nominative and accusative cases in association with subject and object function predominate, where there is a clear distinction between all these gender paradigms. Even where nominative case may be used instead of accusative case in the masculine paradigm (see 4.3.2), the form is marked for gender distinctively from the others, so that one cannot talk of a gender error.

In Preyer's data, no gender mistakes occur but it is not a point on which he comments. Examples of the three genders used correctly appear by age 2;9. Stern and Stern claim the correct distinction of the masculine and feminine forms by age 2;6 in Hilde, but they neglect to report whether she used the wrong article with neuter nouns or whether the article was omitted. Scupin and Scupin, however, claim that when the definite article first was in frequent use in their son at age 2;3, he made many errors, using all three forms quite unsystematically. They do not give examples of such errors however and from the utterances reported over the following period in the diary, a different picture emerges. It must not be forgotten that Scupins' diary consists of almost daily entries which are not summarized or collated at any point, so that it is not clear over what period of time the observations apply. In the majority of utterances recorded, Scupins' son does not make mistakes with the gender of the definite article.

The errors which do occur with the definite article suggest an overgeneralization of the form *die*. Scupins' data include three such errors over the period 2;3 to 2;8: *die Hochstein* (MASC) 'the summit', *die Mann* (MASC) 'the man', *die Truthahn* (MASC) 'the turkey'. Only one other mistake is reported and, in this instance, the neuter is used *das Kopf* (MASC) 'the head'. Stern and Stern's data contain five gender errors (up to age 2;8), all of which indicate overgeneralization of *die*. Günther's reported utterances contain two errors: *die bebau* (= *Wau-*

Wau, Hund (MASC)) 'the dog' at age 1;2 and **die ding* (NEUT) 'the thing' at 2;7. Three errors made by Hilde were when using the definite article *die* as a demonstrative pronoun but quite clearly in the context of referring to a non-feminine noun *Keks* (MASC) 'cake', *Papier* (NEUT) 'paper', *Papa* (MASC) 'Daddy'. Data from spontaneous utterances of Down's Syndrome children support this finding that *die* is overgeneralized (Schaner-Walles, personal communication).

In an experimental study (Mills, 1978), children aged 5 to 10 were required to assign the definite article to ten familiar nouns (all names of toys). This test was carried out in the context of a study examining the relationship between natural and syntactic gender. They were presented with the three gender possibilities for example **der Buch, das Buch, *die Buch* 'the book' and asked to choose the correct form. Even under these highly artificial conditions, the children made very few mistakes. Mistakes were only made by the 5- and 6-year-olds. The feminine gender nouns had the highest percentage of correct responses, as can be seen from Table 2.4. An overgeneralization of *die* was also relatively common, and more frequent than the overgeneralization of *der* and *das*.

The selection of the correct gender seemed also to be dependent on the noun. The greatest number of mistakes were made on the masculine and neuter animate nouns, as opposed to the masculine and neuter inanimate nouns and feminine animate and inanimate nouns. This difference is possibly due to the referents being animate but not clearly of one sex or the other, therefore the semantic possibility of female sex is increased. This point will be taken up again later in a discussion of natural and syntactic gender.

Inspection of the scores of individual children also reflected regularities on this task. Two children (boys) substituted *der* for all their errors, 3 children (1 boy, 2 girls) substituted *das* and 5 children (3 girls, 2 boys) substituted *die*. Only

TABLE 2.4
Percentage of Correct Responses
and Substitutions in Choice
of Grammatical Gender
by German Children Aged 5–6 Years
(from Mills, 1978)

	Correct Grammatical Gender		
Response	*der* *n = 144*	*die* *n = 144*	*das* *n = 192*
der	82	3	10
die	10	94	8
das	8	3	82

one child made a large number of completely mixed substitutions. Three factors seem to influence the results in this task: a tendency to overgeneralize *die,* an influence of the animacy of the noun, and an individual overgeneralization strategy. There is not enough evidence from the diary studies to suggest the role the latter two factors might play in spontaneous production. They may possibly be artifacts of the task.

MacWhinney (1978) tested gender assignment to real and nonce words in children aged 3 years to 12 years (see Table 2.5). The words were selected in order to examine the effects of inherent semantic gender and phonological endings, the real and nonce words being given the same structure. They were presented in three conditions: with no overt cuing, and with overt cuing through previous mention of either the indefinite article in accusative case or the pronoun in accusative case. MacWhinney found that age improved performance on the task. The older children were more able to make use of overt cuing and phonological information, especially in the nonce words. The older children used *das* more frequently, especially with the nonce words. Phonological information was most readily used in the feminine nonce words.

MacWhinney concludes that children in German make little use of inherent semantic gender to determine syntactic gender, since this is of limited applicability. He also compares German children's use of analogy with that of Hungarian children and draws the conclusion that German children use analogy less, since the regularities are fewer. He does not offer any explanation for the

TABLE 2.5
Real and Nonce Words Used by MacWhinney
(1978), Endings Underlined

Real Noun	Meaning	Nonce	Meaning
1. der Mann	man	der Gann	samurai archer
2. der Soldat	soldier	der Molat	barbapapa doll
3. der Hammer	hammer	der Fammer	turtle
4. der Teppich	rug	der Leppich	green man
5. der Korb	basket	der Norb	orange figure
6. der Baum	tree	der Faum	dinosaur
7. die Frau	woman	die Lau	fairy
8. die Kuh	cow	die Puh	barbapapa doll
9. die Pfeife	pipe	die Neife	june bug
10. die Schweinerei	mess	die Teinerei	noise maker
11. die Hand	hand	die Gand	ichthysaurus
12. die Uhr	clock	die Muhr	tyranosaurus rex
13. das Kind	child	das Pind	octopus
14. das Pferd	horse	das Nerd	stick figure
15. das Scheusal	monster	das Heusal	fire engine
16. das Stühlchen	chair	das Nülchen	robot
17. das Bett	bed	das Rett	kiwi
18. das Glas	glass	das Schnas	mouse

overgeneralization of *das* by older children, which does not fit with the results reported earlier.

MacWhinney's material is however problematic with respect to his classification of the test words. Some words which he claims to be linked with a particular gender because of their phonological or morphological structure cannot be so clearly classified. In the group of words which should have arbitrary gender assignment, some regularities were overlooked.

The explanation of the selection by the older children of *das,* as opposed to *die* as might be expected from previous results, can be explained by the monosyllabicity of the majority of items. Monosyllabicity is strongly associated with masculine and neuter genders, not with feminine genders. Masculine and neuter gender also seem closer to each other and quite distinct from feminine gender. Some loan words are used with different genders, but disagreement occurs mainly as to whether nouns should be masculine or neuter, not as to whether they should be masculine or feminine, neuter or feminine (Carstensen, 1980).

Much more investigation needs to be made of the phonological regularities in German and their accessibility to children on the lines of the work in French by Tucker et al. (1977) and by Karmiloff-Smith (1979). Work is being currently conducted by Zubin and Köpcke on the existence of regularities in gender assignment (Zubin & Köpcke, 1981; Köpcke, 1982; Köpcke & Zubin, 1982). They have already established the existence of rules based on semantic, morphological, and phonetic properties. The results of their work will make it easier to look for the use of regularities in children (Mills, 1984).

The early overgeneralization of *die* noted in the spontaneous production data can be accounted for by the frequency of the form *die.* From Table 2.1, it can be seen that this form accounts for 50% of the nominative and accusative case forms. Children would also seem to be aware of the influence of syllabicity in gender assignment. MacWhinney's results indicated no use of semantic cues by children, but until this is correctly controlled for in variation with other phonological and morphological regularities, it cannot be eliminated. The evidence for use of phonological cues by children in assigning gender is as yet unclear. Since the regularities as yet described (e.g. Zubin & Köpcke, 1981) relate to relatively small categories of nouns, it could well be expected that the use of phonological cues will develop slowly in accordance with MacWhinney's principle of production applicability. The size of the child's lexicon and the status of particular items in the lexicon well may influence the regularities to be first used.

Parallel to the overgeneralization of the feminine definite article, the feminine form of the indefinite article *eine* also appears to be overgeneralized in the early stages. Park (1976) reports this and there is supporting evidence from the diary studies. Scupin and Scupin note **eine strump* (MASC) 'a sock' at age 2;0. The possessive adjectives are declined in the same way as the indefinite article, and here too the feminine form is overgeneralized. Stern and Stern record **meine appele* (NEUT) 'my little apple' at age 1;10 and *meine* referring to *Mäntelchen* (NEUT) 'little coat' at 2;6. The dominance of this form, however, cannot be explained by the frequency principle. *Eine* and related forms may be more salient than *ein* because they are polysyllabic, for example.

Quite obviously, Greenberg's (1966) proposed universal that masculine forms are unmarked and the associated acquisition principle that unmarked forms are acquired before marked forms is inappropriate here. This principle may be relevant when syntactic gender is related to natural gender (see Deutsch & Pechmann, 1978, and subsequent discussion).

Although it seems more than a coincidence that the feminine gender forms in three forms should be overgeneralized, namely the adjective ending *-e*, articles *die* and *eine*, I do not think the explanation has any basis in the form being that of feminine gender. Frequency and saliency would seem to provide a sounder explanation (see Mills, 1984 for a detailed discussion of gender in German).

4.3.2. *Nominative and Accusative Case.*

Case is marked on articles, adjectives, and pronouns as an integral part of the form. The form of case marking is dependent on the gender of the noun in the noun phrase (see Tables 2.1 and 2.2). The marking of nominative, accusative, dative, and genitive will be discussed in the subsequent sections, followed by case marking after prepositions since this is a more complex issue.

The case form of the article which first appears is the nominative case form. Nominative case marking is overgeneralized to accusative case (this is only observable in masculine gender nouns) with considerable frequency. There is evidence, however, that the two cases are sometimes distinguished before articles are regularly used, through the correct use of adjective endings. Scupin and Scupin report, at age 2;2, the two sentences:

(95) Scupin (2;2) *groß* *-en*   *Ball*   *sehen*
                    big   MASC:ACC   ball:MASC   see
                    '(I want) to see the big ball'

(96) Scupin (2;2) *groß* *-er*   *Ball*   *kommt*
                    big   MASC:NOM   ball:MASC   comes
                    'the big ball is coming'

Stern and Stern also report early use of accusative case. The frequent error of substituting nominative for accusative case persists, however, until quite late. Sterns' data still contain such errors at age 3;2.

(97) Stern (3;2)
        hab   **der*   *Stuhl*   *(g)e-*   *hau*   *-t*
        PAST.AUX   DEF.ART: chair:MASC   PAST   hit   PAST
                        MASC:SG:NOM
        'I have hit the chair'

Scupins' data contain such errors as late as 4;7. Even within the same sentence the child can produce the correct and incorrect form.

(98) Scupin (4;4)

da	muß	ich	andermal	*der
there	must	I	another:time	DEF.ART:MASC:SG:NOM

Operngucker	mit-	nehmen
opera:glasses:MASC:SG	with [PARTICLE]	take

'I must take the opera glasses with me another time'

(99) Scupin (4;7)

jetzt	hab	ich	*der	auch	tot
now	PAST.AUX	I	DEF.ART: MASC:SG:NOM	also	dead

ge-	schossen,	weil	er	den	ander-	en
PAST	shot	because	he	DEF.ART: MASC:SG:ACC	other	MASC:SG: ACC

Soldaten	tot	ge-	schossen	hat
soldier:MASC	dead	PAST	shot	PAST.AUX

'I shot that one dead now, because he shot the other soldier dead'

As the above examples show, the overgeneralization of nominative case is not limited to nouns in initial position, so that word order does not appear to be the sole factor. In the last example, the fact that the article *der* is used as a demonstrative pronoun and in a position of emphasis may well be factors contributing to the error. There is only one report of accusative articles being overgeneralized to nominative and that is in Hildegard Leopold around 5;0. The fact that only articles with masculine gender nouns are marked distinctively for nominative and accusative case is probably the main factor in this error. The child may well take longer to perceive the rules governing use of accusative case because of its less frequent marking, and secondly he may well regularize the system so that it is symmetrical across all three gender paradigms.

In the indefinite article (and the negative *kein* and possessive adjectives *mein, dein*, etc., which follow an identical declension pattern) the same overgeneralization of the nominative form occurs. Grimm (1973, p. 99) also notes this. It is reported as late as 5;6 by Scupins and 5;1 by Sterns. Where the article appears with an adjective following, however, which is comparatively rare in the data, the adjective is marked for accusative case. It is rare that such a marking occurs in nominative case forms. This suggests that this error is not due to a lack of distinction between nominative and accusative cases but that a regularization of the article system produces the error. The first example of the correct accusative form of the indefinite article noted by Scupin and Scupin is as late as 4;2.

(100) Scupin (2;4) *Bubi hat *kein*   *Hunger*
                   Bubi   has   NEG.ART: hunger:MASC
                              MASC:SG:NOM

                   'Bubi isn't hungry'

(101) Scupin (2;6)

      hab' ich so   *ein   groß -en*
      have   I   such   INDEF.ART: big   MASC:SG:ACC
                         MASC:SG:NOM

      bös -en   *Finger*
      bad   MASC:SG:ACC   finger:MASC

      'I have such a big bad finger'

(102) Scupin (4;2)

      ich hab' einen   *Spazierstock*   *und   du*
      I   have   INDEF.ART: walking:stick:MASC   and   you
                  MASC:SG:ACC

      hast keinen
      have   NEG.ART:MASC:SG:ACC

      'I have a walking stick and you have none'

(103) Scupin (5;3)

      hat die *ein   so   voll -en*   *Bauch*
      has   she INDEF.ART: such full MASC: stomach:MASC
                 MASC:SG:NOM   SG:ACC

      'she has such a full stomach'

(104) Scupin (5;1)

      für den   *Vater*   *ein*
      for   DEF.ART: father   INDEF.ART:
            MASC:SG:ACC   MASC:SG:NOM

      *schönen -en   *Gruß*
      beautiful   MASC:SG:ACC   greeting:MASC

      'a big hello to daddy'

MacWhinney's claim that it is the citation form which is overgeneralized might apply in the instances of articles occurring alone with nouns but in the instances where the adjective is correctly declined, this explanation cannot apply. Unfortunately there are no recorded instances of the definite article, inappropriately in nominative case, with a following adjective. Scupins' data also contain a few examples of the adjective in nominative case after the indefinite article having an incorrect -*n* ending. The child might well be regularizing the masculine gender paradigm at this stage to *ein* ADJ + -*n* for both nominative and accusative case. In adult fast speech the accusative -*en* ending on the indefinite article is often contracted so that it is very difficult to perceive the ending except as a lengthened consonant *n*. This would support the child's regularization of the paradigm.

An early distinction is made between nominative and accusative forms of the first pronouns to appear: *ich* 'I' and *du* 'you'. Case forms are marked quite distinctly:

ich (NOM)   *mich* (ACC)   *mir* (DAT)
du (NOM)   *dich* (ACC)   *dir* (DAT)

The first uses of the accusative are very limited in context, that is, they are used only with certain verbs, frequently as a reflexive. These would appear to have been learned by rote.

(105) Scupin (2;1)   *schäm   mich   nicht*

embarrass   me:ACC   NEG

'I am not embarrassed'

(106) Scupin (2;2)   *stoß   dich   nicht*

bang:IMP   you:ACC   NEG

'don't bang yourself'

This is also true of the first instances of the dative form *mir*. Most authors report the early use of *gib mir* 'give to me'. The nominative forms, especially *ich,* are not so limited to the context of particular verbs, and the first uses are correct for case.

(107) Lindner (2;1)   *ich   fort-jagen   Fliege*

I:NOM   away-chase   fly

'I will chase the fly away'

(108) Scupin (2;3)   *ich   gehe   in   die   Schule*

I:NOM   go   in   the   school

'I go to school'

The child is producing utterances with those forms at the same time as utterances using the proper names and third person for himself and addressee; Scupin's child, for example, was still regularly using his own name (Bubi) to refer to himself at the age of 2;8. Since the pronoun forms are not in wide use or productive, it is difficult to know how much analysis to attribute to the child. The case functions are, however, to some extent differentiated, and this might indicate that the notion of case is available early on. Since the pronouns are monosyllabic and carry more stress, it may be easier to learn the forms appropriate for use in the appropriate function. As mentioned above, the articles are often contracted, especially in fast speech, so that the information distinguishing the case-marked forms is lost. The paradigms for pronouns´do not overlap in forms marking case, so that it is easier to associate form with function. The articles are particularly problematic in this respect.

The importance of nominative/accusative case marking on the article, as opposed to word order, for determining agent and object in active declarative sentences was tested in a comprehension experiment with children aged 6 to 9 years (Mills, 1977a). Active sentences were presented in a picture selection task. These sentences had a high degree of reversibility (Slobin, 1966). The sentences varied according to the relative order of the agent and object and according to the position of the article (masculine gender only) which was marked for case. The other article was unmarked (feminine or neuter):

(109) *der*　　　　　　*Hund sieht die*　　　　　　　*Katze*
　　　 DEF.ART:　　　　 dog　 sees　DEF.ART:　　　　　 cat
　　　 MASC:SG:NOM　　　　　　　　　 FEM:SG:NOM/ACC
　　　 'the dog sees the cat'

(110) *das*　　　　　　*Mädchen schlägt den*　　　　　*Mann*
　　　 DEF.ART:　　　　 girl　 hits　 DEF.ART:　　　　　 man
　　　 NEUT:SG:NOM/ACC　　　　　　　 MASC:SG:ACC
　　　 'the girl hits the man'

(111) *den*　　　　　　*Jungen ruft das*　　　　　　　*Mädchen*
　　　 DEF.ART:　　　　 boy　 calls　DEF.ART:　　　　　 girl
　　　 MASC:SG:ACC　　　　　　　　　 NEUT:SG:NOM/ACC
　　　 'the girl calls the boy'

(112) *das*　　　　　　*Mädchen ruft der*　　　　　　*Mann*
　　　 DEF.ART:　　　　 girl　 calls　DEF.ART:　　　　　 man
　　　 NEUT:SG:NOM/ACC　　　　　　　 MASC:SG:NOM
　　　 'the man calls the girl'

All the children found the sentence with agent in first position, that is with SVO order, easiest to interpret correctly. In the sentences with OVS order, those sentences with the marked article in initial position (like sentence 111) were easier to interpret than those sentences with the marked article in final position. Performance on the OVS sentences improved with age, so that it can be seen that a reliance on a word-order strategy decreases as the child is able to use case information to determine relations. The fact that the marked article in initial position facilitates comprehension can be explained by the saliency of initial position. When the unmarked form is in initial position, the word-order strategy creates the expectation of a following accusative, so that the case information is not so readily perceived. These results strongly suggest the importance of the canonical word order (SVO) in comprehension (see Slobin & Bever, 1982), even if it is not clear that it is more frequent in spontaneous productions (see earlier discussion). From the few examples Ramge observed in school beginners, self corrections in case reveal an association of initial position with nominative case, that is the child will begin with a noun in nominative case but then change the case as he realizes it is inappropriate for the construction. For example, when referring to *der Blumentopf* 'the flower pot':

(113) (ca. 6;0)	*und*	**der*	*de*	*den*	*kann*
	and	DEM.PRO: MASC:SG:NOM		DEM.PRO: MASC:SG:ACC	can
	gar	*nicht*	*gießen*		
	EMPH	NEG	pour		

'and that one you can't water at all'

4.3.3. Dative Case.

The dative case is commonly used to mark the bene-factor. This usage is established relatively early. From one example of an adjective being used in the dative case, without a preceding article, it would appear as though the form chosen is the one appropriate when an article is present. The weak -*n* form is used.

Scupin (2;4)

Papa	*gibt*	*nich*	*arm-*	**en*	*Mama*	*Kussel*
Daddy	gives	NEG	poor		Mummy	kiss + DIM

'Daddy won't give poor Mummy a kiss'

The first examples of dative case in articles suggest that the accusative case is overgeneralized. Caution in interpretation is advisable here, however, since in several dialects, for example that of Berlin, dative and accusative case are frequently interchangeable. (see Kurt Schwitters (1965) poem "An Anna Blume": *O du, Geliebte meiner siebenundzwanzig Sinne, ich liebe dir*).

(114) Scupin (2;6)						
	ich	*will*	*Briefe*	*ins*	*Haus*	**die*
	I	want	letters	into:the	house	DEF.ART: FEM:SG:NOM/ACC

> *Mama   schicken*
> Mummy   send
> 'I want to send letters to mummy in the house'

(115) Scupin (2;9)

mach	**den*	*Mann*	*Beine*
make:IMP	DEF.ART:	man	legs
	MASC:SG:ACC		

'make legs for the man'

The correct dative form of the definite article appears quite early. Scupin and Scupin record many utterances around 2;9 and Stern and Stern at 3;2. Scupin and Scupin, interestingly enough, appear not to have noted these utterances as containing the dative, because they first comment on the use of the dative at age 3;5. At this stage, their son overgeneralized the masculine/neuter form to the feminine which he had previously correctly distinguished. From this one recorded utterance, it is not clear that this was a common occurrence:

(116) Scupin (3;5)

ich	*bin*	**'m*	*Mama*	*sehr*	*gut*
I	am	DEF.ART:	Mummy:FEM	very	good
		MASC/NEUT:SG:DAT			

und	*'m*	*Papa*	*ganz*	*gut*
and	DEF.ART:	Daddy:MASC	quite	good
	MASC:SG:DAT			

'I am very good to (for) Mummy and quite good to (for) Daddy'

Plural nouns in the dative require a suffixed -*n* on the noun itself. Utterances containing such dative plurals are rare in the diary material. When Scupin and Scupin first record such a sentence, at age 4;11, the usage is correct. This is an area which often produces error in adults, however, not only in spoken language. The phrase *Schokolade mit *Nüsse* 'chocolate with nuts' has been seen in print. Errors could be expected to be frequent in child speech for some time therefore.

It is rare for the dative to be used instead of the accusative. Stern and Stern report one use at age 3;2.

(117) Stern (3;2)

haste	**mir*	*ge-*	*kratz*	*-t*
you:have	me:DAT	PAST	scratch	PAST

'you have scratched me'

Verbs which require dative case in the object, such as *helfen* 'help', appear to be first used with accusative case.

(118) Scupin (2;8)

ich	werde	*dich	helfen	auf-	zu-	stehen
I	FUT.AUX	you:ACC	help	up	to	stand

'I will help you stand up'

The dative case, when generally learned, appears here too, however.

(119) Scupin (2;11)

helf	mal	'm	Bubi
help:IMP	just	DEF.ART: MASC:SG:DAT	Bubi:MASC

'help Bubi'

There are no recorded instances of nominative case being used instead of dative case, in so far as that is determinable from the data. This might be attributable to the fact that dative case is distinctively marked from nominative and accusative in all gender paradigms. The context for this form may be more easily learned. Certainly the dative form is acquired only a few months after the use of articles becomes more frequent. Unfortunately there is no body of data on the group of verbs which have the direct object in the dative case.

4.3.4. *Genitive Case.* Genitive case is very rare amongst the diary data and is limited to nouns preceding a noun phrase and is then marked by a suffixed *-s*. Marking of genitive in articles is not recorded at all, which implies for Scupins' child that this emerged after age 6;0, when the diary finishes.

The first use of genitive case involves proper names suffixed by *-s*, which corresponds to adult usage. This use is acquired quite early, around age 2;6.

(120) Scupin (2;8) *in Papa-s Kragen* 'in daddy's collar'

(121) Scupin (3;0) *in Mama-s Kopf* 'in mummy's head'

(122) Stern (2;4) *Hilde-s Suppe* 'Hilde's soup'

Scupins' son later extends this form erroneously to nouns which are not proper names.

(123) Scupin (3;1)

das	ist	Männer	*-s	Wagen
that	is	men	GEN	car

'that is the men's car'

(124) Scupin (4;3)

hier	ist	Männer	*-s	Wohnung
here	is	railway	GEN	house

'this is the railway's house'

(125) Scupin (4;4) *da   tut   Männern *-s   Bauch   weh*
                     there make   men   GEN   stomach hurt
                     'the men's stomachs hurt'

The correct form here is to mark the case on an article and to position the noun phrase in genitive case after the first noun phrase. For example:

(126) *der*   *Wagen*   *der*   *Männer*
DEF.ART: car:MASC   DEF.ART: men:PL
MASC:SG:NOM   PL:GEN

Some noun compounds are also formed by adding an *-s* to the first noun, for example: *Räumung -s -verkauf* 'clearance sale' (see later discussion 4.3.6). This would be another formal pattern, NOUN + *s* + NOUN, which could lead to the child's overgeneralization, although there is no possessive relationship involved.

Over the same period of time, Scupins' son also uses the prepositions *von* 'from, of', which is correct, and *zu* 'to', to express the possessive relationship.

(127) Scupin (3;3) *wo   sind   von   den   allens   Kindeln*
                     where are   of   the   all   children
                     die   Mamales
                     the   Mummies
                     'where are all the children's Mummies?'

(128) Scupin (4;7) *das   ist   der   Schornstein   von   mein*
                     that is   the   chimney   of   my
                     brauner   Baukasten
                     brown   building:box
                     'that's the chimney from my brown building box'

(129) Scupin (3;7) *wo   ist   denn   aber   die   Großmama*
                     where is   then   but   the   grandma
                     *zu   den   Affe?
                     to   the   monkey
                     'but where's the monkey's grandma?'

The first system is clearly an overgeneralization of a standard pattern. The second system of marking, through use of a preposition, makes the possessive relationship explicit, which would support the principle that semantic relationships should be clearly and explicitly marked.

It is permissible in standard German to use the dative case to express the possessive form, especially where the relationship is close to the benefactive. The noun phrase in the dative case is usually ordered before the noun phrase in accusative case.

(130) *ich* *putzte* *dem* *Mann*
I   cleaned DEF.ART: man:MASC
           MASC:SG:DAT

den *Tisch*
DEF.ART: table:MASC
MASC:SG:ACC

'I cleaned the man's table'/'I cleaned the table for the man'

As in the above example, this use of dative case can express either the possessive or the benefactive with no possessive relation. In some dialects, this form is very common, especially with a proper name followed by a redundant marking of the possessive pronoun. If no article precedes the proper name, there is no marking of dative case; it is only indicated by position.

(131) *das* *ist* *Heinz* *seine* *Tasse*
that is Heinz:DAT his cup
'that is Heinz' cup'

Sterns' data contain two examples of this form. The semantic relationship is clearly indicated by the ordering of the nouns and the possessive pronoun.

(132) Stern (2;6)
   is'n *de* *Hilde* *ihr* *Stühlchen*
   is DEF.ART Hilde her chair:DIM
   'it's Hilde's chair'

(133) Stern (3;6) *mit* *klein* *Hilde* *seine* *Schere*
          with little Hilde his scissors
          'with little Hilde's scissors'

Again the redundancy of the marking, through the noun in dative case and the possessive pronoun, means that the semantic relationship is explicitly and clearly marked.

In all these examples from children the possessor is ordered before the thing possessed, unless the relationship is made explicit through the use of a preposition. Word order would seem to be important here for marking this relationship.

In a repetition experiment, with children aged 2;6–6, Grimm (1973, p. 182) found that this word order was always preserved, although up to 4 years old the morphology was often greatly changed.

4.3.5. *Cases After Prepositions.*   This is a complex area since the child must know which case is appropriate after which preposition AND must be able to mark the case in the correct way.

Firstly, it is common for articles to be omitted after prepositions, even at an age when they are in frequent use. This observation was confirmed in my own data and in the data of Stern and Stern (1928), Scupin and Scupin (1910), and Grimm (1973). This was mainly observed with the prepositions *an* and *in,* but since these are commonly used in the early stages, errors of omitting the article were frequent.

> (134) Scupin (3;1)   *da regnet 's an *Schlafzimmerfenster*
> 'there it's raining at (the) bedroom window'

I think that this is not simply due to an uncertainty of case or simplification of a complex construction. An additional factor is the phonetic similarity of the prepositions *an, in,* and the amalgam, PREP + ART:DAT (MASC/NEUT), namely *am* and *im*. There are two arguments in support of this explanation. Firstly, the omission of the article occurs with the prepositions *an* and *in* only when followed by a masculine or neuter noun. Secondly, in one utterance from Scupin's son, the dative was marked on the noun by suffixing *-e* which is an optional form.

> (135) Scupin (3;6)   *sind die Lockerle in Halse drin?*
> 'are the curls inside the neck?'

The marking of the dative on the noun would seem to indicate that the child was not omitting case marking in this context. Paprotté (1977) also suggests that the phonetic similarity of *n* and *m* as endings played a role in the comprehension of case endings, as will be discussed below.

With prepositions which require accusative case only, there appear to be few errors, although it must be remembered that there are few prepositions in this category. Preyer (1882) reports one example of dative after *für,* as do Stern and Stern:

> (136) Preyer (2;4)   *für*   **'m*   *Axel*   'for Axel'

> (137) Stern (3;2)   *für*   **dir*   'for you'

It cannot be said that this is a general trend, however, from the few examples available.

With prepositions which require dative case only, many errors occur, until age 5 at least. Scupins' data provide the fullest picture of development and the following analysis is based on their son's acquisition pattern. Caution in interpretation is advised again here, however, because of the possible influence of dialect, which in certain circumstances may allow a substitution of accusative for dative case and vice versa. Errors occur with Scupins' child in all gender paradigms at first until age 2;11, which is the time the dative case as benefactive becomes established. Correct forms are used about 50% of the time.

It might be expected that the nominative case form as the "citation allomorph" would first be used after prepositions. Scupins' data contain only one such example. This occurs at age 4;7 (see sentence 128 above), however, which makes it seem likely that the error had occurred earlier but had not occurred in the utterances recorded. Grimm's data (1973, p. 100) contain one such example, which she cites as a typical error of lack of case agreement, but it is not clear how often this occurred with masculine nouns.

(138) Grimm (ca. 3;0)

der	*geht*	*auf*	**der*		*Stuhl*
he	goes	on	DEF.ART:		chair:MASC
			MASC:SG:NOM		

'he climbs onto the chair'

More data are needed before it can be claimed that the citation form is used in this context. For the purposes of simplifying explanation, it would be nice if it was.

The errors indicate an overgeneralization of accusative case, since with masculine nouns the distinct accusative form is used.

(139) Scupin (2;5)

will	*bei*	**die*		*Lottel*	*spielen*
want	at	DEF.ART:		Lottel	play
		FEM:SG:NOM/ACC			

'(I) want to play at Lottel's house'

(140) Scupin (2;8)

die	*Milchtasse*	*von*	**-s*		*Piepvögele*
the	milkcup	of	DEF.ART:		bird:DIM:NEUT
			NEUT:SG:NOM/ACC		

'the bird's milkcup'

(141) Scupin (2;8)

ich	*mach*	*neben*	**'n*		*Kopf*
I	make	near	DEF.ART:		head
			MASC:SG:ACC		

eine   feine   Frisur

a   fine   hairstyle

'I am making a fine hairstyle on the head'

After age 2;11, only errors with masculine and neuter nouns occur. This suggests that the phonetic similarity of accusative *n* and dative *m* in the masculine paradigm may cause some confusion. The neuter nouns should provide evidence of whether the continuing errors are due to the overgeneralization of accusative or due to *n/m* confusion. In fact, of the five errors involving neuter nouns in Scupins' data, both explanations are supported. Two errors involved overgeneralization of the accusative, as sentences 140 and 142 indicate. Interestingly enough, this second sentence reflects the uncertainty about the correct form, since the correct and the incorrect forms are side by side in parallel constructions.

(142) Scupin (4;11)

da   denke   ich   mir   immer   ein   viel   schöneres

there   think   I   me:DAT   always a   much nicer

Bild   mit   einem   gut   -en   Schwein

picture with   INDEF.ART: good NEUT:SG:DAT   pig:NEUT
         NEUT:SG:DAT

aus,   bloß   wenn   du   mir   so   ein   häßliches

out   just   when   you   me:DAT   such a   ugly

*Bild   mit   *ein   bös   -es*

picture with   INDEF.ART: bad   NEUT:NOM/ACC
         NEUT:SG:NOM/ACC

Schwein,   da   kann   ich   das   nicht

pig:NEUT   then can   I   that NEG

'I always invent a much nicer picture with a good pig, just when you show me such an ugly picture with a bad pig, then I can't do it!'

This example, together with the following example from my own data, suggest that the prepositional phrase may be learned as a unit as a kind of formulaic speech. The errors occur when a new noun has to be used in the context.

(143) MOTHER: *mit wem hast du gespielt heute?*

'who did you play with today?'

CHILD (3;7)   *mit   dem   Rainer,   mit*

with   DEF.ART: Rainer:MASC   with
       MASC:SG:DAT

dem	Frank	und	mit
DEF.ART: MASC:SG:DAT	Frank:MASC	and	with

der	Julia
DEF.ART: FEM:SG:DAT	Julia:FEM

'with Rainer, with Frank, and with Julia'

MOTHER: *und Barbara?*
'and Barbara?'

CHILD:

nee,	mit	*die	Barbara
no	with	DEF.ART: FEM:SG:NOM/ACC	Barbara:FEM

hab	ich	nicht	gespielt
have	I	NEG	played

'no, I didn't play with Barbara'

The child has the correct case in the article used with names of children he regularly plays with. He has probably frequently reported activities with these friends. With the name of a different child he produces the article in citation form, possibly because he has never used the name with the preposition before. This is a very tentative explanation of such errors, however, and far more data are needed.

The remaining three errors with neuter nouns, of the five errors referred to earlier, suggest that the *n/m* confusion is also important.

(144) Scupin (2;8)

mit	*den	Schießgewehr
with	DEF.ART: MASC:SG:ACC	gun:NEUT

'with the gun'

(145) Scupin (4;9)

von	*den	Häusel
from	DEF.ART: MASC:SG:ACC	house:DIM:NEUT

'from the house'

(146) Scupin (5;1)

war	das	aber	nicht	ulkig	von
was	that	but	NEG	funny	of

*den	Vögerle
DEF.ART: MASC:SG:ACC	bird:DIM:NEUT

'wasn't that funny of the bird?'

All nouns were being clearly used in the singular. A gender mistake is possible but, as we discussed above, gender mistakes are rare and in sentence 146, the child correctly produced *das Vögerle* in the adjoining linguistic context. In support of the *n/m* confusion is the fact that *zum* (*zu* + *dem*) is also frequently produced as **zun* (*zu den*), which is an impossible form. An example of the indefinite article in dative case supports this *n/m* confusion, since the form *einen* was used with a neuter noun.

(147) Scupin (3;4)

du	*hast*	*sie*	**einen*	*klein*	*-en*
you	have	them	INDEF.ART: MASC:SG:ACC	little	MASC:ACC/NEUT:DAT

Kindel	*gegeben*
child:DIM:NEUT	gave

'you gave them to a little child'

Neugebauer's child revealed his awareness of the possible confusion of *m* and *n* at age 3;0:

(148) Neugebauer (3;0)

unten sind ganz kleine Schäumerle-
ich meine keine Scheune, ich meine Schaum

'down there are really little bubbles -
I don't mean "Scheu*n*e" ('barns'), I mean "Schau*m*" ('foam')'

Two factors seem to be involved, therefore: the overgeneralization of the accusative case and the confusion between *n* and *m* forms.

The case-marking following prepositions which can take accusative or dative case according to directional or stative meaning follows the same pattern as described for accusative and dative only prepositions. That is, the directional use (accusative) was always correct except where the article was omitted.

Preyer reports his son describing the movements of a fly all with the correct accusative form at age 2;9:

(149) Preyer (2;9) *in die Zeitung* 'into the paper'
(150) Preyer (2;9) *in die Milch* 'into the milk'
(151) Preyer (2;9) *unter den Kaffee* 'under the coffee'

Far more errors occur when dative case must be used with stative meaning. As described above, the early use seems to indicate overgeneralization of accusative and therefore no indication of marking a distinction in the two meanings. The later errors, however, can all be attributed to the *m/n* confusion. It is not clear that the distinction in meaning is mastered, although Scupins' son produced one contrast with the same noun in the same context.

(152) Scupin (3;2)

wenn	*wir*	*auf*	*'n*	*Molkefelsen*	*gehen . . .*
when	we	up:DIRECT	DEF.ART: MASC:SG:ACC	Molkefelsen	go

'when we go up the Molkefelsen . . .'

(153) Scupin (3;2)

auf	*'m*	*Molkefelsen*	*gibt*	*'s*
on:STAT	DEF.ART: MASC:SG:DAT	Molkefelsen	gives	it

keine	*Semmel*
no	roll(s)

'there are no rolls on the Molkefelsen'

Paprotté (1977) experimentally tested the comprehension of this difference in meaning. He tested the comprehension of prepositions *in* 'in', *auf* 'on', *über* 'over', and *unter* 'under', which can all involve both directional and stative meaning. He used verbs which were either stative or dynamic. With the dynamic verbs, he used the prepositions followed by both cases to give a stative and directional reading. Nouns were used in the singular and plural, but only masculine nouns with the zero plural morpheme were tested so that ambiguous sentences resulted. Sentences 154–159 give examples of the type of sentences used.

(154) *der Clown sitzt in dem Kuchen* (STAT.VERB + DAT:SG)
'the clown is sitting in the cake'

(155) *der Clown hüpft in den Kuchen* (DYN.VERB + ACC:SG)
'the clown hops into the cake'

(156) *der Clown hüpft in dem Kuchen* (DYN.VERB + DAT:SG)
'the clown is hopping in(side) the cake'

(157) *der Clown sitzt in den Kuchen* (STAT.VERB + DAT:PL)
'the clown is sitting in the cakes'

(158) *der Clown hüpft in die Kuchen* (DYN.VERB + ACC:PL)
'the clown hops into the cakes'

(159) *der Clown hüpft in den Kuchen* (DYN.VERB + DAT:PL)
'the clown is hopping in(side) the cakes'

Sentences 155 and 159 are ambiguous. The subjects aged 6 to 12 years had to match the spoken sentences to picture material. A hierarchy of complexity emerged, the sentence type in first position being easiest:

1. stative verbs + DAT
2. dynamic verbs + ACC:PL
3. dynamic verbs + DAT:SG

On the ambiguous sentences, the preferred interpretation was that of dynamic verb + accusative singular. It is concluded that the stative verbs + dative are easiest because the information from the verb makes the information from case marking redundant. This implies that children are already using the category "stative." The marking on the article was important in these cases for distinguishing number, and the majority of errors were to interpret the plural noun as singular. This would fit in with Operating Principle E (Slobin, 1973) according to which underlying semantic relations should be marked overtly and clearly. Since the realization of the plural in this case is the zero morpheme, the child easily assumes that this is the singular form. The forms of the definite article are also phonologically similar *dem* and *den,* as discussed above, so that confusion may be easier here.

With the dynamic verb the correct comprehension of ACC:PL was easiest. The form of the article *die* is distinctly marked as plural, if the gender of the noun is known to be masculine or neuter. It is interesting that the largest number of errors with this sentence type was to interpret it as ACC:SG. Since *die* can be accusative for feminine gender singular as well as for plural, it would appear that the gender is not so well established. The lack of clear plural marking (see above) may make this confusion easier.

The dative singular and accusative singular and dative plural have similar forms of the article, so that phonological confusion can explain the frequency of mistakes. The direction of interpretation was significant, however, in that the largest number of errors with the dative singular and the most frequent perception of the ambiguous sentences was as accusative singular. Again this may be explained by Principle E mentioned above. A further experiment using nouns of different genders and nouns with marked plural forms would possibly disentangle the strategies involved here. It is not possible to conclude that the directional interpretation is the first learned and overgeneralized with dynamic verbs until the other factors have been accounted for. No data are available from natural dialogue to investigate whether this complexity leads to misunderstanding or whether pragmatic and semantic information are regularly used to determine meaning in these instances. I would guess that the latter is the case.

4.4. Adjective Morphology

4.4.1. *Case and Gender.*   Adjective declension involves even more complex rules than articles. The endings are determined by what precedes the adjective within the noun phrase. If the adjective is not preceded by any article or demonstrative adjective, the endings are "strong." If the adjective is preceded by a definite article, demonstrative adjective, or *alle* 'all', they have "weak" endings. When preceded by the indefinite article, the negative article *kein* and the possessive adjective *mein*, etc., the adjective has a mixture of weak and strong endings (see Table 2.2).

In predicate position, endings are rarely used, which supports the first root allomorph principle of MacWhinney. In attributive position, the errors reported are quite varied. It is rare that an ending is omitted altogether but a few such errors occur in the early stages. In Miller's (1976) data the adjective ending is commonly left off *ander* 'other', possibly because the root ends in *-er* and appears to have an ending. With other adjectives there are only two examples of an uninflected adjective.

Firstly, as described earlier, adjectives are used in attributive position before articles appear in the noun phrase. In these circumstances, that is, preceded by no article, the strong endings are appropriate. Preyer has examples of correct strong endings in nominative case at age 2;7 in his son, before articles appeared in frequent use at 2;9.

(160) Preyer (2;7) *dumm -es*   *Ding*
                    stupid   NEUT:SG:NOM/ACC   thing:NEUT
                    'stupid thing'

(161) Preyer (2;9) *neu -er*   *Papa*
                    new   MASC:SG:NOM   daddy:MASC
                    'new daddy'

(162) Preyer (2;9) *du   lieb -e*   *Zeit*
                    you   dear   FEM:SG:NOM/ACC   time:FEM
                    'goodness!'

Miller has such examples at age 1;10, Scupins at age 2;2, Sterns at age 2;6 for Hilde and 2;4 for Günther. A common error recorded, however, is that the adjective ending *-e* is overgeneralized in pre-nominal position at this stage, when articles are missing (Miller, 1976; Park, 1974; Scupin & Scupin, 1910; Stern & Stern, 1928). MacWhinney seeks to explain this overgeneralization by the frequency principle, since the *-e* ending accounts for 5/8 of the endings in the weak paradigm and 2/8 in the strong paradigm. An alternative explanation, which would need careful investigation to substantiate, would be that the ending is selected according to a presupposed definite or indefinite article but that the article is omitted. To explore this, detailed information would be needed about context to attempt to ascertain which article would be appropriate. It would explain the presence of strong endings marking gender and case correctly on the one hand, since those are appropriate after indefinite articles, and, on the other

hand, the overgeneralization of -e neglecting case and gender which is appropriate after the definite article. The more likely explanation would, however, seem
to be that of the frequency principle.

When articles are used, mistakes in adjective morphology seem to be fairly
rare. Stern and Stern claim the weak and strong forms were distinguished in
Hilde by age 3;2. In Scupins' son, the two paradigms are used and mainly
correctly in accusative and nominative case, although two errors occur with the
ending -n after the nominative indefinite article:

(163) Scupin (2;10)   *ein*   *groß*   *-en*
                        INDEF.ART: big   MASC:SG:ACC
                        MASC:SG:NOM
                        Stein
                        stone:MASC
                        'a big stone'

(164) Scupin (3;9)   *das   ist   kein*
                        that   is   NEG.ART:MASC:SG:NOM
                        *richtig   *-en*   *Löffel*
                        correct   MASC:SG:ACC   spoon:MASC
                        'that is not a proper spoon'

This may be part of the attempt to regularize the system making nominative and
accusative in the masculine paradigm identical. Schädel (1905) and Grimm
(1973) report overgeneralization of the weak form after indefinite articles.
Lindner (1898) on the other hand reports the overgeneralized use of strong
endings in early usage:

(165) Lindner (2;2)
                        das   *groß -*es*   *Glas*
                        DEF.ART: big   NEUT:SG:NOM/ACC   glass:NEUT
                        NEUT:SG:NOM/ACC   ['strong']
                        'the big glass'

Lindner's son also added strong endings to the indefinite article itself and the
similar forms (*kein, mein*, etc.). I have similar examples in my data.

(166) Lindner (2;3)
                        mein   *-*er*   *gut   -er*   *Papa*
                        my   MASC:SG:NOM   good MASC:SG:NOM   Daddy:MASC
                        [POSS.ADJ]
                        'my good Daddy'

(167) Lindner (2;3)

das	ist	ein	-*er	Brief
that	is	INDEF.ART: MASC:SG:NOM	MASC:SG:NOM	letter:MASC

'that is a letter'

(168) Mills (5;0)

eur	-*es	Baby
your:PL [POSS.ADJ]	NEUT:SG:NOM	baby:NEUT

'your baby'

These forms actually occur in pronominal use in adult speech, i.e. when not followed by a noun. The next sentence illustrates this.

(169)

Gib	mir	den	Stift.
give:IMP	me:DAT	DEF.ART: MASC:SG:ACC	pencil:MASC

Er	ist	doch	mein	-er.
PRO:MASC: SG:NOM	is	EMPH	mine [POSS.PRO]	MASC:SG:NOM

'Give me the pencil. It is mine.'

This appears to be an alternative attempt to regularize the system, that is that all elements preceding the noun should be marked for gender and case in the same way.

The dative case form after indefinite and definite articles is in every paradigm (masculine, feminine, neuter, and plural) -n. This appears to be quickly learned. I could find only one example of an adjective in dative case not preceded by an article where strong endings would be appropriate (see p. 183) from Scupins' child at age 2;4. This is an early use but I would guess that -n would commonly be generalized in this position.

Adjective endings are overgeneralized to other forms occurring in pre-nominal position, for example numbers and the quantifier all which should have no endings.

(170) Scupin (4;6)

die	all	-*en	Männer
DEF.ART:PL	all		men

instead of all die Männer 'all the men'

(171) Lindner (2;10)

gibt	mir	die	zwei	-*en Äpfel
give:IMP	me:DAT	DEF.ART:PL	two	apples

'give me the two apples'

Both numbers and *all* appear in certain contexts to behave like adjectives, so that this regularization is quite likely as well as indicating the strong tendency to establish patterns in the system.

On the whole the marking of the adjective as related to case and gender is fairly well established by age 3;0 to 3;6.

4.4.2. *Comparative.*

A different morphological problem related to adjectives (and adverbs) is the formation of the comparative. Comparative adjectives are constructed, as in English, by taking the root and adding *-er,* often with an umlaut form of the root. There are exceptions however, as in English. *Mehr* 'more' is the first comparative reported (Preyer, 1882; Lindner, 1898; Stern & Stern 1928), but it is not entirely clear that it is used in the cases where an *-er* ending on the adjective would be appropriate. Other forms used to intensify the adjective are *noch* and *viel.* Schädel also reports the reduplication of the adjective as a method of intensifying.

(172) Schädel (2;6)

eine	klein-e	klein-e	Puppe
INDEF.ART: FEM:SG	small	small	doll

'a very small doll'

It is not clear, however, that the concept of strict comparison is involved in the use of any of these forms. Since these forms appear first, however, this supports Wode's claim (1978) that free forms are acquired before bound forms. When the morphological form of the comparative is used, it is also often commented by the observer that no clear comparison is evident but rather a general form of intensification. Pregel (1970) however found that 50% of the comparatives used by children aged 6–9 years were formed with *mehr* which suggests that this form is preferred since it is semantically clear.

Overgeneralization of the regular form of the comparative occurs frequently, for example

| *gut-er* | from *gut* 'good' | instead of *bess-er* 'better' |
| *hoch-er* | from *hoch* 'high' | instead of *höh-er* 'higher' |

In the last case there is a difference between the predicative form *hoch* and the attributive form *hoh-.* It is significant that it is the predicative form of the adjective which is taken as the root, not the attributive form. This supports

MacWhinney's claim that citation forms are taken as first root allomorphs. Frequency of use also seems to play a part here though. According to Pregel's (1970, p. 137) analysis of 6–9 year olds' language, adjectives can be divided into those used primarily in attributive position and those used in predicative position, although the predominant use overall is attributive. *Hoch* was used primarily in predicative position, hence possibly the error in forming the comparative.

The comparative ending *-er* is also extended to adverbs or verb particles which are not derived from adjectives and therefore cannot have this ending. Commonly the intensifying adverb *noch* 'still' precedes such use and a comparative sense is clear.

(173) Stern (3;2)   *noch*   **rein*   *-er*
                     still   into [VERB.PARTICLE]   COMPAR
                     'still further in'

(174) Stern (3;3)   *noch*   **zusammen*   *-er*
                     still   together   COMPAR
                               [ADV]
                     'still more together'

(175) Scupin (4;6)   *noch*   **rauf*   *-er*
                     still   up   COMPAR
                               [VERB.PARTICLE]
                     'still more up'

This usage, which is quite clear semantically, indicates that the child has not separated out adverbs into the two classes necessary for correct use of the suffixed form.

Scupins' son also reduplicated the suffix *-er* at around age 4;6 e.g. *größ-er-er*. It is not clear under what circumstances this occurred, whether for example additional intensification was intended. The problem may have been one of determining the adjective root; *-er* clearly is identified as an intensifier over this period but its relationship to the concept of comparison is unclear where the comparison remains unexpressed.

4.5. *Prepositions*

Children under 3;0 frequently omit prepositions completely (Stern & Stern, 1928; Grimm, 1973). When prepositions are used, certain ones predominate, leading to incorrect use in locative and temporal expressions. According to the data reported by Grimm (1975), the prepositions most frequently used in locative expressions by children between 2;6 and 6;0 match those which are most frequent in adult speech (Meier, 1964). Table 2.6 shows the frequency of the children's use based on 1102 occurrences. Frequency of usage may be a factor in

TABLE 2.6
Frequency of Occurrence
of Spatial Prepositions
in Children Aged 2;6–6;0
(Adapted from Grimm,
1975, p. 101)

Preposition	Gloss	Frequency
in[1]	'in'	44.4
auf	'on'	19.6
zu	'to'	9.4
bei	'at'	8.9
an	'at'	4.3
nach	'to'	2.9
von	'from'	2.8
aus	'out of'	1.8
durch	'through'	1.1
neben	'beside'	0.8
vor	'in front of'	0.8
hinter	'behind'	0.7
über	'above'	0.7
unter	'under'	0.7
bis	'to'	0.4
um	'around'	0.4
gegen	'against'	0.1

[1] I have put together the figures for the prepositions *in* and *im* which Grimm listed separately. *im* is not a distinct preposition but is an amalgam of *in* and the definite article *dem* which can only be used with stative meaning in association with masculine and neuter singular noun. *in* can be used in both a directional and stative sense.

explaining which prepositions are first acquired. Cognitive simplicity of the relations to be expressed also seems relevant, as will be discussed in more detail below (see 8.6).

The prepositions most frequently used were overgeneralized to produce errors in usage. According to Grimm's classification of the prepositions using semantic features, the children generally use a simpler preposition than a more complex one, for example *rübergehen* *in Straße* 'go over the street' intead of *über die Straße gehen*. This overgeneralization shows that the restrictions on the use of the simpler prepositions have not been acquired, even though the spatial relations they encode may be the simpler to learn.

Temporal prepositions were much rarer in Grimm's data than locative prepositions, and appeared later. The errors that were made consisted mainly of using the most frequent locative prepositions, for example, *gehen* *in Samstag* instead of *am Samstag gehen* 'to go on Saturday'. Grimm attributes these errors to the spatial/temporal undifferentiation in the preoperational child as defined by Piaget. The child is attempting to impose the categories used to distinguish locative prepositions on to the temporal dimension. This can also be explained by the fact that the temporal prepositions also are used as locative prepositions; the homonymity makes it more difficult to learn the specifically temporal features involved.

Grimm's data also include uses of verbal particles which have the same form as prepositions, for example *Angst haben vor* 'to be afraid of'. The use of these verbal particles frequently has little relationship to the meaning of the preposition in its locative or temporal usage. The most usual errors which the children make are to substitute a particle which fits the semantics of the verb, for example *Kopf zerbrechen *gegen* literally 'hit head against' instead of *Kopf zerbrechen über* 'rack one's brains over'. This suggests that children want semantic relationships to be marked clearly, here also concretely, and for each form to have a clear semantic function.

4.6. *Passive*

The passive construction is used quite rarely by children. In German, the passive is distinct from an adjectival construction with the past participle through the use of a different auxiliary, *werden* as opposed to *sein*. For example:

(176) | *die* | *Tür* | *wird* | *ge-* | *strichen* |
|------|------|------|------|------|
| the | door | AUX | PAST | paint:PAST |

'the door is being painted'

(177) | *die* | *Tür* | *ist* | *ge-* | *strichen* |
|------|------|------|------|------|
| the | door | AUX | PAST | paint:PAST |

'the door is/has been painted'

In the case of an agentless passive, the distinction between these two constructions depends entirely on the use of the correct auxiliary. Until the child starts using auxiliaries, therefore, it is difficult to be certain of the use of the passive in spontaneous productions.

Grimm (1973) reports only one passive in the group up to 3;0. The passive was used much more frequently by the group aged 4;7 to 5;0, but in all the groups recorded up to age 6;0 only agentless passives were reported. In the repetition experiment Grimm conducted with these children, a frequent error in repeating an agentless passive was to replace the auxiliary *werden* with a form of *sein,* which would suggest that the passive and the adjectival construction are perceived as similar, if not identical.

In the task of comprehension it has been shown that German children behave very similarly to English children in their understanding of passive sentences with agents. That is, firstly their comprehension is affected by the semantic and pragmatic content of the sentences in their choice of which noun should be agent regardless of the formal structure. Secondly, a word-order strategy based on the order of active sentences is evident in younger children.

Grimm (Grimm et al., 1975) tested children between the ages of 3;0 and 7;12 in a manipulation task. The test material consisted of reversible and irreversible passive sentences (Slobin, 1966) with a variation in the degree of reversibility. For example:

(178) reversible:

> *Hans wird von Ursula ge- küß- t*
> Hans AUX by Ursula kissed
> 'Hans is kissed by Ursula'

(179) less reversible:

> *das Baby wird von der Mutter ge- pfleg- t*
> the baby AUX by the mother cared for
> 'the baby is cared for by the mother'

(180) irreversible:

> *der Boden wird von Hans ge- küß- t*
> the floor AUX by Hans kissed
> 'the floor is kissed by Hans'

(181) semantically anomalous:

> **Hans wird von dem Boden ge- küß- t*
> Hans AUX by the floor kissed
> *'Hans is kissed by the floor'

It was found that the youngest group of children (mean age 3;6) relied very heavily on a word-order strategy which assigns the functions actor, action, object to an NVN sequence (Bever, 1970). In a passive sentence, this strategy leads to an interpretation which reverses the roles of agent and object. This word order strategy was so dominant in the youngest group of children that they made the actor-action-object interpretation even in irreversible sentences. The reliance on this strategy declined in the older children who started to use semantic information to determine interpretation. That is, irreversible passive sentences became easier to understand, since the semantic information supported the passive interpretation. The completely reversible passive sentences were the most difficult, since the semantic information offered no cue to interpretation. Only the oldest age group (mean age 7;2) was able to interpret the semantically anomalous passive sentences correctly, that is they were using only the formal structure to determine their interpretation. Mills (1977a) also obtained similar results in a comprehension task using only reversible passive sentences. Children up to the age of 7;0 were still using the actor-action-object interpretation in some of these sentences.

These results are very similar to those obtained in English (Bever, 1970; Maratsos, 1974; Turner & Rommetveit, 1967a,b), where it was found that children around age 4 relied more heavily than younger children on the actor-action-object strategy which meant that their performance on passive sentences was worse than that of the younger children. Since the youngest German children tested were around age 3;6, it is impossible to determine whether such a dip in performance also occurs.

Grimm also tested imitation of passive sentences containing agents with the same group of children as in the comprehension test. She reports that the youngest children (up to age 4;5) made a large number of random mistakes. Older children made more systematic errors in their imitations. They frequently changed the positions of agent and object in the passive sentences, even though they reproduced the auxiliary, preposition, and past participle. This was done even with irreversible passive sentences. For example:

(182) *der   Vater   wird   vom   Teppich   aus-ge-klopf-t
     the   father   AUX   by:the   carpet   beaten
   *'the father was beaten by the carpet'

was the imitation of the sentence *der Teppich wird vom Vater ausgeklopft* 'the carpet was beaten by the father'. Grimm explains this through a tendency to place the agent of the sentence in first position. The children aged 4;6 to 5;0 performed worse on the imitation test than younger children, but it is not clear from the results what the explanation for this might be.

The same group of children were asked to transform active sentences into passive sentences and vice-versa. The younger children failed to understand the task. The children older than 5;6, when they understood the task, primarily changed the positions of agent and object preserving the original active or passive structure. This would suggest that the word order difference is the first aspect of the active-passive relationship to be learned. Grimm fails to point out, however, that active sentences can have an order other than SVO. The children's rule of changing the positions of subject and object does not necessarily lead to a difference in meaning, especially if case marking is ambiguous. The use of this strategy in this test in German might be increased by the fact that the semantic content is then preserved. This could not be the case in English, for example, and so it might be the case that English children would not use such a strategy.

4.7. Relative Clauses

The first relative clauses reported in the diary studies are from Sterns' children at the age of 2;6. These relative clauses do not contain a relative pronoun, so that their classification as relative clauses could be in doubt. The verb is in final position, however, as is correct for a subordinate clause and semantically the interpretation as a relative clause is acceptable. Stern and Stern also claim that the intonation was appropriate for a relative clause. For example:

(183) Stern (2;6)   *Papa   sieh   mal   *   Hilde   mach-t   hat*
      Daddy   look   just   Hilde   do:PAST   AUX
      'Daddy, look (what) Hilde has done'

(184) Stern (2;6)   *siehe   *   auf-   (g)e-   hängen   hat*
      see   up   PAST   hang:PAST   AUX
      'look, (what) (I) have hung up'

Their son Günther went on to insert a meaningless syllable instead of the relative pronoun until around age 3 years. For example:

(185) Stern (2;10)   *meine   Blume   eigentlich   ist,   *e*
       my   flower   really   is
       Hans   (g)e-   gib- t   hat
       Hans   PAST   give:PAST   AUX
       'that's really my flower that Hans gave'

(186) Stern (3;2)   *das   ist   ein   Pilz   *mm   in   Walde   ist*
       that   is   a   mushroom   in   wood   is
       'that is a mushroom which is in the wood'

Obviously no information is available about cases from these meaningless forms or where the relative pronoun is omitted. It would appear as though the semantic and pragmatic information in the clause is sufficient to make the meaning clear. The child does not seem to be hindered in any way in his production of relativ clauses by not being able to produce the correct case inflected forms of the relative pronoun.

This suggestion is supported by other observations from Grimm (1973). She reports that the younger children in her sample (3–4 years) predominantly used *wo* as the relative pronoun in the clauses they produced. In Standard German, *wo* is the form of the locative interrogative pronoun 'where' and is also a possible form of the relative pronoun used with a preposition. For example:

(187)   *das   Thema,   wo   -rüber   er   spricht*
        the   topic   REL.PRO   about [PREP]   he   talk:PRES
        'the topic he is talking about'

In some dialects, however, *wo* is also used as the relative pronoun in subject and object function. It is this use which predominates in the children's relative clauses. For example:

(188) Grimm	*das*	*ist*	*ein*	*Mädchen,*	*wo*		*in*	*die*
	that	is	a	girl	REL.PRO		in	the
	Schule	*geht*					
	school	goes					
	'that is a girl who goes to school'						

(189) Grimm	*aber*	*die*	*Puppa,*	*wo*		*die*	*Uschi*	*hat*
	but	the	doll	REL.PRO		the	Uschi	has
	'but the doll which Uschi has'						

Grimm took her sample of children from the Heidelberg area which uses *wo* in this way in the local dialect. The same usage is reported in children from Göttingen, but I have not been able to establish whether the local dialect has this form. It is obviously relevant to establish what the influence of the local dialect is. It could be the case that all children use this form, independent of dialect usage, since it is uninfluenced by case inflections. As in the early examples from Stern and Stern, no case information is available from this relative pronoun form.

Around age 4, Grimm reports, the children produce an intermediate form combining *wo* and the standard relative pronoun *der, die, das,* etc. For example:

(190) Grimm

ich	*hab*	*ein*	*Heinzelmann,*	*der*	**wo*
I	have	a	Heinzelmann:MASC	REL.PRO:	REL.PRO
				MASC:SG:NOM	
so	*mach*	*-e(n)*	*kann*		
thus	do	INF	can [MOD]		
'I have a Heinzelmann who can go like this'					

A possible explanation for this double use is that the children are unsure of the formal correctness of the *der,* etc., forms, since their case inflections make these more complex. Both are used until the child feels confident of the case inflected forms according to the principle that semantic relations should be overtly and clearly marked. One error with the relative pronoun, observed in an older child (5 years)[5], suggests that the child has more problems when the relative pronoun should have a case form different from a preceding definite article. In the follow-

---

[5]I am grateful to Werner Deutsch for this example.

ing example, the child has repeated the form of the preceding definite article as
the relative pronoun.

(191) (ca. 5;0) *ich habe das mit der*
I   have   that with DEF.ART:
FEM:SG:DAT

Schere,   **der*   *ganz*
scissors:FEM:SG   REL.PRO   very
FEM:SG:DAT/
MASC:SG:NOM

scharf schneidet, gemacht
sharp   cuts   made

'I have made that with the scissors that cut really sharp'

This could be interpreted as a gender mistake, since *der* is a nominative form in
the masculine paradigm. Possibly the preceding article and the existence of this
form in the nominative both contribute to produce this error. The child may adopt
a strategy of simply copying a preceding definite article as the relative pronoun,
as in fact was the case in Old English, for example. More data are necessary on
error in this area.

Experimental work with relative clauses has produced evidence that the position of the relative clause, the function of the relative pronoun within the clause,
and the position of case-marking inflections are all relevant in the stage of
acquisition. Park (1976) conducted an imitation experiment in which the children
were tested with three types of relative clause: final right-branching, initial left-
branching, and initial right-branching. The following sentences illustrate these
structures:

(192) final right branching—

ich brauche eine Sekretärin,   die   gut   tippt
I   need   a   secretary:FEM REL.PRO: well   types
FEM:SG:NOM

'I need a secretary who can type well'

(193) initial left branching—

wer   das schreibt, muß vollkommen besoffen sein
REL.PRO   that writes   must completely   drunk   be

'whoever writes such things must be completely drunk'

(194) initial right branching—

der Mann   ,der   Würste   verkauft, ist mein
the   man:MASC   REL.PRO: sausages sells   is   my
MASC:SG:NOM

Vater

father

'the man who is selling sausages is my father'

Park only considers the factors of position of the relative clause in respect of the main clause and the direction of the branching. His results indicated that children found it easier to imitate relative clauses in final position rather than in initial position. In the initial clauses, left-branching clauses were easier than right-branching. These results can be attributed to the principle that an interruption in the elements of the same clause will cause that structure to be more difficult to interpret.

Grimm and Wintermantel (Grimm et al., 1975) tested comprehension of relative clauses in a toy-moving task with younger children (4;0–5;4) and in an interview procedure with older children (6;0–7;4). The clauses tested were all right-branching. The conditions which they varied in the material were position of the relative clause and the relative pronoun being in subject or object function. The following examples are taken from the test material:

(195) final,REL.PRO.subject—

der	*Bär*	*beißt*	*den*	*Igel*	*,der*		*den*	*Vogel*
the	bear	bites	the	hedgehog	REL.PRO: MASC:SG:NOM		the	bird:ACC

streift

touches

'the bear bites the hedgehog that touches the bird'

(196) final,REL.PRO.object

die	*Kuh*	*haut*	*die*	*Katze*	*,die*		*der*	*Vogel*
the	cow	hits	the	cat:FEM	REL.PRO: FEM:SG:ACC		the	bird:NOM

anstößt

bumps

'the cow hits the cat that the bird bumps into'

(197) initial,REL.PRO.subject—

der	*Elefant*		*,der*		*den*	*Hasen*	*streichelt,*
the	elephant:MASC		REL.PRO: MASC:SG:NOM		the	rabbit:ACC	strokes

tritt *den* *Esel*

kicks the donkey

'the elephant that strokes the rabbit kicks the donkey'

(198) initial,REL.PRO.object

die	Giraffe	,die	der	Hase	packt,	beißt
the	giraffe:FEM	REL.PRO: FEM:SG:ACC	the	rabbit:NOM	grabs	bites

die	Ente
the	duck

'the giraffe that the rabbit grabs bites the duck'

To summarize their results: the responses to the interview were difficult to evaluate but in general agreed with the results of the manipulation test. Initial subject clauses were easier than final subject clauses, final object clauses were easier than initial object clauses. Sentences where the relative pronoun was subject of the clause were easier than where it was object of the clause. In these results the position of embedding, initial or final, was not shown to influence interpretation independently. There are several possible explanations of these results. The ordering of initial subject before final subject and final object before initial object is explained by Grimm and Wintermantel by the extent to which the sentences deviate from what they regard as the standard order, namely actor-action-object. It is not clear from the argument presented how this deviation is measured in order to predict this sequence of difficulty.

These results also match the results obtained by Sheldon (1974) working with English. Her proposed explanation is that of a "parallel function" hypothesis. According to this hypothesis, it is easier to interpret sentences in which the relativized noun phrase has the same function in the main clause as it does in the relative clause, hence the order obtained above. Results which do not support this hypothesis, however, have been obtained for English (de Villiers et al., 1979) and for German (Mills, 1977a,b) (see later discussion).

The result that relative clauses with the relative pronoun as subject of the clause are easier than where it is object of the clause can also be explained in several ways. The explanations are also possibly related to one another. Keenan and Comrie (1977) proposed an Agreement Hierarchy according to which the possibility of relativization from a particular function is ranked in relation to other functions. Subject function is in first position on the hierarchy, followed by object, indirect object, object of preposition, possessive, and object of comparison. In German, relativization is only allowed from the first five positions on the hierarchy. It is claimed that relativization becomes more difficult the further down the hierarchy you go. If the Agreement Hierarchy has psychological reality, it would predict that relative clauses with the relative pronoun in subject function should be easier to process. Since nominative case is closely associated with subject function, it would predict in this study that relative pronouns in nominative case would be easier than those in accusative case.

Nominative case also seems to be associated with first position in the clause, for which some evidence has been presented earlier. Since the relative pronoun is the first element in the clause, this association would explain the correct interpretation of clauses with the relative pronoun as subject.

If relative pronouns occur with high frequency in nominative case, this frequency may facilitate interpretation. The use of the most frequent form may be quite independent of the factors which cause that form to be the most frequent. In this case, the complexity predictions of the Agreement Hierarchy or the association of nominative case with first position may account for a high frequency of nominative case in relative pronouns, but it may be only the frequent occurrence of nominative case in the relative pronoun which facilitates this interpretation. In order to examine the explanation more closely, it had to be ascertained whether nominative case did occur frequently in relative pronouns.

For this purpose three different types of written language from adults (philosophy text, newspaper, and popular novel) were analyzed and compared with one another for frequency of function, etc. The results of this analysis are reported in Mills (1981a). To summarize: Relative pronouns occur far more frequently in nominative case than in any other case. Although the Agreement Hierarchy's prediction is met for subject function (associated with nominative case), the other cases are not in the order predicted, so that the Hierarchy as an explanation of the order of complexity in interpretation is put into doubt. The frequency of relative pronouns in nominative case and the general association of subject with first position are clearly related and both probably contribute towards making the interpretation of subject relative clauses easier.

The most common error in Grimm and Wintermantel's results was to take the first noun in the sentence to be the actor in both the main and relative clause. This strategy leads to a correct interpretation in initial subject clauses (see sentence 197) which might well explain why this type of sentence was the easiest to interpret. This interpretation strategy leads to error in the other three sentences types and this error was made in all three types. In sentence 195, for example, the bear was made to bite the hedgehog and touch the bird. This strategy suggests that the children have difficulty recognizing the relative clause structure, possibly because of the similarity between the relative pronoun and the definite article. The interpretation by the children that the first noun is actor of both clauses supports the suggestion made earlier that first position is strongly associated with actor/subject.

Grimm and Wintermantel also tested the children's comprehension of the same four types of sentence but with *wo* inserted after the relative pronoun. This compound form is the deviant form which the children in the Heidelberg area themselves produce in spontaneous utterances (see earlier discussion). This compound form, in general, improved comprehension. The insertion of *wo* clearly marks the previous form as a relative pronoun and eliminates the possibility of it being a definite article, which should make the subsequent processing of the clause easier.

The comprehension of the same four types of sentence was tested in a picture selection task with older children (5;11–8;11) (Mills, 1977a). As well as testing for the influence of the position of the relative clause and for the influence of the case of the relative pronoun, the test material was constructed so that the form clearly marking nominative and accusative case (masculine gender) was used EITHER as the relative pronoun OR as the definite article in the second noun phrase in the relative clause. For example:

(199) initial, REL.PRO:SUBJ, REL.PRO marked, DEF.ART unmarked

| *der* | *Mann,* | *der* | *das* | *Mädchen* |
| the | man:MASC | REL.PRO:
MASC:SG:NOM | DEF.ART:
NEUT:SG:NOM/ACC | girl:NEUT |

| *ruft,* | *folgt* | *dem* | *Jungen* |
| calls | follows | the | boy |

'the man who calls the girl follows the boy'

(200) initial, REL.PRO:SUBJ, REL.PRO unmarked, DEF.ART marked

| *die* | *Frau,* | *die* | *den* | *Mann* |
| the | woman:FEM | REL.PRO:
FEM:SG:NOM/ACC | DEF.ART:
MASC:SG:ACC | man:MASC |

| *erschießt,* | *schlägt* | *den* | *Polizisten* |
| shoots | hits | DEF.ART:
MASC:SG:ACC | policeman |

'the woman who shoots the man hits the policeman'

The results indicated that all three factors were relevant in the interpretation of the clauses. Finally-embedded clauses were easier to interpret than initially-embedded clauses. This is the same result as Park found in his imitation test and can be explained by the non-interruption principle. Clauses where the relative pronoun was subject of the clause were easier than where it was object, as Grimm and Wintermantel also found. The exact order of complexity of the four types was: final subject < initial subject < final object = initial object. These results do not fit the prediction of Sheldon's parallel function hypothesis. The difference between Grimm and Wintermantel's and these results can be explained if it is the case that the older children in this study were not relying on the interpretation strategy of taking the first noun as actor for both clauses. The older children seem to have fewer problems in separating the relative clause from the main clause.

The older children still have problems using the case information within the relative clause. For all sentence types, the marked article rather than the marked relative pronoun facilitated interpretation of the clause. A possible explanation of this is based on a surface structure interpretation model which is discussed in detail in Mills (1977a, p. 145). To summarize: The relative pronoun can only be identified as such when it is obvious that it is not a definite article, that is relatively late in the clause. The definite article in these clauses, however, can be easily identified as such because of the noun following immediately after it, and can therefore be analyzed more easily for case information than the relative pronoun.

The importance of the position of the relative clause and the tendency to associate subject with first position in a clause were examined again using ambiguous relative clauses (Mills, 1977b). The clauses were constructed so that the relative pronoun and the definite article with the second noun were unmarked for case.

Adults and children aged 6 to 13 years were tested on their interpretation of these relative clauses. Semantic and pragmatic information which might disambiguate the clause was reduced to a minimum. The following sentences are taken from the test material and illustrate the high degree of reversibility (Slobin, 1966):

(201) initial, REL.PRO and DEF.ART ambiguous

die   *Katze,*   *die*

DEF.ART: cat:FEM   REL.PRO:
FEM:SG:NOM   FEM:SG:NOM/ACC

das   *Mädchen*   *sieht,*

DEF.ART: girl:NEUT   sees
NEUT:SG:NOM/ACC

beißt   *den*   *Hund*

bites   DEF.ART: dog:MASC
       MAS:SG:ACC

'the cat $\left\{ \begin{array}{l} \text{which sees the girl} \\ \text{which the girl sees} \end{array} \right\}$ bites the dog'

(202) final, REL.PRO and DEF.ART ambiguous

der   *Hund*   *sieht*

DEF.ART: dog:MASC   sees

das   *Mädchen,*   *das*

DEF.ART: girl:NEUT   REL.PRO:
NEUT:SG:NOM/ACC   NEUT:SG:NOM/ACC

die   *Krankenschwester*   *ruft*

DEF.ART: nurse:FEM   calls
FEM:SG:NOM/ACC

'the dog sees the girl $\left\{ \begin{array}{l} \text{who calls the nurse'} \\ \text{who the nurse calls'} \end{array} \right\}$

If semantic and pragmatic information cannot guide interpretation, it would be expected that 50% of the subjects would choose nominative case and 50% accusative case.

In every age group, the relative pronoun was interpreted as being in nominative case significantly more often than in accusative case. The frequency of this preferred interpretation was not affected by the position of embedding of the relative clause.

These results again suggest that subject is strongly related to first position in the clause, possibly in association with the canonical word order SVO of main clauses, as discussed earlier. This is also the case in French (see Clark, 1985). Frequency of usage must also be taken into account, possibly as an independent factor, or possibly related to the principle above.

4.8. Infinitival Complements

The only data on acquisition of these structures come from comprehension experiments conducted by Grimm and Schöler (Grimm et al., 1975). Children were tested on their comprehension of sentences containing the causative verbs *lassen* 'to cause', *erlauben* 'to allow', and *befehlen* 'to order'.

These three verbs can have an infinitival complement in which the verb can be intransitive or transitive with an object of the main verb, in dative or accusative case according to the verbs used. The following sentences illustrate these possible sentence types with the verb *erlauben*.

(203) *Maria   erlaubt   Hans   zu   arbeit   -en*
      Maria   allows   Hans   to   work   INF
      'Maria allows Hans to work'

(204) *Maria   erlaubt   Hans   Uschi   zu   hol   -en*
      Maria   allows   Hans   Uschi   to   fetch   INF
      'Maria allows Hans to fetch Uschi'

The verb *lassen* does not have the marker *zu* before the infinitive.

The verbs *erlauben* and *befehlen* also allow a complement construction with *daß* 'that', so that sentences 203 and 204 can also have the following form with very similar semantic content:

(205) *Maria   erlaubt,   daß   Hans   arbeitet*
      Maria   allows   that   Hans   works
      'Maria allows Hans to work'

(206) *Maria   erlaubt,   daß   Hans   Uschi   holt*
      Maria   allows   that   Hans   Uschi   fetches
      'Maria allows Hans to fetch Uschi'

The verb *lassen* can also be used with an active infinitive but with the agent and object reversed to produce a passive meaning. For example:

(207) *Maria   läßt   Uschi   von   Hans   hol   -en*
      Maria   makes   Uschi   by   Hans   fetch   INF
      'Maria causes Uschi to be fetched by Hans'

Grimm and Schöler tested comprehension of such structures in a manipulation task with children aged 5;0 to 6;4.[6] Reversibility was controlled for across all construction types by including a noun in the complement clause which could not semantically function as agent. The verbs *erlauben* and *lassen* were tested with the infinitive complement and the verb *erlauben* with the *daß* complement. The verb *versprechen* 'to promise' was also included with an infinitival complement. As in English, this verb requires the selection of the agent of the main clause as agent in the infinitival complement.

Reversibility was shown to be an important factor in correct interpretation of all construction types. The non-reversible clauses were easier in every case. The complements with *daß* were easier than the infinitival complements. The suggested explanation is that *daß* clearly marks the beginning of a subordinate clause, so that the elements of that clause can be more easily identified as belonging to a unit for the purposes of analysis. The infinitival complement has no such marking at the beginning, although a pause between the main clause and complement clause can mark the subordination. This would fit with the proposed explanation for difficulties in processing relative clauses (4.7) which are not clearly marked at the beginning because of the similarity between the relative pronoun and definite article.

Grimm and Schöler state that the performance with *lassen* in non-reversible infinitival complements was worse than with *erlauben*. They attribute this to the more general semantic content of *lassen* since it can have the meaning of 'allow' and 'cause'. However, they overlooked a formal ambiguity in their test sentences which may have produced the different result.

It is also possible that the particle *zu* before the infinitive helps to mark the clause as a subordinate clause. *Lassen* has no *zu* before the infinitive, and in this respect is like modal verbs, where the agent of the modal is always the agent of the infinitive. As suggested above, the main problem in comprehension may be the grouping of elements in infinitival clauses into a unit. This lack of marking with *lassen* could lead to errors in interpretation. Without detailed results these possibilities cannot be unravelled.

The sentences with *versprechen* were the most difficult. Grimm and Schöler attribute this difficulty, in part, to the fact that the construction with this verb cannot be interpreted according to the Minimal Distance Principle (Rosenbaum, 1965; C. Chomsky, 1969) which, they say, can be used to interpret infinitival complements in German. According to this principle, the noun immediately

---

[6]Grimm and Schöler conducted a second experiment with these verbs using an interview technique. The results are however unclear because of difficulties in experimental design and are therefore not discussed here.

preceding the verb in an infinitival complement is taken to be the agent of that verb. This principle produces a correct interpretation for English and for German sentences of type 203 which have no other nouns in the clause. It does not work for sentences such as 204 however, where the principle would make *Uschi* the subject of the verb *holen*. It cannot be stated therefore that *versprechen* is an exception to this principle, since the principle only works for a limited structure in German. Since no information is given about the type of errors made in this and other verbs, it is difficult to discuss possible explanations except hypothetically.

If the Minimal Distance Principle is involved, it would be expected that the object of the complement clause would be selected as agent, since it is next to the verb. This did not happen with relative clauses, however (see 4.7), which have the same ordering of object before the verb. If the errors follow those of the relative clauses, it would be expected that younger children take the first noun of the sentence, that is the main clause, to be agent of every verb according to the principle of associating subject with first position, since they have difficulties indentifying a subordinate clause within the main sentence, as discussed earlier. This would in fact lead to a correct interpretation of the *versprechen* sentences. When they can identify the elements of the subordinate clause, it would be expected that they take the noun nearest to the subordinate clause to be subject. This leads to a correct interpretation for the majority of verbs; *versprechen* is then an exception.

A detailed study of these constructions in spontaneous speech and through careful experimentation would throw some light on the dependence of interpretation strategies on the word order possibilities allowed and most frequently used within a language.

5. Error-Free Acquisition

5.1. Verb Morphology: Person

The acquisition of the inflections marking person on the verb, appears to involve relatively little error. This may seem a surprising claim when the data are first examined. Stern and Stern (1928) refer to the infinitive stage of the verb in the two and three word utterances, since the verb frequently has the *-en* ending characteristic of the infinitive. In the discussion above on word order, it was mentioned that when the child first produces two- and three-word utterances, he commonly uses a verb-final rule. The suggested explanation for this was the frequency of final infinitive forms, that is *-en* forms, in caretakers' speech to children. The prevalence of this ending in children therefore suggests that it is a directly imitated form which is unanalyzed. When the verb occurs in non-final position, the verb is finite and must therefore have the ending determined by the person and number of the subject. An analysis of Miller's data (1976)[7] collected

---

[7]I am indebted to Ingrid Münnig for her help with this analysis.

TABLE 2.7
Distribution of Verb Endings
in Two- and Three-Word Utterances
from Miller's Data
(Miller, 1976, p. 171–196)

Order of Elements	Endings of Verb				
	-(e)n	-e	-t	-∅	Total
Agent (X) Verb	26	13	30	14	83
non-Agent (X) Verb	81	92	15	23	211
(X) Verb Agent Agent Verb (X)	5	8	24	13	50
(X) Verb non-Agent	13	12	30	21	76
Total	125	125	99	71	420

from two children aged 1;4–1;10 suggests that in children's two- and three-word utterances, when the verb is in non-final position, the -en ending becomes far less common and the -t ending (3SG/2PL) begins to dominate. This -t ending is correct, if it is assumed that where the subject is not named, a proper name (3SG) would occur rather than first or second person singular. In Miller's data (Miller, 1976, p. 171–196), there were 420 occurrences of verbs which could have morphological endings, (see Table 2.7).

The two children were still predominantly placing the verb in final position and the -en ending dominates. One of the children, however, much more frequently used the -e ending than -en. The -e ending is correct for first person singular but there was no evidence that the child was using it to mark this person. It appears rather to be a variation of -en. The deletion of final -n occurs in many dialect forms, although it is not clear that this aspect is significant here. This analysis is supported by the fact that the same child produced a few sentences with modal verbs and infinitives and again used an -e ending for the main verb, for example:

(208) Miller (1;10)   *mag   nicht   ess   -e*
                        want   NEG   eat
                        'I don't want to eat'

The distribution of the -t endings is of most interest however. The -t endings are rare in the cases where the verb is preceded by an element which is not in agent function. In the other cases, where the -t ending is more common, the agent is adjacent to the verb or would immediately precede it, if present. The -t ending would appear to be correctly used as soon as a link is made between subject and verb in terms of word order, that is making subject and verb adjacent.

The diary studies do not report any errors in person inflections, with the exception of one error by Scupins' child, which seems however to be due to wrong segmentation. The child at age 1;10 produced the form *sieh-*ste* for the second person singular of *seh-en* 'to see' in a declarative utterance instead of *sieh-st*. The most probable explanation for this error is the frequent use of the interjection *siehst du* 'you see' in which the *du* in fast speech is pronounced as /ə/. The child has assumed this /ə/ is part of the verb inflection in the second person singular. He only uses it in the context of this one verb, however, and it soon disappears, presumably as the child learns the general rules of person inflections.

Clearly more data are needed from more children but the evidence suggests that the acquisition of person in the verb, as it appears in present tense, is quick and involves little error. This may be explainable by the principle "pay attention to the ends of the words" but also by the fact that the inflections marking person have little duplication of form matched with function.

5.2. Verb Negation

The correct form of negation and its ordering in the sentence appear quickly and with little error. Wode (1977) describes the stages of acquisition of the negative. Firstly *nein* 'no' is used in non-anaphoric negation and placed in initial position. This is quite quickly replaced around age 2;0 by the form *nicht*. As was described earlier, the rules in adult German are broadly as follows: *nicht* is placed after the finite verb (Stickel, 1970) in main clauses (sentence 209), although the exact position of *nicht* amongst the elements following the verb is governed by complex rules. When the sentence contains a modal or auxiliary, however, the *nicht* is ordered before the main verb (participle or infinitive) in clause-final position (sentence 210).

(209) ich   tanze   nicht
     I   dance   not
     'I don't dance'

(210) ich   sollte   seinem   Vater   die   Geschichte   nicht
     I   should   his:DAT   father   the:ACC   story   NEG
     erzähl   -en
     tell   INF
     'I shouldn't tell his father the story'

Wode did not present data on the ability to distinguish these two rules but described the quick acquisition of the first rule.

Park (1979) collected more data on negations. He found examples of negated utterances containing *nein* which were both anaphoric and non-anaphoric. The *nein* was predominantly in initial position in both the anaphoric and non-anaphoric uses. The utterances with *nicht* were few, and since the other parts of speech are not described, it is not possible to categorize the ordering as an error or not.

Clahsen (1981a, 1981b) differentiates Wode's stage of sentence-internal negation. The three children he investigated, aged 2;8 and 2;2, first positioned *nicht* immediately before or after the verb. Two months later they ordered *nicht* only immediately after the verb. At the age of 3;5 the two eldest children had a rule of ordering *nicht* at the end of the sentences.

An analysis of Miller's data shows the strength of the rule positioning *nicht* after the finite verb. 51 utterances contained a negation. The following table shows the breakdown:

nein V	1
nein N	3
N *nein*	1
V *nicht*	34
N *nicht*	5
nicht N	1
nicht ADJ	2
nicht N V	2
misc.	2

There were only two instances of *nicht* preceding a verb, and significantly these were in cases when the verb could be interpreted as being in infinitive form. The placement would therefore be correct. The rule of placement of *nicht* after the finite verb seems to be learned easily, but experimental evidence from Grimm and Wintermantel (Grimm et al., 1975) suggests that this order may be over-generalized by children around 4–5 years and lead to error. The simplicity of the system can account for the ease by which it is learned, since the negative morpheme is a free morpheme and involves no changes in the verb, etc. No data are available for other stages of the acquisition of negation, for example the negative article *kein* 'no' or the negative pronoun *nichts* 'nothing'.

5.3. *Gender*

Relatively few errors have been recorded in the acquisition of gender, as discussed earlier. Gender marking is often correct in the adjectives which are used before articles are part of the child's speech. When the full form of the articles is produced (not the abbreviated forms *de* or *'n*), gender is also usually correct. Primarily the nominative case or citation form is used in the early utterances with the articles and here gender is correct. MacWhinney (1978) suggests that the articles are first learned as an amalgam with the noun and that this rote learning continues for a long time in German children because of the absence of morphophonological regularities in German. As discussed earlier, MacWhinney did not consider the regularities available to the child in enough detail. The correct assignment of gender may well be supported by these regularities. Some work has been done on what such regularities may be in German (Altman & Rättig, 1973; Neumann, 1967). Adults' assignment of gender to loan-words indicate some of the regularities actually used (Arndt, 1970; Carstensen, 1980). Zubin and Köpcke (Zubin & Köpcke, 1981; Köpcke, 1982; Köpcke & Zubin, 1982) have more recently investigated regularities in German and have established numerous rules where gender has been claimed to be arbitrarily assigned (Maratsos, 1979).

Böhme and Levelt (1979) tested usage of gender using the child's ability to discriminate *sein* 'his/its' as referring to masculine or neuter gender nouns from *ihr* 'her' as referring to feminine gender nouns. The results with inanimate nouns will be presented here since these indicate syntactic gender usage. They used three nouns, one of each gender: *der Würfel* (MASC) 'die' (singular of 'dice'), *die Gießkanne* (FEM) 'watering can', and *das Boot* (NEUT) 'boat'. The child's task was to complete the sentence, for example *ihre Farbe ist . . .* 'her/its color is. . .' . Children were tested in three age groups, mean ages 3;11, 4;9, and 5;5. It was found that children in the younger age group had just over 50% correct usage which rose to 70% correct in the oldest group with a slight dip in the middle. Böhme and Levelt claim that the children achieved such high scores by using morphophonological regularities which mark *Kanne* clearly as feminine, not masculine or neuter (-*e* ending and polysyllabicity), and *Würfel* and *Boot* as non-feminine (-*el* ending and monosyllabicity). In a second part of the test, the children were presented with a wrong statement and asked whether it was possible, e.g. 'can I say: "her color is black"?' Subsequently they were asked why it was not possible to say this. The awareness of gender was low in the younger age groups but reached the level of usage in the oldest group. Explanations given by the younger groups were typically linked to natural gender, for example the die belongs to a boy. Little intralinguistic reference was possible. The usage scores are not particularly high, even for the oldest age group. This may be explained by the fact that *sein* and *ihr* are commonly confused in production, even at a time when gender on articles, etc., is correctly marked (Scupin & Scupin, 1910; Stern & Stern, 1928). Most commonly, *sein* is the overgeneralized form.

Ramge (1973), in his statistical collection of self-corrections in 6-year-old children, found few examples in the area of gender. Those he did note were usually to be explained by a false start, that is the child changed his mind about which noun to use.

The results reported above stress the importance of the child's use of morpho-phonological regularities to determine syntactic gender and may account for the few errors reported in this area. Although the child may make an error in case, the choice of form of article, etc., seems to stay within the gender paradigm.

5.4. Grammatical Intonation

The only work in this area has been done by Wode (1980). By the term "grammatical intonation" he means the area in which pitch, stress, and pause are related to linguistic structures. In this connection Wode collected and analyzed data from his own son, Lars, up to the first part of the two-word stage. At the one-word stage, which lasted up to age 1;6 approximately, Lars had already learned four aspects of intonation. He formed the intonation center in the individual lexical items. Multisyllabic items were stressed initially under neutral conditions but, for special emphasis or for fun, other stresses would be added or the stress put on another syllable. He had acquired falling and rising pitch but it was not clear if there was any association with particular meaning, that is the distinction between statements and questions. Emphatic level intonation had also been learned. Before the two-word stage is reached, children will repeat the same word several times after one another. Lars treated these as an intonational whole, making a fall or rise on the final item of the string, for example with:

(211) Wode (1;8)   *decke decke decke*
                   'blanket, blanket, blanket'

Also at this stage Lars would produce admonitions, such as *Mann* 'goodness' or *Mensch* 'heck', with a correct falling intonation. Admonitions in initial position must have such a falling intonation.

Before reaching the two-word stage, the child made systematic use of post-contour intonations by age 1;10. Their use was clear in connection with vocatives. The child used the intonation possibilities correctly according to the position of the vocative. That is, in utterance-initial position, the vocatives formed independent intonations or formed part of the pendant; in other positions they formed postcontours.

According to these data, the child learned the three intonational constituents in the order defined by their hierarchical status (Wode, 1972), that is the intonation center is acquired before the pendant, with postcontour last. He quickly learned to associate morphosyntax with intonation and the restrictions imposed by morphosyntactic structures. As Wode points out, very little has been done in this area in German and equally little in other languages, so that crosslinguistic comparison is impossible.

5.5. Nominal Compounds

German is famous for its long words, and this reputation can be attributed, at least in part, to the possibility of forming multiple nominal compounds such as *Donau-dampf-schiff-fahrt-s-gesellschaft* 'Danube-steam-ship-sailing-company'. Nominal compounds however have their own morphology. There are four basic suffixes that can be post-fixed to the first noun of a compound (determinans): *-en-*, *-(e)s-*, *-er-*, and *-e-*. There can also be a zero suffix. For example:

(212) *Hühn-   er-   ei*
    hen   egg
    'hen's egg'

(213) *Pferde-   e-   stall*
    horse   stable
    'horse stable'

(214) *Kuh-   stall*
    cow   stable
    'cow stall'

(215) *Zeitung-   s-   junge*
    paper   boy
    'paper boy'

(216) *Staat-   s-   mann*
    state   man
    'statesman'

Most suffix forms used are the same as forms which occur in the declensional paradigms of the determinans, *Hühn-er* for example is the plural of *Huhn*, *Staat-s* is the genitive of *Staat*. The exception is *Zeitung-s* since *Zeitung*, as a feminine noun, does not have a *-s* in its paradigm. This *-s* form is a common suffix on feminine nouns in compounds. There are very few regularities in the selection of the suffix. The few rules which can be formulated have numerous exceptions (Augst, 1975; Plank, 1976). The clearest regularity is that the form of suffix in the compound coincides with forms occurring in the declensional paradigm of the noun involved, but, as is seen above, there are exceptions even to this.

Plank (1976) tested 7- and 10-year-old children on the juncture suffixes they would use in specific compounds. The compounds all had a feminine noun which ended in a consonant as the first element. The children were given two nouns and asked to form the compound and to indicate whether they knew the compound or not. In a second experiment, adults were presented with the forms of compounds selected by the children and asked to rate these for well-formedness. The results of these two experiments show that there is considerable diversity among the children, and adults as to the selection or evaluation of the correct form in a particular case. Some compounds produced a high level of agreement amongst subjects; that is, most agreed, for example, on a zero suffix in *Schachtel-macher* 'box-maker'; in other cases there was little agreement. Some subjects showed a preference for a particular suffix across all compounds; others, when tested a second time, selected a different form. Plank concludes that learners acquire "an increasing number of lexical entries of nominal compounds, which are identified and segmented by the learner, rather than being taken as unanalyzable wholes" (Plank, 1976, p. 217). He goes on to argue that in the case of the compound not being reproducible from memory, the child will seek an analogy with a compound containing a similar first noun. As he increases the number of lexical compounds in his memory, he learns the constraints which exist on the possible forms.

Augst (Augst et al., 1977) comes to the same conclusion as Plank from his analysis of the nominal compounds in a 6-year-old's lexicon. Of the complex words in the child's lexicon, more than 68% were nominal compounds as opposed to 56% of the complex words listed in the dictionary (Wahrig, 1968). Despite the complex rules and irregularities in compounding, the child showed no signs of avoiding such constructions, rather the opposite. The child made few errors in the selection of the juncture suffix. In the majority of nominal compounds the child produced, the determinans appeared at least once in a compound entered in a dictionary or used in the immediate speech community. The child could draw on these examples therefore in forming new compounds by the process of analogy. In the examples where this was not the case, the suffixes used followed the rules proposed by Augst (1975). There were very few examples which did not fall in either category. The lexical innovations the child produced were judged to be well-formed in the majority of cases, although Augst does not enter into a discussion of the variability in adults' judgments in this respect.

The lack of error in this area is surprising considering the lack of clear rules. The explanation proposed by Plank and Augst seems plausible. Since adult language contains a large number of compounds, the child has a good chance of hearing the determinans in a compound and being able to use it as a base for analogy. The lexical entry for the individual noun must therefore contain the information on the juncture suffix to be used when it occurs as a determinans. More data are needed from younger children to explore this explanation.

6. Timing of Acquisition

6.1. Precocious Acquisition

6.1.1. *Verbal Particles.* As in English, verbal particles appear very early and are common in two-word utterances (Miller, 1976). The particles which do occur, such as *weg* 'away', *auf* 'up', can be analyzed as part of a verb of which the main part has been omitted. For example in *Katja weg* 'Katja away', *weg* could be part of *weg-gehen* 'go away'. These are usually separable prefixes to the verb and are in sentence-final position as discussed earlier. If they occur with the verb, they take primary stress. I would argue that frequent occurrence in final position and stressed position makes these particles highly salient so that they assume the function of the full verb and appear early.

6.1.2. *Tag Questions.*

Unfortunately there are only data from one bilingual child (English/German) on acquisition in this area (Mills, 1981b). As was discussed earlier, the tag form in German is very simple in comparison with English, since only one word or set phrase is added after the main clause. The form of this word or phrase is independent of the structure of the clause, unlike English where tag questions involve the selection of the right verb and, most commonly, a reversal of the polarity of the main clause. In both English and German, tag questions can have two different functions: interrogative function and confirmatory function. The latter function is so-called because the speaker expects a particular answer, so that the addressee has merely to confirm the expectation. These two functions are distinguished by a difference in intonation in both languages. In German, the difference is indicated by a low-rise (confirmatory) as opposed to a high-rise (interrogative). In English, the contrast is between a fall (confirmatory) and a rise (interrogative).

The child, my son Nicky, learned the German tag form of the local dialect, *gell,* well before structurally well-formed tag questions appeared in English. When he first produced *gell,* around 3;0, he started using the form *uh* in English, both with the low-rise or level intonation and apparently with the same confirmatory function. Intonation seems to be learned early in connection with this function, as discussed earlier (5.4). Although the component structural rules for forming tag questions in English were present in Nicky's speech, tag questions did not start to be used to any extent until age 3;9. They contained many errors until after age 4;0. The greater complexity of the English construction seems to lead to a delay in acquisition, although the function has been marked earlier. Since no data are available for the acquisition of tags in monolingual German and English children, it is impossible to sort out whether the use of the simple form *uh* is common in English or whether Nicky was influenced from German to look for a way of marking the confirmatory question function. Monolingual English children may mark the function in different ways or it may not appear until the more complex structure is acquired. The simple form in German may make it easier to perceive the function in the tag question form.

6.1.3. *The Auxiliary* werden: *Future and Passive.*

The auxiliary *werden* is used to form the future tense and the passive. In the first case the main verb is in the infinitive; in the second case the main verb has the past participle form. If it is the case that a one-to-one mapping between form and function facilitates acquisition, then it might be expected that the acquisition of these structures would be delayed in comparison to languages where this is not the case. It could also be the case that one structure would be learned well before the other.

In general both structures start to appear around the age 3;0. In Scupins' child the first examples of future and passive with *werden* are at the age of 2;3 and 2;4, respectively. In this child the recorded utterances with future tense remain infrequent for the first six months and then become more regular, though still not frequent. Up to that point the usage also appear to be highly context-bound and possibly imitations of adult utterances.

(217) Scupin (2;3) (*Himbeeren*)   *wird*   *gleich*   *alle*   *sein*
                                    AUX.FUT   soon   allgone   be
                    'the raspberries will soon be all gone'

(218) Scupin (2;6)
      wern   *uns*   *jetzt*   *samn*   *setzen*
      AUX.FUT   REFL.PRO:1PL   now   together   sit
      'we'll sit down together now'

(219) Scupin (2;6)
      Mann   *wird*   *mit*   *die*   *großen*   *Schere*   *kommt*
      man   AUX.FUT   with   DEF.ART   big   scissors   come
      und   *Beindel*   *ab-*   *deschneidet*
      and   legs   off   cut
      'man will come and cut off (my) legs'

Utterance 219, for example, was a regular threat from the parents to the child, when he put his feet on the table, and so appears to be repeated by the child in this context.

The passive appears very infrequently in the recorded utterances until around age 5;4, when more examples can be found. This may be a bias of the samples however, although the use of passive is generally infrequent.

(220) Scupin (2;4)
      Mann   *wird*   *aus-*   *ge-*   *zogen*
      man   AUX.PASS   un   PAST   dressed
      'man is undressed'

(221) Scupin (2;6)
      jetzt   *werd't*   *ihr*   *schön*   *ge-*   *fahren*
      now   AUX:PASS:2PL   you:PL   nicely   PAST   driven
      'now you will be taken for a nice drive'

In 220 the child describes a waiter who already has his waistcoat open, so that the correct adult usage to describe a state should be with the auxiliary *sein*. The latter constructions are already common in the child's speech. This error suggests that it may be a problem for the child to separate the two constructions according to the principle of state and action. All the passives recorded from Scupins' child are agentless passives, which is the finding in most acquisition data.

Both the future and the passive do not appear to be delayed in their appearance, but their use stays relatively infrequent. The principle of one-to-one mapping does not appear to be important in this area. The fact that both constructions can be expressed periphrastically, however, might explain their comparative rarity. The future can be expressed by a present-tense verb and a time adverb; this is common before the age of 3;0. Topicalization, one function of the passive, can be expressed by fronting the noun to be topicalized in an active sentence, for example:

(222) *den*   *Ball*   *hat*   *Heidi* *geworfen*

DEF.ART: ball:MASC   PAST.AUX.   Heidi   thrown

MASC:SG:ACC

'Heidi threw THAT ball'

This word order also occurs in children younger than 3;0, but the data are insufficient to be sure that clear topicalization is involved. Through an elicitation study it might be possible to determine whether these constructions are avoided, as is reported for the passive in Hebrew (Berman, 1985), in preference for the periphrastic construction. In terms of comprehension, the passive is acquired as quickly as in English (compare Turner & Rommetveit (1967a) with Grimm (Grimm et al., 1975) and Mills (1977a)). The rarity in production therefore does not necessarily reflect a difficulty in acquisition but rather a preference in production for a simpler structure.

6.2. *Delayed Acquisition*

6.2.1. *Casemarking.* The complexity of the case system and the use of one form for several functions makes the acquisition of the morphology of articles and adjectives late considering the full range of the paradigms. The morphology associated with nominative case is learned quickly by age 3;0. Only the masculine nouns provide evidence of a distinct accusative case; errors with this form are common till age 5;0 or even later. The dative case emerges early but its correct marking in articles and adjectives continues to be problematic for some time, probably because of the similarity of -*n* and -*m* endings. Although case-marking is word final in articles and adjectives, these inflections are unstressed as are the articles in many circumstances, so that case information may be unclear in the input speech. The difficulty of establishing which case follows a preposition makes acquisition of case here even more problematic. Errors are common until 4;0 on average. The problem of case selection after prepositions which may take accusative or dative does not appear to be a particular problem but is in general associated with the problem of correct morphological marking. In production, the usage seems quite clear. The contrastive concept of stativity and directionality would seem to emerge quite late according to Paprotté's results, so that possibly formulae are built up in relationship with certain verbs, for example, *ins Wasser fallen* 'fall into the water' but *im Wasser schwimmen* 'swim in the water'.

Casemarking would seem to be critical in relative clauses, where it appears on the relative pronouns and articles, etc., in the clause, since the verb is in final position and fewer word order rules can be applied to establish case relationships. This does not have a delaying effect on the acquisition of relative clauses, as compared to English. They emerge around 3 years. When they first appear, the relative pronoun is frequently missing (Stern & Stern, 1928) or replaced by a form *wo* which is not marked for case (Grimm, 1973) as was discussed in detail earlier (see 4.7). Case information does not appear critical at all for production. In all examples found, the semantic and pragmatic content of the clause makes it quite clear what the case relationships are.

6.2.2. *Noun Plural Forms.*   Plurals are, on the whole, learned late. Mistakes are quite common in 4-year-olds. Ramge (1975) reports mistakes in 7-year-olds even in common words, e.g. *Hünde* instead of *Hunde* 'dogs'. MacWhinney (1978, pp. 55–56) describes the regularities of the German system, but there are many alternative rules and many exceptions. In spontaneous utterances, plural forms appear around the age 2;6 and overgeneralization of *-en* form, which is the most highly applicable form, is reported (Scupin & Scupin, 1910, Park 1978). Some researchers report few errors however (Schädel, 1905; Stern & Stern, 1928). MacWhinney's experimental results with real and nonce words indicate that only one ending, *-en,* which is the result of two production rules, is fully productive before age 11;0. The other rules do not all become productive by adulthood; only one (zero allomorph with specific word endings) becomes fully productive because it produces no exceptions.

These results fit MacWhinney's claim that the earliest rules will be those which apply correctly to the greatest number of forms. MacWhinney found, as have other experimental researchers in this area, (Mugdan, 1977; Schaner-Wolles, 1978; Park, 1978), that a very frequent response was the use of singular form or zero allomorph. It is not clear what the status of this response may be since German does have plural forms which are realized by the zero allomorph. MacWhinney found the use of this form more common with nonce forms and argues that it is not an overgeneralization of the production rule. Mugdan (1977) proposes that the use of the zero allomorph constitutes an escape route when the correct answer is not known. In Mugdan's experimental results the zero allomorph was common even amongst the oldest children tested (9;8). This would go against Slobin's (1973) principle that underlying semantic relations should be marked overtly and clearly.

The data from spontaneous utterances are few, so that it is difficult to establish whether zero marking is an artifact of the experimental situation. Stern and Stern report correct plurals early, at age 2;0, and in nouns which do not always occur in the plural, for example *Bild-er* 'pictures', *Büch-er* 'books', and *Bäum-e* 'trees'. It is nevertheless possible that these were learned by rote. Around age 4;0 Scupins' child marked plurals on nouns which should have the zero plural morpheme, suggesting that the principle of clearly marking semantic relations is important at this stage, if not earlier. For example:

(223) Scupin (3;9) *Karnickel-* *s 'rabbits'

                  Onkel- *s 'uncles'

(224) Scupin (4;8) *Teller-* *n 'plates'

Their importance of clearly marking relations leading to overmarking was also observed in French by Karmiloff-Smith (1979).

The overgeneralization of the most frequent plural form *-n* is recorded until age 5;0 in Scupins' child. Analogy is clearly used where there can be no general rule. In the following example, the word *Nikolaus,* a proper name which can have no plural, is treated as if it consisted of *Niko* and *Laus* 'louse' and the plural is formed of the second word.

(225) Child (7;5) *der   Nikolaus   war   heute   da   im*

               the   Nikolaus   was   today   there   in+the

               Kindergarten;   eigentlich   gibt   es

               playschool   actually   gives   it

               *mehrere   *Nikoläuse*

               several   Nikolaus:PL

               'Father Christmas was in playschool today; actually there are several Father Christmases (Christmice?)'

The complexity of the system and the lack of regularity makes the system appear late and to continue to be problematic for a considerable time.

7. Reorganizations in Development

There is no clear evidence of any major reorganization. Stern and Stern (1928), however, comment from the study of their two children that after age 3;0 the complexity of syntax increased quickly and greatly. Modals and auxiliaries began to be used as well as some subordinating constructions. This is also the impression to be gained from the other diary studies. From the fairly fixed word order of the two-word stage the number of variations increase and appear to coincide with the acquisition of case-marking on articles, etc., which is necessary to establish syntactic relations. The relationship between these two aspects needs to be carefully investigated.

8. Lexical Innovations

In connection with this area, perhaps more than with any other, it seems inappropriate to use the term "error" (Givón, 1985). In so far as the child creates a new word, where there is a perfectly adequate word in the adult language, because he does not know or cannot recall the adult word, one can speak of an error. In the cases, however, where the child invents a word to express a concept which has not been lexicalized in the adult language (see Clark, 1980, for a discussion of "lexical gaps"), the term "error" implies a correct form, which does not exist. Both instances will be discussed together here, however, since they indicate the way the lexicon is organized in acquisition, what the productive devices are, etc.

The main collection of data in the acquisition of the lexicon was made by Stern and Stern (1928) and Augst (Augst et al., 1977). Stern and Stern documented the development of their two children until age 6; Augst carried out a deatiled study with one child aged 6 years. The observations made are similar in most aspects. Both studies report the largest grammatical cateogry in the vocabulary of the children as being that of noun. This was also the largest category of lexical innovations.

It was rare for a completely new lexical item to be produced; the majority of innovations were compounds or derivative forms. Augst reports only one such example, *muck* meaning 'satiated', and in this instance the child revealed his awareness that the word did not exist by commenting that he had invented it. Children seem to be aware early on that they cannot make an independent arbitrary association between form and meaning.

Compounds accounted for the largest number of lexical innovations. In Augst's data, over 82% were compounds compared with 15% derivatives. Compounds were also strongly represented in the child's total vocabulary. It is not clear how this relates to adult usage, but the principles of compounding are clearly productive for the child (see 5.5).

The suffixes and prefixes which the child uses in new derivatives may involve two principles: firstly, the frequency in the child's own use and possibly adult usage, although reliable data are not available here, and secondly, the association of the affix with a particular meaning, "one form-one meaning." According to Augst's data, the child uses only 16 affixes in innovations as opposed to the 73 occurring in his standard vocabulary. There may be a relationship between the frequency of occurrence of a derivation affix and the production of this affix. There are unfortunately no data on adult usage, so that the role of frequency and productivity in the input language remains unclear. In one case an innovation clearly has nothing to do with the frequency of adult usage. Both Scupins' and Lindner's children produced innovations with the prefix *maus(e)-* 'mouse' which only occurs in one standard word *mause-tot* 'dead as a mouse, stone dead'. The children used the prefix in their innovations *mause-alle* 'completely gone', *mause-ausgetrunken* 'completely drunk up', *mause-trocken* 'completely dry' as an intensifying adverb without, apparently, relating the prefix to the word for mouse.

The affixes used in the innovations are those which have a clear function. The prefix *er-*, for example, is used with verbs and has a vaguely intensifying function but this is not clearly defined. *Er-* prefixed to *finden* 'to find', means 'to invent', whereas prefixed to *geben* 'to give' means 'to result in'. It appears in 17 words of the child's vocabulary but does not appear in a single innovation. On the other hand, the suffix *-er* marking an agent or instrument was frequently used in innovations. The two principles of frequency and clear function seem important and interact which explains the small number of affixes used in innovations. Affixes are extremely important in German grammar, especially verbal prefixes (see 1.2.4). This would be an interesting area to collect acquisition data to examine the interaction of form and function.

From the lexical innovations and from the metalinguistic information which the child gives about lexical items, he is analyzing words to an ever increasing extent beginning around age 3;0. Again the principle of clear meaning seems important since the child questions items in which the meaning of the parts does not match the meaning of the whole. For example:

(226) Augst (6;0) Father: *das   Kind   hat   Sommer-   sprossen*

                                           summer   sprouts

                                           (from *sprießen*

                                           'to sprout')

               'the child has freckles'

          Child: *warum hat das Kind denn Sommersprossen?*
                   jetzt ist doch Winter

                   'why has the child got freckles?
                   it's winter now'

The child can also be led to make a wrong segmentation where this analysis would also make semantic sense. Scupins' child aged 4;11 analyzed the word *Papageis* 'parrots' into *Papa-* 'Daddy' and *-geis,* and named different colored birds, white cockatoos, as if they were the female of the species **Mama-geis.*

9. Cognitive Pacesetting of Language Development

9.1. Semantic Content of one-word and two-word Utterances

Anders (1980) conducted an analysis of the semantic functions of one-word and two-word utterances in two children between the ages of 1;3 and 2;1.[8] At the beginning of the study the children were described as being in the second half of the one-word stage (Greenfield & Smith, 1976) or in Brown's Stage I. In the one-word phase he found the same developmental sequence of semantic functions as Greenfield and Smith found in their work with English. That is, the relations first expressed involved only one entity; utterances involving two entities emerge later. Anders also found, as did Greenfield and Smith, that the children frequently expressed indicative and volitional objects before the age 1;6. This contradicts Bloom's (1973) claim that relational terms such as *more* and *there* dominate at this age and that nouns only start to dominate when object permanency is achieved, usually after the age 1;6.

The most frequently produced functions were those for object, action, appearance/existence/demonstrative, negation, and position. Those rarely produced were for agent, dative, possession, and disappearance. There was a discrepancy between the children, however, in the extent to which modification was produced. There is the same discrepancy in this area between the results of Greenfield and Smith and of Bloom. Anders proposes that this is due to individual "cognitive style" (see later discussion, Section 12).

In the two-word phase Anders reports the same developmental sequence observed by Bloom, Lightbown and Hood (1975) in English children. The first functional relations to be expressed are demonstrative/appearance/existence. The discrepancy which had existed between the two children with respect to expressions of modification in the one-word stage continued in the two-word stage. The one child made early and frequent use of the functional relations, analogy (*auch* 'too'), recurrence (*mehr* 'more') and alternation (*ander* 'another'), whereas these were rare and late in the other child. Both children made reference to actions before states, as Bloom et al. also observed. The instrumental relation and conjunction appeared in only one child at the end of the observation period.

9.2. Questions

Question words appear in a similar order to English and other languages (Wode, 1971). Firstly the locative interrogative pronoun *wo* 'where' appears. It is first used for stative location, then overgeneralized to directional location before the distinct locational interrogative *wo-hin* 'where-to' and *wo-her* 'where-

---

[8]This study used the same data base as Miller (1976).

from' pronouns appear (Greenhalgh, 1976). This would suggest, if considered together with Paprotté's results on prepositions, that the concept "stative" is in some way acquired before "directionality." Secondly, identification interrogative pronouns *was* 'what' and *wer* 'who' are acquired. Within this category the nonpersonal form *was* is acquired first but is used as both personal and nonpersonal. Personal forms appear later. The sequence then continues with modality *wie* 'how', causality *warum* 'why', and lastly time *wann* 'when'.

9.3. *Personal Pronouns*

Personal pronouns can be described in terms of three general contrasts: proximal/nonproximal, singular/nonsingular, and speaker/nonspeaker, with the prediction that the first named of the pair will be acquired first. Deutsch and Pechmann (1978) tested the production of German pronouns in a naming task requiring the dative form. The order that emerged indicated the precedence of proximal/nonproximal over the singular/nonsingular contrast. Unfortunately there are little data from spontaneous utterances but Stern and Stern (1928) report the use of *ich* 'I' before *du* 'you' (SG) which fits the predicted speaker before nonspeaker order.

In general, the diary studies report the pronouns *ich* and *du* to be in use around age 2;6. This is also the usual age in English and in French (Clark, 1985). It has been claimed that the emergence of these pronouns reflects the cognitive ability to represent the self abstractly and coincides with the emergence of representational play (Zazzo, 1948; Fraiberg & Adelson, 1973). Bates (1979, pp. 172–177) has also proposed a link between symbolic play and language acquisition using data from younger children. Fraiberg and Adelson observed the emergence of pronoun use and representational play in English-speaking blind children. In every case they recorded a delay in the acquisition of I/you pronouns and representational play, although they judged the children's language development to be within the range of sighted children in other aspects. In one child, I/you appeared as late as 4;10. It may seem plausible that cognitive development has such an effect on language acquisition until the data from a language such as Kaluli (Schieffelin, 1985) are considered. In this language, the pronouns for *I* and *you* emerge much earlier than 2;6 and the obviously correct explanation for this is the fact that adults in this culture do not use the baby talk feature of referring to the speaker and addressee in a discourse in the third person. The pronouns for 1st and 2nd person are used from the outset. The role of input would seem to be highly significant, therefore, and since neither Zazzo nor Fraiberg and Adelson considered this aspect, no firm conclusions can be drawn about the influence of cognitive factors in this area of acquisition.

9.4. *Natural and Syntactic Gender*

The German syntactic gender system on the whole reflects the natural gender distinction where natural gender is appropriate. Where there is a glaring mismatch, for example, *das Mädchen* 'the girl' is neuter gender, reference will be made as soon as syntactically possible to the natural gender of the noun (see Corbett, 1979; Mills, 1978, 1984). It is obvious that the concept of natural gender distinctions must be acquired before the linguistic system in the cases where it directly reflects those distinctions. There is frequently a delay, however, before the linguistic forms are acquired.

There is evidence that the concept of natural gender may precede the acquisition of the linguistic system but that it does not necessarily facilitate it. Böhme and Levelt (1979), as discussed in detail above (5.3), tested the comprehension of reference with toys reflecting natural gender and three objects distinguished only by syntactic gender. Children aged 3–5 years performed worse on the toys with natural gender as a cognitive cue than on the toys distinguished by syntactic gender. The concept of natural gender did not seem to aid comprehension of the linguistic forms. This agrees with Annette Karmiloff-Smith's results for French (1979) that morphophonological regularities were used as a cue to gender before semantic cues. However, from the few data from the diary studies on the use of third person singular pronouns, the predominant use was in reference to animate objects with natural gender. There may be a difference in comprehension and production here.

As mentioned above, Greenberg (1966) proposed that masculine forms were unmarked as opposed to feminine forms. There is a claim that unmarked terms will be acquired before marked terms, in this case then masculine forms should be acquired before feminine forms. This I would argue is rather simplistic. From experimental evidence (Mills, 1978), it would seem as though masculine natural gender dominates feminine gender in that German and English children and adults all more frequently assigned masculine gender to toys than feminine gender. *He* is also reported as being frequently acquired first and overgeneralized (Chiat, 1978) in English. In German, Deutsch and Pechmann (1978) found that children produced the masculine pronoun *ihm* before the feminine form *ihr*. Scupin and Scupin, and Stern and Stern, also report the use of *sein* 'his/its' instead of *ihr* 'hers'; Scupin and Scupin as late as 5;11. In these cases, there is evidence of the dominance of the masculine form only where natural gender is the concept behind the linguistic form. There is no evidence that masculine forms in general are acquired first. In fact, as discussed earlier (4.3.1), in the definite article the feminine form, if any, was overgeneralized. It is therefore possible that it is an overgeneralized concept which affects the acquisition of the linguistic form.

9.5. Conjoined Sentences

Clancy et al. (1976) found a general order of acquisition of conjoined sentences in a crosslinguistic study of German, Italian, English, and Turkish. The German data were taken from diary studies. The earliest conjoined sentences involve notions of causality, antithesis, sequence, and symmetric coordination.

Later, notions of conditionality emerge. Later still, clauses with 'when' are used both conditionally and temporally. Lastly 'before' and 'after' appear as subordinating conjunctions. They conclude: "The data we have analyzed strongly suggest the existence of a universal cognitive order of emergence in the acquisition of notions underlying conjoined statements" (1976, p. 80).

9.6. *Locative Prepositions*

The relationship between cognitive development and locative prepositions has been the subject of much research which is too extensive to discuss in detail here. If prepositions are classified according to the complexity of the conceptual relationships encoded in them, the resulting order of complexity could predict the order of acquisition (see Piaget & Inhelder, 1967; and Clark, 1977; Johnston & Slobin, 1979; Parisi & Antinucci, 1970, for supporting evidence). This classification will predict, for example, that the preposition expressing the notion 'in' will be learned before that expressing 'between'.

Johnston and Slobin (1979) consider the importance of linguistic factors in relationship to the conceptual complexity predictions in the acquisition of locative prepositions. They present experimental production evidence from English, Italian, Serbo-Croatian, and Turkish children that the linguistic factors of position of the preposition (pre-position < post-position), lexical diversity (one term/one relation < many terms/one relation), clear etymology, morphological complexity (single morphemic < multimorphemic forms), and homonymity (one term/one relation < one term/many relations) all contribute together with conceptual complexity to determine the order of acquisition.

The only data available on this area for German are the frequency and error data collected by Grimm (1975) as discussed above (4.5). If the errors in the use of locative prepositions are subtracted from the total use, as set out in Table 2.6, the relative frequency remains very similar. The frequency is also in the same proportions across the age groups (2;6–6;0), so that frequency can be used to a certain extent as a guide to the order of acquisition. From Table 2.6, it can be seen that *in* 'in' and *auf* 'on' are the most frequently used prepositions, as would be predicted according to the conceptual complexity argument. *Unter* 'under' is far less frequent, although it has a similar level of conceptual complexity, but it is difficult to disentangle the factor of context. It is possible that this relationship is less frequently expressed; the figures from Meier (1964) for adult usage would suggest that. Unfortunately it is impossible to pursue comparison any further since the data are not described in enough detail to separate out uses of different relations. More data are needed to disentangle the influence of linguistic and cognitive factors.

The influence of context on the ability to use prepositions has been shown by Paprotté. Paprotté (1979) tested the comprehension of the locative prepositions *in* 'in', *auf* 'on', *über* 'above', and *unter* 'under' in situations where the child had to place objects in relation to one another. He found that the interpretation of the prepositions was greatly facilitated when the objects were in a cardinal relationship to one another, for example a saucer under a cup, as opposed to unusual situations where a saucer is on a cup. This use of this pragmatic information is based on the prior acquisition of the cardinal relationships between objects. Other research has shown this appears to be learned at a very early age (Freeman & Sinha, 1980).

Weissenborn (Weißenborn, 1981) also showed the significance of context as a factor in determining production of locative prepositions. In an experimental study, children (4;0–10;0) were asked to give directions to another child to enable him to find hidden objects. Weissenborn found that the fact of the child having to project his use in space had an important effect on his use of prepositions. The youngest children, for example, used only nondeictic prepositions. Weissenborn emphasizes the importance of considering the pragmatic conditions of use in describing acquisition.

10. Linguistic Pacesetting of Cognitive Development

10.1. Contrastivity

In German there are two connectives, *sondern* and *aber,* which express contrastivity equivalent to 'but' in English. *Sondern* and *aber* are used under different conditions, however, and present the child with two different tasks in their acquisition. The sentence P *sondern* Q must be constructed so that P is an explicitly negated statement and so that Q corrects that statement. For Q to correct P, the elements in contrast have to be from the same area of meaning. Sentence 228 is unacceptable for this reason; sentence 227 illustrates correct use.

(227) *der Mann ist nicht klug, sondern er ist dumm*
    'the man is not clever but he is stupid'

(228) **der Mann ist nicht klug, sondern er ist dick*
    'the man is not clever but he is fat'

The sentence P *aber* Q, however, requires that Q contradicts a proposition which is not explicit in P but which is inferred from P in a particular context. The context can be linguistic and/or nonlinguistic. In the following example, the proposition derived from the statement P that the man is not clever is that people who are not clever do not earn a lot of money. This proposition is contradicted in Q.

(229) *der Mann ist nicht klug, aber er verdient viel Geld*
    'the man is not clever but he earns a lot of money'

A more detailed description of these sentences appears in Pusch (1975) and Asbach-Schnitker (1979).

Kail and Weissenborn (1980) investigated the acquisition of these connectives in an experimental situation. They tested German and French children to examine the possible difference produced by the structure of the language, since French, like English, has only one form, *mais,* for the functions of *aber* and *sondern.* The children, aged 7;6 to 10;3, were presented with a context and asked firstly to complete expressions with the structure 'P but . . .' and '. . . but Q' to make a good end to the story. Later the children were asked to judge sentences as to whether they fitted the context.

Kail and Weissenborn found that the children, both French and German, adopted a common strategy for the interpretation of the sentences. The younger children interpreted the relationship between P and Q as coordination, older children interpreted it as implication. This has been the general finding with connectives in English. Kail and Weissenborn had predicted that sentences with a *sondern* contrast in German and French would be easier than those with an *aber* contrast, because the former have less propositional complexity. That is, the children have only to carry out one operation of inference, as opposed to two for the *aber* contrast. They also predicted that the *sondern* contrast would be easier since it is cognitively simpler and requires an explicit negated element in P which can serve as a cue that Q is to be interpreted as a correction of P. It is more difficult to interpret these as P *and* Q. These predictions were confirmed for the French and German children. The cognitively less complex structure was easier. Kail and Weissenborn had also predicted that the lexical differentiation in German would help the German children to distinguish between coordination *und* 'and' and contrastivity *aber*, *sondern* at an earlier age than the French children. This was not clear in the results, however, although the youngest German children were ahead in the judgment of acceptable use of *aber, sondern*. Further work is needed in this area, possibly with younger children using a different task, to establish any possible linguistic pacesetting.

10.2. *Natural and Syntactic Gender*

Beit-Hallahmi et al. (1974) found early development of gender identity in Hebrew-speaking children which they related to the explicit gender-marking on the verb. Since natural gender is reflected in the syntactic gender system but is not distinct from it, it might be expected that sex-identity in German would develop later than in English where the gender-marking of pronouns strongly correlates with natural gender. There are no data as yet on this aspect of German.

11. Input and Adult-Child Interaction

11.1. *Word Order in the Two-word Phrase*

The regularity of verb in final position and with *-en* ending in two- and three-word utterances has already been discussed (see 4.1.1 and 4.2.4). It was argued that caretakers' speech to children contains a high percentage of utterances with the main verb in this position and with this ending, since this is characteristic of sentences in which modal verbs or auxiliaries occur, and of certain types of imperatives. The high percentage of such utterances in the adult seems to be linked to the structure of adult-child discourse. The adult is very frequently making suggestions, giving indirect commands or direct commands, and these all involve the syntactic forms described above. Syntactic baby-talk (see example 230) and use of the auxiliary *tun* is also quite common, at least in Southern Germany (Mills, in prep.), so that in declarative sentences the main verb will also appear in final position. This feature of adult speech to children needs to be further investigated but it appears to have a clear influence on the child's derived word-order rule.

11.2. *Third Person Singular Verb Forms*

The third person singular verb form in the present tense appears after the -*en* ending, before the endings associated with other persons of the verb. This is clearly related to the caretaker's tendency to refer to the child and to him or herself in the third person (Oksaar, 1977). This apparent simplification in reference is common in many language communities, but not all (Schieffelin, 1985).

11.3. *Phonological and Lexical Properties of Baby-talk*

Baby-talk has not been fully investigated in German. What little has been done on phonetic properties (Zöppritz, 1976) has found the common features of cluster reduction, fronting, etc. For example, *nuckel* for *Schnuller* 'dummy', *fiege* for *Fliege* 'fly', *buxe* for *Hose* 'trousers', *pussi* for *Kuß* 'kiss'. The influence of dialect must be carefully investigated here.

Adult-child interaction is accompanied by special nursery terms, but it must be emphasized that there is considerable variation in the extent to which these terms are used in individual families. There is also considerable dialectal variation. These terms are connected with the activities which characterize adult-child interaction such as feeding, body functions, play, etc. They are commonly reduplicative. For example:

NURSERY TERM	STANDARD TERM	GLOSS
adda	*spazierengehen*	go for a walk
heia	*schlafen*	sleep
nam-nam	*Essen*	food
bäuer-chen (*machen*) (from *Bauer* 'yokel')	*aufstoßen*	burp
pi-pi	*Harnwasser*	urine
aa-aa/ka-ka (from *kack-en* 'to defecate')	*Stuhlgang*	faeces
stinker (from *stink-en* 'to stink')	*Stuhlgang*	faeces
pfui	*schmutzig*	expression of disgust

Names of animals are frequently onomatopoeic such as *quaak-quaak* 'frog' or *wau-wau* 'dog'. Nursery terms are used in games such as *guck-guck* 'pee-ka-boo' in hide-and-seek. When a child falls down or knocks something down, *hoppela* or *hopsa* is used; *hey-op* is used when a child gets up. There is a very close resemblance between these terms and the Hebrew nursery words (Berman, 1985) which suggests that German or Yiddish (historically a dialect of German) has had a strong influence on Hebrew in this sphere.

It is also common for diminutives to be used in speech to children, for example *Tisch-lein* 'little table', *Püpp-chen* 'little doll'. The actual form of the diminutive is subject to dialectal variation. These diminuitives have the effect of making the noun neuter in gender. This doesn't apparently have any effect on the acquisition of the morphology marking gender (see 4.3.1).

11.4. *Structuring of Dialogue*

A large amount of work has been done in this area in English, especially in the last 10 years (see Andersen, 1977, for a commentated bibliography). The work that has been done with German children has not shown any cultural or language-specific differences to the phenomena described for English. Some of this work has extended the findings of work in other languages; a few examples are discussed here.

Jochens (1979) investigated the use of questions in mother-child dialogue. She found that they are one of the symptoms of there being an unequal balance in mother-child dialogue, since mothers ask far more questions than children. They are used to elicit speech from the children. She also emphasizes, in contrast to Blount (1972) and Mishler (1975), the way that the choice of question is directed by the objects of the child's attention, so that the dialogue is influenced by both parties concerned rather than dominated by one.

Miller and Weissenborn (1979)[9] examined the acquisition of local reference with respect to the pragmatic factors involved. They found inter alia that adults adapt the level of their where-questions to the level of the children's ability to make non-local reference.

Anders (1980)[9] traced the development of adult speech with two children aged 1;2 to 2;1 in terms of the role of expansion, extension, and repetition. He found that, although the children were from different social backgrounds, the percentage of expansions, etc., and the development in the relative proportion of these forms across the period of investigation was the same in the speech to both children. Across the period of investigation, the number of expansions reduced (20% to 10%), the number of extensions increased (10% to 15%), and the number of repetitions declined slightly (8% to 5%). There are large differences in the percentages reported in the literature for English so that it is not possible to draw any conclusions from comparison. When the child was producing two-

---

[9]This study used the same data base as Miller (1976).

word utterances, the number of extensions increased, especially syntactic extensions, indicating that the adult is increasing both the semantic and syntactic information offered.

Anders emphasizes the role of imitation in the child, in contrast to Greenfield and Smith (1976). He stresses the importance of sequences in which the child imitates part of a preceding adult utterance and the adult subsequently expands upon the child's utterance. For example:

(230) Anders (1;7)   Adult: *hör mal zu! soll'n wir'n bißchen ada gehn, wir beide?*

'listen! shall we go for a little walk, we two?'

Child: *ada*

Adult: *mit Maxe ada gehn, hae? hattste Lust? auf die straße gehn?*

'go for a walk with Max, eh? do you want to go? go in the street?'

Child: *dage (= Straße)*

'street'

Adult: *wir beide? hae? gehn wir'n bißchen ada auf die straße?*

'we two? eh? shall we go for a little walk in the street?'

Anders describes a development from the one-word stage to the two-word stage. The child's utterances in the one-word stage first occur in a conversational sequence (Greenfield & Smith, 1976), that is the verbal reply of the adult prompts the second utterance. They later occur in non-conversational sequences, that is where the child's utterance is dependent on the non-verbal context, before the two-word phase begins. The sequences move from having the pattern of imitation and expansion to sequences without this pattern. Anders concludes that the adult structuring of the dialogue is an important factor in producing the progression from conversational to nonconversational sequences and then two-word utterances.

12. Individual Differences

Since the data from spontaneous utterances are so limited in German, and in most studies restricted to one or two children, it is very difficult to know whether the description of one child is typical or a special case. In presenting the data in previous sections, there have been instances when individual strategies appear. For example, two children apparently applied a rule of past participle or simple past formation on the basis of the vowel in the verb stem. There is some regularity in the strong verbs which makes this a possible basis for a rule. Possibly some children are more aware of the properties of vowels than others; possibly all children use this at some stage but drop it more quickly, so that it escapes notice. It is important to be able to determine the extent to which a different rule was used before trying to categorize children into different acquisition types.

Park (1971a) reported one child who apparently overmarked person on all parts of the verb. Typically this seems to be an area where few errors occur (see 5.1). In the one example cited, the child marks both the modal and the main verb:

(231) Park

kann	-st	du	sieh	-st?
can	2SG	you	see	2SG

'can you see?'

It is possible that this is a phase which all children go through, once modal verbs are used and once verbs are placed in relation to the subject. It is not clear from the one example, however, whether the child is influenced by the subject *du* being directly adjacent to both verbs. If this were the case, data of this kind would suggest that adjacency emerges at some stage as an important principle in morphological agreement.

Stern and Stern (1928) report that their son was quite different in respect to the older daughter in the early stages of language acquisition. He inserted a nonsense syllable /e/ between the words of his utterance. For example:

(232) Stern (2;5)

e	hosser	e	heller	e	hünter	e	heine	e	hilde
	big		plate		Günther		small		Hilde

'Günther (has a) big plate, Hilde (has a) small (one)'

Since this was at the stage where the child was omitting functors, articles, etc., it is possible that he was aware of there being missing information in terms of the rhythm of the utterance. The syllable /e/ was then inserted to preserve the rhythm. Some children are possibly more aware of intonation and rhythm as aspects to be acquired than others who concentrate on structural properties.

Anders (1980) observed a difference in the number of utterances in particular semantic categories in two children at the one- and two-word stage. One child used far more *nochmal* 'again', *auch* 'too', and *mehr* 'more'. Anders attributes this to a difference in "cognitive style." This, in my opinion, emphasizes the problem of considering individual differences in language acquisition or any other field. The danger exists that any behavior which does not fit into the general rule will be thrown into the waste-bag "individual differences." In the above example, it should be necessary to examine other areas of behavior to see if there is any independent justification for attributing the child with a different cognitive style before such an explanation can be put forward seriously.

13. Theoretical Implications

It is the intention in this concluding section to discuss those principles of language acquisition which seem most important in explaining the data presented in the preceding sections. This does not mean that only these principles are important for language acquisition in every language, although every attempt has been made to formulate them in general terms. Data are missing on many aspects of the acquisition of German, so that some principles may not emerge as important until these aspects are described.

The principles will be discussed individually, although, as has been obvious from the presentation of the data and as will be obvious from the following discussion, it is rarely clear that data are to be explained by one principle alone. Where more than one principle can account for the data, it can either be the case that really only one is involved, or that all contribute in the process of acquisition. Principles also vary in their relative importance according to the age of the child. The result is a complex interaction which it often seems impossible to unravel.

13.1. *Stressed Syllables and Words are Salient and will be Acquired First*

At the two-word stage, it is characteristic that the unstressed words and syllables are omitted, for example the articles, prepositions, and the past prefix *ge-* on the past participle. The information which these words or syllables would carry is conveyed for the most part via the context. Prepositions have the same form as verbal particles which are stressed and occur in final position. In contrast to prepositions, these particles are frequent at this stage. Stress seems important here, although the final position in the clause could also influence acquisition (see 13.2). Adjective endings are also unstressed and so, it might be expected, would be omitted. This is rarely the case, however, again probably because they are in final position on the adjective.

13.2. *Final Syllables and Words are Salient and will be Acquired First*

As mentioned above, verbal particles are stressed and in final position in the input speech. These are frequently used at the one- and two-word stage and function as full verbs. The past participle occurs in final position and is acquired early. The principle also seems to be relevant within the past participle form as well, since the suffix marking past on the past participle is acquired far before the prefix. The endings marking the simple past and person are all acquired with little error. This may also be the case because the different persons and the simple past are clearly marked by different forms (see 13.9). Although the inflections marking simple past in regular verbs are learned with little error, the simple past is acquired late because it is less frequently used (see 13.7).

13.3. *Word Order is Quickly Associated with the Expression of Semantic Notion*

13.3.1. Verb.   The verb is associated early with final position in the clause, apparently through the influence of particular structures in the input speech at that stage. It is later strongly associated with second position in the sentence. The past participle is correctly placed in final position. When subordinate clauses start to be used, the verb here is also correctly placed in final position. Few word order errors with the verb occur, except when there are several verbal elements in a subordinate clause. The rules in this case are very complex.

13.3.2. Subject Function.   The notion "agent" and the related subject function are strongly associated with first position. Reversed sentences with the structure OVS were interpreted by young children as though they had the structure SVO; case information was mostly ignored by the younger children. Passive sentences were interpreted and imitated as though they were active sentences, that is with agent-action-object order. It could be argued that there appears to be a canonical order in German, SVO, which is the basis of these interpretations. The verb occurs in final position in several environments, however, but this does not seem to present particular difficulty, as might be expected if a canonical order is posited. The more general association of subject with first position can account for the data together with verb positioning rules. From the data with reversed sentences, it would seem that in older children a form clearly marked as non-subject in initial position can block this word order strategy more easily than information in other parts of the sentence.

Relative clauses were easier to interpret when the relative pronoun was subject of the clause. A common error in younger children was to interpret the first noun of the sentence as agent of both the main clause and relative clause. Until the structure of the relative clause can be perceived, the principle will lead to this error. This principle still affects adults in comprehension and production of relative clauses. It also interacts with pragmatic and semantic information which will be discussed below (13.8). Zubin (1975, 1977) claims that the association between subject and first position should be attributed to discourse focus, as defined in his own terms. Focus is associated with nominative case. There are no data from acquisition that this particular aspect is relevant in children, but it needs to be explored.

13.3.3. Negative.   The sentence internal negator is quickly placed in the correct position after the verb in main clauses.

13.3.4. *Possession.* This relationship is expressed in the majority of cases by ordering the possessor before the thing possessed. The relationship is however usually morphologically marked in addition to the word ordering either by the suffix -*s* on the possessor or by the use of the possessive pronoun in addition to the full noun. In general, strategies of interpretation or production based on word order interact with the child's increasing control of the inflections marking case.

13.4. *Adjacent Elements are in Relation to One Another*

Before the two-word stage, a sequence in which the same noun is repeated is produced with an intonation contour across the whole sequence. They are treated as belonging to one unit. When the agent is expressed before the verb in two-word utterances, it becomes more common for person to be marked on the verb. This adjacency seems to be perceived as a relationship between the two elements. The inflections marking person can then be perceived as standing in relation to the subject and the rules for the individual forms acquired.

In sentences containing infinitival complements, the noun adjacent to the infinitival clause is taken to be subject of the clause. Errors occur in comprehension where this is not the case. This can be seen as an extension of Rosenbaum's (1965) Minimal Distance Principle.

Where elements which are usually adjacent to one another are separated, it becomes more difficult to process the units involved. Slobin (1973) formulates this as an interruption principle. Sentences containing centrally-embedded relative clauses are more difficult to process than finally-embedded clauses. In an analysis of text samples from adults (Mills, 1981a), this consequence of the above principle is shown to affect production in that finally-embedded clauses were far more common than centrally-embedded clauses. This also may interact with semantic and pragmatic factors (13.8). Use is made of the possibility of reversing SVO sentences, so that a relative clause on the subject of the main clause, which would normally be centrally-embedded, is then finally-embedded.

13.5. *A Basic Form is First Learned before the Possible Variations*

Here the main problem is to decide on what grounds the form first learned can be described as "basic." Secondly, it must be determined what factors contribute towards that form being perceived as "basic." The first forms of the articles to be acquired are frequently reduced forms which do not mark gender or case. Gender is an arbitrary classification in most nouns; the information conveyed by case marking is usually contained in word order or is clear from the semantic or prgamatic context. It is difficult to perceive the rules of case marking and the functions marked, since the paradigms are irregular. The reduced forms first produced by children occur in fast speech from adults and therefore appear the most systematic of the possible forms.

The first relative pronoun to be used by some children is a form which is not marked for case or gender. This form occurs in dialect use and as a possible relative pronoun with prepositions and again would appear the most systematic form. The perception of the forms of the relative pronoun is probably made more difficult by its similarity to the definite article (see 13.9).

The first locative pronoun to be learned is used in both a stative and directional meaning, although it is only appropriate in a stative sense in adult speech. The directional forms also encode the direction of the motion away from or towards the speaker and are therefore more complex. This information is encoded in a suffix on the stative locative pronoun, so that this form occurs in all three pronouns and is therefore perceived as basic. The directional pronouns are also probably less frequently used (see 13.7).

When full forms of the articles are produced, the nominative case form is frequently used where other case marking would be appropriate. This "citation allomorph" (MacWhinney, 1978) is a frequent form within the paradigm, since feminine and neuter gender do not distinguish nominative and accusative case. Nominative case is also frequent in use, since every sentence has a subject. The continued use of this basic form goes against the principle of one-to-one mapping (see 13.9).

The predicative form of the adjective appears to be learned as the basic form. In the case of the adjective changing its form in the predicative and attributive, the predicative form was taken as the basis for forming the comparative. It is not clear how this relates to use. In older children, adjectives used attributively were more common than those used predicatively, but individual adjectives were preferred in a particular function.

In verb morphology the basic form appears to be the root as it occurs in the infinitive. With irregular verbs children frequently add inflections to this form rather than to the other forms of the root. They seem to have abstracted a rule for determining what the root should be.

13.6. *Patterns, Once Perceived, are Used Wherever Possible*

This principle poses two questions: under what conditions the pattern is perceived and to what range of structures it is extended. This principle clearly interacts with frequency in the input speech (13.7).

In verb morphology, the irregular verbs, which can change their root in the past tense, past participle, and some parts of the present tense, are produced as if they followed the pattern of the regular verbs. This pattern is not perceived immediately; in the first uses of the past participle the irregular root forms are often correct. At a later stage, confusion remains within the past forms as to the root changes involved. By this time the range of the regular patterns has been restricted. There are a few verbs which seem to have a vowel change in the root predictable by rule. Two children appeared to select this pattern briefly but quickly abandoned it, probably as soon as they perceived the many exceptions.

With case inflections, it is difficult to perceive the regularities. Different attempts seem to be made to establish a pattern. In the definite and indefinite article, children make no distinction between nominative and accusative case in the masculine paradigm on a parallel with the feminine, neuter, and plural paradigms. With the adjective, the accusative form is used for both nominative and accusative by some children. The strong adjective endings are taken as the general pattern by some children and extended to possessive adjectives.

The most transparent rule for forming the plural, that is the -*en* suffix, is often applied to all nouns, but quickly abandoned because of the number of exceptions. This remains an area of error for considerable time because the rules are so complex.

After prepositions, the accusative form of the articles is commonly overgeneralized. The pattern after prepositions seems to be perceived as different from the other case forms, otherwise it would be expected that the nominative masculine form be overgeneralized here too.

Rote learning is, in my opinion, the learning of a very restricted pattern. Pronouns in correct case forms after certain prepositions or constructions are acquired quite early, probably because these set phrases occur frequently in the input speech. This is also most likely the case when prepositions with the correct form of the article appear early in connection with certain nouns and verbs, for example *ins Wasser fallen,* where the phrase *ins Wasser* 'into the water' is frequently used with the verb of motion *fallen* 'to fall'.

Few errors occur with the morphology of compound nouns. It would appear as though the possible forms of the determinans are learned from whatever compound nouns occur with that determinans or one with similar structure in the input speech. As the child's lexicon increases, the number of possible forms decreases.

13.7. The Most Frequent Items are the First Learned

This principle poses the problem of the framework within which frequency is perceived by the child. It does not appear to be an independent principle, since the most frequent items must also have a clear meaning or function before they will be acquired. For example, the affixes used in lexical innovations had to fulfill two conditions: being the most frequent in the child's standard lexicon and having a clear meaning.

The definite article *die* is frequently overgeneralized to nouns of other genders. Considering the paradigms, it is the most frequent form overall but it is clearly the most frequent form in the nominative and accusative cases which are again the cases most frequently used. Two kinds of frequency seem to be involved here. The same argument applies to the overgeneralization of the adjective ending -*e,* since this is the most frequent form in nominative and accusative cases in the strong, weak and mixed paradigms.

The early locative questions reported from two children had the correct subject-verb inversion but they only contained the verb *sein* 'to be'. This can be explained by the frequency in the input, since stative locative questions are the most frequent type asked by adults. With this frequent pattern, the inversion rule was learned.

The regular inflections in verb morphology are also the most frequent in that they occur in the greatest number of different environments, i.e. verb stems. This frequent use facilitates the perception of a pattern.

The relative pronoun being subject of the relative clause was a condition which improved interpretation of such clauses. Text analysis shows that relative pronouns are used most frequently as subject of the relative clause. It is possible that children are influenced by this frequency or that they are influenced by the factors which produce this frequency in adult usage, probably the association of subject with first position. It is impossible to disentangle the two.

13.8. *Meaning is More Important than Form*

In comprehension tasks with complex structures, children start to rely on the semantic and pragmatic content of a sentence, after having passed through a stage of relying heavily on a word-order strategy for interpretation. It is not clear from spontaneous speech whether such a development still holds or whether children use semantic and pragmatic content much earlier than experimental results would suggest. This would seem more likely.

In production of these structures, the complexity of the form causes some elements to be omitted in the early stages, such as the relative pronoun or the passive auxiliary. The child does not appear to perceive any difficulty for the addressee in establishing the meaning of the construction. With ambiguous relative clauses the semantic and pragmatic information makes the agent-object relations clear in most cases. Adults show no signs of avoiding such constructions, apparently relying on this to be the case.

Zubin (1979) argues that the element most like the speaker is salient and will therefore be encoded in nominative case. He predicts therefore that animate entities will be in nominative case more frequently. In relative clauses, this can interact with the association of subject with first position. Zubin also argues that the information in relative clauses is defocused, since they have the status of subordinate clauses. Inanimate entities are defocused and are associated with object function. It is therefore predicted that relative clauses on the object of main clauses, that is finally-embedded clauses, will be more frequent. This is the case in adult speech (Mills, 1981a) but it can also be attributed to a preference for non-interruption. Results from English suggest that animacy is relevant in acquisition (Limber, 1973) but this needs to be examined in detail for German.

Recent work (Mills 1984) has shown that meaning is relevant to the acquisition of gender at least in relation to the learning of natural gender terms. Acquisition of morphophonological regularities is taking place concurrently, however, so that no dominance of meaning over form can be claimed.

13.9. One-to-one Mapping Between Function and Form

Where there is a clear relationship between meaning and form, acquisition will be quicker in this area. Where one form is used with more than one function or one function has more than one form, acquisition will involve more error. The child will impose a restriction on form or function to try to preserve the one-to-one relationship. This principle obviously depends on the child perceiving the functions and forms involved.

The similarity between the definite article and the relative pronoun appears to cause problems in comprehension. In production, some children choose a form which is quite distinct from the definite article. Before they use the definite article alone, they combine the two forms so that the relative pronoun is still distinct.

The similarity between -n (marking accusative) and -m (marking dative) as case endings seems to cause difficulty in the acquisition of accusative and dative case.

The inflectional suffix -er is used for the comparative and as a gender/case ending in the context of an adjective. The adpositional morphemes mehr and noch are commonly used to mark the comparative as opposed to the suffix -er, thus marking the distinction clearly. The older child often marks the comparative with a reduplicated -er. This is possibly also attributable to this principle.

Prepositions are also used to mark the possessive relation before the genitive article is acquired. An adposition seems clearer than an affix form, although word order and a suffix are also used to express this relation.

Nouns which have a zero plural morpheme are often marked incorrectly with a plural form. The child has perceived that plural is linguistically encoded and applies this to all forms. Since it appears that German children earlier do not mark plural, this principle could imply that they have not perceived that plural is linguistically encoded. More data are needed to substantiate such a claim.

The possessive adjective sein which is appropriate for masculine and neuter gender is overgeneralized for all singular use. The other possessive adjective ihr which is appropriate for feminine and plural is used only for plural. The separation of these two forms for the clear semantic distinction singular/plural, rather than the formal gender distinction, is a clear example of this principle.

Where a form is used for more than one function by the child, although the language has more than one form available, it must be the case, according to the principle, that the function has not been perceived. This argument would seem relevant to explain the use of the stative locative pronoun for both stative and directional use. That is the child has not yet perceived that this distinction is linguistically encoded. Morphological complexity will also interact with this principle however, as was discussed above (see 13.5).

The perception that a distinction is linguistically encoded presupposes that the child is aware of such a distinction in general cognitive terms (see 9.0). On the other hand, the linguistic data can form part (or all) of the data base for the child's acquisition of the general concept (see 10.0). This fits in with this general principle: Where there is one function/underlying concept look for the linguistic form; where there is one linguistic form, look for the function/underlying concept.

14. Suggestions for Further Study

All the way through this chapter it has been obvious that data are missing in most areas from spontaneous productions and from detailed experimentation. In my view, a combination of data from BOTH sources is likely to give the most insight into acquisition of a particular area. A few areas will be mentioned here.

14.1. *Phonology*

There have been no detailed studies of the acquisition of phonology in German on the lines of Smith (1973) for English. Although Stern and Stern recorded observations in this area, their transcription system is difficult to follow. Morphophonology has not been studied to any great extent in acquisition. There are many aspects which could be researched, for example the acquisition of the devoicing of final labial and dental plosives at a morpheme boundary, with the exception of plurals. Compare *Hand* /hant/ 'hand', *hand-lich*/hantllX/ 'handy', and *Händ-e* /hɛndə/ 'hands'. Is the devoicing rule extended to plurals at any stage? Does the child reveal perception of what is linguistically described as the basic form with voiced final consonant?

14.2. *Word Order and Case Strategies*

The complex development of word-order strategies and use of inflections needs further exploration and detailed study in individual children. There are large gaps in the data, as has constantly been mentioned above. Since the case-marking system is complex in German, involving multifunctional forms, word order is clearly more important for a longer period of time than in a language such as Turkish, but it is far less important than in a language such as English, which has few inflections. Pragmatic uses of word order in topicalization, etc., need to be investigated in detail.

14.3. *Natural and Syntactic Gender Mismatch*

There is sometimes a mismatch between formal gender and natural gender, for example *die Maus* 'mouse' is feminine gender but may be male in the context of the story. Where this occurs, there is a general tendency to switch to the natural gender. Languages have different requirements as to the elements which must have syntactic gender agreement and which can have natural gender agreement. Corbett (1979) describes an agreement hierarchy according to which the switch to natural gender agreement can most readily be made in personal pronouns, then in relative pronouns, predicates, and lastly attributes. Russian, for example, allows the switch in all elements, whereas German allows the switch in the first two elements only. This hierarchy reflects a concept of syntactic distance, as Corbett discusses, which is not identical to surface structure distance. It would be possible to explore the acquisition of the concept of syntactic distance via such cases of gender mismatch comparing acquisition in different languages. The results may also indicate whether at any stage semantic agreement overrides all syntactic restrictions.

14.4. *Modal Particles*

German makes use of modal particles such as *doch, immerhin,* to express certain notions such as concession, strong assertion, etc., whereas English, for example, uses many different devices to express the same notions (Weydt, 1977, 1979), such as auxiliary and intonation. It would be interesting to know whether children acquired these notions of sentence modality at the same time in the two languages, or to what extent the acquisition of these notions was dependent on the formal devices used to express them.

14.5. *Familiar and Polite Pronouns*

German, like many other languages, makes a distinction in second person pronouns between familiar and, what are usually called, polite forms. The use of these forms is associated with notions of social distance, authority, and so on. Linguistically these pronouns have a different status in different languages. In German the polite *Sie* is identical with the third person plural form but is used for second person singular and plural; in French the polite *vous* is identical with the second person plural familiar form but is used for polite singular and plural; in Italian the polite forms *Lei* (SG) and *Loro* are identical with third person forms but they are distinct from other pronoun forms in that they are obligatorily mentioned in the sentence, whereas other pronouns usually only occur when stressed. The acquisition of such pronouns across languages might be compared with the acquisition of social concepts such as politeness and their expression in other linguistic forms such as indirect commands, etc. It might be possible, although very difficult, to tease out the effects on acquisition of the pronouns' differing linguistic status.

14.6. *Ambiguous Infinitival Complements*

The infinitival complement constructions, as described above (4.8), can be ambiguous as to which noun of the main clause functions as their subject. This depends on the verb of the main clause. They can be interpreted as if they had as subject either the object of the main clause or the subject of the main clause (Thiem, in prep.).

(233)	*mein*	*Bruder*	*teilte*	*mir*	*mit,*	*den*	*Preis*
	my	brother:NOM	informed	me:DAT	PARTICLE	the:ACC	prize
	ge-	*wonn*	*-en*	*zu*	*hab*	*-en*	
	PAST	win	PAST PARTICLE		AUX	INF	

'my brother informed me that he had won the prize'
'my brother informed me that I had won the prize'

Sentence 233 can be interpreted as if 'my brother' had won the prize or as if 'I' had won the prize. Such sentences allow the testing of word-order rules in child and adult subjects in terms of preferred interpretation. Such sentences can also be used as a test of the interpretation of pragmatic information and linguistic context to determine which noun functions as subject of the complement clause and the importance of this information with regard to the syntactic principle.

With some verbs it is also possible to omit mentioning the object of the main clause which would then function as subject of the infinitival complement. In sentence 234, for example, it would be necessary to interpret from context or pragmatic information who is to increase wages.

(234)	*die*	*Gewerkschaften*	*fordern,*	*die*	*Löhne*	*um*
	the	unions:NOM	demand	the	wages	by
	10%	*zu*	*erhöh*	*-en*		
	10%	PARTICLE	raise	INF		

'the unions demand that wages be increased by 10%'

(235)	*die*	*Regierung*	*ordnete*	*an,*	*den*	*Vorfall*
	the	government	ordered	PARTICLE	the:ACC	incident
	zu	*untersuch*	*-en*			
	PARTICLE	investigate	INF			

'the government ordered that the incident be investigated'

With a few verbs it is obligatory to omit the object of the main clause and therefore the subject of the infinitival clause. In sentence 235, for example, it must be interpreted who should investigate the incident. Such sentences again provide the possibility of testing the use of linguistic context and pragmatic information.

REFERENCES

Altmann, G., & Rättig, V. Genus and Wortauslaut im Deutschen. *Zeitschrift für Phonetik, Sprachwissenschaft und Kommunikationsforschung,* 1973, *26,* 297–303.

Anders, K. *Von Worten zur Syntax: Spracherwerb im Dialog.* Unpublished doctoral dissertation, Universität Frankfurt, 1980.

Andersen, E. S. Bibliography. In C. E. Snow & C. A. Ferguson (Eds.), *Talking to children: Input and acquisition* (pp. 357–369). Cambridge: Cambridge University Press, 1977.

Arndt, W. W. Nonrandom assignment of loanwords: German noun gender. *Word,* 1970, *26,* 244–253.

Asbach-Schnitker, B. Die adversativen Konnektoren aber, sondern und but nach negierten Sätzen. In H. Weydt (Ed.), *Die Partikeln der deutschen Sprache* (pp. 457–468). Berlin: de Gruyter, 1979.

Augst, G. Über das Fugenmorphem bei Zusammensetzungen. In G. Augst, *Untersuchungen zum Morpheminventar der deutschen Gegenwartssprache* (pp. 71–153). Tübingen: TBL, 1975.

Augst, G., Bauer, A., & Stein, A. *Grundwortschatz und Idiolekt.* Tübingen: Niemeyer, 1977.

Bartsch, R., & Vennemann, T. *Semantic structures. A study in the relation between semantics and syntax.* Frankfurt: Athenäum, 1972.

Bates, E. *The emergence of symbols.* New York: Academic Press, 1979.

Beit-Hallahmi, B., Catford, J. C., Cooley, R. E., Dull, C. Y., Guiora, A. Z., & Raluszny, M. Grammatical gender and gender identity development: Cross-cultural and cross-lingual implications. *American Journal of Orthopsychiatry,* 1974, *44,* 424–431.

Berman, R. The acquisition of Hebrew. In D. I. Slobin (Ed.), *The crosslinguistic study of language acquisition* (Vol. 1). Hillsdale, NJ: Lawrence Erlbaum Associates, 1985.

Bever, T. G. The cognitive base for linguistic structures. In J. R. Hayes (Ed.), *Cognition and the development of language.* New York: Wiley, 1970.

Bierwisch, M. Grammatik des deutschen Verbs. *Studia Grammatica;* 2. Berlin: Akademie-Verlag, 1973.

Bloom, L. *One word at a time: The use of single word utterances before syntax.* The Hague: Mouton, 1973.

Bloom, L., Lightbown, P., & Hood, L. Structure and variation in child language. *Monographs of the Society for Research in Child Development,* 1975, *40,* No. 2.

Blount, B. G. Parental speech and language acquisition. Some Luo and Samoan examples. *Anthropological Linguistics,* 1972, *14,* 119–130.

Böhme, K., & Levelt, W. Children's use and awareness of natural and syntactic gender in possessive pronouns. *Paper presented to the Conference on Linguistic Awareness and Learning to Read,* Victoria, Canada. 1979. (To appear in the *Proceedings*).

Bowerman, M. *Early syntactic development: A cross-linguistic study with special reference to Finnish.* Cambridge: Cambridge University Press, 1973.

Brown, R. *A first language. The early stages.* Cambridge, MA: Harvard University Press, 1973.

Carstensen, B. The gender of English loan-words in German. *Studia Anglica Posnaniensia,* 1980, *12,* 3–25.

Chiat, S. *The analysis of children's pronouns: An investigation into the prerequisites for linguistic knowledge.* Unpublished doctoral dissertation, University of London, 1978.

Chomsky, C. *The acquisition of syntax in children from 5 to 10.* Cambridge, MA: MIT Press, 1969.

Clahsen, H. *Der Erwerb der Syntax in der frühen Kindheit*. Doctoral dissertation, Universität Wuppertal, 1981. (a) Published as *Spracherwerb in der Kindheit. Eine Untersuchung zur Entwicklung der Syntax bei Kleinkindern*. Tübingen: G. Narr, 1982.

Clahsen, H. Kurzbericht über die Studie 'Der Erwerb der Syntax in der frühen Kindheit'. *Paper presented to the DFG Kolloquium Kindersprache/Spracherwerb*. Hannover, June 1981. (b)

Clancy, P., Jacobsen, T., & Silva, M. The acquisition of conjunction: A cross-linguistic study. *Papers and Reports on Child Language Development* (Department of Linguistics, Stanford University), 1976, *12*, 71–80.

Clark, E. Strategies and the mapping problem in first language acquisition. In J. Macnamara (Ed.), *Language learning and thought*. New York: Academic Press, 1977.

Clark, E. *Lexical innovations: How children learn to create new words*. Unpublished paper, 1980.

Clark, E. The acquisition of Romance, with special reference to French. In D. I. Slobin (Ed.), *The crosslinguistic study of language acquisition* (Vol. 1). Hillsdale, NJ: Lawrence Erlbaum Associates, 1985.

Corbett, G. G. The agreement hierarchy. *Journal of Linguistics*, 1979, *15*, 203–224.

Curme, G. O. *A Grammar of the German language*. New York: Ungar, 1964 (2nd rev. ed. of original 1904).

Deutsch, W., & Pechmann, T. Ihr, dir, or mir? On the acquisition of pronouns in German children. *Cognition*, 1978, *6*, 155–168.

de Villiers, J., Flusberg, H., & Cohen, P. Children's comprehension of relative clauses. *Journal of Psycholinguistic Research*, 1979, *8*, 499–518.

Felix, S. *Linguistische Untersuchungen zum natürlichen Spracherwerb*. München: Fink, 1978.

Ferguson, C. A., & Slobin, D. I. (Eds.) *Studies of child language development*. New York: Holt, Rinehart & Winston, 1973.

Fraiberg, S., & Adelson, E. Self-representation in language and play. Observations of blind children. *The Psychoanalytic Quarterly*, 1973, *42*, 539–562.

Freeman, N. H., & Sinha, C. G. Scaling functional relations between linguistic comprehension and nonlinguistic knowledge. *Paper presented to the Child Language Seminar, Manchester*, 1980.

Givón, T. Function, structure, and language acquisition. In D. I. Slobin (Ed.), *The crosslinguistic study of language acquisition* (Vol. 2). Hillsdale, NJ: Lawrence Erlbaum Associates, 1985.

Greenberg, J. H. (Ed.) *Universals of language* (2nd ed.). Cambridge, MA: MIT Press, 1966.

Greenfield, P. M., & Smith, J. H. *The structure of communication in early language development*. New York: Academic Press, 1976.

Greenhalgh, S. *Erwerb und Entwicklung der Interrogativpronomen in der Kindersprache am Beispiel des Deutschen*. Unpublished M.A. thesis, Universität Kiel, 1976.

Grimm, H. *Strukturanalytische Untersuchung der Kindersprache*. Bern/Stuttgart/Wien: Hans Huber, 1973.

Grimm, H. On the child's acquisition of semantic structure underlying the wordfield of prepositions. *Language and Speech*, 1975, *18*, 97–119.

Grimm, H., Schöler, H., & Wintermantel, M. *Zur Entwicklung sprachlicher Strukturformen bei Kindern. Forschungsbericht zur Sprachentwicklung I: Empirische Untersuchungen zum Erwerb und zur Erfassung sprachlicher Wahrnehmungs- und Produktionsstrategien bei Drei- bis Achtjährigen*. Basel: Beltz, 1975.

Helbig, G., & Buscha, J. *Deutsche Grammatik. Ein Handbuch für den Ausländerunterricht*. Leipzig: VEB Verlag Enzyklopädie, 1972.

Jochens, B. 'Fragen' im Mutter-Kind Dialog: Zur Strategie der Gesprächsorganisation von Müttern. In K. Martens (Ed.) *Kindliche Kommunikation*. Frankfurt: Suhrkamp, 1979, 110–132.

Johnston, J. R., & Slobin, D. I. The development of locative expressions in English, Italian, Serbo-Croatian and Turkish. *Journal of Child Language*, 1979, *6*, 529–545.

Kail, M., & Weissenborn, J. A developmental cross-linguistic study of the processing of lexical presuppositions: French 'mais' and German 'aber' vs. 'sondern'. *Paper presented to the Fifth Annual Boston University Conference on Language Development*, Oct. 1980.

Karmiloff-Smith, A. *A functional approach to child language*. Cambridge: Cambridge University Press, 1979.

Keenan, E. L., & Comrie, B. Noun phrase accessibility and universal grammar. *Linguistic Inquiry* 1977, *8*, 63–99.

König, G. *Strukturen kindlicher Sprache*. Düsseldorf: Schwann, 1972.

Köpcke, K. *Untersuchungen zum Genussystem der deutschen Gegenwartssprache*. Tübingen: Niemeyer, 1982.

Köpcke, K., & Zubin, D. Die kognitive Organization der Genuszuweisung zu den einsilbigen Nomen der deutschen Gegenwartssprache. *Zeitschrift für germanistische Linguistik*, 1983, *11*, 166–182.

Leopold, W. *Speech development of a bilingual child*. Vol. 3, *Grammar and general problems*. Evanston, IL: Northwestern University Press, 1949.

Limber, J. The genesis of complex sentences. In T. E. Moore (Ed.), *Cognitive development and the acquisition of language* (pp. 169–186). New York: Academic Press, 1973.

Lindner, G. *Aus dem Naturgarten der Kindersprache*. Leipzig: T. Grieben, 1898.

MacWhinney, B. The acquisition of morphophonology. *Monographs of the Society for Research in Child Development*, 1978, *43* (1–2, Serial No. 174).

MacWhinney, B. Hungarian language acquisition as an exemplification of a general model of grammatical development. In D. I. Slobin (Ed.), *The crosslinguistic study of language acquisition* (Vol. 2). Hillsdale, NJ: Lawrence Elrbaum Associates, 1985.

Maratsos, M. Children who get worse at understanding the passive. *Journal of Psycholinguistic Research*, 1974, *3* 65–74.

Maratsos, M. Learning how and when to use pronouns and determiners. In P. Fletcher & M. Garman (Eds.), *Language Acquisition*. Cambridge: Cambridge University Press, 1979.

Martens, K. (Ed.) *Kindliche Kommunikation*. Frankfurt: Suhrkamp, 1979.

Mater, E. *Rückläufiges Wörterbuch der deutschen Gegenwartssprache*, 2nd ed. Leipzig: Bibliographisches Institut, 1967.

Meier, H. *Deutsche Sprachstatistik*. Hildesheim: Olms, 1964.

Miller, M. *Zur Logik der frühkindlichen Sprachentwicklung*. Stuttgart: Klett, 1976. (English trans. by R. T. King: *The logic of language development in early childhood*. Berlin/Heidelberg/New York: Springer-Verlag, 1979.)

Miller, M., & Weißenborn, J. Pragmatische Voraussetzungen für den Erwerb lokaler Referenz. In K. Martens (Ed.), *Kindliche Kommunikation* (pp. 61–75). Frankfurt: Suhrkamp, 1979.

Mills, A. E. *Parallel studies in first and second language acquisition*. R. O. U. Strauch (Ed.), Ludwigsburg Studies in Language and Linguistics, 2. Ludwigsburg: 1977. (a)

Mills, A. E. The perception of ambiguous relative clauses in German. In G. Drachman (Ed.), *Salzburger Beiträge zur Linguistik*, 4. (pp. 351–363) Salzburg: Neugebauer, 1977. (b)

Mills, A. E. Linguistic and psychological aspects of gender in English and German. *Paper presented to the Linguistic Association of Great Britain*. Autumn, 1978.

Mills, A. E. Cases, case marking, and the interpretation and production of German relative clauses. In E. Hopkins & R. Grotjahn (Eds.), *Studies in language teaching and language acquisition. Quantitative linguistics* (Vol. 9, pp. 204–220). Bochum: Brockmeyer, 1981. (a)

Mills, A. E. It's easier in German, isn't it? The acquisition of tag questions in a bilingual child. *Journal of Child Language*, 1981, *8*, 641–647. (b)

Mills, A. E. *The Acquisition of Gender in English and German*. Unpublished Habilitationsschrift, University of Tübingen, 1984.

Mills, A. E. *Syntactic properties of caretakers' speech to children in German*, in preparation.

Mishler, E. G. Studies in dialogue and discourse. An exponential law of successive questioning. *Language and Society*, 1975, *4*, 31–52.

Mugdan, J. *Flexionsmorphologie und Psycholinguistik.* Tübingen: Narr, 1977.

Neugebauer, H. Aus der Sprachentwicklung meines Sohnes. *Zeitschrift für angewandte Psychologie und psychologische Sammelforschung,* 1915, *9,* 298–306.

Neumann, W. Notizen zur Genusbestimmung der deutschen Substantive und zur Definition des Wortes. *Deutsch als Fremdsprache,* 1967, *4,* 16–22.

Oksaar, E. *Spracherwerb im Vorschulalter. Einführung in die Pädolinguistik.* Stuttgart: Kohlhammer, 1977.

Paprotté, W. Zum Erwerb der lokativ/direktionalen Präpositionen *in, auf, über, unter. Kongreßberichte der 8. Jahrestagung der Gesellschaft für angewandte Linguistik* (pp. 167–180). Mainz: 1977.

Paprotté, W. Zur Interaktion sprachlicher und nicht-sprachlicher Strategien im Erwerb der lokativen Präpositionen *in, auf, unter.* In H. Weydt (Ed.), *Die Partikeln der deutschen Sprache* (pp. 201–214). Berlin: de Gruyter, 1979.

Parisi, D., & Antinucci, F. Lexical competence. In G. B. Flores d'Arcais & W. J. M. Levelt (Eds.), *Advances in Psycholinguistics.* Amsterdam: North Holland, 1970.

Park, T.-Z. *The acquisition of German syntax.* Working paper. University of Bern, Psychological Institute, 1970.

Park, T.-Z. *Acquisition of German morphology.* Working paper. University of Bern, Psychological Institute, 1971. (a)

Park, T.-Z. *The acquisition of German verbal auxiliaries.* Working paper. University of Bern, Psychological Institute, 1971. (b)

Park, T.-Z. *A study of German language development.* Mimeo. University of Bern, Psychological Institute, 1974.

Park, T.-Z. Imitation of grammatical and ungrammatical sentences by German-speaking children. In W. von Raffler-Engel & Y. Lebrun (Eds.), *Baby talk and infant speech* (pp. 202–217). Amsterdam: Swets & Zeitlinger, 1976.

Park, T.-Z. Plurals in child speech. *Journal of Child Language,* 1978, *5,* 237–250.

Park, T.-Z. Some facts on negation: Wode's four-stage developmental theory of negation revisited. *Journal of Child Language,* 1979, *6,* 147–151.

Park, T.-Z. *The development of syntax in the child with special reference to German. Innsbrucker Beiträge zur Kulturwissenschaft,* Sonderheft 45. Innsbruck, 1981.

Piaget, J., & Inhelder, B. *The child's conception of space.* New York: Norton, 1967.

Plank, F. Morphological aspects of nominal compounding in German and certain other languages: What to acquire in language acquisition in case the rules fail? In G. Drachmann (Ed.), *Salzburger Beiträge zur Linguistik,* 2. (pp. 201–219). Tübingen: Narr, 1976.

Pregel, D. *Zum Sprachstil des Grundschulkindes.* Düsseldorf: Schwann, 1970.

Preyer, W. *Die Seele des Kindes.* Leipzig: T. Grieben, 1882.

Pusch, L. Über den Unterschied zwischen aber und sondern oder die Kunst des Widersprechens. In I. Battori et al. (Eds.), *Syntaktische und semantische Studien zur Koordination* (pp. 45–62). Tübingen: Narr, 1975.

Ramge, H. Spontane Selbstkorrekturen im Sprechen von Schulanfängern. *Diskussion Deutsch,* 1973, *12,* 165–190.

Ramge, H. *Spracherwerb,* 2nd ed. Tübingen: Niemeyer, 1975.

Rickheit, G. *Zur Entwicklung der Syntax im Grundschulalter.* Düsseldorf: Schwann, 1975.

Roeper, T. W. *Approaches to a theory of language acquisition with examples from German children.* Unpublished doctoral dissertation, Harvard University, 1972.

Roeper, T. W. Theoretical implications of word order, topicalization and inflections in German language acquisition. In C. A. Ferguson & D. I. Slobin (Eds.), *Studies of child language development* (pp. 541–554). New York: Holt, Rinehart & Winston, 1973.

Rosenbaum, P. S. *A principle governing deletion in English sentential complementation.* IBM Research Paper RC-1519. Yorktown Heights, N.Y., 1965.

Schädel, E. *Das Sprechenlernen unserer Kinder.* Leipzig: Friederich Brandstetter, 1905.

Schaner-Wolles, Ch. Der Gebrauch substantivischer Pluralallomorphe bei Kindern mit Down-Syndrom. *Wiener linguistische Gazette*, 1978, *18*, 37–52.

Schwitters, K. *Anna Blume I: Dichtungen*. Zürich: Arche, 1965.

Schieffelin, B. The acquisition of Kaluli. In D. I. Slobin (Ed.), *The crosslinguistic study of language acquisition* (Vol. I). Hillsdale, NJ: Lawrence Erlbaum Associates, 1985.

Scupin, E., & Scupin, G. *Bubis erste Kindheit*, Vols. 1 & 2. Leipzig: Dürr, 1907, 1910.

Sheldon, A. The role of parallel function in the acquisition of relative clauses in English. *Journal of Verbal Learning and Verbal Behavior*, 1974, *13*, 272–281.

Slobin, D. I. Grammatical transformations and sentence comprehension in childhood and adulthood. *Journal of Verbal Learning and Verbal Behavior*, 1966, *5*, 219–227.

Slobin, D. I. Cognitive prerequisites for the development of grammar. In C. A. Ferguson & D. I. Slobin (Eds.), *Studies of child language development* (pp. 175–276). New York: Holt, Rinehart & Winston, 1973.

Slobin, D. I., & Bever, T. G. Children use canonical sentence schemas: A crosslinguistic study of word order and inflections. *Cognition*, 1982, *58*, 265–289.

Smith, N. V. *The acquisition of phonology*. Cambridge: Cambridge University Press, 1973.

Stephany, U. Werden sprachliche Relationen in der Zweiwortphase durch die Wortstellung signalisiert? In G. Drachman (Ed.), *Salzburger Beiträge zur Linguistik, 2.* (pp. 235–246). Tübingen: Narr, 1976.

Stern, C., & Stern, W. *Die Kindersprache: Eine psychologische und sprachtheoretische Untersuchung*, 4th ed. Darmstadt: Wissenschaftliche Buchgesellschaft, 1975. (Reprint of 1928 edition.)

Stickel, G. *Untersuchungen zur Negation im heutigen Deutsch*. Braunschweig: Vieweg, 1970.

Thiem, R. *Untersuchungen zu deutschen und englischen Infinitivkonstruktionen*. Unpublished doctoral dissertation, University of Tübingen, in preparation.

Tucker, G. R., Lamberg, W. E., & Rigault, A. A. *The French speaker's skill with grammatical gender: An example of rule-governed behavior*. The Hague: Mouton, 1977.

Turner, E. A., & Rommetveit, R. Experimental manipulation of the production of active and passive voice in children. *Language and Speech*, 1967, *10*, 169–180. (a)

Turner, E. A., & Rommetveit, R. The acquisition of sentence voice and reversibility. *Child Development*, 1967, *38*, 649–660. (b)

Twain, M. The awful German language. In M. Twain *The tramp abroad* (Vol. 2, App. D). New York: Harper, 1879.

Wahrig, G. *Deutsches Wörterbuch*. Gütersloh: Bertelsmann Lexikon-Verlag, 1968.

Weißenborn, J. *L'acquisition des prépositions spatiales: Problèmes cognitifs et linguistiques*. 1981. Unpublished paper.

Weydt, H. (Ed.) *Aspekte der Modalpartikeln*. Tübingen: Niemeyer, 1977.

Weydt, H. (Ed.) *Die Partikeln der deutschen Sprache*. Berlin: de Gruyter, 1979.

Wode, H. Some stages in the acquisition of questions by monolingual children. *Word*, 1971, *27*, 261–310.

Wode, H. Zur Erzeugung der Tonhöhe englischer Syntagmata. *Acta Univ. Carol.* (philol.) *Phonetica Pragensia*, 1972, *3*, 271–280.

Wode, H. Four early stages in the development of L1 negation. *Journal of Child Language*. 1977, *4*, 87–102.

Wode, H. Free vs. bound forms in three types of language acquisition. *ISB-Utrecht*, 1978, *3*, 6–22.

Wode, H. Grammatical intonation in child language. In L. R. Waugh & C. H. Schooneveld (Eds.), *The melody of language* (pp. 331–345). Baltimore: University Park Press, 1980.

Zazzo, R. Image du corps et conscience de soi. Matériaux pour l'étude expérimentale de la consience. *Enfance: Psychologie, Pédagogie, Neuropsychiatrie, Sociologie*, 1948, *1*, 29–43.

Zöppritz, M. Babysprache im Deutschen. In D. Lehmann, et al. (Eds.), *A Punch of Mayflowers—Broder Carstensen zum 50. Geburtstag am 27. Mai 1976*. Paderborn: 1976. Pp. 269–271.

Zubin, D. A. On the distributional properties of surface morphology and their consequence for semantic analysis. In W. Diver (Ed.), *Columbia Working Papers in Linguistics,* 1975, *2,* 189–219.

Zubin, D. A. The semantic basis of case alternation in German. In R. W. Fasold & R. Shuy (Eds.), *Proceedings of the Third Conference on New Ways of Analysing Variation* (pp. 88–99). Washington, D.C.: Georgetown University Press, 1977.

Zubin, D. A. Discourse function of morphology: the focus system in German. In T. Givón (Ed.), *Syntax and Semantics* (Vol. 12, pp. 469–504). New York: Academic Press, 1979.

Zubin, D. A., & Köpcke, K. Gender: A less than arbitrary grammatical category. *Chicago Linguistic Society,* 1981, *17,* 439–449.

3 The Acquisition of Hebrew

Ruth A. Berman
Tel-Aviv University

Contents

This chapter is dedicated to the children of the Middle East and to my daughter, Shelli, who at age six-and-a-half provided me with yet another good example when she turned to me and said: ima, yesh lax od kova'ot, kova'im, kova'ey purim? (*'Mommy, do you have any more* hats - *inappropriate feminine plural* - hats - *appropriate masculine plural* - Purim hats - *appropriate masculine plural genitive form of* hats'*)*

INTRODUCTION

Modern Hebrew affords an interesting case for the study of child language for sociohistorical reasons, as well as on internal linguistic grounds. Thus, the children reported on in this chapter represent at most the third generation of native speakers growing up in a Hebrew-speaking environment, as a result of the revival of Hebrew as a spoken vernacular by the Jews of pre-state Israel, which formed part of the nationalist revival movement that started some 100 years ago. Hence the first generation of children for whom Hebrew was a mother tongue—now in their sixties or so—acquired their language from speakers of Arabic, German, Hungarian, Russian, Yiddish, and the many other tongues spoken by those who emigrated to Palestine in the late 1800s and early 1900s. What is remarkable is that all these children, like all subsequent native-born Israeli children or those coming to the country in early childhood, have a distinctive form of pronunciation and usage, recognizable as such by even the untutored ear, irrespective of the mother-tongue of their parents.[1]

From the point of view of language-acquisition research, the sociohistorical circumstances of Hebrew as a language which (a) was recently revived as a means of everyday spoken communication and which (b) serves an immigrant society, a large proportion of whose members are themselves not native Hebrew speakers, are relevant in several ways. Firstly, there is a strong normativist, purist tradition, upheld in the schools and by such bodies as the Hebrew Language Academy and the Israel Broadcasting Authority, as well as by some Israeli linguists, which stipulates as mandatory the usage of Biblical Hebrew (c. 1200–300 B.C.) or Mishnaic Hebrew (c. 300 B.C.–600 A.D.), or else, more marginally, that of medieval and early Modern, 19th and early 20th century writings. Yet colloquial usage diverges considerably from these "norms" in lexicon, syntax, morphology, and pronunciation; and it is the everyday forms which are the main source for children's usage, and which frequently incorporate usages first manifested by native-speaking youngsters. Secondly, owing to the nature of its revival, modern Hebrew evinces very rapid, accelerated processes of language change, so that words, forms, and locutions are constantly being innovated—to some extent by official dictate, more generally in a spontaneous manner by the speakers themselves, where major innovators are found among preschool and school-age children, as well as such institutions as the army, the press, and the media in general.

In consequence, children's "errors" often reflect usages found in less normative segments of the adult population, too, so that the relationship between child language and more general language change is particularly relevant in the acquisition of Hebrew, and is an issue to be addressed at different points throughout this chapter. Moreover, children's innovations and "misusages"—particularly in the area of word-formation processes—provide rich insight into less self-conscious construals of structural properties of the language.

---

[1]This is particularly true of the dominant dialect, the one described in this chapter, for which Blanc (1964a, 1964b) coined the term "General Israeli Hebrew." This refers to the speech of native Israelis of so-called "Ashkenazi" or European-American extraction as distinct from those of Arabic-speaking and other "Sefardi" backgrounds (Berman 1978a), although on the disappearance of "Arabicized" Hebrew among schoolage subjects from different sociocultural backgrounds, see Schwarzwald (1981).

1. Descriptive Sketch of Modern Hebrew

1.1. Syntax

The basic word-order of what Givón (1985) terms the "neutral/canonical clause-type" is SVO—e.g. *ron maca kadur*[2] *'Ron found (a) ball'*. However, the language also has several verb-initial constructions, which include: (i) VS type sentences for the expression of possessives–e.g. 'be to me a new hat' = 'I have a new hat'—and with presentative type predicates—e.g. 'appeared suddenly a ship' = 'a ship suddenly appeared'; (ii) Subjectless sentences, including a highly productive impersonal construction with third-person plural verb, as well as sentences where English might have a dummy 'it'; and (iii) Use of dative-marking with *le-* 'to' or benefactive 'for' to encode experiential predicates—e.g. *kar lo* 'cold to-him' = 'he's cold', *avad li ha balon* 'got-lost to-me the balloon' (= 'I lost the balloon' or 'the balloon went and got lost on me'). In general, Hebrew has many of the properties associated with verb-initial languages: Prepositions serve to mark case-relations as well as adverbials of time, location, and so on; the genitive order is possessed-possessor, that is, head-modifier in all cases; all noun modifiers such as relative clauses, adjectives, and demonstratives follow the head noun, with the single exception of prenominal quantifiers; and within the verb phrase, auxiliaries and modals precede the main verb, but complements follow it.

Ordering of major constituents is pragmatically determined in discourse, with much flexibility in the fronting of nonsubject nominals for purpose of contrastive focus, to yield the equivalent of 'with Ronnie I don't want to play' or 'this game I know well'. Hebrew also makes free use of left-dislocation with pronoun copying in order to offset the topic—as in the equivalents of "Ronnie, I don't want to play with him' or 'my teacher, her little boy is sick'; and it also allows for right-dislocation—as in 'I already gave to him the book, to Ronnie'. Postverbal elements, too, allow of re-ordering, with indirect dative objects and instrumentals and other obliques preceding the direct object when the former are more

---

[2]In representing Hebrew items, broad phonetic transcription is generally adopted. Thus, the following non-English conventions are used:

x = *ch* as in the name *Bach*
c = *ts* as in the word *tsetse*
š = *sh* as in *show*—also rendered by *sh* where convenient
' = a glottal stop or brief intake of air inside a word, usually between vowels
ə = unstressed schwa, as in the first syllable of *among*; for convenience sake, this is generally represented as *e* in the text

In representing root consonants, the following signs are used:

ʔ = glottal stop, called "alef"
' = voiced pharyngeal fricative, called "ayin"
ḥ = voiceless pharyngeal fricative, called "chet"

For further detail, see my reference grammar *Modern Hebrew Structure* (Berman, 1978a).

highly referential or presupposed—e.g. 'I gave to him the book' or 'He went with my sister to town' in English translation. Thus in general Modern Hebrew is closer to the pragmatic than to the grammatical end of the scale of word-order types (Thompson 1978), by contrast with English.

Hebrew verbs take two main kinds of sentential complements: infinitives with prefixal *le-* 'to' marking on the verb, and 'that' clauses subordinated by the marker *še-* 'that'. These also function as the complements of impersonal predicates, in constructions where English might use a dummy 'it' subject, as in the equivalent of '(it's a) pity that he left' or '(it) was hard to find him'. Relative clauses follow the head noun in all the same positions as allowed by English; they are initiated by the invariant relative marker *še-* 'that' and require a pronoun copy whenever the relativized noun is oblique (not a subject or direct object)—e.g. the equivalent of 'the boy that I was playing with *him*', 'that girl that *her* bicycle got stolen'. Adverbial clauses generally follow the main clause, or are backgrounded by fronting, as in English. They are introduced by prepositions or special conjunctions subordinated by the marker *še-* 'that'—e.g. *texake ad še ani avo* 'wait until that I come', *hu baxa mipney še hu nafal* 'he cried because that he fell'. Conjoining in Hebrew is largely similar to English—e.g. *ron ve rina báʔu* 'Ron and Rina came'[3]; *tishte shoko o xalav* 'drink cocoa or milk'; *hu yodéa, aval lo yagid* 'he knows, but (will) not say'.

Hebrew has no special verb meaning 'have'. Possessives are formed with the verb *haya* 'be'[4] or the invariant existential particle *yesh* 'there be' in the present tense, combined with dative marker on the possessor—e.g. *yesh le ron sandalim* 'be to Ron sandals' (= 'Ron has sandals'); *haya li raʾeyon* 'was to-me (an) idea' (= 'I had an idea'). The same verb *haya* 'be' is used in copula sentences, much as in English, but without any form in the present tense. In such cases, 'be' is expressed either by zero or by a pronoun suppletive—e.g. *ha óxel (hu) al ha shulxan* 'the food (he) on the table' (= 'the food is on the table') or *ze shavur* 'it broken' (= 'it is broken'); compare *ha óxel haya sham* 'the food *was* there', *ze yihye kashe* 'it *will-be* hard'.

The definite marker takes the form of prefixal *ha-*. It generally has the same range of senses as English 'the', but it can also be used with generics, thus *ha yéled ba* 'the boy came'[5] is equivalent to the English version, compared with,

---

[3]Stress is normally word-final in Hebrew. When this is not the case, it is indicated by an *accent aigu'* on the penultimate syllable.

[4]In citing Hebrew verbs, which have no unequivocal basic or citation form, I adopt the convention of using the morphologically simplest form of Past Tense, 3rd masculine singular, except where otherwise specified.

[5]Several grammatical markers are prefixed to the following word, both in conventional orthography and in their phonological patterning. These include:

ha-	'the'	*be-*	'in, at'	*le-*	'to'
še-	'that'	*ve-*	'and'	*kše-*	'when'

In my transcription, I usually represent these as separate ''words'' for ease of exposition and more direct translation into English.

say, *ha histórya xozéret al acma.* 'the history repeats itself' or *ha zahav ze matéxet* 'the gold it (=is) a metal'. The fact that a noun phrase is definite requires use of the case-marker *et* with direct objects—e.g. *ra'íti yéled* 'I-saw (a) boy' vs. *ra'íti et ha yéled* 'I-saw DO the boy', or *ra'íti et ron* 'I-saw DO Ron'. Definite marking is incorporated into the two bound prepositions *le-* 'to' and *be-* 'in, at'—e.g. *le xaverim* 'to friends' vs. *la xaverim* 'to-the friends', *be makom* 'at (a) place' vs. *ba makom* 'at-the place'. Nondefinite nouns may occur alone, as Hebrew has no equivalent of English 'a/an', although in colloquial usage unstressed *exad* 'one' may be used in this sense—e.g. *ra-íti sham kélev exad* 'I-saw there dog one' (= 'I saw a dog there'). But in general, and this is true of caretaker instructions to children, too, nouns are named in isolation—e.g. *ma ze?* 'What's that?' / *ze kof* 'it monkey' (= 'it's a monkey').

1.2. Lexico-Morphology

Perhaps the most characteristically Semitic feature of contemporary Hebrew is its word-formation processes. Thus, the bulk of the content vocabulary of the language—all verbs without exception, and most nouns and adjectives—can be characterized as a combination of Root + Pattern. The root is most typically composed of three consonants, and it carries the semantic core of the words formed out of it; the patterns take the form of vocalic infixes plus syllabic CV(C) prefixes and/or (C)V(C) suffixes, and they serve to modify the core meaning in a variety of ways, as illustrated in (1) below. Verbs are formed according to seven such patterns, termed *binyan-im* 'conjugations' (the five most productive of which for children's language are shown below), while nouns and adjectives may occur in any of several dozen patterns, termed *mishkal-im* 'weights', thus:[6]

(1) Words formed from the roots *k-t-b* and *s-p-r* in verb and noun patterns

VERBS

CaCaC	*katav*	'write'	*safar*	'count'
niCCaC	*ni-xtav*	'be written'	—	
CiCeC	—		*siper*	'tell, narrate'
hitCaCeC	*hitkatev*	'correspond = write+Reciprocal'	—	

[6]Note the following with respect to the forms listed in (1):
a. The alternations between the stops /k,b, p/ and the spirants /x,v, f/ are governed by complex morpho-lexical rules discussed further below.
b. The verb-patterns or *binyanim* are traditionally labelled according to the root *p-ʕ-l* meaning 'do, act'. For ease of exposition, these are labeled P-n in the rest of this chapter. Only the five main patterns are listed in (1), to exclude the two passive patterns *pu'al* and *hof'al*, which are marginal in children's usage.
c. Noun and verb patterns alike are entered here and elsewhere by the following convention: C stands for the root consonant, and affixes are specified by consonant and vowel phonemes.
d. Blanks indicate accidental gaps for these roots in these patterns. The listing also excludes homonyms deriving from historically different roots—*s-p-r* also has the sense of 'cut (hair)'—e.g. the agent-noun form CaCaC *sapar* 'barber' or the noun *tispóret* 'haircut'; and historical *q-t-b* occurs in the noun *kótev* 'pole' and also *kituv* 'polarization'.

hiCCiC	*hixtiv*	'dictate = write+Causative'	—	
NOUNS/ADJ				
CaCuC	*katuv*	'written, non-oral'	*safur*	'several, some'
CaCaC	*katav*	'reporter'	—	
CoCeC			*sofer*	'writer, author'
CCaC	*ktav*	'script'	—	
CCiC	*ktiv*	'spelling'	—	
CaCCan	*katvan*	'typist'	*safran*	'librarian'
CCiCa	*ktiva*	'writing'	*sfira*	'counting, enumeration'
CiCCiya	*kitviya*	'writing-kit'	*sifriya*	'library'
CVCóCet	*któvet*	'address, inscription'	*sipóret*	'narrative, fiction'
miCCaC	*mixtav*	'letter'	*mispar*	'number'
taCCiC	*taxtiv*	'a dictate'	—	

Similarly, the root *g-d-l* yields the verbs *gadal* 'grow (INTRANS)', *gidel* 'grow (INTRANS)', *higdil* 'enlarge', *hitgadel* 'self-aggrandize', and nouns such as *gdila* 'growing', *gidul* 'a growth, tumor', *gdula* 'greatness', *gódel* 'size', and an adjective such as *megudal* 'over-grown' as well as *gadol* 'big, large'.

The verb patterns—with a fair degree of irregularity in form-meaning relations—are the basis for morphological marking of such predicate-argument relations as: transitivity vs. intransitivity, causativeness, passive vs. middle vs. active voice, reflexiveness, reciprocality, and inchoativeness. The noun patterns show an ever greater degree of irregularity, and serve to specify lexical classes such as action nouns, agents, instruments, places, abstract states, collective nouns, etc. In gaining command of the lexicon, then, the Hebrew-speaking child needs to acquire a sense of the consonantal root as the morphological and semantic core in the formation of all verbs and most nouns and adjectives in the language, on the basis of a quite fixed set of morphological patterns—a competence which is manifested by adult speakers in the way they construe new or unfamiliar items in the rapidly changing Hebrew vocabulary.

1.3. Morphophonology

Hebrew is rich in inflectional and other bound morphology, although case is marked by prepositions rather than in the forms of nouns and their modifiers. Several grammatical markers are prefixed to a following word (as illustrated in fn. 5), with the normative requirement of change in vowel quality depending on the following consonant—e.g. *ve-* 'and' = historical /w-/, is supposed to be pronounced *u-* before labials.

Numerous grammatical categories are inflectionally affixed in Hebrew. These include, for NOUNS: Gender—all nouns being either masculine or feminine, e.g.

MASC. *shulxan* 'table' vs. FEM. *mita* 'bed', with a semantically motivated contrast in animate nouns, e.g. *ish* 'man' vs. *isha* 'woman', *tarnegol* 'rooster' vs. *tarnególet* 'hen'; and Number—which is either singular or plural, with the masculine suffix *-im* and feminine *-ot,* e.g. *kadur-im* 'ball-s', *buba - bubot* 'doll-s', and there is a marginally productive dual form with the suffix *-áyim* used for paired body-parts, e.g. *yad-áyim* 'hand-s', clothing, e.g. *mixnas-áyim* 'trouser-s', and time-periods, e.g. *sha'a* 'hour', *sha'ot* 'hours', *she'atáyim* 'two hours'. Nouns also alternate between the free or ''absolute'' form and a bound, genitive form used before possessive suffixes or as the heads of noun compounds—e.g. *báyit* 'house' vs. *bet-o* 'his house', *bet yeladim* 'children's house'; *yeled* 'child' vs. *yald-exa* 'your child', *yaldey ha kfar* 'children-of the village' (= 'the village children').

ADJECTIVES and demonstratives agree with their head nouns in number and gender as well as definiteness—e.g. *yéled gadol ze* 'boy big this' (= 'this big boy') vs. *yalda gdola zot* 'this big girl' vs. *ha yelad-ot ha gdol-ot ha éyle* 'the girl-s the big-PL the these' (= 'these big girls').

VERBS agree with their subject nouns in number, gender, and person, and they are also marked for tense—present, past, or future—and for mood, taking special forms in imperative and infinitive, compare, for the root *š-t-y* 'drink': Imperative *shte,* Infinitive *li-shtot,* Present *shote,* Past *shata,* Future *yi-shte.* In past and future tense—but not in the present tense, since this was historically a participial rather than a tensed form—person marking is incorporated in the verb-form for 1st and 2nd person, e.g. *haláx-ti* 'I went' vs. *haláx-ta* 'you (MASC:SG.) went', *nelex* 'we'll go' vs. *telxu* 'you (PL.) will go'. Compare, too, gender marking in: *ron holex* 'Ron is-going' vs. *rina holéxet* 'Rina is-going', *ata haláx-ta* 'you (MASC:SG.) went' vs. *at halax-t* 'you (FEM:SG.) went'.

PRONOUNS also take a complex array of inflections. They take a free form only as as surface subjects—e.g. *ani* 'I', *hem* 'they'—and in all other contexts pronouns are suffixed to prepositions, e.g. *im + ata* 'with you' = *itxa, al + hu* 'on he' = *alav* 'on him'. Nouns can also take possessive pronoun suffixes, as in the examples of 'his house' and 'your child' given earlier, although everyday usage prefers an analytic form with the genitive particle *shel* 'of'—compare *bet-éynu* 'house our' with *ha báyit shel-ánu* 'the house of-us', both meaning 'our house' in formal and casual style respectively.

The child thus needs to gain control of a rich and complex array of largely synthetic inflectional markers, including some that have no semantic correlates, particularly the marking of nonanimate nouns as masculine or feminine; many affixes incorporate more than one grammatical category—e.g. the suffix *-ot* on nouns and adjectives as well as present-tense verbs marks both plural and feminine; and there are several instances of syncretism—e.g. the *t-* prefix in future tense verbs marks both 2nd masculine and 3rd feminine, as in *telex* meaning both 'you'll go' and 'she'll go'.

The task of acquiring this set of forms is further complicated by the leveling of historical phonological distinctions which are still manifested in the orthography, and which still have crucial morphophonemic consequences—even though they are not found in the pronunciation of normal Israeli speech today, of either adults or children. The listing in (2) below represents the 22 consonantal letters of the Hebrew alphabet (vowels being indicated by diacritics only in poetry, the Bible, and stories and readers for young children). All these letters represent historically distinct phonemes, compared with the way they are pronounced today, and the cross-lines indicate where neutralization occurs in current Hebrew speech.

(2) Hebrew consonantal system (in alphabetical order)

Letter-name		Historical	Current
alef	א	ʔ	Ø or ʔ
bet, vet	ב	b ~ v	b ~ v
gimel	ג	g	g
daled	ד	d	d
heh	ה	h	Ø or h
vav	ו	w	v
zayin	ז	z	z
chet	ח	ḥ	x
tet	ט	ṭ	t
yod	י	y	y
kaf, chaf	כ	k ~ x	k ~ x
lamed	ל	l	l
mem	מ	m	m
nun	נ	n	n
samech	ס	s	s
ayin	ע	ʕ	Ø or ʔ
pe, fe	פ	p ~ f	p ~ f
tsade	צ	c	c
kof	ק	q	k
resh	ר	r	r
shin, sin	ש	š ṣ	š s
tav	ת	θ	t

The levelings shown in (2) focus on phonemically relevant distinctions rather than on details of articulation (e.g. classical front /r/ vs. current velar-uvular /r/ is considered irrelevant here). These neutralizations include: historical glottal stop *alef*, pharyngeal stop *ayin* and usually also /h/ are pronounced as zero today in word-initial and word-final position, and either as ø or as a glottal stop between vowels (depending on how "careful" the speaker); thus phonetic *arim* today represents the three words: historical /ʔarim/ 'I will raise' as in *rom* 'height'; /ʕarim/ 'towns' from singular *ir;* and also /har-im/ 'mountains'. The sound *k* today is used both for historical uvular stop /q/ and the velar stop /k/, but only the latter still alternates with spirant /x/—usually after a vowel—while the sound *x* is used both for this spirant alternant of /k/ and for the historical pharyngeal /ḥ/. Compare, for instance: with initial q *kir* 'wall' and *be-kir* 'in a wall'; with initial /k/—*kis* 'pocket' and *be-xis* 'in a pocket'; with initial /ḥ/— *xek* 'lap' and *be-xek* 'in a lap'. Other consequences of such neutralizations are shown below for the multiply ambiguous word *kara,* the 3rd person masculine singular form meaning, respectively, 'happened, read, tore, dug, knelt'.

(3) Historical root   Contemporary form
    of *kara*   of infinitive

q-r-y	*li-krot*	'to happen'
q-r-ʔ	*li-kro*	'to read'
q-r-ʕ	*li-króa*	'to tear'
k-r-y	*li-xrot*	'to mine, dig'
k-r-ʕ	*li-xróa*	'to kneel down'

Similarly, as shown in (2) above, surface *v* derives from both historical /w/ which alternates with /u/ and from the spirantized version of the labial stop /b/—e.g. *le-vater* means either 'to concede' as in the noun *vitur* or 'to cleave' as in the noun *bitur;* while surface *t* derives from both the historical emphatic /ṭ/ and from the feminine marker /t/, which is usually affixal rather than a root consonant—compare *taklit/taklit-im* 'record-s' with the former, and *sak-it/sak-iyot* 'little bag-s' with the latter. Thus, these historical distinctions are still relevant to the morphophonological processes that determine the surface shape of words, even though they have no phonetic reality today. It follows that the child thus has no concrete physical cues to guide him in deciding what kinds of alternations apply to which words—such as in forming the infinitive of all the "different" instances of a verb like *kara* in (3) above.

It is not surprising, then, that the pattern of development traced below shows that Israeli children gain fairly rapid and error-free command of the main syntactic structures in their language, their progress from simple sentences to conjoining and various kinds of subordinate structures often being maturationally rather than linguistically determined. The acquisition of Hebrew morphophonemic alternations and inflectional systems, by contrast, constitutes a formidable instance of what Karmiloff-Smith (1979b) has characterized as "language as a formal problem-space" for the young preschooler.

2. Sources of Data

There is little published research on the acquisition of Hebrew, despite the interest that the special sociohistorical circumstances affecting this process might have aroused. This paucity may be attributed both to the restricted scope of psycholinguistic research in Israel and to the normative tradition of Hebrew scholarship, which engenders the view that spoken usage in general, and that of children in particular, is some kind of aberration not worthy of serious investigation.

The earliest, prestate—prior to 1948—documentation which I found includes teachers' listings of children's "errors" and "foreignisms," with some reference to lexical innovations. Of interest in such articles (e.g. Barless, 1937; Dolzhanski, 1937) is that most of these "misusages" and many of the "new words" are perpetuated in Hebrew child speech today. One noteworthy exception in both attitude and methodology is the work of the educational psychologist Rivkai (1933, 1938), who took detailed notes of children's spoken and written usage from ages 3 to 10, specifying the context in which certain forms were used, as well as the part of the country and the type of settlement (urban, rural, or communal) and the age of the children documented. His data, which accord well with more recent findings as well as with earlier studies as summed up in Avineri (1946), all concern morphology and lexis, with hardly a single reference to syntax—as is to be expected of that period in general.

Educationists have concerned themselves with children's language mainly at kindergarten and especially school-age, with the focus since the 1950s on comparisons of the usage of so-called "culturally disadvantaged" children, usually of lower-income Middle and Near Eastern extraction, with that of middle-class children of more established European and American backgrounds. Such studies include Ortar's (1975) work on the relationship between mothers' speech and children's verbal intelligence, on the one hand, and Stahl's (1977) detailed treatment of the language used by schoolchildren of largely nonliterate backgrounds. The data base for our own work, however, is taken almost exclusively from the usage of children of middle-class backgrounds, where Hebrew is the language of the home as well as of the neighborhood, and investigations of older children, with an educational or sociological motivation, is only marginally referred to in the discussion which follows.

On the other hand, as a reference point for how and to what extent children's usage reflects more general so-called "deviations" from normative requirements, we do have available a few careful studies of various aspects of current Israeli speech and written usage. The major such sources are: Schwarzwald's carefully designed investigation of the verb-forms of middle and lower-class Israelis aged 10–11, 13–14, 17–18, and 20+ (1978, 1981); Donag-Kinrot's large-scale study (1978), based on research conducted through written essays and questionnaires of students from Grades 8, 10, and 12; and Nahir's (1978) interviews with Israeli college students.

To date, the most broadscale study of children's Hebrew is Bar-Adon's voluminous dissertation (1959), findings of which are reported in English in Bar-Adon (1964b, 1971, 1977), accompanied by a strong, and as yet largely unattended plea for serious investigation of the emergent children's dialect of Hebrew (1964a). I have leaned heavily on Bar-Adon's original data, which focus largely on a description of verb-forms used by his own three children at different ages and by scores of preschoolers through teenagers, based on meticulous observations and notes taken over a period of some 10 years.

To the best of my knowledge, there are no fullscale diary studies available—and none that have been published—on any Hebrew-speaking children. I have, however, had access to the detailed documentation conducted by Yisrael Sagi of his grandchild's language from the second through the eighth year of life, which proved helpful mainly in the area of lexical innovation (Berman & Sagi, 1981). I have published case studies of my own child's phonology and verb-usage at the one-word stage (Berman, 1977, 1978b), on her re-acquisition of Hebrew after a year spent in the United States between ages 3 and 4 (Berman, 1979a), and on her narrative discourse style at around age 6 (Berman, 1981d). Findings of these studies are clearly consistent with data from other sources outlined below, even though my child grew up in a partly English-speaking environment. The only truly detailed case study known to me is that of Dromi (1982), an indepth longitudinal investigation of her child's development during the one-word stage.

Other published material referred to below includes: Dromi's (1979) study of the development of prepositions and locative markers by children aged 2 to 3; Berkowitz and Wigodsky (1979)—a study of interpretation of noncoreferential pronouns by children aged 9 to 11; Ariel's (1975) study of negating expressions used by 1-year olds; and the study by Goshen and Eyal (1976) on children's understanding of question-words, based on a structured task given to 18 children aged 2;6 and 3;6—the latter two in Hebrew. Input studies include Zeidner's (1978) sociolinguistic description of "baby talk"; Ninio's (1980) study of mother-child interaction with babies in their second year; and Buium's (1976) case study of parental input to a 2 year old. Frankel et al. (1980) provide a carefully designed study of the role of word order in sentence comprehension at different ages. My own noncase studies to date focus on the acquisition of lexico-semantics through the system of verb-pattern alternation (Berman, 1980, 1982) and the nature of children's lexical innovations, based on naturalistic and more structured data (Berman & Sagi, 1981, and Clark & Berman, 1984, respectively), as well as the acquisition of the inflectional systems and other aspects of morphophonological patterning (Berman, 1981a, 1981b, 1981c, 1983; Berman & Dromi, 1984). Reference is also made below to a revision of Dromi's (1977) model for calculating MLU in Hebrew (Dromi & Berman, 1982), as validated by performance of the 38 subjects on a developmental scale of 12 syntactico-semantic elements in the speech of 2- to 3-year olds.

Much of the data reported on below is based on unpublished material, as follows:

(a) My analysis of transcripts of children's speech recorded in approximately 1-hour-long partially structured elicitation sessions, as follows: 35 children aged 4–5 recorded by Anita Rom for her study of verbal and nonverbal interaction between normal and language-impaired Israeli children (Rom, 1979); 30 children aged 2–4 recorded by Sara Eyal and Haya Salzburg as background to their studies of the acquisition of questions and negatives (Eyal, 1976; Salzburg, 1976); and of 24 children recorded once each every month for a period of 4 months, between ages 1–4, conducted by Myrna Hirsch as part of a joint project for adaptation of the LARSP language-assessment scale for use with Hebrew-speaking children (Berman, Rom, & Hirsch, 1982). I have also used longitudinal recordings of a single child conducted by Lily Dagan of her daughter between ages 23–39 months and by Dafna Kaplan of a girl recorded every 2 to 3 weeks for a year, from age 1;5. I am deeply grateful to all the above for making this material available to me.

(b) The doctoral dissertation of Yonata Levy (1980), including a longitudinal study of her child's acquisition of gender and of verb-forms between the ages of 1;10 and 2;10 and experimental testing of 32 children of average age 2;7 on the acquisition of plural marking; and of Zvia Walden (1982) on innovative vocabulary usage.

(c) Masters' theses of graduates of the Tel Aviv University School of Communications Disorders, consisting mainly of transcripts of around one hour of free speech combined with more structured experiments with between 20 and 60 children, as follows: at the one-word stage, longitudinally, Zonshain (1975); between ages 2 to 3; evaluation of MLU and 12 syntactic and semantic elements, with 38 children, Dromi (1977); two-word utterances, Rabinowitch (1974); telegraphese, Ben-Yitzchak (1979); acquisition of questions Eyal (1976), and of negatives, Salzburg (1976); as well as findings of adaptations of American tests on children aged 3–6 (Greenwald, 1979), aged 4–7 (Ben-Aroya, 1979), and aged 3–7 (Atsmon, 1979). Other masters' theses are: a study of the cognitive and linguistic development of three spatial concepts-terms with 60 children aged 18–30 months (Aviezer, 1979); two structured investigations of school-age comprehension of more complex structures (Ziv, 1976; Wigodsky, 1977); a comparison of the language proficiency of institutionalized compared with home-raised children aged 4–5 and 7–8 based on specially devised elicitation procedures (Yif'at, 1981); an indepth study of the development of a wide variety of morpho-syntactic elements of 40 children aged 1;10 to 3;6 (Kaplan, 1973); and of definiteness marking at ages 2–12 (Zur, 1983).

(d) A wide variety of qualifying or "seminar" papers, usually in the form of structured studies of specific language features of some 20 to 30 children studied cross-sectionally—made available to me by Sara Eyal and Shoshana Rabinowitch, Tel Aviv University; graduate term-papers of my own students; and transcripts of the free speech of nursery-school children at play, made available to me by Ora Schwarzwald of Bar-Ilan University and Andrew Cohen of Tel-Aviv University.

(e) Incidental examples of children's utterances made available to me from observations of their own children or close relatives by: Mira Ariel, Dafna Kaplan, Barbara Josman, Dorit Ravid, Ronit Shoshani, and Tzvia Walden.

(f) Results of pilot-studies conducted as part of graduate research in progress, as follows: comparison of the Hebrew proficiency of bilingual English-Hebrew and monolingual Hebrew-speaking children aged 3 to 5 (Shoshana Rabinowitch); the relationship between child language and language change (Dorit Ravid); and children's construals of noun compounding in Hebrew (Roni Bi-Lev).

(g) Detailed longitudinal observation and recording of my daughter, aged 7;4 at the time of writing, both alone and in interaction with her peers and other children at home and elsewhere in a close-knit village community.

In sum, the data are biased in favor of the language of 2 to 3 year olds. They relate almost exclusively to children whose background is middle-class or higher—the latter being cases where parents have college-level education—and they include children of both rural (kibbutz and moshav cooperative) as well as urban forms of settlement where, with the exception of my own child, Hebrew is the first and main language of the home. These children have typically attended daily nursery-school 6 days a week for 4 to 5 hours a day at least since around age 2, and hence they are strongly affected by peer-input from early on in their language development. The studies in question focus to a very large degree on production rather than on comprehension, and they provide far more detailed information on the acquisition of lexical and morphological aspects of the language than on syntactic structures.

3. Overall Course of Development

3.1. One-Word Stage

This stage which, following Peters (1983), should perhaps be termed the "one-unit" stage, for it includes such unanalyzed strings as *ma ze* 'What('s) that' and *od paam* 'another time' (= 'again'), follows much the same developmental pattern as attested to in the literature for English and other languages. Children usually produce their "first words" at around age 1 year to 15 months, and their repertoire typically includes the following kinds of items:

(a) Nouns used in the unmarked singular form—except in cases where the noun is more generally referred to in the plural, e.g. *naalayim* 'shoes', *xaruzim* 'beads', *kubiyot* 'blocks'. Such nouns typically refer to foods, toys, animals, clothing, body-parts, and other objects familiar from the child's everyday surroundings.

(b) Onomatopeic forms and other nursery-words for objects and activities—e.g. *hau hau* 'woof woof' for a dog, *gaga* for a duck, *kukuriku* for a hen, *dyo* for a horse and also for games of "riding" like English *giddy-ap;* and for other rituals such as greetings *bay-bay* (akin to English *bye,* although no such word exists in conventional Hebrew), *kuku* 'peek-a-boo', and *opala* 'all fall down'. Some such nursery-terms, as analyzed by Dromi (1982), seem to refer to an entire nonreferential frame or gestalt—e.g. *áyta* for putting on a jacket, a buggy, going outside, and other objects and activities associated with going for a walk; *am* for food, eating, bottle, meals, kitchen, etc., where the nursery-term bears no obvious resemblance to any single word in adult Hebrew.

(c) Deictic terms—most particularly *ze* 'it, this, that', the generalized pointing word, often heard—perhaps as a kind of precursor—as early as the babbling stage, pronounced something like [ᵉdzᵉe], so that it sounds like a blend of the object marker *et* plus *ze;* and also *hiney* to indicate appearance or presence, rather like adult French *voici,* where English-speaking children might use (their version of) *there* or *this.*

(d) A small set of other functors, representing generalized kinds of speech acts. These include the negative existential particle *eyn* to express nonexistence, disappearance, or completion, as when a bottle or dish is empty, when a child can't find a toy, and so on—rather like English *allgone; day*—literally meaning 'enough', to express protest, the wish for an activity to discontinue; and *od*— literally 'more, over (again)' to express desire for repetition or continuation of an activity, such as playing a game with an adult who has desisted, or for addition, for instance when the child wants more candy or another toy.

(e) Verbs differ from the other forms noted for the one-word stage, since they have no clear basic or citation form in Hebrew. That is, all verbs must take some inflection for mood, and if marked for tense, they will also indicate number, gender, and person. The initial form of verbs is quite typically in the IMPERATIVE with an instrumental kind of function, to express the child's wish to have people do things for him, or to get something done for himself. Imperatives often take the unmarked masculine form in the use of boys, and the more marked feminine form with the suffix *-i* when used by girls, [e.g. *bo* vs. *bó'i* 'come!', *ten* vs. *tni* 'give!', or *(tista)kel* vs. *(tista)kli* "look!'] showing the important role of input in the child's initial perception of what is "basic" as a verb form. A form which shows up shortly after the first imperatives is the INFINITIVE, where children usually omit the infinitive marker *le-* or *li-* 'to' initially, and where they have no need to mark gender, number, or person—e.g. *(li)shon* '(to) sleep', *(la)rédet* 'to get down', *(le'e)xol* 'to eat'. The choice of whether an imperative rather than an infinitive form is used may be pragmatically determined, so that if the child wants to do something himself, such as to get down or to go to sleep, he will use the infinitive, whereas if he wants someone else to perform an action such as moving over or looking at something or giving him something, he will use the imperative, but this is a topic that requires further study. At all events, it is clear that throughout early child language, well into the third and even fourth year, children "over-use" infinitives, as the most typical way of expressing requests, desires, and prohibitions. Again, this may be a function of input, for infinitives are widely used in adult nursery style as a way of formulating directives more obliquely than through straightforward imperative forms—e.g. a parent may say *lishon* 'to sleep' when telling a child he must go to bed; or *lashévet* 'to sit-down' serves as a standard instruction of nursery-school teachers. Moreover, most adults in addressing children, and all children themselves, use the negative word *lo* 'no, not' plus infinitives to express prohibition—e.g. *lo lingóa* 'not to-touch', *lo lakum* 'not to-get-up' in place of the more normative use of *al* plus a future-tense verb—e.g. *al tiga* 'don't touch', *al takumi* 'don't get-up: FEM'. This construal of infinitives as somehow "basic" by caretakers and children alike may be formally motivated, since infinitive forms require no inflectional marking beyond prefixal *le-* 'to', and they seem to serve as a conveniently indirect way of issuing commands. Besides, infinitives are also found in very casual or intimate adult interactions, too—e.g. *nu, xevre, la-zuz kvar!* 'Well, fellows, to-move' = 'let's get going already!'. Whatever their source, overextension of infinitives—where normative requirements call for imperatives, negative plus future forms of prohibitions, or even tense-marked verbs—is one of the most pervasive features of Hebrew child language; and it affords one of the many instances noted throughout this chapter where the question of what constitutes the real, or relevant, input to children needs to be carefully accounted for.

3.2. *Acquisition of Tensed Verbs*

Imperatives and infinitive forms of verbs are shortly followed—usually as early as the one-word stage—by present and past tense forms, with future tense verbs showing up somewhat later. The issue of tense/aspect acquisition has not been studied in any depth for Hebrew, but there is some indication that at the earliest stages, tense-marking on verbs is associated with the semantics of specific verb-types (Antinucci & Miller, 1976; Bloom et al., 1980). Thus, initially children use present-tense forms for durative activities such as *boxe* 'cries, is-crying', *mesaxek* 'is-playing', as well as for statives such as *roce* 'want' and *yodéa* 'know (how to)', whereas past-tense is used initially with end-state or punctual verbs such as *nafál(ti)* '(I) fell' or *nishbar* 'broke, got broken'. Future-tense forms occur somewhat later, from around age 2½ usually, and they seem to first encode immediate rather than more remote future, as was found by Harner for English (1976, 1981), with much early use of present-tense verbs together with a time-adverb such as *axshav* 'now' serving to encode the next immediate step in a series of activities. Again, early future-tense forms seem linked to activities typically projected onto future events common in the child's world, such as threats—e.g. *arbic lexa* 'I'll-hit you'—or promises—*yiknu li* 'they'll-buy for me'. By around age 3, Hebrew-speaking children typically do have command of tense-marking in their language, as evinced by their ability to assign all three tense forms—present, past, and future—to the same verb, irrespective of its inherent aspectual or pragmatic content, e.g. *shote* 'is-drinking' as well as *shata* 'drank, has drunk' and *yishte* 'will-drink, is-going-to-drink' may be used by the same child (see, too, Berman 1983, Berman & Dromi, 1984).

A more detailed analysis of tense/aspect in Hebrew child language (for that matter, in general adult usage as well as input to children) would need to take into account the fact that while tense is encoded in the tripartite division of verb forms into present, past, and future, other properties of events are encoded either in the morphological *binyan* verb-patterns—including verbs, transitivity, causativeness, inchoativeness, etc., and in a few isolated verbs also iterativeness—or in lexical time adverbials used to specify aspectual distinctions. Among the earliest such "time words" used by young children are: *az* 'then' in the sense initially of French *alors,* later also of *puis* (Karmiloff-Smith, 1979a) and also *axarkax* 'then' (= 'afterwards') used as a kind of discourse conjunction (Bowerman, 1979). Children also very early on use *axshav* 'now' to refer to immediate future, later differentiated to include *od me'at* 'soon'; the word *kódem* 'earlier, beforehand, first' is used to express prior action, with *pá'am* 'once' standing for a generalized kind of "far past" by contrast with *kvar* 'already' as the marker par excellence of perfectivity, as well as *kol ha yom* 'all the day' used by children in preference to more normative *kol ha zman* 'all the time' to express continuality or habituality. During the third year, use also emerges of *etmol* 'yesterday' and *maxar* 'tomorrow' as cover-terms for past and future time-periods respectively, at a stage where the verb-tense will be appropriate to the situation being described, but the time-word need not be—e.g. **maxar halάx-ti* 'tomorrow I-went' may be used to describe a past action. This entire area is currently under detailed study in Hebrew, where it is of crosslinguistic interest in view of the fact that while tense distinctions are encoded in the verb form, aspect marking is primarily achieved through separate lexical items (Berman & Dromi, 1984).

A sense of the relatively very rapid acquisition of a contrastive set of five verb-forms—imperative and infinitive, present, past, and future—is yielded by the following excerpt from the transcript of a child aged 2;5 playing in the bathtub and talking to his father. Note that the child in question, whom I myself have observed, and as described to me by his mother, Dafna Kaplan, a trained speech clinician, is a quite typical 2½ year-old Israeli in his language development. Below, verb-forms are italicized, and slashes indicate separate utterances.

(4) *roce lexol* otánu   / *lex* mi po ! /
   . . . hu (=ha sfog) *barax* li, hu bambátya /
   . . . (ani) *noten* lambátya *lishtot* .   /
   (ax)shav ani *ikax* ta dag haze / . ha oniya *shάta*/
   (a)náxnu *misaxakim* / aba *asa* li péca /
   (a)naxnu *misaxakim* še hu (= ha dag) *yashut* le sham/
   kol ha dagim *ba'im* le sham/

   '(he) *wants*-PRES *to-eat*-INF us / *go-away*-IMP from here! /
   . it (=the sponge) *has-run-away*-PAST from-me, it's in-the-bath /
   . (I) *am-giving*-PRES to-the-bath *to-drink*-INF /
   now I *will-take*-FUT this fish / the boat *is-floating*-PRES /
   we *are-playing*-PRES / Daddy *made*-PAST me a hit (= hurt me) /
   we *are-playing*-PRES that he (= the fish) *will-float*-FUT to there /
   all the fishes *are-coming*-PRES to there /

It seems to me that this early, relatively rapidly acquired proficiency in marking verbs distinctly for all five forms noted above may be attributed to a number of interrelated factors: The Hebrew-speaking child cannot resort to any simple, unmarked form of the verb akin to English basic forms like *jump* or *forget,* but must immediately mark each verb for mood or tense. While he gets some mileage out of initial overextension of infinitive forms, he can then move into present/ past/future distinctions which are generally clearly and saliently marked by specific inflectional forms of verbs (see Berman, 1983 and also section 4.2.4 below); and he can do so without concern for internal marking of such complex aspectual parameters as perfectivity, durativity, or perfectness in the actual form of verbs.

3.3. *Initial Syntax*

Two-word combinations usually show up some time before the second birthday, and the pattern is again largely similar to what has been reported on for other languages. Certain of the functors noted at the one-word stage are widely used now in combination with another word—e.g. *ze* 'it, this, that' followed by a noun for the function of nomination; *hiney* 'here (it is)' with another word to indicate the presence or appearance of some entity, by contrast with *eyn* '(there) isn't' and another word to specify nonexistence or disappearance of an entity or discontinuation of an activity. The negative word *lo* is used with infinitives to express resistance to doing something or to prohibit, and the present-tense verb *roce* 'want' or feminine *roca* is combined with another word to express desires or else protest (e.g. *lo roce* 'I don't want').

Many of children's early two-word and longer utterances are wellformed, however, owing to the following formal properties of Hebrew, which serve to make numerous "here and now" kinds of statements structurally identical in children's and in standard usage: Hebrew has no present-tense form of the copula 'be', nor an indefinite article like English *a,* so that the 2-year old's utterance *iney kélev* 'here dog' is wellformed in the sense of 'there's a dog here'; the same word *ze* is used for 'it', 'this', and 'that', so that the child's *ma ze* 'what('s) this?' and *ze kélev* 'it('s a) dog' are also acceptable in standard Hebrew; sentence-negation simply requires *lo* 'no, not' to be inserted before the verb, so that the 2-year-old's *lo roce* 'not want-MASC' or *lo roca* 'not want-FEM' is an acceptable version of adult 'I don't want'—particularly since object-noun omission is often acceptable in Hebrew discourse when the referent is clear from the context—as it usually is with the verb 'want', or in an utterance like *hu kvar maca* 'he (has) already found'. A relevant example is found in the following "well formed" excerpt from a child aged 3;4 talking about her experiences with a friend at the swimming pool, when she says: *aba amar lo le haxnis ta raglayim la mayim, aval roni ken hixnis* 'Daddy said (=told us) not to put our legs in-the water, but Ronnie yes (=did) put-in'. This is perfectly acceptable, even though there is no explicit pronoun marking the object 'his legs' in the last clause. Other features of Hebrew which render relatively more of the child's initial strings syntactically wellformed than their English counterparts might be are: non-distinction of simple vs. progressive or perfect aspect in verb-forms; use of simple rising intonation for yes/no questions; fronting of question-words with no auxiliary manipulation or other word-order changes; and, corresponding to negation by placing *lo* 'no, not' before the verb, affirmation by placing *ken* 'yes' in the same position—as in the earlier example of Ronnie's 'yes' = 'in fact' having put his legs into the water.

Apart from these simplifying features of simple-clause formation in Hebrew, omissions and substitutions similar to those that have been noted for so-called "telegraphic" speech in English are found in the speech of Israeli 2- to 3-year-olds. These include: omission of the infinitival prefix *le-* 'to' and the definite marker *ha-* 'the', of prepositions—initially indicated by some children by a general kind of syllabic vowel such as *e* or *a*—all of which are perceptually nonsalient, since Hebrew words normally have final stress—as well as of the possessive marker *shel* 'of' and the general subordinator *še-* 'that'. Substitutions include use of the child's own name instead of the personal pronoun 'I' in the nominative free form as well as in case-marked contexts following a preposition, and also overuse of the basic locative preposition *be-* 'in, at', taking the form *be-* before a definite noun—e.g. at age 2;3 *nixnas ba mayim* 'goes-in in-the-water' in place of *la mayim* 'to-the water'; age 2;5 *sheli nafla ba kise* 'Shelli fell-FEM in-the chair' in place of *me ha kise* 'from the chair'; age 2;7 *hu roxev ba ofanáyim* 'he's riding in-the bike' rather than *al ha ofanáyim* 'on the bike—these three examples being from three different children.

3.4. *Inflectional Affixes and Other Morphemes*

A major acquisitional task at the stage of initial syntax is to gain control of the complex inflectional system of Hebrew, which is achieved in essence by around age 3 years (Berman, 1981a, 1981b; Dromi, 1977; Kaplan, 1983, Levy, 1983), with exceptions to be discussed in more detail later in this chapter. As noted, 3-year-olds use the full range of verb forms—imperative, infinitive, and then present, past, and future. During their third year, children also acquire the basis for use of the grammatical elements noted as missing from their telegraphic utterances: use of *ha-* 'the' to mark definiteness and use of the object-marking preposition *et* before definite noun phrases; use of *ve-* 'and' initially as a discourse conjunction, then to combine nouns or adjectives, and later on clauses; and use of prepositions—*le-* 'to' marking dative and possessive relations, later also directionality, and the locatives meaning in', 'on', and 'under' in that order (Aviezer, 1979; Dromi, 1979; Johnston & Slobin, 1979), as well as comitative or instrumental *im* 'with' followed by other prepositions such as benefactive *bishvil* 'for', ablative *mi-* 'from', comparative *kmo* 'like', as well as locational (and afterwards, also temporal) *axarey* 'behind, after' and *lifney* 'in front of, before'.

The third year also marks emergence of PRONOUNS, children first using first and third person singular pronouns, followed by second person and plural pronouns. A clear developmental step is manifested when the typically anaphoric pronouns of the third person start to be used in place of the formerly ubiquitous and inherently deictic *ze* 'it, this, that'. Children quite rapidly acquire the gender distinctions between singular third person *hu* 'he' and *hi* 'she', with rather more fluctuations in distinguishing singular second person masculine *ata* from feminine *at* 'you', but they never make gender distinctions in the plural forms of pronouns, using masculine *hem* 'they' and *atem* 'you-PL' all through even where feminine *hen* or *aten* might be required. This latter neutralization may be due to the phonetic similarity between the final dental and labial nasals, but it may also reflect more general adult usage in spoken Hebrew, and the crosslinguistic tendency for within-paradigm leveling of gender marking in favor of the less marked, more neutral masculine forms (Bybee, 1979). Thus, third person plural verbs in past tense take the same form in masculine and feminine (cf. singular *halax* 'he went' vs. *halxa* 'she went' but plural *halxu* 'they went'), and current usage has extended the masculine form throughout second and third person plurals in the future (e.g. *telxu* 'you'll-go-MASC:PL' is also used today in place of the feminine form *teléxna* in the plural).

Non-subject pronouns invariably take a bound form, as suffixes on case-marking and other prepositions—e.g. *hu sam oto alav* 'HE put HIM ON-HIM'. These tend to occur first with the very basic prepositions marking dative and possessive *le-* 'to, for' and *shel* 'of'—largely in the first person forms at the initial stages, e.g. *li* 'to me', *sheli* 'of me' (= 'my, mine'). The rest of the system is acquired in steps, (see Berman, 1981a, in press-a), proceeding from free juxtaposition of two elements, as in *al hu* 'on he' via an immature blending of the two into a single form such as *alo* 'on-him' to the appropriate form *alav* 'on-him'.

Perhaps the most complex morphosyntactic task for the Israeli child, and one which is as crucial as a developmental criterion for Hebrew as is the acquisition of auxiliary patterning in English, is the learning of grammatical AGREEMENT—from subject to main-verb in number and gender and, in past and future tense, also in person, as well as from the head noun to adjectives and demonstratives in number, gender, and definiteness. The general pattern which emerges (Kaplan, 1983, Levy, 1983a, 1983b) is that number agreement precedes gender agreement, masculine agreement precedes feminine marking, and that this is found first in subject-verb concord, subsequently in internal noun-phrase concord. Thus, by the end of the third year, children generally mark subject-verb agreement correctly, not only for human—and hence semantically motivated—subject nouns such as *tinok oxel* 'baby is-eating' vs. *rina oxél-et* 'Rina is-eating: FEM', or *yeladim box-im* 'children are crying' vs. *yeladot boxot* 'girls are crying: FEM' (Waks, 1978; Schachar, 1978), they are also able to make such distinctions for non-animates—e.g. *kadur nafal* 'ball fell' vs. feminine *mita nafl-a* 'bed fell', *ha balon hitpocec* 'the balloon burst' vs. *ha balonim hitpocec-u* 'the balloons burst-PL.' By around age 3 to 3½ children can also assign number and gender agreement from nouns to adjectives—e.g. *séfer adom* 'book red' (= 'a red book') vs. feminine *maxbéret aduma* 'red notebook'.

As noted, children encounter more difficulty with the marked feminine forms in both singular and plural—where gender distinctions are semantically unmotivated in all nonanimate nouns—and, in experimental designs, with nonsense words children have more difficulty than with familiar words or real-language items (Levy, 1980; Pardo, 1980). They evidently approach this task very much along the lines of a "formal problem space," as discussed for gender assignment in French by Karmiloff-Smith (1979a, 1979b), and as analyzed in some detail for Hebrew-speaking children aged 2;2 to 2;11 by Levy (1983). Word-final /a/ is taken as the sign par excellence of feminine gender—a much later realization being that this must be stressed *-a* as in *nocá* 'feather' and not unstressed *-a* (deriving from historical root-final *ayin* or *heh*) as in *kóva* 'hat', where the former but not the latter is in feminine gender—and see, in this connection, the example from my own child at age over 6 at the outset of this chapter. The next suffix which children recognize as feminine is unstressed *-et* as in *délet* 'door', *rakévet* 'train'—this perception perhaps being facilitated by the fact that verbs, too, take stressed *-a* as a feminine suffix in past tense, and unstressed *-et* in present tense—e.g. *ha mita nishber-a* 'the bed broke-FEM', *ha délet nisgér-et* 'the door is-closing-FEM'. Subsequently, children recognize *-it* as a feminine suffix commonly found in girls' names such as *dalit, ronit, nurit*, later on also *ut*, as in *xanut* 'store'. In general, formal cues in terms of the shape of word endings seem to carry more weight than semantic factors, which would make animate, certainly human nouns more easily inflected than inanimates. And factors of familiarity and frequency of the items in the language used and heard by the child seem to be of crucial importance, too, in children's acquisition of gender and number marking, and in their ultimate ability—from the fourth or even fifth year onwards—to make appropriate adjustments in the form of noun stems—e.g. a feminine noun such as *kapit* 'teaspoon' may first be pluralized by adding the unmarked masculine plural ending to yield **kapit-im,* then take the feminine ending **kapit-ot,* then be modified to yield correct *kapi-yot* 'teaspoons', while *simla* 'dress' will first be regularized to **simlot,* and only around age 4 or 5 modified to yield normative *smal-ot* 'dresses' (Berman, 1981c).

Children also start using the definite marker *ha-* quite early in their third year, with a tendency for overuse of *ha-* at around age 2;6, evidently because the child assumes that whatever is known to him is known to the hearer, too (Zur, 1983). The definite direct-object marker *et* seems to be acquired at the same time as *ha-* in post-verb positions, so that the contrast between *balon hitpocec* 'a balloon burst' and *ha balon hitpocec* 'the balloon burst' occurs together with, or very shortly before, the contrast between *ron roce balon* 'Ron wants a balloon' and *ron roce et ha balon* 'Ron wants OBJ the balloon'. By around age 4, children seem to use *ha-* appropriately, with certain specific exceptions such as in noun compounds and genitives in general (as discussed further below). Thus, the acquisition of definiteness—both conceptually and through its morpho-lexical encoding by *ha-* and *et ha-*, with its associated contracted form *ta* (compare *ten li et ha bakbuk* 'give me OBJ the bottle' with *ten li ta bakbuk*)—is an area which shows both Hebrew-specific and more universal features.

3.5. *Word Order*

Hebrew-speaking children seem to have little difficulty in mastering word-order constraints in their language. This may be due to the largely pragmatic determination of the ordering of major constituents with respect to one another in Hebrew, while comprehension may be facilitated by the fact that case-marking prepositions differentiate nouns according to syntactic function (compare, for instance, *ron ohev et rina* 'Ron loves OBJ Rina' with *et rina ron ohev* 'OBJ Rina Ron loves' referring to the same state of affairs), and gender marking also helps to disambiguate—as in the above example, where the verb 'loves' is masculine in gender, so that Ron rather than Rina must be the subject—as does number marking (compare, for instance, *et rina ohavim ha yeladim* 'OBJ Rina love-PL the children' = 'the children love Rina'). Young children seem to be addressed mainly in canonical SVO order in input (Buium, 1976), and to rely on this in comprehension (Frankel et al., 1980) and in production (Rotstein, 1980; Shoham, 1980). There is some evidence that prototypical transitive events with animate subjects and inanimate objects (Slobin, 1979, 1981) occur earliest in both comprehension and production, while the semantics of human possessors and inanimate possessees seems to be all-important in the interpretation of possessive sentences—e.g. *yesh le dani kóva* 'be to Danny a hat', *yesh kóva le dani* 'be a hat to Danny', and *kóva yesh le dani* 'a hat be to Danny' are all correctly taken to mean that 'Danny has a hat'.

Early on in their syntactic development, children start to manifest increased flexibility of word order for pragmatic purposes, and this can be taken as a sign of early linguistic maturation. In 2- to 3-year-olds, one finds use of left-dislocation—e.g. *ziva, eyn la kóax* 'Ziva, she has no strength', *ha buba, bo'i nikax ota* 'the doll, let's take it'—as well as of right-dislocation (see Clark, 1985)—e.g. *lama hi boxa, ha yalda?* 'why's she crying, the little girl?', *hiney hu oxel, ha tinok* 'look he's eating, the baby'—both evidently motivated by a communicative need to make sure that the interlocutor knows who or what is being commented on. Children start somewhat later to use fronting of non-subject nominals—for purposes of contrastive focusing on some other nominal, e.g. *im rina ani lo roca lesaxek* 'with Rina I don't want to play', *et ha kélev haze negaresh mi po* 'OBJ that dog we'll kick out of here', and fronting of adverbials for purposes of scene-setting or providing background information is also found in 3- to 4-year-old conversation, e.g. *ecel anat sixáknu be loto* 'at Anat ('s house) we played lotto'. Increased, and increasingly appropriate use of grammatically wellformed, but pragmatically marked, noncanonical re-orderings of major constituents is another topic which requires detailed study in a language like Hebrew, as a possibly quite crucial indicator of children's developing discourse competence.

3.6. *Predicate Types: The* binyan *System*

Acquisition of the *binyan* system of verb-pattern alternation is a source of great potential insight into Hebrew language development for several reasons. It highlights language-specific issues of how such notions as causativeness, reciprocality, passive, and middle voice, transitivity, etc. are lexicalized within the verb-pattern system of morphology in a Semitic language like Hebrew. It also touches on quite general developmental issues, representing a special interface of "cognitive, semantic, and syntactic development" (Bowerman, 1974), focusing in Hebrew on the role of lexicalization in the linguistic encoding of such concepts. These issues have been studied extensively for English causatives by Bowerman (1974, 1978, 1981), and noted for different types of predicate relations by Lord (1979), while the general developmental patterns noted in this chapter for Hebrew-speaking children are discussed in detail in Berman (1980, 1982, in press-a; Berman & Sagi, 1981).

(5) Overall development of verb-pattern alternation:
    I (Age around 2–3): A given verb root is used in only one pattern, often correctly—e.g. *ani oxélet glída* 'I'm eating ice cream', but also incorrectly, through leveling of a required distinction—e.g. *ima *oxelet oti hayom* 'Mommy is-eating me today' in place of required *ma'axila* 'is-feeding' in a different pattern based on the same root *ʔ-k-l*. At this phase, verb root and pattern occur as unanalyzed, rote-learned lexical "amalgams" (MacWhinney, 1985), much like words such as *play* or *fell* for English-speaking children.
    II (Age around 3–4): Initial variation of verb patterns occurs with certain common verbs, and neutralization or leveling is rare, as children begin to alternate between their earlier, for them "basic" verbs and semantically more complex verbs based on the same root—e.g. *oxel* 'is-eating' alternates with causative *ma'axil* 'feeds'; reflexive *mitraxec* 'washes-oneself' alternates with transitive *roxec* 'washes' from the root *r-x-c;* and intransitive, middle-voice *nishbar* 'broke, got-broken' alternates with transitive *shavar*. While such alternations of a given verb root show that the child can by now use the correct lexical form in different contexts, there is no evidence that he has a clear perception of the more general processes involved in expressing causation, reflexivity, etc. through the verb system of his language.
    III (Age around 4–5): Patterns are varied for numerous roots, and in many different contexts; and errors in the form of substituting one pattern for another and of lexical innovations provide evidence of a systematic grasp of

the principle of root plus pattern variation to mark semantic and syntactic distinctions. That this knowledge is systematic is shown, inter alia, by the fact that children substitute one pattern for another within but not across the boundaries of transitivity (Berman, 1980).

IV (Age around 5–6): Children manifest command of the system through appropriate *binyan* assignment to most of the verbs in their lexicon, while resorting to (wellformed) analytic periphrasis for certain predicate types, mainly passives and inchoatives.

The development thus shows increasing liberation from specific, rote-learned lexical items, most strongly evidenced at the "stage of acquisition" from around the fourth year—after tense-marking and other inflectional modifications of verbs for number, gender, and person are already well-established. At this point, children seem to realize a major distinction along the axis of transitivity, with mixing within but not across the two typically transitive patterns for verbs, and the two typically intransitive patterns, as though they divide event types into the major dichotomy of active, transitive, causative versus passive, intransitive, reflexive; and they treat the most "basic" pattern—the one which is commonest in children's output, perhaps in the language in general, and which is used freely for both transitive and intransitive verbs—as though it were "non-negotiable," except where it is sometimes assigned higher transitivity (Hopper & Thompson, 1980) by being used in the largely causative verb pattern in cases where no such form exists in the current lexicon (e.g. instead of straightforward *doxef* 'pushes', children sometimes use causative *madxif* 'make-be-pushed'). At the later stage of consolidation, children's lexical formations accord with those established by current convention for general Hebrew usage—and where children's forms continue to differ through school-age, possible changes may be predicted for the adult lexicon eventually.

Children's use of the *binyan* system seems to follow a fairly clear cognitive path. (i) At the initial "unanalyzed" or rote stages, a given verb stands for a general, undifferentiated kind of "whole" action or event; (ii) initial emergence of distinct verb forms marks mainly the difference between causative/noncausative and the related transitive/intransitive types of actions—involving the very basic concepts of Actor-Action-Patient; (iii) shortly after, special reflexive forms of verbs appear in relation to such familiar physical activities as dressing and washing, as well as a few isolated reciprocals, mainly for verbs meaning 'join' or 'get together' and 'fight (one another)'—in accordance with Piaget's observation that the concept of reflexive and reciprocal actions in general emerge later than those of transitivity and causation; (iv) older children express the notion of change of state through an auxiliary verb of becoming used with a familiar adjective, indicating that they have internalized the distinction between 'be' and 'get' = 'become', but not how it can be conventionally lexicalized in Hebrew. Avoidance of passives continues well through grade school; but the idea of an action being carried' out, and of a patient undergoing or being affected by an event, is acquired much earlier, with children—like older speakers—reformulating situations where the passive might be appropriate by means of subjectless impersonal sentences, through fronting of a nonagent NP, or through dative marking of the experiencer as affectee.

Each of these generalizations needs to be qualified in the case of specific, highly familiar verbs, which are acquired early on as "unanalyzed cognitive wholes" (Bowerman, 1974) or as rote "amalgams" (MacWhinney, 1978). In such instances, children may use a causative, reflexive, reciprocal, or passive verb form earlier than its conceptually simpler stative or transitive counterpart. Here, too, then, there is an interplay between a generalized more abstract construal of a given linguistic subsystem and the concepts which it encodes, on the one hand, and the particular exemplars which a child is familiar with from the language he hears around him, in the input as well as output of caretakers and peers.

3.7. *Other Syntactic Constructions, Later Acquisitions*

By the middle of their third year, Hebrew-speaking children have mastery of the form of basic NEGATIVE sentences—by placement of the negative marker *lo* before the verb. Two later developments are: (i) constituent-negation—as in the equivalent of 'I'm playing with Ron not with Rina', which is both conceptually and structurally difficult in terms of conjoining of contradictions; and (ii) negation of indefinite pronouns such as 'somebody' or 'something', which are formally complex since they require suppletive forms—e.g. *mishehu* 'somebody' vs. *af exad* 'nobody', *mashehu* 'something' vs. *shum davar* 'nothing'—as well as double marking with the negator *lo* 'not', even though they occur only in negative constructions. Besides, these expressions contain quantifiers, which are in general rare before around age 3. Semantically, negation proceeds as documented, for instance, for English—with the expression of nonexistence followed by protest or rejection, and then denial (Rom, 1977).

QUESTIONS are also correctly formed by around the middle of the third year, yes/no questions by means of rising intonation, and then information questions which have initial question words and no other manipulation of word order or other syntactic elements. The order of acquisition of question types is, again, semantically determined, and accords with the findings for other languages: 2-year-olds ask yes/no questions and questions with *ma* 'what', subsequently distinguished from *mi* 'who', and also questions with *éfo* 'where', and then *le'an* 'where to', only later with *káma* 'how much, how many', *matay* 'when', *ex* 'how'.

Three to four year olds show the beginnings of productive mastery of causation and the distinction between transitive and intransitive events, as noted earlier. They also begin to make free use of causal and temporal linking of clauses; of non-irrealis conditionals—e.g. 'if you'll hit me, I'll tell my mommy' in literal translation; and of various kinds of relative clauses—e.g. 'the kid that hit me' and also, again in literal translation, 'the kid that I played with-him'. Acquisition of sentence types again seems to be cognitively determined, and follows the general pattern observed in the literature, as summed up in Bowerman (1979) for English. Initial juxtaposition of clauses is followed by coordination with *ve-* 'and' and also with *ve-az* 'and then', only later by use of *aval* 'but', and later development is manifested in increasing use of subordinate rather than coordinate clauses. The subordinator *še-* 'that' is initially overextended to mark temporal and other adverbial relations, which are later differentiated to indicate reason by means of *kiy* or *biglal še-* 'because', followed by later encoding of more complex relations such as those expressed by *ad še-* 'until (that)', *lamrot še-* 'although'. While relative clause formation seems to depend on more strictly structural factors—such as the need for a resumptive pronoun obliquely attached to a prepositional in some but not all such clauses—adverbial clauses are all very straightforward in syntactic construction, the order in which they develop being dependent on the type of semantic relationship expressed between the main clause and its associated subordinated expressions.

In verb-complement structures, VV combinations with the second verb in the infinitive show up initially with the verb *roce,* and later on also include an indirect object, as in *hu amar li la-vo* 'he told (to) me to-come'. The type of verbs which take infinitive complements seem to be semantically determined with respect in order of appearance, so that *roce* 'want' is followed by modal-type verbs taking infinitives, such as *yaxol* 'can', *carix* 'must', *yodea* 'know how to', and other statives such as *ohev* 'like', *xoshev* 'think'' in the sense of 'plan, mean to', as well as verbs of saying; aspectual type verbs such as *hitxil* 'begin', *hispik* 'manage' (= 'have time to'), or *himshix* 'continue' appear still later. Verb complements in the form of *še-* 'that' clauses are used as early as the third year, following simple juxtaposition, as in the Hebrew version of 'I know that he'll come', 'She wants that I'll do it', while embedded questions taking the same surface form, but with a question word such as 'why' or 'how' instead of 'that' occur not much later than these.

Lexical development is manifested by less reliance on ''general purpose verbs'' (Clark, 1978). Two very common verbs at the initial syntax stage are the general-action verb *asa* 'do, make' and the general-motion verb *halax* 'go', which is soon augmented by verbs specifying direction—e.g. 'go in', 'go out', 'go up', 'go down', which are all distinct lexical items in Hebrew—and also manner of movement—e.g. verbs meaning 'run', 'float', 'fly', and so on. Increasing specification is found in use of appropriate verbs for activities such as cutting, washing, wearing, or riding—which in Hebrew tend to be lexically specified in accordance with the type of object they refer to. Children's lexical innovations, mainly from around age 4 show, as noted earlier, increasing awareness of verb-pattern content, and also the start in use of specific noun patterns and/or suffixes to encode such noun classes as agent, instrument, collectives, or abstract nouns, as well as in innovative formation of statal adjectives.

Five-to-7-year-old development, with the beginning of more formal schooling, reflects increased awareness of a more literary or "higher" style of usage, such as is typical of most storybooks and children's literature in Hebrew to this day. This is reflected in children's attempts to use such devices as noun compounding with morphological adjustment of the head noun, bound forms of possessives, VS word order, and special discourse connectives in their own story-telling activities. Systematic data are not available on various aspects of school-age production, but the trend is that errors in anomalous types of morphological patterns—in verb-forms, requiring stem adjustment for plural formation, in gender agreement, etc.—are either stabilized as such by around age 8 or 9, and hence reflect less puristic usage in general, possibly also constituting a more likely source of subsequent language change than forms which are corrected by around age 5 (and see Karmiloff-Smith, 1979c on the nature of developments between ages 5 to 9 approximately); or else such "errors" are corrected by early grade-school age to conform with standard usage. There is, additionally, experimental evidence indicating that comprehension of certain types of complement and relative-clause structures, as well as of pronominal reference, may be deferred to as late as age 11 to 12 (Berkowitz & Wigodsky, 1979; Ziv, 1976).

THE DATA

4. Typical Errors

Many of the error-types noted below are in the area of morphology—due to the complexities of the system as noted in Sections 1.2 and 1.3 above, and because morphological processes have been documented in more detail than syntactic or semantic acquisition, in line with the general tradition of Hebrew studies, which tend to focus on morphology.

Errors NOT noted below include phonological types of "contractions" which are found not only in children's usage, but which seem to characterize Hebrew fast-speech phenomena in general (Kupferberg, 1976). These can be attributed to difficulties of segmentation at the preliterate stage (Peters, 1983), as well as in actual physical perception of phonetically weak or unstressed elements. Such "blurrings" include the following: (i) treating V(ʔ)V sequences as a simple single vowel, particularly when the two vowels are the same—e.g. shomát 'hears-FEM' for shomá'at; baron for ba'arón 'in-the-closet'; nelam for ne'elam 'disappears'; or mil for mə'il 'coat'; (ii) general elision of /h/, particularly but not only in word-initial position—e.g., inéyabubá for hiney ha buba 'here's the doll', likanes for ləhikanes 'to come in', liyot for liheyot ('to be'; (iii) the tendency to give a regular vowel quality to schwa—e.g. lidaber 'to talk', melamed 'teaches' have a historical, or normative, schwa in the first syllable;

(iv) elision of unstressed /e/ in the feminine suffix -et, so that feminine *holéxet* 'is walking' is pronounced *holext* and *nehedéret* 'wonderful' becomes *nedert;* (v) contracted forms of words very common in children's input and output—e.g. *cerixa* 'must-FEM' with a velar to uvular /r/ is pronounced *cixa; axar kax* 'afterwards' becomes *axakax; ma-še-hu* 'what that he' (= 'something') and *mi-še-hu* 'who that he' (= 'someone') become *máshu* and *míshu* respectively; *ha ába shelí* 'the Daddy of me' (= 'my father') is pronounced *ábsheli* or even *ápshli;* while a compound like *yom hulédet* 'day-of birth' (= 'birthday') is pronounced *ymelédt;* and (vi) perhaps the most typical instance of a "contraction" in Modern Hebrew, which is found in the rapid speech of young adults for sure, and which in 3 year old children does alternate with a "full" form, is the combination of the object-marker *et* plus definite *ha-* 'the' to the single element *ta-* or even *t-* alone—e.g. *ten li et ha bakbuk* 'give me OBJ the bottle' becomes *ten li ta bakbuk,* while *ani carix et ha iparon* 'I need OBJ the pencil' becomes *ancix tiparon.*

Another class of "errors" not noted here, since they are pervasive in all but the most normative speech today, is nonobservance of the historical rule requiring spirantization of /b, p, k/ following a prefixal vowel. Thus we do not consider here such forms as *le-betsefer* 'to school' vs. normative *le-vetsefer,* or *be-kadur* 'with (a) ball' vs. normative *be-xadur.*

The entire issue of what constitutes an "error" in Hebrew child language is exceedingly problematic, for rather different reasons than those noted in relation to this question by Ochs (1985). Firstly, lack of detailed input research makes it unclear what precisely constitute real and relevant sources of language use for the children of largely middle-class backgrounds reported on here. Secondly, the great gulf between normative requirements and how people actually speak, coupled with the heterogeneous nature of the Israeli population noted in Section 1 above, means that there is a danger of interpreting as juvenile errors forms and usages which are in fact widespread in certain segments, or even in large parts, of the adult population. Thus, except in the case of forms which are clearly childish and quite shortlived, many "errors" may in fact be deviations from unreal norms, since they may be found in non-preschool usage as well, ranging from the younger generation of teenagers and college students to that of uneducated, less standard speech on the one hand, or of less careful speech in general (with some data on such populations available from the studies of Donag-Kinrot, 1978; Nahir, 1978; and Schwarzwald, 1978, 1981). A crucial question here is just which errors are transient and hence truly characteristic of the acquisitional process, and which are evidence of more pervasive directions of change in the language in general. Yet the latter category cannot merely be dismissed in children's output as a function of "imperfect" input on the part of adult caretakers or older siblings since our data, as noted, derive mainly from middle-class children who come from homes and who attend nursery schools and kindergartens where a "standard" or relatively well-educated kind of speech obtains. The view we take is, rather, that in many instances, faced with the anomalies and opacities of the system noted in Section 1 above, children and older speakers alike come to similar construals quite independently. And we regard such "errors" as self-perpetuating, as a function of the relatively great role of peer input in the Israeli setting, as discussed in 9.4 below, given that children spend many hours each day at nursery school from age 2, and that they interact extensively with their peers after school hours, too.

In the following discussion, accordingly, we try to indicate whether errors are truly transient, hence clearly developmental, or whether they reflect—possibly, are reflected in—more general usage. But this remains an open issue in the current state of Hebrew research, one which should provide a rich source of insight into the more general relationship between child language and language change, as well as into the psycholinguistic factors which underlie the distinction between transient errors and those which persist past early childhood.

4.1. *Morphophonemic Errors*

4.1.1. *Stop or spirant across environments.*   Children have immense difficulty working out when to use the stops /p,b,k/ or their spirant alternants /f,v,x/ respectively. Rules governing these alternations were phonologically well-motivated in Biblical Hebrew, by means of processes which are no longer phonetically manifested in the language, such as consonant gemination or the distinction between long and short vowels (Schwarzwald, 1976). In current Hebrew, spirantization is governed by a complex interaction between morphological, lexical, as well as phonologial factors, producing what appears to be a largely unmotivated series of alternations. For instance, root-medial /p/ in the root *s-p-r* is a spirant intervocalically in one verb-pattern, as in *safar* 'counted' but not in another verb-pattern, as in *siper* 'told' nor in the noun *sapar* 'barber, hairdresser'—since the medial consonant was historically geminate in the latter two words. Similarly, in an example parallel to that of *kara* in (3) above, *katav* 'wrote' alternates with *li-xtov* 'to write' by contrast with *kataf* 'picked' vs. *li-ktof* 'to pick'—because the /k/ of 'write' is one which historically alternates with /x/, whereas the /k/ of 'pick' is based on historical /q/, which has no spirant alternant.

The strategy initially adopted by children seems to be the following. They settle on one invariant consonantal root for a given lexeme, taking a given word as their point of reference—the choice of this word probably being due to input factors of the relative familiarity of this word compared with others from the same root.[7] Once a child has made this choice, he uses it as the basis for all other

---

[7]This is a matter which requires further study. Some choices of a "base-word" seem to be widespread across children, whereas other instances of adherence to either a stop or spirant may be confined to individual children only. In order to settle this issue, large numbers of children at different ages and from different backgrounds would need to be compared to see which stop/spirant neutralizations (alternatively, overextensions) are common across children and which are idiosyncrat-

words based on that root. For example, for the historical root *k-t-b* 'write', children may take *katav-ti* 'I wrote' as their reference point, and then extend "their" root k-t-v to yield *li-ktov* 'to write' in place of *li-xtov,* or *ti-ktevi* 'write- FEM:FUT' in place of *ti-xtevi;* for the root *sh-b-r,* children typically take intransitive *nishbar* 'broke, got broken' as a basic form, to yield *shabar-ti* 'I broke', *shober* 'breaks', and *shburim* 'broken-PL', where adults would use a medial /v/ all through. Conversely, children may pick on the spirant rather than the stop as basic—e.g. given the familiar *kafac* 'jumped', they will construe the root as invariably *k-f-c* rather than as underlying *k-p-c,* to yield *li-kfoc* 'to jump' (a form common among adults, too, as noted below), *makfeca* 'a diving board', *makfic* 'make-jump, bounce', and *mekafec* 'hops', where medial /f/ replaces /p/. Examples of both kinds—where either a spirant or a stop is taken as the invariant segment in all words based on a given root—abound in children's usage (Ben-Horin & Bolozky, 1972; Berman, 1981b; Schwarzwald, 1976, 1981).

Children clearly perceive words in which a stop and spirant alternate as versions of the same item, all the evidence indicating that from a very early age they have no difficulty in processing these alternations in comprehension. That is, they construe *p-f, b-v,* and *k-x* as single "phonemes" in perceptual terms. Moreover, this knowledge is deeply ingrained from an early age, as shown by the four-year old who said *ba-xufsa* 'in-the box', even though *kufsa* 'box' has as its initial stop historical /q/, which never alternates with /x/; and my own child at around age five would talk about the little boy she called /kristofer ravin/, from stories by A. A. Milne which had been told to her only in English.[8] Thus, children have no way of knowing what to do with these alternations when it comes to their own output, owing to the extreme opacity of the rules governing them. The fact that the strategy adopted by children, of taking a given WORD as the basis for all the items they produce with a given root, is not necessarily all that "immature" is shown by the fact that adults, too, take a given word as their source in innovative denominal verbs—e.g. the noun *koxav* 'a star' yields the neologistic *le-kaxev* 'to star (in a movie)', although historical rules would require it to be pronounced *le-xakev;* similarly, the noun *rexilut* 'gossip' has given rise to the new verb *le-raxel* 'to gossip' rather than normative *le-rakel,* and nearly everyone uses the verb *le-talfen* 'to phone' from *telefon,* compared with puristic *le-talpen.*

---

ic; and this distribution in turn would need to be compared carefully with precise adult data, of the kind which are largely lacking to date.

[8]Experimental investigation of children's acquisition of agent and instrument nouns indicates that these alternations are largely "ignored" by responses of children as young as age 4. For instance, given the innovative agent-noun *pazar,* children readily interpret this as referring to someone who does what they call *me-fazer* 'scatters'; and when asked to give a name for someone whose job is *li-shpox* 'to spill', they come up with either *shapxan* or *shafxan,* just as readily as they do when given as a stimulus verb the less normative but very common form *li-shfox* 'to spill' (Clark & Berman, 1984).

The specifically "childish" features of spirant/stop errors is hard to pinpoint, since adults also violate historical requirements very widely, more so in some instances or environments than in others (Fischler, 1975). It is virtually standard adult speech, for example, to have a syllable-initial spirant rather than the normative stop in the infinitive of verbs in the first pattern or conjugation, especially after a root-initial stop—e.g. *li-tfor* 'to sew' vs. normative *li-tpor, li-kvor* 'to bury' vs. normative *li-kbor*. Conversely, adults rarely use a medial stop with verbs in this same pattern, although children very often do—compare children's *shabur* vs. adult *shavur* 'broken', children's *soper* vs. adult *sofer* 'is-counting'. The reason may be due to older speaker's greater awareness of the distinctions between different morphological patterns or classes of verbs, as well as the influence of school-tutoring, where speakers are taught that medial stops are rendered in spirants in the *kal* pattern, but as stops in the so-called "double" patterns *pi'el* and *hitpa'el*—as in *shover* 'breaks' vs. *shiber* 'shattered'; *safar* 'counted' vs. *siper* 'told', the stop in the latter cases being due to historical gemination.

Neither children nor adults ever use stops in word-final position, but that is because post-vocalically, spirants are always required, and hence they never alternate if root-final (e.g. *katav* 'wrote', *saraf* 'burnt', *halax* 'went'). Less clear is the rule that stops are always required in word-initial position, however, because root-initial stops do occur after vowels as spirants—e.g. *pizer* 'scattered' vs. *le-fazer* 'to scatter' (things like blocks or toys, hence a word known to young children), or *bikesh* 'asked' vs. *mevakesh* 'asks'. In such cases, only children use /f/ in word-initial position, to yield such clearly childish forms as **fizár-ti* 'I scattered', **firák-nu* 'we broke-up (the game)', where initial /p/ is used by older speakers. Adults evidently "know" that /f/ is inadmissible in word-initial position (for instance, many render the loan-word *festival* as *pestival*). But a more complex situation exists with respect to the alternations between *b, V* and *k,x*—since it is possible to have words that start with the spirants *v* and *x* when these derive from historical /w/ and pharyngeal /ḥ/ respectively— as in *varod* 'pink' or *xalom* 'dream'. Hence, many adults, as well as children, say things like **xisa* 'covered' for normative *kisa,* or **vikesh* 'asked' instead of *bikesh*. That is, adults seem to have a much better idea than children of possible environments for the stops and spirants respectively—either in phonetic or morpho-lexical terms—but they are often as confused as children regarding the historical source of a given /x/ or /v/ in their language.

Children's errors in spirantization, then, can be attributed to the immense opacity of the data and to the inaccessibility of "rules" which have no concrete synchronic motivation. Where such errors are no longer found in standard adult usage, older speakers' re-analysis of the system can be attributed to increased exposure to a wider range of alternating forms as well as to a greater variety of levels and styles of usage, on the one hand, and to greater appreciation of rules applying to certain morphological patterns or lexical classes as well as school-learning of the rules of Biblical Hebrew and the cues provided by knowledge of conventional orthography, on the other.

4.1.2. Lack of Phonetic Cues.

Under this heading we refer to two main sources of processing difficulty which, like those noted in the preceding subsection, lead to errors of production rather than of comprehension. Firstly, neutralizations of historical distinctions, of the kind charted in Section 1.3 above, mean that the child has no way of figuring out whether, say, the x sound in a given word needs to be treated as a historical pharyngeal /ḥ/ and thus incur vowel-lowering, or as a spirantized version of the stop /k/. Thus, the past tense of the roots m-r-ḥ 'smear' and m-sh-k 'pull' share the same pattern—marax and mashax—but the present tense yields masculine moréax, feminine moráxat for the first verb, as against moshex and moshéxet for the second. A second source of difficulty lies in the fact that the language has many weak or "defective" roots, in which the historical three root consonants do not all show up in the surface forms of words based on such roots—which may include the "low" consonantals alef, ayin, and /h/, the historical glides /y/ or /w/, or root-initial /n/. Thus, for instance, the "full" roots l-m-d 'learn' and l-b-sh 'wear' yield the future-tense forms yi-lmad, yi-lbash by contrast with defective roots such as n-t-n 'give', n-s-ʕ 'travel', r-w-b 'quarrel', which take the future forms yi-ten, yi-sa, and ya-riv respectively.

Consequently, in relation to the first factor noted above, that of historical distinctions which have been leveled in current speech, young children may overregularize to use, say, the paradigmatic form of CoCéC-et for present-tense feminine. Thus, following the regular pattern of words like moshéx-et 'she pulls', holéx-et 'she goes', loméd-et 'she walks', one finds children saying * lokéx-et 'she takes' and *potéx-et 'she opens'—where historical root final pharyngeal /ḥ/ requires vowel-lowering to yield the forms lokáx-at, potáx-at. Interestingly enough, this is a short-lived error, not found among older children; yet the converse, where the x that incurs vowel-lowering is somehow viewed as "basic," is widespread in the speech of older children and less standard adult usage. For instance, one often hears such forms as *shofáx-at 'she spills', *somáx-at 'she relies', *oráxat-din 'woman-lawyer', replacing standard forms such as shoféx-et, soméx-et, oréxet-din. The immature strategy adopted by young children, then, is to extend the paradigmatic cases where vowel-lowering is not incurred across the board. Older speakers, by contrast, realize that final x sometimes requires vowel-lowering, and, where in doubt, they take the one that requires vowel-lowering as "basic," and overextend it to inappropriate environments. Further evidence for this claim is the widespread tendency of less normative adult usage to treat root-initial alef, which lowers the vowel of infinitives to e—as in le'exol 'to eat' vs. paradigmatic li-zxol 'to crawl'—as though it were a pharyngeal ayin, which lowers the vowel to *a,* so that one often hears forms like *la'asof* 'to collect' or *la'aroz* 'to pack', in place of normative *le'esof, le'eroz.*

A second, related source of difficulty arises where not all elements of the historical root are manifested in the surface forms of words. Here, children seem to adopt two main types of strategies. They may take the paradigmatic "full" forms—of verbs based on nondefective roots—as their reference point. For instance, they know *shavár-ti* 'I broke' and *haláx-nu* 'we went' with the paradigmatic CaCaC stem; so they come up with forms like *shatá-ti* 'I drank' or *kaná-nu* 'we bought', although here root-final /y/ requires the vowel *i* in the open stem-final syllable, as in *shatí-ti, kaní-nu.* Similarly, in another verb-pattern, children know the third person forms *diber* 'talked' and *ciyer* 'drew' with a CiCeC stem; accordingly, with verbs with root-final /y/ they may come up with *nike* 'cleaned' or *kise* 'covered', where final *a* is required to yield *nika, kisa.* Another way in which children cope with the complexities of stem-final "open" syllables deriving from weak or defective root-final elements is to take some other form of the same verb which seems to them to have a full set of three consonants, For instance, verbs with root-final /y/ form the infinitive and the feminine with a suffixal *t;* compare for *s-x-y* the forms *li-sxot* 'to swim', *sax-ta* 'she swam' with the full root *s-g-r* yielding *li-sgor* 'to shut', *sagr-a* 'she shut'. Children often take the suffixal *t* of verbs like 'swim' to be a root-final consonant, to yield forms like *soxét-et* 'she swims' along the lines of nondefective *sogér-et* 'she closes' in place of required *soxa;* or they may give the plural *saxt-u* 'swam' as in *sagr-u* 'shut' in place of defective *sax-u.* These are typically childish errors, and they are generally corrected by late preschool age, as children acquire greater familiarity with more exemplars, and as they acquire more sense of different types of paradigms.

In some cases, however, the underlying or historical root is so inaccessible that even adults commit the same kinds of "solecisms" as children. This often occurs when a given root element is not phonetically realized in any inflectionally related form of the word. Thus, the canonical, full form of the *hif'il* verb pattern in present tense is maCCiC—e.g. *matxil* 'begins', *mastir* 'hides'. Where the root has a medial glide /y/ or /w/, the present-tense form is me-CiC, e.g. *mevin* 'understands', *merim* 'lifts'; but where the root has an initial, elided /n/, the present-tense is ma-CiC, e.g. *mazik* 'harms', *makir* 'knows'. And the situation is further complicated by the alternation of the vowels *e* and *i* rather than *a* in the first syllable of the past-tense forms of such verbs. Both the roots and how they pattern inflectionally are so opaque that children may use canonical *a* for present and *i* for past tense throughout, to give, say *mavin,* 'understand', *hivin* 'understood' (cf. normative *mevin, hevin*), or they may extend initial *e* across the board, as in *mekir* 'knows', *hekir* 'knew' (cf. normative *makir, hikir*). It is not surprising that, given the absence of surface phonetic cues in such cases, many adults as well as young children have no way of knowing which is the "correct" vowel to choose in the stem-initial syllable of verbs in this pattern based on defective roots.

There thus appear to be two classes of morphophonological errors at issue here: those which are typically juvenile and transient (such as treating suffixal *t* as though it were a root consonant) and those which are also quite typical of much adult usage (such as inappropriate choice of stem-initial vowels). In the former case, children evidently do have eventual recourse to rules for how stems are modified before suffixes in certain word classes—as analyzed for noun classes in Berman (1981c). In the latter case, however, choice of one form over another appears so totally unmotivated—e.g. whether an initial ''zero'' element (historical ayin or alef respectively) does or does not require vowel-lowering to *a* in the infinitive, or which vowel should occur in the stem-pattern mVCiC of certain verbs—that ''errors'' remain fossilized in the usage of older children, and they are widespread in much adult speech, as well.

4.2. Inflectional Paradigms

4.2.1. *Neutralization of 1st Person Future.* Person-marking in the future tense takes the form of a CV prefix, the consonant alternating according to person, the vowel according to verb pattern or *binyan,* as shown below.

(6)

		VERB PATTERN				
		KAL		PI'EL		HIF'IL
	ROOT: *s-g-r* 'to close'		*c-y-r* 'draw'		*s-t-r* 'hide'	
PERSON	SG	PL	SG	PL	SG	PL
1	*e-sgor*	*ni-sgor*	*a-cayer*	*ne-cayer*	*a-stir*	*na-stir*
2 MASC	*ti-sgor*	*ti-sgeru*	*te-cayer*	*te-cayru*	*ta-stir*	*ta-stíri*
3 MASC	*yi-sgor*	*yi-sgeru*	*ye-cayer*	*ye-cayru*	*ya-stir*	*ya-stíru*

The first person singular prefix is /ʔV/, but the glottal-stop is not pronounced today. Moreover, all children use the 3rd masculine singular prefix /yV/ for first person, too—e.g. *ani yisgor* 'I will-close+3rd', *ani yecayer* 'I will-draw+3rd', *ani yastir* 'I will-hide + 3rd'. This is clearly due to phonetic assimilation of an off-gliding /y/ at the end of the first person pronoun *ani* 'I' which blends with the vowel-initial part of the prefix that follows, thus: *ani + y + esgor* becomes [aniy(i)sgor]; yet the prefix-vowel is given the quality of the THIRD person, even when it is not *i*, as in: *ani + y + astir* which becomes [aniyastir]. While this leveling is clearly phonetic in origin, it occurs in all children's usage today, including in environments where the verb does not immediately follow the final off-glide of *ani* 'I'—e.g. *ani bétax yigmor* 'I certainly will-finish+3rd', *ani téxef yatxil* 'I right-away will-start + 3rd'.

This error is of interest for several reasons. It provides a further instance of the relative weight of the unmarked 3rd masculine singular as the source for intra-paradigm leveling in language (Bybee & Brewer, 1980). Besides, while children do retain the *t*- and *n*- prefixes in 2nd person and in 1st person plural of the future, they fully "regularize" to 3rd person singular not only by extending the initial *y*- in 1st person singular, but also by using the basic prefixal vowel *i* and *e* in the *kal* and *pi'el* patterns respectively, thereby eliminating the need for historical *e* and *a* incurred by vowel-lowering to the initial glottal stop in these environments. A second point to note here is that this overgeneralization is another instance of the production vs. perception split noted with respect to spirantization in Section 4.1.1 above. Children do understand the vowel-only prefix as having first-person reference when they hear it, either because it is used with the pronoun *ani* 'I' or because of available pragmatic cues. Thirdly, this error is so widespread—Bar Adon (1959) claims all children talk this way—that it affords a good example of where a morphological simplification attributable to children's early, independent analysis of input is likely to incur a general change in the language. This is plausible, since today all speakers generally make overt mention of the subject pronoun, even though it is also overtly marked on the verb and hence redundant. Thus in contemporary Hebrew, unlike at earlier stages of the language, ambiguity due to neutralization of the 1st/3rd person distinction in the verb is obviated. Moreover, many younger Israelis of high-school and even college age make the same "error"; but with older speakers, this leveling tends to be confined to certain very common verbs which are often used in the future— e.g. *yagid* 'will tell', *ya'ase* 'will do'—whereas among children this phe- nomenon occurs "across the board" for all verbs they use.

This last point seems to me crucial with respect to developmental patterns in Hebrew, and it is reflected, too, in other changes in inflectional paradigms as noted in Sections 4.2.2 and 4.2.3 below. Deviations from normative require- ments tend, among older speakers, to be confined to lexical items commonly used with a particular inflection (future tense, imperative mood, or plural number respectively); among young children, these errors apply across the board, to all the words at their disposal which they choose to mark with a given kind of inflection.

4.2.2. *Imperatives.*   As noted in Section 3 above, children use imperative forms very early on in Hebrew. These are based on the 2nd person future stem in the unmarked masculine singular, with a suffix to indicate feminine gender or plural number. In negative imperatives, the special negative morpheme *al* 'do not' occurs with the ordinary future form of the verb, which takes a *tV*- prefix— e.g. *al tisgor* 'don't close', *al tecayer* 'don't draw', *al tastir* 'don't hide' for the verbs in (6) above. In early child input and output, however, the general negator *lo* 'no, not' is used with the infinitive to express prohibitions—e.g. *lo le-cayer al ha kirot* 'not to-draw' (= 'don't draw on the walls'). The situation is further complicated by the fact that in casual adult usage, future-tense forms are widely used in place of normative imperatives—where imperatives, infinitives, and future forms share the same stem across different verb patterns.

Given the variability of usage across these three forms to express requests, commands, and prohibitions, children reanalyze the entire system to derive a set of forms that are neither imperative nor future in form, as shown below.

(7)   Children's re-analysis of imperative forms

Pattern of Verb		Normative Imperative		Future = Adult's Casual Imperative	Children's Imperative
kal	MASC	*shtok*	'be quiet'	*ti-shtok*	*shtok*
	FEM	*shitk-i*		*ti-shtek-i*	*shtek-i*
	MASC	*ptax*	'open!'	*ti-ftax*	*ftax*
	FEM	*pitx-i*		*ti-ftex-i*	*ftexi ~ fetxi*
nif'al	MASC	*hikanes*	'come in'	*ti-kanes*	*kanes*
	FEM	*hikans-i*		*ti-kans-i*	*kans-i*
	MASC	*hizaher*	'be	*ti-zaher*	*zaer*
	FEM	*hizahar-i*	careful'	*ti-zahar-i*	*zaar-i*
pi'el	MASC	*kase*	'cover!'	*te-xase*	*xase*
	FEM	*kas-i*		*te-xas-i*	*xas-i*
	MASC	*bakesh*	'ask'	*te-vakesh*	*vakesh*
	FEM	*baksh-i*		*te-vaksh-i*	*vaksh-i*
hitpa'el	MASC	*hitraxec*	'wash'	*tit-raxec*	*traxec*
	FEM	*hitraxac-i*		*tit-raxac-i*	*traxac-i*
	MASC	*histalek*	'get out'	*ti-stalek*	*stalek*
	FEM	*histalk-i*		*ti-stalk-i*	*stalk-i*

What children are doing is to lop off prefixes in forming imperatives—either the normative stem prefix of hV- in the *nif'al* and *hitpa'el* verb patterns, or the tV-prefixes of the future form used in the colloquial imperative of all patterns, yielding a special kind of imperative that consists of the future stem without any prefix. Strong evidence for this is the fact that where the normative imperative requires a word-initial stop as in *ptax* 'open!', *kase* 'cover!' or *bakesh* 'ask!', children typically use a stem-initial spirant. Moreover, in the *hitpa'el* pattern, prefixal *hit-* of imperatives or *tit-* of future—where root-initial sibilant *s* metathesizes with the prefixal preceding to yield *hi-s-talek* 'get out!' from the root *s-l-k* (see section 5.1.1 below)—is only partially lopped off, the prefixal *t* being retained in the "new" imperatives of children as part of the stem.

There is a great deal of variation in actual usage, both within and across children, as is to be expected of a system in transition. Moreover, some of these "truncated" forms are found among older speakers, too—e.g. *kanes* 'come in!' and *azvi* 'leave off!' (cf. imperative *izvi*, future *ta'azvi*) are widespread among all but the most self-conscious adults; and the form *varxi* 'bless-FEM' (cf. imperative *barxi*, future *te-varxi*) is common in religious girls' high schools, where prayer is required at meal-times. This, then, indicates what we pointed out regarding future-tense person levelings in the preceding section: that children may be the forerunners of a more general change in the language, where adults will first adopt such forms for only those lexical items which commonly occur in that particular form in actual usage. Note, further, that this truncation is found in the four verb-patterns illustrated in (7) above, but not in the causative *hif'il* pattern, where children, too, keep to future-tense forms in the infinitive—e.g. as against imperative *hatxel* 'begin!' or *hafsík-i* 'stop!-FEM', they will use future *tatxil*, *tafsík-i* respectively, and not truncated *txil or *fsík-i—evidently because of the different stress and rhythm patterns induced by such forms, as analyzed by Bolozky (1979b).

Despite these qualifications regarding the distribution of these "new imperatives," note that children ARE quite generally exposed to normative imperatives, either because they have very "careful" speakers as nursery school teachers or even parents, or through storybooks and children's verses. Thus first-graders understand normative imperatives in their early readers, but they will follow the pattern delineated in (7) above in their own usage. One reason for this may be that many of the earliest verbs used by children at the one-word stage—quite typically in an imperative function—are based on defective roots in the *kal* verb pattern, where the normative imperative and the truncated, prefixless future form happen to be identical, as in *shev* 'sit down!', *zuz* 'move over!', *kax* 'take!' (Berman, 1978b). Whatever its origins, this innovative tripartite system of Formal Imperative / Future / New Imperative represents an interesting process of children's simplification in fact leading to elaborative change. As noted, this seems to be an instance where child language sets the pace for more general change across the language, as shown by its occasional, lexically restricted occurrence among older speakers, too. Moreover, this reanalysis interacts with changes now under way with respect to speakers' construals of the processes of spirantization (Section 4.1.1 above) and also metathesis of prefix-final *t* and root-initial sibilants in the *hitpa'el* pattern (Section 5.1.1 below).

4.2.3. *Noun Plurals.* The basic rule of adding *-im* to masculine nouns and *-ot* to feminine nouns as well as to present-tense verbs and also adjectives to form the plural is acquired along with initial syntax, during the third year. The masculine, unmarked ending is acquired earlier, before the synthetic *-ot,* which combines both feminine gender and plural number in a single affix. The pattern of this acquisition has been studied in depth for 2 to 3 year olds by Levy (1980), and I will focus here on two main types of errors which seem to be of some general crosslinguistic interest, as two rather different instances of overregularization.

(i) Regularization across noun-classes: A study of plural formation in two sets of noun patterns (Berman, 1981c)—feminine nouns with the form CiCCa as in *tikra* 'ceiling', *simla* 'dress' and masculine nouns with the form CaCaC as in *gamad* 'dwarf, *gamal* 'camel'—showed that 3 year olds consistently observed Clark's (1980) principle of simplicity, to the effect that "the less a word-form changes, the simpler it is." That is, the younger subjects across the board avoided changes in the stem, simply adding *-ot* to feminine nouns to yield the correct alternation *tikra/tikr-ot* 'ceilings' but also incorrect *simla/*siml-ot* 'dresses', *ricpa/*ricp-ot* 'floors' in cases where—for complex morphophonological reasons that adults are not usually aware of—most nouns in CiCCa require a stem-change to yield CCaC-ot in the plural, as in *smal-ot* 'dresses', *rcaf-ot* 'floors'. Similarly, children simply added *-im* to the stem to form the plural of CaCaC masculine nouns, to yield correct *gamad-im* 'dwarfs', *panas-im* 'flashlights' but also incorrect *gamal-im* 'camels', *shafan-im* 'rabbits', where penultimate stem-vowel reduction should yield *gmal-im, shfan-im*—again, for reasons which are not phonologically obvious in current Israeli Hebrew as they were in Biblical language. With greater exposure, children do by age 6 correct all of the commonest nouns in their vocabulary, although neither they nor adults observe the historical rule in all words. Thus 3 year olds and adults alike generally say *mishx-ot* 'salves' rather than normative *mshax-ot* from singular *mishxa*, as well as masculine *pagaz-im* 'shells' rather than normative *pgaz-im* from singular *pagaz*. The findings of this study seem important for the issue of children's errors in general, since they reflect the interaction between competing sets of principles which operate in children's construal or morphological alternations in their language. Formal simplicity explains why at all age-groups fewer errors occurred with masculine than with feminine plurals (going from *gamal* to *gmal-im* 'camels' requires application of a general phonological rule of penultimate vowel reduction before a stressed suffix, by contrast with the extreme modification of the stem in going from *siml-a* to *smal-ot* 'dresses' or *ricpa* to *rcaf-ot* 'floors'). The pragmatic factor of familiarity engendered by frequency of usage of certain plural forms in set, formulaic expressions as well as in general child and adult usage explains why some words do take the "correct" forms in 6 or 12 year old usage, while others remain fossilized as errors. And a more formal, abstract recognition of different word classes in the languages enables 12 year olds and adults to make fewer errors than 6 year olds across a given noun class. In other words, as we saw with respect to a quite different subsystem of the language in Section 4.1.2 above, young preschoolers typically regularize to the paradigmatic case across the board; older children apply different strategies based on the combined factors of greater familiarity with more exemplars and greater knowledge of formal properties of the system;

and certain "errors" persist as a result of the immense opacity of the rules whose historical motivations are irrelevant for current speakers.

(ii) Regularizations of lexical exceptions: There are many quite common nouns in Hebrew that have irregular plurals in the sense that a masculine noun takes the feminine *-ot* and a feminine noun takes the masculine *-im*. The asterisked examples below are taken from the usage of 4 to 5 year olds.

		Singular Noun Forms		Expected = Children's Plural Forms	Conventional Plural Forms
(8)					
MASC:	*tinok*	'baby'		*tinok-im*	*tinok-ot*
	mazleg	'fork'		**mazleg-im*	*mazleg-ot*
	kir	'wall'		**kir-im*	*kir-ot*
	arye	'lion'		**arye-im*	*aray-ot*
FEM:	*beyca*	'egg'		**beyc-ot*	*beyc-im*
	shana	'year'		**shan-ot*	*shan-im*
	mila	'word'		**mil-ot*	*mil-im*
	isha	'woman'		**ish-ot*	*nash-im*

Clearly, the rule children are applying here is a formal strategy to the effect that if the word ends in *-a,* change this to *-ot* in the plural, and simply add basic *-im* everywhere else; and this will work correctly for the large majority of words that end in stressed *-a* in the language (although not for unstressed *-a,* as in the example of *kóva* 'hat' yielding **kovaót* rather than required *kova-ím* given right at the outset of this chapter). Such lexical exceptions are generally given the correct plural form by early school-age—although persistent agreement errors are found in the marking of adjectives with such nouns, as noted in Section 4.4.1 below. Given that formal knowledge of a rule is a hindrance rather than an aid in the case of irregular lexical items, the factors of familiarity and frequency of exposure to the plural forms will dictate which of these nouns acquire the conventional plural at an early age, and which errors will persist till later.

(iii) Back-formations: A third phenomenon relating to plural formation is that of back-formations, which occur mainly when a given word is more familiar in the plural than in the singular form, for pragmatic reasons of actual language use, so that children render the singular noun as the plural stem minus the plural suffix. Common examples in child speech include: (a) *cdafim* 'sea-shells' yields **cdaf*—as in *klaf-klafim* 'cards', although the conventional singular is *cédef*, following the alternation between singular CéCeC vs. plural CCaC-im as in *kélev—klav-im* 'dogs', *yéled—ylad-im* 'children': (b) plural *dma'ot* 'tears (from the eyes)' yields childish **dma'a,* where the conventional singular is *dim'a,* based on the alternation of CiCC-a and plural CCaC-ot noted in subsection (i) above; and (c) plural *acam-ot* 'bones' yielding singular **acama* in place of required *écem* 'a bone', a form that persisted in my child's usage well through first grade.

4.2.4. Verb-Class Forms.

Hebrew verbs tend to manifest fewer lexical exceptions than nouns, where by "lexical exception" we mean a given group of words which have no underlying morphophonological or semantic properties to motivate their difference from paradigmatic forms. For instance, verbs in the *kal* pattern normally take the future-tense stem CCoC, as in *yi-gmor* 'he'll finish', *ni-msor* 'we'll give'; a few common verbs take a stem-vowel *a* rather than expected *o*, and children may regularize these to yield **yilbosh* 'he'll wear' for *yi-lbash*, or **ni-lmod* 'we'll learn' for *ni-lmad*. And, the same verb pattern usually has the stem CoCeC in present tense, e.g. *gomer* 'finishes', *lovesh* 'wears'; a few verbs still take the Biblical stem vowels CaCeC, today normally reserved for adjectives such as *kaved* 'heavy', so that many adults and all children regularize normative *yashen* 'sleeps' and *gadel* 'grow' to **yoshen*, **godel*. These are two kinds of regularizations which are likely to spread across all usage eventually, even though the actual words to which they apply are high-frequency items which are common in children's language, and might thus be predicted as more resistant to change (Schwarzwald, 1979).

A special kind of error in verb forms is widespread among all, but only, children at the stage of early syntax. We refer to overextension of prefixal *m-* in two specific environments: present-tense occurrences of *nif'al* pattern verbs to yield childish **mi-kanes* 'goes in', **mi-radémet* 'is-falling-asleep-FEM' in place of required *nixnas, nirdémet* respectively; and in the present-tense of defective roots for verbs in the *kal* pattern, e.g. **mesim* for *sam* 'puts' and **mariv-im* for *rav-im* 'quarrel-PL'. Elsewhere (Berman, 1983), we explained this as a result of children's need for overt marking of the present tense in the two unique instances where present and past-tense forms are not distinct in current Hebrew pronunciation of verbs. The choice of prefixal *m-* for this function is highly plausible, given that three out of the five verb patterns commonly used by young children do, in fact, distinctively mark present tense in this way, as shown below.

(9) Present vs. past tense marking for the five main verb patterns

Pattern	Present Tense	Past Tense	Gloss
kal "full"	*soger*	*sagar*	shut, close
	holex	*halax*	go, walk
kal "weak"	*shar*	= *shar*	sing
	sam	= *sam*	put
nif'al	*nixnas*	= *nixnas*	go in
	nizhar	= *nizhar*	take care

Pattern	Present-Tense	Past-Tense	Gloss
pi'el	*me̱saxek*	*sixek*	play
	me̱kabel	*kibel*	get
hitpa'el	*mi̱traxec*	*hitraxec*	wash
	mi̱stakel	*histakel*	look
hif'il	*ma̱txil*	*hitxil*	start, begin
	ma̱lbish	*hilbish*	dress

Note that apart from the middle-bloc in (9) above, present-tense forms are distinctly marked by the various *m-* prefixes; and in the first, *kal* pattern, the one accounting for well above half of children's verbs, the vowel infixes for present compared with past are very clearly and distinctively *o-e,* irrespective of whether the first or last consonants are pronounced or not, as below:

(10) Verbs in the *kal* pattern with o-e vs. a-a vowel alternation

	CVCVC	VCVC	CVCV	VCV
Present *o-e*	*soger, holex* shut go	*omed, oxel* stand eat	*roce, bone* want build	*ose, ole* do go-up
Past *a-a*	*sagar, halax*	*amad, axal*	*raca, bana*	*asa, ala*

It is thus only with respect to the problematic middle bloc, of *kal* verbs, with a weak medial root glide, and *nif'al* verbs that children add the *m-* prefix as a marker of present tense. Elsewhere they can rely on vowel alternations to distinguish present from past tense. Moreover, past-tense forms are distinctly marked by person suffixes—e.g. *haláx-ti* 'I went' vs. *haláx-ta* 'you went'; *dibár-tem* 'you:PL spoke' vs. *dibár-nu* 'we spoke'; *histakl-a* 'she looked' vs. *histakl-u* 'they looked', in three different verb patterns. And future-tense forms, as shown in Section 4.2.1, are distinct from both present and past by their associated prefixes for person-marking (although future tense in general emerges later than either present or past in the speech of 2 to 3 year olds, and is hence not so relevant as the present/past distinction here). Strong supporting evidence that *m-* is in fact chosen as a marker of present tense by 2 year olds when they initially move into tense-marking in Hebrew is the fact that this overextension of *m-* is confined to verbs whose semantic aspect is durative, hence more likely to be encoded initially in present tense, rather than the punctual end-state types of verbs which initially prefer past-tense marking—as shown for French by Bronckardt & Sinclair, 1973; for Italian and English by Antinucci & Miller,

1976; for English by Bloom et al., 1980; as well as for Hebrew by Kaplan, 1983. Thus, of the defective verbs in the *kal* pattern, children overmark with *m-* for verbs meaning 'put,' 'sing,' and 'fight' which typically refer to durative activities; and in the *nif'al* pattern, they add *m-* for process verbs like those meaning 'go in', 'take care', 'go to sleep', 'get wet' but NOT when they use typically end-state verbs in the same pattern, like those meaning 'break' = 'get broken', 'be spilt' or 'get spilt', intransitive 'tear', or 'get hurt'.

This error is of interest for several reasons, discussed at some length in Berman (1983). Firstly, it is a classic example of what we have termed a transient or shortlived error, in that it is widespread among very young children in the initial stages of morpho-syntactic development, but it gives way to the conventional forms once children freely alternate between the three tenses—present, past, and future—across a wider range of verbs. As such, *m-* extension offers a good example of an interim rule, one which is quite plausible in terms of the formal properties of Hebrew tense-marking as shown in (9) above, that is adopted by children as a bridge strategy in moving from rote-learned unanalyzed forms to the full range of formal alternations required by the verb system of their language. Secondly, it provides an instance where rather different explanations might be provided for the same surface phenomenon in child speech, as evidenced by the fact that I had originally interpreted this error as a result of phonetic overgeneralization of a related type of pattern (as discussed in detail in Berman, 1981a). My re-analysis in light of further data from Hebrew and from other languages—in terms of *m-* being extended as a highly salient marker of present-tense verbs—indicates the need to interpret children's errors by comparison with a wide range of other paradigms and other subsystems in the language (the three tenses and the five verb patterns respectively), rather than simply in relation to one other set of superficially similar forms.

4.3. Verb-Pattern (Binyan) Alternation

The way in which children acquire the *binyan* system of verb-pattern alternations, as outlined in Section 3.6 above, is crucial in the development of Hebrew as a Semitic language, and is of crosslinguistic interest in that it reflects an interplay between morpho-lexical, semantic, and syntactic knowledge of their language. Since I have described these processes in some detail elsewhere (Berman, 1980, 1982a; Berman & Sagi, 1981), the discussion below is confined to two types of errors in verb-pattern usage among Israeli children. Both error-types take the form of leveling of distinctions, but the first type, which occurs at the phase of initial syntax, is viewed as "immature" and pre-analyzed, while the second type of error, from around age four, is taken as evidence that the child has acquired the system *qua* system, but not achieved full, adult-like command of conventional lexicalizations within the system.

Below, we adopt the following annotation for ease of reference to the five *binyan* verb patterns under discussion: P1 = *kal* or *pa'al,* the basic or unmarked pattern, with the highest frequency in children's language, used for transitive verbs like *lakax* 'take', *shavar* 'break' and intransitives like *yashan* 'sleep', *baxa* 'cry' (and see fn. 4 on the convention of using past-tense 3rd masculine singular forms for citation); P2 = *nif'al*, typically passive as in *nilkax* 'be-taken', *nishbar* 'be-broken: INTRANS break' or middle-voice intransitive as in *nifca* 'get hurt', *nikra* 'tear, be/get torn'; P3 = *pi'el*, typically transitive, used mainly for action rather than state verbs like *ciyer* 'draw, paint', *sixek* 'play'; P4 = *hitpa'el*, often the middle-voice, intransitive reflex of active verbs in P3, e.g. P3 *perek* 'break-up'/P4 *hitparek* 'be broken-up', P3 *siyem* 'end' (= 'bring to an end')/ P4 = *histayem* 'end' (= 'come to an end'), and also in reflexives such as *hitlabesh* 'dress (oneself)' *hitraxec* 'wash (oneself)' and reciprocals such as *hitnashku* 'kiss each other'; and P5 = *hif'il*, most often causative as in *hilbish* 'dress someone', *hirkid* 'make dance', *hicxik* 'make laugh' = 'amuse', and also some-times inchoative as in *hishxir* 'blacken' (= 'make black/ become black'). Note that the traditional names for these patterns are all based on the root *p-'-l* meaning 'do, act', as used in the word *pó'al* 'verb', *po'el* 'a worker', *pe'ula* 'action'.

4.3.1. *Neutralization of semantic distinctions.* Beginning with the one-word stage, children use verbs as unanalyzed lexical items in all of the five verb patterns noted above, e.g. Pl *natan* 'give', *halax* 'go, walk'; P2 *nishbar* 'break-INTRANS', *nixnas* 'come in'; P3 *sixek* 'play', *siper* 'tell'; P4 *histakel* 'look'; and P-5 *hitxil* 'begin'. That is, they early on acquire instances of verbs in each pattern, even though initially they may adjust the surface shape of these verbs to their immature output processing strategies to yield, say, *fal* for Pl *nafal* 'fell', *bar* for P2 *nishbar* 'broke', or *kiy* for P4 *tistakli* 'look!' (Berman, 1977; 1978b). That is, such verbs are available to them as lexical amalgams in much the same way as an English-speaking 2 year old "knows" words like *go, look, broke.* Initially, however, Hebrew-speaking children typically use a given verb-root in only one pattern, in the form which for them is "basic." In many instances, this particular form is appropriate to the syntactic and semantic context in which it is used, as shown in the examples in (11-a) below; but in some cases it is extended to other, inappropriate contexts too, as shown in the examples in (11-b).

(11) (i) Basic / Causative   Adult Form   Root

     a. dina   *oxél-et* P1   banána
        Dina   is:eating-FEM   a banana

     b. ima   *oxel-et   oti   hayom   P5 *ma'axil-a*   ʔ-*x-l*
        Mommy   is:eating-FEM   me   today   is:feeding

    (ii) Transitive / Intransitive:

     a. uri   *zarak* P1   et   ha   nyar
        Uri   threw:away   OBJ   the   paper

b. ha   nyar   *zarak ba   pax   P2 *nizrak*   z-r-k
   the   paper   threw in:the basket   got:thrown

(iii) Intransitive / Transitive:

a. ha   simla sheli   *hitlaxlex-a* P4
   my   dress   got:dirty-FEM

b. ani   *hitlaxláx-ti*   et   ha   simla   P3 *lixláx-ti*   l-x-l-x
   I   became:dirty   OBJ   the   dress   made:dirty

(iv) Transitive / Reciprocal:

a. ani   *mexabek* P3   et   ha   dubi
   I'm   hugging   OBJ   the   teddy:bear

b. anáxnu   *mexabk-im*   P4 *mitxabk-im*   x-b-k
   we're   hugging:TRANS   are:hugging
                                        (each other)

Neutralizations such as those in the (b) examples above—and we have dozens of similar examples from a wide range of children aged around 2 to 2½ years old—correspond to the kinds of levelings noted for English causatives by Bowerman (1974) and for other predicate-argument relations by Lord (1979). However, Hebrew does NOT generally admit of the same verb pattern in different syntactic environments and for different predicate-argument relations (with very few exceptions, such as *hitxil* 'begin', which is used in both 'the lesson began' and 'the teacher began the lesson'). Thus, the Hebrew-speaking child cannot be assumed to be overgeneralizing from verbs that have the same shape in both transitive and intransitive environments, such as English *I broke the vase/the vase broke, they're spinning the top/ the top is spinning, you'll burst the balloon/ the balloon will burst,* nor yet from use of the same verb form in pairs like *I'm washing the dolly / I'm washing (myself)* or *they hugged the baby / they hugged (each other)*. On the contrary, sentences like those in (11-b) above are very un-Hebrew in sound indeed, and are not found among older children— although foreigners learning Hebrew as a second language do make precisely the same kinds of errors as these, as shown in a study by Kantor (1978).

These levelings of verb-pattern distinctions are not due to the relative formal complexity of the patterns which children avoid in such cases for, as noted, children of age 2 use verbs in all the five patterns at issue here. Moreover, children may in one context avoid the very pattern which they overextend in another context—as shown by comparing the examples in (b) of (11-iii) and (11-iv) above. Rather, it seems that at the point where children already use a verb in the appropriate semantic and syntactic context, they do not as yet have free "mental space" to also attend to the appropriate lexical class of the verb by using a *binyan* pattern other than the one most familiar to them for that specific verb. Subsequently, usually later on in the third year, children will start to vary the pattern they use for a few very familiar verbs, to yield, for instance, both basic *oxel* 'eat' and causative *ma'axil* 'feed', both transitive *roxec* for washing something or someone and reflexive *mitraxec* for washing themselves, or both intransitive, middle-voice *nishbar* 'get broken' and transitive *shavar* 'break'. A yet later development, around age 4, is when children begin to perceive certain general relations expressed by use of a given verb pattern, indicating that they have abstracted out such notions as causative, intransitive, or reflexive, as realized through verb-pattern alternations in their language. Such knowledge is manifested in the kinds of errors noted next.

4.3.2. *Pattern Substitution.* This kind of error is common between around ages 4 to 6, when children have already moved into the system conceptually, but do not always know how a given concept happens to be lexicalized in the conventional usage for a given verb-root. Errors of this kind are illustrated in (12) and (13) below, where the forms on the left list other verbs with the same root which these children already know, while the forms on the right are the ones used in the standard lexicon of current Hebrew.

(12) Transitive Verbs:

    a. *saméax* P1 —ze tamid *masmíax P5 oti cf. *mesaméax* P3
       be:happy   it always makes:happy me   make:happy

    b. *ne'elam* P2 —ha kosem *ilem P3   et hashafan
       disappear   the magician made:vanish the rabbit
          cf. *he'elim* P5
             make:invisible, conceal

(13) Intransitive Verbs:

    a. *pogesh* P1 —kan hem*mitpagsh-im P4 cf. *nifgash-im* P2
       meet:TRANS   here theymeet (each other)   meet, join:RECIP

    b. *mefarek* P3 —kol ha migdal *nifrak P2 cf. *hitparek* P4
       take:apart   all the tower came:apart   come:apart,
                        break:up

These errors, as may be true of "late errors" in general, give as much insight into what children do know as into what they do not know about their language. Errors of this kind are all within the boundaries of transitivity appropriateness, in the sense that children may use an intransitive P2 verb form where a P4 verb is required (13b) or an intransitive P4 verb in place of required P2 (13a); and they may use a transitive, causative P5 form in place of P3 (12a) or vice versa (12b). But they will not make haphazard, implausible kinds of errors, cutting across the transitivity axis, as it were. Rather, these errors reveal that children divide events up into two major types—transitive, active, causative versus intransitive, passive or middle-voice, reflexive or reciprocal—and they assign verb-pattern values accordingly. What children may still not know at late preschool age is which of the two patterns—transitive P3 and P5, intransitive P2 and P4—happens to be used in contemporary Hebrew for lexicalizing such concepts as causativity or reciprocality, say, with respect to a given verb-root. Once again, the few such errors which are widespread across children, and which persist on to school-age, may be indicative of more general lexical change in the language.

That "transitivity" is taken as crucial by children is further shown in the errors they make in their use of the basic P1 pattern, which we have claimed is uniquely "non-negotiable," since not only does it not encode any additional semantic content such as causation, reciprocality, inchoativeness, etc., but it alone is used freely for both transitive verbs like those meaning 'do' or 'make', 'give', 'take', 'want', 'see', and 'find' and for intransitive verbs like those meaning 'come', 'laugh', 'cry', 'sleep', and 'walk'. Where older preschoolers do occasionally err with P1 verbs, it is by rewording them in the P5 pattern, which typically expresses causativity, and is thus highly transitive in content. They do so in order to give verbs which are transitive in P1 an effect of heightened, causative type transitivity, as where P5 *mahafix* replaces P1 *hofex* 'turn upside down', P5 *himriax* replaces P1 *marax* 'smear, cover with goo', or P5 *le-halxic* 'to press, push down on' replaces conventional P1 *li-lxoc* from the same root. Such extensions of the P5 pattern indicate that children are using it to render conventional P1 transitive verbs more intensely transitive and causative in impact in an innovative fashion which is highly plausible, given the morpho-semantics of the *binyan* verb-pattern system of their language.

4.4. *Agreement Errors*

As noted in Section 1 above, agreement phenomena are widespread in Hebrew, and they constitute an important source of insight into how children tackle a system of marking which is formally quite complex and which is semantically largely unmotivated, or at best redundant. Initial acquisition takes place along with the bulk of other morphosyntactic development during the third and early part of the fourth year, with subject-verb agreement being controlled earlier than noun-adjective agreement, and number agreement before gender agreement by and large (Levy, 1983; Kaplan, 1983). Following this early acquisition, three types of agreement errors seem particularly ingrained, in some cases persisting beyond early school-age: in adjective agreement of gender with nouns which are lexical exceptions, in use of gender marking on numerals, and in number and gender marking on verbs in verb-initial strings with a following subject.

4.4.1. *Singular-Plural Gender Conflicts.*   Persistent errors of agreement are caused by nouns which are masculine in form—lacking, for instance, typical feminine endings such as stressed *-a* or unstressed *-et*—but which happen to be feminine in gender assignment. Thus, children may say *esh xazak* 'fire strong' (= 'a big fire') when *esh xazak-a* is required; or *éven gadol* 'stone big' (= 'a big stone') in place of *éven gdol-a*. Such errors are corrected, once the specific nouns are learned as isolated lexical exceptions, on the basis of a wider exposure to more examples, and possibly also familiarity with very common, almost formulaic noun-adjective combinations, such as *dérex aruk-a* 'way long-FEM' (= 'a long way'), *ir gdol-a* 'a big city'.

A more complicated type of agreement conflict is incurred by irregular nouns of the kind noted in Section 4.2.3 above, where a masculine noun takes a feminine plural *-ot* ending or, conversely, a feminine noun takes a masculine plural *-im* ending. In such cases, children adopt the following strategy: if the plural noun ends in *-im,* so does the adjective, if the plural noun ends in *-ot,* so does the adjective—even though in fact agreement is dictated by the SINGULAR gender of the noun. In interpreting (14) below, recall that initially children regularize the plural form of the noun in isolation (Section 4.2.3, example (8) above), so that subsequently the plural marker they assign to adjectives will depend on whether they use the correct plural of the noun—as in (ii)—or whether it is still regularized- as in (i) below.

					Adjective Agreement Marking	
					Children	Adults
(14)	MASC	Noun	+ FEM:PL			
	kir	'wall'	*kir-ot*	(i)	**kir-im lvan-im*	*kir-ot lvan-im*
					OR	white walls
				(ii)	*kir-ot *lvan-ot*	
	FEM	Noun	+ MASC:PL			
	beca	'egg'	*bec-im*	(i)	**bec-ot triy-ot*	*bec-im triy-ot*
					OR	fresh eggs
				(ii)	*bec-im *triy-im*	

The asterisked forms represent regularization of agreement marking with the same suffix used for both noun and adjective, as a way of resolving the complex grammatical requirement of going from singular masculine noun with feminine plural ending to a masculine plural adjective, or the other way round for singular feminine nouns that are irregular in plural formation. This requires children to abstract out gender and number marking, where these are conflated within a single morpheme, *-im* for masculine and plural, *-ot* for feminine and plural. Moreover, this type of conflict runs counter to the widespread phenomenon of "suffix harmony" in the language—e.g. *yeled gadol diber* 'a big boy talked' vs. *yald-a gdol-a dibr-a* 'a big girl talked' vs. *yelad-im gdol-im medabr-im* 'big children are talking'.

It seems to me that here, too, as in several other types of later repairs of errors, children first move into the grammatically correct formulations in their use of formulaic, very frequent and familiar types of combinations—as in the common expressions *shulxan-ot arux-im* 'tables laid' in the sense of tables that have been set up for a party or celebration, as well as *mil-im xadash-ot* 'new words' or *zug-ot boded-im* 'single pairs', familiar to children from early school and play.

4.4.2. *Gender of numbers.*   A related conflict may account for the widespread violation of gender agreement of numerals with the nouns which follow them, a usage which continues through high school, and which affords another instance of incipient change in the language (Bolozky, 1979a). Numbers precede nouns, except for *exad, axat* 'one: MASC,FEM', and the masculine numbers generally take the *-a* ending—e.g. FEM *shalosh* vs. MASC *shlosh-a* 'three', FEM *xamesh* vs. MASC *xamisha* 'five'. Elsewhere, however, stressed *-a* is the basic marker of feminine gender in nouns, adjectives, and past-tense verbs, and it is the one first perceived as such as children. It is thus not surprising that young children, as well as many older speakers, resolve the problem by using the morphologically unmarked FEMININE form of the numerals across the board, especially as this is the form that is used in citation and in counting.

4.4.3. *VS sentences.*   As noted, children acquire subject-verb agreement for number, gender, and person by around age 3. In verb-initial strings, however, there is a persistent tendency to leave the verb in the unmarked 3rd person masculine singular, as shown by the following examples from the speech of 4 to 5 year olds.

(15) **haya* sham hamon balonim —cf. hem *hayu* sham
     was there many balloons   they were there

     *nafal lo et ha mitriya —cf. ha mitriya shelo *nafl-a*
     fell him OBJ the umbrella   his umbrella   fell-FEM

     *nishpax al-ay máyim —cf. ha máyim *nishpex-u* alay
     spilt on-me water   the water spilled-PL on me

The children's utterances to the left are wellformed except for the fact that the verb remains in the neutral masculine singular, by contrast with their possible SV counterparts to the right. By age 4, children do already observe agreement from subject to verb, and they also know the number and gender of the nouns in (15) as shown by data taken from the same contexts, such as *balon-im adum-im* 'red balloons', *mitriya shxor-a* 'black umbrella-FEM'. But there is a strong tendency to pick on the neutral form of the verb when it is sentence-initial, even when children are asked to repeat such VS constructions with the verbs in the correct plural and/or feminine forms—as reported to me by Barbara Josman, who conducted such an experiment with 3 to 6 year olds.

This clearly indicates that for Hebrew-speaking children agreement works forward—as is typical in moving from subjects to the verbs they control, and from head nouns to their following modifiers across the language. Evidently the child has the noun he wishes to refer to in mind when he starts talking, but while he is busy focusing on producing the verb, he will ignore the grammatical features of the noun which is to follow. That is, even though the verb will be in the appropriate pattern and tense, it will not carry ''non-autonomous'' features that are triggered by a following subject-noun. While this leveling of verb-subject agreement is more marked in children's usage, it does sometimes occur in verb-initial constructions in adult speech as well, again indicating a possible reorganization in the language. However, children's reanalysis here is so widespread and, as shown by the repetition task noted earlier, so resistant to correction, that this neutralization of backwards agreement can in no way be attributed solely, or even mainly, to input.

4.5. *Anaphora and Deixis*

These are topics which have not been studied in any depth for Hebrew child language, but some typical errors do emerge from our different sources of data.

4.5.1. *Definite Marking.* Prefixing of *ha-* 'the' to a noun to mark it as definite is acquired early, by around age 3, although initially children tend to overextend it to contexts where the content of the referent is known to themselves but not necessarily to their interlocutors, as has been found for English and other languages. One kind of persistent error is semantically based, where children treat names of toys—e.g. *dubi* 'teddy-bear' and *buba* 'doll'—and of family members such as *axot* 'sister', *dod* 'uncle', as though they were proper nouns, which is what they may well be for children. Thus, in describing a picture, a child will say *dubi yashen* 'teddy-bear is-sleeping', or he will tell what happens *ba báyit shel dod sheli* 'in-the house of uncle of-me' (= 'my uncle'), instead of saying *ha dubi, ha dod* respectively.

Another type of error is more formal in origin. Adjectives follow their head nouns and agree with them in definite marking, a rule which children acquire by the time they start using adjectives freely during their fourth year. Noun compounds, however, which also take the form of head + modifier, violate the expected order of *ha*-head + (*ha*) modifier, thus: *naaley ha-báyit* 'shoes:POSS *the*-house' (= 'the slippers'), definite marking being attached to the modifier noun alone. Children regularize these to yield such forms as **ha naaley-báyit* 'the shoes:POSS-house' ('slippers'), or **ha mexabey esh* 'the extinguishers:POSS fire' (= 'the firemen') in place of required *mexabey ha esh*. This is clearly because children do not freely produce novel compounds until about age 5 or even 6, the compounds which they do use—as in those meaning 'slippers' or 'firemen'—being initially confined to those lexicalized as such in the language. Thus, children simply prefix *ha-* 'the' to the entire compound, which they perceive as unanalyzed amalgams, even where the morphology explicitly marks the head noun as having a bound, genitive form. Evidence that this is the case is provided by the fact that children also sometimes pluralize lexicalized compounds as though they were single words—e.g. *yom hulédet* 'day:POSS birth' (= 'birthday') is given the plural form **yomuladet-ót* in place of required *yemey hulédet,* and *béged yam* 'wear:POSS sea' (= 'bathing suit') is pluralized by young children as **begedyám-im* in place of required *bigdey yam.*[9] In fact, it is only around early school age, when children can quite freely produce innovative compounds for different semantic relations and with different morphological modifications of the initial, head noun (as shown by a pilot study conducted by Barbara Hecht and myself with second-graders) that they also first show knowledge of the complex grammatical requirement for marking definiteness on the second, modifying noun rather than on the initial head noun of compounds.

Note, moreover, that children have difficulty in assigning the definite marker to genitives in general, not only to those which take the form of bound compound nouns. Thus, even after children are clearly able to use the definite marker correctly with nouns and their associated adjectives, they will still say things like *naaláyim shel ima* 'shoes of Mommy' instead of *ha naaláyim shel ima* to mean 'Mommy's shoes', or *hiney báyit shel xavera sheli* 'here's house of friend of me', whereas 'my friend's house' should take the definite marker to yield *ha báyit shel.* Perhaps because genitives are inherently definite in reference, children do not seem to feel the need to mark this explicitly by adding *ha-* 'the' to the head noun which initiates such strings. Again, with reference to family members, even adults say things like *aba sheli* 'daddy of me' (= 'my father'), rarely normative *ha aba sheli.*

4.5.2. *Pronouns: Nominative and Inflected.* The first type of "pronominal" used by all Hebrew-speaking is the typically deictic item *ze* meaning 'it, this, that', which remains unmarked for number or gender until well into the third year. By the middle of the third year, children freely use first person singular marking by *ani* 'I', as well as the beginnings of some type of anaphoric reference through *hu* 'he', followed somewhat later by *hi* 'she' with reference both to females and to feminine inanimate nouns. Second person marking with *ata* and *at* in the masculine and feminine singular respectively is at first highly variable, stabilizing around the age that third and second as well as first person plural pronouns start being used freely. Through to school age, however, children extend the use of the masculine plural pronouns *atem* 'you' and *hem* 'they' to contexts where feminine *aten* and *hen* may be required. The error is not conceptually based, for 3 year olds do distinguish between masculine and feminine in the singular pronouns for 'he' vs. 'she' and subsequently also for 'you'.

---

[9]Further evidence that highly lexicalized compounds are perceived very much as indivisible units is provided by the first-grader who wrote the word for 'school', a compound formed of *bet* + *sefer* 'house-poss + book', not with the required five consonantal elements *b t s f r,* but as a fused form with the letters representing *b c f r* respectively.

Rather, it relates to the more basic or less marked nature of masculine gender in general. Thus, children acquire the masculine plural *-im* before *-ot,* and they use masculine forms of adjectives before the feminine in both singular and plural. In terms of formal marking in the language, feminine gender is marked by the addition of a suffix to the masculine stem or citation form for animate nouns and all adjectives as well as verbs. Where leveling occurs, it is in favor of the masculine form—for instance, past tense has a single, nonfeminine suffix in the third person plural, and current usage has adopted the masculine form of future tense for both second and third person plural. Syntactically, masculine nouns determine concord of verbs with subjects to yield, say, 'one boy and five girls are walking + MASC.', and of adjectives with head nouns; and, finally, inattention to agreement constraints such as those noted in Section 4.4.3 above with respect to verb-subject agreement, will always be in the direction of unmarked masculine forms.

A more complex set of formal alternations is provided by the oblique pronouns, that is, all instances where a pronoun functions as other than the grammatical subject, so that it is inflectionally affixed to a preposition. Compare, for instance, the forms of third masculine singular in a sentence like: *hu lakax et shel-o ve diber it-o al-av* 'he took OBJ his and talked to-him about-it = him'. An early error, when children first start using prepositions, is use of the free, subject form of the pronoun after a preposition—as in Column I below. Subsequently, children learn to blend preposition plus pronoun strings into a single, fused form, but this often differs from the standard form used in the language, as shown by comparing Columns II and III below.

(16) Errors in forms of oblique pronouns following prepositions

I. Immature Free Form (initial syntax)	II. Intermediate Fused Form (age 3 to 4)	III. Standard Form (age 4–5)
al hu 'on he'	**alo*	*alav* 'on him'
mi at 'from you:FEM'	**miménax*	*mimex* 'from you'
bishvil anáxnu 'for we'	**bishvilánu*	*bishvilénu* 'for us'
ecel hem 'near they'	**eclehém*	*eclam* 'near them'

As far as we can tell from naturalistic data, children do not have difficulty in comprehending the fused forms of prepositions plus pronouns—so that this system provides a further instance of errors that seem confined largely to production (as in stop/spirant alternations noted in Section 4.1.1 and verb-pattern *binyan* changes noted in Section 4.3.1). Moreover, the initial type of error noted in (16) above, where children use free forms of prepositions followed by free forms of pronouns, is shortlived, even though there are other systems in the language where children continue to prefer a nonbound or analytic formulation through to school age (as in the extended use of the genitive particle *shel* 'of' to mark possession, rather than the bound, noun-compound form noted in Section 6.2.3 below). One reason is that this subsystem, like the system of tense-marking on verbs or number and gender agreement discussed earlier in this chapter, is by way of constituting a "formal imperative" for speakers of Hebrew. That is, even though there may be no semantic motivation for this, the fact is that the grammar of Hebrew makes it obligatory to inflect all pronouns as suffixes on prepositions just in case they are oblique, that is, in nonsubject position in the sentence. Moreover, both prepositions and their associated pronouns constitute a relatively restricted, closed set of high-frequency items in the language. The importance of this latter point is shown by the fact that even very young children invariably fuse prepositions and pronouns in the case of those combinations which show up earliest in their usage—specifically with dative and possessive-marking *le-* 'to' in forms like *yesh li* 'be to me' (= 'I have') or *tni li* 'give (to) me'; with the possessive marker *shel* 'of' in forms like *sheli* 'my, mine' or *shelánu* 'our, ours'; and with the object marker *et* in forms like *oti* 'me', *oto* 'him, it' (Dromi, 1979; Kaplan, 1983).

Errors which do persist in this subsystem, as shown in the middle column of (16) above, can be attributed to the complexity of historically determined factors which specify the specific shape of both the prepositional base and its pronoun suffix across the system. These include the fact that (i) the preposition sometimes changes form before a pronoun suffix—compare object marking *et* in its free form with *ot-o* 'him', *ot-ánu* 'us', or the free form of *im* 'with' and its bound form in *it-o* 'with him', *it-ánu* 'with us'; (ii) some pronouns take a singular form, others a plural form when following prepositions—e.g. *shel-i* 'of me' (= 'my') compared with *al-ay* 'on me', *bishvil-o* 'for him' but *bil'ad-av* 'without him'; and (iii) there may be confusion between pronouns affixed to prepositions and those affixed to nouns to form bound possessives—e.g. *bet-ex* 'your house' but *ot-ax* 'ACC-you', *bet-énu* 'our house' but *ot-ánu* 'us'. It is not surprising, then, that it takes children several years to master the specific details of these forms, and that many of their errors are similar to those found in less standard adult usage as well (e.g. many high-schoolers use a singular suffix in the form of **al-ex* 'on you' rather than required *al-áyix*, or they "regularize" accusative 'you' so that it has the same suffix as the possessive form of nouns to yield **ot-ex* and not normative *ot-ax*). Some of the most difficult combinations are not mastered at all by preschoolers, e.g. *bli + ani* 'without I' should yield *bil-ad-ay* 'without me', and even 5 year olds may say **kmo hi* 'like she' rather than the fused form *kamóha* 'like her'. Nonetheless, 5 year olds do show rich control of most of this system, as shown by the following set of examples from my child at age 5;3, when playing a game of 'If I were':

(17) If I was a cup, people would drink from me: *mi+ani*   → *miméni*
     If I was coffee, people would drink me: *et+ani*   → *oti*

If I was eyes, people would see through me:	*dérex+ani*	→ *darki*
If I was a bench, people would sit on me:	*al+ani*	→ *alay*

These were clearly not acquired as rote items; both this 5 year old, and other 4 to 5 year olds whose spontaneous speech has been recorded, do show use of a wide range of such combinations as: *al + hi = aléha* 'on her'; *axarey + hu = axarav* 'after him'; *leyad + anáxnu = leyadénu* 'next to us'. The ability to make such rich use of this complex system by late preschool age can be explained by the factors both of the "formal imperative" noted earlier and the wide variety of syntactic constructions which require oblique pronouns in Hebrew—including ones like those in (17), as well as the occurrence of resumptive pronouns in relative clauses—to yield the equivalent of 'the kids that I was playing *with-them* '—and left-dislocated clauses—as in 'that chair, you can't sit *on-it*'.

4.5.3. *Pronoun Deletion and Copying.*   The rules governing pronoun deletion—e.g. of subjects of an embedded clause coreferential to a main clause noun as in *ron amar še- yelex* 'Ron said that will-go' (= 'that Ron will go') or of objects that are understood from the general context as in *aval hu kvar natan li* 'but he already gave me Ø'—are rather complex, and have not been studied for Hebrew discourse in general (see, for instance, Clancy, 1985, on problems of pronoun ellipsis in Japanese). The situation is also far from clear with respect to pronoun copying or resumption, which is obligatory in oblique environments in relative clauses and in left-dislocations, as noted in the preceding subsection. Here, children seem to give major consideration to communicative clarity and transparency, rather than to strictly grammatical constraints. The examples in this subsection are from children around age 5, and they typically manifest semantically redundant repetition of subject pronouns following a fully specified subject noun, thus:

(18) a. ha   yéled   *hu*   mesaxek   im   ha   galgal
        the   boy   he   is:playing with the   wheel

   b. ha   anashim   *hem*   mexakim   la   otobus
        the   people   they   are:waiting for   the bus

   c. aval   ima   *hi*   omeret   li   le   hoci
        but   Mommy   she   tells   me   to   take:out

      kcat   et   ha   sroxim
      a-bit   OBJ   the   laces

Similarly, research in progress by Shosana Rabinowitch with children of late preschool age indicates that in forming relative clauses they consistently tend to copy the subject pronoun, even though this is not done in standard usage—e.g. *ha yéled še hu nafal ba máyim* 'the kid that *he* fell in-the water', *ha isha še hi ra'ata et ha naxash* 'the woman that *she* saw OBJ the snake'. Pronoun copying of the subject in free clauses as in (18) seems to derive from children's need to give themselves time out to decide what they are going to say about the topic, or to give a contrastive impact to the topic noun, as in (18c). As noted, however, this is an area which requires systematic study for children's language in Hebrew, on the basis of parallel investigation of such constructions in adult discourse.

Conversely, children sometimes fail to pronominalize where this might be preferred in discourse—although in general lexical repetition is a far more acceptable rhetorical device in Hebrew than it is, say, in English (Berman, 1979b). The repetitions noted below may be due to difficulty of processing, or because children sense that a pronoun may reduce uncertainty of reference, as discussed in Karmiloff-Smith (1979a).

(19) a. ha *kof* kafac al ha keresh ve axarkax ha yeladim natnu la *kof* le-exol

'the MONKEY jumped on the plank and afterwards the kids gave to-the MONKEY to-eat (= gave him some food)'

   b. ha yeled shote *xalav,* aval ha *xalav* nofel al haricpa ve ha xatul melakek et ha *xalav*

'the boy is:drinking MILK, but the MILK fell on the:floor and the cat is:licking OBJ the MILK'

Alongside of redundant pronoun copying as in (18) and pronoun avoidance through lexical repetition as in (19), Hebrew children's language shows very many instances where object pronouns are omitted. This often happens where the referent of the object-pronoun is clear from context, even though grammatically it needs to be explicitly mentioned. Examples of such ellipsis include:

(20) a. ve hi lo yodat mi hevi *et ze,* ve hi xoshevet še ha shem ohev ota ve hu hevi Ø

'and she doesn't know who brought IT, and she thinks that God loves her and he brought Ø'

   b. axarkax hu herim Ø ve az hi tafsa et ha kadur

'afterwards he picked:up Ø and then she caught OBJ the ball'

   c. ha ish shaxax et ha mitriya, az ha yéled rac la tet lo Ø

'the man forgot OBJ the umbrella, so the boy ran to give him Ø'

It thus appears that although by age 4 to 5 children have formal control of the pronoun system, they do not yet master constraints governing (i) where a pronoun is grammatically redundant, though it may function as a way of focusing on the topic; (ii) where a pronoun is grammatically preferred, although repetition of the lexical item makes reference less ambiguous; and (iii) where a pronoun is necessary, even though reference is clear when it is omitted. Preschoolers thus show a sense of discourse requirements of clarity, transparency of reference and so on, but for them such pragmatic considerations override formal constraints of when and where pronominalization is required by the grammar of their language.

4.6. Syntax

Hardly any research has been conducted on developing syntax in Hebrew, although the general impression is that it is relatively error-free from around age 3. This may be because more complex structures, such as complement and adverbial clauses, are maturationally determined in terms of the lexical and conceptual content of the relation between main clauses and their associated subordinate clauses, rather than being in any strict sense more "syntactically complex." Besides, as noted in Section 1.1 above, Hebrew word order is largely pragmatically dictated and allows for great flexibility within and across major constituents. Again, the use of word order in discourse has not been studied for either children's or for adult Hebrew, so that below we confine our remarks to two types of word-order errors and one common error in early subordination (Sections 4.6.1 and 4.6.2 followed by Section 4.6.3)

4.6.1 *NVN order.*   Young children seem generally to adhere to basic SVO order across the board. This may lead to error in the case of possessive sentences, which may first be treated as ordinary SVO in order—e.g. *ron yesh peca* 'Ron be (a) sore', *buba eyn nalayim* 'doll not-be shoes', followed by fronting of the existential particle to yield *yesh ron eca, *eyn buba nalayim, before appropriate use of dative-marking on the possessor noun to yield wellformed *yesh le ron peca* 'be to Ron (a) sore' = 'Ron has a sore', *eyn la buba nalayim* 'not to-the doll shoes' = 'the doll hasn't any shoes'. This error can be explained by early avoidance of NN strings, which two-year olds have difficulty in processing in terms of the semantic relations of possessor vs. possessee, as discussed, for instance, in Shoham's (1980) case-study of a two-year old's spontaneous productions and her interpretation of experimentally-designed strings. (See, also, Braine's (1976) claims about the limited range of semantic relations distinguished at this age.) Even slightly older children may mix the order of possessor and possessee nominals, to yield, for instance, *ha yéled shel ha kóva* 'the boy of the hat' rather than 'the hat of the boy' to mean 'the boy's hat', or *dalit shel kélev* 'Dalit of dog' rather than 'dog of Dalit' to mean 'Dalit's dog'. And Bar-Adon (1971) reports a child at the stage of early syntax who alternated between *kóva buba ina* 'hat dolly Rina' and *buba ina kóva* 'dolly Rina hat' in talking about the doll Rina's hat, which is standard as *ha kóva shel buba rina*.

In general, early word combinations manifest considerable fluctuation in the ordering of elements, so that a two-year old may say both *aba halax* 'Daddy went' or *halax aba* 'went Daddy', while at age 2;1 my daughter said *sími buba kóva* 'put doll hat' and a few minutes later she said *sími kóva buba,* both intended to get me to put the hat *on* the doll. Yet such noncanonic orders may occur even among young children who already do introduce markers of grammatical relations such as locative or dative prepositions, as in another example given by Bar-Adon (1971) of a child saying *uga a-tet le aba 'cake a-give to Daddy' where normally one might expect the verb to come first, as in la tet uga le aba 'to give cake to Daddy'.

Except for very clear instances of acquisitional variability such as these, it is hard to pinpoint strictly grammatical violations of word order constraints on major constituents since these, as noted, are by and large pragmatically flexible, and children's variations on canonic SVO order can only be evaluated in relation to their role in ongoing discourse. For example, in longer strings with more than two post-verb constituents, dative or oblique objects can easily be brought round before the direct object where the former is "highly individuated" in the sense of Hopper and Thompson (1980), or nondominant, as discussed by Erteschick-Shir (1979)—and for Hebrew, see Berman (1982b). Thus, to use Bar-Adon's example, both of the following are equally wellformed, depending on what is taken as background and what as new or more dominant information: natáti et ha buba le aba 'I-gave OBJ the doll to Daddy' and natáti le aba et ha buba 'I-gave to Daddy OBJ the doll'. What young children, however, tend to do more than adults is to place pronouns at the end of an utterance, after fully-specified lexical objects, as in, say, *natáti et ha buba lo 'I-gave OBJ the doll to-him', or *nasim et ha kubiyot ba 'we'll-put OBJ the blocks in-her = in-it', where normally the pronoun lo 'to-him' or ba 'in-it' would come before the direct object, given that pronouns are so highly referential and presupposed, hence nondominant.

It may be that ordering of elements in early child speech manifest a complex interplay between their emerging knowledge of the canonical or neutral grammatical organization of elements in a string, on the one hand, and their tendency to first verbalize what is foremost in their minds at the moment of utterance, leaving all the rest for later on. That is, they are unable to preplan how all the elements they wish to refer to in a given utterance will eventually be ordered with respect to one another. Given the flexibility of word order in Hebrew, this seldom involves them in gross ungrammaticalities across major constituents. But this short-term processing may well explain quite clear instances of deviant word order within constituents, as noted in the subsection which follows.

4.6.2. NP Internal Ordering.   Nouns take post-nominal modifiers except for quantifiers. The number 'one', however, follows nouns, as in yom exad 'day one' (= 'one day') vs. shney yam-im 'two days'. One expected error, hence, which is made by 4 year olds as well, is that they regularize 'one' so that it precedes the head noun just like other numbers, e.g. *hiney exad kof gadol ve exad kof katan 'here's one monkey big and one monkey small' instead of kof exad gadol for 'one big monkey', and kof exad katan for 'one small monkey'.

Inside the noun phrase, ordering of post-nominal modifiers is: Adjectives, Demonstratives, Possessives, but children often reorder these, as shown in the following examples from two 5 year olds.

(21) a. *hu   sam   et   ha   xulca   shelo   ha   kxula
he   wore   OBJ   the   shirt   his   the   blue
(cf. *ha xulca ha kxula shelo* 'his blue shirt')

b. *afílu   et   ha   séfer   haze   ha   gadol
even   OBJ   the   book   this   the   big
(cf. *ha séfer ha gadol haze* 'this big book')

This type of error may be explained by the influence of highly familiar routines, since possessives like *shelo* 'his' in (21a) and demonstratives like *haze* 'this' or 'that' in (21b) are so common immediately after a head noun used without any adjective. In that case, then, this error would be due to the effect of "linear ordering" strategies, in the sense of MacWhinney (1985). It may, however, be due to children's perception of possessives and demonstratives, as deictic elements, as more intimately connected to the noun than the more inherent, yet external properties denoted by adjectives such as 'blue' or 'big'.

4.6.3. *Overextension of* še- *'that'.* The single morpheme *še-* 'that' functions as the subordinator par excellence in current Hebrew, serving as: (i) a complementizer—e.g. *xashavti še- hu nafal* 'I-thought that he fell', *xaval še- hu halax* '(it's a) pity that he went'; (ii) the relative-marker—e.g. *ha yéled še-hirbic li* 'the kid that hit me', *ha meil še- ron natan li* 'the coat that Ron gave me'; and (iii) the adverbial marker, often combining with a preposition to form subordinating conjunctions—e.g. *xake ad še ani avo* 'wait until that I-come', *baxí-ti biglal še- ka'av li* 'I-cried because that (it) hurt me'.

Children typically overextend this marker to inappropriate contexts, in a way similar to that noted for overuse of *que* in French (Clark, 1985). Such contexts include the following. (i) Children use *še-* alone rather than *kše-* 'when', in turn contracted from more formal *ka'asher*—e.g. *aba lo haya še bá-ti* 'Daddy was not (there) that = when I-came'. This may be due to lack of distinction between the cluster in *kše-* and the form *še-*, although there is no evidence that children do not understand the difference between, say *kše amár-ti* 'when I said' and *še amár-ti* 'that I said'. This seems so pervasive, that it is likely that *kše-* may fall into general disuse in casual speech eventually. [10] (ii) Children also often use *še-* alone in place of explicit lexical marking of other adverbial relations as well—e.g. *baxí-ti še ka'ast alay* 'I cried that = because you were mad at me' (cf. *kiy, mipney še-* 'because') said by a child in answer to a "why" question; or *hu lakax mitriya še lo yitratev* 'he took (an) umbrella that he won't get wet' (cf. *kdey še-* 'so that'). Both the syntax and pragmatic context show that here, too, children possess the concepts of reason and purpose—as of time with 'when'—but they

---

[10]That this may be the case is evidenced by a note I saw written by an 18 year old high-school graduate, who asked a friend to meet him *še-agía* 'that (sic) I-arrive'.

omit the appropriate lexical marker in favor of simple 'that'. (iii) Children until well on in school age also add *še-* to question words to form subordinate clauses—e.g. *hu ose mikláxat, matay še hu kam* 'he takes (a) shower, when that he gets-up', *hu oxel lama še- hu ra'ev* 'he's eating why that he's hungry', one of the most typical manifestations of juvenile, and some less standard older, syntax in Hebrew.[11]

In each case, the context is such that children seem to have a clear idea of the logical and semantic relations obtaining between the different propositions. Their overuse of *še-* seems, rather, to be a simply surface collapsing of these different relations by means of one all-purpose subordinator, either by using *še-* in place of or without any other morpheme as in (i) and (ii) above, or by adding it to some other morpheme to express the same sense—of time, cause, and so on—as in (iii) above. Note, moreover, that this overuse of a single marker occurs after the very initial stage of syntax, when clauses tend to be simply juxtaposed without any overt connecting device at all. Thus in marking inter-clause relations as in other areas of grammatical development, we find that initially children will not mark relations by any overt means at all; they then proceed to overuse the most basic, least specific marker of all—in this case 'that', in another case, masculine plural *-im* or a single verb pattern for causative; while at the later, more mature stage of development, they can overtly mark a wide variety of relations by distinct and appropriately varied lexical and grammatical devices.

To sum up this section on "typical errors," a key issue with respect to Hebrew child language would be to specify, and try to explain, which are strictly developmental and hence transient, and which occur—with what degree of spread, at what ages, and for which sections of the native-speaking population—among older speakers, too. Even where details of such data are lacking, however, it seems clear that the kinds of errors noted above cannot be dismissed as largely the product of "input," unless this notion is reinterpreted in terms of the kind of input which seems particularly relevant for the Israeli child: the language which he hears, and learns, from his peers and other children (Section 9.4 below).

5. Error-Free Production

This is an important source of information on processes and strategies in language acquisition, one which has been largely disregarded for Hebrew, as for other languages (although see in this connection, Maratsos, 1978). Clearly errors are more noticeable, and more noted, than the less perceptible, neutral norm, so

---

[11]The pervasiveness of 'that' marking in juvenile Hebrew was manifested by my daughter, on returning to Hebrew dominance after a year in the United States. Thus, at about age 4;6, one of the earliest and most persistent errors of Hebrew interference in her formerly native-like English was overuse of the word *that,* so that she would say things like *because that I'm tired, when that I'll be (sic) ready, even that you say so* (Berman, 1979a).

that the data discussed below under this heading should be viewed as tentative, and, unless this is specifically noted, the data here refer to systems which are relatively rather than totally free of developmental errors. There may also be instances where I have identified error-free development with precocious acquisition, given the lack of indepth longitudinal studies of Hebrew-speaking children moving from the one-word to the initial syntax stage, or from points analagous to Brown's (1973) Stage I to II, II to III, etc., on the one hand, and the absence of Hebrew-based measures of development such as Lee & Canter (1971) or Crystal, Fletcher, & Garman (1976), on the other.

5.1. *Morphophonology*

5.1.1. Hitpa'el *Metathesis.* The *hitpa'el* verb-pattern, which is typically intransitive, middle-voice, or reflexive/reciprocal in content, incurs a metathesis that applies to all sibilant-initial verbs in this pattern as well as to related nouns and adjectives, but to them alone. The stem-prefix of this pattern is *Cit,* with the stem-initial consonant *m-* in the present tense, *h-* (usually zero) in past tense, and alternating for person in the future tense—e.g. *mit-raxec* 'is-washing', *hit-raxec* '(has) washed', *nit-raxec* 'we'll wash'. Just in case the root-initial is a sibilant— *s, z, sh,* or *c*—the prefixal *t-* metathesizes with the sibilant, and agrees with it in voicing, thus:

(22) Nonsibilant Root Initial   Sibilant Root Initial

r-x-c	*mit-raxec* 'washes'	*s-r-k*	*mi-s-t-arek* 'combs'
x-p-s	*hit-xapes* 'dressed up'	*sh-p-x*	*hi-sh-t-apex* 'spilled'
k-l-f	*nit-kalef* 'we'll peel'	*c-l-m*	*ni-c-t-alem* 'we'll photograph'
p-r-k	*le-hit-parek* 'to break up'	*z-r-z*	*le-hi-z-d-arez* 'to hurry up'

The rule is morphological, as it is confined to verbs in the *hitpa'el* pattern and their derivatives. Thus, dental stops and following sibilants do NOT metathesize within words—e.g. from the root *n-t-sh,* one gets expected *natsh-u* 'they left'; nor across morpheme boundary—e.g. from the root *z-w-z,* one gets the noun *t-zuza* 'moving', pronounced as phonetic *cuza;* nor across words, such as in the compound *bet-sefer* 'house-(of)-book' (= 'school').

I know of no instance where a child, whether at the one-word stage or later, fails to apply metathesis to a word that requires it in the *hitpa'el* pattern nor, conversely, do children overextend this metathesis to some other, inappropriate environment. That is, one never hears, say, **hit-sarek* for 'comb one's hair' or **hit-shatef* for 'take part', although these are pronounceable sequences in the language, and although they yield a far more transparent version of the prefix plus root, or stem, elements than their metathesized counterparts. The explanation seems to be as follows: Initially, children acquire verbs in this, as in other patterns, by rote, without any analysis into their component elements (Section 4.3.1 above). This is phonologically well-motivated, since children typically "pay attention to the ends of words" (Slobin, 1973), which in Hebrew—inflectionally a suffixing more than prefixing language—quite generally have main stress. An early verb is *le-histakel* 'look' from the root *s-k-l*, which is used in the imperative as an attention-getter, in the form *kel* or with the imperative suffix *-i* in the feminine, to yield something like *kyi* or *kli*, in place of the fully articulated *tistaké, tistaklí* 'look!'. At the stage of early syntax, as noted in Section 4.2.2, children lop off the imperative *cum* future suffix quite generally in forming imperatives. As a result, the imperative forms they come up with for the *hitpa'el* pattern include, for a verb with a nonsibilant root-initial consonant, *traxec* 'get washed!' in place of *tit-raxec* 'you'll wash' and, with common verbs that have a sibilant initial, forms like *stalek* 'get out!' vs. full *ti-s-talek, stakli* 'look!-FEM vs. full *ti-s-takli*, or *zdarez* 'hurry up!' vs. full *ti-z-darez*. Thus, what the older child has extracted is a "stem" which consists of the root-sibilant plus the prefix-dental as a package, in that order. Further evidence that children are in fact operating with their own kind of "stem" is provided by the many times they coined the agent-noun **stalk-an* 'runner-away' when asked to name someone who tends *le-histalek* 'to run away' from the root *s-l-k* (see, further, Clark & Brown, 1984).

This "pseudo-stem" extraction as a morphological device seems, however, to conflict with the semantics of the verb system of Hebrew. Thus, although the verb *le-histakel* 'to look' has no other related forms from the root *s-k-l*, other verbs used by children in the *hitpa'el* pattern do have such alternants. For instance, 4 year olds know both the *pi'el* pattern verb *shatef* 'include', make part of' and its *hitpa'el* counterpart *hi-sh-tatef* 'take part'; they may know both *le-salek* 'to kick out' and its *hitpa'el* version *le-his-t-alek* 'to get out'; both *le-zarez* 'to hurry someone' and *le-hiz-d-arez* 'to be in a hurry'; and even 3 year olds know both the transitive *pi'el* pattern verb *le-sader* 'to fix, tidy, arrange' and its intransitive *hitpa'el* counterpart *le-histader* 'to get into order, to get fixed up' from the root *s-d-r* (as in the noun *séder* 'order'; and see, too, for the root *s-r-k* 'comb someone's/one's own hair', the related noun *masrek* 'a comb'). What seems to be happening is that children initially work with some kind of "stem" element for these kinds of words, rather than the more abstract consonantal root. By the time they reach a point where they can generalize about the semantic basis for such alternations as transitive *pi'el* pattern verbs by contrast with their intransitive *hitpa'el* counterparts, as discussed in Section 4.3 above, they have already internalized the prefixless stem of *hitpa'el* verbs as starting with a sibilant plus dental consonant cluster. Formal recognition of the fact that transitive-intransitive pairs of verbs as well as semantically related nouns share a given, sibilant-initial root is a later development, and as such irrelevant to early pronunciations of these words.

5.1.2. *Past-Tense Vowel Deletion.* A pervasive phonological rule of Hebrew is that the stem-final vowel of verbs is reduced before a stressed suffix that starts with a vowel—as in *gomer* 'is finishing' vs. *gomr-im* 'are finishing'; *halax* 'he went' vs. *halx-a* 'she went'; *histalek* 'he ran away' vs. *histalk-u* 'they ran away'. Children invariably, as far as I can tell, observe this rule, even though in the present and past tense of most verbs, particularly those in the very common, basic *kal* pattern, this involves a departure from the otherwise unvarying stem form of CoCéC for present and CaCáC for past tense (as noted in Section 4.2.4 above). Consider, for instance, the following past-tense forms of the verb *gamar* 'finish'[12]

(23)		SG	PL
1		*gamár-ti*	*gamár-nu*
2 MASC		*gamár-ta*	*gamár-tem*
	FEM	*gamár-t*	*gamár-ten*
3 MASC		*gamár*	*gamr-ú*
	FEM	*gamr-á*	

Clearly, the base-form here is the unmarked third masculine singular CaCaC; and in fact the second plural forms *gamár-tem, gamár-ten* are regularized versions in general speech today, departing from normative, but asymmetric *gmar-tém/tén*. Yet children like adults do observe stem-vowel deletion before the open prefixes *-a* of 3.FEM-SG and *-u* of 3.PL, so that one never hears them saying things like **gamár-a* or **gamár-u*. This may be a phonological process which is so deeply ingrained in the language, and so closely tied in with the rhythmic stress patterns of its alternating stressed and "closed" syllables (Bolozky, 1979a), that it is by way of being a "predisposition" in the sense in which the term is suggested by MacWhinney (1985).

5.2. *Morphosyntax*

Here the decision whether to specify a system as relatively "error-free" or to include it under the heading of precocious acquisition was particularly difficult. Our decisions, which are bound to be arbitrary to some extent, were governed by a subjective reaction, when working through transcripts and other sources of data, at not finding errors where a more formally motivated analysis of a given subsystem (such as in Berman, 1978a) makes it appear quite complex and/or opaque to the linguist adult.

5.2.1. *Tense Assignment.*   After a very short initial period of fluctuation, children seem at the stage of early syntax to assign present and past, and later future-tense markings to verbs quite appropriately, despite the conceptual complexity of these distinctions and the wide morphological variability of Hebrew verbs. In transcripts by Sara Eyal of 30 children aged 1;9 to 2;9 in question-

---

[12]I am grateful to Joan Bybee for having drawn my attention to this potential, though non-realized, source of children's error.

answer sessions, and of 35 children aged 1;9 to 3;0 with various devices for eliciting free speech by Dafna Kaplan, we found virtually no errors in use of the appropriate tense in relation to a given pragmatic situation. The children did sometimes use an inappropriate time-word—such as 'yesterday' with present-tense verbs or the words for 'next week' with past-tense verbs, but they did NOT say things like *haláx-ti* 'I went' to talk about a future event, nor *elex* 'I'll go' when talking about something that was in the middle of happening, and so on.

The relative ease with which young children move into this system can be explained in several interlocking ways. Firstly, in semantic terms, as was noted in Section 3.2 above, children initially choose to encode certain events or event-types in one tense rather than another. Hence, their formulations may be conceptually, even lexically, restricted for a time, allowing them to move quite gradually into the system as a whole, once they start using all three tenses freely for a wide range of different verbs and event-types by around age 3. Secondly, by contrast with English and other of the languages discussed in this volume, Hebrew does not show a great diversity of tense/aspect forms at all, so that the only choice children need to make beyond the initial preference for imperatives and infinitives is between present, past, and future—all in a single unmarked aspectual form. Thirdly, as was noted in some detail in Section 4.2.4 above, the form of Hebrew tensed verbs allows children to settle on an unambiguous structural schema as a heuristic device: for the basic, most common verb pattern *kal*, they can rely on vowel alternations between present and past-tense forms, and elsewhere they relate to *m-* as an overall marker of present, past and future being distinguished, respectively, by specific person suffixes and prefixes. Besides, as noted earlier, Hebrew verbs have no basic or citation form, so that children learning the language are from the start forced to use some type of inflection, as a kind of "formal imperative" dictated by their language, along the lines noted with respect to oblique pronoun-marking in an earlier section (Section 4.5.2 above).

5.2.2. Definite-Object Marking.

Hebrew, like other, unrelated languages, requires a special case-marker on direct objects just in case they are definite—that is, they have the definite article *ha-* 'the' or a possessive suffix, or else they are proper nouns—and occur in clauses with "high transitivity" (Hopper & Thompson, 1980). Once Hebrew-speaking children start to use *ha-* freely, around the middle of their third year, the accusative preposition *et* is rarely omitted in contexts where it is obligatory. Rather, children often treat the combination of *et* + *ha-* as a single element, as shown below.

(24)

ten	li	*ta*	sfog		aba	lakax	*ta*	kadur
give	me	OBJ:the	sponge		Daddy	took	OBJ:the	ball
ani	roca	*ta*	bakbuk		shapáx-ti	*ta*		mayim
I	want	OBJ:the	bottle		I spilt	OBJ:the		water

This blending of the direct-object marker *et* with following *ha-* 'the' (pronounced typically without initial *h* at all) may correspond to English-speaking children's preference for contractions prior to the full forms noted by Brown (1973). Yet this does not explain why children consistently use *ta-*—or the full form *et ha-*—and not simply *(h)a-* in environments like those in (24) above.

One reason might be that by the time children are producing longer utterances, they take as canonical strings of the form S-V-Prep-O, as though whatever follows a verb must be overtly marked in some way. This is a plausible strategy for Hebrew, where many common verbs govern semantically unmotivated prepositions (as discussed in Section 5.2.3 below). Besides, adult usage, too, has extended *et* marking to non-normative post-verb position in possessives—which are very common sentence types in early child usage, too—to yield, for example, *yesh li et ze* 'be to-me OBJ it' (= 'I have it'), *haya le ron et ha séxel* 'was to Ron OBJ the sense' (= 'Ron had the sense') And *et* often shows up in non-normative positions following a verb in other constructions, too-e.g. *rashum li et ze* 'is-noted to-me OBJ it' (= 'I've got it noted down'); and children often say things like *nafal li ta kos* 'fell to-me OBJ-the cup' in the sense of 'I dropped the cup', in place of required *nafla li ha kos*. In general, children seem to identify postverbal *ha-* as always requiring a preceding *et*.

Moreover once the semantic concept of "object affected by an action" is established, the grammatical notion of direct object is not hard to acquire. Initially children may generalize by using *et* in any postverbal context followed directly by a definite noun, but they do subsequently develop a strong grammatical basis to their use of *et*. This is shown, for instance, by correct retention of the object marker in conjoining, as when a child aged 3;11 said *hi tola et ha xitulim ve gam et ha garbáyim* 'she's hanging (up) OBJ the diapers and also OBJ the socks'.

5.2.3. *Governed Prepositions.*

Many common verbs govern prepositions, even though semantically they express action-patient relations in the same way as do verbs that take direct objects. Compare, for instance, *hu hika et ha xamor* 'he beat OBJ the donkey' with *hu hirbic la yalda* 'he hit TO-the girl'; *hu ca'ak al ron* 'he shouted on = at Ron' but *hu caxak mi ron* 'he laughed from = at Ron'; and note such other common verb + preposition combinations as: *ba'at ba kadur* 'kicked IN-the ball', *azar la yeled* 'helped TO-the boy', *histakel al ha tmuna* 'looked on = at the picture'. Children make very few errors in choice of prepositions assigned to specific verbs, although this is an area where non-native speakers of Hebrew make numerous mistakes, and one which seems to distinguish middle-class children from those from less educated home backgrounds.

It seems that in this connection, input is particularly important in enabling children to designate a given preposition as going with a particular verb, where there is no clear semantic basis to the choice. Rather, what children do is learn the preposition as part of their lexical entry for specific verbs, so that any form of *hirbic* 'hit' is followed by *le-* 'to', any form of *naga* 'touch' takes a following *be-* 'in, at', and any form of *ka'as* 'be angry' takes a following *al* 'on'. This is evidently a successful learning strategy, which may have its origins in very common or incidental, almost formulaic exemplars, and which probably corresponds to the kinds of entries which adult speakers entertain for verb plus preposition combinations in their mental lexicon.

5.2.4. *Other Error-Free Systems.*   Other relatively error-free systems include the following: (i) Certain OBLIQUE PRONOUNS (Section 4.5.2) are fused with preceding prepositions very early on, without error. These include the bound prefixal preposition *le-* 'to', which has no free form, and which expresses several different semantic relations which are central to child language—e.g. possessives as in *yesh li kóva* 'be to-me hat' (= 'I have a hat'), datives as in *ten li kóva* 'give me a hat', and experientials as in *kar li* 'cold to-me' (= 'I'm cold'). Other oblique pronouns which are used correctly from early syntax are ones following *shel* 'of' and the object-marker *et,* initially first acquired by rote, as unanalyzed forms which, like *li* 'to me', are high in frequency in early child input and output—and this would explain why they occur without error unlike, say, *al-ay* 'on me' or *it-i* 'with me', which are first used at a rather later age, and give evidence of being perceived as combinations of preposition plus pronoun, rather than as rote-learned amalgams.

(ii) The fact that there are relatively few errors in WORD ORDER has been noted earlier—though see Section 4.6 above—and can be explained by Hebrew's being fairly high on the scale of "pragmatic word order" languages (Thompson, 1978), so that children can by and large refer to what interests them in the order they perceive as relevant. (iii) Indication of SEQUENCE OF TENSES is also quite error-free once children make use of more complex sentences, since this does not generally involve conflict between grammatical tense and real time, as well as because of the simple three-way choice to be made in the embedded verb, compared with English, Romance, or Slavic. Examples of such constructions which can be heard from quite young children include: *xikíti ad še bá-ta* 'I waited till (that) you-came' vs. *axake ad še- ta-vo* 'I'll-wait till (that) you'll-come', while the neutral present tense is quite generally retained in complement clauses—e.g. *yadati še hu yaxol* 'I-knew that he can', *hem xashvu še ze naxon* 'they thought that it (is) right'. (iv) Relatedly, CONDITIONAL CONSTRUCTIONS are quite straightforward in structural terms, so that once a child is ready to encode such notions conceptually, he will generally do so without error—e.g. *ec'ak im tarbic li* 'I'll-yell if you'll-hit me'. Irrealis conditionals, which are a later acquisition, all take the form of past-tense *haya* 'be' plus a present-tense, participial verb in both clauses—e.g. *hayí-ti ba im hayí-ta mazmin oti* 'I-was come/coming if you-were invite/inviting me' means the equivalent of both 'I would come if you invited me' and 'I would have come if you had invited me'.

Although later acquisition in general requires more detailed study for Hebrew, my impression is that more complex sentences produced at the age of late preschool are in general quite error-free. This may be attributed in part to the relative formal simplicity of various kinds of embedding devices in Hebrew on the one hand (Section 1.1 above), as well as to children's ability to resort to appropriate periphrastic constructions in order to avoid syntactically complex formulations—e.g. by use of impersonal sentences or fronting of non-subject nominals in order to avoid use of the passive, or by using finite 'that' clauses rather than more abstract lexical nominalizations, as in *ka'ásti al ze še hu lo hiskim* 'I-was-angry about it that he didn't agree' which is generally preferred in colloquial style to *ka'ásti al iy-haskama-to* 'I-was-angry about non-agreement-his'. In general, it seems that infelicities in later speech output are not due to strictly syntactic factors so much as to discourse issues of topic marking and topic maintenance, appropriate use of rhetorical connecting devices, or the relations between foregrounded and backgrounded elements of discourse.

6. Precocious and Delayed Acquisition

6.1. Precocious Acquisition

Where acquisition of a given system is precocious, or where it appears error-free, in the sense noted at the beginning of Section 5, the explanation may lie in its relative formal simplicity in Hebrew. A general impression is that the early syntax of Hebrew-speaking children, from around the middle of the third year, is rather "advanced" compared with findings for their English-speaking peers. This could be attributable to sociolinguistic factors of amount and range of input sources, as discussed in Section 9 below. It might also relate to the great deal of word-level complexity in Hebrew, which means that syntax per se can be ignored in the encoding of numerous semantic and grammatical categories which are relevant to early child speech. Thus, it should be borne in mind that the bulk of inflectional marking is mastered by around age 3, as noted in Section 3, and that, moreover, many early two-word utterances are relatively wellformed when compared with their English-speaking counterparts, for reasons outlined in Section 3.3. above.

6.1.1. *Number and Gender Marking.*   Two explanations may account for the fact that by age 3, children make so few errors in marking singular/plural distinctions. One is that conceptually, there is usually a good one-to-one fit between singular meaning 'one' and plural 'more than one' in Hebrew, so that children can hang on to the (stressed, and hence perceptually quite salient) endings -*im* and feminine -*ot*—acquired in that order—as clear markers of specific semantic content. In structural terms, we have noted that number agreement is pervasive across the language, from subject to verb and from noun to adjective; moreover, the same markers -*im* and -*ot* are used for both nouns and adjectives, as well as for all present-tense verbs in the plural, while the plural markers on past and future-tense verbs take the form of the suffix -*u,* or of an affix that partially reiterates the pronoun in first and second person (e.g. *anáxnu macá-nu* 'we found', *anáxnu ni-mca* 'we'll find'). This means that there is not a complex or opaque array of affixes for children to choose from as plural markers. And since agreement typically works forward in Hebrew, a child can quite reliably adopt the straightforward strategy of assuming that once a plural noun is used, whatever follows—a verb or adjective, say—will also be marked for plural.

The acquisition of masculine/feminine gender distinctions is a harder task, as it is semantically unmotivated except for animate nouns. Yet here, too, distinctions are manifested very early on, the most difficult part of the system being the case where both the plural and the feminine are fused in a single -*ot* morpheme. By age 3, children make the relevant distinctions most of the time, with subject-verb agreement being acquired prior to noun-adjective agreement, possibly because in general children only start to use a wider range of adjectives from around age 3. This early proficiency on the part of Hebrew-speaking children is explained, correctly in my opinion, by Levy (1983a) as the result of a formal strategy, whereby children come to realize that specific word endings encode feminine gender: initially, and primarily, final -*a*, sometimes overgeneralized to any final open syllable, and subsequently final -*t*. Thus, in this respect, the children's strategy is comparable with what has been noted by Karmiloff-Smith (1979a) for children learning French. Here, too, we may seek an explanation in terms of the notion of a "formal imperative" in the sense of knowledge dictated by a pervasive structural property of the language being learned. Because so-called "gender" is the basic way of categorizing nouns in the grammar of Hebrew, and because all nouns fall within this binary system, the distinctions are crucially ingrained in the language, and they have far-reaching formal consequences—for agreement between nouns and their associated verbs, adjectives, and demonstratives (though not for articles as in French and German, nor for case-marking as in the Slavic languages). The child is therefore impelled to encode them very early on, in a way which may perhaps be analogous to the early occurrence of tense-marking on Hebrew verbs (Section 3.2 above). Besides, input may play a role here, too. Thus children will have both a father who says *ani roce* 'I want' and a mother who says *ani roca* 'I want', and from around age 2 they are grouped together with their peers in mixed-sex nursery schools, and are addressed by parents and other caretakers in either masculine or feminine forms of verbs. Hence children are familiarized from very early on with the fact that verbs change according to who is being talked to or about (and canonical sentence-subjects are generally animate), and they will have numerous exemplars of the changes incurred by the two major classes of inanimate nouns in their language, as when someone asks them for *xaruz adom* 'a red bead' but *kubiya aduma* 'a red block'.

6.1.2. *Questions.* By age 3, children have acquired the main features of question formation in Hebrew. Thus Eyal (1976) notes that "77.8% of the children in our study, aged 21–30 months, with an MLU not over 1.2 to 2.6 in range, produced wellformed question sentences compared with English-speaking children, who only begin to master question forms at around 38 months, at MLU approximately 3.5.'' This can be explained by the relative structural simplicity of question formation in Hebrew, certainly by contrast with English subject-auxiliary inversion and the need for *do* support. In Hebrew, yes/no questions merely impose rising intonation on a declarative, something which children certainly do by the two-word stage.[13] Information questions merely require sentence-initial question words to replace the missing information—e.g. *ma hu ose* 'what he does, what he is-doing?'; *éfo rína yoshévet* 'where Rina sits/is-sitting?'; *láma ha yéled barax* 'why the boy ran away?' (= 'Why did the boy run away?'). There are occasional reports of children around age 2 not fronting the queston word— e.g. **ha yéled oxel ma?* 'the boy is-eating what?', which is exactly like its English equivalent in import—but these are not common, and they are short-lived. In input, too, very young children are asked things like *ma ze* 'what's this?', *mi ze* 'who's this/that?', *efo X?* 'where's X?' (Ninio, 1980). Thus, children may be aided in perceiving question words as always coming first, so that by the time they start to ask questions about non-subjects, they may already have internalized this "question word first" as a general strategy. The fact that case-marking and other prepositions are preposed with the question word—e.g. *im mi rina holexet?* 'with who Rina is-going?', *al ma ha yeled yoshev?* 'on what the boy is-sitting?'—may also be a facilitating factor, although this requires further study. In fact, few of the children in Eyal's (1976) study had any diffi-culty in understanding such questions. Moreover, although adult questions may entail subject-verb inversion, with the effect of making the verb more topic-like than the subject—e.g. *im mi holéxet rina?* 'with who is-going Rina?', *al ma yashav ha yeled?* 'on what sat the boy?'—it is safe to assume that in input to children the neutral, basic SVO order is maintained throughout in the form of questions. It thus appears that the formal simplicity of these constructions in both input and output accounts for the relatively early acquisition of question-type sentences by Hebrew-speaking children.

6.1.3. *Negatives*. Construction of wellformed negative sentences also seems to occur early in Hebrew child language. Thus Salzburg (1976) found that the large majority of her subjects, with an average age of 28 months and average MLU of 2.58, understood all the negative constructions investigated, except for the negation of a constituent inside of a conjoined sentence, such as 'Rina is-sitting and not is walking'. Her subjects were also able to produce all the following constructions, listed in descending order of frequency of appearance in spontaneous usage: main-verb negation—e.g. *rina lo boxa* 'Rina not is-crying';

---

[13]A more formal option, with the overt sentence-initial interrogative marker *ha'im* 'the if' = 'whether' does not occur until school age, since it is rare in colloquial speech in general. Thus, for children as for older speakers, rising intonation alone seems sufficient as a communicative marking of yes/no questions.

possessive negation—e.g. *eyn lánu praxim* 'not to-us flowers' (= 'we don't have (any) flowers'); and existential negation—e.g. *eyn praxim ba acic* '(there are) no flowers in-the vase'. This, too, can be explained by the relative structural simplicity of these mechanisms in Hebrew. The straightforward rule of placing the negative marker *lo* 'not' before the first verb will work in the vast majority of sentence types in Hebrew; and the morpheme itself is familiar from the one-word stage, where it is used in the sense of 'no' for rejection or protest. Use of this single morpheme in conjunction with verbs in any tense is the norm except in highly formal or literary Hebrew today, although formerly, the negator *eyn* was required in present-tense contexts, since these were nonfinite or participial forms in the classical language. (Compare, in this connection, Japanese children's use of the same morpheme for both past and present tense negatives noted by Clancy, 1985.) The only overextension of a negative marker, as noted in Section 3.1 above, occurs at the time of initial syntax, when children overuse *lo* with infinitives to indicate prohibition and lack of desire in general, before they begin to use the special marker *al* meaning 'don't' in negative imperatives.

Children also very early on form negative possessives and existentials correctly, by using the negative existential particle *eyn* in present tense, or the verb for 'be' negated by the ordinary *lo* elsewhere. Again, the morpheme *eyn* is familiar from the one-word stage, where it serves as the general marker of nonexistence or disappearance, so that children merely need to add suitable arguments to this as a negative predictor in order to produce syntactically wellformed utterances—e.g. *eyn máyim* '(there) isn't water', *eyn li máyim* '(there) isn't to-me water' (= 'I haven't got any water'). Recall, too, that Hebrew has numerous verb-initial type sentences, which children start producing quite freely during their third year. Thus, the familiarity of the negative morphemes from the pre-syntax stage; the fact that the two major negative markers *lo* and *eyn* are used with quite distinct types of semantic propositions; and the surface simplicity and regularity of the syntactic structure of sentences with a negative meaning combine to explain the rapidity with which children acquire command of sentence negation in Hebrew.

6.1.4. *Relative Clauses.*   The acquisition of relative clauses has not been the subject of investigation among Hebrew-speaking children for either comprehension or production. Our data do, however, show that 3 year olds use relative clauses on embedded subjects quite freely—e.g. *ha yalda še boxa* 'the girl that is-crying', *peca še koev li* '(a) cut that hurts me'. All children need to do in such cases is to insert the invariant, and very familiar, multifunctional subordinator *še-* 'that' (Section 4.6.3 above) between the head noun and the modifying clause. Besides, the head-modifier order is canonical for all noun-phrase types in Hebrew, as in *yalda yafa* 'girl pretty' (= 'a pretty girl'), *ha yalda ha tipsha* 'the girl the fool' (= 'the foolish girl'), and also with present-tense participials as in *péca koev* 'cut hurts' (= 'hurting cut' = 'a cut that hurts'). Thus, construction of relative clauses requires no special processing in terms of reordering of elements. Relative clauses on embedded direct objects are also structurally quite simple— e.g. *buba še ani macáti* '(a) doll that I found', *ha jula še hu lakax* 'the marble that he took'. The most difficult type of construction is with embedded oblique noun phrases, where pronoun copying is required—e.g. *ha yéled še ani sixákti it-o* 'the boy that I played with-him', *miflécet še ani mefaxed mimé-na* '(a) monster that I'm afraid of-her'. Even these constructions appear accessible to children's production from quite an early age, evidently because they, too, make use of the all-purpose subordinator *še-* 'that'; the pronoun copy remains in clause-final position and does not need to be moved; and it is affixed to a preposition in forms which are independently familiar to children for inflecting oblique pronouns (Section 4.5.2).[14]

Thus, again, structural regularity, in the dual sense of not requiring complicated restructuring of basic SVO type strings and of being consistent with forms and phrase-types required independently in the language, can account for the relative ease with which Hebrew-speaking children move into the task of relative-clause production at early preschool age.

6.2. *Delayed Acquisition*

Late acquisition of a system can be attributed not only to relative formal and/or conceptual complexity, but also to the availability of periphrastic options. These enable children to encode given semantic relations and pragmatic functions by various other means of expression (as in the case of passives, discussed in Section 6.2.2 below), and they also allow children to rely on more colloquial, often analytic devices to avoid constructions which will be acquired later, with added exposure to more formal registers (as noted for possessives and accusatives in Sections 6.2.4 and 6.2.5 below). Various kinds of late acquisitions can, moreover, be attributed to the impact of Israeli school-learning: (i) Literacy provides an aid in segmentation of strings into words, affixes, and so on, and it also helps speakers to recognize historically distinct segments which, while neutralized in today's pronunciation, incur morphophonemic alternations, and are still manifested in the writing system. (ii) Access to the written language also provides exposure to a more formal, literary style, often based on classical norms, where the gap between everyday spoken usage and the style of written texts of all kinds is particularly marked in Hebrew.(iii) Formal school study of "grammar" (consisting mainly of rules for vocalization of Biblical Hebrew, rules for word formation in distinguishing between different patterns of deriva-

---

[14]A more extensive survey of preschool Hebrew syntax currently under way (by the author in cooperation with Esther Dromi) indicates that relative clauses may be used quite sparingly until school-age. And an experimental study confirms that in fact relative clauses with deleted subjects— *the boy that fell*—are far easier for children to produce as late as age five than are ones with deleted direct objects—*the boy that I met (him)*—or with obligatory pronoun copying on obliques—*the boy that I played with him* (Herzberg 1983).

tional morphology and inflectional paradigms, and correction of "solecisms" in the sense of ordinary colloquial rather than literary, normative forms of usage) also has an impact on speakers' knowledge of their language. That is, as I have tried to argue elsewhere (Berman, 1981b, 1981d), school-learning tends to promote a restructuring of the grammar—or certain parts of it, at least—particularly among youngsters of more established, better educated sociocultural backgrounds (as has been noted for 10 to 15 year-olds by Schwarzwald, 1978, 1981).

6.2.1. *Negation of Constituents.* We noted earlier that, in contrast with the rapid acquisition of sentence negation, children of around age 3 seem to have difficulty in even understanding such strings as *ha yalda yoshévet, lo holéxet* 'the girl is-sitting, not walking'. This may be due to the conceptual difficulty of such contradictions, and the nature of logical choice. For instance, I asked a highly intelligent child of nearly 4 years old: *at roca la léxet habayta, o lehisha'er po?* '(do) you want to go home, or to-stay here?', and she looked at me quite blankly; but when I then said *at roca la léxet habayta?* '(do) you want to go home?', she replied quite firmly: *lo, roca le hisha'er po* 'No, (I) want to stay here'. It thus seems that the processing of conjunction reduction with negatives, as in the earlier example, or as in *ani mesaxek im ron lo im rina* 'I'm playing with Ron not with Rina' is something which children cannot handle till quite late.

Formal complexity, by contrast, seems to underlie the late acquisition of negation of indefinite pronouns. These require redundant use of the marker *lo* 'not', to yield a kind of "double negative," and they also take lexically suppletive forms. Compare, for instance: *macá-ti máshehu* 'I-found something' with *lo macá-ti shum davar* 'not I-found no thing' = ('I didn't find anything'); or *míshehu ba* 'someone's coming' with *af exad lo ba* 'no one not is-coming' (= 'nobody is coming'). The actual expressions *af exad* 'nobody' or *shum davar, klum* 'nothing' are acquired around the fourth year as lexical elements with a negative meaning, together with a growing repertoire of quantifying types of expressions. But these are not used correctly with the redundant particle *lo* 'not' until age 5 or 6. This is shown by a child aged 5;3 who said *ani roca af xalav* 'I want NEG:QUANT milk'; she left out the negative particle *lo* before the verb, and she also used *af* instead of *shum,* which is usually required before a mass noun—compare wellformed *ani lo roca shum xalav* 'I don't want no milk' with *ani lo roca af sefer* 'I don't wany any book'.

6.2.2. *Passives.* A pilot study conducted by Mira Ariel indicates that children as old as 8 consistently avoid passive constructions even when these are required by the context (or the experimenter's prompt), and that even 10 year olds fail to use passives with an agent 'by' phrase. Two reasons may account for the rare occurrence of passives in the usage of even older children. Firstly, in morphological terms, the verb requires a special passive-voice *binyan* pattern, and this varies depending on the pattern of its active counterpart, as follows:

(25) (i) a. ron   *lakax* P1   et   ha   séfer
              Ron   took   OBJ   the book

       b. ha   séfer   *nilkax* P2   (al yedey ron)
           the book   was:taken   (by Ron)

   (ii) a. ha   ish   *tiken* P3   et   ha   bérez
            the man   fixed   OBJ   the faucet

       b. ha   bérez   *tukan* P3:PASS   (al yedey ha ish)
           the faucet was:fixed   (by the man)

  (iii) a. ha   yéled   *higbir* P5   et   ha   kol
             the boy   raised   OBJ   the volume

       b. ha   kol   *hugbar* P5:PASS   (al yedey ha yéled)
           the volume was:raised   (by the boy)

A few P2 passive-form verbs do occur among the earliest of children's verbs, but they are acquired as rote forms in such intransitive verbs as *nishbar* 'broke', *nikra* 'tore', and P2 is not used freely in its more productive, passive sense, children often preferring the middle-voice intransitive P4 pattern instead (Berman, 1980b). Similarly, the two strictly passive verb forms of P3:PASS and P5:PASS illustrated in (25) are rarely heard as such in children's speech. In fact, passive forms account for a relatively high proportion of morphophonological errors in adult usage, too (Schwarzwald, 1978). However, morphophonological complexity alone cannot account for this avoidance on the part of children, particularly as they tend quite generally to overuse the present-tense passive participial form of the P3:PASS pattern, meCuCaC. Thus, not only do children early on use this form for lexicalized adjectives such as *meshuga* 'crazy', *menumas* 'polite', they later extend it to form their own statal-perfective adjectives quite productively between ages 3 and 6—for example, *ha telefon metufas* 'the phone is-engaged' vs. standard *tafus; ani kvar merudem-et* 'I'm already asleep' vs. standard *redum-a;* or *hu od lo merugal la ze* 'he's not yet used to it' vs. standard *ragil* 'accustomed'.

The explanation for passive avoidance needs, rather, to be sought in two interrelated facets of Hebrew structure and usage. Firstly, passives are relatively restricted in Hebrew, certainly in everyday spoken usage. Given the more formal register associated with passives in general, its non-use by children could be a function of the fact that they so rarely encounter it in ordinary conversation. Besides, Hebrew allows clear structural options for performing the functions associated with passives in English and other languages. Thus a non-subject nominal can easily be topicalized by simple fronting, as in *et ha mixnasáyim ha'eyle ani lo roce* 'OBJ those pants I don't want' or by left-dislocation with a pronoun copy, as in *ha mixnasáyim ha'eyle, ani lo roce otam* 'those pants, I don't want them'. Such constructions are freely used by 4 year olds; and this was just what the children whom Ariel investigated did, when forced to start a sentence with a semantic non-agent or experiencer. Moreover, downgrading of the agent when the latter is unimportant or unidentified can be achieved by the productive mechanism of impersonal subjectless sentences with third-person plural verbs—e.g. *orzim et ha tapuzim be argazim* 'are-packing OBJ the oranges in crates', *banu kvar et ha báyit* 'have-built already OBJ the house'. Three year olds use these plural impersonals quite freely, and they are easily understood when used in experimental designs with even younger children. For instance, in pointing to a picture, the investigator will tend to ask questions such as: *ma osim po?* 'what are-doing here?' in the sense of 'what is being done here?', or *ma ro'im ba tmuna?* 'what see-PL in-the picture?' in the sense of 'what can be seen in the picture?'. Again, the children in Ariel's study, including the youngest subjects who were aged 5, avoided agent mention by this perfectly appropriate, deeply ingrained device.

Use of passives is thus delayed in Hebrew acquisition as a combined function of their being so rare in input to children, their relative morphological markedness, and the existence of well-established periphrastic alternatives for achieving the discourse functions typically associated with passive constructions.

6.2.3. *Bound Possessives.* As children move out of the highly elliptical forms of expression typical of initial syntax, they start to use the possessive particle *shel* 'of', usually with the pronoun form as in *(ha) buba shel-i* '(the) doll of-me' (= 'my doll'), and subsequently before full nouns, too, as in *(ha) báyit shel ron* '(the) house of Ron' (= 'Ron's house'). More formal style has a bound form of this construction, which often requires that the initial, head noun changes form—e.g. analytic *ha báyit shel-i* 'the house of-me' vs. *bet-i* 'house-my', both meaning 'my house', or *ha tmuna shel ron* 'the picture of Ron' vs. *tmunat ron* both meaning 'Ron's picture'. Pre-kindergarten children never use these formal, bound forms, except when they are acquired as rote units. These may be nouns commonly used with a pronoun suffix—e.g. *bit-i* 'my daughter' (cf. *ha bat shel-i*) as an address form with little girls, or *tor-xa* 'your turn' used in playing games; and they may be lexicalized noun compounds such as *naaley báyit* 'shoes-house' (= 'slippers') or *xadar óxel* 'room-food' (= 'dining room') (see Section 4.5.1 above).

Even quite young children, however, seem able to understand these bound possessives and other genitives when they occur in stories read to them by caretakers. And with initial schooling, around age 5 to 6, children begin to recognize the dual possibility of using both the analytic form with *shel* which is familiar to them from everyday conversation and also the bound, compound form as a stylistic option for expressing the same kinds of semantic relations. This arises along with school-age exposure to, and awareness of, a more formal, literary-sounding style, of the kind used in all first-grade stories and in most children's literature in general. The following examples are from my daughter's spontaneous narratives between ages 5½ and 6½, in situations where she is in a special, story-telling frame, and hence deliberately trying to use a more high-flown, non-everyday turn of speech (Berman, 1981d).

(26) a. hu   *xaver-i* ha   nexmad,   hu ha xaver   ha   xi   yakar *shel-i*
        he's friend-my the nice,   he's friend the most dear   of-me

        'he's my [bound] nicest friend, he's my [free] dearest friend'

    b. ha   xataltul   hitkonen   le   tiyul,   hu   yaca
       the   kitten   got:ready for   a:walk,   he   went:out

       im   *begad-av*
       with   his-clothes

       . . . hu   himshix   be   *dark-o*
       . . . he   continued on   his-way

The conventional bound form is often not yet known, as when my daughter, aged 6;3, again in her formal, narrative register, said that *hem kámu al *regley'am* 'they got-up on their-feet' cf. correct *ragley-hem* from *régel* 'foot'/*ragláy-im* 'feet'. And for a long time, she double-marked possession on the word for 'house', saying things like **bet bet-am* 'house house-their' for simple *bet-am* 'their house'. That is, the correct morphological marking of bound forms of nouns in different derivational patterns and different inflectional paradigms takes a very long time for Hebrew-speaking children to master. But first-graders like my daughter and other children whom I have observed do attempt to use these bound possessives in their own production, not in everyday interactions, but as a mark of a more literary register.

Relatedly, there is strong evidence that it is around age 5 to 6 that children first try to form compounds nouns for items which they feel might be lexicalized as a single unit, as in such novel forms as when my daughter, aged nearly 6, talked about her *pijamat sport* 'sports pyjamas'' (the free form of the head noun is *pijama,* genitive *pijamat-*) to refer to a pair of her pyjamas which have pictures of footballers. And 7 year olds will create novel combinations such as saying *at bazbezanit oxel* 'you're (a) waster-of food', *ze sinar ha ofe sheli* 'that's apron the baker of-me' (= 'that's my baker('s) apron'). In other words, productive use of compounding as a device for a special type of lexical innovation occurs at late preschool age, followed even later by knowledge of the morphological conventions for marking the bound head noun.

Genitives also take a third form in Hebrew, in addition to the bound NN and the analytic N *shel* N constructions. These are the so-called ''double genitives'' in the form N-Pro$_i$ *shel* N$_i$—e.g. *saarot-éha shel rína* 'hair-her of Rina' (= 'Rina's hair'), *sipur-av shel ron* 'stories-his of Ron' (= 'Ron's stories'). Although such constructions are very common in more formal, literary style and are also found quite widely in speech, children seem to avoid them entirely in their own output. This may be due to the structural complexity of such forms, which require the kind of possessive marking on nouns that we have noted as a late acquisition. Moreover, this type of genitive construction is inherently redundant, since it double marks the possessor-modifier—once as suffixed to the head noun in pronominal form, once as a lexically specified noun following the genitive particle *shel* 'of'; and to form this construction, the speaker needs to process the latter noun for its grammatical properties of number, gender, and person before he produces the noun itself, in a semantically redundant form of backwards pronominalization. Finally, although it seems that the double genitive is used only where the second, modifying noun is fully referential and definite, it is not at all clear what kind of constraints—semantic, stylistic, or other—govern choice of the double genitive rather than the free genitive with *shel* alone linking the two nominals. The fact, then, that children confine their usage to forms like *ha saarot shel rina,* and that production of the totally synonymous double genitive *saarot-éha shel rina* for 'Rina's hair' is a very late acquisition indeed, can be explained by the interaction of numerous features of the latter construction: It constitutes a paraphrase of an early-acquired type of structure which is morphologically less complex, semantically nonredundant, stylistically less marked, and easier in terms of on-line processing with no requirement of backward pronominalization.

6.2.4. *Bound Accusatives.* An instance similar to children's avoidance of inflectional marking of possessive pronouns noted above is found in the case of enclitic, incorporated accusative pronouns; for instance, *re'iti-v* alternates with *ra'iti oto* 'I-saw him', as does *sgarnú-m* with *sagárnu otam* 'we-closed them'. The more analytic, latter forms are the only ones found in everyday speech, hence the only ones used by young children, for the bound form is highly literary, almost archaic-sounding. Yet grade-schoolers do have a recognition knowledge of these forms, and they may try to use them to create their own version of a "literary" register. This is shown by the following examples from a study by Ilana Dor, in which 7- to 8-year-old second-graders were asked to retell a story from one of their school readers.

(27) a. anáxnu lo   *moce'á-hu   cf. *moc'im otam*
        we (do) not find-them

     b. hem   *hiciló-hu   cf. *hicílu oto*
        they saved-him

     c. le *xalc-a et   ragl-o   cf. *le xalec*
        to save-it OBJ foot-his (= 'his leg')

The forms noted here are morphologically incorrect, no doubt because they are so rare in input, and because of the complexity of the rules governing their formation, which are inaccessible to many adult speakers, too. Of note here is the fact that these children, in their second year of school study, recognize the existence of an inflected option for their normal, productive analytic form of expression, and that they try to produce these bound forms, which they view as appropriate to the bookish register of formal story-telling tasks.

6.2.5 *Avoidance of Intensifiers.*   Adjectives and adverbs can be intensified in Hebrew, much as in English, by use of words like *me'od* 'very', *nora* 'terribly, awful'. All younger children, as well as 4 to 5 year olds, to a lesser degree, achieve this effect by using what Jakobson has termed the "typical nursery device" of repetition. Examples from our transcripts include: *katan katan* 'small small' (= 'very very small, tiny'); *maher maher* 'quickly quickly (= 'very quickly'); *harbe harbe* 'lots lots' (= 'an enormous amount'), *raxok raxok* 'far far' (= 'very far away'). Lexical repetition is a deeply ingrained device in Hebrew (Berman, 1979b), including in many set formulae such as *le'at le'at* 'slowly slowly' (= 'gradually'), *yom yom* 'day day' (= 'day in day out'). But the examples given before are of productive, innovative use of this device, and they do not sound at all odd, as they do in English. The device is also widespread in Israeli baby-talk, as when people say to a child *ata yeled matok matok* 'you're (a) child sweet sweet' (= 'you're a really cute child'), *tasim et ze bifnim bifnim* 'put it inside inside' (= 'stick (your spoon) right deep into your mouth'), or a doctor's instruction to patients to *linshom amok amok* 'breathe deep deep' (= 'very deeply'). This kind of repetition is thus not really deviant in Hebrew, but it is typically juvenile in tone and effect, and it seems to entail a delay in preschoolers' usage of more normative lexical means of intensification.

6.2.6. *Comprehension of complex structures and coreference relations.*   In a study adapted in part from Carol Chomsky's (1969) investigation of school-age syntax, Ziv (1976) found that the referents of relative clauses are understood by second grade (age 7–8 years), as shown by correct answers to the question 'who fell into the hole?' in response to the sentence *ha kélev nashax et ha xatul še nafal la bor* 'the dog bit OBJ the cat that fell in the hole'. Verb complement reference is mostly understood by third grade (age 8–9), as shown by correct responses to the question 'Who will buy milk?' when given the sentence *moshe mevakesh mi dan li-knot xalav* 'Moshe asks = requests of Dan to-buy milk'.[15] And pronominalization in embedded clauses is correctly interpreted by fourth grade (age 9–10 years), in correct responses to the question 'Whose are = who has the lessons?' when given the sentence *moshe sha'al et uri im hexin et ha shi'urim* 'Moshe asked OBJ Uri if (he) had-prepared OBJ the lessons'. However, when tests included pragmatically misleading items—e.g. for relative clauses, the

---

[15]Hebrew has two separate verbs for 'ask' meaning 'request' and 'inquire' respectively. Although *le-vakesh* 'to request' is acquired early on, 3 to 4 year olds confuse *li-sh'ol* 'to inquire' with the verb meaning 'tell'. For example, a 4 year old might say **tagidi le aba ex kor'im lo* 'tell (to) Daddy what he's called' when he wants the addressee to ASK his father someone's name, and so should have used the verb *tish'ali* 'ask = inquire'.

question 'Who stood in the corner?' was based on a cue-sentence of the form 'the teacher that the pupil shouted at (him) stood in the corner', and for complements, the question 'Who'll play football?' followed a sentence to the effect 'the little boy asks of Mommy to play football'—children tended to respond incorrectly to the first type of construction as late as fourth grade, and to the second type as late as sixth grade. This study strongly indicates that children are able to rely on formal, morphosyntactic cues such as word order and gender and number marking as overriding conflicting semantico-pragmatic cues only as late as around age 11 or 12, even in the case of a language like Hebrew, where gender-number agreement is so pervasive a processing device. That is, Hebrew-speaking children, too, until around the age of puberty, tend to give major weight to real-world feasibility, such as who normally bakes cakes, plays football, or is put in the corner, and hence disregard relevant formal linguistic cues.

Related findings emerge with respect to the difficulty encountered by children under the age of 11 to 12 in correctly interpreting non-coreferential pronouns (Wigodsky, 1977; Berkowitz & Wigodsky, 1979). Such later developments are clearly not language-specific, and they are in line with findings of related studies for English. Yet these results are, perhaps, of special interest in a language like Hebrew, where the centrality of number, gender (optionally, person) agreement from subjects to verbs, from nouns to adjectives, and in all pronominalizations, provides learners with a wide range of formal cues to which they may—in fact, must—attend in order for appropriate processing to occur (as noted, too, in Frenkel et al., 1980). Nonetheless, it takes Hebrew learners a long time to attend exclusively to these formal cues when they conflict strongly with expectations about the way things usually are in real life, and hence in linguistic output, too.

THE SETTING OF LANGUAGE ACQUISITION

7. Cognitive Pace-Setting of Linguistic Acquisitions

This section focuses on several acquisitional patterns which seem consistent with what is known from research on development in other languages, particularly English. In such instances, crosslinguistic data should reveal similarities that override language-specific features of structure and form. There are numerous issues of potential interest for this question which I cannot address at present, owing to lack of available data and research with Hebrew-speaking children. Such areas include, for instance: (i) The developmental order of "grammatical encoding of EVENT TYPES" (Slobin, 1979, 1981); there is some evidence from my data that this is, in fact, cognitively determined, with basic transitive events of animate agents acting upon inanimate objects being among the earliest to be encoded, while possessive sentences that relate an animate possessor to an inanimate possessee are also produced, and understood, earlier than others. (ii) Numerous studies from different languages, including Hebrew (Section 3.2), indicate that TENSE-ASPECT marking on verbs tends initially to tie present-tense forms to duratives and statives, past-tense forms to end-point punctives; however, there are no data from Hebrew to indicate the internal, conceptually-based content of aspectual distinctions proceeding, say, from immediate via recent to more remote past or future marking; nor, relatedly, do we have data to back up our assumption that the emergence of aspect-marking adverbials such as those meaning 'now'—usually first used in the sense of 'next thing on the program'— 'already', 'in a little while', 'all the time' and so on is cognitively determined, and hence that these lexical items will show up at a period of development consistent with overt indication of similar aspectual distinctions across typologically quite different languages. (iii) Relatedly, it is reasonable to assume that the developmental order of acquisition of different types of ADVERBIAL CLAUSES—which in Hebrew are syntactically quite straightforward, and acquired early on—would also be cognitively based, so that 'when' and 'because' clauses will emerge well before those indicating relations of purpose or concession. (iv) While there are certain language-specific facts which might determine the relative difficulty of different clause-internal structures (Section 6.1.4), it is reasonable to assume that for Hebrew-speaking children, too, RELATIVE CLAUSES will first be used to modify sentence-final nominals, only later being centrally embedded to modify initial, subject nominals.

7.1. Negatives

As early as the one-word stage, children seem universally to have a way of expressing nonexistence, often conflated with disappearance, cessation, or loss in general. In Hebrew, this is achieved by means of the invariant, negative particle eyn 'there isn't' (since 1975), which precedes the use of the affirmative existential particle yesh '(there) is' (= French il y a). And the use of highly emphatic day, literally 'enough', to express refusal, protest, or rejection seems to precede the occurrence of od 'more, over (again)' to express desire for continuation or addition. These in turn precede propositional negation or denial by means of lo 'no, not', although at the very early stages of speech, a child may use the single term lo in place of eyn and day to express both nonexistence and rejection.

In a comparative study of the use of negative utterances by nine American children and nine Israeli children aged 19–35 months, at Brown's Stages II to II in terms of MLU, Rom (1977) concludes that "English and Hebrew subjects used the three semantic functions of negation with similar frequencies. The most frequently used function was nonexistence, followed by rejection, and then denial." These findings, which correspond to the order of negative functions as they emerged in Bloom's (1970) study of three English-speaking children, strongly indicate that the cognitive underpinnings of different types of negation determine order of acquisition as being similar in English and in Hebrew, where the structural properties of different types of negative sentences are so divergent in the two languages.

7.2. Questions

The type of questions which children ask is also in line with what has been found for corresponding developments in English, indicating that there is a cognitive basis to their order of acquisition. Thus, the first question asked is formulaic *ma ze* 'What's this/ that', often at the one-word stage, followed some time later by *mi ze* 'Who's this/that' once children make a distinction between asking about the identity of a person rather than an object, subsequently by questions with *éyfo* 'where'. Comprehension of questions was tested by Goshen & Eyal (1976) in terms of appropriateness of responses to pictures, with subjects aged 2;3 to 2;10 and 3;4 to 3;6. There were no errors in either group in response to yes/no questions and questions with *mi* 'who' relating to a subject noun; the younger but not the older subjects made occasional errors in answer to questions with *eyfo* 'where (plus static location)'; and the younger group made relatively more errors on the following question types, whereas the older children, aged around 3½, showed almost full comprehension (85% to 95% correct answers): *im mi* 'with who(m)'—83% correct answers, *le'an* 'where to'—79%, *káma* 'how much, how many'—54%, *matay* 'when'—41%, *eyx* 'how' (manner, method, instrument)—25%, lama 'why'—21%, *káma zman* 'how-much time' (= 'how long')—17%. This hierarchy of difficulty is similar to the one found in Ervin-Tripp's (1970) study of how English-speaking children answer questions. Moreover, an analysis of the syntactic complexity of the different questions shows that this did NOT correlate with order of acquisition in either comprehension or production (Eyal, 1976). For instance, the two questions *eyfo ron yashen* 'where (does) Ron sleep?' and *matay ron yashen* 'when (does) Ron sleep? have the same surface form, and they can be answered in superficially similar ways, too, as by *ba mita* 'in-the bed' and *ba láyla* 'in = at night' respectively. Yet children understand and produce 'where' questions much earlier than 'when' questions. These findings thus indicate that the kinds of questions which are understood and asked by children at different stages of their development are conceptually rather than linguistically or syntactically determined.

7.3. Locative Terms

Hebrew-speaking children acquire spatial prepositions in an order consistent with that noted for other languages. Thus, in Aviezer's (1979) study of 60 children aged 18 to 30 months, the order of the three terms tested was 'in', then 'on', then 'under', and in each case conceptualization of the spatial relationship, as tested by a language-free method, preceded comprehension, which in turn preceded production of these three terms in Hebrew. Her findings accord with those of Dromi (1979) for 2 to 3 year old production, when several other locative prepositions also begin to occur. A study conducted with children aged 1½ to 4½ (Kolman, 1979) revealed the following order in both comprehension and production tasks: 'on', 'in', 'under', 'next to', 'behind', and 'in front of', with the terms dividing up into two developmental groups—'in', 'on', 'under' and then 'next to', 'behind', and 'in front of', while Yif'at (1981) found that 4 to 5 year olds still had difficulty with the preposition *beyn* 'between, among'. These findings are highly consistent with those of Johnston & Slobin (1979) for English, Italian, Serbo-Croatian, and Turkish. Moreover, similar developmental patterns are shown for comprehension of spatial terms in Ben-Aroya's (1979) adaptation of the BTBC and in Greenwald's (1979) adaptation of the ACLC. Note, too, that the order of acquisition of pairs of dimensional adjectives such as 'big-small', 'long-short', and 'wide-narrow'—which develop in that order in both comprehension and production—closely parallels the findings of research on this subsystem in English. Such correspondences between developments in Hebrew and other, typologically different languages clearly indicate that cognitive grasp of spatial and dimensional relations dictates developmental order, and that conceptualization of these relations precedes the linguistic encoding of such distinctions.

7.4. Predicate Relations Through Verb Patterns

A crucial developmental task of the Hebrew-speaking child, discussed in Sections 3.6 and 4.3 above, is appropriate lexicalization of predicate-argument relations through variation of verb-pattern morphology. We have noted that acquisitional order cannot be explained on the grounds of relative complexity of morphophonological form, since children use all five major verb patterns from early speech. Rather, once they are beyond the stage of initial syntax, children make a developmental breakthrough in the realization that the same global event can be encoded differently, depending on the precise content of predicate-argument relations which are expressed—say, P1 *oxel* 'eats' can contrast with P5 *ma'axil* 'feeds', P2 *nishbar* 'break-INTRANS.' may alternate with P1 *shavar* 'break (something)', or P4 *hitlaxlex* 'get-dirty' with P3 *lixlex* 'make-dirty'. Subsequently, children come to realize that such alternations can be generalized to express quite definite sets of semantic relations, such as basic versus causative acts, transitive compared with intransitive or reflexive actions, unchanging states versus inchoative processes, and so on.

The claim I wish to emphasize here is that the sequence in which children learn to encode these notions within the verb-pattern system is governed by a complex interplay between cognitive prerequisites and language-specific facts (some of the latter being outlined in Section 8.1 below). The earliest, conceptually-based distinction is made between transitive-active-causative events—in which someone performs an action on or to some outside entity—and intransitive, passive, or reflexive events—in which some entity undergoes an event or process with no outside agency specified. The fact that the first type of event is quite soon established as distinct may be attributed to the nature of Agent-Action-Object types of occurrences as basic or canonical in the real world, hence in language, as discussed by Hopper & Thompson (1980) and Slobin (1979, 1981). The fact that intransitives are soon set apart by children may be explained by the familiarity of one-place predicates such as 'cry', 'run', or 'sleep' in early child language, and in their real-world experience. Acquisition of causatives precedes reflexives, for general conceptual reasons, although encoding of reflexive actions is facilitated since in Hebrew, as in many languages (Faltz, 1977), lexicalized reflexives are confined to everyday physical activities such as washing and dressing, which are familiar to children from common routines. Reciprocals are evidently conceptually more difficult, and they are acquired later, again with the exception of actions which are most typically reciprocal, such as meeting in the sense of joining, hugging, kissing, or quarreling—where in the latter case, children aged 3 to 4 quite often recast the ordinary P1 verb *la-riv* 'to fight, quarrel' in a P4 reciprocal-reflexive form to yield *mitrav-im* 'are quarreling'. Late acquisition of inchoatives—again, with some common, lexicalized exceptions which show up quite early, such as the verbs meaning 'get tired', 'become angry'—may be explained by the conceptual difficulty of distinguishing between being in a state and entering into a state. However, as was noted in Section 6.2.2 above with respect to passives, once children are cognitively ready to encode the notion of inchoativity, they can do so by a productive analytic periphrasis with an auxiliary verb, to yield, for instance, *nihya shamen* 'got fat' in place of normative P1 *shaman* or colloquial P5 *hishmin, naasa kacer* 'became short' in place of P4 *hitkacer*.

In general, then, conceptual grasp of the relevant notions—such as causativeness, reflexivity, reciprocality, passiveness, inchoativity—must precede encoding of these semantic relations via verb morphology. And children's construal of the system of verb-patterns qua system seems to proceed in several maturationally conditioned steps. Initially there is an ability to alternate verb patterns for an increasing number of familiar verbs and the event types typically associated with them; subsequently learners extract out the relevant semantic concepts realized through the system, proceeding from causation via reflexivity to reciprocality and inchoativeness, etc.; and, finally, speakers acquire a metalinguistic knowledge of the system of verb-pattern alternation as a highly abstract formal apparatus, coupled with conventionalized lexical knowledge of the many instances where this system does not manifest a one-to-one relation between form and function in the current lexicon of Hebrew.

8. Linguistic Pace-Setting of Cognitive Acquisition

The discussion in this section is highly speculative, and comments here are meant to provide certain tentative hypotheses regarding areas of acquisition which seem to warrant further crosslinguistic study.

8.1. *Verb-Pattern Lexicalization of Predicate Relations*

With very few exceptions, different predicate-argument relations are explicitly marked in the verb in Hebrew, which has no equivalent to English: he tires me vs. he tires easily—P3 *me'ayef* vs. P4 *mit'ayef;* John broke the vase vs.

the vase broke—P1 *shavar* vs. P2 *nishbar;* she is washing (herself) vs. she is washing the baby—P4 *mitraxec-et* vs. P1 *roxec-et:* or he continued the story vs. the story continued—P5 *himshix* vs. P2 *nimshax.* I would like to suggest that this system might facilitate Hebrew-speaking children's perception of the relevant semantic relations involved herein. Firstly, the fact that such notions must be explicitly encoded within the actual form of the verb may make them more transparent than in the kind of input available to English-speaking children, say, for lexicalized material is not only more accessible for retrieval, it may have higher salience in general (Brown, 1958). Moreover, the fact that these distinctions are encoded within the verb rather than in the arguments of the predicate, as in an ergative language like Kaluli (Schieffelin, 1985) may explain why children do not make these distinctions overtly in their early productions; but it may also force children to attend to these notions relatively early in their development. As against this claim, one might argue that analytic forms such as are provided by English auxiliaries like *make* for causatives or *get* for inchoatives, as well as *-self* pronouns for reflexives and *one another* for reciprocals, might be conceptually easier, since a given semantic relationship is marked by a separate, free morpheme. Yet this is a topic which needs further investigation, since for English-speaking children, the very multiplicity of functions associated with verbs like *make* and *get* may hinder rather than facilitate children's internalization of the distinct notions of causative, inchoative, and passive.

Secondly, the fact that a common semantic core is retained through a shared verb-root—for young children, some kind of shared "consonantal skeleton" favoring the perceptually salient ends of words such as *pizer* 'scatter'/*hitpazer* 'be/get scattered', *nixnas* 'go in' / *hixnis* 'put in', *yashav* 'sit' / *hoshiv* 'seat'— may force Semitic-speaking children to an earlier cognizance of such relationships than in other languages (relevant data are available for Moroccan Arabic [Badry, 1983] as well as Hebrew [Clark & Berman, 1984]). That is, the Hebrew-learning child has concrete evidence for the semantic properties shared by such pairs as English *eat-feed* in the forms *oxel-ma'axil,* or *drop-fall* in the forms *nafal-hipil, come-bring* in *lavo-lehavi.* Some evidence that this is in fact the case is provided by children who as young as age 3 fill in accidental lexical gaps by using a different verb pattern in relation to a known verb, in coining, for example, P5 *le-hashtot* 'give to drink' from P1 *li-shtot* 'drink', or P5 *le-hashin* 'put to sleep' from P1 *li-shon* 'sleep'.

8.2. Sex Identity

A crosscultural study (Beit-Hallahmi et al., 1974) found that half of the Israeli children investigated had established gender identity by the age of 30 months, rather earlier than their American counterparts. We have also noted (Section 6.1.1) that by the second half of the third year, children correctly use a feminine form of the verb for (third person) female subjects and a masculine form for male subjects, a finding which is supported by Levy's (1980) experimental study with respect to inanimate noun-verb agreement, too. It may be that the explicit, formal encoding of sex differences as heard, and subsequently produced, by Israeli children in relation to doers of actions and to attributes of people and animals (e.g. *ata yeled matok* 'you're a cute boy-child' vs. *at yalda-a metuk-a* 'you're a cute girl-child') may compel them to make these cognitive distinctions earlier than, say, their English-speaking counterparts. The importance of such distinctions, as linguistically encoded, is evidenced by a 4 year old boy to whom I said: *ze ha kélev shelxa?* 'is that your dog?', whose response was *lo, hi kalba, lo kélev* 'no, it = she's a she-dog, not a dog'. I do not wish to imply that this entails any generalization of sex distinctions to the grammatical category of gender, since inanimate nouns are arbitrarily masculine or feminine in Hebrew as in, say, French. That is, the sexual connotations of objects will be perceived similarly by Israeli children as by speakers of a language like English or Italian (Ervin-Tripp, 1962). This is shown by results of a study of Guiora & Acton (1979), "whose findings offered clear evidence that five-year old Israeli children [like adults—R.B.] will be guided by the assumed sexual connotation of the words denoting them, and not by their grammatical gender." Nonetheless, the fact that a 2½ year old Israeli child will say, respectively, *sharon hirbic li/ hirbic-a li* 'Sharon hit me' depending on whether Sharon is a boy or a girl, may force him to pay attention to the sex identity of the referent relatively quite early on—and this hypothesis deserves further crosscultural and crosslinguistic investigation.

8.3. *Time Reference*

In Section 5.2.1 above, we noted the relatively error-free acquisition of tense-marking on verbs. I attributed this, in part at least, to the existence of clear formal cues in the shape of vowel patterns for the present versus the past-tense of the most common P1 verb-pattern, the use of *m-* to mark present tense in other patterns, and the use of distinct suffixes and prefixes to distinguish between past and future, which together constitute facilitating kinds of schemata which children can rely on in encoding tense differences (Section 4.2.4). Here I would like to suggest that the way in which tense is encoded in the language may enable Hebrew-speaking children to specify events as current, or as prior or subsequent to the time of speaking, relatively early in their development. It might be argued that English-speaking children have similar structural correlates in the form, say, of final dental stop for past, or *gonna* for future. Yet the Hebrew-speaking child has no basic or citation form of verbs which he can resort to until he reaches the point where he is ready to encode tense distinctions, so that his language forces him to make a choice from very early on. Moreover, since aspect is not encoded within the verb system at all, being distinguished usually by lexical adverbs such as the words meaning 'now', 'beforehand', 'soon', or 'already', the Hebrew-speaking child need not specify aspectual properties of an event in order to give an appropriate indication of the temporal relation between the event and the moment of speaking. Thus the language seems to make it "easy" for the child—as well as more or less obligatory—to divide up events along the time axis of present, past, and future. (See, further, Berman & Dromi, 1984.)

8.4. *Marking of Topic and Focus by Word Order*

As noted in Sections 3.5 and 4.6 above, Hebrew has several very productive devices for topicalization and other kinds of pragmatic foregrounding of arguments by departure from the canonical SVO order. Even 2 to 3 year olds tend to right-dislocate quite freely in discourse, to yield utterances equivalent to (well-formed) 'She's crying, the girl' or 'Don't take it, my ball', so as to make it perfectly clear to their interlocutor what or whom they are talking about. Somewhat later, they also begin to freely left-dislocate in order to establish quite clearly who or what the topic of their comment is, as in utterances equivalent to 'that girl, I hate her' or 'my dolly, she fell down and hurt herself'. Hebrew-speaking 3-year-olds also quite freely front a nonsubject nominal which they are focusing on in discourse, as in the perfectly wellformed equivalents of 'with him I won't play any more', 'to her I already gave one', as well as in backgrounding time and place expressions such as 'at Anat's (house) we always play lotto'. Such formal shifts are deeply ingrained in Hebrew, and very natural at all levels of discourse; and they do not require structural modifications of the kind involved in, say, English passives or clefting. The pervasiveness, and structural simplicity, then of word order shifts in Hebrew may assist children learning the language to come to an early recognition of such notions as "THAT's what I'm talking about," or "What matters to me isn't who or what did something, but who or what it happened to." That is, because their language can so easily mark just about any nominal as the topic or point of relative focus (Berman, 1982b), these notions might relatively early on achieve conceptual saliency for Israeli children, possibly for children speaking "pragmatic word order" languages like Hungarian, Slavic, or Turkish in general, by· contrast with those learning languages whose word order is more grammatically constrained, like English or French (Thompson, 1978).

8.5. *Affectee vs. Agent Roles*

There are numerous constructions in Hebrew which take the form of a predicate followed by a dative-marked nominal, where the latter is perceived as the experiencer or affectee rather than the performer (Berman, 1982c). Examples found early in children's usage include expressions like *kar li* '(it's) cold to-me' (= 'I'm cold'), or *lo nóax lánu* 'not comfortable to-us' (= 'we're not comfy'). From very early syntax, children's speech makes liberal use of the dative marker *le-* 'to' or 'for' in relation to the person who is affected by the event, either as benefactee or malefactee. The examples in (a) below are from the speech of children aged around 3, with hypothetical SV agent-marking paraphrases given in the (b) sentences.

(28) (i) a. ha   yalda   sama   *lo*   pérax   ba   af
            the   girl   put   to:him   (a) flower   in:the   nose

      b. ha   yalda   sama   pérax   ba   af   *shelo*
          the   girl   put   (a) flower in   his   nose

  (ii) a. nikra   *li*   ha   daf
           got:torn to:me   the   page

      b. *ani*   karati   et   ha   daf
          I   tore   OBJ   the   page

 (iii) a. nafal   *la*   tinok   (et)   ha   bakbuk
           fell   to:the   baby   OBJ   the   bottle

      b. *ha*   *tinok* hipil   et   ha   bakbuk
          the   baby   dropped OBJ   the   bottle

  (iv) a. nebad   *lá-nu*   et   ze
           got:lost to-us   OBJ   it

      b. *anáxnu* ibádnu   et   ze
          we   lost   OBJ   it

In the first example in (28), the child marks the affectee of having a flower shoved up his nose datively, rather than with ordinary possessor marking, and this is very common in all colloquial usage, as in the equivalents of 'Mommy buttoned to-him the sweater', 'tie to-me the shoes', 'he painted to-them the house = their house'. In the other examples in (28a), specification of the agent-doer is evaded by means of dative-marking of a participant as affectee of the event—of a page getting torn, of the bottle falling, of losing something, and so on. The widespread use of datives to encode the affectee role in Israeli speech affords children with an easy device—structurally familiar to them from other constructions, such as possessives, used in early syntax—for not having to assign responsibility for an action. And this is particularly useful when children themselves have done something "wrong," since they can then say things like 'my shirt (went and) got-dirtied on = to me' rather than the more direct 'I dirtied my shirt', 'the milk got-spilt to us' rather than 'we spilt the milk'.

We suggest here that the fact that children from a young age use a casemarked form to express the affectee or experiencer of an event or state might mean that this cluster of concepts is well-established for them, and clearly distinguished from the familiar notion of agent as performer of the action. And perhaps children whose language does not afford such an accessible means for distinguishing agent/doer from affectee/experiencer—both of which are typically surface subjects in English—may not achieve this conceptual distinction so easily or rapidly. This assumption might be tested by presenting children with a non-linguistic task in which they are required to distinguish the agent/experiencer along a given continuum. Our experience shows that on picture-describing tasks, where young Israeli children are asked, for instance, 'What happened to the man?', and the man in question is shown chasing a balloon, they are very likely to respond by saying *barax lo ha balon* 'fled to-him (= from-him) the balloon', using a predicate-initial construction with dative marking on the man as affectee of the event.

8.6. *Identification of Noun Classes*

Hebrew noun classes manifest even greater inconsistency in form-meaning relations than do the *binyan* verb patterns discussed at various points in this chapter (Sections 3.6, 4.3, 7.4, and 8.1), in part because noun patterns are far more numerous than those for verbs (Ravid, 1978). Nonetheless, children's spontaneous innovations indicate that from around age 4, Hebrew-learning children seem to distinguish semantic classes of nouns according to certain preferred morphological patterns (Berman & Sagi, 1981). The examples below are of forms recorded from children aged 4 to 5, compared with the conventional lexical items in the language.

(29)		PATTERN	CHILDREN'S WORD	ADULT WORD
	AGENTS:	CaCC-an		
		rakd-an dancer	**sapran-it* barber-FEM	*sapar-it*
		saxk-an player, actor	**bany-an* builder	*banay*
	INSTRUMENTS:	maCCeC-a		
		maxresha plough	**maglexa* shaver (= 'razor')	*mxonat gilúax* machine-of shaving
		mamtera sprinkler	**mashkela* weigher (= 'scales')	*moznáyim* balances

Similarly, a single suffix *-ut* is often added by children to a base-word to create innovative abstract nouns (cf. conventional *briy-ut* 'health', *shovav-ut* 'naughtiness'), as in coinages like **cmi-ut* in place of conventional *cima'on* 'thirst', **ke'evut* 'hurtingness' from *ke'ev* 'pain', or **mazi-ut* 'sweat-ness' in place of *haza'a* 'sweating'.

We suggest that the very structured nature of Hebrew word-formation processes as noted in Section 1.2—by means of a consonantal root or skeleton plus a restricted set of possible affixation patterns—may enable children to achieve an early apprehension of noun classes, divided semantically into such notions as agent-doer, its inanimate counterpart of instrument, as well as abstract state or process or place and collective types of nouns. Clearly, Hebrew affords very different devices for word formation than does English, with its preference for compounding, zero conversion, or a suffix such as *-er* (Clark, 1980; Clark & Hecht, 1982). Comparative research on comprehension and production of agent and instrument nouns in Hebrew among children aged 3 to 7 as against 11-year-olds and adults (Clark & Berman, 1984) indicates a very general preference for transparent devices of stem-plus-affix, with suffixes being far commoner than prefixes, and very little use made at all of stem-internal vowel alternation alone (compare *ciyer* 'painted'/*cayar* 'a painter', *shavar* 'broke' / *shéver* 'a fracture'). But further crosslinguistic study is needed to test my hypothesis that Israeli children conceptualize semantic distinctions such as agent vs. instrument, abstract state vs. process, or collective vs. place nouns relatively early on, and that they are aided in so doing by the structural regularities of how such notions are lexicalized in Hebrew.

As noted at the outset of this section, discussion of possible linguistic pacesetting of cognitive acquisition in such areas as predicate-argument relations and semantic classes of objects and events, of time-reference and sex-identity, of semantic roles of affectee versus doer, or of pragmatic functions of topic and focus, is bound to be speculative in the absence of carefully constructed, perhaps language-free crosslinguistic tasks for comparison. At this stage of research, the areas noted in this section seem at the very least compatible with the notion of "precocious acquisition," in that the early marking of the relevant distinctions by young children in their spontaneous output indicates clearly that they are able to give linguistic expression to complex conceptual contents which a priori one might not have attributed to them at a given period of their development.

9. Input and Adult-Child Interaction

There are almost no linguistic or anthropological studies of these issues in Hebrew, so that our discussion is largely sociological and educational in orientation. It also follows that the suggestions regarding the role of multiple interaction with adults and peers in Sections 9.3 and 9.4 below must, in the absence of suitable research, be viewed as tentative.

9.1. *Socioeconomic Background Variables*

Several studies have been undertaken with the aim of lessening the so-called gap between different segments of the Israeli preschool and school-age population. For instance, work of Ortar (1975a, 1975b) on the nature and effects of working-class mothers' speech to early preschoolers—in terms of variables such as number of total utterances, amount of repetition, proportion of "enriching" utterances, and whether parental input relates to caretaking activites, expresses emotion, or is instructional—is concerned with the relation between parental input and level of children's verbal intelligence, and is motivated, in part at least, by the practical aim of instructing less-educated mothers in how to enrich their children's verbal environment woth affectively and intellectually. Studies have also been undertaken on the language of so-called "culturally deprived" children, mainly beyond early school-age. These are reviewed in Stahl (1977), in terms of the vocabulary usage and written expression of youngsters whose backgrounds are mainly of an oral tradition by contrast with the literate, primarily European background of the more established segments of the Israeli population. Such studies aim to both explain and remedy the relative lack of achievement of students from the former kind of background in their formal schoolwork. By contrast, studies by Caisse (1974) and Davis (1976, 1978), within a sociolinguistic, Labov-type framework, show adolescents of such "disadvantaged" backgrounds to be highly proficient in oral interaction with their peers on topics of immediate interest and concern to them.

In a carefully designed study of 40 mother-infant dyads, Ninio (1980) attempts to trace some antecedents of the "intellectual deficit, which is well-established by four years" of children from lower-class backgrounds. Her findings, based on comparison of mothers' interactions with children aged 17 to 22 months, reveal both a qualitative and quantitative difference between the input of mothers from high compared with lower socioeconomic backgrounds. An extreme instance of such deficit is studied by Yif'at (1981), where 4 to 5 year old children from disadvantaged backgrounds who are raised in an institutional setting manifested as much as two years delay in such linguistic tasks as constructing complex sentences, the range of modal verbs used with infinitives, range of dimensional and other adjectives, use of lexically-marked causative verbs, innovative application of plural and feminine gender suffixes, and a wide reliance on investigator-prompting as well as on use of deictic terms and gestures rather than lexical specifications by comparison with children of the same age raised in lower to middle-class homes. Similar deficiencies were manifested by 7 to 8 year old children raised in an institution by comparison with their home-raised peers. The general inability of institutionalized children at both age groups to provide task-elicited lexical innovations and to extend known grammatical processes to unfamiliar contexts revealed by Yif'at's study accords well with Ninio's findings for children in their second year, to the effect that "high-SES infants had a bigger productive vocabulary, and low-SES infants had a bigger imitative vocabulary."

Other studies comparing the language of children from different sociocultural backgrounds reveal similar discrepancies. Thus Stern (1977) found inferior use of contrasting sets of adjectives among lower SES children aged 5 to 6; Greenwald (1979) found that children aged 3;0 to 3;5 performed significantly differently on a comprehension test of language skills in relation to socioeconomic background; and Ben-Aroya (1979) found that on a comprehension test given to 4 to 7 year olds, there was a consistent gap in the achievements of the two socioeconomic levels tested, in favor of children from the higher one.

The material reviewed in this chapter to date, however, has largely disregarded sociocultural variables of this kind, both because of the paucity of data available, and as a matter of deliberate choice. Our data are based almost entirely on the usage of middle-class children whose parents have at least a high-school level of education, and who have grown up in homes with a tradition of literacy. The discussion in the remainder of this section, accordingly, focuses on the kind of population whose children, and parents, are taken to constitute the receivers and transmitters of what we feel safe to view as a kind of "standard" Hebrew usage.

9.2. *Hebrew Baby-Talk*

The only study known to me that relates specifically to the nature of Hebrew "baby-talk" is Zeidner's (1978) characterization of phonological and lexical features of adult input based on observations of adult-child interactions combined with questionnaires and interviews inquiring into adults' attitudes to and use of baby talk. His findings show that there is clearly an Israeli version of baby-talk cum nursery-language, which manifests the features associated with this register in other cultures—such as higher pitch, exaggerated intonational contours, slower tempo, plentiful repetitions, and wide recourse to accompanying gestures.

Such properties are accompanied by a wide range of special nursery terms found in most Israeli homes, where in many cases the etymology is not at all clear, by contrast with common onomatopoeic forms in both input and output such as: *hau-hau* for 'dog', *gaga* 'duck', *me* 'cow, sheep', or *kukuriku* 'cock, hen' (Section 3.1 above). Israeli nursery-terms include the following:

(30) Nursery Form	Meaning = Extension	Standard Terms
am	eating, food, meal	*oxél* 'eat', *óxel* 'food'
áyta	going out, taking a walk, ride in a buggy	*haxuca* 'outside', *le-tayel* 'take a walk'
fúya	'yucky', distaste	*meluxlax* 'dirty', *mag'il* 'disgusting'
nu-nu-nu	disapproval, prohibition	*lo* 'no, don't', *asur* 'not allowed'
céci	pacifier, baby's "dummy"'	*mocec* 'sucker' (= 'pacifier')

Taboo terms also have specific forms, including *pipi* and *kaka, cíciz* or *cickalax* for breasts, bosom, nipples (possibly from Yiddish) versus normative *shadáyim* 'breasts', *ptamot* 'nipples'; and the penis is called *chupchik* 'little appendage' from Yiddish-Slavic, or *búlbul*, the Arabic name for a familiar bird, also jocular for 'silly'. Children's games and rituals also have special appelations, such as: *kuku* 'peek-a-boo', for playing hide and seek; *ópala* 'all fall down'; *hey-ops* 'upsy-daisy'; *uww-ah* for giving or getting a hug; or *dyo* 'giddy-ap' for playing 'horsie'. These are partly onomatopoeic, and in some cases are taken from the corresponding terms in the languages of origin of parents and grandparents.

Baby-talk also includes numerous pet-terms for addressing children, by contrast with the relative lack of such terms as 'darling' or 'honey' among middle-class Israeli adults, where personal feelings are generally not overtly expressed in public. Endearments in addressing young children include: *búbele, bubi* from *buba* 'doll' with a Yiddish deminutive ending in the first one, also found in pet terms for *ima, aba* 'Mommy, Daddy' diminutivized by both parents and children as *imale, abale* in many homes; *motikinz* 'sweetie', from *matok* 'sweet', again with a foreign ending; *mami, mamale* perhaps relating to *ima* 'mama'; also *puci, puchi, pucinyu* from Yiddish-Slavic—all pronounced with the Yiddish-based, non-Hebrew penultimate stress that is general for personal names—as in the name *xáyim* vs the common noun *xayím* 'life'. This may be indicative of the very child-centered, child-adoring nature of Israeli society, which regards it as normal and expected to shower endearments on children of all ages and both sexes. And a related feature may be the wide use of nicknames in all peer groups throughout school age and subsequently, where these childish appelations are often perpetuated in adulthood—e.g. *dudi* for *david, yoni* for *yonatan* 'Jonathan', *tuti* for *rut* 'Ruth', *mimi* for *miryam* 'Miriam'.

The above, and many other examples could be added, reflect the impact of foreignisms on Israeli baby-talk; for even where the parents are native speakers of Hebrew, the nursery talk of their parents, and the children's grandparents, in Yiddish, Russian, Ladino, Arabic, and so on, is perpetuated in monolingual homes as well. For instance, my husband and I, as native English speakers fluent in Hebrew, having spent well over half our lives in Israel, resort to Yiddish-based endearments with the children in the family, our own parents having been Russian-Yiddish and Lithuanian-Yiddish by origin. As a result, then, some features of baby-talk, particularly in the rich class of endearments and intimate terms, tend to differ somewhat in families of different language background. On the other hand, as shown by the examples in (30) above, there is by now a large range of shared nursery terminology which is unique to Hebrew child language.

9.3. *Multiple Interaction with Adults*

Israeli children typically interact quite intensively with adults other than the mother, for fathers play an important part in child-rearing in nearly all strata of the society, and social contexts beyond the nuclear family are highly developed, and tend to include children as a natural part of the scene. In middle-class homes, where most mothers go out to work when the child is 3 months or at most 1 year old, infants also interact with two main kinds of female caretakers: the grand-mother, who is herself often a non-native speaker of Hebrew, and a *metapélet* 'looker-after, caretaker' employed to tend the child while the mother is away from home. From age 2 onwards, most children also have another major source of linguistic input in the form of the *ganénet* 'nursery-school teacher' and her associates, and she will often use a special kind of "teacherese," using rather exaggeratedly high pitch and careful articulations as well as a selfconsciously "correct" type of locution.

From a young age, then, the Israeli child is exposed to a wide range of adult registers, from the highly affective input of parents, grandparents, and other relatives to the more normative, less personalized style of his official caretakers outside the family circle. The frequency with which Israeli children interact with people outside the immediate family and the variation of linguistic input available to them may, clearly, have an effect on their linguistic development, as is suggested in Bowerman's (in press) review of related factors; and it may account for the rather precocious development of young Hebrew speakers when compared with their English-speaking counterparts, as noted at the outset of this chapter. Even though no controlled research is available on such questions, it is quite clear from casual observations that 3 year old Israeli children, much like their American counterparts, adopt a different register and speech style when role-playing with their dolls and teddy bears, when talking to their pets, to young babies, to their older siblings, or to their teachers. Note, moreover, that the relative informality of Israeli social interaction in general involves less differentiation in forms of address and in stylistic level according to social setting and participant status than one will find among children of more traditional or highly formalized societies such as Japan or even Western Europe. We would like to suggest, then, that the combination of multiple interaction with adults and relatively nondifferentiated styles of address in standard Hebrew serves to facilitate the Israeli child's acquisition of sociolinguistic norms.

9.4. Role of Peer Input

A highly typical feature of Israeli child language is the central role played by peer input and by peer norms, in keeping with the generally peer-oriented nature of the society, where from early preschool age, children establish groups with whom they interact intensively during school hours 6 days a week, as well as in the neighborhood, at home, and in the playground; and this intense peer interaction continues through grade and high school, in the army, and often well into adult life. The most extreme instance of this type of interaction is found on the kibbutz, where children spend the bulk of their time from birth in what is termed 'the children's house' with others of their age; but this accounts for only about 3% of the total population (and the source of data for three of the studies reported on here: Dromi, 1977, Eyal, 1976, and Salzburg, 1976). However, intensive peer-interaction is typical for most Israeli children, in urban as well as in other types of non-kibbutz, rural settings.

The crucial importance of peer input in children's language development is noted by many (for instance, Baron, 1977 and Weinreich et al., 1968), although I am not familiar with comparative research in this area. It seems to me that in some very basic sense, Israeli children at all events get their language from other children, and that it is the peer group which establishes the forms and usages that become perpetuated as the Hebrew typical of younger speakers. This may account for the fact that even where Hebrew is not the only, or the main language spoken at home, by the time of emergent syntax the bilingual child is getting what he needs of Hebrew from his peers, if not from his parents. This impression is borne out by results of research in progress by Shoshana Rabinowitch, comparing the linguistic proficiency in Hebrew of monolingual 3 to 5 year olds with their English-Hebrew bilingual peers. Her subjects seem to lag behind the monolingual speakers mainly in range of lexicon rather than in morphosyntactic proficiency or in pragmatic functions of the language, and the deficiencies of the bilinguals seem quite negligible by the time they are ready to start first grade.

One specific piece of evidence indicating the importance of peer input is provided by my own child in first grade, when her teacher had evaluated her as having an unusually rich command of the language. In conversation with me she used, within the same discourse turn, the two words *firuk 'breaking up' in place of standard piruk or peruk and *soprim 'are counting' in place of standard sofrim, thus twice violating the roles for spirant-stop alternation noted in Section 4.1.1 above. None of the adults whom I know her to come in contact with in the village setting in which she has grown up—parents, uncles and aunts, grownup siblings, nursery-school and regular school teachers—use forms like these. Yet I have heard several of Shelli's friends, around ages 5 to 7, making identical mistakes, so that the only conclusion one can draw here is that the child's language forms are feeding on, and into, those of her contemporaries.

Recall that the first generation of native speakers of Hebrew less than a 100 years ago had to create their own peer-talk, so to speak. And this is still evident in the largely loan-based terminology evolved for playing games like marbles or hopscotch (Bar-Adon, 1977), one of the few areas in which regional usage differs from one city to another, or from town to country. The rich lexicon of such games is distinguished by Yiddish-Ashkenazi penultimate word-stress compared with ordinary word-final stress; for instance, the word klaf-ím 'cards' is pronounced kláfim when talking about the game, the words rishón and shení 'first' and 'second' become ríshon, shéni and so forth when counting out in games, and so on (Bolozky, 1978a). Related evidence of the central role of peer-group activity is attested to in Yakir's (1973) study of no less than seven "secret languages"—of the pig-Latin sort—reported on by her informants. They are characterized as "children's lore (traditions transmitted from child to child) as opposed to nursery lore (traditions transmitted from adults to children)," and Yakir notes that her informants without exception "claimed to have learned the variety from another child in school or neighborhood. Many felt that they and their playmates had invented the languages to speak secretly, and were unaware that children in different parts of the country and of different generations had used almost exactly the same techniques of disguise. None of the adults in the sample had used the varieties after adolescence."

In the absence of research on child-child interaction (one exception being the study of Rom, 1979, which was not concerned specifically with the linguistic form of such interchanges), or comparisons with, say, child-parent, child-teacher, and child-older child interactions, these claims remain largely impressionistic. Nonetheless, the following do seem to apply to input factors as having an important role in the development of Hebrew child language. Firstly, the richness of nursery language and baby-talk, which depart considerably from standard Hebrew forms, may be a function of the highly child-centered nature of the community, coupled with the non-native origins of its initiators. Secondly, the relative precocity of Hebrew language development, in the sense of early emergence of syntax, and early control of bound morphology, may be a function of the interrelated circumstances of children's wide exposure to a variety of adults and intensive as well as extensive peer-interaction from an early age. Moreover, the role of peer input in Israel combined with the special sociohistorical circumstances of the revival of Hebrew as a native, spoken language, which engender an accelerated rate of language change together make children in a very real sense the major carriers of language change, as the true originators-creators of a new language and its most prolific innovators.

9.5. *Role of Formal Schooling*

The "naive" speaker of Hebrew is not really all that naive once he goes to school. There are almost no illiterates among native speakers of Hebrew, certainly not in the middle-class contexts focused on in this chapter. From age 4, children are "taught" names of geometric shapes, analogies, contrasts, and other labels as part of the official curriculum for preschoolers; and they are told stories and their people's history, narrated in a literary, often archaic-sounding style. From first grade on, children are familiarized with the consonantal orthography of their language, and this provides them with a perceptible aid in recognizing phonetically opaque forms in terms of their consonantal root plus affixes. That is, they quite early on start on the conscious road to "consonant extraction" so central to a Semitic, root-based language like Hebrew (and see, in this connotation, Bentur, 1978; Bolozky, 1978b). Moreover, from fourth grade on, children are given intensive drilling in Hebrew "grammar," including mainly methods of vocalizing consonantally represented forms and word-formation prcesses according to Biblically-based rules, as well as laws of "correct usage" which denigrate colloquial Hebrew, hence their own usage, as opposed to literary norms of the past. Thus, for instance, while 5 year olds will use verb-pattern alternations or will coin innovative nouns in an intuitively appropriate way for expressing semantic distinctions, 12 year olds will tend more widely to interpret unfamiliar forms according to the "rules" taught them at school, even if these depart from actual contemporary usage.

We are not claiming that formal schooling is so "successful" that Israeli adolescents talk like the books say they should. But it does explain the difference between truly naive and natural preschool learning and the later development of linguistic consciousness. Schooling may have a positive effect in clarifying abstract phonological alternations through the medium of orthography, and in making speakers aware of the role of consonantal roots plus affixal patterns in word formation in their language. Yet it also has a deleterious effect in making teenage and college-level students feel that theirs is not really a legitimate "grammar" at all, so that they come to mistrust their own intuitions and to scorn their judgments about a language which they speak natively. And, to reiterate a theme recurrent in this chapter, one which impinges on Givón's observations (1985) about what constitutes real and relevant input for child language development, the impact of the normative-colloquial divide is so exacerbated by school language studies that it makes the task of deciding what constitutes immature usage and is developmentally dictated as against what is general colloquial usage and hence the basic source of input to children a peculiarly difficult undertaking.

10. Individual Differences

There are to the best of my knowledge no studies available on individual differences in children's acquisition of Hebrew. Anecdotal observations of parents often relate to marked differences in both rate and methods of acquisition among siblings, to the effect, for instance, that one child started speaking very late but then "came out with whole sentences" whereas another was highly precocious and talked a lot "with a lot of mistakes" from a very early age. Parents have also commented to me that one child engaged in a great deal of word play and tended to regard language as an object for comment and analysis, whereas others did not show such tendencies. One notable area of difference seems to be in the case of children who either do or do not engage in so-called "developmental jargon" by resorting to lengthy chunks of what I have elsewhere termed "speech without words" (Berman, 1979a) in the initial stages of acquisition. In addition, preschool-age educators have often pointed out to me one child as having a "very rich language," another as not talking at all well.

This entire topic thus still requires careful study for Hebrew-speaking children along the lines suggested in current research into individual differences (Lieven, 1980). And it needs, further, to be considered in light of sociocultural differences in home background, an area which we noted in Section 9.1 above as having been largely neglected with respect to preschool-age children. Current research on institutionally-raised children aged around 4 compared with their lower to middle-class home-raised peers indicates that the former manifest a developmental gap of some two years on a wide range of language tasks, and that this gap lessens but does not disappear by around age 8 (Yif'at, 1981). Studies such as those of Ninio (1980) of mother-child interaction against the background of different SES groups need to be extended from infancy through to the early grade-school years. It follows that the issue of individual differences and the related area of social variation need still to be included under the heading of "topics for further study" considered in the next section below as far as Hebrew-language acquisition is concerned to date.

CONCLUSIONS

11. Suggestions for Further Study

In light of the relative paucity of both experimental and naturalistic research in Hebrew child language, as noted in Section 2 above, the suggestions which follow are numerous and multifaceted. While this is not formally indicated below, the contents of this section are organized to relate, firstly, to more general issues with respect to which the study of Hebrew child language seems to be of particular interest for crosslinguistic and crosscultural purposes; secondly, to specific areas of linguistic knowledge which have not been researched for Hebrew child language; and thirdly, to similar areas which are particularly relevant to late, school-age acquisition.

11.1. *Comparison with other Semitic Languages*

Characteristically Semitic properties of Hebrew should be investigated by comparison with the acquisition of one or more dialects of spoken Arabic. Such properties might include the use of morphological verb patterns to encode relations of passive, causative, inchoative, etc.; the nature of the consonantal root as a lexical prime; and the alternation of subject-verb and verb-initial order in basic sentence types. There is evidence that colloquial Arabic is undergoing similar processes of change and "Europeanization" as are found in Modern Hebrew (Blau, 1976), and it would be interesting to see how such processes are reflected in children's acquisition of these languages. (See, too, Badry, 1983.)

11.2. *Child Language and Language Change*

A recurrent theme throughout this chapter has been the question of which of children's errors are transient, hence typically "juvenile," and which usages that deviate from normative requirements occur among school-age children, adolescents, and older speakers. A study comparing patterns of stem-change in the formation of plurals by 3, 6, and 12 year olds compared with adults indicates that some errors are in fact the result of immature strategies and occur "across-the-board," whereas others are due to factors of familiarity with set forms and remain fossilized in the usage of educated adults, too (Berman, 1981c). Careful study is required of a wide range of linguistic phenomena to investigate the duration as well as the extent of error among speakers of different ages and backgrounds, so as to pinpoint the relative role of children's usage in evolving forms which are eventually adopted as standard compared with the effect of input. Thus, detailed descriptive accounts are needed to characterize both potential and occurrent directions of change, particularly in view of the unique sociohistorical facts of the emergence of Modern Hebrew, as noted in Section 1 at the outset of this chapter.

11.3. *Nature and Role of Input*

In order to provide some yardstick for deciding which deviations from normative requirements are largely developmental and which may merely reflect general input from the surroundings, input studies need to be made of Israeli speech to children of different ages and sociocultural backgrounds, and in different settings. Ideally, crosscultural input studies would be needed to test the claims made in Sections 9.3 and 9.4 above regarding the importance of multiple interaction with adults and of peer input respectively. Yet even without such research, much could be gained from study of mothers' speech to children of different ages compared with that of nursery-school and other teachers, of fathers, and other caretakers and adults, on the one hand, and how such input relates to peer-group speech, on the other.

11.4. *Impact of Childhood Bilingualism*

In an immigrant society such as Israel, numerous children are exposed to languages other than Hebrew from infancy, but no studies are available on the effects of such exposure in either early or subsequent acquisition of Hebrew. A large-scale study is currently in preparation comparing the Hebrew proficiency of Israeli 3 to 5 year olds from English-speaking homes with that of their monolingual peers (Rabinowitch, in progress), and there is clear indication that the gap between the two groups lessens with age, and that it is particularly strong in highly language-specific areas of Hebrew knowledge. This study needs to be extended to school-age children to see how bilingualism affects or is affected by formal studies. Account needs to be taken of the relation between relative proficiency in the home language and in the general language of the culture, Hebrew. Such issues need to be considered not only in terms of morphosyntax and lexical proficiency—as in the study noted earlier—but also from the point of view of general communicative competence and discourse skills. Finally, similar study is needed of children whose background is other than English (associated as it is with high prestige and above-average socioeconomic status). For instance, there are no data available on the nature and effect of exposure to Arabic in the homes of children whose parents—and by this stage, more typically grandparents— came to Israel from Middle Eastern countries of Arabic-speaking extraction. Parents of more educated backgrounds—today most often of English, Spanish, or Russian-speaking extraction—are plagued by the question of whether and how to use their native tongue with their children who, as noted, from a very early age indeed are absorbed into all-Hebrew speaking peer groups and educational settings. But there are no sociolinguistic, let alone acquisitional, studies available to back up intuitions and familiarity with the findings of relevant research on early bilingualism from outside the Israeli scene.

11.5. *Measures of Language Development*

A need is constantly expressed for clinical and educational as well as for theoretical purposes to evolve standardized measures and developmental scales of children's language in Hebrew, but to date nothing much has been done beyond attempts to "translate" currently available measures for English-speaking children. Research is now under way on an attempt to adapt the LARSP procedure (Crystal, Fletcher & Garman, 1976) for use with Hebrew-speaking children, taking into account the rich processing at the "word level" entailed by the developmental task in Hebrew compared with English. Calculation of MLU for Hebrew was attempted in Dromi (1977) and a revised measure of what we termed "morpheme per utterance" was then evolved on this basis (Dromi & Berman, 1982). Account was taken of the special properties of a synthetic language like Hebrew, where additional morphemic complexity is not always reflected in additional length of utterance. In principle, we favored developmental over strictly structural criteria; for instance, *para* 'cow' was counted as one morpheme even though it is composed of *par* 'bull' plus the feminine suffix -*a,* because children normally acquire the word for 'cow' long before they know the word for 'bull'. Among the many difficulties we encountered were the fact that, at some more abstract level, vowel infixes are also morphemes—e.g. *soger* 'shuts' vs. *sagar* has shut' vs. *sgor* 'shut!'; whether to credit alternating verb patterns for isolated instances—e.g. P2 *nixnas* 'go in' vs. P5 *hixnis* 'put in', which might be rote-learned for our 2 to 3 year old subjects; and how to credit synthetic morphs such as -*ot,* which indicates both feminine and plural. Our measure correlated highly with the scores of the same 2 to 3 year olds on various syntactic and semantic elements, indicating that it may be a valid means of establishing relative linguistic maturity at the stage of early syntax. Further study is needed in several directions, including: detailed comparisons of similar measures for other languages which might pose related, non-English types of problems, as in the Slavic languages; ways of establishing developmental criteria in other areas of language use, such as lexico-semantic and pragmatic, communicative skills; and construction of effective developmental scales for Hebrew-speaking children from the one-word period and through to stages where morphosyntax is so highly developed that morphemic counts are no longer relevant.

11.6. *Awareness of "Roots"*

The answer is not at all clear to what is perhaps the most intriguing issue in the study of Semitic child-language: how and when speakers acquire knowledge of the consonantal root as the morphological and semantic core of most of the content words in the language, and how this interrelates with their perception of different morphological patterns as assigning specific lexico-semantic content to various classes of words. There is evidence that from around age 4 children do begin to relate to some kind of consonantal "skeleton" as representing a given core of meaning, and as a way of construing words with the same root as semantically related (Clark & Berman, 1984). In the later preschool years, children manifest this knowledge by extracting the consonantal core of known words to coin innovative verbs and nouns which accord by and large with the morphological patterns of the standard language (Berman, 1980; Berman and Sagi, 1981); and other research too (Walden, 1982), shows that 5 year olds will explain familiar nouns by means of verbs based on the same consonantal root. Crosslinguistic research is necessary to ascertain whether the reliance on root consonants as semantic and structural primitives facilitates or complicates the task of vocabulary acquisition. And much detailed research is needed to establish how cognizance of consonantal roots is first manifested, how it evolves developmentally, when this knowledge takes the form of conscious awareness, and how it becomes articulated. The issue of the "psychological reality of the root" is a complex one for both adult and developmental psycholinguistic investigation, yet it seems well worth pursuing in some depth.

11.7. *Knowledge of Word Patterns*

The pattern of acquisition of the *binyan* verb patterns has been studied in some detail for Hebrew, as discussed in Sections 4.3, 7.4, and 8.1 above. No such detailed research is available for acquisition of the far more numerous and semantically less predictable set of nominal patterns in Hebrew, although preliminary investigation of naturalistic data does indicate some quite clear developmental trends, as noted in Section 11.8 below. In morphological terms, many noun and adjective patterns alternate differently in ways which have no contemporary phonetic motivation. Examples include: plurals of CiCCa nouns—compare *tikva/tikv-ot* 'hope/s' *pitma/ptam-ot* 'nipple/s'; plurals of CaCaC nouns—compare *pasal/pasal-im* 'sculptor/s' vs. *bacal/bcal-im* 'onion/s'; plurals of monosyllabic nouns, compare *kof/kof-im* 'monkey/s' with *tof/tup-im* 'drums'; feminine of bisyllabic adjectives, compare *katom/ktum-a* 'orange' with *karov/krov-a* 'near'. In many cases, such alternations are unmotivated for adults, too, and they make fewer errors than children because of greater exposure and more familiarity with actual instances; while the "errors" which remain in older speakers become part of standard usage. However, there is some evidence that older speakers can and do resort to more formal kinds of knowledge including of general morphophonological processes of stem penultimate vowel reduction before a stressed suffix and spirantization of stops in non-word-final position, as well as of semantic classes—such as that agent nouns with the form CaCaC do not incur stem-vowel reduction in the plural, or that color adjectives replace stem-final /o/ with /u/ before a stressed suffix, but other adjectives do not. Much more detailed study is needed of a wide variety of such alternations in order to establish whether and when young speakers achieve an awareness of phonological processes as applying to certain morphological patterns and to specific semantic classes of words.

11.8. *Word-Formation Processes*

Closely related to the preceding questions are other aspects of knowledge of word-formation processes which require further examination for Hebrew child language. Lexical innovations are a particularly good source of information on how children, and adults, perceive the wordstock of their language. Preliminary analysis of naturalistic data (Berman & Sagi, 1981) indicates that children first show awareness of the two classes of agent and instrument nouns—in line with experimental evidence for English by Clark & Hecht (1982) as well as Hebrew (Clark & Berman, 1984). Thus, from age 3 on, children mark agent and instrument nouns by means of a suffixal *-an,* and they show a marked preference for the prefix plus suffix pattern maCeCCa for instruments, while a conceptually more developed stage is manifested by the marking of abstract state and action nouns with the suffix *-ut.* These data are of interest because they show that children have a clear perception of these lexico-semantic classes, which they mark off in distinct ways in their own innovative, hence non-rote-learned forms, and that this knowledge is manifested crucially from around the fourth year. Moreover, these investigations show that children do not make use of the typically Semitic process of vowel-alternation alone—although vowel infixes are used in constructing certain classes of nouns in Hebrew (e.g. CaCaC as in agent nouns like *pasal* 'sculptor', *tayas* 'pilot'; CéCeC in instrument nouns like *bérez* 'faucet', *méteg* 'bridle'; or CóCeC in abstract nouns like *kóšer* 'fitness', *lóven* 'whiteness'). This is clearly due to the greater perceptual salience of prefixes and suffixes as lying outside of the stem in marking semantic content compared with vowel-infixing alone. Careful study of children's innovations in spontaneous output combined with experimental study of both production and interpretation-segmentation of a wide range of lexical classes is needed to ascertain how children formwords to cover concepts and combinations (for instance, through compound nouns and blends) which are not lexicalized in their language. Such studies should try to tap whether and how children relate to certain morphological patterns as carrying certain meanings and what weight they give to certain patterns or affixes by comparison with others which are less productive for them. And again, such studies should compare children's strategies with those of adolescents and adults, who may have more or different kinds of lexical knowledge available.

11.9. *Diminutives*

In considering "baby-talk" in Section 9.2 we noted certain typical diminutives which children seem to use very early in their development. Brown (1973) did not count diminutives in his analysis, but this does not seem correct for early child language in Hebrew, where 2 to 3 year olds do seem to manifest a contrast between, say, *šafan/šafan-i* 'rabbit/little rabbit', *pil/pil-on* 'elephant/baby elephant'. Moreover, the naturalistic data culled from children from their fourth year noted in the two preceding subsections indicate that they use a wide variety of devices for diminutivizing and giving pet-names—including five or six different suffixes as well as, at a slightly later age, various reduplications (as in normative *kélev/klavlav* 'dog/puppy-dog' and in my 5 year old's request not for *mangina* 'tune' but for *manginón-et* 'a little tune'). As an area which is richly develped in Hebrew usage, further investigation would be of interest in specifying not only the morphological devices used, but also the pragmatics of how such forms function for emotive purposes.

11.10. *Semantic Acquisition*

Apart from the kinds of lexico-semantic knowledge noted in the preceding subsections, the entire area of semantic development has been almost totally neglected in Hebrew child language studies. Even if much of such knowledge is conceptually anchored, hence likely to be shared crosslinguistically in developmental terms, data from Hebrew are needed to provide evidence for or against this hypothesis. There is, for instance, evidence from data from 40 2 to 3 year olds studied by Dafna Kaplan (1983), that the younger children tend to use "general purpose verbs" (in the sense of Clark, 1978) such as *la'asot* 'to do, make', *la-léxet* 'to go, walk', *li-šbor* 'to break' far more extensively, whereas older children use more lexical specification, such as *li-vnot* 'to build', *li-nsóa* 'to go by vehicle', *li-króa* 'to tear' instead. Similar increasing lexical specification with age is noted with respect to dimensional adjectives—such as *gadol* 'big' for, say, *arox* and *raxav* 'long' and 'wide'—and for evaluative adjectives—such as *yafe* 'nice, pretty' for *mesudar* 'tidy', *šalem* 'whole', *yašar* 'straight', etc. Interestingly enough, this general vs. specific trend is also manifested in comparisons of children of the same age but of different social backgrounds (Yif'at, 1981), while a reverse trend seems to be manifested in schoool-age children who have spent a year or two in an English-speaking country once they return to Israel. In the latter case, as loss of English sets in, the children once again resort to less specific terms as lexical retrieval of words they formerly knew in English becomes more difficult (Berman & Olshtain, 1981). These, then, are topics in semantic acquisition which require further study. The only other study known to me is the as yet unpublished doctoral research of Esther Dromi (1982) on the semantics of her own child at the one-word and initial syntax stage—a rich and detailed investigation which provides invaluable data for crosslinguistic comparison of early semantic development. But no work at all has been done in the area of propositional semantics, to indicate what kind of events children encode first and which later. These are of great relevance, given the peculiar morphosyntactic devices used by a language such as Hebrew in expressing, say, possession through use of 'be' plus a dative-marked nominal rather than with a *habere* verb; relative freedom of word order for pragmatic purposes; morphological marking of event-types within the *binyan* verb system and by means of prepositional case-marking; and the wide occurrence of verb-initial sentences in adult usage. This entire area, too, is still a topic for further study in Hebrew.

11.11. *Dative Marking*

We noted in Section 8.5 above that the dative marker *le-* is widely used in Hebrew to distinguish experiencer from agent, and in general to mark off the affectee of an event. Research is required to ascertain whether children show a consistent preference for Verb-Dative or for Subject-Verb constructions (e.g. 'got-lost to-me X' vs. 'I lost X', 'broke to-Ron the teddy' vs. 'Rina broke Ron's teddy'), and if there is such a trend, what its semantic-pragmatic correlates might be. This might make it possible to compare Hebrew-speaking children's construals of notions of experiences or benefactee/malefactee with that of children acquiring a subject-dominant language like English, where a wide variety of different semantic roles are realized as the surface subject (a way in which English differs, too, from both Polish and Japanese, say).

11.12. *Tense and Aspect*

Details on this topic are not generally available for Hebrew (as for other languages, by and large), although as noted earlier there is some evidence that end-state verbs such as 'fall' and 'break' tend to show up first in past tense, whereas durative and stative verbs, such as 'cry', 'sleep', or 'want', 'like' show strong preference for present tense. It is not at all clear whether these findings for Hebrew (as for other languages in studies such as Antinucci & Miller, 1976; Bloom et al., 1980) are a function of the inherent aspectual semantics of such verbs or largely determined by the input forms favored for such verbs in language addressed to children. And this is one reason why any such study must address the issue of the form of input verbs to children as a possible factor in acquisition. Preliminary analysis of the verb forms occurring in the free speech of 2 to 3 year olds based on data from a study by Dafna Kaplan (1983) shows, in fact, that children use all three Hebrew tenses simultaneously—although future forms are far less common at age 2 than early in the fourth year—and that they alternate verb-form usage across all three tenses right from the start precisely for the commonest, semantically least specific verbs such as the prototypical action verb meaning 'do' or 'make', the movement verb meaning 'go' or 'walk' and the transfer verbs meaning 'give' and 'take'. In other words, study of tense forms in Hebrew-speaking children needs to take into account a rather complex range of semantic and pragmatic variables which may be interacting in acquisition, in order to test such hypotheses as whether the association between a given verb and a given tense form is particularly strong only in the very initial stages of acquisition, and only for some rather than all kinds of events and predicates. Moreover, detailed study is needed to ascertain how the development of tense forms interacts with the acquisition of lexical time-adverbs marking aspectual distinctions—based upon prior study of the emergence of such adverbs as, say, the words for 'now', 'afterwards', 'soon', etc. This, in turn, would make it possible in crosslinguistic terms to investigate how the existence of a limited set of three tense-marked verb forms, coupled with early overextension of the infinitive form as noted earlier in the chapter, which are then complemented by a wide range of time adverbials, either facilitates or hampers acquisition of tense and aspect, by contrast with languages which mark both parameters within the verb system.

11.13. *Word Order*

This was also noted earlier in the chapter as not seriously studied for Hebrew (except for experimental investigation of comprehension strategies by Frankel et al., 1980). Children's speech should be studied—along lines suggested in subsection 11.11 above—to investigate the nature and function of SV and VS orders respectively, both by experimental design and in spontaneous usage, to see if the relative frequency of the two orders tends to change with age. A related question is how and when various devices for establishing discourse topics and for foregrounding and backgrounding of material come into productive use. For instance, is it really the case that right-dislocation is used earlier than left-dislocation or than fronting of non-subject nominals, and how might such patterns be accounted for? On the basis of such information, crosslinguistic study would be needed to test our hypothesis that the very existence of such syntactically straightforward and very rich devices for pragmatic foregrounding and backgrounding might make Hebrew-speaking children aware of such concepts at an earlier stage than children acquiring a language higher on the scale of "grammatical word order" types (Thompson, 1978).

11.14. *More Complex Structures*

The dearth of studies on later acquisition in general, and of more complex types of semantic-syntactic structures, has been noted at various points in this chapter. Three specific topics come to mind in this connection. (i) RELATIVE CLAUSES—findings from an experimental study (Herzberg, 1983) indicate that the following developmental pattern occurs with respect to the three different types of clause-internal relatives found in Hebrew: those with no clause-internal subject, as in *ha séfer še nafal* 'the book that fell' and hence no pronoun-copy; those where the clause-internal direct object may be deleted or copied, as in *ha séfer še ron lakax (oto)* 'the book that Ron took (it)'; and those where pronoun-copying of an oblique phrase is obligatory, as in *ha séfer še ron hityaxes el-av* 'the book that Ron referred to-IT'. But almost nothing is known of when and how children use these constructions in spontaneous speech output in different discourse settings. (ii) COMPLEMENT AND ADVERBIAL CLAUSES—Children first combine two predicates by means of a simple verb plus infinitive phrase, as in *roce la-léxet* 'want to-go', but it is not clear when children first use 'that' clauses as complements of a finite verb as in *ani roce še ron yelex* 'I want that Ron will-go' (= 'I want Ron to go') or with an indirect object as in *ani amarti le ron še ani elex* 'I said to Ron that I will-go', nor how this usage develops for different verb types which require such complements. With respect to adverbial clauses such as *ani baxíti kše / axarey še / biglal še / lamrot še ron kibel glida* 'I cried when / after / because / although Ron got ice cream' or *ani evke im ron yekabel glida* 'I will-cry if Ron will-get ice-cream', it is reasonable to assume that the developmental pattern is similar to what has been noted for English and other languages, and that conceptual complexity determines the way and stage of emergence of these different relations. Yet in the absence of detailed investigation of these structures in Hebrew-speaking children, it is impossible to specify when each of these emerges in either comprehension or production, and what kinds of knowledge entailed by such structures may be deferred to quite late in the child's history. (iii) DERIVED NOMINALS—There is some preliminary experimental evidence (from a class paper by Esther Felzenshtein) that 5 to 7 year olds do not have full command of a task which requires them to provide action and state nominals to describe events such as 'washing clothes', 'climbing a rope', etc. on the basis of their related verbs. This is a morphologically complicated set of forms in Hebrew, as action-nominals generally but not always take a specific form depending on the *binyan* pattern of the related verb. Moreover, Hebrew does not have a verbal form such as English *-ing* which can be used to describe actions and states, but makes use of a vareity of forms to express both the gerundive *arriving* and the nominalized *arrival* of English. This entire area warrants further study as a good source of information concerning a complex lexico-syntactic development which may be developmentally deferred both because Agent-Action descriptions are more easy to process in general than embedded nominal phrases (compare 'I had lunch after my mother arrived' with 'I had lunch after my mother's arrival', where in Hebrew there is a reversal of SV order between *imi higíya* 'my-mother arrived' and *haga'at imi* 'arrival-POSS my-mother') and, relatedly, because the former is the norm in colloquial conversation, the latter restricted to literary or newspaper usage. Hence, both in terms of linguistic structure and of processing strategies as well as of formal vs. colloquial register, the study of abstract nominals should provide important insight into later acquisitions in Hebrew.

11.15. *Pragmatics and Discourse Register*

Pragmatic issues concerning the development of conversational competence and discourse strategies have, again, not been investigated for Hebrew. Yet they should be undertaken because Hebrew manifests a peculiar kind of dualism in this respect. On the one hand, if one compares Israeli conversational interaction with that of, say, Japanese or Samoan, as discussed by Clancy and Ochs respectively (1985), the Hebrew-speaking child's task is very easy indeed: There are very few register differences—even when compared with a language like American English—which the Israeli child has to take into consideration when addressing his or her mother or father, grandparents or siblings, schoolteacher or class-mates (Blum-Kulka, in press); he or she does not even have to use different address terms such as *tu* compared with *vous* (Clark, 1985). The assumption that this lack of social differentiation might facilitate the acquisitional task for Hebrew-learning children requires careful prior study of the type of language that children at different ages use when addressing peers, caretakers, adults of differ-ent stations, etc. (where all the latter except for parents and grandparents tend to be addressed by their first names, even if they are quite elderly!). Only then could crosscultural comparisons be undertaken to ascertain whether this assump-tion is well-founded. Yet the Israeli child does have a formidable "register-bound" task to face in a rather different sphere, and that is the distinction between ordinary spoken Hebrew and the more formal, literary—sometimes archaic—register of written Hebrew, including that of children's narratives and fairy tales. A case study of the stories and dramatizations of my own child aged around 6;2 to 6;6 when a firstgrader (Berman, 1981d) showed that in these "formal" storytelling situations, she switched from her everyday colloquial usage to what she construed as a more "elegant" or high-style language—in pronunciation, morphology, syntax, and the lexicon. However, at this young age, when she herself had first learned to read (and firstgrade primers and readers, as well as stories parents read to 3 year old children, are largely in this very literary style), my child did not as yet have command of the requisite devices, so that she mixed together highflown classical words with slang ex-pressions; she overused the verb-initial syntax favored in narratives to instances where the product was ungrammatical; she tried to use bound forms of genitives and accusative pronouns even when she did not know the correct way to formu-late these; she mixed in frozen formulas familiar to her from storybooks with her own modifications of these; and so on. What these findings clearly indicate is that by first grade, Israeli children—at all events, those from middle-class homes who are used to being read to—are aware of a different register which they perceive as "literary," although command of that register will not be acquired for several years to come (perhaps never will be, to judge from complaints of high-school and college teachers!) Of research interest, then, is to extend such studies to preschool and older grade-school children in order to trace when this "other" register first begins to be recognized, and what the stages are in its development. Comparative studies would then need to test my assumption that this kind of knowledge may be particularly culturally bound, and that children of less literate backgrounds and/or lower SES might not have this potential "di-glossia" develop as early or as well.

11.16. *The Role of Orthography and of Formal Schooling*

It seems that knowledge of the writing system, acquired usually in first grade between ages 6 and 7, may have a direct impact on children's construal of the complex morphophonemic alternations in their language (as discussed in Berman, 1981b). On the one hand, Hebrew literacy entails a great deal of complex syntactic and morpho-lexical analysis, since most texts are written with only the consonants being represented (although children's primers, storybooks, and all poetry, include diacritic marks representing the vowels). The ability to read thus involves a great deal of linguistic knowledge to provide cues for disambiguating consonantal strings which in isolation could represent quite different things— e.g. the letters *s-p-r* could stand for the nouns *sfar* 'border', *séfer* 'book' or *sapar* 'barber' or for the verb *safar* 'counted'; the letters *h-r-g-l* could stand for *hergél* 'habit' or *ha régel* 'the leg'; and the letters *s-ʕ-r* could stand for *še'ér* 'that (is) awake', *šá'ar* 'gate', or *se'ar* 'hair' as well as *še'er* 'assumed'. This indicates that careful study is needed to ascertain how and when children make use of various kinds of linguistic as well as extralinguistic cues to become proficient readers. On the other hand, the consonantal alphabet represents many historical distinctions which are phonetically neutralized today, as noted in Section 1.3 above, and this may aid children who have acquired the writing system in disentangling the numerous morphophonological opacities of the language. A study such as that of Bentur (1978) should be extended considerably, to compare how preschoolers and first-graders construe morphophonemic alternations compared with older children who may have access to the historical root via the written representation of familiar words—which should then be compared with words having similar phonetic properties which children will not have encountered in their written form at all.

Research should also be undertaken concerning how, if at all, the study of "grammar" from the early years of grade school—in the form of so-called rules of correct usage and of Biblically-based morphophonology—affects young speakers' intuitions about their language. Studies might be designed to probe their perceptions of the conflict between their own usage and the system imposed on them in their school grammar lessons, as well as of the difference between incidental exceptions and historically rule-based alternations. One outcome of such studies might then be deeper insight into possible distinctions between the preschooler's geniunely "naive" intuitions and the older child's more conscious, hence perhaps more "cluttered" views of the workings of the language which they share.

12. Theoretical Implications

Study of Hebrew child language affords potential insight into crosslinguistic issues along a number of parameters. In language-specific structures, note has been made of the richly synthetic, bound morphology of Hebrew and the Semitic feature of consonantal root plus set patterns of affixation, including vowel infixes, in the construction of the lexicon. A quite different typological property that has been noted is the relative freedom of word order as pragmatically determined, making the acquisitional task in this respect more like that of a child learning, say, Hungarian or a Slavic language rather than English. Along the diachronic access, the intense acceleration of processes of change in contemporary Hebrew makes the interrelation between child language and language change particularly noteworthy. One facet of this relationship is that in many areas, general colloquial usage opts for an analytical periphrasis in place of more normative, classical bound forms. Examples include inchoatives such as *nihya xiver* 'became pale' versus lexicalized *hexvir* 'paled', possessives such as *ha sfarim shel ron* 'the books of Ron' versus bound *sifrey ron* to mean 'Ron's books', and use of nonspecific verbs with a fully-specified object noun as in *asa ta'ut* 'made (a) mistake' versus lexical incorporation in the verb *ta'a* 'erred'. This trend in general informal usage provides children with a syntactic option which represents form-meaning relations in a more transparent, one-to-one fashion than through bound morphology, and children invariably rely initially on such analytic periphrasis. A second facet of this relationship is the fact that many morphophonological alternations have no clear phonetic motivation in terms of contemporary pronunciation. Examples include the contrast between verbs in the *hif'il* pattern with defective roots to yield normative *mevin, hevin* 'understand, understood', but *mazik, hizik* 'harms, harmed'; rules governing stop/spirant alternations; and inflectional paradigms for historically distinct stems, contrasting *pasal, pasal-im* 'sculptor-s' with *bacal, bcal-im* 'onions'. Such synchronically unmotivated distinctions burden the young child with a great deal of seemingly arbitrary lexical learning, while the underlying rules which govern these alternations are so opaque that they are often not mastered by adult speakers either.

In sociolinguistic terms, one should consider the unique role of young children as the first native speakers of Modern Hebrew some three or four generations back, and the importance of peer interaction in creating and/or perpetuating current usages. It is hard to make clear claims about these processes, given the fact that careful and extensive studies of input are generally lacking to date (Section 11.3 above). It thus remains to be seen whether, as I suggest would be the case, Hebrew child language can provide a particularly rich source of information concerning the role of sociocultural factors, multilingualism, and nature of peer as well as adult-child interactions in acquisition.

Crosslinguistic consideration of Hebrew data suggests that it might be profitable for each language or language type to establish certain areas of "language as a formal problem-space for children" (in the sense of Karmiloff-Smith, 1979b) as criterial or in some sense particularly central to the task of acquisition. Thus, for Hebrew as for Romance languages for instance, nonsemantic gender is crucial to grammatical acquisition. While for English, command of auxiliary structure and position is of major importance across different constructions, and for Slavic languages case-marking on nouns and their associated modifiers carries major formal weight—these features are irrelevant to Hebrew. Rather, control of the complex system of subject-verb and noun-modifier agreement is an important aspect of normal language development for Hebrew, and one which shows clear developmental patterns for the features of number, gender, and person. A second criterial area for Hebrew acquisition is the development of lexicalization of predicate types through the *binyan* system of verb patterns, as discussed in some detail in this chapter and elsewhere (Berman 1980b, 1982a). There is some indication that the ability to lexicalize such relations as causative, reflexive, or reciprocal appropriately within verb-pattern alternations provides a particularly clear criterion of language proficiency in children, as shown by the differential results on tests of this ability given to bilingual English-Hebrew vs. monolingual Israeli children aged 3 to 5 (Rabinowitch, in prep.) and to institutional vs. home-raised children aged 4 and 8 (Yif'at, 1981). An anthology such as the present volume should, hopefully, indicate across languages which specific structural features need to be focused on within rather than across language types.

Another parameter which seems particularly fruitful for establishing language-specific criteria is that of discourse register. This is discussed, for instance, in relation to "social distance" in the chapter by Ochs on Samoan and in relation to interlocutor relationships in Japanese by Clancy (1985). Here, the acquisitional task is far more complex than for the Hebrew-learning child, for whom it is by and large socially appropriate to use much the same kind of register—without so much as a *tu/vous* distinction—irrespective of whom he is addressing (although sociolinguistic research is needed to establish whether this claim holds equally across rural and urban settings, in homes of a more patriarchal rather than a Western background, in religious, traditional rather than secular backgrounds, etc.). Hopefully, some kind of continuum might be established with respect to degree of register differentiation required of children in different cultures and language groups—with Japanese, say, being high on the continuum of differentiation, English far lower down (possibly American English even "lower" than British in this respect), and Hebrew even further to the other extreme. On the other hand, as I noted in Section 11.16 above, Israeli children between the intermediate ages of around 5 to 9 do have to acquire a register very different than their normal conversational style as part of the process of acquiring literacy, failing which children's storybooks, fairy tales, and school primers will not be accessible to them. The nature of linguistic "diglossia" as a sociolinguistic variable thus warrants further investigation and crosslinguistic comparison in order to evaluate the nature of the acquisitional task of the young child.

Turning now to the issue of strategies of acquisition, or of children's "operating principles," our Hebrew data confirm many of the principles articulated in the literature—particularly by Slobin (1973, 1980, 1985) and MacWhinney (1975, 1978, 1985). Among these we find numerous instances where the child observes Eve Clark's (1980) principle of "simplicity," adding affixes with no stem-change—e.g. in adding the masculine plural -*im* and subsequently feminine plural -*ot,* or in retaining the regular /o/ stem vowel in future tense forms even where /a/ is required. To explain the transition from these overregularizations to normative forms of the standard grammar we have noted recourse to rather different kinds of knowledge. One concerns the acquisition of more sophisticated types of "rules" which take into account classes of items as patterning in a certain way on the basis of phonological, morphological or word-class, or semantic types of commonalities—that is, the emergence of formal knowledge as the basis for construing classes of items as behaving in a certain way. A rather different type of knowledge has its source in "familiarity," not merely with real-world referents but with the occurrence of specific items in actual language use—as a result of increased exposure to given forms of words in certain linguistic and/or pragmatic contexts. Note that the notion of familiarity cannot be explicated in simple terms of "frequency" for at least two reasons: Firstly, a given alternation may be quite rare in terms of word types in the general lexicon, but it may yet form the basis for regularizations if it is more transparent or less complex than alternations governing more numerous word types; and secondly, current frequency lists are unhelpful so long as no distinction is made between the lexical composition of input to children and general language use. Rather, "familiarity" needs to take into account such concepts as the notion of "haphazard examples" as discussed by Carey (1978) as well as the notion of "prototypicality" (Bowerman, 1978; Fillmore, 1978; Mulford, 1979). It seems to me that child language studies could benefit by extending these concepts not only to the acquisition of word meaning, but also to the development of alternating word forms (Berman, 1981c, 1984, in press).

Our data provide insight into certain rather special instances of what might be termed "rote learning" (as discussed, inter alia, in the works of MacWhinney cited earlier). We have noted at least two areas where early word use demonstrates an invariant linking of lexeme-to-form, in the following sense. Firstly, at the stage of very initial syntax, 2 year olds tend to use a given verb root in only one pattern—yielding neutralizations between *axal/he'exil* 'eat/feed', *pocec/hitpocec* 'burst TRANS/INTRANS', or *zarak/nizrak* 'throw/be, get thrown' as noted in an earlier section. At this stage, there is only one lexical verb available to children, although they may inflect it appropriately for number, gender, or person by this stage. Another such "linking" was noted with respect to early use of verb tense, where 2 year olds tend predominantly to favor use of a single tense for a given verb or class of verbs, whereas 3 year olds are free to vary a verb across present, past, and future. This kind of category-invariance for certain lexemes is not always immediately obvious in child-language data, since the favored form is often appropriate to the context of use at a given stage of development. Thus, while the factor of "familiarity" noted above will determine what this favored form is, increased exposure coupled with maturation will serve to sever the bonds of such rote linkings, as the child comes to extract out the notions of causative, reflexive, or reciprocal kinds of predicate relations or of past, present, and future along the time axis, AND to express them appropriately by means of language-specific, rule-bound alternations.

Hebrew-speaking children make clear use of formal cues to establish "schemata"—so that, for instance, suffixal -a is construed as marking feminine gender even when it is not strictly suffixal, but is unstressed and part of the word-stem, as in the example in the quotation from my own child's construal of the word *kóva* 'hat' as feminine (at the outset of this chapter). Here I will also cite a vivid instance of "U-shaped learning" (Bowerman, 1981) in the form of an interchange between three siblings aged 3, 4, and 6 as reported to me by Yedida Haymans: the youngest child said, by rote, *láyla tov* 'night good' (= 'good night'), was corrected by the middle child, who insisted it should be **láyla tová*, whereupon the 6 year old told him that he was being stupid, because of course it should be *láyla tov* (cf. *yaldá tová* 'good girl'). Other such schemata include the overextension of prefixal *m-* as marker of the present tense to verb patterns where this is inappropriate (Section 4.2.4 above); invariable marking of present tense in pattern P1 by the vowels *o-e* as in regular *holex* 'walks' and non-normative **yošen* 'sleeps' and of the past tense of this pattern by the vowels *a-a* as in regular *haláx-ti* 'I talked' and non-standard *šatá-ti* 'I drank'; as well as use of non-root suffixal /t/ as though it were a root-consonant in words based on defective roots—so that corresponding to regular *zoxér-et* 'remembers-FEM' children derive **soxét-et* 'swims-FEM' in place of required, "defective" *soxa*.

Data on children's lexical errors and innovations indicate that they clearly associate one form with one meaning, as in such cases as: use of suffixal *-an* to mark agent-nouns as in **sapran-it* 'hairdresser-FEM' (cf. standard *sapar-it*) or *marbic-an* 'hits-AGENT' in the sense of a child who is always hitting others; *-ut* to mark abstract states or activities as in **cmi'ut* 'thirstiness' (cf. standard *cima'on* from *came* thirsty') or innovative *mazi'ut* 'sweatiness' from *mazía* 'perspires'; the pattern maCCeCa to indicate instruments, as in **maglexa* 'shaver' for 'razor' or *makceca* 'snipper' for 'lawnmower'; and the pattern meCuCaC for statal or passive adjectives, as in **merugal* 'accustomed' vs. standard *ragil* or **merudam* 'asleep' vs. standard *radum,* or innovative *mešu'al* 'coughy, having a cough'. These schemata show that for Hebrew-speaking youngsters, stem-external marking of lexical content by means of prefixes and/or suffixes is a simpler and more accessible device for word-formation processing (though not for verb inflections: see Berman, 1982a) than is the equally common and typically Semitic strategy of alternation of vowel infixes only (e.g. *ha sapar siper oti* 'the barber cut-hair me' (= 'cut my hair'); *daxuk kan biglal ha dóxak* '(it's) crowded here because-of the crowding'; *ron tofer et ha téfer* 'Ron is-sewing the seam'). Clearly, stem-external affixation is perceptually more salient than stem-internal vowel-alternation for young children—although in the verb system they have no choice but to pay attention to such schemata very early on in marking present-past tense distinctions between *holex-halax* 'walks-walked' or *yošev-yašav* 'sits-sat' and dozens of other common verbs.

Reorganizations of entire subsystems which we have noted in this chapter include: reanalysis of imperatives as a three-way system (Section 4.2.2); neutralization of the distinction between first and third person in the future singular (Section 4.2.1); overextension of feminine-form numerals (Section 4.4.2); and mixing between the two transitive patterns of P3 and P5 and the intransitive patterns of P2 and P4 respectively (Section 4.3.2). Where these reorganizations are widespread across children and across ages, there is good reason to predict eventual general language change. This prediction seems to be particularly well-motivated in the instances we have noted where the reanalysis of children tends to be "across the board," while with adult speakers it is confined to a few specific high-frequency lexical items. Our hypothesis in such cases is that adult usage will eventually spread to all except a few items which remain fossilized as classically normative, so that elsewhere a new "rule" is introduced which reflects current child language usage with new "exceptions" being tolerated in the case of very common words.

In general, what emerges from early morphosyntactic development in Hebrew is a situation where children seem to be striving for maximal clarity in the form of (prefix) base-word (suffix), with each element having some clear semantic correlate. This explains many of the errors noted in Section 4 above, including children's tendency to reanalyze morphophonologically opaque forms in a way that is meaningful to them, so that accuracy of surface form may go by the board in the interim, so long as the necessary semantic components are expressed. It explains errors of backformation and of non-segmentation of lexicalized compounds and other set formulas, as well as stem-invariance. Acquisition of the rich bound morphology of Hebrew is rendered perceptually complex by the existence of both synthetic and syncretic affixes, while production is complicated by the opacity of morphophonemic alternations which have no surface phonetic motivation. On the other hand, such complexity may be mitigated by the Hebrew learner's ability to hold on to consonantal skeletons as cores of shared semantic content. Possibly, too, we can seek a "trade-off" explanation for the evident rapidity with which Hebrew-speaking children move into this system by taking into account the relative ease of syntactic acquisition in their language. Thus, as noted in Section 3.3, many initial syntax utterances which might be elliptical or telegraphic in a language like English, are wellformed in standard Hebrew. There is also no need for the child to grapple with aspect-marking in the verb phrase as in English, Romance, or Slavic; word order is quite free, with questions and negatives being formed in an uncomplicated, systematic way; and more complex syntactic structures such as clausal complements or adverbial and relative clauses are embedded by means of familiar morphemes and require little further syntactic elaboration, by contrast with, say, the alternation between different complementizers on English verbs or the requirements of nominalized forms of verbs in relative and complement clauses in Turkish. Besides, as soon as they start using complex sentences, Hebrew-speaking children can and do get a great deal of mileage out of a single subordinator meaning 'that' to express a variety of semantic relations across clauses (Section 4.6.3). It may, therefore, be worthwhile examining the acquisition task across different languages by comparing the relative learning burdens faced by children in gaining command of the morphophonological, syntactic, and discourse register systems respectively of their native tongue.

Finally, crosslinguistic data such as are presented in this volume might be reexamined in light of the central issue of the routes taken by children in proceeding from non-analysis to productive rule application. Thus, our Hebrew data reveal that, with respect to a number of unrelated subsystems in their language, children adopt a kind of "interim" procedure as a bridge between rote learning and adult-like command of the system in question. Examples include overextension of prefixal *m*- to inappropriate present-tense form verbs en route to full mastery of tense-marking in Hebrew (Section 4.2.4); mixing between but not across different verb patterns construed as transitive and intransitive respectively, prior to conventional lexicalization of these distinctions (Section 4.3.2); and choice of either a masculine or feminine plural suffix to mark agreement between irregular nouns and their associated adjectives (Section 4.4.1). Such typically juvenile interim strategies clearly provide evidence of transitional phases of "acquisition in progress." At such points, children are not simply resorting to straightforward overregularization. Rather, they are applying "rules" of their own construal to derive forms which are both formally and functionally well-motivated, but which happen to diverge from the norms of standard adult rules and usage. It seems that such notions as analysis and re-analysis, rote and analogy, productivity and conventionality, might be set on a firmer crosslinguistic basis, both theoretical and empirical, through careful consideration of the nature and role of such interim procedures or "bridging rules" in the child's emerging linguistic competence.

POSTSCRIPT

The passage of time since this chapter was first written, and re-written, has given rise to substantial changes in the study of Hebrew as a mother-tongue, and in my own thinking on the subject. Thus, several large-scale research projects are now well under way from which some findings, and hence new insights are now available. Two such studies arise directly out of cooperation with other contributors to this volume: study of the development of temporality in child discourse with Dan I. Slobin, and work on the acquistion of word formation devices in innovative verbs, nouns, and compounding with Eve V. Clark. As for my own thinking, work with the contents of this chapter, and interaction with colleagues involved in the projects noted earlier (for instance, in analyzing the form and function of early verb usage and preschool syntactic patterning with Esther Dromi) have led me to a re-appraisal of the language acquisition process in both Hebrew-specific and crosslinguistic terms. One result has been the emergence of a quite general model for characterizing language development as a series of steps leading from a more universal, shared, and context-bound pre-grammatical phase on to the acquisition of grammar proper and mastery of the formal, structure-bound rules of morpho-syntax, which in turn forms the basis for a discourse-oriented focus on appropriate usage, communicative effectivity, and the like (Berman 1984, in press). Another direction—one which I would now recommend as a possibly most promising basis for both within-language and across-language study of children's linguistic development—concerns the critical role which may attach to the particular discourse mode or setting within which knowledge of grammar and of language use develops. Careful comparative study now seems called for between given linguistic subsystems as manifested in, say, real-life and fictive narratives compared with peer interactions or other conversational settings, to test the rich hypotheses which are beginning to emerge in this connection.

ACKNOWLEDGMENTS

*I am grateful to my students from the Department of Linguistics and the School of Communications Disorders at Tel Aviv University for their cooperation in providing me with data from their work with Israeli children. Students and colleagues who gave me access to their transcripts have been mentioned as far as possible in Section 2 of this chapter. Esther Dromi, Barbara Josman, and Anita Rom gave me very helpful feedback on an initial draft, while Brian MacWhinney, Ann Peters, and Dan Slobin were of immense help in the revision of a preliminary version of this chapter.

REFERENCES

(Hebrew titles are given in the original, in broad phonetic transcription, followed by an English translation. Authors' names are given in conventional transliteration from the Hebrew.)

Antinucci, F., & Miller, R. How children talk about what happened. *Journal of Child Language*, 1976, *3*, 167–189.

Ariel, S. [haba'at iy-kiyum bediburam šel yladim dovrey ivrit begil šana]. Expression of non-existence in the speech of Hebrew-speaking 1 year olds. *DASH—Speech and Hearing Disorders*, Israel, 1975, *6*, 20–30.

Atsmon, I. [bniyat mivxan sinun hitpatxuti liyladim yisraeliyim begil trom bet sefer al piy ha DDST]. *A developmental screening test for Israeli preschoolers according to the DDST*. Tel Aviv University master's thesis, 1979.

Aviezer, O. *An investigation of the relationship between cognition and language in three spatial concepts*. Tel Aviv University master's thesis, 1979.

Avineri, I. [kibušey ha'ivrit bedorenu]. In *The achievements of modern Hebrew*. Tel Aviv: Sifriyat Hapoalim, 1946, 145–184.

Badry, F. *Acquisition of lexical derivation rules in Moroccan Arabic.* University of California, Berkeley, doctoral dissertation, 1983.

Bar-Adon, A. [lešonam hameduberet šel hayladim beyisrael]. *Children's Hebrew in Israel.* Hebrew University doctoral dissertation, 1959. (2 vols).

Bar-Adon, A. [lešono hameduberet šel hador haca'ir beyisrael kenose lemexkar]. The spoken language of the younger generation in Israel as a subject for research. *Hachinuch,* 1964, 21–25. (a)

Bar-Adon, A. Analogy and analogic change as reflected in contemporary Hebrew. In H. G. Lunt (Ed.), *Proceedings of the IXth International Congress of Linguistics.* The Hague: Mouton, 1964, 758–763. (b)

Bar-Adon, A. Primary syntactic structures in Hebrew child language. In A. Bar-Adon & W. Leopold (Eds.), *Child language: A book of readings* (pp. 433–472). Englewood-Cliffs, NJ: Prentice-Hall, 1971.

Bar-Adon, A. Child bilingualism in an immigrant society. In W. F. Macken & T. Andersson (Eds.) *Bilingualism in early childhood* (pp. 147–166). Rowley, Mass: Newbury House, 1977.

Barless, A. [lisfat hayladim] On children's language. *Leshonenu,* 1937, *8,* 185–198.

Baron, N. *Language acquisition and historical change.* Amsterdam: North Holland, 1977.

Beit-Hallahmi, B., Catford, J. C., Cooley, R. E., Dull, C. Y., Guiora, A. Z., & Paluzny, M. Grammatical gender and gender identity development: Cross-cultural and cross-linguistic implications. *American Journal of Ortho-Psychiatry* 1974, *44* (3).

Ben-Arroya, A. [havanat musagey yesod bekerev šaloš kvucot gil miramot socyoekonomiyot šonot al piy mivxan ha-BTBC]. *Comprehension of basic concepts in three age-groups of different SES according to the BTBC.* Tel-Aviv University master's thesis, 1979.

Ben-Horin, G., & Bolozky, S. Hebrew b k p—Rule opacity or data opacity? *Hebrew Computational Linguistics* 1972, *5,* 24–35.

Bentur, E. *Some effects of orthography on the linguistic knowledge of Modern Hebrew speakers.* University of Illinois doctoral dissertation, 1978.

Ben-Yitzchak, D. [dibur telegrafi šel yladim dovrey ivrit]. *Telegraphic speech of Hebrew-speaking children.* Tel-Aviv University master's thesis, 1979.

Berkowitz, R., & Wigodsky, M. On interpreting non-coreferential pronouns: A longitudinal study. *Journal of Child Language,* 1979, *6,* 585–592.

Berman, R. [hašemot hapo'aliyim ba'ivrit haxadaša]. *Verbal nouns in Modern Hebrew,* Hebrew University doctoral dissertation, 1973. (2 vols).

Berman, R. Natural phonological processes at the one-word stage. *Lingua,* 1977, *4,* 1–21.

Berman, R. *Modern Hebrew Structure.* Tel Aviv: Universities Publishing, 1978. (a)

Berman, R. Early verbs: Comments on how and why a child acquires her first words. *International Journal of Psycholinguistics,* 1978, *5,* 21–39. (b)

Berman, R. The (re)emergence of a bilingual: Case-study of a Hebrew-English speaking child. *Working Papers on Bilingualism,* 1979, *19,* 157–179. (a)

Berman, R. Repetition as a feature of Hebrew grammar and discourse. *Paper read at the 12th Conference of the European Linguistic Society,* Jerusalem, August, 1979. (b)

Berman, R. Lexical decomposition and lexical unity in derived verbal categories of Modern Hebrew. *Journal of Afroasiatic Linguistics,* 1979, *6* (3), 1–26. (c)

Berman, R. Child language as evidence for grammatical description: Preschoolers' construal of transitivity in the Hebrew verb system. *Linguistics,* 1980, *18,* 677–701.

Berman, R. Regularity vs. anomaly: The acquisition of Hebrew inflectional morphology. *Journal of Child Language,* 1981, *8,* 265–282. (a)

Berman, R. Language development and language knowledge: Evidence from the acquisition of Hebrew morphophonology. *Journal of Child Language,* 1981, *8.* (b)

Berman, R. Children's regularization of noun plurals. *Papers and Reports on Child Language Development,* 1981, *20,* 34–43. (c)

Berman, R. [al darxey ha siax begil ca'ir: iyun besipureha šel yalda bat šeš]. Aspects of a Hebrew-speaking child's narrative discourse. In S. Blum-Kulka, Y. Tobin, & R. Nir (Eds.), *Hebrew Discourse Studies* (pp. 177–212). Jerusalem: Akademon, 1981. (d)

Berman, R. Verb-pattern alternation: The interface of morphology, syntax, and semantics in Hebrew child language. *Journal of Child Language*, 1982, *9*, 169–191. (a)

Berman, R. On the nature of oblique objects in bitransitive constructions. *Lingua*, 1982, *56*. 101–125. (b)

Berman, R. Dative marking of the affectee role. *Hebrew Annual Review*, 1982, *6*, 35–59. (c).

Berman, R. Establishing a schema: Children's construal of verb-tense marking. *Language Sciences*, 1983, *5*, 61–78.

Berman, R. On the study of first language acquisition. *Language Learning*, 33, 5. In A. Guiora (Ed.), *An epistemology for the language sciences* (pp. 221–245). Detroit: Wayne State University Press, 1984.

Berman, R. A step-by-step model of language learning. In I. Levin (Ed.), *Stage and Structure: Human Development, Volume 1*. Norwood, NJ: Ablex, in press.

Berman, R. & Dromi, E. On marking time without aspect in child language. *Papers and Reports on Child Language Development*, 23, 1983.

Berman, R., Hecht, B., & Clark, E. V. The acquisition of agent and instrument nouns in Hebrew. *Papers and Reports on Child Language Development*, 1982, *21*, 16–24.

Berman, R. & Olshtain, E. Features of first language transfer in second language attrition. *Applied Linguistics*, 1983, *4*, 222–234.

Berman, R., Hecht, B., & Clark, E. V. Acquisition of word-formation devices in Hebrew: Agent and instrument nouns. *Paper read at Stanford Child Language Research Forum*, March, 1982.

Berman, R., Rom A., & Hirsch, M. Adaptation of the LARSP language assessment and remediation measures to Hebrew. *Annual workshop, Israeli Association of Speech Clinicians*, Tel Aviv, February, 1982.

Berman, R. & Sagi. Y. [al darxey tcurat hamilim vexidushan begil ca'ir]. Word-formation processes and lexical innovations of young children. *Hebrew Computational Linguistics Bulletin*, 1982, *18*. pp. 31–62.

Blanc, H. Israeli Hebrew texts. In *Studies in Egyptology and Linguistic in Honor of H. J. Polotsky* (pp. 132–152). Jerusalem: Hebrew University, 1964. (a)

Blanc, H. The growth of Israeli Hebrew. *Middle Eastern Affairs*, 1964, *5*, 385–392. (b)

Blau, J. [txiyat ha'ivrit utxiyat ha'aravit hasifrutit]. *The renaissance of Hebrew in the light of the renaissance of Standard Arabic*. Jerusalem: Hebrew Language Academy, 1976.

Bloom, L. *Language development: Form and function in emerging grammars*. Cambridge, Mass: M.I.T. Press, 1970.

Bloom, L., Lifter, K., & Hafitz, J. Semantics of verbs and the development of verb inflection in child language. *Language*, 1980, *56*, 386–412.

Blum-Kulka, S. Interpreting and performing speech acts in a second language: A cross-cultural study of Hebrew and English. Hebrew University, Center for Applied Linguistics, in press.

Bolozky, S. Some aspects of Modern Hebrew phonology. In R. Berman, *Modern Hebrew Structure* (pp. 11–68). Tel Aviv: Universities Publishing, 1978. (a)

Bolozky, S. Word formation strategies in the Hebrew verb system: Denominative verbs. *Journal of Afroasiatic Linguistics*, 1978, *5*, 111–136. (b)

Bolozky, S. *Remarks on rhythmic stress in Modern Hebrew*. Amherst: University of Massachusetts, 1979 (ms.). (a)

Bolozky. S. On the new imperative in colloquial Hebrew. *Hebrew Annual Review*, 1979, *3*, 17–24. (b)

Bowerman, M. 1974. Learning the structure of causative verbs: A study in the relationship between cognitive, semantic, and syntactic development. *Papers and Reports on Child Language Development*, 1974, *8*, 142–187.

Bowerman, M. Systematizing knowledge: Changes over time in the child's organization of word meaning. *Child Development*, 1978, *49*, 977–987.

Bowerman, M. The acquisition of complex sentences. In P. Fletcher & M. Garman (Eds.), *Language acquisition* (pp. 285–306). London: Cambridge University Press, 1979.

Bowerman, M. Starting to talk worse: Clues to language acquisition from children's late speech errors. In S. Strauss (Ed.), *U-Shaped behavioral growth*. New York: Academic Press, 1981.

Bowerman, M. Cross-cultural perspectives on language development. In H. C. Triandis (Ed.), *Handbook of cross-cultural psychology*. Boston: Allyn, Bacon & in press.

Braine, M. Children's first word combinations. *Monographs of the Society for Research in Child Development*, 1976, *41*, Serial No. 164.

Bronckart, J. P. & Sinclair, A. Time, tense, and aspect. *Cognition*, 1973, *2*, 107–130.

Brown, R. 1958. How shall a thing be called? *Psychological Review*, 1958, *65*, 14–21.

Brown, R. A first language: The early stages. Cambridge, Mass: Harvard University Press, 1973.

Buium, N. An investigation of the word order parameter of a parent-child interaction in a relatively free word order language. *Language & Speech*, 1976, *17*, 182–186.

Bybee, J. Child morphology and morphophonemic change. *Linguistics*, 1979, *17*, 182–186.

Bybee, J. , & Brewer, M. A. *Explanation in morpho-phonemics: Changes in Provençal and Spanish preterite forms*. Buffalo: SUNY, 1980, ms.

Caisse, J. [mexkarim bilšonam šel te'uney tipaux]. Studies in the language of culturally deprived. Haifa University: *Studies in Education*, 1974, *4*, 109–128.

Caisse, J. [hitnahagut milulit vedarxey xivrut: lešonam šel yladim te'uney tipaux umevusasim]. Verbal behavior and socialization: The language of culturally deprived and well-established children. Haifa University: *Studies in Education*, 1978, *19*, 131–152.

Carey, S. The child as word learner. In M. Halle, J. Bresnan, & G. A. Miller (Eds.), *Linguistic theory and psychological reality*. Cambridge, Mass: M.I.T. Press, 1982.

Chomsky, C. *The acquisition of syntax from 5 to 10*. Cambridge, Mass: M.I.T. Press, 1969.

Clancy, P. M. Acquisition of Japanese. In D. I. Slobin (Ed.), *The crosslinguistic study of language acquisition* (Vol. 1). Hillsdale, NJ: Lawrence Erlbaum Associates, 1985.

Clark, E. 1978. Discovering what words can do. In D. Farkas, W. M. Jacobsen, & K. W. Todrys (Eds.), *Parasession on the Lexicon* (pp. 34–57). Chicago: Chicago Linguistic Society, 1978.

Clark, E. Convention and innovation in acquiring the lexicon. *Papers and Reports on Child Language Development*, 1980, *19*, 1–20.

Clark, E. V. Acquisition of Romance, with special reference to French. In D. I. Slobin (Ed.), *The crosslinguistic study of language acquisition* (Vol. 1). Hillsdale, NJ: Lawrence Erlbaum Associates, 1985.

Clark, E. V. & Berman, R. A. Structure and use in the acquistion of word formation, *Language*, 1984, *60*, 542–590.

Clark, E. & Hecht, B. *Learning to coin agent and instrument nouns, Cognition*, 1982, *12*, 1–24.

Crystal, D., Fletcher, P., & Garman, M. *The grammatical analysis of language disability: A procedure for assessment and remediation*. London: Billing & Sons, 1976.

Davis, L. [lešonam šel te'uney hatipuax: ha'omnam te'una hi tipaux?] Is the language of the culturally-deprived in fact deprived? Haifa University: Studies *in Education*, 1976, *13*, 133–138.

Davis, L. [hamišlav vehora'at halašon lite'uney tipaux]. Register and the teaching of language to culturally-deprived students. Haifa University: *Studies in Education*, 1978, *18*, 61–66.

Dolzhanski, T. [šibušey halašon befiy yladim]. Misusages in children's language. *Leshonenu*, 1937, *8*, 35–48.

Donag-Kinrot, R. [lešonam šel talmidim bevatey hasefer beyisra'el] *The language of students in Israeli schools*. Hebrew university doctoral dissertation. 1978. (2 vols.)

Dromi, E. [ha-MLU kemeded lehitpatxut sfatit bekerev yladim dovrey ivrit begil 2–3]. *The MLU as a measure of language development among Hebrew-speaking children aged 2–3*. Tel Aviv University master's thesis, 1977.

Dromi, E. More on the acquisition of locative prepositions: An analysis of Hebrew data. *Journal of Child Language*, 1979, *6*, 547–562.

Dromi, E. *In* pursuit of meaningful words: A case-study analysis of early lexical development. University of Kansas doctoral dissertation, 1982.

Dromi, E. & Berman, R. A morphemic measure of early language development: Data from Israeli Hebrew. *Journal of Child Language*, 1982, *9*, 169–191.

Ervin-Tripp, S. The connotations of gender. *Word*, 1962, *18*, 249–261.

Ervin-Tripp, S. Discourse agreement: How children answer questions. In J. Hayes (Ed.), *Cognition and the development of language* (pp. 79–107). New York: Wiley, 1970.

Erteschik-Shir, N. Discourse constraints on dative movement. In T. Givón (Ed.), *Syntax and Semantics 12: Discourse and Syntax*. New York: Academic Press, 1979. pp. 441–467.

Eyal, S. [rexišat maba'ey še'ela al ydey yladim dovrey ivrit]. *Acquisition of question-utterances by Hebrew-speaking children*. Tel Aviv University master's thesis, 1976.

Faltz, L. *Reflexivization: A study in universal grammar*. University of California, Berkeley, doctoral dissertation, 1977.

Fillmore, C. J. On the organization of semantic information in the lexicon. In D. Farkas, W. M. Jacobsen, & K. W. Todrys (Eds.), *Parasession on the lexicon* (pp. 147–173). Chicago: Chicago Linguistic Society, 1978.

Fischler, B-Z. [b k p degušot urefuyot šelo kadin ba'ivrit hayisra'elit]. The realization of "beth, kaph, pé" in Israeli Hebrew. In B-Z. Fischler & U. Ornan (Eds.), *Rosen Memorial Volume*. Jerusalem: Council on the Teaching of Hebrew, 1975. pp. 86–99.

Frankel, D. G., Amir, M., Frenkel, E., & Arbel, T. A developmental study of the role of word order in comprehending Hebrew. *Journal of Experimental Child Psychology*, 1980, *29*, 23–35.

Gal, I. [tfisat hasavil becurot nif'al behafaka, havana vexikuy bekerev yaldey gan]. *Preschoolers' perception of passive nif al forms in production, comprehension, and imitation*. Tel Aviv University seminar paper, 1979.

Givón, T. Function, structure, and language acquisition. In D. I. Slobin (Ed.), *The crosslinguistic study of language acquisition* (Vol. 2). Hillsdale, NJ: Lawrence Erlbaum Associates, 1985.

Goshen, R. & Eyanl, S. [seder rexišat hahavana šel sugey še'elot be'ivrit] Order of acquisition of understanding question-types in Hebrew. *DASH—Speech and Hearing Disorders*, Israel, 1976, *7*, 13–16.

Greenwald, R. [ha'araxat havanatam hasfatit šel yladim: hat'amat mivxan ha-ACLC le'ivrit] *Assessment of language comprehension in children: Adaptation of the ACLC to Hebrew*. Tel Aviv University master's thesis, 1979.

Guiora, A. C. & Acton, W. R. Personality and language behavior: A restatement. *Language Learning*, 1979, *29*, 1–24.

Harner, L. Children's understanding of linguistic reference to past and future. *Journal of Psycholinguistic Research*, 1976, *5*, 65–84.

Harner, L. Immediacy and certainty: Factors in understanding future reference. *Journal of Child Language*, 1981, *8*.

Herzberg, D. [mishpatey zika bekerev yladim dovrey ivrit] *Relative clauses of Hebrew—Speaking children*. Tel-Aviv University Seminar Paper, 1983.

Hopper, P. & Thompson, S. Transitivity in grammar and discourse. *Language*, 1980, *56*, 251–299.

Johnston, J., & Slobin, D. I. The development of locative expressions in English, Italian, Serbo-Croatian and Turkish. *Journal of Child Language*, 1979, *6*, 529–546.

Kantor, H. [nituax šel sfat habenayim šel talmidim halomdim ivrit kesafa šniya] *An analysis of the interlanguage of learners of Hebrew as a second language*. Bar Ilan University master's thesis, 1978.

Kaplan, D. [seder harxiša šel yesodot morfo-taxbiriyim begil šnatayim ad šaloš] *Order of acquisition of morpho-syntactic categories among Hebrew-speaking 2 to 3 year olds*. Tel Aviv University master's thesis, 1983.

Karmiloff-Smith, A. *A functional approach to child language.* London: Cambridge University Press, 1979. (a)

Karmiloff-Smith, A. Language as a formal problem-space for children. *Paper prepared for the MPG/NIAS Conference on "Beyond Description in Child Language,"* Nijmegen, June, 1979. (b)

Karmiloff-Smith, A. Language development after five. In P. Fletcher & M. Garman (Eds.), *Language Acquisition.* London: Cambridge University Press, 1979. pp. 307–323. (c)

Kolman, N. [gil harexiša šel milot yaxas merxaviyot šonot be'ivrit]. *Age of acquisition of different locative prepositions in Hebrew.* Tel Aviv University Seminar paper, 1979.

Kupferberg, I. *Rapid speech phenomena and meaning attainment.* Tel Aviv University master's thesis, 1976.

Lee, L., & Canter, S. Developmental sentence scoring: A clinical procedure for estimating syntactic development in children's spontaneous speech. *Journal of Speech and Hearing Disorders,* 1971, *36,* 315–340.

Levy, Y. [hamin bisfat hayladim: mexkar birxišat sfat ha'em] *Gender in children's language: A study in first language acquisition.* Hebrew University doctoral dissertation, 1980.

Levy, Y. It's frogs all the way down. *Cognition,* 1983, 75–93. (a)

Levy, Y. The acquisition of Hebrew plurals: the case of the missing gender category. *Journal of Child Language,* 1983, *10,* 107–121. (b)

Lieven, E. V. M. *Language development of young children.* Cambridge University doctoral dissertaion, 1980.

Lord, C. "Don't you fall me down": Children's generalizations regarding cause and transitivity. *Papers and Reports on Child Language Development,* 1979, *17,* 81–89.

MacWhinney, B. Rules, rote, and analogy in morphological formation by Hungarian children. *Journal of Child Language,* 1975, *2,* 65–78.

MacWhinney, B. The acquisition of morphophonology. *Monographs of the Society for Research in Child Development,* 1978, *43.*

MacWhinney, B. Hungarian language acquisition as an exemplification of a general model of grammatical development. In D. I. Slobin (Ed.), *The crosslinguistic study of language acquisition* (Vol. 2). Hillsdale, NJ: Lawrence Erlbaum Associates, 1985.

Maratsos, M. The use of definite and indefinite reference in young children. London: Cambridge University Press, 1976.

Maratsos, M. New models in linguistics and language acquisition. In M. Halle, J. Bresnan, & G. Miller (Eds.), *Linguistic theory and psychological reality.* Cambridge, Mass: M.I.T. Press, 1978, 247–263.

Mulford, R. Prototypicality and the development of categorization. *Papers and Reports in Child Language Development,* 1979, *16,* 13–25.

Nahir, M. Normative and education speech in Modern Hebrew. *International Journal of the Sociology of Language,* 1978, 18, 49–67.

Ninio, A. Picture-book reading in mother-infant dyads belonging to two subgroups in Israel. *Child Development,* 1980a, *51,* 587–590.

Ninio, A. Ostensive definition in vocabulary teaching. *Journal of Child Language,* 1980b, *7,* 565–574.

Ochs, E. Variation and error: A sociolinguistic approach to language acquisition in Samoa. In D. I. Slobin (Ed.), *The crosslinguistic study of language acquisition* (Vol. 1). Hillsdale, NJ: Lawrence Erlbaum Associates, 1985.

Ortar, G. [markivim bilšona šel ha'em hatormim limnat hamiskal haverbalit šel yeladeha]. Components of the mother's speech contributing to her children's verbal I.Q. *Megamot,* 1975a, *21,* 5–21.

Ortar, G. [xizukim lilšona šel ha'em latinok ke'emca'i limni'at pa'ar tarbuti]. Reinforcement of the mother's speech to the infant as a means of preventing cultural lag. *Megamot,* 1975b, *21,* 269–276.

Pardo, O. [yexoltam šel yladim behat'amat hato'arim 'gadol' ve 'katan' lamin hadikduki šel šemot ha'ecem]. Children's command of agreement of the adjectives 'big' and 'small' to the grammatical gender of nouns. Tel Aviv University seminar paper, 1980.

Peters, A. *The units of language acquisition*. Cambridge: Cambridge University Press, 1983.

Rabinowitch, S. [maba'im du-miliyim šel yladim dovrey ivrit]. Two-word utterances of Hebrew-speaking children. Tel Aviv University master's thesis, 1974.

Rabinowitch, S. [yedi'at ha'ivrit šel yladim du-lešoniyim anglit-ivrit begil šaloš ad xameš behašva's livney gilam haxad lšoniyim be'ivrit]. *Hebrew language proficiency of bilingual English-Hebrew 3 to 5 year olds compared with their monolingual peers*. Tel Aviv University doctoral dissertation, in preparation.

Ravid, D. *Word-formation processes in the Hebrew noun and adjective system*. Tel Aviv University master's thesis, 1978.

Rivkai, Y. [al haspecifiyut halšonit befiy yladeynu be'erec yisra'el]. On the linguistic specificity of the language used by our children in Eretz Yisrael. *Leshonenu*, 1933, *4*, 279–294; 1934, *5*, 73–77, 231–242.

Rivkai, Y. [sfat yladeynu ba'arec]. *The language of our children in this country*. Tel Aviv: Shimoni, 1938.

Rom, A. *The acquisition of negation in a cross-lingual study*. Wayne State University master's thesis, 1977.

Rom, A. *A comparison of verbal and nonverbal communicative skills in normal and language-impaired children*. Wayne State University doctoral dissertation, 1979.

Rotstein, D. [al mašma'am vetafkidam šel musagey 'topic' ve 'comment' bisfata šel yalda bat šnatayim]. *The meaning and role of the notions of topic and comment in the speech of an Israeli two-year old*. Tel Aviv University seminar paper, 1980.

Salzburg, H. [mišpatey šlila ecel yladim dovrey ivrit]. *Negative sentences of Hebrew speaking children*. Tel Aviv University master's thesis, 1976.

Schieffelin, B. B. Acquisition of Kaluli. In D. I. Slobin (Ed.), *The crosslinguistic study of language acquisition* (Vol. 1). Hillsdale, NJ: Lawrence Erlbaum Associates, 1985.

Schwarzwald, O. [gišot te'oretiyot muxašiyot umofšatot benituax b k p be'ivrit]. Concrete and abstract theories in the analysis of Hebrew b k p. *Leshonenu*, 1976, *40*, 211–232.

Schwarzwald, O. The influence of demographic variables on linguistic performance. *Quantitative Linguistics*, 1978, *1*, 173–197. (In *Glottometrika* 1, G. Altmann, Ed.).

Schwarzwald, O. The regularity of irregular forms. *Paper read at the 12th Annual Conference of the European Linguistic Society*, Jerusalem, August, 1979.

Schwarzwald, O. [binyaney hapo'al uzmaney hapo'al al piy toc'ot mexkar ba'ivrit bat yameynu]. Verb patterns and tenses as reflected in the results of a study of current Hebrew. Jerusalem: Hebrew University, *Ben Hayyim Jubilee Volume*, 1980.

Schwarzwald, O. [dikduk umeci'ut bapó'al ha'vri]. *Grammar and reality in the Hebrew verb*. Ramat-Gan, Bar Ilan University Press, 1981.

Shachar, N. [gil havanat hahevdel ben zaxar unkeva befo'aley kal]. *Age of understanding the difference between feminine and masculine in verbs in the kal pattern*. Tel Aviv University seminar paper, 1978.

Shoham, L. *Further evidence on comprehension: A study of sentence types in the usage of a 2 year old Israeli girl*. Tel Aviv University term paper, 1980.

Slobin, D. I. Cognitive prerequisites for the development of grammar. In C. A. Ferguson & D. I. Slobin (Eds.), *Studies of child language development* (pp. 175–208). New York: Holt, Rinehart, & Winston, 1973.

Slobin, D. I. *The role of language in language acquisition*. University of California, Berkeley, 1979, ms.

Slobin, D. I. Operating principles in child language. *Paper prepared for Berkeley conference on crosslinguistic study of child language*, November, 1980.

Slobin, D. I. The origins of grammatical encoding of events. In W. Deutsch (Ed.) *The child's construction of language* (pp. 185–200.) London: Academic Press, 1981.

Slobin, D. I. Crosslinguistic evidence for the Language-Making Capacity. In D. I. Slobin (Ed.), *The crosslinguistic study of language acquisition* (Vol. 2). Hillsdale, NJ: Lawrence Erlbaum Associates, 1985.

Stahl, A. [lašon vexašiva šel yladim te'uney tipuax beyisra'el]. *Language and thought of culturally deprived children in Israel.* Tel Aviv: Otsar Hamoreh, 1977.

Stern, I. [hašva'at ha šimus bešemot to'ar ecel yladim te'uney tipuax viyladim mevusasim]. *Comparison of the understanding and use of adjectives among culturally-deprived and advantaged children.* Tel Aviv University seminar paper, 1977.

Thompson, S. Modern English from a typological point of view: Some implications of the function of word order. *Linguistische Berichte*, 1978, *54*, 19–36.

Waks, O. [rexišat ntiyot hamin bapó'al bizman hove] *Acquisition of masculine and feminine inflections on present-tense verbs.* Tel Aviv University seminar paper, 1978.

Walden, Z. The root of roots: Children's construction of word-formation processes in Hebrew. Harvard University doctoral dissertation, 1982.

Weinreich, U., Labov, W., & Herzog, M. I. Empirical foundations for a theory of language change. In W. P. Lehmann & Y. Malkiel (Eds.). *Directions for historical linguistics* (pp. 95–195). Austin: University of Texas Press, 1968.

Wigodsky, M. [havanat kinuyim baaley ko-referencya umexusarey ko-referencya ecel yladim bney teša ad šteym esrey šanim.] *Comprehension of coreferent and non-coreferent pronouns by 9 to 12 year old Israeli schoolchildren.* Tel Aviv University master's thesis, 1977.

Yakir, R. Secret languages of Israeli children. Hebrew University: *Language Behavior Papers*, 1973, *2*, 29–39.

Yif'at, R. [kišurey lašon bekerev yladim hagdelim bemosad behašva's liyladim hagdelim babayit begil arba ušmone). *Language skills of institutionalized and home-raised children aged 4 and 8.* Tel Aviv University master's thesis, 1981.

Zeidner, M. [aspektim psixolingvistiyim šel mišlav sfat hatinokot be'ivrit.] Psycholinguistic aspects of the "baby talk" register in Hebrew. Haifa University: *Studies in Education*, 1978, *20*, 105–120.

Ziv, E. *Acquisition of syntactic structures among Hebrew-speaking grade-school children.* Tel Aviv University master's thesis, 1976.

Zonshain, Y. [maba'im xad-miliyim šel yladim dovrey ivrit begil 12, 15, and 18 xodašim.] *One-word utterances of Hebrew-speaking children aged 12, 15, and 18 months.* Tel Aviv University master's thesis, 1975.

Zur, B. [al rxišat hayidua bekérev yladim dovrey ivrit]. *On the acquisition of definiteness by Hebrew-speaking children.* Tel-Aviv University master's thesis, 1983.

4 The Acquisition of Japanese

Patricia M. Clancy
University of Southern California

INTRODUCTION

1. Grammatical Sketch of Japanese

The origin and genetic affiliations of the Japanese language are matters of considerable interest and debate. Japanese appears to be genetically related to Korean (cf. Martin, 1966; Miller, 1967b); the two languages are remarkably similar in morphology and syntactic structure. One hypothesis is that both Japanese and Korean are members of the large Altaic language family, which includes the Turkic, Mongol, and Tungus branches (Miller, 1967a). However, many layers of extensive contact and borrowings from other languages, includ-

373

ing Melo-Polynesian languages and Chinese, have contributed to the formation of Japanese, and it may be wrong to seek a single parent language (Aoki, 1981). There are numerous Japanese dialects, some virtually unintelligible to speakers of the Tokyo dialect, which constitutes the modern standard.

Japanese shares many morphological and syntactic features with Altaic languages such as Turkish, but also exhibits many features which, from the standpoint of the European languages, seem quite exotic, such as the various linguistic reflexes of the pervasive social and sexual stratification of Japanese society. Thus Japanese offers an interesting case study for the crosslinguistic analysis of language acquisition. It provides an opportunity for further testing of hypotheses based on typologically similar languages, and also for investigating dimensions of acquisition which are not so easily explored in languages where pragmatic and sociolinguistic factors have fewer grammatical consequences.

Typologically, Japanese is an SOV language, and exhibits many of the grammatical features consistent with this classification. For example, Japanese makes use of postpositional particles rather than prepositions; nominal modifiers such as adjectives, genitives, and relative clauses precede head nouns; and conjunctions appear at the end of the first of two conjoined clauses, rather than at the beginning of the second, although the latter is an optional possibility. There are several introductory Japanese grammars available in English, such as Jorden (1962–1963) and Alfonso and Niimi (1972), which provide a basic background with many linguistically interesting details. Kuno (1973) presents a linguistic introduction to the important properties of Japanese grammar; Kuno (1978) elaborates on some of the typological characteristics of Japanese. Miller (1967a) treats a wide range of topics, including the history of the Japanese language, as well as its grammar. Another, much briefer, overview, including many interesting psychological and social properties of Japanese, is available in Inoue (1979).

Although the most common word order, and the one which appears in standard grammars, is subject-object-verb, in ordinary Japanese conversation, word order is quite flexible preceding the verb. Furthermore, postposing constituents and even entire clauses after the main verb of a sentence also occurs rather frequently, with definable pragmatic functions. The grammatical roles of each constituent in a sentence are marked by postpositional case particles indicating subject, object, indirect object, genitive, source, location, goal, instrument, etc. A standard textbook sentence in Japanese might be as follows:

> *Taroo   ga   Hanako   ni   hon   o   age - ta.*
> SUBJ*   IO   book   DO   give   PAST
> 'Taroo gave a book to Hanako'.

If the subject or direct object of this sentence were topicalized, the particle *wa* would replace the ordinary case particles; with other nominal arguments, *wa* is

---

*See p. 515 for a list of abbreviations used in this chapter.

added after the regular particle. In the appropriate conversational context, any of the three nouns in the above sentence (or all of them, although this would be rare) could be postposed to sentence-final position following the verb, or re-ordered with respect to one another in preverbal position.

Not only may the order of constituents in this sentence be changed, but in the appropriate circumstances any of the three nouns may also be omitted. Thus in Japanese any or all of the nominal arguments of a predicate, and sometimes the predicate as well, may be ellipted. In fact, the main difference between sentences of spoken Japanese and those which appear in grammars and linguistic articles on Japanese is that in actual usage one or more basic constituents of a sentence is usually omitted from overt mention. The missing constituent is presumably one which the speaker thinks the listener will be able to supply on the basis of background knowledge, the non-linguistic context, or the preceding conversation, that is, it constitutes "old information" (see Chafe, 1976). The situation is further complicated by the fact that case particles can also optionally be omitted. Different particles are ellipted with different frequencies (Tamori, 1977), and the same particle may be ellipted with different frequencies in different semantic functions (Miyazaki, 1979). Ellipsis of verbs also occurs; it is especially common with verbs which are relatively empty semantically, such as *suru* 'do', the copula *da,* and *iru/aru,* the animate and inanimate existentials. Verbs with more semantic content can also be ellipted if there is sufficient information in the linguistic or non-linguistic context to permit comprehension (Hinds, 1976–1977, 1982).

From the standpoint of language acquisition, the extensive ellipsis of ordinary Japanese conversation makes it difficult to evaluate a child's utterances in terms of concepts typically applied in analyzing the early stages of grammatical development, such as "telegraphic speech" and "obligatory context" (Brown, 1973). Japanese child language at the one- and two-word stages is more frequently grammatically complete and correct than would be the corresponding utterances of an English-speaking child, since child language is so dependent upon the "here and now" and in Japanese, ellipsis where pragmatically appropriate is grammatically correct. Thus "acquisition" is more difficult to define, and early telegraphic speech more adult-like in Japanese than in English.

Verb morphology in Japanese is agglutinative, and compared with languages such as Hungarian or Polish, morphophonemic alternations are minimal. Inflectional suffixes mark verbs for tense, aspect, voice, mood, negation, causation, and semantic relations between clauses, such as conditionality. Verbs are not inflected for person and number; personal pronouns are not connected with verb morphology as in Indo-European languages, and are typically omitted. The system of pronouns in Japanese is quite complex, especially in the first and second person, with several options available depending upon the age, sex, social status, and type of relationship between speaker and hearer, as well as the nature of the conversational context. Therefore, the use of pronouns is a highly sensitive matter with sociolinguistic implications, rather than the relatively automatic registering of conversational participants marked or copied on the verb that is typical of Western languages.

In Japanese, verbs may be combined in sequence for various functions. One set of verbs, including *kuru* 'come', *iku* 'go', *shimau* 'finish', *oku* 'put', *aru/iru* 'exist', and *miru* 'see', combine with the non-final form of the preceding verb to convey aspectual nuances. In contracted form, some of these concatenated verbs are reduced to inflectional endings, and acquired as such by children. Another set of verbs, including *ageru* and *kureru* 'give', *morau* 'receive' and their honorific and humble counterparts, combine with the non-final form of the preceding verb to indicate that an action was performed by one person for the benefit of another. The choice of the appropriate verb depends upon the speaker's point of view as well as social status relative to the addressee. Both sets of concatenated verb constructions are very common in ordinary spoken Japanese and, like other common verbal inflections, are not omitted or simplified by mothers in the speech they address to 2-year-olds.

Verbal inflections in Japanese also convey varying degrees of politeness. The basic polite suffix is *-mas* (copula *des-*), which appear in various inflected forms. At high levels of politeness, honorific prefixes and special verbs are also used. Thus verb morphology is sociolinguistically conditioned in Japanese; any verb which does not bear the polite *-mas* inflection is casual and informal, to be used only with social equals and inferiors, friends, and family members. Consequently, every predicate one utters in Japanese necessarily reflects the nature of the social relationship between speaker and hearer. There is also a grammatically based system of honorifics which makes use of different verbal inflections and a special lexicon to indicate respect for certain referents within a sentence of superior status to the speaker, regardless of the social status of the listener. Thus grammatical marking of respect is extended to superiors when they are referred to, as well as when they are addressed.

The pragmatics of speaker and hearer in context is also overtly marked in Japanese through a range of sentence-final morphemes indicating the speaker's attitude toward the information being communicated, presuppositions about the context and the addressee's state of knowledge, the function of the utterance, and the type of response sought from the listener. These particles express, for example, assertion, emphasis, agreement, wondering, questioning, seeking confirmation, etc. Sentence-final particles are also sensitive to sociolinguistic factors. Appropriate use depends upon the formality of the speech context, the relative status of speaker and hearer, the nature of their relationship, the sex of the speaker, and sometimes also that of the hearer. Since certain functions of sentence-final particles may be more socially appropriate for members of one sex than the other, a particle may serve to mark the speaker's sex in addition to its other functions.

As this brief sketch of Japanese suggests, pragmatic and sociolinguistic factors pervade the grammar of the language. Therefore, the child who masters the syntax and morphology of Japanese has also mastered a subtle pragmatic system for regulating the flow of information to listeners in accordance with their needs in the speech context through word order, ellipsis, and sentence-final particles, as well as an elaborate system of socially defined statuses and roles which are expressed in verb morphology, pronouns, and sentence-final particles.

2. Sources of Evidence

As in the United States, the field of child language acquisition in Japan has recently undergone tremendous expansion, and an extensive body of literature on the development of Japanese is now available. Although research has also been conducted in this country, many major works on Japanese acquisition are published in Japanese and are not readily available in this country. Most books and papers written in English are not to be found in the United States. Therefore, in writing this chapter, I have relied upon the cooperation of many Japanese scholars, who have kindly sent me copies of their work; I have also drawn heavily upon those sources which are available in English in this country.

The types of data available on Japanese acquisition are many and varied. Longitudinal studies of individual children as well as cross-sectional investigations of large numbers of children across wide age ranges have been made. Methodologies include parental observations, such as diaries and responses to questionnaires, tape-recordings of naturalistic contexts and semi-naturalistic interviews, and a variety of experimental approaches, including elicited imitation, recognition tasks, and acting-out procedures. Research has been performed on a wide range of topics, including preverbal mother-child interaction, babbling, phonological development, vocabulary and early semantic development, neurological aspects, and other areas which cannot be included here. Hatano's (1980) review article and Sanches' (1974) bibliography provide helpful introductions to this research. In this chapter, I focus primarily on the acquisition of grammar, especially early morphological and syntactic developments, and also consider the potential influences of cognitive and social development upon language acquisition, and vice versa.

Data for this chapter have been drawn primarily from observational studies of the early stages of grammatical development. An extensive longitudinal record is available in Okubo (1967), in which the author traces her daughter's development from 1- to 6-years-of-age, basing her analysis upon monthly tape-recordings. Fujiwara (1977) is a diary study based on the author's notes on the speech of his son and three daughters, as well as his two grandsons and four granddaughters. There is also a monumental diary study by Noji, covering his son's development from birth to 6 years-of-age, which has been published in four volumes (1974–1977). For this chapter, I have not used Noji's data, except for one paper based on parts of this diary (Miyazaki, 1979), relying instead upon Okubo's book for long-term longitudinal information, supplemented by the partial records in Fujiwara's diary. My own data on the early stages of Japanese acquisition consist of 30 hours of spontaneous speech collected from five children between the ages of 1½ and 3½ years. Twelve 1-hour speech samples were collected from a boy aged 1;11–2;4 years. Two to four samples were collected from five other children: a boy of 2;4–2;5, and three girls, aged 2;1–2;3, 3;1–3;3, and 3;5–3;8. The children were recorded in their homes, interacting with their mothers and sometimes also with a young woman who was my assistant, while I took contextual notes.

Many other sources, which provide analyses of specific aspects of development, have also been used for this paper. By far the most information is available on the period from about 1½ to 2½ years-of-age, when verbal inflections, case and sentence-final particles are being acquired. Okubo (1963, 1967) documents these developments in her daughter's speech. Murata (1961a, 1961b, 1965) examines the transition from the one- to two-word-stages, focusing on the use of particles and multi-morpheme utterances in a large sample of 1-year-olds. Miyahara (1973, 1974) examines the development of case, sentence-final, and connective particles in her daughter's speech from 1;8 to 2;2 years-of-age. Sanches' dissertation (1968) analyzes the acquisition of particles, verbal inflections, and word order in three children aged 2;1–2;6 years. Tanouye (1979, 1980) focuses on the one-word stage and the development of verbal inflections in two children aged 1;4–2;4, contrasting her findings with the development of English-speaking children of comparable age. Yamada (1980) analyzes the emergence of particles and verbal inflections in the speech of one child aged 1;11–2;3, and includes an analysis of those features of mother's speech as well. Cook (1985) examines the acquisition of postnominal particles by a child of 2;7 years, comparing his usage with that of his caregivers. Hirayama (1978) studies the development of particles and verbal inflections in a child of 1;9–2;2 years. Rispoli (1981a,b) analyzes the emergence of verbal inflections and request forms in the speech of one child aged 1;6–2;0 years, and also examines the inflections in a sample of mother's speech. Miyazaki (1979) focuses on the acquisition of the topic particle wa and the subject particle ga by the child in Noji's diary study. Hatano (1968) and Iwabuchi and Muraishi (1968) include information on early grammatical developments in the speech of four children, who were studied from birth to 5 years-of-age. Lust and Wakayama (1981) analyze the responses of children aged 2;5–5;10 in an experimental study of the development of word order and coordinate structures. Takahara and Peng (1981) present data on the use of different word orders in the speech of two 2-year-old children.

The development of negation is the focus of McNeill and McNeill (1973), who study one child aged 2;3–2;8 years, Yamamoto (1981), who examines her bilingual daughter's development from 1;7 to 2;11 years, and Ito (1981), who analyzes the development of three sisters, as well as the results of questionnaires answered by 31 mothers of young children. The development of questions is considered in Yoshida (1977), who analyzes one child's responses to questions at 2;4 and 2;7 years-of-age, and is explored in depth by Okubo (1965, 1967), who analyzes the order of emergence of different types of questions in her daughter's speech. The acquisition of aspectual (1981b) and benefactive (1979) constructions is analyzed in detail by Horiguchi, who studied her son's development from 2;0 to 3;1 years-of-age. Uyeno et al. (1978) conducted an experimental study of the comprehension of benefactive constructions by children aged 3–6 years. Okubo (1967, 1983) presents longitudinal data on the development of conjunctions and aspect.

The later stages of development have been studied extensively through cross-sectional and experimental research, although longitudinal information is also available, for example, in Okubo (1967), Fujiwara (1977), and Noji (1974–1977). A National Language Research Institute project has gathered cross-sectional data on later developments in production through interviews with about 300 children of 3;3–6;3 years-of-age. Using these data, Takahashi (1975a) analyzes the morphology of verbs, adjectives, nominal adjectives, and (1975b) the use of case particles. Okubo (1973), using the same data, analyzes the development from simple to complex sentences. The development of coordination has been the focus of attention in some recent research, using an experimental paradigm (Lust & Wakayama, 1981), Hakuta et al. (1982), and combining observational and experimental data (Lust & Wakayama, 1979).

Experimental studies have also documented the development of sentence processing strategies focusing upon case particles and word order, typically using comprehension and imitation tasks. Hayashibe (1975) presents an experiment on the comprehension of simple active sentences with and without case particles by children of 3;0–5;11 years-of-age. Hakuta (1982) analyzes the comprehension, imitation, and production of active and passive sentences in different word orders by children aged 2;3–6;2; Sano (1977) examines these sentence types as well as cleft sentences. Harada (1977) analyzes her daughter's comprehension and imitation of passive, causative, and benefactive sentences, and (1976) sentences with relative clauses, at 2;8–2;10 years-of-age. The role of case particles in sentence processing is examined in Harada (1983), with an emphasis on their discourse functions. In a large experimental study of children aged 5;0–6;10, Kamio and Harada (1979, in press) analyze the imitation of sentences with relative clauses, appositives, complement constructions, and adverbial clauses.

A considerable amount of research has been performed in Japan on early mother-child interaction; however, much of it focuses on the prelinguistic stage and is not considered here. An example of this type of research available in English is Caudill and Weinstein (1974), who compare 30 mother-child pairs in Japan and in the United States when the children were 3–4 months old; they note consistent differences in the frequency and functions of speech addressed to the children in each country. Papers such as Azuma et al. (1979), Conroy et al. (1980), and Hess et al. (1980) report on the findings of a major research project on the influence of maternal variables such as education and communicative style upon cognitive development in 58 Japanese and 67 American mother-child pairs studied from 3;8 to 6 years-of-age; the results include information on contrasting verbal strategies used by mothers in each culture in interacting with their children. Murata and Ohara (1966) describe characteristics of Japanese mothers' speech to 1-year-old children, presenting the relative frequencies of different types of speech acts and of expansions. Okayama (1979) analyzes an entire day of mother-child interaction for a total of 130 children aged 2;2–4;11, and includes information on the frequencies of different speech acts. The structure of the Japanese babytalk lexicon is analyzed in Chew (1969); the development and use of babytalk by 1-year-olds is studied in Murata (1960). Systematic analyses of input from adults who might address young children with speech different from that of their mothers, such as siblings, fathers, or grandparents, would be a valuable addition to the available information on input in Japanese.

The study of individual differences has not been the focus of much research so far, but recently has begun to receive more attention. Okubo (1980, 1981a) compares the early stages of development in a boy and his younger sister, focusing on the different frequencies of nouns and verbs in each child's speech. Komura (1981) analyzes the different developmental paths followed by two different children in acquiring possessives and other types of N *no* N constructions. Sanches (1975) and Matsumoto (1984c) discuss individual differences in the development of numeral classifiers. Certain experimental studies of sentence processing, such as Hayashibe (1975), Sano (1977), and Hakuta (1982) include information on individual differences.

Relatively little research seems to have been performed so far on the acquisition of sociolinguistic aspects of Japanese. Horiguchi (1979b, 1981a) presents information on the emergence and development of sex differences in the forms used for self-reference by three 2-year-old children. Hori (1981) treats the development of sex differences in the use of sentence-final particles in a sample of 2-year-olds, elementary and junior high school children. Ide (1977, 1978, 1978–1979) examines the use of first and second person references in children of 1;6–6;0 years-of-age. Ito (1980) compares interactional strategies in Japan and America, and discusses how these influence the system of address and reference, speech registers, and conversational style which children acquire. Okuda (1979) analyzes the use of polite style and honorifics in first, fourth, and sixth grade children, who performed various tasks and responded to explicit questions about their usage. Ide (1981) also reports on the use of polite and honorific forms by a sample of elementary and junior high school children. Given the sociolinguistic complexity of Japanese, further research on adult linguistic input to children and the acquisition of sex-and status-appropriate speech could greatly add to our understanding of linguistic socialization.

3. Overall Course of Development

The outline of linguistic development presented in this section is composite and hypothetical, based as it is upon partial records from several children of different ages, and only one thorough longitudinal record (Okubo, 1967). Future research will hopefully fill in the gaps, and clarify the typical coordination in time of the development of the different linguistic systems.

As in other languages, the earliest phase of acquisition is the one-word stage, in which the child learns the names of the familiar people and objects in the environment, predicates referring to a few common events, states, and actions, and verbal routines accompanying certain actions, such as *Hai* 'Yes' when handing something to someone. In Japanese, there is an unusual number of reduplicated babytalk forms and onomatopoeic words for sounds at this stage, reflecting the extensive babytalk lexicon and the great development of sound symbolism in the language. Verbs are used in the tense which occurs most frequently for each item, for example, the present tense for references to certain states, such as *Nai* 'Does not exist', and the past tense for events such as *Ochita* 'Fell'. The first negatives, typically *Iya* 'I don't want', *Dame* 'No good', and in some children *Nai* 'Does not exist', appear.

The first stage of grammatical development in Japanese is marked by contrastive use of certain verbal inflections, usually including at least the imperative and the past tense, and the appearance of the three most common sentence-final particles: *yo* (assertive/emphatic), *ne* (seeking/indicating agreement) and *no* (presupposed shared context). This initial stage of grammatical development is typically quite early, before 2 years-of-age. Two-word utterances also begin to appear during this period, but there is evidence that a few verbal inflections are acquired before MLU reaches 2.0. Some children acquire sentence-final particles before, others after, the emergence of two-word utterances. At about the same early period, the genitive particle *no* appears as a marker of possession following single nouns, as in *Maho no* 'Maho's', and *wa,* the topic marker, is used with rising intonation following nouns, either as a question about the location of an absent person or object, as in *Papa wa?* 'What about/where is papa?', or about whether a person (usually the child) is to be included in the handing out of food, toys, etc. Deictics of the *ko* series (close to speaker) emerge, typically *kore* 'this' and *koko* 'here'. Yes/no questions are produced by using rising intonation and the question *Nani?* 'What (is it)?' is acquired.

During the next stage of development, which occurs at about 2 years-of-age, two-word utterances become very frequent. Case particles begin to appear, and the particle *mo* 'also' following single nouns emerges. There is an increase in the number of verbal inflections, and children may begin to combine more than one sentence-final particle in sequence at the end of utterances. The verbal inflections for the present progressive/resultative in *-teru,* for the non-past tense in *-ru,* and the completed past in *-chatta* become fully productive, if they were not already in the prior period. At this time the non-past negative suffix *-nai* and the desiderative *-tai* are also acquired. Several additional sentence-final particles emerge, such as *ka* (question), *kana* (wondering question), and *naa* (exclamatory). Many case particles, such as the subject marker *ga,* the locative *ni,* and the instrumental *de* appear. As more particles are acquired, both *mo* 'also' and the possessive *no* begin to appear in constructions with two nouns, as in N *mo* N *mo* 'N and N', and N *no* N 'N's N'. Two precocious characteristics of this period are the appearance of verbal complements with *iu* 'say/go'[1] to quote speech and report sounds, and the emergence of the first conjunctions, typically for expressing prohibition and permission.

The first half of the third year is spent expanding the child's repertoire of morphological devices within the systems which have been developing thus far. A number of new verbal inflections are acquired, including the completed non-past *-chau,* the cohortative/intentive *-oo,* the past progressive/resultative *-teta* and potentials in *-eru.* Sentence-final particles which are somewhat less common and marked for sex of speaker are acquired, such as *wa* (female). Little boys learn to refer to themselves as *boku* 'I' (male). The case particle *ni* is used to mark datives, and the giver in sentences with verbs of receiving. More complex locatives such as N *no tokoro ni* 'in N's place' appear, along with case markers for goals and sources. The genitive marker *no* begins to be used for a variety of different relations between nouns, and not just the possessive. The direct object marker *o,* which is rare in adult speech, is acquired. Many concatenated verb constructions emerge, including aspectual constructions with *kuru* 'come', *oku* 'put', etc. and benefactive constructions with verbs of giving. The number and semantic range of conjoined sentences is expanded, including the connectives *-te* 'and/and then/and so/-ing', *kara* 'because', *-tara* 'if/when', and sometimes *-temo* 'even though'. Sentences expressing purpose with verbs of coming and going in the V-*i ni* construction appear. The earliest relative clauses may begin to be used at this stage, consisting of single verbs preceding a head noun. The first polite inflections are acquired by some children, usually the non-past in *-masu* and the cohortative in *-mashoo.*

In the months around the child's third birthday, verbal inflections for passive, causative, and obligation in *-nakya* 'must' are acquired. Polite inflections in the past and negative emerge. More sophisticated conjunctions such as *noni* 'although', *node* 'since', and *-nagara* 'while' begin to appear, along with some of the more common optional clause-initial conjunctions such as *soshite* 'and then', *sorede* 'and so/then', and *dakara* 'and so'. By this time, if not earlier, little girls are using the first person pronoun *(w)atashi* 'I' (female). The basics of code-switching with polite verbs and the various forms of first and second person reference may be established in some children. Embedded clauses appear on

---

[1]Japanese uses the same verb, *iu* 'say', not only to report speech, but also for the sounds made by animals and objects, which in English are reported with the verb 'go', as in *Cows go moo.*

certain common head nouns, such as *toki* 'time', *koto* 'thing', *tokoro* 'place', and *hoo* 'way'.

At approximately 3½ to 4 years-of-age, most Japanese children in urban areas like Tokyo begin to attend kindergarten for half a day. (In some areas, nursery schools or day care centers are available even earlier.) This is an important period in children's sociolinguistic development, since they must now deal with new adults of superior status in a formal context, as well as with large groups of children of both sexes of the same age to several years older. This is a time for the development of forms which children may not have had much opportunity to use before; for example, little boys may now become fluent in the use of the "rough" masculine pronouns *ore* 'I' and *omae* 'you'.

Acquisition of the complex system of honorifics, extremely polite speech, and the more formal pronouns, such as *watakushi* 'I' for boys, continues into the junior high school years. Children who leave Japan during their early elementary school years may never fully acquire the adult system of politeness. There is even some concern that children in Japan do not always master the higher stylistic levels and honorifics. Thus although Japanese children's acquisition of certain morphological features, such as verbal inflections and sentence-final particles, seems precocious, certain important sociolinguistic features of the language are acquired as late as the school years, and apparently sometimes are not acquired at all.

THE DATA

4. Typical Errors

4.1. The Continuative Inflection

The system of verbal inflections in Japanese emerges quite early, and errors are not frequently reported. However, there is one error which appears to be quite common, occurring in many children at about 2 years-of-age, when the first inflections are becoming productive: overgeneralization of the verb form in *-te*. This error occurred in each of the 3-year-olds in my sample, and is also reported by Sanches (1968, Chap. 3), Hirayama (1978), and Rispoli (1981a,b).

The *-te* inflection marks the continuative form of the verb, which does not itself indicate any particular tense or aspect, but rather serves as the non-final form in sequences of concatenated verbs and in conjoined clauses. The *-te* form combines with *iru* 'be' to form compound tense/aspects, such as the progressive/resultative, with verbs such as *kuru* 'come', *iku* 'go', and *miru* 'see' to mark aspectual distinctions, and with verbs of giving and receiving to indicate benefactive relations. The *-te* form of a verb, followed by a verb of giving, is frequently used in making requests. It is also possible to use the *-te* form alone as an imperative; this is frequent in mothers' speech to young children, and is the first imperative verb form which children acquire. This imperative use of -te is typically one of the earliest productive inflections which Japanese children acquire. Then, when -te has already been established as an imperative inflection, some children begin to overgeneralize it, using it as if it were a finite tense/aspect form in describing events and states. This error is very frequent in some children; Rispoli (1981a,b) found that 22.7% of the -te forms produced by one child of 18–24 months were not requests.

The majority of children's errors seem to be substitutions of the -te form alone for compound tense/aspects and concatenated verb sequences which incorporate -te. Sanches found that all three of the young 2-year-olds in her sample usually used -te for the progressive/resultative inflection -teru, which is a contraction of -te + iru 'be'.[2] In the following example from my data, a child of 2;2 substitutes -te for -temasu, the polite form of -teru.

Adult: (talking about a toy which has bells inside)
mada   hait - te   - mas - u   ka? kotchi ni.
still   enter CONT POL NONPAST Q   here   in
'Are they still inside here?'

Child: hait - te.
enter   CONT
'(They)'re inside'.

Rispoli and Hirayama have each proposed that uses of -te which are not requests may represent the child's attempt to produce concatenated verb structures of the form V-te V, and there is evidence in my data supporting this view. The clearest cases occur in dialogues in which the child intends to agree with a prior utterance by repeating the predicate, as in the above example, but produces only the -te form from a benefactive or aspectual construction, as in the following examples:

(Child is pretending to cook)

Mother: nani   tsukut - te   kure - ru?
what   make CONT give NONPAST
'What will you make for me?'

---

[2]Sanches proposes a phonetic explanation for this substitution of -te for -teru. In casual speech, Sanches notes, when -teru is followed by the sentence-final particle no, the entire sequence is often contracted to -tenno or -tenn, assimilating -ru. Although this may contribute to the frequency of the -te for -teru substitution, the overall pattern of errors suggests a more general process, in which the child selects out the familiar -te form from a larger verbal construction.

Child: *gohan   tsukut - te.*   2;1 yrs
          rice   make   CONT   F
          'Make rice'.

(Child is flying his toy airplane upside down)

Mother: *nanka   okkot - te   ku   - ru   n ja nai no,*
          something   fall   CONT   come   NONPAST
          sakasama   ni   nattara?
          'Won't something fall out if it's upside down?'

Child: *okkot - te.*   2;4 yrs
          fall   CONT   M
          'Fall'.

Thus during the period when children are overusing *-te*, the inflection appears
not only in imperatives, but also in indicative sentences, such as reports and
descriptions. Sanches apparently found *-te* used consistently instead of the present progressive/resultative *-teru*, but in my data incorrect indicative uses of *-te*
also substituted for aspectual and benefactive constructions, as the above examples show.

In addition, there are uses of *-te* which do not seem to be attempts to imitate
V-*te* V constructions. These examples are very difficult to analyze semantically,
and it often seems impossible to specify the child's semantic intention precisely.
In the following case, for example, the adult rephrases the child's *-te* with a
generic non-past in *-ru*, but it is not clear whether that was the child's intended
meaning.

Adult: (talking about a pull-toy swan on wheels)
          kore   nani?
          this   what
          'What's this?'

Child: *hippat - te.*   2;0 yrs
          pull   CONT   F
          'Pull'.

Adult: *ara,   hippar - u   no?*
          EXCLAM   pull   NONPAST   EP
          'Oh my, you pull it?'

Certain examples, such as the foregoing, may be intended as requests, as descriptions (the child was holding the string, although not using it to pull the toy),

or may even be self-addressed imperatives. Further research will be necessary to clarify the status of -*te* overgeneralizations and to determine whether they serve specifiable semantic functions contrasting with other simple inflections in particular children's speech, as was the case in Sanches' sample.

The overgeneralization of -*te* by Japanese children constitutes an apparent exception to children's general preference for the preservation of a one-to-one correspondence between form and function. By using -*te* as if it were a finite verb form, children who make this mistake add a non-imperative function to a form which initially fills only the imperative function. However, in most cases the children's semantic intention appears to be a compound tense/aspect incorporating -*te*, such as -*teru*, or a V-*te* V benefactive or aspectual construction. Thus children's non-imperative use of -*te* appears to be primarily the result of imperfect attempts at imitating continuative -*te* in the adult model, perhaps based on incomplete or filtered processing of the input. At a stage when they cannot yet produce two verbs in sequence, the only way Japanese children can imitate verbal structures of the V-*te* V type is either to use only the -*te* form, as typically happens, or to use only the aspectual or benefactive auxiliary verb, which did occur in my data, but much less frequently. The latter option is not really possible with a tense/aspect form such as -*teru*, in which the aspectual verb has been contracted into a unitary inflection with the -*te* form. Thus a brief stage of plurifunctionality for the surface form -*te* may be an unavoidable step in the acquisition of these structures, at least for children who do not wait until they can handle the full adult form before attempting to produce complex -*te* structures. The fact that the -*te* form is already familiar to children, since it is typically one of the first inflections to be acquired (as an imperative) apparently helps children to isolate this form when processing complex -*te* structures in the input. And since it is the -*te* form which is the main verb in V-*te* V constructions, children are more likely to focus on this form than the auxiliary aspectual or benefactive verb. Moreover, the -*te* form is extremely frequent in the input, which probably increases its salience for children. Rispoli (1981b) has analyzed a sample of mother's speech to a child of 18 months, and found that if all compound tenses and concatenated verbs are considered, as well as imperatives, the -*te* form occurred almost twice as frequently as the next most common inflection, the non-past -*ru*.

There may be another reason for Japanese children's willingness to accept this temporary plurifunctionality in their verbal system. As Smith (1973, Chap. 4) has found in the acquisition of phonology, children may not even be aware that a particular form has more than one meaning in their speech when the adult "target" forms are different. If most non-imperative uses of -*te* in Japanese children's speech are attempts to produce adult complex -*te* structures, then perhaps the general constraint against plurifunctionality does not apply because the children do not recognize their simplified -*te* version as being homophonous with their current imperative inflection. When complex -*te* forms are acquired, the imperative -*te* will also be restructured as a shortened, but grammatical, version of a V-*te* V construction, namely the imperative benefactive V-*te* *kudasai/choodai/kure* 'do and give'. The stage of plurifunctional -*te,* in which the -*te* form alone serves both imperative and non-imperative functions, thus seems to occur because it would be very difficult to avoid when learning complex -*te* forms, and also because the surface homophony of imperative and non-imperative -*te* occurs only in children's speech, rather than in the adult model. Therefore, -*te* overgeneralizations may not be subject to the same kind of monitoring which leads children to avoid homophonous adult forms, such as certain inflections within case paradigms.

4.2. Case Particles

In general, Japanese children acquire case particles early and without much apparent difficulty. My own data, as well as the studies of Okubo (1963, 1967), Miyahara (1973, 1974), Hirayama (1978), Yamada (1980), and Sanches (1968) indicate that the basic grammatical particles such as *wa* (topic) and *mo* 'also' and the case particles *ga* (subject), *no* (genitive), *de* (instrument), *ni* (locative/dative), *to* (comitative), *kara* (source), *e* (goal), and *o* (direct object) emerge between approximately 1;8–2;6 years–of–age. Errors are not usually reported. The typical course of acquisition is from failure to use a particle where appropriate to a gradually increasing rate of production until the child's frequency approximates adult usage. For example, Miyazaki (1979) reports that the child in Noji's diary study began using *ga* at 2;1 years–of–age, but did not use it with adult frequency until 11 months later. This process is probably hindered by the optional omission of certain particles in casual conversation, especially the ones marking basic grammatical relations, such as *o* (direct object), *ga* (subject), and *ni* (indirect object/locative goal). Particle ellipsis is apparently even more frequent in the speech addressed to young children. Yamada reports that *o* was almost never used in mother's speech in her study, and Miyazaki found that *ga* was omitted in 10.2% and *wa* in 25.5% of potential contexts in adult-adult conversation, whereas the corresponding figures in mother's speech to a 2-year-old were 30% and 70% omission. This feature of Japanese babytalk probably has an important impact on acquisition, especially of the most frequently omitted grammatical particles.

Although most studies of case particles report on early stages in which children use particles less frequently than adults, there is also some evidence for a later stage in which particles may be overused in comparison with the adult model. Cook (1985) reports that one child of 2;7 years used the subject marker *ga* in 90.3% of potential contexts, compared with 83.8% in his caregivers' speech, and used the object marker *o* in 40.6% of potential contexts, compared with his caregivers' frequency of only 17.9%. Cook also notes that this child tended to pronounce the case markers, especially *o,* more clearly than his caregivers, and interprets this as evidence for Slobin's (1973) claim that "children apparently prefer that grammatical functors be not only present whenever possible but also that they be clearly marked acoustically.'' Overgeneralization of the frequency of case particles in Japanese provides interesting confirmation of Slobin's claim that children prefer consistency in grammatical marking. In the speech of at least some Japanese children, then, the acquisition of case particles may show a U-shaped curve rather than a steady increase in frequency, with a stage of overgeneralization preceding the particle ellipsis characteristic of casual adult speech.

Children's errors in using case particles provide interesting insights into their hypotheses about particle functions. The nature of the errors depends upon the stage of acquisition. When a child first begins to use a particle, unsystematic errors may occur, which seem to represent random guesses. For example, a child of 2;4 years old in my sample was just beginning to use the direct object marker *o,* and made errors such as the following:

Mother: *chitchana   hora,   porusha   at - ta   deshoo.*
          little   listen   Porsche   exist PAST COP:PRESUM
         'Listen, there was a little Porsche, wasn't there'.

Child: *porusha   o.*
       Porsche   DO

The mother has omitted the subject particle *ga* after *porusha* 'Porsche', and in agreeing with her utterance by a partial repetition, the child uses *o* where *ga* would have been appropriate. The only case particle this child was using spontaneously with any frequency was *no* (genitive) to indicate possession. He seems to be at a stage where he is realizing that nouns are typically followed by particles, but in cases other than possession does not yet know which particle to use. The unit 'Noun + Particle' is an accepted grammatical and phonological unit in Japanese, one type of *bunsetsu* or phrase (see Hashimoto, 1934). Children apparently recognize and attempt to produce this unit early, even before they have learned the functions of case particles.

At a more advanced stage of acquisition, children make systematic errors which reveal how they are organizing a given particle within their grammar. The particles which cause the most difficulty seem to be those with primarily grammatical functions, especially the subject marker *ga*. In Japanese, *ga* marks nouns having a wide range of semantic functions, including agentive/actor subjects of transitive verbs, experiencers and other subjects of intransitives, as well as certain types of objects. For example, *ga* marks the object of stative predicates such as *suki* 'like', *wakaru* 'understand', and *mieru* 'appear/be visible', the object of verbs in the potential and the object of verbs in the desiderative. Some of these predicates, such as *suki* 'like', are very common in the input to children and are acquired very early in sentences of the form N *ga* Pred, such as N *ga suki*

'(I) like N' or 'N is likeable'. However, as the alternative translations suggest, there is some confusion with predicates such as *suki* 'like(able)' and *kowai* 'fearful' as to whether a *ga*-marked nominal indicates the experiencer or the object of experience. For example, the question *Dare ga kowai?* might mean either 'Who is afraid?' or 'Whom are you afraid of?'. Thus children may be exposed to input in which *ga* marks different case roles even with the same predicate. Given the great diversity of semantic relations between predicate and argument marked by *ga*, it would be difficult for children to formulate a single semantic hypothesis about its functions.

In my data, *ga* appeared in three major functions at about the same time in two different children: marking the agent of transitive verbs, as in *Miki ga nomu* 'Miki will drink', the subjects of intransitives, as in *hana ga aru* 'there are flowers' (lit. 'flowers exist'), and the objects of stative predicates with *suki* 'like'. Since *ga* does not consistently mark agents, and is sometimes omitted, the direct object marker *o* is frequently omitted, and many transitive sentences include only a single nominal argument, Japanese children have difficulty acquiring the case marking for transitive events with agents and affected objects having the surface configuration N-*ga* N-*o* V. One rather common error is to mark both agents and patients with *ga* in transitive sentences, as in the following example from my data:

| **omizu* | *ga* | *ire* | *- ta* | *noni* | 2;1 yrs |
| water | SUBJ | put in | PAST | although | F |

'although she put in water'.

Earlier in this conversation, the child had correctly said:

| *mama* | *ga* | *mizu* | *ire* | *- ta* | *no* | *ne.* |
| mama | SUBJ | water | put in | PAST | EP | AGR |

'Mama put in water'.

This child seems to know that *ga* should mark the agent when both agent and patient are expressed, but also uses *ga* for patients which occur as the only nominal argument of a transitive verb. Fujiwara (1977) cites similar examples, such as (p. 224):

| **mada* | *kore* | *ga* | *ki* | *- teru.* |
| still | this | SUBJ | wear | PRES.PROG |

'I'm still wearing this'.

Although children typically assume that the use of grammatical markers should make semantic sense (see Slobin, 1973), when the input does not permit the formulation of a semantic hypothesis, they will turn to other solutions. The errors which occur with *ga* in Japanese seem to indicate that some children make a syntactic, or positional hypothesis, namely, that *ga* follows the first nominal argument in a sentence.

Substitution of *ga* for *o* can be found not only at the early stages of acquisition, but also in much older children. Fujitomo (1977) found that children of 4- to 6-years-old, who were asked to describe a set of pictures, made many errors in which *ga* was used instead of *o*. Takahashi (1975b) also found that children between 3;3 and 6;6 years old made this error, usually in sentences where the direct object was the only nominal argument. Older children sometimes marked the object with *ga* even when both subject and object were expressed, as in the following case (p. 13):

kuma	*ga*	*ne*	*nezumi*	*ga*	*ne*	*oikake - teru.*	6;4 yrs
bear	SUBJ	AGR	mouse	SUBJ	AGR	chase PRES.PROG	F

'The bear is chasing the mouse'.

Hakuta (1982) has made similar findings on an immediate imitation task, involving 40 children aged 3;8–6;8 years. Even the older children had great difficulty imitating OSV sentences with the configuration N-*o* N-*ga* V, which are much less common in Japanese than SOV sentences. The children either switched the order of particles so that *ga* marked the first noun, or else simply changed the particle on the first noun to *ga*, leaving both nouns with *ga*, as in the above example from Takahashi's production data. Thus problems with *ga* may continue into the early school years.

Fujiwara (pp. 105–108) also cites mistakes with *ga* made by a child who seems to have a more semantically refined version of the positional hypothesis. This child, at 1;9 years old, typically used *ga* instead of *ni* (locative goal) with the verbs *kuru* 'come', *iku* 'go' and *kaeru* 'return'. In most of the cited examples, the child is describing one person's motion towards another person, and uses *ga* to mark the person who is the goal rather than the actor. For example, when her grandmother carried her over to her grandfather, she said:

jiichan	*ga*	*ki*	*- ta*	*kitaa.*
grandfather	SUBJ	come	PAST	

'Grandfather came'.

The child's intention was clearly *ni:* 'came *to* grandfather.[3] This child also used *ga* instead of *ni* with the verb *morau* 'receive', as in:

---

[3]Actually, the correct adult form would be:

jiichan	*no*	*tokoro*	*ni*
grandfather	GEN	place	to

'to grandfather's place'

The difficulty of this construction may be hindering use of *ni,* which does not simply follow the

*Junchan   ga   maat-   ta (= moratta).
             SUBJ   receive   PAST
'Junchan received (it)'.

Again, since the child meant to say 'I received it from Junchan', *ni* would have been appropriate. It is striking that all errors cited for this child in which *ga* replaces *ni* involve two human referents in the same case frame, although only one of these is overtly expressed. Interestingly, most examples of correct use of *ga* which Fujiwara cites for this child involved animate or pseudo-animate subjects, including humans, a dog, and a doll. Thus it appears that this child is learning to use *ga* correctly with animate subjects; her errors indicate that she uses *ga* with animate goals and sources as well. This child seems to be operating on the hypothesis that *ga* marks the first nominal referent in a sentence, with the constraint that the referent must be animate.[4]

In formulating hypotheses about the functions of case particles, children may begin by associating a particle with a particular verb that takes a nominal argument marked by that particle. In such cases, errors show that the child knows that a certain case particle is used with the verb, but does not know which argument of the verb it should mark. For example, Sanches (1968, p. 31) cites the errors of a child at 2;0–2;1 years-of-age, who used the particle *ni* (locative) incorrectly at first. Riding on her father's back, she said:

*Asachan   ni   not - teru.
Asachan   on   ride   PRES.PROG
'(He) is riding on Asachan/me'.

Similarly, she put a jack-in-the-box on a truck and said:

*jakku   ni   not - ta.
jack   on   ride   PAST
'(It) rode on jack'.

However, she did use the particle correctly in the following case:

rinrin   ni   not - ta.
bike   on   ride   PAST
'(I) rode on the bike'.

---

nominal referent in this case. However, the child is making the same substitution of *ga* for *ni* with *morau* 'receive', in which case *ni* marks the source from whom an object was received, and does follow the human referent directly.

[4]In one example (p. 105), this child said *Omikan ga kita yoo* 'Tangerines came', when her grandmother brought several tangerines. Here the child is apparently treating the tangerines as the "actor."

Clearly, the child knows that *noru* 'ride' typically takes an argument in *ni,* but is not sure whether *ni* marks the rider or the vehicle.

Kameyama (1982), analyzing the development of case frames in the speech of one child from my sample from 1;11 to 2;2 years-of-age, has found that certain case particles tend to occur with particular verbs. Although some of the child's case particles were multi-functional even at this early stage of development, each particle actually occurred with only a very limited number of verbs. For example, *ni* was used to mark location with *aru* 'exist' and *hairu* 'enter', to mark the result with *naru* 'become', to mark purpose with *iku* 'go', and to mark the agent/source with *morau* 'receive'. Kameyama proposes that children may go through an initial phase of associating case particles with particular verbs before they start to formulate general semantic hypotheses. These findings from language acquisition are consistent with Hinds' proposal (1976–1977) that Japanese speakers reconstruct ellipted nominal arguments in discourse through their knowledge of the case frames characteristic of different verbs. This organization of verbs in the lexicon in terms of their case frames is apparently being constructed in the early stages of Japanese language development, as the child learns case particles and begins to verbalize the arguments of predicates.

When children formulate a general semantic hypothesis about a case particle, the errors which occur sometimes reflect incomplete understanding of the meaning of a newly emerging particle and inappropriate generalization to the semantic range of other particles in the same domain. For example, Takahashi (1975b, p. 46) cites the following errors produced by 4-year-olds, who were still having difficulty distinguishing between *de,* which marks the place where an action occurs, and the locative functions of *ni.* As a locative, *ni* marks directional goals with verbs of motion, as it should in the first example below, and marks the location of objects and people with verbs of existence, as it should in the second example.

*raion	ne	ee	dokka	de	ne	it - te	ne . . .	4;7 yrs
lion	AGR	uh	somewhere	LOC	AGR	go	CONT	AGR	F

'The lion goes somewhere and . . .'

*okaasan	wa	ouchi	de	i-ru	-ur	no.	4;2 yrs
mother	TOP	house	LOC	exist	NONPAST	EP	M

'Mother is at home'.

Thus sorting out the functions of particles within a single semantic area, such as locatives, may continue beyond the early stages of acquisition.

At later stages of development, children may use a particle in ways which indicate a full grasp of their meaning, but reflect an unfamiliarity with conventional Japanese modes of expression. These errors are interesting in that they reflect natural extensions of the basic meaning of a particle, which can be found in other languages, but which Japanese happens to express differently. For example, Fujiwara (p. 247) cites a child of 3;2 years, who said that her mother got angry at her using the expression:

```
*. . . Kyookochan   ni       okori   - mashi - ta.
       Kyookochan   LOC   be angry   POL     PAST
       'got angry at Kyookochan'.
```

The child uses the locative particle *ni,* which can mark static location, just as English uses *at.* However, in Japanese, this is incorrect: *okoru* 'be angry' takes an abstract direct object. The child should have said:

```
Kyookochan   no    koto     o    okori   - mashi - ta.
Kyookochan   GEN   matter   DO   be angry  POL     PAST
'got angry at the matter of Kyookochan'.
```

Certain errors reflect the basic operating principle that the use of grammatical markers should make semantic sense (Slobin, 1973); children will regularize exceptional functions of case particles. For example, in Japanese, the objects of verbs of involuntary perception, such as *mieru* 'appear/be visible' are marked with *ga,* the subject marker, rather than *o.* In other languages, these nominals are treated like direct objects, and sometimes Japanese children do so as well. A 3-year-old in my sample said:

```
*. . . ohashi       o     mie - na    - i              mienai.
       chopsticks   DO    see   NEG    NONPAST
       'I can't see the chopsticks/The chopsticks aren't visible'.
```

Here the child is regularizing Japanese case marking, eliminating the distinction between objects of stative predicates and other direct objects. Thus late errors with case particles tend to involve exceptional uses which are not semantically consistent with their more common functions.

4.3. *Negation*

In English, the word *no* serves a variety of semantic/pragmatic functions, which in Japanese are expressed with distinct forms. A very common error among Japanese children of about 1½ to 2½ years-of-age is to confuse the different forms used for the functions of rejection (refusal), prohibition, non-existence, and denial. (See Bloom [1970] for a treatment of the development of negation in English which influenced some of the Japanese research.) The development of negation in Japanese has been analyzed by McNeill and McNeill (1973), who report on one monolingual child between 2;3–2;9 years, by Yamamoto (1981), who follows her Japanese-English bilingual child from 1;7–

TABLE 4.1
Single-Word Negative Expressions
in Two-Year-Old Children's Speech

Function	Form	
Rejection/Refusal	*iya*	'no'/'I don't like/want'
Prohibition	*dame*	'no'/'it's no good'/'don't'
Non-existence	*(i)nai*	'doesn't exist/isn't there'
Denial	*chigau*	'no'/'it's not true'

2;11 years, and by Ito (1981), who reports on three Japanese sisters, as well as 31 children whose mothers responded to a questionnaire. Table 4.1 summarizes the single-word negative expressions which these authors discuss and which occurred in my data.[5]

Iya is a nominal adjective which means 'unpleasant/unlikeable', and is used in rejecting objects and refusing suggestions. *Dame* is a nominal adjective which means approximately 'no good/won't work/won't do'; in single-word prohibitions it corresponds to English *Don't!*. The adjective *nai* predicates the absence or non-existence of inanimate objects, *inai* of animate beings. Ito found that *nai* was first used to express disappearance, and later non-existence. *Chigau* is a verb meaning 'differ'; as a general single-word denial, it means, 'The truth is different from what you said'.

The form *nai*, which expresses non-existence, also appears as a bound morpheme which attaches to the roots of verbs and adjectives to inflect them for the negative non-past tense. Predicates inflected with *-nai* can be used to deny the truth of a prior statement and also to express rejection and, occasionally, prohibition. For example, in my data children often, correctly, produced refusals of the form V-*nai*, such as *Tabe-nai* 'I will not eat'. Yamamoto (personal communication) reports cases of V-*nai* used to express prohibition, such as *Naka-nai* 'You will not cry' or 'Don't cry', when the child's mother pretended to cry. The form V-*nai* also occurs in adult speech to express prohibition, although other constructions are more common.[6]

Thus *nai* is a very frequent and salient marker of negation in Japanese. It is not surprising that a common error in the early stages of the acquisition of negation is to overgeneralize *nai* as a single-word negative to functions other

---

[5]McNeill and McNeill also report early acquisition of *iiya* to express denial. This form did not occur in my data, and was not found by Yamamoto or Ito. The form *iie*, a somewhat formal adult denial, also does not seem to occur at this early stage. The 3-year-olds, but not the 2-year-olds, in my sample used the colloquial *uu-un* 'uh-uh' for denials.

[6]If the use of V-*nai* for prohibition is rare in the input, then examples such as Yamamoto's case of *naka-nai* 'don't cry' may be overgeneralizations of the non-past indicative suffix *-nai* as a negative imperative.

than non-existence. For example, Japanese 2-year-olds frequently use *nai* instead of *iya* to express rejection. Ito reports that *iya* was the first negative acquired by 22 of the 31 children whose mothers responded to his questionnaire. However, *nai* is also acquired very early; Tanouye (1980) found that both children she studied used *nai* at the one-word stage. When *nai* emerges, it may start to replace *iya* in expressions of rejection. For example, Fujiwara (1977, p. 29) reports that a child of 1;3 years who was refusing to go indoors after an outing said *Nainai* 'Allgone' instead of *Iya*. Another child of 1;10 years, refusing to say goodbye, said *Baibai nai* 'There is no bye-bye' instead of *Baibai iya* (p. 128). McNeill and McNeill report that the child they studied, at the age of 2;3–2;7 years, used *nai* in 40% of the contexts where *iya* would have been appropriate. Ito found that *nai* was used to express rejection even by children who had not yet begun to use it correctly to express non-existence. As Ito points out, such use of *nai* rather than the previously acquired *iya* to express rejection is consistent with Slobin's (1973) proposal that "new forms first express old functions."

Some children continue to use *nai* for rejection and other functions even after they are also using it appropriately to express non-existence. *Nai* may be overextended to express denials, for example. Ito found that children use *nai* for denials before acquiring the correct *chigau*. This error is an example of Slobin's principle (1973) that "new functions are first expressed by old forms." Some children apparently continue this use of *nai* even after acquiring *chigau;* one child of 1;11 years in my sample was using *chigau* correctly for some denials, but also produced sentences such as the following:

Mother: *kowashi-chatta   Yotchan   ne.*
          break   Yotchan   AGR
          'Yotchan (you) broke it, didn't you'.

Yotchan: **nai.*
          doesn't exist
          'There is none'.

Here *Chigau* 'It's not true' would have been appropriate.

The form *nai* also frequently replaces *ja-nai* 'is not' in denials. The negative of the copula *da* is *de-nai,* but typically the topic particle *wa* is infixed to give *de wa nai,* which is contracted to *ja-nai.* In producing these denials, children usually omit *ja* and use the same sentence pattern as for negative existentials: N *nai* 'There is no N'. The following example from my data is typical:

Adult: (referring to a picture of a helicopter)
        hikooki   kana?
        airplane   Q
        'I wonder if it's an airplane'.

Child: *hikooki   nai   yo.   2;1 yrs
         airplane   doesn't exist   EMPH   F
         'There's no airplane'.

Adult: hikooki   ja   - nai   ne.
         airplane   COP+TOP   NEG   AGR
         'It's not an airplane, is it'.

All three of the 2-year-olds in my sample substituted *nai* for *janai;* this error is
also reported by Yamamoto (personal communication), Ito, Fujiwara (pp. 113,
220), Hatano (1968), and Sanches (1968, p. 76). This mistake probably reflects
not only overgeneralization of *nai*, but also the lack of perceptual salience of *ja*
in its position between a familiar noun and the familiar negative *nai*. Children
probably fail to notice *ja* at first; they certainly do not recognize *ja* as incorporating the copula *da,* which may increase their tendency to filter out *ja* as "noise."

The form *iya,* which indicates rejection, is also sometimes overextended to
denials. For example, one child of 2;0 years in my sample, who had been using
iya appropriately to express rejection and dislike, began using *iya* to deny the
truth of a prior utterance. This child was also correctly using *chigau* for denials at
this stage. In the following exchange, mother and child were looking at a picture
of a popular cartoon character, which the child called *wanwan* 'doggie'.

Mother: wanwan   ka.   araiguma   rasukaru.
         doggie   Q   raccoon   rascal
         'A doggie, huh. It's rascal raccoon'.

Child: *iya   da.
          dislike   COP
         'I don't like/want it'.

Mother: chiga - u?   chigau   no?
         differ   NONPAST   EP
         (Lit., 'Does it differ?') 'Am I wrong?'

Child: un.
         yes
         'Yes (you're wrong)'.

McNeill and McNeill also report the use of *iya* for denials, as in the above
example, although they interpret this finding differently.[7] Ito found that *chigau*

---

[7]McNeill and McNeill claim that in these cases, *iya* is a phonetic variant of *iiya,* and therefore is
semantically appropriate in denials. However, the same error occurs in my data, although *iiya* did not
occur in the input and was not acquired by the children in my sample.

emerged later than the function of denial, which was at first expressed with *nai*. As noted above, in children who have not yet acquired *chigau*, the use of *iya* or *nai* for single-word denials reflects operation of the principle that new functions are first expressed by old forms (Slobin, 1973). Frequency also may be a factor; in general, *iya* occurs much more frequently than *chigau* in child speech. Ito (1981) states that *chigau*, which notes a discrepancy between opinions, is more rational and intellectual than *iya*, which marks an emotional reaction. In situations of conflicting opinions, there seems to be a transition from *iya* 'I don't like', which expresses the child's displeasure in this context, to *chigau* 'it's different', which explicitly denies the truth of the opposing view. *Iya* and *chigau* are similar in that both types of negation are very frequently responses to the addressee's prior utterance, and both express direct conflict with the addressee.

Japanese children also sometimes use *dame* to express rejection and *iya* to express prohibition, instead of vice versa. Ito found that rejection and prohibition were the earliest negative functions to emerge, and suggests that these categories are at first undifferentiated in children's speech. In the early stages of development, the children Ito studied used *dame* and *iya* interchangeably to express rejection. Yamamoto (personal communication) also found that her daughter used *dame* and *iya* interchangeably to mean 'I don't wanna'. Both Yamamoto and Ito found *iya* in contexts of prohibition. It is important to note that in adult usage, this is not necessarily incorrect; each form may actually be used for either rejection or prohibition. For example, the following use of *dame* for refusal in my data was judged to be acceptable by several speakers of Japanese:[8]

(Mother is encouraging 2-year-old to lend his toys to a baby)

Mother:	*fuusen*	*wa*	*dore*	*kashi - te*		*age - ru*		*no,*
	balloon	TOP	which	lend	CONT	give	NONPAST	EP
	fuusen?							
	balloon							
	'Which balloon will you lend to him?'							

Child:	*dame.*		2;0 yrs
	no good		M
	'No'.		

* * * * * *

Adult:	*kore*	*wa*	*ja.*	*kore*	*akachan*	*ni*	*kashi - te*
	this	TOP	well	this	baby	to	lend	CONT
	age - ru,		*gohon?*				
	give	NONPAST	book				
	'Well, what about this. Will you lend this book to the baby?'						

---

[8]This judgment is not unanimous, however, among speakers of Japanese.

Child: *iya*   *da.*
          dislike   COP
          'No'.

The overlap in usage between *iya* and *dame* reflects the pragmatic and emotional overlap between their functions. Both rejection and prohibition entail the speaker's dislike or disapproval, and in many contexts either would be appropriate. For example, if one child were taking another's toys, the owner could say either *iya* to express strong dislike of this behavior, or *dame* to warn the child to stop. Since *iya* strongly implies a first person subject, it does not directly express prohibition, but this would be the obvious implication in such a context. Similarly, *dame,* which actually means 'no good', can be used to express rejection/refusal, even though it is less personal than *iya.* It is not clear how sensitive children are to these subtle distinctions between *iya* and *dame;* in my data, both were often used forcefully and angrily to express rejection in the same context, as in the above example. It seems likely that the process of generalizing *dame* and *iya* from their more common functions to the domains of rejection and prohibition, respectively, is based on pragmatic and emotional factors similar to those responsible for erroneous overgeneralizations.

The availability of distinct forms for each negative function in Japanese helps clarify the semantic, pragmatic, and emotional factors which probably underlie the acquisition of negation in other languages as well. Figure 4.1 summarizes the available data on Japanese children's errors in the acquisition of negation. The findings suggest the hypothesis that rejection and prohibition are the two most similar functions. Ito has proposed that during the earliest stages of development, children do not distinguish rejection and prohibition; instead, rejecting, demanding, commanding, prohibiting, and insisting constitute an undifferentiated semantic complex with an emotional basis that has developed during the prelinguistic period. Even in adult speech, there is overlap between the usage of *iya* and *dame.*

Denial seems to be kept somewhat more separate from rejection and prohibition than the latter two are from one another. *Chigau* 'it's not true' is apparently not overgeneralized to express rejection or prohibition by children. Ito suggests that denial is a more intellectual function than rejection or prohibition, since it requires that the child hold in mind a clear and contrasting alternative to the preceding statement rather than just making an emotional response. Denial seems to have more in common with rejection than with prohibition; prohibition usually responds to the actions rather than the words of the addressee, whereas both denial and rejection are often responses to a prior utterance. The direction of children's errors supports this view: *iya* (rejection) but not *dame* (prohibition) is overextended to denials. However, denial is similar to both rejection and prohibition in that it involves conflict with the addressee, which may be quite emotional; in my data, children often seemed to have a sense of outrage when they heard a

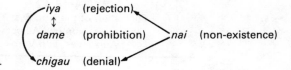

FIG. 4.1.   Children's substitution
errors in the acquisition of negation.

proposition with which they disagreed. It is interesting that rejection, prohibition, and denial are the three functions which in English are expressed with the same word: *no!*

In contrast, non-existence has much less in common semantically and pragmatically with the other three negative functions. Ito has pointed out that in the early stages, when *nai* expresses disappearance, it has affective connotations. However, as an expression of non-existence, *nai* typically lacks the sense of conflict with the addressee which is present with the other three negatives. The overgeneralization of *nai* therefore seems to be based upon its frequency and salience as a negative inflection and its early emergence as both an inflection and an expression of disappearance, rather than upon underlying functional similarities between non-existence and the other negative functions.[9] Evidence for this proposal can be found in the direction of children's errors: although *nai* is used for other negative functions, none of the other forms is substituted for *nai* to express non-existence, not even *iya,* which is acquired before *nai* by many children. Thus non-existence, the only function which cannot be expressed by the single word *no* in adult English, seems to be kept conceptually distinct from other negatives during the course of acquisition by Japanese children.

4.4. *Inflectional Errors*

The inflectional system in Japanese is not extremely complex compared with many other languages, but children do make many errors during acquisition. Several studies of the early stages of language development in Japanese include information about inflectional errors, such as Fujiwara (1977), Hatano (1968), Iwabuchi and Muraishi (1968), Okubo (1967), Sanches (1968) and Yamamoto (1981). Errors typically occur in using the copula, forming the past tense of adjectives, using negative inflections, and determining the grammatical status of a special class of nominal adjectives, which are adjectives semantically, but behave like nouns morphologically.

Table 4.2 summarizes the non-past tense of the different parts of speech in Japanese. The non-past tense of adjectives is marked by the inflection -*i,* of verbs

---

[9]Evidence for this claim can be found in data on the acquisition of Korean. Korean, like Japanese, has distinct single-word negative forms for rejection, prohibition, denial, and non-existence. However, the expression for non-existence, *epse,* bears no resemblance to the negative inflections *an-* and -*ci ane.* Hahn (1981), who studies her daughter's acquisition of negation, found no overgeneralization of *epse* to negative functions other than non-existence.

TABLE 4.2
Formation of the Non-Past Tense
in Nouns, Nominal Adjectives,
Adjectives, and Verbs

Noun	*ringo da/na no*	'is an apple'
Nominal Adjective	*joozu da/na no*	'is skillful'
Adjective	*atsu - i no*	'is hot'
Verb	*tabe - ru no*	'eats'

by *-(r)u;* the tense of nominal adjectives must be indicated by using the copula, as with nouns.

The copula *da* becomes productive early in naming routines of the form N *da* 'It's an N'. Although the copula *da* is optional, when it is followed by the sentence-final particle *no, da* becomes *na,* and may not be omitted. In my sample, one child of 1;11 years consistently omitted *na* before *no,* as in the sentence **Buubuu no* 'It's a car'. The form *na* is less salient perceptually than *da,* since it does not occur sentence-finally, but rather is sandwiched in between the familiar noun and the particle *no.* Furthermore, since *no* follows true adjectives and verbs directly, analogy with these sentences may contribute to the omission of *na* with nouns. This child began using *na* with *no* correctly 1 month later, but 4 months after that, he began to overgeneralize *na,* using it even with verbs, as in:

*de	*- te*	*ki*	*- ta*	*na*	*no?*
come out	CONT	come	PAST	COP	EP

'Did it come out?'

Having acquired *na,* the child is now using it with verbs as he does with nouns. This error may also reflect a segmentation problem: the child may temporarily be treating *na no* as a unitary variant of the sentence-final particle *no.*

Table 4.3 presents the negative inflection in non-past and past tense for each part of speech. As Table 4.3 shows, the negative morpheme in Japanese is *na;* this affix converts verbs to morphological adjectives. Tense marking follows *na;* as with adjective stems, *-i* indicates the non-past, and *-katta* the past tense. At first, children seem to acquire *-nai* as a unitary negative suffix, and do not analyze it as incorporating the non-past tense. A common error in the earliest stage of acquiring negative inflections is to juxtapose *nai* after the noun, nominal adjective, adjective, or verb to be negated, rather than using the correct morphophonemic variants appropriate for each part of speech. The basic model for this X + *nai* pattern is probably the negative existential sentence N *nai* 'There is no N', which is acquired very early.

TABLE 4.3
Negation of Nouns, Nominal Adjectives, Adjectives,
and Verbs in the Past and Non-Past Tenses

	Non-Past	Past	
Noun	ringo ja-na-i	ringo ja-na-katta	'isn't/wasn't an apple'
Nom. Adj.	joozu ja-na-i	joozu ja-na-katta	'isn't/wasn't skillful'
Adjective	atsu - ku-na-i	atsu - ku-na-katta	'isn't/wasn't hot'
Verb	tabe - na-i	tabe - na-katta	'doesn't/didn't eat'

For example, as noted earlier in section 4.3, a very common error among 2-year-olds is to use the pattern N *nai* rather than N *ja-nai* when negating sentences which name objects, saying, for example, *Hikooki nai,* which actually means 'There is no airplane' rather than *Hikooki janai* 'It's not an airplane'. Perceptual factors probably play a role in this error. If we assume that children preferentially attend to the ends of intonational units, and also somewhat to the beginnings (see Peters, Slobin, 1985), then *ja* is probably not being processed at first. In the early stages of acquisition, children surely do not recognize that *ja* contains the copula. Even after *janai* is being used correctly, errors occur which reveal that the form has not been analyzed, such as the following example from Yamamoto (personal communication) produced by a child of 2;9 years:

*Suupaaman   da   ja   - nai.
Superman   COP   COP+TOP   NEG
'It's not Superman'.

Here the child uses the copula *da* redundantly, apparently unaware that it is incorporated in *ja*.

In general, the verb is the part of speech which Japanese children experience the least difficulty negating. The non-past tense, the first to be acquired in the negative, is formed by adding the suffix *-nai* directly to vowel-final verb roots, e.g. *tabe-nai* 'does not eat', and to the root plus /a/ of consonant-final roots, e.g. *nom-a-nai* 'does not drink'. This verbal inflection is usually mastered by children during the first few months of their third year, and errors are not usually reported. However, some children occasionally add *-nai* after an inflected form of a verb. For example, one child of 2;1 years in my sample, who sometimes added *-nai* correctly to verb roots, also produced the following forms:

*tabe - ru   - nai   **deki - ta   - nai*
eat   NONPAST NEG   can   PAST   NEG
'I won't eat'.   'I couldn't do it'.

This child even said *aru-nai* 'there is none'. In Japanese, the negative existential is a distinct predicate from the affirmative: *aru* means 'there is', *nai* 'there is not'. Instead of using *nai* alone, the child is attempting to inflect *aru* for the negative by adding *-nai*. Ito (personal communication) cites the parallel error in the past tense: *atta-nai*. Fujiwara (1977, p. 202) and Ito (1976) also report the suffixing of *-nai* to inflected verbs, as in *kaeru-nai* instead of *kaera-nai* 'I won't return (home)'. One factor underlying this error may be a tendency toward using a single strategy to form all negatives, namely, suffixing *-nai* to a familiar lexical item. Another factor may be these children's failure to analyze *-nai* as incorporating a tense marker. Typically, both the past tense verbal inflection *-ta* and the non-past *-(r)u* are acquired before 2½ years-of-age, but the negative past *-nakatta* does not emerge until later. Children at this stage of development who wish to express both tense and negation simply add *-nai* to a verb inflected for tense. This error thus provides evidence for Slobin's operating principle of one-to-one mapping of form and function (1985), and for MacWhinney's proposals (1985) that combination is one strategy used in acquiring morphology and that the combinations children use need not have a model in the adult input.

Table 4.4 contrasts the non-past and past, negative and affirmative inflections for true and for nominal adjectives. As the table shows, true adjectives consist of a vowel-final root, followed by the tense markers *-i* (non-past) and *-katta* (past). Negating adjectives is more difficult than negating verbs in Japanese, and errors are much more common. To negate true adjectives, *-ku* is affixed to the adjectival root; this *-ku* also converts adjectives to adverbs (e.g. *naga-i* 'long', *naga-ku* 'for a long time'), and is used in causative (e.g. *naga-ku suru* 'make long') and inchoative (e.g. *naga-ku naru* 'become long') constructions. The negative morpheme *na,* marked for tense, follows *-ku*. Thus negative inflections are somewhat different for verbs and adjectives. The comparative frequencies of verbal and adjectival inflections are also quite different. In a 1-hour sample of mother's speech to a child of 1;6 years, Rispoli (1981b) found the following frequencies of verbal and adjectival inflections. The verbal inflections *-(r)u, -ta,* and *-nai* are generally acquired quite early, but adjectives are initially perceived

TABLE 4.4
Non-Past and Past Tenses
of True vs. Nominal Adjectives
in the Affirmative and Negative

	True Adjectives	*Nominal Adjectives*
Non-past	*atsu - i* 'hot'	*joozu da* 'skillful'
Past	*atsu - katta*	*joozu datta*
Negative non-past	*atsu - ku-na-i*	*joozu ja-na-i*
Negative past	*atsu - ku-na-katta*	*joozu ja-na-katta*

TABLE 4.5
Frequency of Verbal and Adjectival Inflections in One Mother's Speech
to Her Child at 1;6 Years (From Rispoli, 1981b)

	Verbal Inflections			Adjectival Inflections		
Non-past	V - (r)u	47.4%	(55)	Adj - i	79.1%	(34)
Past	- ta	32.8	(38)	- katta	14.0	(6)
Negative non-past	- nai	19.0	(22)	- kunai	7.0	(3)
Negative past	- nakatta	.9	(1)	- kunakatta	—	(0)

as unitary lexical items, and used only in their non-past inflection. Obviously, the much lower frequency of adjectival compared to verbal inflections in the input plays a major role in their delayed acquisition.

Based on the available data from several different children, it is possible to construct a hypothetical sequence of development for adjectival inflections. In the first stage beyond the use of the most common non-past form of adjectives, Japanese children negate true adjectives by adding *-nai* to the non-past inflection, producing forms such as **atsui-nai* rather than the adult *atsu-kunai* 'is not hot'. This error appears to be almost universal in Japanese children of about 2 years-of-age; it occurred in the speech of all three of the 2-year-olds in my sample, and is also reported by Okubo (1967, p. 147), Ito (1976), and Yamamoto (personal communication). At this stage, both *-nai* and the non-past tense of adjectives are unanalyzed, and children are following the same pattern as with nouns: X + *nai*. Perceptual factors probably play a role in the early omission of *-ku*. Like *ja* in negative sentences with nouns and nominal adjectives, *-ku* is a semantically opaque formative sandwiched between the recognizable adjectival root and *nai;* it is probably filtered out at first in perception by young children. At this stage, nominal adjectives, which should be inflected with *janai,* are also negated simply by adding *nai.* A typical error is **Suki-nai,* produced by a child of 2;1 years in my sample, instead of the correct *Suki janai* 'I don't like it'.[10]

---

[10]Similar errors occur in the acquisition of inchoative constructions, which usually occur in the past tense with *natta* 'became'. Inchoatives in Japanese are formed by adding the particle *ni* to nouns and nominal adjectives, and the *-ku* inflection to true adjectives, as in the following examples:

Noun	tomodachi	ni	naru/natta	'become/became a friend'
Nominal Adjective	joozu	ni	naru/natta	'become/became skillful'
Adjective	atsu	-ku	naru/natta	'become/became hot'

There is evidence that children at first form inchoatives by simply adding *natta* 'became' to nouns and nominal adjectives, omitting *ni*, just as they initially form all negatives by simply adding *nai*. For example, Fujiwara (1977) cites the errors *oshimai natta* 'became the end' (p. 142) and *kiree natta* 'became clean' (p. 160), in which *ni* is omitted and *natta* follows directly after the noun and nominal

In the development of adjectival inflections, the next stage after the ADJ + *nai* pattern is the acquisition of *-kunai* to express negation, and somewhat later *-katta* to mark the past tense. Some children acquire these inflections before learning the correct segmentation of adjectives into root plus *-i* (non-past). Thus a common error is to add *-kunai* or *-katta* to the non-past form of an adjective. For example, errors such as *samui-kunai* for *samu-kunai* 'is not cold' are cited by Hatano (1968) and Yamamoto (1981). Okubo (1967, p. 147) reports that at 1;10 years her daughter said *abunai-katta* instead of *abuna-katta* 'was dangerous'; the same error occurred in the speech of a 3-year-old in my sample.

At the stage when *-kunai* and *-katta* are being used with true adjectives, a very common error is for children to add these inflections to nominal adjectives as well, which should take *janai* and *datta* for the non-past negative and past affirmative, respectively. (See Table 4.4 contrasting true and nominal adjectives.) For example, Hatano (1968) reports that a child of 2;4 years said *kiree-kunai* instead of *kiree janai* 'is not pretty/clean' and *kiree-katta* instead of *kiree datta* 'was pretty/clean'. These errors reveal that nominal adjectives have been aligned with true adjectives rather than with nouns for inflectional purposes. It is interesting that although the class of nominal adjectives includes some of the most frequent adjectives in children's speech, such as *suki* 'like(able)', *kiree* 'clean/pretty', *kirai* 'hateful', and *ippai* 'full', children consistently operate on a semantic basis, and inflect nominal adjectives incorrectly as if they were true adjectives. The generality of this error, which occurred in my data and is reported by Fujiwara (1977, p. 288), Hatano (1968), Okubo (1967, p. 146) and Yamamoto (personal communication) provides strong support for Slobin's proposal (1973) that children try to construct their grammars on a semantic basis, following the principle that "the use of grammatical markers should make semantic sense."

In the next stage of development, children segment adjectives correctly into root plus *-i*, and add inflections to the root rather than the non-past inflection. At this stage, a very common error is to segment nominal adjectives in the same way wherever possible. Many of the common nominal adjectives which children use mimic the morphophonological structure of true adjectives, as do *kirai* 'hateful' and *ippai* 'full'. If a nominal adjective ends in two vowels, of which the second is *-i*, children will analyze this *-i* as the non-past inflection, and will drop it, adding inflections to the root they have thus created. Fujiwara (1977, p. 233) and Yamamoto (personal communication) both cite *ippa-kunai;* the children have

---

adjective, respectively. Again, there is a strong tendency toward the use of a single construction to convey a particular meaning (see Slobin, 1985, Vol. 2). Since *ni* occupies the medial position in inchoative constructions, lack of perceptual salience is probably also a factor in its omission. Unfortunately, data on true adjectives are sparse. Okubo (1967, p. 147) cites the following isolated error in her daughter's speech at 2;1 years: *ooki natte kara* 'after becoming big (growing up)'. Here the child has failed to attach the *-ku* inflection to the stem *ooki-*, although typically she produced inchoatives correctly with true adjectives.

dropped the final -*i* of the nominal adjective before adding the negative inflection.[11] (The correct form is *ippai janai* 'is not full'). This error may be quite persistent; Okubo (1967, p. 146) reports that her daughter was still producing such forms at 5 years-of-age. This error is consistent with MacWhinney's prediction (1985) that children are being misled by their semantically based assignment of nominal adjectives to the class of true adjectives, and also by the phonological structure of certain nominal adjectives.

The most difficult of the inflections considered here, and the least frequent in the input, is the negative past -*nakatta*, which attaches to verb roots and to adjectives in -*ku*. Before children acquire this suffix, they first may try to use old forms for this new function, in keeping with Slobin's (1973) proposal. One option is to make do with forms that do not express the child's full intention. For example, a child of 2;3 years in my sample used the negative non-past inflection -*nai* instead of -*nakatta*, as in the following case:

Mother: *nai - ta?*
        cry   PAST
        'Did you cry?'

Child: *naka - nai.*
        cry   NEG
        'I don't cry'.

Another option is to combine familiar morphemes to express all the semantic distinctions intended. The verbal past tense inflection -*ta* and the negative non-past forms -*nai* (verbs) and *janai* (nouns) are acquired before -*nakatta*, and may be combined to form the negative past. As noted earlier, one child of 2;1 years in my sample said *deki-ta-nai* for *deki-nakatta* 'I couldn't do it'. Ito (1976) cites *hie-ta-nai* for *hie-na-katta* 'did not get cold' at 2;2 years. At a somewhat later stage, when the adjectival inflections -*kunai* (non-past) and -*katta* (past) have been mastered, children may combine these forms to express the negative past of adjectives. Hakuta (personal communication) cites a 3-year-old who said *oishi-katta-nai* instead of *oishi-ku-na-katta* 'wasn't delicious', and Fujiwara (p. 288) cites a child of 3;1 years who said *yo-katta-ku-nai* instead of *yo-ku-na-katta* 'wasn't good'. It is interesting that all of the errors cited follow the sequence PAST < NEGATIVE, although the correct inflection, -*nakatta*, actually has the reverse order. In the correct form the negative morpheme *na* is infixed between the verb root and the past tense inflection -*katta*. Apparently, children prefer to increase the salience of the negative marker by placing it in word-final position.

---

[11]Okubo (p. 146) and Yamamoto (personal communication) also report the same error with *kiree* 'pretty/clean'. In this case, since long /e/ tends to become narrower as it is pronounced, in some speakers tapering into a glide, children apparently segment it as the non-past inflection -*i*.

This makes sense, since the main point of a statement in the negative past is the negation, not the tense.

Another important factor in children's novel morpheme combinations is the preference for analytic over syncretic options. For example, in Japanese the form *janai* 'is not' follows nouns and nominal adjectives, that is, complete lexical items rather than roots. In negating verbs, children sometimes use *janai* after an inflected form instead of adding *-nai* to the verb root. For example, a child of 2;4 years in my sample said *nomu janai* instead of *noma-nai* 'I will not drink'. Fujiwara (p. 173) cites *kaetta janai* for *kaera-nakatta* 'I didn't go home' at 2;0 years. Thus children may seize upon *janai* as a means of avoiding the inflection of verb stems.[12]

Another interesting case occurred in the speech of a child in my sample who was using the verb *chigau* 'differ' to express denials. In adult speech, the pattern N *to chigau* 'It differs from N' has a meaning close to 'It's not an N'. At 2;2 years-of-age, this child was using *chigau* for denials in the pattern N *chigau*, omitting the particle *to*. In adult speech, *chigau* cannot occur with true adjectives, which must be negated by adding *-kunai* to the adjectival stem. However, this child used the following sentence, **Hazukashii chigau* '(I'm) not ashamed', instead of the correct *hazukashi-kunai*. Since *-kunai* was not yet fully productive in her speech, this may be a case of old forms for new functions (see Slobin, 1973). However, preference for the more analytic option may also be playing a part. *Chigau* is an independent verb rather than an inflection; as in the overextensions of *janai* from denials with nouns to negating verbs, using *chigau* with the adjective *hazukashii* avoids the problem of segmenting a root and suffixing a bound morpheme. Such errors provide support for the operating principle proposed by Berman (1985) that children will select more analytic options wherever possible.

4.5. *Prenominal Modifiers*

An error which occurs in the speech of many Japanese 2-year-olds is overgeneralization of the genitive particle *no* in prenominal modifiers. This particle is required when the modifier is a noun, but is ungrammatical when the modifier is an adjective. In Japanese, as in English, adjectives simply precede the noun they modify. However, on the model of N *no* N constructions, which express a variety of semantic relations between nouns, including the extremely common notion of possession, children frequently produce ungrammatical **ADJ *no* N constructions. See section 7.1 for a more complete discussion of this common error.

---

[12]Another potential model for this overextension is the adult use of *janai* in constructions of the form S *no janai* 'isn't it the case that S', in which an entire sentence is nominalized with *no* and then *janai* is added. In these cases, the child may hear *janai* following true adjectives and inflected verbs, but fail to perceive the nominalizer *no*, which is often reduced to *n*.

4.6. Benefactive Constructions

In Japanese, when one person performs an action which benefits another person, the situation is described with constructions using verbs of giving and receiving. For example, if Hanako buys a book for Taroo, the following sentences could be used:

Hanako	*ga*	*Taroo*	*ni*	*hon*	*o*	*kat - te*	*age - ta.*
	SUBJ		IO	book	DO	buy CONT	give PAST

'Hanako gave buying a book to Taroo'.

Taroo	*ga*	*Hanako*	*ni*	*hon*	*o*	*kat - te*	*morat - ta.*
	SUBJ		AGT	book	DO	buy CONT	receive PAST

'Taroo received buying a book from Hanako'.

Thus benefactive relations are expressed as the giving or receiving of actions. Benefactive constructions are quite common in Japanese and are used in many cases which would not be phrased with a beneficiary in English. The verbs of giving and receiving used in benefactive constructions are the same as in simple sentences describing the giving and receiving of objects, and the case marking is also the same. As the above sentences show, the configuration of case markers is the same whether a verb of giving or of receiving is used: 'N-*ga* N-*ni* N-*o* V'. However, it is important to note that the semantic interpretation of the case particles is different. As Uyeno et al. (1978) have pointed out, with verbs of giving, the subject particle *ga* marks the agent or source and the particle *ni* marks the recipient or goal. In contrast, with verbs of receiving, *ga* marks the recipient/goal and *ni* marks the agent/source. This interpretation of the particle *ni* also appears in passive sentences, where *ni* marks the agent, as *by* does in English passives.

In expressing benefactive relations, the speaker's point of view plays an important part. There are two different verbs of giving which may be used in benefactive constructions, *ageru* and *kureru*.[13] Selection of the appropriate verb depends upon whether the speaker is taking the viewpoint of the giver, in which case *ageru* is used, or of the recipient, in which case *kureru* is used. If the speaker or member of the speaker's in-group, such as family or friends, are participants in the event being described, the speaker must take that point of view. Thus if the speaker or someone close is the giver of the favor, *ageru* must be used, if the recipient, *kureru* must be used. Kuno and Kaburaki (1975) have

---

[13]The verbs used in benefactive constructions also have honorific counterparts: *sashi-ageru* for *ageru* 'give', *kudasaru* for *kureru* 'give', and *itadaku* for *morau* 'receive'. These verbs are used in referring to favors received or requested from social superiors. Except for the polite *kudasai,* a fixed form meaning approximately 'please', 2-year-olds do not use these verbs with any frequency, and so I will consider only the more common *ageru, kureru,* and *morau* here.

described these constraints in terms of "empathy." Speakers must empathize with themselves or in-group members. In syntactic terms, the focus of empathy is the subject with *ageru,* and the indirect object with *kureru.* There is only one verb of receiving, *morau,* but point of view is similarly constrained; when *morau* is used, the speaker or in-group member must be the recipient of the favor. Thus with *morau,* as with *ageru,* the focus of empathy is the subject. In describing events involving third parties who are equally unrelated to the speaker, *ageru* or *morau* will be used. Thus *kureru* is the most strongly constrained verb with respect to empathy.

In Japanese, there is no person-marking on verbs, and references to first and second persons are often omitted. However, due to constraints on empathy or point of view, the verbs *ageru, kureru,* and *morau* actually incorporate information about first and second person deixis. Thus if both speaker and addressee are participants in the event being described as a favor, *ageru* means 'I give to you', *kureru* 'you give to me', and *morau* 'I receive from you.' Therefore, these verbs serve different functions in discourse, and are used to perform different types of speech acts. For example, one offers to do favors with *ageru,* and requests favors with *kureru* questions.

Table 4.6, based upon Uyeno et al. (1978) and Horiguchi (1979a), summarizes the grammatical relations, case marking, semantic relations, and empathy focus involved in the different benefactive constructions.

Clearly, the expression of benefactive relations is one area of Japanese grammar in which the child is presented with several different forms to fill one semantic function. As predicted by the principle of one-to-one mapping (Slobin, 1985), mastering benefactive constructions is very difficult, and errors are frequently reported. Typically, *ageru* and *kureru* are confused; this occurred in my data and is reported by Okubo (1967, p. 79) and Fujiwara (1977, pp. 171, 191,

TABLE 4.6
Grammatical Relations, Semantic Relations,
Case Marking, and Empathy Focus in Sentences
with Benefactive Constructions
(Adapted from Uyeno et al., 1978
and Horiguchi, 1979a)

SUBJECT/AGENT	*ga*	INDIRECT OBJECT	*ni*	V-*te*	*ageru.*
Giver		Recipient			give
Empathy Focus					
SUBJECT/AGENT	*ga*	INDIRECT OBJECT	*ni*	V-*te*	*kureru.*
Giver		Recipient			give
		Empathy Focus			
SUBJECT	*ga*	AGENT	*ni*	V-*te*	*morau.*
Recipient		Giver			receive
Empathy Focus					

TABLE 4.7
Benefactive Constructions in the Speech
of One Child from 2;0–3;1 Years-of-Age[a]
(From Horiguchi, 1979a)

Giver	Recipient	V-*te ageru* (449) 'I give'		V-*te kureru* (101) 'give to me'		V-*te morau* (32) 'I receive'	
I	you/3rd p.	87.3%	(392)	*42.6%	(43)	* 9.3%	(3)
you/3rd p.	I	* 6.3	(28)	56.4	(57)	68.7	(22)
you/3rd p.	3rd p.	4.2	(19)	—		22.0	(7)
3rd p.	you/3rd p.						

[a]Errors are marked with asterisks, and absolute frequencies are given in parentheses. A small number of other uses occurred for *ageru* and *kureru*, which are not presented here.

198) as well. The most comprehensive analysis of errors in production data is presented by Horiguchi (1979a), who analyzes her son's use of verbs of giving and receiving, both in simple sentences and in benefactive constructions, from 2;0 to 3;1 years-of-age.

Horiguchi reports that in her data, as well as the longitudinal studies of Okubo and Fujiwara, *ageru* emerged first; *morau* and *kureru* were acquired in different order by different children. In Horiguchi's data, *ageru* was the verb used most frequently in benefactive constructions and with the fewest errors. *Morau* was acquired next, was used least frequently, and had a higher percentage of errors than *ageru*. *Kureru* emerged last, and was used quite frequently, but with an extremely high rate of errors. Table 4.7 summarizes Horiguchi's findings on the comparative frequencies and rate of errors with verbs of giving and receiving in benefactive constructions. The first row indicates contexts in which the child should have used *ageru*, since he was the giver, and the second row gives contexts in which the child received a favor, and *morau* or *kureru* would have been appropriate.

As Table 4.7 shows, this child used verbs of giving rather than of receiving to express benefactive relations. In about 95% of his benefactive constructions, the child was either the giver or recipient of the favor being described, usually the giver. When the child was the giver, *ageru* was used most of the time, but errors with *kureru* and *morau* also occurred, as in:

Hirochan *mama* *ni* *gohon* *mot* - *te* *ki* - *te*
               IO   book   carry CONT come CONT

kure - *ru*.
give NONPAST
'Hirochan will give bringing a book to mama'.

In this sentence, *kureru* takes the point of view of the indirect object *mama* rather than the speaker Hirochan, and so is ungrammatical. In the following case, Hirochan uses *morau,* which takes the viewpoint of the subject; since Hirochan is the indirect object, this is also ungrammatical.

*Mikichan	Hirochan	ni	fearedii	zetto	kat	- te*
*		AGT	Fairlady Z		buy	CONT

*mora	- u*		*no	yo.*
receive	NONPAST		EP	EMPH

'Mikichan will receive buying Fairlady Z from Hirochan'.

The reverse error also occurred. Hirochan sometimes described events in which he was the recipient of a favor with *ageru,* which reflects the viewpoint of the subject/giver:

*Hirochan	ni	Miyukichan	ga	torakku	kashi	- te*
*	IO		SUBJ	truck	lend	CONT

*age	- ta*		*no	yo.*
give	PAST		EP	EMPH

'Miyukichan gave lending a truck to Hirochan'.

Hirochan should have taken his own point of view and used *kureru,* which places the focus of empathy on the indirect object.

As the table shows, the most frequent errors were confusions between the two verbs of giving, *ageru* and *kureru.* This is consistent with the principle of one-to-one mapping of form and function, since the meanings of *ageru* and *kureru* are the most similar. The pattern of errors was strongly asymmetrical; *ageru* was rarely used incorrectly, whereas *kureru* is incorrect almost half of the time it occurs. One factor contributing to this asymmetry is frequency: *ageru* is used in benefactive constructions much more frequently than *kureru,* and *ageru* contexts (speaker = giver) apparently occur much more frequently than *kureru* contexts. Another important factor is the nature of adult-child interaction, which contributes to the high frequency of errors with *kureru.* When an adult requests a favor with *kureru* 'will you give to me', the child must use *ageru* 'I will give to you' in his response. In Japanese, children frequently answer yes/no questions by repeating the predicate from the question with declarative intonation. However, with benefactive constructions, this strategy will lead to error, as in the following typical case from my data:

(Child is placing imaginary people in a toy truck)

Mother:	*mama	nose	- te*		*kure	- na	- i*		*no?*
		put	CONT		give	NEG	NONPAST		EP

'Won't you put mama in it?'

Child: *un.*

       'Yes'.

       (English: *no*—In Japanese, one says, 'Yes, I will not'.)[14]

Mother: *ara.*   *neechan*   *wa?*

        EXCLAM older sister TOP

        'Oh my. What about older sister?'

Child: **nose - te*   *kure - ru*   *no.*   2;4 yrs

       put   CONT give NONPAST EP   M

       'I'll put her in it'.

The child should have used *ageru* 'I give', but repeats *kureru* from his mother's utterance. This is apparently a very common error among Japanese children; Fujiwara (p. 204) cites a similar example, and Horiguchi notes that her son consistently responded to *kureru* questions with *kureru,* never the correct *ageru.* These are clear cases of what MacWhinney (1985) has called "discourse analogy." MacWhinney cites very similar errors of Hungarian children, who answer 'Do you want?' questions with verbs marked for the second rather than the first person. Confusion of *ageru*/*kureru* occurs even without discourse analogy; children have great difficulty mastering the constraints on person deixis which apply to each form. (See Okubo [1983] for further examples of these errors.)

The empathy constraints on *ageru, kureru,* and *morau* provide a particularly striking example of underlying semantic distinctions which are not clearly marked on the surface (see Slobin, 1973). Since there is no person-marking on Japanese verbs, there is no formal marker for the child to associate with *ageru* and *kureru* that would clarify the underlying person deixis. In ordinary Japanese conversation, overt references to first and second person are frequently omitted, since these referents are typically presupposed in the speech context. This makes it even more difficult for the child to associate *ageru* with first person subjects and *kureru* with first person indirect objects. It is not surprising that confusion of *ageru* and *kureru* is common and very persistent; Horiguchi found that errors occurred throughout the 13 months she studied her son's production.

The lower rate of error with *ageru* may indicate that the particular combination of syntactic and semantic roles with empathy constraints is simpler or more natural with *ageru* than with *kureru* or *morau.* Horiguchi (1979a) has proposed that *ageru* is the easiest form for children to acquire because with this verb, the roles of speaker, subject, and agent are combined. This interpretation is con-

---

[14]In Japanese, when one agrees with a negative question, such as 'Isn't it?', the answer is 'Yes, (it's not)'. In my data, even the youngest child of 1;11 years was able to answer negative questions appropriately with *un* 'yes'. The acquisition of appropriate answers to negative questions provides an interesting case for crosslinguistic comparison. Akiyama (1979) reports that it is more difficult for Japanese children aged 3–6 years to answer negative questions with the correct *un* 'yes (it's not)' than for English-speaking children to answer these questions with *no* (it's not).

sistent with Givón's proposal (1979, p. 58) that the roles of agent and subject tend to coincide in human language; constructions such as passives which "demote" the agent to other case roles tend to be marked and infrequent. Horiguchi's explanation is also consistent with the view of empathy constraints set forth in Kuno and Kaburaki (1975). These authors propose that there is a "surface structure empathy hierarchy," according to which it is easier for the speaker to empathize with the referent of the subject than with referents having other grammatical roles. They also propose a "speech-act participant hierarchy" which states that it is easier for speakers to empathize with themselves than with their hearers, and with hearers than third parties. If these proposals accurately reflect general tendencies in the way languages are constructed, then constructions with *ageru* '(I) give' may fit a kind of natural prototype: the agent is the subject of the sentence, the subject is the focus of empathy, and the speaker is the subject. *Morau* '(I) receive' preserves the speaker/subject empathy focus, but is more difficult because the agent is not the subject of the sentence. With *kureru* 'gives (to me)', the agent is the subject of the sentence, but the speaker, the most natural focus of empathy, must be the indirect object rather than the subject, and cannot be the agent. Thus *kureru* departs from the hypothetical prototype more radically than *morau;* this is consistent with Horiguchi's finding than *kureru* is the most difficult form for children to acquire.

Although *kureru* may be more difficult than *morau* for children to produce correctly, tests of comprehension indicate that *morau* 'receive' poses special problems with respect to processing strategies. As noted above, the surface configuration of case markers in sentences with *morau* is the same as with *ageru* and *kureru,* but with *morau, ga* marks the recipient or goal rather than the agent, and *ni* marks the agent or source rather than the recipient/goal. Thus the ordinary interpretation of *ga* and *ni* is different—in fact, more or less reversed—in sentences with *morau*. The effect of this reversal of ordinary case roles is clear in the results of comprehension tests with *morau*. Harada (1977) tested her daughter's comprehension of benefactive sentences with *morau,* and found that at 3;11 years-of-age, the child systematically misinterpreted them. For example, the child was presented with the sentence:

otoosan	*ga*	*okaasan*	*ni*	*obentoo*	*o*	*tsukut - te*
father	SUBJ	mother	AGT	lunch	DO	make CONT

morat	*- ta.*
receive	PAST

'Father received making lunch from/by mother'.

When asked who made lunch, the child answered that the father did, although this goes counter to ordinary expectations. Harada concludes that at this stage the child is using a processing strategy in which the first, *ga*-marked nominal is taken to be the agent, and the second, *ni*-marked nominal to be the indirect object. Uyeno et al. (1978) made similar findings in experiments with children aged 3–6 years, who matched pictures with sentences presented, and acted out sentences with *ageru, kureru,* and *morau.* These children performed significantly worse on sentences with *morau.* (The point of view difference between *ageru* and *kureru* was not investigated in this study.) In the acting-out experiment, passive sentences were also used; passive sentences, like benefactive constructions with *morau,* mark the agent of the action with *ni.* Children's performance on passive sentences was nearly the same as on sentences with *morau.* The authors conclude that *ga* is acquired earlier as a marker of agents, and children take the nominal marked by *ga* in passive sentences and benefactives with *morau* as agent, reversing the interpretation of the sentence. Difficulties with case marking, as well as the availability of other means of expressing benefactives, may be contributing to the very low frequency with which *morau* was used in benefactive constructions by Horiguchi's child.

4.7. *Numeral Classifiers*

Counting in Japanese is complicated by the existence of two sets of numerals and a system of numeral classifiers. Table 4.8 gives the different numbers available for counting from one to ten. One set is of native Japanese origin, the other is Sino-Japanese. (Above ten, Sino-Japanese forms are used.) The choice of numeral set is generally conditioned by the origin of the classifier; Japanese classifiers are used with Japanese numerals and Sino-Japanese classifiers with Sino-Japanese numerals. Except for *too* 'ten', the Japanese forms do not occur without a classifier suffix; the Sino-Japanese numerals occur without suffixes in doing arithmetic and counting in the abstract. In my data, both sets were used by mothers in counting routines with their young 2-year-olds; typically, the children could not go beyond three without help. Mothers never mixed the Japanese and

TABLE 4.8
Japanese
and Sino-Japanese
Numerals from One to Ten

	JAPANESE	SINO-JAPANESE
'one'	*hito-*	*ichi*
'two'	*futa-*	*ni*
'three'	*mi-*	*san*
'four'	*yo-*	*shi*
'five'	*itsu-*	*go*
'six'	*mu-*	*roku*
'seven'	*nana-*	*shichi*
'eight'	*ya-*	*hachi*
'nine'	*kokono-*	*kyuu/ku*
'ten'	*too*	*juu*

Sino-Japanese forms; they counted either *hitotsu, futatsu, mittsu,* etc. or *ichi, ni, san,* etc.

When counting specific referents in Japanese, the numerals may not be used alone; a classifier must be suffixed to either the Japanese or Sino-Japanese numeral, as in *hito-kire* 'one slice' or *ichi-mai* 'one (thin flat object)'. Classifiers such as these embody a categorization of referents on the basis of characteristics such as shape, size, arrangement, and function. There is a classifier for human beings, *-nin,* which is used with Sino-Japanese numerals for three or more people; Japanese numerals are used for *hito-ri* 'one person' and *futa-ri* 'two people'. There are various classifiers for animals, including the general classifier *-hiki,* as well as *-too* for large animals, and *-wa* for birds. The largest number of classifiers is for inanimate objects. Certain classifiers are used for specific, culturally salient objects, such as flowers, *-rin;* others are generally applicable to large categories of objects, such as *-mai* for thin, flat objects. There are classifiers for measures, such as *-hun* (minutes); for abstract concepts, such as *-ken* (incidents, events); for processes and their results, such as *-kire* (slices) from *kiru* 'to cut'; for objects which share a particular function, such as *-soku* (pairs of footwear); and for shape, such as *-hon* (long, thin objects). If no specific classifier exists, Japanese numerals with the suffix *-tsu* are used; some speakers also treat the Sino-Japanese classifier *-ko* (small, three-dimensional objects) as a default option. While certain traditional classifiers, such as *-bi* for fish, are dropping out, new ones, often adopted from foreign languages, are being added at a rapid rate, such as *-torakku* for tape tracks (Downing, 1984). The number of classifiers used by adults has been estimated at from 28 (Sanches, 1977) to 81 (Downing, 1984, pp. 13–15).

The acquisition of Japanese numeral classifiers has been studied by Sanches (1977) and by Matsumoto (1984a,b,c). In her study of 100 children of 9–12-years-old, Sanches found that, in addition to the unmarked Japanese classifier *-tsu,* most children by 6 years-of-age had acquired from two to six forms from the basic list of Sino-Japanese classifiers in Table 4.9. Of these classifiers, Matsumoto has found that among classifiers for animates, the classifier for human

TABLE 4.9
Numeral Classifiers Acquired by Most 6-Year-Olds
(Adapted from Sanches, 1977)

CLASSIFIER	SEMANTIC CATEGORY	EXAMPLES
nin	human beings	
hiki	animals	dogs, cats
hon	long, thin objects	pencils, carrots
mai	thin, flat objects	paper, leaves
dai	man-made/mechanical objects	cars, sewing machines
ko	small, three-dimensional objects	balls, pieces of candy

beings (-*ri* or -*nin*) is acquired before -*hiki* (personal communication), and among classifiers for inanimates, -*ko* is acquired before -*mai* and -*hon*, which precede -*dai* (1984b).

The system of numeral classifiers in Japanese presents a striking case in which there is no simple one-to-one correlation between form and function. Based on experiments in which 5- and 6-year-olds performed various counting tasks, Matsumoto (1984a,b,c) has analyzed the types of errors which commonly occur in the acquisition of the numeral classifier system. These include using the wrong numeral plus classifier series, e.g. using a Sino-Japanese numeral and classifier where Japanese forms are required; mixing numerals from one series with classifiers from the other, e.g. suffixing a Japanese classifier to a Sino-Japanese numeral; and using the wrong classifier, typically substituting a general classifier for one having a more specific meaning. The former two errors give insight into the operating principles which Japanese children bring to bear in dealing with the extremely complex relationship between form and meaning embodied in the morphology of Japanese numeral classifiers.

Errors in the selection of the appropriate numeral plus classifier series usually involve overgeneralization of the Sino-Japanese forms. For example, in an experiment with 70 children, Matsumoto (1984b) found that in counting mountains and clouds, which take Japanese numerals with -*tsu*, 66% of children aged 5;0–6;3 and 44% of children aged 6;4–7;11 years used the Sino-Japanese series. Similarly, in counting days of the month up to the fifth, which take the Japanese series, only 13% of the younger children used the correct forms, and 37% used Sino-Japanese numerals and classifiers. The older children reversed this trend, with 47% using the appropriate Japanese forms, and 35% overgeneralizing the Sino-Japanese forms. Thus Matsumoto's subjects apparently acquired the Sino-Japanese forms first, and substituted them for Japanese numeral expressions.

In keeping with this tendency to favor Sino-Japanese forms, Matsumoto found that a frequent error in combining numerals and classifiers was to suffix a Japanese classifier to a Sino-Japanese numeral. For example, when the children were asked to count with Japanese classifiers that they did not know, such as -*kire* 'slice' or -*mune* 'building', they suffixed them to Sino-Japanese rather than Japanese numerals. (This error was made even by some children who were familiar with these classifiers.) Thus it appears that many children regard Sino-Japanese numerals as the forms which should be used in combination with classifiers.

Appealing to Clark's recent formulation of operating principles for word formation (Clark, 1980, 1981; Clark & Hecht, 1982), Matsumoto attributes these errors to two morphological properties of the classifier system. First of all, he claims, the Sino-Japanese numerals have greater generality, since they can be used for counting both above and below ten, whereas the Japanese series is limited to numbers below ten. Secondly, he proposes that the Sino-Japanese numerals are more transparent semantically in that they can occur alone as independent morphemes. This makes it easier for children to segment the Sino-Japanese numerals from the classifier suffixes. Children also have much more experience segmenting the Sino-Japanese numerals since the overwhelming majority of classifiers, as well as the first classifiers to be acquired (with the exception of -*tsu*), are Sino-Japanese and suffixed to the Sino-Japanese numerals. Errors such as *futa-tsu-kire* 'two slices', in which the Japanese classifier -*kire* 'slice' was suffixed to the Japanese numeral plus -*tsu,* rather than to the bound morpheme *futa* 'two', support Matsumoto's claim that segmentation of the Japanese numerals causes problems for young children.

Japanese children's problems with numeral classifiers provide support for the view that systems which do not exhibit a one-to-one correspondence of form to function will be difficult for children to acquire (Slobin, 1985). The specific errors which occur indicate that many children attempt to isolate one set of numerals, the Sino-Japanese ones, to be combined with classifier suffixes. Selection of the Sino-Japanese numerals for this function is consistent with the proposal that children prefer more analytic over syncretic options (see Berman, 1985, and Slobin, 1985), and with Clark and Hecht's (1982) adaptation of this proposal, which states that children prefer to combine free rather than bound morphemes in word formation.

5. Error-Free Acquisition

5.1. Questions

In Japanese conversation, a statement can be converted to a question simply by using rising intonation. Optionally, a question may be marked as such with the sentence-final particle *ka*. Women do not use *ka* as frequently as men, unless they are also using polite verb forms (See Yamada, 1980); instead they typically use the particle *no,* which is discussed in section 6.1.2 below. Since *no* can also occur in declarative sentences, yes/no questions in the input to children are frequently formally identical with statements, differing only in intonation.

WH-questions are formed with a series of question words which usually have corresponding deictics, e.g. *koko/doko* 'here/where'. These question words are simply placed in a sentence at the point where the "missing constituent" would usually occur. Question words are followed by the same case markers as ordinary nominal constituents, e.g. *dare no* 'of whom', *doko ni* 'to where'. Since word order in questions is the same as in declarative sentences, question formation does not involve any syntactic complications. Pronouns are usually ellipted in ordinary conversation, and hence children do not have to master the alternation of personal pronouns in question/answer sequences which occurs in many Western languages. Since there is such extensive ellipsis in Japanese conversation, the form of questions can be extremely simple, and children's earliest one-word questions, such as *Nani?* 'What?' meaning 'What is this?' are actually grammatically complete and correct in casual conversational style. In essence, Japanese presents the child with a language in which it would be very difficult to make a mistake in forming a question.

The following are examples of the type of questions which typically occur in adult speech to children and in children's early production. The corresponding declarative sentences are given to show the great similarity between questions and declaratives in Japanese.

QUESTION	DECLARATIVE
ik - u? go NONPAST 'Are you going?'	*ik - u.* go NONPAST 'I'm going'.
tabe - ru no? eat NONPAST EP 'Will you eat?'	*tabe - ru no.* eat NONPAST EP 'I will eat'.
kore ·wa nani? this TOP what 'What is this?'	*kore wa buubuu.* this TOP car 'This is a car'.
kore wa dare no? this TOP who GEN 'Whose is this?'	*kore wa Maho no.* this TOP Maho GEN 'This is Maho's'.
papa wa doko ni papa TOP where LOC *i - ru?* exist NONPAST 'Where is daddy?'	*papa wa kaisha ni* papa TOP company LOC *i - ru.* exist NONPAST 'Daddy's at work'.
kore wa doo su - ru? this TOP how do NONPAST 'How do you do this?'	*kore wa koo su - ru.* this TOP this way do NONPAST 'You do it this way'.
akachan wa nani baby TOP what *shi - teru no?* do PRES.PROG EP 'What is the baby doing?'	*akachan wa nenne* baby TOP sleep *shi - teru no.* do PRES.PROG EP 'The baby is sleeping'.

The grammatical structure of questions in the adult input and in children's speech becomes progressively fuller as they grow older, with the copula, nominal constituents, and case particles provided with increasing frequency. Thus, due to the great simplicity and consistency of the grammar of questions in Japanese, children typically make no errors in production, and their questions develop grammatically along with their declarative sentences.

Because questions are so similar to declarative sentences in Japanese, one problem which children face is identifying questions in the speech which is addressed to them. Yoshida (1977) analyzes one child's reactions to the questions addressed to him during 2 half-hour sessions with his mother at the ages of 2;4 and 2;7 years. The findings suggest that the child was at first heavily dependent upon rising intonation to identify questions. The child's mother seems to have been aware of this; in the session at 2;4 years, she used rising intonation in 86.4% of her questions, but 3 months later she used rising intonation only 64.9% of the time. At 2;4 years old, the child responded to questions with sentence-final *no* and the topic marker *wa* 'what about/where' much more frequently if rising intonation was also used. Three months later, he answered almost all questions with *no* and *wa,* and 75% of questions with *deshoo,* the presumptive form of the copula meaning approximately 'isn't it?', even if falling intonation was used. Yoshida concludes that younger children rely more heavily upon intonation contours to grasp illocutionary force. This must be especially true in Japanese, where several of the most common morphological markers in questions addressed to children, such as *no, wa,* and *deshoo,* also occur in declaratives. Young Japanese children's ability to respond to questions with these markers when they receive rising intonation supports the view that a very early operating principle is to pay attention to intonation, and to assume that differences in intonation contours signal important linguistic information.

5.2. *Word Order*

Typologically, Japanese is classified as an SOV language. On the basis of experiments on syntactic perception with adult subjects, Uyeno and Harada (1975) have postulated that the canonical form of a Japanese sentence is: subject—adverbial[15]—indirect object—direct object—verb. In formal written language, the verb-final constraint is strictly observed. However, in ordinary conversation, constituents are freely ellipted and re-arranged in accordance with pragmatic factors, such as the speaker's sense of what constitutes new and old information at any given point in a discourse. Thus in the spoken language, word order is quite flexible, and constituents may even appear after the verb, with special intonation contours which add them on to the finished sentence.

---

[15]There is some evidence that the canonical position of adverbs, at least time and place adverbs, may be to the right of the subject (see Shibamoto, 1979, pp. 93–4).

In Japanese, constituents which are placed after the main verb are typically described as afterthoughts, which the speaker adds on to the sentence at the end, having belatedly realized that the listener will need more information to understand the sentence (see Hinds, 1976; Kuno, 1978; Takahara & Peng, 1981). Given the frequency of postposed elements in casual conversation, and the fact that postverbal constituents often occur in very short utterances with no pause or other sign of hesitation, it seems likely that postposing[16] does not always reflect a lapse in planning on the speaker's part. Rather, postposing may have become integrated into Japanese syntax as a deliberate defocusing device for material which has low saliency or is highly presupposed in context. Since this is precisely the type of material which a speaker might forget to mention, this view is not inconsistent with the afterthought interpretation.

In fact, an examination of the types of constituents which are postposed supports a defocusing account. Takahara and Peng (1981) and Shibamoto (1979, Chap. 5) report that the most frequently postposed constituents in adult speech are adverbials, such as *yappari* 'after all/as expected' and *chotto* 'a little', which do not convey very important information. Similarly, subordinate clauses, especially those providing reasons for material given in the main clause, are very frequently postposed; this information may be important, but is not as essential as that in the main clause. Another frequently postposed constituent is the sentence subject or topic; authors such as Chafe (1976), Givón (1979), and Bates and MacWhinney (1979) have pointed out that subjects tend to be "given" information, and this is even truer of sentence topics. Thus the types of constituents which are postposed frequently in Japanese are either inessential or the kind of information which tends to be presupposed.

The following examples of postposing from the speech of three mothers in my sample to their 2-year-olds illustrate the use of postposing in Japanese, and show its relationship to presupposition and defocusing.

1. *papa no kuruma ni notta deshoo ne.   suki,   papa no kuruma?*
   'You rode in papa's car, didn't you.   Do you like it,   papa's car?

2. Child: (making his toy car fly)

   osora   tobu.
   sky   flies

   'It flies in the sky'.

   Mother: *Maachan datte tobitai deshoo,   osora.*
   'You would like to fly too, (in the)   sky.

---

[16]I do not intend to imply that sentence constituents are actually generated in canonical position and then postposed to the end of the sentence by a process having psychological reality. "Postposing" is simply meant as a descriptive term for post-verbal location of a sentence constituent.

3. (referring to a glass of soda on the table)

   dare ga nomu no,   kore?
   'Who will drink it,   this?'

4. *onaka ga ponkeponopon deshoo   Yotchan wa ne.*
   Lit., 'The stomach is probably full,   as for Yotchan (= you)'.
   (This is a "double subject" sentence of the type N-*wa* N-*ga* . . . 'N-topic N-subject . . .', with the topic postposed.)

5. *papa ni tanomoo ka,   odenwa shite?*
   'Shall we ask papa,   calling him on the phone?'

6. (Mother and child have been talking about the child's toy car)

   kooen ni oite kita deshoo,   sunaba ni.
   'Didn't you leave it in the park,   in the sandbox?'

The first four examples illustrate the postposing of sentence constituents which are highly presupposed in the speech context. Such referents may have been previously mentioned, as in (1) and (2), may be present on the scene (3–4), or may be participants in the conversation (4). Example (5) involves a postposed clause expressing the means by which the main action will be accomplished, and is a typical case of subordinate information. The last sentence differs from the others in that the postverbal element could not simply be transferred to a preverbal position. As Hinds (1976) has pointed out, in such cases the postposed constituent represents a more precisely specified reference to an element appearing preverbally; here *kooen ni* 'in the park' is elaborated in postverbal position as *sunaba ni* 'in the sandbox'. Again, postposing gives the impression that this detail is being mentioned parenthetically.

Since Japanese children's primary linguistic input seems to be their mother's speech (Okayama, 1979), it is interesting to note that female speakers use a higher frequency of postposing than male speakers. Shibamoto (1979, Chap. 5) reports that in informal conversation, female speakers produced sentences with postposed elements 2.54 times as often as male speakers. This is consistent with women's more frequent use of the sentence-final particle *no* (See section 6.1.2), which also reflects presupposition of shared information. Thus a speech style featuring various expressions of presupposition seems to be characteristic of Japanese women.

Evidence from several sources indicates that postposed word orders are used very early by Japanese children. Murata (1961a) notes postposing in the two-word utterances of children under 2;0 years; Fujiwara (1977, pp. 94, 130, 149) cites early examples of postposing by three children of 1;8–1;11 years. Sanches (1968, Chap. 2) reports that the three children in her study, aged 2;0–2;3, were using postposed as well as standard verb-final order, and were using appropriate intonation patterns for each type. Takahara and Peng (1981) cite several examples of different types of postposed constituents in the speech of two children during their third year. Postposing was quite common, occurring in approximately 25% of the sampled utterances for each child. As in adult speech, the most frequently postposed sentence constituents were subjects (36.6% of all postposed elements for one child, 23.8% for the other) and adverbs (35.2% and 18.6%, respectively); objects and nominal modifiers were postposed much less frequently. Both children postposed entire subordinate clauses, with those expressing reasons appearing after the main verb very frequently (14.7% and 30.2%, respectively). Experimental data also support the notion that Japanese children are sensitive to word order at an early stage, and have learned the relationship between postposed and standard orders. Lust and Wakayama (1981) found that children of 2;5–2;11 years old, when imitating sentences with postposed coordinate subjects and objects of the form N *to* N 'N and N', spontaneously re-ordered the entire postposed constituent to preverbal position 27% of the time. Since in the experimental context there was no reason for these constituents to be presupposed, re-ordering them to preverbal position also shows children's sensitivity to the functions of postposing.

In my sample, three children of 1;11–2;4 years old were using both verb-final and postposed word order, and the types of constituents which were postposed were similar to those in their mothers' speech, as the following examples illustrate:

1. (Adult and child are looking at a picture of a jumping bear)

   Adult: *kono panda nani shi - ten no?*
   this panda what do PRES.PROG EP
   'What is this panda doing?'

   Child: *shi - ten no, shiten no, panda - chan wa.*
   do PRES.PROG EP panda DIM TOP
   'He's doing it, he's doing it, the panda'.

2. (People had been talking about a picture drawn by the child's sister)

   tsukut - ta no, are.
   made PAST EP that
   'She made it, that'.

3. (My coat was wet and child's mother was taking it from me)

   nure - teru no, oneechan no.
   wet PRES.PROG EP older sister GEN
   'It's wet, older sister's'.

4. (looking at a picture of a baby)

akachan,   kore.
baby   this

'It's a baby, this'.

5. (talking about his father, who went to work in a car)

it - ta   no, buun   tte.
go PAST EP   sound of motion QUOT

'He went, (the car going) "buun" '.

Like their mothers, these children postpose referents which have just been mentioned (1–2), which are present in the context (2–4), and clauses which refer to subordinate information parenthetically (5). Although it is difficult to be certain without more information about context than is available, the examples of postposed word order cited by Fujiwara, Sanches, and Takahara and Peng seem to follow similar patterns. Postverbal constituents refer to familiar people or animals, objects or actions apparently present in context (i.e., referred to with deictics such as *kore* 'this' or *koo* 'like this'), referents mentioned in the prior discourse, or parenthetical information.

In his analysis of postposing in Japanese, Hinds (1976) also notes a pattern in which a preverbal constituent is repeated without modification in postverbal position. This word order pattern was common in adult speech to children in my sample, and was also used by the 2-year-olds. The mothers in my sample frequently produced sentences of the following type, when trying to get their children to name an object: *Kore nani, kore?* Lit., 'This is what, this?'. As Hinds has pointed out, the basic motivation for this pattern is emphasis; this is obvious in cases in which the mother holds or shakes the object, trying to focus the child's attention on it. In adult narrative discourse, this pattern can be found at points where subject or topic reference changes; mentioning the new referent twice apparently reflects the speaker's wish to emphasize the change for the listener (Clancy, 1980). Children also sometimes use this pattern with a whining, insistent intonation when their mother is not paying close attention to what they are saying. In the following example, a child of 2;1 years uses repeated reference appropriately for emphasis. She had been giving out imaginary pudding to various people, and was asked whether it was also pudding that she was giving to her doll:

purin   ar - u   no, purin.
pudding exist NONPAST EP   pudding

'There's pudding, pudding'.

The early acquisition of standard and alternate word orders in Japanese is similar to Bowerman's (1973) finding with respect to Finnish; the two children in her study also used the dominant and alternate word order patterns of Finnish even before reaching MLU 2.0, and used them in frequencies similar to their mothers'. Japanese data also provide evidence for the claim that children "pay attention to the order of words" at the early stages of language development (Slobin, 1973).

To understand the early acquisition of postposing in Japanese, it is probably important to consider the relationship between word order and ellipsis, which also involves presupposition of shared information. In Japanese, there are at least four different possibilities for dealing with a referent: (1) placing it both in preverbal and postverbal position for emphasis, (2) placing it in preverbal position,[17] (3) placing it in postverbal position for defocusing, and (4) omitting it completely. These options seem to represent a pragmatic continuum from strong emphasis to total presupposition, reflecting a range of attitudes towards the addressee's need for explicit information at a given moment in the discourse. (See Givón [1979] and Bates & MacWhinney [1979] for further discussion of the notion of such a pragmatic continuum.)

Children's usage of these options seems to have the same basis as in adult speech. For example, in my data, a mother and child were looking at a picture of people riding on a train, and the mother was making up a story about them, identifying them as the child and people he knew. At this point, the following exchange took place:

Yotchan: *doko   ni   ik - u   no?*
          where to   go   NONPAST   EP
          'Where am (I) going?'

Mother: *un?*
          'Huh?'

Yotchan: *doko   ni   ik - u   no,   Yotchan?*
          where to   go   NONPAST   EP   Yotchan
          'Where is Yotchan going?'

Initially, the child assumes that his mother will realize he is referring to himself, as she usually is able to do even when he does not use either a pronoun or his name. However, either because of the imaginary context, her absorption in the story she was creating, or the fact that questions do not usually have first person subjects, his mother did not understand. When the child repeats the question, he

---

[17]There are actually a variety of options for pre-verbal position, the canonical one and any one of several others as well. The conditions governing different pre-verbal word orders, such as SOV vs. OSV, have not been systematically investigated. It seems likely that similar factors relating to presupposition and focus may be relevant.

includes a postposed reference to himself. Thus the postposing of defocused constituents apparently can serve as a more explicit alternative to ellipsis,[18] and may develop naturally out of early patterns in which presupposed information is omitted. If this interpretation is correct, there may be an ontogenetic parallel for Hinds' (1976) claim that in adult speech, "postposing starts out as noun phrase deletion."

In the "here and now" in which a mother and child typically communicate, it is quite safe for the child to assume that the mother shares the same information that she does. At first, therefore, children are free to follow their own focusing and attentional tendencies in verbalizing new information and omitting old information. Greenfield and Smith (1976, Chap. 4.3) have found that at the one-word stage, the word which a child will verbalize from among the various possibilities in a given situation is the one which encodes the aspect of a situation containing the most information, i.e. which is the least predictable from the child's point of view.[19] Bates (1976, Chap. 4) traces the ability to distinguish new and old information back to the early orienting patterns and pointing gestures of the sensorimotor period. The child's first verbal productions, Bates claims, build upon already established attentional patterns identifying figure and ground. If this is true, then the ability to treat referents differently depending upon whether they are new or highly presupposed in a particular context is a skill which the child has already developed before the two-word stage. The early and error-free acquisition of postposed word orders with presupposed referents in Japanese provides support for this hypothesis. If "free" word order in other languages has a similar pragmatic basis as in Japanese, then young children's "attention to the order of words" probably reflects not only their cognitive ability to process and store different syntactic patterns, but also their sensitivity at an early stage to linguistic correlates of presupposition. Evidence on pragmatically appropriate use of varying word orders in the acquisition of Turkish (see Aksu-Koç & Slobin, 1985) supports this view.

It would be wrong to imply, however, that Japanese children always use ellipsis appropriately. Yamada (1980, p. 17) cites an example of a one-word utterance in the speech of her daughter at 1;10 years of age which she was unable to understand. Clearly, not all single-word utterances communicate adequately, even in a language which permits extensive ellipsis, and Japanese children must learn to verbalize a sufficient amount of material to be comprehensible to their

---

[18]Postposed word order is sometimes described as emphatic (Sanches, 1968, p. 33), and in this example, the use of postposed self-reference is emphatic compared with the ellipsis of the original sentence. However, the highly presupposed nature of postposed referents in general argues against an interpretation of this pattern as emphatic. Rather, it represents a more explicit, and hence potentially more emphatic, point on the continuum of presupposition compared with ellipsis.

[19]Greenfield and Smith (1976) noted that there is a difference between the concept of new/old information and their notion of informativeness, which is based on the comparative uncertainty of a referent from the child's point of view, rather than the status of the referent with respect to the addressee's knowledge. However, they state that the perception of information is, in general, the psychological basis for the given/new contrast.

listeners. The adult language presents Japanese children with a model which supports their early tendency to omit presupposed information, but the limits on this process must be acquired gradually.

It is especially interesting that older Japanese children may under-use ellipsis, and produce too much information from an adult point of view. Ito (personal communication) reports that 3- and 4-year-old Japanese children sometimes fail to use ellipsis where appropriate, creating redundant sentences. Smoczyńska (personal communication) has noted a similar tendency in Polish children beyond the early stages of language acquisition, as has Slobin (personal communication) in Turkish. The development of ellipsis in Japanese has not been investigated; it may show a U-shaped curve, with ellipsis being used less adequately by older children before it is used appropriately by adult standards. There is an interesting parallel here with Slobin's claim (1973) that when a child first controls the full form of a linguistic entity which can undergo contraction or deletion, for a while only the full form will be used. Clearly, much further research is necessary before any strong claims can be made about the relationship between ellipsis at the one- and two-word stage and the acquisition of postposed word order. At present, it appears that whatever presuppositional abilities Japanese 2-year-olds have at the two-word stage are sufficient to allow them to acquire word orders with postposed constituents and to use them appropriately.

6. Timing of Acquisition

6.1. Early Acquisition

6.1.1. *Verbal Inflections.*   A striking feature in the acquisition of Japanese is the precocious control of verbal inflections. Studies by Hatano (1968), Okubo (1967), Rispoli (1981a,b), Sanches (1968, Chap. 3), Tanouye (1980), and Yamada (1980) indicate that Japanese children typically are using several different inflections by the age of 2 years. The order of emergence and relative frequencies differ across children, but the earliest inflections typically come from among those listed on Table 4.10. Rispoli (1981a) and Murata (1961c) report an initial contrast between -*te* (imperative) and -*ta* (past tense) in children of 1;6 years. The desiderative -*tai*, and in some children, the negative -*nai*, tend to be acquired later than the other inflections. The inflection -*teru* is actually a contraction of -*te* + *iru* 'be', and -*chatta* is a contraction of -*te* + *shimatta* 'finished', but these are heard and acquired by children as unitary suffixes. Rispoli found that -*teru* appeared both as a present progressive, e.g. *yon-deru* 'is reading', and as a resultative, e.g. *hait-teru* 'is inside' from *hair-u* 'enter', at approximately the same time. The -*chatta* inflection adds special connotations to the past tense, such as completion and totality, e.g. *tabe-chatta* 'ate all up', or an implication that the event was unfortunate, e.g. *koware-chatta* 'got broken'.

Verbal inflections at first are not used productively. Sanches (1968) and Rispoli (1981a,b) give the verb roots on which different inflections first appeared, and it is clear that typically a given verb root will occur with only one

TABLE 4.10
Children's Earliest Verbal Inflections

-te	imperative
-ta	past tense
-teru	present progressive/resultative
-ru	non-past tense (present states, habitual or future actions)
-chatta	completed past
-nai	negative, non-past tense
-tai	desiderative, non-past tense

inflection. For example, Rispoli found that at 1;6 years old, one child used the past inflection -ta on several verbs, some of which never occurred with other inflections, such as ochi-ta 'fell' and ori-ta 'got off' (although a few verbs at this stage did occur with both -te and -ta, as noted above). Thus there is support for MacWhinney's proposal (1985) that "meanings associated with affixes will appear in amalgams before they are used in isolation." Sanches (1968) and Tanouye (1981) report that each inflection tends to be used with a particular subclass of verbs in the early stages.

The progression from amalgams to productive combination of verb roots and inflections in the acquisition of Japanese seems typical, but the precocity of the process is unusual. Tanouye notes that in English, acquisition proceeds from single-word to two-word utterances, and only then do grammatical morphemes, such as verbal inflections, emerge. For example, Brown (1973, p. 178) reports that before MLU 2.0, the use of grammatical morphemes in English was "very infrequent and apparently uncomprehending." Bloom, Lifter, and Hafitz (1980) found that grammatical morphemes first emerged at MLU 1.5–2.0. In contrast, Tanouye reports that in the two Japanese children she studied, verbal inflections were used productively before MLU 1.5. Tanouye used the following criteria for productivity: an inflection was counted as a separate morpheme only if the inflected verb root also occurred with other inflections in the same or previous speech samples, if the inflection occurred with other verb roots, and if the verb root plus inflection were used appropriately. Since grammatical morphemes do not, presumably, contribute to MLU in English-speaking children before about MLU 1.5, Tanouye measured MLU in her samples by words to facilitate comparison with the English data. On the basis of this word count, Tanouye found that one child had two productive inflections at MLU 1.03 and four by MLU 1.34. The other child had two productive inflections at MLU 1.13 and four by MLU 1.43.[20] Thus these children began to use verbal inflections productively at a time when the majority of their utterances still consisted of only a single word.

---

[20]Tanouye also counted MLU by morphemes. Using that measure, the first child had two productive inflections by MLU 1.42 and four by MLU 1.43. The second child had two productive inflections by MLU 1.51 and four by MLU 2.34. With this measure, however, it is the productive inflections themselves which are the main source of increased MLU.

There are several reasons for the early acquisition of verbal inflections in Japanese. There is no "base" form of Japanese verbs, so that every verb which the child hears is necessarily inflected for some tense/aspect.[21] Japanese verbal inflections are suffixes, and since the most common word order is verb-final, these inflections are often utterance-final. Their early acquisition provides evidence for Slobin's proposal that children pay attention to the ends of intonational units, apply segmentation strategies to final syllables, and attempt to interpret them as grammatical functors (see Peters, 1985; Slobin, 1985). Thus, as Tanouye points out, the structure of Japanese makes the verb perceptually salient. Since ellipsis of nominal referents is so common, many of the sentences which children hear consist of single inflected verbs. Verbs are not "sandwiched" in between an obligatory subject and object as they are in English, and there are no separable verbs in Japanese. Furthermore, all verbs are inflected regularly in Japanese, even the most common ones, such as *suru* 'do' or the copula *da*. Stem changes do occur with different inflections, and for some verbs these changes are irregular, but the inflectional ending does not change. Verbal inflections consist of at least one stressed syllable, and the only phonetic modification which they undergo is voicing assimilation of the initial consonant for *-te, -teru, -ta* and *-chatta* and contraction of *-teru* before sentence-final *no* to *-tenno.*Only two early forms, *-teru* and *-ru,* have more than one related semantic function, and only *-te* is plurifunctional. Thus verbal inflections in Japanese are perceptually salient, morphologically regular, usually semantically distinct, and are very frequent in the adult input to children. Tanouye suggests an additional reason for the early emergence of verbal inflections in Japanese: inflecting a verb may be cognitively simpler than combining two words. If so, we can expect that children learning languages with favorable structures will acquire verbal inflections before their MLU reaches two words. Evidence from Turkish on the productive use of inflections on both nouns and verbs at the one-word stage supports this position (see Aksu-Koç & Slobin, 1985).

6.1.2. *Sentence-Final Particles.*   In Japanese, a very early morphological development is the appearance of sentence-final particles. As Uyeno (1971, Chap. 4.1) points out, these particles are essential in face-to-face interaction in Japanese. There are many different sentence particles, which serve to mark illocutionary force, convey the speaker's attitude and feelings, and reflect presuppositions. Appropriate use of sentence-final particles, as Uyeno notes, depends upon the nature of the context, as well as the relative sex, social status, and type of relationship between speaker and hearer.

Sentence-final particles are quite common in Japanese casual conversation and in the speech addressed to young children. Yamada (1980) reports that about

---

[21]The only potential exceptions are verbs formed from a noun plus *suru* 'do', which are rather common in babytalk, e.g. *nenne suru* 'do sleep'. These may appear in the input without *suru,* in which case they would constitute uninflected verbs.

50% of one mother's utterances to her daughter at 1;8–3;8 years of age ended with a sentence particle. She notes that according to the Kokuritsu Kokugo Kenkyuujo (Japanese National Language Research Institute), the three most common sentence-final particles in adult speech are *ne, yo,* and *no;* these were also the most common in the mother's speech in her sample. There have been many studies documenting the emergence and early development of sentence-final particles in Japanese. Here I will rely upon Fujiwara (1977), Miyahara (1973, 1974), Murata (1961a,b, 1965), Okubo (1967), Yamada (1980), and my own data, and will consider only *ne, yo,* and *no,* which are always among the first sentence-final particles to emerge.

Typically, the first sentence-final particle appears between 1;6–2;0 years; about five to seven different sentence particles emerge during the next 3 months. In general, these particles emerge at about the same time as the earliest two-word utterances. Yamada and Okubo found the first sentence-final particles in the same month as the first two-word utterances; Miyahara (1974) and Murata (1961a) report a lag of 2 or more months between the onset of two-word utterances and the appearance of the first sentence-final particles. Although productivity has not been measured, it seems likely that at least some children can use sentence-final particles productively while the majority of their utterances still consist of a single word. It is particularly striking that these particles, which are extremely difficult for foreigners to master and use naturally, are acquired so early by Japanese children. A consideration of the functions of these particles gives insight into the types of non-lexical, non-relational meanings which children can consistently and correctly encode at the transition point between one- and two-word utterances.

Of the three most common sentence particles, perhaps the easiest for Westerners to understand is *ne,* which is rather similar to a tag question. Uyeno (1971, Chap. 4.7) describes *ne* as a particle of rapport, which expresses agreement with the addressee, or seeks some expression of confirmation or approval from the addressee. As with English tag questions, the exact nuance of *ne* varies with the context and the speaker's intonation. Uyeno states that with a short vowel, *ne* seeks the listener's agreement or confirmation; an appropriate response to this usage would be *Hai* 'Yes'. With a long vowel and falling pitch, *ne* more strongly assumes the listener's concurrence, rather like a tag question with declarative intonation in English. A common response for the listener is to repeat the utterance with *ne* to indicate agreement. Thus the basic function of *ne* is to seek confirmation of information which the speaker presupposes the listener knows and will agree with.

An examination of the early contexts in which *ne* appears reveals the types of information which children assume to be shared, or seek to share, with the listener. In my data, many early instances of *ne* are partial repetitions of adult utterances with *ne.* As already noted, this is an appropriate response to obvious generalizations and opinions marked with *ne.*

Adult: (pointing out various flowers in the room)

koko   ni   mo   ar - u   ne.
here   at   also exist NONPAST AGR
'There are some here too, aren't there'.

Child: *koko   ar - u   ne.*   1;11 yrs
here   exist NONPAST AGR   M
'There are some here, aren't there'.

Such repetitions may serve as a kind of prototypical case of shared information, with mother and child repeating and agreeing with each other's utterances.

Even without overt prior mention, children just beginning to acquire *ne* can use it appropriately in expressing an opinion or making a comment whose truth is obvious in the context. For example, pointing to a very large boat in a picture illustrating many kinds of boats, a boy of 1;11 years said:

ookii   ne.
big   AGR
'It's big, isn't it'.

At the same age this child also used *ne* in stating information which he had heard from his mother many times, and knew she would agree with. For example, playing with a toy airplane, he said:

buun tte, buun tte, buun   tte   tob - u   no   ne.
sound of flying   QUOT fly NONPAST EP   AGR
'It flies (going) "buun, buun, buun," doesn't it'.

Ne can also occur in presenting new information which is not available to the addressee; when *ne* is used in this way, it seeks to secure the listener's acceptance of the information or speech act. *Ne* is often used with requests, apologies, and in imparting information which the listener may not be pleased to hear, in an attempt to convey a sense of fellow-feeling, reduce any negative impact, and gain the listener's compliance. For example, Miyahara (1973) cites the following uses at 18–19 months:

gomen   ne.
sorry   AGR
'I'm sorry, OK?'

mata   ab - oo (= asoboo)   ne.
again   play COHRT   AGR
'Let's play again'.

Uyeno points out that *ne* softens imperatives by seeking reassurance that it was alright to give the command, and turns an imperative into a request. Fujiwara (p. 93) cites such an example at 1;8 years:

papa,	mi	- tete		ne.
papa	look	PRES.PROG:IMP		AGR

'Papa, watch'.

Thus from its earliest occurrences, *ne* is used appropriately in different types of speech acts to express or seek agreement with the addressee.

The particle *yo* is in certain ways the converse of *ne*. It conveys "the speaker's emphasis in giving a piece of information to the addressee" (Uyeno, 1971, p. 109), and often presupposes that the addressee did not already know the information being communicated. Accordingly, *yo* is common in making claims, expressing opinions, giving advice, warnings, etc. While *ne* presupposes shared information and attitudes, *yo* is used when speakers have reason to believe that the addressee does not share knowledge or opinions, or when speakers wish to indicate that, regardless of the addressee's state of mind, they have certain information and views of their own. *Yo* and *ne* thus express two basic contrasting attitudes of a speaker communicating information to a listener: wanting to impose or emphasize the information (*yo*), and anticipating agreement or confirmation (*ne*).

Like *ne*, *yo* seems to be used correctly from its earliest occurrences. In my data, one of the most common early uses of *yo* was in answer to questions; in this case, the prior utterance specifies for the child that the listener does not know the information which is to be provided. The following example at 2;1 years is typical:

Child: (giving mother some imaginary soup)

        kore   suupu
        this   soup
        'This is soup'.

Mother: *hun.   oishii   kana.*
        oh   delicious   Q
        'Oh. I wonder if it's delicious'.

Child: *oishii   yo.*
        delicious   EMPH
        'It's delicious'.

One child at 1;11 years in my sample used *yo* frequently in contradicting the prior speaker. In such cases, since the child is contrasting his statement with that of his addressee, the sense of *yo* becomes clearly emphatic, as in the following case:

Adult: (referring to a toy ambulance)

kore	*wa*	*na*	*n*	*deshoo.*		*kore*	*wa*	*nani?*
this	TOP	COP	EP	COP:PRESUM		this	TOP	what

'What could this be? What is this?'

Child: *buubuu.*
        car
        'A car'.

Adult: *buubuu*   *soo*   *nee.*   *kyuukyuusha.*
        car   right   AGR   ambulance
        'A car, right, isn't it. An ambulance'.

Child: *buubuu*   *yo!*
        car   EMPH
        'A car!'

Having acquired the "babytalk" word *buubuu,* this child strongly resisted attempts to teach him specific adult terms for different kinds of vehicles. Contradictions provide a common context for the emphatic use of *yo;* in such cases, children know they are conveying new information because they already know that the addressee holds a different opinion.

There are also early examples in which children are able to determine, without any verbal cues, that their utterances constitute new information to the hearer. Miyahara (1974) cites the following example at about 1;6 years:

mama,   *oki*   *- ta*   *yo.*
           get up   PAST   EMPH
    'Mommy, I got up'.

In my data, a child of 2;4 years was watching a garbage truck from the window and said to the adults sitting inside the room:

it   *- chatta*   *yo.*
go   COMPL:PAST   EMPH
'It went away'.

Statements about the speaker's internal states also constitute new information, and Fujiwara (p. 91) reports that a child of 1;8 years used *yo* in statements such as

kowai   yo.
fearful   EMPH
'I'm scared'.

Yo can also occur with imperatives, conveying a tone of urging and insistence. Uyeno points out that imperatives with *yo* are actually weaker in force than without *yo*, since *yo* is used when the speaker cannot presuppose compliance, and feels it necessary to insist to overcome the addressee's reluctance. Obviously, this is a typical context for children's imperatives, and *yo* can be found very early in cases such as the following, cited by Fujiwara (1977, pp. 91):

ame   choodai   yo.
candy   give   EMPH
'Please give me some candy'.

The functions of the sentence-final particle *no* are more difficult to specify. Sentence-final *no* is actually an abbreviation of the "extended predicate" (EP) construction (see Jorden, 1963, Part 2, 23.1), in which *no desu* (*no* plus the copula) follows the predicate of a sentence; the literal translation is 'it is that'. Since the copula is frequently ellipted in Japanese conversation, *no* tends to occur sentence-finally.[22] This is especially common in the speech of women; use of the plain form of the copula, *da,* is characteristic of men's casual speech. *No* can occur both in declarative and interrogative sentences, and a wide range of meanings has been attributed to this construction, including indirectness and softening (Jorden, 1963), politeness, reservation, and emphasis (Martin, 1975), explanation or amplification (Alfonso & Niimi, 1972), evidence (Kuno, 1973), and emotional connotations such as concern, surprise or reprimand (Mizutani & Mizutani, 1977). See Noda (1981, Chap. 1.2) for a summary of these views.

Noda (1981, Chap. 2) analyzes *no* in terms of the speaker's presuppositions. The basic distinction between use and non-use of *no,* she claims, is that adding *no* overtly recognizes the existence of shared or shareable information between speaker and hearer in the speech context. *No* occurs when the speaker believes

---

[22]Since *no* is actually part of the extended predicate construction, it is somewhat different from the other sentence-final particles grammatically. In a sequence of sentence-final particles, *no* must always come first, since nothing may intervene between the predicate which it nominalizes and *no*. Children, however, probably are not aware of the special grammatical status of *no;* for them, the ordering of *no* is probably on a par with other ordering conventions, such as the fact that *yo* always comes before *ne.* Thus the sequence of the three earliest sentence final particles is *no* < *yo* < *ne.* Ordering errors with these particles are not reported in the literature. However, in my data, one child of 2;2 years produced sentences ending in the sequence *yo da,* with the copula *da* incorrectly following sentence-final *yo.* At this stage, the child seems to have identified *da* as an emphatic (perhaps masculine) sentence-final particle, although actually, the copula should precede all other sentence-final forms, including *no.*

the proposition to be true; it indicates that the proposition is an inference derived from information which the addressee shares. This information may be linguistic, e.g. prior mention in the discourse, or non-linguistic, e.g. common knowledge or something directly observable in the context of utterance. According to Noda, *no* always recognizes some situation which the listener is assumed to be aware of, or can become aware of, upon hearing the speaker's proposition. *No* takes on a range of emotional connotations, Noda claims, depending upon the implications of such overt recognition of shared information in a particular context, such as great intimacy between speaker and hearer, or a sense of rebuke if the situation in question is one which the listener has been ignoring.

In yes/no questions, *no* implies that the speaker seeks confirmation of the proposition, while marking it as an inference from available information. As Kuno (1973, p. 226) points out, if the addressee is dripping wet, one might ask *Ame ga futte iru no?* 'Is it that it's raining?'. *No* is also very common in WH-questions, where it implies that the speaker has inferred all but the information being questioned. Thus when one encounters a friend walking down the street, it is appropriate to say *Doko e iku no?* 'Where is it that you are going?', since it is obvious that the addressee is going somewhere. As Noda (Chap. 2.5.2) points out, the closer the relationship between speaker and addressee, the more information they share, and the more likely that *no* will be used. Therefore, *no* is very common in mother's speech to children, because mothers usually have fairly complete information about their children's behavior and states.

Yoshida (1977) and Yamada (1980) both report that *no* was much more frequent than *ka* as a question marker in mother's speech to young children. These authors, as well as Okubo, found that children acquire *no* earlier than *ka*, and use it much more frequently in their questions. In my data, *no* was used appropriately in children's questions from an early stage. For example, a girl of 2;1 years was preparing imaginary food, when an adult asked if she planned to drink tea. She responded:

ocha?	*ocha*	*nom - u*		*no?*	*hai.*
tea	tea	drink	NONPAST	EP	yes

'Tea? Will you drink tea? Here'. (handing over some imaginary tea)

The child heard the mention of tea as a request, and her use of *no* appropriately reflects her presupposition that the addressee wants to drink tea.

One of the earliest uses of *no* in declarative sentences in my data was in answer to questions with *no,* as in the following example:

Adult: (showing child a picture of a boy playing with blocks)

Yotchan,	*nani*	*shi - te*		*ason - den*		*no?*
Yotchan	what	do	CONT	play	PRES.PROG	EP

'Yotchan, what is he doing (and) playing?'

Yotchan: *tsumiki   not   - ten   no.*   1;11 yrs
           blocks   get on   PRES.PROG   EP   M

           'Blocks are on (top of each other)'.

In this context, it is apparent to both mother and child from the picture what the
boy is doing, and use of *no* recognizes this shared information. Although the
child's utterance is an answer to a question, *yo* would not be appropriate because
the adult already knows the answer.

Very young children are also capable of using *no* when it has not appeared in
the previous utterance. For example, a child of 2;0 years in my sample looked in
a basket for his toy cars, which he had already emptied out, and said:

nai   no.
doesn't exist   EP

'There are none'.

The use of *no* reflects the shared context, in which the addressee can also see that
the basket is empty. In such cases, *no* is similar to *ne* in its recognition of shared
information, but does not call for any response from the listener.

As is often noted, *no* tends to occur in explanations; in this case the shared
context to which *no* refers tends to be the speaker's own behavior or condition.
This is one of the first uses of *no,* as in the following case:

Mother: (urging child to eat an apple)

          tabe - nasai   ne.
          eat   IMP   AGR

          'Please eat it'.

Child: *ira - nai   no.*   1;11 yrs
          need   NEG   EP   M

          'I don't want it'.

Here the child's utterance explains why he is not taking the apple; *no* refers to
this shared context.

Children also use *no* on declarative sentences expressing desire/intent. Fujiwara (1977, p. 86) and Miyahara (1973) cite such examples among the earliest
uses of *no*. In my data, a child of 2;0 years wanted to watch television during the
recording session; when his mother refused to allow him, he said, whining:

mi - ru   nooo!
see   NONPAST   EP

'I will watch (TV)'.

In such cases, *no* refers to the shared context of the child's obvious desire and attempts to achieve his goal; the statement with *no* constitutes a demand. Since the adult is ignoring this obvious situation, the child's reference to it with *no* is a reproach and expression of frustration. This is a clear case in which *no* takes on emotional connotations derived from its basic implication of shared information.

In many ways, the sentence-final particles *ne, yo,* and *no* are optimal candidates for early acquisition. They occur sentence-finally, and so will be perceptually salient to children paying attention to the ends of intonational units (Slobin, 1973; Peters, 1985). They are syllabic, stressed, and do not change shape except for optional vowel lengthening, which creates subtle differences in nuance, such as heightened affect. The intonational possibilities for each particle are many, but they are often distinct from the rest of the utterance intonationally, with rising or falling pitch. Sentence-final particles are extremely frequent in the adult input to children, and figure prominently in some of the earliest conversational routines, such as naming.

In addition, these particles are probably acquired so early because correct usage has a pragmatic and emotional basis. The development of the linguistic expression of affect has not yet received much attention, although this may well be the basis for the early acquisition of intonation patterns. The precocious acquisition of sentence-final particles in Japanese suggests that very young children may be especially sensitive to simple linguistic correlates of their own emotional states. *Yo* is used when children are encountering resistance or lack of mutuality, and feel they can impose their information or will on the addressee; *ne* is used when children are in rapport with their addressees, agreeing with them or expecting their confirmation or approval. The emotional content of *no* is less fixed than *yo* and *ne;* typically *no* seems to be fairly neutral in affect, occurring in the ordinary give and take of information shared in the speech context. Using each of these particles appropriately also reflects some ability to deal with presuppositions about shared/unshared information. It is interesting that, as with word order, this is apparently within the cognitive capacity of children aged 1½ to 2 years. Perhaps these particles are so difficult for Westerners learning Japanese as a second language because their usage is so context-dependent that ordinary classroom instruction cannot duplicate the appropriate conditions for acquisition.

6.1.3. *Case Particles.*   Soon after Japanese children can combine words within a sentence, case particles begin to emerge. The development of case particles, and the errors which typically occur in the course of acquisition, are discussed in detail in section 4.2. Although case particles appear at an early stage of Japanese language development, there are other languages in which the acquisition of casemarking is more precocious. In Japanese, the ellipsis of case particles in casual speech, and especially in babytalk, as well as the semantic inconsistency in the uses of certain particles, such as the subject marker *ga,* may delay the acquisition of case particles compared with the Slavic languages or Turkish. For example, studies of children's sentence comprehension, which are discussed in section 7.2.1, have shown that Turkish children can use inflections as the sole cue to grammatical relations earlier than Japanese children. This is apparently because in Turkish, word order is freer than in Japanese and inflections cannot be omitted. Thus language-specific factors influence the timing of acquisition for production and comprehension of casemarking.

6.1.4. *Reported Speech.* In general, the content of very young children's speech in Japanese seems quite similar to that of English-speaking children. One striking difference, however, is the great frequency in Japanese of words referring to the sounds that are made by objects as well as animals. This is not a peculiarity of child speech, but rather reflects the very large and colorful lexicon of onomatopoeic words in Japanese. These words are extremely common in colloquial speech, and in the input to very young children. Onomatopoeic words represent both actual sounds and noises (*giseigo*), and the manner in which activities are performed or events occur (*gitaigo*). Japanese 2-year-olds typically know a great number of animal sounds, such as *wan-wan* 'bow-wow' and *kya-kya* (monkeys' cry), words for familiar noises, such as *pipo-pipo* (sirens) and *baan* 'bang', and many expressions symbolizing manner, such as *para-para* (sprinkling, scattering) and *kuru-kuru* (spinning). (See Okubo, 1981b, on the acquisition of onomatopoeic words by one child.) A significant amount of mothers' speech to Japanese children consists of explicit instruction in onomatopoeic words. Japanese mothers typically call their children's attention not only to the sounds in their environment, but also to the speech of other people. Furthermore, they frequently tell their children what to say in particular situations.

In this light, it is not surprising that one of the earliest grammatical forms to emerge in Japanese is sentence-final *tte,* after reported speech and sounds. *Tte,* or its more formal equivalent *to,* is the complementizer used with verbs of saying and other non-factive predicates, like English *that;* it is the general "quotation mark" used in citing speech and reporting sounds. In Japanese, direct and indirect quotations can be distinguished only if the embedded sentence incorporates forms such as sentence-final particles or polite verb inflections, which indicate that the speaker's exact words are being quoted. As Uyeno (1971, Chap. 3.1) points out, in colloquial Japanese, the verb of saying is often omitted from quotations; in such cases the tense and mood of the ellipted verb must be deduced from context. Thus the simple sentence

arigatoo   tte.
thank you   QUOT
' "Thank you" '.

may mean 'S/he says/said, "Thank you"' or 'Say, "Thank you,"' depending upon the context. Mothers frequently use such sentences in telling children what to say or in calling their attention to a sound or to someone's utterance.

In the earliest cases of reported speech, the child simply gives the word or sound being quoted followed by *tte;* Okubo (1967, p. 87) cites such a case at 1;6 years. In the next stage, which began at 1;8 years in Okubo's daughter (p. 89), sentences of the following type appear:

aan	*tte*	*nai - teru*	*no.*
waa	QUOT	cry PRES.PROG	EP

'(S/he) cries (going) "aan"'.

In the earliest recordings of one child in my sample, at 1;11 years, such examples also occurred:

buun	*tte*	*tob - u*	*no.*
sound of flying	QUOT	fly NONPAST	EP

'It flies (going) "buun"'.

These are actually conjoined sentences in which the verb of saying in the first conjunct, which would follow *tte,* has been omitted. This reduced form is very common in casual Japanese conversation, where it is the typical way of describing a thought, utterance, gesture, or sound accompanying some action. It is interesting that Japanese children find this pattern simpler than a conjoined sentence. In my data, such sentences occurred before the earliest instances of conjoined sentences with *-te* 'and'; Okubo's daughter used both types of sentences at the same age. Perhaps reduced conjuncts with *tte* may constitute a kind of adverbial on the sentence describing the main action before children learn the full pattern S_1 *tte itte,* S_2 'Saying S_1, S_2'.

In my data, the same child of 1;11 years who could produce the above pattern of reduced conjuncts with *tte* could also produce quotations of speech with explicit verbs of saying. In the following case, an adult had failed to understand his pronunciation:

uupapa	*tte*	*it - ten*	*no.*
supercar	QUOT	say PRES.PROG	EP

'I'm saying, "supercar"'.

Fujiwara (1977) reports quotations with the speaker overtly mentioned in the speech of a child of only 1;10 years. For example, when this child overheard her grandfather in the bath, she reported to her grandmother (p. 124):

jiichan   ga   atsui   tte.
grandfather SUBJ   hot   QUOT
'Grandfather (said), "It's hot"'.

The earliest quotations tend to appear at about the same time as multi-word utterances; sentences quoting speech were among the most syntactically complex and longest sentences produced by children of 1;11–2;4 years-of-age in my sample. For example, the following exchange took place with a girl of 2;1 years old, who had not yet spontaneously produced any conjoined sentences:

Child: *okashi   tabe - ru?*
          sweets   eat   NONPAST
          'Will you eat sweets?'

Adult: *un.*
          yes
          'Yes'.

Child: *okashi   tabe - ru   tte   yut - ta.*
          sweets   eat   NONPAST QUOT   say   PAST
          'She said that she'll eat sweets'.

English-speaking children do not seem to acquire linguistic means for reporting speech at such an early stage of development. Eisenberg and Renner (1981), for example, examined the development of complement structures, with or without complementizers, in the speech of five American children, and found that reports with verbs of communication such as *say* and *tell* emerged in only three of the children, at 2;8–3;0 years-of-age. Bloom, Lahey, Hood, Lifter and Fiess (1980) did not find *say* among the complement-taking verbs used by the four American children in their study. These four children started using complements with verbs of communication and the complementizer *that* between 2;8 and 3;2 years-of-age; at this time, temporal, causal, and coordinate conjunctions were being used in conjoined sentences, and object specification patterns, including relative clauses, had become productive. However, Bloom et al. do note that sentences such as *Tell him wake up* without complementizers emerged at the same time or before conjoined sentences with *and*. Limber (1973) reports that *say* and *go* were used by children aged 1;11–2;5 years in reporting direct speech and noises, e.g. *Cows go "moo."* It is difficult to compare these findings with the Japanese data, since Limber does not elaborate on the types of reported speech which he found at different stages, and Bloom et al. do not analyze reported speech without complementizers in detail. However, it appears that Japanese children report speech and sounds more frequently, and at an earlier developmental stage, than American children. In my data, *tte* was used to mark quoted speech and sounds before any other complement types or any conjoined sentences were being used, at 1;11 and 2;1 years-of-age in two children, respectively.

The early acquisition of reported speech in Japanese seems to have both a linguistic and cultural basis. The grammar of quotation is much simpler in Japanese than in English; at first the use of *tte* is a morphological rather than syntactic development, comparable to the use of sentence-final particles. Structures which could be embedded in verbs of saying can first be practiced as simple sentences ending in *tte,* with the verb of saying omitted. With embedded quotations, there is no grammatical distinction between direct and indirect speech in Japanese, with problematic rules for sequence of tense, as in English. Early acquisition of reported speech in Japanese probably also depends upon the frequency of reported speech and sounds in mother's speech to young children. This frequency reflects both the much more developed onomatopoeic lexicon in Japanese, and the cultural emphasis on instructing children in what to say, and calling their attention to what others have said.

The contrasting data on quoted speech in Japanese and English raise a methodological issue. If children are observed primarily in interaction with their mothers, there will be less opportunity for quoted speech than if other active participants are present. In my samples with frequent quoted speech, a native speaker of Japanese was usually present and actively interacting with the mother and child while I was taking contextual notes. This context probably increased the likelihood that the Japanese mothers would quote speech and the children report speech.

6.1.5. *Conditional and Concessive Conjunctions.*   The acquisition of conditional and concessive conjunctions in Japanese seems to be quite precocious, and to contradict the course of semantic development found in studies of other languages, such as Bloom et al. (1980) and Clancy et al. (1976), who investigated English, Italian, German, and Turkish. For example, Okubo (1967, p. 104) cites the emergence of *-tara* 'when/if' in her daughter's speech at 1;10 years, and in other children at 2;3 and 2;2 (Okubo, 1983), at 2;3 years of age, each only 1 month after starting to conjoin sentences with *-te* 'and/and then/and so'. Another surprisingly precocious acquisition is the concessive conjunction *-temo* 'even though/although'. This conjunction appeared at 2;3 years in the speech of two children in my sample, as well as Okubo's daughter (p. 105). Another child cited by Okubo even used *-temo* at the same time as *-te*. All these children were using *-temo* earlier than *kedo* 'but',[23] and much earlier than conjunctions of comparable meaning in other languages. Clancy et al. (1976) found that conditional conjunctions did not emerge in the earliest stage of development of conjunctions;

---

[23]Iwabuchi and Muraishi (1968) report that *-temo* appeared in one child's speech at 2;1 years-of-age, 1 month after *kedo* 'but', so it appears that *-temo* is not always the first adversative conjunction.

Bloom et al. (1980) do not report either conditional or concessive conjunctions among those being used productively by four American children studied to the age of 3 years.

One reason for the early acquisition of these conjunctions is linguistic: *-te, -tara* and certain other Japanese connectives are actually verbal inflections; *-temo* is formed by simply adding the particle *mo* 'also/even', which is a very early acquisition, to the *-te* form of the verb. The early acquisition of connective inflections provides further evidence for the operating principle "pay attention to the ends of units" (Slobin, 1973; Peters, 1985); since these conjunctions are verb-final and intonationally part of the verb, they are perceptually salient. Since these connectives are also clause-final, occurring at the ends of major intonation contours, they are probably more perceptually salient to children than the clause-initial conjunctions of English.[24] Since the acquisition of verb inflections in Japanese begins during the one-word stage, it is not surprising that verb-final conjunctions also appear precociously.

However, from a semantic point of view, the early emergence of these conjunctions in Japanese seems anomalous. One would expect conditionals and concessives to be beyond the conceptual grasp of children in the initial stage of acquiring conjoined sentences, even if the linguistic forms are perceptually salient and grammatically simple. The explanation lies in pragmatics, the way these conjunctions are typically used in the speech addressed to very young children. In Japanese, conjoined sentences are used to express some of the most common speech acts in the adult input to 2-year-olds: permission, prohibition, suggesting, and warning.

For example, in granting permission, Japanese mothers typically conjoin a clause with the verb describing the action in question to a clause consisting of the adjective *ii* 'good', as in:

tabe - te   i   - i.
eat   CONT   good   NONPAST
'It's alright to eat it'.

Children use this pattern very early in requesting permission, sometimes before 2 years-of-age (e.g. Fujiwara, 1977, p. 103). An alternative form of the conjoined sentences with *ii* 'good' granting permission uses the conjunction *-temo* 'even though' rather than *-te*. A mother might say, for example,

tabe - temo   i   - i.
eat   CONC.   good   NONPAST
Lit., 'Even eating it is alright'.

---

[24]Japanese also has clause-initial conjunctions, but these are optional, whereas all conjoined clauses must be marked by a clause-final connective at the end of the first clause.

In my data, these were the only types of sentences in which children of 2;0–2;4 were using -*temo;* this is also the earliest usage cited by Okubo (1967, p. 94) at 2;3 years-of-age. Fujiwara (1977, p. 103) reports that one child was using the pattern with -*te ii* at 1;8 years, and 1 month later started using -*temo* in sentences expressing permission (p. 108). Semantically, -*temo* does not seem to be significantly different from -*te* in this construction, although the other functions of these conjunctions in adult speech are as different as English *and* and *although*.

A similar explanation applies to the early instances of conditional conjunctions in Japanese. In sentences expressing prohibition, the first clause ends with -*te,* typically realized as -*cha,* which is a contraction of -*te* plus the topic marker *wa.* The second clause usually consists of a single word, such as *dame* 'no good' or *ikenai* 'won't do'. Whereas an American mother would say *Don't touch it,* a Japanese mother says,

sawat - cha   *dame.*
touch   CONT+TOP   no good
'Touching it is no good'.

The conjunction -*te* may be used instead of -*cha* in this construction, but -*cha* is much more common, and is probably acquired by children as a separate verbal inflection for use in prohibitions. It is also possible, of course, to use negative imperatives in Japanese, but this is not the typical way of expressing prohibition.

As with sentences expressing permission, there is an alternate form of prohibition which uses a more sophisticated conjunction than -*te;* in this case, the conjunction is -*tara* 'when/if'. Thus a mother might also say:

sawat - tara   *dame.*
touch   if   no good
'If you touch it, it's no good'.

In my data, the conditional -*tara* first appeared in one child's speech at 2;3 years-of-age in such prohibitions with *dame* 'no good'. This is also the first use of -*tara* cited by Fujiwara (p. 123) at 1;10 years.

Thus the evidence suggests that Japanese children's conceptualization of -*tara* and -*temo* is at first limited to the pragmatic domain of permission/prohibition. Japanese does not have a grammatical system comparable to modals, which in English express such meanings as *may* and *should;* instead, conjoined sentences are used. If acquisition of conditionals and concessives in Japanese is compared with that of English modals, the Japanese children no longer appear so advanced. Brown (1973, p. 270) reports that "semi-auxiliaries" such as *wanna, hafta,* and *gonna* are fairly frequent in the speech of American children at Stage II, which sometimes begins before 2 years-of-age. In English, it would be very difficult for children if permission and prohibition were expressed in conjoined sentences, since subjects cannot be ellipted. In Japanese, however, these speech acts can be expressed in two-word sentences, and it is at a stage when two-word utterances are becoming common that *-tara* and *-temo* appear, shortly after *-te,* in these constructions. Apparently, there is nothing about sentential conjoining per se, as a linking of two concepts, which is beyond the cognitive capacity of the two-word stage child, provided that the meanings encoded are accessible, the linguistic structure simple, and the total number of words required within the child's productive capacity. Semantically, *-te* is similar to an infinitival construction in English when used to express permission or prohibition, e.g. *it's alright/not alright to do it.* When *-tara* and *-temo* are used, there is an additional flavor of conditionality or concession, respectively, but it seems unlikely that children are aware of this until they acquire these connectives in other types of sentences.

6.1.6. *Polite Style.* In Japanese, verbal inflections express different degrees of politeness, as well as tense/aspect. Plain forms, such as the non-past in *-(r)u* and the past in *-ta,* are used to addressees of equal or lower social status; polite forms in *-mas,* such as *-masu* (non-past) and *-mashita* (past), are used to addressees of superior social status to the speaker (Uyeno, 1971, Chap. 2.2.1). The nature of the conversational context and of the relationship between speaker and hearer are also extremely important. According to Ito (1980), the choice between plain and polite registers is determined by the distinction between in-group vs. out-group: polite forms are used to people outside the speaker's group, and plain forms to in-group addressees such as family members and peers. Thus teachers usually use *-mas* forms to their students and employers to their employees, even though they are of higher status, because their relationship is formal, rather than personal (Uyeno, 1971). The *-mas* level of speech is the register used in official conversations and formal situations.

It is difficult to assess the timing of the acquisition of polite speech in Japanese with respect to other languages; the *tu/vous* distinction in Indo-European languages affects a much smaller portion of the verbal system. However, it does seem that acquisition of *-mas* forms, which begins at about 2 years-of-age and in some cases is fairly well-established by 3, is precocious.[25] Okubo (1967, p. 127) reports that her daughter began using polite inflections quite early, such as *-masu* at 2;1 years and *desu* (the polite form of the copula *da*) at 1;11 years-of-age.

---

[25]An interesting comparison can be found in the Luo children studied by Blount (1977). These children at about 3 years-of-age "learn to use deferential, respectful speech, signalled by lower volume and brief, clear remarks." This style is acquired in certain formal contexts; for example, beginning at about 3-years-old, boys must eat dinner with their older brothers and father, and use this style. Use of this speech register in Luo seems to be more common and to reflect more extreme social distinctions than that of polite style in Japanese, which is not used within the family extensively in modern times.

Fujiwara (1977) also cites early examples of polite forms, such as *desu* at 1;9 years (p. 109). In my sample, one boy of 2;0–2;2 was beginning to use *-mas* forms in set formulas which he had been explicitly taught, such as *Itadaki-masu* 'I will receive it', which is said as one is about to begin eating, and *Itte mairi-masu* 'I go and will come back', which is said as one leaves, as well as in memorized phrases from storybooks. A girl of 2;1 years in my sample was beginning to use *-masu* spontaneously.

Since *-mas* forms are used in polite and formal speech, one might wonder how a child under 3 years-of-age, who does not yet go to kindergarten or have much experience with formal situations, learns this stylistic level. Moreover, since most 2-year-olds are probably of inferior social status to everyone who addresses them, it seems unlikely that they would hear *-mas* forms frequently enough to acquire them so early. However, an examination of mother's speech to 2-year-olds in my sample revealed that there are several well-defined circumstances in which mothers use *-mas* forms to very young children.

One early context in which mothers used this register was when reading storybooks to their children. In my data, *-mas* forms were at first interspersed among plain forms in reading to children, but were used with increasing frequency as the children grew older. Mothers also used *-mas* forms when they imitated authority figures such as doctors and quoted their speech. For example, one mother, reminding her son of his visit to the doctor, quoted: *Yotchan genki DESU ka tte. Genki ni asobi-MASU ka?* 'Is Yotchan healthy (he said). Does he play actively?'. Interestingly, the mothers in my sample also used polite forms when quoting my speech or my assistant's to their children, even if we had not used polite forms in addressing the children. This usage apparently serves to express politeness to the quoted person indirectly; it also gave these children experience with the *-mas* level of speech in the context of visitors.

In my data, the longest stretches of polite speech occurred during certain routines, which mother and child treated as games. For example, one mother had a set routine in which she and her child would talk to his grandmother on a toy telephone. After giving the child the phone, she would feed him his lines, which he would repeat into the phone. At first, when he was only 1;11 years old, the mother did not use any *-mas* forms, but by the time he was 2;1 years-of-age, she began to interject polite forms for him to repeat in this routine. Iwabuchi and Muraishi (1968) report the spontaneous use of *-mas* forms in an imaginary telephone conversation produced by a 2;8-year-old boy.

Another routine in which mothers use *-mas* forms is hostess/guest role-play. Two mothers in my sample had fairly elaborate routines in which the child would play host/ess, and serve food to her and the other adults. In the context of these "pretend" sequences, mothers would switch to *-mas* forms themselves, and would sometimes explicitly tell the child what to say using polite forms, as in the following case:

Mother: *Yotchan kikanakya, oneechan,   nani   ga   ii,   nani*
                                older sister what SUBJ good what

     ga   ii   desu   ka tte   kikanakya.
     SUBJ good COP:POL   Q

'You must ask, "Older sister, what will you have, what would you like?" you must ask'.

Child: *juusu?*   1;11 yrs
     'Juice?'   M

Mother: *juusu desu   ka?*
     juice COP:POL   Q

'Will it be juice?'

Child: *juusu su (= desu) ka?*
     juice COP:POL   Q

'Will it be juice?'

Here the mother tells the child exactly what to say, *Nani ga ii,* literally, 'What is good' using the plain non-past form of the adjective *ii* 'good', and then adding the polite copula *desu.* When the child simply asks the question with the word *Juusu?* 'Juice?', she expands it for him using a polite form, *desu,* and he attempts to repeat it.

In my data, mothers also sometimes switched to -*mas* forms for a single sentence; these cases seemed to be briefer, more subtle instances of the shift in roles which characterized the longer routines. For example, mothers sometimes used the -*mas* level in requesting that the child perform, as in *Nani o utatte kureru n* DESU *ka?* 'What will you sing for us?' or *Midori wa dore* DESU *ka?* 'Which is the green one?' addressed to a girl of 2;1 years. In such contexts, the mother seems to step momentarily out of her ordinary role to become a kind of teacher, and these situations have the feel of assumed formality which characterizes the longer routines. Mothers seem to enjoy these playful code-switching sequences, in which they briefly adopt a different attitude or role towards their child; clearly, both mothers and children enjoyed the long role-playing routines.

Polite style was also used by the mothers in my sample when they were implicitly or explicitly correcting their child's behavior, or when the child had corrected them. For example, when one child of 2;1 years repeatedly sat on his mother's lap, she said, *Mata dakko* DESU *ka? Iya* DESU *ne* 'Are you sitting on my lap again? I don't like it, you know'. When referring to the fact that the child (at 2;4 years) had broken the nose off his Snoopy toy, this mother said, *Ikenai* DESU *ne* 'That's not nice, is it'. Mothers also sometimes used the more formal *Sumimasen* 'Excuse me' rather than the usual *Gomen* 'I'm sorry', when their children complained or corrected them. In the following example, such code-switching occurs when the child disagrees with his mother's identification of a panda in a picture as a bear:

Child: wanwan deshoo? 2;1 yrs
 doggie COP:PRESUM M
 'It's a doggie, isn't it?'

Mother: a, wanwan DESU ka?
 oh doggie COP:POL Q
 'Oh, is it a doggie?'

Here the mother has switched to the polite register with *desu* in responding to the child's correction. The use of polite forms in mother's speech can apparently have a distancing function, marking a shift in mood towards affected formality, as the mother pretends to take her child's correction seriously, as in the above example, or adopts a more formal, authoritative stance in correcting a child who is misbehaving.

Children's first uses of polite forms are often merely repetitions of what their mothers have said or told them to say. As the use of *-mas* forms becomes productive, it appears in precisely those contexts in which it has occurred in mother's speech. For example, the girl of 2;1 in my sample, who was beginning to use polite style spontaneously, used it when playing hostess with her doll:

Kyuupi - san tabe - mas - u.
Kewpie HON eat POL NONPAST
'Miss Kewpie will eat'.

The hostess/guest routine is apparently a common context for role-playing and the early use of polite forms by Japanese children. Iwabuchi and Muraishi (1968) cite a monologue in which a girl of 2;0 playing dolls by herself takes the roles of both hostess and guest:

gomen kudasai. irasshaimase.
sorry please welcome.
'Hello'. 'Come in'.

mina - san o - genki hai. o - genki desu.
everyone HON HON healthy yes HON healthy COP:POL
desu ka? 'Yes. We're fine'.
COP:POL Q
'Are you all well?'

kore	rika	tte	yuu	namae
this	Rika	QUOT	say	name

maa,	ookiku
my	big

desu.
COP:POL

'This one's name is Rika'.

nari	- mashi - ta	ne.
become	POL PAST	AGR

'My, how big she's gotten'.

In this monologue, the polite formulas of greeting appear, along with the honorific prefix *o-*, the suffix *-san,* the polite *hai* 'yes', and the verbal inflections *-masu* and *desu.* (The child uses *o-* incorrectly in the response *O-genki desu* 'We're fine'; *o-* cannot be used for references to the speaker or speaker's group.) Okubo (1967, p. 223) cites a similar example from her daughter's speech at 2;1 years-of-age. Such cases show the beginnings of sensitivity to the kind of formal social situations which require polite style. Fujiwara (1977) also reports early uses of polite inflections by children to family members in contexts of ritualized formality, such as *Han (= gohan) desu yo* 'Dinner is ready', spoken by a child of 1;11 years (p. 134), and at 2;3 years *Naokochan desu yo* 'It's Naoko', said when knocking on a door (p. 207). Thus the earliest uses of polite inflections are apparently all contextually appropriate.

Although children of 1;11–2;4 in my sample were just beginning to acquire polite inflections, a child of 3;1 exhibited much greater control of this register, and could switch from plain to polite levels with ease. She used *-mas* in polite formulas, when reading books, in role-play routines serving food, playing doctor, and imitating her mother's speech. In her role-playing, she also demonstrated full control of the non-verbal accompaniments of polite style in Japanese. Imitating her mother speaking to me, she stood much straighter, bowed, pursed her lips slightly, and spoke with higher pitch. This child would also switch to *-mas* if addressed with a *-mas* form. Thus by 3 years-of-age, she could not only create her own make-believe contexts for using polite speech, but could respond appropriately to the level of politeness used by her addressee.

The ability to use polite forms in appropriate social contexts apparently develops after a fairly long period during which the child practices using this register with family members in contexts of ritualized role-playing and affected formality. Given the nature of these contexts, an important factor underlying the early acquisition of *-mas* may be the special affect accompanying these experiences. In these sequences, mothers' intonation changes and becomes sing-song, with lengthened vowels, higher pitch, and clearer articulation, signaling the shift in atmosphere. The early acquisition of polite style may therefore provide further support for the hypothesis that very young children will be quite sensitive to any correlation between linguistic forms and affect. As children become older and pay more attention to adult speech which is not addressed to them, and participate more actively in adult conversations, their experience with polite speech is extended to real social interactions. Okuda's (1979) study reveals that by 3- to 5-years-of-age, Japanese children are sensitive to the social factors governing use of polite style; 46–73% of the children in this age range in her sample invented dialogue using polite forms for a child addressing a doctor in a cartoon, and 80% used polite forms for a girl asking directions from a stranger. Thus pre-schoolers are responsive to social status differences and to the in-group/out-group distinction conditioning the switch to polite style. It has often been noted that Japanese children are allowed a relatively long period of freedom from social constraints, followed by the imposition of the rather rigid limitations of adult social stratification at about 7 years-of-age (see Benedict, 1946, Chap. 12). Perhaps one aspect of this socialization process is extending the sense of feigned formality first acquired in play as a 2-year-old to a sense of true constraint in social contexts calling for polite style. Okuda's data indicate that this process is under way in the years between 3 and 5.

6.2. Late Acquisition

6.2.1. *Honorifics.* In addition to the polite forms and inflections used to show respect to the addressee, Japanese also has a system of honorifics, which express the speaker's deference toward referents mentioned in the sentence, regardless of the relationship between speaker and hearer. Thus an honorific verb may occur with plain rather than polite inflections when, for example, the speaker is referring to a social superior in conversation with a friend.[26] Although there is not much data on this topic as yet, the available evidence suggests that honorifics are acquired very late, well after what is typically regarded as the primary period for language acquisition. There are a few intriguing examples in longitudinal studies citing isolated, and probably non-productive, uses of honorifics by 2-year-olds (Okubo, 1967, p. 223; Fujiwara, 1977, p. 197). However, it is common knowledge that even junior high school students may have problems using honorifics correctly.

In recent years, it has even become a matter of public concern that some children fail to master honorifics at all (Harada, 1980a). Evidence for the late acquisition of honorific forms can be found in Okuda's (1979) study of 335 children in the first, fourth, and sixth grades. In inventing dialogue for a cartoon of a mother addressing a doctor over the telephone, only 5.7% of the first graders, 8.9% of the third graders, and 20.4% of the sixth graders used honorific forms. These results are supported by the findings of Ide (1981), who reports that virtually no honorifics occurred in the speech of elementary and junior high school children in interviews with an adult. However, these interviews were not designed to elicit honorifics, and so further research is necessary to ascertain the extent of school children's knowledge of honorifics.

One reason for the delayed acquisition of honorifics is the extreme linguistic complexity of the system. Honorifics, called *keigo,* have traditionally been clas-

---

[26]Actually, in casual speech honorifics may not be used very frequently; friends are more likely to use them when referring to honored referents known to both speaker and listener.

sified into *sonkeigo* 'respect words' and *kenjoogo* 'humble words'. The more elaborated system is *sonkeigo,* which includes a variety of linguistic devices for indicating respect for the subject referent of a sentence, who may not be the speaker or a member of the speaker's in-group. *Kenjoogo,* on the other hand, show respect for a non-subject referent, often a direct or indirect object, by lowering the subject referent, often the speaker or a member of the speaker's in-group. In a transformational analysis of honorifics, S. I. Harada (1976) has termed these "subject honorifics" and "object honorifics," respectively.

Sonkeigo, or linguistic means of honoring the subject referent, include an honorific prefix *go/o-,* two different verbal inflections, and a number of lexical substitutions for common verbs. The honorific prefix may be attached to nouns, adjectives, and the infinitive (*renyookei*) form of verbs. Typically, although there are exceptions, the prefix *o-* is used with words of native Japanese origin, and *go-* with Sino-Japanese vocabulary. This prefix is not fully productive, and so speakers must memorize which vocabulary items can occur with it. The *sonkeigo* honorific inflections are *o*-INF *ni naru* and V-(*r*)*areru;* the following examples illustrate their usage:

gakusei	ga	hon	o	yom - u.			(Plain)
student	SUBJ	book	DO	read	NONPAST		

'The student will read the book'.

sensei	ga	hon o	o	- yomi	ni	nar	- u.	(Honorific)
teacher			HON	read	to	become	NONPAST	

'The teacher will read the book'.

sensei	ga	hon	o	yom - are	- ru.	(Honorific)
				read HON	NONPAST	

'The teacher will read the book'.

The -(*r*)*are* suffix, which is somewhat less formal, is homophonous with the passive, and for vowel-final stem verbs, also with the potential. *Sonkeigo* lexical substitutions affect some of the most common verbs, such as *iu* 'say', which is replaced by *ossharu* to show deference to the subject referent. Substitutions are also made for other parts of speech, for example, *kata* for *hito* 'person' and *donata* for *dare* 'who'.

Kenjoogo 'humble words' include similar linguistic devices, such as lexical substitutions and the verbal inflection *o*-INF *suru,* which uses the honorific prefix plus infinitive with *suru* 'do'. The following example illustrates the formation of the 'humble' verbal inflection, which is used when the subject referent is of lower status than the non-subject referent:

gakusei	ga	sensei	ni	hon	o	o	- kaeshi	su	- ru.
student	SUBJ	teacher	IO	book	DO	HON	return	do	NONPAST

'The student will return the book to the teacher'.

Table 4.11 lists some of the most common lexical substitutions used in honorific language. As this table shows, there are many irregularities in the honorific forms. As S. I. Harada (1976) points out, either an entire predicate, or just the infinitive, may have a lexical replacement (e.g. *go-ran* instead of *o-mi* from *miru* 'see'). Honorific forms are also sometimes irregular semantically, neutralizing semantic distinctions marked by plain verbs. Thus *nomu* 'drink' and *taberu* 'eat' both become *meshi-agaru,* and *iru* 'exist', *kuru* 'come', and *iku* 'go' may all become *irassharu.* Matters are further complicated by the existence of polite and hyper-polite speech styles for showing deference to an honored addressee; in these styles the polite *-mas* inflections are added to honorific verb stems. Thus there are many structural and semantic features within the system of Japanese honorifics which probably contribute to the late acquisition of these forms.

As this very incomplete discussion of honorifics indicates, the system involves many morphological, semantic, and social complexities which could delay acquisition. Irregularities and exceptions in the use of the honorific prefix and lexical substitutions require that many honorific forms must simply be memorized. Moreover, the morphology of honorific inflections runs counter to certain basic operating principles which have been proposed. As K. Harada (1980a) has pointed out, the subject honorific pattern *o-INF ni naru* involves discontinuous morphemes; Slobin (1973) has proposed that children tend to avoid such interruption of linguistic units. In the case of subject honorifics, two different inflec-

TABLE 4.11
Some Common Honorific Lexical Substitutions
(Adapted from S. I. Harada, 1976 and Martin, 1975,
pp. 348–51)

		SONKEIGO	KENJOOGO
da	'be' (COP)	*de irassharu*	*de gozaru*
iru	'be' (AUX)	*irassharu*	*oru*
iru	'exist'	*irassharu / o-ide ni naru*	*oru*
kuru	'come'	*irassharu / o-koshi ni naru*	*mairu*
iku	'go'	*irassharu / o-ide ni naru*	*mairu*
shiru	'know'	*go-zonji da*	*zonjiru*
miru	'see/look'	*go-ran ni naru*	*haiken suru*
suru	'do'	*nasaru*	*itasu*
nomu	'drink'	*meshi-agaru*	*itadaku*
taberu	'eat'		
iu	'say'	*ossharu*	*moosu*

tions are available to fill a single function, whereas children tend to prefer a one-to-one correspondence between form and function (Slobin, 1985). Honorific forms also violate the principle of one-to-one mapping in another way: the construction Noun/Adj. + *ni naru* and the inflection *-(r)are* have both already been acquired at an early age in different meanings, which probably makes their acquisition as honorifics more difficult. The pattern with *ni naru*, which is similar to the honorific pattern, is acquired by 2-year-olds as an inchoative construction; *-(r)are* is mastered by 2- and 3-year-olds as the passive, and for certain verbs, also as the potential. Furthermore, as a passive inflection, *-(r)are* has actually been acquired with diametrically opposed semantic functions. In non-honorific speech, *-(r)are* is one of the cues of a passive sentence, in which the subject should be interpreted as the patient rather than the agent. As an honorific, *-(r)are* is in the active voice, and therefore the subject will often be an agent.

Not only is the system of honorifics grammatically difficult, it also presents the child with a new concept, namely, that linguistic expression of deference is required upon the mere mention of a socially superior person and not just when addressing that person face-to-face. The special feeling of speaking with a superior must be extended to contexts where that person is not even present, in which the social constraint which this presence might create may not be felt very deeply, if at all. Thus the pragmatic and affective basis for the acquisition of polite speech is lacking in the case of grammatically based honorifics, and this may be an additional barrier to their acquisition.

Furthermore, it is probably difficult to separate the notions of politeness toward an addressee and respect toward a socially superior referent, since in many situations the honored person being referred to in a sentence is also the addressee. This overlap may contribute to the trend noted by Harada (1980a) for the younger generation to use the polite *-mas* inflection instead of honorifics, saying, for example, *Sensei ga kaki-mashi-ta* instead of *Sensei ga o-kaki ni nat-ta* 'The teacher wrote'. As Harada points out, compared with the o-INF *ni naru* pattern, the *-mas* inflection is more regular and fully productive, and so these young people are substituting regular for irregular patterns. This change is also an instance of Slobin's (1973) principle that "new functions are first expressed by old forms," since the *-mas* inflection is acquired much earlier than honorific inflections.

In accounting for the late emergence of honorifics, it is also important to consider the nature of the input. In my data, there appeared to be ample opportunity for children to acquire the polite *-mas* level of speech in direct interaction, but I did not find mothers in my sample using honorifics to their children, even in role-playing. This is in accordance with Okuda's (1979) findings on maternal expectations with respect to the time at which honorifics should be acquired. In Okuda's survey of mothers, only 10.1% thought that honorifics should be used before 6 years-of-age; 75.1% felt that honorifics should start being used between

6- and 10-years-of-age. It may well be that by the time a mother might feel her child is linguistically and socially advanced enough to deal with honorifics, the kind of role-playing which fosters acquisition of *-mas* forms no longer is part of mother-child interactions. Perhaps the main exposure to honorifics which young children receive is passive, that is, observing interactions among adults who are using *keigo*. It is not clear how frequent such input is or how much direct instruction children receive from their parents on the usage of honorifics. It is easy to imagine that there would be extensive individual differences in exposure to honorifics, depending upon the social class and kinds of interactions typically engaged in by a child's family members. It is likely that out-of-context instruction and second-hand input are less effective sources of input than the face-to-face exchanges typical of the child's early experience with *-mas*. Thus the nature of children's exposure to honorifics, as well as the linguistic difficulties inherent in the system itself, contributes to their late acquisition.

6.2.2. *Pronouns.*   Compared with the Indo-European languages, the development of pronouns is very late in Japanese. Brown (1973, p. 210) reports that in Stage I, at 1;6–2;3 years-of-age, the three American children in his sample were using the personal pronouns *I, you, it,* and *my.* In my data, in contrast, none of the three children aged 1;11–2;4 were using second person pronouns. The two little boys occasionally referred to themselves as *boku* 'I', but at 2;2 years-old, the girl still had not spontaneously referred to herself with a pronoun, although her linguistic development was certainly no less advanced than that of the boys. These children usually referred to themselves by name, as Japanese children continue to do, at least occasionally, until the age of 6 years (Ide, 1977). This is a very general finding in the data on Japanese language acquisition. For example, Horiguchi (1979b, 1981a), based on longitudinal records of three children, reports that the earliest and by far most common form of self-reference was nickname + *-chan,* the diminutive suffix. This form of self-reference accounted for 99% of all sampled self-references for one boy during his third year, and 94.2% for one girl. Most little boys, however, use *boku* 'I' for self-reference (Ide, 1978), as the two boys in my sample were beginning to do.

Fischer (1970) regards this usage of names for self-reference as one of several instances in which Japanese families differ from American families in permitting developmentally earlier ways of speaking to be continued for a longer time. To understand this belated acquisition of pronouns, it is important to recognize that the system of Japanese personal reference is very different from that of Indo-European languages. For example, within the family, parents and older siblings are addressed with kinship terms, such as *otoosan* 'father', *okaasan* 'mother' (*papa* and *mama* in the earliest stages of development), *oniisan* 'older brother' and *oneesan* 'older sister'. These family members also often refer to themselves by these kinship terms where appropriate within the family. One's children and younger siblings are usually addressed and referred to by their first name or nickname plus the diminutive suffix *-chan*. Thus within the Japanese family, names and kinship terms often substitute for personal pronouns. (See Fischer [1964] for a description of personal reference within Japanese families.)

Not only do nouns frequently substitute for pronouns in Japanese, but often any overt form of personal reference will be omitted. In Japanese, person is not marked in the morphology of verbs, and pronouns are entirely optional. Ide (1977, 1978, 1978–9) has analyzed the forms used for first and second person reference in the speech of 18 children from 1½ to 6 years-of-age. After these children's speech was observed at a nursery school, detailed questionnaires were sent out to 150 mothers of children from 1 to 6 years old, and filled out during one week of observing their children's use of first and second person references in a variety of contexts. Ide found that the most frequent form of reference to first, second, and third persons was ellipsis; person deixis is thus usually understood from context. This creates many difficulties for speakers of Indo-European languages (confusions between first and second person can be particularly disastrous!). However, Ide (1977) reports that a dozen Japanese children can play together for half an hour at a time without using a single first or second person reference. Similarly, Horiguchi (1979b) reports that overt first person references occurred with increasing frequency in the speech of her two children during their third year, but the percentage was only 6.5–13.2% in the boy and 13.5–24.9% in the girl. (Second children in Japanese families apparently feel more need to use explicit self-references; see also Okubo, 1981a.) Since titles and names, which Westerners typically regard as third person references, generally substitute for first and second person pronouns in Japanese, the frequency of personal pronouns in the input to Japanese children is extremely low compared with Indo-European languages.

Moreover, in Japanese there are several different options available for first and second person pronouns, and these are conditioned, not grammatically, as in English, but socially, by such factors as the age, sex, and relative social status of speaker and hearer, and the nature of the conversational context. Children hear different pronouns from different people, and hear the same people referring to themselves with different pronouns in different contexts. Thus Japanese pronouns constitute a good example of many forms being used for a single function; their late acquisition is consistent with Slobin's (1985) proposal that children prefer a one-to-one mapping of form and function.

Table 4.12 lists some of the most common Japanese pronouns, following Uyeno (1971, p. 16). It is also possible to add plural markers, such as *-tachi*, to several of these pronouns. The third person pronouns seem similar to English ones in marking number and gender. However, they are used very infrequently, and have somewhat different functions. For example, *kare* 'he' and *kanojo* 'she' may mean girlfriend and boyfriend, although this usage is less common nowadays (Okubo, personal communication). As more neutral referential forms, Japanese third person pronouns tend to be used in quasi-academic or formal style

TABLE 4.12
Some Common
Japanese Pronouns
(From Uyeno, 1971)

First Person	Second Person	Third Person
watakushi		*kare* 'he'
watashi	*anata*	*kanojo* 'she'
atashi	*anta*	*karera* 'they' (M)
boku	*kimi*	*kanojotachi/kanojora* 'they' (F)
ore	*omae*	

(Aoki, personal communication). None of the children in my sample ever used third person pronouns, and Okubo's daughter at the age of 6 years had still not acquired them (Okubo, 1967, p. 72).

As Uyeno (1971, Chap. 2.2.2) discusses, the first and second person pronouns listed above are restricted in usage by the sex of the speaker and sometimes also of the hearer, as well as by their social relationship, relative status, degree of intimacy, and the speech context. Following Uyeno, the pronouns are listed in order of decreasing formality. Certain pronouns are paired at the same stylistic levels; thus *ore* 'I' and *omae* 'you' are at the same, extremely casual level of speech. The more formal pronouns, *wata(ku)shi* 'I' and *anata* 'you' can be used by either male or female speakers to addressees of either sex, although actually these pronouns are used much more frequently by women. *Atashi* 'I' is used only by women to addressees of either sex; *boku, kimi, ore,* and *omae* are used only by men. Women use *an(a)ta* to their husbands, boyfriends, to their female friends, and, in certain contexts, to their children. *Omae* 'you' is how a man addresses his wife or girlfriend, his buddies, and, sometimes, his children. Although *wata(ku)shi* 'I' is formal enough to use in conversation with a superior, *anata* 'you' is not; superiors are always referred to by title or last name plus title. *Boku* 'I' may be used by boys even in formal situations, although they learn to use *wata(ku)shi* by the time they enter junior high school (Ide, 1977). *Kimi* 'you' is appropriate for a man to use only when addressing social equals or inferiors whom he knows fairly well. Both *ore* 'I' and *omae* 'you' are limited to particular contexts with peers or inferiors. There is thus an interesting discrepancy between the sexes in their use of pronouns. Women are limited to the more formal options, and if they address their husband and children with pronouns, they use the more formal *anata*. In contrast, men's options cover the full range of formality/informality, and the pronoun they use to their wives, girlfriends, or children is the least formal one available.

In my data, the earliest and by far the most common form of reference used when speaking to a child was his or her name, usually nickname, plus the diminutive suffix *-chan*. For example, the mother of a boy of 1;11–2;0 years always addressed him using this form as a second person reference; at 2;1 years-of-age, she began calling him *boku* 'I', as in the following example:

(while reading her child a Winnie the Pooh story)

boku,   Puu - san   mi   - te.
I   Pooh HON   look IMP

Lit., 'I, look at Pooh'.

As Ide (1977) and Fischer (1970) have pointed out, *boku* or *boku-chan* tend to function as alternate proper names for little boys. Fischer (1964) proposes that this usage originated as a way of teaching little boys to call themselves *boku*. In my sample, about 2 months after the mother in the above example began to use *boku* as a second person reference, her son also began to refer to himself as *boku* 'I'. This boy's mother also would model the use of *boku* as a first person pronoun for him. For example, one time when the child (at 2;2) had been awaiting my arrival, his mother said to him, BOKU *matte ta n da yo tte iwanakya* 'Say, " I was waiting" '.

The mothers of 2-year-old boys in my sample used *boku* frequently as a vocative and second person reference, and both boys were beginning to use *boku* for self-reference. In contrast, the mother of the 2-year-old girl in my sample rarely referred to her as *watashi* 'I', and this child at 2;3 years had not spontaneously used *watashi* to refer to herself. In her survey of Japanese mothers, Ide (1978–79) found that girls generally started using *watashi* later than boys used *boku*. The use of *watashi* as an alternative name seems to be more limited than *boku;* for example, the suffix *-chan* which appears with names cannot be used with *watashi,* although it occurs with *boku.* Iwabuchi and Muraishi (1968) report acquisition of *watashi* as late as 2;8 years in one girl. However, there are apparently great individual differences in this domain. Okubo (1967, p. 71) reports that her daughter was using *atashi* 'I' for self-reference at 1;10 years old, and Fujiwara (1977, p. 130) cites this form in the speech of a girl of the same age. On the other hand, Horiguchi's son was not yet using *boku* for self-reference by 2;11 years, although most boys acquire this form much earlier.

The way pronouns are used in the input to different children probably plays an important role in the timing of their acquisition. Except for the type of modeling described above for *boku,* parents' speech does not seem to be as important for the acquisition of pronouns as the speech of other children. This is because, as Horiguchi notes, parents do not usually refer to themselves with pronouns in front of their children. If a child has older siblings, their usage will lead to earlier acquisition of pronouns in the case of same-sex siblings, and to imitation of inappropriate pronouns when the sibling is of the opposite sex. For children who do not have older siblings of the same sex, entering nursery school or kindergarten and coming into contact with children outside the family circle leads to acquisition of the appropriate pronouns. Horiguchi reports that her son began to use *ore* at 2;10 years, when a boy with an older brother joined his class; her daughter began using *watashi* at 2;2 years, when she entered nursery school and heard this form in the speech of a classmate with an older sister. Horiguchi proposes that consistently correct use of Japanese pronouns for self-reference is not established until about 3 years, when the child's consciousness of sex differences is also firmly established.

As different forms of self-reference are acquired, children also begin to use them selectively in different contexts. For example, one boy of 2;4 years in my sample, who had an older sister, called himself *oniichan* 'older brother' when playing with his toy Pooh bear. Okubo (1967, p. 71) reports that her daughter called herself by name when speaking to her parents, but used *atashi* 'I' when speaking to her friends. Examples cited by Fujiwara (1977, p. 246) from a girl of 3;0 years old indicate that she called herself by name in sentences in which she was using plain verb forms, but used *watashi* 'I' in sentences with polite inflections. Similarly, Horiguchi's 2-year-old daughter frequently used *watashi* in sentences ending with the feminine sentence-final particle *wa;* this child also used certain non-verbal components of female style in these cases. Although this child did not always combine elements of female style consistently (*watashi* also occurred with the more masculine sentence-final *n da yo*), early examples of *watashi* reflect some preliminary awareness of the different features appropriate to a particular speech style.

This kind of code-switching has been documented in detail by Ide (1977, 1978). Ide found that the use of different forms of first and second person reference was governed by both inter-personal factors such as relative age, sex, social status, and personal relationship between speaker and addressee, and by "intra-personal" factors, i.e. psychological or behavioral factors such as self-assertion or dependency. Boys and girls used their name plus *-chan* for self-reference (boys also used *boku-chan*) within their families in a mood of *amae* or dependency. (See Doi, 1973, for a discussion of this fundamental Japanese concept, which refers to a wide class of behaviors and feelings which presume upon the indulgence of another.) Girls in Ide's study switched to (*w*)*atashi* 'I' or *oneesan* 'older sister' to express an attitude of *kidori* 'affected maturity' especially with younger friends or children. Boys switched to *ore* 'I' to show solidarity with a peer group. Ide states that "in a group situation, the word *ore* becomes a kind of 'password', a verbal reflection of an important psychological attitude." Younger boys use *ore* to gain acceptance into a play group of older boys, who use this form in active play, when showing off, bossing their peers around, or seeking the admiration of younger children. Horiguchi's son also used *ore* when showing off or calling attention to his strength, when he was still only 2-years-old and occasionally using the female pronoun.

Second person pronouns seem to be acquired even later than first-person pronouns, probably at about the time children enter kindergarten or begin spending time in peer groups. For example, when a boy is referring to himself as *ore*, he will typically be addressing his friends as *omae*. Errors in the use of second person pronouns help provide insight into the factors underlying their acquisition. *Omae,* for example, is sometimes used inappropriately by kindergarten boys. The 4-year-old son of a friend of mine, who usually referred to me as *Patorishiya-san* would switch to *omae* 'you' when involved in active play and rough-housing. His mother said that he did the same with her, and she invariably corrected him, asking *Omae tte dare?* 'Who is "omae"?'. In these cases, the child was apparently allowing the affect associated with the behavioral context to take precedence over inter-personal social factors, such as the age and status of the addressee, in selecting a second person reference.   As with the use of polite -*mas* inflections, it seems that young children may at first rely heavily upon their own affect in a particular context in deciding what linguistic forms to use.

The second person pronoun *an(a)ta* also emerges late. Okubo (1967, p. 71) reports that her daughter began using *anta* 'you' to her friends regularly at 4 years-of-age. In my data, mothers of 2-year-olds used *an(a)ta* to their children very rarely, typically when instructing, criticizing, or otherwise distancing themselves somewhat, as in the following cases:

(telling her boy of 1;11 years to give my assistant an apple)

doozo	*tte.*	*anata*	*sanzan*	*sawat - ta*	*no*
please	QUOT	you	completely	touch PAST	one

ja	*- naku - te.*
COP+TOP	not CONT

'(Say), "Help yourself". Not one that you completely touched'.

(to her daughter of 2;1 years who calls all colors pink)

anta	*pinku*	*shika*	*wakara - na*	*- i*	*no.*
you	pink	except	know NEG	NONPAST	EP

'You only know pink'.

Horiguchi (1979b, 1981a) reports only a few instances of *an(a)ta* in the speech of her son and daughter during their third year, to one another and, inappropriately, to their mother. Ide's data indicate that boys learn to identify *anata* as a woman's word, perhaps because they are never addressed this way by their fathers. Ide points out that *anata* 'you', the second person pronoun which girls acquire, reflects a formal attitude, whereas *omae,* the second person pronoun which boys first acquire, reflects a coarse, extremely casual attitude. *Kimi,* the more formal second person pronoun for boys, is not acquired until about 5–6 years-of-age, later than girls acquire *anata*. Apparently, as Ide suggests, boys first learn to relate to their peers in an attitude of rough solidarity, the *ore* 'I'/*omae* 'you' mode, and girls in an attitude of affected maturity and formality, the *atashi* 'I'/

an(a)ta 'you' style. Boys must proceed to acquire another, more formal level, whereas there are no less formal options for girls to master.

The late acquisition of pronouns in Japanese can be attributed to their low frequency of occurrence, the large number of forms, and most importantly, to the social and psychological complexity of appropriate usage. Pronouns form part of the sociolinguistic structure of Japanese; their use requires code-switching, just like selection of appropriate verbal inflections. The type of input required may preclude the acquisition of pronouns outside of certain contexts, such as peer group, same sex situations, which may not be available to some children until kindergarten. Japanese children must learn to be sensitive to the relevant attributes of the addressee vis-a-vis themselves, and must also learn to use different forms of self-reference in different moods and contexts. Japanese pronouns do present some problems for the language learner, but in contrast with the acquisition of honorifics, there do not seem to be any cases of children who fail to acquire pronouns. This is partly because pronouns occur more frequently than honorifics and in a wider variety of contexts, but also because pronouns in Japanese are strongly linked to the child's developing sense of identity, both personal and social.

7. Reorganizations in Development

7.1. Prenominal Modifiers

The development of prenominal modifiers in many Japanese children undergoes an interesting reorganization in the course of development. In Japanese, many types of relations between nouns, such as possessive, appositional, and sometimes locative, are expressed by the genitive particle *no* in constructions of the form N *no* N, in which the modifier plus *no* precede the head noun. In contrast, adjectives precede the noun they modify with no special grammatical marker; the same is true of relative clauses, since there are no relative pronouns in Japanese. The following examples illustrate these three types of prenominal modifiers:

Noun	*otoosan*	*no*		*kuruma*
	father	GEN		car
	'father's car'			

Adjective	*ookii*	*kuruma*		
	big	car		
	'a big car'			

Relative clause	*otoosan*	*ga*	*kat - ta*	*kuruma*
	father	SUBJ	buy PAST	car
	'the car that father bought'			

One of the earliest case particles which children acquire is the genitive *no,* which they first use to indicate possession in sentences of the form N *no* 'It's N's'. Okubo (1967, p. 89) and Miyahara (1974) both found that *no* emerged at 1;8 years-of-age, as in the following example from Miyahara:

Noriko-chan   no.
               GEN
'It's Noriko's (= mine)'.

In the next stage of development, many children begin to produce both the modifier and the head noun in two-word constructions. In my sample, one child of 1;11 years was at this stage. This child used two types of nominal modifiers: nouns and adjectives. Both were formed simply by juxtaposing the related words in the order: MODIFIER - HEAD. Thus this child correctly produced adjectival modifiers, such as,

akai   buubuu
red   car
'a red car'

but omitted the obligatory genitive marker in constructions with nouns, such as:

*neechan   buubuu
older sister   car
'older sister's car'

This child even omitted *no* in repeating N *no* N constructions from the immediately preceding adult utterance at this stage.

At 2;2–2;4 years-of-age, this child began to use *no* productively in N *no* N constructions indicating possession. *No* was never omitted where appropriate, and began to occur in constructions with body parts, locations, and other types of relations between nouns, such as:

Yotchan   no   o-chinchin
Yotchan   GEN   penis
'Yotchan's penis'

Oosaka   no   ojiichan
Osaka   GEN   grandpa
'grandpa who lives in Osaka'

During the same period, this child also produced the following constructions with adjectival modifiers:

*aoi   no   buubuu
blue   GEN   car

'a blue car'

*chitchai   no   buubuu
tiny   GEN   car

'a tiny car'

It seems to be very common for Japanese children to go through a stage of overgeneralizing *no* with prenominal adjectives.[27] Fujiwara (1977, pp. 124–5, 157, 218) notes this error in the speech of three different children, aged 1;10–2;4 years, and Iwabuchi and Muraishi (1968) cite similar examples from a child of 1;8 years old. Okubo's daughter, however, is an exception to this trend ((Okubo, 1967, p. 108).

Harada (1980b) found the same course of reorganization which appeared in my data. Her daughter first used the N *no* N pattern without *no;* at a later stage, when she was using N *no* N correctly, she produced ADJ *no* N constructions as well. Harada's daughter continued this mistake even after acquiring relative clauses, and added *no* between relative clauses and head nouns, as in:

*kaijuu   ni   nat   - ta   no   onna no ko
monster   to   become PAST GEN   girl

'the girl who became a monster'

*usachan   ga   tabe - ta   no   ninzin
rabbit   SUBJ   eat   PAST GEN   carrot

'the carrot that the rabbit ate'

Thus many Japanese children initially treat nominal and adjectival modifiers in the same way, simply placing them before the head noun.[28] When N *no* N constructions have been acquired, children often apparently notice the discrepancy between the formation of modifying constructions with nouns and adjec-

---

[27]Nominal adjectives such as *kiree* 'pretty/clean' take the *na* form of the copula rather than *no* as prenominal modifiers, e.g. *kiree na hana* 'pretty flowers'. At first, like *no, na* may be omitted. Okubo (1976, p. 216) cites *kiree hana* at 1;8 years in her daughter's speech; *na* was used correctly by 2;2 years. Iwabuchi and Muraishi (1968, p. 157) found omission of *na,* and also overgeneralization of *no,* as in *kiree na no densha* 'clean/pretty streetcar' at over 2½ years old. Apparently, as with true adjectives, an early pattern of simple juxtaposition, Modifier + Noun, is used, followed by overgeneralization of *no* in some children.

[28]Not all children go through a stage of producing *NN genitive constructions, however. Komura (1981) describes the development of one child who developed N *no* N constructions directly from N *no* constructions, without an intermediate stage of *NN. (See section 10.2 for a fuller discussion of Komura's findings.)

tives, and overgeneralize *no* so that all prenominal modifiers are again formed in the same way. At this point, it seems that these children have recognized the single grammatical category of nominal modifiers, and see the functional similarity between the two patterns of noun modification which have been developing, one with nouns and one with adjectives. The reorganization of adjectival modifiers with *no* provides strong support for Slobin's operating principle (1985) that children prefer to use a single form for a single function. At this stage of development, it seems that the N *no* N pattern is too firmly established in familiar constructions, such as the possessive, for the child to resolve the discrepancy in form between nominal and adjectival modifiers by returning to juxtaposition for nouns. In my data, N *no* N constructions are more frequent than prenominal adjectives, and this difference in frequency may also favor the use of *no* with adjectives. The overgeneralization of *no* is also consistent with Slobin's operating principle that "underlying semantic relations should be marked overtly and clearly," and provides strong support for his prediction that "if a category is sometimes marked by Ø and sometimes by some overt phonological form, the latter will, at some stage, also replace the Ø" (Slobin, 1973). Obviously, in achieving adult competence, Japanese children who overgeneralize *no* have to go through another phase of reorganization, in which they distinguish nominal from adjectival and sentential modifiers.

7.2. Word Order and Case Particles

In English, the subject and object of sentences are indicated by word order; in many languages with freer word order, such as Turkish, inflections are used to indicate grammatical relations. Japanese is interesting in that it represents a kind of middle ground, using both options, but neither one entirely consistently. The canonical word order is SOV, but OSV is also possible,[29] and either subject or object may optionally be placed after the verb. Grammatical relations are marked by postpositions such as *ga* (subject) and *o* (direct object). However, certain postpositions, including *ga* and *o,* may be omitted in casual conversation, and this ellipsis occurs even more frequently in the speech addressed to very young children (see section 4.2). The strategies which Japanese children develop for sentence production and comprehension reflect the importance of both word order and case particles in the adult language. As children figure out the relationship between these devices, various reorganizations take place. These have been documented primarily in experimental studies.

7.2.1. *Simple Active Sentences.* Since case particles typically do not emerge until after multi-word utterances are being produced, and then appear only gradually, the developmentally earlier strategy for marking grammatical

---

[29]Kuno (1978) cites a large-scale study of modern Japanese sentence patterns in journalistic writings which found that the ratio of SOV to OSV word order was 17:1.

relations is word order. Miyahara (1973) documents an interesting reorganization which occurred in the speech of her daughter. At 1;11 years, this child used object-verb utterances in fixed order, although it is possible to postpose objects after the verb in colloquial speech. Rigid OV order was maintained until the child acquired the direct object marker *o;* only then did postposed objects begin to appear, as in:

ire	- *ta*	*yo*	*aiai*	*o.*
put in	PAST	EMPH	monkey	DO

'I put it in, the monkey'.

It would be grammatical to omit the object marker in postposed position, as in preverbal position. This child was apparently at first using word order to indicate the object-verb relation; when the object marker was acquired, the word-order strategy could be relaxed. Miyahara's finding is very similar to Slobin's observation that one Russian child preserved a more rigid subject-object word order than the adult language until he acquired the accusative inflection, at which point he began producing both subject-object and object-subject sentences (Slobin, 1966), and similar to findings of Radulovic (1975) in Serbo-Croatian.

Experiments on the comprehension of simple active sentences document reorganizations in the roles of word order and case particles in children's strategies for processing sentences. Hayashibe (1975) and Hakuta (1982) found that at approximately 4 years-of-age, Japanese children will impose a consistent interpretation upon strings of two nouns and a verb, taking the first noun to be the agent. In each of these studies, children were presented with semantically reversible and irreversible sequences of the form NNV, NVN, and VNN with no case particles, and were asked to act them out. Testing 60 children between 3;0 and 5;11 years-of-age, Hayashibe found that an agent-patient strategy for interpreting the nouns appeared at about 4 years-of-age, regardless of the position of the verb. Hakuta, testing 30 children between 3;3 and 6;2 years-of-age, reports a statistically significant increase in preference for interpreting the first noun as agent at 4;2–5;2-years-old. In both studies, even the 3-year-old children had no difficulty acting out semantically irreversible sequences; thus the earliest strategy appears to be semantic/pragmatic, based upon the likelihood of a certain referent being the agent of a particular action. The strategy of taking the first noun as agent, which emerges at about 4–5 years-of-age, appears to be derived from the dominant adult SOV word order of Japanese. However, this strategy is not sensitive to the position of the verb; Hakuta found that NNV sequences were no more likely to receive an agent-patient interpretation than NVN or VNN strings. Apparently, the focus of the syntactic strategy is the first noun itself, rather than its position relative to the other noun or verb. Thus by about 4 years-of-age, Japanese children have acquired a sensitivity to word order in the absence of semantic or morphological cues.

Experiments with simple active sentences incorporating case particles reveal the early preferences of Japanese children for the standard adult SOV word order. Various studies have assessed the performance of children in acting out semantically reversible and irreversible simple active sentences in SOV and OSV order, such as Hayashibe (1975), testing 30 children from 3;0 to 5;11 years old; Hakuta (1982), who tested 48 children between 2;3 and 6;2-years-old; and Sano (1977), who studied 80 children between 3;3 and 6;8 years. Again, semantically irreversible actives were generally well understood by even the younger children, but developmental trends were apparent in the interpretation of reversible sentences. Each of these studies found that in the dominant SOV order, sentences were acted out correctly more frequently. In each study, there were a few children who consistently interpreted all OSV sentences as if they were SOV, ignoring the case particles completely. Analyzing errors, Hayashibe found that only the older children in his sample (mean age 5;0 years) could interpret both SOV and OSV reversible actives correctly, showing that they were able to rely upon case particles even when these did not occur in the expected word order. Hayashibe concludes that word order is a developmentally earlier strategy than case particles; the former seems to develop at about 4 years-of-age, the latter at about 5. Similarly, Hakuta (1977) found that OSV sentences were acted out correctly by about 5;4 years-of-age. Thus, one reorganization which must take place in the development of processing strategies is a shift in emphasis away from word order toward case particles.

It is interesting to compare these findings with crosslinguistic data on sentence comprehension. Hakuta (1982) contrasts his results with those of Slobin (1982) on Turkish. Unlike Japanese children, from the age of 2 years, Turkish children are able to comprehend sentences with all six possible orders of subject, object, and verb. In Turkish, word order is quite free and inflections are obligatory. Thus inflections provide a more consistent cue than in Japanese, where the direct object marker *o* is frequently omitted, and the subject marker *ga* may also occasionally be omitted. Moreover, since Turkish word order is so variable, children are forced to rely primarily upon inflections to interpret sentences, whereas in Japanese, the dominant SOV word order leads children to form a fallible agent-patient-action strategy. Hakuta concludes that in languages which utilize both word order and inflections to mark grammatical relations, children formulate processing strategies which incorporate the two variables, and find it difficult to comprehend sentences which violate the expected correlation between them.

The findings on Japanese children's strategies for processing sentences are borne out by studies of imitation, reported by Hakuta (1982) and Sano (1977). Hakuta had 14 children aged 3;8–6;8 imitate simple active sentences with case particles, in SOV and OSV orders. There were no errors with SOV sentences, whereas only 63.4% of the OSV sentences were correctly imitated. Of the errors, 85.4% retained the order of nouns, but switched the particles to create canonical

SOV sentences, or changed the first particle to the subject marker *ga,* so that both nouns were marked by *ga.* Clearly, Japanese children expect the first noun of a sentence to be a *ga*-marked subject. The children in Sano's study also imitated SOV actives correctly, but changed the particles in OSV sentences to create canonical SOV sentences. These findings are supported by the results of a production task conducted by Hakuta (1982), in which 48 children between 3;3 and 6;2 produced only 2.2% OSV actives. Most sentences were canonical SOV actives, with *ga* marking the subject 90% of the time by the age of 3;9 years. Thus imitation data provide further evidence for Hakuta's proposal that Japanese children expect agreement between case particles and their location within a sentence.

7.2.2. *Passive Sentences.* As in English, Japanese passive sentences reverse the semantic roles of sentence subject and object, and provide special case-marking for the agent, and a special inflection on the verb. The following examples illustrate the contrast between active and passive sentences in Japanese:

Active: *Taroo* *ga*   *Hanako* *o*   *but - ta.*
                SUBJ   DO hit PAST
      'Taroo hit Hanako'.

Passive: *Taroo* *ga*   *Hanako* *ni*   *but - are* *- ta.*
                SUBJ   AGT hit PASS PAST
      'Taroo was hit by Hanako'.

In the active sentence, *ga* marks the subject, which is also the agent, and *o* marks the direct object or patient. In the passive sentence, the patient is now the subject, and the agent is marked with *ni,* which also marks indirect objects, locatives, certain sources, as well as the agents of causative sentences. The verb takes the passive suffix *-(r)are* before tense marking. Like active sentences, passives may appear in both SOV and OSV order; for example, the above passive could also be phrased *Hanako ni Taroo ga butareta* 'By Hanako, Taroo was hit'.

As expected, Japanese children acquire active sentences, at least in the standard SOV order, before passive ones. In the earliest stage documented by experimental research, Japanese children are able to discriminate passive sentences from active ones, but do not know how to interpret the passive sentences correctly. Harada (1977) reports that at 3;11 years-of-age, her daughter's comprehension of passive sentences was still random. Both Sano (1977) and Hakuta (1982) found that children of about 3½ years old performed randomly when acting out passive sentences, but acted out SOV actives correctly about 70% of the time. The fact that very young children do discriminate between actives and passives shows some early sensitivity to the special morphology of passive sentences: the case particle *ni* and the passive inflection on the verb.

In the next stage of development, many Japanese children begin to interpret passive sentences consistently, but incorrectly, as if they were actives. It is interesting that this development takes place at about the same age at which children will impose an SOV interpretation on strings of two nouns and a verb, approximately 4 years old. Hakuta (1982) found a U-shaped curve for the acquisition of passive sentences by Japanese children. Grouping his 48 subjects by their mean length of morphemes in a production task (a measure which correlated highly with age), Hakuta found that the group with the lowest production scores interpreted passives randomly, but the next group, which had a mean age of 3;9 years, consistently misinterpreted SOV passives as SOV actives. In the third group, interpretations again became random; the fourth group, with a mean age of 5;4 years, interpreted SOV passives correctly over 70% of the time. Thus, as in the development of passive sentences in English (see Bever, 1970), there is a stage in which the interpretation of SOV passives in Japanese is consistently reversed.

However, as Hakuta's analysis reveals, this misinterpretation of Japanese passives is not merely the result of applying an SOV word order strategy to all passive sentences. As Hakuta points out, if Japanese children were relying solely upon a word order strategy, in which NNV sequences were interpreted as agent-patient-action regardless of case-marking, then we would expect them to perform well on OSV passives, since an agent-patient-action interpretation would be correct. Instead, Hakuta found that performance on OSV passives was significantly worse than on SOV actives. Furthermore, the children did not perform any better on OSV passives than on OSV actives and SOV passives, which have the reverse semantic sequence, patient-agent-action. Sano (1977) made similar findings in a study of 80 children aged 3;3–6;8; their ability to act out SOV actives correctly was much superior to their performance on OSV actives, but there was no such difference between SOV and OSV passives. Hakuta concludes that if the subject marker *ga* is not on the first noun of a sentence, children cannot take advantage of the semantic information in the particle in interpreting OSV actives. If the semantic sequence is agent-patient-action, but the agent is not marked by *ga*, as in OSV passives, children are unable to benefit from the correspondence of the sentence to the canonical semantic sequence. Apparently, the presence of the agent marker *ni* after the first nominal in OSV passives blocks the agent-patient-action interpretation assigned to SOV actives beginning with a *ga*-marked nominal. Thus Japanese children's reversal of passive sentences is not based upon a fixed word order strategy, as appears to be the case in English, but rather, Hakuta concludes, upon the correlation between word order and case particles in expected positions. It is interesting to note that Slobin and Bever (1982) have made similar findings on the processing of sentences by Serbo-Croatian children. These children performed better on OVS sentences with accusative marking on the first noun than on OVS sentences with an unmarked first noun (neuter zero) and a marked subject (feminine nominative) on the second noun. These authors also conclude that a noun with nonstandard case-marking in initial position blocks the canonical sentence-processing strategy.

To acquire passive sentences, Japanese children must learn to re-interpret *ga* as marking the patient rather than the agent when passive morphology occurs later in the sentence. A critical factor in this reorganization may be focusing upon the *ni*-marked nominal, which indicates the agent in passive sentences. Sano (1977) found that when imitating sentences with passive verbs, children often supplied the particle *ni* if it was omitted from the model sentence, or substituted *ni* for some other particle in the sentence. As noted above, both Hakuta and Sano failed to find the large difference between SOV and OSV order with passives that is found with actives. It is interesting that a number of children acquire OSV passives before SOV passives, although this is extremely rare with actives. For example, in Hakuta's data, a higher percentage of children in group three, with an average age of 5;1, controlled OSV than SOV passives. Perhaps this is because OSV order in passives places the *ni*-marked nominal in sentence-initial position, where it can serve as an early trigger for applying a different processing strategy.

The role of specific morphological cues in developing processing strategies can be seen by comparing Japanese children's comprehension of passive sentences with their performance on OSV actives in which the initial object nominal has been topicalized. As noted earlier, in passive sentences, children must learn to take the *ga*-marked nominal to be the patient; this reinterpretation takes place in the context of the passive inflection on the verb, and, frequently, a *ni*-marked nominal somewhere in the sentence. Thus, there are morphological cues to indicate that *ga* will not have its typical interpretation as the agent marker in a transitive sentence. Experimental data from Sano's (1977) study suggest that it may be more difficult to re-interpret a familiar case particle when there are no such overt morphological cues to rely upon. In Japanese, any argument of a predicate may be topicalized with the particle *wa*. When subject or direct object is topicalized, the case particles *ga* and *o* are omitted and only *wa* appears on the surface. (In other cases, the original particle is retained and followed by *wa*.) Sano reports that the children in her sample tended to treat *wa* as an alternate subject marker; they understood SOV actives in which the subject was marked by *wa* just as well as sentences in which the subject was marked by *ga*. If instead an initial object nominal were topicalized, children had tremendous difficulty interpreting the sentence. The number of correct responses on O-*wa*SV actives was lower than other actives across the entire 3;3–6;8 year age range in Sano's study. Moreover, the responses on these sentences were even lower than on any type of passive sentence. Most probably, this is because N-*wa*NV sequences, which are common enough, typically do not have a patient-agent-action interpretation. For example, in what may be the most common sentence type with this configuration, *wa* marks the subject and *ga* marks what is sometimes analyzed as the underlying object of a transitive stative predicate, as in the following:

mama	*wa*	*ebi*	*ga*	*suki.*
mama	TOP	shrimp	SUBJ	like

'Mama likes shrimp'. (Lit., 'As for mama, shrimp are likeable'.)

In these sentences, *wa* marks the experiencer, which is semantically somewhat similar to an agent, and *ga* marks the object of experience. Thus OSV actives having the semantic sequence patient-agent-action with *wa* marking the patient force the child to re-interpret, in fact almost reverse, the meaning of this familiar configuration of case particles, although there are no overt morphological cues to trigger a new strategy. The extreme difficulty of these sentences as compared with passives suggests that it is easier to reorganize processing strategies when there are new local morphological cues which can be taken as signals to switch to the new strategy, as there are in passive sentences.

7.2.3. *Relative Clauses.* Experiments on the comprehension of sentences with relative clauses also indicate that children must undergo reorganizations in their strategies for sentence comprehension. Several studies in which children acted out and/or imitated sentences with relative clauses give insight into the strategies which children follow during this process of reorganization: Harada et al. (1976), K. I. Harada (1976), Hakuta (1981), Asano (1979).

In Japanese, relative clauses precede the head noun with no relative pronoun. There are only minimal cues as to the syntactic structure of sentences with

TABLE 4.13
Sample SOV Sentences with Relative Clauses
(From Harada et al., 1976)

SS:	(*kirin*	*o*	*taoshita*)	*zoo*	*ga*	*shika*	*o*	*nadeta.*
	giraffe	DO	knocked down	elephant	SUBJ	deer	DO	patted

'The elephant that knocked down the giraffe patted the deer.'

SO:	(*zoo*	*ga*	*taoshita*)	*kirin*	*ga*	*shika*	*o*	*nadeta.*
	elephant	SUBJ	knocked down	giraffe	SUBJ	deer	DO	patted

'The giraffe that the elephant knocked down patted the deer.'

OS:	*zoo*	*ga*	(*kirin*	*o*	*taoshita*)	*shika*	*o*	*nadeta.*
	elephant	SUBJ	giraffe	DO	knocked down	deer	DO	patted

'The elephant patted the deer that knocked down the giraffe.'

OO:	*zoo*	*ga*	(*kirin*	*ga*	*taoshita*)	*shika*	*o*	*nadeta.*
	elephant	SUBJ	giraffe	SUBJ	knocked down	deer	DO	patted

'The elephant patted the deer that the giraffe knocked down.'

TABLE 4.14
Surface Configuration of Case Markers
in Complex Sentences with SOV and OSV Word Order
in the Matrix Clause (From Hakuta, 1981)

	Matrix SOV Order				Matrix OSV Order		
SS:	(N-*o* V) N-*ga*	N-*o* V		SS:	N-*o*	(N-*o* V)	N-*ga* V
SO:	(N-*ga* V) N-*ga*	N-*o* V		SO:	N-*o*	(N-*ga* V)	N-*ga* V
OS:	N-*ga*	(N-*o* V)	N-*o* V	OS:	(N-*o* V)	N-*o*	N-*ga* V
OO	N-*ga*	(N-*ga* V)	N-*o* V	OO:	(N-*ga* V)	N-*o*	N-*ga* V

relative clauses: the embedded verb can only appear in plain, not polite, inflections, the topic marker *wa* is avoided, and the subject marker *ga* may be replaced with the genitive particle *no*. The examples on Table 4.13, taken from Harada et al. (1976), illustrate the formation of sentences with relative clauses in Japanese. There are four types of sentences, those with embeddings on the matrix subject, which also serves as the subject of the relative clause (SS), those with embeddings on the matrix subject, which also serves as the object of the relative clause (SO), those with embeddings on the matrix object, which also serves as the subject of the relative clause (OS), and those with embeddings on the matrix object, which also serves as the object of the relative clause (OO). The surface structure of these sentences, which have SOV word order in the matrix clause, is presented on the left side of Table 4.14.

Experimental studies conducted in English have tested children's ability to process sentences of these four types, but conflicting results have been obtained in different experiments, such as Brown (1971), deVilliers et al. (1979), Sheldon (1974), Smith (1974), and Tavakolian (1981). See Hakuta (1981) for a summary contrasting the results of these studies. The theories which have been proposed to account for these findings have been based on grammatical and/or perceptual factors, and make different predictions about comprehension. For example, Sheldon (1974) has set forth the "parallel function hypothesis," according to which sentences will be easier to understand if the relativized noun serves the same grammatical function in both the matrix and the embedded clauses. According to this hypothesis, SS and OO sentences should be easier to comprehend than OS and SO. An account in terms of perceptual constraints has been proposed by Slobin (1973), in the form of the operating principle "avoid interruption or rearrangement of linguistic units." This "anti-interruption" principle predicts that sentences in which the relative clause is center-embedded, interrupting the matrix clause, will be more difficult to process. Thus in English, SS and SO sentences, which have center-embedding, should be harder to comprehend than the right-branching OS and OO sentences. Since consistent results have not been obtained in English, Japanese data provide an interesting test of these hypotheses.

Results of experiments in Japanese indicate that the first types of embeddings which children can process are left-branching subject embeddings. Using semantically irreversible sentences, K. I. Harada (1976) found that her daughter was able to comprehend and imitate SS sentences correctly at 2;9–2;10 years-of-age. Using semantically reversible sentences, Harada et al. (1976) tested 98 children between 3;6 and 10;11 years-of-age, and found that children over 5 years-old performed correctly on sentences with subject embeddings, that is, SS and SO sentences, much more frequently than on OS and OO sentences. In the great majority of cases, children's errors were based upon failure to recognize a clause boundary between the first and second noun phrase in the center-embedded OS and OO sentences. Instead, they interpreted these as if they were conjoined sentences, for example, interpreting the OS sentence given above as if it were: 'The elephant knocked down the giraffe and patted the deer'. As the table of Japanese surface structures shows, the initial segment of OS and OO sentences follows the word order of simple NNV sentences; the children processed the initial NNV sequence as if it were an independent clause. This was more frequent in the case of OS than OO sentences, since OS sentences mimic not only the NNV word order of a simple sentence, but also the N-*ga* N-*o* V sequence of particles in a standard SOV active sentence. Harada et al. conclude that these findings are consistent with Slobin's anti-interruption principle, and also with the "juxtaposition hypothesis," namely, that complex sentences are at first processed as if they were juxtaposed clauses. (See Tavakolian's "conjoined-clause analysis," 1981.) Apparently, one way of avoiding interruption is to apply a conjoined-clause interpretation.[30]

Two further studies have confirmed these findings with statistical analyses. Asano (1979) tested 45 Japanese children aged 2;11 to 6;7 years, and found that children over 4;6 years old correctly acted out sentences with left-branching relative clauses, SS and SO, significantly more often than center-embedded OS

---

[30]In Japanese, the occurrence of ellipsis, especially of subject ellipsis, means that even complex sentences which do not begin with an NNV sequence may be interpreted as conjoined. Thus sentences with the configuration NVNNV may be analyzed as conjoined clauses of the form NV-NNV, with ellipsis in the first rather than the second conjunct. Taking into consideration the naturalness of this kind of ellipsis and of the resulting configuration of case particles, SS/SOV sentences seem the most likely candidates for this analysis. Thus the SS/SOV sentence from Table 4.13, *Kirin o taoshita zoo ga shika o nadeta* 'The elephant that knocked down the giraffe patted the deer', may receive a conjoined-clause interpretation, meaning approximately 'Having knocked down the giraffe, the elephant patted the deer'. This interpretation will yield the correct assignment of nominal arguments to predicates, and is probably responsible for the superior performance on SS/SOV sentences which has been noted in the Japanese studies of relative clause processing. It would be difficult to formulate predictions based on the application of a conjoined NV-NNV analysis to other sentence types, however, since certain combinations of first conjunct ellipsis and case particles are quite unnatural, and probably do not occur frequently enough in the input to children to serve as the basis for development of a conjoined-clause processing strategy which could be applied to sentences with relative clauses.

and OO sentences. Hakuta (1981) tested 12 children between 5;3 and 6;2 years old and also found significantly better performance on left-branching than center-embedded sentences. Again, there is support for the anti-interruption and juxtaposition hypotheses, whereas the superior performance on SO than OO sentences runs counter to Sheldon's parallel function hypothesis.

These findings leave open the possibility that grammatical role is the crucial factor in comprehension, since subject relatives in Japanese are consistently easier to process than object relatives. Since both SOV and OSV word orders are permitted in Japanese, it is possible to analyze the effects of grammatical role and center-embedding separately. Table 4.14 above, right side, summarizes the surface structure configuration of sentences with relative clauses which have OSV word order in the matrix clause. As the table shows, in these sentences, it is the subject relatives which are center-embedded and the object relatives which are left-branching. Harada et al. (1976), Asano (1979), and Hakuta (1981) have all investigated the role of grammatical vs. perceptual factors in experiments using sentences with OSV matrix order. Again, the results of these studies show that it is the sentences with center-embedding which are the most difficult; in each experiment, OS and OO sentences were correctly interpreted significantly more often than SS and SO sentences. Again, Slobin's perceptual anti-interruption principle, rather than an explanation based on grammatical role, is supported. The authors of these three investigations conclude that Slobin's proposal is the only one to date which can claim crosslinguistic validity.

The processing difficulty which sentences with relative clauses pose for the Japanese child can be understood by examining the sequences of case particles which occur in these sentences. Hakuta has proposed that in interpreting sentences with relative clauses, it is the "stacking" of case particles which children find difficult, rather than center-embeddedness per se. In SOV sentences, OO embeddings create a sequence of two *ga*-marked nouns; in OSV sentences, SS embeddings create a sequence of two *o*-marked nouns. Asano reports that some children over 4½ years-of-age in her study, when trying to act out OO sentences with matrix SOV order, would point out that they could not figure out which toy should perform the action because there were two *ga*'s in a row. The lack of particle stacking in SS/SOV sentences probably played a part in K. I. Harada's (1976) finding that her daughter acquired SS sentences before SO sentences. In SOV matrix order, only SS sentences allow the child to process constituents as they are heard, without being confused by repeated particles, or sequences of particles which mimic simple SOV sentences.

Hakuta (1981) investigated the effects of stacking in an experiment in which the second matrix noun of each stimulus sentence was postposed. This un-stacks the particles in complex sentences so that no two nominals with the same case-marking occur in immediate succession. Table 4.15, which presents configurations of surface structures from Hakuta's experiment, illustrates how postposing un-stacks particles; in these cases, the second matrix noun with its embedded

TABLE 4.15
Surface Configuration of Case Markers
in Complex Sentences With and Without Postposing
(From Hakuta, 1981)

	STANDARD	POSTPOSED
SS/OSV	N-*o* (N-*o* V) N-*ga* V	N-*o* V, (N-*o* V) N-*ga*
OO/SOV	N-*ga* (N-*ga* V) N-*o* V	N-*ga* V, (N-*ga* V) N-*o*

clause, is postposed. Hakuta analyzed the performance of 5;4–6;3-year-old children on SS/SOV, SS/OSV, OS/SOV, and OS/OSV sentences in both standard and postposed conditions. Comprehension of the center-embedded structures OS/SOV and SS/OSV was significantly better in the postposed condition, in which the particles were un-stacked. Hakuta concludes that it is the stacking of case particles which makes sentences with center embeddings difficult for Japanese children to process, leading them to make erroneous assignments of nouns to verbs in sentences of the configuration N(NV)NV.

Thus between the ages of 5 and 10 years, Japanese children reorganize their strategies for processing complex sentences, abandoning early attempts to process them as simple, conjoined sentences. This reorganization probably involves learning to recognize that successive noun phrases marked by the same case particle may be a local cue for embedding, and that finite verbs inflected for tense which do not occur at a clause-final intonation contour are always a sign of embedding. This reorganization must await development of short-term memory to the point where the assignment of nouns to verbs can be suspended until two clauses have been stored.

THE SETTING OF LANGUAGE ACQUISITION

8. Cognitive Pacesetting of Linguistic Development

8.1. Locatives

One type of evidence for the cognitive pacesetting of linguistic development can be found by comparing the order in which similar concepts emerge across different languages. Johnston and Slobin (1979) have analyzed the acquisition of locative expressions by children acquiring English, Italian, Serbo-Croatian, and Turkish, and found the following order of acquisition in the four languages: IN, ON, UNDER, BESIDE < BACK$_f$, FRONT$_f$, BETWEEN < BACK, FRONT. (Objects with inherent fronts and backs, such as trucks and houses, were called "featured objects.") This order of acquisition, the authors propose, reflects both cognitive complexity and language-specific linguistic complexities.

Although Japanese data on this topic are rather sparse and unsystematic, there is some evidence that Japanese children acquire locatives in a stable sequence.

My own data on one child between 1;11–2;4 years-of-age, as well as Miyahara (1974) and Okubo (1963, 1967, Chap. 2) provide some information on the order of emergence of case particles, including locatives. Usually the first locative to be acquired is *ni*, which covers the semantic range of English *in* and *on*, as well as *at* and *to*. Shortly afterwards in my data, but at the same time in some children (Okubo, 1967), the directional *e* 'to/toward' begins to be used. In my data, the next locative to emerge was *de*, which marks the place at which an action is being performed. The next two locatives which appear are *made* 'until/up to' and *kara* 'from'. *Kara* emerged first in my data, Miyahara's child, and one child cited by Okubo; these two locatives were acquired in reverse order by Okubo's daughter.

In my data, after several simple postpositions had emerged, locatives which are linguistically and cognitively more complex began to appear, such as the Japanese equivalents of 'beside', 'inside', etc. These expressions are formed by using the genitive marker *no* plus a series of nouns referring to specific locations, such as *ue* 'top', *naka* 'middle, inside', *shita* 'bottom', *soba* 'side', and *tokoro* 'place', followed by the locative *ni*, as in:

N   *no*   *shita*   *ni*
N   GEN bottom LOC
'under N'.

Since these forms are constructed in a manner quite similar to the corresponding Turkish locatives, Japanese would provide an interesting test case for the course of acquisition proposed by Johnston and Slobin (1979). Unfortunately, systematic data on the acquisition of these expressions by Japanese children are not yet available.

8.2. *Conjunctions*

On the basis of a variety of longitudinal and cross-sectional data from English, German, Italian, and Turkish, Clancy et al. (1976) hypothesized that there is a consistent, cognitively based order of emergence of the notions underlying sentence conjunction across languages. The authors found that the earliest relations between sentences included notions of symmetric coordination, antithesis,[31] sequence, and causality. Next, conditional notions emerged, followed by

---

[31]Clancy et al. (1976) categorize as antitheses cases in which the child rejects one proposition and asserts an alternative, as in *No mangiae gioco io* 'no eat I play', from an Italian child of 1;6 years. Since the authors were concerned with the meaning relations between clauses rather than specific conjunctions, they did not analyze the emergence of other types of adversative relations, which appear later. In contrast, Bloom et al. (1980) did not analyze such antitheses, which they classified as "anaphoric negation." In their English data, adversative relations were late in emerging, and the connective *but* did not appear until 2;8–3;2 years-of-age. Okubo (1967) does not cite examples of antithesis; her data on the emergence of explicit adversative connectives in Japanese are consistent with the findings of Bloom et al.

conditional and temporal uses of conjunctions corresponding to English *when.* The last development was the acquisition of *before* and *after.* Using detailed longitudinal data from four English-speaking children, Bloom et al. (1980) also found a consistent order of emergence of semantic relations in conjoined sentences (considering only those with explicit connectives): additive < temporal < causal < adversative. The first conjunction acquired by all the children was *and;* the other connectives, however, emerged in different orders in the different children.

At present, there is comparatively little longitudinal information available on the order of emergence of conjunctions in Japanese. However, the longitudinal data in Okubo (1967, Chap. 2) and Fujiwara (1977), as well as my own sample, are generally consistent with the crosslinguistic findings. The first conjunction acquired by the Japanese 2-year-olds in my sample, and by Okubo's daughter, was *-te,* which, like English *and,* covers the broadest semantic range of any connective. In adult speech, *-te* 'and/then/so' includes the meanings of coordination, temporal sequence, and causality, as well as instrumental and manner relations between clauses.

In my data, the earliest examples of *-te* occurred in sentences conjoining a main action with a clause expressing the manner or means in which the action was performed. For example, describing how to place one piece of a game on top of another, a child of 2;1 years said:

koo	*shi - te*	*nose*	*- ru*		*no.*
like this	do and	put on	NONPAST		EP

'You put it on like this'.

These sentences seem semantically similar to certain English sentences with object complements cited by Limber (1973), such as, *I show you how to do it,* which he found at about the same time as the earliest conjoined sentences. Other examples of the earliest uses of *-te,* such as the following sentence from Fujiwara (1977, p. 169), are instrumental:

basu	*n (= ni)*	*not - te*	*kaer*	*- u*	*no.*	2;0 yrs
bus	on	ride and	return (home)	NONPAST	EP	F

'I'll go home by bus'.

Apparently, certain of the earliest functions of conjoined sentences with *-te* in Japanese would not be expressed by conjoined sentences in languages such as English, making it difficult to compare the timing of their acquisition.

Other early instances of *-te* express the kinds of temporal and causal relationships which can be found among the early uses of English *and,* and the first conjunctions in other languages. For example, Fujiwara (p. 121) cites the following case, which is strongly causal/temporal as well as instrumental:

ocha non - de naor - u.
tea   drink and recover NONPAST

'I'll drink tea and recover'.

This sentence was produced by a child of 1;10, who had eaten something sour. Such use of *-te* to express sequence and causality is consistent with the findings of Bloom et al. (1980), who report that *and* was used for temporal and causal meanings before any other conjunctions were acquired.

Shortly after the emergence of *-te*, *kara* 'because' also begins to appear in conjoined sentences.[32] As discussed earlier in section 6.1.5, both *-te* and *-temo* 'even though' may occur at this stage to express permission and *-tara* 'when/if' to express prohibition. Ignoring these early uses, the next conjunction to emerge in Okubo's data and mine was *-tara* 'when/if' expressing temporal sequence and conditionality, as in the following example from Okubo at 2;1 years:

kaze hii - tara komar - u   deshoo.
cold catch if trouble NONPAST COP:PRESUM

'It will be too bad if I catch a cold'.

This initial phase of development, with *-te, kara,* and *-tara,* typically occurs during the first months of the child's third year, or somewhat earlier. The meanings expressed—manner, sequence, and causality—are similar to those found in other languages at this stage. The lack of coordination, or "additive" meanings with *-te,* which does serve this function in adult speech, is unexpected. Perhaps symmetric coordination with *-te* is not very frequent in Japanese compared with other languages, or perhaps this negative finding simply reflects the paucity of data on Japanese connectives at this point. The use of *-tara* in conditionals is precocious compared with English and other Indo-European languages, but such examples do occur very early in the more typologically similar Turkish (see Clancy et al., 1976). The lack of adversative connectives (other than *-temo* 'even though' in permission sentences) is also consistent with the findings of Bloom et al.

The next development which Okubo reports is the emergence of *-tari,* the alternative or representative inflection (see Jorden, 1963, Part 2, 27.1) used in presenting a series of similar actions or states. It is like additive *and* in English, except that it strongly implies 'and so on'. The earliest examples cited by Okubo use the same verb, as in:

omame ka - i   ni it - tari, nanka   kat - tari,
bean   buy INF to go REP something buy REP

---

[32]One child in my sample was using *kara* 'because' at the end of single clauses even before the first spontaneous examples of S-*te* S 'S and S'. As discussed in section 12.1.4, *kara* typically appears on single clauses before being acquired as a conjunction between two clauses.

oume	kat - tari,	jidoosha	kat - tari	su - ru		no	yo.
plum	buy REP	car	buy REP	do	NONPAST	EP	EMPH

'I will go to buy beans, and buy something, and buy plums, and buy a car'.

Thus this child's first use of -*tari* is quite similar to English *and* as a simple coordinator of interchangeable actions. The late emergence of -*tari* reflects its infrequency and greater semantic complexity compared with *and*. -*Tari* is also more difficult grammatically; it is typically used in a series of clauses, each marked by -*tari*, with *suru* 'do' as the main, tensed verb at the end of the list, as in the above example.

In the next stage of development, more sophisticated temporal connectives are acquired, including *to* 'when/whenever/if', which expresses both sequence and conditionality, and *toki*, a noun meaning 'time' which functions as a conjunction similar to English *when*. The earliest use of *toki* which Okubo (p. 228) cites at 2;3 years-of-age expressed both temporal sequence and conditionality, as do the early uses of *when* in English and other Indo-European languages (see Clancy et al., 1976):

mata	kureyon	na	- ku	nat	- ta	toki	kat - te	ne.
again	crayon	not exist		become	PAST	time	buy IMP	AGR

'When the crayon is used up, buy (one) again, alright'.

The earliest use of *to* at 2;5 years was similar:

Yachiyo (= Yachiko)	mama	soba	ne	- teru		to
Yachiko	mama	side	sleep	PRES.PROG		when

naka - na	- i		no.
cry	NEG	NONPAST	EP

'When mama sleeps beside me, I don't cry'.

A very late acquisition was -*nagara* 'while', at 3;8 years. Thus, the sequence of development for temporal connectives is generally consistent with the crosslinguistic finding that 'when' appears first in temporal sequences and conditionals, with later acquisition of conjunctions expressing simultaneity, such as 'while'.

The adversative connectives *noni* 'although' and *kedo* 'but' emerged at 2;4 and 2;5, respectively, Okubo reports. The examples cited indicate that both were used to express semantic opposition and/or denial of expectation, as in:

Yachiyo (= Yachiko)	takusan	tabe - ru		noni	akachan
Yachiko	a lot	eat	NONPAST	although	baby

tabe - na   - i   no.
eat   NEG   NONPAST EP
'Although Yachiko eats a lot, the baby doesn't eat'.

The emergence of adversative connectives after coordination, sequence, and causality is consistent with the findings of Bloom et al. (1980) on English. Although the data are sparse and somewhat inconsistent (Okubo cites various differences in the order of emergence of conjunctions in another child), the development of these clause-final connectives in Japanese seems similar enough to findings from other languages to warrant further investigation from the standpoint of cognitive universals. (See, also, Okubo, 1983, for further information on the acquisition of conjunctions.)

It is interesting that the order of emergence of the optional, clause-initial connectives in Okubo's daughter followed the same semantic sequence, at a somewhat later age. The first set of clause-initial conjunctions to be acquired were those expressing temporal sequence, *soshite* (2;2 years) and *soshitara* (2;3) 'and then'. Next came *sorede* (2;4), which implies causal and temporal sequence. At 2;7 years, *dakara* 'and so/therefore' appeared. The conditional *sorenara* 'if so' emerged at 3;2, and at 3;5 the temporal/conditional *suruto*. The last group of clause-initial connectives was the adversatives: *soredemo* 'even so' at 3;5 and *dakedo* and *demo* 'but' at 4;0 (Okubo, 1967, Chap. 1.4.4). Again, this parallels the sequence found by Bloom et al., with temporal, causal, and adversative conjunctions emerging in that order. Thus the development of clause-initial connectives in Japanese provides further evidence for cognitive pacesetting of the acquisition of conjunctions.

8.3. *Questions*

For many years, crosslinguistic evidence has been accumulating for a cognitively based order of emergence of question types. Studies of English-speaking children, such as Ervin-Tripp (1970) and Tyack and Ingram (1977) have suggested the following sequence of development: *what* < *where* < *why* < *how* < *when*. Ervin-Tripp proposes the sequence *what do* < *whose* < *who* between *where* and *why;* Tyack and Ingram suggest a later acquisition for *who*. Using detailed longitudinal data from Serbo-Croatian, Savić (1975) divided her twins' acquisition of question words into four stages. Each child followed the general sequence: I *what* < II *where* < III *who* < *how* < IV *why* < *which* < *when*, with *what kind* and *whose* appearing in Stage III in one child and stage IV in the other. One child acquired *how much* in stage IV.

Fortunately, there are detailed longitudinal data available from Japanese for comparison. Okubo (1965, 1967) provides a very complete description of her daughter's acquisition of different types of questions over the course of more than 3 years. In acquiring different types of questions, it is clear that this child

TABLE 4.16
Order of Emergence of Question Forms in One Child's Speech
(Based on Okubo, 1967, p. 167)

1;8	*nani*	'what'
	doko	'where'
	nani shiteru	'what doing'
1;11	*dare*	'who'
2;1	*dore*	'which' (of more than two)
2;3	*doo*	'how'
	donna	'what kind of'
2;5	*dooshite*	'why' (can also mean 'how')
2;6	*dotchi*	'which' (of two)
	(*dare no*[a]	'whose')
3;0	*naze*	'why' (more formal, less frequent than *dooshite* in speech to young children)
4;0	*ikura*	'how much'
4;10	*dono*	'which' (ADJ)
	itsu	'when'

[a]This form is not from Okubo's daughter, but occurred in other data (Okubo, personal communication).

followed a developmental sequence similar to that which has been found in other languages. Table 4.16 gives the age and order of emergence of these forms in Okubo's daughter. On the basis of data from several children, Murata (1968, p. 145) reports that the first question asked is *nani* 'what', which typically appears around 1;9–1;11 years-of-age. Iwabuchi and Muraishi (1968), examining the emergence of a more limited set of questions in the speech of one child, found a somewhat different sequence of development from Okubo. The child in their study used *nani* 'what', *doko* 'where', and *dare* 'who' at 1;8 years-of-age, and used *doo* 'how' as early as 1;7 years. However, *doo* 'how' was apparently not used again after its first occurrence until the child was 2;0-years-old. *Dore* 'which' emerged at 1;9, *dotchi* 'which' at 1;11, and *donna* 'what kind' at 2;8 years. Obviously, further research will be necessary to determine the extent of individual differences in the acquisition of different question types in Japanese.

However, in general, the Japanese data do fit the crosslinguistic order of emergence quite well. The data also suggest that there may be language-specific, as well as individual, differences in the emergence of question types. Thus in English *why* seems to precede *how*, whereas in Japanese (as in Serbo-Croatian), the reverse order holds. Also, although Ervin-Tripp proposes the sequence *whose* < *who* for English, the Japanese data show a clear lag between *who* and *whose*. As Okubo has pointed out (personal communication), in Japanese *dare no* 'whose' is morphologically complex, combining the question form *dare* and the genitive case particle *no*. Therefore, it seems unlikely that a Japanese child would acquire *dare no* 'whose' before the simple *dare* 'who'. Although data from a larger number of Japanese children would be necessary before any definitive claims can be made, the striking correspondence between the order of emergence in Japanese and in other unrelated languages provides further evidence for the cognitive pacesetting of the acquisition of different question types.

9. Linguistic Pacesetting of Cognitive Development

9.1. Numeral Classifiers

As noted in section 4.7, Japanese has numeral classifiers which categorize referents that are being counted on the basis of various dimensions, such as animacy, size, and function. The most detailed categorization occurs with inanimate objects, and among the different dimensions employed, shape or form is clearly one of the most important. For example, in the prototypical case, the classifier *-mai* is used for thin, flat, one-dimensional objects such as sheets of paper, *-hon* for long, thin, two-dimensional objects such as pencils, and *-ko* for small three-dimensional objects such as apples. Matsumoto (1984a, 1984b, 1984c) analyzes *-ko* as the unmarked Sino-Japanese classifier for inanimate objects in general, and *-mai* and *-hon* as shape classifiers. In any event, it is clear that shape is the earliest dimension to be acquired for inanimates; Matsumoto (1984b) found that *-ko, -mai,* and *-hon* are the first three Sino-Japanese classifiers to emerge for objects. Matsumoto (1984a,b) has found that the Japanese classifier *-tsubu,* which is used for tiny, grainlike objects and thus classifies by both shape and size, emerges next, followed by the function-based Sino-Japanese classifier *-dai,* which is used for cars and other land and air vehicles, furniture, machines and appliances.

It is possible that acquisition of these classifiers, which provide a linguistic organization of familiar objects into semantic categories, might have an influence upon children's conceptual development. Carroll and Casagrande (1958) tested this hypothesis in an experiment with Navaho children of 3–10-years-old. In Navaho, when using verbs of handling, it is obligatory to use one of a set of verbal forms depending upon the shape or form of the object being handled, such as long, rigid objects vs. round objects. In the experiment, children were shown two objects, and then were asked to tell the experimenter which of the two went best with a third object. As expected, children who were "Navaho-dominant" based their choices on similarity in shape or form, in accordance with the verb-stem classification in Navaho, rather than on size or color. The tendency to classify by form increased with age in both Navaho-dominant and English-dominant children, but the Navaho-dominant children based their judgments on form significantly more often and at an earlier age. A group of English-speaking children in Boston who performed a similar task also consistently chose form in preference to color and size at an early age; the authors suggest that this reflects early and frequent practice with toys of the form-board variety. Children's cognitive development, the authors conclude, can be influenced either by language or by appropriate cultural experiences. Japanese children, who begin to acquire form classifiers by about 2½–3 years-of-age, and who also play with modern toys emphasizing shape, might be expected to show an even earlier and stronger sensitivity to form over other dimensions of classification compared with American children. Clever investigation of conceptual organization and development in Japanese children acquiring classifiers might be able to provide evidence for linguistic pacesetting of cognitive development in the area of object classification.

9.2. *Social Cognition*

A language such as Japanese, which forces speakers to make many grammatical choices on the basis of social factors, probably has a strong effect upon the development of social cognition in children. The linguistic structure of Japanese, including such features as verbal inflections, pronouns, and sentence-final particles, informs children of important distinctions among people of different social roles and statuses, and of the inherent formality of certain kinds of interactions, such as those with people outside the child's family or peer group. Okuda's sociolinguistic survey (1979) of first-, fourth-, and sixth-graders shows that they differentiate linguistically between addressees of the same age and one year older than themselves at school, between members of the same and opposite sex, between family members and outsiders, and between adults with relatively high status occupations, such as the school principal, and those with lower status, such as bus drivers. Japanese children are exposed to linguistic differences correlated with social variables from a very early age, and are probably more sensitive to the social factors which trigger linguistic differences in Japanese, such as relative age, sex, and status of speaker and hearer, than are American children of comparable age. Furthermore, this sensitivity reaches the level of conscious awareness quite early in Japanese children. Horiguchi's data (1979b, 1981a), for example, show that the beginnings of such awareness emerge in some children before their third birthday; the girl of 3;1 years in my sample was obviously aware of stylistic differences in speech having a social/sexual basis. Okuda reports that even first-graders could answer questions about their use of *hai* 'yes' (polite) vs. *un* 'yes' (casual), as well as their use of polite verbal inflections with different addressees. In fact, the need to make the relevant linguistic choices in verbal interactions may be a major factor in bringing social structure to the conscious attention of Japanese children at an early age.

9.3. *Personal Identity*

The effects of the sociolinguistic structure of Japanese upon the child's developing sense of personal identity are probably most evident in the area of first person pronouns. As Ide (1978) points out, the act of self-reference has a great potential effect upon one's self-image. The Japanese system of pronouns makes social, sexual and contextual distinctions not only in how others are referred to, but also in how people refer to themselves. Therefore, acquisition of this system will probably affect the child's developing sense of identity, especially in the area of social and sexual roles. Ide concurs with the view that "personal identity is more consistent in the case of speakers of Indo-European languages, because 'I' is 'I' wherever one is and whomever one is talking to, whereas in Japanese personal identity is flexible and dependent on the position of speaker in relation to hearer within a given situation." The Japanese system of self-reference, by allowing different options, lets a person function in several different roles, and the existence of a special linguistic form for a particular range of social and emotional situations probably delineates each persona for the speaker. Since the form of self-reference chosen depends in part upon the addressee, there is in Japanese a very literal identification of oneself in terms of others.

Based on her findings on the forms of self-reference used by children from 1½ to 6 years-of-age, Ide (1977, 1978) analyzes how the Japanese system of pronouns shapes the child's developing sense of identity. Children's earliest sense of self, Ide assumes, is expressed in the forms which they first hear and use in referring to themselves: NAME + -chan for boys and girls, and also boku-chan 'I' for boys. (Recall that Japanese adults use boku 'I' as a form of second person reference in speaking to little boys, saying, for example, 'Does boku want to play?'). Ide considers the first developments away from these basic forms of self-reference to be indications of how the child's sense of identity develops, shaped by the available linguistic options. In her data, for little boys the next form of self-reference to develop was ore, which is based upon awareness of both speaker and hearer as masculine, emphasizes solidarity with a same-sex peer group, and occurs frequently in contexts where the child is swaggering and showing off, or involved in active play. For little girls the next form of self-reference to be acquired was (w)atashi, which reflects a formal attitude, at least compared with ore, and/or an affectation of maturity, as well as an awareness of themselves as female. Girls referred to themselves as oneechan 'older sister' outside the family, whereas boys did not extend oniichan 'older brother' in this way in Ide's data. Thus the familial, nurturing role was emphasized in the system of self-reference for girls. The affect and behavior associated with the pronouns girls and boys acquire is quite different: atashi is mature and well-behaved, ore is rough and rather wild. Ide points out that these developments away from the child's initial forms of self-reference lengthen the psychological distance between speaker and hearer for girls and shorten it for boys, since the girls' option, (w)atashi, is more formal than ore, which emphasizes a boy's solidarity with his peers.

At first, both boys and girls may occasionally use inappropriate first person pronouns which they hear frequently in their surroundings. For example, Horiguchi (1979a) reports that when they were 2-years-old, her son and daughter each sometimes used the first person pronoun appropriate for the opposite sex; thus, hearing her older brother use ore, the daughter imitated his usage, although only very rarely. Beyond such early imitations, especially after becoming aware of the sex differences governing correct usage at about 3 years-of-age, children usually stick to the first person pronoun appropriate for their sex.

Ide (1977) has suggested that the Japanese system of self-reference plays an important role in supporting and reinforcing stereotyped notions of male and female in Japanese society, since acquisition of this system fosters a definition of oneself in terms of these notions. What happens to the child who finds, in acquiring this system, that the linguistic options available do not coincide with his or her favorite persona? There is evidence that children are aware of the implications of the available forms of self-reference for the shaping of one's identity and behavior, namely, the existence of children who resist acquiring sex-appropriate forms of self-reference or who deliberately choose to use the first person pronoun of the opposite sex, at least on occasion. It is interesting that this seems to happen mostly with girls, who sometimes prefer to refer to themselves as *boku*, the most common first person pronoun for boys, rather than using the feminine (*w*)*atashi*. Ide (1977) found that girls of 5–6 years-of-age used *boku* to draw attention to themselves, especially when talking to their mothers.

In my data, there was a much more extreme case, a little girl of 3½ years who steadfastly insisted upon calling herself *boku* or *boku-chan* all the time, and not just for special effect. This girl had no brothers, just a very ladylike older sister; she herself was a tomboy with many friends among the little boys at kindergarten. The following dialogue was part of a continuing struggle in which her mother tried to get her to refer to herself as (*w*)*atashi* (*atashi* is a less formal variant, used only by women).

Mother: *watashi.*

Child: *boku.*

Mother: *watashi   deshoo.*
          I   COP:PRESUM
          'It should be *watashi*'.

Child: *boku   deshoo.*
          'It should be *boku*'.

As this example suggests, the use of appropriate male and female pronouns for self-reference is one of the few areas of grammar in which Japanese parents correct their children's errors. Fujiwara (1977, p. 151) also cites a case in which a girl of 1;11 years called herself *boku* and was immediately corrected by her father. The other 3-year-old girl in my sample used *atashi* very frequently, in fact, somewhat more often than an adult probably would. This child apparently enjoyed being *atashi* and liked to carry a toy pocketbook, imitate her mother's speech, etc. In contrast, the girl of the above example seemed to be rebelling rather violently against the social behavior characteristic of *atashi*, preferring to identify herself as *boku*, and allowed to engage in the loud, active behavior which kindergarten boys enjoy. Despite discussions and arguments such as the above, which certainly brought the issue to her conscious attention, this girl used *boku* very frequently and naturally in her conversation, just as the other child used *atashi*. Clearly, she was not just using *boku* to get a reaction from adults, but had acquired the form instead of *atashi* as her ordinary means of self-reference.

Use of *boku* by females sometimes continues well past the age of primary language acquisition. I have observed girls in the third grade refer to themselves as *boku* when playing active games with the boys. There is much anecdotal evidence that girls of even high school or college age refer to themselves as *boku*, usually among friends. Very rarely, a woman regularly refers to herself as *boku*; this is interpreted as a personal mannerism and/or an indication of pro-liberation sentiments. It will be interesting to see whether the pronoun *boku* gradually yields to this pressure from discontent females, who are reluctant to be limited to *atashi*. The current situation may reflect an early stage of linguistic change, which may lead to the addition of another first person option for Japanese women, who now have a more limited range of accepted linguistic (and social) choices than men.

10. Individual Differences

Although individual differences have not been a major focus of Japanese research in language acquisition, there are many examples of such differences in the literature. Unfortunately, it is usually very difficult to determine whether these are due to input differences, subtle linguistic differences between the examples being cited, as in the area of case particles, or differences in linguistic level across children of similar age. However, there are a few studies documenting different acquisition strategies used by individual children; recent papers, such as Okubo (1980, 1981a) and Komura (1981) may reflect an increasing interest in this topic among Japanese scholars.

10.1. *Noun-Dominant vs. Verb-Dominant Children*

Okubo (1981a) proposes that there are two main strategies which children follow in the transition process from the one-word to the two-word stage. This fundamental difference can be seen in the relative proportion of nouns to verbs in the speech of children during this period. The data for Okubo's study consist of approximately 14 hours of speech recorded during the course of a typical day from two siblings when they reached 2 years-of-age. The motivation for the comparative analysis came from Okubo's observation that the language development of a boy she had been studying was quite different from that of his younger sister.

The words of each child were divided into 15 parts of speech; nouns were the most frequent type for both children. However, the boy was clearly "noun-dominant" compared to his sister. In a type/token analysis, 72% of all his vocabulary items were nouns, and 45.5% of the total number of words he used in the sample were nouns. In contrast, only 58.0% of his younger sister's vocabulary consisted of nouns, and only 38.3% of the total number of words in her sample were nouns. The comparative frequencies of verbs were also strikingly different; the "verb-dominant" girl used a total of 23.9% verbs, whereas the boy used only 5.2%. Thus when the girl wanted to be read a storybook, she would say *Yonde* 'Read', using the imperative inflection; her older brother at that stage made the same request with the babytalk nominal *Jiji* 'Characters/writing'. Thus the same situation can be expressed using either a noun or a verb. It is interesting to note that Tanouye (1979) has found Japanese children to be verb-dominant compared with American children.[33] Language-specific patterns of encoding situations and structural factors such as word order may cause languages to differ along the dimension of noun vs. verb dominance, with individual differences existing within the range for any particular language.

These different strategies had implications for the acquisition of various other linguistic features. The girl, for example, had a greater variety of verbal inflections, which she used more frequently; she was also more advanced with respect to sentence-final particles, which typically follow the verb in adult Japanese. The boy, although more limited in the predicate position of his sentences, had more complex nominal arguments, including modifiers such as color terms.

These differences in noun vs. verb dominance also had interesting effects upon the nature of early two-word utterances in the children's speech. Okubo (1980) reports that the verb-dominant girl tended to use *kore* 'this' and people's names as fixed "pivots" in her two-word utterances, with a wide range of predicates and sentence-final particles. In contrast, the noun-dominant boy used a few simple predicates, such as *nai* 'does not exist' and *akai* 'red' as "pivots," and predicated these of a wide range of different nouns. Thus the patterns established during the one-word period continued into the next stage, and provided each child with a different means of breaking into the creation of productive two-word combinations. These findings are quite similar to those made by

---

[33]Tanouye (1979) analyzes the utterances of two children acquiring Japanese, and gives the percentage of "function," "action," and "substantive" forms. Although various studies of English-speaking children have found that verbs are acquired later than nouns, Tanouye found that at the one-word stage (MLU 1.1 for one child, 1.08 for the other), only 16% and 22%, respectively, of all utterances were substantives. Furthermore, in Japanese, the "function" of existence is expressed by the verbs *iru/aru* 'exist', and non-existence by the adjective *nai*. Also, in contrast with English, the great majority (94%) of all "action" forms in Japanese were verbs. Thus there is a very high frequency of verbs in early Japanese language development. (At a later stage, the frequency of substantives in the children in Tanouye's sample increased to a level comparable with the children of 2;0 in Okubo's study.)

Lieven (1980), who has also investigated individual differences and the continuity between one- and two-word stages, using data from three children acquiring English.

Certain differences between the two children in Okubo's study may have been the result of birth order. For example, within the category of nouns, the boy more frequently labeled objects and their colors; in contrast, the girl had a much higher frequency of references to people. This suggests an early pattern of mother-child interaction focusing on objects with the first child, but more social contacts with the second; such a difference could obviously result from the presence of another child and his friends. Similarly, the girl frequently used the quotative particle *tte* as a sentence-final form; at 2 years, her brother did not use this particle even once. As Okubo points out, the older brother probably did not have as much opportunity to report the speech of others to a third party as his sister did, who would frequently be in a context including her brother and another person. The girl referred to herself by name 145 times as compared with only 25 examples in her brother's data; she also had a much higher frequency of request forms in *-te*. Both differences Okubo attributes to birth order. As the second child, the girl probably had a greater need to distinguish herself from her brother and emphasize her own wishes. In fact, this motivation for acquiring the *-te* inflection, which marks requests, may have contributed to the girl's early focus on verbs.

Thus early environmental differences may foster the development of different approaches to language acquisition. Once the child has focused upon a particular type of language use, such as labeling objects, reporting speech, or requesting actions, this may lead to the development of certain grammatical areas over others. Thus a child who reports speech with a sentence-final particle may become more interested in other sentence-final particles; a child who is not interested in objects may not be motivated to acquire grammatical means of expressing object attributes with modifiers. Clearly, the social context of language acquisition, as well as personality and cognitive differences, must be taken into account in understanding individual differences in language development.

10.2. Genitive Constructions

Komura (1981) analyzes the differences between two children in their acquisition of genitive N *no* N constructions, focusing primarily upon possessives. Each child was recorded at 1–2 week intervals from 1 year-of-age to somewhat over 2 years. Two different courses of development were observed. One child first expressed possession by single nouns referring to possessors while pointing at the object possessed. Next, the genitive particle *no* emerged and was used after the possessor, as in *Toochan no* 'Daddy's'. Then constructions with two nouns emerged, first simply juxtaposed, as in **neechan tokei* 'older sister's watch', or with a vague sound between the nouns. Later, the full adult form *neechan no tokei* 'older sister's watch' emerged. Thus in this child, the acquisition of genitive constructions with two nouns did not seem to be derived directly from the temporally prior stage of N *no*. In this child, the sequence of development was: N < N *no* < NN < N *no* N. In contrast, the other child started using both single possessor nouns and N *no* at the same time. Next, full N *no* N forms emerged without the intermediate step of NN. Juxtaposed nouns did appear, but only after N *no* N had been acquired; they were very rare and dropped out quickly. In each child, other types of genitive constructions, such as those expressing apposition, time, place, quantity, etc., emerged later than possessives, but followed the same sequence of development.

Thus for the first child, the acquisition of genitive constructions apparently involved an extra step, in which adult N *no* N was first simplified by omission of the linking *no* before the full construction emerged. As noted in section 7.1, this is apparently a very common course of development in Japanese children. It is interesting to note that the second child, who skipped this stage, showed an extremely rapid pace of acquisition. The first child used single nouns at 1;5 years, N *no* at 1;6, NN at 1;7 and N *no* N at 1;8, whereas the second child used both N and N *no* at 1;4, and was using N *no* N later in the same month. Moreover, the frequency of the construction in each child's speech was quite different. The first child did not have five instances of N *no* until 1;8, or of N *no* N until 1;11, whereas the second child used at least five instances of both N *no* and N *no* N within the first sample in which each construction appeared.

Thus in the slower, and perhaps more typical, course of development, children gradually learn to add explicit surface markers of semantic intention to unmarked nominals; in these children, the semantic intention clearly precedes the ability to express that intention grammatically (see Slobin, 1973). The omission of *no* in two-noun constructions after it has been acquired with single nouns suggests the continued pressure of a slowly lifting cognitive ceiling on the linguistic means of expressing semantic intentions in production. In children who are developing more slowly, the limits of this ceiling apparently apply first to the production of an unmarked semantic relation, then to the production of the grammatical marker, creating four stages in the acquisition of genitive constructions: N < N *no* < NN < N *no* N.[34] When the acquisition process is greatly accelerated, the constraint on production seems to apply in only two stages, to single nouns and then to two-noun constructions. In this case, overt surface marking of the intended semantic relation does not seem to appreciably increase the cognitive demands, and the grammatical marker appears as soon as the "content words." This makes sense, since grammatical morphemes often, as in Japanese genitive constructions, merely mark redundantly what is already being

---

[34]As expected, this production constraint seems to apply only at the early stages of development. Komura reports that both children acquired N *no* before N *no* N in sentences which contained only a single constituent, such as *Watashi no* '(It's) mine' or *Watashi no hon* '(It's) my book'. In each child's speech, N *no* also emerged before N *no* N in two-constituent sentences, e.g. ones including both subject and predicate, but N *no* N became frequent earlier in these sentences. By the time three-constituent sentences were being used, N *no* N appeared before N *no*.

adequately conveyed in context by more telegraphic means (see Brown, 1973). As the individual differences in Komura's study suggests, the addition of a content term in a semantic relation presents children with a more difficult cognitive task than the addition of redundant morphological markers.

10.3. *Numeral Classifiers*

As noted earlier in section 4.7, one of the problem areas for Japanese children is the acquisition of numeral classifiers. Matsumoto (1984c) reports on individual differences which he found in children's use of numeral expressions in various experimental tasks. In these counting tasks, children generally tended to prefer Sino-Japanese numerals and classifiers to the native Japanese forms. However, individual children differed in their degree of preference for the Sino-Japanese forms. In one counting task, children were asked to count cups and erasers, which can take either Japanese or Sino-Japanese forms, and mountains and clouds, which take only Japanese numerals with the unmarked *-tsu* classifier. On the basis of their responses, Matsumoto divided the children into two groups: a "Sino-Japanese group," who used Sino-Japanese numerals, alone or with the classifier *-ko,* which Matsumoto analyzes as the unmarked Sino-Japanese classifier for objects, on 6 or more of the 8 items, and a "Japanese group," who used Japanese numerals with the unmarked Japanese classifier *-tsu* on 6 or more of the 8 items. Of the 25 Tokyo first-graders in one experiment, 11 preferred Japanese forms, and 16 Sino-Japanese; in an experiment on 31 Kyoto children aged 5;6–6;5 years, 6 preferred Japanese forms and 12 Sino-Japanese. The children's preferences were manifest in certain of the other counting tasks as well. The "Japanese group" correctly attached the Japanese classifiers *-ka* for days and *-tsubu* for small, grainlike objects to Japanese numerals, whereas the "Sino-Japanese group" was more likely to make errors overgeneralizing Sino-Japanese forms, saying, for example, *san-nichi* instead of *mik-ka* 'the third day (of the month)', or attaching a Japanese classifier like *-tsubu* to a Sino-Japanese numeral.

Counting in Japanese provides an interesting case in which more than one form is available for the same function. Matsumoto's findings indicate that, faced with two different series of numeral expressions for counting, children tend to stick to either the Japanese series or the Sino-Japanese one. Thus there is support for Slobin's claim (1985) that children prefer a one-to-one correspondence between form and function. Sanches (1977) also reports that some of the young children in her study of numeral classifiers stuck to the Japanese forms with *-tsu;* others, however, began using Sino-Japanese numerals and classifiers for lower numbers while relying on the Japanese forms with *-tsu* for numbers above two or three. This finding, as well as the differences in degree of preference among Matsumoto's subjects, suggest that some children may adhere more strongly than others to the one form-one function principle. It would be interesting to investigate whether different children's degree of adherence to the principle of one-to-one mapping results in consistent profiles of individual differences in the acquisition of various linguistic subsystems.

10.4. Processing Strategies

Both Hakuta (1982) and Sano (1977) report individual differences in the sequence in which different types of sentences are acquired. Both authors found that most children had acquired SOV active sentences by about 3½ years-of-age. However, of children who controlled two types of sentences, some had mastered OSV passives, but not OSV actives, whereas other children had mastered OSV actives, but not passives. These individual differences may reflect cognitive differences shaping the kinds of processing strategies which children formulate. Some children may be more sensitive to specific local morphological markers, whereas others rely more heavily upon word order in processing sentences. Children who acquire passive sentences before OSV actives apparently find it easier to formulate an entirely new processing strategy, using different morphological cues, such as the agentive particle *ni* and the passive inflection, than to change the word order of their existing agent-patient-action strategy. Children who acquire OSV actives before passives apparently experience greater difficulty in dealing with a new configuration of morphological markers and/or greater flexibility in changing the word order of an existing processing strategy.

There is some striking evidence of differing degrees of dependency upon word order from the experiments on sentence processing. Hayashibe (1975) reports that three children in his study of active sentences consistently interpreted all OSV sentences as if they were SOV, ignoring case particles completely. In their studies of active and passive sentences, Sano (1977) found two children, and Hakuta (1982) found three, who correctly interpreted all SOV actives and all OSV passives, and consistently reversed the interpretation of all OSV actives and SOV passives. Clearly, these children had formulated an extremely rigid agent-patient-action strategy for processing sentences and were oblivious to morphological cues such as the case markers on the nouns and the inflections on the verbs. The other children in Hakuta's study were usually sensitive to at least the subject marker *ga* when it appeared on the first noun in a sentence.

Of course, longitudinal data would be necessary to verify that these findings represent real individual differences rather than different stages in the same course of development or simply experimental "noise." However, at this point it seems likely that some children focus upon more global, gestalt aspects of linguistic input, such as relative word order, whereas others rely more upon local cues. Such individual differences would probably have definable influences throughout the course of acquisition. Ultimately, they might prove to be dependent upon very general aspects of cognitive style, such as field dependency, which could be measured independently and correlated with linguistic findings.

11. Input and Adult-Child Interactions

At this stage, there is various research available on the nature of adult input to Japanese children, but little on the effects of typical patterns of adult-child interaction upon language development. It is often pointed out that Japan, like the United States, is a "child-centered" society (see Fischer, 1970), and certain aspects of the linguistic input to very young children, such as frequent use of directives, questions, and expansions in both countries, reflect this orientation. As in America, it seems that the primary source of verbal input to Japanese children is usually their mother; Okayama (1979) reports that 83.9% of the mothers of 31 2-year-olds in her study said that the person who talked to the child most was the mother.

In keeping with the greater emphasis in Japan upon differentiating social status linguistically, the babytalk register is much more developed than in America, and is used by mothers to a later age (Fischer, 1970). Fischer suggests that this is indicative of the Japanese indulgence of dependency, as contrasted with the American push for precocity, which reflect the very different attitudes toward children in each country. As Fischer proposes, extensive use of the babytalk register in Japan emphasizes the status of the child as such, which is consistent with the more hierarchical nature of family and social structure in Japan. Chew (1969) analyzes the structure of the babytalk lexicon in Japanese, and Murata (1960) examines the use of babytalk words in a large sample of 1-year-olds. Sanches (1968, Chap. 3) discusses the morphology and acquisition of babytalk forms by three 2-year-olds.

In this section, I will consider those features of mothers' speech to Japanese 2-year-olds which may have an influence upon their acquisition of grammar, and their development of the characteristically Japanese indirect communicative style.

11.1. *Expansions and Paraphrases*

Two features of English-speaking mothers' speech which are frequently assumed to facilitate children's grammatical development are paraphrases and expansions. As Brown (1973, p. 106) points out, expansions provide children with a complete, grammatical version of their semantic intention at the moment when they are concentrating on expressing that intention with their current, limited grammatical means. Similarly, Cross (1977) suggests that mothers' self-repeating paraphrases, which frequently juxtapose both full and abbreviated versions of the same message, provide the child additional opportunity to process the original utterance, and also illustrate ways of encoding the same intention at different degrees of complexity. Hearing these different options while trying to understand a particular message may be important in revealing to the child the functions of certain forms, such as verbal inflections.

Research on mother-child interaction in Japan indicates that both expansions and paraphrases occur in the input to 1-year-old children. For example, Murata and Ohara (1966) recorded 41 mothers interacting with their 1-year-olds, and found that they repeated their children's speech very frequently. Almost all of these were "corrective imitations" or expansions. Mothers of children aged 1;3–1;5 expanded 14.5% of their children's utterances, and mothers of children aged 1;6–1;8 expanded 25.4% of their utterances. Thus as children reached the stage where grammatical development usually begins, at about 1½ years-of-age, the frequency of maternal expansions increased. Studies of English-speaking mothers have found different frequencies of expansion: Cross (1977) reports that expansions constituted 20.5% of maternal input to the 1;7–2;8-year-old children in her sample, whereas Newport et al. (1977) found only 6% expansions in the speech addressed to children of 1;10–2;6 years. Although it is not possible to compare frequencies with the data available, it is clear that expansions are an important feature of mothers' speech to Japanese, as to English-speaking, children.

Data on English-speaking mothers also indicate a high frequency of self-repetitions or paraphrases. Newport et al. (1977) report that 23% of the mothers' utterances in their sample were exact or partial renditions of the same content; Cross (1977) found a rate of 28.2%. In my sample, many such sequences occurred in the mothers' speech to 2-year-olds. As Newport et al. and Cross also found, paraphrases were especially common in sequences of imperatives, where they served to ensure comprehension, or, as Gleason (1977) has discussed, to guide and direct the child's behavior. Thus sequences such as the following were typical:

(to her daughter of 2;1 years old)

ja,	*sono*	*teeburu*	*katazuke - te*		*choodai.*
well	that	table	clean	CONT	please

soko	*ja*	*- nai,*	*hako*	*no*	*naka*	*ni*	*ire - te*
there	COP+TOP	NEG	box	GEN	inside	in	put CONT

ki	*- te.*
come	IMP

hako	*no*	*naka*	*ni*	*mada*	*mada*	*mada,*	*hako*	*no*	*naka*	*ni*
box	GEN	inside	in	still	still	still	box	GEN	inside	in

ire - te		*ko*	*- nakya.*
put	CONT	come	OBLIG

mada,	*motto,*	*asoko*	*no*	*ue*	*katazuke - te*		*choodai.*
still	more	there	GEN	top	clean	CONT	please

ja,   o-katazuke   shi - te.
well   cleaning   do   IMP

'Alright, please clean up that table.
Not there, put them inside the box.
Inside the box, still still still, you must put them inside the box.
Still, more, please clean up on top of that.
Alright, clean up'.

In this sequence, the imperative in -*te* is modeled repeatedly, with and without the polite *choodai* 'please'. Both the ordinary imperative *katazukete* 'clean up' and the special babytalk form *o-katazuke shite* 'do cleaning' with the *o-* nominal prefix, verb stem, and *suru* 'do', appear. The concatenated VERB + *kuru* 'come' construction appears twice, both in the affirmative *irete kite* 'put in and come' and the negative of obligation *irete konakya* 'must put in and come'. (The form *ko-nakya* is short for *ko-nakya ike-nai/nara-nai/dame* 'not coming won't do', which roughly corresponds to English *must*.) As this example suggests, the verbal inflections appearing in sequences of paraphrases are extremely varied. In two hours of tape, I found the following verb forms exemplified in sequences of paraphrases in the speech of the mother of the above example to her 2;1-year-old daughter: the imperatives -*te* and -*nasai,* optionally with *yo* (emphatic) or *choodai* (casual) and *kudasai* (formal) 'please'; the non-past V-*ru* 'you will V'; benefactives with *ageru/kureru* 'give'; conditionals with -*tara* and -*(r)eba* 'if'; aspectual concatenated verbs, such as V-*te miru* 'V and see' or its babytalk equivalent V-*te goran;* conjoined sentences with V-*cha dame* 'V-ing is no good' and V-*nakute mo ii* 'not V-ing is alright'; questions of the type V *n ja nai* 'isn't it that one V's' and V *deshoo,* the presumptive form of the copula meaning approximately 'shouldn't one'; the cohortative -*oo* 'let's'. Thus sequences of paraphrased directives served as a kind of substitution drill for verbal inflections, with several major forms contrasted in sequence for the child. Since these are precisely the inflections which are being mastered by young 2-year-olds, the tendency to paraphrase directives with these forms may well facilitate their acquisition.

Paraphrases may also play a role in the acquisition of different speech styles. In my data, paraphrases addressed to young 2-year-olds who were not yet using polite inflections productively sometimes juxtaposed both plain and polite verb endings. For example, as the above mother was playing "hostess" with her daughter using polite inflections, she said:

tsukat - te   ii   desu   ka? tsukat - te   ii?
use   CONT   good COP:POL Q   use   CONT   good
'Is it alright to use it? Is it alright to use it?'

In the first question, the polite form of the copula, *desu,* is used after the adjective *ii* 'good', which is how adjectives are inflected for politeness. The second question simply uses the plain style *ii* 'good'. The question marker *ka* appears in the first sentence. As noted in section 5.1, *ka* is used by women when they are using polite inflections; in plain style, it is common in men's speech. Thus this sequence also exemplifies the use of *ka* in polite style and its omission in plain style in women's speech.

11.2. *Directives*

A striking feature of the speech of Japanese mothers to their 2-year-olds in my sample was the high frequency of explicit directives, as illustrated above with respect to paraphrases. Murata and Ohara (1966) report that an average of 12.7% of mothers' utterances to children of 1;3–1;5 years old and 17% of utterances to children of 1;6–1;8 were *yookyuu* 'requests', a category which included questions as well as imperatives. These frequencies seem roughly comparable to the 18% frequency of directives reported by Newport et al. (1977) and the 7.4% found by Cross (1977). Okayama (1979), however, found a higher frequency of directives, 22.5%, in the speech of mothers to 31 2-year-olds who were taped during the course of an entire day's activities. Apparently Japanese mothers are, if anything, even more directive than American mothers.

The high frequency of directives in Japanese mothers' speech, along with their high percentage of questions (see section 11.4 below), reflects a style which seeks to keep children involved in interaction and to control their behavior. Azuma et al. (1979) have analyzed the relationship between a highly directive maternal communicative style and the performance of Japanese children on a number of cognitive measures. In an analysis of "control strategies," 58 Japanese mothers were given a set of hypothetical situations calling for adult intervention, and were asked to respond with exactly what they would say if their child were present. Direct physical intervention and demands for compliance made with no rule or reason were categorized as "appeals to authority." Use of this authoritative strategy correlated positively with the children's performance on seven different cognitive tasks, such as number conservation, literacy, and spatial ability. In contrast, in a sample of 67 American mother-child pairs from the same study, reliance upon "appeals to authority" correlated negatively with children's performance on six out of the seven tasks. From a social point of view, one might speculate that in a society which emphasizes conformity and hierarchical relationships, maternal input which is highly directive is a good preparation for successful functioning, whereas in a society which emphasizes individualism and independence, excessive emphasis upon obedience to authority figures puts children at a disadvantage. On the personal level, the meaning of an authoritarian style may be quite different in each culture, reflecting different attitudes toward the child, which in turn have different effects upon cognitive development.

11.3. *Verbal Instructions*

In my sample, many of the directives which Japanese mothers addressed to their 2-year-olds consisted of explicit instructions in what the children should say in various situations. These instructions occurred either in the course of ordinary interactions or within role-playing routines. Much of this instruction was aimed at teaching children the many polite verbal formulas in Japanese, which are much more numerous than in English, and cover a much broader range of situations. The verbal formulas taught to 2-year-olds include greetings such as *Ohayoo* (*gozaimasu*) 'Good morning', *Konnichi wa* 'Good day', *Oyasuminasai* 'Good night', and the polite expressions *choodai* or *kudasai* 'please' for requests. Japanese children also learn many formulas with no fixed English equivalents, such as *Itadakimasu* (Lit.) 'I receive it', said before eating, *Gochisoosama deshita* 'It was a fine meal', said after eating, *Doozo* 'Please/help yourself/go ahead', *Tadaima* 'I'm home', and *Itte kimasu/mairimasu* 'I go and will come back', said upon leaving the house. Mothers in my sample said these formulas for their children in appropriate situations, attributed them to characters in picturebooks, and called their children's attention to the forms when they were used by other people. The mothers frequently prompted their children to use polite formulas when the occasion arose. In the following case, when my assistant had picked up something for a child of 1;11 years, his mother said, *Hora, ochichatta yo. Arigatoo wa? Oneechan ni arigatoo tte yuu deshoo* 'Look, it fell. What about thank you? You should say "thank you" to older sister'. Mothers seemed to take every opportunity to comment on and reinforce the use of polite formulas, as in the following case, when the same child at 1;11 was talking about his father's departure that morning:

Child: *Bai-bai tte itta no.*
           'He said "bye-bye"'.

Mother: *Itta no ne. Papa nante itta? Itte mairimasu tte itta deshoo. Itte mairimasu.*
           'He said it, didn't he. What did papa say? He said, "I go and will come back," didn't he. "I go and will come back"'.

The finding that mothers of 2-year-olds provide so much instruction in the use of these verbal formulas is consistent with the research reported in Hess et al. (1980). In this study, Japanese mothers expected earlier mastery of social courtesy, such as greetings, than American mothers.

Japanese mothers also provide children with a considerable amount of instruction in appropriate verbal behavior which is somewhat less stereotyped than polite formulas. In role-playing routines in my data, mothers created certain types of social interactions, and then demonstrated to their children, with explicit instructions, how to behave and what to say. For example, after starting to eat, it is polite to comment that the food is delicious. If a child does not say *Oishii* 'It's delicious' spontaneously, the mother may ask whether the food is delicious. In the following exchange, the mother demands that her child of 2;1 years make this comment, when she had been eating without saying anything:

Mother: *Oishiku nai no? Tabenai de ii yo. Moo gochisoosama shite choodai. Sore moo ii kara.*

          'It's not delicious? You don't have to eat it. Please finish eating. You've had enough of that'.

Child: *Iya!*

          'No!'

Mother: *Soshitara oishii tte iwanakya.*

          'Then you must say, "It's delicious"'.

Child: *Oishii.*

          'It's delicious.'

Mother: *Oishii nee.*

          'It's delicious, isn't it?'

Children are also instructed in the proper behavior for a host/ess serving guests. In my data, 2-year-olds were taught to ask their guests what they wanted to eat, to say *Doozo* 'Help yourself' when offering food, to ask *Oishii?* 'Is it delicious?' after the guests began to eat, to ask if the food was too hot or cold, and whether the guests wanted more to eat. In role-playing routines, children were also taught how to speak on the telephone. For example, one mother would demonstrate to her child what to say to his grandmother on the phone, teaching him to inquire about her health and to invite her to visit. Such play included instruction in the use of polite style through modeling, as in the following example to a child of 2;2 years:

Mother:	*o*	*- genki*	*desu*		*ka*	*tte*	*chanto*	*iwa - nakya,*
	HON	healthy	COP:POL		Q	QUOT	properly	say OBLIG
	hora.							
	listen							

'Listen, you must say, "How are you?"'.

Here the mother uses the honorific prefix *o-* on the word *genki* 'healthy', and the polite form of the copula, *desu,* with the question particle *ka,* as is typical of questions in polite speech. Thus instructions in what to say in particular situations incorporate information about which speech register should be used as well.

11.4. *Question-Answer Sequences*

Another major feature of the child-centered verbal input to English-speaking children is a very high frequency of questions. Newport et al. (1977) cite a frequency of 44%, and Cross (1977) gives 33.4%. Figures for Japanese indicate a somewhat lower frequency of questions: Okayama (1979) reports 18.7% in her sample of mothers' speech to 2-year-olds. Since the studies on English found lower frequencies of imperatives than Okayama, it may be that English-speaking mothers phrase directives in question form more frequently than Japanese mothers.

Aksu-Koç & Slobin (1985) have pointed out the role of question-answer sequences in exemplifying grammatical morphology to Turkish children. Noting that inflectional suffixes remain the same across both question and answer, they propose that this kind of interaction may direct the child's attention to the morphology. In Japanese, the importance of question-answer sequences in ex-emplifying verbal inflections may even be greater, since questions often consist of a single predicate, with the nominal arguments ellipted. Moreover, an ex-tremely common response to a yes/no question in Japanese is a full predicate, rather than a single-word 'yes' or 'no' answer, as is common in English. Jap-anese children, for example, if asked *Taberu?* ''Will you eat?', very often reply *Taberu* 'I will eat' and not just *Un* 'Yes'. Children apparently learn to answer questions this way very early. Tanouye (personal communication) has found that mothers of Japanese children just over 2 years old often answer their own questions with full predicates, which may be how children acquire this pattern of response. Having learned to answer questions in this way, Japanese children incidentally receive a tremendous amount of practice in a variety of verbal inflections simply by answering their mothers' questions. In my transcripts of 2-year-olds, most imitative utterances were answers to yes/no questions. Further-more, these answers seemed to be grammatically progressive in the youngest child in my sample, a boy of 1;11 years. New inflections tended to appear first and to be most common in answers to questions, with spontaneous usage appear-ing a few weeks later.

The Japanese pattern of asking questions about alternatives may also contrib-ute to the acquisition of verbal inflections. In Japanese, the typical way of asking questions about two contrasting possibilities does not involve verbal ellipsis as in English sentences, such as *Will you eat an apple or a tangerine?*. Rather, two distinct sentences repeating the predicate are used, as in the following:

ringo	*tabe - ru?*		*mikan*	*tabe - ru?*	
apple	eat	NONPAST	tangerine	eat	NONPAST

'Will you eat an apple? Will you eat a tangerine?'

This pattern serves to increase the frequency of verbs and verbal inflections in the input to Japanese children. In cases of affirmative and negative alternatives, the

Japanese child receives explicit modeling of the contrast between the difficult
negative inflections and the more common affirmative forms, as in the following
example from my data:

oishi	- i?	oishi	- ku	na	- i		no?
delicious	NONPAST	delicious		NEG	NONPAST		EP

'Is it delicious? Is it not delicious?'

Clearly, such questions could be valuable to the child who is having difficulty
acquiring the negative inflection of adjectives with -ku.

Question-answer exchanges may also play a part in the acquisition of case
particles in Japanese. For example, in my data, it was clear that these sequences
were fostering acqustion of the topic marker wa in one girl of 2;1 years. This
child at first used wa only in one-word questions, such as Papa wa? 'What
about/where is papa?'. In declarative sentences, this child used wa only in the
answers to questions with wa, such as the following:

(Child is giving out blocks)

Mother: *mama   wa?*
           mama   TOP
           'What about mama?'

Child: *mama   wa   kore.*
           mama   TOP   this
           'Mama gets this one'. Lit., 'As for mama, this one'.

(pointing to characters in Heidi storybook)

Adult: *kotchi   wa   dare?*
           this   TOP   who
           'Who is this?'

Child: *kotchi   wa   neesan.*
           this   TOP   older sister
           'This is older sister'.

Thus in her replies to questions with wa, this child builds her sentence upon the
preceding utterance. This strategy produces grammatical results, since the topic
of a sentence in Japanese, unlike the subject, is not restricted to a limited set of
semantic relations with the predicate. The child probably developed this strategy
by observing the responses to her own N wa? 'What about N?' questions.

Question-answer sequences of this type exemplify the grammatical structure of sentences with topics, and probably facilitate their acquisition.

11.5. Communicative Style

Compared with Western languages, the typical style of communication in Japanese is intuitive and indirect. The basis of this style is a set of cultural values which emphasize *omoiyari* 'empathy', and are so widely shared that overt verbal communication often is not required. Thus in Japan, the ideal interaction is not one in which speakers express their wishes or needs adequately and addressees understand and comply, but rather one in which each party understands and anticipates the needs of the other and fills them before any verbal communication becomes necessary. Silence is more highly valued in Japan than in the West; if all is going well, there should be no need for speech. Ito (1980) points out that excessive verbalism has traditionally been looked down upon in Japan, especially for men. This attitude, he notes, is revealed in traditional sayings, such as *Iwanu ga hana* 'Silence is better than speech'. If verbal communication enters in, it will not be explicit; rather the speaker will rely upon the hearer's ability to realize what s/he means, often in spite of what is actually said. This style of communication can cause tremendous problems for Americans, who discover to their frustration that 'yes' often means 'no', but cannot figure out when. (See Loveday, 1982, and Ueda, 1974, who gives "Sixteen ways to avoid saying 'no' in Japan.")

In Japan, people are often consciously aware of these differences in communicative style, and most Japanese who have had contact with Americans can articulate these values explicitly, on the basis of many misunderstandings. For example, Japanese visitors to this country often point out that in Japan, an offer of food should ideally be refused three times before accepting. Of course, the host must realize that the guest is actually hungry and merely exhibiting appropriate *enryo* 'reserve'. Most Japanese who come to America can expect to suffer a period of hunger before learning that offers of food will be made only once, and will probably raise a few eyebrows by their unseemly boldness in accepting offers quickly upon returning to Japan. Clearly, the Japanese system of communication can work only in a homogeneous society, in which people actually can anticipate each other's needs and wants. Universal expectation of empathy fosters *amae*, dependency or relying upon the indulgence and patronage of others. Doi (1973) has analyzed how this concept pervades both individual and social psychology in Japan.

How does a Japanese child learn this intuitive, indirect style of communication? Studies of early mother-child interaction have revealed patterns emphasizing non-verbal communication at an extremely early stage. For example, in a study of 30 Japanese and 30 American infants of 3–4 months old, Caudill and

Weinstein (1974) have found that Japanese mothers talk to their children significantly less often than American mothers, and Japanese children had significantly lower rates of "positive vocalization" than the American children. On the other hand, the Japanese mothers were together in the same room with their children, even while they were sleeping, significantly more often than American mothers, and responded quickly to soothe and care for their child's needs upon any negative vocalization. Caudill and Weinstein conclude that "it is as if the majority of the American pairs had reached an 'agreement' to be talkative, while the majority of the Japanese pairs had reached an 'agreement' to be silent." Thus, as early as 4 months-of-age, Japanese infants have developed a pattern of silent togetherness with their mothers, whereas American infants have learned to interact with their mothers vocally.

My data on a much later stage of development reveal patterns of verbal interaction with 2-year-old children which could foster acquisition of an intuitive, "mind-reading" style of communication. Japanese mothers teach their children to pay attention to the speech of others, to intuit and empathize with their feelings, to anticipate their needs, and to understand and comply with their requests, even when these are made indirectly.

For example, in my data, the 2-year-olds would sometimes become engrossed in their own actions and fail to notice the attempts of others to engage them in conversation. The mothers did not allow this to continue; when their children failed to respond to someone, they would explicitly focus the children's attention upon the person who was trying to interact. Mothers often repeated other peoples' utterances,[35] indicating to their children that they must pay attention and respond to the speech which is addressed to them. It was common for mothers to repeat questions which their child had failed to answer, as in the following case:

> (Child is serving imaginary food on toy dishes)

> Adult: *Mahochan nanika tabeten no? Koko nani ga haitten no?*
>   'Are you eating something? Is there something in here?'

> Child: (doesn't respond)

> Mother: *Nani ga haitten no kana. Oneechan nani ga haitten no tte kiiteru yo.*
>   'I wonder what's in it. She's asking, "What's in it?"'

If someone made a request, mothers frequently repeated it, indicating that the child must comply immediately.

---

[35]Pye (1982) reports that Mayan mothers also often repeat the speech addressed to their children. The Mayan mothers also frequently spoke for their children, and this occurred in my data as well, although not as frequently as attributing speech to others.

Indirect speech is especially characteristic of certain types of polite interactions, such as between host/ess and guest. In my data, 2-year-olds received practice and instruction in the use and interpretation of indirect speech in role-playing host/ess-guest routines with their mothers. In these routines, a mother would often explicitly tell her child what to say to the guests or to prepare and offer a certain type of imaginary food. In expressing requests for themselves, however, mothers frequently simply stated a wish, such as, Mama suupu mo hoshii naa 'Gee, I'd like soup too'. The sentence-final particle *naa* often follows expressions of inner feelings and wishes, and conveys a sense of monologue. Sing-song intonation with a very long vowel also occurs, adding to the impression of talking to oneself. Mothers sometimes even affected indifference to the presence of the child, even gazing away. However, the 2-year-olds seemed quite aware that these wishes were actually to be treated as imperatives, perhaps because they were sometimes accompanied by an explicit directive, as in the following case:

mama	*supagechi*	*ga*	*ii*	*naa.*	*tsukut - te*	*kudasai.*
mama	spaghetti	SUBJ	good	EXCLAM	make CONT	please

'Gee, I'd like spaghetti. Please make some'.

If a child failed to understand an indirect request, the mother might "translate" it into a more explicit expression. For example, on one occasion my assistant wished to end a routine in which a child of 2;1 years kept serving her food, and the following interaction took place:

Adult: *moo   ii   desu.*
         already good COP:POL

         (Lit., 'It's already good'.) 'I've had enough'.

(Child continues serving imaginary food)

Mother: *moo   ii   tte   oneesan.*
         already good QUOT   older sister

         'She said, "I've had enough"'.

(Child continues serving)

Adult: *hai. moo   onaka   ippai desu.*
         yes already stomach full COP:POL

         'Thank you. I'm full'.

Child: (serving) *mii.*
                   milk

         '(Here's some) milk'.

Adult: *doomo gochisoosama deshi   - ta.   a,   kondo   kore*
        very   fine meal   COP:POL PAST   oh   this time   this

        wa   mii   desu   ka?
        TOP   milk   COP:POL   Q

        'Thank you for the fine meal. Oh, now is this milk?'

Child: *suupu   na   no.   suupu.   suupu.*
        soup   COP   EP   soup   soup

        'It's soup. Soup. Soup'.

Adult: *hai,   hai,   hai.*
        yes   yes   yes

        'Thank you. Thank you. Thank you'.

Child: *jaa,   jaa,   jaa.*
        alright alright alright

        'Here. Here. Here'.

Mother: *moo   oneesan   iya tte,   moo   ii   tte*
        already   older sister no   QUOT   already   good QUOT

        mii   wa.
        milk   TOP

        'She said, "I don't want anymore, I've had enough milk" '.

At this point, the child discontinued the game. In this sequence, the mother begins by repeating the phrase *moo ii* without the polite *desu* for the child. When the child ignored this, and continued serving despite the more explicit *Moo onaka ippai desu* 'My stomach is full', and the polite *Gochisoosama deshita* 'It was a fine meal', which is said at the end of a meal, the mother intervenes again. In her last utterance, she quotes my assistant as having said *iya,* which is a very strong refusal meaning approximately 'I don't want it'. She juxtaposes this with the less direct expression *moo ii* 'already good', my assistant's first utterance, clarifying for the child that this should have been interpreted as *iya* 'I don't want it'. Thus Japanese mothers teach their children to read behind the polite statements of others, understanding them as expressions of strong feelings and wishes with which the child must comply.

Not only do children learn to comply with explicit and implicit requests, they are also taught to anticipate the needs of others, before anything is actually said. One common behavior for all three mothers of 2-year-olds in my sample was to attribute speech to people who had not actually spoken, in order to indicate to the child what they might be thinking and feeling. For example, when children played host/ess, their mothers would attribute requests for food to other people.

They also often did this when the child was eating something alone. For example, when one child of 1;11 years was eating a tangerine, his mother suddenly said, *Oneesantachi mo tabetai tte* 'The girls also say, "We want to eat," although we had not said anything. Thus Japanese mothers train their children to anticipate the unspoken wishes of others.

Empathy is especially important in order to avoid inconveniencing or annoying other people. The mothers in my sample were quick to point out cases in which a child had caused someone trouble; again, this was often done by attributing thoughts or speech to someone who might appear to be silently content. When a child imposed upon someone, even if the person willingly complied, the mother might indicate that such behavior is not appreciated. For example, when a child of 1;11 years asked my assistant to peel a tangerine for him, and she was doing this very amiably, his mother said, *Oneechan jibun no muite taberu tte ne* 'Older sister says she'll peel and eat her own'. Such examples indicate to the Japanese child that there may be a difference between what people seem to feel and what they are really thinking.

Mothers frequently attributed feelings of pain to others, especially if the child was responsible but had failed to notice or apologize for causing the pain. For example, when the toy dishes of a child of 2;1 years fell on my assistant, her mother immediately said, *Neechan itai-itai tte* 'Older sister says "ouch, ouch" ' before anything had been said. Feelings were even attributed to inanimate objects. When a child of 1;11 years kept dropping apples on the floor, his mother said, *Sonna koto suru n dattara ringo-san itai itteru wa yo* 'If you do that kind of thing, Mr. Apple says "ouch" '. As these examples suggest, mothers often attributed speech to others as a way of correcting their child's behavior. For example, when a boy of 2;4 years was getting very loud, pretending that he was firing guns, his mother attributed a request that he stop to his stuffed animal *Kikochan: Kikochan bikkuri shiteru yo. Kikochan yamete kudasai tte. Gomennasai tte. Kikochan ga itai tte* 'Kikochan is amazed. Kikochan says, "Please stop." Say, "I'm sorry." Kikochan says "ouch." ' Mothers often pointed out to children when they were misbehaving that others did not approve of their behavior, attributing very direct statements of disapproval or correction to people who had not spoken. For example, on one occasion when a child of 2;1 years was loudly refusing to sing a song and yelling *Dame!* 'No!', his mother said: *O, kowai, Yotchan, oneechan kowai tte. Yotchan kowai naa, Yotchan dame nante yuu kara, kowai, kowai* ' "Oh, I'm afraid of Yotchan," older sister says, "I'm afraid. Gee, I'm afraid of Yotchan because he says 'no'. I'm afraid, I'm afraid." '

Consistent with these findings, Azuma et al. (1979) and Conroy et al. (1980) report that "appeals to feeling" function as a control strategy among Japanese mothers, who invoke the feelings of others as the rationale for a child's good behavior. In a study of 58 Japanese and 67 American mother–child pairs, each

500 Clancy

mother was given a set of hypothetical situations, such as being in the super-market with a disruptive child, and was asked to respond as she would if the child were actually present. In analyzing the results, Azuma et al. report, the category "appeals to feelings" had to be created because of its frequency among the Japanese mothers, who used this strategy at a frequency of 22%, compared with only 7% among the American mothers. In these responses, Japanese mothers said that they would ask the child to consider how they felt as the mother, or how the child would feel if someone else did the same thing. As in my sample, this study found that Japanese mothers appealed to the feelings of third parties and even of inanimate objects, as in "The wall will feel sad." Although these appeals to feelings often function as control strategies, they can also be viewed as providing children with explicit training in empathy, lessons in how to guess what others are thinking and feeling even when they have not spoken. It is consistent with the very different styles of verbal communication in Japan and America that American mothers thought of using this strategy so much less frequently than Japanese mothers.

Through their training in empathy, Japanese mothers teach children not only to be sensitive to the needs and desires of others, but also to fear their criticism and disapproval. Benedict (1946) has discussed how Japanese children are inculcated with a fear of ridicule and ostracism. As Ito (1980) points out, familial approval is dependent upon more general social approval, upon children's conducting themselves in a manner which will uphold their family's good name. Japanese mothers, Ito notes, often threaten a misbehaving child with the ridicule of other people, saying *Hito ni warawareru* 'You will be laughed at by other people'. This strategy locates the source of disapproval and constraint outside the mother, in society at large.

Japanese mothers also frequently convey their own reactions directly to their children, yet in these cases too, the reactions tend to incorporate the opinion of Japanese society. In my sample, the clearest examples of this were mothers' use of the words *okashii* 'strange' and *hazukashii* 'shameful/embarrassing'. These reactions label for the child the behaviors which are not expected and/or socially disapproved, and indicate how to feel in such situations. For example, when a 2-year-old boy was asked to bring over some toy cars, he refused, whined, and started to cry. His mother said,

okashii   yo,   nai - tara.
strange   EMPH   cry   if
'It's strange, if you cry'.

The word *hazukashii* frequently means 'shy', and children are often asked if they feel *hazukashii* in situations where they are the focus of attention, as when they have been asked to perform for guests. The word is also used with a sense closer to 'ashamed' when a child has misbehaved in front of other people. In such cases, mothers will simply say *hazukashii*. Typically no explicit subject is used; *hazukashii* conveys both the mother's own feeling and the strong implication that the child should feel the same way. For example, when a girl of 2;2 years in my sample was about to leave the house with her parents and guests, she wet her pants, and then ran away from her mother as she was trying to wash her. Her mother pointed out that everyone was watching, and repeatedly said *hazukashii*.

Kasahara (1974) suggests that Japanese child-rearing practices, which attempt to control the child's behavior by appealing to the disapproving gaze of others, may contribute to a fear of eye-to-eye confrontation, which is common among young adults in Japan, but virtually unknown in the West. In this neurosis, people experience a phobia of being stared at by others, and in severe cases, fear that they cannot control their own eyes, and prevent their stares from inflicting undue pain upon others. The strong emphasis on *Hito ga miteru* 'People are watching' from early childhood, Kasahara proposes, may foster the development of personalities which incessantly watch, and dread being watched, by those outside their family circle.

In this light, it is interesting to note that very young children in Japan may at first strongly resist internalizing their mothers' *hazukashii* and the disapproval of watching eyes. For example, the 2-year-old in my sample who wet her pants responded to her mother's *hazukashii* with a resounding, *Hazukashii chigau!* 'I'm not ashamed!'. This is probably because Japanese adults do not actually expect very young children to measure up to the social norms of self-restraint and discipline until the school years. As Benedict has pointed out, the "arc of life" in Japan is a U-curve with the greatest freedom and indulgence enjoyed by babies and the elderly, and the low point of greatest restriction during the prime of life, especially just before marriage. From an American point of view, child-rearing in Japan tends to be permissive. An American's blood will boil to watch the boyish temper tantrums which Benedict describes, in which a child of 3- or 4-years-old screams and pummels his mother, while other family members stand patiently by. Yet an examination of mothers' interactions with 2-year-olds reveals that, in their comments and attitudes toward their children's unrestricted or selfish behaviors, they are already sowing the seeds for the social constraints to be imposed by the watching eyes of *hito* 'other people'. The permissiveness of the early years actually increases mothers' opportunities to present such evaluations over a long period of time. When the period of early indulgence is finally over, Japanese children will be quite familiar with which behaviors are *okashii* 'strange', and which should make them feel *hazukashii* 'ashamed'. Early training in empathy thus leads Japanese children to understand the feelings and expectations of others, and also to experience the expected feelings themselves. This sets the stage for successful functioning of the Japanese indirect, intuitive mode of communication.

CONCLUSIONS

12. Theoretical Conclusions

Slobin (1973) has proposed that certain constraints on children's perception and production of speech, and on their organization and storage of linguistic rules, can be formulated in terms of universal operating principles which are brought to bear in acquiring language. The data on Japanese acquisition provide evidence for certain basic tendencies underlying the encoding and decoding of speech, and the organization of form and function in developing grammars. In addition to cognitive pacesetting, Japanese data reveal the importance of affect and pragmatic developments in the early stages of language acquisition.

12.1. *Encoding/Decoding Principles*

12.1.1. *Perceptual Salience.* Slobin (1973) has suggested that children have a tendency to pay attention to the ends of units, acquiring word-final elements, such as suffixes and postpositions, earlier than word-initial elements, such as prefixes and prepositions. There is considerable evidence in the data on Japanese acquisition for a perceptual bias favoring the ends of units. The earliest grammatical acquisitions are those which occur not only at the ends of words, but also at the ends of utterances, as do sentence-final particles. Verbal inflections, which become productive late in the one-word stage, very frequently occur at the ends of sentences, since Japanese is usually verb-final. Certain very early case particles, such as the genitive *no* and the topic marker *wa,* also frequently appear at the ends of sentences, as in *Papa wa?* 'What about/where is papa?' and *Papa no* 'It's papa's'.

At an early stage, this perceptual bias may have discernible effects throughout a child's speech production. In my sample, one child of 1;11 years produced a rather large number of utterances which were almost completely incomprehensible except for the last syllable, usually a verbal inflection or sentence-final particle. In a smaller number of utterances, only the first and last syllables were clearly articulated. The frequency of both types of utterances decreased over the course of about 2 months, but it was clear that this child's initial focus was upon producing the ends of units correctly.

Selective attention to the ends of units, and to a lesser extent the beginnings of units, leaves medial position as the most vulnerable. The acquisition of morphology in Japanese provides ample evidence for children's failure to process morphemes which are "sandwiched" between familiar elements. For example, the form *ja,* which is a contraction of the copula *da* plus the topic marker *wa,* is typically omitted in sentences of the form N *ja-nai* 'It's not an N', where it is sandwiched between a familiar noun and the negative predicate *nai.* Similarly, the particle *to* may at first be omitted from the construction N *to chigau* 'It's not an N/it's different from N', and the genitive *no* is often omitted from N *no* N constructions. The -*ku* inflection, which is suffixed to the stem of adjectives preceding the negative inflection, seems to be omitted by all children in the early stages of negating adjectives.

The only striking exception to this general tendency to omit morphemes in medial position is -*te,* the continuative inflection. This inflection appears in medial position in compound tense/aspects, such as the present progressive/resultative -*teru,* and in concatenated verb structures, such as benefactive and aspectual constructions of the form V-*te* V. In this case, children have already acquired the -*te* form of many common verbs as a verb- and often utterance-final imperative. Therefore, the V-*te* form is familiar and salient, whereas the following verb may be unfamiliar, and at first even not understood. Moreover, the form of the verb preceding -*te* cannot occur alone; due to phonological processes such as voicing, place of articulation assimilation, and consonant gemination, this form would be unpronounceable, and has never been heard in the input. Thus familiar morphemes which form a single phonological unit with the preceding element may be exempt from the general vulnerability of medial position. Similarly, the familiarity of *no* as a possessive in N *no* constructions may be responsible for the fact that some children do not omit it in N *no* N constructions. Thus familiarity and/or semantic salience can over-ride the filtering process, but usually children do not attend to medial position as well as initial or final position when processing input.

12.1.2. Intonation.   In addition to these biases, it appears that non-segmental, gestalt aspects of linguistic input, such as intonation and word order, have a perceptual advantage over local, segmental cues in the acquisition of certain areas of Japanese grammar. For example, in the development of questions in Japanese, there is some evidence that intonation may be processed earlier than morphological markers. Yoshida (1977) found that one child responded to certain types of questions at the age of 2;4 only if they were uttered with rising intonation. Three months later, he was able to respond to these questions even if falling intonation was used, apparently because he had learned to recognize the sentence-final morphemes as potential question markers regardless of intonation. Yoshida proposes that it may be easier for young children to focus upon intonation than upon morphology. Intonation is probably also an important factor in the early acquisition of sentence-final particles in Japanese.

12.1.3. Word Order.   The data on Japanese acquisition supports Slobin's (1973) proposal that children are sensitive to the sequential order of input words and morphemes at a very early age. Japanese children at the two-word stage are already producing sentences with constituents postposed after the verb, as well as sentences with the canonical verb-final order. This finding, which is consistent with the crosslinguistic data, provides further support for the view that a capacity for processing and storing sequential aspects of linguistic input may be inherent in the child's mechanisms for perceiving and storing information.

There is also some evidence in the Japanese data for the primacy of word order over case particles in processing sentences; this is consistent with findings on German acquisition (Mills, 1985). Hayashibe (1975) reports that in his study of SOV and OSV active sentences, comprehension based on case particles emerged later than word order strategies. Frequent ellipsis of the direct object marker *o,* and the semantic inconsistency of the subject marker *ga,* probably contribute to children's greater reliance upon word order in Japanese. In languages such as Turkish, where inflections are regular but word order is much more variable than in Japanese, children are able to rely upon inflectional endings at an extremely early age (Aksu-Koç & Slobin, 1985). In Japanese, where word order is more consistent, it is apparently preferred over morphological strategies at an early age.

12.1.4. *Contextual Support.*   In language production, one factor which affects children's ability to encode information is the availability of contextual support, as Slobin (1985) proposes. In my data, a clear example of this can be found in the acquisition of the conjunction *kara* 'because'. In Japanese, *kara* is often used elliptically; the speaker presents a reason and leaves it to the listener to deduce the statement or request which follows from it. For example, if the addressee is resisting accepting a favor, it is common to say *Ii kara* 'Because it's alright', leaving implicit 'let me do it'. In my data, the first uses of *kara* were of this type. For example, one child of 2;1 years accidentally tore a page in his sister's book, and in the resulting uproar, as his mother sought to appease his sister, he said:

(h)att   age - ru   kara,   mama.
paste   give   NONPAST   because   mama
'Because I'll paste it for her, mama'.

Here the child is ellipting the conclusion that everyone should stop getting excited, and gives only the reason: that he will paste the page together again.

This elliptical use of *kara* also emerged first in the speech of another 2-year-old in my sample. For example, talking to her father, who was practicing English with me and not paying attention to her, this child angrily said,

dame   kara[36]
no good   because
'Because it's no good'.

---

[36]Since *dame* is a nominal adjective, it should be followed by the copula *da* before adding a conjunction. Therefore, the correct form is actually *Dame da kara,* with the copula *da* preceding the conjunction *kara.*

leaving implicit the conclusion that he should stop speaking to me. Similarly, Okubo (1967) reports that her daughter used *kara* at the end of a single clause at 1;10 years old, 1 month before its first appearance as a conjunction between two clauses. Thus the earliest instances of *kara* are linked to a context in which the ellipted proposition is obvious, rather than to another explicit clause.

In my data, one 2-year-old reached the next stage, in which *kara* appeared in single-clause responses to *dooshite* 'why' questions. In these cases, the child's subordinate clause is linked with the proposition in the prior utterance. Aksu (1975) has found that causal connectives in Turkish emerged in response to adult questions before appearing in conjoined sentences. Thus the course of acquisition of *kara* in Japanese suggests that it is easiest for the child to link a proposition to the nonverbal context, somewhat harder to conjoin a proposition to a prior utterance, and most difficult to produce both clauses of a conjoined sentence without contextual support.[37]

12.2. *Form/Function Principles*

The crosslinguistic data suggest that children have certain inherent preferences for the organization of form and content in grammars. Many of the errors which occur follow directly from the basic principles that underlying semantic notions should be overtly and clearly marked, and that the use of grammatical markers should make semantic sense (Slobin, 1973). However, the Japanese data suggest that in certain cases, either form or content may take precedence, and the child may temporarily ignore one or the other in the early stages of acquisition.

12.2.1. *Surface Structure Configuration.* For example, in the very early stages of acquiring case particles, Japanese children may use newly emerging particles in a random way. At this stage, the children seem to know that in Japanese, a noun is typically followed by a case particle, which together form a single intonational unit. When children come to recognize NOUN + PARTICLE as a typical surface structure configuration, they may add case particles after nouns even when they do not know which particle is required. It is interesting that this tendency to create a canonical surface structure seems to take precedence, at least in some children, over Slobin's principle that "the use of grammatical markers should make semantic sense." Perhaps this provides further evidence for the relative importance of intonation compared with morphology in the early stages of language development.

---

[37]In contrast, Bloom et al. (1980) report that in three English-speaking children, the use of connectives to chain a child utterance to the nonlinguistic context developed at the same time as syntactic uses linking two clauses. A fourth child acquired contextual before syntactic uses. It should be noted, however, that contextual use of *kara* 'because' in Japanese is much more frequent in colloquial adult speech than contextual use of *because* in English. Bloom et al. also found that two of these children first used *because* both in answer to adult *why* questions, and to connect clauses within a single sentence. The other two children first used *because* in answers to *why* questions, as did the one child in my sample who advanced beyond the stage of contextual sentence-final *kara*.

12.2.2. *Semantic/Pragmatic Processing.*   The reverse tendency can be observed in the early stages of acquiring sentence processing strategies. Experimental data on Japanese 3-year-olds show that they tend to ignore morphological markers, such as case particles, and syntactic devices, such as word order, and process input on the basis of semantic/pragmatic factors. Hayashibe (1975), Hakuta (1982), and Sano (1977) all report that even before the age at which morphological or syntactic processing strategies emerge, children interpret sentences by picking out the most likely agent of the action from the two nouns given. Similarly, K. I. Harada (1976) found that at 2;8–2;10 years-of-age, her daughter was able to understand sentences with relative clauses which described experiences which had occurred in her own life, but misinterpreted complex sentences which were not consistent with her experience. These findings, which are not, of course, limited to Japanese, support the priority of semantic/pragmatic processing over morphological/syntactic strategies in the timing of language acquisition. Thus whereas form may sometimes take precedence over function in the speech production of very young children, in their processing of linguistic input, formal devices may be ignored in the search for meaning.

12.2.3. *Semantically Transparent Marking.*   There is considerable evidence in the Japanese data for the proposal that children prefer clear and overt marking of semantic information (Slobin, 1973). The errors which occur indicate that children acquire semantically empty or opaque forms late, prefer overt to zero morphemes, replace syncretic with analytic options where possible, and have difficulty acquiring discontinuous morphemes and interrupted linguistic units.

In the early stages of acquiring Japanese morphology, children tend to eliminate semantically empty or opaque forms, probably at first filtering them out in perception as well as production. For example, in the negative *-kunai* inflection on adjectives, the *-ku* has no real semantic function, since *-nai* marks negation and non-past tense. The data indicate that children go through a stage of omitting *-ku* and suffixing *-nai* directly to the non-past form of adjectives. Similarly, allomorphs which are not recognizable to the child are typically omitted, such as *na,* the form of the copula *da* which precedes sentence-final *no,* and *ja,* the form of the copula contracted with the topicalizer which precedes the negative inflection. (As noted above, the perceptual "sandwiching" effect contributes to the vulnerability of these morphemes.) Similarly, the non-past inflection of adjectives,*-i,* is very different from the more common verbal non-past marker, *-(r)u,* and children do not recognize *-i* as a tense marker at first, either on adjectives, or on the negative inflection *na-i.* This vowel is not omitted, since it is taken as the base form of adjectives, but is not analyzed as the non-past inflection for a long time.

12.2.4. *Overt Marking.*   Slobin (1973) has proposed that zero morphemes violate the "clear and overt" constraint, and that "if a category is sometimes marked by Ø and sometimes by some overt phonological form, the latter will, at some stage, also replace the Ø.'' There is a striking example from Japanese acquisition which supports this proposal: the extremely common overgeneralization of the genitive particle *no*. When a noun is modified by another noun, it must be preceded by the genitive particle *no* in the construction N *no* N. In contrast, adjectival and relative clause modifiers simply precede the head noun with no overt morphological marker. Japanese children very often go through a stage of extending *no* to follow adjectival as well as nominal modifiers. Thus *no* is strongly preferred to zero marking of prenominal modifiers.

Children's preference for overt marking can also be observed in the development of processing strategies for different types of sentences. The Japanese data suggest that it is easier for children to change an established processing strategy if there is some overt morphological cue to signal that a change is necessary. For example, passive sentences have two overt morphological cues indicating that the subject should not be interpreted as the agent: the agent marker *ni* on a nominal other than the *ga*-marked subject, and the passive inflection -*(r)are* on the verb. In constrast, OSV actives with topicalized objects do not incorporate any new particles or inflections, but do require the child to interpret a *wa*-marked noun as the patient, although *wa* does not usually mark patients. Sano (1977) has found that passive sentences are comprehended earlier than O-*wa*SV actives; one reason may be the overt markers available to trigger passive processing strategies.

12.2.5. *Analytic vs. Syncretic Marking.*

Japanese data also provide evidence for the view that children prefer analytic over syncretic marking. For example, in denials of the form N *janai* and N *to chigau* 'It's not an N', the negatives *janai* and *chigau* follow independent forms and do not require segmentation and affixing. Japanese 2-year-olds who have learned to use *janai* and *chigau* in denials may overextend them, adding them on after finite verb forms instead of suffixing a negative inflection to the verb root. Similarly, in expressing the negative past, 2-year-olds will sometimes simply add the negative nonpast -*nai* after a finite verb in the past tense rather than affixing the conflated form -*nakatta* to the verb root.

12.2.6. *Contiguous Marking (The ''Anti-Interruption'' Principle).*

There is support in the Japanese data for Slobin's proposal that children tend to preserve the structure of linguistic units, and to process one unit at a time. This principle is clearly operative in Japanese children's acquisition of complex sentences. Since Japanese does not have relative pronouns, the only mark of embedding is repetition of case particles and optional genitive marking on the subject. Several studies have shown that sentences with center-embedded relative clauses are interpreted as if they were conjoined sentences. That is, children assume that they are processing an uninterrupted main clause, and treat the initial NNV segment in sentences of the form N(NV)NV as a single unit. The anti-interruption principle, which presumably reflects very general constraints on perception and short-term memory in young children gives an explanation of certain findings on complex sentences in English which is also applicable to the Japanese data.

12.2.7. *Formal Consistency.* Perhaps the simplest and clearest type of marking which a grammar may have is a one-to-one correlation between form and function. Slobin (1985) proposes that if a language has more than one form for expressing a particular function, or different means of expressing more differentiated aspects of a basic notion, then the child will try to use one form for all instances. On the other hand, if a particular form has two or more related functions, the child will avoid that form or attempt to restructure the system so as to distinguish its functions.

In several areas of Japanese grammar, there are many forms to express subtle differentiations within the domain of a single basic concept. In these cases, children typically overgeneralize at least one of the available forms, and may try to use a single form for all functions. For example, in the area of negation, distinct forms are available for the concepts of prohibition, rejection, non-existence, and denial. The development of negation is characterized by repeated overextensions of the earliest and most common negative forms: *nai,* which expresses non-existence and serves as the non-past negative inflection, and *iya,* which expresses rejection and is typically the earliest negative to be acquired. Ito (1981) notes that there is a tendency for *nai* to be used as an "omnibus" negative.

In the expression of benefactive relations, there are two verbs of giving as well as a verb of receiving which may be used. The most frequently confused forms are those with the most similar function, the verbs of giving *ageru* and *kureru.* The most common verb, *ageru,* was overextended in Horiguchi's data (1979a) to a large percentage of cases where a different verb would have been appropriate, including 44.9% of all contexts calling for *kureru.* In the acquisition of counting, some children go through a phase of overextending Japanese numerals with the unmarked *-tsu* classifier where specific classifiers would be appropriate. Thus the more semantically differentiated options are temporarily avoided. Another area of Japanese grammar with a many-to-one relation between form and function is the expression of respect or deference. Polite speech, which is marked by *-mas* verbal inflections, shows respect for the addressee; honorific speech, which is marked by lexical substitutions and three special verbal inflections, shows respect even for referents other than the addressee. In the acquisition of respect terms, polite forms are sometimes overgeneralized as honorifics. Also, some speakers are eliminating one of the two available inflections for subject honorification. Thus there is a strong tendency throughout Japanese grammar for a single form to be generalized within a semantic domain, eliminating the subtle distinctions marked by the different forms available.

In other cases, alternate forms within a particular domain express grammatical rather than semantic distinctions. For example, in Japanese morphology, a single semantic notion may be realized by different surface forms with different parts of speech. This is true of negation, where nouns and nominal adjectives are negated with *janai,* adjectives with *-kunai,* and verbs with *-nai.* Children generally use a single form, *nai,* to negate these different parts of speech in the first stage of acquiring negatives. Similarly, Japanese grammar distinguishes true adjectives from nominal adjectives, which are treated like nouns for marking politeness, negation, etc. Japanese children go through a phase of treating nominal adjectives like true adjectives and using the same inflectional endings for both. Form class distinctions are also ignored in the acquisition of prenominal modifiers. Japanese children often overextend the genitive particle *no,* which precedes head nouns modified by other nouns, and use it also with adjectival modifiers, which should simply precede the noun they modify.

In these cases, a single form is selected and applied to all instances of a semantic category without regard to the distinctions between different parts of speech made by the adult grammar. The greater generality, consistency, and persistence of these errors suggest that the principle of one-to-one mapping of form and function is adhered to more strictly when different forms mark purely grammatical distinctions than when they mark subtle semantic distinctions. This is consistent with Slobin's principle that "the use of grammatical markers should make semantic sense."

12.2.8. *Semantic Consistency.* There is some evidence from Japanese acquisition that children prefer forms to have a consistent semantic function. Many production errors are reported in the literature for case particles which serve a variety of semantic functions, such as the subject marker *ga.* The results of comprehension studies indicate that children tend to apply the one form-one function principle to *ga* during processing. In simple active sentences with transitive verbs, *ga* marks the agent. In comprehension experiments using transitive sentences, some young children assume that *ga* on the first nominal marks the agent, even in SOV passive sentences, where *ga* marks the patient, and in benefactive sentences with *morau* 'receive', where *ga* marks the recipient. Similarly, the topic marker *wa* frequently marks the subject of a sentence, and in transitive sentences therefore often marks the agent. Simple active OSV sentences in which *wa* marks a sentence-initial object are very poorly understood by Japanese children. Thus it is difficult for children to attribute semantically inconsistent functions, such as agent and patient, to a single morpheme.

However, there are also cases in which Japanese children do not maintain the principle of one-to-one mapping of form and function. These examples provide evidence for the constraints which limit that general principle. One example from Japanese data is the overgeneralization of the *-te* form in the acquisition of the verbal system. In their attempts to produce complex adult forms incorporating the continuative *-te,* such as the present progressive/resultative *-teru* and benefactive and aspectual V-*te* V constructions, children who are already using *-te* as an imperative (correctly) may begin to overgeneralize *-te* to non-imperative contexts as well. Thus -*te* ends up serving more than one function in some children's speech. The surface homophony resulting from this overgeneralization seems unavoidable if a child who cannot yet produce adult complex -*te* structures attempts to imitate them, or substitutes -*te* for them in spontaneous production. This apparent violation of one-to-one mapping may be tolerated partly because the children's underlying semantic intent and the adult target form are actually different. That is, since the homophony occurs only in the child's output, it may not be subject to the same kind of monitoring which leads to the avoidance of adult homophonous forms.

A more striking case of tolerated homophony occurs with *no*, which functions both as a sentence-final particle and a possessive marker in the earliest stage of Japanese grammatical development. This'form is plurifunctional in the adult input, but is acquired in both functions and used very frequently by Japanese children even before the age of 2 years. Here, the fact that the two *no*'s belong to completely different grammatical subsystems probably accounts for children's willingness to tolerate the plurifunctionality. The two functions of *no* are extremely different pragmatically and semantically, and also differ in their distributional patterns. Both uses occur sentence-finally at the earliest stage, but possessive *no* at first follows only the names of people, whereas sentence-particle *no* frequently occurs after verbal and adjectival predicates. Slobin (1985) has suggested that the constraint against a single form having more than one function applies to forms having similar functions; in this case, the two early functions of *no* are apparently sufficiently different that the constraint does not apply.

Another interesting case is the acquisition of the subject particle *ga*. As discussed in section 4.2, many Japanese children do not attempt to assign a single semantic function to the subject marker *ga*. This particle serves a wide range of semantic functions in adult speech, including agent, experiencer, recipient in benefactives with *morau* 'receive', patient in passive sentences, causee in causative sentences, and what is sometimes analyzed as the object of transitive stative predicates, such as *suki* 'like'. In the early stages of acquiring *ga*, some children seem to ignore its semantic functions, and simply place *ga* after the first noun in their sentence. Apparently, one factor which limits the tendency toward semantic consistency is a tremendous amount of "noise" in the input. When a single semantic function cannot be found for a very frequent form, children may abandon semantics and attempt to formulate a consistent syntactic (positional) hypothesis.

12.3. *Other Pacesetters*

12.3.1. *Affect.*   For many years, research on language acquisition has emphasized the role of cognition as a pacesetter of linguistic development. Japanese data suggest that affect, another highly developed faculty which children bring to the task of learning language, also plays a major role in shaping the course of language acquisition. Many of the earliest acquisitions in Japanese grammar have a basis in the child's expression of internal emotional states. In all languages, early sensitivity to affect may contribute to the acquisition of intonation patterns. In Japanese, correct use of many grammatical morphemes, such as sentence-final particles, depends upon the speaker's attitude or feelings, e.g. *yo* (assertive, potentially conflicting) and *ne* (seeking or expressing agreement).

Ito (1981) has emphasized the role of affect in the acquisition of negation in Japanese. The emotional basis for use of the different negative forms in Japanese, such as *iya* (rejection) and *dame* (prohibition), evolves during the pre-linguistic period, Ito suggests, as an initially undifferentiated semantic complex of emotions involved in insisting, demanding, and forbidding. As children acquire different negative expressions, the emotional similarities among certain forms contribute to the many confusion errors which occur.

Later acquisitions continue to be influenced by emotional factors. For example, the use of polite -*mas* inflections, which in my data first appeared in contexts of assumed formality and role-playing, has special affective connotations which may be important in their acquisition. At about 3–4 years-of-age, when children are interacting in social groups, sensitivity to affect is necessary for mastering the distinctions among forms of first and second person reference, such as the difference between the ordinary masculine first person pronoun *boku* 'I' and the rougher, more casual *ore* 'I'. As errors with the corresponding rough second person pronoun *omae* 'you' show, affect may precede and over-ride social constraints in young children's acquisition of grammatical forms conditioned both by affect and by sociolinguistic factors. Although affect probably plays a major, as yet largely unexplored, role in the acquisition of all languages, Japanese children will find more obvious and consistent grammatical correlates of their emotions than children acquiring many other languages.

12.3.2. *Presupposition.* Somewhat more crosslinguistic information is available on the development of pragmatics, and the early effects on language acquisition of children's capacity for presupposition, another faculty which apparently develops in the pre-linguistic period. There is evidence from the data on Japanese acquisition that children are sensitive to linguistic expressions of presupposition from the earliest stage of grammatical development. For example, presupposition underlies the use of different word orders in Japanese, and variations in word order are used appropriately in context from the two-word stage. Presupposition also plays a part in the acquisition of sentence-final particles, such as *yo,* which typically presupposes that new information is being conveyed, and *ne,* which often presupposes shared information. The early acquisition of presuppositional devices raises an interesting question with respect to egocentrism, since they seem to require taking the addressee's point of view. Perhaps, as Greenfield and Smith (1976, Chap. 4.3) and Bates (1976, Chap. 4) suggest, children first base apparent presuppositions about old/new information upon their own point of view, which in the "here and now" of early interactions often is the same as that of the addressee. Careful investigation may show this to be true of Japanese ellipsis and postposing rules. Affect and sensitivity to different types of speech acts may account for many of the early uses of sentence-final particles. However, this would be an interesting area for further study with respect to presupposition, since appropriate use of sentence-final particles does seem to require that the children be able to recognize, at least to some extent, the similarity or difference between their own state of knowledge and/or attitude compared with the addressee. Children's ability to recognize and make presuppositions seems to be an important factor in early language acquisition, and probably continues to influence the course of development throughout later stages as well.

13. Suggestions for Further Study

13.1. Particles

Although there are many studies of the acquisition of case particles, it would be very helpful for crosslinguistic comparison if detailed longitudinal data were analyzed in terms of the specific semantic functions served by each particle, since many have several distinct uses. For example, the particle *ni* marks stative and directional locatives, datives, agents in passive and causative sentences, adverbials, etc. Since several, but not all, case particles are plurifunctional, a contrastive analysis of their acquisition would serve as an interesting test case for Slobin's hypothesis that children prefer a one-to-one mapping of form and meaning. The particle *e*, for example, has the single function of marking direction towards a location, which might lead children to prefer it to *ni*, which has so many other functions as well. Such an analysis should provide insight into the factors which may influence the operation of the one-to-one mapping principle, such as frequency.

Since data on the acquisition of locatives in several languages are available, an analysis of Japanese locative particles and constructions would be a valuable addition to the crosslinguistic data. It would be especially useful if the methodology of Johnston and Slobin (1979) could be followed in a study of the comprehension of complex locatives, such as N *no ue ni* 'on top of N'. Since the grammatical formation of these locatives is very similar in Japanese and Turkish, Japanese data would provide a good test of the cognitively based sequence of development proposed by Johnston and Slobin.

A detailed longitudinal analysis of sentence-final particles, focusing on their functions in different types of speech acts, would be extremely interesting from a crosslinguistic standpoint. The discussion presented in section 6.1.2, a composite picture based upon several different children, provides only a few suggestions about the strategies which individual children might follow in acquiring sentence-final particles, such as associating a particular particle with a certain type of speech act, for example, *yo* with contradictions. Since overt morphological expression of the pragmatic and emotional functions served by Japanese sentence-final particles does not occur in languages which have been extensively studied to date, such research should provide valuable insights into the role of affect and presupposition in the earliest stage of language development.

13.2. *Sociolinguistic Features*

From a crosslinguistic point of view, one of the most interesting aspects of Japanese is the extensive sociolinguistic conditioning of grammatical forms. This is also an area of Japanese acquisition which has not yet received much attention. One topic deserving further analysis is the acquisition of polite *-mas* inflections, which would be interesting to study in depth with longitudinal data from a pragmatic and sociolinguistic standpoint. In section 6.1.6 it was suggested that children may first associate *-mas* inflections with the special affect of certain ritualized, pseudo-formal contexts, and only later develop an understanding of the relevant interpersonal factors, such as age and social status, which govern the selection of *-mas* by adults. Future research might analyze the contextual factors conditioning the use of polite style from the appearance of *-mas* forms in 2-year-olds to code-switching in appropriate social contexts among older children. Although it would be valuable, of course, to study children's use of polite style in actual social interactions, role-playing techniques could probably elicit information about children's knowledge of the social factors governing polite style at a very early age. For example, the methodology of Andersen (1978), in which child and experimenter used puppets to act out interactions between such conversational partners as doctor-patient, would probably yield extremely interesting results with Japanese children. It would then be interesting to compare findings about children's knowledge of polite speech with their own usage in social contexts calling for polite inflections.

As noted in section 6.2.1, the acquisition of honorifics has not been investigated longitudinally, probably because they are used so rarely, and are not mastered until the school years. Okuda's (1979) study suggests that role-playing might be a very effective methodology for analyzing children's knowledge of honorifics as well as polite style. The children in Okuda's study were able to invent dialogue, incorporating honorifics in some cases, for characters depicted in cartoons. Direct verbal role-playing, such as that used by Andersen, might tap unconscious knowledge more extensively and at an earlier age. Okuda's findings suggest that investigation of the acquisition of honorifics should extend in age range at least through junior high school.

Another major area for sociolinguistic investigation is the acquisition of the differences between male and female speech in Japanese. The studies of the acquisition of first and second person reference by Ide (1977, 1978, 1978–79) and Horiguchi (1979b), and Hori's (1981) study of sentence-final particles, are valuable contributions on this topic. Since Japanese is so rich in male/female differences, detailed longitudinal research on the acquisition of those areas of grammar with sex-based options would be an important addition to the crosslinguistic literature on the acquisition of sex-appropriate speech. Again, role-playing at different ages would probably be a valuable methodology for experimental investigations in this area, especially for eliciting information about children's knowledge of the speech of the opposite sex.

13.3. *Input*

Another interesting area for research is a comparison of ordinary adult speech and the speech addressed to young Japanese children. The relevant comparison here should be the speech used among adult family members or close friends, to reduce the linguistic effects of social distance between speaker and hearer. Miyazaki's (1979) study of the acquisition of *wa* and *ga,* Yamada (1980) and Cook (1985) have shown that Japanese input to young children has at least one distinctive characteristic which may have a direct bearing on language acquisition, namely, an extremely high frequency of particle ellipsis. Other differences might include the frequency of nominal and verbal ellipsis, of particular verbal inflections, such as -*chatta,* the "vivid" past (see Rispoli, 1981b), and of certain patterns of word order, such as repeated, postposed nouns.

Since there are so many speech styles in Japanese, the linguistic input to children will be significantly different depending upon the composition of their families. Given the differences between male and female speech, Japanese "motherese" may be quite distinct from father's input. If a child lives in an extended family, s/he will receive input from the grandparents, which will be different from the speech of younger people in various ways, e.g. perhaps a higher frequency of polite style in grandmother's speech. If children have siblings of the opposite sex, they may hear forms which they would not otherwise experience so directly, such as certain pronouns used in the siblings' peer groups. If there are older siblings of the same sex, their input may encourage earlier acquisition of sex-appropriate speech.

One important question with respect to input and Japanese language acquisition is Oedipal. If the primary linguistic input to both boys and girls comes from their mothers, when and how do little boys learn to use masculine style, eliminating or reducing the frequency of female forms heard from their mothers? Little girls do not have to undergo this shift in identification, although they may reject at least certain parts of the female linguistic model, as problems in the acquisition of *atashi* 'I' (female) in certain cases indicate. Since sex-appropriate speech is so important in Japan, mothers may adapt their speech according to the sex of their child; it would be interesting to study what differences may exist between mothers' speech to sons as compared to daughters.

A thorough investigation of the input to Japanese children should also consider the role of at least two other types of input: the speech of peers, and indirect or overheard input, not addressed to the child. Interaction with peers, especially once the child has entered kindergarten and is exposed to large groups of children, probably has significant effects upon the acquisition of male/female speech, and register differences governed by in-group vs. out-group factors such as age. In the acquisition of polite, and especially of honorific speech, indirect or overheard input may be important. Okuda's (1979) study suggests that children have extensive knowledge about polite and honorific speech derived from their observation of adult interactions. My data suggest that at least some Japanese mothers engage in direct role-playing with polite speech, but children's observation of mothers' speech to visitors and other adults may also be important. One other source of indirect or passive input which deserves investigation is the television, which has apparently become a major source of linguistic input for Japanese children. Okuda reports that there was a significant inverse correlation between the number of hours per day spent watching television, and children's use of polite speech in various tasks; modern children's programs do not typically use the *-mas* style. Each of the different sources of input will contribute to the range of registers in children's repertoires, which will be an important factor in their ability to function successfully in Japanese society.

LIST OF ABBREVIATIONS

ADJ   Adjective
AGR   Seeking/expressing agreement
AGT   Agent
COHRT   Cohortative
COMPL   Completed past
CONC   Concessive
CONT   Continuative
COP   Copula
DIM   Diminutive
DO   Direct object
EMPH   Emphatic
EP   Extended predicate
EXCLAM   Exclamatory
GEN   Genitive
HON   Honorific
IMP   Imperative
INF   Infinitive
IO   Indirect object
NEG   Negative
NONPAST   Non-past tense
OBLIG   Obligation

PASS   Passive
PAST   Past tense
POL   Polite
PRES. PROG   Present progressive
PRESUM   Presumptive
Q   Question
QUOT   Quotative
REP   Representative
SUBJ   Subject
TOP   Topic

ACKNOWLEDGMENTS

I am grateful to the many scholars in Japan and the United States who helped me with this work, corresponding with me, sending advice, suggestions for references, and copies of their own research, especially Akiyo Asano, Kenji Hakuta, Kazuko Harada, Robert Hess, Sumiko Horiguchi, Sachiko Ide, Katsutoshi Ito, Megumi Kameyama, Barbara Lust, Kooji Murata, Ai Okubo, Akiko Okuda (Kawasaki), Matthew Rispoli, Taroo Takahashi, Ellen Tanouye, Tazuko Uyeno, Akiko Yamada, and Masako Yamamoto. I greatly appreciate the time and trouble of those who commented on and corrected earlier versions of this work, including Ruth Berman, Pamela Downing, Kenji Hakuta, Morio Hamada, John Hinds, Katsutoshi Ito, Megumi Kameyama, Yoshiko Matsumoto, Ai Okubo, Dan Slobin, and Masayo Yamamoto. I especially appreciate the efforts of Katsutoshi Ito, Ai Okubo, and Masayo Yamamoto, who gave me many helpful examples and comments from their own data. I also wish to thank Haruo Aoki, Kiko Yamashita, and Mamoru Saito, who answered many questions about Japanese; Masayoshi Hirose, Yumiko Yoshimura, and Akiko Okuda (Kawaski), who helped me find Japanese references; and Yoshizo Itabashi, who helped me read many of them. I am grateful to all those who helped me with my own research on Japanese child language, especially Kazuko Harada, who found subjects for me, Akiyo Asano and Miyako Namikawa for their assistance at the recording sessions, and Janet Akaike-Toste, for her patient and painstaking transcription. Special thanks are due to Yukiko Kurihata (Nishimura) and her family, for their help and friendship during my stay in Tokyo, and to the mothers and children who participated in my research.

The early stages of this work were carried out at the University of California at Berkeley; it was completed at the Center for Cognitive Science at Brown University.

This research was supported in part by a Fulbright-Hays Doctoral Dissertation Research Abroad Fellowship, a Social Science Research Council Postdoctoral Fellowship, a National Science Foundation National Needs Postdoctoral Fellowship, and an Alfred P. Sloan Postdoctoral Fellowship in Cognitive Science.

REFERENCES

Akiyama, M. Yes-no answering systems in young children. *Cognitive Psychology,* 1979, *11,* 485–504.

Aksu, A. Development of the expression of cause-effect relations in Turkish. Unpublished paper,

Department of Psychology, University of California, Berkeley, 1975. (Abbreviated version available as Aksu, A. The acquisition of causal connectives in Turkish. *Papers and Reports on Child Language Development* (Department of Linguistics, Stanford University), 1978, *15*, 129–139.)

Aksu-Koç, A. A., & Slobin, D. I. The acquisition of Turkish. In D. I. Slobin (Ed.), *The crosslinguistic study of language acquisition* (Vol. 1). Hillsdale, NJ: Lawrence Erlbaum Associates, 1985.

Alfonso, A., & Niimi, K. *Japanese: A basic course* (5th revised ed.). Tokyo: Takayama Printing Co., 1972.

Andersen, E. S. Will you don't snore please. *Papers and Reports on Child Language Development* (Department of Linguistics, Stanford University), 1978, *15*, 140–150.

Aoki, H. *Lecture on the history of the Japanese language.* Department of Linguistics, University of California, Berkeley, Spring quarter, 1981.

Asano, A. On strategies for processing Japanese relative clauses. In *Attempts in linguistics and literature: Papers in honor of Kazuko Inoue* (Vol. 6). Society of Linguistics and Literature, International Christian University, 1979.

Azuma, H., Hess, R. D., Kashigawa, K., & Conroy, M. Maternal control strategies and the child's cognitive development: A cross-cultural paradox and its interpretation. *Paper presented at the International Congress of Psychology,* Leipzig, 1979.

Bates, E. *Language and context: The acquisition of pragmatics.* New York: Academic Press, 1976.

Bates, E., & MacWhinney, B. A functionalist approach to the acquisition of grammar. In E. Ochs & B. Schieffelin (Eds.), *Developmental pragmatics.* New York: Academic Press, 1979.

Benedict, R. *The chrysanthemum and the sword.* New York: Meridian, 1946

Berman, R. A. The acquisition of Hebrew. In D. I. Slobin (Ed.), *The crosslinguistic study of language acquisition* (Vol. 1). Hillsdale, NJ: Lawrence Erlbaum Associates, 1985.

Bever, T. G. The cognitive basis for linguistic structures. In J. R. Hayes (Ed.), *Cognition and the development of language.* New York: Wiley, 1970.

Bloom, L. *Language development: Form and function in emerging grammars.* Cambridge, MA: MIT Press, 1970.

Bloom, L., Lahey, M., Hood, L., Lifter, K., & Fiess, K. Complex sentences: Acquisition of syntactic connectives and semantic relations in complex sentences. *Journal of Child Language,* 1980, *7*, 235–262.

Bloom, L., Lifter, K., & Hafitz, J. Semantics of verbs and the development of verb inflection in child language. *Language,* 1980, *56*, 386–412.

Blount, B. G. Ethnography and caretaker-child interaction. In C. E. Snow & C. A. Ferguson (Eds.), *Talking to children: Language input and acquisition.* Cambridge: Cambridge University Press, 1977.

Bowerman, M. *Early syntactic development: A cross-linguistic study with special reference to Finnish.* Cambridge: Cambridge University Press, 1973.

Brown, D. H. Children's comprehension of relativized English sentences. *Child Development,* 1971, *42*, 1923–1936.

Brown, R. *A first language: The early stages.* Cambridge, MA: Harvard University Press, 1973.

Carroll, J. B., & Casagrande, J. B. The function of language classifications in behavior. In E. E. Macoby, T. M. Newcomb, & E. L. Hartley (Eds.), *Readings in social psychology* (3rd ed.). New York: Holt, Rinehart, and Winston, 1958.

Caudill, W., & Weinstein, H. Maternal care and infant behavior in Japan and America. In T. S. Lebra & W. P. Lebra (Eds.), *Japanese culture and behavior: Selected readings.* Honolulu: University Press of Hawaii, 1974.

Chafe, W. L. Givenness, contrastiveness, definiteness, subjects, topics, and point of view. In C. Li (Ed.), *Subject and topic.* New York: Academic Press, 1976.

Chew, J. J. The structure of Japanese baby talk. *The Journal of the Association of Teachers of Japanese,* 1969, *6*, 4–17.

Chomsky, C. *The acquisition of syntax in children from five to ten.* Cambridge, MA: MIT Press, 1969.

Clancy, P. M. Referential choice in English and Japanese narrative discourse. In W. L. Chafe (Ed.), *The pear stories: Cognitive, cultural, and linguistic aspects of narrative production.* Norwood, NJ: Ablex Publishing Corp., 1980.

Clancy, P. M., Jacobsen, T., & Silva, M. The acquisition of conjunction: A cross-linguistic study. *Papers and Reports on Child Language Development,* (Department of Linguistics, Stanford University), 1976, *12,* 71–80.

Clark, E. Convention and innovation in acquiring lexicon. *Papers and Reports on Child Language Development* (Department of Linguistics, Stanford University), 1980, *19,* 1–20.

Clark, E. Lexical innovations: How children learn to create new words. In W. Deutsch (Ed.), *The child's construction of language.* New York: Academic Press, 1981.

Clark E., & Hecht, B. Learning to coin agent and instrument nouns. *Cognition,* 1982, *12,* 1–24.

Conroy, M., Hess, R. D., Azuma, H., & Kashigawa, K. Maternal strategies for regulating children's behavior. *Journal of Cross-Cultural Psychology,* 1980, *11,* 153–172.

Cook, H. Minegishi. Frequency of nominal markers in the speech of a Japanese child and his caretakers: A case study. *Descriptive and Applied Linguistics,* (International Christian University), 1985, *18,* 13–24.

Cross, T. C. Mothers' speech adjustments: The contribution of selected child listener variables. In C. E. Snow & C. A. Ferguson (Eds.), *Talking to children: Language input and acquisition.* Cambridge: Cambridge University Press, 1977.

deVilliers, J. G., Tager-Flusberg, H., Hakuta, K., & Cohen, M. Children's comprehension of relative clauses. *Journal of Psycholinguistic Research,* 1979, *8,* 449–518.

Doi, T. *The anatomy of dependency.* (Tr. by J. Bester.) New York: Harper and Row, 1973. (Originally *Amae no koozoo.* Tokyo: Kodansha.)

Downing, P. *Japanese numeral classifiers: A semantic, syntactic and functional profile.* Unpublished doctoral dissertation, University of California, Berkeley, 1984.

Eisenberg, A., & Renner, T. Acquisition of complex sentences in English: Similarity and variation across children. *Paper presented at the Sixth Annual Boston University Conference on Language Development,* Oct., 1981.

Ervin-Tripp, S. Discourse agreement: How children answer questions. In J. R. Hayes (Ed.), *Cognition and the development of language.* New York: Wiley, 1970.

Fischer, J. L. Words for self and others in some Japanese families. *American Anthropologist,* 1964, *66* (pt. 2), 115–126.

Fischer, J. L. Linguistic socialization: Japan and the United States. In R. Hill & R. Konig (Eds.), *Families in East and West: Socialization process and kinship ties.* The Hague: Mouton, 1970.

Fujitomo, Y. Kodomo no kotoba no kenkyuu (I). *Hokkaidoo Kyooiku Daigaku Kiyoo* (Dai-ichibu), 1977, *28,* 59–63.

Fujiwara, Y. *Yooji no Gengo Hyoogen Nooryoku no Hattatsu.* Hiroshima: Bunka Hyoron Publishing Co., 1977.

Givón, T. *On understanding grammar.* New York: Academic Press, 1979.

Gleason, J. B. Talking to children; Some notes on feedback. In C. E. Snow & C. A. Ferguson (Eds.), *Talking to children: Language input and acquisition.* Cambridge: Cambridge University Press, 1977.

Greenfield, P. M., & Smith, J. H. *The structure of communication in early language development.* New York: Academic Press, 1976.

Hahn, K. *The development of negation in one Korean child.* Unpublished doctoral dissertation, Department of Linguistics, University of Hawaii, 1981.

Hakuta, K. Word order and particles in the acquisition of Japanese. *Papers and Reports on Child Language Development* (Department of Linguistics, Stanford University), 1977, *13,* 110–117.

Hakuta, K. Grammatical description vs. configurational arrangement in language acquisition: The case of relative clauses in Japanese. *Cognition*, 1981, *9*, 197–236.

Hakuta, K. Interaction between particles and word order in the comprehension and production of simple sentences in Japanese children. *Developmental Psychology*, 1982, *18*, 62–75.

Hakuta, K., deVilliers, J., & Tager-Flusberg, H. Sentence coordination in Japanese and English. *Journal of Child Language*, 1982, *9*, 193–207.

Harada, K. I. Acquisition of Japanese relative clauses: A case study on a two-year-old. *Annual Reports* (The Division of Languages, International Christian University, Tokyo), 1976, *1*, 1–16.

Harada, K. I. The acquisition of passive, causative, and *te moraw* constructions in Japanese: A case study on a two-year-old. *Annual Reports* (The Division of Languages, International Christian University, Tokyo), 1977, *2*, 1–16.

Harada, K. I. Notes on honorifics for seminar in crosslinguistic language acquisition, Prof. D. I. Slobin. *The Summer Institute of The Linguistic Society of America*, Albuquerque, New Mexico, 1980. (a)

Harada, K. I. Notes on the acquisition of the genitive particle *no* for seminar in crosslinguistic language acquistion, Prof. D. I. Slobin. *The Summer Institute of the Linguistic Society of America*, Albuquerque, New Mexico, 1980. (b)

Harada, K. I. The acquisition of Japanese case particles: A new look. In Y. Otsu, H. van Riemsdijk, K. Inoue, A. Kamio, & N. Kawasaki (Eds.), *Studies in generative grammar and language acquisition*. Tokyo: International Christian University, 1983.

Harada, S. I. Honorifics. In M. Shibatani (Ed.), *Syntax and semantics 5: Japanese generative grammar*. New York: Academic Press, 1976.

Harada, S. I., Uyeno, T., Hayashibe, H., Yamada, H. On the development of perceptual strategies in children: A case study on the Japanese child's comprehension of the relative clause construction. *Annual Bulletin of the Research Institute of Logopedics and Phoniatrics*, (University of Tokyo) 1976, *10*, 199–224.

Hashimoto, S. *Kokugohoo yoosetsu*. Tokyo: Meiji Shoin, 1934.

Hatano, E. Gengo kakutoku. In *Yooji shinrigaku no shimpoo*. Tokyo: Kaneko Shoboo, 1980.

Hatano, K. Kotoba no hattatsu shinri. In E. Iwabuchi (Ed.), *Kotoba no tanjoo: Ubugoe kara gosai made*. Tokyo: Nihon Hoosoo Shuppan Kyookai, 1968.

Hayashibe, H. Word order and particles: A developmental study in Japanese. *Descriptive and Applied Linguistics*, (International Christian University), 1975, *8*, 1–18.

Hess, R. D., Kashigawa, K., Azuma, H., Price, G., & Dickson, P. W. Maternal expectations for mastery of developmental tasks in Japan and the United States. *International Journal of Psychology*, 1980, *15*, 259–271.

Hinds, J. Postposing in Japanese. *Eoneo* (The Journal of the Linguistic Society of Korea), 1976, *1*, 113–125.

Hinds, J. Ellipsis in Japanese. *Papers in Japanese Linguistics*, 1976–1977, *5*, 63–97.

Hinds, J. *Ellipsis in Japanese*. Edmonton, Alberta: Linguistic Research, Inc., 1982.

Hirayama, M. *Acquisition of Japanese particles by a child: Aged from one year and nine months to two years and two months*. Unpublished bachelor's thesis, International Christian University, Tokyo, 1978.

Hori, M. Shuujoshi no shuurui. In F. C. Peng (Ed.), *Nihongo no danjosa: Male/female differences in Japanese*. Tokyo: The East-West Sign Language Association, 1981.

Horiguchi, S. Nenshooji no jukyuu hyoogen. In F. C. Peng & M. Hori (Eds.), *Brain function and language acquisition: Kotoba no Hattatsu*. Hiroshima: Bunka Hyoron Publishing Co., 1979. (a)

Horiguchi, S. *Nisaiji no hanashikotoba ni mitateru danjo no sai*. Paper presented at the Sixth International Christian University Linguistics Symposium, August, 1979. (b)

Horiguchi, S. Ichininshooshi, nininshooshi, koshooshi. In F. C. Peng (Ed.), *Nihongo no danjosa: Male/female differences in Japanese*. Tokyo: The East-West Sign Language Association, 1981. (a)

Horiguchi, S. Nenshooji no asupekuto. In M. Hori & F. C. Peng (Eds.), *Aspects of language acquisition: Gengo shuutoku no shosoo.* Hiroshima: Bunka Hyoron Publishing Co., 1981. (b)

Ide, S. Sex and personal referents of Japanese children. *Proceedings of the Symposium on Japanese Sociolinguistics,* Summer Institute of the Linguistic Society of America, Honolulu, University of Hawaii, July, 1977.

Ide, S. Nihongo ni okeru seibetsu to ninsho daimeshi—yooji no baai. In F. C. Peng (Ed.), *Development in verbal and nonverbal behavior: Hattatsu to shuutoku ni okeru gengo koodoo.* Hiroshima: Bunka Hyoron Publishing Co., 1978.

Ide, S. A sociolinguistic analysis of person references by Japanese and American children. *Language Sciences,* 1978–1979, *1,* 273–293.

Ide, S. Keigo. In F. C. Peng (Ed.), *Nihongo no danjosa: Male/female differences in Japanese.* Tokyo: The East-West Sign Language Association, 1981.

Inoue, K. Japanese: A story of language and people. In T. Shopen (Ed.), *Languages and their speakers.* Cambridge, MA: Winthrop Publishers, 1979.

Ito, K. Yooji ni totte 'ayamari' to wa nani ka. In F. C. Peng (Ed.), *Development in verbal and nonverbal behavior: Hattatsu to shuutoku ni okeru gengo koodoo.* Hiroshima: Bunka Hyoron Publishing Co., 1976.

Ito, K. Towards an ethnopsychology of language: Interactional strategies of Japanese and Americans. *Bulletin of the Center for Language Studies* (Kanagawa University), 1980, *3,* 1–14.

Ito, K. Two aspects of negation in child language. In P. S. Dale & D. Ingram (Eds.), *Child language: An international perspective.* Baltimore, MD: University Park Press, 1981.

Iwabuchi, E., & Muraishi, S. Kotoba no shuutoku. In E. Iwabuchi (Ed.), *Kotoba no tanjoo: Ubugoe kara gosai made.* Tokyo: Nihon Hoosoo Shuppan Kyookai, 1968.

Johnston, J. R., & Slobin, D. I. The development of locative expressions in English, Italian, Serbo-Croatian, and Turkish. *Journal of Child Language,* 1979, *16,* 531–547.

Jorden, E. H., with the assistance of H. I. Chaplin. *Beginning Japanese (Parts 1–2).* New Haven, CT: Yale University Press, 1962–1963.

Kameyama, M. *Development of verb use in Japanese: Early case frames.* Unpublished paper, Department of Linguistics, Stanford University, 1982.

Kamio, A., & Harada, K. *Children's processing of complex sentences in Japanese: An interim report of a repetition experiment.* Kenkyuu hookoku: Nihongo no kihon koozoo ni kansuru rironteki-jisshooteki kenkyuu, International Christian University, 1979.

Kamio, A., & Harada, K. Children's processing of complex sentences in Japanese. In K. Inoue, E. Kobayashi, & R. Linde (Eds.), *Issues in syntax and semantics: Festschrift for Prof. Masatake Muraki.* Tokyo: Sanshuusha, 1983.

Kasahara, Y. Fear of eye-to-eye confrontation among neurotic patients in Japan. In T. S. Lebra & W. P. Lebra (Eds.), *Japanese culture and behavior: Selected readings.* Honolulu: The University Press of Hawaii, 1974.

Komura, A. Shoyuu hyoogen no hattatsu. In M. Hori & F. C. Peng (Eds.), *Aspects of language acquisition: Gengo shuutoku no shosoo.* Hiroshima: Bunka Hyoron Publishing Co., 1981.

Kuno, S. *The structure of the Japanese language.* Cambridge, MA: MIT Press, 1973.

Kuno, S. Japanese: A characteristic OV language. In W. P. Lehmann (Ed.), *Syntactic typology: Studies in the phenomenology of language.* Austin: University of Texas Press, 1978.

Kuno, S., & Kaburaki, E. Empathy and syntax. In S. Kuno (Ed.), *Harvard studies in syntax and semantics* (Vol. 1). Published by the Department of Linguistics, Harvard University, Cambridge, MA, 1975.

Lieven, E. Different routes to multi-word utterances? *Papers and Reports on Child Language Development* (Department of Linguistics, Stanford University), 1980, *19,* 37–44.

Limber, J. The genesis of complex sentences. In T. Moore (Ed.), *Cognitive development and the acquisition of language.* New York: Academic Press, 1973.

Loveday, L. Communicative interference: A framework for contrastively analysing L2 communicative competence exemplifed with the linguistic behavior of Japanese performing in English. *International Review of Applied Linguistics,* 1982, *XXII,* 1–16.

Lust, B., & Wakayama, T. K. The structure of coordination in first language acquisition of Japanese. In F. Eckman & A. Hastings (Eds.), *First and second language learning.* Rowley, MA: Newbury House, 1979.

Lust, B., & Wakayama, T. K. Word order in first language acquisition of Japanese. In P. Dale & D. Ingram (Eds.), *Child language: An international perspective.* Baltimore, MD: University Park Press, 1981.

MacWhinney, B. Hungarian language acquisition as an exemplification of a general model of grammatical development. In D. I. Slobin (Ed.), *The crosslinguistic study of language acquisition* (Vol. 2). Hillsdale, NJ: Lawrence Erlbaum Associates, 1985.

Martin, S. Lexical evidence relating Korean to Japanese. *Language,* 1966, *42,* 185–251.

Martin, S. *A reference grammar of Japanese.* New Haven, CT: Yale University Press, 1975.

Matsumoto, Y. The child's acquisition of Japanese numeral classifiers. *Paper presented at the International Congress for the Study of Child Language,* Austin, July, 1984. (a)

Matsumoto, Y. Hito--futa--mi vs. ichi--ni--san: Kodomo no suuchi--josuushi koozoo no keitai ni miru soosa gensoku. In F. C. Peng, K. Akiyama, & T. Kondo (Eds.), *Gengo no dainamikkusu.* Hiroshima: Bunka Hyoron Publishing Co., 1984. (b)

Matsumoto, Y. Gengo shuutoku ni okeru wakan suushi keiretsu: Kisokusei to bunsekisei. *Paper presented at the 90th Meeting of the Society for the Study of the Japanese Language,* Tokyo, June, 1984. (c)

McNeill, D., & McNeill, N. B. What does a child mean when he says 'no'? In C. A. Ferguson & D. I. Slobin (Eds.), *Studies of child language development.* New York: Holt, Rinehart, & Winston, 1973.

Miller, R. A. *The Japanese language.* Chicago: University of Chicago Press, 1967. (a)

Miller, R. A. Old Japanese phonology and the Korean-Japanese relationship. *Language,* 1967, *43,* 278–302. (b)

Mills, A. The acquisition of German. In D. I. Slobin (Ed.), *The crosslinguistic study of language acquisition* (Vol. 1). Hillsdale, NJ: Lawrence Erlbaum Associates, 1985.

Miyahara, K. *Language development in a young Japanese child—acquisition of particles.* Unpublished paper, Kyuushu University, 1973.

Miyahara, K. The acquisition of Japanese particles. *Journal of Child Language,* 1974, *1,* 283–286.

Miyazaki, M. *The acquisition of the two particles wa and ga in Japanese—A comparative study of L1 acquisition and L2 acquisition.* Unpublished master's thesis, University of Southern California, 1979.

Mizutani, O., & Mizutani, N. *An introduction to modern Japanese.* Tokyo: Japan Times, 1977.

Murata, K. Ikujigo no kenkyuu: Yooji no gengo shuutoku no ichijooken to shite. *Shinrigaku Kenkyuu,* 1960, *31,* 33–38.

Murata, K. Gengo koodoo no hattatsu I: Issaiji-K no danwa ni okeru bun. *Japanese Journal of Psychology,* 1961, *32,* 1–13. (a)

Murata, K. Gengo koodoo no hattatsu II: Hahaoya no kansatsu kiroku ni motozuku issaiji no danwa no hattatsuteki kenkyuu. *Japanese Journal of Psychology,* 1961, *32,* 10–23. (b)

Murata, K. Gengo koodoo no hattatsu III: Yookyuu katsuwa no gengo keishiki narabi ni kinoo no shoki hattatsu katei. *Japanese Journal of Educational Psychology,* 1961, *9,* 32–41. (c)

Murata, K. Gengo koodoo no hattatsu V: Shoki rengo hatsuwa no koozoo bunseki no kokoromi. *Japanese Journal of Psychology,* 1965, *36,* 67–75.

Murata, K. *Yooji no gengo hattatsu.* Tokyo: Baifuukan, 1968.

Murata, K., & Ohara, T. Gengo koodoo no hattatsu VII: Issaiji to no 'taiwa' ni okeru hahaoya no yakuwari. *Japanese Journal of Psychology,* 1966, *37,* 67–73.

Newport, E. L., Gleitman, H., & Gleitman, L. R. Mother, I'd rather do it myself: Some effects and non-effects of maternal speech style. In C. E. Snow & C. A. Ferguson (Eds.), *Talking to children: Language input and acquisition.* Cambridge: Cambridge University Press, 1977.

Noda, M. *An analysis of the Japanese extended predicate: A pragmatic approach to the system and pedagogical implications.* Unpublished master's thesis, Cornell University, 1981.

Noji, J. *Yoojiki no gengo seikatsu no jittai* (Vols. 1–4). Hiroshima: Bunka Hyoron Publishing Co., 1974–1977.

Okayama, Y. Ko to haha no taiwa ni okeru 'kotoba' no kinooteki bunrui—2, 3, 4-saiki no hikaku. *Oosaka Shiritsu Tanki Daigaku Kyookai Kenkyuu Hookokushuu, 1979, 12,* 109–122.

Okubo, A. Yooji no joshi no hattatsu—ichiyooji no choosa kara. *Kokugogaku 55.* Musashi no Shoin, 1963.

Okubo, A. *Yooji no gimon hyoogen no keishiki to sono hattatsu—yooji no gengo choosa 3.* Kokuritsu Kokugo Kenkyuujo Ronshuu 2, Kotoba no Kenkyuu Dainishuu. Shuuee Shuppan, 1965, 255–271.

Okubo, A. *Yooji gengo no hattatsu.* Tokyo: Tokyodoo, 1967.

Okubo, A. *Yooji no bunkoozoo no hattatsu: Sansai—rokusaiji no baai.* Kokuritsu Kokugo Kenkyuujo Hookoku 50, 1973.

Okubo, A. Koobun no hattatsu. In J. Orii et al. (Eds.), *Kotoba no hattatsu to sono shoogai.* Osaka: Osaka Kyooiku Daigaku, 1976.

Okubo, A. Gengo shuutoku no kojinsa—kyoomai ni arawareta chigai. *Yoonen Jidai, 1980, 10,* 22–31.

Okubo, A. Gengo shuutoku no hooryaku. In M. Hori & F. C. Peng (Eds.), *Aspects of language acquisition: Gengo shuutoku no shosoo.* Hiroshima: Bunka Hyoron Publishing Co., 1981. (a)

Okubo, A. Kotoba no kakutoku to onmanego. In M. Hori & F. C. Peng (Eds.), *Aspects of language acquisition: Gengo shuutoku no shosoo.* Hiroshima: Bunka Hyoron Publishing Co., 1981. (b)

Okubo, A. *Dooshi to sono kasetsugo no hattatsu no jittai: Danji no nisai kara sansai zenban made.* Kokuritsu Kokugo Kenkyuujo Hookoku 74: Kenkyuu Hookokushuu 4, 1983.

Okuda, A. *Kodomo to taiguu hyoogen.* Unpublished master's thesis, Tsukuba University, 1979.

Peters, A. Language segmentation: Operating principles for the perception and analysis of language. In D. I. Slobin (Ed.), *The crosslinguistic study of language acquisition* (Vol. 2). Hillsdale, NJ: Lawrence Erlbaum Associates, 1985.

Pye, C. Mayan motherese. *Paper presented at the Seventh Annual Boston University Conference on Language Development,* Oct., 1982.

Radulovic, L. *Acquisition of language: Studies of Dubrovnik children.* Unpublished doctoral dissertation, University of California, Berkeley, 1975.

Rispoli, M. *The pragmatic and paradigmatic in language acquisition: A case study from Japanese.* Unpublished paper, University of Pennsylvania, 1981. (a)

Rispoli, M. *The emergence of verb and adjective tense-aspect inflections in Japanese.* Unpublished master's thesis, University of Pennsylvania, 1981. (b)

Sanches, M. *Features in the acquisition of Japanese grammar.* Unpublished doctoral dissertation, Stanford University, 1968.

Sanches, M. Recent publications in Japanese on language acquisition. *Anthropological Linguistics, 1974, 13,* 120–127.

Sanches, M. Language acquisition and language change: Japanese numeral classifiers. In B. G. Blount & M. Sanches (Eds.), *Sociocultural dimensions of language change.* New York: Academic Press, 1977.

Sano, K. An experimental study on the acquisition of Japanese simple sentences and cleft sentences. *Descriptive and Applied Linguistics,* (International Christian University), 1977, 10, 213–233.

Savić, S. Aspects of adult-child communication: The problem of question acquisition. *Journal of Child Language*, 1975, *2*, 251–260.

Sheldon, A. The role of parallel function in the acquisition of relative clauses in English. *Journal of Verbal Learning and Verbal Behavior*, 1974, *13*, 272–281.

Shibamoto, J. *Language use and linguistic theory: Sex-related variation in Japanese syntax.* Unpublished doctoral dissertation, University of California, Davis, 1979.

Slobin, D. I. The acquisition of Russian as a native language. In F. Smith & G. A. Miller (Eds.), *The genesis of language: A psycholinguistic approach.* Cambridge, MA: MIT Press, 1966.

Slobin, D. I. Cognitive prerequisites for the development of grammar. In C. A. Ferguson & D. I. Slobin (Eds.), *Studies of child language development.* New York: Holt, Rinehart, & Winston, 1973.

Slobin, D. I. Universal and particular in the acquisition of language. In E. Wanner & L. R. Gleitman (Eds.), *Language acquisition: The state of the art.* Cambridge: Cambridge University Press, 1982.

Slobin, D. I. Crosslinguistic evidence for the Language-Making Capacity. In D. I. Slobin (Ed.), *The crosslinguistic study of language acquisition* (Vol. 2). Hillsdale, NJ: Lawrence Erlbaum Associates, 1985.

Slobin, D. I., & Bever, T. G. Children use canonical sentence schemas: A crosslinguistic study of word order and inflections. *Cognition*, 1982, *12*, 229–265.

Smith, M. Relative clause formation between 29–32 months: A preliminary report. *Papers and Reports on Child Language Development* (Department of Linguistics, Stanford University), 1974, *8*, 104–110.

Smith, N. *The acquisition of phonology: A case study.* Cambridge: Cambridge University Press, 1973.

Swan, M. Yamamoto. *The semantic development of negation in English and Japanese in a simultaneously bilingual child.* Unpublished master's thesis, University of Hawaii, 1981.

Takahara, P. O., & Peng, F. C. Gojun toochi. In F. C. Peng (Ed.), *Nihongo no danjosa: Male/female differences in Japanese.* Tokyo: The East-West Sign Language Association, 1981.

Takahashi, T. *Yoojigo no keitaironteki na bunseki.* Kokuritsu Kokugo Kenkyuusho Hookoku 55, 1975. (a)

Takahashi, T. *Yoojigo no rengoronteki na bunseki—Meishi no kaku no yoojoo.* Kokuritsu Kokugo Kenkyuujoo, Gengo Taikei Kenkyuubu Daiichi Kenkyuushitsu, 1975. (b)

Tamori, I. NP and particle deletion in Japanese discourse. In E. O. Keenan & T. L. Bennett (Eds.), *Discourse across time and space.* Published by the Department of Linguistics, University of Southern California, 1977.

Tanouye, E. K. The acquisition of verbs in Japanese children. *Papers and Reports on Child Language Development* (Department of Linguistics, Stanford University), 1979, *17*, 49–56.

Tanouye, E. K. *Language development in two Japanese-speaking children: A cross-linguistic study.* Unpublished qualifying paper, Teacher's College, Columbia University, 1980.

Tavakolian, S. The conjoined-clause analysis of relative clauses. In S. Tavakolian (Ed.), *Language acquisition and linguistic theory.* Cambridge, MA: MIT Press, 1981.

Tyack, D., & Ingram, D. Children's production and comprehension of questions. *Journal of Child Language*, 1977, *4*, 211–224.

Ueda, K. Sixteen ways to avoid saying 'no' in Japanese. In J. C. Condon & M. Saito (Eds.), *Intercultural encounters.* Tokyo: Simul Press, 1974.

Uyeno, T. *A study of Japanese modality: A performative analysis of sentence particles.* Unpublished doctoral dissertation, University of Michigan, Ann Arbor, 1971.

Uyeno, T., & Harada, S. I. Perception of syntactic structure in Japanese. *Annual Bulletin of the Research Institute of Logopedics and Phoniatrics* (University of Tokyo), 1975, *9*, 171–192.

Uyeno, T., Harada, S. I., Hayashibe, H., & Yamada, H. Comprehension of sentences with giving and receiving verbs in Japanese children. *Annual Bulletin of the Research Institute of Logopedics and Phoniatrics* (University of Tokyo), 1978, *12*, 167–185.

Yamada, A. *The development of syntactic devices for communication in the early stages of the acquisition of Japanese: A case study.* Unpublished master's thesis, University of Hawaii, 1980.

Yamamoto, M. (See Swan 1981.)

Yoshida, K. The acquisition of question and request forms in a Japanese child. *Paper presented at the Second Annual Boston University Conference on Language Development,* Oct., 1977.

5 The Acquisition of Kaluli

Bambi B. Schieffelin
University of Pennsylvania

Contents

KALULI LANGUAGE AND CULTURAL CONTEXT

1. Kaluli Language Description

Kaluli is one of the more than 700 languages spoken in Papua New Guinea. It is a non-Austronesian language which is part of the Central and South New Guinea Stock of the Trans-New Guinea Phylum (Voorhoeve, 1975). Within this Phylum are 67% of all Papua New Guinea languages, and 82% of all speakers of Papua New Guinea languages. On the basis of word lists and phonological inventories (Shaw, 1973), Kaluli has been classified as one of the five languages of the Bosavi family. There are four dialects of Kaluli, but they will not be discussed in this chapter.

In several important ways Kaluli resembles other non-Austronesian languages that have been described for Papua New Guinea. It is a verb-final language marking case relations postpositionally on nouns. Subject marking is suffixed on the verb through bound person markers and follows a nominative-accusative pattern. One bound person marker may denote two or several different persons.

This is common, especially in distinguishing 1st from 2–3 person, but there is variation in the pattern depending on sentence type. Li and Lang (1979, p. 109) point out that "those Papuan languages which have case systems are mostly ergative." In Kaluli there are two casemarking systems for nouns, neutral and ergative/absolutive. Casemarking on nouns follows a semantically motivated split ergative system. In terms of marking the semantic functions of nouns, Kaluli has a mixed word-order and inflectional system. That is, sometimes word order and other times casemarking is used to indicate semantic function. Kaluli has two allowable word orders for agent and object, AOV and OAV, each of which is used for different pragmatic ends. As with other split ergative languages found in this area, there is no passive.

Like other languages in this Phylum, there is considerable morphological complexity and irregularity in the verb system. The complex morphological system has elaborate affixation and inflection. Transparency is often veiled through morphophonemic changes. Unlike some of the other languages in the Trans-New Guinea Phylum, there is no object marking in the verb through bound markers, but the verb may carry information about the action (frequency and duration).

Kaluli nouns are not marked for gender, nor are they morphologically marked for plurality or definiteness. There are two sets of independent personal pronouns known as nonfocused and focused pronouns. Nonfocused pronouns are multi-functional and are used as subjects and experiencers of intransitive verbs, agents of transitive verbs in AOV utterances, and as objects. Focused pronouns are found in (O)AV utterances, when the agent is in focus. Some of these pronominal forms are marked for number (singular, dual, plural), inclusive, exclusive, as well as for other pragmatic and semantic properties.

Subordinate clauses precede the main clause. However, unlike English, which has a variety of lexical conjunctions such as *and, before, because, when,* and *if* to join clauses, Kaluli uses a variety of morphosyntactic constructions, called medial verb constructions. These, in relation to final inflected verb constructions, express the meanings of purposive and temporal conjunctions. These constructions, more than any other, give Papuan languages a characteristic stamp as different from those spoken in other parts of the world and build the types of sentences used in "clause-chaining" (Haiman, 1979; Longacre, 1972; Olson, 1978). Through additional morphological markers on the verb, speakers must signal whether the following clause will have the same or different subject. This system, SWITCH REFERENCE, is found in most Papuan languages.

Possession is indicated in several ways: through casemarking suffixes on nouns and demonstratives, through possessive adjectives, and through modified forms of the personal pronouns. The genitive construction typically has the order Genitive + Head. Unlike the more common pattern of noun phrase ordering in verb-final languages (as described by Greenberg, 1966), modifiers follow the head noun. All adverbial modifiers of the verb precede it. When an adjective follows the noun, it carries all of the inflectional material of the noun phrase. However, in contrast to English, Kaluli has relatively few adverbs and adjectives in its lexicon.

Negation is signaled lexically and by both prefixing and suffixing. Nominals are negated with one set of suffixes. Verbal negation varies according to the form of the verb, with imperatives taking only suffixes, and other forms taking a variety of prefixes and suffixes, depending on pragmatic as well as structural constraints.

Kaluli employs an elaborate system of emphatic and evidential particles. These particles are suffixed in word-final and sentence-final position, with evidential particles preceding emphatic particles when they co-occur. These particles encode nonrelational meanings, but are extremely important in conveying information about how speakers feel about what they are saying, and how they know about what they are saying.

Kaluli allows a great deal of deletion and ellipsis in all genres of talk. Utterances may consist of a single verb, or a verb with one or more other sentence constituents. When a person opens a discourse all major NPs are usually specified, but if one NP does not change, and there is no likelihood of ambiguity, that NP will probably not be repeated.

1.1. *Linguistic Research on Kaluli*

Like most of the other languages spoken in Papua New Guinea, there is no written grammar of Kaluli. The first work on this language was done by missionary linguist Murray Rule in the mid-1960s. Rule, working through translators speaking related languages, spent 6 weeks in the Bosavi area and put together a short preliminary grammatical sketch. This was designed to help Australian missionaries who would be sent into Bosavi, and was the first time the language was written.

Since that time the only other linguistic work in Bosavi has been carried out by myself while doing ethnographic and linguistic fieldwork on the development of communicative competence (1975–1977). Additional insights and assistance were provided by E. L. Schieffelin and S. Feld in the course of their anthropological fieldwork among the Kaluli. The linguistic analyses which follow must be considered work in progress since additional fieldwork is necessary to untangle a number of remaining linguistic puzzles.

Learning a language for which there is no grammatical description of the adult language does not present any serious problems to the child who is acquiring it as a first language. Describing the language acquisition processes of a language for which there is no grammatical description does present a serious challenge to the researcher. One not only must worry about how one is getting to one's destination, but what the destination itself looks like.

Working back and forth between adult and child language use in constructing grammatical and pragmatic analyses of Kaluli has been an instructive task. There is much to be learned from child language about the structure and function of linguistic systems. Through children's misanalyses and oversegmentations, underlying forms are made apparent. Systematic error patterns reveal the distribution of pragmatic forms which otherwise would be difficult to elicit. Adult misunderstandings, corrections, and laughter offer insights into what is and is not grammatically acceptable and pragmatically appropriate language. These are some of the essential cues that a non-native speaker must rely on in doing this type of research in a monolingual situation.

1.2. *Data Base for Language Acquisition*

This study represents the first child language acquisition research carried out in Papua New Guinea. For the present analysis I have examined two types of data: diary notes and observations made from November 1975 until April 1977 on a number of Kaluli children of different ages and the longitudinal tape-recorded and transcribed conversations I collected from three Kaluli children and members of their families from January 1976 until April 1977. At the beginning of the study these three children, two boys (Abi and Wanu) and one girl (Mɛli), were about 24 months old. One child (Wanu) was using mostly single words, and the other two were using single and multiword utterances. Spontaneous speech samples were collected at 4–6 week intervals and averaged over 3 hours per sample. Eight samples were recorded for two children and seven samples were recorded for the third child. In addition to the three focus children, several samples were taken of a fourth child, Suela, Abi's half sister, who was several months younger than Abi.

The language was recorded in the everyday familial settings in which it was being learned, so as to document the contexts of language acquisition as well as the acquisition process itself. The language that comprises these samples therefore is naturalistic and spontaneous, and captures the communication of the child with those individuals, both adult and child, with whom he or she regularly interacted. Working from an ethnography of speaking framework, extensive contextual notes and ethnographic observations were recorded both during and after recordings. In addition, in-depth interviews were carried out concerning general socialization practices and beliefs about language acquisition. This information was used to understand and interpret the meanings of utterances as well as the meanings of interactions.

After recording each sample, the mothers of the children and other native assistants helped me understand the language that was being spoken. This lengthy transcription process included the discussion of linguistic as well as cultural material. A total of 83 hours of taperecorded family interactions were transcribed and annotated. These tapes, along with tape recordings of other types of verbal genres (e.g. traditional and personal stories) supplemented by more formal linguistic elicitation with adults served as the basis for the current linguistic analysis of Kaluli. (For details about method and samples see Schieffelin, 1979.) Because the framework of this study was the spontaneous use of language in naturalistic contexts, the findings reported here concern language production. At this point there are no comprehension data available.

1.3. *Cultural Sketch*

The Kaluli people (population 1200) live in a tropical rain forest just north of the slopes of Mt. Bosavi, on the Great Papuan Plateau in the Southern Highlands Province of Papua New Guinea. They are one of four small groups who collectively refer to themselves as *Bosavi kalu* 'people of Bosavi' and to their language as *Bosavi to* 'Bosavi language'. Except for a few of the young men who have been out of the area (Bible school or through contract labor on plantations) and have learned some Tok Pisin or other local languages, the majority of Kaluli speakers are monolingual. They are traditionally nonliterate, though in the last decade, a few individuals have become literate in Kaluli and Tok Pisin through their association with the Christian mission in the area.

The Bosavi people live in about 20 longhouse communities, each separated by an hour or so walking distance through primary and secondary rain forest. Villages are composed of 60–90 individuals who traditionally lived in one large longhouse with no internal walls. Currently (1982), while the longhouse is maintained, many families are living together in smaller dwellings so that one or more extended families may live together. It is not unusual then for at least a dozen individuals of different ages to be living together in one house which consists essentially of one semipartitioned room. (See E. L. Schieffelin 1976 for detailed ethnographic account.)

Kaluli are swidden horticulturalists maintaining large gardens of pandanus, bananas, and breadfruit. Their staple starch is sago derived from wild palms. They hunt and fish extensively as well as keep domestic pigs. Kaluli society is generally egalitarian, lacking the "big man" patterns of social organization so common in the New Guinea Highlands. Men and women utilize extensive networks of obligation and reciprocity in the organization of work and sociable interaction. Everyday life is overtly focused around verbal interaction. Kaluli think of and use talk as a means of control, manipulation, expression, assertion, and appeal. Talk gets you what you want, need, and feel owed. Talk is a primary indicator of social competence and a primary way to be social. Learning how to talk and to become independent are major goals of socialization.

Customarily Kaluli observe a division of labor, and men and women's activities are for the most part cooperative, complementary, but usually separate. Child caregiving is exclusively in the domain of women. Since it is important to understand something of the cultural basis for the ways in which Kaluli act and speak to their children, I will sketch selected aspects of the cultural dimensions of language acquisition.

1.4. *The Cultural Context of Language Acquisition*

Kaluli describe their infants as helpless, 'soft' (*taiyɔ*) and 'having no understanding'. They take care of them, they say, because they feel sorry for them. Mothers, who are the primary caregivers in the first 3 years, are attentive to their infants and physically responsive to them. However, while nursing their infants they are often involved in other activities such as cooking, making netted bags, and conversing with others. Given their belief that infants 'have no understanding', Kaluli do not treat them as partners (speaker/addressee) in dyadic communicative interactions. While mothers greet their young infants by name and use expressive vocalizations, they rarely address other types of utterances to them.

Mothers encourage sibling interaction with infants by holding the infant up, faced outwards while they speak for the infant in a high-pitched nasalized voice. These triadic exchanges, which continue until an infant is between 4–6 months, are primarily for the benefit of the older sibling and help create a relationship between the two from an early age. It is important to point out that in these exchanges, the mother's utterances "as the baby" are not based on, nor do they originate with anything that the infant has initiated—either vocally or gesturally. After all, how could someone with 'no understanding' initiate appropriate interactional sequences?

However, there is an even more important and enduring cultural construct that helps make sense out of the mothers' behaviors in these situations and many others as well. Kaluli say that "one cannot know what another thinks or feels." Now, while Kaluli obviously interpret and assess one another's available behaviors and internal states, these interpretations are not culturally acceptable as topics of talk. Individuals often talk about their own feelings. However there is a cultural dispreference for talking about or making claims about what another might think or feel, or what another is about to do, especially if there is no evidence. These culturally constructed behaviors, which are related to other forms of language use, have important consequences for the ways in which Kaluli caregivers verbally interact with their children.

As infants become older (6–12 months) they are addressed by adults to a limited extent. They are greeted by a range of names and receive a limited set of both negative and positive imperatives. Rhetorical questions such as "Is it yours?!" (meaning, it is not yours!) are used when a child reaches for something that is not theirs to take. The language addressed to the preverbal child consists largely of "one-liners" which call for no verbal response. Either an action or termination of an action is the appropriate reaction. Other than these utterances, very little connected discourse is directed to the young child by adult caregivers.

This pattern of adults not treating infants as communicative partners continues even when babies begin babbling. Kaluli recognize babbling (*dabedan*) but say that this vocal activity is not communicative and has no relationship to speech that will eventually emerge. Adults and older children occasionally repeat vocalizations back to the young child (ages 12–16 months), reshaping them into the names of persons in the household or into kinterms. However, adults do not expect that children this age will be able to produce closer approximations of these names, and there is no pressure on them to do so. Thus, throughout the preverbal period very little talk is directed to the child, except for imperatives, rhetorical questions, and greetings. A child who by Kaluli terms has not yet begun to speak is not expected to respond either vocally or verbally. What this means is that in the first 18 months or so very little sustained dyadic verbal exchange occurs between adult and infant.

All this does not mean that Kaluli children grow up in an impoverished verbal environment. Quite the opposite! The verbal environment of infants is rich and varied, and from the very beginning infants are surrounded by adults and older children who spend a great deal of time talking to one another about what they are doing. In addition, the infants' on-going activities such as standing and what they are eating are topics of talk between members of the household. All of this talk about the here-and-now is available to the infant though it is not talk addressed or directed to the infant. For example, in referring to the infant's actions, siblings and adults will use the infant's name or a kinterm. They will say, "Look at Seligiwo! He's walking by himself." Thus children may learn from these contexts to attend to and learn from the verbal environment in which they live.

Every society has its own ideology about language, including when it begins and how children acquire it. The Kaluli are no exception. Kaluli claim that language begins at the time when the child uses two critical words, *nɔ* 'mother' and *bo* 'breast'. The child may be using other single words, but until these two words are used, the beginning of language is not recognized. Once a child has used these two words, a whole constellation of interrelated behaviors is set into motion. Kaluli claim that once a child has begun to use language, he or she then must be 'shown how to speak' (*to widan*) (Schieffelin, 1979). Kaluli show their children language by using a teaching strategy. They provide a model for what the child is to say, followed by the word *ɛlɛma,* an imperative meaning 'say like that'. Mothers use this method of direct instruction to teach the social uses of assertive language (teasing, shaming, requesting, challenging, reporting). However, object labeling is never part of an *ɛlɛma* sequence, nor does the mother ever use *ɛlɛma* to instruct the child to beg or appeal for food or object. Begging, the Kaluli say, is natural for children. They know how to do it, and need not be taught. In contrast, a child must be taught to be assertive through the use of particular linguistic expressions and verbal sequences.

A typical sequence using *ɛlɛma* is triadic, involving the mother, child (between 20–36 months) and other participant(s). For example,

Mɛli 26 months, her cousin Mama 40 months, and her mother are sitting around the house. The two girls have been talking and teasing each other about a large carton in the room.[1]

Mama → Mɛli: *ge   bokisi -ya   diɛfenɔ*
                you box   LOC put:1:FUT
                'I will put you in the box.'

Mɛli → Mama: *ne   bokisi -ya   diɛfenɔ*
               I/me
               ?'I will put in the box'

Mother → Mɛli ⇒ Mama: *gi   bokisi -yɔ   hɛ?!*
                               your box   NEUTRAL what about
                               ɛlɛma.
                               say:IMP
                               'What about your box?!' say like that.

Mɛli → Mama: *gi bokisi -yɔ hɛ?!*
               'What about your box!'

Mama (pointing to box) → Mɛli: *giyɔlɔ hɛ?!*
                                     yours   what about
                                     'What about yours?!'

Mother → Mɛli ⇒ Mama: *niyɔ   dalab   ɛlɛma.*
                               mine   have:3:PRES say:IMP
                               'I have mine' say like that.

Mɛli → Mama: *niyɔ   dalab*
               'I have mine'

Mother → Mɛli ⇒ Mama: *niyɔ   halo   ɛlɛma*
                               mine up there   say:IMP
                               'Mine is up there' say like that

---

[1]Ages for all children are given in months and weeks. For example, 25.3 means 25 months and 3 weeks. Transcription conventions for speaker/hearer in triadic exchanges are as follows: single arrow → indicates addressee, double arrow ⇒ indicates intended addressee.

Mɛli → Mama: *niyɔ   niyɔ   hado-wɔ   hɛ?   Mama!   giyɔ   hado-wɔ*
              mine   raw Q   huh?   yours raw Q
            'Mine, mine is raw? huh? Mama! is yours raw?'

(Mama and Mother laugh at Mɛli's mishearing and Mɛli starts another teasing routine, claiming that Mama's sweet potatoes (not present) are not cooked.)

In this situation, as in many others, the mother does not modify her language to fit the linguistic ability of the young child. Instead her language is shaped so as to be appropriate (in terms of form and content) for the child's intended addressee. Consistent with the ways she interacts with her infant, what a mother instructs her young child to say usually does not have its origins in any verbal or nonverbal behavior of the child, but in what the mother thinks should be said. The mother pushes the child into ongoing interactions that the child may or may not be interested in and will at times spend a good deal of energy in trying to get the child verbally involved. This is part of the Kaluli pattern of fitting (or pushing) the child into the situation, rather than changing the situation to meet the interests or abilities of the child. Thus mothers take a directive role with their young children, teaching them what to say so that they may become participants in the social group.

In addition to instructing their children by telling them what to say in extensive interactional sequences, Kaluli mothers pay attention to the form of their children's utterances. They will correct the phonological, morphological, or lexical form of an utterance or its pragmatic or semantic meaning. Since the goals of language acquisition include a child becoming competent, independent, and mature sounding in his language, Kaluli use no Baby Talk lexicon, for they said (when I asked about it) that to do so would result in a child sounding babyish which was clearly undesireable and counter-productive. The entire process of a child's development, of which language acquisition plays a very important role, is thought of as a hardening process and culminates in the child's use of "hard words," speech that is well-formed and situationally appropriate (Feld & Schieffelin, 1982).

The cultural dispreference for saying what another might be thinking or feeling has important consequences for the organization of dyadic exchanges between child and caregiver. For one, it affects the ways in which meaning is negotiated during an exchange. For the Kaluli the responsibility for clear expression is with the speaker, and child speakers are not exempt from this. Rather than offering possible interpretations or guessing what a child is saying or meaning, caregivers make extensive use of clarification requests such as "huh?" and "what?" in an attempt to elicit clearer expression from the child. Since responsibility for communication lies with the speaker, children are also instructed with ɛlɛma to request clarification (using similar forms) from others when they do not understand what someone is saying to them.

Another important consequence of not saying what another thinks is the absence of adult expansions of child utterances. Kaluli caregivers will put words into their children's mouths, but these words originate with the caregiver. They rarely elaborate or expand utterances initiated by the child. Nor do they jointly build propositions across utterances and speakers except in the context of sequences with ɛlɛma in which they are constructing talk for the child.

All of these patterns of early language use, such as the lack of expansions or verbally attributing an internal state to an individual, are consistent with cultural conventions of adult language usage. The Kaluli avoid gossip, and often indicate the source of information they report. They make extensive use of quoted speech in a language that does not allow indirect quotation. They utilize a range of evidential markers in their speech to indicate the source of speakers' information: for example, whether something was said, seen, heard, or gathered from other kinds of evidence. These patterns are also found in early child speech and affect the organization and acquisition of conversational exchanges in this society. (See Ochs & Schieffelin, 1984.)

OVERALL SKETCH OF DEVELOPMENT

2. Early Language (20–24 months)

By 20 months Kaluli children have acquired the names of common foods (*mɛn* 'sago/food', *jun* 'asparagus', *galen* 'crayfish', *magu* 'banana', *hɔn* 'water'), animals (*gasa* 'dog', *kabo* 'pig'), body parts (*dagi* 'hand', *bo* 'breast'), and household objects (*as* 'bag', *helebe* 'knife', *i* 'wood/stick'). However, this aspect of language, the saying of names, is downplayed in Kaluli families. There are no labeling games to facilitate or encourage the learning of object names. This is primarily due to the linguistic ideology of the culture. It is only in families who are acquiring literacy that one sees any attention paid to saying the names of objects, and this activity is initiated by the child when the mother is looking at books. When extended by the child to other contexts, the mother's response is disinterest.

In contrast, because of the cultural importance placed on learning the proper names and kinterms of the individuals with whom they interact, Kaluli children are consistently encouraged to master a large number of proper names, kinterms, and other relationship terms. They are corrected if the name is misapplied or mispronounced and told to repeat it correctly. While children have little problem in addressing their parents (*nɔwɔ* 'my mother', *dowɔ* 'my father'), when referring to the parents of others they have difficulty shifting to the correct forms (*gɔwɔ* 'your mother', *gɔlɔ* 'your father', *ene ano* 'his/her mother', *ene inya* 'his/her father'). Errors in reference continue with this set of kinterms, which is applied to a large set of individuals (not just biological parents, but classificatory parents) at 30 months. Such errors include switching terms for mother and father

(3rd person) and switching 1st and 2nd person terms in reference, but never in address. Children are usually corrected when this occurs.

In terms of linguistic development it is important to emphasize that Kaluli children learn selected aspects of particular linguistic systems, such as a restricted set of tense markers or only the 1st person of a given pronoun set. Therefore one must talk fairly specifically about which tenses and for which persons any particular aspect of language is being learned. One cannot say that the young child, for example, uses the verb *dimina* 'give'. One must specify which forms are used at any one time.

Kaluli children use the nonfocused form of the 1st and 2nd person subject pronouns by 22 months. Most early nouns lack any casemarking. Young language learners also use deictics and demonstratives (*we* 'this/here', *ko* 'that/there'), though errors distinguishing proximal/distal occur well beyond 24 months.

Possessive relationships for 1st person are expressed with possessive adjectives in combination with a limited set of deictics and nouns. For 3rd person the order of nouns expresses possession before casemarking is used. Possessive pronouns are used in the 1st person in assertions of ownership (*nɛnɔ* 'mine'), and with an interrogative particle added to 2nd person (*gɛnɔwɔ?* 'is it yours?!') used in challenges of ownership.

Locative relations are always marked by a general locative casemarking suffixed to a range of lexical items including deictics and nouns.

we	-*na*	*ɛn*	-*a*
this/here	LOC	it	LOC

'on this, on here, on it'

a	-*ya*		*as*	-*a*
house	LOC		bag	LOC

'in/at/to (the) house'   'in/on (the) bag'

Function words such as 'gone' (*ane* for animates) and 'none' (*aundoma* for inanimates) are frequent, both as single words and in two-word utterances. However, the animate/inanimate distinction is not always applied correctly. An additional form is *nowɔ* 'another'. (Animacy is not distinguished in Kaluli for this form.)

Early negation is expressed in a variety of ways: as a verb of affect/internal state (*mɔbeab* 'unwilling', rejection of object/action/proposition); as a negative imperative (*diɛsabo* 'don't take'); and with several lexical items expressing negation which can only be used as single words (*a* 'no', *ɛm*, 'no', *mɔ* 'no, not'). Kaluli children have a range of other affective expressions using verbs (*ne tagidab* 'I'm afraid') as well as both positive and negative expressive words (*yagidi* 'yikes!').

The first verbs include a limited number of imperatives (*hamana* 'go', *mena* 'come', *dimina* 'give', *bɔba* 'look') and a restricted set of verbs in selected forms such as 'take:1:PRES', 'see:2:PRES:Q', 'eat:PAST, 3:PRES, PRES:IMP', and 'go:PAST, 3:PRES'. One never hears an uninflected verb form, though one hears incorrectly inflected forms and misanalyzed stems.

Requests are important in early language. However many requests are pragmatically limited and are not expandable to more complex structures. Only the word order in these constructions provides "building blocks" for other types of constructions. One frequent request consists of the 1st person dative form *nelɔ* 'to me'. Since this is the only dative form at this time and is restricted to requests, it should be considered a formulaic expression that appears in limited syntactic constructions with a restricted set of nouns (mostly foods) and deictics. It also is correctly used with a single verb, *nɔl* 'eat:1:PRES' meaning 'I want to eat', literally 'to me I eat'. Later it is used with only a few verbs, and its use is restricted to begging requests even in adult usage. Another early request is *nowɔ ne* 'some to me'. This formulaic expression does not take dative casemarking.

While there is no Baby Talk lexicon, there is one imperative form *mɔ/mo* 'give' used only by children when whining and begging for food and for the breast. Children will use the fuller form *dimina* or *mina* when not whining, and select the reduced form when whining until about 27 months, at which time only the full form is used (in all contexts). None of the above request forms are instructed since they are in a begging mode. However, Kaluli children have ample opportunity to hear other youngsters using these begging forms and probably acquire them through that exposure.

In addition to these aspects of language, there are a number of discourse level features that Kaluli children use in their early utterances. To many of their early single and multiword utterances, such as deictics, possessive pronouns, and various verb forms, they attach word final (and sentence final) emphatic particles. These particles indicate several different degrees of emphasis. Homophonous with several nominal casemarkers (ergative, instrumental, genitive), they are phonologically conditioned (-*ɛ*/-*yɛ*/-*wɛ*) and are stable forms across all word classes, except past tense of verbs, where a vowel change indicates tense agreement. Children under 24 months only use the nonpast form.

There are other discourse level features of language that children master early on. In Kaluli, as in all other societies, individuals must acknowledge when they are called, indicate compliance with or refusal of requests, reply affirmatively or negatively to questions, and request clarification. All of these speech acts must be accomplished in culturally specific ways. In Kaluli two of these responses *o* 'huh?', 'okay' have the same phonological shape, and changes in the intonational contour convey the intended meaning. Kaluli children learn to use these single-word utterances early. While these openings, closings and acknowledgments are not usually reported in other acquisition studies, they are crucial for children to learn if they are to engage in discourse with others. The fact that these lexical items are explicitly instructed shows the importance Kaluli place on their use.

Lacking in early Kaluli speech are adjectives, colors, adverbs, and numbers.

2.1. *The Development of Syntax (24–30 months)*

It is difficult to distinguish a clear single word from a multiword stage in Kaluli since early language includes formulaic phrases (mostly requests and rhetorical questions), a range of multi-word expressions such as those with agents/actors accompanying verbs inflected for person/tense, nouns and deictics with emphatic and evidential particles, as well as with limited casemarking (though locative is always marked). In addition, given the amount of ellipsis in the language, and the infrequent use of three constituent utterances in casual adult speech, Kaluli child language even in its early productive usage, appears to sound relatively mature compared with the utterances of children speaking English. Single words and two constituent utterances are very common in adult-adult casual speech and adult-child speech. While the children's earliest samples were dominated by single words, by 25 months, multiword (two-word utterances) were increasing. Even in the latest samples (32.2 months) single words are frequently and appropriately used. Single words in Kaluli, therefore, have a somewhat different status than they do in languages in which deletion and ellipsis are not major discourse factors.

With regard to casemarking on nouns, at about 25 months most nouns in the role of agent/actor, instrument, or direct and indirect object lack any casemarking or have neutral casemarking which is not correct by adult standards. However, between 25 and 28 months several markers were being used, if inconsistently. The genitive casemarker (which is homophonous with agent and instrument as well as with certain emphatic particles) was the first to be used with any regularity, though it was not used in all obligatory contexts until about 30 months. Following its use for genitive marking, the same morpheme was used to mark ergatives, instrumentals (body parts), and finally other instrumentals (objects such as knives, sticks), in that order. One error that occurred during this time (26–30 months) was double casemarking on NPs that were composed of nouns modified by demonstratives, deictics, and directionals (especially with locatives, indirect objects, and less frequently, ergatives). Only the modifier should carry the inflected material for the noun phrase, but children were casemarking both the noun and its modifier.

However, children very rarely put the wrong casemarking on nouns, and used neutral or zero marking rather than incorrect marking. The neutral or absolutive case markers (-ɔ/-wɔ/-yɔ) were often dropped in fast speech by children and adults or difficult to hear when they did occur. It is not possible at this time to present an acquisition pattern for the Neutral/Absolutive set of morphemes.

By about 25 months possessive relationships are indicated simultaneously in several ways. For 1st and 2nd person, possessive adjectives (*ni* 'my', *gi* 'your') are followed by proper and common nouns and deictics. For example,

ni	gasa	gi	babo		ni	ko
my	dog	your	mother's brother		my	that

For 3rd person, possession is expressed by genitive casemarking (*-ɛ* with phonological conditioning) on nouns such as,

Abi-yɛ	*Abi-yɛnɔ*
GEN	GEN
'Abi's'	'It is Abi's'

and by word order (Noun + – genitive casemarking + Noun—Possessor + Possessed). Children during this time period do not take the 3rd person pronominal options that are available in the language and use only the possessor's name.

However, segmentation was a problem with some of these forms, and both Abi and Wanu made errors of oversegmentation. For example,

Wanu 25.1 *Babi wɛ   -yɔ   we   (= *we Babi-yɛnɔ*)
                 GEN NEUTRAL this   this   GEN
           'This is Babi's'

Abi 25.1 *Babi-yɛ   we   (= *we Babi-yɛnɔ*)
                 GEN   this
           'This is Babi's'

           *i   -yɔ   wɛ   we   -yɔ   (= *iyɛ we*)
           stick NEUTRAL   INST this NEUTRAL
           'with this stick'

Abi 28.2 *go   wɛ   wɛnɔ   (= *gowɛnɔ*)
                 mother GEN GEN   'mother's'

           *abe ɛnɔ-wɔ   (= *abɛnɔwɔ*)
           who   it Q   'whose is it?'

In the first two examples we see that when there is difficulty in forming the genitive it is due to using the deictic (*we* 'this') instead of adding the suffix *-ɛnɔ* which is composed of the genitive (*-ɛ*) and the word *ɛnɔ* 'it'. This sample pattern interfered with Abi's early formation of the instrumental. Oversegmentation errors, such as found in Abi 28.2 show the child's analysis of the underlying morphological forms. Forms segmented in this way are never heard in adult speech.

The general locative morpheme continues to be used with a range of nouns in syntactic constructions with the specific locative meaning derived from verbs as in adult usage. A limited number of spatial terms which take the locative suffix (*wɛl* 'top', 'above', *uš* 'inside', 'under', and *hɛg* 'side') are added. An additional suffix *-lɔwa* 'to the place of' is added to proper names and kinterms. During this time period, the child acquires a large number of place names (names of specific streams, grounds) used when talking about the whereabouts of individuals.

In addition to locatives, Kaluli employs an elaborate set of directionals indicating culturally important ways of conveying spatial relationships. These include orienting notions from the perspective of the speaker with regard to a referent such as 'up/down hill', 'up/down stream' as well as 'above' and 'below'. Through a regular set of infixed consonants these directional terms also mark the referent that they modify in terms of animate/inanimate, and if animate, whether or not it is moving. These directionals (which may occur alone) also combine with the deictic system for additional specificity. At about 28 months a limited set of directionals is added. However, many of these are incorrectly used, and distinctions between animate and inanimate are not made consistently.

Kaluli do not employ a large elaborated set of adjectives, adverbs, or quantifiers. While their use is infrequent between 24–30 months, they do occur. Adjectives (which must occur with the head noun) include *lɛsu* 'small', *badyo* 'large', *sambo* 'long'. Quantifiers (which can be used as single words) include *hɛlu* 'little/few' and *alan* 'large-sized'. (The word *modɔ* 'many' is not used during this time.) In addition, these terms combine with one another, and children do use them as nominal modifiers such as *hɛlulɛsu* 'very small' and in existential constructions such as *we alan badiyɔ* 'This is very big.' The main adverbs used are *hɛsɛ* 'slowly', *bɔbɔge* 'quickly', *wɔnɔle* 'secretly'. There were occasional reversals in the order of words in noun phrases. For example, children incorrectly produced constructions with modifiers preceding (rather than following) the head nouns and deictics.

The majority of interrogative constructions involve no syntactic alteration of the word order found in declarative utterances. There are three types of interrogative suffixes which are added to the final syllable of the last word of the utterance. One set of suffixes is exclusively for verbs and is used for interrogatives that are direct questions and require an answer. While verbs in declarative utterances follow a two-way split in person markers (1st and non 1st person), verbs in interrogative utterances have a three-way distinction (1st, 2nd, and 3rd person). Because children tend to follow the pattern for declarative sentences, they have difficulty in using these interrogative suffixes correctly, due to the additional distinction made.

The second type of interrogative suffix is for lexical items that take nominal morphology. A single suffix (-ɔ with morphophonemic alternations) makes any noun or pronoun an interrogative. This suffix is acquired by 25 months.

The third interrogative particle is also formed by a single suffix (-ɛlɛ) and is applied across all word types and in verbs after the 1st person or 3rd person tense inflection. It has the gloss, 'I wonder (if it is mine, where he is going' etc.) or 'Is it really . . .'. When used, a listener is not under the same obligation to answer as one is with the direct interrogative sentences. This form presented difficulty for one child, Abi (25–27 months). Rather than using the verbal interrogative suffixes, he attached the -ɛlɛ suffix directly to the stem material of the verb producing incorrect utterances such as,

A 25.1   *ge   ɔba   *han - ɛlɛ*   (= *ge ɔba hana-ya*)
         you   where   go   Q   go:2:PRES:Q
         'Where are you going?'

There are several ways to form questions involving the equivalent of 'wh' words. One may use constructions such as,

do   ɔba   or   *do   hɛ*
father   where   what about
'Where's father?'   or   'What about father?'

we   ɔba
this   what
'What's this?'

These types of constructions require no inflections and no verb. They are frequent in casual conversation and are acquired by 24 months without errors. Other interrogative constructions may be formed using verbs such as,

do   ɔba   sab -a   or   *do   ɔba   sab-ɛlɛ*
father   where   is:3:PRES:Q   Q
'Where is my father?'   or   'I wonder where my father is?'

These presented more difficulty and Abi produced utterances such as

A 25.3   **aba   -lab   -ɛlɛ*   (= *aba sabɛlɛ*)
         where   *   Q
         'I wonder where he/she is?'

         *ɛnɔ-   ba-   lab-ɛlɛ   (= *ɛnɔbɛlɛ*)
         it   what   *   Q
         'I wonder what it is?'

```
*we   abe / /*we   abe-   ɛlɛ/ /*ko   abe-ɛlɛ
this  who                 Q    that    Q

(= ko/we     abɛnɔwɔ    or    abɛnɔwɛlɛ)
   that/this whose             who:it:Q
'Whose is it/this/that?'
```

Through these errors we see Abi's misanalysis of the formation of certain types of interrogative structures. He has suffixed a single form -ɛlɛ to interrogative pronouns and to part of the verb-stem material. In some cases he inserted other verb-like morphemes such as -lab which are found in Kaluli but not in this type of construction. While Mɛli made no errors of this type, Wanu produced utterances with redundant expression such as,

```
W 26.3   *abe   abɛnɔ-wɔ      (= abɛnɔwɔ)
         who    whose is it    'whose is it'
```

'When' and 'why' questions (as true information seeking questions) are almost never asked at all by either parents or children. 'Why' questions are rhetorical and not meant to be answered. Children do not produce rhetorical 'why' questions until they are over 5 years.

Other questions used at this time are rhetorical questions and formulaic expressions which are instructed through ɛlɛma sequences and produced spontaneously as well as imitatively. Some of these do not involve any morphological means to indicate interrogative (ge ɔba?! 'Who are you?') while others do (genɔwɔ?! 'Is it yours?!'). Finally, interrogative particles were suffixed to nouns and possessive pronouns in clarification requests following the usage patterns of Kaluli adults. These interrogatives used the identical morphosyntactic forms as did the rhetorical questions, but followed a different intonational contour.

The number of different verbs increased during this time as did the distribution of tense inflections. Verbs (as in the adult language) always appeared with inflected material and were used as single words and in multiword constructions.

At this time imperatives were used with and without subject pronouns and direct objects. Children showed a predictable acquisition of a large number of transitive, intransitive, and stative verbs. In addition to simple verbs ('come', 'go', 'give') children used a restricted set of concatenated verbs. These verbs express sequential and purposive action, and in a number of cases stress disambiguates otherwise similar surface forms due to contraction. Initially these verbs were treated as single lexical items and there was no evidence of analysis of the two different underlying forms of the suffixes (sequential action and purposive action). Purposives were the first complex verbal relationship to be expressed morphologically. (Verbs used include sieniane 'went in order to pick', and diɛ (ni)hɔnɔl 'I'm going in order to take'. Consecutive past action verbs, which followed, included omɛ or omina 'having chewed give', and diɛ(gɛ)-mena 'having taken come' or 'bring'.

The use of the quotative verb 'say:3' preceded by a sentential object to report the speech of others is frequent from the age of 26 months. Direct quotation is frequently used to report speech, and children are encouraged to contribute a turn of talk in this manner. The verb 'say' is used in both past and present.

Aspect is expressed in Kaluli through prefixes, infixes, and lexical items. Infixes are infrequent before 30 months. Around 30 months, one of several preverbal particles became productive. This prefix, -ɔ 'still' is used to indicate duration. Other expressions of aspect by lexical and morphological means were acquired after this period.

Additional means of verbal negation were acquired between 24 and 30 months. In addition to an increase in different negative imperatives, children correctly prefixed the negative morpheme *mɔ-* to verbs in the past, future, and habitual tenses in simple verbs, and correctly placed the negative prefix on the initial verb in complex forms taking auxiliary verbs. They continued to use less complex forms of lexical negation in pragmatically appropriate ways. By 30 months they were adding the negative suffix (*-ba/-ma*) to nominals and deictics.

At the discourse level, emphatic particles marking degree of intensification were added across a wider range of utterance types, especially on 1st and 2nd person possessive pronouns and imperatives in requests, and when repeating utterances that are not understood. However, between 28–30 months children changed the final vowel of a word to the emphatic suffix, which is not correct. For example,

    nowɔ 'another' *nowɛ   dowɔ 'was' *dowɛ

In addition, one of a set of evidential particles becomes productive, *-lɔb,* which indicates visual evidence, such as *welɔb* 'it's here' said when finding something that was previously out of sight. Emphatic particles may be attached to this evidential. For example, by 25 months children produced utterances such as *welɔbɛ* 'it's really here!' By 28 months, children use the past form of the emphatic for verbs and following the evidential *-lɔb* 'I see evidence' on deictics and existential forms, such as *aundoma* 'there is none' to change the tense of that word. For example, *aundoma* 'there is none', *aundomalɔb,* 'there is none (I see)' and *aundomalɔbe* 'there was none (I saw)'. By 28 months they use several emphatic forms in sequence to intensify their utterances.

Different sets of nominal and verbal suffixes are used depending on whether one is close or distant from the addressee. Different intonational contours are used if someone is saying something for the first, second, or third time. These different aspects of language use are acquired by 28 months. However, children do tend to use different evidential and discourse suffixes as general emphatics, without the correct pragmatic force.

Only those word orders found in adult speech were used by Kaluli children. Initially utterances with the following word orders were produced: OV, AV, SV,

O DAT (noun/deictic + 'to me'), DAT V, LOC V, A LOC V, S LOC V. However, for three children all word orders were produced with higher frequency with 1st person agents than with 3rd person agents. Once three constituent utterances were established, OAV utterances were produced with higher frequency than AOV for all children.

2.2. *Later Acquisition (30+ months)*

As noted above, Kaluli has a rather elaborate set of directionals which through infixing also encode animate/inanimate. A further distinction is made within the category of animate: +/−movement. These forms emerged around 30 months but were not used correctly. The animacy/inanimacy distinction was usually not acquired until later.

Even at 30 months (and beyond) there was a pattern of deletion in ergative casemarking in AV utterances for certain verbs, but obligatory casemarking was used in OAV utterances.

After 30 months children acquired more complex forms of negation, including a set of suffixes for verbs and nominals used to counter assertions and actions.

Children began to use a limited set of future imperatives, both positive and negative, including infixes that express plurality in both present and future imperative. Aspect was beginning to be expressed morphologically (by infixing) and lexically.

Rather than just using the verb 'say' preceded by the quoted speech, around 30 months children quoted speech by bracketing the sentential object (the quoted speech) with the agent (marked with the ergative) and the inflected verb.

There were no relative clauses used before 32 months. Children used two separate propositions to express the coordination of two actions by two different agents before morphosyntactic means were used. Complex constructions are limited to same agent/actor (for both dependent and independent clauses). There was no morphologically marked switch reference before 32 months.

Around 32 months a fuller range of evidential markers are used to indicate source of evidence: 'having heard', 'inferred from evidence' emerged and children began to use these more specifically for their evidential features, not as generalized emphatics.

WORD ORDER

3. The Pragmatics of Word Order

Kaluli has two allowable word orders: OAV and AOV. Except in situations where speakers believe that listeners have not understood what they are referring to, the verb is always final. When such self-repair sequences occur and a NP appears after the verb, there is a marked pause followed by the clarification of the referring expression. For example,

ko	ni	mɔnɔ	siabulu	-wɔ
that	I	eat:PAST	sweet	ABS
			potato	

'I ate that . . . the sweet potato.'

Word order is used for pragmatic focus. "The constituent with the most salient or important pragmatic information" is in focus (Givón 1975, p. 185). In Kaluli focus can be thought of from two perspectives. In utterances that have two NPs, the second NP is in focus and the first NP is not. Thus the NP that is in preverbal position indicates what is in focus, what is at issue, or what is being contrasted by the speaker in the discourse. In other words, in utterances with two NP constituents, the second NP has the relatively new information. It can be seen as the informational highlight of the sentence. Therefore in sentences in OAV order, the agent is in focus; sentences in AOV order, the agent is not in focus.

Furthermore, given the pragmatics of these word orders, each one is selected and used by speakers in different speech genres and registers, for different speech acts. OAV, with the agent in focus, is used in a variety of speech acts, such as requests, teasing, tattling, and in arguments over who shall perform a specific action. For example,

Three people are sitting around and one spots a cucumber. Speaker 1 reaches for it.

Speaker 1:
yagan	-ɔ	ni	diɛnɔ.
cucumber	ABS	I	take:1:FUT

'I'll take the cucumber.'

Speaker 2:
a!	yagan	-ɔ	nisa	diɔl.
no	cucumber	ABS	I (not	take:1:PRES
			you)	

'No! I take the cucumber!'

In this example Speaker 1 is a potential agent and uses OAV order in claiming the cucumber. Both agent and object are expressed since a new topic is being introduced. Speaker 2 challenges the claim and uses another focused pronoun which is more specific ('I not you'). Since the agent is what is the issue, or informational highlight of the sentence, OAV order is used. For emphasis, both agent and object are expressed by Speaker 2.

Utterances with AOV order are used to announce or report an action, in narratives and stories, or when the speaker is focusing on or contrasting the object. For example,

Abi's older sister (age 9) sees him drinking dirty water. Calling to her mother to inform her,

Abi	-yɔ	hɔn	mɔgagɔ	-wɔ	nab	-o
	NEUTRAL	water	bad	NEUTRAL	eat:3:PRES	EMPH

'Abi is drinking bad water!'

It is alright for Abi to drink, but not dirty water. The object he is acting on is problematic, in focus and placed directly before the verb.

In these examples we can see how the pragmatic concerns of the speaker are reflected in the way in which elements of the utterance are arranged. Pragmatic concerns and context determine the word order selected by speakers. In turn, word-order selection communicates the concerns of the speaker to the listener.

These pragmatic functions are also conveyed in the use of two-constituent utterances. AV utterances are those in which the agent is less topical, information about the agent is relatively new, in focus, and more specified. However, from the speaker's perspective the outcome for the agent is less certain. In OV utterances, information about agents is referenced in the verb through bound person suffixes and further information is presumed to be given.

In addition to the order of NP constituents, the number of expressed constituents in Kaluli follows discourse constraints. Three-constituent utterances, especially those with full nouns expressing agent and object, are relatively infrequent in everyday conversational discourse. One 4-hour language sample was analyzed in order to compare the relative frequency of three-constituent utterances in child and adult speech. The sample that was chosen was the last sample from Mɛli (32.2 months) since that was the most advanced child language sample. In addition, during this taping a number of adults were present and their conversations with her as well as with each other were quite extensive. In that sample five adults produced of 1476 utterances which included 29 utterances with expressed agent and object. Mɛli produced 1514 utterances of which 49 utterances had expressed agent and object. This suggests that a higher number (and proportion) of three-constituent utterances does not mean greater linguistic competence.

When three-constituent utterances do occur their use is patterned. They are used to introduce a discourse topic when talk has not yet been established. For example,

A group of people return to the house having left a food packet containing *yɛsi* (a small marsupial) warming on the coals. Finding it gone and seeing a couple of bones on the floor one exclaimed,

yɛsi	-yɔ	gasa	-yɛ	mɔn	-ga
	ABS	dog	ERG	eat:PAST	EVID

'The dogs/A dog obviously ate the *yɛsi*'

Three-constituent utterances are often used as initial requests, threats, and tattles—as seen in the examples above. In all of these speech acts the order would be OAV. Three-constituent utterances are frequently found in counter-assertions (as in the example above). In addition, the use of both agent and object adds emphasis to the speaker's utterance.

Three-constituent utterances are also found in contexts where a speaker tries to change the topic of ongoing discourse, attempts to establish his place in the conversation, or tries to break into the turn of another speaker. They also occur when a speaker changes addressee in conversation without the use of a vocative.

In addition to these uses in conversation, three-constituent utterances are also found as expansions following clarification requests and as self-repair on utterances by a speaker when he has some reason to believe that his message has not been conveyed with adequate clarity. A common pattern is for a single-constituent utterance (usually the inflected verb) to be expanded to a two-constituent utterance following some need for clarification, and for a two-constituent utterance to be expanded to three. Almost without exception, expansion takes place to the left of the expressed constituents, that is in an AV utterance, expansion would be to OAV. Speakers do not insert constituents into a two-constituent utterance.

Finally, in addition to the order and number of constituents occurring in the discourse, the distribution and choice of new and old information conveying lexical forms (nouns, pronouns, deictics) in the expression of NP constituents is important. The use of two full nouns is usually reserved for utterances that introduce a topic, when the addressee is out of the immediate visual context and would not be able to adequately identify the referents through deictics or demonstratives, or when there is reason for emphasis. Otherwise, speakers use non-focused forms of the pronouns in AOV utterances and deictics, demonstratives, and other given information markers as objects in OAV utterances, such as the following:

Two women are reaching for the same stalk of asparagus,

Speaker 1:   *ko   niba   dagumiɛni*
             that I (not you) peel:INTENT 1
             'I am about to peel that.'

3.1. *Acquisition of Word Order Patterns*

Kaluli children, in keeping with the adult model of verb-final syntax, produced only verb-final utterances. This pattern was established at the outset and continued throughout all samples. In terms of the order of elements within the utterance, children consistently (correctly) placed locatives and adverbs before the verb when only one of the two major constituents was expressed (agent/object). There were occasional errors in order when both major constituents were expressed.

With only two exceptions, children's use of AOV utterances was pragmatically appropriate. They were used to announce intended actions and describe ongoing activities where the agent was not in focus. OAV utterances were also used appropriately in teasing, tattling, shaming, and requesting. Children used word order pragmatically appropriately before they used grammatical casemarking correctly. There is strong evidence from two-word utterances that children were encoding agent and verb when the agent was in focus. When it was not, they encoded object and verb. The reason that pragmatic usage in word order precedes grammatical casemarking is most likely due to the fact that word order is tied to pragmatic function. Word order is more salient than casemarking, in that alternative word orders are more obvious than the presence or absence of a one-syllable casemarker. Any language (such as Kaluli) which uses word order for pragmatic purposes will have an interaction between discourse and syntax. The Kaluli data suggest that children from an early age are sensitive to that interaction and the meaning conveyed by different word orders. However, to become competent speakers, children must use the morphological devices of their language as well.

Comparing the frequency of OAV and AOV 1st person declarative utterances, for all children OAV utterances were of considerably higher frequency than AOV utterances (17 of 25 samples, 3 samples having equal frequencies). This is not surprising, considering that OAV utterances are used in requests and situations where the child wants something for him/herself. OAV 3rd person utterances were of higher frequency in only 9 of 25 samples, with 9 samples equal. However, OAV (combined 1st and 3rd person) utterances were consistently more frequent than AOV utterances throughout all samples (17 of 25 samples, 2 samples being equal). Given that this OAV order is used for tattling, teasing, arguments, all parts of family interaction that include children, it is not surprising that children's word order reflects this fact.

The pattern is somewhat different for two-constituent declarative transitive utterances. The AV/OV pattern is reversed for 1st person. OV were more frequent than AV utterances in 15 of 25 samples, with 2 samples equal. But for 3rd person, AV utterances were more frequent in 10 of 25 samples, but 9 samples equal. Comparing the combined 1st and 3rd person two-constituent utterances, OV was higher frequency in 13 of 25 samples, with 2 samples equal.

Slobin has suggested (following Lehmann, 1973) that the verb and object constitute "a kind of perceptual Gestalt which resists interruption" (1975, p. 197). Ochs's analysis of the acquisition of word order in Samoan confirms Slobin's hypothesis in that "young Samoan children prefer to keep the verb and

patient sequentially contingent, placing the agent either before or after this unit''
(1982, p. 663).

Kaluli children's word order patterns (declaratives only) were analyzed to see
if an OV strategy was preferred. The total OV and AOV utterances for each child
were combined for each sample (referred to hereafter as OV), as were the AV
and OAV utterances (AV). The most striking pattern is one of individual variation. There is no preference in general or developmentally for (transitive) AV or
OV word-order pattern. For Abi, 5 of 8 samples showed higher frequencies of
OV with no developmental trend favoring one pattern over another. For Mɛli, 7
of 8 samples showed higher frequencies for AV, with the 1 sample favoring OV
being at 24.3. Wanu's samples split, with the first three samples (25.1–27.3)
having higher frequency OV (though numerically the samples were close) and
the last three samples (29.–32.1) having higher frequency AV. Given these
findings, there seems to be no overall pattern of word order preference for the
three children.

These findings do not support Slobin's hypothesis nor are they consistent with
Ochs's Samoan data regarding the OV unit.[2] Considering the nature of the
pragmatic functions of word order in Kaluli, the child data suggest that these
three different acquisition patterns have more to do with the particular types of
speech acts that children were using in a given sample rather than indicating a
cognitively based word-order preference. Since requests, challenges, threats,
and tattles are expressed with (O)AV word order, if a child was in interactions
where those speech acts were being used, (O)AV utterances would be produced,
since children did tend to use word order in pragmatically appropriate ways.

The appropriate use of ellipsis in speaking is another important component of
communicative competence. The fact that three-constituent utterances were less
frequent than two-constituent utterances in child speech is not indicative of a lack
of competence. Three-constituent utterances are not more adultlike than two-
constituent utterances. While there is a general developmental trend in the increase of three-constituent utterances, by 31 months there is a decrease in the use
of three-constituent elements. In these later samples the use of three-constituent
utterances tends to be governed by discourse related, rather than language acquisition related issues. While children did not always mark new topics with
three-constituent utterances, when they used them they were almost always
appropriate. The children did follow the parallelism of question word order in
their responses, answering 'who' questions with AV order and 'what' questions
with OV order as in the following example.

Mɛli 32.2 is climbing a tree, out of her mother's sight.

---

[2]Slobin (1977) points out that in OV languages, verbal modification follows the verb and nominal
modification precedes the noun, thus keeping the object and verb together as a unit. This is not the
case in Kaluli and many other verb-final Papuan languages.

Mother:	*ge*	*ɔba*	*dia*		*-yɛ*
	you	what	do:2:PRES		Q:EMPH

'What are you doing?'

Mɛli:	*ne*	*adam*	*-ɔ*	*sulɔl*	*-o*
	I	guava	NEUTRAL	pick:1:PRES	EMPH

'I'm picking guava.'

Depending on the type of talk, number of participants, spatial arrangement of participants, the attention paid to different speakers—the number of three-constituent utterances will vary. Children learn these discourse rules, including deletion and parallelism, by 30 months and produce discourse appropriate speech.

PERSONAL PRONOUNS

4. Personal Pronoun Sets

Like other related languages that have been described for the Trans-New Guinea Phylum, Kaluli has two sets of independent personal pronouns known as focused and nonfocused forms (Wurm 1975, p. 192; Rule, unpublished). In Kaluli the selection of one or another of these pronoun sets depends primarily on how the speaker wishes to express 1st or 2nd person agents or subjects. The selection of one or the other pronoun sets co-occurs with the selection of a specific word order. In brief, nonfocused forms are multifunctional, while focused forms serve only agent functions. Nonfocused forms have distributional parallels with the neutral casemarking system found in AOV utterances. Focused forms are found only in (O)AV utterances as agents, and for the most part are distributed along ergative/absolutive dimensions. While there are dual/plural and inclusive/exclusive forms for some members of both sets, gender is not encoded in any of these pronominal forms.

In order to appropriately use these forms, children must be able to minimally assess the situation, to understand what is being asked of them, and what is being done around them. Children have to learn when it is correct to assert that they will do something themselves, or that they, not someone else, will do the task. Children must learn which forms can be used to initiate something in the discourse and which forms must be used to respond to something in the discourse. What has gone on in the prior discourse and nonverbal context must be taken into account.

4.1. *Nonfocused Pronouns*

There is only one basic nonfocused pronominal form for each person in the singular. These forms are: *ne* 'I/me', *ge* 'you', *e* 'she/he/her/him/it'. There are additional forms marking dual/plural, inclusive/exclusive, but since they are rarely used by children under 3 years they will not be considered here. In addition, in everyday conversation the singular form is used unless duality or plurality is being emphasized. As mentioned briefly above, nonfocused forms have several functions. They are used as the agents of transitive verbs in utterances when the agent precedes the object (AOV), as subjects of intransitive verbs, as experiencers of verbs of affect and internal states (SV), and as objects of transitive verbs. In order to form the dative, the nonfocused form takes a dative suffix *-lɔ* or *-mɔ* as in *nelɔ* 'to me'. Thus, nonfocused forms are not only multifunctional, but they do not distinguish different case relations. For example,

e	*ne*	*sandab*	(AOV)
he/she	me	hit 3:PRES	

'He/she hits me.'

ne	*e*	*sondɔl*	(AOV)
I	him/her	hit:1:PRES	

'I hit him/her.'

However, it is extremely rare in adult or child speech to hear a three-constituent utterance with two nonfocused pronouns, especially with AOV order. Because subject agreement is marked on the verb, and discourse constraints operate on the number of constituents that are expressed, nonfocused agents (in three-constituent utterances) may be deleted, and often are. The preferred form is OV. In fact, the usual pattern in conversation is to delete most NPs which are to the left of a focused NP or a dative. Nonfocused forms are also used in existencial constructions without verbs, such as,

ne	*wego*
I	here

'I'm right here.'

ge	*ɔba*
you	who

'Who are you?'

4.2. Acquisition of Nonfocused Pronouns

The 1st person nonfocused form, *ne,* is used in early syntactic expressions first as an agent of transitive verbs (AOV/AV) and as a subject (actors, experiencers) of intransitive verbs (SV). Soon after being used with transitive and intransitive verbs, it is used to express the experiencer with verbs of affect and internal state (such as 'I'm afraid', 'I'm hungry'). The 2nd person form *ge* is used as agent in a limited number of routines and formulaic questions as well as with imperatives. The third person form *e,* which like the other forms is unmarked for number and gender, is used infrequently in both the child and adult samples, deletion being the usual option.

The nonfocused agent forms were acquired before any of the more semantically specific focused agent forms (discussed below) were used. That is, the most general, least semantically specified pronoun forms that could be used with both transitive and intransitive verbs and which are the most frequent in adult speech, are the first to be acquired. In AOV utterances, only nonfocused forms were used to indicate agent. That is, children did not use focused forms for agents followed by objects. This suggests that children in their early syntactic expressions distinguished between focused and nonfocused forms and their correct arrangement with regard to other NPs. Furthermore, as we shall see below, children treated nouns and pronouns differently in terms of semantic role. That is, the semantic role of pronouns was indicated by their position in the sentence, sometimes supported or disambiguated by agreement in the verb. Nouns took additional casemarking to indicate semantic role.

Nonfocused forms were also used as direct objects. However, in the early samples these children did not use the 1st person to express direct objects in imperatives, preferring to use the verb alone, *dimina!* 'give!' much like adults. Nonfocused forms appear later in the samples as direct objects, initially with imperative forms, such as *ne galima* 'carry me'. Use of the 1st person nonfocused form as direct object is relatively infrequent compared to the 2nd person, which is used in threats, such as *ge sɛmɛnigɔl* '(I'm) gonna hit you!'. In fact, use of *ne* 'me' as direct object is infrequent even in later samples, given that it can only occur with 2nd/3rd person verb forms (when the agent is not 1st person). The use of the 3rd person form is quite rare, both for agents and objects, as third persons are indicated by other lexical forms (proper names, kinterms, etc.). Compared with 1st and 2nd person, children have a much lower frequency of 3rd person agents. And in those cases when an object is specified, it is rarely the 3rd person pronoun *e,* but rather a full noun, deictic, or demonstrative. This restricted use of nonfocused forms of the pronoun does not hold for 2nd person, as in certain frequent utterances like '(I) hit you', '(I) carry you'. However, throughout the samples of adult conversational data, the frequency of nonfocused pronouns used as direct objects surprisingly is low. While they are allowed in the language, they do not seem to be a form of choice. The child data reflect this pattern.

As an indirect object *ne* 'me' is used by 20 months. It is used both as a single word and in syntactic expressions such as *nowɔ ne* 'some to me', and *nelɔ* 'to me' (usually begging). Both children and adults use it with nominals in requests such as *mɛn nelɔ* 'food to me' without a verb. It is frequently used with the verb 'give' (especially 3rd person past) in reporting who something was given to (such as *nemɔ miabe* 'gave to me, not someone else'). In this as well as other syntactic contexts (which are not yet fully determined) it appears as *nemɔ*. The dative form is not used for 2nd or 3rd person 'to you', 'to him/her' until the child is at least 3 years of age since children do not seem to talk about individuals giving things to persons other than themselves.

Therefore, while the nonfocused pronouns can serve a variety of functions, they are in fact somewhat restricted by both developmental and pragmatic constraints. In the earliest samples they are predominantly used in the 1st/2nd person to express agent/actor, and in the samples that follow to express 1st and 2nd person direct objects. When used as indirect objects, they may be marked with dative casemarking depending on the social and linguistic context of their occurrence (*-lɔ* or *-mɔ*).

One error children made in using these forms was the occasional selection of a dual or plural form, or an inclusive or exclusive form when that did not seem to be referentially or pragmatically correct. However, in every case when this occurred, children selected forms from within the same person category that would have been correct. This maintenance of person category was probably due to the fact that all 1st person forms, regardless of semantic role are n-initial, all 2nd person forms are g-initial, and the majority of 3rd person forms are e-initial. The similarity of phonological form lends support for learning the broad category of person in pronominal forms.

While children had no difficulty using focused forms in three-constituent utterances, they did have some difficulty in two-constituent utterances, usually with imperatives. In scattered examples until about 30 months, children would use nonfocused pronouns when there was a clear demand for focused forms, as in the last line of the example that follows. Mɛli should have used the focused pronoun back to her mother, *giba*, 'you not I'. However, the category of person was always correct.

Mɛli 28.3 with mother while cooking bananas.

Mɛli: nɔ   siɛfin ko   -mɛ   balema
        mother   tongs   those INST   turn:over:IMP
        'Mother, turn (them) with those tongs.'

Mother: no   niyɔ   giba   balemesea
         and   mine   you (not I) turn:be:IMP
         'and mine, you keep turning'

         ne   de   -yɔ   ɔ-   gidɔ   -kɛ
         I   fire NEUTRAL ASP   light:1:PRES EMPH
         'I'm still lighting the fire.'

Mɛli: *ge   balemesea, nɔ
        you   my:mother
        'You keep turning, mother.'

4.3. *Focused Pronouns*

In many important semantic, syntactic, and pragmatic aspects, focused forms differ from nonfocused forms. First of all, instead of one basic form for each person, there are five focused forms. For 1st person these forms are:

ni	'I'
nɛ	'I emphatic'
nɔnɔ	'I without assistance'
niba	'I not you'
ninɛli	'I alone'

For 2nd person initial g- substitutes for initial n- and all contrasts are between 1st and 2nd persons.

In terms of NP functions, focused forms are used by adults only as agents of transitive verbs, except for one of these forms *ninɛli* 'I alone' which may also be used as actor with intransitive verbs. None of the focused forms may be used to express experiencer with verbs of affect or internal states. Furthermore, for all forms except for *ni* and *ninɛli*, there are restrictions on use with past tense due to pragmatic constraints. Three of these forms (*ni/nɛ/nɔnɔ*) also function as genitives when followed by nouns. Thus they, as well as other focused forms, can only be followed by locatives, adverbs, verbs, and other lexical items that cannot be modified to avoid misinterpretation as a possessive relationship. As we have seen, while focused pronouns do share many features of a set, there is enough variation among these forms (in terms of co-occurrence restrictions with tense/negation/transitivity) to indicate that they do not form a totally homogeneous set.

Unlike nonfocused pronouns, focused forms are restricted both in the semantic functions which they can serve and in their location vis-à-vis the verb. Focused pronouns are used when the agent follows the object and precedes the verb in transitive constructions (OAV) and in AV utterances in response to 'who' questions. These forms are more semantically specific and pragmatically restricted than the nonfocused pronouns. They are used when the agent is the focus of the utterance—the new information—and often appear in utterances with deleted objects (AV) or as single words.

4.4. *Acquisition of Focused Pronouns*

Ascertaining the developmental pattern for focused pronouns was a difficult task. First, in transcription it was often difficult for informants as well as the researcher to determine whether a child was using the unfocused form *ne* 'I' or the focused form *ni* 'I' appropriately. When listening to the speech of young children, native speaker judgment favored the nonfocused form, even in contexts where the focused form was appropriate. Another complication in determining the exact form of this pronoun was that Kaluli adults never corrected it in OAV or AV utterances. Since OAV/AV utterances were often requests or protests uttered in high pitched, whining voices with rapid delivery, it was difficult to determine the exact phonological shape of the vowel.

However, the use of the four other focused forms was much easier to determine because of their phonological distinctness. Before 26 months of age, use of these forms was infrequent. By the age of 27 months, *nɔnɔ* 'I without assistance' and *niba* 'I not you' were established for three children, and *nɛ* 'I emphatic' was being used by two. The two earliest forms (*nɔnɔ* and *niba*) were high frequency forms throughout the samples for all children, while *nɛ* and *ninɛli* 'I alone' were relatively infrequent. Once these forms were acquired, the frequency of their use was determined by the pragmatic demands of the situations in which children found themselves. The children were using *nɔnɔ* 'I by myself' to emphasize that they wanted to perform actions by themselves without the assistance of others (like eating, putting objects on themselves) and used this form when refusing or resisting help from others. This form usually occurred with future or intentive tense markers. The second most frequent form, *niba* 'I not you' was used in arguments over who was going to act on something. The use of this form presupposes an assertion (or action) made by someone else; it is not used as an initial assertion. It is often preceded by *a!* 'no!'. This form cannot be used with past tense, and children never made this type of error.

The last two forms (*nɛ*/*ninɛli*) were used by the children less frequently, but in all cases use was appropriate. In order to use any of these forms correctly, the child must attend to prior situational and discourse contexts and control the different restrictions according to tense, negation, and transitivity. In almost all cases, children used focused forms in two-element utterances (AV) before using them in three-element utterances (OAV). When there was an exception, use was simultaneous.

The children made none of the following errors:

1. In using both 1st and 2nd person focused forms, adult word-order rules were followed. There were no cases where the child used a focused form followed by an object (AOV).

2. The restricted semantic role of focused forms was adhered to. Focused forms were used only as agents, never as direct or indirect objects.

3. Pronouns and nouns were treated differently. Casemarking suffixes were never added to these pronouns in spite of their analogous syntactic position and pragmatic function to nouns that received obligatory ergative casemarking.

4. The distinction between agent of transitive verb, and subject of intransitive verb or experiencer was made. Children did not use focused forms with intransitive verbs or verbs of affect and internal states, but only with transitive verbs. This distinction is further supported by evidence in the use of casemarking on nouns.

5. Children were sensitive to the tense restrictions on some of the focused forms. These forms were not used with verbs in the past tense.

The pattern of acquisition of the focused forms taken together with the errors that do not occur suggest that this is an area where acquisition might be "speech act specific." If the child has some sense of the paradigmatic nature of word order, then focused pronouns can be "mapped" onto the same pragmatic conditions laid out for OAV utterances. This makes their acquisition easier than if the child had to figure out a totally new pragmatic distinction underlying focused pronoun selection. The fact that children followed adult usage regarding tense restrictions is further evidence for the acquisition of the focused pronouns through their association with particular speech acts, since correct usage would fall out from their speech act classification. For example, children did not use *niba* 'I not you' when reporting events in the past, but instead used that form in pragmatically appropriate requests and challenges.

In contrast with data reported on English-speaking children (Bloom, Light-bown, & Hood, 1975, among others), Kaluli children never referred to themselves (as either agent, object, beneficiary, etc.) using anything other than a 1st person pronoun, regardless of verb type or speech act. As noted earlier, mothers and other caregivers never addressed their children using that child's name (such as "Is Abi eating sugar cane?") nor did they ever refer to themselves using anything other than one of the 1st person pronominal forms. In addition, in direct instruction sequences with *ɛlɛma,* caregivers always instructed the child to use one of the appropriate 1st person forms when speaking about him or herself. Perhaps the consistency in both speaking to the child and modeling language for the child explains why there were no errors occurring with the acquisition of the "shifters"—the first and second person pronouns—in any of the Kaluli child data. American mothers, by using both the child's name and personal pronouns, put their children in a "many forms for one function" situation. Children, given such a choice, may stick to their own name, which never changes, rather than trying to use to shifters which do not consistently refer to themselves.

NOMINAL CASEMARKING

5. Casemarking on Nouns

Nouns in Kaluli, as in the majority of languages in the Trans-New Guinea Phylum (Wurm, Laycock, & Voorhoeve, 1975), are not morphologically marked for gender, number, definiteness, or indefiniteness. Nominal morphology is regular, and case relations are indicated through a series of suffixes on proper and common nouns, deictics, and demonstratives. Proper and common nouns, demonstratives, and deictics take the following casemarking suffixes. Phonologically conditioned alternations are indicated in parentheses.

Absolutive	-ɔ	(-wɔ/-yɔ)
Neutral	-ɔ	(-wɔ/-yɔ)

Ergative	-ε	(-wε/-yε)
Instrumental	-ε	(-wε/-yε)
Genitive	-ε	(-wε/-yε)
Comitative	-ɔliε	
Locative	-a	(-wa/-ya/-na)
Dative	-lɔ/-mɔ	

In addition to these casemarkers, nouns, deictics, and demonstratives take discourse and affective particles to indicate emphasis, evidence, and repetition among other discourse level functions.

5.1. *Casemarking on Agents, Actors, and Objects*

As in many other non-Austronesian ergative languages, only full nouns—that is proper nouns, common nouns, deictics, and demonstratives that refer to animate agents—receive agent casemarking. Nonfocused personal pronouns receive casemarking but only for locative and dative case. One of the focused personal pronouns, *ni* 'I' (the least semantically specified) takes neutral casemarking, but only when it is left-dislocated.

Kaluli uses two casemarking systems on noun phrases, each related to word order. AOV is the unmarked case and agents and objects are usually marked with neutral casemarking (see Comrie, 1978, p. 331 for the use of these terms). In addition, actors or experiencers with intransitive verbs may only be marked with the neutral casemarking. OAV is the "agent-focus" word order and ergative marking on the agent is obligatory. Object casemarking in OAV is the same as in AOV. The only exception to this casemarking paradigm is AOV when both agent and object of the sentence are either proper nouns or kinterms. In those sentences, the agent is marked with the ergative casemarker. This split ergative casemarking paradigm is illustrated below.

(A)OVtrans word order   (O)AVtrans word order

agent:	-ɔ	(NEUTRAL)	agent:	-ε	(ERGATIVE)
	-ε	(ERGATIVE)	object:	-ɔ	(ABSOLUTIVE)
object:	-ɔ	(NEUTRAL)	subject:	-ɔ	(ABSOLUTIVE)
			of intransitive verbs		

phonologically conditioned alternation: -ɔ   -yɔ/-wɔ
                                           -ε   -yε/-wε

The neutral casemarking is the "unmarked form," identical to (homophonous with) the absolutive and the form given as the citation form in elicitation. In casual or fast speech, such as commonly spoken in family interactions, these neutral casemarkers are often omitted. This is consistent in both adults' speech to children and adults' speech to each other.

The neutral forms of agent and object casemarking can be used on both nouns as in the following example.

Abi -*yɔ*   *siabulu*   -*wɔ*   *mɛnigab.*
    NEUTRAL   sweet potato   NEUTRAL   eat:3:INT2
'Abi is about to eat a sweet potato.'

While AOV usually follows a neutral casemarking system, ergative case-marking can occur. When both the agent and object are expressed by proper names and/or kinterms, ergative casemarking is used to mark the sentence initial agent. For example,

Abi -*yɛ*   *Suela* -*yɔ*   *sandab*
    ERG   ABS   hit:3:PRES
'Abi hits Suela.'

As we shall see, the selection of one or the other casemarking systems in AOV depends on the animacy hierarchy of nouns used to encode agent and object.

Dixon (1979) and Silverstein (1976) have discussed what types of lexical items are most likely to occur as agents. A hierarchy of agents, from most likely to least likely, shows that first and second person pronouns are highest in this animacy hierarchy; animate common nouns follow; while inanimate common nouns are the lowest (Dixon, 1979, p. 85). Proper nouns fall in the middle of this continuum, that is, they are just as likely to be acted upon by an agent as they are to be agents.

In Kaluli AOV utterances, when both agent and object are expressed by proper names or kinterms, this can be seen as the context of maximum ambiguity in the animacy hierarchy. The ergative paradigm is used to indicate which equally potential agent is in fact controlling the action. The ergative marker grammatically disambiguates the function of each proper noun in the utterance. Only in AOV utterances of this type can the ergative casemarker appear, and its use is obligatory.

In recent discussions on ergativity (Comrie, 1978; Dixon, 1979; Silverstein, 1976) it has been pointed out that in all split ergative languages the ergative casemarking system applies under certain conditions, and not under others, e.g. with certain word orders, tenses, person/number of agents. Just as the pro-nominal forms (focused/nonfocused) are selected according to whether or not the agent is in focus (position vis-à-vis the object), the ways in which nouns are marked for semantic role of agent varies according to their position in the sentence, that is whether or not the agent is the new information or is being emphasized or focused. In Kaluli (O)AV utterances (3rd person) which have the agent in focus, ergative casemarking is obligatory for proper and common nouns, deictics and demonstratives.

5.2. *Acquisition of Casemarking in AOV Utterances*

Recall that for adult speech, AOV order uses neutral casemarking on both nouns in most contexts; that is, both nouns are marked identically and word order signals semantic role. In casual speech, one or both of these neutral case suffixes may be omitted. Only when both nouns are expressed as proper nouns or kinterms must ergative casemarking be used with sentence-initial agents. To mark agents in any other way in AOV utterances is incorrect.

Children essentially go through three stages once they start producing AOV utterances (3rd person). First, agents are not marked at all; then the ergative marker is added to sentence-initial agents (when objects are not proper nouns or kinterms), producing incorrectly marked utterances. Finally, sentence-initial agents are marked with neutral or sometimes zero casemarking. At this time, the use of the ergative marker is restricted to OAV order, and to those infrequent occurrences of AOV order with proper noun and kinterm in both agent and object role. The following example is from the first stage, zero casemarking.

Abi 25.1 is watching me eat pandanus, a tropical vegetable. Announcing this to his mother,

Babi   oga   nab
         pandanus   eat:3:PRES
'Babi eats pandanus.'

This is the correct word order (AOV) since he is reporting an event, and a three-constituent utterance is appropriate since he is opening a new topic of discourse. All three children produced this type of utterance without any casemarking on the agent or the object.

For two of the three children, within a month of producing correctly marked agents in OAV utterances, there was an overgeneralization of the ergative marker to agents in sentence-initial position. Wanu did not follow this pattern exactly, but he was using the ergative marker correctly with two-element (AV) constructions, which might have influenced his incorrect extension of the ergative marker in sentence-initial position. None of the children produced utterances in which both nouns were proper nouns at this time. Therefore, all sentence-initial agents were being marked incorrectly. All three children produced this type of error.

Wanu 29.3 is with his father, who is taking salt out of a box. To his sister,

*do   -wɛ   sɔlu   diab
my father   ERG   salt   take:3:PRES
'My father takes the salt.'

Again, the word order is correct since Wanu is reporting his father's action, and three-constituents are appropriate since it is a new topic of talk. However, the ergative casemarker is on the agent in sentence-initial position, followed by the object, which is incorrect.

The use of utterances where both agent and object were expressed by proper names and kinterms was infrequent. With a total of 41 AOV utterances produced by the three children, only two utterances of this type were produced and both were correctly marked. These occurred in samples over 30 months. By 30 months two of the three children were consistently marking AOV utterances correctly. Only Mɛli made occasional errors. By 32 months all three children were consistently controlling both word order and the casemarking system. These Kaluli children used word order pragmatically appropriately before using casemarking correctly. Ergative casemarking was used independently of word order to mark transitive agents. All three children overextended its use in AOV utterances, producing grammatically incorrect utterances before learning to restrict its use to the correct word order, OAV. However, the ergative marker was never extended to the actors of intransitive verbs, keeping separate the transitive/intransitive verb distinction important in this split ergative language. This suggests that children may not have a general notion of actor/agent which is applied across all verb categories.

5.3. *Acquisition of Ergative Casemarker in OAV Order*

There are two issues in the acquisition of the ergative casemarking in OAV and AV utterances. One concerns the use of ergative casemarkers in three-constituent utterances to clearly mark the semantic roles of agent and object. The other concerns issues of transitivity as seen in AV utterances where particular verbs do not "elicit" the obligatory ergative casemarking on agents in child speech.

For all children, ergative casemarking was used in AV utterances before they were producing any OAV utterances at all. All children produced ergatively marked AV utterances before producing ergatively marked OAV utterances. In all cases, children produced more correctly marked AV utterances per sample than OAV utterances per sample. For Mɛli both correctly and incorrectly marked (meaning zero casemarking) OAV utterances were produced about a month after ergatively marked AV utterances were being used. Abi produced ergatively marked AV utterances two months before correctly marked OAV utterances; and Wanu produced correctly marked AV utterances four months before using OAV utterances.

There was individual variation in the acquisition of appropriate casemarking on three-constituent utterances. Once children begin producing these utterances with 3rd person nominal agents, they go through two stages in acquiring the obligatory ergative casemarker. One child, Abi, produced no three-constituent utterances until 27.2, at which time he produced utterances with the ergative marker correctly placed. With only two exceptions, he correctly marked all remaining nouns (in three-constituent utterances) for the duration of the study. Wanu initially produced three-constituent utterances without any casemarking at all until 30.3 months, at which time he produced only correct forms and continued to do so thereafter. The third child, Mɛli, used ergative casemarking correctly from 26 months, but within the same sample had utterances in which it was not added through 32.2 months when sampling terminated. In Mɛli's last five samples, the number of correct markings was always greater than the number of neutral and zero casemarkings. Her casemarking errors tended to cluster around her use of particular verbs (discussed below), and these caused Abi problems as well. When children omitted an obligatory ergative casemarker, mothers often told them to say it again properly after providing the correct model for them to imitate.

Children marked not only proper nouns (names, kinterms) with the ergative marker (in OAV utterances), but correctly marked a variety of animate agents, referring to them with common nouns, as well as deictics and demonstratives. For OAV 3rd person utterances, in only one example in the entire corpus (77 tokens) was an incorrect casemarker, the absolutive used on the agent. In all other examples there was either zero casemarking, which was not correct, or correct ergative casemarking.

Children used ergative casemarking and the concomitant word order to correctly contrast agents within their own turns of talk, as well as across speaker turns. For example,

Mɛli 27.3 is taking one sandal and her brother S is taking the other. To her mother,

nodo	*-wɔ*	*nisa*	*diɔl*
one side	ABS	I	take:1:PRES

'I take one side.'

nodo	*-wɔ*	*S*	*-wɛ*	*diab*
			ERG	take:3:PRES

'S takes one side.'

Wanu 31. and his sister are talking. She is holding a net bag.

Sister: *as* *-ɔ* *we* *Daibo* *-wɛ* *dimiabe*
        bag ABS this   ERG give:RECENT.PAST

        'Daibo gave this bag.'

Wanu: *we* *Babi* *-yɛ* *dimiabe*
       this   ERG

       'Babi gave this.'

5.4. *Inconsistency of Ergative Casemarking in (O)AV Utterances*

While the pattern of inconsistency of ergative casemarking is pervasive only for Mɛli in three-constituent utterances, it is the rule rather than the exception in the ergative casemarking for two-constituent utterances for all three children. In every sample the number of agents without ergative casemarking is greater than the ergatively marked forms. The majority of these agents have neutral casemarking while in every sample there are some agents that have no casemarking at all. In some samples, even the later ones, the number of agents without ergative casemarking is twice the number of marked agents. This pattern strongly contrasts with the pattern of marking agents with the ergative casemarker in three-constituent utterances. For example,

zero casemarking on agent:
*Abi   dilɔb
    take:PAST:EVID
?'Abi took'   or   ?'(someone) took Abi'

neutral casemarking on agent:
*Abi   -yɔ   dilɔb
    NEUTRAL

ergative casemarking on agent:
Abi   -yɛ   dilɔb
    ERGATIVE
'Abi took'

In examining the data for possible explanations of this pattern, one strong possibility is that casemarking may be interacting with tense. In many ergative languages (and in other split ergative languages) casemarking and tense interact, in that ergative casemarking may be restricted to only certain tenses. For example, in Georgian as well as other South Caucasian languages, in many modern Iranian and Indo-Aryan languages (Bechert, 1979) as well as in Chol (a Mayan language of Mexico), the tense/aspect basis of split ergativity in present tense follows a nominative-accusative pattern while the past tense follows an ergative-absolutive pattern (Comrie, 1978, p. 352). This, however, is not the case for Kaluli. Tense does not restrict the application of ergative casemarking in transitive verbs. In spite of this, once children begin to use ergative casemarking, they mark agents more frequently when those agents accompany verbs that are in past tense forms. That is, there is a preference to mark the agents of past action, rather than present or future actions with ergative casemarking. This is most evident in the verb 'give', where present and future tense agents are erratically marked, and past tense agents are more consistently marked. In later samples (over 28 months) other verbs in the past tense tend to take ergatively marked agents while their corresponding present and future tense forms have agents with neutral or zero casemarking, which is incorrect. These verbs include 'take', 'hit', 'bite', 'light (a fire)', 'cut', 'eat', 'cook', 'touch'—all relatively high in transitivity. In addition, while there are not enough examples for a more conclusive analysis, it appears that another factor affecting inconsistent marking in child speech is negation. Verbs that are negated also tend to have neutral or zero-marked agents.

For the duration of the study (until the children were 32 months old) all children produced AV utterances with neutral or zero casemarking on agents at the same time as they were correctly marking agents with the ergative casemarker. An analysis of these AV utterances (transitive verbs requiring ergative marking on agents directly preceding them) was carried out. While there is some individual variation, there are general developmental patterns in acquisition.

The marking or nonmarking of the ergative casemarker on nouns is not randomly distributed throughout the verbs that co-occur with those nouns. Certain verbs, in spite of their high frequency in both adult and child usage, seem to present difficulties for children. Two of these verbs are *sama* 'speak/say', and *ɛngab* 'does like that'.

The verb 'speak/say' is used frequently in the imperative as well as the habitual and past. These tenses rarely take 3rd person agents. The most frequently used form taking 3rd person agent (in the context of children) is in threats, where 'speak' is in the 3rd person future and the agent is specified by name. This usually takes the following form,

do   *-wɛ*   *samɛib*
my father   ERG   speak:3:FUT
'My father will speak/say (something)!'

This common threat never takes an object, that is, unlike reported speech, no one ever says what anyone will in fact say. While adults always use the ergative casemarker on the agent with this verb, it is not until children are over 30 months that they do the same. Until that time, the agent receives zero, neutral, or ergative casemarking. Similar patterns occurred for related verbs such as 'call out'. Ergative casemarking was never used when the verb was negated. Rather than input being the issue here, the verbs of saying may appear to be low in terms of transitivity to the child speaker since they never appear with an object (except in quoted speech) nor do they carry action to an affected object, like the more typically high transitive verbs.

The second verb that consistently presented difficulty, and which along with *sama* 'speak/say' accounts for a high percentage of neutral and zero casemarked agents, was *ɛngab* 'does' and *ɛlɛngab* 'does like that'. This verb was often used when the child did not remember or know the more specific verb for the action he or she was referring to. When the child used these less specific verbs it was sometimes difficult to identify what aspect of the action or situation the child was referring to. For example, upon hearing the strumming of a guitar, one child said, *Seligiwo ɛngab,* 'Seligiwo does that', but it was unclear whether that meant he hits the strings or he makes the noise. All children tended to mark agents when this verb was in the past tense, while not marking agents when the verb was in the present and future tenses. (This verb as well as 'speak/say' was not used with 1st person, so there is no evidence from pronominal usage.) Given the consistency of child use, there seems to be a constellation of factors which inhibit agents accompanying this verb from taking the ergative casemarkers. Clearly two factors to consider are the relative transitivity of the verb and the extent to which it takes an object.

Hopper and Thompson (1980) have outlined ten parameters of transitivity, each of which suggests a scale according to which clauses can be ranked. An examination of the Kaluli child data on the use of ergative casemarking to indicate agency suggests that Kaluli children are sensitive to at least four of these parameters of transitivity. These are (1) Aspect—children tend to mark agents of completed rather than noncompleted actions, (2) Mode—children tend to mark agents with past action, rather than action that is currently or has not yet occurred, (3) Affirmation—children tend to mark affirmative but not negated clauses and (4) Kinesis—the agent of the verb 'say' was usually not marked. Data on the acquisition of languages with ergative features would be especially interesting to examine for these relationships.

5.5. *Expressing Agents: Comparing Focused Pronouns and Ergative Casemarking*

Focused pronouns and ergatively marked nominals have a number of structural parallels that make them interesting to compare in terms of the acquisition data. First, both focused pronouns and nouns with ergative casemarkers (except when both agent and object are proper nouns in AOV utterances) occupy the same position in the sentence, in that they both must follow the object. Both mark the agent as the new information or the informational highlight of the sentence. Both, in terms of core semantic roles, can only be agents. However, one important difference between focused pronouns and ergatively marked nouns is that nouns with nonergative casemarking can express a range of roles other than agent, as determined by their different casemarking, while focused pronouns can only be agents. They have no other semantic function. The question is what is the relationship between the correct use of focused pronouns and ergatively marked nouns in the child language data.

Wanu first produced AV utterances (3) at 25.1, and at 26.3, three different focused pronouns were used. Mɛli used ergative casemarking on AV utterances (2) at 24.3 and one focused form appeared at 24.1 mo. In Mɛli's next sample, two focused forms became productive. Abi used ergative casemarking in only one AV utterance at 25.1 mo. and one focused form appeared at 25.3 mo. At 27.3 three different focused forms were productive, and AV utterances began to be produced at 28.2.

There is no clear pattern to the order of emergence of focused pronouns and ergative casemarking. However, focused pronouns are used correctly in AV utterances before ergative case is consistently marked on nouns in AV utterances. In fact, with two-constituent utterances, the 90% obligatory context rule cannot be met for two of the three children at 32 months because of their inconsistent use of the ergative casemaker! (It is met however for the three-constituent utterances for all three children.) However, if we compare these findings with the use of 1st and 2nd person focused pronouns that occupy the same position and semantic role as the ergatively marked forms, the picture is very different.

Unlike the ergatively marked nominals, focused pronoun form usage has an acquisition pattern with very few errors, especially in three-constituent utterances. This is for several reasons. Each pronominal form has an independent semantic meaning, unlike the ergative suffix which has no meaning by itself, and is homophonous with the instrumental, genitive, and one set of emphatics. As a lexical item the pronominal form may occur alone. It is more salient than the suffix, though both are tied to word order. As will be presented below, there are errors in ergative casemarking on nouns followed by direct objects (AOV). Errors of word order are not found with focused pronouns in that their use does not violate word-order rules; that is, they are not found preceding an object. In addition, 1st and 2nd person pronouns are used more frequently than ergatively marked nouns, and are pragmatically relevant to the child over a range of contexts. Thus, when we examine the acquisition of notions relevant to ergativity (agency, transitivity) using only nominal casemarking data, we find one set of patterns and errors and some of these vary with the number of constituents (two or three) in the utterance. However, when we examine the focused pronouns in terms of errors due to agency and transitivity, a different pattern emerges—one which is a great deal more consistent, and most importantly, does not reveal some of the potentially interesting problems concerning the interaction of various aspects of language (such as transitivity, tense, and negation) that are problematic for Kaluli children. Without errors or inconsistencies, we cannot see how the child is constructing the language at any given point in time. However, we need to examine how the different systems (pronouns/nouns) and complementary linguistic resources available in a language present different and sometimes inconsistent types of information about the developing linguistic system.

More data for further research are needed in this area. It is important to emphasize that in samples before 30 months, there is lower frequency for 3rd person in general, unlike 1st and 2nd person forms, which are frequent and more varied.

5.6. *Locative and Dative Casemarking*

The single locative suffix (*-a* 'to', 'in', 'at', and 'on') was used in the earliest of samples of all three children, around 24 months. It was added to deictics, demonstratives, and directionals, and used with a restricted set of verbs including *mesea* 'sit', *diɛ-foma* 'put', and *hamana* 'go'. Locative expressions were used with high frequency with intransitive verbs and in noun phrases. More specific locative words, such as 'inside' and 'top', appeared at 26–27 months, and they too took the general locative casemarking.

The first errors in locative marking appeared in Mɛli's speech at 26 months and in Abi's about a month later. Errors were of several types, but most involved overmarking of location and/or direction. Children's errors were of the following types and were high frequency from 26 to 29 months:

Use of two contradictory locatives:

M 26   **ya   ka   mesea*
here   there   sit:IMP

*'Sit here there.'

Use of a locative and a deictic/direction where only one is needed, marking both:

M 26   **i   wɛl   -a   we   -na   diɛfoma*   (= *i wɛla diɛfoma*)
wood   top   LOC   this   LOC   put:IMP   (= *i wena diɛfoma*)

'Put (it) on top of the wood'   or   'Put (it) on this wood'

A 28.2   **isasub   -a   holo   -na*
under house   LOC   down there   LOC

delin   (= *isasuba delin*)
be:RECENT PAST   (= *holona delin*)

'It was under the house'   or   'It was down there'

*id   a   -ya   ɛn   -a   dowɔ   (= *id a ena dowɔ*)
shit   house   LOC   there   LOC   be:PAST

'It was at the shit house'

For these children, the casemarking was added to both the noun and the unnecessary deictic. Other errors included mixing directionals for locatives such as *wena* 'on this' for *hono* 'that one over there (to the west or south)'.

While the majority of overmarking errors occurred with locatives, similar patterns occurred with the dative, genitive, and, to a lesser extent with the ergative. The following example illustrates an error with dative marking and the word order of the noun phrase.

Mɛli 27.3 is with her mother, the researcher (BBS) and several children including the researcher's namesake, Babi. Thus there are two people named Babi present. Mɛli is giving her mother some sugar cane and says,

*hono   Babi-mɔ   dimina
that one over there   DAT   give:IMP

*Babi-mɔ   hono   dimina
    DAT

*Babi-mɔ   hono-mɔ
    DAT   DAT

Mother: Babi   hono-mɔ   dimina   ɛlɛ salan
                      DAT   like:that say:HAB

  ' "Give to that Babi over there" one says like that'

In this example, the first error made by Mɛli is in the order of demonstrative and noun, an error that was made by all children occasionally until 28 months. The dative marker is suffixed to the noun. No one responds to Mɛli's utterance and in her next turn she reverses the word order, which is correct, but incorrectly attaches the dative to the noun, not the demonstrative (which like all nominal modifiers should carry the casemarking information). With still no pickup from her mother, she formulates another utterance, this time attaching the dative to both noun and modifier. Her mother provides the correct model for this utterance, but Mɛli does not repeat it.

While these Kaluli children did not correctly attach (the homophonous) ergative, genitive, or instrumental suffixes to pronouns, they correctly added dative and locative suffixes to nonfocused forms of the pronouns.

VERBS

6. General Background on Kaluli Verbs

In contrast to Kaluli nominal morphology, which is regular and relatively non-elaborated, verbal morphology is irregular and complex. Kaluli verbs are composed of stem material plus an inflectional suffix marking person and tense. Except for imperatives, number is not marked through bound suffixes, but is indicated through the use of separate pronominal forms. There is no single base form of the verb nor is there an infinitive.

Kaluli distinguishes the following major tenses: past, recent past, habitual, present, intentive 1, intentive 2, future. All tenses follow a regular pattern of inflectional suffixing. Person is marked in all tenses except recent past, nonrecent past, and habitual, which have single forms. In declarative utterances inflections for person follow a two-way split: 1st and non-1st (2nd/3rd). In present tense interrogatives, inflections follow a three-way split: 1st, 2nd, and 3rd person. In future interrogatives, the two-way distinction that is marked is 1st/2nd versus 3rd. Unlike nominal morphology which follows two casemarking paradigms, verbal morphology only follows a nominative-accusative pattern.

Aspect is infixed between the stem and the inflectional suffix. It may be expressed lexically and with a limited set of prefixes as well. Negation is marked by both prefixation and suffixation in all forms except imperative, where it is marked only through suffixation.

Imperatives indicate information through suffixation about (1) number (singular/dual/plural), (2) time of expected action (present/future), and (3) duration (+/−continuous), which is marked by infixing. In negative imperatives, the negative suffix changes according to number/time.

There are two different types of verb constructions: medial and final. Final forms are found in independent clauses, receive tense-person inflection, aspect, and emphatic and other discourse-level particles. They are sentence final. Medial forms are found in dependent clauses and do not carry information about person but do carry information about tense. If the agent/actor in the independent clause is different from that of the dependent clause, that change must be signalled by a particular form of the medial verb. This type of reference marking is known as "switch reference" and is found in languages that connect clauses by "clause chaining." The particular form of the medial verb in dependent clauses in conjunction with final forms in independent clauses indicates the temporal relationship between the clauses: purposive, sequential, simultaneous. Several medial forms (dependent clauses) may be chained together followed by a final form (independent clause).

A number of verbs are formed by concatenation of a medial and final form. For example 'take away' is constructed from *diɛgɛ* + *hamana* 'having taken + go'; 'bring' is from *diɛgɛ* + *mena* 'having taken + come'. In fast speech, the final syllable of the medial form is dropped. Other complex verbs are constructed by using inflected forms plus stative verbs.

While the linguist is able to determine the boundaries between what is stem material and what are inflectional endings, the child is not always able to make this distinction. In the section that follows, these two components of the verb will be treated separately.

6.1. *Verb Stems*

Verb stems in Kaluli undergo considerable change when the various verbal suffixes are added. Predicting the form of a given verb stem is difficult for individuals learning Kaluli as a first or second language. According to Rule (1966), in many of the Central and South New Guinea Stock languages which are geographically adjacent to Kaluli (such as Huli, Foe) it is possible to obtain from one verbal form, the stem or root of the other verb forms. In a number of languages in this area of Papua New Guinea, present singular imperative without any suffix is the base form which may be taken as the stem. From this form, all other grammatical forms of the verb can be determined by adding the appropriate suffix to that stem, either as it is, or after one or two slight morphophonemic changes have been made.

In Kaluli, however, there are many radical changes in the stem between one grammatical form and the next. In his analysis of 100 verbs (with 10 different grammatical forms for each), Rule found that certain groups of these grammatical forms were determined by adding the appropriate suffix to one particular form of the stem. Similar stem forms:

—The future imperative, negative imperative, present declarative (1st and non-1st), and recent past are all based on the same form of the verb stem. The rest of the forms can be determined if the future imperative is known.
—The future declarative (1st, 2nd/3rd) and the 1st person purposive forms are all based on the present imperative form of the stem.
—The past tense form is completely irregular.

Thus, once the linguist knows the present and future imperative, 1st person future declarative, and past tense, other tense forms can be derived for many verbs.

However, there is a sizable group of verbs for which these rules simply do not apply, where the stem is completely changed for every form. These verbs include some of the most common verbs such as *mena* 'come', *hamana* 'go', *mesea* 'sit', *maya* 'eat', *melea* 'stay', and *doma* 'have', among others.

Rule tentatively described six patterns of stem vowel and consonant change, and the variations found within each group. Particularly complex are the changes in stems which are multisyllabic. One major reason that they are so difficult to master is that these verb groups are not organized by any apparent semantic principles. A second reason is that there is no clear phonological pattern which determines the membership of a particular form for a given class of verbs. To date, no phonological analysis is adequate to describe the changes for any single group of verbs.

The following short sample of verb paradigms of common verbs in six proposed classes should provide the reader with a sense of the possibilities of stem changes for each form.

	Imperative Present	Imperative Future	1st Person Future	Past (nonrecent)
1.				
blow	*foloma*	*folɛbi*	*fomɛnɔ*	*folɔ*
tie up	*melema*	*melɛbi*	*memɛnɔ*	*melɔ*
2.				
go	*hamana*	*hɛnɛbi*	*hɛnɛnɔ*	*ane*

	Imperative Present	Imperative Future	1st Person Future	Past (nonrecent)
come	*mena*	*yɛbi*	*miɛnɔ*	*miyɔ*
sit	*mesea*	*sɛbi*	*mesɛnɔ*	*sen*
eat	*maya*	*nɛbi*	*mɛnɔ*	*mɔnɔ*
3.				
speak	*sama*	*sɛlɛbi*	*sɛmɛnɔ*	*siyɔ*
put on (clothes)	*kama*	*kɛlɛbi*	*kɛmɛnɔ*	*kɔlɔ*
put into (bags)	*disɛma*	*disɛlɛbi*	*disɛmɛnɔ*	*disɛ*
4.				
cook	*sɔfa*	*sɔdɛbi*	*sɔfɛnɔ*	*sɔfɛ*
hit	*sanama*	*sandɛbi*	*sɛmɛnɔ*	*sɔnɔ*
5.				
take	*dima*	*diyɛbi*	*diɛnɔ*	*di*
give	*dimina*	*miyɛbi*	*miɛnɔ*	*dimi*
6.				
put down (objects)	*diɛfoma*	*diɛsɛbi*	*diɛfɛnɔ*	*difɛ*

6.2. *Acquisition of Verb Stems*

Imperative forms (both positive and negative) were used with high frequency by all children. Imperatives were used as single words and in multiword constructions from 25 months. Imperatives were formed even when a child did not know or had forgotten the stem. Taking the "word" *ege* which is the hesitation particle but also means 'watcha ma call it?', the child would add the suffix *-ma* (*egema* for affirmative) or *-sabo* (*egesabo* for negative). (*Ege* is infected for tense and receives nominal cases in syntactic constructions by children and sometimes adults when the specific word is not forthcoming.) Children were not corrected when they used *ege* as a noun or verb.

An analysis of the errors in early verb usage suggests that although Kaluli does not have a single base form of the verb, Kaluli children do use one form as such. Taking the present imperative as a base form they alter the final vowel. For example, when a child did not use the correct form of the 1st person present of the verb, one strategy was to use the imperative as the 1st person, with or without the 1st person pronoun and to change the final vowel (usually *-a*) to *-ɛ*.

*ne	*menɛ*	correct	*ne*	*yɔl*
I	come:IMP	form:	I	come:1:PRES
			'I come'	or 'I am coming'

This morpheme (*-ɛ*) is not one of the possible person/tense inflectional endings, but the highest frequency verb final emphatic marker. Wanu, whose acquisition of verbal morphology was somewhat slower than the others, provided the data for the majority of these errors, especially during the time he was 25–28 months. However the other two children had examples of this type of error, especially in samples before 27 months.

A variation on this type of error was to use another emphatic particle, *-loga* (meaning 'I said' but because of contraction this meaning is not available to the child), suffixed to the present imperative or all but the final syllable of the imperative. These errors suggest the saliency of these final particles and their possible confusion as inflectional endings. For example, while performing the following actions Mɛli said,

	ERROR		*BASE	BASE	FORM
M 24.3	*ne*	**diɛfoga*	*diɛfoma*	*diɛtɛbi*	*diɛtɔl*
	I	put down	PRES:IMP	FUT:IMP	1:PRES
	'I put down'				
M 26	*ne*	**timologa*	*tima*	*tiɛbi*	*tiɔl*
	I	take out of fire	PRES:IMP	FUT:IMP	1:PRES
	'I take out of fire'				

The second type of evidence to support the present imperative as the child's base form comes from errors made when attempting to form 1st person present tense. These show a close approximation of the correct inflection, added to a stem that is modeled from the present imperative rather than the future imperative, which is correct. For example, while commenting on his own ongoing actions Wanu said,

	ERROR		*BASE	BASE	FORM
W 25	**dagulo*		*daguma*	*dudɛbi*	*dudɔl*
	peel/shell		PRES:IMP	FUT:IMP	1:PRES
	'I peel'				
W 26.3	*ne*	**gadolo*	*gadama*	*gidɛbi*	*gidɔl*
	I	put together	PRES:IMP	FUT:IMP	1:PRES
	'I put together'				

As mentioned above, the future imperative, which is the basis for the present tense, is not used with high frequency by parents, nor is it used by children under 30 months. However, there is no clear evidence that children are learning verb paradigms or the rules of stem formation based on particular forms as in the linguistic description above.

Other errors appeared throughout the tenses, not just first person present tense. For example, there were errors for all children in the use of the verb *daguma* 'peel' which is used to request or talk about peeling bananas and other fruits as well as shelling crayfish. In the first example (M 27.3) the present imperative was used for the stem.

	ERROR	*BASE	BASE	FORM
M 27.3	*daguabeyɔ	daguma	dudɛbi	dudabeyɔ
'peel'	RECENT PAST	PRES:IMP	FUT:IMP	RECENT PAST
M 30.2	*dagumɛnɔ		daguma	dubɛnɔ
'peel'	1:FUT		PRES:IMP	1:FUT

In the second example (M 30.2) Mɛli's guess is a good one, 1st person future is usually based on present imperative but this verb has an additional stem change. This error, made at a later period, suggests that Mɛli is using the paradigm to form the future tense, but this form, like many others is irregular.

Other problems with stem formation are due to too much or too little stem material. For example,

M 27.3 *kamama from kama 'put on clothing'

There are no imperatives that have the canonical shape Consonant + *amama*. However, numerous imperatives follow Consonant + *ama* and Consonant + *anama*. In this example Mɛli has lengthened the bisyllabic stem adding -*ma* (part of the imperative ending) to the imperative *kama*.

In this example there is not enough stem material for the formation of the 1st person present.

M 26.	ne	*folɛ	from	foloma	(= folɔl)
	I	blow		blow:PRES:IMP	1:PRES 'I blow the fire'

When these types of errors occurred, they were almost always corrected by the adult.

While children did make a number of errors in choosing the form of the past tense, such as M 26 *dimiya for dimi/mi 'give:PAST', there was only one example of the addition of inflectional material (recent past) to that past form. The utterance, which was repeated by the child several times, was not understood and dropped. The lack of overgeneralization of inflectional material to past tense forms of the verbs suggests that Kaluli children may be learning these single past forms as separate lexical items, and do not involve them in the morphological processes of other verb tenses.

Stem errors were no more frequent in certain verb classes than others, though forms that were irregular produced the highest number of errors. There was no systematic error pattern based on the phonological shape of the verb. One problem that faces the child concerns picking the correct form on which to base the stem. An important point to emphasize is that in Kaluli the present imperative is usually the base form for the future tenses, including intentive 1 and 2. The present declarative is based on the future imperative. This "mismatch" in the temporal basis of stem formation is an important factor in errors in stem formation for the child.

	ERROR	*BASE	BASE	FORM
W 29	*halɛmɛni	halɛbi	hama	hamɛni
	'rub':INT:1	FUT:IMP	PRES:IMP	INT:1
	'I am about to rub.'			

M 27.3	jun	kɔs	-ɔ		*gidɛfɛnigɔ- bale
	asparagus	leaf	NEUTRAL		burn:1:INT:2 EMPH
	(= gilimɛnigɔbale)				
	'I am about to burn asparagus leaves'				

Both children chose the future stem for intentive 1 and intentive 2, which was not correct. The stem should have been based on the present imperative.

While some stem errors had to do with the incorrect selection of a consonant, other errors were due to incorrect vowels as in *bɛdɔl for bɔdɔl 'I see' where 3rd person is bɛdab. Some errors did show resemblance to their imperative stems; others were simply misshapen and often misunderstood by those to whom they were directed.

6.3. Tense Inflections

If one has the basic four stems that are presented above, one can add the following tense inflections to form declarative Kaluli sentences.

Recent past:	1st/2nd/3rd	-abe		
Present tense:	1st	-ɔl	2nd/3rd	-ab
Intentive 1:	1st	-ɛni	*2nd/3rd	
Intentive 2:	1st	-gɔl	2nd/3rd	-gab
Future tense:	1st	-mɛnɔ/-iɛnɔ/-ɛnɔ	2nd/3rd	-mɛib/-ɛib
Habitual:	1st/2nd/3rd	-an		

As one can see from the above inflectional paradigm, the tense endings are regular and do not change according to verb class. Tense inflections may be followed by a variety of discourse particles marking, for example, successive degrees of emphasis (with past tense agreement), repetition, and quotation.

6.4. *Acquisition of Tense Inflections*

For this analysis, three children's spontaneously produced verbs (from both single and multiword utterances) were examined for patterns in the acquisition of tense inflection. Both transitive and intransitive verbs were analyzed and only utterances that were situationally appropriate were included. The verbs were divided into two categories, 1st person and 3rd person agents/actors. The 2nd person was not considered since the majority of 2nd person utterances were present imperatives.

For all children, only inflected verbs were produced and they appeared simultaneously as single words and in syntactic constructions. There was no sequential pattern. This does not seem to be an artifact of sampling since for Mɛli there were no 1st or 3rd inflected intransitive forms in the first sample, while in the following sample, there were both, with a majority of inflected forms appearing in syntactic constructions.

Perhaps the most interesting finding from this analysis is the distribution of tense inflections within each sample according to 1st and 3rd person verb inflection. Five tenses were considered: past (single form for 1/2/3), present, intentive 1 (or inceptive, 'about to', restricted to 1st person and used when agent/actor announces own intentions but has not yet initiated action), intentive 2 ('starting to', action has been initiated or there is evidence that it is about to be, in contrast to intentive 1, this is not restricted to 1st person), and future. For all children in all samples, there are striking differences between 1st and 3rd person usage.

For 3rd person forms, usage was concentrated in two tenses, past and present. Out of 23 samples (combined samples of three children) only two samples had over 7% of their utterances in tenses other than past or present tense forms, and these exceptions were in later samples (over 30 months). This means that most of the time when children are using verbs and talking about others, they are talking about completed or ongoing action. They infrequently talk about what other people are about to do (intentive 2), or what others will do (future). When they do talk about what others will do, one finds threats ("someone will say something") or responses to queries about the future actions about others. In addition, following adult patterns of use children never extended use of the intentive 1 tense to the third person. Thus, when talking about 3rd persons, children talked about what was certain and observable, and most of this talk concerned the past and ongoing actions of others. Finally there is an additional cultural issue that may be a factor. Kaluli adults claim that one does not know what another person thinks. This is realized by a dispreference for talking about what another person might think or what they will be doing. Adults do not frequently speculate or talk about these topics; to do so could be considered gossip. However, without further research it is not possible to ascertain whether this cultural pattern affects acquisition patterns, or whether cognitive and pragmatic constraints carry the explanation.

When children talked about themselves as agents or actors in the earliest samples, the majority of their utterances were in the present tense as they described their own actions. However, by about 27 months use of the five tense inflections was distributed more evenly throughout each sample. Talk of already initiated and future actions dominated the speech of all three children. Between 10% and 15% of their talk concerned past actions. Talk about what they were going to do, but had not yet begun (intentive 1) ranged between an average of 5% for Meli and 12% for Abi and Wanu. Again, these children preferred to talk about what was observable and knowable. As agents, they knew their own intentions and future actions best and these were the topics of talk.

What is clear from this analysis is that Kaluli children are not using verbs inflected for all persons and all tenses. Before the age of 30 months, there are gaps in the verb paradigms that a linguist would construct. Due to cognitive and pragmatic constraints, children use only certain forms of a given verb, and not others when they begin to acquire the verbal system. This is particularly clear in a language like Kaluli where each verb is always inflected for person and tense. It is less clear in a language that lacks this type of verbal morphology. The children in this study used, for example, *dimina* 'give' in the present imperative, but not in the 1st person present or the negative imperative. The verb *dima* 'take' was used in the 1st person present, with the negative imperative, and with a 3rd person agent in the past, but rarely in the imperative or the future. Thus while inflected forms are produced from the beginning of the child's use of language, they are restricted to a limited set of verbs. Furthermore, for each verb there may be a particular set of inflectional forms which the child uses, and others that he or she does not. For example, the verb *omina*, 'having chewed give', only occurred in the imperative, since children asked their parents to chew and give food, but had no other pragmatic function to express with that verb.

Overall, the inflectional verb endings do not pose major problems in acquisition. Two of the three children did not have difficulty with their use in declarative utterances. The reasons for this relative ease of acquisition are as follows. Kaluli verb inflections do not change form according to verb stem class. Inflections are both word and sentence final. In addition, the use of emphatic particles following the inflection may highlight the perceptual saliency of the tense inflections. This is supported by evidence from early use of tense inflections followed by different emphatic forms as illustrated by *hɔnɔl* 'go:1:PRES' showing different emphatic endings *hɔnɔkɛ* and *hɔnɔlo*. Moreover, there is a high proportion of single inflected verbs used as sentences in both casual adult-adult verbal interaction, and adult-child speech as well.

However there were a number of recurring errors in the data for all three children. Before 28 months two children produced utterances of the following type: **ne diabo* 'I take' instead of *ne diɔl* when referring to their own actions. They used 1st person pronouns and inflected the verb for 3rd person *-ab* adding the final particle *-o* used in calling out. The reverse error (the use of 3rd person forms for incorrectly referring to the self) did not occur. It was clear from the context and the corrections of adults that children were speaking about their own actions. This error in inflection occurred with a number of verbs in several different verb classes, for example *yabo (= yɔl) 'come' *hɛnabo (= hɔnɔl) 'go', *bɛdabo (= bɔdɔl) 'see/look', *alilabo (= alilɔl) 'lie down', *adulabo (= adulɔl) 'step on', among others. There is no clear single cause of these errors, and I suggest several possible related causes. First, this error may be related to the fact that verbs of affect and internal state (ne tagidab 'I'm afraid', ne mayab 'I'm hungry') which occur at this time, only take 3rd person inflection and children may be overgeneralizaing from those forms. They never inflected those forms for the 1st person. Alternatively, the 1st person ending -ɔl may appear phonologically similar to the nominal case endings (absolute and neutral case, both signalled by -ɔ), whereas the 3rd person -ab is more distinctive and occurs only with verbs. Therefore, the 3rd person may be seen as less ambiguous than the 1st person inflection. A third possibility is that children misanalyze the stem of the verb as in the case of diab 'take' (instead of di-) and add the emphatic marker -o as the final inflectional material. While the form diab is grammatically correct in some contexts, it is not correct in conjunction with a 1st person pronoun nor when referring to one's own actions. Errors regarding correct inflection for 1st person persisted in certain verbs for Abi until 31.2 and for Wanu until 32.1 months.

Another systematic error occurs with inflectional endings on present tense interrogative utterances. While declarative sentences make a two-way distinction for marking person/tense inflection (1st versus non-1st person), interrogatives makes a three-way distinction, adding a different 2nd person subject ending before adding the interrogative particle. In their use of interrogatives, Kaluli children do not make this three-way distinction and base all of their inflectional patterns on the present declarative. Therefore, when they are addressing someone and use the 2nd person pronouns they use the 2nd/3rd person declarative inflection along with the 3rd person interrogative particle. This error pattern does not occur in 2nd person formulaic interrogatives, but only in non-formulaic expressions until about 28 months. Another departure from the most common paradigm (1st/non-1st person) is found in future interrogatives. In these utterances, 1st/2nd person is marked identically, with 3rd person marked differently, unlike the usual 1st—2nd/3rd pattern of future declarative. While only a few future 2nd person interrogatives were produced, they were incorrectly inflected for 3rd person until 29 months. Thus children were overgeneralizing from the declarative tense inflections across sentence types, which in most cases was not correct.

Other overregularization occurred as children tried to make specially inflected verb forms conform to their developing knowledge of inflections. This is clearly seen when children try to regularize certain formulaic expressions which do not conform to the paradigmatic use of the inflectional system.

There is a set of teasing formulae which one uses when offering food or an object without the intention of ever giving it to the person. It is used to tease people who beg for or want something you have when you wish to taunt them with the fact that they cannot have it. Instead of using a form with a negative, such as 'you don't eat/take' etc., Kaluli has a special construction without a negative, used only in these teasing and confrontational contexts. It is composed of a focused form of the 2nd person pronoun, *gi* 'you', with the 3rd person form of the verb minus the final consonant. This results in the following forms:

	REGULAR FORM		TEASING FORM	
PRESENT	*gi nab*	'you eat'	*gi na*	'you don't eat'
	gi diab	'you take'	*gi dia*	'you don't take'
FUTURE	*gi mɛib*	'you will eat'	*gi mɛi*	'you will not eat'
	gi diɛib	'you will take'	*gi diɛi*	'you will not take'

The following teasing exchange comes from Mɛli 28.3. In this example we see how Mɛli is trying to make this special form into an inflected form during a sequence of teasing and direct instruction using *ɛlɛma*.

Mɛli's Grandfather has brought a small marsupial (*yɛsi*) to the house and has given it to Mɛli. Mɛli, her mother, and mother's sister, Faili are sitting around the fire. After talk about how Grandfather had killed it and given it to Mɛli, Faili reaches for it.

(1) G'fa → Mɛli ⟹ Faili: *a!   mɔ-   miɛnɔ   -kɛ!   ɛlɛma.*
                           no! NEG give:1:FUT EMPH say:IMP
                          'No! I will not give! say like that.'

(2) *ninɛli   mɛnɛ   ninɛli   mɛnɔ. Faili, gi   na!   ɛlɛma.*
      I alone   eat:1:FUT   you (don't) eat   say:IMP
      'Only I will eat. Only I will eat. You don't eat! say like that.'

(3) Mɛli → Mother: *nɔ!   Faili we   sanama!*
                    mother   this   hit:IMP
                    'Mother! Hit this Faili!'

(4) G'fa → Mɛli ⟹ Faili: *gi   na!   ɛlɛma.*
                           'You don't eat! say like that.'

(5) Mɛli → Faili: *gi   nan   -kɛ!*
                you   eat:HAB EMPH
                'You usually eat!'

(6) Mother → Mɛli ⇒ Faili: *gi   mɛi!*   *ɛlɛma.*
                              you   will (not) eat. say:IMP
                              'You will not eat! say like that.'

(7) Mɛli → Faili: *gi   mɛib   -kɛ!*
                    you   eat:3:FUT EMPH
                    'You will eat!'

(8) G'fa → Mɛli ⇒ Faili: *gi mɛi! gi nɛli!*   *gi na!*
                                       will (not) keep eating
                           'You won't eat! You will not keep eating! You
                           don't eat!'

In her first turn in this exchange (3), Mɛli does not correctly repeat the form that
her grandfather has said, *gi na* 'you don't eat', but instead she tells her mother to
hit Faili. Her grandfather repeats his instruction to Mɛli (4) telling her to say the
teasing expression to Faili. Instead, Mɛli utters the phonologically similar habitual form of the verb plus an emphatic particle (5). Her mother then tells her to
say *gi mɛi* 'you will not eat' (6) and Mɛli produces the 3rd person future with an
emphatic particle (7). None of Mɛli's utterances convey the appropriate meaning, as she produces utterances with the regular inflectional endings rather than
the phonologically similar teasing forms. Then her grandfather uses this teasing
construction in three different forms (8), future, future + continuative aspect,
and present. Mɛli does not repeat. The discussion then turns to the details of the
animal, followed by further exchanges instructing Mɛli in using these formulaic
teasing expressions. She not repeat them, but instead produces forms with the
regular inflectional endings (future and habitual) as she has done before. Finally
her mother makes an important link for Mɛli in a discourse sequence that has
been documented elsewhere for the development of rhetorical questions used for
teasing (Schieffelin, in press). She says,

nainɔ yɛsi -yɔ   *e -lɔ*   *miɛ*   *-sabo!*
our   NEUTRAL   3P:DAT give   NEG:IMP
'Don't give our *yɛsi* to her!'

ni   yɛsi -yɔ   *gi   mɛi-kɛ*   *ɛlɛma!*
my   NEUTRAL   you   eat EMPH   say:IMP
'You (won't) eat my *yɛsi*! say like that!'

Here we see the meaning and consequences of the teasing form made explicit by
sequencing the negative imperative and the teasing, 'we won't give it, and
say. . .'

The talk then turns to all the reasons why Faili cannot have the *yɛsi,* followed by another set of *ɛlɛma* instructions to repeat these formulaic expressions, which Mɛli still does not do. Instead she tells her mother to hit Faili to prevent her from taking the *yɛsi.* This is not acceptable to the adults. Later when Faili starts to beg for the *yɛsi* from Mɛli, her grandfather again instructs her to say, *gi na!* and Mɛli finally says it with the appropriate force of delivery several times in succession. Her grandfather then yells with delight, "She says *'gi na'!"*

In addition to this example providing evidence about the child's attempted regularization of irregular formulaic expressions, we see how Kaluli adults assist their children in mastering the use of routine expressions and how this enables the child to participate in culturally appropriate ways. Family members provide different cues to help the child understand the meaning of this particular expression, which has a negative force without any surface negative marking. Without actually explaining the form to her, adults are persistent in encouraging her to say this expression correctly through the use of *ɛlɛma,* direct instruction. Its use is contextualized within a recurring framework of teasing. The child is encouraged to think that her correct performance is critical to the desired outcome of the immediate situation. For the Kaluli, the appropriate use of these expressions, and many others like them, are important indicators not only of linguistic competence but social competence as well.

While the following type of error did not occur frequently, it illustrates what the child does when trying to express a more complex form of the tense without knowing the morphological devices for doing so. In this case the child resorts to lexical means.

Mɛli 27.3 has found a crayfish shell on the floor. Showing it to her mother:

Mɛli:	nɔ,	galen	we	ne	*nɔl	kɔmɔ	-lɔb
	mother	crayfish	this	I	eat:1:PRES	finish	EVID

'Mother, I eat finish this crayfish'

Mother:	gilɔ	nalogo
	you	ate:already:2nd/3rd

'You ate already'

Mɛli:	ne	*nalogo	(= nɔlogo)	ne	*nalogo-lɔb	-e
	I	ate already:3		3:		EVID	EMPH:PAST

In this example, Mɛli is trying to express something other than the simple or recent past, since that form of the verb was already in her productive vocabulary and used many times in the same sample. The verb phrase she constructs is not used in the adult language, and has several errors in it. It is a combination of 1st person present tense and the word *kɔm* meaning 'the end, finish, enough' with the evidential particle meaning 'I see'. The present tense which indicates on-going action cannot be used with the word meaning completed. The evidential cannot be used with the 1st person present tense since one cannot claim that one observes one's own ongoing action. However, the evidential is often used with the word *kɔm*. Her mother's response uses a verb with an inflection that Mɛli is not familiar with. Mɛli repeats it with the 2nd/3rd person inflection and then again with the evidential particle followed with an emphatic particle, creating an incorrect utterance. After Mɛli's several incorrect attempts to use this form of the verb, her mother responds with a simple question:

Mother: *no   gilɔ   mɔnɔ   -wɔ?*
           it   you   eat:PAST   Q
           'Did you eat it?'

Child: *Ni   mɔnɔ*
           I   eat:PAST
           'I ate'

They then proceeded to discuss who had given the crayfish to Mɛli and from what river it had come, all culturally important aspects of the topic.

Mɛli did not attempt to use that particular past form of the verb until 30.2. It was still not under her control at that time. However, she was working on it by trying to change the stem and inflectional material but continued with the verb in the 3rd person.

nowɔ   ni   *nɛliyogo/nowɔ   ni   *nalilolo   (= *nɔlogo*)
another   I   *eat:3   eat:1
 'I already ate another (one)'

6.5. *Other Problems with Verbs*

Kaluli has many verbs within particular semantic domains. For example, in English the meaning of the verb 'put' is altered by changing the preposition, *put on/off/in/over/down*, etc. In Kaluli, each of these distinctions is indicated by different lexical items. Some of the differences include animate/inanimate, nature and number of objects, duration of action, end result of affected object, and location. Some verbs which are semantically related have minor pho-nological differences, such as *tima* 'pick leaves', 'take food out of fire' and *tuma* 'pick (certain) fruits'. Others involve single infixes, multiple infixes, prefixes, changes in suffixes and combinations of the above. Other forms bear no re-semblance at all to one another in spite of some of the same close semantic relationships that one finds signalled morphologically in other verbs. The tre-mendous amount of complexity and variation that one finds in the verbal system gives children difficulty well after 30 months. Wanu, in particular, had extensive errors involving verb semantics.

Errors in choosing the correct verb were made by all children for several reasons: The child might not know the form at all, producing the wrong stem and ending. This resulted in a virtually incomprehensible utterance. Alternatively, if the child did not know the specific verb, *ege* was used and inflected accordingly. Or, a single form would be overextended to cover too much of a given semantic field. For example, Wanu used the verb *fagema* meaning 'untie' to refer to all acts of opening as well as closing and tying. Wanu used this single verb to refer to actions covered by four different verbs at 26.3 months, listed below. He was always corrected.

fagema for *sogoma*	'untwist'
fagema for *hagoma*	'pick off tree bark'
fagema for *melema*	'tie up'
fagema for *kɔlama*	'open up (a door)'

However, by 28 months, this type of problem was seldom encountered.

Other error patterns with verbs came from several sources. A child could choose a verb which was (1) phonologically close to the correct form, but semantically unrelated, (2) phonologically close and semantically related, (3) semantically related, but phonologically different, (4) within the correct semantic domain but an antonym ('fire dies down' 'fire flares up') and (5) totally unrelated. The first pattern was a relatively early strategy and virtually disappeared by 28 months. All children produced utterances of the 2nd, 3rd, and 4th type through the latest samples, over 32 months. These would usually be corrected and the child would be asked to repeat the correct form. Only Wanu produced a fair quantity of utterances of the 5th category, but by 27 months they were only occasional.

The tasks that the linguist faces in understanding these verbs is very different from the child's task. First, the linguist seeks regularities within verb paradigms, and determines the morphophonological relationships between the various parts of the paradigms. A second task is to determine whether verbs fall into major classes, with the hope of establishing some predictability of forms. As we have seen, if certain forms are known, such as the imperative in both the present and future forms, other parts of the paradigm can be filled in.

The child faces a very different set of tasks. He or she cannot approach the task paradigmatically, as can the linguist. As a result, due to cognitive, linguistic and pragmatic factors, children are learning the verb system piece by piece. For example, they have little basis upon which they can predict the stem of the verb from one form to another. The "mismatch" between present and future tenses for stem formation causes the child to make errors in trying to set up a logical system based on temporal similarity.

Another "non-facilitating factor" comes from the verbal input. In clarification sequences, the form of the 1st person declarative has little resemblance to the 2nd person imperative or the past tense. The child cannot be assisted by the similarity of forms across turns that one would get in clarification sequences in some languages. For example, in English if the child says "come!" to someone who then requests clarification, that speaker will usually say, "come?". In Kaluli, however, except for the past and the habitual forms, if the child says, *mena!* 'come:PRES:IMP' the clarification request will be *yɔlo?* 'come:1:PRES:Q'. Before the child has the appropriate inflected interrogative form, he or she repeats the adult's utterance with some modification to the final syllable which is where inflection occurs. The most common modification is to change the final vowel and keep everything else intact. This of course is incorrect, but it does indicate that the young child is aware of inflections before controlling them and knows that the form has to change, especially the inflectional ending. Only through the direct instruction sequences involving *ɛlɛma* does the child get the "adjusted" form. This facilitates acquisition.

6.6. Aspect

Aspect is complex in Kaluli, and to date there is no detailed account of this system. Aspect is predominantly signalled through infixes between the stem and inflectional material, though it is also indicated through prefixes. Unlike tense inflection, which is obligatory, aspect is optional and may be used when a speaker wishes to highlight some feature of the situation. Children under 33 months only infrequently mark aspectual information, and much of the time they do so incorrectly. One way in which children mark duration is through repetition of the utterance. For example, when watching a leaf float downstream, children would say, *hɛnabo, hɛnabo* 'it goes, it goes' etc., until it was out of sight. Repetition is used in adult narratives as a stylistic device for expressing duration, while in conversation, morphological means of expressing aspect are more usual.

One of the earliest morphological forms used to express aspect is the prefix *ɔ-* meaning 'still, in the process of' as when commenting on one's own or another's actions. At 30.2 Mɛli was prefixing many verbs this way, some appropriately and some not. The prefix was clearly being overused, which was indicated by her mother asking, "Why are you saying *ɔ-* all the time?!"

6.7. Complex Verbal Constructions

So far our discussion of verbs has concerned simple verbs and single independent clauses. However, this is only one part of the verbal system. In addition to simple verbs, Kaluli combines verbs to form serial and complex verbs. These will be discussed below. Another aspect of the verbal system that will be examined is the system of clausal relationships. In English, two or more clauses are joined together by conjunctions. The verbs in these clauses are not very different from one another. Coordination and subordination are indicated through lexical means. In Kaluli, like other non-Austronesian languages, the organization of combining clauses is quite different. Longacre (1972, p. 2) describes this "clause-chaining" as follows.

In place of sentences that are composed of several coordinated clauses joined together by verbs of equal rank in all clauses, we find sentences which contain a clause with a distinctive verb form occurring but one in the entire sentence (usually at the end) preceded by other clauses with verbs of other structure. We may say we have a structure with an engine at the end and a bunch of cars hooked on preceding it.

If the agent/actor of the two verbs is the same in two adjoining clauses, there is one set of verbal suffixes. If the agent/actors are different in the adjoining two clauses, another set of suffixes is used. The verbal suffix in the first dependent clause not only carries the temporal information about that predicate, but indicates that the following clause (dependent clause) has a different agent/actor. This is called switch reference.

Examples of complex clause chaining and switch reference are not found in the speech of children under 3 years. They are rarely used in direct instruction sequences with ɛlɛma, though they are used in speech to children. Instead of using the morphosyntactic devices found in clause chaining with switch reference, children from about the age of 30 months sequence propositions as in the following example.

Mɛli 32.2 is opening a piece of wire used as a gate to keep puppies in a particular area of the house.

gasa   we   -na   sab
dog   this   LOC   sit:3:PRES
'(The) dogs stay in here'

gasa   we   -na   tandomɛib
                    cross:3:FUT
'(The) dogs will cross on here'

asidɔ   -kɛ
close:1:PRES EMPH
'I close (it)'

While Mɛli's utterances are not "wrong," they are not linked using Kaluli morphosyntactic devices. They sound, in fact, "childish." An adult would chain these propositions in the following way,

gasa   wena   mesɛiki   tok   ami   tandolowabɛniki   asifɛnɔ.
'So dogs stay here, so (they) won't cross (the) door, I'll close (it).'

The ability to use clause chaining (and switch reference) is one of the achievements of a competent speaker. It is what makes the language sound "Kaluli."

Speakers use clause chaining not only in longer stretches of discourse, but in fairly short expressions as in the example above.

In Kaluli there are complex, serial verb forms that express notions of purpose, as well as the temporal relations of simultaneity and sequence. These notions are not expressed lexically, but morphosyntactically. Young children use these verbal constructions with a single agent/actor in both clauses from about 27–28 months. They seem to be the building blocks of more complex syntactic constructions in Kaluli before switch reference is used. Since data are only available for children who used the same agent/actor, background material for only those structures will be given. Data from older children are needed to document the development of complex clause chaining, one of the most distinctive aspects of language development in Kaluli.

6.8. Subordinate Verbs of Purpose

Subordinate verbs of purpose are used to express the reason or goal of an individual's actions. For example,

oga	mɛni	meno!
pandanus	eat:PURP	come:IMP

'Come (in order) to eat pandanus!'

Ne	a	-ya	sɔfɛni	hɔnɔl
I	house	LOC	cook:PURP	go:1:PRES

'I am going to the house to cook.'

The medial verb is a constant form and is identical to the tense intentive 1 (which alone can only be used for 1st person). The final verb can be inflected for any tense. In rapid speech, the two verbs are concatenated and the final syllable of the medial form (-ni) is deleted (except when followed by a vowel-initial final verb). When the subject of the two verbs is not the same, a different form of the medial verb is used.

6.9. Acquisition of the Purposive

The first complex verbal forms produced by children express purposive relations. These forms emerged between 24–26 months. They were used frequently in direct instruction with ɛlɛma as imperatives. The children in this study expressed purposive relations only in utterances where the subject was the same for both verbs. Purposive utterances with different subjects for each verb are more complex linguistically as well as cognitively, and were relatively late acquisitions (after 32 months).

When purposive verbs are first used, they occur with only three medial verbs, dima 'take', mesea 'sit', sanama 'hit'. Medial verbs have a single underlying form which is identical to intentive 1. When children use these medial verbs in combination with final verbs, they contract the medial verb, deleting the final syllable (-*ni*) except with vowel-initial final verbs. However, because of contraction and the infrequent occurrence of vowel-initial final verbs, it is unclear whether in the early stages of acquisition children realize that the forms for the medial verb and for intentive 1 are the same. They had no difficulty using this same verb form as a single verb or a concatenated one later. This may be due to the similarity of the meanings of the two, intention and purpose.

While adults and older children use a variety of final verbs, children combine medial forms with only two final verbs, *hamana* 'go' and *mena* 'come'. The final verbs occur predominantly as imperatives, 1st person present, and 3rd person past. For example, children produced the following utterances:

Mɛli 24.3   *diɛ*   *-hɔnɔl*
             take:PURP   go:1:PRES
             'I'm going (in order) to take'

Wanu 25.1   *mesɛ*   *-meno!*
             sit:PURP   come:IMP
             'Come (in order) to sit!'

Mɛli 26   *jun siɛni*   *-ane*   *-yo?*
                 pick:PURP   go:PAST   Q
             'Did (she) go to pick jun?'

It is important to mention that when children use a concatenated verb with 'go', they are referring to change of location, and as in the example above, are talking about their own or other people's movement and the reason for it.

Almost all medial verbs used were transitive verbs. As children increased their knowledge of inflectional endings for simple verbs, these inflections were also used on the final verbs in concatenated forms. The children in this study did not add final verbs other than 'come' and 'go' during the course of taping (to 33.2 months), but did increase the number of medial verbs. For all children, in spite of the limited combinations, purposive relations were the most frequently expressed complex forms in all samples.

6.10. *Past Consecutive Action*

Past consecutive action is also expressed using serial verbs. For this, the medial verb is based on the future imperative minus the imperative ending plus the suffix -*ɛsɛgɛ* (+/−morphophonemic changes). The final verb is inflected according to the usual procedures. For example,

kɛ   nɛsɛgɛ   yɛbi
fish   eat:PAST:CONSEC   come:FUT:IMP
'Having eaten fish, you will come'

diɛsɛgɛ   *miɛnɔ*
take:PAST:CONSEC   come:1:FUT
'Having taken I will come.'   (= 'bring')

diɛsɛgɛ   *hɛnɛnɔ*
take:PAST:CONSEC   go:1:FUT
'Having taken I will go.'   (= 'take away')

gulɛsɛgɛ   *mina*
break:PAST:CONSEC   give:IMP
'Having broken in half, give.'

These medial forms are usually contracted in fast speech, dropping *-sɛgɛ*, except when the final verb is vowel-initial or when the imperative is in the future. In all of the examples, the subject is the same for both verbs. When there is a switch, both forms of the verbs undergo morphological changes.

6.11. Acquisition of Past Consecutive Action

Serial verbs expressing past consecutive action emerged about one month later than purposive verbs, around 25–27 months. One medial verb dominated these utterances, *dima* 'take', especially in combination with two final verbs, *mena* 'come' and *hamana* 'go'. As in the examples above, these two verbs were used to talk about the change of location of objects, their being taken away 'having taken + went' and being brought to different individuals. There were no errors in deixis. One reason for this may be that in Kaluli the deictic verbs 'come' and 'go' are part of the surface form of the serial verb and the meaning is explicit. As with verbs of purpose, additional medial verbs were added. Only one additional final verb, 'give', was used with high frequency for all children.

6.12. Other Complex Constructions

Additional complex constructions did not become productive before 30 months. Around this time children used formulaic expressions, such as 'Do you see him going there?' which were composed of an interrogative + verb. Different constructions used correctly with auxiliary verbs (in 3rd person), were used in both positive and negative constructions, such as,

Mɛli 30.2 trying to chew something tough,

mɔ-   *omɛnɔ*   *dowab*
NEG   chew:1:FUT   do:3:PRES
'I am unable to chew'

de   *-yɔ*   *gilimɛnɔ*   *dowab*
fire   NEUTRAL   light:1:FUT   do:3:PRES
'I want to light the fire'

However, due to the lack of data beyond 32 months it is not possible to discuss the development of productive forms. Clearly in Kaluli, language acquisition after 32 months would show the development of additional complexity. What the current data demonstrate are the foundations of this development. This is only the beginning of a complex acquisition pattern.

EMPHATIC AND OTHER DISCOURSE PARTICLES

Kaluli has an extensive range of emphatic, affective, and discourse particles. They are suffixed to almost all parts of speech, are utterance final, and serve a range of functions. Emphatic and other discourse particles are among the earliest morphemes to be acquired. While emphatic particles are used correctly in some contexts from their earliest production, there are errors due to overgeneralization. As mentioned above, one set of emphatic particles was incorrectly used with imperatives as a means to inflect the verb. Another type of error occurs when children use too many emphatics strung together.

M 27.3   *ge   bes   -ɔ   *ɛlɛngɔ
         your   teeth NEUTRAL   like:this

         dugumɛnigɔl   -ɛ   -balo
         pull:out:1:INTENT 2   EMPH   EMPH

         'I'm going to pull your teeth out like this!'

There are several errors in this utterance. Mɛli has used a subject pronoun (*ge*) instead of a possessive adjective (*gi*). There is an error in the deictic term concerning proximity of action (=*wɛngɔ*). The verb is correct, but has two emphatics which cannot co-occur. For all the children, but especially for Mɛli, the period between 27 and 30 months was a time with a great deal of overmarking. Overmarking occurred not only with emphatics, but in the casemarking system on nominals.

The evidential particle -*lɔb* 'I see' was acquired early and in some contexts used correctly, but it was often used as an emphatic and not with its more specific evidential meaning. The particular discourse constraints of the use of the evidential were not always apparent in child language. It was used incorrectly as an emphatic co-occuring with the 1st person present tense, and in other instances it was used incorrectly with negatives and with interrogatives.

Mɛli 28.3   ne   *mɔ   -gɛlimɛnɔ   -lɔb
            I   NEG   carry:1:FUT   EVID

            *'I obviously will not carry'

Abi 28.2   nɔwɔ   *ane   -lɔb   -ɛlɛ
            my:mother   go:PAST   EVID   Q

            *'I wonder if my mother obviously went?!'

Another type of error making use of this evidential as a more general emphatic was its occurrence with the verb 'see', which is not correct.

Mɛli 30.2 is with her cousin Mama, age 45 months.

Mama: *ɛn   -a   bɛbɛ   -ke*
        there LOC   see:PAST EMPH:PAST
        'I saw (it) on there'

Mɛli: *ne   bɛbɛ-lɔb -ke*
        I   EVID   EMPH:PAST
        *'I saw (it) obviously'

If Mɛli wanted to escalate the degree of emphasis, she could have added an additional emphatic particle *-ye* to the already present emphatic particle (as is done by more mature speakers), but it was not correct to add the evidential.

Another frequent error was in the use of the quotative verb in confrontational rhetorical questions. Rhetorical questions are frequently used to challenge another's rights to objects or actions. Speakers (whether in fact they have said anything or not) use utterances such as *Dima ɛlabeyɔ?* 'Did I say 'take'?!' (meaning 'I didn't say take so you can't take!'). The errors made by children were due to using this form as an emphatic with the wrong pragmatic force. For example,

Mɛli 27.3 was looking for a lost spoon.

Mother: *ko   -na   sulufɔtinabe   -ke*
         there LOC   fall:RECENT PAST   EMPH:PAST
         'It fell there!'

Mɛli: *ɛh?   ɔba   *sulufotinɛbi-yɔ   ɛlabeyɔ*
         huh?   where   fall:IMP:FUT Q   'did I say'
         *'Huh? Where fall, did I say?'

Since this is the first clarification request in this sequence, there is no real need for Mɛli to use any emphatics at all. However, she uses the formulaic expression with the quotative verb as part of her query, which is not correct. In addition she has used the future imperative form instead of the past tense of the verb. These types of errors with the use of quotatives as emphatics continued through 29 months. At 32 months they inappropriately re-emerged in situations where Mɛli was angry and she used them to mark her anger. This use was challenged by her classificatory mother who asked, ''What's with all this 'did I say'? '' as everyone laughed at Mɛli. This suggests that children overgeneralize to similar affective content much like they overgeneralize in other areas of language acquisition.

The quotative verbs were also used correctly during this time period in non-challenging contexts of reported speech.

In addition to emphatics and evidentials, there are other discourse based particles in Kaluli. For example, if one speaker wishes to immediately repeat the words of another to a third person (other-repetition) there are two ways to do so. The speaker can use a quotative construction with the verb *sama* 'say'—which is frequently done. Use of the verb 'say' has no time constraints and all participants need not be present. A second option is less flexible. The pragmatic constraints on this form, *-do,* are as follows. All speakers must be present and the repetition must be in the next turn. A speaker cannot use this particle for self-repetition or repetition at a later time. The repetition particle, *-do,* is suffixed to the utterance; sometimes there are slight morphophonemic changes before the suffix is added. For example,

| Speaker A to Speaker B: | *sagalima!* | 'put on:IMP' |
| Speaker C to Speaker B: | *sagalindo!* | 'put on:IMP:REPET' |

The pragmatic distinctions between self- and other-repetition markers were not made by young children, who used this other-repetition particle as an emphatic on their own repeated utterances. Errors such as the following occurred,

Mɛli 26 to her mother,

| *magu* | *diɛ* | *-hamana* |
| banana | take:PURP | go:IMP |

'Go get a banana'

(no response from mother)

| *nɔ* | **diɛ* | *-hama-ndo!* |
| mother | take:PURP | go:IMP:REPET |

'Mother, go get a banana!'

After 27 months this particle was no longer used, either correctly or incorrectly, until 30 months, when it was correctly, though infrequently, used.

We see similar error patterns in the acquisition of emphatic and discourse particles as we see in other parts of the linguistic system. Certain salient and highly frequent forms are used early and appropriately in many contexts. However, there are errors caused by overgeneralization. In Kaluli, evidentials and other-repetition devices are used by young children as general emphatics, without the specific functions that are found in adult language use. By 30 months, however, the majority of these errors disappear.

CONCLUSIONS

While many different aspects of Kaluli children's language acquisition have been discussed in the body of the chapter, a few concluding thoughts remain. They are of two types. First, support is offered for a number of Slobin's Operating Principles (1985) based on the developmental patterns and processes presented above. Second, several questions based on the Kaluli acquisition data will be raised with the hope that answers will be forthcoming at a future date.

Kaluli children's early use of variable word order in pragmatically appropriate ways provides evidence for two of Slobin's (1985) Operating Principles. They are OP (STORAGE): UNITS and OP (MAPPING): VARIABLE WORD ORDER. Furthermore, given the Kaluli data, these two principles appear not only to interact with one another, but to strengthen one another. Young children must not only store the different word orders of the language that is both directed to them and that they overhear in their everyday experiences, but they must also "tag" those word orders with information about the relevant context in which they occur. The relevant context may include the linguistic environment (phonological, morphological, etc.) or the social environment (speaker/addressee relationship, speech event, mood, etc.). One type of context which determines word-order choice in Kaluli is the speech act that is being expressed. For Kaluli children, this tagging process mentioned above could match different word orders with particular speech acts. Thus Kaluli children may draw on those consistent relationships existing between word order and speech act type, facilitating the acquisition process.

The early acquisition of pragmatically appropriate word order may be only one of several areas in which contextual support is in the form of pragmatic function. Another concerns the acquisition of personal pronouns. For example, the relatively error free acquisition of focused and nonfocused pronouns may be further evidence of the interaction of the two Operating Principles (stated above) with the net effect of mutual reinforcement. The two sets of personal pronouns are also tagged by specific speech act contexts and specific word orders, and their acquisition may be guided through the support of the pragmatic context. In particular, if one considers the errors in pronoun acquisition that might have been made, but did not occur, we see the conceptual basis for certain aspects of morphological development and the importance of several kinds of contextual support, including pragmatic support.

Several sets of errors in different areas of the linguistic system provides evidence for overextension, or Slobin's (1985) OP:EXTENSION. In terms of casemarking on noun phrases, the young Kaluli child tries to mark notions consistently even within the component parts of noun phrases. One consistent pattern of Kaluli child language errors involved the addition of nominal casemarking on both the noun and its modifier (deictic, demonstrative, directional). This occurred during a limited time period after the initial emergence of casemarkers, especially with the locative on noun phrases in conjunction with verbs of location and change of location, with the dative, and less frequently, with the ergative casemarker.

Overextension occurred in other areas of the linguistic system. For example, children overgeneralized from the declarative tense inflections across sentence types, which in most cases was not correct. In addition, when children encountered unfamiliar formulaic expressions that were phonologically similar to already productive forms, they used the incorrect, but similar form before producing the correct formulaic expression.

The acquisition of correct verb stems for different forms of the verb provides strong evidence for another one of Slobin's (1985) Operating Principles, OP (UNITS): WORD FORMS. Kaluli children tried to change word forms through the suffixation of the most salient word final phonological morpheme (the emphatic markers), producing incorrect forms. This can be seen as an example of an interim production strategy, where the child tries to produce an appropriate sounding inflection by "stealing" from another part of the grammar. There are other examples of the use of this same strategy, also in verb formation, where children use other less frequent but salient verb final particles as possible inflectional forms in constructing a verb-like word.

In addition, in acquiring the extremely complex system of verb stem changes, Kaluli children frequently picked one form as basic (the stem of the present imperative) and attempted to add the tense endings to that form. Recall that in Kaluli there is a mismatch in the temporal basis of stem formation in that the present declarative is based on the future imperative. Following the Operating Principle that children prefer the use of grammatical markers that make semantic sense (Slobin, 1973), in their selection of one form as basic, Kaluli children incorrectly pick the present imperative as the base for present tense forms. Later, as they acquire additional verb forms, they incorrectly base future forms on the future imperative. In languages with extensive and irregular morphology one would expect to find these strategies used well beyond the age of three years.

Evidence from the distribution of verb forms used by Kaluli children supports the view that some aspects of the acquisition process may rely more heavily on function and context. In fact, the acquisition of some forms of the verb may be seen as context specific and pragmatically based. Given that verb forms which differ in tense/person and sentence type are morphologically marked, Kaluli children may not initially be learning verbs in general or verbs in a paradigm, but verb forms in particular. Thus we may want to be more specific when we discuss the acquisition of verbs. If the child does not use all of the forms of a given verb, we should investigate in more detail the extent to which particular forms in the verbal paradigm are used. Given a language that has rich and complex morphology in the verbal system, we should examine the distribution of verbs according to person, tense and when relevant, sentence type. In the acquisition of verbs, the child may be learning pieces of the paradigm, that is, specific forms for specific functions before he or she is able to generalize to other forms in the paradigm.

Questions generated from the Kaluli data suggest further areas of investigation concerning not only the acquisition of Kaluli but concerning child language research in general. For example, considering the early acquisition data, Kaluli resembles those languages for which we already have a significant amount of information. It is the more complex verbal constructions (clause-chaining and switch-reference) that distinguish Kaluli from other types of languages. Once we look at more complex syntax, the differences between Kaluli language acquisition and acquisition in other languages will probably appear greater. One question, then, concerns how we locate the building blocks and bridges between relatively simple syntax and more complex constructions. Data focusing on these aspects of development will help us understand how the child comes to sound like a speaker of his or her language, not just a speaker of "Child Language."

In all languages complementary linguistic resources present different and inconsistent information about the language system to the language acquiring child. In Kaluli, for example, verb agreement follows a nominative-accusative pattern while nominal morphology is split between a neutral system and an ergative-absolutive system The syntactic structure of the language is not ergative, but part of the morphological structure is. We need to understand how these systems interact in the development of the child's linguistic hypotheses and the expressions reflecting those hypotheses. Another area in which this type of interaction is found is in Kaluli personal pronoun and nominal casemarking systems. As we have seen, the acquisition of pronouns for expressing agents is more consistent and precocious than the acquisition of correct casemarking of nouns as agents. Therefore, the acquisition of expressions of agency varies according to which part of the linguistic system is examined. Does this mean that the nominal and pronominal systems do not interact? The Kaluli data suggest that we should investigate how different linguistic resources are used to express the same notions in the system.

Another issue that needs be addressed in future child language research is the role played by ellipsis. Languages with extensive ellipsis, such as Kaluli, are more difficult to analyze in terms of canonical clause forms, since the full forms are less common even in the input than reduced clauses. However, the rules of ellipsis seem to be one aspect of the language acquired relatively early by young speakers.

Finally, as this chapter and others in this volume (for example Ochs, Clancy) have shown, researchers investigating child language acquisition need to attend to the importance of affective and discourse components (whether morphological, lexical or syntactic) in the acquisition process. These components are important to consider for what they tell us in contexts of both appropriate and inappropriate use. Affective and discourse particles are linguistic resources that enable the child to more effectively communicate and accomplish some of the interpersonal and expressive goals of language. They must be considered along with the phonological, morphological, syntactic and semantic aspects of development in the crosslinguistic study of language acquisition.

ACKNOWLEDGMENT

I would like to thank institutions as well as individuals for the different kinds of support necessary in order to prepare this chapter. Funding for the fieldwork among the Kaluli was from the National Science Foundation (pre-doctoral research grant #GS 43769) and the Wenner-Gren Foundation for Anthropological Research, New York (grant-in-aid # 3054). A University of Pennsylvania Faculty Summer Grant (1982) facilitated the analysis and preparation of the chapter. Many non-Kaluli speaking friends generously provided detailed comments which improved all aspects of this work. In particular I want to thank Pat Clancy and Gillian Sankoff for their critical suggestions and extensive encouragement. Elinor Ochs and Dan Slobin kept certain fires going throughout the cooking process for which I am grateful. Cherie Francis assisted in the final preparation of the chapter. Of course I wish to thank my Kaluli-speaking friends for their assistance in this project—Buck Schieffelin, Steve Feld, and the Kaluli people of Bona village. And Zachary, thanks for your patience with it all.

REFERENCES

Bechert, J. Ergativity in the constitution of grammatical relations. In F. Plank (Ed.), *Ergativity*. London: Academic Press, 1979.

Bloom, L., Lightbown, L., & Hood, L. Structure and variation in child language. *Monographs of the Society for Research in Child Development*, 1975, serial no. 160, *40*(2).

Comrie, B. Ergativity. In W. P. Lehmann (Ed.), *Syntactic typology*. Austin: University of Texas Press, 1978.

Dixon, R. M. W. Ergativity. *Language*, 1979, *55*, 59–138.

Feld, S. *Sound and sentiment*. Philadelphia: University of Pennsylvania Press, 1982.

Feld, S., & Schieffelin, B. B. Hard words: A functional basis for Kaluli discourse. In D. Tannen (Ed.), *Text and talk*. Washington: Georgetown University Press, 1982.

Givón, T. Focus and the scope of assertion: Some Bantu evidence. *Studies in African Linguistics*, 1975, *6*, 185–205.

Greenberg, J. H. Some universals of grammar with particular reference to the order of meaningful elements. In J. H. Greenberg (Ed.), *Universals of language*. Cambridge, MA: M.I.T. Press, 1966.

Haiman, J. Hua: A Papuan language. In T. Shopen (Ed.), *Languages and their status*. Cambridge, MA: Winthrop Publishers, 1979.

Hopper, P. J., & Thompson, S. A. Transitivity in grammar and discourse. *Language*, 1980, *56*, 251–299.

Lehmann, W. P. A structural principle of language and its implications. *Language*, 1973, *49*, 47–66.

Longacre, R. F. *Hierarchy and universality of discourse constituents in New Guinea languages: Discussion*. Washington, D. C.: Georgetown University Press, 1972.

Li, C. N., & Lang, R. The syntactic irrelevance of an ergative case in Enga and other Papuan languages. In F. Plank (Ed.), *Ergativity: Towards a theory of grammatical relations.* London: Academic Press, 1979.

Ochs, E. Ergativity and word order in Samoan child language. *Language,* 1982, *58,* 646–671.

Ochs, E., & Schieffelin, B. B. Language acquisition and socialization: Three developmental stories and their implications. In R. LeVine & R. Shweder (Eds.), *Culture theary: Essays on mind, self, and emotion.* New York: Cambridge University Press, 1984.

Olson, M. L. Switch reference in Barai. *Proceedings of the Fourth Annual Meeting of the Berkeley Linguistic Society,* 1978, *4,* 140–157.

Rule, M. *A statement of the alphabet and grammar of the Kaluli language of Bosavi, Papua.* Unevangelized Field Mission, Lake Kutubu, Papua New Guinea. 1964, Unpublished.

Schieffelin, B. B. Getting it together: An ethnographic study of the development of communicative competence. In E. Ochs & B. B. Schieffelin (Eds.), *Developmental pragmatics.* New York: Academic Press, 1979.

Schieffelin, B. B. *How Kaluli children learn what to say, what to do, and how to feel: An ethnographic study of the development of communicative competence.* Unpublished doctoral dissertation, Columbia University, 1979. (Cambridge University Press, in press).

Schieffelin, B. B. Teasing in Kaluli children's interactions. In E. Ochs & B. B. Schieffelin (Eds.), *Language socialization across cultures.* New York: Cambridge University Press. In press.

Schieffelin, E. L. *The sorrow of the lonely and the burning of the dancers.* New York: St. Martins Press, 1976.

Shaw, R. D. A tentative classification of the languages of the Mt. Bosavi region. In K. Franklin (Ed.), *The linguistic situation in the Gulf district and adjacent areas, Papua New Guinea. Pacific Linguistics,* no 26, series C, 1973, 187–224.

Silverstein, M. Hierarchy of features and ergativity. In R. M. W. Dixon (Ed.), *Grammatical categories in Austrialian languages.* Canberra: Australian Institute of Aboriginal Studies, 1976.

Slobin, D. I. Language change in childhood and history. In J. Macnamara (Ed.), *Language learning and thought.* New York: Academic Press, 1977.

Slobin, D. I. Cognitive prerequisites for the development of grammar. In C. A. Ferguson & D. I. Slobin (Eds.), *Studies of child language development.* New York: Holt, Rinehart & Winston, 1973.

Slobin, D. I. Crosslinguistic evidence for the Language-Making Capacity. In D. I. Slobin (Ed.), *The crosslinguistic study of language acquisition* (Vol. 2). Hillsdale, NJ: Lawrence Erlbaum Associates, 1985.

Voorhoeve, C. L. Central and western Trans-New Guinea Phylum languages. In S. A. Wurm (Ed.), Papuan languages and the New Guinea linguistic scene. *Pacific Linguistics,* no 38, series C, 1975, 345–460.

Wurm, S. A. Personal pronouns. In S. A. Wurm (Ed.), Papuan languages and the New Guinea linguistic scene. *Pacific Linguistics,* no. 38, Series C, 1975, 191–218.

Wurm, S. A., Laycock, D. C., & Voorhoeve, C. L. General Papuan characteristics. In S. A. Wurm (Ed.), Papuan languages and the New Guinea linguistic scene. *Pacific Linguistics,* no 38, Series C, 1975, 171–190.

6 The Acquisition of Polish*

Magdalena Smoczyńska
Jagiellonian University
Kraków, Poland

Contents

INTRODUCTION

1. Descriptive Sketch of Polish

1.1. General Typological Characteristics

Polish is an Indo-European language, belonging to the Slavic branch. Within the Slavic branch, Polish represents one of the North Slavic languages, as different from South Slavic (Serbo-Croatian, Bulgarian, etc.). The North Slavic group

*The present chapter includes some sections written by Dr. Richard M. Weist, who was asked to give a first-hand account of his research conducted at Adam Mickiewicz University and SUNY College, Fredonia. These sections are indicated by [WEIST] at the beginning and end of each section. Due to the communication problems caused by the situation in Poland during the completion of work on this book, Dr. Weist undertook the job of developing and editing the first draft of my chapter as a favor to me. He has contributed enormously to the final formulation of my text, and I would like to express my deepest gratitude for his cooperation. I would also like to thank my colleague and friend, Dr. Elżbieta Tabakowska from Jagiellonian University, Kraków, who helped me with the English formulation of the original draft.

is further subdivided into West Slavic languages including Polish, Czech, Slovak, etc., and East Slavic (Russian, Ukrainian, etc.).

Like other Slavic languages, Polish represents an inflecting, or fusional type of language, in which single grammatical morphemes combine several functions: case, gender, and number in noun forms; person and number in verb forms. However, Polish is less close to the ideal model of an inflecting language than Czech or Slovak. Lotko (1979) gives many examples of replacing synthetic means of expression by analytical ones in contemporary Polish. In general, the Polish grammatical system closely parallels that of Russian.

Because Polish retains a rich inflectional system, morphology is the main device for expressing syntactic distinctions. Word order has grammatical functions only to a limited extent, and hence it can serve other purposes, namely, it performs pragmatic functions. Deviations from the standard (unmarked) SVO order serve the purposes of topicalization; and combined with focal stress, word order expresses special emphasis on certain elements, in a way independent from discourse structure. Furthermore, the rich inflectional system makes it possible to apply ellipsis to a much larger extent than in English. A selective outline of Polish morphology and syntax is provided in Sections 1.2 and 1.3. The interested reader will profit from Schenker's (1967, 1973) comprehensive and well-organized description of Polish grammar and Fisiak, Lipińska-Grzegorek, and Zabrocki's (1978) Polish-English contrastive grammar.

1.2. Morphology

There are some relevant differences between Slavic and English morphology. In English, the basic word form is the stem. The same stem can constitute the basic form of both noun and verb, e.g. *change, drink*. The form STEM + Ø usually performs numerous functions, and the use of inflectional endings is greatly limited. The form STEM + ENDING occurs in opposition to the basic form, e.g. *ball-s/ball, Mommy-'s/Mommy, drink-s/drink, want-ed/want*, etc. Thus, in English one can talk about the acquisition of particular grammatical morphemes, as is actually done in Brown (1973), de Villiers and de Villiers (1973), and others.

In Slavic languages, bare stems, i.e. forms with a zero ending, are rare, and in most cases, the word stem can never occur alone. Hence, the concept of a word stem is a mere abstraction which can be formed by cutting off the common part that occurs in various forms of a word from the array of possible endings. Even those forms which are functionally unmarked, e.g. nominative singular of nouns or infinitive of verbs, have specific endings, and a given ending explicitly specifies the grammatical category of the word. Moreover, in view of the rich variety of inflectional forms of a word, a given form occurs in opposition to the whole inflectional pattern, rather than to the basic form only. Therefore, morphological development should be conceived of as the acquisition of the ability to REPLACE grammatical morphemes according to the rules of language, rather than the ability to ADD them to basic forms when required.

In consequence, although Polish children can very easily split a word form into a stem and an ending (as illustrated by their own morphological formations, differing from adult forms), the basic unit of the text is a WORD rather than a morpheme. In Polish this is additionally strengthened by fixed penultimate word stress. In contrast to Polish, word stress is mobile in Russian and Serbo-Croatian. Free morphemes are not numerous in Polish, and their status is entirely different from that of bound morphemes. Furthermore, most Polish endings are syllabic, whereas in English many of them are nonsyllabic. Thus their presence does not affect the prosodic shape of the word (equal to stem).

The purpose of this section on morphology is to provide the reader with a sketch of the declensional and conjugational patterns of Polish. Hence, the description which follows has been simplified in many ways. In some areas, the nature of the simplification will be identified so that the reader can appreciate the complexity of the overall system. However, in many instances the relationship between this brief sketch and the full system will not be identified. The reader seeking an understanding of the full system should consult another source, such as Schenker (1973).

1.2.1. *Nouns.*   Nouns are marked for gender, and they are inflected for case and number. The relationship between the cases and their most typical semantic and syntactic functions is presented in Table 6.1, and the basic regular declensional patterns are outlined in Table 6.2. Gender serves as the basis for the classification of nouns into declensional patterns. Singular nouns have one of three genders: feminine, masculine, or neuter. The masculine and neuter patterns are relatively similar as contrasted with the feminine pattern. In the plural, there are two genders: virile (VIR) and nonvirile (NVIR), where virile includes the

TABLE 6.1
The Polish Cases and Their Most Typical Functions [WEIST]

Case	Semantic Function	Syntactic Function	Key Wh Question
Nominative (NOM)	Agent	Subject	Who
Accusative (ACC)	Patient	Direct Object	Whom
Genitive (GEN)	Possessor	Possessive	Whose
Dative (DAT)	Receiver	Indirect Object	To whom
Locative (LOC)[a]	Location	Adverbial	On what/where
Instrumental (INSTR)	Instrument/Comitative	Adverbial	With what/whom
Vocative (VOC)	The case used when addressing someone		

[a]The locative case is also referred to as the prepositional case.

TABLE 6.2
The Basic Declensional Patterns

	Singular (SG)		
Case	Feminine (FEM)	Masculine (MASC)	Neuter (NEUT)
NOM	-a	-ø	-o/-e
ACC	-ę	[AN] = GEN/[INAN] = NOM	= NOM
GEN	-y/-i [SFC]	-a/(-u)	-a
DAT	-e/-i [SFC]	-owi/(-u)	-u
LOC	= DAT	-e/-u [SFC]	-e/-u [SFC]
INSTR	– ą	-em	-em

Plural (PL) with Virile (VIR)/Nonvirile (NVIR)

NOM	-y/-i, (-e) [SFC], -a [NEUT], -owie [VIR]		
ACC	[NVIR] = NOM/[VIR] = GEN		
GEN	-ø [−MASC]		-ów/(-y/-i) [+MASC]
DAT	-om		
LOC	-ach		
INSTR	-ami (-mi)		

[ ] = criterion, e.g. animate [AN].
SFC = stem final consonant (hard/soft or other).
( ) = less frequent suffix.

features masculine and human.[1] In the plural, the dative, locative, and instrumental suffixes are identical, regardless of gender. The nominative and accusative suffixes are conditioned by the virile versus nonvirile distinction and the genitive endings depend on the masculine versus non-masculine distinction. Throughout the declensional system specific suffixes are sometimes controlled by the morphophonological properties of the noun stem, e.g. hard versus soft stem-final consonants. Furthermore, it is important to note that the speaker's task consists not only in the selection of an appropriate ending but also in performing necessary modifications of the phonological form of the stem. Some of such stem alternations result from general phonological rules. In most instances, however, they are governed by narrow morphophonological rules only.

1.2.1.1. **[WEIST]** *Cases and Functions.*   One of the basic problems that the child (or any other listener) faces is to extract information about semantic functions, e.g. agent versus patient, from the surface structure. If a simple

---

[1]Polish seems to be the most sex-biased of all Indo-European languages. Russian has the animate/inanimate distinction in plural for all nouns and Serbo-Croatian preserves the masculine, feminine, and neuter distinction.

transitive sentence contains two feminine singular nouns, there is no ambiguity within the basic declensional pattern as shown in sentence 1.[2] In sentence 1,

(1) *Dziewczynk-a*   *pcha*   *matk-ę*
    girl-FEM:NOM:SG   pushes mother-FEM:ACC:SG
    '(A) girl is pushing (the) mother.'

(2) *Dziewczynk-i*   *pchają*   *matk-i*
    girl-NVIR:NOM/ACC:PL push   mother-NVIR:ACC/NOM:PL
    'Girls are pushing mothers'   or   'Mothers are pushing girls.'

(3) *Chłopiec-ø*   *goni*   *ojc-a*
    boy-MASC:NOM:SG   chases father-MASC:ACC:SG
    '(A) boy is chasing (the) father.'

(4) *Samochód-ø*   *goni*   *autobus-ø*
    car-MASC:NOM/ACC:SG chases bus-MASC:ACC/NOM:SG
    '(A) car is chasing (the) bus'   or   '(A) bus is chasing (the) car.'

the word *dziewczynk-a* 'girl' has the nominative singular suffix *-a* which indicates (in this context) that the girl is the one who is initiating the action, and the word *matkę* 'mother' has the accusative singular suffix *-ę* which specifies that the mother is somehow affected by the action. The meaning is the same if we change the word order: *Matkę pcha dziewczynka, Pcha dziewczynka matkę,* etc. Ambiguity can arise if these nouns are plural nouns since the nominative suffix is the same as the accusative for nonvirile nouns, as demonstrated by sentence 2. If the two nouns in a transitive sentence are masculine singular and animate, the nominative and accusative suffixes are distinct, e.g. *chłopiec* and *ojciec* in the nominative case and *chłopca* and *ojca* in the accusative case. However, if the masculine nouns are NOT animate the suffixes in the nominative and the accusative case are identical as shown in sentence 4.

(5) *Siostr-a*   *Michał-a*   *zjadła*
    sister-FEM:NOM:SG Michael-MASC:GEN:SG ate

    ciast-o   *pod*   *stoł-em*   *w*
    cake-NEUT:ACC:SG under table-MASC:INSTR:SG in

    kuchn-i
    kitchen-FEM:LOC:SG
    'Michael's sister ate (the) cake under (the) table in (the) kitchen'

(6) *Chłopc-y*   *zjedli* *ciast-a*   *z*
    boy-VIR:NOM:PL ate   cake-NEUT:GEN:SG with

---

[2]For a guide to pronunciation, see Appendix A.

rodzynk-ami.
raisin-NVIR:INSTR:PL
'The boys ate some cake with raisins'

(7) *Michał-ø*   *nie jadł ciast-a*
Michael-MASC:NOM:SG   not   ate   cake-NEUT:GEN:SG
palc-ami.
finger-NVIR:INSTR:PL
'Michael did not eat (the) cake with (his) fingers'

(8) *Chłopiec-ø*   *poszedł do sklep-u*   *z*
boy-MASC:NOM:SG   went   to shop-MASC:GEN:SG   with
siostr-ą.
sister-FEM:INSTR:SG
'(The) boy went to the shop with (his) sister'

(9) *Dziewczynk-a*   *czytała brat-u*   *o*
girl-FEM:NOM:SG   read   brother-MASC:DAT:SG   about
zwierzęt-ach.
animal-NVIR:LOC:PL
'(The) girl read to (her) brother about animals.'

The above examples serve to demonstrate that the functions of cases are not limited to those presented in Table 6.1. The genitive, for instance, is not only the Possessor's case (as in sentence 5) but also expresses the Partitive (sentence 6), the Direct Object of negated sentences (sentence 7), the Location in the expression 'to the shop' (sentence 8), etc. Similarly, the instrumental is not only the expression of Instrument (as in sentence 7: 'with fingers') but also a Comitative: 'with raisins' and 'with sister' (sentences 6 and 8), as well as the Location 'under the table' (sentence 5). The locative not only expresses Location (as in sentence 5) but also figures in a prepositional phrase 'about animals' which is not a Location (sentence 9). As for the locative case, which is also referred to as the prepositional case, it is worth noting that both its names are misleading: in fact, other cases serve to express location as well, and other cases are used with prepositions. For instance, while *na* 'on' and *w* 'in' require the locative to express static location, when used with the accusative they express dynamic notions of 'onto', 'into'. Prepositions *do* 'to', *od* 'from' require the genitive, while *pod* 'under', *nad* 'over', *za* 'behind' govern the instrumental case. The same prepositions, however, when used with the accusative express motion: 'to go under/over/behind something'. Among Polish cases, it is the genitive which has the widest range of functions, while the use of the dative is relatively the most limited, i.e. Receiver, Beneficiary, Experiencer. In addition to these points concerning the relationships between the cases and semantic and syntactic functions, sentences 1–9 show clearly the sense in which Polish is an inflecting language. Each suffix combines the concepts of gender, case, and number. Furthermore, the individual suffixes can only be understood within the context of a declensional pattern. Hence, the suffix -*a* [a] has the nominative singular function in the feminine pattern, the genitive (and/or) the accusative function in the masculine pattern, and the accusative and nominative plural function in the neuter pattern. [**WEIST**]

1.2.2. Adjectives. Adjectives agree in case, number, and gender with the noun they modify. The declension of adjectives is relatively regular: there are five different patterns corresponding to the five genders (three in singular, two in plural). Comparative and superlative degrees are formed also rather regularly by adding special suffixes and prefixes. With some classes of adjectives only analytical forms can be used.

1.2.3. Adverbs. Adverbs are primarily derived from adjectives by means of suffixes. They are not declined. Comparative and superlative degrees are formed according to rules similar to those for adjectives.

1.2.4. Numerals. While ordinals are declined according to the regular adjective pattern, the declension of cardinal numerals is a loose collection of exceptions rather than a system. Every honest native speaker of Polish would confess making occasional mistakes with these forms or at least admit that the choice of the correct form requires an intensive intellectual effort on his or her part.

1.2.5. Pronouns. Most pronouns are declined according to the regular adjectival pattern, but the case forms of personal pronouns are highly idiosyncratic. Furthermore, oblique cases of personal pronouns have special enclitic short forms, distributed according to special rules.

Another peculiarity is the existence of special reflexive pronouns, which replace the personal or possessive pronoun when the person to which it refers coincides with the sentence subject. For instance, the English sentences *I think about myself, You think about yourself, They think about themselves* are translated into Polish as *Myślę o sobie, Myślisz o sobie, Myślą o sobie,* where a single reflexive pronoun, *sobie,* is used with no distinction for number or gender. Similarly, the following set of sentences reveals the contrasts for possessives: *On bierze moje książki* 'He takes my:1SG books', but *Biorę swoje książki 'I:take my:REFL books';* and compare *Biorę jego książki* 'I:take his:3SG:MASC books' with *On bierze swoje książki* 'He takes his:REFL books'. The use of the third person singular pronoun in the last example (*On bierze jego książki* 'He takes his books') would specify that the owner of the books and the agent are two different persons.

In general, possessive pronouns are used less frequently than in English. For instance, in the above examples the possessive reflexive is most frequently omitted and such terms as body parts or kinship terms are usually used without possessive pronouns, unless the "possessor" happens not to be identical with the agent. Thus, a literal translation of the English, *I wash my hands,* would seem queer in Polish, unless the speaker wanted to stress that he is not washing somebody else's hands. Furtheremore, many English constructions with a possessive are rendered in Polish by means of a construction with the benefactive (in dative): *I wash his hands,* translates as *Myję mu ręce* 'I:wash to:him hands'.

1.2.6. *Verbs.* Finite and nonfinite forms of the verb are marked for aspect. Finite forms are inflected for tense, mood, person, number, and in some instances gender.

1.2.6.1. *Aspect.* The major aspectual distinction in Polish is between perfective and imperfective, and Polish also has an iterative aspect. These distinctions are clearly marked in the morphology (see Majewicz, 1982). While the meaning of perfectivity is still debated (e.g. Ferrell, 1951; Ridjanović, 1976), we will take the position that perfective verbs specify the notion of a completed situation, i.e. a situation which has a beginning, a continuation, and a termination (see Comrie, 1976). The imperfective aspect is neutral and the imperfective verb form does not specify whether the action is completed or not. The selection of aspectual form depends on perspective. Given that a situation is in fact completed, the speaker may refer to that situation with a perfective or imperfective verb form. The perfective form is chosen if the speaker intends to identify the property of completion in the situation. However, if reference is made to a situation which is not completed, only an imperfective verb can be used.

For most verbs, the imperfective form is morphologically simpler, and the perfective form is derived from it. This is done by means of adding either a prefix, e.g. *pisać/na-pisać* 'to write' (IPFV/PFV) or a suffix, e.g. *kop-a-ć/kop-ną-ć* 'to kick' (IPFV/PFV). For some aspectual pairs, both terms do not differ in morphological complexity. Each of them includes a stem and a suffix, and the aspectual opposition is indicated by the kind of suffix used, e.g. *strzel-i-ć/strzel-a-ć* 'to shoot' (PFV/IPFV). For many verbs of this group the suffix alternation is accompanied by the stem alternation as well, e.g. *otworz-y-ć/otwier-a-ć* 'to open' (PFV/IPFV). Suffix alternation usually implies the shift of the verb to another conjugation type. For a dozen other verbs, the basic form is perfective and the imperfective form is derived from it, e.g. *dać/dawać* 'to give' (PFV/IPFV); *wstać/wstawać* 'to get up'' (PFV/IPFV).

As has already been said, for most verbs perfective forms are derived from the imperfective and the number of verbs in which the derivation goes the other way is rather limited. There is, however, another (very frequent) process which consists of deriving imperfectives from prefixed perfective forms. In the example cited above, *pisać/na-pisać* 'to write' (IPFV/PFV), the prefix *na-* is added to the simple imperfective form to make a perfective form. This particular prefix does not carry any particular meaning except for that of perfectivity. There are, however, other prefixes which can be added to the imperfective *pisać* and which serve two functions at one time. They perfectivize the verb and carry additional meanings roughly corresponding to those expressed by verbal particles in English, e.g., (1) *pod-pisać* 'to sign' (PFV) *pod-* 'under', (2) *wy-pisać* 'to write out' (PFV) *wy-* 'out', (3) *prze-pisać* 'to copy' (PFV) *prze-* 'through', (4) *przy-pisać* 'to ascribe' (PFV) *przy-* 'at', (5) *w-pisać* 'to write in' (PFV) *w-* 'in', (6) *do-pisać* 'to add to' (PFV) *do-* 'to', and (7) *od-pisać* 'to crib' (PFV) *od-* 'from'. Since all these verbs are perfective and their meanings differ from that of the imperfective simple verb *pisać,* their aspectual counterparts are derived from them by means of suffixation, e.g. *pod-pis-ywa-ć, wy-pis-ywa-ć,* etc. Such forms are called secondary imperfectives. Finally, aspectual pairs can be suppletive, each of the terms based on a different stem, e.g., *brać* (IPFV)/*wziąć* (PFV) 'to take,' *widzieć* (IPFV)/*zobaczyć* (PFV) 'to see'.

1.2.6.2. *Finite Forms.*   The conjugation of the Polish verb is illustrated in Table 6.3, where all the finite forms of the verb *pisać/napisać* 'to write' are given.

There are three moods in Polish: indicative, conditional, and imperative. The tense system is very simple and it involves three tenses only: present, past, and future. The tense distinction appears in the indicative mood only, and its full realization concerns imperfective verbs. Perfective verbs lack the forms of present tense, since the notion of perfectivity precludes the simultaneity of action with the moment of speaking; thus they have only past and future forms. For perfective verbs, forms corresponding to those of present (in imperfective verbs) are used to express futurity, while for imperfective verbs a separate analytic construction is used. It involves the auxiliary *będę* 'I:will' followed either by the "past participle" (see below): *będę pisał* (MASC), *będę pisała* (FEM), *będzie pisało* (NEUT), *będziemy pisali* (VIR), *będziemy pisały* (NVIR) or by the infinitive: *będę pisać, będziemy pisać,* with no distinction of gender. The choice of the form (past participle vs. infinitive) is optional.[3]

It should be noted that each verb has at least two stems. Stem I, called the "present tense stem" (here: *pisz-*) appears in present forms (both "true" present of imperfective verbs, and "formal" present, in fact, future of perfective verbs) and in imperative forms. Stem II, called, the "infinitive stem," occurs in past tense indicative forms (including the "past participle" of the analytic future) and in conditional forms. What is more, many verbs require additional stem alternations WITHIN a given inflectional paradigm, e.g. *bior-ę* 'I-take' but *bierz-esz*

---

[3]In Polish, the analytic future is ungrammatical with perfective verbs, while in Serbo-Croatian it is a regular form.

TABLE 6.3
Finite Forms of the Verb *pisać/napisać* 'to write'

	Aspect	
	Imperfective (IPFV)	*Perfective (PFV)*

Indicative Present

SG
1. *pisz-ę*
2. *-esz*
3. *-e*

PL
1. *pisz-emy*
2. *-ecie*
3. *-ą*

Future

SG
1. *będ -ę   pisa-ł-* $\begin{Bmatrix} \phi \\ a \\ o \end{Bmatrix}$ MASC FEM NEUT
2. *będzi-esz* or
3. *-e   pisa-ć*

1. *na-pisz-ę*
2. *na-pisz-esz*
3. *-e*

PL
1. *będzi-emy pisa-* $\begin{Bmatrix} l\text{-}i \\ ł\text{-}y \end{Bmatrix}$ VIR NVIR
2. *-ecie* or *pisa-ć*
3. *będ -ą*

1. *na-pisz-emy*
2. *-ecie*
3. *-ą*

Past

SG
1. *pisa-ł-* $\begin{Bmatrix} \phi \\ a \\ o \end{Bmatrix}$ *+ m* MASC FEM NEUT
2. *+ ś*
3. *+ ø*

1. *na-pisa-ł-* $\begin{Bmatrix} \phi \\ a \\ o \end{Bmatrix}$ *+ m* MASC FEM NEUT
2. *+ ś*
3. *+ ø*

PL
1. *pisa-* $\begin{Bmatrix} l\text{-}i \\ ł\text{-}y \end{Bmatrix}$ *+ śmy* VIR NVIR
2. *+ ście*
3. *+ ø*

1. *na-pisa-* $\begin{Bmatrix} l\text{-}i \\ ł\text{-}y \end{Bmatrix}$ *+ śmy* VIR NVIR
2. *+ ście*
3. *+ ø*

Conditional

SG
1. *pisa-ł-* $\begin{Bmatrix} \phi \\ a \\ o \end{Bmatrix}$ *+ by-m* MASC FEM NEUT
2. *-ś*
3. *-ø*

1. *na-pisa-ł-* $\begin{Bmatrix} \phi \\ a \\ o \end{Bmatrix}$ *+ by-m*
2. *-ś*
3. *-ø*

PL
1. *pisa-* $\begin{Bmatrix} l\text{-}i \\ ł\text{-}y \end{Bmatrix}$ *+ by-śmy* VIR NVIR
2. *-ście*
3. *-ø*

1. *na-pisa-* $\begin{Bmatrix} l\text{-}i \\ ł\text{-}y \end{Bmatrix}$ *+ by-śmy*
2. *-ście*
3. *-ø*

Imperative

SG
1. —
2. *pisz-ø*
3. —

1. —
2. *na-pisz-ø*
3. —

PL
1. *pisz-my*
2. *-cie*
3. —

1. *na-pisz-my*
2. *-cie*
3. —

'you-take', with the alternation /b'or/ : /b'ež/ within Stem I, as opposed to Stem II: /bra/ in *bra-ć* 'take-INF' (cf. stem alternation in the auxiliary *będę/będziesz* in Table 6.3). Stem selection is the major difficulty in Polish conjugation. In respect to stem alternations, Tokarski (1973) distinguishes among 11 groups of verbs, some of them further subdivided. For many of those "regular" groups it is not sufficient to know the infinitive and the present tense form in order to be able to predict all the alternations involved. Moreover, a number of verbs are quite irregular.

The forms which are especially interesting are those of the past tense and of the conditional mood. Their peculiarity consists of their agglutinative structure (Tokarski, 1973), quite atypical for Polish. In these forms, each category is expressed by a separate morpheme. The rule of past tense formation can be phrased as follows:

[INFINITIVE STEM + PAST + GENDER] + PERSON

e.g.	*pisa-*	*-ł-*	*-a-*	*-ś*
	write	PAST	FEM	2SG

The conditional is derived from the past tense form by inserting the special article *by,* which results in:

[INFINITIVE STEM + PAST + GENDER] + [CONDITIONAL + PERSON]

e.g.	*pisa-*	*-ł-*	*-ø-*	*-by-*	*-m*
	write	PAST	MASC	COND	1SG

Yet another peculiarity lies in the fact that these forms are not fully synthetic: they are composed of the "past participle" (PP): [INFINITIVE STEM + PAST + GENDER] and the movable ending: PERSON in past tense forms, and [CONDITIONAL + PERSON] in conditional forms. The past participle forms a prosodic entity: it is regularly stressed on the penultimate syllable, whether followed by the ending or not, and it is an autonomous word (e.g. when used with the auxiliary *będzie* to form the analytic future).[4] Past participles: *pisał* (MASC), *pisała* (FEM), *pisało* (NEUT), *pisali* (VIR), and *pisały* (NVIR) coincide with the third person past forms, since these forms have a zero marker for PERSON. On the other hand, past and conditional forms are not analytic either, since the movable endings are not words *per se*. They can either follow the participle, without altering its stress, or they are moved towards the beginning of the clause, usually to follow the first stressed unit, e.g. *Co ty napisała-ś?* or *Co-ś ty napisała?* 'What have you written?'

---

[4]Even if the ending follows the verb, its presence does not affect the regular penultimate stress pattern of the past participle: *pisáli-śmy, písał-bym, pisáła-bym,* etc.

The endings which are most frequently moved to the front of the clause are the syllabic ones, which are enclitic. These include the first and second plural of the past tense -śmy, -ście, and all the conditional endings: −by-m, -by-ś, -by for singular and -by-śmy, -by-ście, -by for plural. In spoken language, *Dlaczego-śmy to napisali?* is more natural than *Dlaczego to napisali-śmy?* 'Why did we write that?' and *Ja by-m to napisała* is much more frequent than *Ja to napisała-bym* 'I would write that'.

All these peculiarities result from the fact that the Polish past tense historically comes from an analytic construction (*pisał jeśm*), and the present state is that of a transitional form, neither fully analytic nor fully synthetic. In Serbo-Croatian the corresponding forms preserve their analytic status, e.g. *ja sam pisao, ja bih pisao,* with regular auxiliaries. In Russian the auxiliary disappeared completely, and the person distinction is expressed by the pronoun only, e.g. *ja pisal, ty pisal,* etc. It is worth noting that Polish marks person in the endings of all the finite forms, and this is why personal pronouns are not used unless special emphasis is required. English *I write* or *I am writing* translates simply as *Piszę,* while *Ja piszę* would mean 'It is I who am writing' or 'As for me, I am writing'.

Synthetic imperative forms exist for second singular and first and second plural, while the third person forms, as well as that of first singular, are formed periphrastically, e.g. *niech on pisze* 'let him write'. It should be noted that the imperative form is not considered impolite among familiar speakers, and it is used much more frequently than in English.

It has already been noted that the main difficulty of Polish verb inflection consists in stem selection. The choice of endings does not present major problems. Linguists distinguish three conjugation types, based on the present tense vowel: -e, -i/-y, or -a. Some linguists treat it as stem final vowel, while other consider it as a part of ending, as we did in Table 6.3. Except for the vowel, the sets of endings used in the three conjugation types are very similar. The exception is the first singular ending of the present tense, where two alternative endings occur: -ę or -am (*pisz-ę* 'I-write' vs. *czyt-am* 'I-read'). (see Table 6.7.)

1.2.6.3. *Nonfinite Forms.* Indeclinable forms comprise infinitives (e.g. *pisać* or *napisać* 'to write') and two gerunds. The present gerund, e.g. *pisząc* (only IPFV) is equivalent to the adverbial clause 'while writing'; and the past gerund, e.g. *napisawszy* has the meaning 'having written' (only PFV). The past gerund is almost never used in spoken language. Apart from these, there are verbal nouns e.g. *pisanie* or *napisanie* '(the action of) writing' (both PFV and IPFV) and two adjectival participles. They are the active participle, e.g. *piszący* 'writing (person)' (only IPFV) and the passive participle, e.g. *pisany* or *napisany* 'written' (both IPFV and PFV). Verbal nouns and adjectival participles are regularly declined according to respective noun and adjective patterns. What has been referred to as "past participle" in Section 1.2.6.2 is only a part of some finite verbal forms and does not occur independently.

Passive participles are used in passive voice constructions. In spoken language, however, these have a limited range of use, as word order flexibility is sufficient for expressing focus, and a number of subjectless active constructions can be used for subject downgrading. Those occurring in spoken language typically involve perfective participles, used in order to refer to a resulting end state of some action, performed by an unspecified agent which is either unknown or evident or simply irrelevant. These cannot be called truncated passives, as full passives are practically never used. They are rather a subclass of attributive sentences making statements about objects.

1.3. Syntax

1.3.1. *Simple Sentences.* Most of the basic constructions correspond to those in other Indo-European languages. Thus I will point only to some idiosyncratic structures. There are a number of subjectless constructions with either special impersonal forms used, such as the reflexive verb form *pisze się* or the impersonal participle *pisano* 'one:wrote', or the third plural form without a subject, *piszą* 'they:write' (= 'somebody writes').

Another specific structure is the existential sentence, in which the verb *być* 'to be' is used in the sense of 'to exist, to be present', e.g. *Jest chłopiec-ø* 'is boy-NOM' (= 'There is a boy' or 'The boy is here'), with the negated version *Nie ma chłopc-a* 'not have boy-GEN' (= 'The boy isn't here').

Specific structural patterns are those involving an experiencer in dative, e.g. *Jest mi zimno* 'is me:DAT cold' (= 'I am cold'), *Jest mi smutno* 'is me:DAT sadly' (= 'I am sad')[5] or *Leci mi krew* 'is falling me:DAT blood' (= 'I am bleeding') (cf. Berman, 1985, for a description of identical constructions in Hebrew). The dative experiencer can also be used instead of the nominative subject (i.e. agent) in order to express the lack of a definite agentive intention. Compare *Stłukła mi się filiżanka* 'the cup broke itself to me', uttered by an involuntary agent, with *Stłukłem filiżankę* 'I broke cup' on the one hand, and *Filiżanka się stłukła* 'cup itself broke', where no agent is mentioned, on the other.

1.3.2. *Negation.* The negation system is simple. Unlike Russian, where anaphoric and sentential negation have two distinct forms (*nyet* and *ni*), in Polish there is only one negative particle, *nie*. In negated sentences *nie* immediately precedes the verb or the auxiliary, and in constituent negation it immediately precedes the constituent in question, e.g. *Czy Jan idzie do szkoły?–NIE.* 'Does John go to school?'–'No.', *Jan NIE idzie do szkoły* 'John not go to school' (= 'John doesn't go to school'), *Jan idzie NIE do szkoły* 'John goes not to school (but . . .)', and *NIE Jan idzie do szkoły* '(It is) not John (who) goes to school (but . . .)'.

---

[5]The copula *jest* can be deleted, which results in *Zimno mi, Smutno mi*, etc.

A peculiarity of Slavic languages is that of converting the object of a negated verb into the genitive form, e.g., *Czytam książk-ę* 'read book-ACC' (= 'I am reading the book') but *Nie czytam książk-i* 'Not read book-GEN' (= 'I am not reading the book'). The same transformation is applied to subjects of negated existential sentences.

Unlike English, Slavic languages display multiple negation, e.g. *Jan nigdy z nikim nie idzie* 'John never with nobody not goes' (= 'John never goes with anybody').

1.3.3. *Questions.*   Question formation is also simple. Yes-no questions require either rising intonation alone or preposing the particle *czy* 'whether', e.g. *Piszesz?/Czy piszesz?* 'Do you write?'. Wh-questions are formed by preposing a given wh-word or a prepositional phrase with the wh-word (the "stranding" of prepositions is not allowed). No additional transformations are needed for questions.

1.3.4. *Modals.*   Polish verbs whose semantic content corresponds to that of English modals should be treated as full verbs rather than auxiliaries in view of their syntactic properties (cf. Fisiak et al., 1978, for details). Therefore sentences with modals are embedded constructions rather than simple sentences with a complex predicate, e.g. *Musz-ę napisa-ć list* 'Must-1SG write-INF letter' (= 'I must write a letter') or even *Mog-ę musie-ć wyjść* 'can-1SG must-INF leave-INF' (= 'I could be obliged to leave'). In these examples, the past or future tense forms of the "modal" could be used. Moreover, there are a number of impersonal modals used in subjectless constructions, e.g. *można* 'one:can', *wolno* 'one:is:allowed:to', *trzeba* 'it:is:necessary:to', etc.

1.3.5. *Complex Sentences.*   A detailed analysis of syntactic differences between Polish and English complex sentences is given in Fisiak et al. (1978). In the present discussion, I will point only to some of the most general characteristics of Polish syntax. The major difference is that Polish constructions are more transparent. It would be premature to say that surface realizations of clauses are closer to the deep structure than their English counterparts, since we still do not know what the deep structure in fact is like for adult speakers, much less for children. But we can say that Polish complex sentences are easy to process, since the surface form of constituent clauses is much like that of simple sentences, and the abundance of explicit local cues facilitates the processing of internal relationships holding between clause constituents, with clauses being clearly delineated by explicit boundary markers. This "transparency" of Polish complex sentences is manifested in various aspects, which are discussed below.

1.3.5.1. *Clear Marking of Clause Boundaries.*   Except for some coordinate clauses which can be simply juxtaposed without any connective, complex sentences must be clearly divided into separate clauses, not only by pauses (or commas in writing) but also by overt markers. This feature is a natural consequence of the freedom of word order. Constituents can be permuted within a given clause, but the clause as a whole must be "bracketed" in some way to prevent relating a given constituent to the predicate of the neighboring clause. Therefore connectives in relative and complement clauses cannot be deleted. The English *He said (that) he was there* is rendered by *Powiedział, ŻE tam był* with the obligatory complementizer *że* 'that'. The English *The boy (whom) I met was hungry* translates into Polish in the form *Chłopiec, KTÓREGO spotkałem, był głodny* with the obligatory relative pronoun *który* 'whom', in the accusative case.

The main clause which follows the subordinate clause is usually preceded by the empty particle *to* 'it'; for instance, the English *When I came, you were sleeping* translates as *Jak przyszedłem, TO ty spałeś;* and the English *If it rains, I'll stay at home* is rendered by *Jeśli będzie padać, TO zostanę w domu.* The empty particle is not used when the main clause comes first; e.g., *Zostanę w domu, jeśli będzie padać,* where the connective *jeśli* 'if' is a sufficient boundary marker. Although not obligatory, *to* is widely used in spoken language. It occurs also with center-embedded relative clauses to mark the beginning of the second part of the interrupted matrix clause, e.g., *Ten chłopiec, KTÓREGO spotkałem, TO był głodny.* In this way the inserted relative is placed within "brackets" formed by *który* and *to.*[6]

1.3.5.2. Clear Marking of Syntactic Relations.
Polish lacks certain rules that result in semantically opaque constructions, at the same time providing overt local cues that facilitate interpretations. This can be illustrated by the following examples.

The first point concerns restrictions on infinitivization rules. Polish lacks constructions of the "accusativus cum infinitivo" type. Where English uses a infinitival construction, Polish frequently requires a full clause with the finite verb form, e.g. *I saw him go(ing)* = *Widziałem, że szedł* 'I:saw that he:was:going' or *Widziałem (go), jak szedł* 'I:saw (him) as he:was:going'. Similarly, *I asked him to go* = *Prosiłem (go), żeby poszedł* 'I:asked (him) that he:goes'. If the verb can take an infinitival complement, the other complement appears in dative form, e.g. *I ordered him to go* = *Kazałem mu pójść* 'I:ordered he:DAT go:INF'. Fisiak et al. (1978) cite the verb *uczyć* 'to teach' as the only exception, since it takes both the accusative and the infinitival complements, e.g. *Uczę go śpiewa-ć* 'I:teach he:ACC sing-INF' (= I teach him to sing).

It is worth noting that Polish lacks a periphrastic causative construction of the *make*+VERB type. The causative meaning is conveyed mostly by lexical causatives, e.g. *usypiać/spać* 'make sleep'/'sleep', *rozśmieszać /śmiać się* 'make laugh'/'laugh', *zasmucać/być smutnym* 'make sad'/'be sad', or by means of the nonreflexive/reflexive contrast, e.g. *złamać/złamać się* 'break'/'break

---

[6]The distribution of Polish *to* seems quite similar to that of *ia* in the creole Tok Pisin language, as described in Sankoff (1974), quoted by Slobin (1977).

itself' as in *Chłopiec złamał patyk* 'boy broke stick' vs. *Patyk złamał się* 'stick broke itself'. Another device used in Polish is that of employing complex sentences with subordinated clauses of purpose, introduced by *żeby* 'so:that' (nonfactive). Typically, the main clause verb specifies the KIND of action performed in order to realize the PURPOSE specified by the subordinate clause as the intended result of the main clause action. Therefore, more information is conveyed than in English, *Make it pretty* or *Make it hold,* which do not specify the manner of obtaining the causative results, cf. Polish counterparts of the above sentences: *Pomaluj to, żeby było ładne* 'paint it so:that (it) be pretty' or *Umocuj to, żeby się trzymało* 'fix it so:that itself (it) held'. On the other hand, using a general term for causative action as in *Zrób, żeby się trzymało* 'make so:that itself (it) held' is not equivalent to the English periphrastic causative, since it conveys additional information, 'I don't know how to do it' or 'Do it, whatever means you employ'.

The second factor involves demonstrative elements in the matrix clause. In the matrix clauses for embedded relatives, demonstrative pronominal antecedents occur, which serve as "auguries" of the following subordination, e.g. *Zrobię to WTEDY, KIEDY będę mieć czas* 'I:shall:do it THEN WHEN I:will have time', *Znalazłem to TAM, GDZIE to położyłeś* 'I:found it THERE WHERE you:put it', *Znalazłem TO, CO chciałeś mieć* 'I:found THAT WHAT you:wanted to:have'. Such pairs comprising the demonstrative antecedent and the relative pronoun provide cues for establishing correct relations between the matrix and the relative clause.

The third point concerns the abundance of local cues (endings). In simple sentences, the large range of gender/number/case agreement may seem redundant. Its usefulness, however, can be best seen in complex sentences. Compare the following English sentence with its Polish counterpart:

The cow that the elephant kissed kicked the lion.

Krow-a	*którą*	*pocałował-ø-ø*
cow-FEM:NOM:SG	which-FEM:ACC:SG	kissed-MASC:3SG

słoń-ø	*kopnę ł-a-ø*	*lwa*
elephant-MASC:NOM:SG	kicked-FEM:3SG	lion-MASC:ACC:SG

Apart from casemarking on nouns, which separates the agents in nominative 'cow' and 'elephant' from the patient 'lion' and corresponds to the information conveyed in English by word order, gender agreement in past tense verbs makes the situation clear at first glance. It is only the cow that can be the agent of kicking as the past-tense verb *kopnęła* is marked for feminine and the word 'elephant' is masculine. Analogically, the cow is precluded as an agent of kissing, since *pocałował* is marked for masculine. Furthermore, the relative pronoun *który* occurs in the accusative feminine singular form, *którą.* Thus it agrees in gender and number with its antecedent 'cow', while its case form is governed by the predicate of the relative clause 'kissed'. It is not difficult to guess that only the cow could be kissed and that the only possilbe agent of kicking is the elephant.

In relative clauses, another relative pronoun the indeclinable *co* 'that' can be used. In such cases a shadow pronoun appears in an appropriate case form in order to make explicit the relation clause-antecedent,[7] e.g. *Chłopiec, co GO spotkałem* 'boy that HIM I:met', *Chłopiec, co NA NIEGO czekałem* 'boy that FOR HIM I:was:waiting' (cf. similar constructions in Hebrew in Berman, 1985).

Another example of clear marking is the form of nonfinite verbs. Infinitives are clearly marked as such, due to their specific endings (in English, although they are sometimes preceded by *to,* their form itself is homonymous with finite forms). Polish counterparts of the ambiguous *-ing* form are also clearly differentiated, e.g. *pisanie* 'writing (books)', *piszący* 'writing (people)', *pisząc* '(while) writing' with additional cues provided by casemarking in verbal nouns and case/gender/number marking in adjectival participles. Thus, Poles do not have such problems with visiting relatives as typical for English-speakers (and, especially, for linguists).

The fourth issue is direct temporal reference. The use of tenses is not restricted by any formal rules (i.e. there is no "consecutio temporum"); for instance, *Powiedziała, że PISZE list* 'She:said that (SHE):IS:WRITING letter', where a complement clause in the present tense is embedded in a main clause in thepas the past tense. It means that she said 'I am writing'. On the other hand, the Polish counterpart of the correct English sentence *She said that she was writing*— *Powiedziała, że PISAŁA*—would mean that she referred to a past event and said 'I was writing'. Similarly, an *if*-clause which refers to a future event occurs in future tense form, e.g. *Jeśli będzie padać* 'if (it):will rain', cf. English *If it rains.* Polish use of tenses preserves the one-to-one correspondence between tense form and temporal characteristics of external reality.

Finally, we must consider factive/nonfactive reference. Like the use of tense discussed above, mood is not formally restricted, and any proposition considered by the speaker as nonfactive is put into conditional mood. In conditional sentences, all possible combinations of mood and tense can occur. If the speaker conceives both events as nonfactive (only possible or truly hypothetical), both clauses occur in conditional mood e.g. *Jeśli by-ø padał-o, poszedł-ø-by-m do teatru* 'If COND-3SG rain:PP-NEUT, go:PP-MASC-COND-1SG to theater:GEN' (= 'If it-would-rain, I-would-go to the theater;), cf. English *If it rained . . . ,* where the past tense is used according to a purely formal rule.

There is a specific type of conditional mood used in nonfactive subordinate clauses introduced by *żeby.* It is called "entangled" because of the impossibility

---

[7]In colloquial speech the shadow pronoun can be omitted if the relation clause-antecedent is unambiguous, e.g. *To krzesło, co ja (na nim) siedziałem* 'this chair that I (on it) was:sitting', as the usual relation between the chair and sitting is that of sitting on it.

of detaching the conditional particle *by* from the proper connective *że*. In accordance with the general rule concerning conditionals (cf. Section 1.2.6.2), *żeby* must be immediately followed by a person suffix, while the remaining verbal form is that of the "past participle," e.g. *Ona chce, że-by-m poszł-a,* 'She wants, that-COND-1SG go:PP-FEM' (= 'She wants me to go') or *Ona chce, że-by-śmy poszl-i* 'She wants, that-COND-1PL go:PP-VIR' (= 'She wants us to go'). To summarize, tenses and moods in Polish tend to carry clear and nonarbitrary semantic information concerning temporal relations of events and factive/nonfactive evaluation of the propositional content which is made by the speaker.

The above outline of Polish presents some main features of the system as a whole, with more detailed discussions of the formal features which are significant for the following analysis of the acquisition process. The structures that I have discussed and the examples that I have provided are those of the normal colloquial use of the language.

2. Sources of Evidence

Unlike some other languages discussed in this volume, most of the evidence concerning the acquisition of Polish is provided by naturalistic data. Experimental studies dealing with strictly grammatical questions are scarce.

2.1. *Naturalistic Data*

2.1.1. *Diary Studies.*   There exists a large corpus of raw data collected 100 years ago (1885–1904) by the eminent Polish linguist Jan Baudouin de Courtenay, which comprises detailed diaries of the speech of his five children.[8] In 1974, extracts from one of those diaries were edited by Maria Chmura-Klekotowa. Those extracts (10% of the whole diary) prove that Baudouin's data still have more than merely historical value (see Zarębina, 1976, and Savić, 1975).

Polish diary studies published so far are presented in Table 6.4. The authors are mainly linguists who recorded and analyzed their own children's speech, concentrating on the earliest stages of language development. Particular analyses differ with respect to scope and delicacy. The monographs by Kaczmarek, Smoczyński, and Zarębina contain the most detail. Later periods of the grammatical development find a less complete documentation in diary studies. There are two short works: (1) a paper by Siatkowscy (1956) with some observations of the authors' son of age 2;6 and (2) a paper by Wójtowicz (1959), who reports "formations by analogy" in her duaghter's speech from 4;0 to 5;0. The diary studies provide copious evidence on the acquisition of the basic system; however, because of the well-known shortcomings of diary studies in general, the data are frequently difficult to interpret from a psycholinguistic point of view.

---

[8]The manuscript (13,000 pages) is kept in the Polish National Library.

TABLE 6.4
Polish Diary Studies

Author	Date	Children-Age	Description
Rzętkowska	1908	girl 0–4;6	vocabulary, remarks on morphology and syntax (33 pages)
Rzętkowska	1909	boy 0–3;0	vocabulary, somewhat more detailed discussion of grammar, and a comparison with the older girl's development (54 pages)
Brenstiern-Pfanhauser	1930	girl 1;0–2;3 boy 1;0–2;3	phonetics, morphology, syntax (56 pages)
Wawrowska	1938	boy 0–2;3	vocabulary, general remarks on grammar, psychological analyses (57 pages)
Skorupka	1949	girl 0–2;0	general remarks (39 pages)
Kaczmarek	1953	girl 0–3;6 plus casual observations on three older children	full linguistic description (90 pages, summary in German)
Smoczyński	1955	girl 0–3;0 boy 0–3;0	most detailed analysis of phonology and semantics of first words, remarks on morphology and early syntax (230 pages, summary in French and in Russian)
Zarębina	1965	girl 0–2;3 plus casual observations on two younger children	full description of phonology, morphology and syntax, vocabulary (100 pages, summary in French)

The monograph by Chmura-Klekotowa (1971), concerned with children's neologisms, is based on longitudinal data of several children (including early Kraków data, see Section 2.1.2) as well as experimental data of elicited word-formations.[9] It provides a detailed and systematic analysis of 5000 neologisms recorded in children's speech. To the best of my knowledge, it is the most exhaustive published study of derivational processes in child language.

2.1.2. *The Szuman Project: Early Kraków Data.*   A separate group of naturalistic longitudinal data are those recorded in Kraków in 1950–1960 as a part of a research project on language and thinking directed by Stefan Szuman (Jagiellonian University). Although the samples were recorded by the mothers of the subjects in handwriting (or sometimes in short-hand), they differ significantly from classic diary data. The observers did not record isolated utterances, selected for some reason or other, as was the case with classic diaries. On the contrary, the observers collected short sections of discourse which covered the entire

---

[9]Chmura-Klekotowa used also data from Baudouin's children. She found significant differences between productive suffixes which they used to form neologisms and those employed by contemporary children.

chronological sequence of utterances addressed to the child as well as the child's productions. Changes in behavioral and situational context were also observed and recorded. Every day several samples were taken, with the observers trying to make the fullest account possible of what they considered to be typical situations. Daily samples were collected for several years of the child's life, and in the case of children studied for the longest periods, they comprise up to about 20,000 utterances. All the children studied had at least one parent with a higher education degree, with most mothers being psychologists. Four girls and four boys were studied through the following period of development: (1) Inka 1;0-8;0, (2) Basia 1;5-8;0, (3) Kasia 1;3-3;1, and 3;9-4;0 (Kasia is Michał's younger sister), (4) Tenia 1;5-1;7 (Tenia is Inka's younger sister), (5) Jaś 1;6-6;0, (6) Michał 2;0-6;0, (7) Miś 2;9-5;10, and (8) Janek 4;2-7;3 (Miś and Janek are two brothers, observed simultaneously).

Szuman's project was carried out in collaboration with Maria Przetacznikowa and Lidia Geppertowa. One part of the project was concerned mainly with vocabulary development: its input consists of Szuman's (1955) work on nouns and verbs, Przetacznikowa's (1956, 1959) studies on adjectives and adverbs, and Geppertowa's (1968) monograph on the acquisition of prepositions and conjunctions. Another part of the project dealt with syntactic development and is represented by Przetacznikowa's (1968) study of the syntactic structure and function of child utterances. This work is based on the corpus of all declarative utterances recorded for Jaś over the period 1;6 to 6;0. The data were classified according to a taxonomy used by Polish grammarians, and detailed quantitative analyses show the structural development of the child's syntax. Qualitative analyses, however, reflect the approach of the whole Szuman project; that is, they concentrate on the ways in which children's thoughts are expressed through language rather than on the process of learning the grammatical structure itself (Przetacznikowa, 1976, 1978).

Although the children who were studied are now more than 20 years old, the data are still used for various kinds of analyses, concerning psycholinguistic and psychological problems. My own dissertation on early syntax (Smoczyńska, 1978a; also see papers written in English: 1976a, 1976b, 1978b, 1980, 1981) was based on the early data of five of those children. The same corpora were analyzed by Przetacznikowa (1975) within the framework of Fillmore's case grammar. Other detailed studies on these data involve negation (Kubit, 1977), a functional analysis of children's questions (Ligęza, 1979), and a number of other works in preparation.

2.1.3. Tape-Recorded Discourse: Late Kraków Data and Other Research.
In Kraków, at Jagiellonian University, new data were collected in the 1970s within a child language project directed by Maria Przetacznikowa. Tape recordings of several children were made by their mothers, who were mainly members of the project. In order to collect relatively continuous data, the recordings were

made two to four times a week in the early stages. The frequency of recording decreased with age. The following children (one girl and five boys) were recorded: Agnieszka, Witek, Szymon, Przemek, and twin brothers, Michał S. and Maciek from the beginnings of syntax to about 3;0 (with some extra samples collected later).

Grace W. Shugar at Warsaw University collected data from two children over the period 1;6 to 3;0. Those data were analyzed in her study on relations between language structure and activity structure (Shugar, 1972, 1974, 1976a, 1976b, & 1978). These data also served as a basis of the report on grammatical development of Polish children found in Slobin (1973).

At Adam Mickiewicz University in Poznań, Richard M. Weist conducted a research project which combined longitudinal and cross-sectional experimental designs. In the longitudinal phase six children were tape-recorded twice a month for about 6 months and two children for shorter periods. The observations include detailed contextual notes which were integrated with the discourse. The naturalistic observations concentrated on the period from 1;6 to 2;6. Two of the children began participation at 1;7, two at 1;9 and two at 2;2 (Weist, Wysocka, Witkowska-Stadnik, Buczowska, & Konieczna, 1984).

2.2. Experimental Studies

Although many experimental studies concerning child language have been carried out in Poland, those which are relevant for the present discussion are few. Smoczyńska (1972) investigated the control of the singular noun declension forms in 3-, 4-, 5-, and 6-year-old children (10 children per age group) using elicitation techniques for real and nonsense words. Olszowska-Guzik (in preparation) investigated selected aspects of the control of the linguistic system by 6-year-old children with respect to environmental differences (4 milieux × 30 children). She used various experimental procedures such as elicitation techniques, grammaticality judgments, etc. Mystkowska (1970) analyzed 6-year-old children's productions (story narration on the basis of a series of pictures) which were then compared with parallel data obtained from 11-year-olds and adults. Weist (1980, 1983a,b) used comprehension and production tests in studies of tense and aspect and of word order with ten 2;6-year-old and ten 3;6-year-old children. All subjects were also tape recorded in naturalistic situations for one 45 minute session.

2.3. Sources of the Data Used in This Paper

While examining the existing data concerning the acquisition of Polish from the point of view of their relevance for the present paper, I discovered that only a few of the previous studies could be directly utilized. As far as morphology is concerned, only the diary studies proved useful. However, even in the case of the diary studies the data are limited to the acquisition of the basic system up to about 2;3, and the authors (mainly linguists) were interested in the emergence of adult categories. These investigators did not attempt to identify the rules that the child could have formed for himself. Typically, several examples of the first correct use of a form were given followed by instances of erroneous usage. Thus, the reader is not able to estimate the ratio of correct/incorrect forms for a given linguistic expression.[10] As for syntax, it has been investigated by the Kraków psychologists but, in view of their cognitive orientation, they centered on referential meaning. The acquisition of the linguistic forms themselves was given only marginal attention.

Consequently, I undertook the task of exploring the corpora of the Kraków children. The first step consisted of extracting all erroneous forms from the data of several children aged 2 to 6. I determined the morphological and syntactic forms which were especially difficult for Polish children. Subsequently, the corresponding instances of correct use of those forms were singled out in order to establish the significance of the errors, i.e. whether they were consistent or only sporadic. Sometimes it was necessary to go back to the period preceding the occurrence of the first error in order to trace the emergence of the category itself. When no erroneous forms were attested, I tried to find out whether this was so because the child used the form correctly or because he did not employ it at all. Because of the short time at my disposal, I could not do this for all kinds of errors, and I chose only those which seemed to be of theoretical interest. Regarding case for instance, errors in totally irregular exceptional forms are less interesting than those occurring with more or less complex yet regular forms. I also gathered all utterances in which the conditional mood appeared, as well as those containing relative clauses. These two structures are interesting in themselves, both from the cognitive and the strictly formal point of view.

Another part of this study consisted of analyzing the emergence of basic linguistic categories and forms in the data of three children covering the period from the very beginning till the age of 2;6. This analysis was carried out as a supplement to the diary studies in order to obtain detailed knowledge concerning consecutive steps in the acquisition of the basic system.

This research provides the basic data of the present paper. The results obtained by other authors were frequently confirmed, which I shall point out at relevant points. The analysis of the raw data helped me to form a general outlook concerning the acquisition of Polish which can be compared with what is known about other Slavic languages. Additional arguments were provided to confirm my strong opinion that the acquisition of a language (especially in later stages) cannot be reasonably accounted for if we try to divide it into the acquisition of particular forms or subsystems, since the various parts of the linguistic system are interlinked. The interrelationship is inherent and organic so any analysis should be carried out within the broader framework.

Another important point of caution to be made here concerns INDIVIDUAL DIFFERENCES. The analyses I carried out made me realize that there can exist

---

[10]This criticism refers to Gvozdev's (1949) work on Russian as well.

immense differences between the individual paths children take to arrive at roughly the same final result, i.e. mastery of the full system. It is not the case that one child acquires all forms more quickly than another, but rather that the order of acquisition of the correct adult forms is never the same for two different children. An investigation of these individual ways of arriving at the full adult system would require a very thorough study. Having analyzed the data of more than ten subjects, all that I can say about Polish children in general is that there are linguistic forms whose acquisition is LIKELY to cause some difficulties for varied intervals of time somewhere between the age of 2 and 6. With one child this interval can last 3 months, and with another 3 years, and with still another child the predicted difficulty may not appear at all. Some scholars assume that if errors attested in the data of one child are not found in other children, they must have gone unnoticed. The nonselective and continuous daily sampling used with the Kraków children makes me preclude such a possibility. The absence of a predicted difficulty is most puzzling, especially if the source of difficulty can be easily accounted for. That is why I prefer to discuss individual children rather than to make general statements. On the other hand, the observations concerning individual variation call for great caution when generalizing the results obtained from a diary study based on the data from a single child.

3. Overall Course of Linguistic Development

At the one-word stage there is no evidence for productive use of any inflectional forms, with no significant changes being observed in this respect in the earliest two-word combinations. Indeclinable words used in this early period are either specific baby talk items, e.g. *am* 'food, to eat' and onomatopoeias, e.g. *hau-hau* 'dog, to bark' or adult words. In the latter case, nouns occur in the nominative singular, or sometimes in one of the oblique cases as "citation forms." Verbs occur in the third singular present tense form or in the imperative or the infinitive form. Zarębina's (1965) daughter, for example, began to use the imperative form at 1;0, e.g. [es'] = *weź* 'take' and [Xuc' or oć] = *chodź* 'come on', and the third singular indicative form at 1;3, e.g. [gʰa] = *gra* 'plays', [pxa] = *pcha* 'pushes', [c'ita] = *czyta* 'reads', etc. Zarębina reported that Hania used the imperative form to express demands and desires and used the indicative form to make statements. While these verbs have a pragmatic value, they are syntactically frozen forms. We do not find contrasting verb forms at this stage of development, e.g. *chodź* 'come on!' versus *idzie* 'he:is:going' or *pcha* 'he:pushes' versus *pchaj* 'push!' In my data verbs with the imperative form occur MOSTLY in requests, and verbs with the indicative form occur MOSTLY in the declarative context. However, if children happen to use one of these verbs in the less frequent context, they do not change the form of the verbs. Sometimes several forms are used in free variation, e.g. *da, daj, dam, dać,* or *damy-damy,* 'give'. All these forms of the verb 'to give' were used interchangeably by one of the children studied.

The development of the syntactic structures of multiword utterances, recorded in five children during the six months after the emergence of first word combinations, was described in Smoczyńska (1978a). It was found that by the end of the period studied the children had arrived at full control over most of the basic simple sentence patterns. Assessment was made according to three criteria: (1) the ability to produce a number of complete sentences of a given type; (2) pattern generalization, as revealed by a relatively large variety of predicates (Smoczyńska, 1981); and, (3) automaticity of pattern generation, as evidenced by the lack of replacement sequences on the one hand, and examples of expanded patterns on the other. An example of the developmental analysis with respect to the transitive sentence pattern is given in Smoczyńska (1976a).

As for morphological development, it usually starts in the third month of the two-word stage. Regarding nouns, the initial contrast is accusative and genitive singular as opposed to nominative, with vocative appearing at the same time or slightly earlier. In verbs, the second singular of the imperative emerges as opposed to the third singular of the present tense. The infinitive is found a little later. The next step is the emergence of the nominative plural and the accusative plural, followed by the instrumental singular, the locative singular (in locative phrases with the preposition omitted) and the dative, which is typically mixed with the genitive (see Section 4.3.2.1). The following new verb forms appear more or less simultaneously—all of them mostly in the third singular: perfective future (formally identical with the imperfective present tense form), past tense (mostly perfective, but also imperfective, see Section 6.1.2) and a little later, also the analytic imperfective future. Thus tense and aspect emerge very early and simultaneously. The above list of forms characterizes the average level of morphological development of a 2-year-old. The sequence was established on the basis of the data of three children (Kasia, Jaś, and Basia), and it is consistent with the findings reported in Zarębina (1965) and Kaczmarek (1953).

It should be said, however, that such an overlap of morphological and syntactic development is not always observed. With some children, the acquisition of morphology is slowed down, probably due to individual phonological difficulties, cf. the data in Smoczyński (1955) and in Baudouin de Courtenay's diary (1974). Also Smoczyńska (1978a) reported a contrastive example of two of her subjects (Jaś and Tenia). In the fourth month after the first word combinations emerged both children reached the same level of syntactic development. However, while Jaś's morphological development was fairly advanced, Tenia still tended not to make inflectional contrasts.

As far as the acquisition of specific case endings is concerned, most of them are used correctly from the very moment of emergence of a given category, as opposed to Russian, where "inflectional imperialism" (Slobin, 1966) is common. This is due to the early mastery of grammatical gender in the singular, which determined assigning a given noun to an appropriate declensional pattern (see Section 6.1.1). Overgeneralization occurs mainly when an irregular ending competes with a regular one, and less frequently within regular patterns (see Section 4.3).

In the third year of life new tasks appear. The child learns the remaining elements of the declensional pattern, especially plural case forms of nouns which have not been used so far. During this period of development children expand various noun phrase constituents, begin to use oblique case forms of adjectives, and master the whole declensional pattern of adjectives. Przetacznikowa (1968) computed the percentage of noun modifications in all kinds of expansions occurring in simple declarative sentences produced by Jaś, and she found that attributes appeared in about 20% of expanded sentences from 1;6 to 3;0. Their number systematically increased with 36% from 3 to 5 years and 42% from 5 to 6 years.

At the same time, the child learns how to combine basic patterns that he had previously acquired to form various types of complex sentences. The ratios of different kinds of declarative sentences recorded for Jaś are presented in Table 6.5. It can be seen that coordination precedes subordination and occurs more frequently in the early years. Jaś started using conjunctions relatively early. With "telegraphic" children, however, who omit conjunctions over a relatively long period, the dominance of parataxis would be even stronger since mere juxtapositions must normally be interpreted as coordination. Another important development shown in Table 6.5 is the growing ability to combine more than two clauses. The different structural patterns of such constructions have been described by Przetacznikowa (1968), and a detailed discussion of complex sentences can be found later in this paper (see Sections 6.1.4 and 6.2).

TABLE 6.5
The Proportions of Declarative Sentences[a]
of Varying Complexity in the Speech of Jaś
(Based on Przetacznikowa, 1968)

Age	1;6–2	2–3	3–4	4–5	5–6
simple sentences[b]	94%	78%	64%	52%	46%
coordinate clauses	6%	13%	18%	25%	29%
main & subordinate	—	7%	13%	14%	12%
more than 2 clauses[c]	—	2%	5%	9%	13%
Total	100%	100%	100%	100%	100%
N	372	2365	2223	1484	2243

[a]The proportions would be somewhat different if imperative sentences were included since some kinds of subordinate clauses typically occur first with requests.

[b]including expanded.

[c]subordinate or mixed.

Another important task for the 2-year-old involves mastering the distinction of person in verbs. The first-person form emerges in opposition to the third-person form, which was initially used for self-reference as well as for the second and third person. Later on the second person is also introduced. The acquisition of the rules of deictic switching takes several months and is followed by the mastery of the pronominal declension pattern, as well as the discourse rules of pronominalization. All these processes are gradual. During the third year of life, many examples can be found in the child's utterances of some of the required forms but not all of them. While the conjugation patterns of the indicative are supplemented by adding first- and second-person forms, the conditional mood emerges, first in its entangled form in subordinate clauses, and later in main clauses with some typical formal difficulties (see Section 4.6.3). Also, passive constructions are used from the age of 2 without explicit mention of the agent.

By the end of his third year of life the child masters the syntax of complex sentences as well as discourse rules which makes it possible for him to construct longer texts in a more coherent and economical way. This textual function is realized by means of a complex system involving pronominalization, reflexivization, ellipsis, word order, focal stress, etc., all these elements being related to each other. Finally, after 3 years of age, the child learns the devices for compacting information in still more economical although less transparent form, which involves infinitivization, nominalization, etc.

THE DATA

4. Typical Errors

The present chapter gives a relatively complete outline of errors that were found in naturalistic data of 10 children aged 1;6 to 6;0. Although several kinds of erroneous forms are reported in earlier diary studies, the studies lack sufficient information concerning frequency of occurrence and the ratio of correct versus incorrect forms. It is only when these aspects are taken into account that an exact evaluation of the range of erroneous forms can be made and the following kinds of errors distinguished: (1) consistent errors; (2) inconsistent erroneous usage of forms in their earliest appearance, resulting from unsuccessful attempts at quoting a particular form or reconstructing its general shape; (3) mistakes, i.e. sporadic occurrences of erroneous forms after the given rule has been learned, attested by a prevailing number of correct uses (these errors constitute a 10% margin which remains after the 90% criterion has been met); (4) free variation of correct and incorrect forms; and, (5) totally isolated occurrences of erroneous forms which do not follow typical structural patterns.

Another classification is related to the character of the adult norm with which the error is compared, where the norm we refer to is that of spoken language as used by educated native speakers. Some morphological patterns that occur in a language are RULE GOVERNED (or regular). Some of these rules are simple and others are complex. Regardless of the complexity of the rule the distribution of forms is based on some explicit grammatical criteria, for instance, a group of words sharing certain features (criterion A) takes the form a, whereas another group of words which satisfies the criterion B takes the form b. On the other hand, there are IRREGULAR morphological patterns with no criteria for their application, for instance, a list of words: $C_1, C_2 \ldots C_n$ which do not share any common feature takes the form c. The latter is found to be less interesting than the former, as in such cases learning the correct form consists of rote-memorization of a list of exceptions, although the strategies that the child employs in such cases can prove to be of some interest, e.g. overgeneralization, looking for distributional criteria where there are none, etc.

The distinction between the complexities of the regular system on the one hand and the irregularities on the other has not received adequate attention, in spite of its crucial relevance. For instance, many authors claim that Slavic children are not able to acquire the declension system before the age of 5 or even 7. If however the term "system" is taken to mean a given set of rules excluding irregularities, then in fact, the system itself is mastered much earlier. In his discussion of Russian, Slobin (1966, 1968) emphasized certain aspects that must have been unknown to those investigating the acquisition of English. Slobin discussed morphological complexities and irregularities which the child must face and with which—much to the amazement of scholars—he finally manages to cope. In this place, however, I would like to introduce the distinction between a set of rules and the exceptions to these rules in order to make the acquisition of Slavic languages more easily understood and a little bit less amazing.

We shall therefore try to classify particular types of errors in terms of the relation between children's productions and the norms of the language. The simplest kind of error, very common with English-speaking children, but considerably less so with Polish children, is that of omitting a grammatical morpheme in an obligatory context. The opposite kind of error is overmarking. Still another type consists of using correct adult forms in improper contexts.

Sources of difficulties can be found in different characteristics of the adult norm: (1) complexity of the criteria for rule application; (2) complexity of the rules themselves, i.e. when the rule involves a combination of several operations; and, (3) given a simple criterion and a simple rule, a difficulty can arise from a mismatch between the system acquired so far by the child and the rule under acquisition.

Consequently, the following situations can be distinguished: (1) disregard—or lack of recognition—of adult criteria of form distribution which results in overgeneralization or formation of an idiosyncratic or simplified rule which does not exist in the language; (2) acquiring all rules without learning the criteria of their distribution, which results in free variation of the forms in question; and, (3) difficulties in the complete application of a complex rule after the criteria of its use have been learned, i.e. partial application of a rule.

All these types are attested both among early and late errors. While the early errors can be explained in terms of operating principles (whether cognitive or strictly linguistic), the later errors should be related to the entire system of the language. We must attempt to discover the discrepancy between a given rule (or the criteria of its application) and the distinctions already acquired, rather than some isolated operating principles. A discrepancy of this kind can result in U-shaped developments such as the blurring of some well-learned distinctions due to the acquisition of a rule which contradicts the distinctions. Moreover, it seems that there exists another type of U-shaped development in which the child, in his attempt to create a maximally economical system, gets rid of an already acquired sub-rule and overextends the one that he had just learned.

4.1. *Omission of Obligatory Functors*

In view of the general morphological structure of Polish, only the following free grammatical morphemes are potential candidates for telegraphic reduction: prepositions, conjunctions, the copula *jest*, the future tense auxiliary *będzie*, two enclitic particles (i.e. the reflexive *się* and the conditional *by*) and possibly also enclitic movable endings of the plural past tense forms (i.e. *-śmy, -ście*). In the earliest data the children studied omitted prepositions and the reflexive particle *się*. The copula *jest* was also deleted, however, it is not obligatory in Polish. In the case of other candidates for reduction, omission could not occur in the earliest utterances because of the lack of appropriate obligatory contexts. Later, the children can be clearly divided into "telegraphic" versus "non-telegraphic" types with most of the children falling in the latter category. Two of the children studied (Basia and Inka) persistently omitted some obligatory morphemes. With the development of syntax, new obligatory contexts emerged for other free morphemes and Basia and Inka now omitted the new set of free morphemes. With these two "telegraphic" children (as with English-speaking children) the appearance of the morphemes that had been omitted earlier was a gradual process taking place during the third year, for instance, at the given moment the children were using some conjunctions and omitting others, even though they were building sentences with both kinds of obligatory contexts. Typically, asyllabic prepositions (*w* 'in', *z* 'with') were omitted for a longer time than the syllabic ones (*do* 'to', *na* 'on'). This is due more to phonetic reduction of an initial consonantal cluster than to processes discussed here. In the case of the remaining children, prepositions and the particle *się* appeared before the age of 2, and the remaining free morphemes were used from the moment of the emergence of appropriate contexts, and their usage satisfied the 90% criterion from the point of emergence.

Let us turn to the data of the "telegraphic" children. Establishing obligatory contexts for conjunctions and other connectives is not very easy since in some kinds of complex sentences their use is optional. However, with complement clauses, "complementizers" are obligatory, and Basia and Inka omitted them. The resulting utterances would be correct in English but not in Polish, e.g. Inka (2;4) *Tatuś powiedział jestem grzeczna* 'Daddy said I:am good', cf. correct *Tatuś powiedział, ŻE jestem grzeczna* 'Daddy said THAT I:am good'.

Another obvious example is the omission of the conditional particle *by*, resulting in utterances in which the predicate occurs in a past-tense form while they clearly refer to some hypothetical future events, e.g. Basia (2;6) refused her friend's invitation to climb a hill and said, *Ja nie pójdę, ja spadłam, moja mamusia płakała* 'I not will:go, I fell, my Mommy cried'. Since Basia had never fallen down a hill before, and thus her mother could never have cried for that reason, it is obvious that the girl actually meant to say, *Ja BY-m spadła, moja mamusia BY płakała* 'I WOULD-1SG fall (and) my Mommy WOULD cry'. Omissions of the conditional *by* are easy to detect in Basia's utterances as early as 2;0 because Basia had already demonstrated an understanding of the correspondence between tense and temporal reference at an earlier phase of development (see Section 6.1.2). Hence, we know that a word like *płakała* is not intended as a past form but rather as a past participle with conditional particle *by* omitted (cf. *by pł akała* or *płakałaby*).

Among the candidates for omission listed above, two behave differently in that one is seldom omitted and the other is often omitted irrespective of whether the child demonstrates "telegraphic" tendencies or not with respect to other functors. First of all, the future tense auxiliary *będzie* appears very early in all children. This can be explained both by its clear semantic function, and by the fact that unlike other free morphemes, the auxiliary *będzie* is polysyllabic and receives normal penultimate stress. As such it can be more easily given the status of a "normal" word. While the periphrastic future is formed quite early, some investigators have observed the omission of *być* 'to be' during the emergence of the form. In the earliest data, I found examples such as *Basia spa-ć* 'Basia sleep-INF' (= 'Basia to sleep') which could have been due to the omissions of either the future auxiliary *będzie* or the verb *chce* 'want'.

When considering truncated forms of the periphrastic future one must be careful to evaluate the discourse context because some contexts provide the option of deleting the auxiliary. Excluding elliptical examples, I found no examples of auxiliary deletion with the past participle, e.g. *pisała* instead of *będzie pisała* 'she:will write (be writing)'. Weist (personal communication) has found such truncated forms but very infrequently. In contrast to Polish where the polysyllabic auxiliary is seldom omitted, Kolarič (1959) has found auxiliary deletion in Slovenian where the auxiliary is monosyllabic. This shows that the poly- versus monosyllabic nature of this functor is responsible for its resistance to omission.

Secondly, the movable ending *-śmy* of the first person plural past tense is omitted both by "telegraphic" and "non-telegraphic" children. The use of this ending involves some quite special problems which are discussed in Section 4.4.4. The second person ending *-ście* is very rare.

4.2. *Overmarking*

Redundant marking appears most clearly with movable endings. In the process of learning acceptable positions of an ending, frequently a transitional stage occurs, when it is used twice. With conditional forms, one kind of error consists of using the particle *by* twice. For instance, when Basia began to use explicit marking at 2;7, she introduced the particle *by* which had been omitted before. She used the particle in two positions, e.g. after she was told by her mother not to take her shoes off, she said, *Bo co? Bo zaziębiłam-BY się BY?* 'Because what? Because I-would-get-a-cold would?' Such final repetition of *by* is limited to the very early examples. Later on, the particle appears twice in each of the two alternate correct positions, i.e. as an enclitic and postverbally, e.g. Basia (2;11) *A moja mamusia też BY miała-BY ładne włoski* 'And my mommy also would have would pretty hair' (cf. correct *by miała* or alternatively *miałaby*). Such errors can be found in other children, and they are also reported for Russian in Gvozdev (1949).

Another kind of error with conditionals involves overmarking for person. As will be shown below (Section 4.6.3), children tend to attach the person suffix to the past participle and not to the particle *by*. While learning the correct position of the person suffix, they frequently use it twice (once with the past participle and with *by*), e.g. in the context where mother said, *Nie pojeździł-by-ś na koniku?* 'Not ride:PP-COND-2SG on horse' (= 'Wouldn't you (like to) ride a horse?'), and Jaś (3;0) replied, *Nie pojeździł-em by-m* 'Not ride:PP-1SG COND-1SG' (= I wouldn't (like to) ride.) cf. correct *Nie pojeździł-by-m.*

In case of the analytic future with the past participle, analogous examples of person overmaking can be found, but they are significantly less frequent, e.g. Jaś (2;7) *W spodenkach będzie-m leżał-em* 'in trousers will-1SG lie:PP-1SG' (= 'I will lie down with my trousers on'), cf. correct *będę leżał*. Siatkowscy (1956) reported such errors in their son's speech at 2;5. However, there is no information on how consistent the error was. In my data, it should be treated as a mistake or a slip of the tongue rather than a consistent error. Finally, another case of overmarking is that of using a sequence of two conjunctions as *bo żeby* 'because so:that', *bo dlatego* 'because because' or two connectives in comparisons as in *większy niż od ciebie* 'bigger than from you'.

4.3. *Overgeneralization*

This strategy is applied first of all when an irregular ending competes with a regular one, the latter being overextended to include irregular cases. Some examples are presented below in Section 4.3.1. Another process is the overgeneralization of one of the two regular forms, i.e. when the child fails to discover relevant criteria (see Section 4.3.2).

4.3.1. Irregular Versus Regular Form

4.3.1.1. *Genitive Singular of Masculine Nouns: the Irregular* -u *Replaced by the Regular* -a *Ending.* The class of masculine nouns with the genitive -*u* suffix is quite large. There exist some vague criteria, such as [—animate], e.g. *pociąg* 'train' or [+ mass noun], e.g. *cukier* 'sugar' or [+ loan word], e.g. *papier* 'paper', but they are not adequate since not all nouns having one of these features take the -*u* ending in the genitive singular. Children show a tendency to overextend the regular -*a* ending. The reverse overextension is rare. It should be noted, however, that the number of words to which the -*u* ending is applied correctly constantly grows with age, and the errors of overextension of -*a* quickly become infrequent. I am unable to explain the way in which the children elaborate a rule which grammarians have been so far unable to make explicit. Yet if not rule governed, the children would have to retain the information for each item separately. This seems unlikely since the number of words that take the -*u* ending is large. One of the factors facilitating the acquisition of correct forms may be the high frequency of genitival forms as it is the grammatical case that has the largest range of functions.

4.3.1.2. *Regularization of the Irregular Feminine Nouns Which End in a Consonant in the Nominative Singular.* The irregular feminine declensional pattern is as follows in the singular: NOM & ACC -ø, GEN, DAT & LOC -*y*/-*i*, and INSTR -*ą*. Here the child faces a conflict situation. While the adjective and verb agreement indicates the feminine gender, the lack of an ending suggests the masculine gender. These nouns constitute quite a large class. One of the options chosen by children is that of avoiding these forms and using regular diminutive forms, e.g. *mysz* 'mouse' becomes *myszka*. Diminutive forms are also used by adults when they address children and even *krew* 'blood' becomes *krewka* in the baby-talk register.

If the child does not avoid the base form, he will either treat it as masculine and decline it accordingly (together with appropriate agreement) or else he will provide it with the regular -*a* ending and treat as a regular feminine noun. The selection of one or another pattern is subject to free variation. The child can say *Widziałem kolej-ę* 'I:have:seen train-FEM:ACC:SG' using the regular feminine accusative ending -*ę*, and immediately afterwards say *Ten kolej jechał-Ø* 'this:MASC:NOM:SG train was:going-MASC' with the demonstrative *ten* and past tense *jechał* marked for masculine.

Smoczyńska (1972) found that children over 4;0 know this special declensional pattern, but they are not likely to apply it when there is a clear diminutive correspondent of a noun, e.g. *mysz* is replaced by overregularized *mysz-a* (under the influence of *mysz-k-a*) yet the noun *kość* 'bone' is declined correctly since its diminutive *kostka* has a different meaning.

4.3.1.3. *Irregular and Infrequent Forms.*   The dative singular form *-u* with masculine nouns and the instrumental plural *-mi* can serve as examples of irregular and infrequent forms. They are used for a very limited number of words without any explicit criteria so that they are marginal with respect to the overwhelming number of words that take the respective regular endings (*-owi* and *-ami*). Overgeneralization of the regular pattern is most typical in such cases. Smoczyńska (1972) did not find any progress in 5- and 6-year-olds as compared with 4-year-olds with respect to the dative in *-u*. Olszowska-Guzik (personal communication) has supplied me with her data concerning the acquisition of irregular forms in 6-year-olds. Using elicitation techniques she tested 120 children from four different social backgrounds and found that some items of the kind described above were incorrect in nearly 100 percent of responses, irrespective of the social background of the child. In some other instances, social background proved to be significant.

4.3.2. Competition of Regular Forms

4.3.2.1. *Genitive Case Instead of the Dative (and Vice Versa).*   According to Slobin (1973), so far no scholar has reported consistent mixing of two cases or using one case instead of another. Gvozdev (1949, vol. 2, p. 84) explicitly states that such errors never occur in his data. According to my Polish data, however, several children went through a transitional period of substituting the genitive case for the dative. The overextension of the genitive case usually follows some early correct uses of dative forms, and it can persist for some time, e.g. 1;7 to 1;10 in Kasia and 1;9 to 2;5 in Basia.

In order to explain this phenomenon, several features of the Polish declensional system should be presented. First of all, the dative case in Polish has a very restricted range of functions and all of them referring to animate beings. Receiver, Benefactive, and Experiencer are the most typical functions.[11] In child speech, the dative contexts appear quite early but usually only after the genitive has been acquired. Such early occurrences are primarily strictly limited to forms of the names of family members with the child himself included, and less frequently, the names of some animals or animal toys occur. No doubt the cause of the presently discussed generalization is the homonymy of the genitive and the dative endings in one class of feminine nouns, i.e. stems ending in a soft consonant. This set of nouns includes frequently used nouns such as *mamusia* 'mommy', *babcia* 'granny' or the child's name, e.g. *Basia* and *Kasia*. The

---

[11]Unlike Russian, where the notion of 'movement towards' is expressed by the preposition *k* + DAT, in Polish it is expressed by means of *do* + GEN, which accounts for the absence of dative contexts for inanimate nouns.

homonymous genitive-equals-dative forms for these examples are: *mamusi, babci, Basi,* and *Kasi.* Because of the very restricted use of the dative, this homonymy is not counterbalanced by a sufficient number of other forms where the genitive is not identical with the dative. Some of these counterexamples which do occur in the data include the following: from the nominative *mama* 'mom' there is the dative *mamie* and the genitive *mamy,* from NOM *tatuś* 'daddy' DAT *tatusiowi* versus GEN *tatusia,* from NOM *miś* 'teddy-bear' DAT *misiowi* versus GEN *misia,* etc. The children tend to use the genitive form in dative contexts, e.g. *misia* not *misiowi.*

One of the three children studied, Jaś, did not reach the level of mixing the two cases. Probably his own name, which takes the dative form *Jasiowi* as different from the genitive *Jasia,* and which was used very frequently in dative contexts, helped to avoid this confusion. However, there was a short period (from 1;10 to 1;11) when the *-i* ending became generalized and was used also with some nouns requiring *-e* or *-owi.* The examples were not numerous: (1) *mami* for dative, cf. correct *mamie,* versus the genitive *mamy* 'mom', (2) *babi* for dative, cf. correct *babie,* versus the genitive *baby* 'grandma', and (3) *pieski* for dative cf. correct *pieskowi,* versus the genitive *pieska* 'doggie'. One month later the correct distribution was established. This example, however, points to the importance of the homonymous *-i* ending.

Zarębina (1965) quotes similar examples from her daughter's speech in the last months of the second year. They are followed, after the age of 2, by several examples of reversed substitution, where the dative is used instead of the genitive in the sense of possession, e.g. *tatusiowi jest lekarstwo* 'to:Daddy is medicine'—quite unusual in Polish but typical for Latin (e.g. *Mihi est liber*) or Hebrew (cf. Berman, 1985). Similar examples of the possessive dative are given in Siatkowscy (1956), e.g. *książka tatusiowi* 'book to:Daddy' instead of the correct *książka tatusia* 'book of:Daddy'. The Siatkowscy examples were collected during the period from 2;0 to 2;6. In my data such errors are only sporadic.

The homonymy alone cannot adequately account for these substitutions since it is fairly frequent in the whole declensional system and still never leads to such results. What seems necessary for this homonymy to result in the mixing of the two cases is the close semantic proximity of the possessive genitive and the dative cases, the only difference between the Possessor and the Receiver being that of the stative versus dynamic notions.

The cases are occasionally mixed in locative phrases when a directional expression is used instead of a stative one (or vice versa), e.g. 'to the tram' instead of 'in the tram', or 'at the shop' instead of 'to the shop'. Such examples occur sporadically in my data, and similar ones have been cited by Zarębina (1965).

4.3.2.2. *Genitive Plural -ów Instead of ø Ending in Feminine and Neuter Nouns (Grammatical Gender Criterion).* This overextension represents the only obvious instance of "inflectional imperialism" in the acquisition of Polish.

The adult rule is quite simple, i.e. in the genitive plural masculine nouns have the ending *-ów* while feminine and neuter nouns have a zero ending. In addition to this regular pattern, some masculine nouns take an irregular *-y/-i* ending.[12]

The majority of the children studied used the *-ów* ending irrespective of the noun gender. Typically, this ending appeared in the first contexts for genitive plural (about the age of 2) and was persistently and exclusively used for differing periods of time, for instance, till 3;0 for Kasia, 3;4 for Michał, 3;9 for Jaś, and 4;6 for Basia.[13] This is a typical "late error" since all the remaining REGULAR case forms are mastered by the age of 2;6 or before. It is also worth noting that in the Russian data for Zhenya, the corresponding *-ov* ending persisted much longer than other "imperialistic" endings, which were no longer overextended after the age of 2;9 (Gvozdev, 1949, vol. 2, p. 87).

There are five factors which should be taken into account as possibly responsible for the "inflectional imperalism" of *-ów*. First of all, the zero ending in feminine and neuter nouns contradicts the principle of overt marking (see Slobin's (1973) Operating Principle E). This argument, however, does not provide a sufficient explanation of the persistence of this error. Furthermore, this argument does not explain why other *-ø* endings are NOT replaced by overt markers with similar consistency, e.g. the accusative singular of inanimate nouns or the second person imperative for the verb.

Secondly, the form with the zero ending is one (or even two) syllable(s) shorter than the remaining forms of the noun, e.g. nominative singular *lampa* 'lamp' has the genitive plural form *lamp* and the instrumental plural *lampami*. The significance of this factor is supported by the finding that diminutive forms, e.g. *lamp-(e)k-ø* 'lamp-DIM-GEN:PL' which for phonetic reasons acquires an additional syllable with the insertion of /e/ between the stem and the *-k* suffix usually appear earlier than bare stem forms. Hence the child who uses the correct form *lamp(e)k* will continue to say *lamp-ów* instead of *lamp*. It is possible that the child conceives /ek/ as a kind of ending for genitive plural. While the first and second factors are concerned with the form of the rule, the third and fourth factors refer to the criteria of rule application.

Thirdly, in case of genitive plural, the criterion of grammatical gender distinction between feminine and neuter nouns on the one hand and masculine on the other is in two ways inconsistent from the point of view of the declension system. First, in plural the distinction between masculine/feminine/neuter, relevant for singular, is abolished to be replaced by the virile/nonvirile gender distinction. While this is true for adult language, in early child language this conflict of double gender distinction does not actually occur because the virile/nonvirile

---

[12]The *-y/-i* ending occurs also with some irregular feminine nouns. This fact will not be taken into account here, as these nouns were not found to occur in the data.

[13]After this age, *-ów* continued to be overextended to replace the irregular *-y/-i* of masculine nouns, but this phenomenon is similar to those discussed in Section 4.3.1. There were also sporadic instances of its use with feminine and neuter nouns but the correct use was much more frequent.

distinction with all its implications is acquired long after the appearance of the genitive plural forms (see Section 6.3.1).[14]

Moreover, in singular, masculine and neuter nouns form the nonfeminine gender as opposed to the feminine, while in the case of genitive plural it is the neuter together with the feminine that are opposed to the masculine. This disproportion justifies the prediction of special difficulties with neuter nouns, which would therefore be likely to behave as masculine nouns, rather than take the same ending as feminine nouns. This prediction is confirmed in the data of Basia, who used *-ów* as the only genitive plural ending until the age of 4;6, while later, from 4;6 to 5, she applied it only to neuter nouns (apart from its correct use with masculine nouns), with feminine nouns having the correct Ø ending. Thus, the factor seems to be significant, although not from the very beginning of the acquisition of genitival form.

The fourth factor concerns the fact that the basic system of the plural declension as elaborated by small children seems to be much simpler than that of adults. There is a clear tendency for one-to-one correspondence between case and ending with no gender distinction at all, i.e. nominative has two allomorphs *-i/-y*, accusative equals nominative,[15] dative takes *-om*, instrumental *-ami* and locative *-ach*. This apparent regularity of the system can contribute to the child's expectation that the genitive also has a unique form.

The fifth and final factor concerns the role of agreement. Agreement forms can also be of some importance for establishing gender distinctions. Table 6.6 shows the neutralization of gender in plural, where all the nouns except [+ virile] take the same agreement forms in both adjective and verb. The importance of this factor was revealed to me by a strange metalinguistic problem set forth by one of the subjects studied, Miś (3;4): *Mamusiu, płatek to on?* 'Mommy, is *płatek* (petal) a he?' *Płatek, jak jeden, to on?* '*Płatek,* when there is one, is it a he?'. Mother: *Tak.* 'Yes.' Miś: *A dwa?* 'And (if there are) two (of them)?' Mother: *To płatki.* 'Then (they are) *płatki*' Miś: *A sto?* 'And a hundred (of them)?' Mother: *To płatków* 'Then—*płatków*'. Rather than the form itself, the child wanted to learn the grammatical gender. Miś's use of 'he' and 'she' was a technique that he employed as early as 2;11 to ask questions about gender. What is interesting here is the occurrence of two separate questions, i.e. 'What is the gender of *płatek* in singular?,' and then 'What is its gender in plural?'. It could mean that Miś constructed a hypothesis on the metalinguistic level concerning the change of gender in plural. He could have noticed that *płatek,* which in singular behaved like a boy, undergoes a sharp transformation in plural and begins to behave like

---

[14]There are, however, numerous early examples of the correct nominative plural *-a* with neuter nouns, which could be treated as evidence that the tripartite gender distinction can work in plural as well. However, the nominative form is somewhat more basic than those of oblique cases, and as such it can be learned more easily.

[15]Children use mostly inanimate plural objects, which are nonvirile. The use of virile objects, where accusative equals genitive, comes much later.

TABLE 6.6
Gender Agreement in Adjectives and Past Tense Verbs in Singular and Plural

Singular				Plural			
Gender	Noun	'was'	'pretty'	Gender	Nouns	'were'	'pretty'
MASC	chłopiec 'boy'	był	ładny	VIR	chłopcy	byli	ładni
MASC	kotek 'cat'	był	ładny	NVIR	kotki	były	ładne
FEM	matka 'mother'	była	ładna	NVIR	matki	były	ładne
FEM	zabawka 'toy'	była	ładna	NVIR	zabawki	były	ładne
NEUT	jabłko 'apple'	było	ładne	NVIR	jabłka	były	ładne

girls, and thus it takes the adjective and verb forms proper to female human beings. It could be then that children perceive the non-virile gender simply as a kind of feminine which is due to their tendency to refer to natural sex differences in their metalinguistic reasoning (cf. Karmiloff-Smith, 1979).

The combination of all these factors can provide an adequate explanation of the phenomenon described above. What I found to be most difficult to account for is the case of three children among my subjects who had no problems with the genitive plural. With two of them, the distribution of ø and -ów was correct from the very beginning (2;0 to 2;2). The third one, Inka, seemed to avoid zero forms until 2;5 using -ów exclusively and only with masculine nouns. Next, from 2;5 to 3;3 she used the Ø ending but only with diminutive nouns (when this involves /e/-insertion). Eventually after the age of 3;3, she also used bare stem forms. Such a stategy of avoiding difficulties is interesting in itself, but it goes beyond the problem presently under discussion. When trying to account for the data from these children, I would claim that the first two factors can also be the very cause of the EARLY acquisition of zero forms. Word forms which do not have any overt marker and are shorter than usual seem strange to all children. This peculiarity can be rejected by some children which results in replacing the zero ending with an overt marker. In contrast other children would notice the zero ending just because of the perceptual salience of the lack of an ending, and they would accept it resulting in the establishment of distributional criteria.

4.3.2.3. *Accusative Singular of Masculine Nouns: Overextension of -*a *(the Animate/Inanimate Criterion).* In the accusative singular, masculine nouns subdivide into animate and inanimate, with the former ending in -*a* and accusative equal to genitive and the latter having the Ø-ending and accusative equal to nominative. The distribution of forms is identical to the parallel distribution in Russian, where it has been reported as a late acquisition by Gvozdev (1949) and Slobin (1966). Polish data are unclear in this resepct. The picture is obscured by the interference of another factor. In contemporary spoken Polish, there is a strong tendency to use the -*a* ending also with inanimate nouns in some limited but not very well-defined contexts. So far, the research carried out by Polish linguists has not led to any clear conclusions concerning either the kinds of words which are likely to take the -*a* ending, or typical contexts in which it occurs. Hence, no adequate explanation of the phenomenon has been provided.

On the one hand, Polish children seem to acquire the -*a* versus ø distinction very early (about 2;0), but at the same time, they use the -*a* ending with inanimate nouns to a much larger extent than adults do, although some contexts prove that they know the distinction. It is difficult to state anything definite without clear information on adult usage. What seems to be the case here is the overextension of some adult rule rather than the simple overgeneralization of the -*a* ending. Typically, child language more explicitly reflects a change that the language undergoes at a given time (cf. Slobin, 1977).

4.3.2.4. *Locative Case of Nonfeminine Nouns: Overextension of the Ending* -u *(Morphophonological Criterion).*   The distribution of the two alternative endings -*u* and -*e* depends on the character of the stem final consonant. Furthermore, while adding -*u* does not require any transformation of the stem, the -*e* ending involves softening of the stem final consonant, e.g. the shift from [v] to [v'] in *drzew-o* vs. *na drzewi-e* 'tree'. When there is no palatal counterpart of the consonant, it is replaced by another consonant according to a clearcut pattern, e.g. *rower* vs. *na rowerze* 'bike'; *zeszyt* vs. *w zeszycie* 'copybook', with /r/ - /ž/ and /t/ - /ć/ alternations.

In some children one can find a dozen or so examples of overextended -*u*, e.g. *na roweru, w zeszytu,* but the -*u* ending is never found to predominate to such an extent as to drive out the -*e* ending completely; cf. also examples in Wójtowicz (1959). This overextension results in the avoidance of stem alternations. Furthermore, in some children, the vocative ending -*u* undergoes an analogous overextention. Russian has similar endings but their distribution differs from that of Polish, and in view of differences in the phonological system, no similar stem alternations are involved. In fact Gvozdev (1949) finds a reverse tendency to overextend -*e* at the cost of -*u*.

4.4. *Idiosyncratic Rules*

Idiosyncratic rules are somewhat different than overgeneralizations. Idiosyncratic rules involve a simplified procedure invented by the child in order to cope with a diversity of rules. This is not identical to overextending a rule that exists in the adult language. On the other hand, an idiosyncratic rule is usually related to one of the existing rules, or else it can be based on a single linguistic form which serves as a model for overgeneralization.

4.4.1. *Present Tense: First-Person Form Equals Third-Person Plus* -m.
Among present-tense forms the first to emerge is the third-person form. When shifting to the use of first singular for self-reference, children must establish the

TABLE 6.7
Present Tense Forms in Singular

Person	Conjugation I (-e-)		Conjugation II (-i-)		Conjugation III (-a-)
1	pisz-ę	bior -ę	rob-i-ę	widz -ę	czyt-a-m
2	pisz-e-sz	bierz-e-sz	rob-i-sz	widz'-i-sz	czyt-a-sz
3	pisz-e	bierz-e	rob-i	widz'-i	czyt-a
	'write'	'take'	'do/make'	'see'	'read'

distribution of the two endings -ę and -m. Table 6.7 presents the distribution of these endings. Most of the children studied acquired these rules quickly and made no consistent errors. One boy (Jaś), however, used a simplified rule of adding -m to the third-person form in all verbs, e.g. *pisze-m, bierze-m, robi-m* and the correct *czyta-m*. It is worth noting that this invention made it possible for the child to avoid specific options related to the application of -ę, i.e. replacing the stem vowel by -ę (as in *pisz-e/pisz-ę*) versus adding the ending to it (as in *rob-i/rob-i-ę*), or finally stem alternations (e.g. *bierz-/bior-, widź/widz-*). Jaś applied the rule from the age of 2;0 to 3;6. A slightly different rule which involves adding -em was used by the child reported in Siatkowscy (1956) from 2;0 to 2;6.

4.4.2. *Sentence External Negation:* nie + *Sentence.*   Most Polish children do not have any difficulties with sentence internal placement of the particle *nie.* In general, the negation system is mastered early. One child (Basia), however, displayed the strategy of NEG + S commonly used by English-speaking children (see Bellugi, 1967). This case was reported in Smoczyńska (1978a), where it was pointed out that Basia's overall syntactic development was much slower than that of the other four children studied. Basia used this rule in her early negated sentences, e.g. *Nie Basia śpi* 'not Basia sleeps'. The context clearly indicated that such utterances involved sentence negation rather than the anaphoric *nie* + positive statement, which is contrary to Bloom's (1970) claim. Furthermore the negations were used not only for rejection, as claimed by de Villiers and de Villiers (1979), but also in declarative negative statements and questions, e.g. *Nie tu brudno?* 'not here dirty?' (= 'It's not dirty here?'). Later on, Basia continued to place *nie* in sentence-initial position but moved the verb to the second position, which results in correct sentences, e.g. *Nie śpi Basia* 'Not sleeps Basia'. Eventually, she arrived at sentence-internal placement of *nie,* e.g. *Basia nie śpi* 'Basia not sleeps' (= Basia isn't sleeping'). On the other hand, Kaczmarek (1953) gives several examples of placing *nie* after the verb, e.g. (1;6) *płacze nie* 'cries not'; (1;8) *mamusia kopać będzie nie* 'Mommy dig will not'. Similar examples occur sporadically in Kasia's early negations.

Children learning English introduce multiple negation into their language. If this is a general tendency for children, Polish (with its multiple negation) should be an ideal language to learn. Yet this is not the case. While American children reconstruct the multiple negation, nonexistent in their language, Polish children do exactly the opposite. With Kasia and occasionally also with other children, the use of a negative pronoun involved the deletion of *nie*. This deletion resulted in literal counterparts of English sentences of the kind *I will say nothing*, *Nic powiem*, 'nothing I:will:say' while the correct Polish form is *Nic nie powiem*. Moreover, when the particle *nie* was used, the pronoun was not converted into its negative form,[16] e.g. Kasia (2;3) said, *A Jezus to zawsze nie gryzie* 'But Jesus always not bites' where *nigdy* 'never' should be used instead of *zawsze* 'always'. Rzętkowska (1980) reported the use of emphatic *wcale* 'at all' as a negative marker, e.g. (1;10) *Jadziusia wcale płacze* 'Jadwiga at all cries'.

4.4.3. *Syllabic Prepositions and Prefixes Realized as a Reduplication of the First Syllable of the Word.*   This individual strategy was used by my own twin sons whose early speech was systematically recorded (see Section 2.1.2).[17] The twins began to combine words at the age of 2;4. At the beginning, they omitted all prepositions, using only appropriate case endings. At the age of 2;7 one of them, Michał S., began to produce strange forms of nouns with reduplicated first syllable, e.g. *ma-mamy, (s)to-tole* or *kup-kupkach*. The context, as well as case endings, clearly indicated that a prepositional phrase was intended, such as *do mamy* 'to Mom' *na stole* 'on table' and *po kupkach*, used in *Nie wolno chodzić po kupkach* '(One is) not allowed to:walk on (cow) excrements'. Immediately after the emergence of these forms, I tried to make the child repeat various kinds of prepositional phrases. This procedure revealed that the reduplication technique was consistently used to replace syllabic prepositions, while the asyllabic ones were continually omitted, e.g. the phrase *z mamą* 'with Mommy' was produced *mamą* with the preposition *z* deleted and *w lesie* 'in forest' was produced as *lesie*. Later on, the reduplication rule was extended to include syllabic verbal prefixes indicating perfectivity and/or modulation of verb meaning, e.g. *je-jechał* meant either *po-jechał* 'went', *wy-jechał* 'left', or *przy-jechał* 'arrived'.[18] The same procedure began to be used by the other twin, Maciek, 3 months later and it persisted in both of them for several months.

It is more than probable that the rule was based on a single instance, namely the frequently used phrase *do domu* 'to home', in which the phonetic form of the

---

[16]Contrary to the English *some/any/no* tripartite distinction, Polish has the binary opposition, e.g. *ktoś/nikt* 'somebody/nobody'.

[17]From informal sources I have learned about three other cases of applying such a rule. Unfortunately, data were not collected.

[18]I noted one case of erroneous morphological analysis, in which the initial stem syllable of the word *wysoki* 'high' was treated as a prefix, which resulted in *so-soki* (cf. the prefix *wy-* in *wyjechał*, above).

preposition happens to be the same as that of the first syllable in *domu*. Since the rule was applied only in case of syllabic morphemes, it cannot be treated as a strictly grammatical rule, but rather as a procedure used to render an approximate prosodic shape of the prefixed form. There was no attempt to differentiate specific semantic content of various prepositions and prefixes. All received exactly the same treatment.

4.4.4. *First-Person Plural of the Past Tense: Total or Partial Identification of the Movable Ending with the Personal Pronoun.*

First of all, it should be said that the first-person plural forms of the past tense appear relatively late (usually after 2;6) and due to the lack of appropriate context, they are rarely used. When referring to past actions carried out together with other persons, young children are more likely to use a singular subject and a comitative, which is acquired relatively early. Past forms of the first-person plural begin to be used more frequently about the age of 5 in the case of only children, and somewhat earlier if the child has siblings or attends a nursery school.

The Polish enclitic and movable ending -*śmy*, which is the unique marker for first-person plural of the past tense in all verbs, appears to cause specific difficulties for all children. As it happens, the phonetic shape of -*śmy* partially coincides with that of the respective personal pronoun *my* 'we'. As a consequence of this coincidence, two kinds of erroneous interpretation appear in the data. The first one consists in the identification of *my* and -*śmy*. The latter is considered as an allomorph of the former. Children correctly use -*śmy* in sentences which do not contain a pronoun, e.g. *Wczoraj poszli-śmy* 'yesterday went-1PL'. In contrast, when the pronoun is present, they omit the ending and say; *Wczoraj my poszli*, cf. correct *Wczoraj my poszli-śmy* or the more natural, *Wczoraj my-śmy poszli*.

Another interpretation is based on an erroneous analysis of the morpheme -*śmy* into two morphemes, i.e. the ending -*ś* and the pronoun *my*. Here again sentences without pronouns seem to be correct, but for children the form *poszliśmy* consists of three morphemes (PP + -*ś* + PRO) rather than two (PP + -*śmy*) as in adult language. This can be seen in such utterances as *My poszli-ś* or *My-ś poszli*. In the latter example, the idiosyncratic -*ś* ending is given the status of a movable suffix. For some children, such forms as *poszli* (first interpretation) or *poszli-ś* (second interpretation) appear also in sentences with no pronoun used. This indicates that children can correctly apply the pronoun ellipsis rules, but they delete the pronoun from the suffix -*śmy* where it is supposed to be placed. With some children, examples of overmarking can be found, e.g. *My-śmy poszli-śmy*. Finally, evidence for the full control of the adult form is found in utterances such as *My-śmy poszli* in which both the pronoun and the ending are present. In other cases, the erroneous rule can result in apparently correct forms.

In general, the kind of error presently under discussion is typically a late error. The omission of -*śmy* which results in forms like *My poszli* can also be found in the substandard Polish of adults with a low educational level. The role of incorrect input is evident in the case of Inka, who (at some period) used correct forms when referring to actions carried out together with her mother, but who used the *my* + PARTICIPLE form when reporting what she was doing with the children in the yard.

It would be interesting to compare the acquisition of the ending *-śmy* with that of *-ście* for second person plural which does not coincide phonetically with the corresponding pronoun *wy*. Unfortunately, contexts involving addressing several persons are even more rare than those referring to jointly performed past actions, and the second-person plural past-tense form is extremely infrequent in the data. The forms found in the data occurred late and were correct except for one case of overmarking in Witek (4;5) *Wy-ście przebierali-ście się* 'you-2PL changed-2PL REFL' (= 'you changed yourselves').

From the theoretical point of view, these errors provide evidence for the significance of prosodic features in establishing what is a word and what is not. Such errors would never occur if *-śmy* were not enclitic. A contrastive test-case is provided by the present-tense first-person plural ending *-my,* which is phonetically identical with the pronoun *my,* e.g. *czyta-my* 'read-1PL'. However, it is neither enclitic nor movable, cf. the stress pattern of *czytámy* with that of *czytáliśmy*. Conseqeuntly, children never try to identify this ending with the pronoun and use correct forms from the very beginning, with no errors at all.

4.4.5. *An Idiosyncratic Causative Construction.*   This is also an individual case. When he was 2;11, my youngest son, Wawrzont, invented a syntactic construction which does not exist in Polish. He used the verb *karmić* 'to feed' in an overextended causative sense, e.g. *Mama mnie pokarmi umyć rączki* 'Mommy me will:feed to:wash hands'. He meant that he wanted Mommy to wash his hands instead of him doing it by himself. Other examples involved 'feeding him' to eat something although the meaning of 'eat' is normally included in that of 'feed', i.e. 'make eat'; 'feeding him' to put on his clothes; 'feeding him' to wee-wee; or even 'feeding him' to draw a dog after he declared he was unable to do it. In all these instances, a simple transitive sentence would have been quite appropriate, e.g., 'Mommy will wash my hands' or 'draw a dog for me'. What the child intended to convey by his causative constructions was a special emphasis on his refusal to do something by himself, that he was in fact able to. Hence these constructions had a definite pragmatic sense which was narrower than that of the English *make* + VERB structure. This pragmatic sense emerged in response to a specific situation. I was very busy for several weeks and although I was present at home, other people had to take care of the child. The origin of this construction can be found in a concrete proportion, i.e. 'I am eating by myself': 'Mommy is feeding me.' The word 'feed' became a causative auxiliary. An especially interesting aspect of this construction is that it represents the 'accusativus cum infinitivo' type which is practically nonexistent in Polish. In other words Wawrzont added an infinitival complement to the accusative object normally governed by *karmić*. This construction was strongly productive for a limited period of time, and disappeared simultaneously with the disappearance of the appropriate context, that is, as soon as I finished my work.

4.5. Free Variation

This kind of error occurs when the child has acquired alternative forms without learning specific criteria of their distribution, which are either irregular or too complex or inconsistent with his present system.

4.5.1. *The Choice of Present (PRES) vs. Infinitive (INF) Stem Form of the Verb.* Establishing which verb stem should be used with a given form takes over two years. From 2 to 4, the erroneous choice of the stem is clearly the most frequent error with all children. As noticed in Zarębina (1965), the number of such errors increases with age in proportion to the growth of vocabulary. From 4;0 on, the number of errors diminishes, but those involving especially complicated kinds of verbs persist till 6;0 and over.

Considerable complexity, and also irregularity of the adult system in this respect has been discussed in Section 1. While in some verbs the phonetic realization of the stem does not change, e.g. *czyta/czytać* 'read' (3SG:PRES/INF), others require complex transformations, e.g. *rysuje/rysować* 'draw', *pierze/prać* 'wash', and *weźmie/wziąć* 'take'.

According to Brenstiern-Pfanhauser (1930), the child displays a tendency towards building all verb forms from the stem that he learned first. On the other hand, Zarębina (1965) claims that this is true only for the early stages. After the child has learned both stems, he builds the given form in an ad hoc way using one or the other stem. Thus one can observe two types of errors occurring simultaneously: imperfective present tense or perfective future tense forms created from infinitive stems and past tense forms created from present tense stems. For instance, the present tense form *rysowa* '(he):draws' is built on the infinitive stem (*rysowa-ć* 'draw-INF') instead of the correct *rysuje*. For the verb *prać* 'to:wash' we find on the one hand the past tense form *pierzy-ł* '(he):washed' obviously based on the present tense *pierz-e* '(he):washes' instead of the correct *pra-ł* (cf. infinitive *pra-ć*). On the other hand, however, present tense forms happen to be based on the infinitive, e.g. *pra* or *praje* instead of *pierze*.

As shown by the following examples from Inka, when coping with such problems, children do not avail themselves of the correct model, and even if they do, it is only to produce an ad hoc correct form; soon afterwards they revert to the old one. At 2;7 Inka asked her father: *Co to rysowa-sz tatusiu?* 'What are you drawing, Dad?' (cf. correct *rysuj-esz*). Father: *Nie rysuj-ę, tylko pisz-ę.* 'I am not drawing, but I am writing'. Inka: *Co pisa-sz?* 'What are you writing?' (cf. correct *pisz-esz*). At 2;4 Inka's grandmother said: *A babcia ci coś przywioz-ł-a* 'Granny has brought you something'. Inka: *Co przywioz-ł-a-ś babciu?* 'What have you brought, Granny?' *Kolejkę przywiezia-ł-a-ś mi?* 'A train did you bring me' (cf. correct *przywiozł-a-ś*).

Early examples of such errors have been reported in all diary studies, and those for later periods can be found in Siatkowscy (1956) and Wójtowicz (1959). Gvozdev (1949) has presented a detailed discussion of similar errors in Russian, and Guillaume (1927) has done the same for French. The phenomenon should be investigated systematically in order to establish which kinds of verbs are especially difficult, and to look for some rules which could underlie this overall picture of free variation. In all these cases, the verb is clearly marked for tense and aspect although the given realization of these categories does not correspond to the adult norm. From the theoretical point of view, however, this phenomenon—in spite of its wide range—is of relatively little interest, as the irregularity of the system (if it can be considered a system at all) is immense.

4.5.2. Cardinal Numeral 'Two': Feminine Form dwie *Versus Nonfeminine* dwa. Unlike the errors discussed above, the occurrence of a free variation pattern in this case is extremely interesting. The cardinal numeral 'two' when used with reference to nonvirile nouns[19] has two distinct forms: *dwie* for feminine nouns and *dwa* for masculine and neuter, where the latter form is unmarked (e.g. used while counting: *jeden, dwa, trzy . . .*). Most of the children studied had problems establishing the correct distribution of these forms in spite of the fact that it is determined by a very simple rule which is based on grammatical gender, and gender is a category which is acquired a long time before numerals come in use. Initially, children use the unmarked form *dwa* regardless of gender. Later on, both forms are found to occur in free variation.

For Jaś, this error persisted even in the latest recordings (6;0). His case is especially interesting. Jaś was very interested in numbers, and numerals were unusually frequent in his speech.[20] Not only did he frequently speak about thousands and millions, but even his nostrils were numbered and received specific labels as 'the first one' and 'the second one'. His data provide obvious support for the claim that training does not help to acquire even such a simple rule if it happens to be blocked for some mysterious reasons. When trying to find some rule governing the distribution of *dwa/dwie*, I was able to analyze more than 200 examples of 'two' + NOUN constructions recorded from 2 to 6. Still, I failed to find any rule. Clearly, both forms were used in free variation with a tendency to use the same form at a given moment, e.g. at (3;5) he said *dwi-e bramk-i i dwi-e domk-i* 'two-FEM gate-FEM:PL and two-FEM house-MASC:PL' (= 'two gates and two houses') cf. correct *dwie bramki i dwa domki*. After he was corrected by

---

[19]Virile nouns involve complicated rules of numeral agreement, which will not be discussed here.

[20]The data were collected more than 20 years ago, and it might be of some interest to add that those early interests prevailed, since he is a statistician by now.

his mother ('One doesn't say *dwie domki* but *dwa domki*'), he corrected himself with *dwa domki i dwa bramki,* with the incorrect form of 'two' for *bramki* this time. As adults started correcting his utterances, he began analyzing the problem on the metalinguistic level. The only result of this was "correcting" adults, that is, providing erroneous forms with the correct argumentation concerning gender, e.g. 'Auntie, you should say *dwi-e numerk-i* 'two-FEM number-MASC:PL' because one says *ten numerek* 'this:MASC:SG number:MASC:SG'. He also began to produce both forms at the same time, leaving the option to the listener, e.g. *Znalazłem dw-a czy dwi-e szmatk-i* 'I:found two-MASC or two-FEM rag-FEM:PL' (= 'I found two or two rags').

For other children, this error did not persist for such a long time, but still it could be considered as a typical late error, for instance, it appears in the Baudouin data. I am unable to provide an adequate explanation for this error although three factors can be demonstrated to be of some importance. Firstly, among plural cardinal numerals only 'two' displays such a gender distinction in addition to the opposition of virile/nonvirile forms; 'three' and 'four' having only the latter differentiation. If this factor were the only one at play, one would expect the children to ignore the distinction *dwa/dwie* and use only *dwa* in order to preserve paradigmatic relations among numerals. In fact, this distribution does occur, but only in the early stages.

Secondly, the nonvirile nominative plural form of adjectives ends in *-e,* e.g. *duż-e klock-i, piłk-i, ciastk-a* 'big-NVIR:NOM:PL, block-NVIR:MASC:PL, ball-NVIR:FEM:PL, biscuit-NVIR:NEUT:PL'. If the child were to treat *dw-a/dwi-e* as a kind of adjectival form (by analogy to *jeden-ø/jedn-a/jedn-o* 'one', which takes regular adjective declension forms), he would be expected to use the form *dwie* exclusively for all nonvirile nouns—a prediction that is not supported by the data. Finally, it could be hypothesized that children simply refuse to take into account the masculine/feminine/neuter distinction when using plural forms. This would be congruent with one of the explanations offered in connection with their generalizing of the genitive plural *-ów* ending (see Section 4.3.2.2)[21] Note, however, that the distribution of 'two' forms is consistent with the main distinction within the singular (feminine vs. nonfeminine), whereas that of *-ów/ø* is not. Yet in the case of Jaś, the latter rule is acquired EARLIER than the former. That is why I am unable to produce any definite explanation.

4.5.3. *Using Masculine or Feminine Forms of Adjectives and Past-Tense Verbs in Free Variation.*   This kind of error differs considerably from those described above. The rules are neither too complex nor incompatible with the system. On the contrary, they are simple and consistent, but the child simply does not know them yet. The occurrence of these errors is limited to the earliest

---

[21]Children, however, are perfectly aware of the gender of the noun in singular, e.g. *dw-a śrub-y, jedn-a . . . drug-a . . .* 'two-MASC screws-NVIR, one-FEM . . . other-FEM'.

instances of using adjectives and past tense forms, e.g. *tatuś mił-a* 'Daddy nice-FEM', *babcia poszedł-ø* 'Granny went-3SG:MASC'. At the very beginning, *miła* or *poszedł* can be simply the only form of the word that the child knows. These errors disappear completely long before the age of 2 (see Section 6.1.1).

4.6. Partial Application of a Rule

These errors reveal difficulties in the complete application of a complex rule which involves performing several operations. The problem does not consist of learning the criteria, but rather it concerns technical difficulties in producing a correct form.

4.6.1. *Nouns: Correct Ending Added to an Incorrect Stem Form.*   Errors of this type occur infrequently in all children. The basic noun form is nominative singular. The child tends to build other forms from the nominative form. However, there are stem alternations in the nominative singular, and oblique cases have a different stem. In Polish there is a phonological rule according to which the opposition of voiced/voiceless becomes neutralized in word final position, e.g. /χlep/ versus /χleba/ 'bread' for nominative versus genitive but /χu̯op/ : /χu̯opa/ 'peasant'. In order to know whether the final voiceless consonant in the nominative form alternates with its voiced counterpart, the child must memorize the form that a given stem takes in oblique cases. The phonological rule is acquired early and errors such as *chlepa* instead of *chleba* typically occur very early. When this kind of error occurs at a later stage of development, it occurs when the child has just heard the nominative form for the first time.

Another rule requires that *-e-* be inserted between consonants in order to avoid an unacceptable word-final cluster. It appears typically in diminutive masculine nouns with the *-k* suffix, e.g. *kot-k-a* 'cat-DIM-GEN' but *kot-(e)k-ø* 'cat-DIM-NOM'. Because of the abundance of diminutive forms, this rule is acquired very early, and children normally delete the inserted *-e-* when producing oblique case forms. Errors such as *kotek-a* appear only in the earliest period. Other forms with the *-e-* inserted into the stem itself prove more difficult especially if the stem is relatively short (one or two syllables), e.g. the genitive of the word *lew* /lef/ 'lion' is frequently realized as *lew-a* (cf. correct *lw-a*) or even *lef-a* if the unvoiced /f/ is preserved and *ogień* 'fire' results in *ogienia* (cf. correct *ognia*).

Sometimes stem-internal consonants and/or vowels alternate following definite alternation patterns. What seems to be most difficult for the child is the case when several phonemes alternate according to distinct patterns. The following example will make this clear. Michał (2;4) wanted to say 'Good morning, eagle!' *Dzień dobry, orle!*, where the vocative *orle* contrasts with the nominative *orzeł*. He began with *Dzień dobry, orzele* /ožele/ then corrected himself with *orzle* /ožle/, and eventually, he gave up and used the nominative *orzeł* /ožeu̯/ instead. Producing the correct version required three transformations of the nominative stem form, i.e. /u̯/ to /l/, deletion of /e/, and /ž/ to /r/. The sequence of forms that he produced demonstrates that he was able to perform one transformation at a time. Although he failed to perform the third one, the fact that he reverted to the more safe nominative form (also acceptable in the vocative function) proves that he was not satisfied with the form he arrived at. Wójtowicz (1959) noted that errors of preserving the nominative singular stem in oblique cases are much more frequent than those involving the reverse process, e.g. an incorrect nominative singular form *ojc* 'father', based on the genitive singular *ojc-a,* (cf. correct nominative singular *ojciec*).

4.6.2. *Preserving Case Forms in Negated Sentences.*   The rule of converting the accusative object of transitive sentences into genitive when the predicate is negated is likely to create difficulties at least for some children. Sometimes the rule is grasped at the earliest period, e.g. for Michał not a single error was found for the period 2;0 to 6;0, while other children tend to preserve the case ending used in non-negated sentences and they say *Nie czytam książk-ę* 'not I:read book-ACC' instead of *książk-i* 'book-GEN'. This can be seen in the early data for Basia, who used the genitive case correctly with possessives, as well as in contexts involving the preposition *do* 'to', but failed to use it with negated existential sentences with *niema* 'there:is:no' and preserved the nominative form typical for subjects of positive existential sentences. Similarly, after she began constructing negated transitives, the object appeared in the accusative case. Eventually, she learned the adult rule, but she frequently failed to apply it in negated sentences with modals. Such errors occurred also with other children.

4.6.3. *Conditional Forms: Wrong Placement of the Person Suffix.*   This error can be found to occur in practically all the children studied for at least a short period. According to the adult rule, the person suffix for first and second person in singular and plural must follow the conditional particle *by* regardless of the place in which this particle happens to occur, that is, whether it follows the past participle (e.g. *pisał-BY-m*), precedes the verb (e.g. *Ja BY-m pisał*), or constitutes a part of the connective *żeby* (e.g. *żeBY-m pisał*).

A widespread error concerning the use of conditional forms is that of placing the suffix immediately after the participle (which results in a regular past-tense form) while leaving the particle *by* either to follow it or to occur in an enclitic position, e.g. *pisał-(e)m-by* or *Ja by pisał-(e)m* 'I would write'. Here the children apply the rule: Add *by* to the past-tense form, with the option of moving *by* to an enclitic position. This contrasts with the adult rule: Insert *by* between the participle and the person suffix so that *by* + PERSON forms an enclitic. This erroneous rule is probably due to the influence of the third-person forms, in which the past participle is identical to the past-tense form where both rules lead to the same correct result, i.e. the child's *pisał* + ϕ + *by* equals the adult's *pisał* + *by* + ϕ (see also Section 6.1.3).

With some children this error was typical only during the early uses of the conditional form while in others it was more persistent. In the case of Jaś, for instance, the correct order of morphemes had not been acquired by the age of 6. Early errors involving the incorrect order of morphemes and/or overmarking for person (see Section 4.2) can be accounted for if we propose that the child builds the conditional form on the basis of the past-tense form, and not the past participle.[22] As to late errors, some additional factors can contribute to their persistence. Jaś, for instance, was more likely to use the correct form in main clauses than in subordinate clauses, and he was especially reluctant to attach the person suffix to the connective *żeby*. It could be hypothesized that children avoid applying a verbal suffix to a morpheme which is not a verb, and the morpheme *by* (even though, historically, it comes from an aorist) does not have the status of an auxiliary verb. For *żeby*, it can be even more difficult for the child to accept the rule which requires that a connective be conjugated. Therefore, the adult rules can be rejected because they violate the well-established distinction of word classes.

4.6.4. *Self-Reference: Using Feminine Forms.*

This error appears frequently with boys when they begin using the first-person form of verbs. It has nothing to do with gender agreement, since the latter is firmly established before the occurrence of these errors.[23] In my data the following sequence can be found. After the emergence of feminine forms of first person in past-tense verbs, e.g. feminine *pisał-a-m* instead of masculine *pisał-ø-(e)m*, the use of the feminine form was overextended in two ways to include: (1) adjectives referring to the child himself, e.g. *Jestem głodn-a* 'I:am hungry-FEM, cf. correct *głodn-y* 'hungry-MASC', and (2) the third-person past-tense form of verbs but only in self-reference, e.g. *Michał pisał-a*, 'Michael wrote-3SG:FEM', (cf. correct *pisał -ø*, 'wrote-3SG:MASC'). Earlier, these forms had the correct gender marking. These overextensions quickly disappeared while the feminine first-person forms persisted for several more months, occurring in free variation with correct masculine forms. Eventually, the masculine form became the only one used by the child when referring to himself. This phenomenon was sometimes accompanied

---

[22]It is not the case, however, that children are unable to single out the past participle form, since they use it very early in correct future tense forms in which the person is marked on the auxiliary by means of special endings and not added to the participle, e.g. *będ-ę pisał, będzie-sz pisał* 'will -1SG write:PP, will-2SG write:PP') or overmarking for person (e.g. *będ-ę pisał-(e)m* 'will-1SG write:PP-1SG') are extremely rare. But on the other hand, a strange form *mogł(e)-by-m* (correct *mógł -by-m*), produced by Jaś in his effort to order morphemes correctly, is clearly based on the past tense form *mogł-(e)m* 'I-could', as revealed by the presence of phonetic (e).

[23]Gvozdev (1949) reports quite a similar phenomenon in Zhenya's speech, noting that gender agreement with nouns was mastered by the age of 2;6, while feminine past-tense forms with self-reference continued to be used till as late as 3;0.

by the use of the masculine second-person form irrespective of the sex of the person addressed (see also Rzętkowska, 1909, and Brenstiern-Pfanhauser, 1930).

It is quite clear that when learning the rules of person switching, the male child employs the first-person form which he hears most frequently from his mother, while for the second person he selects the masculine form used by adults when addressing him. For girls, unless they are brought up by their fathers, the task is more simple because boys must perform an additional operation to arrive at the correct form. This error is rare with boys who have elder male siblings, since elder brothers provide the correct model.

4.7. Summary

The above presentation of grammatical errors can be considered as complete, in the sense that it gives an account of all systematic errors found in the data, regardless of their duration and of whether they were made by most children studied or only one of them. Special attention was given to errors occurring with respect to regular adult language categories, while the children's problems with irregular categories were only mentioned, even if they produced a large number of erroneous forms. If a category is not reported here or in the section on U-shaped developments (Section 5) or delayed acquisition (Section 6.3), it means that its acquisition is error-free and does not cause any problems to children. The comparisons of what is difficult for children with what is easily acquired allow for some generalizations on children's strategies presented in Section 7.

5. U-Shaped Developments

5.1. Possessive and Attributive Modifiers

In Polish, possession is expressed by means of a genitival construction, while attribution is realized mostly by an adjective modifying the head noun.[24] In the earliest stages of syntactic development, two distinct patterns appear (attribute plus head and possessive genitive plus head) which are subsequently used as constituents of expanded sentences (Smoczyńska, 1978a).

During the third year of life, children learn adjectival declension, and they try to reduce the number of rules of noun modification by replacing genitival possessors with denominal adjectives. Chmura-Klekotowa (1971) reports a wide use of such possessive adjectives, e.g. *mamusin, mamusiny,* or *mamusiowy* instead of the genitive *mamusi* 'Mommy's'.

---

[24]Although denominal possessive adjectives exist in Polish, they are not widely used by adults, the genitival form being much more common. In Serbo-Croatian and Russian the situation is different: possessive adjectives are used much more frequently than genitival forms.

On the other hand, the data from Kasia, who did not use such possessive adjectives, provide interesting examples of adding other case endings to the genitive form of the noun in order to achieve agreement in case with the head noun. Normally, the genitive modifier preserves its form regardless of the case of the head. Kasia, however, treated it as if it were an adjective, e.g. *w pokoj-u Anul-i-m* 'in room-LOC Anula-GEN-LOC' or *Anul-emi kredkami* '(with) Anula-INSTR:PL pencils:INSTR:PL' (cf. correct *w pokoju Anuli* and *Anuli kredkami*). Chmura-Klekotowa (1971) has cited similar examples.

After the children have established separate rules for both kinds of noun modification and learned possessive pronouns, another kind of regularization appears. The Polish system is inconsistent in that the function of possessive is performed by possessive adjectives for the first and second person (as well as the reflexive) while in the third person, genitival forms of the personal pronoun are used, which do not agree with the head. In the following set of examples the first three show agreement and the second three do not: *Moj-a książk-a* 'my-NOM book-NOM', *moj-ą książk-ę* 'my-ACC book-ACC', and *w moj-ej książc-e* 'in my-LOC book-LOC' contrast with *jego książk-a* 'his-GEN book-NOM', *jego książk-ę* 'his-GEN book-ACC', and *w je-go książc-e* 'in his–GEN book-LOC'.

The regularization made by children consists of using the genitive form of the personal pronoun of first and second person instead of the possessive adjective, e.g. *Michał chce do MNIE łóżka* 'Michał wants (to come) into ɪ's bed' (cf. correct: *do MOJEGO łóżka* 'into MY bed') or *Gdzie jest CIEBIE rączka?* 'where is YOU's hand?' (cf. correct: *TWOJA rączka* 'YOUR hand'), cited by Rzętkowska (1908). Typically, instead of using a specific question word *czyj?* 'whose?' children incorrectly employ the genitive question word *kogo?* 'of:who?'.

5.2. Embedded Infinitival Complement Replaced by a Full Clause

Similar to English-speaking children, the earliest kind of embedded constructions with the verb 'want' is that with coreferential subjects ('I want' plus infinitive). When the two subjects are not coreferential, a construction with an embedded *żeby*-clause is used, equivalent to the English 'I want him' plus infinitive.

With Jaś, infinitival clauses emerged at 2;0, e.g. *Chcem pić dżem w słoiku* 'I:want to:drink jam in jar', and the explicit *żeby*-clauses appeared three months later, e.g. Mother: *Co ty chciałeś?* 'What do you want?' Jaś: *Żeby mamusia szła do kuchni z Jasiem* 'that Mommy goes to kitchen with Jaś'. From this time on, constructions of both kinds were frequently used, without errors. Surprisingly enough, within the period of 3;1 to 3;4, a number of examples were recorded in which the explicit *żeby*-clause was used with coreferentiality, e.g. *Ja chcę, żeby miałem kotka* 'I want that I:have cat' (cf. correct *Ja chcę mieć kotka* 'I want to:have cat'). Although the infinitival construction acquired a long time earlier was not completely ruled out by the *żeby*-clause (the errors constitute about 25% of all instances of coreferential 'want' sentences), the proportion is important enough to infer that an attempt at reducing the variety of rules had taken place.

6. Timing of Acquisition

This section is concerned with those linguistic categories which are mastered by Polish children either especially early or especially late. There is a difficulty with what should be taken as the reference point with which the Polish acquisition pattern could be compared in order to evaluate precociousness or delay in the mastery of particular categories. A common option here is to take the acquisition of English as the reference point, since it is best described and widely known. This option, however, would lead us, for instance, to state that for most languages the mastery of negative and interrogative sentences is precocious, while in fact, it is in English that it is delayed because of the formal complexity of these transformations in that language. Therefore I will limit myself to presenting only those categories which seem to be mastered in Polish significantly earlier or significantly later than in several other languages.

6.1. *Precocious Acquisition*

The categories reported here are: grammatical gender, which is acquired earlier than in Russian (Section 6.1.1); tense and aspect, both of which are acquired simultaneously and very early as compared with other languages (Section 6.1.2, presented by Richard Weist); and hypothetical reference, which appears in Polish children two years earlier than in English-speaking subjects (6.1.3). As for the acquisition of complex sentences, it takes place in Polish either at the same time as in other languages or slightly earlier, or—with some types of temporal clauses—later. In order to present the data on complex sentences in a more or less systematic way, I included a separate section (6.2), which follows the present section.

6.1.1. *Grammatical Gender: Declensional Patterns and Gender Agreement.*[25]   The acquisition of grammatical gender has been reported to occur late in Russian children, both with respect to the establishment of noun inflectional patterns and to the control of gender agreement in adjectives and past-tense verbs (Gvozdev, 1949; Zakharova, 1973; Popova, 1973; Slobin, 1966, 1968, 1973). A phenomenon typical in the acquisition of Russian is that of ''inflectional imperialism.'' The child seizes upon one ending for a given case and uses it for all

---

[25]The present discussion is limited to the acquisition of the gender distinction in singular (masculine/feminine/neuter); the plural distinction into virile/nonvirile, which is acquired late, is discussed in Section 6.3.1.

nouns irrespective of their gender. Later on, he selects another "imperialistic" ending to drive out the initial "imperialistic" ending. Slobin (1966, 1968) gave a detailed description of this phenomenon, trying to establish the determinants governing the selection of the given ending as dominant. As far as gender is concerned, he concluded that this category seems to be difficult because of its arbitrariness.

My analysis of the early data of several Polish children, together with careful reading of Polish diary studies, reveals that the acquisition of gender is precocious in Polish children. Most of the children have acquired this distinction before the age of 2. First, when a case category emerges, several endings appear simultaneously according to the gender of the noun; thus, there is no inflectional imperialism. Second, the occurrence of inappropriate gender agreements is limited to a very short period when adjectives, past-tense forms, or pronouns begin to appear, and it should be attributed to the lack of knowledge of possible differentiation of these forms rather than of that concerning noun gender. (Using feminine forms when referring to oneself (Section 4.6.4) is quite a separate phenomenon, which consists in treating the first person-form used by the mother as the only one in existence.)

The early acquisition of gender in Polish is even more puzzling if one takes into account the close similarity of the Polish and the Russian declensional systems. The distribution of endings in the singular is almost identical. The Polish declension looks as if the Russian endings were translated into the Polish phonological system. In both languages the criterial nominative singular endings are ø for masculine, -a for feminine, and -o/-e for neuter. Moreover, both languages have a limited number of masculine nouns ending in -a which take feminine case forms and masculine agreement, and a large class of irregular feminine nouns ending in ø in the nominative singular having a special set of case endings. Two apparently minor factors appear to cause a considerable delay in Russian acquisition. First, the fact that the Russian unstressed o is pronounced as a; and second, the existence of diminutive masculine forms which end in -a and are declined like feminine nouns, e.g. mishka/myedvyed 'bear', zayka/zayats 'hare', and, very frequently, boys' first names such as Zhenya, Sasha, Kolya. These two apparently minor facts seem to be the cause of the whole confusion. While most of the nouns ending in -a to which Polish children are exposed are regular feminine nouns, the input to the Russian child contains different declension and agreement patterns, e.g. mama 'mommy' with a feminine declension and agreement, Zhenya 'boy's name' with a feminine declension and masculine agreement, and yábloko [yáblaka] 'apple' with a neuter declension and a neuter agreement (-o is identical to the feminine -a when unstressed). Such an inconsistent input makes it impossible for the Russian child to discover the criteria of grammatical gender, while Polish children can tolerate the limited amount of inconsistency to which they are exposed, simply regularizing irregular instances according to the tripartite gender distinction (see Section 4.3.1.3).

Early acquisition of gender in Polish shows that the child is able to learn rules which are based on totally arbitrary criteria, provided these criteria are consistent and clear enough to be discovered, and that selecting one salient (or phonetically unique) ending is only a strategy that Russian children apply when faced with the impossibility of discovering adult criteria.

6.1.2. *Tense and Aspect* **[WEIST].**   Weist, Wysocka, Witkowska-Stadnik, Buczowska, and Konieczna (1984) and Weist (1983a) have conducted the most intensive investigation of tense and aspect in child Polish. Given that tense expresses a deictic relationship between speech time and event time, Antinucci and Miller (1976), Aksu (1978), Stephany (1981), and others proposed that the initial tense morphology in languages such as Italian, Turkish, and Greek was "defective" in its function. According to the strongest form of this "defective tense" hypothesis (see Antinucci & Miller), children between the ages of approximately 1;6 and 2;6 cannot express temporal deictic relationships because they lack the necessary abstract conceptual capacity. It was proposed that when tense morphology emerges it codes the aspectual distinction between completed and ongoing situations rather than a relationship between speech time and event time. Hence tense morphology was supposed to be coding an aspectual distinction, not a tense distinction. The research on Polish challenges this hypothesis.

The defective tense hypothesis involved three lines of argumentation and can be viewed as having the following three components: (1) semantic—only telic verbs will be inflected in the past tense because a prior change of state with a speech-time resulting state is required; (2) syntactic—aspectual distinctions will not be made independently of tense distinctions, and present versus past morphological distinctions will correspond in a one-to-one manner with the situational properties "completed" versus "ongoing"; and (3) temporal—children will refer only to the immediate past. Evidence supporting each component of the argument can be found in the research of Antinucci and Miller (1976), Stephany (1981), and Szagun (1979), respectively. In fact, none of these components of the defective tense argument are supported by the evolution of tense and aspect distinctions in child Polish—nor any other Slavic language for that matter.

When considering the semantic component of the argument, one must first draw attention to the problem of defining subcategories of verbs which are relevant to verbal aspect (or *Aktionsart*). Since defining categories of verbs according to the situations to which they refer leads to a hopelessly circular argument, objective definitions are needed. Weist et al. used a contemporary version (Dowty, 1979) of Vendler's classification schema, which was shaped for Polish with the guidance of Cochrane's (1977) work on Serbo-Croatian and Miller's (1970) work on Russian. Growing out of this framework, objective distinctions were made between state versus dynamic verbs, atelic (or activity) versus telic verbs, and achievement versus accomplishment verbs. From the initial period of tensed language, Polish children use imperfective activity verbs in the past, producing such utterances as the following: (1) Marta (1;7): *Leciał samolot* 'fly:IPFV:PAST plane' (= 'The plane was flying'), (2) Bartosz (1;8): *Pływała się* 'swim:IPFV:PAST', and (3) Paulina (1;11): *Jadłam* 'eat:IPFV:PAST'. The production of activity verbs with past-tense inflections can be found in other research on Polish (Smoczyńska, 1978a), research on Russian (Gvozdev, 1961), and on Serbo-Croatian (Radulović, 1975). This phenomenon is by no means unique to Slavic languages, e.g., Spanish (Eisenberg, 1982), Greek (Stephany, 1981), Japanese (Rispoli, 1981), and Finnish (Toivainen, 1980).

Regarding the syntactic component of the defective tense hypothesis, tense and aspect morphology emerge simultaneously in Polish. During the acquisition of the verb system, there is an early period during which children use only frozen forms. There is some evidence (e.g. Zarębina, 1965) for a primitive distinction in mood at this point, since indicative forms are typically used to make statements and imperative forms to make requests. The indicative forms are typically imperfective verbs in the present tense and in the third-person singular. Zarębina has shown that this third-person form is generally applied making reference to second as well as third person. Typically when children are between about 1;6 and 1;9, they begin to use past-tense inflections and perfective verb forms. References to the future are made at that time or soon thereafter. Since the present perfective meaning is impossible in Polish, the combination of three tenses and two basic aspects produces five possible verb forms. Only the periphrastic future form for imperfective verbs is sometimes missing (or difficult to identify) in the initial set of tense/aspect combinations. These distinctions appear to emerge without errors in Russian (Gvozdev, 1961) and in Serbo-Croatian (Radulović, 1975) as well as in Polish. There is no evidence WHATSOEVER that tense morphology codes the aspectual distinction between perfective and imperfective or that tense morphology emerges as a redundant appendage.

When considering the temporal component of the overall argument, the first obvious finding is that the resulting state of a previous change of state is not required for children to make reference to past events. At 1;7, for example, Marta was talking to her grandmother about their recent trip to the seashore and in response to the question *A co panowie robili?* 'And what were the men doing [IPVF]?', Marta replied *łowili* 'They were catching [IPFV]'; and in response to further questioning, *rybki* 'fish'. *Łowili . . . rybki* is an imperfective accomplishment verb phrase and as such a clear terminal point is implied, yet the child did not need any specific retrieval cues much less the resulting catch to refer to this event. Weist et al. partitioned all of the utterances which made reference to a prior situation into the categories "modeled" versus "spontaneous" and "immediate" versus "moderately remote" (more than two turns in the discourse). During the early period of tensed language, more than one-fourth of the utterances of the children were both spontaneous and moderately remote. In summary, tense and aspect emerge simultaneously and from the initial period of tensed utterances, Polish children produce activity verb phrases in the past, imperfective as well as perfective past forms, and moderately remote references to the past. Experimentation within the cross-sectional component of the research design only confirms this general conclusion.[26] **[WEIST]**

In general, my data support Weist's findings. After the earliest period of the very emergence of tense/aspect distinctions, no instances were found of inappropriate use of tenses. Aspectual errors do occur, but they are insignificant in proportion to the total frequency of verbs (Polish children are forced to make an aspectual option each time they use a verb); for instance, sometimes the analytical future form occurs with a perfective verb (e.g. *będę na-pisać* 'I:shall PFV-write' cf. correct PFV *na-piszę* or IPFV *będę pisać*), but it should be treated as a mistake, since children frequently correct themselves after having produced such a form.

[WEIST] Considering children who are somewhat older, there are two sources of data which attest to the child's control of aspectual distinctions in comprehension and production. Weist (1983a) used a sentence-picture matching task to evaluate the capacity of children to comprehend tense and aspect distinctions which were made either by prefixation or by suffixation. Two groups of ten children at age levels 2;6 and 3;6 participated in the experiment. The problems concerning aspectual distinctions contrasted pictures of completed versus incomplete situations and sentences differing only in the form of the verb, e.g. *zjadł/jadł* PFV/IPFV 'ate/ate, was eating' or *zamknął/zamykał* PFV/IPFV 'closed/closed, was closing'. The children in both groups were able to comprehend the aspectual distinction.

Regarding productive capabilities, Chmura-Klekotowa (1967, 1968) has contributed important insights from her work on neologisms. Polish children use prefixation and suffixation processes to invent aspectual contrasts.[27] At 3;4, one child invented the imperfective form *zwyczaić* 'to:get:used:to'. For the adult, the aspectual pair is *przyzwyczaić/przyzwyczajać się* PFV/IPFV. The child appears to have used the perfective form as the basis for a prefix deletion in the formulation of his imperfective form. In the next example, the process of suffixation was used by a child at 4;0 to create the form *łaskotnę* 'I:will:tickle'. In contrast to the adult's aspectual pair which is based on prefixation *łaskotać/połaskotać* IPFV/PFV, the child invents the perfective form *łaskot-ną-ć* 'tickle-PFV-INF' by suffixation. Gvozdev (1961, pp. 424–427) has shown that Russian children

---

[26][WEIST] This section replaces an earlier section which Smoczyńska based on the preliminary findings of this research which were reported in Kraków (Weist, 1980). In this research on tense and aspect, the classification of verbs always included verb phrase context (see Verkuyl, 1972). [WEIST]

[27][WEIST] Slobin (personal communication) has made the interesting observation that Polish and Russian children create neologisms differently, depending on whether a tense distinction or an aspect distinction is being constructed. When making a tense distinction, children appear to be searching for a common stem (see Section 4.5.1). However, when making an aspect distinction, children try to construct two different forms. [WEIST]

also use prefixation and suffixation to invent aspectual pairs. The form *zdravil* 'congratulated' observed at 6;10 was derived by prefix deletion from the perfective form *po-zdravit'*. The adult's aspectual pair is *pozdravit'*/*pozdravlyat'* PFV/IPFV. At 2;10 the form *katnúl* 'rolled' was observed. The perfective form *katnut'* was constructed from the imperfective *katat'*, by *-nu* suffixation. For the adult the aspectual pair is formed by prefixation *katat'*/*vykatat'*. [**WEIST**]

Adverbs which point to aspectual and temporal characteristics of events also emerge very early. Among the earliest adverbs used are those indicating completion vs. duration of an action: *jeszcze* 'more, again, still' is a pivot word for recurrence, but it is also used to express imperfectivity (cf. also *jeszcze nie* 'not yet'), and the opposite term is *już* 'already' (Przetacznikowa, 1956; Smoczyńska, 1978a). Another very frequent adverb is *teraz* 'now', which is used mostly to mark immediate futurity. In some children, numerous temporal adverbs are used in early speech, e.g. Kasia at 1;9 used *dziś* 'today', *jutro* 'tomorrow', *niedługo* 'soon', *potem* 'afterwards', and even asked *kiedy?* 'when' questions. These time words were used appropriately in that they referred to a kind of temporal notion; however, their specific meanings were not yet acquired. As a matter of fact, such notions are mastered very late: during the whole period under study, numerous examples were found of using 'tomorrow' instead of 'yesterday', 'afterwards' instead of 'before', etc., whereas tense-marking on the verb was always correct. Words expressing 'timelessness' such as *zawsze* 'always' and *nigdy* 'never' emerge before the age of 3 that is, much earlier than in English-speaking children (cf. Cromer, 1968).

6.1.3. *Hypothetical Reference.*   Brown (1973) states that the hypothetical use of past-tense forms comes very late in English-speaking children. Cromer (1968) did not find any reference to hypothetical events, even inappropriately expressed, in the data of the Harvard children until the age of 4;6. Kuczaj and Daly (1979), who used eliciting techniques in naturalistic and experimental situations, obtained a number of hypothetical statements from younger children. They found that such early uses are more often implicit than explicit and other-initiated than self-initiated. They refer to single hypothetical events rather than to a sequence of such events, and reference to future hypothetical events is prior to that to past ones.

Gvozdev (1949) and Slobin (1966) have pointed out that relative to the emergence of imperative and indicative moods, the conditional mood develops somewhat late, e.g. Zhenya was observed to produce conditional clauses with *esli* 'if' at 2;9. While this may be relatively late for Russian, it is relatively early when compared to English. The onset of conditional forms in Russian occurs almost 2 years earlier than in the English-speaking Harvard children, and it is preceded by the emergence of non-factive subordinate clauses introduced by *štob(y)* which closely correspond to the Polish *żeby*-clauses.

In my data, *żeby*-clauses are found at about 2;0 (with some children as early as 1;9 or even 1;7).[28] Causal clauses providing a hypothetical reason appear at the same time, e.g. Jaś (2;1):

Nie	*rzuca-m*	*piórk-a*		*do*	*wody*		*bo*
Not	throw-1SG	feather-NEUT:GEN		to	water-FEM:GEN		because

mokr-e	*by-ø*	*był-o*
wet-NEUT	COND-3SG	be:PP-NEUT

'I don't throw a feather into the water because it would be wet'. Note that the future tense form (*bo będzie mokre*) would have worked as well, but Jaś did not avoid the conditional mood form in spite of the existing option. Later on, the first 'if'-clauses are used in indicative mood, and somewhat later hypothetical conditional clauses appear. They are not as frequent as at the age of 5; nevertheless, several examples can be found in the spontaneous speech of all children before the age of 3. The following examples, provided with detailed glosses, can serve not only as evidence for hypothetical conditionals but also as illustration of some phenomena which appear typically from 2 to 3:

Agnieszka (2;0)

Jak	*ty*	*by-ś*	*chcial-a,*	*to*	*by-m*
If	you	COND-2SG	want:PP-FEM	PARTICLE	COND-1SG

ci	*dał-a*
you:DAT	give:PP-FEM

'If you wanted (it), I would give (it) to you.'

Kasia (2;6)

Ja	*ma-m*	*dw-a*	*kieszonk-i.*		*A*	*jak*	*by-ø*
I	have-1SG	two-MASC	pocket-NVIR:FEM:PL.		And	if	COND-3SG

był-a	*jedn-a*	*to*	*by-ø*	*brakowal-o.*
be:PP-FEM	one-FEM	PARTICLE	COND-3SG	be:missing:PP-NEUT

'I have two pockets. And if there was one, (something) would be missing.'

(The neuter *-o* in *brakował-o* expresses the impersonal 'something would be missing'.) Note the erroneous *dw-a* instead of *dwi-e*.

The following two examples from Kasia 2;9 involve double hypothetical implications of a hypothetical condition:

Jak	*by-m*	*wylazł-a*	*na*	*płot-ø*	*to*	*jeszcze*
If	COND-1SG	climb:PP-FEM	on	fence-ACC	PARTICLE	even

---

[28]With "telegraphic" children, conditional mood clauses can be deprived of their specific markers, i.e. *by* and conjunctions, the only cue to the non-factive or hypothetical reference being the inappropriate use of past tense forms (see Section 4.1).

by-ø   *mnie*   *bab-a*   *skrzyczał-a*   . . . *Może*
COND-3SG   me:ACC   old:hag-FEM   scold:PP-FEM   Perhaps

by-ø   *mnie*   *porwał-a?*
COND-3SG   me:ACC   kidnap:PP-FEM

'If I climbed the fence, the old hag would even scold me . . . Perhaps she would kidnap me?'

Jak   *by-m*   *poszł-a*   *bez*   *misi-a*
If   COND-1SG   go:PP-FEM   without   teddy:bear-MASC:GEN

to   *miś-ø*   *by-ø*   *płakał-ø.*   *I*
PARTICLE   teddy:bear-MASC:NOM   COND-3SG   cry:PP-MASC.   And

wołał-ø-by-ø   *Kasi-u!*
call:PP-MASC-COND-3SG   Kasia-VOC

'If I went without my teddy-bear, the teddy-bear would cry. And he would call: Kasia!'

The following four examples illustrate not only the hypothetical conditionals but also typical difficulties with the person suffix placement, as described in Section 4.6.3. These difficulties appear with respect to the first and second person only, but in view of the special rule children use, the third person forms have to be glossed differently, as compared with the examples cited above, and with adult use.

Kasia (2;7)

Jak   *by*   *ukroił-a-m*   *to*   *by*   *się*
If   COND   cut:PP-FEM-1SG   PARTICLE   COND   REFL

skaleczył-a-m.   *Krew-ø*   *by*   *mi*   *leciał-a-ø.*
hurt:PP-FEM-1SG   Blood-FEM:NOM   COND   me:DAT   fall:PP-FEM-3SG

'If I cut (it), I would hurt myself. I would bleed.' Literally: 'Blood will fall to me'—correct in Polish! Cf. adult 3SG form:

by-ø   *leciał-a*
COND-3SG   fall:PP-FEM

Note the presence of two implications.

Miś (2;10) [After his brother told him he would not let their mother enter the school, he said]:

Jak   *by*   *ja*   *chodził-ø-(e)m*   *to*   *by*   *mamusi-ę*
If   COND   I   go:PP-MASC-1SG   PARTICLE   COND   mommy-ACC

wpuścił-ø-(e)m.
let:in:PP-MASC-1SG

'If I were going (to school), I would let mommy in.'

Miś (3;0)

Mamusi-a		*by*	*płakał-a-ø*		*jak*	*by*	*ja*
Mommy-FEM:NOM		COND	cry:PP-FEM-3SG		if	COND	I

był-ø-(e)m		*w*	*spółdzieln-i.*	*I*	*ja*	*by*	*płakał-ø-(e)m*
be:PP-MASC-1SG		in	shop-LOC	And	I	COND	cry:PP-MASC-1SG

sam-ø	*w*	*spółdzieln-i.*
alone-MASC	in	shop-LOC

'Mommy would cry if I were in the shop. And I would cry in the shop alone.'

Jaś (2;10)

Jak	*by*	*Jaś-ø*	*powalał-ø-ø*		*się*
If	COND	Jaś-MASC:NOM	smear:PP-MASC-3SG		REFL

klej-em	*to*	*by*	*był-ø-(e)m*	*klej-ø*	*a*
glue-INSTR	PARTICLE	COND	be:PP-MASC-1SG	glue-NOM	and

nie	*Jaś-ø.*
not	Jaś-NOM

'If Jaś smeared himself with glue, I would be glue and not Jaś.'

Note the coexistence of two perspectives in self-reference. Jaś uses here both first and third person while speaking about himself. This phenomenon, typical of the third year of life, is also illustrated in the next sentence, where the 1SG possessive pronoun 'my' is used, although the verb occurs in 3SG.

Jaś (2;10)

Jak	*by*	*Hani-a*	*stoił-a*		*na*	*wózk-u,*	*to*
If	COND	Hania-FEM	stand:PP-FEM-3SG		on	pram-LOC	PARTICLE

by	*Jaś*	*musiał-ø-ø*		*kupi-ć*	*wózek-ø*	*za*
COND	Jaś:MASC:NOM	must:PP-MASC-3SG		buy-INF	pram-ACC	with

moj-e	*pieniądz-e.*
my-PL	money-PL

'If Hania stood on the pram, Jaś would have to buy a (new) pram with my money'. Note the incorrect stem in *stoi-ł-a* (= *sta-ł-a*). In the above example, as well as in the following one, we cannot credit Jaś with the adult glossing of the 3SG conditional forms. If I insist on that, it is mostly in order to stress that the apparently correct surface structure must not necessarily reflect a correct underlying rule.

Jaś (2;10) [After having been scolded for locking a neighbor in the bathroom, he explains that no harm was done.]

Jak	by	pan-i		zamykał-a-ø	się	sam-a,
If	COND	lady-FEM	(= she)	lock:PP-FEM-3SG	REFL	self-FEM

to	by	się	też	boił-a-ø.
PARTICLE	COND	REFL	also	frighten:PP-FEM-3SG

'If she locked her up herself, she would also be frightened.' Note the incorrect stem in *boi-ł-a* (= *ba-ł-a*)

A few more observations on conditionals are relevant here. As seen from the above examples, the children refer not only to sequences of hypothetical events (condition-implication), but often two hypothetical conditions or implications are mentioned. Sometimes the logical order is reversed, e.g. Jaś (2;10) said, *Jak by brałem zastrzyki, to by byłem chory i miałem katar* 'If I took injections, I would be ill and would have a cold'. One of the children studied, Michał, began asking hypothetical questions at 2;1, e.g. *Jak by kto Michałowi urwał rączki, to co?* 'If somebody tore off Michał's hands, then what?', and then he frequently carried out "experiments," presenting two alternate versions of events, e.g. [putting his hand close to a candle] Michał (2:2): *A jak bym się sparzyła?* 'And if I burned myself?' Mother: *To by było źle* 'It would be bad'. Michał : *A jak by nie?* 'And if not?'. Similarly at the age of 2;3: *A jak by nie miałem głowy?* 'And if I had no head?' Sister: *To by cię nie było* 'Then you wouldn't exist'. Michał: *A jak bym była z głową?* 'And if I were with a head?' Sister: *To byś był. To jesteś* 'Then you would exist. You exist'. Michał: *A jak bym nie była z głową?* 'And if I were not with a head?' Finally, at the age of 3;1 the following complex reasoning was recorded: Michał: *Co by było, gdyby Pana Boga nie było?* 'What would happen, if there was no God?' Mother: *To by i nas nie było* 'Then we wouldn't exist either'. Michał: *A jak by Pana Boga nie było, a śmy byli?* 'And if God didn't exist and we did?'

To summarize, the only overlap with Kuczaj and Daly's results is that reference to future hypothetical events appears before that to past hypothetical events. In all other respects, the development of Polish children is decidedly precocious when compared with their English speaking peers.

There are three factors that can account for this finding. First of all, the conditional particle *by* is a salient and a unique marker for nonfactive events (hypothetical events included). Secondly, the first distinction to be made is that between factive versus nonfactive reference, and the conditional mood is introduced first in *żeby*-clauses, which have an explicit structure. In contrast, the above distinction is not marked at all in English, and the counterparts of Polish *żeby*-clauses are opaque infinitival constructions. Thirdly, English conditional clauses are expressed by means of the purely conventional use of the past-tense form in the subordinate clause and a *would* + VERB construction in the main clause. The parallel distinction in Polish is realized in terms of transparent constructions in which every single occurrence of nonfactivity is clearly and consistently marked by conditional mood.

6.2. *Acquisition of Complex Sentences*

In general, the acquisition of complex sentences matches the universal pattern described by Clancy, Jacobsen, and Silva (1976), as well as that for English presented in Limber (1973) and Bowerman (1979). At some points, however, it seems to be precocious. In this section I try to present the data on complex sentences in a more or less systematic way. Complex structures which appear before the age of 2 involve coordination, antithesis, sequence, infinitival embedded clauses, and causal adverbial clauses. While conjoined structures seem to develop in a manner which is similar to other languages (cf. Clancy et al.), the two latter ones deserve special attention.

With children who formulate their requests as "desires" rather than as "orders" (Smoczyńska, 1980), the earliest embedding verb is *chce* 'want', e.g. Tenia (1;6): *Jabłko chce jeść* 'apple want to:eat', Kasia (1;7): *Iść na dół chce Kasia* 'to:go on down wants Kasia', Kasia (1;9): *Kasia chce budzić babcię* 'Kasia wants to:wake:up Granny'. These sentences seem more complex than those reported for English at the same age.[29] Before the age of 2, sentences involving a non-coreferential subject of the embedded verb are not used or used incorrectly, e.g. Kasia (1;9): *Kasia nie chce kaszlesz* 'Kasia not wants you:cough', in which the second-singular present-tense form is used instead of a *żeby*-clause (cf. correct *Kasia nie chce, żeby-ś kaszlał-a* 'Kasia not wants that-2SG cough:PP-FEM' (= 'Kasia doesn't want you to cough')).

Another type of early embedding involves the Polish "modals" (or better "pseudo-modals"), both personal and impersonal; e.g. Jaś (1;10): *Można łyżeczką pić herbatkę?* 'One:can with:spoon to:drink tea?'. These were extremely frequent with Kasia, who freely employed a number of constructions with "psuedo-modals" before the age of 2,[30] e.g. Kasia (1;9): *Trzeba przykryć mamę naszą . . . poduszką* 'one:should to:cover mommy our . . . with:pillow', or the following sequence recorded at 1;9 (note the variability of word order): *Musi Kasia jeść obiadek. Musi obiadek jeść. Myć naczynie Kasia musi. Musi Kasia naczynie myć. Garnuszek musi Kasia myć.* 'Must Kasia to:eat lunch. Must lunch to:eat. To:wash:up dishes Kasia must. Must Kasia to:wash:up dishes. Cup must Kasia to:wash:up.' These constructions also seem to appear a little earlier than in English (cf. Limber, 1973).

The earliest adverbial clauses are those providing "reasons" for requests. In "telegraphic" children these are realized by means of mere juxtaposition, e.g. Basia (1;9): *Babciu, zdjąć to, ba to, tu dziura* 'Granny, take it off, ugly this, here hole' [Basia wants Granny to take off her apron because it is dirty and has a hole in it.] In other children the conjunction *bo* 'because' appears, e.g. Kasia (1;8): *Umyć rączkę, bo brudna* 'to:wash hand, because dirty' (This utterance is quite

---

[29]As in English, these are preceded by simpler forms such as 'want apple' or 'want eat'.

[30]It should be noted, however, that Kasia, who began combining words at 1;3, manifested precocious development.

TABLE 6.8
The Proportions of Various Kinds
of Subordinate Clauses
Within Complex Declarative Sentences
Recorded for Jaś
(Based on Przetacznikowa, 1968)

Type of Clause	Age			
	2–3	3–4	4–5	5–6
Complement clauses				
object	21%	9%	12%	14%
Adverbial clauses				
cause	21%	36%	37%	33%
purpose	10%	8%	4%	2%
condition/time	25%	26%	26%	29%
Relative clauses	12%	17%	14%	14%
Other	1%	4%	7%	8%
Number of sentences	165	290	203	280

correct in adult Polish!). It is only later that *bo*-clauses become attached to declarative statements. A *bo*-clause usually follows the main clause. Thus the order of events mentioned is reversed. *Więc* 'so'-clauses which reflect temporal sequence of events are marginal in both child and adult speech.

As for later developments, I shall concentrate on subordinate clauses. Table 6.8 shows the quantitative development of subordinate clauses in declaratives over the period from 2 to 6 years. The figures would be somewhat different if all kinds of utterances were taken into account. Some types of clauses are especially frequent with requests, e.g. cause and purpose adverbials, or with questions, e.g. conditional questions of the kind 'Why if so-and-so, then so-and-so?'. The development of particular kinds of subordinate clauses will be discussed below.

6.2.1. *Complement Clauses.* Object complement clauses emerge at about 2 years. The complement-taking verbs used correspond to those listed in Limber (1973). The most frequent are verba dicendi and sentiendi. With "telegraphic" children, sentences have an English-like structure (see Section 4.1), but most children use a whole range of appropriate connectives, e.g. factive *że* 'that', nonfactive *żeby* 'that', *jak* 'as', etc., as well as a number of wh-words in indirect questions.[31] Errors in the choice of factive versus nonfactive complementizers are extremely rare although examples can be found, e.g. Kasia (2;9): *Obiecuję,*

---

[31]Embedded questions are formally identical to direct questions since neither kind involves inversion.

żeby Michał był grzeczny w szkole 'I:promise so:that Michał would:be good at:school'. This error was obviously caused by the lack of understanding of the verb 'promise'.

As far as the 'ask/tell' problem is concerned, Polish displays certain peculiarities. The meaning of the English *ask* is realized by two distinct verbs, i.e. *zapytać* 'ask:a:question' and *prosić* 'ask:a:favor'. However, another ambiguity arises with *tell* since Polish has no *tell/say* distinction and only the verb *powiedzieć* is used followed by *żeby*-clauses in the sense of 'order' and factive *że* or wh-clauses for 'tell/say'. Although children do not mix the two meanings and use appropriate complementizers, it is often the case that they use *powiedzieć* 'tell/say' instead of *zapytać* 'ask:a:question', e.g. Basia (4;0): *Ale powiem mamie jak trzeba ciąć* 'but I:shall:tell to:Mommy how one:should cut', when *zapytam* 'I:shall:ask' was intended. It could be explained by the semantic relationships between the two verbs: 'asking' constitutes a subclass within a broader class of 'telling'/'saying', and the child can simply use the more general term in the matrix clause without specifying that what he says is a question.

Subject complement clauses emerge later. They occur with some special constructions, e.g. *zdaje mi się, że* 'seems to:me that', *śniło mi się, że* 'dreamed to:me that' (= 'I dreamed'), *prawda, że* 'true that', and they are very infrequent.

6.2.2. *Adverbial Clauses.*   Clancy et al. (1976, p. 74) stated that, "Even in adult language the three concepts of cause, time, and condition are closely related and overlap to some extent." One could argue that these concepts are in fact aspects of a broader category which could be called something like "relationships holding between events" and that the partitioning of the particular meanings among these "concepts" differs from one language to another. Moreover, in the case of Polish, another "concept" is clearly marked, namely that of purpose, as expressed by means of *żeby*-clauses.

Indeed, the means of expressing "relationships between events" are not limited to subordinate adverbial clauses. For instance, what Italian children express by conditional clauses with *senno* 'if not' is translated into English by means of coordinate clauses with *or* (Clancy et al., 1976, p. 78). In Polish the same meaning will be rendered by a *żeby*-clause with the verb negated indicating "a purpose to avoid," for instance, *Nie ruszaj tego, żebyś się nie sparzył* 'Don't touch it, so that you wouldn't burn yourself,' or by a causal *bo*-clause with the verb in future tense, for example, *Nie ruszaj tego, bo się sparzysz* 'Don't touch it because you will burn yourself', with the implicit 'If you do it'; in English one would say *Don't touch it or you will burn yourself.* Similarly, many of Polish *żeby*-clauses will be rendered in English or Italian by means of a causative construction. Each language therefore makes a different categorization of possible relationships, and the same event can be shaped differently by speakers of different languages. It would be interesting to investigate how these linguistic differences affect cognitive development.

6.2.2.1. *Cause.* Causal adverbial clauses emerge in Polish children before the age of 2, and they constitute the most frequent category of subordinate clauses throughout the whole period under study (see Table 6.9). Their functions, however, undergo certain significant changes. Geppertowa (1968), who analyzed the meanings of the conjunction *bo* 'because' as used by several children, distinguished between the following usages: (1) motivational "reasons" (both objective and less frequently, subjective) used to justify actions and requests; (2) statements of objective causality; and (3) beginnings of logical reasoning. Table 6.9 presents the change of meaning of causal adverbial clauses in Jaś, as analyzed in Przetacznikowa (1968). It can be seen that motivational reasons dominate until 4 at which time statements of objective causality begin to prevail. The logical reasoning category can be found at about the age of 3 and becomes more frequent with age.

In the data there are two examples which indicate that there can be nothing causal about *bo*-clauses used as "reasons" for requests, their only function being that of strengthening the request itself, e.g. talking to her mother who was laughing at her, Kasia (2;1) said: *Nie śmiej się mamusiu, bo . . . jest ślisko. Nie wolno się śmiać* 'Don't laugh, mommy, because . . . it's icy. One:is:not:allowed to:laugh' and this example from Miś (2;9): *Ubierz mnie, bo szyby się stłuką.* (Mother: *Dlaczego?*) *Bo szyby się stłuką, jakby mnie się potem ubierało.* 'Dress me, because window will:break' ('Why?') 'Because window will:break, if one dressed me later'. Both were uttered when the child was so angry that he could not look for a more appropriate "reason," and just picked up the first one *bo*-clause he could think of.

6.2.2.2. *Purpose.* Clauses of purpose are reasonably frequent in early stages (see Table 6.8). They are also used to express "reasons," e.g. Michał (2;9): *Ja pluję na indyki, żeby się obraziły* 'I spit on turkeys so:that they:get:of-

TABLE 6.9
Meanings of Causal Adverbial Clauses
in Declarative Utterances of Jaś
(Based on Przetacznikowa, 1968)

	Age			
Categories	*2–3*	*3–4*	*4–5*	*5–6*
motivational reasons	73%	59%	33%	39%
objective causality	25%	26%	42%	39%
logical reasoning	2%	15%	25%	22%
Number of sentences	52	104	76	93

fended'. In fact, both kinds of meanings overlap, which frequently makes the children use a sequence of conjunctions, e.g. Michał (2;3): *Mamo, zapal lampę, BO ŻEBY widziałem, bo jest ciemno* 'Mommy, put the light on, BECAUSE SO:THAT I:see, because it's dark'. Sometimes the purpose clause is quite superflous, e.g. Jaś (3;2): *Chcę tu przyjść, żeby tu byłem* 'I:want to:come here so:that I:am here'. A detailed analysis of various meanings of *żeby* as used by children is given in Geppertowa (1956).

6.2.2.3. *Time/Condition.* Except for hypothetical conditional sentences which are clearly marked as such (see Section 6.1.3), it is impossible to distinguish between temporal and conditional clauses since both are introduced by the conjunction *jak* 'as'. The question should be asked whether this reflects the parental tendencies to use only *jak* when talking to their children, since normally the spoken language provides the option for distinguishing between the two meanings, i.e. *kiedy* 'when/while' and *jeśli* 'if'. If the hypothesis were not confirmed, it would be somewhat surprising if children did not prefer the clear marking of temporal sentences with the connective *kiedy* instead of plurifunctional *jak*. This expectation is supported by the fact that *kiedy* is also a question word for time while *jak* is a question word for manner ('how') as well as a comparative term 'like, as', a complementizer 'as', etc.

Clauses introduced by *jak* emerge early. They usually occur in sentence initial position with the main clause introduced by the semantically empty particle *to*. In Polish, the distinction 'when/while' is not marked in the conjunction. It is expressed through the aspectual marking of verbs in both clauses. The imperfective aspect of the subordinate clause points to simultaneity of events. The perfective verb form indicates that the event referred to in the subordinate clause occurred first. In the sentence *Spotkałem Zosię jak kupowałem chleb* 'I:met:PFV Zosia while I:was:buying:IPFV bread' the past tense *kupowałem* of the imperfective verb *kupować* is used and the word *jak* means 'while'. However, in the sentence *Spotkałem Zosię jak kupiłem chleb* 'I met Zosia when I:bought:PFV bread' the word *jak* is now interpreted as 'when' or 'after' because of the perfective verb *kupić* which appears in the past form *kupiłem*. The perfective aspect of the adverbial clause points to the fact that the action of buying bread occurred first, and the meeting with Zosia, second. It is not marked in the sentence whether the meeting took place at the very moment when the buying was completed ('when') or some time later ('after'). If the clauses are reversed, with the *jak*-clause coming first, the order of mention matches the temporal order of events, and in fact this order prevails in children's data. Temporal sentences with the main clause coming first are usually those referring to simultaneous events (where the order of mention is irrelevant). Further research would be needed to establish which of the two meanings ('when' vs. 'while') appears earlier, nonsimultaneous temporal sentences are more frequent but a large part of them could be better described as conditional clauses.

As for other temporal clauses, the meaning of 'after' is usually rendered by aspectual marking in the *jak*-clause and no special construction is needed. There is, however, a nominalized form of the 'after'-clause involving *po* 'after' plus a verbal noun in locative case. Such constructions are not recorded in the data, except for two examples in Michał (4;1) [asking his mother to give him her pen] Mother: *Nie mogę, bo piszę* 'I:cannot because I:am:writing' Michał: *Na chwilkę albo po pisaniu* 'For a moment or after writing' Mother: *Ale ja teraz piszę* 'But I am writing now' Michał: *To po napisaniu* 'Then after having:written'; and Michał (5;1): *Żołnierz po zwyciężeniu idzie* 'Soldier after having:won goes'. An incorrect use was recorded in Wawrzont at (3;7): *Ja nie chcę za jajkiem od-poczywać* 'I not want after egg to:rest' (= 'I don't want to have a rest after I eat my egg') in which the wrong preposition is used, i.e. the spatial *za* 'after' or 'behind' instead of the temporal *po* 'after'. The gerundial form *napisawszy* 'after:having:written' was not attested in the data. Most probably it is hardly used in spoken language. It occurs, however, in "short stories" written by a 9-year-old.

The meaning of 'before' cannot be rendered by *jak*-clauses, and the special conjunction *zanim* is required which introduces a regular clause with a finite verb. However, I did not find examples of this structure in any of the data studied. The only example is that of an inappropriate use, recorded from Wawrzont at (3;8): *Kto mi wytrze tyłek, zanim ja zrobię kupkę?* 'Who will wipe off my bottom before I pass my B.M.?', where the natural order of events referred to shows that he meant 'after' and not 'before'. This example provides negative evidence, yet the fact that the child tried to use *zanim* can be a signal that he has noticed the structure and will soon learn it.

The notion of simultaneity involves two kinds of transformed structures which are infrequently found in the data. One of them is *przy* 'at' plus verbal noun in the locative case found in Michał as early as (2;6): *Dlaczego przy leżeniu na brzuszku nie chlupnie krwi?* 'Why at lying on belly blood won't spurt (from the nose)?' and in Wawrzont at (3;8): [sitting in his bed and reading books] *Dobrze się czuję przy spaniu* 'I feel well at sleeping'. Another construction involves the present gerund, and it is reported in Rzętkowska's daughter before the age of (4;0): *Wracając do domu spotkałyśmy Czesię* 'While:going:back home we:met Czesia'; in Witek (3;7): *Boś ty nie widziała rozmawiając z ciotką wtedy* 'Because you didn't see (it) while:talking to Auntie then', and also in Wawrzont at (3;11): [Mother had promised him that she would go to sleep at the time when he is going to sleep, but she continues to read a book] Wawrzont: *Śpisz?* 'You:sleep?' Mother: *Ja tak śpię czytając* 'I am:sleeping while reading?' Wawrzont: *Ty tak śpisz czytając?* 'You are:sleeping while:reading' Mother: *Tak* 'Yes' Wawrzont: *To ja będę nie czytając spał, tylko zamknę oczka* 'So I will not while:reading sleep, but I:shall:close eyes'. It seems that the meaning of simultaneity is more available to Polish children than that of 'before' (constructions with 'after' are not necessary since *jak* works equally well).

6.2.3. Relative Clauses

6.2.3.1. *Production.*   In all the children studied the first relatives appear about 2;0, following an adult question 'Which one?' or 'Which kind of?', asked in order to obtain additional information about one of the referents previously mentioned by the child. Children usually answer by using an isolated relative clause, or they precede it with the demonstrative antecedent 'this (one)', e.g. Kasia (2;0): *Daj mi chustkę* 'Give me handkerchief' Mother: *Jaką?* 'Which (one)?', Kasia: *CO LEŻY* 'THAT IS:LYING', and Michał (2;2): *Daj mi tu laski moje* 'Give me my walking-sticks' Mother: *Jakie laski?* 'Which walking-sticks?' Michał: *TE CO SA W MOIM KACIKU* 'Those THAT ARE IN MY ROOM'.

At the same time children learn to construct full complex sentences and to use them when they suppose that some additional information is needed to establish unique reference, e.g. Michał (2;3): *A gdzie te naczyńka CO JE WYJMOWAŁEM?* 'And where are those dishes THAT THEM I:WAS:TAKING:OUT?' and Kasia (2;5): [comments on a picture] *O, goły chłopczyk. A te CO SIE BAWIA to nie są gołe.* 'Oh, a naked boy. And those THAT ARE:PLAYING are not naked', also Kasia (2;6): [to her parents who came back home after an absence] *Zdechła jedna rybka. A te CO NIE ZDECHŁY to pływają.* 'Died one fish. And those THAT NOT DIED are:swimming'. As can be seen from the above examples, contrary to Limber's (1973) observation concerning English-speaking children, Polish children produce subject-embedded relatives early on. Note the use of the empty particle *to* at the beginning of the second part of the main clause.

Children frequently use relatives also to explain what they mean if they do not know the name of an object, e.g. Jaś (4;0); [explains what he wants to play with] *Taki z długą rączką CO MA DZIURKE, taki chcę CO WCZORAJ* 'Such with a long handle THAT HAS A HOLE, such I:want THAT YESTERDAY'. Note that such an incomplete elliptical relative as 'THAT YESTERDAY' instead of 'THAT I HAD YESTERDAY' could be also used in adult Polish. (To satisfy the reader's curiosity, I will say that the object referred to was a strainer.)

All the examples quoted above refer to some knowledge that the listener is supposed to have. If a relative carries some new information about a referent, it is embedded in a kind of "introductory" matrix clause, e.g. Kasia (3;0): *A ja jestem byk potworny CO ZJADA DZIECI, a mamusia byczek mały CO NIE ZJADA DZIECI* 'And I am bull terrible THAT EATS CHILDREN, and Mommy bull little THAT NOT EATS CHILDREN', Jaś (2;10): *Ja mam szoferkę CO MA OKNO* 'I have cab THAT HAS WINDOW', Kasia (2;10): *Ja widziałam takiego psa CO GRYZIE i mnie nie ugryzł i patrzył* 'I saw such dog THAT BITES and (he) me not bit and looked', and Michał (2;2): *Był sobie taki Jacuś CO SIE BAWIŁ CÓRKA* 'Once there was such Jacuś THAT PLAYED WITH:DAUGHTER'. Moreover, although less frequently, relatives of place appear early, simultaneously with the attributive type exemplified so far; e.g. the following complex construction, involving a hierarchical combination of both types, Michał (2;6): *Czy Janek jest w kuchni GDZIE JEST STARY*

ZEGAR CO ROBI TIK-TAK? 'Is Janek in kitchen WHERE IS OLD CLOCK THAT SAYS TICK-TOCK?'

Most children employ almost exclusively the relative pronoun *co* which is indeclinable, and it requires a shadow pronoun or an antecedent copy to make explicit case relationships, although in unambiguous contexts they can be omitted. The relative pronoun *który* which requires case marking and a gender/number agreement with its antecedent occurs only sporadically. These requirements seem to cause special difficulties in constructing prepositional phrases such as 'in which', 'on which', etc., e.g. Michał (2;1): *Jaki wspaniały koń! Ja go kiedyś narysowałem KTÓRY SIĘ NA NIM JEŹDZI* 'What a splendid horse! I him once drew WHICH RIDES ON HIM'. Note the lack of a case marker on *KTÓRY* and the shadow pronoun *NA NIM,* cf. correct *NA KTÓRYM SIĘ JEŹDZI* 'on which one rides'. At 3;2, while looking for the car that he has lost, Jaś said *Ono było na szafie malutkiej KTÓREJ MAM RZECZY NA TEJ* 'It was on cupboard little WHICH I HAVE THINGS ON THAT'. In Jaś's statement there is a correct case ending and gender/number agreement (*KTÓREJ*), but the child could not front the preposition and introduced a shadow pronoun instead, cf. correct *NA KTÒREJ MAM RZECZY* 'on which I have things'. It seems that English forms involving "stranding" of prepositions would be easier to produce.

Among the children studied it is only Michał who mastered the correct use of *który* and employed it frequently in later stages (also with prepositions); other children avoided it throughout the whole period studied, e.g. Jaś (4;3): [telling his mother what he has seen] *Mamusiu, widziałaś ten autobus CO W TYM AUTO-BUSIE NIE BYŁO KIEROWCA* i *ten autobus CO W TYM AUTOBUSIE NIE BYŁO KIEROWCA ciągnął drugi autobus?* Mother: *Pewnie jeden się zepsuł.* Jaś: *Nie zepsuł się tylko nie było w tym autobusie kierowca CO CIĄGNAŁ DRUGI AUTOBUS.* Jaś: 'Mommy, you:saw that bus THAT IN THAT BUS THERE WAS NO DRIVER and that bus THAT IN THAT BUS THERE WAS NO DRIVER was:pulling another bus?' Mother: 'Probably one broke down'. Jaś: 'It not broke down, only there was in that bus no driver THAT WAS:PULLING ANOTHER BUS.' Note the numerous repetitions of the whole antecedent.

The data recorded in writing do not provide adequate cues for the restrictive versus nonrestrictive distinction, which in Polish is clearly marked by different intonation contours. However, in view of the contexts in which the recorded relatives occur, it is highly improbable that any of them could be classified as a definitely nonrestrictive.

6.2.3.2. *Comprehension.* The large corpus of relatives recorded from the Kraków children needs a thorough analysis before the developmental tendencies can be systematized. General properties of children's production of relatives as described above can shed some light upon numerous comprehension studies which result in conflicting observations (see Bowerman, 1979). In the case of Polish, it can be expected that *który*-relatives although difficult to produce, do not involve difficulties in parsing, because of the large amount of explicit cues they provide. The only experimental study concerning Polish relatives is that of Zabielski (1974), who tested comprehension of different kinds of sentences with 3-, 4-, 5-, and 6-year-olds (20 subjects in each age group). For relatives he used the five following items:

1. *Kazik głaszcze psa, który je kiełbasę.*
   'Kazik is stroking a dog that eats sausage'
2. *Tata rozmawia z Jackiem, który trzyma piłkę.*
   'Daddy is talking to Jacek, who is holding a ball'
3. *Jaś goni kota, który uciekł na drzewo.*
   'Jaś is running after a cat which had climbed a tree'
4. *Mama podaje jabłka, które przyniosła na talerzu.*
   'Mommy is serving apples that she had brought on the plate'
5. *Kasia spotkała Jacka, którego boli głowa.*
   'Kasia met Jacek whose head is aching'

For each item three pictures were presented, and the children had to choose the one which corresponded to the sentence uttered by the experimenter. Unfortunately, there is no exact information on the pictures used, except for one example (item 4), where the two "wrong" pictures were those of a boy serving some apples on a plate to a woman and a boy holding an empty plate, being given some apples by a woman (with no plate). The ratios of the correct choice for all the five items were: 65% with 3-year-olds, 60% at 4, 78% at 5, and 90% at 6. These global results indicate that the level of comprehension as measured by Zabielski was relatively high with children aged 3–4, and then gradually increased to reach 90% criterion at 6.

In view of these results, and expecting that Polish *który*-clauses would be easy to understand, I arranged an experiment investigating my son at age 3;10, who freely produced *co*-relatives whenever required by the context. Although only one child was tested, and in a quite informal way, the result obtained is surprising enough to be reported. When presented with four classical types of reversible *który*-relatives (SS, SO, OS, and OO, e.g. 'The cow that kissed the horse kicked the rabbit', etc.) and asked to repeat each of them, he did not make any errors.[32] However, when asked to act-out the same sentences, in most cases[33] he was unable to do so, although additional information was supplied by gender marking in past tense verbs. In his wrong answers he used all kinds of "strategies," described in the literature and summarized by Bowerman (1979). What I found

---

[32]On the other hand, he was quite unable to repeat utterances in which *który* was preceded by a preposition.

[33]Some positive answers were obtained with SS sentences, but they were not consistent enough.

most puzzling, however, were not his scored answers but the nonscored behavior which accompanied the performance. If he used the strategy of main-clause-only, he acted it out quickly and, quite satisfied, looked at me asking for approval. In all the remaining cases, his behavior showed total confusion and apparent inability to retain the whole information given in the sentence. He asked me to repeat the sentence several times or asked 'Who kissed?', 'Who kicked?', etc. after he had performed one of the actions, and still he was unable to solve the task correctly. Clearly, what he found difficult was not sentence processing but rather information processing.

An experimental situation is of course artificial in some way, and significant discrepancies can occur between correct performance in natural contexts and correct solving of experimental tasks. In natural conversation, relatives are understood (and produced) when they are necessary to transmit a message. It can be of no significance to the child whether it is the cow who did the kissing or the rhinoceros. A more relevant fact, however, is that the acting-out task is not congruent with the very function of relative clauses, which usually serve to downgrade one clause with respect to another. When both clauses are equally important, and both provide new information, they are coordinated. The relative transformation reduces one clause to the function of an attribute, which either refers to some prior knowledge or points at some observable features of the referent. In both cases it serves to help the listener in identifying the referent uniquely. Thus the matrix clause usually contains new information (to be remembered or acted out), whereas the relative clause contains the information to be retrieved from memory (old information) or perceptually checked. Even if it is new information, as in the latter case, it is not intended as a message to be remembered, it is totally instrumental with respect to identifying the referent of its antecedent. Now, the experimental task of acting out BOTH actions is comparable with testing the comprehension of *The black cow is swimming* in which the child would be scored for painting the cow black. If the child does not pay equal attention to both clauses, it is precisely because he knows the function of relatives. The strategy of acting-out the main clause only is the most intelligent answer to an inappropriate task requirement.

I carried out another "experiment" in which Wawrzont (3;10) had to choose by means of a relative clause the correct toy out of 10 toys presented to him. The relative clause referred to an action which had been performed by one of the toy-animals before the presentation of the sentence, e.g. 'The animal which has fallen down kissed the elephant' and, subsequently, 'The cow kicked the animal that kissed the elephant' or even 'The animal that the elephant kicked kissed the animal that jumped over the lion'. The child made some errors, but in general his responses were correct and what is most important, there were no signals of confusion while processing these sentences.

All these observations point to the fact that the acting-out tasks do not check comprehension of relatives but much more beyond that. In view of the existence of copious naturalistic data in Polish, and also because of the relatively easy structure of the relatives, it would be profitable to carry out regular experiments with Polish children in which not only the form of relative clauses but also their function were taken into account.

6.3. Delayed Acquisition

Two kinds of phenomena can be discussed here. One is the "late mastery" of forms which emerged relatively early, which is revealed in "late errors." Another phenomenon is that of late emergence of a category which is present in the child's input. Typical late errors involve difficulties with all kinds of irregular forms, the choice of verb stem being the most frequent error of this type (see Section 4.5.1). Among regular forms, most difficult categories—frequently not yet fully mastered by the age of 3 or 4 or beyond—are the following: (1) the genitive plural of nouns (Section 4.3.2.2), (2) the order of morphemes in conditional forms (Section 4.6.3), (3) the first person plural of the past tense (Section 4.4.4), and (4) the distribution of *dwa/dwie* 'two' (Section 4.5.2). It is perhaps worth noting that the very same forms appear as innovations in various Polish country dialects (cf. Bartnicka-Dąbkowska, 1965). As far as late emergence is concerned, apart from some kinds of temporal clauses, which have been discussed in Section 6.2.2.3, several categories will be discussed below.

6.3.1. *Virile vs. Nonvirile Gender Distinction (in Plural).* The distinction of virile/nonvirile gender is relevant for the following linguistic forms: (1) nominative plural (where virile nouns have a specific and highly irregular distribution of endings), (2) accusative plural (with accusative identical to nominative for nonvirile nouns, and accusative identical to genitive for virile), (3) gender agreement in adjectives, pronouns and past tense verbs (see Table 6.6), and (4) forms of numerals.

I have not yet wholly analyzed the data concerning this distinction. All that can be said at this point is that virile nouns and the problems involved in their use do not occur in the child's speech from the very beginning. Note that potential referents for virile gender (men in plural) are rather limited in number, as opposed to all other elements of reality which have nonvirile gender. Moreover, the use of specific virile nouns requires broader social knowledge (in early stages only the plural of the semantically "neutral" *pan* 'man, sir' occurs, which is typically *pany* instead of *panowie*). In general errors emerge after 3 or 4 years, and they occur with respect to all the forms listed above. Mystkowska (1970) reports gender-agreement errors in plural forms as typical for 6-year-olds.

The most interesting category is the accusative. The rule is inconsistent with that for singular where all animate masculine nouns have the accusative-equals-genitive pattern. It can be therefore predicted that the names of animals of masculine gender will cause difficulties in the accusative plural since they are

[+ MASC] and [+ AN] but [- HUM], and therefore [- VIR]. Indeed such errors are frequent, e.g. Janek (6;6) [speaking about snakes]: *Żeby ich zabić* 'in:order them to:kill' (= 'to kill them'; cf. correct *Żeby je zabić*). Here Janek uses the genitive plural *ich* 'them' following the accusative-equals-genitive pattern, rather than the correct nominative plural *je* 'them', according to the appropriate accusative-equals-nominative for nonvirile nouns. The results obtained for Polish could be then compared to those for Russian and Serbo-Croatian. All three languages have the same distribution of accusative forms in singular with clear-cut differences in plural. In Russian all [+ AN] nouns, irrespective of gender, have the accusative-equals-genitive pattern, and in Serbo-Croatian all masculine nouns, irrespective of animacy, have a specific accusative plural ending which is distinct from both the nominative and genitive plural, whereas feminine and neuter nouns have the accusative-equals-nominative pattern. Such a contrastive analysis could perhaps elucidate more general principles of language acquisition.

6.3.2. *Concessive Clauses.* These appear rather late in the data, and not in all children. Przetacznikowa (1968) noted some single instances in Jaś during his sixth year. In other data they were not found except for Miś at (3;7), e.g. *A zając jest on, choć zając wcale nie jest chłopakiem* 'And a hare is a he, although hare is not a boy at all', and Michał, who even tried to use a concessive clause at 3;0 with the following result: *Ja nie wiem jak się robi most, choć umiem to robić* 'I don't know how to make a bridge, although I can do it', but from 3;8 Michał produced correct forms, e.g. (4;1): *Biedny wilczek. Chociaż on jest niedobry, to ja jego żałuję* 'Poor wolf. Although he is bad, I pity him'; (4;1): *Ale ja widziałem jak z zabitego ktoś ściągał skórę, chociaż był dobrym człowiekiem.* 'But I saw somebody skinning a killed one, although he was a good man'; (4;2): *Bardzo ich lubił, choć ich nie znał. Nieznajomych miłował.* 'He liked them very much, although he didn't know them. He loved the strangers.'; and (5;3): *Te ryby w beczce się nie pozjadają, choć mają dopływ do siebie* 'Those fishes in the barrel won't eat one another, although they can reach one another'.

These data show that concessives are cognitively not as difficult as was expected. The failure to observe concessives in the data could be caused either by their low frequency (as compared with other kinds of adverbial clauses), or by the fact that parents do not use them when speaking to their children. Additional evidence for this claim is supplied by Zabielski's (1974) comprehension tests. Children aged 4 succeeded in 40% of the answers consisting of choosing the right picture out of three presented for each of five sentences, e.g. *Piesek uciekł mimo że był przywiązany do drzewa* 'The dog ran away although he was tied to a tree'. This result approximated the chance expectation. Five- and 6-year-olds did much better giving correct responses—in 62% and 82% cases, respectively. Similar results were obtained with nominalized versions of concessives, e.g. *mimo przywiązania do drzewa* 'in:spite:of being:tied to (a) tree'.

6.3.3. *Comparison, Comparatives, and Superlatives.* The earliest occurrences of comparative degree involve the form *większy* 'bigger' as an egocentric expression of power, e.g. Michał (2;1); *Ja jestem większy od tatusia.* 'I am bigger than Daddy' [disappointed by the reaction of his listeners, he looks around, notices a pair of scissors and says] *Od nożyczek jestem większy* 'I am bigger than the scissors'; Michał (2;4) [after he said that his cousin, Paś, is a little boy] Mother: *Paś jest większy od ciebie* 'Paś is bigger than you' Michał: *Tak. Paś jest większy ode mnie, ale ja jestem większy od Pasia* 'Yes. Paś is bigger than me, but I am bigger than Paś'; Michał (3;0): [to his father, who is drawing] *Ładniej rysujesz niż mamuma* 'You draw better than Mom' Father: *Mamuma też ładnie rysuje* 'Mom can also draw well' Michał: *Tak. Mamuma ładniej od ciebie rysuje, ale ty ładniej od mamumy* 'Yes. Mom draws better than you, but you (draw) better than Mom'. While the example of 2;4 could involve an egocentric meaning 'He is bigger, but I am more important', the latter example clearly shows that the notion of comparison itself is misunderstood, and the comparative degree is used in an absolute sense.

All the children studied made errors that consisted of using the positive form in comparative constructions, e.g. Janek (4;3): *Ja jestem duży niż wujek Staś* 'I am big than uncle Staś'; and, Janek (4;3): *Miś ma mało wody niż ja* 'Miś has little water than I'. On the other hand, the following utterance was recorded from Michał, which made explicit the relative value of compared terms: Michał (3;9): [giving cake to his mother] *Ja ci to dam. To jest większe, a ja sam mam mniejsze. Ale też duże* 'I'll give you this one. It is bigger, and I have a smaller one myself. But (it is) also big'. Even so, later on he continues to use the incorrect form: Michał (4;2): *Pies to głuptas od wilka* 'A dog is a fool than a wolf'. Such errors persist all throughout the period studied, besides correct forms, also for the superlative.

Another case is that of the expression of "sameness." Unlike English or French, studied by Karmiloff-Smith (1977), Polish has two separate expressions for the two meanings: 'same one' is expressed by *ten sam* 'this same'; 'same kind' by *taki sam* 'such same'. Surprisingly, children happen to make mistakes when using these forms, although the correct use normally prevails, e.g. one of my twin sons at 3;8 said, *Zobacz, taki sam!* 'Look, the-same-kind-of!' when noticing the person we had met two hours earlier. And, at 5;5 he asked, *Czy pani jest sama?* which literally means 'Is the lady alone?'. He obviously meant to say *taka sama* as he intended to ask whether the pregnant woman seen in the shop was as pregnant as his mother was at the moment.

Such isolated occurrences of the incorrect use of those expressions indicate that there can be someting difficult in the cognitive distinction between the two kinds of sameness. Thus Karmiloff-Smith's (1979) interpretation, which attributed the errors made by French-speaking children mainly to linguistic factors, should perhaps be tested against experimental results obtained for a language like Polish which makes the distinction more clearly.

CONCLUSIONS

7. Universal Operating Principles and the Acquisition of Polish

The data presented in preceding sections will now be compared with what have been claimed to be universal principles used by the child while processing linguistic information (Slobin, 1973). Some comparisons will also be made with available data on other languages.

7.1. *Operating Principle A: "Pay attention to the ends of words."*

Slobin's Operating Principle A refers to receptive processes ("pay attention") but it is mostly based on the data on production and not on comprehension. As for Polish children, they seem to obey this principle in production. They produce word endings earlier than preposed grammatical morphemes (prepositions and prefixes). It is reasonable to assume that if the endings are produced early, they must have been noticed before, according to the general rule that comprehension precedes production. One cannot, however, preclude the possibility that preposed grammatical morphemes are noticed equally early, but for some reason or other they are not used in production until later.[34]

In the Polish language the modification of a word ending is the most widespread pattern of grammatical marking, with inflectional endings being used much more frequently than preposed morphemes. In this situation it is impossible to say whether the facts observed are due to a universal a priori principle, to which Polish happens to fit, or to the child's prior experience with this particular language, which has led to a similar generalization. If we had the acquisition data of a language which uses mainly preposing, and if children, who learn such a language, ignored the commonly-used device for a less frequent postposing device, we could regard Operating Principle A as proven.

Although it does not apply directly to the beginning and ends of WORDS, there is some less clear-cut evidence which challenges the universal validity of Operating Principle A. It can be found in the acquisitional sequence of 14 English grammatical morphemes as established by Brown (1973) and de Villiers and de Villiers (1973). Why are the PREPOSITIONS *in* and *on* among the earliest grammatical morphemes to appear (rank order 2 and 3)? Why are the PREPOSED articles *a* and *the* (rank order 8) acquired earlier than the regular past ending *-ed* (rank order 9) and the third-person ending *-s* (rank order 10)? The answer to these questions can be found in the general characteristics of the English language, in which preposed and free grammatical morphemes are used relatively frequently.

---

[34][WEIST] We are now analyzing the prefixation in the aspectual and locative systems. Our preliminary findings indicate that children from 1;6 to 2;6 develop prefixes surprisingly rapidly, given what has been said about the child's preference to pay attention to the ends of words. [WEIST]

As demonstrated above, English-speaking children discover this morphological pattern relatively early in comparison to Polish children, even if this does not fit the universal Operating Principle A.

7.2. Operating Principle B: "The phonological form of words can be systematically modified."

As was demonstrated above, children not only know THAT the forms of words can be modified, but also HOW they are usually modified in a particular language. We should try to trace back the genesis of this knowledge by analyzing the stages which precede the productive use of morphological markers.

Once the child has gained some basic knowledge of phonology which makes it possible for him to recognize sequences of sounds, his efforts concentrate on segmentation of the flow of speech. This early segmentation cannot be done on the whole string of sounds except for some rough procedures of establishing prosodic units. What the child is most interested in is to extract those sounds which can be paired with some referents present in the situation. This task can be more or less difficult depending on the language the child is dealing with. In some languages, the sounds for such referents as 'dog' or 'wash' do not vary depending on the syntactic context except for the fact that they are sometimes accompanied by some additional sounds which precede or follow the word without affecting its phonological and prosodic shape. In other languages, there is more or less considerable variation WITHIN the word conceived as a prosodic unit. The word can be divided into a constant part (a lexeme) and another part which is subject to variation (a grammatical morpheme). In some languages the constant part itself can include some amount of extra variation (stem alternation, etc.). In order to recognize the meaningful referential parts of the flow of speech, such as 'dog' or 'wash', the child must have developed stategies of IGNORING possible variation involved in their forms (cf. Berman, 1985). Paradoxically enough, an early strategy used by Polish children can be formulated as: "Ignore the ends of words," since it is precisely the ends of words which are subject to variation in most cases. Once the child is able to detect lexemes with some ease, his attention can be turned to what has been ignored so far.

What is puzzling is that in spite of enormous differences between particular languages as to the amount of morphological variation involved, the one-word stage does not seem to be especially protracted in any particular language. In my opinion, it is at the end of this stage that every child has gained passive knowledge of the most widespread patterns of morphological variation used in the language under acquisition. This knowledge is used in later stages, when the child starts to make productive use of morphology.

I would like to emphasize the important role of the FREQUENCY of morphological (or syntactic) PATTERNS used in a language. This factor has not usually been taken into account as only the frequency of particular forms or words has been investigated. To make this point clear, let us compare morphological development in English and in Polish. One would expect the morphology of English, being relatively simple and involving a limited number of grammatical morphemes, to be easier to learn than the complex and highly irregular morphological system of Polish. The facts do not confirm such an expectation, as Polish children start to use inflections productively much earlier than English-speaking children do. They do so because they are forced to notice that the most frequent pattern is WORD = STEM + ENDING. English-speaking children frequently hear forms where WORD = STEM, and instances of WORD = STEM + ENDING are relatively less frequent. On the other hand, Turkish children, who deal with a language characterized by a highly regular agglutinative morphology, use inflections productively as early as the one-word stage (Aksu-Koç & Slobin, 1985).

7.3. *Operating Principle C: "Pay attention to the order of words and morphemes."*

There is one preliminary objection as to the formulation of this Operating Principle, and that is that the word order within an utterance and the order of morphemes within a word are two distinct things. This objection is confirmed by acquisition data from many languages. There are no instances of incorrect ordering of morphemes within a word, whereas examples of the wrong word order are rather numerous. This demostrates that children organize their utterances by taking words as basic units instead of by ordering morphemes like beads on a string. We cannot analyze a child's utterances in terms of morphemes without taking into acount the status of particular kinds of morphemes with respect to words. There are lexemes which are equal to words and lexemes which are not autonomous words. There are grammatical morphemes which cannot occur independently (bound) and those which can be used as words (free). Moreover, since most words are also prosodic units—since they have independent stresss—special attention must be paid to clitics, which have the status of words without this prosodic feature.

I have not tried to describe the use of word order by Polish children. The task is very hard, since the rules governing its use in adult language are so complex that they are not sufficiently well described in linguistic literature. All that can be said at this point is that there are large individual differences with respect to adherence to a rigid word order. Anyway, the freedom of word order is much larger than in English-speaking children, who seem to discover the grammatical relevance of the word-order device very early. As for the pragmatic use of word order by Polish children, it needs further detailed study.

[WEIST] There is no question about the fact that children can process word-order information, and children learning English rapidly acquire a strategy which involves the use of word-order information to recover basic relations. It has been argued that the basic conceptual relationships which are fundamental to sentence processing are ordered, e.g., agent-action-object-recipient (Bruner, 1975, p.

17). The hypothesis implies that those patterns of nouns and verbs which correspond to the ordered basic relations lend themselves to a "natural" one-to-one mapping. It follows from this argument that order information should precede inflectional information as a cue for basic relations. This argument has been made explicitly for a Slavic language by Radulović (1975, p. 117): "Coordination of SVO word order is a prerequisite to the recognition of structural relationships which may be varied in productive language by the use of inflections."

In Polish, word order has the discourse function of distributing given and new information. According to Szwedek (1976), the least marked sentence pattern is GIVEN INFORMATION IN INITIAL POSITION AND NEW INFORMATION IN FINAL POSITION WITH HIGH STRESS. Syntactic and semantic functions are related to the case system as described in Table 6.1 earlier. If word order is naturally related to ordered semantic functions, children learning Polish should be faced with the predicament of first learning to express and retrieve semantic functions with word order and then later learning the discourse function of word order and at the same time having to discover the relationship between the case system and syntactic-semantic functions. Weist's (1983b) experiment on the role of word order, inflectional information, and given-new discourse patterns is relevant to this issue.

Ten children at two age levels (2;6 and 3;6) participated in an experiment in which the children were required to act out sentences with toys (cf. Slobin, 1982). The children were presented with a sequence of two sentences: a context sentence followed by a test sentence. The context sentence established the given information. The test sentences were semantically reversible. One half of the test sentences were inflected and the other half were "uninflected" (i.e. inflected with a zero morpheme where the nominative equals the accusative case). The following two sentences were typical of the inflected and uninflected target sentences: (1) *dziewczynk-a obudzi-ł-a-ø chłopc-a* 'girl-NOM:FEM:SG wake:up-PAST-FEM-3SG boy-ACC:MASC:SG' (= 'The girl woke up the boy') and (2) *autobus-ø stukną-ł-ø-ø samochód-ø* 'bus-NOM/ACC:MASC:SG hit-PAST-MASC-3SG car-NOM/ACC:MASC:SG' (= 'The bus hit the car' or 'The car hit the bus'). Thus, the children received the following six types of problems: (1) given-new & SVO, (2) given-new & OVS, (3) new-given & SVO, (4) new-given & OVS, (5) given-new & $N_1 VN_2$, and (6) new-given & $N_1 VN_2$.

When the test sentences contained unambiguous inflectional information (problems 1–4), the children primarily used the strategy NOMINATIVE CASE = AGENT with the following accuracy: 2;6 at 87% and 3;6 at 92%. When the test sentences were uninflected (problems 5 & 6), the children used priority in word order, i.e. an N_1 = AGENT solution, with the following performance levels: 2;6 at 78% and 3;6 at 82%. The manipulation of given and new information did not have a strong impact on the outcome of the experiment. It is possible, however, that the procedure failed to maintain contextual relevance throughout the period of acting out the target sentences with toys. In any event, the children demonstrated the capacity to use inflectional information as well as word-order information, with no indication that the word-order strategy is more primitive. If anything, precisely the opposite is true. Children who are approximately 2½ years old and learning highly inflected languages such as Polish or Turkish (Slobin, 1982) are more accurate in their capacity to process affixes than American or Italian children are in their capacity to process order information.

We have begun to analyze the longitudinal component of the Poznań research project in ways which will shed some light on the relevance of word-order information for children from about 1½ to 2½ years of age. Some of the preliminary findings have been reported (Weist, 1982). We are working with the hypothesis that child language involves pragmatic, semantic, and syntactic distinctions beginning with the one-word phase. Proportionally, pragmatic distinctions (e.g. statement versus request) and semantic distinctions (e.g. agent versus patient) are the most prominent aspects of this early phase of language acquisition. However, Polish children begin to show evidence for a primitive concept of the syntactic function SUBJECT at about 1½ years old. At this age, children begin to use the subject properties of case, agreement, priority (subject before object), and animacy. Other potential subject properties are absent (see Keenan, 1976). In order to understand the relevance of word order for Polish children, we have to look at the property of priority in the context of other properties of subjecthood.

The nominative case emerges first in Polish, but we cannot argue that it marks the notion of subject until it contrasts with other cases. As the case system evolves, we can be more confident that the nominative case is a productive marker. The nominative, accusative, vocative, and genitive cases are normally found before 1;6. The locative, instrumental, and dative cases evolve somewhat later, e.g. for one of the Poznań children, Bartosz, the last two cases were instrumental (found at 1;8) and dative (at 1;9), and for Zarębina's (1965) Hanna, the last two cases were dative (at 1;8) and locative (at 1;10). Agreement has as its point of departure a frozen third-singular form. In singular, the first-, second-, and third-person distinctions are found with numerous varied examples during the period from 1;7 to 1;10, and with the tense-aspect system emerging at a similar time, agreement in gender in the past and future is added. For Zarębina's Hanna, the distinction between second person and third person occurred between 1;7 and 1;9 and the distinction between second person and first was found at 1;11. Hence, as for case and agreement, the initial signs of these subject properties are found at 1½ years and the full system is productive in many children before 2 years-of-age.

In contrast, priority is not a salient feature of the child's early notion of the subject function. Table 6.10 was taken from our preliminary analysis of the productions of two children (see Weist, 1982). During the period from 1;7 to 2;8 the most frequent utterances containing a finite verb are single word utterances with the subject pronoun deleted. Utterances with two nouns and a verb are relatively infrequent. Given verbs in the indicative mood, the set of single noun

TABLE 6.10
Verb Plus Noun Combinations in the Indicative Mood
Produced by Two Polish Children
in 45-Minute Caretaker-Child Interactions
(from Weist, 1982)

Pattern	Bartosz					Wawrzon					
	1;7	1;8	1;9	1;11	2;0	2;2	2;4	2;5	2;6	2;7	2;8
NOUN:NOM—VERB	15	4	5	2	1	6	1	8	11	14	20
VERB—NOUN:NOM	13	1	2	1	2	5	1	8	5	3	9
NOUN:ACC—VERB	5	10	5	8	4	14	4	5	4	0	2
VERB—NOUN:ACC	3	6	4	9	1	16	11	7	6	8	6

plus verb combinations during this period is sufficiently large to provide a basis for comparison, and the following noun-plus-verb combinations were distinguished: NOUN:NOM + VERB, VERB + NOUN:NOM, NOUN:ACC + VERB, and VERB + NOUN:ACC.[35] Given the combinations with a noun in the nominative case, the noun failed to gain priority in 41% of the sentences for Bartosz and in 34% of the sentences for Wawrzon. In spite of conclusions to the contrary, Radulović (1975) reported similar findings for children learning Serbo-Croatian. While Polish (or maybe Slavic) children develop a priority bias for nouns in the nominative case, there is no period during which word order is artificially restricted. Word order is NOT used as a remedial device to deal with the subject function while inflectional apparatus is being acquired. On the contrary, the acquisition of inflectional distinctions appear to precede the priority bias. Our preliminary work indicates that Polish children have a tendency to place new information in initial position (see also Bates, 1976). During the period from 1;6 to 2;6, children change from a NEW-GIVEN to a dominant GIVEN-NEW pattern. The nominal element with the subject function is often the given information. Hence, the development of a subject priority bias may come about coincidentally because children are learning how to distribute given and new information. [WEIST]

7.4. Operating Principle D: "Avoid interruption or rearrangement of units."

The evidence given in Slobin (1973) as support for this Operating Principle is not satisfactory, since other explanations can be given for the facts cited. Inversion rules are difficult because they contradict other rules which have been

---

[35][WEIST] Verbs in the imperative mood occur most frequently with nouns in the accusative case (see also Smoczyńska, 1976a), and while we have found both verb-ACC and ACC-verb patterns, verb-ACC patterns are clearly dominant. [WEIST]

acquired earlier. It is the contradiction itself which causes difficulties and not the rearrangement of word order as stated in the Operating Principle D.

The evidence quoted as support for the Universal D2 ("whenever possible, discontinuous morphemes will be reduced to, or replaced by continuous morphemes") concerned with discontinuous morphemes is not convincing, since many other factors interfere. For instance, in the French formula of negation *ne* . . . *pas* only the element *pas* is stressed, and in colloquial adult language the element *ne* is practically absent. The fact that Slavic children omit prepositions and not the endings has to do with the status and frequency of free vs. bound morphemes as well as those of preposed vs. postposed morphemes. In general, discontinuous morphemes are used only marginally and as such they can be reduced to one part in order to conform with other more frequent morphological patterns.

Insertion of a word into an already established pattern does not seem to be difficult in any language. There are no cases of adding a preposition to a sentence as a whole instead of placing it before the appropriate word, nor of adjective modifiers placed at the beginning or the end of a sentence instead of being placed close to the head. The only example is that of sentence-external negation appearing in some English-speaking children (Bellugi, 1967). The account of this phenomenon, however, is not conclusive (cf. Bloom, 1970; de Villiers & de Villiers, 1979).

It should also be noted that in an agglutinative language such as Turkish, where long strings of grammatical morphemes occur, the ongoing acquisition of morphology involves the insertion of newly acquired morphemes into the word form used earlier (thus, interruption of a linguistic unit) and this fact does not seem to create any serious difficulties.

7.5. Operating Principle E: "Underlying semantic relations should be marked overtly and clearly."

The role of perceptual salience, as indicated in the Universal E1 ("A child will begin to mark a semantic notion earlier if its morphological realization is more salient perceptually (ceteris paribus)"), would predict that longer endings should be acquired before shorter ones. Accordingly, Polish children should acquire such endings as the dative singular masculine *-owi* or the instrumental plural *-ami* before other, mostly monosyllabic endings, but this is not the case. It should be noted that the formulation itself of this universal points at the receptive, perceptual properties of some markers, whereas facts given as support for the universal concern production. In order to explain those facts we should rather take into account the prosodic consequences of using an ending or omitting it. If an ending is SYLLABIC, which is the case for most Polish inflections, its omission affects the general prosodic shape of the word form. On the other hand, omitting asyllabic endings does not involve such deformations. This factor cannot be ignored when comparing morphological development in various languages.

As for the Universal E2 ("There is a preference not to mark a semantic category by Ø ("zero morpheme"). If a category is sometimes marked by Ø and sometimes by some overt phonological form, the latter will at some stage, also replace the Ø"), it should be said that the lack of tolerance for zero-endings is typical for those languages which have overt syllabic endings in most word forms. English-speaking children are much more tolerant in this respect than Polish children. If they were not, they should not only replace *two deer* by *two deers,* which is a simple regularization, but also invent the missing markers for, say, the first and second person of verbs, which they do not. The explanation is rather simple: for Polish children zero-endings are exceptions, whereas for English-speaking children it is rather the overt marking which is exceptional. Children's behavior therefore can be explained on the basis of Operating Principle F: "Avoid exceptions."

Universal E3 ("If there are homonymous forms in an inflectional system, those forms will tend not to be the earliest inflections acquired by the child; i.e. the child tends to select phonologically unique forms, when available, as the first realization of inflections") does not seem to be supported by the data. English-speaking children should be reluctant to use the multifunctional *-s,* but they are not. Likewise in Polish, the ending *-i,* which serves a number of functions in the noun-declension system (see Table 6.2), is among the earliest endings used by children.

7.6. *Operating Principle F: "Avoid exceptions."*

This Operating Principle is without any doubt universal. Its universality, however, is by no means restricted to language acquisition, but is present in every domain of cognitive development in which the child is trying to generalize on the basis of common experience, while ignoring exceptional instances.

On the other hand, particular universals given under the heading of this principle concern two distinct things. Some of them refer to true exceptions (i.e. instances where a rule is not based on any explicit criteria), while others are concerned with subrules valid for a narrower range of cases than that of a superordinate rule and based on some explicit criteria (cf. the discussion of irregularity vs. formal complexity in Section 4). Exceptions—and I mean true exceptions—are a nuisance for the child and he copes with this difficulty simply by ignoring them or by overregularizing correct irregular forms which have been learned earlier as separate items.

Quite a different problem is that of dealing with formally complex systems, i.e. those which involve a large number of subrules and/or complicated hierarchies of subrules to be applied. The number itself of rules involved does not seem to be especially relevant. What is important is the INTERNAL COHERENCE of the given (sub)system. A system is internally coherent if its subrules do not contradict more general rules and if some proportions are preserved throughout the whole system. For instance, an English-speaking child, who has already learned SV order, will find the inversion rules used for questions difficult since VS contradicts SV. After this rule has eventually been acquired, another difficulty arises with embedded questions that have the surface form of questions, except for the fact they are not inverted.

In order to make this point clear, let us analyze the case of the Egyptian Arabic plural system, which has been repeatedly quoted as a canonical example of formal complexity (Slobin, 1973; Clark & Clark, 1977) and which in fact involves not only formal complexity but also irregularity and incoherence. If the Arabic system has three numbers, i.e. singular, dual, and plural, this is only a sign of greater formal complexity than that of a language like English, for example, which has only two numbers. If plural nouns accompanying numerals above 10 do not take normal plural forms but a zero ending (typical for the singular) this still is a sign of formal complexity and—what is more—an instance of incoherence since a zero ending is already used for the singular. The complexity, as manifested by the existence of two subrules for plural forms, is not in itself the cause of difficulty since a similar situation can be found in Polish and the rules are acquired early and without any problems. (Polish nouns with numerals from 2 to 4 take the regular nominative plural form while those accompanied by numerals above 4 take the genitive plural ending.) The source of difficulty is therefore to be found in the contradiction of using a zero (singular) form to mark a noun for plural. Finally, the fact that most nouns have totally unpredictable irregular plural forms has nothing to do with formal complexity but is a sign of irregularity. To conclude, it seems that choosing the Arabic number system as a canonical example of formal complexity has led to confusion rather than to clarification.

The evidence that complex systems can be acquired easily, provided they are coherent enough, can be found in Polish data on the acquisition of singular declension, where the tripartite gender distinction—masculine/feminine/neuter—is preserved in the whole paradigm with some more subtle subdivisions introduced at some places. On the other hand, the plural paradigm, which involves fewer endings (and fewer rules) than the singular, is more difficult because the proportion is destroyed. In some cases there is no gender distinction at all, and in others, a new distinction of virile/nonvirile gender is introduced, contradicting the distinction between masculine animate vs. inanimate nouns introduced in the accusative singular. Finally, in the genitive, the tripartite distinction is maintained, but neuter nouns are grouped together with feminines, and not with masculines, as they were in the singular.

It is not only the lack of internal coherence of the plural noun declension which makes this subsystem difficult to learn. Another factor is what can be called ''external coherence''—the relation of a subsystem to other (possibly related) subsystems within a language. In this case, rules governing the distribution of endings in plural contradict the rules of a previously acquired related subsystem, namely, that of singular.

Any subsystem is acquired as part of the whole system of a language and its acquisition cannot be analyzed in isolation. If the structure and function of forms under acquisition are coherent with those of related parts of the system, and if the same criteria are maintained across subsystems, these forms are much easier to acquire than in cases where contradictions and incoherences are present. In any system of language there are weak points, incoherences, which are usually the focus of ongoing and future linguistic change, as reflected in adult errors, as well as in dialectal regularization. Child language is especially sensitive to these incoherences, which appear to be the main source of late errors. Child language study may help to detect and interpret them, as children's forms are more systematic and clear than occasional adult modifications.

As far as irregularity is concerned, an important question to be answered in further study is: What are the limits of the child's tolerance for irregularity? What amount of irregularity can be ignored without causing confusion and forcing the child to use "avoidance strategies" such as the inflectional imperialism strategy used by Russian children, who are unable to discover the regular distribution of endings?

7.7. Operating Principle G: "The use of grammatical markers should make semantic sense."

While questioning the validity of this Operating Principle, I do not mean that the child is not sensitive to semantic criteria of rule application. In fact, children usually look for such criteria, since in most cases formal distinctions can be found to correspond to semantic distinctions present in a language. What I want to say is that if there are no semantic criteria of formal distinctions, even purely formal criteria can be easily captured, provided the children needs to use the given forms and the criteria are consistent enough. Whether they are semantic or formal is less important than whether they are consistent or not. Therefore Universal G3—"Semantically consistent rules are acquired early and without significant errors"—is valid because it is a narrow instance of another universal, which says: "ANY consistent rule is acquired early and without significant error" (provided the child needs to use forms involving these rules, which is not necessarily the case). This broader universal, however, is nothing else than a positive formulation of Operating Principle F: "Look for consistencies" instead of "Avoid exceptions." As has already been said, there is nothing specifically linguistic about this operating principle.

The main argument for the easy acquisition of a formal system is presented in Section 6.1.1, where the acquisition of Polish gender is discussed and compared with that of Russian. Other examples are provided by the early acquisition of the distribution of endings based on the phonological form of the stem or the fact, already mentioned, that the formal rule of using the genitive plural of nouns with numerals above four is acquired easily and without errors. In fact, one could reasonably claim that the whole acquisition of phonology is the most convincing case of easy learning of purely formal rules. There is nothing semantic in basic phonological oppositions; they can only be used for semantic purposes, but they are not semantic in themselves.

8. Language Acquisition Strategies: Universal or Language Specific?

The analysis presented above demonstrates that children learning Polish proceed as if they conform to some Operating Principles proposed by Slobin (1973); whereas they are reluctant to do so with respect to some other Operating Principles. Whether they obey or not depends on the features of the particular language they learn. It can be said that these features contribute either to strengthening the validity of a particular Operating Principle, or to weakening (or even abolishing) it. This result contradicts Slobin's assumption that the acquisition of devices which do not fit the universal principles will be delayed. What appears in the data is that children are more likely to reject an Operating Principle which does not fit the particular language rather than to reject a particular linguistic device which does not fit their Operating Principles. Should we therefore admit that the Operating Principles are not independent of the ongoing process of acquisition, but that they are being tested against the data of a particular language and revised according to the results of this verification?

In order to answer this question we have to discuss the origin of the Operating Principles. Slobin is not explicit as far as this problem is concerned, since he avoids discussing the nativism vs. empiricism issue in language acquisition. However, he qualifies the Operating Principles as something which every child brings to bear on the problem of language acquisition (1973, p. 197)—as something preexisting with respect to the process of acquisition. The question I would like to ask is whether the child actually obeys some of the preexisting Operating Principles or does he just behave AS IF he were doing so. To put it another way, are the Operating Principles actually brought to the task of learning a language as something which existed prior to the acquisition process? In view of what has been said above, it seems simpler to propose that the Operating Principles the child is obeying are nothing else than the outcome of his LINGUISTIC EXPERIENCE. Hence, they are the generalizations about a particular language he has made on the basis of prior learning rather than the effect of testing preexisting principles against the specific data. Therefore, the claim is that all the Operating Principles are totally LANGUAGE SPECIFIC, as they are built upon the child's experience with a particular language. Some strategies are universal in the sense that they are present in the acquisition of any language, e.g. "Avoid exceptions" (or, better, "Look for regularities and ignore the remainder"). We should, however, take into account the fact that every language is more regular than irregular, and also that "looking for regularities" is the only economical way to build any kind of knowledge. It is a strategy which is used by the child in many other domains of learning and a long time before he starts to speak.

Another aspect which is not taken into account in Slobin's procedure of establishing language acquisition universals is the system-like nature of human language. The child not only discovers that the language he hears is rule-governed but also that the rules are interrelated to form a system. What is more, while building his own language the child does not memorize a list of unrelated rules but also builds up a system. Here too, there is nothing specifically linguistic about this, since any knowledge is systematized in a similar way. When analyzing the data we are frequently tempted to forget this and to isolate one category (or one rule or one subsystem) and to relate its acquisition to one Operating Principle. However, something can be difficult for the child because it cannot be easily integrated into the already existing NETWORK of rules. In such a case, the rule can be modified to fit the system, or its acquisition can be postponed until the child is able to rebuild his system in order to create a place for the rule in question. In the first case, that of creating an "erroneous" rule which fits the child's system but not the adult's, its genesis should be analyzed in terms of the system as a whole rather than be attributed to a single factor as the necessary and sufficient reason of its formation. As I have tried to demonstrate at many points in this paper (Section 4), the formation of such a rule seems to be due to the joint action of several factors which altogether form the necessary and sufficient reason, although none of them taken alone can be said to be sufficient by itself.

There is still another assumption of Slobin's procedure which is not supported by the data. As demonstrated by Judith Johnston (1985), cognitive development does not seem to be the main pacesetter of linguistic development. It is true that the child cannot express a notion which is not cognitively available at a given moment, but the fact that he is able to grasp a notion does not necessarily involve the appearance of its linguistic expression in his speech. In fact, many semantic categories are not used at the time they are cognitively available, and their emergence in the child's speech should be attributed to other factors.

We are often tempted to conceive of language acquisition as an activity comparable to those of a linguist who is trying to discover the rules of an unknown language. This metaphor does not take into account the obvious fact that the acquisition of language is not an activity per se (as linguists' investigations are) but it is only a marginal outcome of the child's efforts to USE an unknown language. If we look for pacesetters of language development, it is therefore reasonable to expect to find them in the domain of language use. Rules which are acquired early must be not only cognitively available (this being the necessary although not sufficient condition) but also, and foremost, USEFUL. Sometimes the particular language forces the child to acquire a rule early, although its use is based on relatively difficult criteria. In such cases we can think about the influence of language on cognitive development. The rules which are most useful are those which involve frequently-used structures. In this sense the role of frequency must be taken into account.

In order to build a system the child must start by learning the most basic rules of the language. These basic rules are at the same time those which are frequently used since they are present in simple constructions, as well as in more complex ones which are derived from them. In his discovery procedures the child is helped by the special features of the adult language addressed to him, simplified at the beginning and growing more and more complex as the child's linguistic competence develops. We should bear in mind, however, that the adult interlocutor is shaping his utterances according to the child's presumed PASSIVE competence, which significantly outgrows what he is able to produce at a given stage. Therefore, if we investigate the child's speech at the moment when he starts to put words together, we can assume that he knows much more about putting words together than he demonstrates in his early two-word sentences. Yet it is very difficult to establish his passive knowledge, as comprehension techniques are difficult to use at very early stages. On the other hand, we should not assume that all that adults say is processed by the child; an error commonly made by investigators of the input language. The child probably has his own selection procedures, which help him to pay attention to particular features in turn while ignoring the remainder. These procedures are also very difficult to investigate.

As far as early child language is concerned, we should also take into account the fact that most of the exchanges occurring between the child and the adult refer to ongoing activities and objects present in the situation. At this stage, utterances cannot be ambiguous since their meanings can be easily discovered from the situation itself, and this is in fact what both child and adult do without paying much attention to grammatical markers present in utterances. At this stage grammatical markers are quite superfluous since successful communication could be achieved as well if they were not used at all. Most students assume, however, that the child starts to use inflections, word order, or other marking devices in order to disambiguate his utterances. In my opinion, this is not so until much later, when the child starts to talk about other places and other times than those of the speech situation. His early marking devices are introduced only because he wants his utterances to resemble the adult model, and since the word as prosodic unit seems to be the main element of his utterance organization, those markers which are parts of words (and not autonomous morphemes) and which have a prosodic value (syllabic) seem to be the easiest to acquire. This is the only result of crosslinguistic studies performed so far which I would call universal and specifically linguistic. Nevertheless, I do not claim this to be innate but rather resulting from the situation of communication at early stages, which is similar for all children.

To summarize, the child learning a language elaborates a set of processing procedures, which are determined by general cognitive principles on one hand, and the nature of the specific language on the other. These procedures change as the child's linguistic system develops. New procedures appear to deal with new problems and they are always based on the linguistic experience the child has at a given stage. Crosslinguistic study should take into account the dynamic aspects of child language development. We should compare DEVELOPMENT of various systems rather than single out particular facts to be compared without paying attention to their systematic and developmental contexts unless we actually believe in innate linguistic capacities which specify with much detail the order of acquisition. In my opinion, however, there are no data to support such a claim, and the efforts to account for the mysteries of child language development by innate propensity result in explaining ignotum per ignotum.

APPENDIX A

Tips on Polish Phonology and Pronunciation: Grapheme, Phoneme, and English Word [WEIST]

	Stops[a]		
	Bilabial	Dental	Velar
Voiced	b /b/ bad	d /d/ dog	g /g/ gas
Voiceless	p /p/ pan	t /t/ tap	k /k/ karp

[a]Bilabial and velar stops have palatalized and nonpalatalized pairs such as /k/ in *kosz* 'basket' vs /k'/ in *kiedy* 'when'.

	Fricatives[b]			
	Labiodental	Dental	Alveolar	Velar
Voiced				
Nonpalatal	w /v/ van	z /z/ zoo	rz or ż /ž/ treasure	
Palatal	wi /v'/		zi or ź /ź/	
Voiceless				
Nonpalatal	f /f/ fog	s /s/ sod	sz /š/ sheep	h or ch /χ/ loch
Palatal	fi /f'/		si or ś /ś/	hi or chi /χ́/

[b]English palatal fricatives and affricates as in treasure, sheep, loch, jump, reach are pronounced somewhere between the Polish alveolar nonpalatal and the dental palatal counterparts.

		Affricates	
		Dental	Alveolar
Voiced	Nonpalatal	dz /ʃ/ fads	dż /ʄ/ jump
	Palatal		dzi or dź /ʃ/
Voiceless	Nonpalatal	c /c/ cats	cz /č/ reach
	Palatal		ci or ć /ć/

Resonants

		Bilabial	Dental	Alveolar	Palatal
Nasal	Nonpalatal	m /m/ man	n /n/ note		
	Palatal	mi /ḿ/	ni or ń /ń/		
Medial (glides)		ł /u̯/ win			j /i̯/ young
Lateral (liquid)		^	l /l/ leaf		^
Trill				r /r̄/ room[c]	

[c]The Polish r is "rolled."

Vowels[d]

	Front		Back
High	i /i/ peek		u or ó /u/ book
Lower high	y /i̵/ sit		
Mid nonnasal	e /e/ ten		o /o/ mole
Mid nasal	ę /ē/		ą /õ/
Low		a /a/ father	

[d]The English examples only approximate the Polish vowels, e.g. /i̵/ is between *sit* and *set*.

In general, (1) voiced consonants become voiceless in word final position or when followed by a voiceless consonant, e.g. the phoneme /g/ in *śnieg* 'snow' is pronounced [k], cf. [g] in *śniegu*; (2) when followed by some consonants, nasal vowels /ē/ and /õ/ are pronounced as the nonnasal counterparts plus [m], [n], or [ŋ] depending on the place of articulation of the consonant, e.g. the /ē/ in *ręce* 'hands' is pronounced [r̄ence] while in *ręka* 'hand' it is pronounced [r̄eŋka]; and (3) the stress normally falls on the penultimate (prefinal) syllable of polysyllabic words, *písze* '(he):writes', *autóbus* 'bus', and *portmonétka* 'wallet'.

REFERENCES

Aksu, A. A. *Aspect and modality in the child's acquisition of the Turkish past tense.* Unpublished doctoral dissertation, Department of Psychology, University of California, Berkeley, 1978.

Aksu-Koç, A. A., & Slobin, D. I. The acquisition of Turkish. In D. I. Slobin (Ed.), *The crosslinguistic study of child language* (Vol. 1). Hillsdale, NJ: Lawrence Erlbaum Associates, 1985.

Antinucci, F., & Miller, R. How children talk about what happened. *Journal of Child Language,* 1976, *3,* 167–189.

Bartnicka-Dąbkowska, B. *Podstawowe wiadomości z dialektologii polskiej (z ćwiczeniami)* [Basic information on Polish dialectology (with exercises)]. Warsaw: Państwowe Zakłady Wydawnictw Szkolnych, 1965.

Bates, E. *Language and context: The acquisition of pragmatics.* New York: Academic Press, 1976.

Baudouin de Courtenay, J. *Spostrzeżenia nad językiem dziecka* [Observations on child language]. Ed. by M. Chmura-Klekotowa. Wrocław: Zakład Narodowy im. Ossolińskich, 1974.

Bellugi, U. *The acquisition of negation.* Unpublished doctoral dissertation, Harvard University, 1967.

Berman, R. The acquisition of Hebrew, In D. I. Slobin (Ed.), *The crosslinguistic study of child language* (Vol. 1). Hillsdale, NJ: Lawrence Erlbaum Associates, 1985.

Bloom, L. M. *Language development: Form and function in emerging grammars.* Cambridge, MA: MIT Press, 1970.

Bowerman, M. The acquisition of complex sentences. In P. Fletcher & M. Garman (Eds.), *Language acquisition.* Cambridge: Cambridge University Press, 1979. Pp. 285–306.

Brenstiern-Pfanhauser, S. Rozwój mowy dziecka [The development of child speech]. *Prace Filologiczne,* 1930, *15,* 273–356.

Brown, R. *A first language: The early stages.* Cambridge, MA: Harvard University Press, 1973.

Bruner, J. S. The ontogenesis of speech acts. *Journal of Child Language,* 1975, *2,* 1–19.

Chmura-Klekotowa, M. Neologizmy słowotwórcze w mowie dzieci (I) [Morphological neologisms in the speech of children (I)]. *Poradnik Językowy,* 1967, *10,* 433–445.

Chmura-Klekotowa, M. Neologizmy słowotwórcze w mowie dzieci (II) [Morphological neologisms in the speech of children (II)]. *Poradnik Językowy,* 1968, *1,* 19–25.

Chmura-Klekotowa, M. Neologizmy słowotwórcze w mowie dzieci [Morphological neologisms in the speech of children]. *Prace Filologiczne,* 1971, *21,* 99–235.

Clancy, P., Jacobsen, T., & Silva, M. The acquisition of conjunction: A cross-linguistic study. *Papers and Reports on Child Language* (Department of Linguistics, Stanford University), 1976, No. 12, 71–80.

Clark, H. H., & Clark, E. V. *Psychology and language.* New York: Harcourt Brace Jovanovitch, 1977.

Cochrane, N. J. *Verbal aspect and the semantic classification of verbs in Serbo-Croatian.* Unpublished doctoral dissertation, University of Texas, 1977.

Comrie, B. *Aspect: An introduction to the study of verbal aspect and related problems.* Cambridge: Cambridge University Press, 1976.

Cromer, R. F. *The development of temporal reference during the acquisition of language.* Unpublished doctoral dissertation, Harvard University, 1968.

de Villiers, J. G., & de Villiers, P. A. A cross-sectional study of the acquisition of grammatical morphemes. *Journal of Psycholinguistic Research,* 1973, *2,* 267–278.

de Villiers, P. A., & de Villiers, J. G. Form and function in the development of sentence negation. *Papers and Reports on Child Language Development* (Department of Linguistics, Stanford University), 1979, No. 17, 57–64.

Dowty, D. *Word meaning and Montague Grammar.* Dordrecht (Holland): D. Reidel, 1979.

Eisenberg, A. R. *Language development in cultural perspective.* Unpublished doctoral dissertation, University of California, Berkeley, 1982.

Ferrell, J. O. The meaning of perfective aspect in Russian. *Word,* 1951, *7,* 104–135.

Fisiak, J., Lipińska-Grzegorek, M., & Zabrocki, T. *An introductory Polish-English contrastive grammar.* Warsaw: Państwowe Wydawnictwo Naukowe, 1978.

Geppertowa, L. Rozwój rozumienia i posługiwania się pojęciami stosunków wyrażanymi przez spójnik "żeby" u dzieci do lat pięciu [The development of understanding and usage of notions expressed by the conjunction *żeby* in children up to five years old]. *Przegląd Psychologiczny,* 1959, *3,* 47–81.

Geppertowa, L. Rozwój rozumienia i posługiwania się przez dzieci pojęciami stosunków określanymi przez przyimki i spójniki [The development of children's understanding and usage of notions of relations defined by prepositions and conjunctions]. In S. Szuman (Ed.), *O rozwoju języka i myślenia* [On the development of language and thought]. Warsaw: Państwowe Wydawnictwo Naukowe, 1968. Pp. 149-381.

Guillaume, P. Le développement des éléments formels dans le langage de l'enfant. *Journal de Psychologie Normale et Pathologique,* 1927, *24,* 203–229.

Gvozdev, A. N. *Formirovanie u rebenka grammatičeskogo stroja russkogo jazyka*. Vols. I and II. Moscow: Izd-vo Akademii Pedagogičeskix Nauk RSFSR, 1949.

Gvozdev, A. N. *Voprosy izučenija detskoj reči*. Moscow: Izd-vo Akademii Pedagogičeskix Nauk RSFSR, 1961.

Johnston, J. R. Cognitive prerequisites: The evidence from children learning English. In D. I. Slobin (Ed.), *The crosslinguistic study of child language* (Vol. 2). Hillsdale, NJ: Lawrence Erlbaum Associates, 1985.

Kaczmarek, L. *Kształtowanie się mowy dziecka* [The formation of the child's speech]. Poznań: Towarzystwo Przyjaciół Nauk, 1953.

Karmiloff-Smith, A. More about the same: Children's understanding of post-articles. *Journal of Child Language*, 1977, *4*, 377–394.

Karmiloff-Smith, A. *A functional approach to child language: A study of determiners and reference*. Cambridge: Cambridge University Press, 1979.

Kolarič, R. Slovenski otroški govor. *Godišnjak Filozofskog Fakulteta u Novom Sadu*, 1959, 4, 229–258.

Kubit, D. Kształtowanie się negacji w mowie dziecka [The formation of negation in the child's speech]. *Psychologia Wychowawcza*, 1977, 4, 358–377.

Kuczaj, S. A., & Daly, M. J. The development of hypothetical reference in the speech of young children. *Journal of Child Language*, 1979, *6*, 563–579.

Ligęza, M. Interpersonalna funkcja pytań dzieci w wieku 1;6–6;0 [Interpersonal function of questions of children at the age of 1;6–6;0]. *Zeszyty Naukowe Uniwersytetu Jagiellońskiego*, 599 (Prace Psychologiczno-Pedagogiczne, 31), 1979, 119–135.

Limber, J. The genesis of complex sentences. In T. E. Moore (Ed.), *Cognitive development and the acquisition of language*. New York: Academic Press, 1973.

Lotko, E. Język polski z typologicznego punktu widzenia [The Polish language from a typological point of view]. *Polonica*, 1979, 5, 9–23.

Majewicz, A. F. Understanding Aspect (1). *Lingua Posnaniensis*, 1982, *24*, 29–62.

Miller, J. E. Stative verbs in Russian. *Foundations of Language*, 1970, *6*, 488–504.

Mystkowska, H. Właściwości mowy dziecka sześcio-siedmioletniego [The characteristics of a six-seven-year-old child's speech]. Warsaw: Państwowe Zakłady Wydawnictw Szkolnych, 1970.

Olszowska-Guzik, T. Poziom rozwoju struktur gramatycznych języka dzieci sześcioletnich a środowisko społecznokulturowe [The level of development of grammatical structures of six-year-old children and their socio-cultural environment]. Kraków: Uniwersytet Jagielloński, in preparation.

Popova, M. I. Grammatical elements of language in the speech of pre-preschool children. In C. A. Ferguson & D. I. Slobin (Eds.), *Studies of child language development*. New York: Holt, Rinehart & Winston, 1973. Pp. 269–281.

Przetacznikowa, M. Rozwój i rola przysłówków w mowie i myśleniu dziecka do lat trzech [The development and function of adverbs in the speech and thought of a child up to three years old]. *Biuletyn Polskiego Towarzystwa Językoznawczego*, 1956, *15*, 139–193.

Przetacznikowa, M. *Odzwierciedlenie cech przedmiotów i zjawisk w mowie dzieci w wieku przedszkolnym* [Reflection of the features of objects and phenomena in the speech of preschool children]. Kraków: Uniwersytet Jagielloński, 1959.

Przetacznikowa, M. Rozwój struktury i funkcji zdań w mowie dziecka [The development of structure and function of sentences in the child's speech]. In S. Szuman (Ed.), *O rozwoju języka i myślenia* [On the development of language and thought]. Warsaw: Państwowe Wydawnictwo Naukowe, 1968. Pp. 383–629.

Przetacznikowa, M. Semantyczna interpretacja wczesnych stadiów rozwoju składni u dzieci [The semantic interpretation of the early stages of the development of syntax in children]. *Zeszyty Naukowe Uniwersytetu Jagiellońskiego*, 389 (Prace Psychologiczno-Pedagogiczne, 23), 1975, 7–53.

Przetacznikowa, M. Additive and contrastive relations expressed in preschool children's speech. *Polish Psychological Bulletin,* 1976, *7,* 45–54.

Przetacznikowa, M. Functions of inclusive coordinate constructions in early language development. *Polish Psychological Bulletin,* 1978, *9,* 231–238.

Radulović, L. *Acquisition of language: Studies of Dubrovnik children.* Unpublished doctoral dissertation, University of California, Berkeley, 1975.

Ridjanović, M. *A synchronic study of verbal aspect in English and Serbo-Croatian.* Cambridge, MA: Slavica, 1976.

Rispoli, M. *The emergence of verb and adjective tense-aspect inflections in Japanese.* Unpublished master's thesis, University of Pennsylvania, 1981.

Rzętkowska, J. *Przyczynek do badań nad rozwojem mowy dziecka* [Contribution to studies of the development of child speech]. Warsaw: Vol. I, 1908; Vol. 2, 1909.

Savić, S. Review of J. Baudouin de Courtenay, Spostrzeżenia nad językiem dziecka [Observations on child language]. *Journal of Child Language,* 1975, *2,* 326–328.

Schenker, A. M. *Polish declension.* The Hague: Mouton, 1967.

Schenker, A. M. *Beginning Polish.* New Haven: Yale University Press, 1973.

Shugar, G. W. *Relations of language structure and activity structure in the early developmental period.* Unpublished doctoral dissertation, University of Warsaw, 1972.

Shugar, G. W. Text-constructing with an adult: A form of child activity during early language acquisition. In G. Drachman (Ed.), *Akten des 1. Salzburger Kolloquiums über Kindersprache* (Salzburg, 6–8 December 1974). Tübingen (FRG): G. Narr, 1976, 345–356. (a)

Shugar, G. W. Behavior stream organization during early language acquisition. *Polish Psychological Bulletin,* 1976, *7,* 27–36. (b)

Shugar, G. W. Text analysis as an approach to the study of early linguistic operations. In N. Waterson & C. Snow (Eds.), *The development of communication.* Chichester: Wiley, 1978. Pp. 227–251.

Siatkowscy, E. J. W zwiazku z rozprawą Smoczyńskiego "Przyswajanie przez dziecko podstaw systemu językowego" [A response to Smoczyński's dissertation "The acquisition of the fundamentals of the language system by a child"]. *Poradnik Językowy,* 1956, 330–338.

Skorupka, S. Obserwacje nad językiem dziecka [Observations on child language]. *Sprawozdania z Posiedzeń Komisji Językowej Towarzystwa Naukowego Warszawskiego,* 1949, *3,* 116–155.

Slobin, D. I. The acquisition of Russian as a native language. In F. Smith & G. A. Miller (Eds.), *The genesis of language: A psycholinguistic approach.* Cambridge, MA: MIT Press, 1966. Pp. 129–148.

Slobin, D. I. Early grammatical development in several languages, with special attention to Soviet research. *Working Paper No. 11, Language-Behavior Research Laboratory,* University of California, Berkeley, 1968.

Slobin, D. I. Cognitive prerequisites for the development of grammar. In C. A. Ferguson & D. I. Slobin (Eds.), *Studies of child language development.* New York: Holt, Rinehart & Winston, 1973. Pp. 175–208.

Slobin, D. I. Language change in childhood and in history. In J. Macnamara (Ed.), *Language learning and thought.* New York: Academic Press, 1977. Pp. 185–214.

Slobin, D. I. Universal and particular in the acquisition of language. In E. Wanner & L. R. Gleitman (Eds.) *Language acquisition: The state of the art.* Cambridge: Cambridge University Press, 1982.

Smoczyńska, M. Przyswajanie form deklinacji rzeczownikowej przez dzieci w wieku przedszkolnym [The acquisition of forms of noun declension by preschool children]. *Psychologia Wychowawcza,* 1972, *29,* 515–527.

Smoczyńska, M. Development of the transitive sentence pattern. In G. Drachman (Ed.), *Akten des 1. Salzburger Kolloquiums über Kindersprache* (pp. 221–233). Tübingen (FRG): G. Narr, 1976. (a)

Smoczyńska, M. Early syntactic development: Pivot look and pivot grammar. *Polish Psychological Bulletin*, 1976, *7*, 37–43. (b)

Smoczyńska, M. Wczesne stadia rozwoju składni w mowie dziecka [Early stages of syntactic development in child speech]. Unpublished doctoral dissertation, Uniwersytet Jagielloński, Kraków, 1978. (a)

Smoczyńska, M. Semantic intention and interpersonal function: Semantic analysis of Noun + Noun constructions. In N. Waterson & C. Snow (Eds.), *The development of communication*. Chichester: Wiley, 1978. Pp. 289–300. (b)

Smoczyńska, M. Linguistic expression of requests at the early stages of syntactic development. *Paper read at the XXII International Congress of Psychology*, Leipzig, July 1980.

Smoczyńska, M. Uniformities and individual variation in early syntactic development. *Polish Psychological Bulletin*, 1981, *12*, 3–15.

Smoczyński, P. *Przyswajanie przez dziecko podstaw systemu językowego* [The acquisition of the fundamentals of language system by a child]. Łódź: Łódzkie Towarzystwo Naukowe, 1955.

Stephany, U. Verbal grammar in Modern Greek early child language. In P. S. Dale & D. Ingram (Eds), *Child language: An international perspective*. Baltimore: University Park Press, 1981.

Szagun, G. *The development of spontaneous reference to past and future: A crossslinguistic tudy*. Institut für Psychologie, Technische Universität Berlin, 1979.

Szuman, S. Rozwój treści słownika u dzieci [The development of vocabulary content in children]. *Studia Pedagogicane*, 1955, *2*.

Szwedek, A. *Word order, sentence stress and reference in English and Polish*. Edmonton (Canada): Linguistic Research, Inc., 1976.

Tokarski, J. *Fleksja polska* [Polish flection]. Warsaw: Państwowe Wydawnictwo Naukowe, 1973.

Toivainen, J. *Inflectional affixes used by Finnish-speaking children aged 1–3 years*. Helsinki: Suomalaisen Kirjallisuuden Seura, 1980.

Vendler, Z. Verbs and time. In Z. Vendler, *Linguistics in philosophy*. Ithaca, NY: Cornell University Press, 1967. Pp. 97–121.

Verkuyl, H. J. *On the compositional nature of aspect*. Dordrecht: Reidel, 1972.

Wawrowska, W. Badania psychologiczne nad rozwojem mowy dziecka (od 1;0 do 2;3 lat) [Psycholological studies on the development of child spech (from 1;0 to 2;3)]. In S. Szuman (Ed.), *Prace psychologiczne*. Warsaw: Wydawnictwo Naukowe Towarzystwa Pedagogicznego, 1938.

Weist, R. M. The acquisition of temporal deixis in Polish. *Paper read at the Institute of Psychology*, Uniwersytet Jagielloński, Kraków, June 1980.

Weist, R. M. Cross-linguistic perspectives on sentence processing in early patterned speech. Paper presented at the meeting: *Current trends in cognitive science: Conversations in the disciplines*, SUNY Cortland, March 26, 1982.

Weist, R. M. Prefix versus suffix information processing in the comprehension of tense and aspect, *Journal of Child Language*, 1983, *10*, 85–96. (a)

Weist, R. M. The word order myth, *Journal of Child Langauge*, 1983, *10*, 97–106. (b)

Weist, R. M., Wysocka, H., Witkowska-Stadnik, K., Buczowska, E., & Konieczna, E. The defective tense hypothesis: On he emergence of tense and aspect in child Polish, *Journal of Child Language*, 1984, *11*, 347–374.

Wójtowicz, J. Drobne spostrzeżenia o działaniu analogii w mowie dziecka [Some remarks on the function of analogy in child speech]. *Poradnik Językowy*, 1959, *8*, 349–352.

Zabielski, S. *Rozumienie relacji semantycznych przez dzieci w wieku przedszkolnym* [The understanding of semantic relations by preschool children]. Unpublished doctoral dissertation, Uniwersytet Jagielloński, Kraków, 1974.

Zakharova, A. V. Acquisition of forms of grammatical case by preschool children. In C. A.

Ferguson & D. I. Slobin (Eds.), *Studies of child language development.* New York: Holt, Rinehart & Winston, 1973. Pp. 281–284.

Zarębina, M. *Kształtowanie się systemu językowego dziecka* [The formation of the language system of a child]. Wrocław: Zakład Narodowy im. Ossolińskich, 1965.

Zarębina, M. Review of J. Baudouin de Courtenay, Spostrzeżenia nad językiem dziecka [Observations on child language]. *Polish Psychological Bulletin,* 1976, *7,* 61–63.

7 The Acquisition of Romance, with Special Reference to French

Eve V. Clark
Stanford University

> . . . *D'abord (les enfants) ont, pour ainsi dire, une grammaire de leur age, dont la syntaxe a des règles plus générales que la nôtre; et si l'on y faisait bien attention l'on serait etonné de l'exactitude avec laquelle ils suivent certaines analogies . . .*[1]
>
> —J.-J. Rousseau, *Emile* (1762)

---

[1] "At first (children) have, so to speak, a grammar suited to their age, a grammar whose syntax contains rules more general than ours; and if one pays close attention to their language, one is amazed at how well they follow certain analogies . . ."

INTRODUCTION

The first part of this chapter contains a brief grammatical sketch of French, with occasional comments on how other Romance languages diverge from this picture; a brief account of the sources available on language acquisition by children; and a summary of the overall course of development in children acquiring the major Romance languages. The remainder of the review takes up different facets of the language acquisition process in more detail.

1. Descriptive Sketch of French, with Notes on Other Romance Languages

The Romance languages are Indo-European, direct descendents of the varieties of Latin spoken in different parts of the Roman Empire. Romance is commonly divided into several types, depending on geographic location and history. French is considered part of Gallo-Romance (which includes the various languages and dialects that evolved in the northern and southern halves of modern France); Italian belongs to Italo-Romance; Portuguese and Spanish to Ibero-Romance; and Rumanian to Balkan Romance (see Elcock, 1960; Ewert, 1953).

Standard grammars for the major Romance languages are generally available in English and in the language concerned, but the best reference grammars tend to be in the actual language (e.g. Chevalier et al., 1964; Gougenheim, 1962; Grevisse, 1964; Wagner & Pinchon, 1962; Wartburg & Zumthor, 1958, for French; for a list of major grammars for each language, see McKay, 1979). In the sketch that follows, I simply list some of the main characteristics of French and note some of the respects in which other Romance languages differ from the French model. My sketch focuses on syntactic, morphological, and lexical properties, and ignores most phonological ones. I will follow much the same procedure when I turn to the data on the acquisition of these languages by children.

1.1. *Word Order.*   The basic word order in French, and in most Modern Romance languages, is SVO, but according to Greenberg's (1963) criteria, the Romance languages are mixed rather than pure cases. In French, for example, articles, possessive pronouns, and prepositions precede nouns but adjectival modifiers (with some subtle exceptions) follow them (see Waugh, 1977; Wilmet, 1981), as do relative clauses and possessive noun phrases in possessive constructions:

Mon	*livre*	*noir*	*se*	*trouve sur la table.*
POSS.PRO	book	black	REFL.PRO	find on the table

'My black book is on the table.'

Le chien   que   j'ai vu est à Jean.
the dog   REL.PRO   I-saw is to Jean

'The dog I saw is Jean's.'

Italian, Portuguese, and Spanish follow virtually the same pattern as French in these constructions; in Rumanian, though, the article follows and is enclitic on the noun; possessive pronouns also follow their nouns, and the possessor noun in possessive constructions is further marked by being in the dative or genitive case. (Case marking has vanished, except from parts of the pronoun systems, in the other major modern Romance languages.)

The basic word order in French changes from SVO to SOV when the direct object is pronominalized. Pronominalized indirect objects also precede the verb:

Jean donne   le livre   à Pierre.
Jean gives   the book   to Pierre

Jean   le   donne à Pierre.
Jean   OB.PRO:MASC:SG   gives to Pierre

'Jean gives it to Pierre.'

Jean le   lui   donne.
Jean it   IO.PRO:SG   gives

'Jean gives it (to) him.'

Jean lui   donne le livre.
Jean to:him   gives the book

'Jean gives him the book.'

The relative ordering of direct and indirect objects, in either full or pronominal form, is maintained with imperative verbs, but both follow rather than precede the verb:

Donnez-le   à Pierre.
give-it   to Pierre

'Give it to Pierre.'

Donnez -le   lui.
give   -it   him

'Give it (to) him.'

Donnez-lui   le livre.
give-him   the book

'Give him the book.'

The ordering of direct and indirect object pronouns is further complicated when the indirect object is a first or second person pronoun since it then PRECEDES the direct object in declarative utterances but not in positive imperative ones:

Jean   me le   donne.
Jean   me it   gives
'Jean gives it to me.'

Donnez   -le-moi.
give   -it-me
'Give it (to) me.'

(For further discussion of some of complexities of word order with clitic pronouns, see Gaatone, 1976.)

In formal French, the basic sentential negative is discontinuous, *ne . . . pas*, with the first element preceding the finite verb (and any direct or indirect pronoun objects) and the second immediately following it:

Jean   ne donne pas   le livre à Pierre.
Jean   not gives not   the book to Pierre
'Jean doesn't give the book to Pierre.'

Jean   ne   l'a   pas donné à Pierre.
Jean   not   it-has   not given to Pierre
'Jean hasn't given it to Pierre.'

Negative imperatives—where both direct and indirect pronominal objects precede the verb—keep the same relative ordering of negative and pronoun forms as is found in indicative utterances:

Ne   le   lui   donnez pas.
not   it   (to):him   give   not
'Don't give it (to) him.'

Ne   me   le   donnez pas.
not   (to):me   it   give   not
'Don't give it (to) me.'

In colloquial spoken French, however, the element *ne* is normally omitted (Gaatone, 1971).

Dependent clauses in French—relative, adverbial, and certain complement forms—also normally have SVO word order. Allowable exceptions, though, are those object relative clauses in which a main clause noun phrase occurs as the object of the relative clause. In such clauses, although the commoner order is probably OSV, the subject and verb can be inverted to yield an OVS order instead, as in the second example:

SVO: *L'homme   qui   porte   le manteau   est entré*
      the man   who:SUBJ   carries:V   the coat:OBJ   is entered

      dans la maison.
      into the house

      'The man who is carrying the coat has gone into the house.'

OVS: *L'homme   qu'   a vu   Jean   est entré dans la maison.*
      the man   who:OBJ   saw:V   Jean:SUBJ   is entered into the house

      'The man Jean saw has gone into the house.'

For object relatives with a pronoun subject, the order is invariably OSV. When the relative clause head is the subject of the following verb, it is introduced by *qui;* otherwise, when it is the object, it is introduced by *que* (or *qu'* before a verb beginning with a vowel).

Another factor affecting word order is the frequent reliance in spoken French on both left- and right-dislocation.[2] For instance, a subject noun phrase may follow an utterance with a pronoun subject (right–dislocation):

Il mange tout ce qu'il voit,   cet homme.
he eats all that he sees,   that man

'He eats everything he lays eyes on, that man does.'

Or, having introduced the subject noun phrase, the speaker may continue with a pronominalization for the same referent (left-dislocation):

Cet homme,   il mange tout ce qu'il voit.

'That man there, he eats everything he lays eyes on.'

In discourse, right-dislocation tends to serve as a way of making sure one's addressee has the correct referent in mind for the subject pronoun, while left-dislocation serves more of an emphatic function, picking out a particular referent as given, and then, having established it, going on to comment on some aspect of

---

[2]The terms left- and right-dislocation are used here simply for descriptive simplicity, and are not intended to imply anything about the psychological processes of production or comprehension. The phenomenon of dislocation in French is combined with reliance on clitic subject pronouns (*je, tu, il,* etc.) that occur obligatorily with the verb. In Italian and Spanish, dislocation appears just as pervasive, but since the verb forms in these languages mark both person and number, there is no corresponding reliance on pronouns to fulfill those functions.

it. (In colloquial speech, the left-dislocated noun phrase is often followed by a nonsubordinating *que*.) The two forms just illustrated are very common, but occur mainly with subject noun phrases, less often with object ones (except to "fill in" one's addressee).

In Spanish and Italian, where person pronouns are not obligatorily used with finite verbs, the word order appears superficially to be much freer than in French because both subject and object noun phrases can be ordered to reflect the relative importance or thematic relevance of what's being mentioned. However, speakers normally avoid orders that would be ambiguous in the context of the utterance. In general, word order in Romance is highly sensitive to the pragmatic constraints imposed by discourse and cannot be fully described without taking such factors into account.

The word order in yes-no questions in French is usually the same as in declarative utterances, but the question is marked by a final rise in intonation:

> *La fille   monte l'escalier?*
> the girl   climbs the-staircase
> 'Is the girl going upstairs?'

Yes-no questions can be marked in addition by inversion of subject and verb, although this is rare in colloquial speech (Behnstedt, 1973). Inversion can take one of two forms, either an inverted *est-ce que* 'is it that' preceding the utterance, as in:

> *Est-ce que   la fille monte l'escalier?*
> is-it that   the girl climbs the-staircase
> 'Is the girl going upstairs?'

or a pronominal subject and verb inverted directly:

> *La fille,   monte-t-elle   l'escalier?*
> the girl   climbs- -she   the-staircase

In colloquial French, intonation alone is the device most commonly used to mark yes/no questions. Both intonation and inversion, though, are required for *qu*-questions, introduced by *qui* 'who', *quoi* 'what', *où* 'where', *combien* 'how many, how much', *comment* 'how', *pourquoi* 'why', *quand* 'when', and *quel* 'which' in French, as in:

> *Où   va-t-elle,   la fille?*
> where   goes she,   the girl
> 'Where is the girl going?'

(alongside the common colloquial order, *Où elle va, cette fille?*)

Comment	*se*	*mangent-ils*	*les asperges?*
how	REFL.PRO	eat-they	the asparagus

'How does one eat asparagus?'

Quel chien	*regardes-tu?*
which dog	look:at-you

'Which dog are you looking at?'

In many *qu-* questions, one can use *est-ce que* immediately after the question word, and follow it with declarative order. The inversion required may be complex or simple. For instance, when the subject is a noun phrase rather than a pronoun, the inversion requires the addition of an inverted clitic subject to the verb (as in the first two *qu-* questions above). Otherwise, with pronoun subjects, the subject and verb are merely inverted so that the subject follows rather than precedes. As in English, questions introduced by a question word (unlike yes-no questions) do not have rising intonation.

1.2. *Noun and Verb Morphology.* Nouns in French are marked for definiteness, gender (masculine or feminine), and number, by means of their accompanying articles:

	definite		indefinite	
	SG	PL	SG	PL
MASC	*le*	*les*	*un*	*des*
FEM	*la*	*les*	*une*	*des*

Thus nouns nearly always occur with a definite or an indefinite article. After negatives, the form *des* normally becomes *de* (see further Gaatone, 1971). In spoken French, the articles are the primary source of information about gender and number (Chevalier, 1966; Mok, 1968). This is because (a) gender is not entirely predictable from the phonological shapes of words, and (b) number is not normally marked by any modulation in the form of the noun. (The written changes marking plural on nouns are for the most part purely orthographic. Very few nouns have a plural form that is pronounced differently from the singular. Those that do tend to end in *-al* or *-ail*, e.g., *cheval-chevaux, corail-coraux*).

Adjectives agree in gender and number with the nouns they accompany, whether in attributive or predicative position. In the plural, adjective agreement can provide clues to gender that are lacking from the article alone. However, where plurals refer to a mixed-gender set, all forms of adjectives and articles go to the masculine plural. Most adjectives follow their nouns in French, but a few precede, e.g. *petit* 'small', *bon* 'good', *vieux* 'old'; others may be preposed for emphasis. There is also a small group of adjectives that have different meanings, depending on their position, e.g. *ses propres mains* 'his **own** hands' compared to *ses mains propres* 'his **clean** hands', so that the order noun-adjective is not necessarily very rigid in French (see Waugh, 1977). Two or more adjectives modifying the same noun are usually separated by *et* 'and'.

Possession can be indicated in two ways, one of which requires agreement of the possessive pronoun in person with the possessor, and in number and gender with the object possessed. Gender-marking is explicit in the form of the possessive adjective for first, second, and third person singular possessors, but not elsewhere.

Person	SG:MASC	SG:FEM	PL	SG	PL
1	*mon*	*ma*	*mes*	*notre*	*nos*
2	*ton*	*ta*	*tes*	*votre*	*vos*
3	*son*	*sa*	*ses*	*leur*	*leurs*

Otherwise, possession can be indicated analytically, by naming the object possessed and following it with a prepositional phrase introduced by *à* or *de* with a proper name, noun phrase, or a disjunctive (strong) pronoun form, as in: *Le cheval de Jean est là-bas* 'the horse of Jean is over-there' (= 'Jean's horse is over there'), or *Cette voiture est à moi* 'that car is to me' (= 'That car's mine'). The strong pronoun forms, generally used after prepositions, are *moi, toi, lui* (*soi* for impersonal or reflexive uses), *nous, vous, eux* 'me, you, him, us, you, them'. Finally the pronominal possessive forms, like the possessive adjectives, agree in person with the possessor, but in number and gender with the object possessed; they are always used with articles, as in: *C'est le mien* 'it:is the:MASC:SG mine:MASC:SG', (= 'It's mine'). The different ways of marking possession will be considered further with the acquisition data.

Verbs in French mark person, number, tense and aspect, mood, and in a few constructions gender as well. Person is distinguished primarily by the person pronoun that must co-occur with the verb in the absence of a noun phrase subject (that is, a third person form). The pronoun forms in French are shown below with the regular (first conjugation) present tense forms of *donner* 'to give':

Person	SG	PL
1	*je donne*	*nous donnons*
2	*tu donnes*	*vous donnez*
3	*il, elle donne*	*ils, elles donnent*

For first conjugation verbs, the 1st, 2nd, 3rd singular and 3rd plural forms are all pronounced alike (e.g. /don/); the 1st plural verb has a distinct ending *-ons* (e.g. /donō/), and so does the 2nd person plural, *-ez,* but the latter is indistinguishable in pronunciation from the infinitive form in *-er* (both /done/). The accompanying pronouns therefore play a critical role in indicating person.

Number is also marked by the pronouns (and, for the 1st and 2nd persons plural, by the verb ending as well). Although the 3rd person pronouns, singular and plural, are normally pronounced alike, the plural is distinct from the singular before a verb stem beginning with a vowel since the final *-s* on *ils* or *elles* is then pronounced.

Verbs in French can be assigned to one of three conjugations. The largest and most regular, which contains some 90% of all French verbs, is the first, with verb infinitives that end in *-er* (like *donner*). This conjugation is also the one to which most new verbs, both coinages and borrowings, are assigned. The second conjugation is much smaller—some 300 verbs with infinitives in *-ir,* like *finir* 'to finish', shown here in the present indicative for comparison with *donner:*

Singular: *je finis, tu finis, il finit*
Plural: *nous finissons, vous finissez, ils finissent*

(The three singular verb forms are pronounced alike, /fini/, despite orthographic differences, while the plural forms contrast with both the singular and with each other: /finisõ, finise, finis/.) The third conjugation contains the remaining verbs, all irregular in form, including some 30 in *-ir* that do not follow the *finir* pattern, e.g. *dormir* 'sleep', *ouvrir* 'open', *tenir* 'hold', *venir* 'come'; another 30 or so in *-oir,* e.g. *vouloir* 'want', *s'asseoir* 'sit', *devoir* 'must, ought'; and about 100 in *-re,* e.g. *prendre* 'take', *battre* 'hit', *boire* 'drink', *conduire* 'drive'. Most of the verbs in this irregular or catch-all conjugation are very common in everyday use, and so are more frequent than any first conjugation verbs. They are therefore very likely to be used both to and by children.

Tense and aspect in French are both marked through verb endings, but the two systems are intertwined rather than being separate, as in some languages. The indicative has five commonly used forms: present, imperfect, compound past (*passé composé*) and two forms of future.[3] The present picks out the actual time of utterance, while the imperfect and the compound past pick out times in the past, prior to the time of the utterance. The imperfect also marks incompletive aspect, and is used in narrative for background events and descriptions. The compound past in contrast, marks completive aspect, focusing on the result or product of an activity, as in this sentence where the first verb is in the imperfect, and the next two in the compound past:

Les gens regardaient; le chien a suivi les traces et a trouvé la balle perdue.
'The people watched; the dog followed the trail and found the lost ball.'

---

[3]I am deliberately excluding from this sketch forms that are no longer used in modern spoken French, such as the simple past.

The compound past is constructed with one of the two auxiliary verbs, *avoir* 'to have' or *être* 'to be', carrying tense, plus the past participle.

For talking about the future, there are two options: a periphrastic form constructed with the verb *aller* 'to go' plus an infinitive, as in *Je vais partir demain* 'I'm going to leave tomorrow' and the simple future expressed by an inflection added to the infinitive form of the verb, as in *Je partirai demain* 'I'll leave tomorrow'. However, the two forms of the future cannot always be interchanged, since certain uses of the inflectional (simple) future do not allow substitution of the periphrastic form.

There are several other moods besides the indicative (the only one considered so far). The exact number, however, is a matter of dispute and standard grammars show little agreement on this. For the present sketch, I will consider the conditional, the subjunctive, and the imperative. The conditional is generally used in main clauses for tempus irrealis, whether in the future, present, or past. It can be used for describing supposed facts in general (things one's heard tell) even when they are not dependent on prior conditions, and for purpose where that is dependent on potential facts or conditions. It can be used for the indignant rejection of imputations, for the description of imaginary situations (daydreaming or fiction), and for polite (attenuated) requests. (The imperfect tense can also have the latter function, as in *Je venais vous offrir* . . .'I was going to offer you . . .'.)

The subjunctive, like the conditional, is used for certain kinds of tempus irrealis. In particular, it appears in subordinate clauses following verbs of wanting, ordering, forbidding, or begging; after many verbs of feeling, and after verbs of opinion or perception when what is to be conveyed is considered possible rather than actual by the speaker. The subjunctive is also used in certain adverbial clauses, after conjunctions expressing purpose, and after some temporal and conditional conjunctions. It is also used in certain restrictive relative clauses. However, characterizing the precise domain of the subjunctive is extremely difficult since numerous constructions where one might expect to find it instead take the indicative (see Sandfeld, 1965). Most speakers of French today make use only of the present tense subjunctive in colloquial speech. The imperfect tends to be used only in written French, and even there is often avoided.

The imperative is used for ordering and directing. It occurs only in the two second person forms, and is identical to the indicative (without the pertinent pronouns), e.g. for *donner,* the two forms are *donne* (singular) and *donnez* (plural). Directive utterances are often softened by using the politer conditional, as in *Vous plairait-il de recommencer?* 'you it please + COND to start again,' (= 'Would you like to start over again?'). Some interrogative forms are also conventionally used as (less polite) directives, e.g. *Veux-tu finir?* 'want-you to finish' (= 'Finish, will you?') or *Tu ne t'arrêtes pas?* 'You aren't stopping' (= 'Stop it!').

Although the main properties of verb morphology—the marking of person, number, tense, aspect, mood, and gender—are similar in all the Romance languages, there are also numerous differences. In Spanish and Italian, for example, person can be identified from the verb form alone and person pronouns are therefore optional. As a result, subject pronouns tend to be used more for emphasis than in French. And the fact that both person and number are marked in the verb form itself makes for greater flexibility in the word orders commonly used in both Spanish and Italian. Word order can be varied to mark information as given and new, to mark gradients of emphasis, and to tie a following utterance directly to whatever the preceding speaker had said. This, in turn, suggests one might find more variability in word order, even during the early stages of acquisition, for children acquiring Italian and Spanish than for children acquiring French.

1.3. *Word Formation.* New words—that is, new forms with new meanings—can be constructed either by derivation or by composition in French. Most derivation in French is through the addition of suffixes to the base or root word to make adjectives, nouns, or verbs into nouns: e.g. *cherche* 'look,' [V], *chercheur* 'looker, person who looks; researcher' [N]; to make nouns or adjectives into verbs: e.g. *boxe* 'boxing,' [N], *boxer* 'to box,' [V]; or to make the feminine forms of adjectives into adverbs: e.g., *douce* 'quiet,' [ADJ:FEM:SG], *doucement* 'quietly,' [ADV]. Most derivational suffixes fall into the first group, for forming new nouns, but there are productive suffixes of all three kinds, e.g. nominal *-et* (diminutive), *-eur* and *-ier* (both agentive); verbal *-er* and *-ir* to form nouns and adjectives into verbs (the first conjugation *-er* is the more productive of the two) and adverbial *–ment* to form adverbs from adjectives. Finally, there is some reliance on zero derivation in that the infinitive of any verb, when preceded by an article, becomes a noun designating the pertinent activity, e.g. *le monter* 'the climb', *le peser* 'the weighing'.

Composition or compounding in French is much rarer than in the Germanic languages, but there are many idiomatic or lexicalized compounds in modern French. Moreover, the process of compounding seems to be getting commoner, especially in such domains as advertising. In NOUN + NOUN compounds, the most productive pattern, the modifier follows the head, consistent with the word orders elsewhere in the language, e.g. *commis-voyageur* 'salesman-traveler' (='traveling salesman') or *montre-bracelet* 'watch-bracelet' (='bracelet-watch'). The gender of such compounds is determined by the gender of the head noun. Derivation is favored over composition in the other major Romance languages too, with suffixation being the most usual derivational device.

2. Sources of Evidence

The sources for this chapter range from the general observations found in early diary studies (e.g. Egger, 1887; Perez, 1892, Compayré, 1896), to the more detailed notes kept by observers like Deville (1891) or Vinson (1915), and the broader studies carried out by Bloch (1921, 1923, 1924), Descoeudres (1922), and Guillaume (1927a, 1927b). More recent studies include the extensive diary kept by Grégoire (1937, 1947) and Cohen's (1969) summary of his own observations and his comments on the process of language acquisition. Other published diary sources for French include Aimard (1975), Lightbown (1977), François et al. (1978), and Fondet (1979).

These observational studies are supplemented by a large number of experimental studies of comprehension, production, and imitation. In many cases, these complement the observational research directly and help paint the overall picture of acquisition in considerable detail. I will draw extensively on both observational and experimental studies in discussing the course children follow as they acquire French as a first language.

The data available on the other Romance languages appear to be rather sparser: for Italian there are a few published diary sources that provide some general outlines of early development (e.g. Ferri, 1879; Della Valle, 1931; Frontali, 1943–44). These are supplemented by some recent analyses of longitudinal data collected by Parisi and Antinucci (e.g. Antinucci & Miller, 1976; Antinucci & Parisi, 1973; Antinucci & Volterra, 1975; Bates, 1974, 1976), and by several experimental studies of comprehension and production (e.g. Ammon & Slobin, 1979; Bates & Rankin, 1979; Flores d'Arcais, 1978a, b; Johnston & Slobin 1979; Slobin, 1982, Slobin & Bever, 1982).

For Portuguese, there is little published research. There are some studies being carried out in Brazil, though, as well as in Portugal. De Lemos (1975, 1979) analyzed the emergence, longitudinally, of aspectual contrasts; Costa (1976) and Simões and Stoel-Gammon (1979) did research on inflections; Pinto (1982) worked on locative prepositions; Figueira (1977, 1979) examined several facets of lexical development, and Simonetti (1980) looked at early uses of articles and demonstratives. Since most of these studies are of spontaneous production, there is little information available on children's comprehension of Portuguese in the domains studied so far.

For Spanish, aside from the fairly extensive observations of Gili Gaya (1972a), Montes Giraldo (1974, 1976), and a recent ethnographic study of the earlier stages of acquisition (Eisenberg, 1982), many of the studies available are rather sketchy. Moreover, data collected in the U.S. have mostly been collected from children who are, or are becoming, bilingual (e.g. González, 1970). The observational data on production are complemented by some studies of comprehension (e.g. Bermejo, 1975; Lopez Ornat, 1975; Echeverría, 1978), but there is still relatively little published research available on Spanish as a first language.

Finally, for Rumanian, there have been some observational studies of the acquisition of inflections, of overall development, and of children's dialogues (e.g. Slama-Cazacu, 1961, 1962, 1973), but I have been unable to find any detailed diaries or studies of comprehension.

All the sources I consulted, plus a number of others, are listed in the bibliography at the end of this review. This list contains nearly all the studies of syntactic, morphological, and lexical development I have been able to locate, plus a few studies of input language. Wherever possible, I have cited published sources.

3. Overall Course of Development

Among children's first words in French, those based on adult nouns predominate. The earliest verb forms seem to be based on infinitival forms, but initially these are rare. Two-word combinations begin to appear at about 1;6 or so, and with them come the first inflectional endings on verbs, usually used to mark a resultant state. Irregular verbs at this stage (and for some time to come) may appear with several stems, e.g. *boiv-, boir-,* or *buv-* from *boire* 'to drink', and are frequently regularized, often by being added to the first conjugation.

The word order in two- and three-word utterances is fairly variable and, in some children, rarely seems to match the canonical SVO order of declaratives. This could simply be an incidental result of the fact that the children are not yet using person pronouns, combined with a tendency towards postposing subject noun phrases to produce frequent VOS and VS orders. Other children appear to stick much more closely to an SVO or SV order in nearly all their utterances. The first adverbials—*maintenant* 'now', *aujourd'hui* 'today', *ici* 'here'—tend to appear in final position, but may also occur initially. Expressions like *voici* 'here (is)' are nearly always initial.

Pronouns, articles, and prepositions begin to emerge soon after the first word combinations, but the linguistic subsystems they represent take several years to acquire. For example, the first pronominal forms to be picked up are often the possessives *mon* 'my' and *ton* 'your', between 1;9 or so and 2;0. But for self-reference in talking about actions or states, young children will use *bébé* or their own names, then maybe an emphatic pronoun like *moi* 'me', and only after that begin to make regular use of the pronoun *je* 'I' with verbs. When they do begin to use *je,* it is often in the combination *moi je.* Singular pronouns tend to appear before plural ones, and the first and second person contrasts among pronouns appear before third person ones. The latter may be more difficult because they also require gender agreement to be marked. However, gender marking is typically mastered only after number agreement by French-speaking children.

The definite and indefinite articles also begin to appear at this stage, but adult-like uses may take six years or more to appear. Young children, for instance, overuse definite articles. They often treat facts as if they were known to their addressees, tagging noun phrases with definite articles, instead of new, tagged with indefinite articles. Their article use also reveals some errors of gender—errors that suggest that the pertinent articles may not be acquired along with each noun. Again, children appear to master number before gender, just as they do for pronouns. Children also take a long time to work out the intricacies of article-use in negative utterances.

The first preposition to appear is *à* 'at, to'. It is used in both locative and possessive constructions (it is sometimes hard to distinguish the two at this stage), e.g. *Nini à bout* for *Nini à bouche* 'in Nini's mouth' at 1;7,22, *chaise à Pierre* 'Pierre's chair' at 1;8. Other prepositions like *sur* 'on', *de* 'of, from', and *par* 'by', emerge over the next year or so, but many take longer than that for children to work out their meanings and identify the other terms they contrast with.

Early questions are marked by intonation alone for yes/no forms and by reduced versions of *qu-* words; neither question-type appears with any inversion of the subject and verb. The commonest early *qu-* questions are 'where' and 'what' questions, but the forms used are not always equivalent to the adult's. 'Where' questions are introduced by *où* 'where' or *où 'est* 'where is' combined with a noun, as in *où portenaie?* for adult *Où il est, mon porte-monnaie?* 'where's my purse?' and *Où 'est, ton manteau?* for adult *Où il est, ton manteau?* 'where's your coat'. 'What' questions are introduced by zero, as in *Tu fais?* 'you do' for adult *Qu'est-ce que tu fais?* 'What are you doing?'; by a reduced form of adult *Qu'est-ce que c'est que ça?* 'What's that', as in *Ceça?* from *C'est que ça?* or *Que c'est?*, with later (ungrammatical) uses of *que* alone, as in **Qu'i fait là?* 'What's he doing there?' or by the nonconventional *quoi* 'what for what' as in **Quoi à main quoi?* 'what in hand, what' for *Qu'est-ce que tu tiens?* 'What are you holding?'. Early negatives are usually marked with *pas*, from *ne . . . pas* 'not', *a plus* 'no more', and *non* 'no', either preceding or following the utterance being negated. (The *ne* that goes with *pas* is typically omitted entirely in colloquial adult French.) The placing of negatives within utterances develops later, as do the more complex negative forms like *ne . . . rien* 'not . . . anything', *ne . . . jamais* 'not . . . ever', or *ne . . . personne* 'not . . . anyone'.

In the next year, children also begin to use their first subordinate clauses and complements. The first subordinate clauses tend to be introduced by conjunctions like *quand* 'when' and *si* 'if'. Coordinate clauses at this stage are either juxtaposed with no conjunction or joined by *et* 'and', *et puis* 'and then', or *puis* 'then' alone—the latter particularly in describing sequences of events. Besides adverbial clauses with *quand* and *si,* children begin to use the complementizer *que,* apparently as an all-purpose marker of any subordinate clause, including both subject and object relative clauses. The first complements produced, as in English, tend to be those that follow verbs like *vouloir* 'want', with a first person subject in both clauses. With first person subjects, the complement contains an infinitival verb form rather than a full clause with an inflected verb, e.g. *Je veux venir* 'I want to come' versus *Je veux que Pierre vienne* 'I want Pierre to come'. The latter complement-type also requires the subjunctive for the verb following *vouloir*. Different classes of verbs place different restrictions on the possible complement forms, and children start out with a very limited repertoire of such constructions.

Later acquisitions include some of the compound tenses for talking about recent versus remote past; the conditional and subjunctive moods—used primarily for tempus irrealis; complements and subordinate clauses requiring the subjunctive; certain quantifiers and some functions of articles; partitive articles (used with negatives); and some types of relative clauses. Also fairly late is full mastery of the different word orders required with direct and indirect object clitic pronouns, in affirmative versus negative and in indicative versus imperative sentence forms.

Many of the linguistic subsystems in French, as in other languages, take children several years to acquire. For instance, to integrate tense and aspect with temporal adverbials in French, children must have mastered the various functions of tense and aspect for talking about time relations and for assigning information a role in the foreground or background at different stages in a conversation or narrative. This in turn requires coordination of one's perspective as speaker with that of one's addressee, in light of what each participant in the conversation already knows. Each successive "layer" of forms acquired, for instance the addition of tense and aspect markers to the earlier system of simple adverbials like *maintenant* 'now' and *puis* 'then', leads to reorganization of the system or subsystem as a whole, and each successive reorganization may lead to new kinds of errors in the utterances children produce.

Similar factors play a role in the acquisition of definite and indefinite articles, as well as in the acquisition of other noun modifiers such as possessive adjectives or relative clauses. In each case, mastering forms with multiple functions appears to take a long time. Children may find it difficult to identify all the functions that can be carried by a particular word or construction, and even when they have identified them, they are sometimes unwilling to rely on a single form to express multiple meanings and may temporarily construct ungrammatical forms alongside the conventional adult form to carry some of those meanings (e.g. Karmiloff-Smith, 1979).

Two other systems that appear to be acquired late are complex negatives (e.g. *Personne n'a jamais fait ça,* 'no-one has ever done that') and counterfactual conditions. Children as old as 12 still make errors of form in the latter, using conditional verb forms instead of the imperfect indicative in the 'if' clause, e.g. **s'il aurait* for *s'il avait* 'if he had . . .'. This form, however, does appear in colloquial French. Many of the constructions requiring the subjunctive mood are also acquired late. Investigation of still other systems will probably reveal even more late acquisitions both in French and in other Romance languages.

The overall course of acquisition appears both like and unlike that noted for such languages as English or German. The similarities can probably be attributed to the fact that cognitive development is a major determinant of some aspects of language acquisition, especially during the earlier stages. For instance, the sequence of temporal terms and their integration with tense and aspect in the verb shows strong parallels across French, English, and German.

The differences can often be attributed to differences of formal complexity. For example, French, which marks only number and not gender in noun plurals, or Spanish, which marks number and gender, should both be simpler than Polish, which marks number, gender, and case throughout the noun system, and has three genders rather than two. The Romance languages, of course, also differ from each other, for example, in the constraints governing the placement of clitic pronouns. This in turn makes for different word-order rules across languages for the analogous constructions. While in French one might say *Il veut me le donner* 'he wants to:me it to:give', in Spanish one would say *Quiere dar-me-lo* 'he:wants to:give-to:me-it' (='He want to give it to me'). The object pronouns in both languages are clitic on the verb 'to give', but in French they precede it and in Spanish they follow. Differences like these among the Romance languages offer interesting domains in which to assess the effects of formal complexity. At the same time, domains in which there are strong similarities across the Romance languages tend to produce close similarities in the pattern of acquisition. Such parallels are presumably due both to formal similarities in what has to be acquired, and a common cognitive basis.

THE DATA

In this section I first consider some of the typical errors that have been observed in the early speech of children acquiring Romance languages, and then summarize what is known about error-free acquisition and about the timing of acquisition—which constructions are typically acquired early and which late. I then take up the acquisition of articles and of possessives as examples of domains in which children organize and reorganize what they know as they learn more about how particular forms are used. I conclude this section with a discussion of what children know about lexical structure and word-formation, and how this knowledge is revealed by their attempts to extend the vocabulary they have at their disposal.

4. Typical Errors

What are the typical errors children produce in the course of acquiring French? And are the patterns for French also found in the acquisition of other Romance languages? I will present the different kinds of errors noted for French first and then provide as much comparative data as possible from other Romance languages.

4.1. *Overregularization.* Overregularization is very common, particularly for verbs. For children acquiring French, the preferred model for regularization appears to be the paradigm provided by first conjugation verbs (Hiriartborde, 1973), the pattern carried by some 90% of verbs in French. For instance, for infinitives, 2-, 3-, and 4-year-olds commonly use such forms as *rier*[4] from the

---

[4]Starred examples (*) are utterances or examples unacceptable in the adult language either because the form is incorrect or because another expression is the one conventionally used.

stem *ri-* plus *-er* for *rire* 'to laugh', **buver* from the stem *buv-* for *boire* 'to drink', **batter* from the stem *batt-* for *battre* 'to hit', **tiender* from the stem *tien-* for *tenir* 'to hold', or **éteigner* from the stem *éteign-* for *éteindre* 'to turn off'.

For past particles, they construct forms like **couré* from the stem *cour-* for *couru* 'ran', **coudé* from the stem *coud-* for *cousu* 'sewn', **metté* from the stem *mett-* for *mis* 'put', **mordé* from the stem *mord-* for *mordu* 'bit', **éteindé* from the stem *éteind-* for *éteint* 'turned off', **prendu* from *prend-* for *pris* 'took', **pleuvé* from *pleuv-* for *plu* 'rained', and **buvu* from *buv-* for *bu* 'drank'.

Many irregular verbs have two different stem forms in the present tense, and children may make use of either one, e.g. *boi-* or *buv-* from *boire* 'to drink', *veu-* or *voul-* from *vouloir* 'to want', *tien-* or *ten-* from *tenir* 'to hold'. In fact, the same children show considerable variation in which stem they pick initially as the form to use in regularizing such third conjugation verbs.

The existence of two or more different stems also leads to side-by-side usage by the same child of two forms of an infinitive or past participle, apparently with the same meaning. For instance, one 2-year-old used both **mouri* from *mourir* 'to die' and *mort* 'dead'; another used *pris* and **prendu* 'took' in successive utterances. Another child, aged 3;9, used **tiendre* alongside *tenir* 'to hold', and yet another, also 3;9, used the correct *ouverte* alongside **ouvrie* 'opened' from *ouvrir* (see Deville, 1891; Egger, 1887; Fondet, 1979; Grégoire, 1947; Guillaume 1927b; Suppes et al., 1973; Vinson, 1915–16). How prevalent such fluctuations in form are, and whether children regard the different forms as equivalent in meaning has yet to be established.

One possible reason for the prevalence of regularizations based on the first conjugation pattern is the sheer frequency of that pattern in French. One might therefore expect that first conjugation verbs would predominate in young children's speech, but that turns out not to be the case. Guillaume (1927b) found that although first conjugation verbs were the majority when one counted verb types used by 2- to 4-year-olds, they made up only a third of the tokens PRODUCED by the children he recorded. The distributions, by conjugations, are shown in Table 7.1. Moreover, the most frequently used verbs (with only three exceptions) were all irregular third conjugation ones: *être* 'to be', *avoir* 'to have', *faire* 'to do', *vouloir* 'to want', *mettre* 'to put', *prendre* 'to take', and *voir* 'to see', plus *aller* 'to go,' (irreg.). The only first conjugation verbs used with any frequency were *donner* 'to give', *tomber* 'to fall', and *casser* 'to break'. The effect of frequency, then, is an indirect one. Children hear many different first conjugation verbs and appear to extract a paradigm or schema (Bybee & Slobin, 1982) based on that conjugation that they then impose on frequently used second and third conjugation verbs.

The kinds of overregularization noted for French-speaking children have also been noted for children acquiring Spanish. Verbs are again regularized on the model of the first conjugation (*-ar* infinitives in Spanish), which, as in French, comprises the majority of Spanish verbs. But, again as in French, many of the

TABLE 7.1
Percentages of Verbs from Each Conjugation
in French Children Aged 2 to 4
(Guillaume, 1927b)

Conjugation	Types	Tokens
1 -er	76	36
2 -ir	6	6
3 remainder	18	58

Note: Guillaume's 3rd and 4th conjugation figures have been collapsed to conform to the classification in Grevisse (1964).

verbs used most frequently come from one of the other conjugations. For example, 3-year-olds form infinitives like *traigar from the stem *traig-* for *traer* 'to bring' or *pongar from the stem *pong-* for *poner* 'to put', and, from a 5-year-old: *juegar from the stem *jueg-* for *jugar* 'to play' and *cresar from the stem *crec-* for *crecer* 'to grow'.

Spanish-speaking children also rely on the first conjugation pattern in forming the simple past tense, e.g. *saló for *salió* 'he went out' (INF *salir*), *movó for *movió* 'he moved' (INF *mover*), *metó for *metió* 'he put in' (INF *meter*), *perdó for *perdió* 'he lost' (INF *perder*), and in forming the first person present of common irregular verbs, e.g. *tieno from the stem *tien-* for *tengo* 'I have' (INF *tener*), *teno from the stem *ten-* for *tengo* (ibid.), *sabo from the stem *sab-* for *se* 'I know' (INF *saber*). The same regularizing tendency appears with the present participle, e.g. *tengan(d)o from the stem *teng-* for *teniendo* 'holding' (INF *tener*). There also seem to be some confusions of form between second (-er) and third (-ir) conjugation verbs.

Much as in French, most regularization errors for irregular verbs result from the choice of a single stem for all the forms used, e.g. either *teng-* or *tien-* for *tener*. Regularization errors in Spanish appear very early (Montes Giraldo, 1976) and are still prevalent at 5 and older (Brisk, 1974; Dato, 1971; Gili Gaya, 1972a; Medina-Nguyen, 1978). And, again like French, such errors appear to be particularly frequent with common irregular verbs, notably *hacer* 'to do', *poner* 'to put', and *tener* 'to have'.

The data on such regularizations in Italian are sparser, but Frontali (1943–44) noted that verbs were frequently overregularized by children, again on the first conjugation model (-are), the most widespread one for Italian. For example, his daughters formed first conjugation past participles like *diciato from the stem *dic-* for adult *detto* 'said' (INF *dire*), *cuciato for *cucito* 'sewn, mended' (INF *cucire*), and *leggiato for *letto* 'read' (INF *leggere*). Irregular verbs were often first regularized with the construction of first conjugation past participles, e.g.

spingiato for *spinto* 'pushed' (INF *spingere*). Frontali pointed out that such regularizations usually seemed to follow a period of correct uses on the part of younger children (see also Francescato, 1964, 1978). The same observation has been made for French and other languages (e.g. Kuczaj, 1977). Guillaume (1927b) argued that the initial correct uses were simply forms that had been picked up as whole units, and that regularization errors entered as children began to analyze the verb forms being acquired (see Bowerman, 1978).

Similar overregularizations have been observed for Portuguese, both in spontaneous speech (Simões & Stoel-Gammon, 1978) and in elicitation tasks (Costa, 1976; Mediano, 1976).

Overregularizations of nouns in forming the plural are practically nonexistent in French. This, however, is only because the singular and plural forms of most nouns are pronounced in exactly the same way. (Number is indicated through the form of the article, and in certain cases through verb and adjective agreement.) However, when they get a chance, children acquiring French do regularize noun plurals. For instance, some children pick the singular noun stem *cheval* 'horse' for both singular and plural, while others pick the plural *chevaux* for both (e.g. Suppes, Smith & Léveillé, 1973).

In Spanish, children appear to overregularize nouns so that they conform to the major paradigms as far as gender marking is concerned. For instance, nouns ending in a consonant may have a final vowel added, typically -*a* for feminine and -*o* for masculine. This not only clarifies their gender but also regularizes word stress by placing it on the pre-final rather than the final syllable of the word. Thus, Montes Giraldo (1976) noted one child (2;10) who used *una fola* for *una flor* 'flower' (FEM) and *la mujala* for *la mujer* 'the woman' (FEM). Another child (2;11) used *una mana* for *una mano* 'hand' (FEM), and another (2;6) used *papelo* for *papel* 'paper' (MASC).

4.2. *Gender.*   The acquisition of gender in a language like French would appear to pose certain problems since there is no consistent semantic basis to gender assignments. Natural gender provides a basis for classifying a few nouns, but provides no clues to WHERE in the language gender has to be marked, for example, in articles, adjectives, certain participial forms, and so on. The forms of words, on the other hand, appear to offer a more consistent basis for classification according to gender. Certain endings are typically masculine, others typically feminine. And, according to Tucker et al. (1968), adult speakers of French are good at deciding on word gender from the word form alone.

Some errors of gender marking and agreement appear in the early stages of acquiring French. Lightbown (1977, p. 70), for example, noted a number of occasions where the children she was observing used the wrong gender article with a noun, as in *la petit bouton* 'the:FEM little button' for adult *le petit bouton*, *a bateau à voile* 'the:FEM boat with sails' for adult *le bateau à voile* 'the sailing boat', or *maman fait un maison* 'mummy is making a:MASC house' for adult *maman fait une maison* 'mummy is making a house'.[5] This even occurred immediately after appropriate adult uses, as in the following exchanges:

(a) Mo: *Alors, prends un autre couvercle.*   'Well, take another lid then.'

    Ch: **La couvercle.*   'the:FEM lid' (= *le couvercle*)

(b) Mo: *C'est pas la table; c'est l'assiette.*   'It's not the table; it's the plate.'

    Ch: *C'est l'assiette. *Le 'siette.*   'It's the plate. The:MASC plate.'

    Mo: *L'assiette.*   'The plate.'

    Ch: *L'assiette.*   'The plate.'

Errors in the choice of articles provide evidence against the view that children learn each noun in combination with an appropriate (gender-marked) article. One reason they don't may be that each noun can occur with at least four different forms of the article, e.g., *la chaise, une chaise, les chaises,* and *des chaises* 'the:SG, a, the:PL, some chairs(s)'. It would seem easier for children to start out with what's invariant across these forms, namely *chaise* alone. And, as Lightbown (1977) observed, nouns in early word combinations in French typically occur without any article. By age 3, children appear to make few errors in their choices of articles. Occasional late gender errors are reported by Ervin-Tripp (1974) and Valette (1964) for second-language learners aged 5 or 6, as well as by Grégoire (1947). Reports of such errors in spontaneous usage during the early stages, however, are not as common as errors in adjective-noun agreement, e.g. the use of **gros porte* for *grosse porte* 'big door' at 2;5. Both agreement and article errors are corrected automatically by adults in any repetitions or expansions of what the child has said.

Gender errors with articles also appear during the early stages of acquiring Spanish. Mazeika (1973) for example, observed a 2-year-old who, when he used articles, relied almost exclusively on the feminine singular *la* (53 to 2 in the corpus analyzed). The same child also made errors on the indefinite article, e.g. **un camisa* 'a shirt' for *una camisa* (see also Tolbert, 1978). Brisk (1976) noted a similar over-dependence on the feminine article—for 76% of masculine nouns in spontaneous speech; the feminine article was also the one most over-used in children aged 6 and older in an elicitation task she designed to study knowledge of gender. One possibility is that *la,* the feminine article, is more salient for children because its form is always the same. In contrast, the masculine singular article, *el,* takes on the form *al* in combination with *a* 'at, to' and *del* with *de* 'of, from'. These contractions probably make it harder for children to discern the form *el* in those contexts. (Whether French-speaking children ever choose just one of the articles and overuse it in this way is not clear from the data available.)

---

[5]I am grateful to Patsy M. Lightbown for supplying these examples.

Other gender-linked errors that remain prevalent are errors of agreement between nouns and co-referent pronouns. In French, children tend to rely almost exclusively on the masculine singular pronoun *il* 'he'.[6] For instance, one finds utterances like (2;3,24) *i va nir, i va venir* 'he's going to come, he's going to come' for *elle va venir* 'she's going to come' or (2;4,5) *i a sese des boîtes, la 'tite fille* 'he looked for the boxes, the little girl' for *elle a cherché des boîtes, la petite fille* 'she looked for the boxes, the little girl' (= 'the little girl looked for the boxes') (e.g., Grégoire, 1947; Guillaume, 1927b). In both examples, the pronoun fails to agree in gender with the subject noun phrase. Children typically use *il* in place of *elle* 'she' at least to age 3 and often beyond. They acquire the plural feminine pronoun, *elles* 'they', even later than the singular. Cohen (1927) noted numerous errors—uses of *ils*, the masculine plural 'they,' for *elles*—in children up to age 9. Learning how to mark gender appropriately in this domain is clearly complicated by having to integrate two distinct systems: pronouns on the one hand, where the choice of any third person form is governed by the gender of the antecedent noun phrase (whether explicit or implicit) and articles on the other, which, in French at least, are the primary indicators of gender for their accompanying nouns. (Yet another complication is probably the existence of natural gender, assigned on the basis of sex, for animate referents of certain nouns.)

4.3. *Person and Number.*   Person in French is marked primarily by pronouns and only secondarily by the form of the verb. In French, pronunciation for most verbs does not distinguish between the three singular persons, although it does distinguish the three plural forms. In the other Romance languages, person and number are generally marked directly in the verb form for each person whether singular or plural. And, unlike in French, pronouns are not obligatory, for instance, in Italian or Spanish.

Typical errors of person and number consist of errors in pronoun use, in verb form, and in agreement between subject pronouns or noun phrases and their accompanying verbs. Pronouns start to emerge around age 2. Guillaume (1927b) reported very early uses of the third person singular *il* for both masculine and feminine referents, e.g. *(où) il est maman chérie?* 'where is he, dear mommy', where this use of *il est* is probably formulaic (Fillmore, 1979; Lightbown, 1977). First person pronouns, according to Grégoire (1947, p. 95), emerge around 2;0 to 2;6, with *je* and *moi* 'I, me:EMPH' appearing at the same time (at 2;6 and 2;7 for one child, both together at 2;5 for the other). From then on, these pronouns are usually used together in the form *moi je*.

[6]This form is typically pronounced as [i] and could be regarded as a neutralized pronoun form, with gender unspecified, except that this is also the colloquial adult pronunciation always given to *il*. It always contrasts for adults with that given to *elle* (phonetically [ɛ] or [ɛl]).

The next pronouns acquired are the second and third person—in French *toi* or *tu* and masculine *il* (Cohen, 1969). Although Frontali (1943–44) reported for Italian that his children confused the first (*io,* 'I') and second (*tu,* 'you') person forms for a few months before they began to use *io* in self-reference, such errors in pronoun use tend to be prevalent but poorly documented. Nonetheless, the errors that have been recorded seem to parallel exactly those observed in other languages. The difficulty children seem to have here is with the shifting nature of pronouns like 'I' and 'you' such that 'I' is whoever is speaking and 'you' whoever is the addressee (Clark, 1978a).

The next pronouns to emerge in French are the second and third person plural, with the first person plural appearing later still. Like adult speakers of French, children tend to use the third person impersonal *on* 'one' rather than *nous* 'we, us', from as early as age 3. This probably contributes to the late acquisition of the first person plural pronoun. The emergence of each pronoun form is typically marked by a brief period of confusion where the new form is used inappropriately, presumably as children try to work out where each new form belongs in the pronoun system (Grégoire, 1947).

The order of pronouns in French is similar to the order of emergence for verb forms in Italian, where person is marked directly in the verb. First comes the imperative, then the third person indicative, followed by the first person form, and then, only some months later, the first person plural form. These forms emerge by age 2 or 2½ (Frontali, 1943–44).

Because the third person verb form emerges before the first person one, and because the child appears to start by making third person reference to himself (*bébé,* own name, etc.), there are frequent errors of person agreement from the second year on. For example, Montes Giraldo (1976) noted the following in Spanish: *Le tito caco* for *Me quito el saco* 'he, I get rid of the bag' at 1;11, *La lola* for *Me duele* '(it) hurts her, me' at 2;9, and *Dónde se siento yo?* for *Dónde me siento yo* 'where am he/I to sit' at 4;3. There are similar errors of form (and hence of reference, as in the last Spanish example) for reflexive verbs in French (e.g. Grégoire, 1947), but, on the whole, such errors do not seem to be very prevalent.

Children also make errors in number agreement, but these too tend to be early errors. They are rare for nouns in French because there are so few nouns where the pronunciation changes from singular to plural. All children need do is master the plural definite article, *les,* for both genders. They do make errors of agreement, though, between subject and verb, usually by combining a plural subject with a singular verb, or with inappropriate singular pronoun and verb combinations. The former type of error can only be detected, of course, with second and third conjugation verbs, where the singular and plural third person indicative forms are pronounced differently, as in utterances like *Les chats, il vient* for *ils viennent* 'the cats, he's, they're coming'. Most such errors seem to involve a singular verb with a plural subject, rarely the reverse (e.g. Grégoire, 1947;

LaBelle, 1976). Again, such forms are common in some varieties of colloquial French.

In Spanish, number errors are apparently rare although nouns as well as articles are marked for number (with an added -s in most cases). Note that the overt marking of consonant-final nouns by an -o (MASC) or an -a (FEM) observed by Montes Giraldo (1976) makes plurals easier to form: children have simply to add a final -s to all nouns and to the feminine article (la to las). They do have to learn the form los, though, as the plural for masculine singular el 'the'. And an error that does occur quite commonly is the pluralization of mass nouns. Medina-Nguyen (1978), for example, noted such instances as *tus ropas for tu ropa 'your clothes' at 4;4 and *zacates for zacate 'grass' at 3;0. Errors of this type are common in other languages too (e.g. Gordon, 1982), and generally seem to be the result of overregularization, with singular-form mass nouns being treated as if they too were count nouns marked for number with the regular plural ending.

Overall, number errors are not as common as person errors, although they quite often appear to cause the problem when children make agreement errors. Number appears to be mastered first in nouns and articles for all the Romance languages, and only later in pronouns and then verbs. Number in verbs, of course, may be more complicated since the same inflection typically marks both person and number. Although person and number errors appear and then disappear fairly early, their full range has probably not been mapped for any of the Romance languages. There has also been little analysis of the kinds of referential errors children make with person and number.

4.4. *Word Order.*   There seems to be considerable variation in the word order reported for young children acquiring French, and although some of the variations appear erroneous, the data are difficult to interpret. The two monolingual children observed by Lightbown (1977), for example, differed in the degree to which they observed SV or SVO word order in describing actions. Daniel (aged 1;8 at the start of the study) observed SV order with intransitive verbs over 75% of the time, and kept to SVO order over 90% of the time with transitive verbs. (His other utterances were VS and, presumably, VOS order.) Nathalie (1;10) observed SV order with intransitive verbs only 30% of the time, so her normal order was VS at this stage, but she kept closer to the canonical SVO order with transitive verbs (with SVO used about 75% of the time). One problem, of course, in talking about word order from the two-word stage on is the nature of the sequences—whether the terms fall under the same intonational contour or whether there is any pause between the intransitive verb, say, and the subject. Guillaume (1927a) noted few noncanonical orders, and where he did cite one (*fermée fenêtre* 'shut + FEM:SG window,' = 'window shut'), he suggested that it was based on an adult *Elle est fermée, la fenêtre* 'It's shut, the window', with right dislocation of the subject noun phrase. Such examples make it very clear how carefully one needs to take into account any intonational evidence in assessing word order in a language like French.

Bloch (1924), on the other hand, cited a number of noncanonical orders, e.g. *Chapeau chercher 'hat look:for' '(I) look for hat'), or at 2;1, *Maman let li for maman lettre lire 'Mummy letter read' (= 'Mummy read letter'), with the object noun preceding a transitive verb. He also cited one example of three different orders produced in succession by one child: the SVO Papa couper cheveux 'daddy cut hair', followed a few seconds later by: *Cheveux couper papa, couper cheveux papa (with OVS and VOS orders respectively). Such sequences suggest that the child was trying the variant orders in a further attempt to make himself heard. Descoeudres (1922), like Bloch and Lightbown, noted a number of variants on the normal word order in one child (2;9), e.g. VS in *A passé tram 'went:by tram,' (= 'tram went by') and *Mord le vouvou 'bites the doggie' (= 'the doggie bites'), OVS in *Tout mangé moi 'all eaten me'' (= 'me eaten all'), VSO in *A vu moi le papa de Roger 'has:3SG seen me the daddy of Roger' (= 'I saw Roger's daddy'), and VOS in such utterances as *Sais tout moi 'know everything me' (= 'I know everything') or *Chercher le jus moi 'look:for+INF the gravy me' (= 'me look for the gravy'). All four, of course, might be susceptible to the explanation offered by Guillaume, namely that they are based on the order found in adult dislocated constructions. Such variability in word order appears very common in the speech of children acquiring French (Leroy, 1975; Sabeau-Jouannet, 1975). What is difficult to tell is which variants should be counted as word-order errors and which not. This problem is even more acute when one considers word order in Spanish or Italian where the pragmatically governed variations are even more extensive than in French.

Once children acquire their first pronouns, they begin to use more utterances like the following, all in self-reference (Guillaume, 1927a): *Pierre il fait 'Pierre he does,' (= 'Pierre can do it), *Pierre il sait 'Pierre he knows,' (= 'Pierre knows'), Pierre il peut pas 'Pierre can not' (= 'Pierre can do it'), *Pierre il sait 'Pierre he breaks,' (= 'Pierre breaks'), all at 1;8, and Pierre il pleure 'Pierre he cries' (= 'Pierre is crying') at 1;9. Essentially this child is repeating the subject (Pierre) via the pronoun il 'he' with left-dislocation of the subject noun phrase.

French allows both left and right dislocation, and, according to Virbel (1975), French-speaking 4-year-olds nearly always use such constructions in preference to plain noun phrase subjects. In assertions, they tend to prefer right dislocation, e.g. Il est pas mort le roi! 'he's not dead, the king' from Mathieu, aged 4;0, as they do in qu- questions, e.g. Comment i va faire papa? 'how he is going to manage, daddy' (= 'how's daddy going to manage?'), from Sarah, aged 4;0. In yes/no questions, left- and right-dislocations appear to be equally common. Overall, Virbel found that the usual word order in 4-year-old speech was that of sentences with a right-dislocated subject noun phrase (see also LaBelle, 1976). (It was much rarer for children to extract an object noun phrase, although that did occur occasionally.) The prevalence of dislocation yields only at around age 9 to a larger porportion of plain subject noun phrases (Faïta, 1974). And in adult colloquial spoken French, constructions with extracted noun phrases are much more the norm than many grammars would suggest.

The acquisition data available so far suggest that word order at the two-word stage and even later, before children make really consistent use of articles or pronouns in French, is very variable, especially with intransitive verbs. SV and VS are both common. With transitive verbs, some children appear to stick more closely to a canonical SVO order, while others prefer to move the subject noun rightwards (VOS). What is not clear from the accounts given is (a) how much such variations might be attributed to partial imitation of preceding adult utterances, or (b) whether all such sequences fall under a single intonation contour. If not, they could simply be sequences of single words (e.g. Fónagy, 1972) and thus not represent any violations of word order at all.

Another form of word-order error appears to be due to the acquisition of formulae—set expressions not yet analyzed into their constituent parts by the children speaking (cf. Fillmore, 1976, 1979). For example, Vinson (1915–16) reported that his son at 2;3 used *il y a* 'there is/are' both initially and finally. For instance, in initial position (the appropriate one), one finds *Ana baso zadē boku* [7] (=*Il-y-a oiseaux jardin beaucoup* 'it-there-is bird(s) garden lots') for adult *Il y a beaucoup d'oiseaux dans le jardin* 'there are lots of birds in the garden', or * *Kakā zadē pāt ana* (=*Canards Jardin Plant il-y-a* 'ducks garden plant it-there-is') for adult *Il y a de canards dans le Jardin de Plantes* 'there are ducks in the Jardin des Plantes' [a zoo]. Notice that this child also appears to have made an order error in placing the quantifier *beaucoup* 'lots, many' in the first instance cited here, but this would depend on the intonation used.

Yet another kind of word-order error is common with negative placement, both in imperatives and in indicative assertions. For instance, Guillaume (1927b, p. 214) observed several 3-year-olds use wrong orders with negatives. One, for instance, used *Cache-le pas* 'hide-it not' for (*Ne*) *le cache pas* '(not) it hide not' (='don't hide it') and another (3;6) used *Fais-le pas tomber* 'make-it not fall' for (*Ne*) *le fais pas tomber* '(not) it make not fall' (='don't make him/it fall').[8] The object pronoun in negative imperatives should precede the verb. Negatives like *rien* 'nothing' also cause problems: for example, one child (3;2) said *Je lui ai fait rien* 'I to:him have done nothing' for *Je lui ai rien fait* 'I to:him have nothing done' (='I didn't do anything to him'). The negative element, whether *pas* or *rien,* usually follows the finite verb, which in compound tenses is the auxiliary *avoir* (as in the example just cited) or *être*. However, it may be postponed for emphasis in adult speech.

---

[7]The /n/ in *Ana* suggests this child was aiming at (*Il*) *y en a* rather than *Il y a.*

[8]Word-order errors of this type still appear in the speech of children as old as 9 and it is quite possible such forms are also used by adults, at least when speaking to young children. I would like to thank Annette Karmiloff-Smith and Patsy M. Lightbown for discussion on this point.

Finally, a few researchers have noted spontaneous repairs to word order, even in quite young children's speech. For example, Guillaume (1927b) noted the following sequence from a child aged 2;1: *Il faut moi je l'écrive . . . *il faut moi qu'il écrive . . . *il faut moi que je l'écrive . . . il faut qu'elle écrive, Zézette 'I must write him/her . . . he must write . . . I must write him/her . . . she must write, Zézette' (probably for adult: Il faut que j'écrive à Zézette 'I must write to Zézette') and from another child age 2;5: A non pris . . . Renée . . . ça . . . Renée a pris ça 'didn't take . . . Renée . . . that . . . Renée took that'). Such spontaneous corrections suggest that the children's difficulty may sometimes lie as much with getting the pieces of an utterance straight in production as with word order per se (see further Clark, 1982b; Karmiloff-Smith, 1981).

Word-order patterns, however, have not been studied extensively and the prevalence of actual errors past the two- or three-word stage is poorly documented. Sinclair and Bronckart (1972) looked at the interpretations 3- to 8-year-olds made of bare nouns (without articles) and infinitive verb forms in NVV, VNV, VVN, NNV, NVN, and VNN sequences. The younger children tended to treat the verbs as intransitive, with conjoined subjects, or else as imperative. Only around age 5 or 6, which seems comparatively late, did they begin treating the first of two nouns as a subject and the second as a direct object. These data, though, are problematic because of the absence of all the normal articles and verb inflections. The children in this study may have had recourse to special strategies to cope with such odd-sounding sentences.

Aside from Virbel's (1975) detailed study of the usual sentential structures used by 4-year-olds, both in ordinary conversation and in narratives, there has been little observational or experimental study of word order, changes in word order, or of the problems associated with inserting negative particles and their interactions with other sentential elements like object pronouns. One recent exception is the series of studies by Annibaldi-Vion (1980), who compared syntactic and lexical-pragmatic information in 3- to 6-year-olds' comprehension of word order. Although the younger children showed a greater tendency to rely on pragmatic information, all of them appeared to base their interpretations on both kinds of information, with their choices dependent on the type of non-canonical form to be interpreted. What Annibaldi-Vion did not find was any consistent reliance on positional information to identify grammatical subjects or objects (e.g. first noun phrase, or the noun phrase following the verb). This suggests that even quite young children are aware that word order per se, in French, is not the only or even the best clue to identifying grammatical relations.

Young children acquiring Italian also use variable word orders. For example, Bates (1976) found the orders SV and VS were both used by two children at the two-word stage in Italian, with a statistical preference for the VS order. However, once the children began using longer utterances (with a mean length of three morphemes), their word order fluctuated from one recording session to the next, sometimes being predominantly SVO, at other times VOS (see Bates, 1976, pp.

188–189). With increasing age, though, they made more use of SVO. In comprehension, though, Slobin and Bever (1982) found that young Italian children (aged 2 to 5) relied heavily on order to identify subjects and objects in a toy-moving task.

The picture in Italian for production is complicated by the complexity of the pragmatic options available, which allow for several alternatives to an SVO order. Moreover, since the subject is inferrable from the form of the verb, subject noun phrases and pronouns are frequently omitted. The assignment of subject and object is often dependent on the preceding discourse, on the presence of a clitic pronoun preceding the verb to pick out the object, as in *Il libro lo compro io* 'the book it buy I' (= 'I am buying the book'); on contrastive stress; on semantic distinctions that restrict the role of subject to only one of the entities denoted, as in *La mela mangia Giovanni* 'the apple eats John' (= 'John is eating the apple'); on number agreement in the verb; or on person in the verb (with first and second person assigning speaker or addressee as subject). One or more of these cues is always available in Italian, which may account for the relative lack of reliance on word order per se to mark grammatical relations in the speech of young children (see MacWhinney & Bates, 1978).

In Spanish, the commonest word order in young children's spontaneous speech appears to be SVO, but other orders also appear. For instance, Echeverría (1978, p. 65) cited some 2-year-olds who used both OVS and VS orders, e.g. (2;3) *Hatos chiches tene la tia Pachelita* 'lots:of knick-knacks has the aunt Pachelita' (= 'aunt Pachelita has lots of knick-knacks'), (2;11) *Ta durmiendo un pollito* 'is sleeping a chick' (= 'a chick is sleeping'). To check on children's comprehension of different possible word orders in Spanish, he gave 5- to 9-year-olds instructions to act out with toys, using the verbs *perseguir* 'follow', *pegar* 'hit', and *botar* 'throw', in four different word orders: SVO, SOV, OSV, and OVS. In Spanish, as in Italian, person (and hence the subject) is marked in the verb in all tenses. Moreover, the animate direct object for many verbs is marked by the preposition *a*, e.g. *Veo al hombre* 'I+see to+the man' (= 'I see the man'), *Persigue a su hermano* 'he follows to his brother' (= 'he follows his brother'). Echeverría found that the youngest children understood the SVO and SOV orders best. As children got older, they began to do better on OSV, and eventually on OVS too. (He did not report any analysis of the errors they made.) Noncanonical word orders, of course, may be much more transparent in a discourse setting than when presented in isolation as instructions to move toys. Further information is needed here on how younger children (and adults) use different word orders in conversation, and how pragmatic factors affect the orders used (cf. Bates, McNew, MacWhinney, Devescovi, & Smith, 1982).

4.5. *Pronoun Placement.* The pronominal system in French consists of three subsystems: emphatic or tonic pronouns, on the one hand, used in dislocated noun phrase position and in prepositional phrases (*moi, toi, lui*), and clitic pronouns, on the other, used for subjects (*je, tu, il*) and for objects preceding the verb (*me, te, le, la, les,* etc., for direct objects; *me, te, lui, leur* for indirect ones). With the first and second person indirect objects (IO), the indirect pronouns precede the direct object (DO) ones: *Marie me le donne* 'Marie to:me it gives' (= 'Marie gives it to me'), but with third person indirect objects, the order is reversed to DO before IO: *Marie le lui donne* 'Maries it to:him gives' (= 'Marie gives it to him'). Two bilingual (French-English) children studied by Connors, Nuckle, and Greene (1981) used double clitic pronouns, but tended to avoid third person indirect objects where the order is DO-IO rather than IO-DO used everywhere else. Connors et al. followed up these observations by collecting experimental data in a production task designed to elicit such constructions. Monolingual French-speaking 4-year-olds made frequent order errors. For example, they would say things like **Le monsieur leur le donne* 'the man to:them it gives' instead of *Le monsieur le leur donne* 'the man it to:them gives' (= 'the man gives it to them'). The children also made order errors in an imitation task, and consistently placed the indirect object pronoun before the direct object one. In a survey of 4- and 8-year-olds' spontaneous speech, however, Bautier-Castaing (1977) found no cases of double clitic pronouns being used. In fact, the younger children rarely used even direct object clitics alone. In answering questions, for instance, they typically repeated the full object noun phrase, as in *Qu'est-ce qu'il a fait de ses chaussures?—Il a enlevé ses chaussures* 'What did he do with his shoes?—He took his shoes off'. The older children, though, would reply with *Il les a enlevées* 'He took them off'. These data suggest that clitic object pronouns are a fairly late acquisition.

Children also used tonic forms alone as subjects, where adults use the tonic pronoun in combination with a clitic subject pronoun. For example, Connors et al. reported that one of the 4-year-olds they followed longitudinally used utterances like **Moi l'a oublié* 'me it has:3SG forgotten' instead of *Moi, je l'ai oublié* 'me, I it have:1SG forgotten' (= 'I forgot it') or **Toi le sais* 'you it know' for *Toi, tu le sais* 'You, you it know' (= 'YOU know it'). They also occasionally used *lui,* the tonic form, following the verb, in lieu of the clitic object, *le,* preceding it, e.g. **Deux fois, on avait lui* 'two times, one had it' pointing to a letter T, for *Deux fois, on l'avait* 'two times, one it had' (= 'twice we had it') or, under similar circumstances, *moi* for *me,* e.g. **Là, je vas faire moi* 'there, I go:2/3SG to do me' for *Là, je vais me dessiner* 'there, I go:1SG me to:draw' (= 'there, I'm going to draw myself'). They also used *à elle* 'to her' after the verb instead of *lui* before it, e.g. **Je dis à elle* 'I say to her' for *Je lui dis* 'I to:her say' (= 'I say to her'). Again, such forms do appear in adult colloquial speech too.

Lastly, children make mistakes when they combine clitic object pronouns with imperative verbs. Guillaume (1927b) reported errors like **Cache-le pas* 'hide-it not' for *(Ne) le cache pas* '(Not) it hide not' (= 'Don't hide it'), presumably on the model of the positive imperative plus direct object, *Cache-le* 'hide-it', and **Fais-le pas tomber* 'make-it not to:fall' for *(Ne) le fais pas tomber*

'(Not) it make not to:fall' (= 'don't make it fall'), both from 3-year-olds. Unfortunately, there appear to be no data available on such constructions in other Romance languages, where the rules for ordering clitics generally differ, at least for some constructions, from those for French.

To summarize, the errors children make in pronoun placement appear to reflect generalizations made from more widely-used patterns. The order IO-DO, for instance, holds for all first- and second-person indirect and direct object combinations. Only with third-person clitics is the order reversed. And children make order errors in just those constructions, using IO-DO instead of DO-IO. They could, of course, avoid those constructions by using full noun phrases instead of one or both clitic pronouns. Double clitic constructions with first- and second-person indirect objects, *me* and *te* (e.g. *me le, me la, me les*), however, are quite common in 4-year-old speech. And regularization errors, assimilating third-person indirect object constructions to the first- and second-person pattern, also appear, but how frequently in spontaneous speech has not been well documented.[9] The other order errors they make involve use of tonic pronouns instead of clitics for direct objects, with the word order that would have been used with a full noun phrase: SVO instead of SOV. And, in imperative constructions, they retain the VO order of affirmatives with a clitic object for negatives as well, instead of shifting to an OV order by placing the pronoun before the verb. Clitic pronouns affect word order in all the Romance languages, but the changes in order as one goes from a noun phrase object, say, to a clitic pronoun vary with different constructions in the different languages. What children appear to rely on in the early stages is the predominant order, so their errors consist of relying on the orders used with full noun phrases, and on the dominant orders used with clitic combinations.

4.6. *Complex Sentences.*   Children begin to construct their first complex sentences around age 2 to 2½: they use simple juxtaposition to express cause, condition, purpose, and sequence, omitting any conjunction that might specify the intended relation more precisely (Guillaume, 1927a; see also Sechehaye, 1950).

The first conjunctions to appear are coordinative, usually *et* 'and' or *puis* 'then', for linking two propositions. These first emerge sometime around 2;0. The first subordinating conjunctions appear soon after, with *parce que* 'because' the earliest, followed by *si* 'if' and *quand* 'when'. This pattern of emergence in production is very similar to that for English (Clark, 1970, 1973a) as well as for other languages (Clancy et al., 1976). Another coordinating conjunction that appears around 3;0 is *alors* 'so, then'. Temporal conjunctions like *avant que*

---

[9]Adult speakers of Canadian French, according to Connors et al. (1981), do apparently avoid double clitic constructions with third-person forms.

'before' and adversatives like *bien que* 'although' emerge rather later, usually appearing around age 4 (cf. Chambaz et al., 1975; Grégoire, 1947).

Once children begin to use coordinating and subordinating conjunctions, as well as finite complement clauses, they make a variety of errors. Few of these, though, have been carefully documented from point of onset to point of adult-like acquisition. In relative clauses, for instance, one finds some overuse in production of *qui* 'who:SUBJ' to introduce both subject and object relatives; only a bit later does *que* 'who:OBJ' become established for object relatives. One reason for an initial overuse of *qui* might be the many other functions *que* has, including its earlier general-purpose function of marking all subordinate clauses. It serves to introduce all finite verb complements, e.g. *vouloir que* 'to want to', *dire que* 'to say that'. It forms part of many conjunctions, e.g. *avant que* 'before', *pour que* 'so that', *afin que* 'in order to', and serves as a reduced form for all subordinating conjunctions on the second and subsequent uses within the same utterance, e.g. *Pendant que Pierre est sorti et que Marie n'était pas encore là*, . . . 'While Pierre was out and [while] Marie hadn't yet arrived, . . .'. It also serves as the linking particle in comparative clauses, e.g. *Elle est plus grande que lui* 'She is bigger than him'; and it introduces exclamations, e.g. *Qu'il fait beau aujourd'hui!* 'What a fine day it is today!'. By choosing a single form, *qui*, to mark all their relative clauses, children at this stage could be deliberately avoiding one of the multiple functions of *que* until they have sorted out more of the system.

Children also confuse certain conjunctions with each other, both in production and in comprehension. For instance, Ferreiro (1971) reported that when she asked children to imitate and then act out temporal sequence instructions in a comprehension task, they often substituted the conjunction *avant que* 'before' for *après que* 'after', or the reverse. They made similar errors in their spontaneous speech and in answering questions about sequence (see also Simon et al., 1972–73). Many of these errors appear to be semantic in origin. Children appear to confuse the meanings of closely allied conjunctions. These confusions in turn may result in errors of syntactic form since some conjunctions (e.g. *avant que, pour que,* 'before, in order to') require the subjunctive while others take the indicative.[10]

Many conjunctions appear to be treated initially as if they simply linked two clauses describing sequential events. For instance, Jakubowicz (1978) found that young French children, up to age 5 or so, seemed to have no sense of probability or uncertainty associated with their uses of *si* 'if'. Rather, they simply used it for the sequential relation in structures of the form 'if *p, q*'. But presented with utterances of the form 'if *p, q*, but if not *p*, not *q*', they could be made aware of

---

[10]In adult speech, *avant que* 'before' is followed by the subjunctive (or ought to be, according to normative grammar), while *après que* 'after' is followed by the indicative. Currently, many speakers appear to be confused on this point, and often use the wrong mood for one or both conjunctions.

the uncertainty associated with *p*. Older children seemed to use cues based on the verb forms (imperfect and conditional), and then the conjunction itself in deciding *p* was uncertain. In production, by contrast, even the youngest children (aged 3) produced conditional utterances (including counterfactuals), provided the uncertainty about the events to be described was made explicit. Where uncertainty had instead to be inferred, younger children (up to 5) used *si* apparently to express some kind of regularity holding between the two events, *p* and *q*. Older children (up to age 11) used *si* only for hypothetical situations or ones where there was some uncertainty (see Piéraut-Le Bonniec, 1980a, 1980b).

Children acquiring French and Spanish also make the same kinds of mistakes as English-speaking children when they are asked to identify the subject of complement clauses following such verbs as 'promise'. They treat the nearest noun phrase before the complement verb as its subject (Chomsky, 1969). Goldblum (1972), for French, and Echeverría (1978), for Spanish, found that children under 7 or 8 consistently treated *promettre* and *prometer* respectively as if they belonged to the same class as verbs of saying or ordering (e.g. French *dire* 'to say, tell', *commander* 'to order'; Spanish *pedir* 'to ask,' *ordenar* 'to order'). Echeverría (1978) also looked at Spanish-speaking children's comprehension of *preguntar* 'to ask' (used only for information questions) and *contar* 'to tell', and found that children understood how to interpret the complements of *preguntar* before those of *contar,* a finding apparently opposite to the relative ordering of *tell* before *ask* in English (see also Edelsky & Muiña, 1977). Nonetheless, the patterns of confusions—here, treating *contar* as if it meant *preguntar*—appear similar.

In a further study of children's ability to interpret and then produce complement constructions with the verbs *dire* 'to say, tell' and *vouloir* 'to want' in French, Streri (1979a) asked children between 3 and 6 to report on what certain puppets had said or wanted done. (The tasks were complicated by the children's having to switch point of view as they took the roles of or reported on different participant puppets.) The younger children tended to avoid finite complements with *vouloir* and opted for commentaries like (3;11) *La petite fille, si elle veut pas manager, elle va pas grandir* 'The little girl, if she doesn't eat, she won't grow big', rather than taking the role of the mother puppet directly: *Je veux qu'elle manage* 'I want her to eat', or indirectly: *Elle veut qu'elle (sa fille) mange* 'She wants her (her daughter) to eat'. Streri found that the younger children (3- and 4-year-olds) did much better when asked what particular puppets 'said' than asked what they 'wanted'. *Dire* was consistently better understood than *vouloir*. So it was easier for the younger children, after watching a puppet scene, to report that *La maman dit (raconte) que sa fille dessine* 'The mother says her daughter is drawing' than *La maman veut que sa fille dessine* 'The mother wants her daughter to draw' (see also Streri 1979b, 1980). The errors children made, though, were often errors of omission rather than commission. Complement constructions and subordinate clauses generally require more investigation.

Finally, there has been some research on children's understanding of the presuppositions carried by particular conjunctions such as *mais* 'but' and quantifiers or adverbs like *seul, aussi,* and *même* 'only, too, same' (e.g. Kail, 1979; Kail & Weissenborn, 1980). The conjunction *mais,* for example, appears very early, soon after *et* 'and' and *puis* 'then' in children's spontaneous speech (e.g. Grégoire, 1937, 1947; Fondet, 1979). However, Kail and Weissenborn (1980) found that it was still treated simply as a coordinating device to link two clauses by 7-year-olds. And it wasn't until age 9 that they seemed to take full account of the contrastive meaning of *mais* in a sentence completion task. Children may begin to use such forms, then, long before they appreciate the precise presuppositions they carry with them—in the case of *mais,* that there is a contrast between the two parts of the statement being linked by this conjunction.

Errors in the use of terms like *mais,* of course, are notoriously hard to detect in spontaneous speech. Few, if any, of the diaries available provide adequate information about the context of each utterance or about the surrounding discourse. There are very likely other errors in children's production and comprehension of conjunctions, for example, in the more complex conjunctions like *bien que* 'although', which contradicts prior suppositions. (This conjunction is one that requires the subjunctive mood.) The general patterns of development in children's acquisition of coordinate and subordinate clause constructions are still too sketchy for one to be able to draw general conclusions. Too many of the details remain to be filled in.

Although there has been some research on the acquisition of coordinating and subordinating conjunctions in Italian and Spanish, again there seems to have been little analysis of the precise errors children make. In Italian, the first clause combinations are by juxtaposition alone, with no conjunctions, much as in French (e.g. Frontali, 1943–44; Parisi & Antinucci, 1974). The first coordinating conjunction to appear is *e* 'and', followed shortly by *ma* 'but'. The earliest complements, as in French, are infinitival in form, after such verbs as *fare* 'to do', *volere* 'to want', or *devere* 'to need'. The first subordinating conjunctions are *perchè* 'because' and *quando* 'when', followed later by *affinchè* 'in order to' and *se* 'if' (Parisi & Antinucci, 1974; Flores d'Arcais, 1978a, 1978b). These are followed by other temporal conjunctions like *prima che* 'before' and *dopo che* 'after' (Clancy, Jacobsen, & Silva, 1976). In comprehension tasks, young children act initially as if order of mention rather than the conjunction *prima che* or *dopo che* determines interpretation. So the event mentioned first is treated as the first in sequence (Flores d'Arcais, 1978a), just it is by children acquiring other languages (Clark, 1971; Ferreiro, 1971). Only later do children work out the contrasting meanings of the conjunctions themselves.

The same general patterns of development have been noted for Spanish: the first coordinating conjunctions are *y* 'and', from age 2 on, and *pero* 'but' from age 3 or 4. The first subordinating conjunction is *que* 'that' for introducing complements, as in (3;0) *Mamá dice que vamos (a la) calle* 'Mummy says we're going out' or (3;0) *Tiita no kele (=quiere) que pongo ese vestido* 'Aunty doesn't want me to put on these clothes'. Next, between age 3 and 5, according to Gili Gaya (1972e), children begin to use *porque* 'because', *para que* 'in order to', and *si* 'if'. These examples appear to be typical: (5;0) *Si me lo dice le pego* 'If he says that to me, I'll hit him', and (5;0) *El perro acude pa(ra) que le echen de comer* 'The dog's waiting for them to throw him some food'. However, their early spontaneous uses are often incorrect, and the conjunctions sometimes appear to be used simply to link two or more clauses. This often results in syntactic errors, for example, with the verb used in the indicative instead of the subjunctive. The meanings of some conjunctions may also be confused with each other. Again, this may result in syntactic as well as semantic errors. And still other conjunctions, like *aunque* 'although', are only rarely used even by 8-year-olds. Few studies have looked at children's comprehension of conjunctions, but Galvan (1980) found that children relied on order of mention with the temporal forms *antes de* 'before' and *después de* 'after', just as children acquiring other languages do. He also found that children seemed to understand *antes de* rather earlier than *después de*.

In summary, although the various accounts mention that children make errors in using different conjunctions, relatively few examples of actual errors have been reported, so it is difficult to tell whether there are consistent trends in common, either across children or across the different Romance languages. One of the few domains in which there are some production and comprehension data appears to be that of the temporal conjunctions *avant que* and *après que* in French, *prima che* and *dopo che* in Italian, and *antes de* and *después de* in Spanish.[11] In production, the errors appear typically to consist of overuse of one of the conjunctions (usually 'before') and some confusions; in comprehension, the conjunctions are initially ignored—until about age 4—in favor of an order of mention strategy where children treat the first event mentioned as the first that occurred. Later, they acquire the meanings of 'before' and 'after', and presumably begin to use both conjunctions appropriately.

4.7. Other Typical Errors.   Several other systems that typically elicit errors from children during the course of acquisition are discussed in more detail later in the review. For example, children have considerable difficulty working out the different subsystems used for marking possession, where possessive pronouns and adjectives agree in person with the possessor and in number and gender with the object possessed. Getting the person right in the pronominal system requires that children be able to shift from first to second person, for instance, with a

---

[11]The Spanish data collected by Galvan all pertain to the infinitival construction that follows *antes de* and *después de*. There are no data available on children's comprehension or production of the conjunctions *antes de que* or *después de que*, which are followed by the subjunctive, or, with reference to events in the past, by a simple past participle.

change of speaker. And getting the right possessive construction requires that children take account of which combinations of constructions are permissible, for emphasis, say, and which are not.

Children acquiring French also have some difficulty learning where to use the definite and indefinite articles. Like children acquiring other languages, they tend to overuse the definite. It is not clear, therefore, that these errors are peculiar to children acquiring Romance languages. It seems more likely that they result from children's relative lack of skill in keeping track of what they and their addressees mutually know about any particular topic.

Errors in the uses of determiners in French, whether possessives or articles, are discussed in detail in Section 7.

5. Error-Free Acquisition

There are few subsystems in French and the other Romance languages that children acquire with no errors, but there are several that appear to be mastered early, with only a brief period of erroneous use prior to mastery. Number as indicated by the singular/plural contrast, is one such subsystem: Nouns marked as singular or plural by means of the article are produced with relatively few errors in French. One reason for this is probably that noun forms themselves do not change in pronunciation with a change in number. In Spanish, where number is marked both by the article and by an ending added to the noun, there appear to be more errors, particularly with the forms of nouns ending in consonants.

French-speaking children also appear to make relatively few aspectual errors. Initially, they use the compound past (at first in the form of the past participle alone) for results and changes of state. This form of the verb later comes to contrast with the imperfect, used to describe "background" events and activities with limited duration (e.g. Krafft & Piaget, 1925; Bronckart, 1976). Despite such relatively early acquisitions, there appear to be few systems in French, or elsewhere in Romance, that are acquired entirely without error.

One point to consider: Most of the errors documented in studies of language acquisition are errors of FORM. But children also make numerous errors of reference or CONTENT. For example, they may use a plural noun to pick out a singular object. But the latter errors have rarely been documented thoroughly enough for description. The emphasis in most studies has been on the acquisition of the form rather than on accurate use of each form, given its content. Content errors are very difficult to document post facto: Transcripts without meticulous contextual notes can yield no information about such errors, although research on word-meaning acquisition suggests they are fairly prevalent, especially in the first two or three years of language acquisition.

Finally, errors made during acquisition may be errors of omission or of commission. The former again are difficult to assess. Avoidance of particular constructions or of lexical items could be due to the cognitive or linguistic complexity of the distinctions being encoded. Or they could be due to the caution of the learner. Analyses of acquisition errors have depended almost entirely on errors of commission, in particular on those prevalent in the linguistic sub-systems acquired earlier rather than later in the acquisition process. Do children get more careful as they learn more about a particular linguistic system as a whole? Or do they simply get better at making appropriate inferences about how each new subsystem is likely to work? Analysis of early versus late-appearing errors might yield some insight into the relative amounts of error at different stages of acquisition, as well as any qualitative differences in the kinds of errors made early as opposed to late (e.g Bowerman, 1982c; Karmiloff-Smith, 1979).

6. Timing of Acquisition

In any language, children acquire some words and constructions before others. They also acquire some constructions without apparent error, and others with many errors on the way.

6.1. *Precocious Acquisitions.*   There are no strikingly precocious acquisitions in children acquiring Romance languages, but among early acquisitions in production are gender, number, and person. Children master phonological cues to word gender in French, for instance, by age 3;0 and will assign gender, marked with the appropriate articles, even to nonsense words, as long as the word forms conform to the patterns found in the lexicon as a whole. For example, Karmiloff-Smith (1979) found that 3-year-olds treated nonsense words with typically masculine endings such as *-eau* or *-on* as masculine, and ones with typically feminine endings such as *-elle* or *-aise* as feminine. But when Karmiloff-Smith used indefinite articles incompatible with the word forms, e.g. *une bicron, un forsienne,* children under 5 tended to change the article to match the form, e.g. *le bicron, la forsienne.* Older children, though, would pay more attention to the gender given by the indefinite article and would reply with the equivalent definite article, as in *la bicron* and *le forsienne,* despite the lack of congruence between article and word shape.

Number is mastered early, first in nouns and articles, and then in pronouns. It seems to appear slightly later in verbs, but this may be because both number and person are marked with the same device within the verb system. Children rarely make errors of number in nouns. In French, of course, number for nouns is typically marked only in the article, whereas the other Romance languages mark number on the noun as well. This makes for a contrast between a preposed marker for number in French versus a postposed system of marking in the other Romance languages where number is indicated by the addition of inflections for plural to both articles and nouns.

Agreement for number also differs across the Romance languages in where and how systematically it has to be marked. For example, Spanish marks number agreement very consistently—in the article, the noun, the adjective, and the verb. French essentially marks number in the article and to some extent in the verb. Most adjectives, like most nouns, do not differ in pronunciation according to number, and so rarely mark number overtly. The extent to which agreement is marked could affect how fast children master number as a whole within the language being acquired.

French-speaking children make some errors of number agreement, but these are not very common. They are detectable only with second or third conjugation verbs where the forms for singular and plural third person differ, e.g. *Les chats, il vient* for *Les chats, ils viennent* (= 'the cats, he's coming/they're coming'). Most agreement errors seem to involve a singular verb used with a plural subject, seldom the reverse (e.g. Grégoire, 1947).

Number errors are also rare in Spanish although nouns as well as articles are marked for number. In fact, the overregularizations Spanish-speaking children make for gender—adding a final *-o* or *-a* to consonant-final nouns (Montes Giraldo, 1976)—make plurals easier to form. Children simply have to add a final *-s* to all nouns and to the feminine article *la* (for *las*). They do have to learn the form *los*, though, as the plural of the masculine singular *el*.

Number in the verb is also acquired relatively early, without very many errors. In French, of course, for most verbs, the three singular person forms are pronounced alike (and are usually identical with the third person plural form too). Children's first verb forms appear to be the singular and plural of the imperative, e.g. *donne, donnez*. However, the singular imperative coincides with the three singular forms of the indicative, while the plural one coincides with the infinitive in pronunciation, for most verbs. The latter, then, can only be identified as a plural form on the basis of second and third conjugation or irregular verbs where the infinitive and imperative forms differ, as in second conjugation *finir* 'to finish' and *finissez* 'finish!', or third conjugation *prendre* 'to take' and *prenez* 'take (it)!'. Next to emerge seems to be the second or third person of the indicative, e.g. the third person in *il mange* 'he's eating'. Although the first three persons are pronounced alike for most French verbs, the second and third person forms (usually identical in pronounciation) are distinct from the first person in irregular verbs like *aller* 'to go', *être* 'to be', and *avoir* 'to have'. Evidence from irregular verbs like these suggests that this form is the next to emerge (e.g. Fondet, 1979; Grégoire, 1947; Leroy, 1975).

The pattern of emerging number contrasts for French is similar to those attested for Italian, Portuguese, and Spanish, where a similar sequence of imperative forms followed by a third person indicative marks the first contrast among forms of the verb (e.g. Della Valle, 1931, Frontali, 1943–44; Simões & Stoel-Gammon, 1978; Gili Gaya, 1972c).

Third person verb forms in French may or may not appear with an overt subject. The earliest in verbs in French often appear alone or with a direct object when children talk about their own activities (e.g. Bloch, 1921, 1923), and only occasionally with a subject noun like *bébé* 'baby' or their own names. If the actor is someone else, however, children appear more likely to supply a subject, typically a noun with no article at all (e.g. Bloch, 1924; Cohen, 1969; Guillaume, 1927a; Lightbown, 1977). A similar pattern appears to hold for the other Romance languages at the equivalent stages of development (e.g. for Italian, Antinucci & Parisi, 1973; Bates, 1976; Parisi & Antinucci, 1974; for Portuguese, Scliar-Cabral, 1976; de Lemos, 1975; and for Spanish, Eisenberg, 1982; Rodríguez Brown, 1975). Along with these contrasts among verb forms come the first uses of pronouns. Full mastery of different pronoun systems, though, may take some time.

Another fairly early acquisition is markers for locative relations. Children start to produce some prepositions, typically the terms for relations such as 'in', 'on', and 'under', from age 2 on. However, the forms produced at this age are often used erroneously, with mistakes in both form and content. Mastering all the contrasts among locatives typically takes several years (e.g., Johnston & Slobin, 1979; Le Rouzo, 1977).

Children begin to modulate the forms of words by adding different derivational suffixes from quite an early age. They use diminutive and augmentative endings on nouns (and elsewhere) from around 2;0 to 2;6 in Spanish and Italian, and begin to use other derivational suffixes to modify or change the meaning and grammatical category of word forms at about the same age. Again, though, mastering an adult-like repertoire of possible word forms for coining new lexical items takes several years. (Typical developments in this domain are discussed in detail in Section 8.)

Temporal distinctions marked by the different tenses also begin to emerge early. Children begin to use tense in French from age 2 on, and typically contrast the compound past (probably to mark results or end-states) with the present. From about age 3 or so on, they also contrast the compound past with the imperfect, using the later for background and for ongoing events.[12] They mark future time with *aller* + INFINITIVE 'to be going to', from about age 3;0 or so, and only later begin to use future tense inflections. This pattern for future marking, with a periphrastic future form emerging before the inflected one, appears common to all the Romance languages.

The overall picture for early acquisitions is one of systems that begin to emerge in production relatively early, from age 2 or 3 on. But although children start on many systems early, their mastery of most evolves fairly gradually over the course of several years.

6.2. *Late Acquisitions.* Among notably late acquisitions in French are the subjunctive mood in verbs (acquired considerably later than the imperative and indicative), certain kinds of relative clause constructions, certain complement constructions, and subordinate clauses that require the subjunctive mood. The

---

[12]In Spanish and Italian, children initially use past participial forms for results, but the next tense form acquired is the simple past—a form no longer used in spoken French.

subjunctive, now used mainly in present tense form only in spoken French, appears to take time to acquire both because of the situations in which it is commonly used (after certain verbs and conjunctions as well as for certain hypotheticals) and because of its form. Part of its complexity is undoubtedly due to the difficulty children have in discerning the reasons for its use (e.g. in such arbitrary contexts as 'before' clauses but not 'after' ones), and part of it is probably due to the difficulty they may have in detecting the presence of the subjunctive as a distinct verb form. Since it coincides in form with the indicative in all first conjugation verbs, only second and third conjugation verbs provide overt evidence in input that a non-indicative form is required in certain constructions and contexts.

Remacle (1966) found that the first uses of the subjunctive tended to be produced in a small set of sentence frames that required such forms, e.g. after such expressions as *il faut que* 'it is necessary that, must', *je voudrais bien que* 'I would like', and after the conjunction *pour que* 'in order to'. But even with these favored frames, he noted that the 4- and 5-year-olds he followed used less than one-quarter (19%) of their second and third conjugation verbs in the subjunctive. (All first conjugation verbs were necessarily omitted from this analysis.) And, in a number of other constructions that also required the subjunctive, children consistently used the indicative instead (see also Ferreiro, 1971; Streri, 1979a). The difficulty of learning the subjunctive in French, then, appears to be compounded by the coincidence of forms between the indicative and the subjunctive for all first conjugation verbs.

Relative clauses provide children with a number of difficulties in both production and comprehension. In production, for example, relative clauses that interrupt the main clause are harder for children to imitate than those that don't interrupt it (e.g. Kail, 1975a, 1975b; Deyts & Noizet, 1973). Indeed, the first relative clauses very young children produce spontaneously are nearly always in final position, attached to the object nouns of main clauses. Kail (1975a) also found that relative clauses introduced by *que* (object relatives) were harder to imitate than those introduced by *qui* (subject relatives). This suggests that by age 6 (the youngest children studied by Kail) children have identified *qui* as a relative marker, but since *que* has so many different functions, they are less sure of its status in relative clauses. Moreover, with delayed imitation, slightly older children often substituted *qui* for *que* in their imitations (Kail, 1975b), as if *qui* offered a more consistent cue to the relative nature of the subordinate clause being imitated. (Six-year-olds—the younger children—often omitted the relativizer altogether in this task.)[13] Finally, one further factor that appears to make relative clauses hard to produce is noncanonical word order. Object relatives

---

[13]These data, of course, are in contrast to those from 2- and 3-year-olds who tend to use only *que* in early relative clauses. In these, though, *que* is probably being used to mark any linkage between propositions and should not be considered a relative marker at all (see Bouvier & Platone, 1976).

with OSV order are harder for children to imitate than those with SVO order. Late production errors, then, are nearly always errors involving oblique cases.

The comprehension data make this picture rather more complicated. For example, although subject relatives are harder to produce than object ones, they appear to be easier to understand than object relatives, especially when the latter have noncanonical order (Ségui & Léveillé, 1977; Sheldon, 1977). Otherwise, even the youngest children tested (4-year-olds) appeared to understand all relative clause constructions pretty accurately (Ségui & Léveillé, 1977). In other words, interruptions of the main clause did not seem to make for greater processing difficulty in comprehension. The errors 4-year-olds make with object relative clauses are subject to two interpretations. The first is that they rely on a canonical SVO strategy in interpreting all relative clauses because they have not yet discovered that a local cue (the form of the relativizer) can indicate case and may, as a result, require a change from canonical (SVO) order to OSV or OVS. A second interpretation is that they consistently treat *que* as if it was *qui,* so that they treat object relatives as if they were subject relatives. With noncanonical object relatives (OVS), they interpret the *que* (marking the object) as the subject of the relative clause and the second noun phrase (the actual subject) as its object. In the noncanonical relatives, then, both interpretations make the same prediction: children will impose SVO order on OVS sequences.

The difficulties 4-year-olds have in understanding the cues to oblique case (use of *que* rather than *qui*) in object relatives are paralleled by the difficulties much older children have in producing this type of relative clause. Local cues to case such as those given by the alternations in the relativizer are rare in French, as is OVS order. Combined, they cause children difficulty both in understanding and in producing certain kinds of relative clause.

These studies have documented errors children make when called on to imitate or understand isolated relative clauses. But there has been little research on the functions of relative clauses or how children use them spontaneously. For example, what forms of relative clause do young children use to distinguish one object from another on the basis of history, characteristics, or spatial location? Some preliminary elicitation studies by Bouvier and Platone (1976) suggest that children can produce some relative clauses for such purposes by age 4, but even at age 6 produce many erroneous forms. One child age 5;6, for instance, used relatives like *la voiture que le monsieur arrête* 'the car that the man is stopping' alongside more problematic utterances like *la voiture que le monsieur met une roue* 'the car that the man is putting a wheel' for *la voiture à laquelle le monsieur met une roue* 'the car the man is putting a wheel on'; from a 5-year-old using *où* 'where' as a relative marker, both the appropriate *le camion où on met d' l' essence* 'the truck someone's putting some gas in', and the problematic form *la voiture où l' gendarme l' arrête* 'the car where the-policeman it-stops' for *la voiture que le gendarme arrête* 'the car that the policeman stops'. These elicitation data, where the relative clauses appear with a determiner function, suggest that even 6-year-olds still have a long way to go in learning how to use relative clauses in French.

Relative clauses are also a late acquisition in Spanish. Ferreiro, Othénin-Girard, Chipman, and Sinclair (1976) found that 10-year-olds still made errors in the comprehension of object relatives. In production, relative clauses begin to appear (as they do with French-speaking children) at around age 3. The first ones used are subject relatives. Other relative clause types emerge over the course of the next three or four years (Gili Gaya, 1972e). However, there has been little detailed study of the precise forms produced, and no analysis of the uses to which young children first put them. One note of caution should be added here: Many of the comprehension studies have focused on relative clauses that may be both bizarre and difficult out of a normal conversational context. As a result, there are extensive discrepancies from one report to another. For example, although both French and Spanish children begin to produce relative clauses spontaneously from age 3 or so onwards, they still have difficulty understanding certain forms as late as age 10. The formal difficulties that make for late acquisition appear to be oblique case marking and noncanonical word orders in some relative clause types. The functional difficulties that contribute to late acquisition appear to involve children's discovery of when and where to use relative clauses appropriately. However, aside from Bouvier and Platone (1976), no one has made any serious study of the functions involved.

In summary, I have outlined some of the difficulties children have with two late acquisitions, the subjunctive mood and relative clause constructions. More detailed investigation of other constructions such as object clitic pronouns or the conditional mood will add to what is known about late acquisitions and help uncover in more detail the sources of difficulty children face in acquiring French as their first language.

7. Organization and Change During Development

When children first acquire new words, they use them at first in only a few contexts. For example, *tall* may be applied only to trees (Carey, 1978). These limited uses are often correct. However, as children find out more about the meanings of related words and extend each word in their repertoire, they begin to make errors where they made none before. This pattern of acquisition—correct but limited use followed by errors in use—has been documented, for example, by Bowerman (1978, 1982b, 1982c) in her account of various late-occurring errors in English-speaking children's uses of verbs. This pattern of development appears to be a fairly general one since children allow many different forms to go unanalyzed for some time (e.g. Vihman, 1982; Johnson, 1980, 1981).

There are at least two common types of late-occurring errors in children's speech. The first is errors that appear to result from children's attempts to maintain one-to-one pairings of meanings and forms within their language. The second is errors that result from their overmarking of certain (possibly newly discovered) semantic distinctions.

The first kind of error may arise either with the construction of additional—and usually ungrammatical—forms in order to preserve a one-meaning-to-one-form approach, e.g. *la même vache* 'the same cow' for 'same one' versus **la même de vache* 'the same of cow'—found in colloquial French also—for 'same kind'; or from a specialization of different grammatical forms to convey newly acquired contrasts in meaning, e.g. use of the contracted *de* + ARTICLE for partitive meaning, as in *J'ai du pain* 'I've got some bread' and **Y'a da neige*, with *da* in lieu of *de la* 'there's some snow', in contrast to uncontracted *de* + ARTICLE for possession, as in **le chapeau de le monsieur* 'the man's hat' with *de le* instead of *du*, alongside *le soulier de la dame* 'the woman's shoe'.[14]

The second kind of error that one finds following previously errorless use is overmarking. Children typically overmark by indicating the same semantic distinction in more than one way on a single lexical item, as in English **unthaw*, or by marking it at several different points in the utterance, as in **mon mien de chapeau à moi* 'MY MINE of hat to ME' 'MY hat' or *La fille a poussé un chien et puis aussi le garçon a repoussé encore le même chien* 'the girl pushed a dog and then ALSO the boy RE-pushed AGAIN the SAME dog'.

Why do children begin to make such errors after earlier, apparently correct, usage? One possible answer is that such errors are themselves indicators of children's continuing organization and reorganization within various subsystems of their language. For example, it may well be the realization that one form is carrying two or even more meanings that leads children to construct additional forms. This in turn allows children both to hold on to a one-meaning-to-one-form system and to consolidate their own grasp of the different meanings they are discovering—both necessary preludes to their adopting the pertinent adult system with its more complex pairings of meanings and forms.

Overmarking, then, would be another symptom of adult-like organization in the process of emerging. Children draw on all their resources to make a particular meaning salient by indicating it in more than one way in particular words, phrases, or utterances. In overmarking, children could also be trying to avoid confusions among meanings they have just begun to realize are related to each other. For example, Bowerman (1978) documented the onset of errors in uses of the English verbs *put, give, make,* and *let,* as well as of *put, take,* and *bring,* by her daughters. The children had previously used these verbs quite correctly, but

---

[14]Note that contracted forms are required only when *de* precedes either the masculine singular article, *le,* or the plural article, *les,* for the forms *du* and *des,* respectively, whether partitive or possessive in meaning. French-speaking children as old as 5 still do not consistently contract *de le* to *du, de les* to *des, à le* to *au,* or *à les* to *aux* (LaBelle, 1976; Bautier-Castaing, 1977)).

perhaps in a quasi-formulaic way with restricted meanings. As they began to use these verbs in a wider range of contexts, they started to make errors of substitution and to use inappropriate combinations of noun phrases with each verb. Their errors suggested they had begun to recognize how the different meanings in question were related to each other—and this led to momentary confusions and errors.

These later-appearing errors are particularly important for the information they offer about which meanings children are trying to keep distinct, and how they organize various subsystems in the language being acquired. I will illustrate this phenomenon in two domains where children make later-occurring errors: with articles and with possessive constructions.

7.1. Definite and Indefinite Articles.

7.1. *Definite and Indefinite Articles.*   Observational studies of French (and the other Romance languages) suggest that children begin to use articles around age 2;0 to 2;6 (e.g. Grégoire, 1937, 1947; François et al., 1978). However, the earliest uses are often indeterminate phonetically between a definite and indefinite form, and articles in general are often omitted up to age 3.

Several researchers have looked experimentally at children's article use in order to establish more precisely what they know about specific and nonspecific reference. For example, Bresson, Bouvier, Dannequin, Depreux, Hardy, and Platone (1970) studied 4- and 5-year-olds' ability to use the definite and indefinite articles in a limited set of contexts containing one or more instances of objects from the same class. Their children all used the indefinite appropriately in naming things, e.g. *C'est un mouton* 'It's a sheep'. But when the indefinite article was called for in referring to one or more of a set of like objects, they consistently used the definite article instead. For example, shown a number of sheep, followed by the experimenter removing some of them and asking *Qui est parti?* 'who went away?', 4-year-olds would reply with utterances like **Les moutons sont partis, les moutons sont restés* 'the sheep went away, the sheep stayed' in lieu of *Des moutons sont partis, des moutons sont restés* 'some sheep went away, some sheep stayed'. Four-year-olds used the indefinite *un* 'a:MASC:SG' and *des* 'some:PL' only 50% of the time in such contexts, and 5-year-olds did even worse, using the indefinite only 31% of the time (see also Bresson, 1974; Bouvier & Platone, 1976). French children, then, overuse the definite article, at least up to age 6.

This finding is compatible with Warden's (1976) observations for English over a rather wider range of elicitation contexts. He found that before age 5, children's referring expressions were mostly definite. Between 5 and 9, there was a general decrease in inappropriate uses of the definite and some inconsistency of use overall. Warden concluded that it was only from age 9 that children showed full mastery of the indefinite article for nonspecific references like those needed in answering the question *Qui est parti?*. Overuse of the definite article appears to be the result of children's failures to realize that their addressees do not necessarily know all that they, as speakers, know. Learning how to assess what is mutual knowledge and what is not, and, from that, being able to decide on the appropriate article to use is very complex (e.g. Clark & Marshall, 1981).

Articles also seem to cause children difficulty because of their multiple meanings that vary with context—meanings that children take time to acquire. In a series of ingenious studies of children's production and comprehension of articles and other forms of determiner, Karmiloff-Smith (1977, 1978, 1979) showed that children's initial usage depended heavily on the identification of a single meaning or function for each term. For example, even with the addition of *même* 'same' and *autre* 'other' to the definite *le* and indefinite *un*, 3- and 4-year-olds, asked to act out a series like the following: 'The little girl pushes a duck and then the boy pushes the same duck', consistently treated an expression like *le même canard* 'the same duck' as if it picked out another instance of the same KIND, i.e., another duck, rather than the duck already mentioned and acted upon (Karmiloff-Smith, 1977). With age, children showed a change in interpretation from 'same kind' to 'same one'. With expressions like *un autre canard* 'another duck', most of the children, even 3-year-olds, picked out another duck. However, if the ducks were identical, a few of the younger children refused to choose, apparently because they took this expression also as meaning 'one of another kind' rather than 'another one'.

The transition to adult-like comprehension was accompanied slightly later by a parallel progression in their production of articles with *même* or *autre*. Their initial uses did not reveal obvious errors, but as the children began to switch from the interpretation of 'same kind' to 'same one', Karmiloff-Smith noted that children frequently created new (often ungrammatical) forms to carry the additional meanings they were trying to express. For example, 4- and 5-year-olds tried to introduce into French a distinction between 'same kind' and 'same one'. For 'same kind', for example, upon noticing the toys used in the experiment, they might comment, **Moi j'ai la même de vache* 'I've got the same of cow', instead of relying on the form used by younger children and adults: *J'ai la même* 'I've got (one) the same'. These children reserved *la même* for 'same one' and created a new expression for 'same kind'.

In another experiment, Karmiloff-Smith noted children constructing new forms of article to distinguish the nonspecific reference function of the indefinite, *j'ai une vache* 'I've got a cow' from its numeral function, e.g. **J'ai une de vache* 'I have one of cow' (=I've got one cow). These "new" expressions disappear again when children realize that single expressions can have several different meanings (see Karmiloff-Smith, 1979). The youngest children's production of articles—alone and in combination with *même* and *autre*—showed few errors of form; in contrast, somewhat older children used some apparently correct forms but also created ungrammatical forms to carry some of the adult functions of articles. Finally, from around age 7 or so, children appeared to accept the multiple functions of articles and returned to the use of a single form with several meanings.

It is important to note that while these data on children's production appear to show a U-shaped curve in development, their initial uses of the articles in such contexts combined with *même* and *autre* did not in fact reflect totally adult-like usage (see also Kail, 1978, 1979). But this is only apparent in light of the comprehension data where the youngest children's preference for *le même X* as meaning 'same kind' over 'same one', for example, reveals convincingly that what children say and what they understand do not correspond to adult usage.

There has been little or no research on the acquisition of article systems in the other Romance languages, aside from one observational study by Simonetti (1980) of Portuguese. Simonetti examined one child's spontaneous uses of the different articles and demonstratives from age 1;9 to 2;4 and found that the definite article appeared to be used mainly with direct objects whereas the demonstrative appeared mainly with subjects. This study, though, covers too early a stage for the kinds of errors documented by Bresson or Karmiloff-Smith for French. Given the similarities of the functions marked by articles across different Romance languages, though, it would be surprising if children acquiring the other languages did not follow similar routes in development.

7.2. *Possessive Constructions.* The earliest expressions of possession in French vary in form from child to child. Guillaume (1927b) reported that one of his children used *moi* 'me' on its own at 1;4 in the sense of *à moi* or *pour moi* 'to, for me', and very soon used juxtaposition for the possessions of others, e.g. *taté papa* for *café papa* 'coffee daddy'. By 1;11, this child regularly used the analytic *de moi* 'of me' and *de toi* 'of you', e.g. *la cuiller de papa et celle de moi* 'the spoon of daddy and that of me' (= 'daddy's spoon and my spoon'). By 1;9, the child also made sporadic use of *mon* and *ma* 'my:MASC', 'my:FEM', as well as of *le mien* 'mine:MASC'. And by by 1;11, he added the second person possessor forms: *ton, ta,* and *le tien* 'your:MASC', 'your:FEM', 'yours:MASC'.

Grégoire (1947) reported that initial juxtapositions were followed by reliance on the prepositions *à* 'to' and *de* 'of, from' in possessive constructions, e.g. (2;4,16) *La conyé (=cuiller) à bébé* 'the spoon to baby' (= 'the baby's spoon'), (2;6,22) *La ke:me (=crême) de moi* 'the cream of me' (= 'my cream'), (2;6,23) *Regarde le café de moi* 'look at the coffee of me' (= 'look at my coffee'), and (2;6,25) *Une tasse de moi* 'a cup of me' (= 'my cup, a cup of mine'). In the last three examples, with *de moi*, adults would normally use the adjectival forms: *ma crême, mon café, ma tasse* (or *une de mes tasses*). Prepositional constructions for possession appear to be more analytic than possessive adjectives like *mon* 'my:MASC:SG' in that they mark explicitly the relation between object-possessed and possessor. The same preference for analytic over synthetic forms also appears early in the acquisition of other Romance languages.

In Spanish, as in French, children again rely initially on juxtaposition alone and then begin to mark possession with the preposition *a* 'to' with the possessor, as in *Pato* (=*zapato*) *a Daddy* 'shoe to daddy' from a 2-year-old (Mazeika, 1973). However, the preposition *de* is the one usually used in such constructions by adults. Slightly older children may continue to use juxtaposition but use articles with both the object-possessed and the possessor nouns, as in (2;9) *I liito* (=*el librito*) *la yo* 'the:MASC book+DIM the:FEM (agrees with sex of speaker) I' (= 'my book'), *Popita* (=*sopita*) *ya* (=*la*) *yo* 'soup the I' (= 'my soup'), or (3;6) *La cata* (=*casa*) *le mí* 'the house the me' (= 'my house') (Montes Giraldo, 1976). Only later do children start to use possessive adjectives instead to indicate the possessor. Acquisition of the latter in Spanish may be complicated by the presence of two possible forms: when the possessive precedes the noun designating the object possessed, a "short form" is used, as in *mi libro* 'my book', *tu casa* 'your house', etc.; but when it follows, the construction takes the form ARTICLE + NOUN + POSSESSIVE', as in *el libro mío* 'the book my', *la casa tuya* 'the house your'. These forms are slightly more emphatic and are probably sometimes better rendered in English as *that book of mine* or *that house of yours*. Picking out the object-possessed and the possessor in two separate noun phrases linked by a preposition like 'to' or 'of', appears to be a common analytic stage in the expression of possession.

In Rumanian, possession is marked by use of the genitive case, but in colloquial adult speech, case marking is often replaced by an analytic construction with the preposition *la* 'at, to'. In children, the first expression of possession, according to Slama-Cazacu (1962), is simple juxtaposition. For instance, 2-year-olds use utterances like **coada calu* 'tail horse' in lieu of the adult *coada calului* 'the tail of the horse'. From about age 3, children start to rely on the variety of analytic forms. These continue in common use up to age 6 or 7 when explicit corrections and study of the synthetic (case-marked) forms take over in school. Between 3 and 7, they commonly rely on *la* 'at, to' in lieu of the genitive case, as in (2;2) **Gura la Dorel* for *gura lui Dorel* 'mouth to (of) Dorel' (= 'Dorel's mouth'), or (2;7), in answer to the question 'whose is it?' **La un copil* for *a unui copil* 'to (of) a child' (= 'a child's'). From age 3 on, children come up with a number of different analytic devices they substitute for the genitive case ending. Characteristically, they use the nominative-accusative form of the noun with a preposition: *la* 'at, to' as in the examples already cited, *de* 'of', *de la* 'from', *despre* 'about', all with genitival value in that the resultant prepositional phrases mark the possessor (Slama-Cazacu, 1962, p. 80).

They also rely on analytic forms instead of the dative case, as in (2;5) **Dă și la Sanda* for *dă-i și Sandei* 'give to Sanda too'. When slightly older children start to mark the dative, they appear to do so with a proclitic article which precedes the possessor noun, as in (4;0) *Ii da să mănînce lu căţel,* for dative *căţelului,* or colloquial *lu căţelu* 'he gave to eat to:it dog' (= 'he fed the dog'), or (3;3) *Roata lu maşină,* for genitive *maşinii* or colloquial *lu(i) maşina* 'the wheel to:it car' (= 'the wheel of the car').

Synthetic expressions for possession, then, are systematically replaced by young children who construct analytic forms instead. In doing this, they receive some support from colloquial usage for replacements of the dative, but the children's own constructions are frequently ungrammatical and do not necessarily match those found in adult speech. Rumanian children between 3 and 7, then, spell out by means of prepositions and proclitic articles the relation between the object-possessed and the possessor.

Slama-Cazacu attributed late acquisition of the case forms to the abstractness of the relations expressed by cases. However, the delay noted for Rumanian is not typical in other highly inflected languages. The explanation seems more likely to lie in the existence of a colloquial or spoken standard that relies on some analytic forms alongside the case-marked standard literary language. With two kinds of input for possessive constructions, children presumably first pick up those forms that are most transparent, namely the analytic ones. Since none of the other Romance languages have retained case marking, further comparisons are difficult. However, children acquiring these languages do show a marked preference for constructions with prepositions (usually 'at', 'to', or 'of') to signal possession, and this from an early age.

In French, as in the other Romance languages, there are several different subsystems to be mastered for the expression of possession. Aside from the analytic forms with *à* (*à moi, à eux,* 'to me, to them') and possessive adjectives (*mon, ma, mes,* etc., 'my:MASC, my:FEM, my:PL'), one can also use possessive pronoun forms on their own. Unlike their English equivalents, these pronouns are used with the definite article, agree in person with the possessor, and in gender and number with the object possessed (e.g. *le mien* 'mine:MASC:SG', *la mienne* 'mine:FEM:SG', *le tien* 'yours:MASC:SG', *le sien* 'his:MASC:SG'). This subsystem, though, appears to be acquired later than the other two, and it takes children some time to integrate it with prepositional forms and possessive adjectives. During its acquisition, beginning around 3;6 or 4;0, children may overmark for possession, constructing forms like **Mon mien de chapeau à moi* 'my mine of hat to me' (Karmiloff-Smith, 1977) or identifying the possessor by using phrases like **Le tien de moi* 'yours of me' (= 'mine'), possibly based in part on formulaic forms (Vinson, 1915–16, p. 33).[15]

When children were asked to identify the possessor (themselves, the experimenter, or a third person) of color-coded objects heaped on a table, Depreux

---

[15]Certain combinations, of course, are perfectly acceptable and commonly used, e.g. *Mon livre à moi* 'MY book', with the possessive pronoun (*mon*) combined with the prepositional *à moi* for emphasis.

(1977) found they made frequent mistakes with the possessive pronoun forms. The youngest children (3-year-olds) avoided the possessive pronouns and relied on possessive adjectives and prepositional forms, often in combination, as in the question (3;0) *C'est mon papa à toi? 'it's my father to you' (= 'is it your father'), or identifications like (3;6) Ma voiture à les poupées 'my car to the dolls' (= 'the dolls' car'). At this stage, they appeared to have difficulty in shifting such pronominal forms between first and second person possessors, e.g. (3;6) *mon tien 'my yours' (= 'mine') in lieu of le mien 'mine', or *le mien à toi 'mine to you' (= 'yours') in lieu of le tien 'yours'. They also had difficulty shifting to third person possessor pronouns, e.g. (3;6) *le tien au pâtisseur 'yours to the baker' (= 'the baker's'). If only the possessive adjectives and prepositional forms with à are considered, the children have good mastery of the system. What they still have to learn is how to use this new subsystem of possessive pronouns in conjunction with the two they already know. This is what appears to lead both to overmarking and to the shifting errors just cited. Depreux (1977) found that there was no real synchronization among the different possessive forms until about 5;6.

Acquisition of the different forms, à moi 'to me', mon 'my', and le mien 'mine' is not enough. Children also have to learn how to use them in different contexts. For instance, one could use mon mouchoir 'my handkerchief' where the possessive adjective serves to describe the only handkerchief in sight, or mes voitures 'my cars' to contrast the speaker's cars with toy cars on another lot, where the possessive serves to determine which of two sets of cars should be moved. Karmiloff-Smith (1979) found that different possessive forms were used initially with descriptive functions. Only at age 8 or 9 did children begin to use them with a determiner function as well. As early as age 4, though, children may be aware that possessives, for instance, have some kind of determiner function, but be uncertain how to express it. This is one reason, she argued (1979, pp. 85–114), why children overmark and produce such emphatic expressions as mes voitures à moi 'my cars to me' (= 'MY cars') or the ungrammatical *les miennes de voitures rouges ouvertes 'my cars red open' (= 'my red convertibles'). The different functions of possessive phrases, adjectives, and pronouns are also intricately bound up with other subsystems of descripters and determiners in the language. And children have to acquire not only all the forms but also each of their functions.

In summary, children start their acquisition of possessive forms with the analytic prepositional constructions, then add the possessive adjectives. Some of the errors of contradictory possessor-marking (e.g. *mon papa à toi 'my father to you') that follow this early stage may result from children's combinations of formulaic uses of possessive adjectives with what for them is the "real" way of indicating possession, namely the preposition à followed by a noun denoting the possessor. (Individual children clearly vary, given Guillaume's and Grégoire's data on these two possessive subsystems.) Finally, having mastered the prepositional and adjectival devices, children have to learn and integrate yet another subsystem into their set of markings for possession: the possessive pronouns. They have to re-map the distinctions they already know for the devices acquired earlier and learn both the meanings and the uses to which the new devices can be put. Elaborating each new subsystem and combining it with what they already know takes time and causes errors.

8. Lexical Structure and Word-Formation

When children first start to acquire words their meanings often differ from the adult's (e.g. Grégoire, 1937, 1947; Montes Giraldo, 1974, 1976). Words may be over- or under-extended in meaning (Clark, 1973b), be used only in highly restricted contexts (Carey, 1978), or occur only in formulaic utterances that have yet to be analyzed by the child (e.g. Vihman, 1982). Although there has been some research on lexical domains like that of spatial terms (see section 9.1), there has been comparatively little analysis of young children's lexical structure or of how they build up different taxonomies of terms. My focus in this section will therefore be on how children exploit some of the resources available to them for filling gaps in their current lexicon (Clark, 1983). Essentially, I argue that children rely heavily on what they already know about the lexicon and about relations between words known to them in finding means to talk about categories for which they still lack the conventional vocabulary. I first consider some options children pursue in talking about actions, and then take up those they rely on in talking about objects. In the case of actions, I shall focus on what children know about the relations between intransitive, transitive, and causative verbs, and in the case of objects, on what they know about options for forming new nouns.

8.1. *Doing Things with Verbs.*   Children begin to talk about actions relatively early in the one-word stage, but acquiring the appropriate verbs in many instances takes a long time. Children therefore tend to fill in for verbs they don't yet know by relying, for instance, on general purpose verbs like *do* (Clark, 1978b; Berman, 1978), on more or less iconic gestures, and on extensions of other terms to fill gaps. They use intransitive verbs causatively and causative verbs intransitively, using the verbs in question with the requisite number of arguments; they confuse the meanings of converse verbs; they sometimes coin new verbs from nouns that denote objects involved in the actions they wish to talk about; and they coin negative verbs for talking about the reversal of an action. I will briefly take up the evidence for each of these observations in turn.

English-speaking children often use intransitive verbs as if they were causative, as in *She comed it* (meaning, 'she brought it') beside the intransitive *She comed* for *She came,* or *She crossed us* (meaning, 'she let us, had us cross') beside *We crossed the road.* Bowerman (1974, 1982b) was the first to point out that children made intransitive verbs quite freely into causatives in English, possibly on the model of such pairs as *walk* (intransitive) and *walk* (causative). She argued that children's overregularizations in this domain were evidence for their discovery of the component CAUSE as part of the meanings of causative verbs. The emergence of periphrastic causative forms at the same point in development, with the component CAUSE made quite explicit through use of such verbs as *make* or *get*, lends further support to this interpretation. Lord (1979) observed that children also made causative verbs into intransitives just as freely, as in *They don't seem to see,* from a child looking for sandals. She suggested that children may make a generalization about verb meanings based on the number of surface arguments, such that intransitives have one argument, transitives (often also causative) have two, and bitransitives three. They then use the appropriate schema when they need a verb of the requisite type to convey their meanings. Children, then, presumably make use of whatever verbs they already have in their repertoires and stretch them by combining them with differing numbers of arguments only when needed.

While there has been no systematic study of children's uses of verbs from this perspective in French, examples noted by several observers show considerable resemblance to the English data. For instance, intransitive verbs get used transitively, as in (1;10) *(Je) travaille les cailloux* 'I am working the stones' (= 'I am playing with the stones') from a child unfamiliar with the transitive sense of *travailler,* (2;6,2) *Ne faut pas tomber le livre* 'mustn't fall the book'[16] or (3;2,5) *Tu vas te mourir* 'you're going to die yourself' (Guillaume, 1927a; Grégoire, 1947; Egger, 1887). Another intransitive used transitively, according to François (1978) is *gigoter* 'to fidget', as in (3;6) *Je me gigote* 'I'm fidgeting/wriggling myself' or (3;6) *Tu gigotes ma chaise* 'you're fidgeting my chair'. Older children continue to do this, as in (4;6) *Siffles encore une herbe* 'whistle another grass' said to an adult blowing on a blade of grass, or (6;0) *(Le loup) envole la maison* 'the wolf flies away the house' (Grégoire, 1939, Méresse-Polaert, 1969).

The only other Romance language for which there are data is Portuguese, where Figueira (1979, 1984) analyzed longitudinal records of spontaneous speech and found verb uses virtually identical to those noted by Bowerman (1974) and Lord (1979). For instance, among the intransitive to causative examples the following appear typical: *sair* 'to go away, leave' for *tirar* 'to take away' as in (2;11,15) *Quem saiu este esmalto do dedo, quem?* 'Who went away this polish for fingers, who' (= 'who took away this nail polish, eh?'); *cair* 'to fall' for *derrubar* 'to drop' or *fazer cair* 'to make fall' as in (3;8,15) *Não sei se este balanco vai te cair* 'not:know-1SG if this swing is:going:to you fall' (= 'I don't know if this swing is going to make you fall'); *vir* 'to come' for *trazer* 'to bring' as in (3;11) *A Luisa veio uma menina hoje aquí* 'for Luisa I came a doll today here' (= 'I brought a doll here today for Luisa'); *morrer* 'to die' for *matar* 'to

---

[16]Although this verb can be used transitively in very colloquial speech, meaning 'to seduce' or 'to do in', the child's intended meaning on this occasion had to do with falling, or rather dropping.

kill' as in (4;8,26) *Eu vou morrer essa 'I'm going to die this'; and dormir 'to sleep' for fazer dormir 'to make sleep' as in (4;7,27) *Eu vou dormir ele aquí 'I'm going to sleep him here'. Figueira also found causative verbs used intransitively, for instance, matar 'to kill' used for morrer 'to die', as in (4;8,25) *Apareceu uma pessõa pobre . . . com frio e . . . matou a pessõa 'a poor person appeared . . . with cold and . . . the person died', and tirar 'to take away' for sair 'to go away', as in (4;5,1) *Ela tirou 'she took away' (='she went away').

Overall, these data suggest that children take quite a long time to work out any semantic and grammatical constraints on intransitive, transitive, and causative verb categories. In part, of course, they simply have to acquire enough vocabulary to realize that not all verbs allow movement from one category to another within the language. They also have to learn that transitive and causative verbs agree in person and number (and on occasion gender) with the subject and not with the direct object. For instance, Antinucci and Miller (1976) found that when Italian children first began using the compound past in Italian, at around age 2;0, they made the past participle of the verb agree in number and gender with the noun for the object affected by the action, rather than with the subject. As the children extended their uses of the compound past to verbs for non-change of state activities, however, they shifted to marking agreement with the subject rather than with the direct object. This kind of shift would suggest that these children are coming to understand that transitive and causative verbs differentiate among their surface arguments on the basis of grammatical role such that agreement goes with the subject. Their earlier strategy of having the past participle agree with the direct object, however, is interesting in that it suggests they might have been treating the direct object as if it was related to the verb in the same way the subject of an intransitive verb is. The errors children make in extending their options for talking about actions by adding or removing surface arguments from their current repertoire of verbs needs much more detailed study. Too little is known at present about the development of lexical structure in language acquisition.

Children not only extend their verbs in various ways. They also at times confuse them with each other. For example, a common lexical error for verbs related in meaning is confusion of opposites or converses. In French, children frequently confuse apprendre 'to learn' and enseigner 'to teach', often using apprendre for both meanings. They also make errors with venir 'to come' and aller 'to go', as in (6;0) *(Il dit) "Viens," alors j'ai venu avec lui 'he said "come," so I came with him',[17] or (6;0) *Il faut pas venir à l'école 'we mustn't come to school' where the verb aller (je suis allé avec lui 'I went with him'; aller

---

[17]This child not only used the wrong deictic verb given the context of his utterance, venir for aller, but also the wrong auxiliary, avoir instead of être. Venir, like several other motion verbs, requires être rather than avoir in the compound past.

à l'école 'to go to school') was the appropriate deictic choice in the context of this utterance (Méresse-Polaert, 1969). This particular confusion is consistent with the late acquisition of 'come' and 'go' in other languages (e.g. Clark & Garnica, 1974).

The confusion of opposites in Portuguese presents a very similar picture. *Aprender* 'to learn' is used for *ensinar* 'to teach', and vice versa; *subir* 'to go up' is confused with *llevantar* 'to raise, and so on (Figueira, 1977, 1979). And the same picture emerges for Spanish, with confusions reported between *caer* 'to fall' and *llevar* 'to rise', *preguntar* 'to ask' and *decir* 'to tell', *recibir* 'to receive' and *dar* 'to give', *aprender* 'to learn' and *enseñar* 'to teach', and *venir* 'to come' and *ir* 'to go' (Montes Giraldo, 1976; Echeverría, 1978). A few of these confusions may also involve different numbers of verb arguments, as when the verb 'learn' is used in lieu of 'teach'.

When children need to talk about a particular activity, they sometimes have recourse either to general purpose verbs or to coinage and construct new verbs for particular occasions (Clark, 1982a, 1983). The general purpose verb most used by children acquiring French is *faire*. Even children as old as 6 rely on it heavily, as in such uses as *faire des tentes* for *dessiner* 'to make tents'; 'to draw tents',[18] *faire de la peinture* for *peindre* 'to do painting'; 'to paint', *faire les jardins* for *jardiner* 'to do gardens'; 'to garden', *faire un accident* for *provoquer un accident* 'to make an accident'; 'to cause an accident' *faire la circulation* for *régler* 'to do the traffic'; 'to direct traffic', *faire la boxe* for *boxer* 'to do boxing'; 'to box', and even *faire la marche* for *marcher* 'to do walking'; 'to walk' (see Méresse-Polaert, 1969). The equivalent verbs in Portuguese (*fazer*), Spanish (*hacer*), Italian (*fare*), and Rumanian (*a face*), appear to play the same role in those languages too.

The other option children take is to coin a new verb just for that occasion, by forming a verb from a noun for one of the objects involved in the action. For example, French-speaking children form denominal verbs like **mètrer* (from *mètre* 'ruler') for *mesurer* 'to measure', **pincer* (from *pince* 'paintbrush') for *peindre* 'to paint'; *pantoufler* 'to put one's slippers on' from *pantoufle* 'slipper'; *ensoldater* 'to make into a soldier' from *soldat* 'soldier'; **pianer* (from *piano*) for *jouer du piano* 'to play the piano', and **piper* (from *pipe*) for *fumer* 'to smoke'.[19] A comparison of the categories of verbs coined by French-speaking children with those from English- and German-speaking children shows strong parallels, even though coining verbs from nouns is not as productive a device in

---

[18]The forms with *faire* are generally perfectly acceptable. However, in most instances there is a more specific verb available for the activity being talked about, a verb adults would be more likely to use on such occasions (see further Giry-Schneider, 1978).

[19]Some of these verbs, with the meanings intended by the children, have since entered the lexicon. At the time these innovations were observed, they appear not to have been considered conventional. Many of them, of course, represent perfectly legitimate innovations (see Clark, 1982a), while others are unacceptable with the meanings intended.

French as it is in the other two languages (Clark, 1982a). What appears critical is that children need a verb for talking about some activity, and to fill that gap either rely on a general purpose verb or coin one from an appropriate noun just when they need it (Clark, 1983).

Another type of verb children often coin is one for talking about the reversal of an action just mentioned or observed. In French there is a very productive prefix, *dé-*, that serves to ''undo'' the requisite action, as in the well-established verbs *faire* and *défaire* 'to do, undo'. Children begin to use this device early to construct reversal verbs in French. Among the numerous instances that have been noted from children as young as 2;6 are **désendormir* (from *domir* 'to sleep') for *réveiller* 'to wake up', *déchauffer'* (from *chauffer* 'to heat'), **déprocher* (from *approcher* 'to approach') for *s'éloigner* 'to go away', **déprisonner* (from *emprisonner* 'to imprison') for *libérer* 'to set free, let go', **déssouffler (from souffler* 'to pant, blow') for *dégonfler* 'to deflate', and **délumer* (from *allumer* 'to turn on') for *éteindre* 'to put out, turn off' (Clark, 1981a).

Children acquiring Portuguese display a similar facility in coining reversal verbs, this time with the prefix *des-*. Figueira (1979), for example, cited such instances as *deszipar* (from the innovative denominal *zipar* 'to zip'), **desabrir* (from *abrir* 'to open') for *fechar* 'to shut', **desquentar* (from *quentar* 'to warm') for *esfriar* 'to cool', **desenfiar* (from *enfiar* 'to put on') for *tirar* 'to take off'), and *destampar* (from *tampar* 'to cover with a lid'). She also noted some use of the overtly negative prefix being used redundantly with verbs that already had the requisite reversal meaning, e.g., **desvaziar* for *esvaziar* 'to deflate' and also **desmurchar* (from *murchar* 'to wither, wilt'), again in place of *esvaziar*. As in the case of French, these innovations start to appear relatively early. Although there are no pertinent data available for the other Romance languages, it seems reasonable to assume that there too it should be relatively easy for children to coin reversal verbs when they need them. The commonest setting in which children seem to do this is one in which they are making a direct contrast or comparison between an action and its reversal. This holds for both the French and Portuguese observations reported here.

8.2. *New Words for Objects.*   Children form new nouns for talking about objects and events for which they lack words in their current vocabulary. They begin to do this fairly early in the Romance languages, and rely on a variety of derivational suffixes depending on the kind of noun they need. They coin new terms for agents and instruments (the first category I shall consider in this section), they coin new terms for the objects that result from specific activities, and they coin new terms for talking about particular acts as events in themselves. They also make use of an elaborate system of diminutive and augmentative endings, available in most of the Romance languages, to modify the meanings of nouns along dimensional, affective, and evaluative lines. In each case, children seem to master first those word-formational options that are productive in the language, and the early uses they make of them are largely appropriate. Where children's uses are not appropriate, it is usually because they have coined a word for some category for which there is already a word available. Thus, the coinage with that meaning is pre-empted by a previously established word with that meaning in the language, a word that therefore takes priority (see Clark & Clark, 1979; Clark, 1983). I will take up the data available from each of the four domains in turn.

Agents and instruments differ in animacy, but otherwise appear to be close kin in most languages. The same suffixes can typically mark both agents and instruments, although other suffixes may be specialized for only one of these categories. The kinship between agent and instrument is most apparent in French with the suffix *-eur/-euse* (MASC:SG,FEM:SG). This suffix is currently one of the most productive agentive suffixes, and children seem to rely on it early to coin new agent and instrument nouns. Among the agent nouns observed by such researchers as Grégoire (1947) and Aimard (1975) are: (3;8) *le crêmeur* (from *crême* 'cream'; for 'eater of cream'),[20] *le preneur* (from *prendre* 'to take'; for 'the taker'), (3;11) *le salisseur* (from *salir* 'to dirty'; for 'the dirtier'), (4;3) *le répareur (from *réparer* 'to repair'; for *réparateur* 'repairer'), (4;6) *le réfléchisseur* (from *réfléchir* 'to think'; for 'the thinker'), and (5;4) *l'arrêteur* (from *arrêter* 'to stop'; for 'the stopper').

Earlier records of children's innovative agent nouns suggest children 50 years ago relied more on *-ier* then *-eur* as an agentive suffix, e.g. *le poutrier (from *poutre* 'beam') for *charpentier* 'carpenter', *un marronnier* (from *marron* 'chestnut'; for 'a seller of chestnuts'), or *le cersonnier* (from *cerceau* 'hoop'; for 'the mender of hoops') (cf. Egger, 1887; Decroly, 1932). These observations may reflect a change in the relative productivity of the two agentive suffixes similar to the changes that appear to have taken place in Polish since the 1890s (cf. Chmura-Klekotowa, 1970).

Among the innovative instrument nouns are ones like (3;6) *l'asticateur* (from *astiquer* 'to polish'; for 'the polisher') and (4;0) *une troueuse (from *trou* 'hole'; for *un perforateur* 'a drill'), but children appear to use a wider range of suffixes for instruments than they do for agents. This variety is reflected in examples like (4;6) *un croquoir* (from *croquer* 'to crack'; for *une casse-noisette* 'a nutcracker'), (3;5) *un pendule (from *pendre* 'to hang'; for *un porte-manteau* 'a hanger'), (3;4) *une pesette (from *peser* 'to weigh'; for *une balance* 'a weighing machine'), (2;11) *une fume (from *fumer* 'to smoke'; for *une pipe* 'a pipe'), or (2;10) *la pêche (from *pêcher* 'to fish'; for *une canne à pêche* 'a fishing rod').

---

[20]Note again that many of these innovations are quite legitimate, that is, they fill actual gaps in the lexicon. A few, however, are pre-empted by the existence of another word with that exact meaning or by the existence of the same word with a different meaning. Those cases I have starred. In a few instances, the child's coinage coincides with what has now become a well-established lexical item.

The data available suggest that the younger children tend to drop the infinitival ending on the verb to form a noun, while the older ones add a specific suffix (see Clark & Hecht, 1982, for analogous data from English).

The data on Spanish and Portuguese are sparser, and come primarily from elicitation studies. Kernan and Blount (1966) replicated Berko's (1958) study with Spanish-speaking Mexican children aged 4;0 to 12;0, and asked two questions, both with nonsense stems, to elicit agentive endings. With adult responses to the task as the criterion, Kernan and Blount found that the younger children (4;0 to 7;0) added the *-ador* ending to a nonsense verb stem 67% of the time (versus 93% for the 11–12 year-olds), and the *-ero* ending to a nonsense noun stem only 40% of the time (versus 77% for the oldest children). Again, these data appear to reflect the relative productivity of the different agentive suffixes.

The data for Portuguese are very similar: Costa (1976) also replicated Berko's study, but he asked children (aged 4;0 to 8;0) to form agent nouns from a nonsense verb of first (*-ar*), second (*-er*), or third (*-ir*) conjugation form. He found that the second conjugation form, *-edor,* was the easiest overall (supplied in 68% of the cases), while the third conjugation ine, *-idor,* was the hardest (36%). Although the *-dor* suffixes were preferred overall, children produced several other agentive endings too, e.g. *-eiro, -ista.* However, Costa provided no information about the precise patterns of responses at each age level and did not discuss the relative productivity of the different suffixes. Mediano (1976) reported similar findings. A problem with both the Spanish and Portuguese data is that using nonsense stems may considerably underestimate children's knowledge of word-formation processes (see Clark & Hecht, 1982).

The only data on spontaneous innovations for Spanish or Portuguese come from Figueira's (1977, 1979) studies of Portuguese. She reported only one agent noun, (4;0,19) *sou ajudadeira* 'his helper' for adult *sou ajudado.* The data on spontaneous innovations are even sparser for Rumanian, although Slama-Cazacu (1971) noted such agent nouns as (4;10) *luptari* 'fighters' for adult *luptatori* (from either the noun *lupta* 'fight,' or the verb *a lupta* 'to fight'). (The *-ar* agentive suffix is very productive in Rumanian.) There appear to be no data available on spontaneous coinages in Italian children's speech.

What of other categories of new nouns? Children also coin words for talking about the objects intrinsic to certain activities, or resulting from them, and for the activities themselves as discrete acts or events. In French, for example, children coin nouns from verbs, nouns that pick out particular objects, e.g. (1;10) *une roule* and (3;0) *un rouleau* (both from *rouler* 'to roll') for adult *une balle* 'a ball', (3;0) *du pleuré* (from *pleurer* 'to cry') for adult *des gouttes* 'drops of water', (3;0) *ton coupé* (from *couper* 'to cut') and (3;4) *une saignure* (from *saigner* 'to bleed') for adult *ta/une coupure* 'your/a cut', and (3;6) *le gonflé* (from *gonfler* 'to swell') for adult *le gonflement* 'swelling' (Vinson, 1915–16; Grégoire, 1947; Aimard, 1975; François, 1978). Forms recorded as *du pleuré, ton coupé,* and *le gonflé,* however, should probably have been transcribed as *du pleurer, ton couper,* and *le gonfler;* that is, children were likely to have been forming these novel nouns by means of the article plus infinitive construction, a highly productive option for adults. (The two forms in each case are phonetically indistinguishable.)

The same children also coin nouns for talking about the act of doing something, and they begin to do this, in French at least, by about age 3;0. The following examples are typical: (3;3) **la séchade* (from *sécher* 'to dry') for *le séchage* 'the act of drying', (3;5) **une parlette* (from *parler* 'to talk') for *une causette* 'a chat', (3;7) **une plonge* (from *plonger* 'to dive') for adult *un plongeon* 'a dive', (3;9) **tes brûlements* from *brûler* 'to burn') for the activity of burning weeds, (4;1) **le réparage* (from *réparer* 'to repair') for *la réparation* 'the repair', and (4;2) *la parlation* (from *parler* 'to talk') for a segment of discussion on a TV program following a film.

The only other data available, from Portuguese, appear similar to those noted for French. Figueira (1977) recorded numerous examples of nouns formed from verbs to pick out some object intrinsic to or resulting from some activity. The following are typical: (3;7) **esta pinto* (from *pintar* 'to paint') for, variously, *desenho, risco,* or *pintura* 'design, tracing, picture', (3;10) **o dirigi* (from *diriger* 'to drive') for *o volante* 'the steering wheel', (4;8) **o fuma* (from *fumar* 'to smoke') for *o cigarro* 'the cigarette', and (4;10) **um/meu penteado* (from *pentear* 'to comb') for *um estojo de pente* 'a comb case'. However, there do not appear to be any activity nouns coined of the type noted earlier for French.

Finally, one modification to the meanings and forms of nouns that appears to be acquired fairly early is that brought by diminutive and augmentative suffixes. While these suffixes appear to arrange objects in terms of relative size, the different suffixes vary also in their affective or evaluative overtones. Some diminutives and augmentatives carry a positive weighting, while others carry a negative one. Italian, Portuguese, and Spanish all make extensive use of diminutive and augmentative suffixes, and these suffixes are often among the earliest derivational endings children learn to add to nouns. Bates and Rankin (1979), for example, found that some diminutives were used productively in Italian by age 2;0. The two children whose speech they examined used both adjectival and suffixal diminutives primarily to express size. In a further study with 84 2- to 6-year-olds, they found that comprehension of suffixes like *-ino, -etto, -uccio* (diminutive), *-one* (augmentative), and *-accio* (pejorative) was limited initially to a narrow range of meanings, based mainly on relative size. The evaluative meanings of such suffixes were acquired rather later.

Other researchers who have looked at diminutive and augmentative suffixes have done so in Berko-type studies. For instance, in Portuguese, Costa (1976) elicited the diminutive *-inha* or *-zinha* forms and the augmentative *-ona, -ão,* or *-zão* for a variety of nonsense stems. (The choice of suffix depends largely on the form of the noun being modified.) For most regular nouns forms, the children (aged 4;0 upwards) produced the appropriate form over 80% of the time. Some of the children also used adjectival modifiers for size and even added the appropriate suffixes to adjectives, e.g. *pequeninho, grandão, menorzinho* (= 'little + DIM', 'big + AUG', 'smaller + DIM'). In Spanish, Kernan and Blount (1966) elicited only diminutive suffixes, on two nonsense stems. The younger children (5;0–7;0) produced *-ito* more readily than *-cito* but failed to do very well with either before age 10;0. These findings are in marked contrast to those for Italian and Portuguese. This is particularly surprising given the strong parallels among the three languages in how diminutives and augmentatives are used otherwise.

The data on French and Rumanian are sparser: Slama-Cazacu (1971) reported that diminutives are acquired early and used quite widely, but cited few examples. The situation in French appears slightly different since diminutives are not nearly as productive and hence do not color the vocabulary to the same extent as in Italian, Portuguese, or Spanish (but see Grégoire, 1939). Size modification is generally marked by the adjectives *petit* 'small' and *grand* 'big' from very early on.

To summarize, children rely on well-established words as well as on some word-formation devices to expand their vocabulary from a fairly early age. With verbs, they change forms from intransitive to transitive or causative, and from causative to intransitive; they also add new verbs to their vocabularies by drawing on nouns used to denote objects central to the activity they want to talk about; and they draw on reversal prefixes to talk about the opposites of actions just watched or described. With nouns, they form new words for agents and instruments, they talk about the objects that result from an action, and they talk about the act of doing different actions, relying in each instance on forming an appropriate noun from the verb for the activity in question.

I have emphasized children's innovative word-forms here because they offer important clues to some of the factors underlying lexical organization: their innovations fill gaps, gaps where children have no appropriate conventional word-form to express the meaning intended. The kinds of gaps that get filled allow us to make inferences about lexical organization and structure, and about the principles children may follow in acquiring a repertoire of word-formation devices (Clark, 1980a, 1981b, 1983). For example, children are known to acquire verb meanings rather slowly and their repertoire of verbs appears to lag behind that of nouns (e.g. Goldin-Meadow, Seligman, & Gelman, 1976; Gentner, 1983). Yet young children nonetheless manage to talk about their activities and the activities of others in great detail. How do they manage this with a restricted vocabulary? Reliance on extending known verbs to transitive, causative, and even intransitive schemas offers children one means of talking about varieties of actions; using general purpose verbs—whose meanings are transparent in context—offers another. And forming new verbs for specific actions offers yet another. If we look more at where and for what types of activities children rely on such means, we should find out something both about their underlying concepts of action-types and about their incipient grammatical categories. Equally, study of what children know at different stages about word-formation offers insights into the kinds of acquisitional principles they rely on in building up a repertoire of word-formational devices. Their choices of suffix to mark agent nouns, for instance, could reveal whether they attend to the relative productivity of different agentive suffixes in the language (see Clark & Cohen, 1984). Some word-forms are simpler than others in that they require fewer changes in the constituent parts as they are combined. Again, children appear to acquire simpler word-forms before they master more complex ones that need more adjustments. By looking at spontaneous coinages, one can tease out such factors as semantic transparency, productivity, and simplicity of form, and can then start to look systematically at how they interact with each other and with what children already know about the word-formation options of their language (Clark, 1980a, 1983).

But it is clear from the small amount of data available on Romance that we need much more detailed information about the acquisition both of conventional words and of possible innovative word-forms for use in filling lexical gaps. Little is known about the initial contexts of word acquisition, the gradual growth and structuring of vocabulary, or the restructuring that may take place as children recognize more of the dimensions of similarity and difference within sets of lexical items. Even less is known about how and when children master the available word-formation devices of their first language.

THE SETTING OF LANGUAGE ACQUISITION

In this section, my focus is on some of the elements that make up the setting in which children acquire their first language. The first element is the cognitive development children bring to the task of acquiring language, and the extent to which their cognitive development sets the pace. A second element is the nature of the language children are exposed to, the input language heard from parents, caretakers, and older siblings. And a third is the individual differences among children who are acquiring language, for example, differences in their approach to learning a system.

9. Cognitive Pacesetting in Language Development

To what extent does cognitive development set the pace for language development? In 1973, Slobin proposed that there were two major sources of complexity governing the course of children's language acquisition: the cognitive complexity of the distinctions or concepts being encoded and expressed, and the linguistic complexity of the means available in the particular language being learned. Moreover, if we assume that cognitive development is more or less uniform across cultures, the cognitive complexity of a conceptual domain provides a baseline against which to assess the formal complexity of different linguistic means used for talking about those domains. To look at differences among languages, then, we need extensive comparative data on the acquisition of terms from the same domains, on the one hand, and ways to assess cognitive development in those domains, on the other. Because of this dual requirement, there has been relatively little research on how these two kinds of complexity affect each other. There is, however, a growing body of consistent observations on WHICH distinctions children try to make WHEN during the course of language acquisition. And their first attempts to use some device to mark a particular contrast, whether or not it is the conventional adult one, itself provides important evidence that children have attained and are trying to express certain conceptual distinctions.

Spatial and temporal terms offer two domains in which there has been considerable research on children's production and comprehension of different terms. The findings in these domains for the Romance languages show a number of parallels with data from other languages. And this in turn suggests that these domains may be good candidates for crosslinguistic comparisons of the complexity of the various devices used to encode spatial and temporal notions. In Romance, the devices used for talking about the relations between objects (space) and between events (time) can be grouped formally as prepositions, adverbs, and conjunctions on the one hand, and as inflections added to the verb to mark tense and aspect on the other. But since the latter have received little attention to date (although see Bronckart, 1976; Bronckart & Sinclair, 1973; Sabeau-Jouannet, 1973), I will focus mainly on the various lexical expressions available—the prepositions, adverbs, and conjunctions—first those for space (9.1) and then those for time (9.2).

9.1. *Spatial Terms.*   The earliest locative term to appear in children's spontaneous speech in French are the deictic *là* 'there', usually accompanied by pointing gestures to indicate both proximal and distal objects (cf. Clark, 1978a), and the locative *à* 'at, to'. The latter seems to appear first in possessive or benefactive settings, as in *à moi* 'to me/mine, for me' (e.g. Grégoire, 1937, 1947; Sabeau-Jouannet, 1978; Fondet, 1979). *De* 'of, from' also appears early with animate nouns, to indicate possession. However, the line between possessive and locative is somewhat tenuous in the earliest stages, and very young children may equate the two (cf. Greenfield & Smith, 1976). The next spatial preposition to appear is *dans* 'in', followed soon after by *sur* 'on', which, according to Sabeau-Jouannet (1978), contrasts with both *à* and *dans* in the 2-year-old's speech. The further contrast of *sur* 'on' with *sous* 'under' takes a little longer to emerge. Sabeau-Jouannet also noted that expressions for encoding motion towards, such as *aller à* 'go to' or *porter à* 'carry to', consistently appear before any uses of such verbs with *de* 'from' for motion away from. This ordering is close to that observed for English and for other languages (e.g. Clark, 1973c, 1977).

In comprehension, children appear to master terms that contrast on the vertical axis, e.g. *sur* 'on' and *sous* 'under', *en dessus de* 'on top of' and *en dessous de* 'underneath', before those for the horizontal, front-back axis, e.g. *devant* 'in front of' and *derrière* 'behind' (Piérart, 1977, 1978; Lurçat, 1974). This too generally parallels the English data (Clark, 1980b). Later still, they acquire terms like *entre* 'between' and *au milieu de* 'in the middle of' (Piérart, 1975).

Although the general order of acquisition in production seems to follow that found in comprehension, there are some discrepancies within production when Sabeau-Jouannet's data are compared to Piérart's. For example, the latter found no spontaneous uses of *sous* 'under' in her Belgian children (they did use *en dessous* though) until as much as two years after the age at which Sabeau-Jouannet reported first uses of *sous* in French children (at 2;9 to 3;6). Such discrepancies could be the result of subtle differences in the varieties of French spoken by and to the children, or the result of the elicitation methods used to obtain production data in some experimental settings. Le Rouzo (1977), for example, systematically elicited descriptions of locative actions from children aged 3;6 and older. She found that the younger children tended to code the location of a block they had moved, for example, in absolute rather than relative terms. They would mention only one of two objects, as in *J'ai mis sur, le jaune* 'I put on, the yellow' (= 'I put the yellow (block) on (top of the other one)'). It was only from age 5 or so on that she was able to elicit fully relational descriptions, as in *J'ai mis le cube vert sur le rouge* 'I put the green cube on the red (one)'. It is possible that children are more explicit in their spontaneous utterances on some occasions than others because they are trying to get someone to understand a particular spatial relationship. In experimental elicitation settings, this may often appear unnecessary since the child knows that the experimenter can see the array in question.

In Italian, the main data available are observations of early production, some elicited production, and some data on comprehension. The first locative preposition to appear is *a* 'to, at', at around age 2 (Della Valle, 1931; Ferri, 1879). Frontali (1943–44) reported as first locatives *giu* 'up' and *su* 'down', used in early requests from about 1;6, usually for being picked up or put down. In a crosslinguistic study, Johnston and Slobin (1979) elicited words equivalent to English 'in' (*in, nel, dentro*), 'on' (*sul, sopra*), 'beside' (*vicino a*), 'under' (*sotto*), 'between' (*tra, in mezza a*), 'in front' (*davanti*), and 'behind' (*dietro*), from children aged 2;0 to 4;4. Although the children produced relatively few terms overall, they found a clear order of acquisition. Terms for 'in', 'on', 'under', and 'beside' were the easiest to supply. These were followed by a second group comprised of 'between' and inherent uses of 'in front' and 'behind'. The hardest were noninherent uses of *dietro* and *davanti* (see also Axia & Nicolini, 1979). Johnston and Slobin argued, on the basis of parallels in the order of acquisition for Italian, English, Serbo-Croatian, and Turkish, that conceptual complexity was a major component in accounting for the similarities across languages. But Johnston and Slobin also showed that linguistic complexity—the number of terms available in a language and the variety of uses to which the terms could be put—played a critical role in the speed of acquisition and hence the ease with which children sorted out the contrasts among words for different spatial relations within each language. Finally, Parisi and Antinucci (1970) looked at older children's (4;0–9;0) comprehension of various spatial prepositions in Italian and found they did best on *in* 'in', *su* 'on', *dentro* 'into, inside', and *fuori di* 'out of, outside'. Terms relating to the vertical axis were harder, e.g. *sopra* 'above', *sotto* 'under', *davanti* 'in front of', and *dietro* 'behind'; and hardest of all were terms like *attraverso* 'across' and *lungo* 'along'. These observations parallel the data from French.

The data for Spanish are not as extensive. Montes Giraldo (1974, 1976) reported that among the earliest prepositions used were *a* 'at, to' at 2;3, primarily for possession (see also Mazeika, 1973), followed by *en* 'in' with containers at 2;7, *con* 'with' for instruments, as in *con una yae* for *con una llave* 'with a key', at 2;8 and *de* 'of, from', also for possession at 2;10. He also reported a number of misuses, e.g. of *para* 'by' for *con* 'with', at this early stage of production. The deictics *aquí* 'here' and *allá* 'there' also appear by age 2 or even earlier (Cabrejo-Parra, 1977; Padilla & Lindholm, 1976); and some directional adverbs come in by 2;6, e.g. **Qué va afuera?* 'what goes outside' (= 'who's going outside'), *abajito* 'down+DIM' (= 'down a little'), *cerquita* 'near+DIM' (= 'very close'). Padilla and Lindholm also noted that adverbs that were both locative and directional, e.g. *adentro* 'in front', *atrás* 'behind', *afuera* 'outside', *abajo* 'down', were acquired before those forms restricted to use with locative (non-motion) verbs alone, e.g. *dentro, detrás, fuero,* and *bajo* 'in front, behind, outside, down'. Finally, Lopez Ornat (1975) looked at the uses of *hasta* 'up to, until' in children aged 3;0 to 6;0, and found that the spatial meaning of this term was both understood and produced before the temporal one.

The earliest spatial prepositions acquired, then, are terms for 'at' or 'in', followed very quickly by 'on', 'up' and 'down', and by 'out' or 'off'. These forms enter during the second year, from 2;0 or 2;6 onwards. At this point, presumably, children also begin to acquire the various verbs of motion that contain directional information. In the Romance languages, such verbs typically combine notions of motion with those of direction, e.g. Spanish *subir* 'to go up', *entrar* 'to go in', *bajar* 'to go down' or French *entrer* 'to go in', *sortir* 'to go out'. This is in contrast to English, where verbs usually combine motion with manner rather than direction, e.g. *run, scramble, crawl* (Talmy, 1975). Directional information in English is provided by locative particles like *in, out, on,* or *towards* added to the verb, e.g. *run in, clamber on, crawl up out of,* and so on. Although there has been no systematic study of how young children acquiring a Romance language begin to express motion, direction, and manner, some observations suggest that children acquiring Spanish seem to begin by trying to combine motion and manner in the verb and expressing direction with a locative adverb, e.g. *correr abajo 'to run down' instead of the adult *bajar corriendo* 'to go:down running' (= 'to run down').[21] This aspect of lexical acquisition—how children learn to partition information appropriately, assigning it to verb, participle, locative adjunct, and so on—has received no attention in acquisitional studies of Romance. Yet the interaction of other locative notions with the acquisition of spatial prepositions could shed further light on how children interrelate different subsystems in a language. Their initial generalizations could provide important clues to what may be conceptually more accessible, and hence what might make some terms easier to map onto prior conceptual knowledge than others.

By age 5 to 6, children produce a large number of different spatial terms and are capable of using many of them appropriately (Le Rouzo, 1977; Piérart, 1978). The data from French, Italian, and Spanish for the earlier stages of locative expression show strong parallels in which notions are expressed first and the means children use. These parallels, that hold not only across the Romance languages, but also match the general order of acquisition in other languages, suggest that the conceptual complexity of many spatial notions is a primary factor in when children learn expressions for them in their first language. Complex notions take longer to grasp and so are available only later in development. And children first look for linguistic expressions of those notions already mastered conceptually. In this domain, then, the pace set for the acquisition of spatial terms appears to be largely determined by children's cognitive development.

9.2. *Temporal terms.* The first temporal term to emerge in French is usually *maintenant* 'now'. But this term is used initially in connection with things children want and so probably has no real temporal value (Sabeau-Jouannet, 1973). By 2;6 or so, children begin to contrast *maintenant* with *hier* or *demain* 'yesterday', 'tomorrow' for a present time versus non-present contrast (Grégoire, 1947; Sabeau-Jouannet, 1973). This first contrast is followed soon after by various terms to mark succession, e.g. *d'abord* 'first', *avant* 'before', *ensuite* 'next', *alors* 'then', *après* 'after', *puis* 'then', or *et puis* 'and then' (see Decroly & Degand, 1913; Gendrin, 1973). As I have already noted (section 4.6), children acquire coordinating elements for talking about sequence before they acquire subordinating ones.

The first temporal subordinate marker to emerge is *quand* 'when', which appears soon after *parce que* 'because' and *si* 'if', at around 3;0 to 3;6 (cf. Gendrin, 1973; Chambaz et al., 1975). Next are the conjunctions *avant que* 'before' and *après que* 'after'. In comprehension, these conjunctions appear to be very similar to their counterparts in other languages (e.g. Clark, 1971). Children first depend on an order-of-mention strategy for acting out sequences of events, then master the meaning of *avant que,* and only later *après que* (Ferreiro,

---

[21]I am indebted to Evelio Cabrejo-Parra for these observations.

1971). Ferreiro also looked at children's ability to describe sequences, and at the options they choose when asked to start from the second of two events rather than from the first (Ferreiro & Sinclair, 1973; Ferreiro, 1971). The younger children (aged 3 and 4) had some difficulty when they were asked to describe a sequence OUT OF ORDER, i.e., starting with the second of two events, but most managed to answer *quand* 'when' questions appropriately. With age, they advanced from reliance on sequence markers like *puis* 'then' or *d'abord* 'first' to relational connectives like *avant que* 'before'. She also found a general correlation between cognitive stage, measured on Piagetian tests of reversibility, and linguistic maturity, with "reversible" children doing much better in comprehension.

In Italian, there has been somewhat less research on temporal terms. Ferri (1879) noted that terms like *oggi* 'today', *ieri* 'yesterday', and *domani* 'tomorrow' were acquired around age 3, but didn't mention any errors in use although these appear very prevalent in other languages. She also noted some use of *dopo* 'then' used with the future tense for some sequences. Clancy et al. (1976) looked at records of spontaneous speech for the emergence of different temporal markers and found *desso (for *adesso*) 'now' and *dopo* 'then' appeared around age 2. The first subordinating conjunction to appear is *quando* 'when', between 2;8 and 3;0, along with various other temporal adverbs for sequence like *prima di* 'first'. Later still, around age 4;0–5;0, *prima che* 'before' and *dopo che* 'after' appear as conjunctions. In comprehension, Italian children under 5 or so rely on an order-of-mention strategy for interpreting both temporal conjunctions like these, and causal and purpose ones like *perchè* 'because' and *affinchè* 'in order to'. For example, they consistently act out two-event sequences as if the first event mentioned was the first to occur. And slightly older children, who appear to understand *perchè* and *affinchè*, reveal a similar tendency in their recall of sequences: they usually placed causal clauses before the main clause, and purpose clauses after it, so their own order of mention conformed to the actual order of occurrence (e.g. Flores d'Arcais, 1978a).

In Spanish, as in French and Italian, the first temporal contrast appears to be between the present and non-present. Padilla and Lindholm (1976) recorded *ya* 'now, already' and *ahora* 'now' as the first temporal terms to appear. These were followed by *mañana* 'tomorrow' or *ayer* 'yesterday', both used for non-present, often incorrectly. The first sequence adverbs to appear were *ya* 'already' and *primero* 'first', followed by *después* 'after, later' and *luego* 'then'. These terms begin to appear around 2;0–2;6, and are gradually added to over the next two or three years.

In a more extensive survey of spontaneous speech from children aged 2;0–4;6, González (1980) found a similar order of emergence but reported a greater variety among the terms produced. First came *ya* 'now, already' and *ahorita* 'now+DIM' 'now' at 2;0, with an increase in the frequency of use by 2;6, as well as the appearance of some stock phrases like *hasta la noche* 'towards evening', *hora en la mañana* 'this morning', and the first sequence markers, *pués* (=*después* 'after, then') and *mañana* 'tomorrow'. By age 3;0, more children used *ya* and used it more frequently. There was also some use of adverbs like *todavía* 'still', *entonces* 'then, next', *anoche* 'last night', and *luego* 'then'. In the next six months, children started to use *después* 'afterwards' in short narrative sequences, and made occasional use of *a veces* 'sometimes' and *ayer* 'yesterday', with the latter often used to signal the completion or the result of some action. These uses appeared to contrast by age 2 with uses of the adverb *ahora* 'now' for ongoing activities or requests for an activity from the child. By 3;6, González also noted some incorrect uses of *mañana* 'tomorrow' to mean 'yesterday', and the first appearance of *cuando* 'when' to introduce subordinate clauses. By about 4, children appear to make consistent contrasts between *ahora* 'now' and *mañana* 'tomorrow', the latter now used with a future sense (Gili Gaya, 1972d).

These accounts show considerable consistency in the kinds of forms produced spontaneously from about age 2 on. And the forms produced accord well with the data from French and Italian, as well as with those from other languages. The available comprehension data also show a similar consistency in the findings across languages. Galvan (1980), for example, looked at the acquisition of *antes de* 'before' and *después de* 'after' in Mexican children between 5;0 and 16;0. He presented them with sets of two pictures, one above the other, gave a description, and asked them to pick out the picture of the first event described. His results essentially parallel those reported for French by Ferreiro (1971). Overall, children found *antes de* easier to understand than *después de,* and *después de* used in second position (after the main clause) remained difficult, even for the oldest children.[22]

The temporal markers discussed here, of course, are not the only devices children have to master in talking about time and sequence. They also have to master the tense and aspect systems of their language. The data on French suggest that children initially rely on verb tense to mark the CONTOUR of an event rather than to mark temporal relations per se. For example, Decroly and Degand (1913), in a detailed case study of one child, noted that the first tensed forms tended to be past participles like *fini* 'done, finished', *parti* 'gone', or terms like *voilà* 'there!', used to signal the completion or result of some action. These uses appeared to contrast by age 2 with uses of the adverb *maintenant* 'now' for ongoing activities or requests for some activity. Future forms of the verb were used first for routines, in anticipation of the usual sequence (see Malrieu, 1972–73; Sabeau-Jouannet, 1973). These observations are backed up by Bronckart and Sinclair's studies of French (1973; Bronckart, 1976). They asked children be-

---

[22]The forms *antes de* and *después de* are followed by an infinitive in Spanish. One can also use *antes de que* or *después de que,* with the verb in the subjunctive. The latter forms would presumably be harder, and acquired later, since subjunctive verb forms in Spanish (unlike French) are always distinct from the corresponding indicative ones.

tween 3;0 and 8;0 to describe various actions and action sequences, and found that they used verb forms to contrast results of actions with frequency and duration, rather than to indicate temporal succession or organization.

Antinucci and Miller (1976) made similar observations for Italian. The first past tense forms, around age 2, appeared to be used for results or the outcomes of actions, rather than for past time. Children used past forms initially only on change-of-state verbs (see further Bloom, Lifter, & Hafitz, 1980). Similar findings have also been reported for Portuguese (de Lemos, 1975, 1981), but not for Spanish (Eisenberg, 1982).

Although the data on temporal terms like adverbs and conjunctions are fairly detailed for some Romance languages, and show general agreement across languages, the picture is much clearer for production than it is for comprehension. There has been little examination of which temporal contrasts children understand first. There is even less information available on children's acquisition of tense and aspect, and the contrasts within these systems in the different Romance languages. And there has been hardly any attempt to interrelate children's acquisition of such temporal terms as *maintenant* 'now', *demain* 'tomorrow', or *après que* 'after' with the different tenses and aspects of verbs. Part of the problem, of course, is that tense (but not aspect) is deictic, so the choice of tense depends on the time, place, and circumstances of the speaker's utterance. This presumably makes mastering a system of tense contrasts more complex than mastering a system of aspectual ones.

The general picture of how temporal terms develop, though, is fairly uniform across the different Romance languages. Children begin with a present time marker, and set up their first contrast as one between present and non-present time. Then they start to acquire their first terms for talking about sequence, usually beginning with a term like *d'abord* 'first' and soon after adding one like *puis* 'then, next'. The earliest time terms are all adverbials and appear to be used to "tag" each event separately. Later, they relate one event to another in time, with increasing reliance on conjunctions like *quand* 'when', from around age 3;0 or 3;6. Many of the more complex conjunctions, though, do not emerge for another two or three years.

The parallels among the Romance languages, and the similarity of this general sequence to those observed in other languages, suggests that the acquisition of temporal terms depends on children first acquiring the requisite conceptual distinctions. The pace and the order of emergence of different temporal distinctions indeed seem to be "set" by cognitive development. The same appears to be true for the various spatial terms and the distinctions they encode. Moreover, where the same term has both a spatial and a temporal sense, the spatial one seems to be acquired first (e.g. Lopez Ornat, 1975). The domains of space and time, then, appear to be an area where cognitive complexity plays a major role. At the same time, the Romance languages differ in how many terms they dispose of and hence the precise set of contrasts available for talking about space and time.

More detailed analysis of some of these differences might yield another domain in which to examine differences in formal complexity across languages (see Johnston & Slobin, 1979; Slobin, 1982).

10. Language Input

Adults adjust and try to simplify their speech to young children in Romance languages just as they do in English (Snow & Ferguson, 1977). They use babytalk terms and simplified constructions in talking to 1- and 2-year-olds. In French, for example, they use some special lexical items for various daily routines and activities: *faire dodo* 'to lie down, sleep', *bobo* 'sore', *faire bobo* 'to hurt oneself', *caca* 'dirty'; 'bowel movement', *pipi* 'urine'—both used with *faire* 'to do' for the activity; *mémé* or *mian-mian* 'food, eating',[23] *lolo* 'water', and also for toys and animals, e.g. *oua-oua* or *vou-vou* 'doggie' (equivalent to English *wuff-wuff,* for the noise of barking), and *nounours* 'toy bear, teddy bear' (Grégoire, 1937; Lentin, 1973; Lightbown, 1977; Paradis, 1978).

Spanish babytalk shows a similar range,[24] with special terms for a number of everyday objects and routines, e.g. *el miaú* 'cat', *el guau-gua(u)* 'dog', *el píopío* from *pollito* 'chick', *la papa* 'food, meal' as in *Es la hora de la papa* 'it's time to eat', *la meme,* possibly from *dormir, duerme* 'to sleep', 'sleep!' as in *Es la hora ir a la meme* 'it's time to go to bed', *el titín,* from *calcetín* 'sock', *el papo,* from *zapato* 'shoe', *la teta,* from *tetera* (New Mexico) 'bottle' and *hacer pipí* 'to do pipí'. Like French *faire,* Spanish *hacer* 'to do' supplies a general purpose verb in babytalk for all sorts of actions.

In Rumanian, there are a number of phonetic adjustments in babytalk words compared to their conventional equivalents in the adult lexicon. For example, Avram (1960) noted that fricative consonants were replaced by glottal stops, unstressed syllables were omitted, words were reduced to one or two syllables or to a single syllable that was reduplicated. (The latter is evident in French also, e.g. *lolo* from *l'eau* 'water' and *mémé* or *mian-mian* both possibly from *manger* 'to eat.') And, as in French and Spanish, adults make frequent use of more analytic expressions, e.g. verbs like *a face nani* 'to lie down, to sleep', like French *faire dodo,* instead of *a dormi* 'to sleep', and rely on juxtaposition rather than use of the genitive case to express possession, e.g. *carta mama* 'book mummy', with both nouns in the NOM-ACC case, instead of *cartea mami* 'the:book of:mummy' (= 'mummy's book'). They also use an analytic dative with the preposition *la* 'to' instead of a case marking.

Avram also noted that adults omitted articles, the copula verb, and even *a face* 'to do' in utterances addressed to young children. The indefinite article, *un,* was

---

[23]*Mémé* is sometimes used for 'grandma' or 'granny' too.

[24]The terms cited here are ones current in Mexican Spanish. I am indebted to Elly Pardo for these data. There is probably considerable variation in the repertoire used in different Spanish-speaking countries, just as there is in French-speaking ones (Paradis, 1978).

generally avoided, as was the definite, but he also noted some instances of the latter where adults wouldn't normally use it. There was general avoidance of both first and second person pronouns. Adults replaced them with third person ones—especially in the singular—or with nouns or proper names (see also Wills, 1977). Overall, there appear to be few verbs in Rumanian babytalk, aside from the constructions with *a face* 'to do' or *a da* 'to give', e.g. *a face nani* 'to sleep', *a face nini* 'to cajole', *a face pipi* 'to do pipi'; *a da nana* 'to hit', *a da un pup(ic)* 'to kiss'.

A number of the features noted by Avram are reported by Lentin (1973) in her comparison of middle- and lower-class French speech to young children. (Unfortunately, her sample—one family from each mileu—is too small to know whether the findings really pertain to class differences or rather are characteristic of the particular families studied.) The lower-class parents used babytalk to their 3-year-old, rarely corrected what he said, and used very simple sentences in talking to him. The father spent a good deal of time trying to teach him single words, presented to the child without articles or any larger context. In contrast, the middle-class parents carried on long conversations with their child, correcting number and gender errors by repeating the child's utterances with the appropriate changes, and using a large range of quite complicated sentence structures.

A more detailed quantitative analysis of the kind of utterances used by both mothers and fathers to their children is presented by Rondal (1980). He recorded the speech of five middle-class Canadian French families in three different settings with their only children (who ranged from 1;6 to 3;0 in age) in order to examine the language used by fathers as well as mothers. The older the child in the family, the more lexical diversity in both parents' speech. There was also an increase with age in the average utterance length used to the child, with a concomitant increase in syntactic complexity. There were also fewer imperatives, repetitions, and expansions used to older children. These quantitative findings parallel those for English (see Clark & Clark, 1977; Snow & Ferguson, 1977). Rondal, however, gave no details about the uses of such factors as word order, left- or right-dislocated subjects, uses of pronoun objects, or any other structures peculiar to French as a language.

In her study of children's descriptions, Sinclair (1973) noted that the only departure from SVO word order in children over 3;6 was with right-dislocation of the subject, VOS, as in *Il a poussé les oiseaux le cochon* 'He pushed the birds the pig' (= 'the pig pushed the birds'). Sinclair suggested that this order was normally avoided by adults where it would be ambiguous, and therefore rejected the possibility that children's VOS forms might be based on an adult model. However, the findings reported by both Virbel (1975) and Faïta (1974), together with the frequency of both left- and right-dislocations in adult colloquial speech, suggest that there is an adult model for such noncanonical word orders. Indeed Lightbown (1977) noted several instances where the mothers of the two children she studied used just such utterances. For example, from Daniel's mother (Lightbown, 1977, p. 183):

(a) Mo (looking at a familiar TinTin book with D): *Pourquoi il a tapé le soldat, le gros monsieur?* 'Why he hit the soldier, the big man' (= 'Why did the big man hit the soldier?')

(b) Mo (commenting that D has found the missing cover for a box): *Elle a trouvé son couvercle la petite boîte?* 'it found its lid the little box' (= 'Has the little box found its lid?')

Right-dislocation of the subject appears with both with transitive and with intransitive verbs (1977, p. 184):

(c) Mo (D has thrown a ball): *Elle va vite, la balle.* 'it goes fast, the ball' (= 'The ball goes fast')

(d) Mo (looking at picture book with D): *Elle rit, la petite fille, quand il passe, le garçon.* 'she laughs, the little girl, when he goes by, the boy' (= 'The little girl laughs as the little boy goes by')

With intransitive verbs, there is no ambiguity. Overall, the number of utterances with VOS order (Lightbown gave examples only of right-dislocations, by far the commonest in Virbel's (1976) data) was low. It amounted to only 8% for Daniel's mother and 5% for Nathalie's. At the same time, it was the commonest divergence from SVO order in parental speech.

Lightbown (1977) also noted an almost complete absence of subject and verb inversion in yes/no questions. Both mothers relied on rising intonation alone with the normal declarative word order in utterances intended as yes/no questions. This, of course, is the commonest way to ask such questions in spoken French, both among adults and in adult-child interactions (see Behnstedt, 1973; Redard, 1976). These parents also avoided inversion in *qu-* questions. Again, this absence of inversion is typical of the *qu-* questions asked of children at least up to age 3 (Redard, 1976).

These findings suggest that children's word orders in French, typified by dependence on subject dislocation and absence of inversion in all questions, do have an adult model. But the relatively small proportion of VOS-order utterances reported by Lightbown (1977) would appear to go against frequency as an explanation for children's word orders. However, subject dislocation is often accompanied by heavier stress or greater volume in pronouncing the dislocated noun phrase or emphatic pronoun (*moi, toi, lui,* etc.) and that could make the order in such utterances more salient to young children.

The findings for Italian input are slightly different. Although there is a similar proportion of VOS orders in adult-to-adult speech in Italian, adults talking to younger children use non-SVO orders with explicit noun or pronoun subjects as much as 50% of the time. This heavy reliance by adults on noncanonical but pragmatically salient word orders (Duranti & Ochs, 1979) is presumably a major factor in the highly variable word order produced by Italian children during the earlier stages of acquisition (see also Slobin, 1982; Slobin & Bever, 1982).

There is little direct information available on input for Spanish. Blount and Padgug (1977) reported on a comparison of parental input to five small children acquiring English and four acquiring Spanish (all but one of the children under 1;6). They focused primarily on prosodic features such as breathiness, high pitch, vowel lengthening, and slow tempo, but also looked at several other characteristics of speech to children such as pronoun use, repetitions, and baby-talk words. They found considerable similarity across parents, but the features most favored in the two languages did not always coincide. For example, Spanish-speaking parents made more use of baby-talk words, repetitions of words, and instructions, than English-speaking ones did. And English-speaking ones made more use of affective prosodic features such as exaggerated intonation patterns. Blount and Padgug suggest that some of the differences stemmed from the preference for a direct interactive ''style'' on the part of Spanish-speaking parents. This conclusion is offered strong support by Eisenberg's (1982) ethnographic study on adult input in two lower class Mexican families. Parents and relatives alike focused on appropriate names, address terms, and the things one should say or feel in particular situations. Such ethnographic studies point to a very important aspect of the language adults speak to children: it offers them information not only about the language, but also about the culture, and hence about how to use language in that culture.

To summarize, although there have been a few studies of input language for some of the Romance languages, there has been little attempt to focus in such studies on linguistic features peculiar to Romance. As yet, little is known about the range of modifications made by parents speaking such languages, the variability of parental word order, or the extent to which that variability might be pragmatically predictable. Equally unknown is whether parents avoid clitic pronouns or complex combinations of clitic pronouns, or whether they consistently correct their children's mistakes of gender, number, agreement, or verb form. As yet, there are few answers available for any of these questions.

11. Individual Differences

Individual differences are as poorly documented for the acquisition of Romance languages as they appear to be elsewhere. There has been no research specifically addressed to this question. However, there are a few observations available in the literature that suggest children may vary quite a bit in the precise route they follow in acquiring particular subsystems of their first language. For example, the degree of divergence from a canonical SVO word order in French may depend to some extent on the individual child. Guillaume (1927b) noted few divergences, but Lightbown (1977) found large divergences in one child compared to relatively few in the other. The differences appeared to be related to differences in the relative frequency of transitive and intransitive action verbs. Leroy (1975) also noted highly variable word order in one child compared to stricter adherence to an SVO order in another. The differences in this case were correlated with differential uses of intonation. The variable-order child seemed to rely on intonation as a segmentation device to mark the ends of constituents and produced adult-like intonation sequences with few identifiable words. The SVO child, in contrast, used shorter sequences and more clearly pronounced phonological segments (see Peters, 1977). Lightbown (1977) also found that one of the children she followed was a "pronominal" child while the other was a "nominal" one—that is, one of the children used a higher proportion of pronouns in two-word combinations than the other (see Bloom, Lightbown, & Hood, 1975).

The rate at which different children master different parts of the language also varies considerably. Some children master particular locative and temporal terms as much as a year or more before others, although the order of acquisition tends to be the same (e.g. Grégoire, 1947; Ferreiro, 1971). The range of options open to children acquiring different subsystems, though, has not been directly studied at all. Cohen (1969), like other diarists, pointed to a number of cases in which there is a considerable difference in the length of time to mastery of such subsystems as pronouns, articles, irregular verbs, and relative clause constructions. These differences are also apparent when one compares different diary records (e.g. Grégoire, 1947; Fondet, 1979), but all too often the crucial comparison data are missing. Moreover, for the other Romance languages, there are hardly any diary records available at all. The only longitudinal data available on Spanish, Italian, Portuguese, or Rumanian from the last two or three decades have focused mainly on the earlier stages of acquisition (e.g. Bates, 1976; Eisenberg, 1982; de Lemos, 1975; Scliar-Cabral, 1976). There is little material on later stages suitable for documenting possible individual differences in language acquisition.

Nonetheless, it is possible to speculate about certain dimensions along which there do seem to be individual differences. For example, a comparison of the children studied by Grégoire (1937, 1947) and Aimard (1975) suggests that children may differ considerably in how creative they are with the lexicon—how much they coin new words, how aware they are of rhymes and puns, how much they play with sounds and senses during acquisition. Although all three children coined new words and indulged in a certain amount of word play, Aimard's daughter appears to have done so to a much greater extent than Grégoire's sons. The paucity of diary studies, though, makes such comparisons very difficult.

The domains identified as sources of typical errors (Section 4) are the obvious place to start in trying to document individual differences in the acquisition process. If children differ in their willingness to make inferences about the structures being acquired, one might expect "bold" or "rash" learners to leap in as soon as they've heard one or two exemplars. Such children may generalize very quickly and thus make many more errors initially than those farther towards the cautious end of the continuum. "Cautious" learners could be characterized as those who wait for the evidence to come in before committing themselves. And they should make fewer errors. But, at the same time, one would expect them to avoid the constructions or word-forms they are unsure of so they appear to acquire them later than their "rash" peers. There is some preliminary evidence for just such a continuum among children learning a second language (Fillmore, 1976; Vihman, 1982). Some start in immediately, trying to use whatever they have picked up, while others go much more slowly and cautiously until they are sure of what they are saying. There seems to be no reason not to assume that one source of individual differences in first language acquisition is children's relative caution or boldness in trying out new ways of communicating (see also Nelson, 1980).

The study of individual differences is likely to provide critical information about universals in language acquisition. This is because the range of individual differences provides another source of information about permissible routes in acquisition. Universals of language acquisition do not specify one single route for all children to follow, but rather the bounds on a range of possible routes. And to set these bounds, one needs to look both at what children do in common as they acquire their mother tongue and at what they do differently. Information about individual differences will allow us to chart much more precisely the universals in first language acquisition.

CONCLUSIONS

In the last part of this review, I first take up several theoretical issues, pertinent not only to the present review of Romance acquisition, but also to language acquisition in general. I then make some suggestions about where further research might answer some of the many questions noted so far.

12. Some Theoretical Implications

Common to all research on language acquisition are several theoretical problems. Here I wish to take up just three of them. The first concerns what it means to have ACQUIRED a particular word meaning, linguistic distinction, or syntactic construction. The second concerns the kinds of COMPLEXITY that may play a role in when and how children acquire various parts of their first language. And the third concerns how one tests for or identifies UNIVERSALS in the acquisition process. The resolution of each of these issues has important implications for the study of language acquisition and for claims made both about the course of acquisition followed by children for different languages and about the actual process of acquisition itself.

12.1. *What Does Acquired Mean?*   Most of the data that have been collected on children's language acquisition consist of detailed records of children's spontaneous speech. These production data provide the kind of corpus from which investigators conclude that children have or haven't acquired particular constructions in the language under study.

But what criteria are applied in assessing acquisition? These have varied from simple usage of a form alone in apparently appropriate circumstances, to some minimal frequency of occurrence, say five instances per recording session of a particular construction, or, a more stringent requirement, adult-like use in 90% of the linguistic contexts where an adult speaker would have used that particular form. The difficulty in attributing acquisition in each such case is fairly obvious. Use alone, even in appropriate-seeming contexts, does not assure that a child has real productive control over a particular morpheme, word, or construction. Children use many utterances in a formulaic way in restricted contexts during both early and late stages of acquisition. And this could be true on five or more occasions during a single recording session. The third level of use I mentioned, the 90% criterion, has been applied mainly to the acquisition of grammatical morphemes in English. It too has failings. First, some uses could be formulaic and yet count towards meeting the criterion. Second, taking the linguistic context as the basis for assessing adult use there may not be sufficient. This may often leave out of account errors of content as opposed to errors of form. A child may have intended to designate two dogs, rather than one, with *See the dog,* but there is nothing in the linguistic context that suggests the child has in fact made an error.

The nonlinguistic setting as well as the linguistic context both have to be taken into account. This is because the child's productions need to be matched as far as possible with what he intended to communicate on each occasion. The recognition of this issue has led many investigators to take more careful account of the context of each utterance at the two-word stage, but older children are still all to often taken at face value when they say anything. Investigators who hear conventional forms used apparently appropriately rarely go beyond those uses to check whether the children really have adult-like command of those forms and their functions.

The questions I have raised so far about judging whether some form has been acquired or not apply to forms that children produce. But what about the forms they understand? There seems to be less of a problem in assessing acquisition in comprehension. The data appear slightly more clear-cut (where they are available) in that the obvious criterion is consistent adult-like responses. (One has to guard, of course, against adult-like responses that are not based on linguistic knowledge of the pertinent forms.) The major limitation, as far as comprehension data are concerned appears to lie with the investigator. In many cases, it is hard to devise appropriate experiments to check up on how children understand particular words or constructions. And most have approached the problem by removing any clues that might be offered either by the physical setting or by the surrounding discourse. Comprehension studies in general, then, set a very strict criterion before attributing to children the acquisition of particular forms. And this in turn may make comprehension tasks highly unnatural. For example, it is difficult to tell whether the strategies that show up in such tasks are the ones children normally use, or whether they are called up just to deal with special situations.

But the real problem arises when production and comprehension data from the same child do not match. If a child understands a form but fails to produce it, we do not wish to conclude that the child has not yet "acquired" that form. If we do, we are clearly underestimating the child's linguistic knowledge. How, then, should we characterize such data? Many discussions of acquisition have assumed a representation of linguistic knowledge in the child (and adult) that is neutral between comprehension and production. Such an analysis is clearly called into question when comprehension and production fail to match (see Clark & Hecht, 1983). And mismatches where comprehension precedes or simply doesn't match production are very common.[25] From one perspective, a child HAS acquired the plural article in French, say, but from the other that same child has not. How can this fact be related to a uniform representation of linguistic knowledge that fails to distinguish the processes of comprehension and production? One solution, of course, until this issue is fully resolved in a theoretically satisfactory manner, is to report for each form and function whether it has been acquired in comprehension and in production, or in only one of these modes.

The problem may be even more acute. If the processes of comprehension and production are sufficiently different from one another, it may well be that constructions that are easy in comprehension (and hence simpler by some measure) may be relatively harder than other related constructions in production. A mismatch of this type appears to hold, for example, in the acquisition of relative clauses in French. The two major processes involved in language use may require different criteria for assessing complexity in language acquisition.

12.2. *Kinds of Complexity.*   One issue in accounting for order of acquisition in a language is the measure or measures of complexity used to predict the

---

[25]Such mismatches may play an important role in the actual process of acquisition. If children base their own memory representations on the forms heard from adults, and monitor their own productions, then any mismatches they detect between their representations (used in comprehension) and their own productions of those same forms may provide the impetus for them to attempt to CHANGE their own productions in the direction of the adult's (see Clark, 1982b).

particular order found. While there has been extensive discussion of RELATIVE complexity within various subsystems for both syntactic and semantic development (e.g. Brown, 1973; Clark, 1973b, 1983), there has been much less discussion of what determines an overall order of acquisition. Slobin (1973) came closest to this when he posited two major influences on acquisition as a whole: the cognitive complexity of the distinction being acquired and the formal complexity of the linguistic device or devices used to pick out that distinction in each language. Development of the requisite cognitive distinction places a lower bound on when a child can begin to look for some linguistic means of expression, while the time from this point to the point of acquiring the conventional adult expressions provides a measure of the formal complexity of the pertinent linguistic devices in a particular language. For example, children acquiring English and Arabic begin to talk about plurality at about the same age (around 2), using various unconventional devices (e.g. *two book*). Children acquiring English then go on to master the conventional system of noun plurals by about age 6 while Arabic-speaking children take to age 12 or more. This, Slobin argued, is a direct reflection of the formal complexity of the pluralization system in Arabic for nouns.

For Slobin's proposal to be extended, one needs good measures of cognitive distinctions independent of the language used to express them. This will allow one to equate children acquiring different languages at the point where they are starting to look for the relevant linguistic devices to express particular cognitive distinctions. However, there has been relatively little research taking up this facet of Slobin's argument. There have been several attempts, however, to analyze the linguistic complexity of what children have to acquire in terms of the kinds of acquisition processes children bring to their first language (e.g. Slobin, 1973, 1977, 1985; MacWhinney, 1978, 1985). These acquisition processes have focused on properties of the structures to be acquired—for instance, whether a language uses prepositions or postpositions, whether it is a case-inflected language, whether grammatical relations are indicated by word order, and so on. And there has also been some analysis of factors like productivity (the extent to which a particular word-formation device can be used to form new words, say) and regularity (the size of various paradigms to which various inflections apply, say) in the domain of word formation (e.g. Clark, 1980a, 1981a, 1981b).

These attempts to analyze linguistic complexity have focused mainly on the forms to be acquired. But there are other kinds of complexity that pertain to the conversational uses of such forms. For instance, one dimension of complexity may be the register chosen by the speaker to fit the circumstances—who the addressee is, the topic of conversation, the degree of mutual knowledge about it, the social relations holding between speaker and addressee, and so on. The child has to learn which choices, at the levels of phonology, morphology, lexicon, and even sentence structure, are correlated with particular registers (Ervin-Tripp, 1973).

Another source of complexity that is linked to register choice is the set of rules governing conversational turns (e.g. Sacks, Schegloff, & Jefferson, 1974). While turn-taking with two participants seems to be set up for children in some cultures very early (e.g. Snow, 1977), turn-taking in larger groups is generally much more complex, and children take a number of years to learn how to participate appropriately. Some conversational settings may be more complex than others because of the range of factors to be taken into account. For instance, talking to peers should be simpler than talking to non-peers; talking to family members should be simpler than talking to people outside the family, and so on. While there may be many formulaic expressions learned early on, for instance, in greeting routines (e.g. Clancy, 1985), acquiring conversational "rules" takes time.

Yet another source of complexity within each register and conversation type is the genre of speech required. Many lexical and structural choices depend on the type of discourse—whether the speaker is telling a story that is fictitious, a second-hand report, or an eye-witness account; giving instructions; making arrangements for future actions with several people, and so on. Particular genres themselves often require particular linguistic devices and observe special conventions. The speaker of any language must learn these rules too. Since the young child's repertoire for genre is fairly limited, it seems quite reasonable to suppose that this may provide yet another dimension of complexity in the acquisition process.

Ultimately, cognitive, formal, and interactional kinds of complexity will have to be assessed all together for their relative contributions at different stages during language acquisition. Most studies have limited themselves to a single dimension of complexity, treating it as if it is the only factor affecting the use of a particular linguistic form. But the present list, incomplete as it is, makes it clear that linguistic complexity covers a broader range of phenomena than has been considered so far.

12.3. *Universals of Acquisition.*   What universals are there in the acquisition process? What do children acquiring French, Hungarian, and Navajo do in common as they tackle the problem of mastering a first language? One goal in studying language acquisition is to identify possible universals of acquisition. Reports of the early stages of language acquisition, when children are producing one-word and then two-word utterances, show striking similarities across languages (e.g. Slobin, 1970). However, the task of identifying universals becomes more complex as children begin to master inflectional systems, agreement, word order, and the particular arrays of properties that distinguish one language from another.

Slobin (1973) inspected a large body of data from several languages in arriving at a preliminary list of universals in acquisition. From these he derived various Operating Principles that would account for the tendencies he had observed. For example, he noted that children generally acquired grammatical markers attached to the ends of words before they acquired such markers attached to the beginnings of, or preceding, words, e.g. the plural -*s* on nouns in English before articles or prepositions. This universal, he suggested, could be captured by postulating that children paid attention to the ends, rather than the beginnings of words. However, this particular Operating Principle has then to be reconciled with the fact that when children first try to pronounce words, they generally attempt the first few segments but often omit the final ones. Here then, they appear to be attending to the beginnings and not to the ends of words. Such discrepancies point to two factors that need to be taken into account in the study of such universals: whether the Operating Principle is one for comprehension or for production, and what the current state of the child's knowledge is.

The Operating Principle, "Pay attention to the ends of words," is one that pertains to children who are trying to understand the language being spoken around them. It assumes that they can already recognize word bases or stems but have not yet worked out how combinations of two or more words may be related to each other (as well as to the physical and linguistic contexts). Under these circumstances, this principle would have to be characterized as a principle for comprehension. But what about when children themselves try to talk? It is then that they appear to pay most attention to the beginnings of words. In this case, the inverse Operating Principle, "Pay attention to the beginnings of words," appears to be at work, but the strategy in this case is one that applies to production. If children only pronounced the ends of words, it would be much harder to tell what words they were attempting. This example makes clear the need to consider universals in acquisition from two perspectives, comprehension and production, and to look at the different operating principles that guide the growth of each process.

The operating principles children rely on at any particular point during acquisition will also depend on the actual state of their linguistic knowledge. For example, once they have gained articulatory control of a large vocabulary, they will have less need to focus specifically on getting the beginnings of words right in production. This will have become an almost automatic part of their speaking. And, once they have come to understand the full case system, say, they will no longer have to focus on the ends of words to the same degree in an effort to identify and analyze the meanings of different case endings. Particular operating principles or strategies, then, may apply at different stages, and may be ranked differently among themselves at different points in the acquisition process. The critical question is how children's strategies are organized initially and which take priority over others. Some strategies may make exactly opposite predictions and the issue is to find a principled basis on which to order them and weight them in relation to what a child already knows. Ultimately, the body of strategies children develop for comprehension and production must become equivalent in scope to those that adults rely on.

To identify universals of acquisition requires that we find answers to fundamental questions. The search for these answers offers a major challenge—that of finding out how children really do acquire their first language.

CODA

13. Some Suggestions for Further Study

Of the Romance languages included here, French has been the best studied to date, yet even there, there are many lacunae in the data available. For the other four languages, we know much less. There are few or no diary studies available in print and few experimental studies. And the data that are available on Italian and Spanish, for instance, are often not directly comparable. Nor are they comparable to the more extensive data available for French. There is some documentation of the very early stages of acquisition for Italian, Portuguese, and Spanish, but studies of the later stages of acquisition, or of children over age 3 or 4, are a comparative rarity. Rumanian appears to be the least well-documented language from the point of view of acquisition. Despite some research by linguists, there is no published diary record that documents the acquisition of the one remaining case system in Romance, nor the numerous other details that differentiate Rumanian from the other Romance languages. As a result, it is difficult, despite the materials that are available, to build up a composite picture of the stages children go through as they acquire any one of these languages. The French case, of course, is the best documented, and hence offers plentiful clues to what one might expect in the other Romance languages. Yet even so, there are many unanswered questions.

13.1. *Canonical Word Orders.* Word order in French, as in the other Romance language, is commonly said to be SVO. Yet when one considers colloquial spoken French, with its heavy reliance on subject dislocation, it becomes clear that the usual word order is much more variable than most accounts would suggest: VOS is also frequent, possibly as frequent as SVO, in adult speech. So the question of which order or orders children consider CANONICAL is an important one. The picture is further complicated in French since these two—SVO and VOS—are canonical only for utterances with full noun phrase arguments. As soon as one uses object pronouns for direct and indirect objects, the canonical order changes. For direct object pronouns, the order is SOV or, combined with a right-dislocated subject, (S)OVS. When the indirect object pronoun is added into the account, things get even more complex. First and second person IO pronouns precede the DO pronoun, while third person IO pronouns follow it, to produce the following canonical orders: $S-IO:_{1,2}-DO-V$ and $S-DO-IO:_3-V$. The word orders change yet again when the mood is imperative, with the clitic object pronouns following the verb in the order V-DO-IO, rather than indicative. When negated, however, the canonical imperative word order reverts to that used in the indicative, with the same differentiation of first and second versus third person indirect object orders. Negative placement adds a further complication, where the negative particle (usually *pas* alone in colloquial speech) has to be placed after the finite verb. That often means after the auxiliary *avoir* or *être,* which, in compound tenses, carries tense, number, and (where marked) person. Add to this the canonical word orders in relative clauses, where object relatives allow optional inversion of the subject and verb to produce an OVS order (alongside a OSV one), and the various "stylistic" inversions following particular conjunctions, and it becomes clear that "word order" in French should be far from simple to acquire.

When children acquire adult-like knowledge of the canonical word orders is not at all clear. What we do know is that they make errors in word order at numerous points in the system. Some of these errors appear to result from an over-reliance on a single order, for instance, maintenance of SVO order in both yes/no and *qu-* questions, and also some reliance on SVO with (tonic) pronoun objects. Other order errors appear to result from reliance on a single canonical order for all clitic pronoun combinations, with IO before DO. These regularizations suggest that children acquiring French take some time to sort out the different factors that affect word order, the main ones being negation, tense, mood, and person. The errors documented so far appear predictable if we assume children start with one general word order and impose it as canonical for a variety of situations (see Slobin & Bever, 1982). What we do not know is the extent to which children of different ages impose canonical word order schemata, nor which ones are favored early. To find out will require much more systematic examination of word order in production, and especially of the word orders favored by the younger children.

Canonical word orders and their scope—the range of construction-types each applies to—are therefore one important domain in which we need to ask more systematic questions about the course of acquisition. And, in asking such questions, we also need to look closely at how children who do not yet know the adult word orders convey the grammatical and pragmatic information such orders carry.

13.2. *Tense and Aspect.*   When do children begin to organize their discourse, their conversational turns, along temporal and aspectual lines? Studies of tense and aspect have focused mainly on the mapping of action-type and verb aspect or tense, as in Bronckart's (1976) detailed investigation. But there has been little attention paid to (a) how different tenses and aspects are marked within the conversational setting, (b) which contrasts may be required for highlighting or backgrounding different pieces of information, or (c) the range of contrasts possible among action-types and their outcomes. Tense can also be used to reflect the speaker's perspective and involvement in an event or activity. And there are also conventions on how one tells a story, setting up the salient events and characters against a background of other activities and events. All of these discourse activities are marked by subtle uses of the various tenses and aspects available in the language.

In the experimental work done so far, the forms elicited from children aged 3;0 and up suggest that the youngest children use hardly any tense or aspect markers beyond the compound past or the infinitive, both produced apparently to talk about the activity being observed (Bronckart, 1976). This account, of course, contrasts rather with observations of children's use of temporal markers in spontaneous speech (Section 9.2). From 3;6 to 6;0, Bronckart argued that children used different tense forms to mark aspect, focusing mainly on whether an action was completed (compound past) or not (imperfect). It was only after that, he suggested, that children invested a temporal value in different verb tense forms. However, their spontaneous uses of tense and of temporal adverbs suggests that this development may occur much earlier (e.g. Decroly & Degand, 1913).

What is needed now are studies complementary to the kind of investigation carried out by Bronckart, studies that focus on the uses to which different tense forms are put in a variety of different conversational settings. Only in this way can we arrive at a fuller picture of how children acquire the range of aspectual and temporal options available to them.

13.3. *Discourse Structure.*   Despite several studies of conversation between children or between children and adults (e.g. Slama-Cazacu, 1961, 1966; Goldberg, 1976; Brami-Mouling, 1977; François, 1978e, 1978f; Hudelot, 1980), there has been little research on when or how children start to act as cooperative participants in conversation. When do they acquire the particular devices used in Romance to mark elements as given, or as themes, or as "settings" for subsequent utterances? How soon do children acquire a notion of "relevance" à la Grice? Where do they observe or fail to observe the various maxims Grice (1975) characterized along with the Cooperative Principle? While there are clues to different segments of such developments in the research on definite articles, on tense and aspect, and on word order, there has been little research on discourse itself, either in the form of conversations between two or more participants, or in the form of short narrative "texts" produced spontaneously or with probing, by children of different ages (but see Karmiloff-Smith, 1980).

While discourse would appear to include everything anyone has ever studied in the acquisition of Romance, there is good reason to look at the earliest forms of discourse children participate in. They build up their knowledge of both structure and function in language from the uses to which language is put, that is, from language observed in its social setting (e.g. Ervin-Tripp, 1977). The child's gradual mastery of the principles and conventions governing conversation and narrative, then, may provide insights into his growing mastery over different parts of the language systems being acquired—for example, word order, deictic and anaphoric pronoun use, definite reference, modification, and tense.

13.4. *Language Input.*   Another domain for which little information is available is that of language input. What kinds of modifications do Romance speakers make for young children? In their "baby talk," they clearly make many of the same kinds of modifications to word forms as speakers of other languages. And some of the simplifications reported (reliance on general purpose verbs, omission of articles, prepositions, and copula verbs, replacement of pronouns by noun phrases) are common to other languages too. But virtually nothing is known about the kinds of word order and word-order variation offered as models to young Romance speakers. To what extent are the patterns noted for Italian input (Bates, 1976) typical of parental input to 2-year-olds acquiring the other Romance languages? Would this account for the variable word order noted for some children? To what extent are adult variations in word order tied to register and to pragmatic factors? Indeed, many of the forms identified as erroneous in children's speech are common in current usage in many varieties of colloquial French. It is therefore essential to establish what the input is that children hear.

Another area awaiting investigation is the pattern of pronoun use offered to children. Are adult pronoun uses in input primarily deictic or anaphoric? And what patterns of clitic pronoun combinations occur in input speech? How do adults indicate possession to very young children: analytically, with a preposition plus noun phrase construction, or by means of possessive adjectives or pronouns? Which *qu-* question forms are most used, or used earlier in speech to 1- and 2-year-olds? Which tense forms are commonest in which contexts? Does adult input focus children's attention on such factors as completive or incompletive aspect? Do adult uses of tense and aspect to young children differ from uses to other adults? The myriad questions to which we have no current answers attest to the need for more research in this domain.

13.5. *Word-Formation Options.*   The Romance languages as a family have a rich set of derivational, mainly suffixal, forms available for coining new words. They also allow some compounding, with this becoming a commoner process of word formation than it used to be in a language like French. Languages like Spanish and Italian also rely on a large variety of diminutive and augmentative suffixes, used to talk about both size and affect (positive and negative) as modulations on words for categories or properties. (The suffixes used may be added to nouns or adjectives, or both.) Observation of children's spontaneous speech in French suggests that they know a good deal about the word-formational possibilities in their language by age 3 or 4. The same presumably is true of children acquiring the other Romance languages. However, there has been virtually no systematic analysis of word-formation by children (but see

Aimard, 1975; Clark, 1982a), and no systematic study of what children know about meanings and forms in the coinage of new words.

This domain of research is important for the light it casts on children's knowledge of meaning and form paradigms, on their rule use, and on their observance of such general principles as conventionality and contrast, which govern the lexicon as a whole (Clark, 1980a, 1983). Extensive comparative data are needed in order to identify WHICH general principles play a role in the acquisition of a word-formation repertoire.

These five areas represent those in which new research, in my opinion, would contribute most, both to the overall picture of how children acquire a Romance language, and to more detailed pictures of the acquisition of canonical word orders, clitic pronouns, tense and aspect as organizers of "time-talk," discourse structure, and word-formation as subsystems within the language being acquired. I have focused on these areas because they would offer information about certain forms and functions specific to the Romance languages; because there are few or no data currently available; and because studies in these areas will allow crosslinguistic comparisons not currently possible.

13.6. *Within-Family Comparisons.*   Finally, since the Romance languages differ at a number of points in the details of how particular systems have evolved over time, it would be particularly interesting to do some comparative studies of, say, word order and cliticization, with particular emphasis on where these languages diverge from each other, to see whether such comparisons might cast further light on the kinds of difficulties attributable to "formal" complexity, in the sense used by Slobin (1973). Although there are acquisition data available on some Germanic languages (English, German, Dutch), there has been little or no attempt to look at differences in the course of acquisition for such closely allied systems.

The Romance languages offer several particularly interesting points of comparison. For example, all but Rumanian have preposed articles. In Rumanian, they are postposed. What difference does this make to the acquisition of the article system? All the Romance languages mark gender in nouns and require agreement with adjectives and on occasion with verb participles. What difference do the different numbers of forms within the definite article system make to children's acquisition? In French, for instance, both of the singular article forms, like the plural, begin with /l-/ (*le*-MASC:SG, *la*-FEM:SG), but in Spanish, only the feminine singular form resembles the plural forms: *la*-FEM:SG, *las*-FEM:PL, *los*-MASC:PL. The masculine singular has the form *el,* and thus may not be as easily identified as a member of the article system. The other Romance languages offer yet other points of contrast.

Such comparisons might also be important in considering word formation since they offer a rather similar range of word-formation options, alongside a lexicon that has evolved in rather different directions, for instance, in French with Germanic influence, and in Spanish with some Arabic influence. The extent to which historical factors have influenced current choices of word-formation devices is a topic that has received some attention in the domain of philology, but virtually none in the field of language acquisition.

ACKNOWLEDGMENTS

This review was begun while I was a Fellow at the Center for Advanced Study in the Behavioral Sciences, Stanford; it was supported in part by the National Science Foundation (BNS80-07349) and the Spencer Foundation. I would like to thank all the participants at the conference for which this review was prepared as well as the many colleagues who supplied me with additional references, corrections, reactions, and arguments, particularly Annette Karmiloff-Smith, Patsy M. Lightbown, Clive Perdue, Hava Ben-Zeev Shyldkrot, and Marilyn May Vihman. I also owe special thanks to Margaret Amara of the Center for Advanced Study in the Behavioral Sciences for tirelessly tracking down so many of the articles I consulted. Last of all, I am deeply indebted to Dan I. Slobin for offering me the opportunity of carrying out a project I had long had in mind and for making so many insightful comments and suggestions on earlier versions of the manuscript.

REFERENCES

Aimard, P. *Les jeux de mots de l'enfant.* Villeurbanne: Simép Editions, 1975.

Allain-Sokolsky, G. Interaction adulte-enfant dans la mise en fonctionnement du système syntaxique d'entrainement à l'école maternelle. *Langue Française,* 1975, *27,* 95–104.

Ammon, M. S., & Slobin, D. I. A cross-linguistic study of the processing of causative sentences. *Cognition,* 1979, *7,* 1–17.

Anastasi, A., & de Jesus, C. Language development and nonverbal IQ of Puerto Rican preschool children in New York City. *Journal of Abnormal & Social Psychology,* 1953, *48,* 357–366.

Annibaldi-Vion, M. La compréhension des phrases simples chez le jeune enfant: Une étude expérimentale. Thèse du Doctorat de Troisième Cycle, Université de Provence, Centre d'Aix-Marseille, 1980.

Antinucci, F., & Miller, R. How children talk about what happened. *Journal of Child Language,* 1976, *3,* 167–189.

Antinucci, F., & Parisi, D. Early language acquisition: A model and some data. In C. A. Ferguson & D. I. Slobin (Eds.), *Studies of child language development.* New York: Holt, Rinehart & Winston, 1973. Pp. 607–619.

Antinucci, F., & Volterra, V. Lo sviluppo della negazione nel linguaggio infantile: Uno studio pragmatico. *Lingua e Stile,* 1975, *10,* 231–260.

Avram, A. De la langue qu'on parle aux enfants roumains. In *To Honor Roman Jakobson,* vol. 1. The Hague: Mouton, 1960. Pp. 133–140.

Axia, G., & Nicolini, C. 'Prima-dopo', 'davanti-dietro': Uno studio sperimentale sui termini spazio-temporali in bambini di età prescolare. *Età Evolutiva,* 1979, *2,* 101–108.

Bacri, N., & Boysson-Bardies, B. de, Portée de la négation et référentiation chez les enfants de 4 à 10 ans. *Année Psychologique,* 1977, *77,* 117–136.

Bates, E. The acquisition of conditionals by Italian children. In M. W. LaGaly, R. A. Fox, & A. Bruck (Eds.), *Papers from the tenth regional meeting.* Chicago: Chicago Linguistic Society, 1974. Pp. 27–36.

Bates, E. *Language and context: The acquisition of pragmatics.* New York: Academic Press, 1976.

Bates, E., McNew, S., MacWhinney, B., Devescovi, A., & Smith, S. Functional constraints on sentence processing: A cross-linguistic study. *Cognition,* 1982, *11,* 245–300.

Bates, E., & Rankin, J. Morphological development in Italian: Connotation and denotation. *Journal of Child Language,* 1979, *6,* 29–52.

Bautier-Castaing, E. Acquisition comparée de la syntaxe du français par des enfants francophones et non-francophones. *Etudes de Linguistique Appliquée,* 1977, *27,* 19–41.

Bautier-Castaing, E. La notion de stratégie d'apprentissage permet-elle de rendre compte de l'acquisition d'une langue seconde par des enfants? *Langages,* 1980, *57,* 95–106.

Beaudichon, J., & Lemaire, F. Acquisition de la négation considérée sous différents aspects chez l'enfant de 3 à 8 ans. *Bulletin de Psychologie,* 1972–1973, *26,* 375–382.

Behnstedt, P. *Viens-tu? Est-ce que tu viens? Tu viens? Formen und Strukturen des direkten Fragesatzes im Französischen.* Tübingen: Gunter Narr Verlag, 1973.

Berko, J. The child's learning of English morphology. *Word,* 1958, *14,* 150–177.

Berman, R. A. Early verbs: Comments on how and why a child uses his first words. *International Journal of Psycholinguistics,* 1978, *5,* 21–39.

Bermejo, V. S. Contribución a la ontogenesis de lenguaje. *Revista de Psicología General y Aplicada,* 1975, *30,* 1081–1091.

Bernicot, J. *Le développement des systèmes sémantiques de verbes d'action.* (Monographies françaises de psychologie, No. 53.) Paris: Editions du CNRS, 1981.

Berthoud, I., & Sinclair, H. L'expression des éventualités et de conditions chez l'enfant. *Archives de Psychologie,* 1978, *179,* 205–233.

Berthoz-Proux, M. Aperçu de certains développements récents des recherches sur l'acquisition du langage. *Langue Française,* 1975, *27,* 105–121.

Bideaud, J. Etude génétique de la quantification en situation d'emboîtements concrets. *Enfance,* 1979, *2,* 133–148.

Bloch, O. Les premiers stades du langage de l'enfant. *Journal de Psychologie,* 1921, *18,* 693–712.

Bloch, O. Langage d'action dans les premiers stades du langage de l'enfant. *Journal de Psychologie,* 1923, *20,* 670–674.

Bloch, O. La phrase dans le langage de l'enfant. *Journal de Psychologie,* 1924, *21,* 18–43.

Bloom, L., Lifter, K., & Hafitz, J. Semantics of verbs and the development of verb inflections in child language. *Language,* 1980, *56,* 386–412.

Blount, B. G., & Padgug, E. J. Prosodic, paralinguistic, and interactional features in parent-child speech: English and Spanish. *Journal of Child Language,* 1977, *4,* 67–86.

Bonnet, C., & Tamine, J. Les noms construits par les enfants: Description d'un corpus. *Langages,* 1982, *66,* 67–101.

Bonnet, C., & Tamine, J. Names constructed by children: Description and symbolic representation of the data. *Archives de Psychologie,* 1983, *51,* 229–259.

Bouton, C. P. *Le développement du langage: Aspects normaux et pathologiques.* Paris: Masson/UNESCO, 1976.

Bouvier, N., & Platone, F. Etude génétique de la construction d'une détermination linguistique complexe: L'expression d'un même contenu par des enfants d'âges différents. *Etudes sur le développement du langage de l'enfant,* tome 1, *Centre de Recherche de l'Education Spécialisée et de l'Adaptation Scolaire* (Institut Pédagogique National, Paris), 1976, *16*A, 25–165.

Bowerman, M. Learning the structure of causative verbs: A study in the relationship of cognitive, semantic, and syntactic development. *Papers & Reports on Child Language Development* [Stanford University], 1974, *8,* 142–178.

Bowerman, M. Systematizing semantic knowledge: Changes over time in the child's organization of word meaning. *Child Development*, 1978, *49*, 977–987.

Bowerman, M. Evaluating competing linguistic models with language acquisition data: Implications of developmental errors with causative verbs. *Quaderni di Semantici*, 1982, *3*, 5–66. (a)

Bowerman, M. Re-organizational processes in lexical and syntactic development. In E. Wanner & L. R. Gleitman (Eds.), *Language acquisition: The state of the art*. Cambridge: Cambridge University Press, 1982. Pp. 319–346. (b)

Bowerman, M. Starting to talk worse: Clues to language acquisition from children's late speech errors. In S. Strauss (Ed.), *U-shaped behavioral growth*. New York: Academic Press, 1982. Pp. 101–145. (c)

Boysson-Bardies, B. de, Négation syntaxique et négation lexicale chez les jeunes enfants. *Langages*, 1969, *16*, 111–118.

Boysson-Bardies, B. de, On children's interpretations of negation. *Journal of Experimental Child Psychology*, 1977, *23*, 117–127.

Brami-Mouling, M.-A. Notes sur l'adaptation de l'expression verbale de l'enfant en fonction de l'âge de son interlocuteur. *Archives de Psychologie*, 1977, *45*, 225–234.

Braun-Lamesch, M. M. Le rôle du contexte dans la compréhension du langage chez l'enfant. *Psychologie Française*, 1962, *7*, 180–189.

Braun-Lamesch, M. M. Contexte et catégories grammaticales: Etude génétique chez des enfants de 8 à 13 ans. *Psychologie Française*, 1964, *12*, 118–127.

Braun-Lamesch, M. M. Les contextes des noms et des verbes chez l'enfant. *Journal de Psychologie*, 1965, *62*, 201–218.

Braun-Lamesch, M. M. Remarques sur le caractère global ou analytique de la compréhension du langage chez l'enfant. *Journal de Psychologie*, 1967, *64*, 73–83.

Braun-Lamesch, M. M. Sur l'acquisition du vocabulaire chez l'enfant. *Bulletin de Psychologie*, 1972–1973, *26*, 361–374.

Bresson, F. Problèmes de psycholinguistique génétique: L'acquisition du système de l'article en français. *Problèmes actuels en psycholinguistique/Current problems in psycholinguistics*. Paris: Editions du CNRS, 1974. Pp. 61–66.

Bresson, F. Semantics, syntax, and utterance: Determining a referent. *International Journal of Psycholinguistics*, 1977, *4*, 31–41.

Bresson, F., Bouvier, N., Dannequin, C., Depreux, J., Hardy, M., & Platone, F. Quelques aspects du système des déterminants chez les enfants de l'école maternelle: Utilisation des articles défini et indéfini. *Centre de Recherche de l'Education Spécialisée et de l'Adaptation Scolaire* (Institut Pédagogique National, Paris), 1970, *2*, 3–40.

Brisk, M. E. A preliminary study of the syntax of five-year-old Spanish speakers of New Mexico. *International Journal of the Sociology of Language*, 1974, *2*, 69–78.

Brisk, M. E. The acquisition of Spanish gender by first-grade Spanish-speaking children. In G. D. Keller, R. V. Teschner, & S. Viera (Eds.), *Bilingualism in the bicentennial and beyond*. Jamaica, NY: Bilingual Review Press, 1976. Pp. 143–160.

Bronckart, J.-P. *Genèse et organisation des formes verbales chez l'enfant*. Brussels: Dessart & Mardaga, 1976.

Bronckart, J.-P., & Sinclair, H. Time, tense, and aspect. *Cognition*, 1973, *2*, 107–130.

Brown, R. *A first language: The early stages*. Cambridge, Mass.: Harvard University Press, 1973.

Cabrejo-Parra, E. Quelques aspects comparatifs de l'acquisition du langage. In F. Bresson & H. Sinclair (Eds.), *Genèse de la parole*. Paris: Presses Universitaires de France, 1977. Pp. 259–267.

Cambon, J., & Sinclair, H. Relations between syntax and semantics: Are they "easy to see"? *British Journal of Psychology*, 1974, *65*, 133–140.

Canellada, M. J. Sobre lenguaje infantil. *Filología*, 1968–1969, *13*, 39–47.

Carey, S. The child as word learner. In M. Halle, J. Bresnan, & G. A. Miller (Eds.), *Linguistic theory and psychological reality*. Cambridge, Mass.: M.I.T. Press, 1978. Pp. 264–293.

Carpentier, C. Etude grammaticale du langage des enfants de 3, 4, et 5 ans. Thèse de licence en psychologie, Université de Liège, 1969.

Carrow, E. Comprehension of English and Spanish by preschool Mexican-American children. *Modern Language Journal*, 1971, *55*, 299–306.

Celce-Murcia, M. The simultaneous acquisition of English and French in a two-year-old child. In E. M. Hatch (Ed.), *Second language acquisition: A book of readings*. Rowley, Mass.: Newbury House, 1978. Pp. 38–53.

Chambaz, M., Leroy, C., & Messeant, G. Les "petis mots" de coordination: Etude diachronique de leur apparition chez quatre enfants entre 3 et 4 ans. *Langue Française*, 1975, *27*, 38–54.

Chevalier, J.-Cl. Eléments pour une description du groupe nominale. *Le Français Moderne*, 1966, *34*, 241–253.

Chevalier, J.-Cl., Blanche-Benveniste, Cl., Arrivé, M., & Peytard, J. *Grammaire Larousse en français contemporain*. Paris: Larousse, 1964.

Chomsky, C. *The acquisition of syntax in children from 5 to 10*. Cambridge, Mass.: M.I.T. Press, 1969.

Chmura-Klekotowa, M. Odbicie tendencji slowotwórczych języka polskiego w neologizmach dzieci. *Prace Filologiczne*, 1970, *20*, 153–159.

Clancy, P. The acquisition of Japanese. In D. I. Slobin (Ed.), *The crosslinguistic study of language acquisition* (Vol. 1). Hillsdale, NJ: Lawrence Erlbaum Associates, 1985.

Clancy, P., Jacobsen, T., & Silva, M. The acquisition of conjunction: A cross-linguistic study. *Papers & Reports on Child Language Development* [Stanford University], 1976, *12*, 71–80.

Clark, E. V. How young children describe events in time. In G. B. Flores d'Arcais & W. J. M. Levelt (Eds.), *Advances in psycholinguistics*. Amsterdam: North-Holland Publishing Co., 1970.

Clark, E. V. On the acquisition of the meanings of *before* and *after*. *Journal of Verbal Learning & Verbal Behavior*, 1971, *10*, 266–275.

Clark, E. V. How children describe time and order. In C. A. Ferguson & D. I. Slobin (Eds.), *Studies of child language development*. New York: Holt, Rinehart & Winston, 1973. Pp. 586–606. (a)

Clark, E. V. What's in a word? On the child's acquisition of semantics in his first language. In T. E. Moore (Ed.), *Cognitive development and the acquisition of language*. New York: Academic Press, 1973. Pp. 65–110. (b)

Clark, E. V. Non-linguistic strategies and the acquisition of word meanings. *Cognition*, 1973, *2*, 161–182. (c)

Clark, E. V. Strategies and the mapping problem in first language acquisition. In J. Macnamara (Ed.), *Language learning and thought*. New York: Academic Press, 1977. Pp. 147–168.

Clark, E. V. From gesture to word: On the natural history of deixis in language acquisition. In J. S. Bruner & A. Garton (Eds.), *Human growth and development: Wolfson College lectures 1976*. Oxford: Oxford University Press, 1978. Pp. 85–120. (a)

Clark, E. V. Discovering what words can do. In D. Farkas, W. M. Jacobsen, & K. Todrys (Eds.), *Parasession on the lexicon*. Chicago: Chicago Linguistic Society, 1978. Pp. 34–57. (b)

Clark, E. V. Convention and innovation in acquiring the lexicon. Keynote Address, Twelfth Annual Child Language Research Forum, Stanford University, March 1980. (In *Papers & Reports on Child Language Development* [Stanford University], 1980, *19*, 1–20.) (a)

Clark, E. V. Here's the *top:* Nonlinguistic strategies in the acquisition of orientational terms. *Child Development*, 1980, *51*, 329–338. (b)

Clark, E. V. Lexical innovations: How children learn to coin new words. In W. Deutsch (Ed.), *The child's construction of language*. London: Academic Press, 1981. Pp. 299–328. (a)

Clark, E. V. Negative verbs in children's speech. In W. Klein & W. J. M. Levelt (Eds.), *Crossing the boundaries in linguistics: Studies presented to Manfred Bierwisch*. Dordrecht: Reidel, 1981. Pp. 253–264. (b)

Clark, E. V. The young word-maker: A case study of innovation in the child's lexicon. In E. Wanner & L. R. Gleitman (Eds.), *Language acquisition: The state of the art.* Cambridge: Cambridge University Press, 1982. Pp. 390–425. (a)

Clark, E. V. Language change during language acquisition. In M. E. Lamb & A. L. Brown (Eds.), *Advances in child development,* vol. 2. Hillsdale, NJ: Lawrence Erlbaum Associates, 1982. Pp. 171–195. (b)

Clark, E. V. Meanings and concepts. In J. H. Flavell & E. M. Markman (Eds.), *Carmichael's Manual of child psychology.* vol. 3: *Cognitive development* (general editor, P. H. Mussen). New York: Wiley, 1983. Pp. 787–840.

Clark, E. V., & Clark, H. H. When nouns surface as verbs. *Language,* 1979, *55,* 767–811.

Clark, E. V., & Cohen, S. Productivity and memory for newly formed words. *Journal of Child Language,* 1984, *11,* 611–625.

Clark, E. V., & Garnica, O. K. Is he coming or going? On the acquisition of deictic verbs. *Journal of Verbal Learning & Verbal Behavior,* 1974, *12,* 556–572.

Clark, E. V., & Hecht, B. F. Learning to coin agent and instrument nouns. *Cognition,* 1982, *12,* 1–24.

Clark, E. V., & Hecht, B. F. Comprehension, production, and language acquisition. *Annual Review of Psychology,* 1983, *34,* 325–349.

Clark, H. H., & Clark, E. V. *Psychology and language.* New York: Harcourt Brace Jovanovich, 1977.

Clark, H. H., & Marshall, C. R. Definite reference and mutual knowledge. In A. K. Joshi, B. Webber, & I. A. Sag (Eds.), *Linguistic structure and discourse setting.* Cambridge: Cambridge University Press, 1981. Pp. 10–63.

Cohen, M. Etapes de l'acquisition du mot *poule* par une petite fille. *Bulletin de la Société de Linguistique de Paris,* 1922, *23,* 13–14.

Cohen, M. Sur les langages successifs de l'enfant. In *Mélanges J. Vendryès.* Paris: Champion, 1925. Pp. 109–127.

Cohen, M. A propos de la troisième personne du féminin au pluriel en français. *Bulletin de la Société de Linguistique de Paris,* 1927, *27,* 201–208.

Cohen, M. Sur l'acquisition du langage par les enfants. *Bulletin de la Société de Linguistique de Paris,* 1951, *47,* 35–38.

Cohen, M. Sur l'étude du langage enfantin. *Enfance,* 1969, *3–4,* 203–272.

Compayré, G. *L'évolution intellectuelle et morale de l'enfant.* Paris: Hachette, 1896.

Connors, K., Nuckle, L., & Greene, W. The acquisition of pronoun complement structures in French and English. In J. E. Copeland & P. W. Davis (Eds.), *The Seventh LACUS forum.* Columbia, SC: Hornbeam Press, 1981. Pp. 475–485.

Costa, A. M., & Fonzi, A. *Psicologia del linguaggio: Richerche e problemi.* Turin: Boringhieri, 1967.

Costa, S. R. *Aprendizagem de alguns aspectos da morfologia portuguesa por crianças brasileiros.* Unpublished MA thesis, Universidade de Campinas, 1976.

Cousinet, R. Le monologue enfantin. *Journal de Psychologie,* 1936, *33,* 28–39.

Coyaud, M. Le problème des grammaires du langage enfantin. *La Linguistique,* 1967, *2,* 99–129.

Coyaud, M., & Sabeau-Jouannet, E. Analyse syntaxique de corpus enfantins. *La Linguistique,* 1970, *6,* 53–67.

Cravatte, A. Comment les enfants expliquent-ils les mots? *Langages,* 1980, *59,* 87–96.

Dato, D. P. The development of the Spanish verb phrase in children's second-language learning. In P. Pimsleur & T. Quinn (Eds.), *The psychology of second language learning.* Cambridge: Cambridge University Press, 1971. Pp. 19–33.

Dato, D. P. On psycholinguistic universals in children's learning of Spanish. In D. P. Dato (Ed.), *Developmental psycholinguistics—Theory and applications.* Washington, D.C.: Georgetown University Press, 1975. Pp. 235–254.

Dato, D. P. Development of Spanish interrogatives in children's second language learning. In V. Honsa & J. M. Hardman-de Bautista (Eds.), *Papers on linguistics and child language.* The Hague: Mouton, 1978. Pp. 11–38.

Decroly, O. *Comment l'enfant arrive à parler.* Brussels: Cahiers de la Centrale, 1932.

Decroly, O., & Degand, J. Observations relatives au développement de la notion du temps chez une petite fille. *Archives de Psychologie,* 1913, *13,* 113–161.

Degand, J. Observations sur un enfant sourd. *Archives de Psychologie,* 1911, *11,* 378–389.

Della Valle, G. Le prime fasi dello sviluppo del linguaggio infantile. *Revista Pedagogica,* 1931, *24,* 165–197.

Depreux, J. L'acquisition de la pronominalisation: Etude du fonctionnement du pronom possessif chez des enfants d'âges préscolaires. *Etudes sur le développement du langage de l'enfant,* tome 2, *Section de Recherche de l'Education Spécialisée de l'Adaptation Scolaire* (Institut Pédagogique National, Paris), 1977, *16*B, 5–182.

Descoeudres, A. *Le développement de l'enfant de deux à sept ans.* Paris: Delachaux & Niestlé, 1922.

Deville, G. Notes sur le développement du langage. *Revue de Linguistique,* 1891, *24,* 10–42, 128–143, 242–257, 300–320.

Deyts, J.-P., & Noizet, G. Etude génétique de la production de subordonnées relatives. *Cahiers de Psychologie,* 1973, *16,* 199–212.

Dienes, Z. P., & Lefèvre, B. Exploitation de jeux logico-sémantiques par des enfants de huit ans. *Langue Française,* 1971, *12,* 43–59.

Dubois, J., Assal, G., Ramier, A.-M. Production des phrases dans une population d'âge scolaire. *Journal de Psychologie,* 1968, *65,* 183–207.

Durand, M. De quelques éliminations d'homonyms chez un enfant. *Journal de Psychologie,* 1949, *42,* 53–63.

Duranti, A., & Ochs, E. Left-dislocation in Italian conversation. In T. Givón (Ed.), *Syntax and semantics,* vol. 12: *Discourse and syntax.* New York: Academic Press, 1979. Pp. 377–416.

Echeverría, M. D. *Desarrollo de la comprensión de la sintaxis española.* (Serie Linguistica 3.) Concepción, Chile: Universidad de Concepción, 1978.

Edelsky, C., & Muiña, V. Native Spanish language acquisition: The effect of age, schooling, and context on responses to *dile* and *pregúntale. Journal of Child Language,* 1977, *4,* 453–475.

Eisenberg, A. R. *Language acquisition in cultural perspective: Talk in three Mexican homes.* Unpublished PhD dissertation, University of California, Berkeley, 1982.

Elcock, W. D. *The Romance languages.* London: Faber & Faber, 1960.

Egger, M. E. *Observations et réflexions sur le développement de l'intelligence et du langage chez les enfants.* Paris: Picard, 1887.

Engel, W. von R. *Il prelinguaggio infantile.* Rome: Paideia, 1964.

Ervin-Tripp. S. The structure of communicative choice. In S. Ervin-Tripp, *Language acquisition and communicative choice.* Stanford, Calif.: Stanford University Press, 1973. Pp. 302–374.

Ervin-Tripp, S. Is second language learning like the first? *TESOL Quarterly,* 1974, *8,* 111–127.

Ervin-Tripp, S. From conversation to syntax. Keynote Address, Ninth Annual Child Language Research Forum, Stanford University, March 1977. (In *Papers & Reports on Child Language Development* [Stanford University], 1977, *13,* K1–K21.)

Ewert, A. *The French language.* London: Faber & Faber, 1953.

Faïta, D. *Etude syntaxique du français parlé par des enfants de neuf ans.* Thèse du Doctorat de Troisième Cycle, Université de Provence, Centre d'Aix-Marseille, 1974.

Fantini, A. E. *Language acquisition of a bilingual child: A sociolinguistic perspective.* Brattleboro, Vermont: The Experiment Press, 1976.

Farioli, F. L'identification de la coréférence pronominale chez les enfants de 5 à 11 ans. *Année Psychologique,* 1979, *79,* 87–104.

Ferreiro, E. *Les relations temporelles dans le langage de l'enfant.* Geneva: Droz, 1971.

Ferreiro, E., Othénin-Girard, C., Chipman, H., & Sinclair, H. How do children handle relative clauses? A study in comparative developmental psycholinguistics. *Archives de Psychologie*, 1976, *44*, 229–266.

Ferreiro, E., & Sinclair, H. Temporal relations in language. *International Journal of Psychology*, 1971, *6*, 39–47.

Ferri, Osservazioni e considerazione sopra una bambina. *Filosofia della Scuole Italiane: Revista Bimestrale*, 1879, 155–176.

Figueira, R. A. Aréas de dificuldade na aquisição do léico: Exame do 'corpus' de um (1) sujeito (2;8 a 3;10). *Paper presented at Il Encontro Nacional de Lingüistas*, Rio de Janeiro, October 1977.

Figueira, R. A. *Análise preliminar dos verbos causativos no 'corpus' de um (1) sujeito (2;8 a 5;0)*. Manuscript, Universidade de Campinas, January, 1979.

Figueira, R. A. On the development of the expression of causativity: A syntactic hypothesis. *Journal of Child Language*, 1984, *11*, 109–127.

Fillmore, L. W. *The second time around: Cognitive and social strategies in second language acquisition*. Unpublished PhD dissertation, Stanford University, 1976.

Fillmore, L. W. Individual differences in second language acquisition. In C. Fillmore, D. Kempler, & W. S.-Y. Wang (Eds.), *Individual differences in language ability and language behavior*. New York: Academic Press, 1979. Pp. 203–228.

Flores d'Arcais, G. B. The acquisition of subordinating conjunctions in child language. In R. N. Campbell & P. T. Smith (Eds.), *Recent advances in the psychology of language: Language development and mother-child interaction* (Vol. 4a.). New York: Plenum Press, 1978. Pp. 349–393. (a)

Flores d'Arcais, G. B. Levels of semantic knowledge in children's use of connectives. In A. Sinclair, R. J. Jarvella, & W. J. M. Levelt (Eds.), *The child's conception of language*. New York: Springer Verlag, 1978. Pp. 133–153. (b)

Fónagy, I. A propos de la genèse de la phrase enfantine. *Lingua*, 1972, *30*, 31–71.

Fondet, C. *Un enfant apprend à parler: Récit et analyses d'un apprentissage de la langue maternelle de la naissance à six ans*. Dijon: Les Presses de l'Imprimerie Universitaire, 1979.

Francescato, G. Alcuni esempi di formazioni infantili. *Lingua Nostra*, 1964, *25*, 50–53.

Francescato, G. *Il linguaggio infantile: Strutturazione e apprendimento*. Turin: Einaudi, 1973.

Francescato, G. Appunti per la biografia linguistica dei miei figli. *Rassegna Italiana di Linguistica Applicata*, 1978, *10*, 92–120.

François, D. Du pré-signe au signe. In F. François et al., *La syntaxe de l'enfant avant 5 ans*. Paris: Larousse, 1978. Pp. 53–89.

François, F. Syntaxe, lexique, et contraintes formelles. In F. François et al., *La syntaxe de l'enfant avant 5 ans*. Paris: Larousse, 1978. Pp. 120–136. (a)

François, F. La genèse de la syntaxe: Les énoncés à deux termes. In F. François et al., *La syntaxe de l'enfant avant 5 ans*. Paris: Larousse, 1978. Pp. 137–156. (b)

François, F. Le stade 3: Les structures de base. In F. François et al., *La syntaxe de l'enfant avant 5 ans*. Paris: Larousse, 1978. Pp. 157–169. (c)

François, F. Le stade 4: Evolution et diversification du système. In F. François et al., *La syntaxe de l'enfant avant 5 ans*. Paris: Larousse, 1978. Pp. 170–192. (d)

François, F. Mise en mots et organisation de l'expérience. In F. François et al., *La syntaxe de l'enfant avant 5 ans*. Paris: Larousse, 1978. Pp. 214–231. (e)

François, F. *Syntaxe et mise en mots: Analyse différentielle des comportements linguistiques des enfants*. (Collection des Actions Thématiques Programmées, Sciences Humaines 29.) Paris: Editions du CNRS, 1978. (f)

François, F., François, D., Sabeau-Jouannet, E., & Sourdot, M. *La syntaxe de l'enfant avant 5 ans*. Paris: Larousse, 1978.

Frontali, G. Lo sviluppo del linguaggio articulato nel bambino. *Vox Romanica*, 1943–1944, *7*, 214–243.

Fuster, M. Observations sur le langage de deux petites filles de 4 mois à 3 ans. *Bulletin Mensuel*, 1903, *4*, 253–255.

Gaatone, D. *Etude descriptive du système de la négation en français contemporain*. Geneva: Droz, 1971.

Gaatone, D. Les pronoms conjoints dans la construction factitive. *Revue de Linguistique Romane*, 1976, *40*, 165–182.

Gadet, F. Recherches récentes sur les variations sociales de la langue française. *Langue Française*, 1971, *9*, 74–81.

Galvan, J. L. *The development of aspectual relations in Spanish-speaking children*. Unpublished PhD dissertation, University of Texas, 1980.

Gauthier, M. Etude de l'acquisition et théorie linguistique: Actions en retour. In *Mélanges Emile Benveniste*. Paris: Société de Linguistique, 1975. Pp. 181–196.

Gendrin, J. Aspects du langage de deux enfants de 2 ans et demi. *Etudes de Linguistique Appliquée*, 1971, *4*, 53–76.

Gendrin, J. Quelques observations sur l'apprentissage linguistique chez une fillette suivie entre 3;0 et 4;0. *Etudes de Linguistique Appliquée*, 1973, *9*, 76–90.

Gendrin, J., & Lentin, L. Aspects du langage de deux enfants de deux ans et demi. *Etudes de Linguistique Appliquée*, 1971, *4*, 53–76.

Gentner, D. Why nouns are learned before verbs: Linguistic relativity versus natural partitioning. In S. A. Kuczaj, II (Ed.), *Language development, vol. 2: Language, thought, and culture*. Hillsdale, NJ: Lawrence Erlbaum Associates, 1983. Pp. 301–334.

Gili Gaya, S. *Estudios de lenguaje infantil*. Barcelona: Bibliograf, 1972. (a)

Gili Gaya, S. Imitación y creación en el habla infantil. In S. Gili Gaya, *Estudios de lenguaje infantil*. Barcelona: Bibliograf, 1972. Pp. 9–28. (b)

Gili Gaya, S. Funciones gramaticales en el habla infantil. In S. Gili Gaya, *Estudios de lenguaje infantil*. Barcelona: Bibliograf, 1972. Pp. 31–93. (c)

Gili Gaya, S. La espresión infantil del tiempo. In S. Gili Gaya, *Estudios de lenguaje infantil*. Barcelona: Bibliograf, 1972. Pp. 97–120. (d)

Gili Gaya, S. Nexos de la oración compuesta en el lenguaje activo de los niños. In S. Gili Gaya, *Estudios de lenguaje infantil*. Barcelona: Bibliograf, 1972. Pp. 123–138. (e)

Giry-Schneider, J. *Les nominalisations en français: L'opérateur FAIRE dans le lexique*. Geneva: Droz, 1978.

Goldberg, G. Conduite du discours enfantin et complexité syntaxique. *La Linguistique*, 1976, *12*, 3–34.

Goldblum, M. C. Etude expérimentale de l'acquisition de la syntaxe chez des enfants de 5 à 10 ans. *Langue Française*, 1972, *13*, 115–122.

Goldin-Meadow, S., Seligman, M. D. P., & Gelman, R. Language in the two-year-old. *Cognition*, 1976, *4*, 189–202.

González, G. *The acquisition of Spanish grammar by native Spanish speakers*. Unpublished PhD dissertation, University of Texas, 1970.

González, G. The acquisition of grammatical structures by Mexican-American children. In E. Hernández-Chavez, A. D. Cohen, & A. F. Beltramo (Eds.), *El lenguaje de los chicanos*. Arlington, Virginia: Center for Applied Linguistics, 1975. Pp. 220–237.

González, G. The speech of a chicano child: Spanish grammatical transformation at age 2;6. In A. G. Lonzano (Ed.), *Bilingual and biliterate perspectives*. Boulder, Colo.: University of Colorado, 1978. Pp. 216–225. (a)

González, G. The acquisition of Spanish grammar by native Spanish speaking children. Rosslyn, Virginia: National Clearinghouse for Bilingual Education, 1978. (b)

González, G. The acquisition of verb tenses and temporal expressions in Spanish: Age 2;0–4;6. *Bilingual Education Paper Series* (National Dissemination & Assessment Center, California State University, Los Angeles), 1980, *4*(2).

Gordon, P. Early encoding of the count/mass distinction: Semantic or syntactic? *Papers & Reports on Child Language Development* [Stanford University], 1982, *21*, 71–78.

Gougenheim, G. *Système grammatical de la langue française.* Paris: D'Atrey, 1962.

Greenberg, J. H. Some universals of grammar with particular reference to the order of meaningful elements. In J. H. Greenberg (Ed.), *Universals of language.* Cambridge, Mass.: M.I.T. Press, 1963. Pp. 73–113.

Greenfield, P. M., & Smith, J. *The structure of communication in early language development.* New York: Academic Press, 1976.

Grégoire, A. *L'apprentissage du langage.* (2 vols.) Liège, Paris: Droz, 1937, 1947.

Grégoire, A. *Edmond—Puxi—Michel: Les prénoms et les surnoms de trois enfants.* Liège, Paris: Droz, 1939.

Grégoire, A. L'apprentissage du langage. *Lingua,* 1948, *1,* 162–174.

Grevisse, M. *Le bon usage: Grammaire française avec des remarques sur la langue française d'aujourd'hui.* (8e. édition.) Gembloux, Belgium: Editions J. Duculot, 1964.

Grice, H. P. Logic and conversation. In P. Cole & J. L. Morgan (Eds.), *Syntax and semantics,* vol. 3: *Speech acts.* New York: Academic Press, 1975. Pp. 41–58.

Guillaume, P. *L'imitation chez l'enfant.* Paris: Alcan, 1925.

Guillaume, P. Les débuts de la phrase dans le langage de l'enfant. *Journal de Psychologie,* 1927, *24,* 1–25.(a) [English translation by E. V. Clark in C. A. Ferguson & D. I. Slobin (Eds.), *Studies of child language development.* New York: Holt, Rinehart & Winston, 1973.]

Guillaume, P. Le développement des éléments formels dans le langage de l'enfant. *Journal de Psychologie,* 1927, *24,* 203–229. (b) [English translation by E. V. Clark in C. A. Ferguson & D. I. Slobin (Eds.), *Studies of child language development.* New York: Holt, Rinehart & Winston, 1973.]

Harner, L. *Yesterday* and *tomorrow.* Development of early understanding of the terms. *Developmental Psychology,* 1975, *11,* 864–865.

Hiriartborde, A. Sur la généralisation de quelques marques grammaticales dans le langage d'enfants de 3 ans 1/2. *Etudes de Linguistique Appliquée,* 1973, *9,* 101–124.

Hudelot, C. Organisation linguistique d'échanges verbaux chez des enfants de maternelle. *Langages,* 1980, *59,* 63–79.

Jakubowicz, C. Fait actuel ou fait virtuel? La compréhension d'énoncés conditionnels chez l'enfant. *Année Psychologique,* 1978, *78,* 105–128.

Johnson, C. E. The ontogenesis of question words in children's language. *Paper presented at the Fifth Annual Boston University Conference on Language Development,* October 1980.

Johnson, C. E. *Children's questions and the discovery of interrogative syntax.* Unpublished PhD dissertation, Stanford University, 1981.

Johnston, J. R., & Slobin, D. I. The development of locative expressions in English, Italian, Serbo-Croatian, and Turkish. *Journal of Child Language,* 1979, *6,* 529–545.

Jones, R. M., & Pouder, M. C. Les échanges verbaux chez des enfants de maternelle. *Langages,* 1980, *59,* 63–78.

Kail, M. Etude génétique de la réproduction de phrases relatives. *Année Psychologique,* 1975, *75,* 109–126. (a)

Kail, M. Etude génétique de la réproduction de phrases relatives II: Réproduction différée. *Année Psychologique,* 1975, *75,* 427–443. (b)

Kail, M. Stratégies de compréhension des pronoms personnels chez le jeune enfant. *Enfance,* 1976, *4–5,* 447–466.

Kail, M. La compréhension des présuppositions chez l'enfant. *Année Psychologique,* 1978, *78,* 425–444.

Kail, M. Compréhension de *seul, même,* et *aussi* chez l'enfant. *Bulletin de Psychologie,* 1979, *32,* 763–771.

Kail, M. La coréférence des pronoms: Pertinence de la stratégie des fonctions parallèles. In M. Kail,

J.-P. Bronckart, & G. Noizet (Eds.), *Psycholinguistique de l'enfant*. Neuchâtel: Delachaux et Niestlé, 1983. Pp. 107–122.

Kail, M., & Léveillé, M. Compréhension et coréférence des pronoms personnels chez l'enfant et l'adulte. *Année Psychologique*, 1977, *77*, 79–94.

Kail, M., & Weissenborn, J. A developmental cross-linguistic study of the processing of lexical presuppositions: French *mais* and German *aber* vs *sondern*. *Paper presented at the Fifth Annual Boston University Conference on Language Development*, October 1980.

Karmiloff-Smith, A. More about the same: Children's understanding of post-articles. *Journal of Child Language*, 1977, *4*, 377–394.

Karmiloff-Smith, A. The interplay between syntax, semantics, and phonology in language acquisition processes. In R. N. Campbell & P. T. Smith (Eds.), *Recent advances in the psychology of language: Language development and mother-child interaction*. (Vol. 4a.) New York: Plenum, 1978. Pp. 1–23.

Karmiloff-Smith, A. *A functional approach to child language*. Cambridge: Cambridge University Press, 1979.

Karmiloff-Smith, A. Psychological processes underlying pronominalization and non-pronominalization in children's connected discourse. In J. Kreiman & A. E. Ojeda (Eds.), *Parasession on pronouns and anaphora*. Chicago: Chicago Linguistic Society, 1980. Pp. 231–250.

Karmiloff-Smith, A. The grammatical marking of thematic structure in the development of language production. In W. Deutsch (Ed.), *The child's construction of language*. London: Academic Press, 1981. Pp. 121–147.

Keller, G. D. Acquisition of the English and Spanish passive voices among bilingual children. In G. D. Keller, R. V. Teschner, & S. Viera (Eds.), *Bilingualism in the bicentennial and beyond*. New York: Bilingual Press, 1976. Pp. 161–168.

Kenyereš, A. Comment une petite fille hongroise de sept ans apprend le français. *Archives de Psychologie*, 1938, *26*, 321–366.

Kernan, K. T., & Blount, B. G. The acquisition of Spanish grammar by Mexican children. *Anthropological Linguistics*, 1966, *8*, 1–14.

Kessler, C. *The acquisition of syntax in bilingual children*. Washington, D.C.: Georgetown University Press, 1971.

Kessler, C. Contrasts in the acquisition of syntax in bilingual children. *Rassegna Italiana di Linguistica Applicata*, 1972, *4*, 165–175.

Kraft, H., & Piaget, J. La notion de l'ordre des événements et le test des images en désordre chez l'enfant de 6 à 10 ans. *Archives de Psychologie*, 1925, *19*, 306–349.

Kuczaj, S. A., II. The acquisition of regular and irregular past tense forms. *Journal of Verbal Learning & Verbal Behavior*, 1977, *16*, 589–600.

LaBelle, G. La langue des enfants de Montréal et de Paris. *Langue Française*, 1976, *31*, 55–73.

Lanouzière, J. Compréhension des marques d'appartenance et échec scolaire. *Enfance*, 1979, *1*, 59–80.

Lastra de Suarez, Y. El habla y la educación de los niños de origen mexicano en Los Angeles. In E. Hernández-Chavez, A. D. Cohen, & A. F. Beltramo (Eds.), *El lenguaje de los chicanos*. Arlington, Virginia: Center for Applied Linguistics, 1975. Pp. 61–69.

Lemos, C. G. de, *The use of ser and estar with particular reference to child language*. Unpublished PhD dissertation, University of Edinburgh, 1975.

Lemos, C. G. de, Adult-child interaction and the development of aspectual markers in Brazilian Portuguese. In W. Deutsch (Ed.), *The child's construction of language*. London: Academic Press, 1981. Pp. 57–76.

Lentin, L. Intéraction adultes-enfants au cours de l'acquisition du langage: Un exemple—Etude contrastive du langage de deux enfants entre 3 et 4 ans et de celui de leurs parents (Milieux socioculturels différents). *Etudes de Linguistique Appliquée*, 1973, *9*, 9–50.

Lentin, L. Notes sur l'apparition et l'emploi du comparatif (enfants de 2 à 7 ans). *Langue Française,* 1975, *27,* 55–64.

Le Rouzo, M. Les relations spatiales dans le langage de l'enfant: Référence et énonciation. *Travaux du Centre d'Etudes des Processus Cognitifs et du Langage,* 1977, *10.*

Leroy, C. Intonation et syntaxe chez l'enfant français à partir de dix-huit mois. *Langue Française,* 1975, *27,* 24–37.

Léveillé, M., & Suppes, P. La compréhension des marques d'appartenance par les enfants. *Enfance,* 1976, *3,* 309–318.

Lightbown, P. M. *Consistency and variation in the acquisition of French: A study of first and second language development.* Unpublished PhD dissertation, Columbia University, 1977.

Lightbown, P. M. French L2 learners: What they're talking *about. Language Learning,* 1977, *27,* 371–381.

Lightbown, P. M. The acquisition and use of questions by French L2 learners. In S. W. Felix (Ed.), *Second language development: Trends and issues.* Tübingen: Gunter Narr Verlag, 1980. Pp. 151–175.

Linares-Orama, N., & Sanders, L. J. Evaluation of syntax in three-year-old Spanish-speaking Puerto Rican children. *Journal of Speech & Hearing Research,* 1977, *20,* 350–357.

Lombroso, P. *Saggi di psicologia del bambino.* Rome: L. Roux, 1894.

Lopez Ornat, S. Dinámica de la adquisición verbal. *Revista de Psicología General y Aplicada,* 1975, *30,* 1059–1068.

Lord, C. "'Don't you fall me down'": Children's generalizations regarding cause and transitivity. *Papers & Reports on Child Language Development* [Stanford University], 1979, *17,* 81–89.

Lurçat, L. L'espace inter-objets. *Psychologie Française,* 1974, *19,* 151–167.

McKay, J. C. *A guide to Romance reference grammars: The modern standard languages.* Amsterdam: Benjamins, 1979.

MacWhinney, B. The acquisition of morphophonology. *Monographs of the Society for Research in Child Development,* 1978, *43* (Serial No. 174).

MacWhinney, B. Hungarian language acquisition as an exemplification of a general model of grammatical development. In D. I. Slobin (Ed.), *The crosslinguistic study of language acquisition* (Vol. 2). Hillsdale, NJ: Lawrence Erlbaum Associates, 1985.

MacWhinney, B., & Bates, E. Sentential devices for conveying givenness and newness: A cross-cultural developmental study. *Journal of Verbal Learning & Verbal Behavior,* 1978, *17,* 539–558.

Machado y Alvarez, D. A. Titín: A study of child language. *Transactions of the Philological Society,* 1885–1887, 68–74.

Malrieu, P. Le langage de 1 à 4 ans: Etude différentielle. *Revue Suisse de Psychologie,* 1970, *29,* 224–233.

Malrieu, P. L'expression verbale de la temporalité avant quatre ans. *Bulletin de Psychologie,* 1972–1973, *26,* 340–349.

Malrieu, P. Aspects psychologiques de la construction de la phrase chez l'enfant. *Journal de Psychologie,* 1973, *70,* 157–174.

Malrieu, P., & Larrue, J. Langage et personnalité dans la deuxième année. *Journal de Psychologie,* 1967, *64,* 41–71.

Martínez Bernal, J. A. *Children's acquisition of Spanish and English morphological systems and noun phrases.* Unpublished PhD dissertation, Georgetown University, 1972.

Mazeika, E. J. A comparison of the grammar of a monolingual and a bilingual (Spanish-English) child. *Paper presented at the Biennial Meeting of the Society for Research in Child Development,* Philadelphia, April 1973.

Mediano, Z. D. *Preliminary studies in the acquisition of Portuguese morphology by Brazilian children.* Unpublished PhD dissertation, University of New Mexico, 1976.

Medina-Ngyuyen, S. Overgeneralization in a group of Spanish-English bilingual children. *Paper presented at the Second-Language Research Forum*, Los Angeles, February 1978.

Méresse-Polaert, J. *Etude sur le langage des enfants de six ans.* Neuchâtel: Delachaux & Niestlé, 1969.

Mok, I. Q. *Contribution à l'étude des catégories morphologiques du genre et du nombre dans le français parlé actuel.* The Hague: Mouton, 1968.

Montagero, J. L'apprentissage de la phrase passive. *Archives de Psychologie*, 1971, *41*, 53–61.

Montes Giraldo, J. J. Esquema ontogenético del desarrollo del lenguaje y otras cuestiones del habla infantil. *Thesaurus: Boletín del Instituto Caro y Cuervo*, 1974, *29*, 254–270.

Montes Giraldo, J. J. El sistema, la norma, y el aprendizaje de la lengua. *Thesaurus: Boletín del Instituto Caro y Cuervo*, 1976, *31*, 14–40.

Motta Maia, E. A. *A negação na criança.* Unpublished MA thesis, Universidade Federal do Rio de Janeiro, 1975.

Mottram, F. A baby learns French. *Educational Research*, 1979, *20*, 201–209.

Naerssen, M. M. van, *Acquisition of definiteness and indefiniteness in Spanish as a first language.* Unpublished paper, University of Sourthern California, January 1979.

Naerssen, M. M. van, *Proposed acquisition order of grammatical structures for Spanish as a first language: A comparison of thirteen studies.* Unpublished paper, University of Southern California, September 1979.

Necker de Saussure, A. *Education progressive, ou étude du cours de la vie* (1827). 2 vols. (6e. édition). Paris: Garnier, 1884.

Nanpon, H. Ordre des éléments de la phrase et compréhension chez l'enfant. *Psychologie Française*, 1967, *12*, 133–149.

Nelson, K. Individual differences in language development: Implications for development and language. *Paper presented at the Fifth Annual Boston University Conference on Language Development*, October 1980.

Nyssen, R., & Crahay, S. Les capacités de définition et d'évocation des néologismes d'utilisation récente en fonction de l'âge. In J. Ajuriaguerra et al. (Eds.), *Problèmes de psycholinguistique.* Paris: Presses Universitaries de France, 1963. Pp. 193–204.

Oléron, P., & Herren, H. L'acquisition des conservations et le langage. *Enfance*, 1961, *3*, 201–219.

Padilla, A. M., & Liebman, E. Language acquisition in the bilingual child. *The Bilingual Review*, 1975, *1–2*, 34–55.

Padilla, A. M., & Lindholm, K. J. Development of interrogative, negative, and possessive forms in the speech of young Spanish-English bilinguals. *The Bilingual Review*, 1976, *3*, 122–152. (a)

Padilla, A. M., & Lindholm, K. J. Acquisition of bilingualism: A descriptive analysis of the linguistic structures of Spanish-English speaking children. In G. D. Keller, R. V. Teschner, & S. Viera (Eds.), *Bilingualism in the bicentennial and beyond.* New York: Bilingual Press, 1976. Pp. 97–142. (b)

Paradis, M. Baby talk in French and Québécois. In W. Wölck & P. L. Garvin (Eds.), *The fifth LACUS forum.* Columbia, South Carolina: Hornbeam Press, 1978. Pp. 355–366.

Pardo, E. Semantic prototypes in first language acquisition. *Paper presented at the Annual Meeting of the Linguistic Society of America*, New York City, December 1981.

Parisi, D. *Il linguaggio come precesso cognitivo.* Turin: Boringhieri, 1972.

Parisi, D., & Antinucci, F. Lexical competence. In G. B. Flores d'Arcais & W. J. M. Levelt (Eds.), *Advances in psycholinguistics.* Amsterdam: North-Holland Publishing, 1970. Pp. 197–210.

Parisi, D., & Antinucci, F. Early language development: A second stage. In *Problèmes actuels en psycholinguistique/Current problems in psycholinguistics.* Paris: Editions du CNRS, 1974. Pp. 129–144.

Pavlovitch, M. *Le langage enfantin: Acquisition du serbe et du français par un enfant serbe.* Paris: Champion, 1920.

Penna, A. G. A aquisição da sintaxe pela criança. *Boletim do Instituto de Psicologia*, 1972, *22*, 1–5.

Perez, B. *Les trois premières années de l'enfant*. Paris: Alcan, 1892.

Peters, A. M. Language learning strategies. *Language*, 1977, *53*, 560–573.

Pfister, M. Trois problèmes morphosyntaxiques à la lumière de l'enquête sur le langage de l'enfant français de 10 ans. *Actes du XIII Congrès International de Linguistique et Philologie Romanes*. Québec: Presses de l'Université de Laval, 1971. Pp. 451–466.

Piaget, J. *La formation du symbole chez l'enfant*. Neuchâtel: Delachaux & Niestlé, 1946.

Pichevin, C. L'acquisition de la compréhension entre 2 et 4 ans: Problèmes de recherche. *Psychologie Française*, 1968, *13*, 175–186.

Piérart, B. La genèse de *entre:* "Intuition primitive" ou "coordination des voisinages"? *Archives de Psychologie*, 1975, *43*, 75–109.

Piérart, B. L'acquisition du sens des marqueurs de relation spatiale "devant" et "derrière". *Année Psychologique*, 1977, *77*, 95–116.

Piérart, B. Acquisition du langage, patron sémantique et développement cognitif—observations à propos des prépositions spatiales *au dessus de, en dessous de, sous,* et *sur*. *Enfance*, 1978, *4*, 197–208. (a)

Piérart, B. Genèse et structuration des marqueurs de relations spatiales entre trois et dix ans. *Cahiers de l'Institut de Linguistique de Louvain*, 1978, *5*, 41–59. (b)

Piéraut-Le Bonniec, G. Développement de la compréhension des phrases conditionnelles. *Année Psychologique*, 1980, *80*, 65–79. (a)

Piéraut-Le Bonniec, G. *The development of modal reasoning: Genesis of necessity and possibility notions*. New York: Academic Press, 1980. (b)

Pinto, M. da G. A study of locative expressions in Portuguese. *Paper presented at the Summer Meeting, Linguistic Society of America*, University of Maryland, College Park, Maryland, July 1982.

Reichstein, R. Etude des variations sociales et géographiques des faits linguistiques. *Word*, 1960, *16*, 55–95.

Redard, F. Etude des formes interrogatives en français chez les enfants de trois ans. *Etudes de Linguistique Appliquée*, 1976, *21*, 98–110.

Remacle, L. Remarques sur l'apprentissage du subjontif. In *Mélanges de grammaire française offerts à M. Maurice Grevisse*. Gembloux, Belgium: Duculot, 1966. Pp. 299–305.

Richelle, M. *L'acquisition du langage*. Brussels: Dessart, 1971.

Rodríguez Brown, F. V. *Some aspects of language development in a two-year-old child*. Unpublished PhD dissertation, University of Illinois, 1975.

Rondal, J. A. 'Maman est au courant': Une étude des connaissances maternelles quant aux aspects formels du langage du jeune enfant. *Enfance*, 1979, *2*, 95–105.

Rondal, J. A. Fathers' and mothers' speech in early language development. *Journal of Child Language*, 1980, *7*, 353–369.

Ronjat, J. *Le développement du langage observé chez un enfant bilingue*. Paris: Champion, 1913.

Rothemberg, M. *Les verbes à la fois transitifs et intransitifs en français contemporain*. The Hague: Mouton, 1974.

Roussey, C. Notes sur l'apprentissage de la parole chez un enfant. *La Parole*, 1899–1900, *8*, 791–799, 870–880.

Ruwet, N. *Théorie syntaxique et syntaxe du français*. Paris: Le Seuil, 1972.

Sabeau-Jouannet, E. L'expression des modalités aspectivo-temporelles et son évolution chez des enfants de deux à quatre ans. *Etudes de Linguistique Appliquée*, 1973, *9*, 91–100.

Sabeau-Jouannet, E. Les premières acquisitions syntaxiques chez les enfants français unilingues. *La Linguistique*, 1975, *11*, 105–122.

Sabeau-Jouannet, E. L'expression de l'organisation spatiale et temporelle: Son évolution chez des enfants de 2 à 5 ans. In F. François et al., *La syntaxe de l'enfant avant 5 ans*. Paris: Larousse, 1978. Pp. 205–213.

Sacks, H., Schegloff, E. A., & Jefferson, G. A simplest systematics for the organization of turn-taking for conversation. *Language*, 1974, *50*, 696–735.

Sandfeld, K. *Les propositions subordonnées*. Geneva: Droz, 1965.

Scliar-Cabral, L. Emergência da função reportativa. *Letras de Hoje*, 1975, *19*, 54–74.

Scliar-Cabral, L. *A explanação lingüística em grammáticas emergentes*. Unpublished PhD dissertation, Universidade de São Paulo, 1976.

Sechehaye, A. *Essai sur la structure logique de la phrase*. (Collection Linguistique XX, Société de Linguistique de Paris, paru en 1926). Paris: Champion, 1950.

Ségui, J., & Léveillé, M. Etude sur la compréhension de phrases chez l'enfant. *Enfance*, 1977, *1*, 105–115.

Sheldon, A. The acquisition of relative clauses in French and English: Implications for language-learning universals. In F. R. Eckman (Ed.), *Current themes in linguistics: Bilingualism, experimental linguistics, and language typologies*. New York: Wiley, 1977. Pp. 49–70.

Simões, M. C. P., & Stoel-Gammon, C. The acquisition of inflections in Portuguese: A study of the development of person markers on verbs. *Journal of Child Language*, 1979, *6*, 53–67.

Simon, J., Boxaca, M., Grastilleur, S., & Larre, B. L'expression verbale de l'ordre de succession temporelle de deux événements chez les enfants de 6 à 10 ans. *Bulletin de Psychologie*, 1972–1973, *26*, 350–360.

Simonetti, M. Z. The emergence of determinants in Portuguese: A case study. *Paper presented at the Summer Meeting, Linguistic Society of America*, University of New Mexico, Albuquerque, August 1980.

Sinclair-de Zwart, H. *Acquisition du langage et développement de la pensée: Sous-systèmes linguistiques et opérations concrètes*. Paris: Dunod, 1967.

Sinclair, H. Language acquisition and cognitive development. In T. E. Moore (Ed.), *Cognitive development and the acquisition of language*. New York: Academic Press, 1973. Pp. 9–25.

Sinclair, H., & Bronckart, J. P. SVO—A linguistic universal? A study in developmental psycholinguistics. *Journal of Experimental Child Psychology*, 1972, *14*, 329–348.

Sinclair, H., & Ferreiro, E. Etude génétique de la compréhension, production, et répétition des phrases au mode passif. *Archives de Psychologie*, 1972, *40*, 1–42.

Slama-Cazacu, T. *Relaţiile dintre gîndire limbă în ontogeneză (3–7 ani)*. Bucharest: Ed. Academei, 1957.

Slama-Cazacu, T. Aspecte ale relaţiilor dintre gîndire şi limbaj în insuşirea structurii gramaticale de către copilul antepreşcolar (2–3 ani). *Revista de Psihologie* (Bucharest), 1960, *2*, 43–63.

Slama-Cazacu, T. *Dialogul la copii*. Bucharest: Ed. Academei, 1961.

Slama-Cazacu, T. The oblique cases in the evolution of child language. *Revue de Linguistique*, 1962, *7*, 71–89.

Slama-Cazacu, T. Le dialogue chez les petits enfants: Sa signification et quelques unes de ses particularités. *Bulletin de Psychologie*, 1966, *19*, 688–697.

Slama-Cazacu, T. La régularisation: L'un des universaux de l'acquisition de la langue. *Cahiers de Linguistique Théorétique et Appliquée*, 1971, *8*, 63–92.

Slama-Cazacu, T. *Introduction to psycholinguistics*. The Hague: Mouton, 1973.

Slobin, D. I. Universals of grammatical development in children. In G. B. Flores d'Arcais & W. J. M. Levelt (Eds.), *Advances in psycholinguistics*. Amsterdam: North-Holland Publishing, 1970. Pp. 174–186.

Slobin, D. I. Cognitive prerequisites for the acquisition of grammar. In C. A. Ferguson & D. I. Slobin (Eds.), *Studies of child language development*. New York: Holt, Rinehart & Winston, 1973. Pp. 175–208.

Slobin, D. I. Language change in childhood and history. In J. Macnamara (Ed.), *Language learning and thought*. New York: Academic Press, 1977. Pp. 185–214.

Slobin, D. I. Universal and particular in the acquisition of language. In E. Wanner & L. R. Gleitman

(Eds.), *Language acquisition: The state of the art*. Cambridge: Cambridge University Press, 1982. Pp. 128–170.

Slobin, D. I. Crosslinguistic evidence for the language-making capacity. In D. I. Slobin (Ed.), *The crosslinguistic study of language acquisition* (Vol. 2). Hillsdale, NJ: Lawrence Erlbaum Associates, 1985.

Slobin, D. I., & Bever, T. G. Children use canonical sentence schemas: A crosslinguistic study of word order and inflections. *Cognition*, 1982, *12*, 229–265.

Snow, C. E. The development of conversation between mothers and babies. *Journal of Child Language*, 1977, *4*, 1–22.

Snow, C. E., & Ferguson, C. A. (Eds.), *Talking to children: Language input and acquisition*. Cambridge: Cambridge University Press, 1977.

Solan, L., & Ortiz, R. The development of pronouns and reflexives: Evidence from Spanish. In B. Lust (Ed.), *Studies in the acquisition of anaphora: Defining the constraints*. Dordrecht: Reidel, in press.

Sourdot, M. Identification et différentiation des unités: Les modalités nominales. In F. François et al., *La syntaxe de l'enfant avant 5 ans*. Paris: Larousse, 1978. Pp. 90–119.

Stoel-Gammon, C. Baby talk in Brazilian Portugese. *Revista Brasileira de Lingüistica*, 1976, *3*, 22–26.

Stoel-Gammon, C., & Scliar-Cabral, L. Learning to tell it like it is: The development of reportative function in children's speech. *Papers & Reports on Child Language Development* [Stanford University], 1977, *13*, 64–71.

Streri, A. *Enonciation et référentiation: Etude génétique des productions d'énoncés avec 'vouloir' et 'dire'*. (Monographies françaises de psychologie, No. 48.) Paris: Editions du CNRS, 1979. (a)

Streri, A. Etude génétique des productions d'énoncés avec *vouloir* et *dire* obtenues à partir d'images. *Année Psychologique*, 1979, *79*, 347–361. (b)

Streri, A. Etude génétique des productions et compréhension des pronoms anaphoriques dans une situation de reprise de discours. *Archives de Psychologie*, 1980, *48*, 41–58.

Suppes, P., Smith, R., & Léveillé, M. The French syntax of a child's noun phrases. *Archives de Psychologie*, 1973, *42*, 207–269.

Swain, M., Naiman, V., & Dumas, G. Aspects of the learning of French by English-speaking five-year-olds. In E. M. Hatch (Ed.), *Second language acquisition: A book of readings*. Rowley, Mass.: Newbury House, 1978. Pp. 297–309.

Swain, M., & Wesche, M. Linguistic interaction: Case study of a bilingual child. *Working Papers in Bilingualism* [Ontario Institute for Studies in Education], 1973, *1*, 10–34.

Tabouret-Keller, A. L'acquisition du langage parlé chez un petit enfant en milieu bilingue. In J. de Ajuriaguerra et al. (Eds.), *Problèmes de psycholinguistique*. Paris: Presses Universitaires de France, 1964. Pp. 205–219.

Tabouret-Keller, A. A propos de l'acquisition du langage: Les premiers mots. *Bulletin de Psychologie*, 1972–1973, *26*, 321–331.

Taeschner, T., & Volterra, V. Prime fasi dello sviluppo linguistico di una bambina bilingue. *Rassegna Italiana di Linguistica Applicata*, 1975, *7*, 41–56.

Taine, H. Note sur l'acquisition du langage chez les enfants et dans l'espèce humaine. *Revue Philosophique*, 1876, *1*, 5–23.

Talmy, L. Semantics and syntax of motion. In J. P. Kimball (Ed.), *Syntax and semantics*, vol. 4. New York: Academic Press, 1975. Pp. 181–238.

Tits, D. *Le mécanisme de l'acquisition d'une langue se substituant à la langue maternelle chez une enfant espagnole âgée de six ans*. Brussels: Veldeman, 1948.

Tolbert, M. D. *The acquisition of grammatical morphemes: A cross-linguistic study with reference to Mayan (Cakchiquel) and Spanish*. Unpublished PhD dissertation, Harvard University, 1978.

Toronto, A. *A developmental Spanish language analysis procedure for Spanish-speaking children.* Unpublished PhD dissertation, Northwestern University, 1972.

Toronto, A. Developmental assessment of Spanish grammar. *Journal of Speech & Hearing Disorders,* 1976, *41,* 150–171.

Toye-Dispy, N. *Contribution expérimentale à l'étude de l'acquisition de la morphologie française chez l'enfant.* Thèse de licence en psychologie, Université de Liège, 1967.

Tucker, G. R., Lambert, W. E., Rigault, A., & Segalowitz, N. A psychological investigation of French speakers' skill with grammatical gender. *Journal of Verbal Learning & Verbal Behavior,* 1968, *7,* 312–316.

Valette, R. M. Some reflections in second language learning in young children. *Language Learning,* 1964, *14,* 91–98.

Vihman, M. M. Formulas in first and second language acquisition. In L. K. Obler & L. Menn (Eds.), *Exceptional language and linguistics.* New York: Academic Press, 1982. Pp. 261–284.

Vinson, J. Observations sur le développement du langage chez l'enfant. *Revue de Linguistique,* 1915–1916, *48,* 1–39.

Vion, M. La compréhension des phrases simples comprenant des marqueurs de relation spatiale. *Cahiers de Psychologie,* 1978, *21,* 37–52. (a)

Vion, M. Les résistances pragmatiques à la compréhension de phrases simples chez l'enfant. *Enfance,* 1978, *4/5,* 225–236. (b)

Virbel, M. *Etude du détachement et de l'extraction dans le langage de l'enfant.* Thèse du Doctorat de Troisième Cycle, Université de Provence, Centre d'Aix-Marseille, 1975.

Volterra, V. Il "no": Prime fasi dello sviluppo della negazione nel linguaggio infantile. *Archivo de Psicologia, Neurologia e Psichiatria,* 1972, *23,* 16–53.

Volterra, V., & Taeschner, T. The acquisition and development of language by bilingual children. *Journal of Child Language,* 1978, *5,* 311–326.

Wagner, R. L., & Pinchon, J. *Grammaire du français classique et moderne.* Paris: Hachette, 1962.

Wartburg, W. von, & Zumthor, P. *Précis de syntaxe du français contemporain.* Berne: Francke, 1958.

Warden, D. A. The influence of context on children's use of identifying expressions and references. *British Journal of Psychology,* 1976, *67,* 101–112.

Waugh, L. R. *A semantic analysis of word order.* Leiden: Brill, 1977.

Wills, D. D. Participant deixis in English and baby talk. In C. E. Snow & C. A. Ferguson (Eds.), *Talking to children: Language input and acquisition.* Cambridge: Cambridge University Press, 1977. Pp. 271–295.

Williamson, R., & Rodríguez, O. Asking and telling, a problem of language acquisition: Some data from Mexican children. *Rassegna Italiana di Linguistica Applicata,* 1980, *12,* 73–90.

Wilmet, M. La place de l'épithète qualificative en français contemporain: Etude grammaticale et stylistique. *Revue de Linguistique Romane,* 1981, *45,* 17–73.

8 Variation and Error: A Sociolinguistic Approach to Language Acquisition in Samoa

Elinor Ochs
University of Southern California

Contents

1. WHAT IS AN ERROR?

The isolation of errors in the language of young children has led to general and interesting statements concerning the acquisition process. In discovering differences between child and adult language use, the researcher has been able to present hypotheses concerning conceptual strategies young children implement. These strategies in turn can be related to particular features of languages that enhance or inhibit the process of acquisition. Such analyses have drawn the interests of linguists interested in foundations of certain language universals as well as those interested in cognitive constraints on language change.

The present paper is an attempt to further these goals and achievements by examining the notion of error itself from a sociolinguistic perspective. Specifically, it suggests that the notion of error should be understood in light of the range of variants in use for the feature under consideration. Types of error in the language of young children can be distinguished in terms of whether or not the "error" exists as a variant in the adult speech community and if so, the value attached to that variant by the community. I will demonstrate that the assessment of what counts as an error is affected by data collection methodology, in particular by the way in which adult linguistic norms are established. To establish these points, I will draw on a longitudinal study of Samoan child language carried out by Martha Platt, Alessandro Duranti, and myself. This study was carried out in the village of Falefā on the island of Upolu, Western Samoa, from July 1978 through July 1979.

> If someone uses a sentence structure that is not generated by the grammar, there is nothing to prevent us from setting it aside as a mistake or a dialect difference (Labov, 1972, p. 200).

Pursuing an adequate definition of error is like chasing down a slippery eel. Just as its outline appears to emerge, it disappears into some other conceptual category. It is not an easy notion to assess, and it seems to me that, if only because of these definitional difficulties, those of us considering acquisition strategies ought to turn our collective attention to the ontological status of error. A comparison of errors children do/do not make across languages should be based on a clear and commonly accepted characterization of the nature and properties of an error.

The term *error* is related to the verb *to err,* which in Latin originally meant to wander from and subsequently to be deceived (Partridge, 1966). That which someone or something "wanders from" is an accepted standard or norm. (The term *norm* derives from the Latin *norma,* meaning a carpenter's square, hence a rule of conduct (Partridge, ibid).) A current transformation of *wander from,* used within the social sciences, is *deviation from.* In this interpretation, an error is a type of deviation from an accepted standard. The reader should note the use of the terms *type of deviation,* because not all deviations count as errors. In Canberra, Australia, most people prefer that their cars have steering wheels on the right side. We can say that it is the norm. Some people, however, own and drive cars with lefthand steering. We would not want to say that these people have made an error, even if they have not conformed to the preferred mode of conduct. In contrast, there is an accepted standard (norm) of driving on the left in Australia and if someone does not conform to this standard, that person has committed an error.

What makes one behavior an error and the other solely a deviation? This is a crucial and difficult question to adequately resolve. One lead to its resolution is to bring in the role of negative sanctions and/or correction. A deviation counts as an error if its occurrence is viewed as a VIOLATION of a norm and, as such, warranting negative sanctioning and/or correction. Driving on the right is an error, because its occurrence can provoke the application of negative sanctions by other members of the society (anything from horn-blowing to payment of fines). Note that an error is not defined by the actual implementation of negative sanctions. The status of a deviation as an error depends on members' judgments that the deviation could or should receive some form of negative feedback. In other words, we would want to count driving on the right as an error, even if the driver were unaware of the norm and even if no one saw the behavior or if others happened to ignore the behavior (in isolated cases, but not if the behavior were ignored regularly).

Moving to language, we want to maintain the same criteria. A particular speech phenomenon counts as an error if it (1) DEVIATES from a norm of speaking and (2) warrants (i.e. could provoke) NEGATIVE SANCTIONING, as judged by members of the speech community. In terms of actual implementation of negative feedback, such a response could come from hearers, audiences, or from speakers themselves. Indeed, as demonstrated by Schegloff, Jefferson, and Sacks (1977), in English-speaking communities while others may draw attention to a trouble source, there is a preference for speakers to correct or repair their own errors (i.e. what they themselves or others conceive of as error). As in the earlier example, we do not want to tie the concept of error to invariable implementation of negative feedback. A particular feature of speech (or language use) counts as an error because it is usually or often followed by a negative response and/or it is evaluated as a violation in the consideration of members. Certain slips of the tongue may be good examples of language errors that may not always receive attention by the speaker or others but are nonetheless judged to warrant attention and correction.

The careful reader will have noticed that there is a problem looming in the inclusion of members' judgments in our definition of error. Members may judge a feature of speech to be an error because it is not part of the prestige register of the language. Modern linguistics distinguishes itself by its concern with what speakers CAN say rather than what speakers SHOULD say. That is, grammars should account for what is possible in a language rather than what is the preferred standard of a language (a pedagogical grammar). By implication, the "modern" investigation of ERRORS should be concerned with deviations that are outside the realm of what is linguistically possible in a language (violations of a grammatical rule) rather than with deviations from the formal register(s) of a language.

At this point, the discussion turns to more complex points, because we must consider both an ideal definition of error, and error as it has been treated in the literature. As noted above, the concept of error is closely tied to the concept of grammar. In the modern framework, an error should be OUTSIDE the grammar. Indeed, the research on children's errors assumes this thesis, spelling out the ways in which rules are overgeneralized, undergeneralized, ignored, or otherwise treated by children at different stages in their language development. I do not take issue with such a definition of error (as outside the grammar of a language). The important issue to pursue concerns the KIND of grammar being used to assess errors.

The kind of grammar on which analyses of errors are based tends to be CATEGORICAL in nature (i.e. characterized by categorical rules). Errors are matched against rules that (are felt to) apply to all native speakers, and typically social context is not encoded in the formulation of the rule. However, as pointed out by Hymes (1974), Labov (1972), and others, categorical rules in a language are less frequent than one might suppose. They are far more reflective of the method of collecting linguistic data than they are reflective of the structure of the language itself. Categorical rules are intimately linked to the use of formal elicitation of speakers' judgments of language use. When one turns to naturalistic observation and recording, however, one finds systematic differences in language norms, sensitive to social definitions of speaker, hearer, setting, topic, genre, and the like. Grammatical rules based on grammaticality judgments must be thought of as capturing only a part of the language.

These rules may capture one or more formal registers, for example, structures characteristic of the written language, of formal interviews, or of talk to foreigners (cf. Duranti, 1981 for extended discussion of this point). The important point is that we cannot tell if a linguistic structure is categorical or variable until a sociolinguistic analysis of that structure is carried out. Examining that structure systematically across speakers and situations, we may find sociolinguistic variation or we may find the construction to be invariant across contexts.

In terms of an analysis of errors, it is important to establish soundly the nature of the rule being violated. Is the rule truly categorical and hence the deviation truly outside the scope of what is possible? It could well be that certain child language "errors" are in fact productive constructions for certain groups of adult speakers in particular social settings. If so, the child's speech would reflect a portion of the linguistic repertoire of the speech community in which he participates.

What is needed then, is a definition of error that incorporates sociolinguistic information. The previous definition of error specified that it was a deviation from a norm and that it counted as a violation, i.e. would be judged as warranting negative feedback. From the discussion above, we know that the treatment of norm in this definition is unrefined. We need to specify that A NORM MAY VARY ACROSS SOCIAL CONTEXTS (VARIABLE NORM) OR IT MAY BE INVARIABLE ACROSS SOCIAL CONTEXTS (CATEGORICAL NORM). For example, the norm for dressing in our society varies across social contexts (variable norm); on the other hand, the way we pick up a telephone receiver is minimally sensitive (if at all) to social context (categorical norm). Similarly, the pronunciation of consonant clusters in English varies across speakers and social settings (Labov, 1972) (variable norm), but the placement of the definite article in English is invariable across social contexts (categorical norm). Our definition of error needs to address these two types of norm. The amended definition reads:

For some particular phenomenon to count as an error, it must

    a. be a deviation from either a socially variable or a categorical norm and
    b. warrant negative feedback.

From this definition, we can begin to discuss types of error in terms of types of norm violated. SOCIALLY VARIABLE ERRORS are context-sensitive. They are judged as unacceptable (cf. prior discussion of ways in which judgments may be realized) in some particular social context. But the appearance of the same phenomenon in some other context may not necessarily be so judged, i.e., may not count as an error. Thus, wearing a tuxedo to play baseball is an instance of a socially variable error; it is violation of the norm for that particular set of social circumstances. To wear a tuxedo at most formal balls would not count as an error. Similarly for certain speakers of English, to reduce the consonant cluster /st/ to /s/ (e.g. /faest/ to /faes/) or /nt/ to /n/ (e.g. /want/ to /wan/) may be judged as unacceptable in formal social situations, but in casual situations these reductions will go by unnoticed.

Socially variable errors contrast with CATEGORICAL ERRORS, socially insensitive deviations, whose occurrence is judged as warranting negative feedback across shifting social contexts. Someone who answers the telephone by turning it upsidedown, lifting the body and leaving the receiver to dangle has made a categorical error. Such behavior would be judged as warranting some form of negative feedback regardless of social situation. Similarly, someone who places the definite article after the noun it modifies in English, as in *Boy the cries a lot* has made a categorical error, because such a construction would be judged as unacceptable across settings, speakers, topics, genres, activities, etc.

To be able to assess linguistic features as errors and if so, their status as variable or categorical, the researcher must have a record of language use in different social contexts. It is NOT acceptable to rely on grammatical descriptions of languages, such as those characteristic of traditional grammars or typological surveys. Such descriptions are usually context-restricted, and many features of casual registers are not captured. In the case of children's speech errors, this is particularly significant, as young children are typically primarily exposed to the speech register(s) characteristic of casual family interaction.

The child language researcher may think that certain methodological difficulties associated with intuition grammars can be overcome by the recording of a caregiver's spontaneous speech to the child and to the researcher carrying out the recording. As will be demonstrated shortly, this method is not sufficient. It is likely that speech to the researcher and perhaps even speech to the child represents some formal variant of adult-adult and/or adult-child speech. The researcher is typically not an intimate of the caregiver; therefore, the caregiver's speech to adult intimates must be captured, if possible to both same and different sex listeners. It may sound strange that the language to the child recorded may be formal, but particularly in middle class households, caregivers rarely display anger or annoyance or respond in a distracted manner to their children in the presence of the observer/recorder. Further, typically the caregiver is not carrying out one of the day's necessary tasks other than attending to the child. And, in the typical recording situation, the caregiver's attention is not divided among several charges. Usually the language of one caregiver to one child is captured. If formality of speech can be measured in terms of degree of attention to one's speech (Labov, 1966), then these circumstances of language use are relatively formal.

In the subsequent portions of this paper, I will relate these theoretical and methodological points to research carried out on Samoan language acquisition. As data collection was carried out relatively recently, the discussion will focus on selected features of children's language. Further, as a sociolinguistic grammar is not available and is in fact the object of ongoing research, the sociolinguistic description of adult Samoan will necessarily be rudimentary and not always quantitatively substantiated.

2. A SOCIOLINGUISTIC SKETCH OF SAMOAN

Samoan, a Polynesian language, belonging to the sub-group of Samoic-Outlier languages (Pawley, 1966, 1967; Chung, 1978) contains several sociolinguistic varieties.

2.1. Samoan View of Context

To introduce our sociolinguistic description, I first consider the place of social context in Samoan belief and value systems. This discussion draws on the analysis by Shore (1977, 1982) of contextual constraints on Samoan social behavior.

From a Samoan perspective, the idea that there is one set of norms for speaking makes little sense. As pointed out by Shore (1977, 1982), Samoans do not value consistency across social contexts. Members are expected to adapt themselves to the contingencies of different situations. Persons are not seen as having a particular personality or character, but rather all persons are seen as having many *itū* 'sides' which emerge in different settings. One's *itū* encompass both diverse social roles and diverse states of being. In this sense, one's identity is a consequence of particular social circumstances. The particular status one assumes and the mode of conduct and/or affect one displays are seen as generated by the social situation itself. To the outsider, one of the most outstanding impressions of Samoans is the quickness with which they are able to transform their social posture. The arrival of a stranger in someone's home provokes an immediate shift in demeanor and spatial arrangement of participants. Someone who is quite drunk, when suddenly face-to-face with the local pastor, will conduct himself in a completely sober and appropriately respectful manner. Similarly emotional states rapidly shift. An injury of one party to another may receive an angry response but that response is typically quickly dissipated once compensation is provided. Similarly acts of generosity receive approval at the time they are performed but once the event is completed, they are no longer noted. In general, attitudes towards persons are not enduring—gratitude, grudges and the like rarely overstep the bounds of particular events.

The significance of context for the traditional Samoan is reflected in the range of settings to which behavior is sensitive. One's mode of conduct becomes more ''proper'' the more one is in the public eye (Shore, 1977, 1982): day more than nighttime, center of the village (especially the road) more than the edge of the village or the bush itself, outside one's house more than inside, center of a house more than the edge of a house, front of a house (usually closer to the road) more than back of a house. For example, a woman may leave her shoulders uncovered if inside her house, but on the road she must wear something covering her shoulders. Drinking and eating are to be done seated inside houses but certainly not on the public thoroughfares. Defecation should take place behind houses, as close to the bush as possible. Within one's house, the more dignified interactions take place in the central front area. Typically, interactions among lower status family members take place in the back and periphery of a house when persons of some importance are present.

In addition to the dimension of public versus private, the dimension of Western versus non-Western (i.e traditional) setting strongly constrains social behavior. These institutions introduced by Western societies, such as churches, pastor's schools, and public schools, are associated with a particular code of dress and comportment. Children attending the pastor's school are expected to wear a shirt and those attending the public school wear uniforms. Outside these settings, it is common to find children barebreasted. Adults and children alike wear more clothing at a Sunday church service than at other times and settings in the village. This is the setting for women to wear broad-rimmed hats, and white, European-cut dresses or Samoan two-piece long suits. Men in this setting wear a European style shirt, a suit jacket. In other, non-Western settings within the village, mean and women tend to wear brightly colored floral printed *lavalava*.

Finally, the importance of context is evident in the way in which actions of members are evaluated. An action is not viewed as right or wrong, good or bad, in isolation (i.e. as inherently of this quality). Rather, actions are talked about in terms of the particular social situation in which they are performed. A common way to evaluate an action is in terms of whether or not it *fekaui* 'fits' with the situation. Disapproval is voiced as *E lē fekaui* 'It doesn't fit'. Similarly, something is judged as good or bad with respect to some particular social circumstances. What is bad in some circumstances is good in other circumstances or what is good in some circumstances is bad in other circumstances. For example, it may be bad to throw stones under many circumstances, but it is good to throw stones when the honor of one's family is at stake. Another way of looking at this is to recognize that it would be bad to act "good" (i.e. properly) when aggressive behavior is required.

2.2. The Sociolinguistic Repertoire

2.2.1.Tautala Lelei and Tautala Leaga

The following description draws on a fuller study of Samoan language variation carried out by Duranti (1981) and the ethnographic descriptions of Samoan speech use by Kernan (1974) and Shore (1977, 1982).

It is common knowledge to any speaker of Samoan that there are two major ways of speaking their language. There is what is called *tautala lelei* 'good speech' and *tautala leaga* 'bad speech'. From our discussion above, the reader should realize that these descriptions must be understood as highly contextbound; they do not refer to invariably good or bad qualities of speech.

Tautala lelei and *tautala leaga* are distinguished on many levels of grammar. The most salient dimension is phonological. In *tautala lelei,* there exists a phonemic distinction between /t/ and /k/ and between /n/ and /ŋ/ (written 'g' in Samoan orthography). Thus, in *tautala lelei, tete* means 'shivering' but *keke* means 'cake'; *ana* means 'cave' but *aga* (/aŋa/) means 'conduct' (examples taken from Duranti, 1981, ch. 8). The bulk of the lexical items in which /k/ is used are borrowings from English, such as *kī* 'key', *kukama* 'cucmber', *kalone* 'gallon', *suka* 'sugar'.

In *tautala leaga,* the /t/ is not used and all lexical items that include /t/ in *tautala lelei* are pronounced with /k/. Thus, in *tautala leaga,* both borrowed and non-borrowed lexical items are pronounced with /k/. In *tautala leaga, keke* means either 'cake' or 'shivering'. Similarly the /n/ and /ŋ/ distinction is not made in *tautala leaga,* and lexical items that in *tautala lelei* include /n/ are pronounced with /ŋ/. The lexical item *ana* in *tautala lelei* becomes *aga* in *tautala leaga.*

Another phonological distinction between these varieties is that /r/ in *tautala lelei,* e.g. *Maria,* becomes /l/ in *tautala leaga,* e.g. *Malia.* These lexical items are, like the use of /k/ in *tautala lelei,* largely borrowings.

There is a folk belief, with some external historical evidence (Pratt, 1911), that *tautala lelei* was at one time the language used by high chiefs (*ali'i*), particularly on formal occasions. At the time the Bible was first translated into Samoan, it was the code used by high ranking Samoans to missionaries engaged in this project.

The link with high status and dignity continues in attitudes of many Samoans. Competence in *tautala lelei* is linked to high chiefs rather than to orators among titled persons, and to women rather than to men among untitled persons (Shore, 1977, 1982). Transvestites displaying the behavior of women will exaggerate this image, speaking not only with the /t/ and /n/ and /r/ but moving all sounds towards the front of their mouth. The perception of status and language use does not correspond to actual practice, however.

Currently, within most villages in Western Samoa, *tautala lelei* is primarily associated with Western dominated settings and institutions. It is the preferred variety in church services, church conferences, pastors' schools, village public schools, and any situation in which Samoan is addressed to a European. It is also the variety that villagers hear when they turn on their radios. Finally *tautala lelei* is the variety used not only for the Bible but for literacy materials in Samoan in general, e.g. newspapers, letters, government documents.

With respect to speakers of this variety, one finds that those trained in formal educational institutions beyond the primary school, those who have an important role in church organizations (e.g. deacons, pastors, priests, etc.) and those who have a steady job in the capital are the most frequent users of this variety.

While we have devoted considerable discussion to *tautala lelei,* it is *tautala leaga* that prevails in village social life. *Tautala leaga* is not restricted to particular statuses, but rather is universal to all members of the community. It is the variety used in all formal and informal traditional (i.e. non-Western) social situations in the village—casual interactions among family members and familiars as well as highly stylized deliberations among titled persons interacting in village council meetings. *Tautala leaga* cuts across several genres, ranging from personal narratives, tattletaling and teasing to oratory. In these contexts, *tautala leaga* is not *leaga* 'bad' but *lelei* 'good'.

As discussed by Duranti (1981), these two varieties of Samoan have methodological implications. As *tautala lelei* is linked to Western settings and to talk to a Westerner in particular, it is the medium in which a Samoan would talk to a linguist in a formal elicitation session. Thus far, what has been described of Samoan captures this variety of the language. As will be discussed below, while many features of syntax and morphology are shared, there are important structural distinctions between *tautala lelei* and *tautala leaga (kaukala leaga).* An analysis of errors that is based on data obtained through formal interview between native and non-native speakers runs the risk of counting as error a feature that is productive in everyday language use. That is, a verbal strategy that violates a norm in *tautala lelei* may not count as a violation in *tautala leaga.* (It may be a socially variable language error.) Further, such a procedure would lead the researcher to miss what counts an an error in *tautala leaga,* either in terms of using features of *tautala lelei* (socially variable error) or in terms of using features that do not exist in either register (categorical error).

2.2.2. *The Parameter of Social Distance*

From the above discussion it is apparent that *tautala lelei* and *tautala leaga* are associated with different social relationships among interlocuters. Comparing the two registers, we may say that, relative to *tautala leaga, tautala lelei* is used in socially more distant relationships (Brown & Gilman, 1966).[1] *Tautala lelei* is generally used where relatively impersonal relationships obtain, particularly in cases in which one person addresses a large number. Most literacy materials fall into this category (one author to many readers). It is also used where speakers are not familiar with one another. as in many interactions between Samoans and non-Samoans. Thirdly, it is used where speakers, who in most contexts share an intimate relationship, wish to take distance from their addressees. For example, speakers may switch to *tautala lelei* (/t/ and /n/) to a family member to signal that they are angry with that person. The strategy of switching to the register of social distance prevails WITHIN as well as between two registers under discussion. Within the register of *tautala lelei,* relationships between language users may be more or less socially distant. For example, the relationship between author and reader or most literacy materials (e.g. newspapers, school books) is more impersonal than the relationship between Samoan and non-Samoan causally conversing with one another. Within the register of *tautala leaga,* the relationship assumed in the formal setting of ceremonial events or village councils are more distant (i.e. positional cf. Irvine, 1979) than those assumed among the same individuals engaged in causal activities (e.g. sharing a family meal or relaxing on mats after work).

The parameter of social distance is a very important contextual constraint on language use in traditional Samoan life. The move from less to more distant social relationships has linguistic reflexes in the lexicon and in the morphosyntactic structure of the language. The transition affects the organization of discourse as well, including procedures for participating in particular speech events. However, this dimension will not be considered here, and the reader is referred to Duranti (1980, 1981) for a detailed analysis of these features.

2.2.3. *The Lexicon*

Samoan has a respect vocabulary (see Milner, 1961), used in *tautala lelei* and *tautala leaga* when referring to or speaking to persons of high status, particularly titled persons. It is also used to persons who do not have titles to whom the

---

[1]For every generalization, there are exceptions and in this case, the exceptions are those who, because of strong church alignment, choose to use *tautala lelei* with intimates. Only one such person in the village met this description: the wife of a pastor, who is also the daughter of a pastor and who was educated in a church school in the capital. But even here, it is difficult to say that *tautala lelei* even in its fullest form is employed by this speaker. As in other sociolinguistic studies, a close examination of the speech of this speaker indicates that while /t/ is generally maintained, /n/ is variable and alternates with /ŋ/. Speakers are more self-conscious about the use of /t/ and are able to control its use more than the use of /n/, often producing /t/ and /ŋ/ pronunciation.

speaker wishes to convey deference and respect. For example, it may be used towards an untitled person to whom a particularly important request is being directed. This vocabulary, when used with titled persons, includes many items that are appropriate only to particular statuses of titled persons, e.g., only to orators, only to high chiefs. Other lexical items apply to any person who has a title. The use of these items is not characteristic of relaxed, informal interaction among familiars. A shift into the use of respect vocabulary brings into focus the political/social status of participants in an interaction. This is what occurs, for example, when a non-family member arrives for a visit or is passed on the road. The greeting will include respect vocabulary that implies the positional identity of the addressee. Once the greeting is completed, the social interaction may shift to a more initimate register, in which unmarked lexical items are used.

2.2.4. *Morphology*

2.2.4.1. Ergative Casemarking.   Samoan has been described as an ergative language (Chung, 1978), that is, a language in which subjects of the transitive sentences are distinguished from subjects of intransitive sentences and in which subjects of intransitive sentences and direct objects of transitive sentences are treated (at least in some ways) as a single category (Comrie, 1978; Dixon, 1979). Such a language is fairly unusual and contrasts with the more common, nominative type of language, in which subjects of transitive and intransitive sentences are treated as one category and distinguished from the category of direct object. The difference between the two language types is represented below:

ERGATIVE LANGUAGE   NOMINATIVE LANGUAGE

Key: S = Intransitive Subject
         A = Agent/Transitive Subject
         O = Transitive Object
                 (from Dixon, 1979)

In Samoan, as in most ergative languages, the ergative distinctions are expressed through nominal casemarking. In Samoan, the transitive subject is preceded by the particle *e* when the transitive subject follows the verb (VSO, VOS, OVS). Intransitive subjects following the verb and all direct objects receive no casemarking. The difference in marking is presented in (1) and (2) below:

(1) TRANSITIVE SENTENCE:

       VSO: *'ua*   *fasi*   *e*   *le*   *tama*   *Sina*
                 PAST.PERF   hit   ERG   ART   boy   Sina

VOS: *'ua*   *fasi* *Sina* *e*   *le*   *tama*
            PAST.PERF hit   Sina ERG ART boy
            'The boy hit Sina.'

(2) INTRANSITIVE SENTENCE:

VS: *'olo'o*   *moe* *le*   *tama*
           PRES.PROG sleep ART boy
           'The boy is sleeping.'

This case-marking system is sociolinguistically variable. Its variation is partly but not completely a function of the social distance between language users. Where social relationships are relatively impersonal and distant, there is a greater tendency for Samoans to use the ergative particle. Where intimacy prevails, language users tend not to express the ergative case marker. For example, in literacy materials and in radio broadcasts, the ergative particle is always present in the grammatically feasible environments (i.e. when transitive subject follows the verb). In face-to-face social interaction, the particle is not always expressed. The social distribution of the use of this particle in spoken Samoan is represented in Table 8.1, drawn from an earlier study of this case marker (Ochs, 1982). Table 8.1 indicates that the ergative particle *e* rarely appears in its grammatically feasible environments when the language users are members of one's own household and the setting is casual. Women in these settings use ergative case marking in only 20% of the grammatically feasible environments and men use it only 16.6%. When social distance is increased, the frequency of expressed ergative case marking is also increased. When speaking to non-family members, women more than double and men more than quadruple the frequency of use of this marker. The relation of greater social distance to increased use of the case marking ends at this point, however, given that those participating in highly formal chiefly council meetings do not use the marker more than when they are chatting to friends. It is in this sense that the use of the ergative case marker is partially sensitive to the pole of social distance.

While a statistical analysis has not been carried out for other case markers in Samoan, a first appraisal indicates that the following are also sensitive to the parameter of social distance:

2.2.4.2. *Possessive Case Marking.* Samoan has two ways to express possession. In the first, a possessive modifier is placed before the noun it modifies. The modifier is composed of a determiner (either the specific form *l(e)* or the nonspecific form *s(e)*) and a pronoun, that encodes one of two types of possession (roughly, inalienable/alienable):

TABLE 8.1
Ergative Casemarking in Adult Samoan Speech
(Canonical Transitive Declaratives, Y-N Interrogatives)

Context:	% ECM/Total:	% Ergative Environments/ Total:	% ECM/ Ergative Environments:	% Agents Expressed:
Informal language of women to female adults & to children (family members) (150 total)	4.0% (6)	20.0% (30)	20.0% (6)	40.0% (60)
Informal language of men to female/male adults & to children (family members) (60 total)	5.0% (3)	30.0% (18)	16.6% (3)	40.0% (24)
Informal language of women to female adults (non-family members) (120 total)	13.3% (16)	29.2% (35)	45.7% (16)	52.5% (63)
Informal language of men to male adults (non-family members) (50 total)	24.0% (12)	32.0% (16)	75.0% (12)	40.0% (20)
Formal language of male titled men to one another in discussion portion of village council meetings (56 total)	28.6% (16)	39.3% (22)	72.7% (16)	55.3% (31)

SPECIFIC FORMS:

la'u masi	'my biscuit'	*lo'u lima*	'my arm'
lau masi	'your biscuit'	*lou lima*	'your arm'
lana masi	'his/her biscuit'	*lona lima*	'his/her arm'
etc.			

NON-SPECIFIC FORMS:

sa'u masi	'one of my biscuits'	*so'u lima*	'one of my arms'
sau masi	'one of your biscuits'	*sou lima*	'one of your arms'
sana masi	'one of his/her biscuits'	*sona lima*	'one of his/her arms'
etc.			

The second way to express possession places a full pronoun or noun after the noun modified and marks the possessor with either the particle *a*, for alienable possession, or *o*, for inalienable possession:

le	masi	a	a'u	'my biscuit'
ART	biscuit	POSS	1.PERS	

le	masi	a	oe	'your biscuit'
ART	biscuit	POSS	2.PERS	

le	masi	a	Sefo	'Sefo's biscuit'
ART	biscuit	POSS	Sefo	

le	lima	o	a'u	'my arm'
ART	arm	POSS	1.PERS	

etc.

The second way uses casemarking and is of interest in this discussion of morphological variation. The expression of the possessive markers *a* and *o* varies in terms of whether the social relationship among language users is relatively intimate or distant. THE MORE IMPERSONAL THE RELATIONSHIP THE GREATER THE USE OF THE POSSESSIVE MARKER. In the intimate surroundings of one's family, the marker is often dropped.

2.2.4.3. *Verbal Suffix.*   In all social environments a suffix may be added to intransitive verbs, transitive verbs, and what Chung (1978) calls "middle verbs," e.g. verbs of perception, emotion, desire, cognition. This suffix has a number of forms (*-a, -ia, -ina, -lia, -fia,* etc.).

VERB	VERB + SUFFIX
fai	*faia*
tu'u	*tu'uina*
alofa	*alofagia*
vala'au	*vala'aulia*
tā	*tāia*

For transitive verbs, it tends to appear (Chung, 1978, p. 85) in clauses whose subjects are clitic pronouns, in relative clauses whose subjects have been removed, in clauses whose subjects appear in cleft constructions, and in clauses with deleted generic agents; it is "required" in negative imperatives and negative generic statements (Chung, 1978, p. 91).

Preliminary analysis by Duranti (1981) indicates that the CIA suffix appears both MORE FREQUENTLY and in a WIDER RANGE OF CONSTRUCTION TYPES in the highly formal meetings of chiefs (where positional identities are assumed) than in more causal interaction among men (where more personal identities are assumed. highly formal meetings of chiefs (where positional identities are assumed) than in more casual interaction among men (where more personal identities are assumed. In the formal setting, men use the suffix in the less as well as more predictable grammatical environments; in casual surroundings, the use of the suffix tends to appear only in the more predictable environments (specified above).

2.2.4.4. *Subject-Verb Agreement*. In formal, standard Samoan, many verbs agree with the subject in terms of number, i.e. whether the subject is singular or plural. The most common method of forming the plural consists of reduplicating the penultimate syllable of the singular form of the verb, e.g.

SINGULAR	PLURAL
'ai	*'a'ai*
savali	*savavali*
moe	*momoe*

Other means of forming the plural include reduplicating two or more syllables; adding the prefix *ta-* (as in *tafasi* (singular: *fasi*)) or *fe-* (as in *feinu* (singular: *inu*)); dropping a syllable; and lengthening the vowel in the first syllable of the singlular form (Pratt, 1876). For certain verbs, two different lexical items are used to express the singular and plural forms of the verb. For example, the verb 'go' in the singular is *alu;* in the plural it is *ō.* The verb 'come' in the singular is *sau;* in the plural it is *ō mai.*

The use of subject-verb agreement is more restricted in language used among intimates than in the language of more socially distant interlocutors. As with the use of the CIA suffix, the restriction is in terms of frequency and range of constructions used. IN CASUAL SPEECH, ONE FINDS FEWER INSTANCES OF AGREEMENT AND A MORE RESTRICTED SET OF VERBS THAT ARE ALSO INFLECTED. The most common plural forms in casual speech are those of the verbs 'go', 'come', and 'eat'; outside these verbs, the use of the plural is uncommon in this context.

2.2.4.5. *Tense/Aspect Marking*. The discussion that follows will be quite preliminary, as the semantics of tense and aspect marking has not been fully analyzed.

Formal, standard Samoan is characterized by the use of seven tense/aspect markers. They include:

MARKER	TIME
'e / te	present (habitual), future (*te* restricted to 1st and 2nd person clitic subjects—singular, dual, plural)
'o lo o	present continuous
'ua	imperfect, action just initiated, present (with adjectives)
'o le'ā	future
na	past perfect
sā	past imperfect

These markers appear as particles preceding the verb, e.g.

'o   lo'o   moe   Sina
PRES PROG   sleep   Sina

'Sina is sleeping.'

'*ua*   *alu*   *Sina*
IPFV   go   Sina
'Sina has gone.'

'*e*   *alu*   '*oe?*
FUT   go   you
'Are you going?'

The most common social context for these tense/aspect markers is in literate Samoan, particularly books and newspapers, where language users are socially distant from one another. In spontaneous spoken Samoan, these forms (in *tautala leaga* pronunciation) are used much less frequently, particularly in the casual environment of one's own household. In these latter contexts, two alternatives are characteristic. Either the tense/aspect marker is completely omitted as in (1) below:

(1) P17-051

A: *Ae   vaai,   ou   alifo   ā*
But   see   1.CLITIC   go:over   PARTICLE (TAG)

Laku   laku o   le,   (pause)
go:DEICTIC   go:DEICTIC   there

avaku   le   mea   i   le   oki
give:DEICTIC (take)   the   thing   to   the   dead

'But you see, I went over, you know?

I went—went there, (PAUSE)

took the thing to the dead one.'

or an alternative marker is used. The alternate may be a REDUCED FORM OF ONE OF THE MARKERS used in standard Samoan. Tuitele and Kneubuhl (1978) mention that the marker '*o lo* '*o* may be reduced to '*o* and that '*o le* '*ā* may be reduced to '*ā*. In our transcripts of casual conversation, '*a* is not common; future time tends to be expressed through the particles *la'a, lā* and *la,* producing such utterances as:

$$\left\{\begin{matrix} la'a \\ lā \\ la \end{matrix}\right\} \quad alu$$
  FUT   go

$$\left\{\begin{matrix} I \\ you \\ he \end{matrix}\right\} \quad \text{will go.'}$$

la'u   *alu*
FUT.1.CL   go
'I will go.'

la'e   *alu*
FUT.2.CL   go
'You will go.'

The tense/aspect particles *la'a*, *lā*, and *la* are very frequently used in conversation transcribed in our study. The underlying form of these particles is not clear. One possibility is that they are reduced forms of *'o le'ā*, i.e.,

    (i)   *'o le'ā*
    (ii) ('o → ø) *la'ā*
    (iii) (' → ø) *leā*
    (iv) (*e* → ø) *lā*

A second possibility is that *lā* is to be understood as a distinct morpheme. *Lā* is a deictic adverb or pronoun, meaning 'there' or 'that', 'those' (in speaker's sight, not far away). In this case, *lā* may be combined with the particle *'ā* to form *la'a*, *lā* (deleting glottal stop, which is also common in casual speech) or *la* (reducing vowel length, again a comon process in casual speech).

Support for the second of these hypotheses comes from the use of *la* to mark other dimensions of time. The particle *la* may precede the tense/aspect marker *'e* forming *lae* (again deleting the glottal stop). The particle *lae* is used only for third person subjects and denotes present tense. The sentence *lae moe* means roughly 'There (now) he sleeps'. *La* also may precede the marker *'ua* to become *lāua*, *laua*, or *lauā*. These forms express action (of a third person) that has started but is not completed. Hence, the sentence *laua moe* means roughly 'He/She has just gone to (go to) sleep (but is not yet sleeping)'.

In addition to *la*, the deictic forms *lea* (meaning 'this' or 'that' or 'now') and *loa* ('now') are used before the verb in casual speech instead of the present future tense marker *'e/te*, e.g. *loa alu* can mean '(I) am about to go'. The semantics of these deictic forms has not been sufficiently researched to establish their scope and use as tense/aspect markers.

This brief discussion brings out two important points. First that IN DESCRIBING THE ACQUISITION OF TENSE/ASPECT MARKING, ONE MUST CONSIDER NOT ONLY THE SYSTEM DESCRIBED FOR STANDARD SAMOAN. THE CHILD'S USE OF DEICTIC FORMS FOR EXPRESSING TIME AS WELL AS OMISSION OF ANY MARKING OF TIME IS NOT A CATEGORICAL ERROR BUT PART OF THE LANGUAGE MODEL TO WHICH THE CHILD IS EXPOSED (AND PROBABLY TO WHICH THE CHILD IS MOST EXPOSED).

The second important point to note is that CASUAL SPEECH IS NOT TO BE THOUGHT OF AS A PALER OR LESS ELABORATE VERSION OF STANDARD SPEECH.

Our observations indicate that tense/aspect may receive more complex marking (e.g. deictic forms plus particles) in the speech of familiars than in the speech (and writing) of socially more distant language users.

2.2.4.6. *The Particles* 'i *and* i.   In standard Samoan, the particles 'i and i are used as case markers. The particle 'i marks directionality (goal), causality, instrumentality, and 'aboutness' (Tuitele & Kneubuhl, 1978, p. 61):

(2) Examples of 'i
      (from Tuitele & Kneubuhl, 1978, pp. 57–61)[2]

DIRECTIONALITY:

Tū	'i	luga
stand	DIR	up

'Stand up.'

CAUSALITY:

Na	'ou	sau	'i	le	fa'alevelave
PAST	1.CL	come	CAUS	ART	significant:event

'I came because of the significant event.'

INSTRUMENTALITY (in sense of material from which something is made or changed):

Na	fau	le	fale	'i	laupapa	ma	simā
PAST	construct	ART	house	INSTR	timber	CONJ	cement

'They made the house with timber and cement.'

ABOUTNESS:

Na	'ou	pese	'i	le	Atua
PAST	1.CL	sing	ABOUT	ART	God

'I sang about God.'

The particle *i* marks time; location (not in the sense of goal); the objects of a class of verbs (called semi-transitive (Churchward, 1926), middle verbs (Chung, 1978), and intransitive verbs (Tuitele & Kneubuhl, 1978)) that include verbs of perception, emotion, desire, and cognition, among others; instrumentality; and comparison:

(3) Examples of *i*
      (from Tuitele & Kneubuhl, 1978, pp. 59–60)[3]

[2&3]Only the Samoan examples are taken from Tuitele and Kneubuhl. Word-by-word and free glosses as well as certain sub-headings are not from this source.

TIME:

Na	matou	ō	i	le	lua
PAST	we:EXCL	go	TEMP	ART	two

'We went at two.'

LOCATION:

'Ou	te	nofo	i	Masefau
1.CL	PRES	live	LOC	Masefau

'I live in Masafau.'

OBJECT ASSOCIATED WITH SEMI-TRANSITIVE/MIDDLE/INTRANSITIVE VERB:

'Ou	te	alofa	iā	'oe
1.CL	PRES	love	OBJ	you

'I love you.'

'Ou	te	fa'alogo	iā	'oe
1.CL	PRES	hear	OBJ	you

'I hear you.'

INSTRUMENTALITY (in sense of item used or item that affects one):

Na	'ou	lavea	i	le	fao
PAST	1.CL	cut:TRANS	INSTR	ART	nail

'The nail cut/injured me.'   or   'I was cut by the nail.'

COMPARISON:

'E	sili	Sina	iā	'oe
PRES	beyond	Sina	COMP	you

'Sina is better than you'

While the two particles are distinguished phonologically in careful registers of Samoan, they are not in the more casual social environments of language use. Where interlocuters are familiar with one another and the situation is relatively informal, the glottal stop is deleted, removing the one feature that differentiates the two particles. The dropping of the glottal stop is related not only to relatively less attention paid to speaking but also to increased speed of speech characteristic of casual interactions. With the exception of certain formulaic genres (e.g. kava calling, greetings), formal speech is relatively slower than informal speech.

2.2.5. *Word Order*

Samoan has several possible orderings of full, major constituents. For all constructions, the preferred order is VERB-INITIAL, i.e. intransitives as VERB SUBJECT and transitives (with three full constituents) as either VERB SUBJECT OBJECT or VERB OBJECT SUBJECT. This preference cuts across social distance and degrees of formality of settings (Duranti, 1980). The second major preference when all constituents are expressed is SUBJECT VERB and SUBJECT VERB OBJECT word orders. Other possible, but less frequently used word orders are OBJECT VERB SUBJECT and SUBJECT OBJECT VERB.

(4) Examples of word order

INTRANSITIVES:

VS: 'Ua   sau   Pesio
     IPFV   come   Pesio

SV: 'O   Pesio 'ua   sau
     TOPIC Pesio IPFV   come

'Pesio has come.'

CANONICAL TRANSITIVES:

VSO: Na   usu   e   Tala   le   pese
      PAST   sing   ERG   Tala   ART   song

VOS: Na   usu   le   pese   e   Tala
      PAST   sing   ART   song   ERG   Tala

SVO: 'O   Tala   na   usu   le   pese
      TOP   Tala   PAST   sing   ART   song

OVS: 'O   le   pese   na   usu   e   Tala
      TOP   ART   song   PAST   sing   ERG   Tala

'Tala sang the song.'

SEMI-TRANSITIVES/MIDDLE VERB CONSTRUCTIONS:

VSX:[4] 'E   inoino   le   pālagi   i   le
         PRES   feel:disgust/despise ART   white:man OBJ   ART

         falevao   lale.
         outhouse   there

VXS: 'E   inoino   i   le   falevao   lele
      PRES   feel:disgust/despise   OBJ   ART   outhouse   there

      le   pālagi
      ART   white:man

SVX: 'O   le   pālagi   e   inoino   le
      TOP   ART   white:man PRES   feel:disgust/despise ART

      falevao   lale
      outhouse   there

XVS: 'O   le   falevao   lale   e   inoino
      TOP   ART   outhouse   there PRES   feel:disgust/despise

---

[4]X represents either direct object or indirect object (depending upon whether these constructions are considered as transitives or not).

iai   le   pālagi.
COPY.PRO   ART   white:man
'The whiteman is disgusted at/despises the outhouse over there.'

In Samoan, both intransitive and transitive subjects may be represented by a clitic pronoun as well as by a full pronoun or noun. While full pronoun and noun subjects may appear in any of the above word orders, clitic pronoun subjects have only one possible position, that of before the verb.

(5) Examples of clitic subject word order

SV: *'Ou   te   alu*
       1.CL   FUT   go

       'I will go.'

SVO: *'Ou   te   usu   le   pese*
       1.CL   FUT   sing   ART   song

OSV: *'O   le   pese   'ou   te   usu*
       TOP   ART   song   1.CL   FUT   sing

*VSO: *'e   usu   'ou   le   pese*
       FUT   sing   1.CL   ART   song

Comparing constructions with clitic vs. full subjects, we can see that the notion of error is easier to assess in the former than in the latter constructions. In the case of clitic subject constructions there is only one acceptable position for the clitic pronoun (i.e. before the verb) and the range of possible word orders is restricted. In the case of full subject constructions, the subject pronoun or noun may appear both before and after the verb, yielding a wider range of acceptable word orders.

2.2.5.1. *Word Order and Focus.*   Word order has been widely discussed as responsive to the speaker's intentions and the speaker's perception of interlocutors' knowledge (cf. discussions of topic, new, old, given information in Li, 1976, and Givón, 1979, for example). Word order in Samoan is not the only means of differentiating what is the information focus (Chomsky, 1971) from old, background information. There are intonational means, a wide range of emphatic particles that apply to verbs, adverbs, adjectives, and nominal forms, suffixes that can be added to transitive and middle verbs, reduplication of verb, code switching of single lexical items from *tautala lelei* (t/n) to *tautala leaga* (k/ŋ) or vice versa. Indeed, as will be discussed below, THE EXPRESSION OF ALL THREE MAJOR CONSTITUENTS IS IN ITSELF A MARKED FORM OF LANGUAGE USE AND SIGNALS A TYPE OF EMPHASIS not conveyed when only the verb or verb and one constituent is expressed.

The availability and frequent use of these alternate means of highlighting and backgrounding make it difficult to discuss the relation of word order in Samoan to these informational functions. Placing a full NP in sentence-initial position before the verb with the accompanying topic marker '*o* is a means of focusing on the referent expressed in this position (e.g. *SVO, OVS, IOVOS, LocVS* etc.). This does not mean, however, that the speaker cannot focus on that referent using other word orders. Just as the topic marker '*o* is used to indicate emphasis or focus for items appearing in sentence-initial position, so other markers are used to the same end on items appearing after the verb.

(6) Examples of emphatic particles in verb-initial constructions

(a) Particle *fo'i*: emphasis on verbs[5]
P17-099

A: | *Fiu* | *fo'i* | *guku* | *e* | | *ai* | *mea* | *pālāgi* |
    | fed:up | EMPH | mouths | COMPL | | eat | things | foreign |

| *mea* | *pālāgi* | *mea* | *pālāgi* |
| things | foreign | things | foreign |

'Our mouths are FEDUP with eating foreign food, foreign food, foreign food.'

(b) Particle *a*: emphasis on verb
P8-272

I: | *Sa'o* | *a* | *oe* |
    | Right | EMPH | you |

'You are RIGHT.'

(c) Particle *a*: emphasis on predicate adjective
Iak I-2-272

Iul: | *E* | *ulavale* | *a* | *Vaa* |
      | is | naughty | EMPH | Vaa |

'Vaa is certainly naughty.'

(d) Particle *ia*: emphasis on adjective
Iak I-2-111

P: | *Faikala* | *valea* | *ia* |
    | Say:stories | bad | EMPH |

'She says BAD words.'

(e) Particle *ia*: emphasis on predicate adjective
Iak I-2-271

---

[5]Examples of spontaneous speech are marked by a transcript catalogue number, e.g. P59-062, PV, etc. The transcripts capture fairly closely what speakers actually expressed and will include variable and idiosyncratic ways of speaking. In examples of child language, speech of the child under study is placed to the left of the speech of others participating in the interaction. To represent the velar /ŋ/in Samoan, I use the conventional orthographic symbol "g" adopted by Samoans. Conventions for marking overlap and other conversational phenomena are drawn from conversation analysis (Schenkein, 1978).

Iul: *Au: Kaukalaikiki ia   Vaa*
    ?   cheeky   EMPH Vaa
'Vaa is really cheeky.'

2.2.5.2. *Word Order, Social Identity and Social Distance.* While word order has been discussed with respect to communicative intentions, it has not been discussed in terms of social identity of speakers and/or social relationship obtaining among language users. A preliminary analysis of adult use of word order by Duranti (1981) and Ochs (1980) indicates that there are significant differences in preferred word orders between male speakers and female speakers (social identity) as well as between more and less intimate interlocutors (social distance). These differences are displayed in Tables 8.2, 8.3, and 8.4 below: Table 8.2 presents word order preferences across a range of social contexts for CANONICAL TRANSITIVES with all three full constituents expressed. The data base is exactly that described earlier for the analysis of ergative case marking. Table 8.3 reorganizes these data in terms of sex of speaker and indicates that MEN AND WOMEN DIFFER IN THEIR PREFERENCE FOR VSO AND SVO WORD ORDERS. The most strking difference concerns the use of SVO: the percentage of use of SVO by women is nearly five times that by men (37.5% vs 7.89%). With respect to VSO ordering, on the other hand, the percentage of use by men is one and a half times that by women (44.7% vs 28.1%). Looking at the data in terms of whether or not the speaker is speaking to a family member (collapsing informal and

TABLE 8.2
Word-Order Preferences: Canonical Transitives
with Three Full Constituents

	VSO	VOS	SVO	OVS
Women Family (23)	.217 (5)	.348 (8)	.348 (8)	.087 (2)
Men Family (15)	.266 (4)	.666 (10)	—	.0666 (1)
Informal Women Non-family (14)	.286 (4)	.357 (5)	.286 (4)	.071 (1)
Informal Men Non-family (6)	.666 (4)	.166 (1)	.166 (1)	—
Men Formal Fono (17)	.529 (9)	.176 (3)	.118 (2)	.176 (3)
TOTAL 75	.347 (26)	.36 (27)	.20 (15)	.093 (7)

TABLE 8.3
Word-Order Preferences
and Sex of Speaker

	VSO	VOS	SVO	OVS
Men (38)	.447 (17)	.368 (14)	.0789 (3)	.105 (4)
Women (32)	.281 (9)	.406 (13)	.375 (12)	.031 (3)

formal speaking-out situations, and men's and women's speech), we can see that
VSO IS MORE PREFERRED (2:1) IN SPEAKING-OUT SOCIAL CONTEXTS AND VOS IS
MORE PREFERRED IN SPEAKING-IN CONTEXTS (I.E. IN SPEECH TO OTHER FAMILY
MEMBERS). THE DISPREFERENCE OF VSO BY WOMEN AND IN INTIMATE CON-
TEXTS IS AN IMPORTANT SOCIAL FACT AND WILL BE RETURNED TO LATER IN OUR
DISCUSSION OF THE ACQUISITION OF WORD ORDER PREFERENCES BY YOUNG
SAMOAN CHILDREN.

The reader should note here that these data counter previous typological
accounts of Samoan (Greenberg, 1966; Chung, 1978) in which Samoan (as a
Polynesian language) has been described as having a basic (and most frequent)
word order of verb-subject-object. As can be seen here the idea of BASIC word
order must be reassessed in terms of BASIC FOR PARTICULAR SOCIAL AND LIN-
GUISTIC CONTEXTS. It doesn't appear to be basic in the sense of norm for
speakers and for both men and women in intimate surroundings.

2.2.5.3. *Expression and Non-expression of Subjects and Objects.* While
most studies of word order examine sentences in which all major constituents are
expressed, there are certain languages, like Samoan, in which such sentences are
not that frequent in spoken registers. We can get some idea of the relative
presence of major constituents by examining again the data on transitive assertions across contexts.

TABLE 8.4
Word-Order Preferences:
Speech to Family vs. Non-Family

	VSO	VOS	SVO	OVS
SPEAKING IN (men & women) (38)	.237 (9)	.474 (18)	.211 (8)	.079 (3)
SPEAKING OUT (men & women) (37)	.459 (17)	.243 (9)	.189 (9)	.108 (4)

TABLE 8.5
Percentage of Canonical Transitives
(Declaratives & Yes-No Interrogatives
with Simple Subject, Verb and Object)

	FULL S+V+O	*CLITIC S+V+O*	*TOTAL S+V+O*
Women			
Family			
(150 total)	15.3% (23)	4.70% (7)	20% (30)
Men			
Family			
(60 total)	25% (15)	6.7% (4)	31.7% (19)
Informal Women to Non-Family			
(120 total)	11.7% (14)	2.5% (3)	14.2% (17)
Informal Men to Non-family			
(50 total)	12% (6)	6% (3)	18% (9)
Men to Men in Formal Village Council			
(56 total)	30.3% (17)	10.7% (6)	41% (23)
TOTAL AVERAGE: 436	17.2% (75)	5.3% (23)	22.5% (98)

Table 8.5 displays the relative presence of canonical transitive assertions with subject, verb, and object all expressed. Constructions with clitic and full subjects are represented and analyzed separately as well as together. Combining all contexts, we see that SENTENCES WITH ALL THREE CONSTITUENTS CONSTITUTE ONLY 22.5% OF THE TOTAL CORPUS OF CANONICAL TRANSITIVE DECLARATIVES AND YES-NO INTERROGATIVES. If we look at those constructions with a FULL subject (a full pronoun or noun phrase) and verb and object, we can see that the percentage drops even further to 17.2% of the corpus.[6]

These figures suggest that great care must be taken in comparing pragmatic aspects of word order across languages. IN A LANGUAGE LIKE SAMOAN, THE EXPRESSION OF A SUBJECT AND/OR OBJECT IS IN ITSELF A MARKED STRATEGY. Thus, to mention a referent in these syntactic roles is itself a means of drawing increased attention to that referent. The reader should keep in mind that absence of a subject is usually accompanied by absence of any agreement marking on the verb. Thus, in Samoan, when the subject is not expressed, it is not specified elsewhere through grammatical means. This means that we cannot make a direct comparison with the non-expression of subjects in languages where agreement functions across registers (e.g. Italian).

The relative markedness of expressing both subject and object is also of considerable import to understanding the acquisition of word order by Samoan children. WE CANNOT ASSESS THE INFREQUENT EXPRESSION OF THESE MAJOR

---

[6]For percentages of canonical transitive declaratives and yes-no interrogatives with subjects expressed (i.e. both ± objects expressed), see Table 8.1.

TABLE 8.6
Percentage of Canonical Transitives with Subject,
Verb + Object: Sex of Speaker

	FULL S+V+O	CLITIC S+V+O	TOTAL S+V+O
Women (270)	13.7% (37)	3.7% (10)	17.4% (47)
Men (166)	22.9% (38)	7.8% (13)	30.7% (51)

CONSTITUENTS IN CHILD LANGUAGE AS AN ERROR. We cannot bring to bear a notion such as "deletion transformation" (Bloom, 1970) to account for the nonoccurrence of the constituents under discussion here. Rather, we must look at what children are doing as acquiring the pertinent syntactic features of spoken Samoan. Indeed, if Samoan children were to express agents and patients in the majority of their utterances, we might want to say that then they would have violated a speech norm. In contrast to the many studies of acquisition of word order in English, the relative NON-EXPRESSION OF MAJOR CONSTITUENTS INDICATES COMPETENCE.

Tables 8.6 and 8.7 display the use of all three constituents in canonical transitive declaratives and yes-no interrogatives according to sex of speaker and according to social distance between speaker and addressee.

Glancing first at Table 8.7, we can see that THERE ARE NO SIGNIFICANT DIFFERENCES IN THE USE OF THESE CONSTRUCTIONS AS SOCIAL DISTANCE INCREASES OR DECREASES. This result has interest in that it indicates that an increase or decrease in the amount of shared information between interlocutors does NOT trigger non-expression/expression of subject and/or object. Future research will have to substantiate this point, but it appears as if the expression of all constituents has an emphatic or focusing function rather than a strictly referential function.

TABLE 8.7
Percentage of Canonical Transitives with Subject,
Verb + Object: Speech to Family vs. Non-Family

	FULL S+V+O	CLITIC S+V+O	TOTAL S+V+O
SPEAKING IN (to family) (210)	18.1% (38)	5.2% (11)	23.3% (49)
SPEAKING OUT (to non-family) (226)	16.4% (37)	5.3% (12)	21.7% (49)

Table 8.6 indicates that there are differences between male and female speakers in their use of three constituent transitives. Such constructions account for 17.4% of women's transitives and 30.7% of men's.

2.3. Concluding Remarks on Sociolinguistic Sketch

Considerations of time and space and current state of research have constrained the scope of this sketch. There are many areas of grammatical structure not considered here and the reader is referred to Pratt (1911), Milner (1961, 1966, 1973), Pawley (1966) Tuitele, Sāpolu and Kneubuhl (1978), Tuitele and Kneubuhl (1978), Chung (1978) and Duranti (1981) for fuller descriptions.

In summary, we see that many but not all aspects of the language are sensitive to social distance. Among the most affected features are the use of /t/ and /k/, /n/ and /ŋ/; the glottal stop; respect vocabulary; ergative casemarking; possessive casemarking; transitive suffix; subject-verb agreement; tense/aspect marking; and ordering of subject, verb, and object. Among the least affected by social distance are the case marker *i* (to mark directionality, causality, time, location, objects of middle verbs, etc.) and the extent of expression/non-expression of subjects and objects. We have seen as well that other parameters of social context affect grammatical structure, for example, formality/informality (which is closely related to social distance) and sex of speaker.

A responsible account of acquisition of Samoan has to consider the sociological patterning of language use. Any assessment of error must be based on knowledge of of variable and categorical features of the language. This knowledge is best captured by a sociolinguistic grammar. Such a grammar has not been provided here, simply the outlines of such an endeavour.

3. SOURCES OF DATA

3.1. Setting

As noted in the introduction, the research on which this analysis is based was carried out in the village of Falefā on the island of Upolu, Western Samoa. The village lies about 18 miles from the capital Apia and takes approximately 45 minutes to reach by private vehicle. The village is quite large by Samoan standards, approximately 1200 residents. Slightly over half of the population is under the age of 15, with the average number of children per family being six.

The village contains a number of extended family households. Each family elects certain individuals to hold titles (*matai*) and represent the family in inter-village, village, and domestic affairs. Typically member families of a larger household will live in close proximity of one another, either in a single cleared compound or in neighboring compounds. Each nuclear family usually has a separate dwelling in the compound, but as the traditional dwelling has no walls, families have constant visual and auditory access to one another's homes throughout the day.

3.2. Subjects

In accordance with our disinclination to compare children's spontaneous speech behavior exclusively to accounts of Samoan based on grammaticality judgments, our research group collected and analyzed everyday speech behavior of BOTH adult and child members of this community. In this way, features of children's speech would be matched with the adult speech to which children were exposed. A broad range of adult speakers and settings was captured, representing casual and formal language use of both titled and untitled men and women within the village. A total of 50 hours of audio recording were collected, 26½ hours of which were transcribed and translated *in loco,* in cooperation with participants to the interactions recorded and/or other native speakers. This probject was under the direction of A. Duranti.

The collection of children's speech was carried out by M. Platt and myself. We focused our recording on six children from six different households, ranging from 19 to 35 months at the onset of the study. All of these children had at least one other sibling and a large group of age-mates within their family compounds. These children closely interact with one another, those close in age forming play groups (which, in turn became peer groups on which one relies throughout life). A total of 17 other children under the age of 6 were intermittently present during recording sessions.

3.3. Recording Schedule

Five of the six focus children were recorded every five weeks. Three to four hours of audio and a half hour of video recording were made at each interval. The youngest child (19 months), at the late single word stage, was videotaped each month for 30 minutes. This child was a member of the family compound in which we lived, and our recording was supplemented by daily but casual observation. Three children were recorded over a period of 9 months, two over a period of 8 months and the youngest over a period of 7 months. A total of 128 hours of audio and 20 hours of video recording of these children were collected and transcribed in the field. As in the adult study, transcription and interpretation involved the cooperation of either participants to the interactions recorded or neighbors familiar with the families recorded.

4. OVERALL COURSE OF DEVELOPMENT

The acquisition study focuses on acquisition of two phonological registers (*tautala lelei* and *tautala leaga*), word-order strategies, and expression of ergativity. Young children begin using the phonological features of both registers at the single-word stage, but do not use them in the appropriate social contexts until they are well into the multi-word stage (2–2½ years old).

With respect to word order, younger children display a preference for verb-initial sequences, and for preserving the verb and patient as a contiguous unit. In utterances containing three major constituents, verb-agent-patient order is dispreferred. These preferences and dispreferences match those of adults, particularly women, speaking in intimate contexts. The pattern found in both adult and child word order in this sample runs counter to typological accounts of Samoan, which characterize it as a verb-subject-object language (Greenberg, 1966). Such an account represents most closely careful Samoan (cf. Table 8.4), indicating that word order should be examined as a sociolinguistic variable and register-sensitive.

The very preliminary study of clitic pronouns indicates that children use them in the obligatory grammatical environment (i.e. before the verb) and evidence no errors with respect to their position. The preverbal position of clitic pronouns is a categorical (i.e. socially invariable) norm in adult Samoan speech.

With respect to presence/absence of major constituents, children display a dispreference for utterances containing agents with/without patients. This dispreference matches adult usage patterns as well. Children and adults differ only in the frequency of non-expression of these major constituents. As non-expression of major constituents is a frequent characteristic of spoken Samoan across different social contexts, children's utterances of this type should be seen as well-formed rather than as an expression of linguistic incompetence. In this sense, the correlation of language development with (increasing) expression of major constituents (applied to English) does not apply to Samoan.

The results of the ergativity study indicate that ergative case marking is acquired relatively late. The children in our sample evidenced little or no use of the marker. This could be partially accounted for on the basis of perceptually-distressful surface features of the particle, e.g. that it is preposed, unstressed. However, the most important factor appears to be that the particle is not a distinguishing characteristic of intimate, casual speech nor is it common in the speech of women. These social conditions match closely the environment of the language-acquiring child. Again, the pattern displayed in the speech of young children matches an adult norm for a particular social context. In the setting of the household where women and children are casually conversing, the child's nonexpression of the ergative particle is not an error but a sociolinguistic norm.

On the other hand, these results do not indicate that ergative distinctions are not expressed in the speech of young children. A study of intransitive and transitive word order patterns reveal that children express these distinctions through word order. Children reserve the position following the verb for major arguments of intransitive verbs and for patients (absolutive constituents) but exclude agents (ergative constituents) from this position.

The language errors of young Samoan children can be discussed in terms of two types of error: socially variable errors and categorical errors. Errors of the first type, i.e. errors that are social context-bound, include using *tautala leaga* 'bad speech' where *tautala lelei* 'good speech' register is appropriate; over-generalizing use of /t/ to lexical borrowings which should remain in the /k/ in standard *tautala lelei*. Categorical errors in the speech of young children include the overgeneralization of /t/ to morphemes that should in standard *tautala lelei* take /n/ or some other phonological form; overgeneralization of /ŋ/ to mor-phemes that in standard *tautala lelei* should take /n/. (For certain speakers of Samoan, overgeneralization of /t/ to lexical borrowings with /k/ counts as a categorical error rather than as a socially variable error.)

5. ACQUISITION OF TWO PHONOLOGICAL REGISTERS

5.1. Developmental Sequence

The reader will recall that Samoan has two major registers of speech, *tautala lelei*, in which /t/ and /k/, and /n/ and /ŋ/, are distinguished, and *tautala leaga*, in which only /k/ and /ŋ/ are used (in place of the above distinctions). *Tautala lelei* is associated with Western-introduced situations, although it probably was once associated with the competence of high chiefs. *Tautala leaga* is associated with local, traditional situations, including formal and informal social interac-tions (Shore, 1977, 1982).

Most children will hear predominantly *tautala leaga* in their waking hours. *Tautala leaga* is the norm in interactions within the village. However, every child is brought to church weekly (usually twice each Sunday) from infancy, where she/he hears sermons and hymns in *tautala lelei*. Further, as young children are cared for by older siblings, they will hear lexical items, routines, and songs in *tautala lelei* from the latter's school experience. Many households have radios and the children will hear *tautala lelei* through this medium. They will also hear family members switch into *tautala lelei* (as described in section 2.2.2 above), as an emphatic device. Finally, and perhaps, most importantly, children from a very young age are socialized into PERFORMANCE. They will be taught Bible verses, hymns, the alphabet, and a series of Biblical facts to be memorized and displayed around the age of 2 years. The transmission of this knowledge and its display are couched in *tautala lelei*.

The acquisition of these two registers was first examined by Kernan (1974) and subsequently considered by Shore (1977). Kernan carried out a longitudinal study of language acquisition on the island of Manu'a in American Samoa. His study of these two codes relied on spontaneous language use and an elicited imitation task involving lexical items with the relevant phonological features (/t/ /k/ /n/ /ŋ/). He concluded that children acquired competence in three stages. At Stage I (from 2;2 to 3;2 years), the children could comprehend both registers but in their spontaneous production they used only one register and that register was usually *tautala lelei*. They tended to intimate all items in the register they produced spontaneously. At Stage II (from 3;6 to 4;2 years), children used *tautala leaga* in their spontaneous speech. They were generally accurate in imitating lexical items in both registers but there were errors due to overuse of the /k/ /ŋ/ register. At Stage III (from 3;10 to 5;1 years), children continued to use *tautala leaga* spontaneously. However, in the imitation task, the children made many errors due to overuse of features of *tautala lelei*. In particular, they overgeneralized the rule that shifts /ŋ/ to /n/ in *tautala lelei*. As noted earlier, *tautala lelei* contains both these phonemes, e.g. the word for 'person' in *tautala lelei* is /taŋata/; the word for 'touch/get' is /taŋo/. Hearing in a lexical item with the /t/ and /ŋ/, these children imitated it with /n/.

From the point of view of errors, these results indicate that COMPETENCE IN A REGISTER MAY BE DISPLAYED THEN LOST. Children in Kernan's Stage II displayed fewer errors than those in Stage III. Shore (1977, 1982) relates this phenomenon to the child's emerging understanding of the elicited imitation task as a type of situation that calls for *tautala lelei,* i.e., one of a school-like routine with an outsider present. Children at Stage II do not yet define the task in these terms and are not caught between the specific demands of the imitation task and the cultural demands associated with a social situation.

Many of Kernan's observations were matched in our longitudinal study in Western Samoa. Certain important differences, however, emerged from the data gathered in the latter study. Most importantly, every child in our study had some competence in *tautala lelei* and *tautala leaga* phonological systems. This competence was observed FROM THE SINGLE WORD STAGE ON. AT THE EARLIEST STAGE OBSERVED (LATE SINGLE WORD, 19 MONTHS), THE ALTERNATION BETWEEN /t/ AND /k/ APPEARED TO BE PHONOLOGICALLY RATHER THAN SOCIALLY CONDITIONED. The use of /k/ was overwhelmingly (91.9%) followed by the vowel /a/; the use of /t/ was followed by the vowel /i/ (40%) as well as the vowel /a/ (50.9%). The overriding constraint of the vocalic environment is seen in the child's repetitions of caregiver speech. For example, in (7) below, the caregiver uses the word *kiki,* a borrowing from the English *kick*. As noted earlier, borrowings with /k/ should in standard Samoan (*tautala lelei*) remain in the /k/. As can be seen, however, the child repeats the item as /titi/.

(7) Kalavini, 19 months (/ki/ repeated as /ti/)

Mother: *Kiki*   *Vini*
         Kick   Kalavini
        'Kick it, Vini.'

        Kiki
        Kick
        'Kick it.'

Child: *Ai   titi/*
          See?   Kick.

Similarly, items presented by a caregiver with /t/ followed by /a/ are often repeated by the child as /k/ with /a/. For example, in (8) below, the adult utters the name *Mareta* (the name of one researcher) and the child repeats it as /kakaka/:

(8) Kalavini, 19 months (/ta/ repeated as /ka/)

Mother: *Mareta*
          Mareta

Child: *Kakaka/*
          Mareta

It should be noted here that the particular child observed at the single word stage was far more exposed to *tautala lelei* than any other child in the village. As specified in footnote 1, the child's mother is both the wife and daughter of a pastor and educated in a church school in which *tautala lelei* is the norm. This child spent much of the day with this mother, who used *tautala lelei* with some modification (see footnote 1). His father and younger caregivers in the household tended to use *tautala leaga*. I mention this background to indicate that even in this environment, the child used /k/ about as often as /t/ (and in non-borrowings). In a count of all syllables that contain either a /t/ or a /k/, this child at 19 months produced /k/ for 53% and /t/ for 47% of the corpus.

At 20 months, this child, Kalavini, continued to use both /k/ and /t/ but the conditions of use differ from the earlier data. Familiar, previously learned lexical items are uttered in both /t/ and /k/. New items, particularly those learned in the context of rote repetition from his mother, tend to be produced in the /t/, with only borrowings in the /k/. Unlike his earlier behavior, Kalavini is nearly always accurate in his repetitions of caregiver speech.

By 23 months, Kalavini's speech (now solidly into the multi-word stage) shifts to a much greater use of /k/, although /t/ is maintained as well to some extent. This shift corresponds to a move away from his mother towards greater alignment with peers and child caregivers. Such a shift was occasioned by the birth of a younger sister. Relying predominantly on /k/ pronunciation, Kalavini tends to make many more errors in rote repeition tasks and in formal instruction about Biblical facts (which should occasion use of /t/).

By 2½ years, all the children of this age in our study were able to use both *tautala lelei* and *tautala leaga* in socially appropriate contexts to a limited extent. The phonologically conditioned use of /t/ and /k/, /n/ and /ŋ/ was superseded by socially conditioned use of these phonological variants. This observation indicates a much earlier productive competence in the two registers than was reported in the Kernan study.

5.2. Variation and Error in Use of *Tautala Lelei*

In this section, I discuss deviations from standard *tautala lelei*. I consider both adult and child language deviations. The discussion focuses on deviation as constituting an error or not, and if so, as variable or categorical error. Further, each deviation is described in terms of its relation to a standard norm, e.g. as an underapplication, overapplication, etc. of a norm.

Let us consider the registers *tautala lelei* and *tautala leaga* as sets and the phonological features that distinguish them as members of these sets. In standard *tautala lelei,* the features /t/, /k/, /n/, /ŋ/ all are members. The speaker of standard *tautala lelei* knows which lexical items are to be produced in the /k/ (e.g. borrowings) and /n/ (e.g. /tanata/) and which are to be produced in the /t/ and /n/.

In both adult and child speech, three major deviations from these cooccurring features are found: (1) underuse of /t/ and /n/; (2) overgeneralizations of /t/ and /n/ to exceptions; (3) overgeneralization of /t/ to /n/ and other environments.

5.2.1. *Underuse of /t/ and /n/*

In the first instance, we find adults and children producing utterances that mix features of *tautala leaga* with those of *tautala lelei*. The mixing may involve use of /t/ plus /k/ (in non-borrowing) or use of /t/ plus /ŋ/ (in inappropriate lexical item). The mixing may take place within a single lexical item or within a single utterance or larger unit such as genre (same song, recitation, etc.). Examples of register mixing are provided below:

(9) Example of /t/ plus /k/: Adult
P59-070

(A speaking to daughter):

A:	*Se*	*fai*	*a*		*oe*	*mea!*	
	Please	do	EMPH		you	things	

'Please do your things!'

⟶	(*Tai*)	*ou*	*vae*	*ma*	(*kusi*)	*le*	*api*
	Fold	your	legs	and	write	the	notebook

'Fold your legs and write (in) the notebook.'

(10) Example of /t/ plus /k/: Child
Pesio, 2;9

(Pesio and her classificatory sibling M., are looking at pictures with researcher E. E. speaks in the /t/, M. in the /k/ and P. in both registers.)

Pesio			*Others*
⟶ *i*	(*/štou/*)	*pusi,* (h)	
Here?	your?:PL	cat	

—→ *ma(e) ie 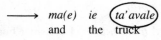*
   and   the   truck

'Here is your cat and the truck.'

> E: *Tavale LAPO'A*
>   Truck   big
>
>   'A BIG truck.'

—→ */ /Tavale e okou/*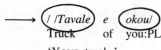
   Truck   of you:PL

'YOUR truck.'

> M: // *Ka'avale laikiki*
>   Truck   small
>
>   'A SMALL truck.'
>
> E: *Telē*
>   Big
>
>   '(It's) big.'

—→ *Tavale makou/*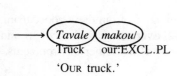
   Truck   our:EXCL.PL

'OUR truck.'

(11) Example of /t/ plus /n/
     N57-055

(The mother (AK) of Sose first calls to her, then tells her sister (SA) jokingly
how much the baby has grown in the time the researchers Alesaga and Elegoa
have been recording the family.)

Context	*Speech*
AK kisses Sose and	((high))
puts Sose on her lap.	AK: *Sose/*
	(Pause.)
	((normal pitch))

—→ AK: *Sa   o   mai   Alesaga   ma*
        PAST   come:PL A.   and

—→   *Elegoa* (Pause)
        E.

        O   pēpē   meamea
        PRED baby   tiny

        'When Alesaga and Elegoa first came (she)
        (was) a tiny infant.'

    SA: *O   pēpē*
        PRED baby

        '(She) (was) a baby.'

—→ AK: *A'o legei ua   ā   legei*
        But now   IPFV EMPH now

⟶   'ua *lo'o matua/*
          IPFV old   lady

'But now, now (she) has become an old lady.'

(12) Example of /t/ plus /ŋ/: Child
     Niulala, 3;3

(Fineaso (1 year, 9 months) had done something naughty. His mother (AK) and F's brother (Niulala) begin listing things that F. will not be given because of this.)

Niulala	*Other*
	AK: *Ma se ā?*
	And a what
	'And (not) what else?'
	F: ((whines))
/ /Ma se -	F: / /o/
And a	(?)
ma - ma se	*ia*
and and a	(?)
ma se (pause)	
and a	
⟶ *ma* *saga* *giu/*	
and NON-SPECIFIC POSS coconut	
'And not any - and - and not any, not any (pause) and not his coconut.'	
	AK: *Ma se ā?*
	And a what
	'And (not) what else?'
⟶ *Ma* *sag'* *ta'avale*	
And NON-SPECIFIC POSS truck	
'And not his truck.'	
	AK: *Oka!* *Oka!*
	INTERJ INTERJ
	'Oh my! Oh my!'

At this point, the question of distinguishing errors from deviations from the standard arises. Not all cases of register mixing are errors. Indeed, the concept of error here must be seen as sensitive to social context, i.e. variably counting as error. In social contexts that demand standard *tautala lelei* (e.g. hymns, songs, formal written Samoan, news broadcasts, etc.) deviations count as errors. To mix /t/ and /k/ counts as an error in reciting the Lord's Prayer, for example. Further, where a speaker wishes to define a social situation as highly formal and socially distant by using standard *tautala lelei* (e.g. in polite interactions with one of our research team, for example), deviations count as errors. On the other hand, there are many contexts in which register mixing is not an error. It is not an error, for example, where sudden switching signals a change in affect or is used to gain attention. It is not an error as well in a range of less formal interactions with outsiders (or insiders, see footnote 1). The transcripts in our corpus show many cases in which interactions with us (outsiders) begin in a formal modality but eventually evolve into more relaxed social encounters. The use of mixed registers in the same utterance or word expresses this decrease in social distance and formality. It indicates that speakers are paying less attention to their pronunciation. Similarly, for our one speaker of *tautala lelei* in informal contexts, the intrusion of "inappropriate" /ŋ/ is not an error. For this speaker, the increase in use of /ŋ/ corresponds to a particular social context (intimate, informal). Rather than calling these phenomena errors, we should consider them as instances of a third register, which might be called NON-STANDARD *TAUTALA LELEI*.

The category UNDERUSE OF /t/ AND /n/ includes as well cases in which none of the features of the t/n register are produced, i.e. underused in the sense of not used at all. While not strictly speaking a type of deviation from *tautala lelei,* this dimension is an important one to note as it accounts for a large proportion of the registral errors among young children. Examples are provided below of the social situations calling for *tautala lelei* (e.g. Bible instruction, school recitation, songs) in which young children produce instead *tautala leaga*. This type of error is rare among older children and adults.

(13) Example of Failure to Use *Tautala Lelei* (Where Required): Child KVII-389

(S. directs Bible question to her son Kalavini, 2;1.)

S: 'O   ai   na
   TOP   who   PAST

   faia   oe.
   make+CIA   you.

   'Who made you?'

⟶ K:

S: 'O   ai   na   ta'ā
   TOP   who   PAST   strike

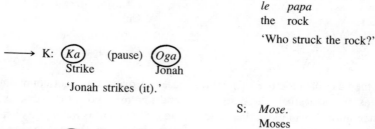

le   papa
the   rock

'Who struck the rock?'

⟶ K: (*Ka*)   (pause)   (*Oga*)
　　Strike　　　　　　Jonah

'Jonah strikes (it).'

S: *Mose.*
　　Moses

⟶ K: (*Ka*)   (pause)   *Mose.*
　　Strike　　　　　　Moses.

'Moses strikes it.'

5.2.2. *Overgeneralization of /t/ and /n/ to Exceptions*

The second major type of deviation from standard *tautala lelei* involves the extremely common process (Shore, 1977, 1982) of overgeneralization. There are two major sub-types, one involving the extension of /t/ to those borrowed lexical items that should in the standard remain in the /k/ and one involving the extension of /n/ to lexical items that should remain in the /ŋ/. This process, characteristic of both adult and child speech behavior, is an instance of HYPERCORRECTION (Labov, 1966). The speaker uses a prestige variant in linguistic contexts in which in the standard that variant is inappropriate.

(14) Example of Overgeneralization: Adult
　　P59-098

(A. to young daughter):

　　Overgeneralization of /n/: *gutu → nutu*
⟶ A: *Ese   peni   ma   le   (nutu)*
　　　Away   pen   from   the   mouth

　　'Take away (the) pen from your mouth.'

(15) Example of overgeneralization:
　　P67-125

(Ameto, 4 years, while drawing, tells researchers (E.) that he is doing school. The term for school is *aoga* /aoŋa/ in standard *tautala lelei* but A. pronounces it with /n/.)

　　Ameto　　　　　　　　　*Other*
⟶ *Fai   la   (ōna/)*
　　Do   the   school

E: / /*Oi*/ (to Ameto)
        Oh

MK: / *Uma* (to baby)
        Finished

As in the case of underuse of features, cases of overuse do not count categorically as errors. Rather, there are social and linguistic conditions that enter into consideration. As in the earlier case, where the standard is required, such as in written Samoan, overuse of /t/ and /n/ counts as an error. On the other hand, in spontaneous interactions with foreigners, these hypercorrections are not considered always as errors. One important social variable is that speakers differ in their judgments concerning this practice. When brought to their attention (as we did, from time to time), certain Samoans will insist that borrowings in the /t/ are correct when speaking (spontaneously) *tautala lelei*. Others will insist the borrowing should remain in the /k/. Further, speakers differ in their judgments concerning different lexical items; for certain speakers all borrowings should go to the /t/; for others a subset (and not the same subset). Future research will examine this phenomenon more carefully, but it appears as if the boundaries of the category of "borrowed word" vary from speaker to speaker and that certain borrowings are treated as Samoan (versus recently introduced).

We have as a consequence a rather complicated sociolinguistic situation, in which the assessment of a construction as an error is not a simple matter. For a certain group of Samoans (as yet undefined), the overgeneralization (from the perspective of the standard) of /t/ and /n/ is a categorical error. For others, it is a variable error but the linguistic conditions under which it counts as error are not universally agreed upon.

5.2.3. *Overgeneralization of* /t/ *to* /n/ *and Other Environments*

In the third type of deviation from standard *tautala lelei,* the feature /t/ is extended to environments in which /n/ or some other phonological variant should be used.

Unlike (1) and (2) above, THIS PHENOMENON IS NOT CHARACTERISTIC OF ADULT SPEECH USAGE. This is not to say that it never occurs, but that it is not common. It appears to be ASSOCIATED WITH THE SPEECH OF YOUNG CHILDREN. Further, this deviation is a CATEGORICAL ERROR, cutting across a range of social contexts.

This type of extension differs from (2) above, where /t/ is extended to environments in which /k/ should be used (in the standard). In the current case, the speaker has switched to the appropriate register set but has selected the wrong feature. For example, instead of switching from /ŋ/ to /n/, the speaker switches from /ŋ/ to /t/. For example, my name in *tautala leaga* is /eleŋoa/ (Elegoa); in *tautala lelei,* it is /elenoa/ (Elenoa). One 4-year-old child whom I had just met addressed me as /toa/ (instead of /noa/, a shortened version of my name). Another child just under three years pronounced my name in the very first session of recording as /eto/.

In other examples, /t/ is used where some other phonological element should be used or where none should be used. For example, in one session, I commented on the drawing by a child of 2;8, saying *fale lapo'a* 'big house'. The child took my utterance as a directive to repeat it (as a school drill task) and said immediately *fale tapoa*. Here the child replaced the feature /l/ with /t/. (In other situations, the child showed productive competence in use of /l/.)

These examples illustrate a quality that distinguishes /t/ from other features that distinguish *tautala lelei* register. Speakers are more conscious of the use of /t/ than they are of the use of /n/ and /r/. *Tautala lelei* is commonly called "Samoan in the T." As demonstrated by Shore's ethnography (1977), speakers are able to talk about errors involving the overuse (hypercorrection) or underuse (e.g., inappropriate /k/) of /t/ to a far greater extent than the over/underuse of /n/ or /r/. Further, speakers associate /t/ (and /k/) with a range of affective and social states (which is much less true of other phonological features).

Given the special salience of /t/ as a feature of *tautala lelei,* it is not surprising that it would be overgeneralized to other phonological environments in attempts to switch into that register. Thus far, I have not found cases in which /n/ is extended to environments which take the /t/ or to other environments.

6. ACQUISITION OF WORD ORDER

With respect to the acquisition of word order, there are two major interests. The first concerns the strategies used by children for the ORDERING OF MAJOR CONSTITUENTS IN TRANSITIVE AND INTRANSITIVE CONSTRUCTIONS (e.g. agent, action, and patient; state and object to which state relates). This concern matches the interest in ordering strategies of subject, verb, and object among adult Samoan speakers. The second interest focuses on the EXPRESSION AND NON-EXPRESSION OF major constituents (such as agent and patient) in Samoan child language.

6.1. Word Order of Major Constituents

As discussed in Section 2.2.3, Samoan has a wide range of possible word orders, with verb-initial orders preferred. With respect to the order of full constituents (not clitics), there is little chance of error. Errors would involve other variables, such as the casemarking appropriate to constituents appearing in particular orders (e.g. the topic marker, the ergative marker).

With such a range of word orders, it is interesting to examine preferences exhibited by language-acquiring children. Is one ordering preferred over others?

TABLE 8.8
Percentage of Verb-Initial Canonical Transitives
(Declaratives & Yes-No Interrogatives)

Child	Age at Onset of Study	Session I	Session III	Session V	Session VII	Average
Matu'u	(2;1)	91.7% (11)	76.2% (16)	95.6% (22)	87.5% (14)	92.7% (76)
Pesio	(2;3)	100% (15)	54.5% (5)	68.9% (20)	91.4% (53)	83.2% (94)
Naomi	(2;10)	90.3% (28)	94.1% (16)	92.3% (24)	97.1% (34)	93.6% (102)
Niulala	(2;11)	80.9% (17)	82.8% (24)	85.5% (53)	94.3% (33)	86.4% (127)

Do the word order preferences of young children match those of adults? Do they match the preferences associated with causal speech among intimates?

Tables 8.8 and 8.9 provide information concerning word order strategies of young Samoan children. As can be seen from these tables, CHILDREN, LIKE ADULT SAMOANS, OVERWHELMINGLY PREFER VERB-INITIAL CONSTRUCTIONS.

Table 8.10 displays word order preferences for canonical transitive declaratives and yes-no interrogatives. The totals for each child are represented because of the low frequency (see below) of constructions with major constituents expressed. As can be seen from this table, THERE IS ONLY ONE CHILD, THE OLDEST, FOR WHOM THE WORD ORDER VERB-AGENT-OBJECT IS PREFERRED. FOR THE OTHERS, THIS WORD ORDER IS DISPREFERRED IN FAVOR OF EITHER AGENT-VERB-PATIENT OR VERB-PATIENT-AGENT WORD ORDERS.

Comparing these results to the adult word-order data, we can see that THEY MATCH MOST CLOSELY THE WORD-ORDER PATTERNS OF WOMEN'S SPEECH (TABLES 8.2 AND 8.3) AND SPEECH TO INTIMATES (TABLES 8.2 AND 8.4). In both of these contexts, verb-subject-object word order is not preferred over others. In the

TABLE 8.9
Intransitives (with Major Argument Expressed)
(Declaratives & Yes-No Interrogatives)
% of Verb-*Major Argument* Word Orders
Compared to *Major Argument*-Verb

Child	Age at Onset of Study	Session I	Session III	Session V	Session VII	Average
Matu'u	(2;1)	100.0% (9)	70.0% (7)	84.6% (21)	71.4% (20)	81.5%
Iakopo	(2;1)	100.0% (1)	85.7% (6)	85.7% (18)	85.2% (23)	85.7%
Pesio	(2;3)	96.1% (25)	80.0% (4)	78.9% (30)	86.5% (45)	85.4%
Naomi	(2;10)	100.0% (16)	70.6% (12)	91.3% (22)	75.8% (25)	84.4%
Niulala	(2;11)	90.9% (30)	77.3% (34)	88.9% (64)	65.8% (25)	80.7%

TABLE 8.10
Canonical Transitives (Declaratives & Yes-No Interrogatives)
Word Order Preferences (Where Verb, Patient (O), and Agent (A) Are Expressed)

Child:	Total UTTS.	VOA	VAO	AVO	AVO CLITIC	OVA	O (VA) RCLAUSE	OAV
Matu'u	16	50.0% (8)	6.3% (1)	25.0% (4)	0	6.3% (1)	12.5% (2)	—
Iakopu	13	38.5% (5)	—	53.8% (7)	—	—	—	7.7% (1)
Pesio	8	37.5% (3)	12.5% (1)	12.5% (1)	37.5% (3)	—	—	—
Naomi	5	—	20.0% (1)	40.0% (2)	40.0% (2)	—	—	—
Niulala	20	25.0% (5)	30.0% (6)	5.0% (1)	25.0% (6)	10.0% (2)	—	—
AVERAGE:	62	33.9% (21)	14.5% (9)	24.2% (15)	17.7% (11)	4.8% (3)	3.2% (2)	1.6% (1)

speech of women, verb-object-subject and subject-verb-object orders are roughly equally preferred.

For children as well as adults, then, verb-agent-patient is not the norm for ordering major constituents. For both adults in intimate contexts and children, THE NORM IS TO PRESERVE THE VERB AND PATIENT AS A CONTIGUOUS UNIT (AVO, VOA, ETC.). This finding supports Slobin's hypothesis that a word order that interrupts the predicate is cognitively distressful and would be acquired relatively late (Slobin, 1977). It indicates that factors of "cognitive ease" are at play in the more relaxed speech of adults as well as in Samoan children's speech. This parallel indicates once again the need to examine a range of adult speech in assessing processes guiding acquisition.

6.1.1. *A Note on Order of Subject Clitic Pronouns*

As noted in the sociolinguistic sketch of Samoan, the placement of subject clitic pronouns is fixed rather than variable (as in the case of full subjects). These pronouns must appear pre-verbally. EXAMINING ONLY THE USE OF CLITICS IN OUR TRANSITIVE DATA BASE, I FIND NO ERRORS WITH RESPECT TO THEIR POSITION BEFORE THE VERB. The subject clitics in declaratives and yes-no interrogatives are relatively slow to be acquired, however, and only the oldest child uses them with any significant frequency. These observations are displayed in Table 8.11 below.

6.2. Expression and Non-Expression of Agent and Patient

One of the earliest observations of child language research is that children's utterances are reduced or telegraphic versions of adult constructions (Brown, 1973; Bloom, 1970; Braine, 1963; for example). This observation has established as a direction of research the investigation of how and when children's utterances get filled in and ultimately match the explicitness of adult sentences. This process is associated with increasing competence. But, as I have shown in

TABLE 8.11
Use of Subject Clitics
in Canonical Transitives
(Agent Clitic-Verb-(Patient))
(Declaratives & Yes-No Interrogatives)

Child	Session I	Session III	Session V	Session VII
Matu'u	—	—	—	—
Pesio	—	—	3	4
Naomi	3	—	—	1
Niulala	1	2	5	2

TABLE 8.12
Canonical Transitives
(Declaratives & Yes-No Interrogatives)
Percentage of Utterances with Agent Expressed
as Major Constituent

Child	Session I	Session III	Session V	Session VII	Average
Matu'u	16.7% (2)	42.9% (9)	30.4% (7)	18.7% (3)	25.6% (21)
Pesio	6.7% (1)	36.4% (4)	20.7% (6)	12.1% (7)	15.9% (18)
Naomi	12.9% (4)	41.2% (7)	3.8% (1)	17.5% (6)	16.5% (18)
Niulala	19.1% (4)	13.8% (4)	25.8% (16)	22.9% (8)	21.8% (32)

the sociolinguistic sketch, this process, at least with respect to major constituents, is not a measure of increasing competence in Samoan. Competence in the adult Samoan model does not demand full expression of major constituents. Sentences very often appear without a subject (see Table 8.1). Constructions with both subject and object expressed are quite infrequent (Table 8.5). Further, this phenomenon does not appear to be conditioned by increased intimacy among interlocutors (Table 8.7). It is a pattern of language that cuts across parameters of social distances.

Tables 8.12 and 8.13 provide information concerning the extent to which young Samoan children express major constituents in utterances containing transitive verbs (declaratives and yes-no interrogatives). Table 8.12 displays the extent to which agents appear as major constituents; Table 8.13 displays the extent to which children produce transitives with both patient and agent expressed as major arguments of the transitive verb.

These Tables show two important patterns. First, they indicate that YOUNG CHILDREN INFREQUENTLY PRODUCE UTTERANCES WITH AGENTS AND EVEN MORE INFREQUENTLY PRODUCE UTTERANCES WITH AGENTS AND PATIENTS BOTH EXPRESSED AS MAJOR ARGUMENTS.

TABLE 8.13
Canonical Transitives
(Declaratives & Yes-No Interrogatives)
Percentage of Utterances with Agent & Patient
Expressed as Major Constituents

Child	Session I	Session III	Session V	Session VII	Average
Matu'u	16.7% (2)	38.1% (8)	30.4% (7)	18.7% (3)	24.4% (20)
Pesio	6.7% (1)	18.2% (2)	13.8% (4)	5.2% (3)	8.8% (10)
Naomi	9.7% (3)	5.9% (1)	3.8% (1)		4.6% (55)
Niulala	19.1% (4)	10.3% (3)	17.7% (11)	5.7% (2)	13.6% (20)

Second, these Tables show that EARLY DEVELOPMENTAL MATURITY IS NOT MATCHED BY INCREASED USE OF AGENTS AND PATIENTS. Looking at each child, we can see that the use of these constituents fluctuates from the first session to the last. In Table 8.13, we can see than in the final session (seession VII), three of the four children actually display fewer three-constituent utterances that in the first session. Further, in both Tables, the youngest child in the Table, Matu'u (2;1 at onset of study), shows the greatest percentage of utterances with agents and patients expressed.

What is the relation of these results to adult language use? Children match the speech behavior of adults in that the expression of all three major constituents (agent, verb, patient) is dispreferred. However, on the average, the expression of agents and agents with patients is less frequent in the speech of young children than in adult speech (see Tables 8.1 and 8.5). In this sense, children's language use does not match adult usage. This difference resembles descriptions of children's speech behavior in English-speaking communities (see above references). As discussed earlier, for English-speaking children the non-expression of these constituents reflects relative competence and counts as an error. With respect to Samoan-speaking children, the meaning of this pattern is not the same. In the case of English, young children are (described as) producing utterances that deviate from adult speech patterns. In the case of Samoan, the children are conforming to adult speech patterns. Differences between adult and child language use are quantitative rather than qualitative. The quantitative difference IN ITSELF can not be interpreted as incompetence or error. Future research is necessary to ascertain if other pragmatic conditions enhance the expression/non-expression of major constituents and the sensitivity of children to these conditions.

7. ACQUISITION OF ERGATIVE CASE MARKING

Having examined the acquisition of *tautala lelei* and *tautala leaga* phonological features and word-order strategies, let us now consider the acquisition of one morphological feature of the language, ergative casemarking. Definitional and formal dimensions of ergativity in Samoan have been discussed in Section 2.2.4.1, along with variation in adult use of the case marker. The analysis of adult and children's use of ergative case marking is drawn from a larger study (Ochs, 1982), to which the reader is referred.

The sociolinguistic sketch of ergative casemarking in adult speech indicated that it is sensitive to the parameters of social distance and sex of speaker. As displayed in Table 8.1, the case marker is far more common in speech to nonintimates than in speech to intimates and more common in the speech of men than in the speech of women.

The most outstanding result of our acquisition study is that Samoan children between the ages of 2 and 4 rarely use the ergative marker *e* in their spontaneous

TABLE 8.14
Agency & Ergative Case Marking
in Spontaneous Novel Canonical Transitives (Assertions & Y-N Qs)[a]

Child	Age at Onset of Study	Total UTTS.	UTTS. w/Agents		Post-Verbal Agents (Erg. Case Mark. Environment)		Erg. Case Marking	
Matu'u	(2;0)	76	22.4%	(17)	14.5%	(11)	0	
Iakopo	(2;1)	50	30.0%	(15)	12.0%	(6)	0	
Pesio	(2;3)	113	13.25%	(15)	4.42%	(5)	0	
Naomi	(2;10)	109	15.6%	(17)	10.1%	(11)	.9%	(1)*
Niulala	(2;11)	148	21.6%	(32)	13.5%	(20)	.7%	(1)
Maselino	(3;3)	86	36.0%	(31)	33.7%	(29)	4.6%	(4)

*Partial repetition.
[a](from Ochs, 1982)

speech. The frequency with which the ergative marker appears in canonical transitives of five children in our sample is displayed in Table 8.14.

We can see from this Table that the three youngest children, Matu'u, Iakopo, and Pesio, used absolutely no ergative case marking whatsoever. The next oldest children, Naomi and Niulala, used the marker in one utterance (each) only, representing .9% and .7% respectively of the total canonical transitives and 10.1% and 13.5% respectively of the transitives with post-verbal agents in their corpora. These extremely low percentages led me to examine the speech of an older sibling, Maselino, who was not one of the ''focal'' children in the study and present only intermittently throughout the recording sessions. The percentage of ergative casemarking was higher in the speech of this child—4.6% of the total canonical transitives and 33.7% of these with post-verbal agents. However, these figures are still extremely low and do not evidence that ergative casemarking is part of the productive competence of the child.

Instances of the children's use of ergative casemarking are presented in examples (16) through (18) below:

(16) Naomi, 2;11

(Naomi hits mother, asks where her mango is:)

Naomi	Mother

ikae   uma   mago/
shit   finish   mango

'Shit, the mango is finished.'

uma   mago   a'u/
finish   mango   my

'My mango is finished.'

tae   tae   uma   mago/
shit   shit   finish   mango

'Shit, shit, the mango is finished.'

uma   mago   a'u/
finish   mango   my

'My mango is finished.'

uma   ai/
finish   eat

'The eating is finished.'

                                ai   e   ai/
                                  eat   ERG   who

                                  'Who ate it?'

(?)/

                                  fea
                                  where

                                  'Where?'

uma/
finish

'Finished.'

⟶ *ai   e   oe*
    eat   ERG   you

'*You* ate it.'

(17) Maselino, 3;8

(Pesio, 2;7 is crying, looking at her father. Another child, Kala, has hit her, though this has not been mentioned. Her father wants her to stop crying:)

Pesio: (Crying)
                                  Father: ((soft))

                                    (*alu   loa*)/
                                    go   now

                                    Paula (female caregiver):

                                    Pesio/

                                    Maselino:

              ⟶ *fasi* / / $\begin{pmatrix} a \\ e \end{pmatrix}$ *Kala/*

                                  hit   ERG   Kala

                                  'Kala hit her.'

                                    Elenoa:

                                    / /*Kala/*

Maselino:

⟶ *fasi e   Kala/*
   hit ERG Kala

'Kala hit her.'

(18) Maselino, 3;6

(Maselino decides to scare another child by using a common scare expression about mother absence. He turns to this child, Gike:)

Maselino:

⟶*Gike! Gike! le   'ua   'ai   e   le/ / pua'a*
             DEICT PERF eat ERG ART pig

Koe/
Koe* (*Gike's mother)

'Gike! Gike! Now the pig ate Koe.'

.
.

Maselino:

fiu   e   sue/
tired COMPL search

'They are tired of searching.'

fiu   e   kue   aku/*   *error
tired COMPL search DEICT

'They are tired of searching around.'

⟶ *le   'ua   'ai   e   le   pu'a/*
   DEICT PERF eat ERG ART pig

'Now the pig ate her.'

.
.

⟶ *le   'ua   'ai   e   le   povi Gike/*
   DEICT PERF eat ERG ART cow   Gike

'Now the cow ate her, Gike'

.
.

⟶ */ /'ua 'ai   e   le   povi a   Koe*
   PERF eat ERG ART cow   PARTICLE Koe

'The COW ate Koe.'

We can see from Table 1 that these results are linked to the low frequency of agents expressed in transitive declarations and yes-no interrogatives (average percentage of agents expressed: 21% (112)). That is, one explanation is that children simply do not often mention agents in their spontaneous speech. This explanation would not account, however, for why marking is not used when agents ARE expressed and appear in the grammatical environment that should host the ergative marker (after the verb). Young children do use constructions in which ergative case marking is required (according to speakers' judgments of "good Samoan"), yet they do not use the casemarking.

It is proposed here that THE RELATIVELY LATE ACQUISITION OF ERGATIVE CASEMARKING IS TIED TO THE SOCIOLINGUISTIC DISTRIBUTION OF THIS MARKING AMONG ADULT SAMOANS and to certain features of the marker in Samoan that may affect its perception. Features that enhance or constrain acquisition have been discussed by Slobin (1973, 1977, 1982). These features and their status with respect to the Samoan ergative case marker are displayed in Table 8.15. Presence of these features, represented by the + sign, facilitates the acquisition of the morphological marker.

As can be seen from this Table, the Samoan ergative particle has six features that could delay acquisition. In particular, it is not postposed, stressed, obligatory, tied to the noun it modifies, or applied to all pro-forms. Further, it has pragmatic functions, such as highlighting a noun and its phrase. It is difficult to weigh the importance of these features, as the ergative particle in another language, Kaluli (Schieffelin, 1979, 1985), has five features that could delay ac-

TABLE 8.15
Samoan and Kaluli Ergative Case Marking Features

Feature:	Samoan	Kaluli
± postposed	−	+
± syllabic	+	+
± stressed	−	(uses tonal contrast, prosodic system not worked out)
± obligatory	−	−
± tied to noun	−	+
± rationally ordered	n.a.	n.a.
± consistent with word order pattern	+	+
± non-synthetic	n.a.	n.a.
± only grammatical functions	−	−
± regular	+	−
± applied to all pro-forms	−	−
± no homonymous functors*	+	−

*"Functor" is here taken to mean "case marker."

quisition, yet Kaluli children acquire the particle relatively EARLY. Four out of five perceptually distressful features of the Kaluli marker match those of the Samoan marker. Kaluli is distinguished by the fact that the particle is postposed and tied to the noun. These features could account for why Kaluli children acquire the ergative marker before Samoan children.

However, there are major differences in the social norms for using the ergative case marker in Kaluli and Samoan. In Kaluli, the case marker is used across speakers and role relationships among interlocutors. It does not vary according to social distance and sex of speakers, as in Samoan communities. The Kaluli child is exposed to the marker in his primary acquisition environment to a much greater extent than is the Samoan child.

The difference in social norms for using the ergative case marker in Samoan and Kaluli has, then, a profound effect on acquisition of these two languages. Further, the difference affects the way in which deletion or low incidence of the marker in children's speech should be interpreted. When a Samoan child does not use the ergative particle in the grammatically feasible environment, that behavior is not necessarily, indeed not usually, an error. If the child is speaking to an intimate under relatively casual conditions, the absence of the ergative case marker is perfectly appropriate. The child has not deviated from adult norms in a qualitative sense (as would be the case, for example, for a Kaluli child in similar social context). Once again, the data indicate that assessment of errors must rely on a sociologically responsible description of the language. To contrast children's speech behavior with typological accounts of languages runs a heavy risk of misunderstanding the nature of the linguistic phenomenon under consideration and the dynamics of its acquisition.

8. ACQUISITION OF ERGATIVITY THROUGH WORD ORDER

The results of the ergative casemarking study should not be taken as evidence that young Samoan children do not express ergative distinctions in their speech. On the contrary, ERGATIVE DISTINCTIONS ARE EXPRESSED QUITE EARLY IN SAMOAN CHILD LANGUAGE. Rather than marked through morphological means, however, THE DISTINCTIONS EMERGE IN EARLY WORD-ORDER STRATEGIES. IN PARTICULAR, YOUNG CHILDREN RESERVE THE LOCATION IMMEDIATELY FOLLOWING THE VERB FOR ABSOLUTIVE CONSTITUENTS—TRANSITIVE PATIENTS AND INTRANSITIVE MAJOR ARGUMENTS—BUT EXCLUDE ERGATIVE CONSTITUENTS—AGENTS—FROM THIS POSITION. (In this way, they treat patients and intransitive arguments as a single category, distinct from agents.)

This pattern can be seen by comparing Table 8.9 (cf. Section 6) and Table 8.16.

TABLE 8.16
Spontaneous Novel Canonical Transitives
(Declaratives & Yes-No Interrogatives)
Percentage of (X)-Verb-*Patient*-(X) Word Orders
(Compared to (X)-Verb-*Agent*-(X))

Child	Session I	Session III	Session V	Session VII	Average
Matu'u	100.0% (12)	94.4% (17)	94.7% (18)	83.3% (10)	92.9%
Iakopo	—	100.0% (2)	93.8% (15)	100.0% (22)	97.5%
Pesio	100.0% (8)	100.0% (3)	91.7% (11)	97.4% (38)	97.3%
Naomi	95.8% (23)	64.3% (9)	100.0% (15)	83.9% (26)	86.0%
Niulala	87.5% (14)	88.9% (16)	88.9% (40)	72.7% (16)	84.5%

The use of post-verbal position for absolutive constituents is most striking in the speech of the youngest children in this sample. In the earliest sessions in which V-NP transitive constructions appear, the NP is a patient 100% of the time. That is, an agent is never expressed in this position. At the same time, for these children, between 96 and 100% of the intransitive major arguments appeared in post-verbal position. For all the children in our sample, the percentage of transitive verb-patient and intransitive verb-major argument orders is extremely high, providing strong evidence for the systematic use of word order to distinguish absolutive from ergative constituents.

The preference to exclude the agent NP from the position immediately following the verb is evident as well in children's constructions that express BOTH patient and agent constituents. The reader is referred to Table 10, which displays the percentages and frequencies of different word order patterns of three constituent utterances present in the corpus. THE FIGURES IN TABLE 10 INDICATE THAT VERB-AGENT-PATIENT AND PATIENT-VERB-AGENT ORDERS ARE HIGHLY DISPREFERRED AMONG THE YOUNGEST CHILDREN IN THE STUDY. If agent and patient are both to be expressed, these children tend to place the agent before the verb or after the patient (e.g. agent-verb-patient, verb-patient-agent). The preference for verb-agent-patient ordering increases with age of speaker, but never accounts for more than a third of the transitive assertions and yes-no questions in which the two major constituents appear.

To summarize, ergative relations are expressed in the early stages of Samoan language acquisition. They are expressed through word order rather than through casemarking. These results are paralleled in the work of Goldin-Meadow (1975), who found that the deaf children she observed used word order to distinguish causative agents from both patients and intransitive entities. These results are also consistent with a number of findings in the child language literature that show children relying on word order as an initial strategy for expressing semantic relations (Bever, 1970; Bloom, 1970; Radulovic, 1975; but cf. Slobin, 1982).

9. RELATING SOCIOLINGUISTICS TO LANGUAGE ACQUISITION

This paper has addressed the issue of what constitues a norm, and hence, an error, in adult and child language. To reach an understanding of how children attain linguistic competence, it is necessary to understand what constitutes competence itself. That is, it is necessary to know the range and structure of adult language. This involves an awareness of language in terms of regional dialects, social dialects, and registers. Typically, child language subjects are drawn from the regional and social dialect that is (best) captured in traditional and typological grammars. But even in such a sample, there are norms of adult language not captured in such grammars. The norms not captured tend to be those characteristic of registers appropriate to intimate and informal social situations, the very situations in which young children are most exposed. How can we capture the relation of child to adult language without knowledge of these registers?

The best grammar for understanding language acquisition is a sociolinguistically responsive one. By this I mean a grammar that captures the range of linguistic structures systematically in use and relates those structures to the social and linguistic contexts in which they are in use. Such a grammar ideally would rank the linguistic and social conditions associated with a particular variant (see Labov, 1972; and Cedergren & Sankoff, 1974, for a detailed discussion of this technique). The grammar would tell us, for example, which social factor most affects the probability of a particular variant being used (e.g. sex of speaker, social distance between speaker and hearer, relative rank of speaker vis-à-vis hearer, social event at hand, genre in use, etc.). An ideal sociolinguistic grammar would provide us with sets of linguistic structures that carry out similar communicative functions under different social conditions. It would also specify for a particular socially significant context, those linguistic structures that regularly cooccur (Ervin-Tripp, 1972). That is, a sociolinguistic grammar should ideally specify the features that characterize and distinguish one register from another, one social dialect from another (Andersen, 1977). The latter goal is the most consuming in that it demands examining phonological, morphosyntactic, and discourse features as they are used in different socially significant contexts.

Such a grammar has a number of advantages for the child language researcher:

1. *It allows for a social context-sensitive comparison of adult and child language.*

With such a grammar, we are able to compare the language behavior of adults in a particular social context with child language in that (or a comparable) context. We can see, for example, the way in which adults speak to family members in informal situations and compare that speech to children's speech under the same conditions. Similarly, we can compare the way in which adults speak in a range of more formal situations to the speech of children in those settings. This methodology has obvious advantages over one in which children's speech is compared to only the careful speech elicited through linguistic interviews or to the speech of a parent addressing only the child or the researcher/outsider.

2. *IT SPECIFIES THE SOCIAL STATUS OF THE LINGUISTIC STRUCTURE BEING AC-QUIRED BY THE CHILD.*

A sociolinguistic description would state whether or not a structure under consideration is socially variable or invariable in the adult linguistic repertoire. As noted by Slobin (1982), whether or not a structure is optional affects when that structure will be acquired. A sociolinguistic description says more than this, however, in that it displays the conditions under which the structure is used and the extent to which it is used. This information provides a crucial source for predicting the point at which a young child will acquire competence in the use (or non-use) of a structure. For example, a structure may be socially variable, but it is a distinguishing characteristic of household vernacular; therefore, its "optionality" is less likely to inhibit its acquisition than if it were restricted to formal or public arenas outside the household.

3. *IT SPECIFIES FOR BOTH ADULT AND CHILD THE FREQUENCY OF USE OF A PARTICULAR STRUCTURE IN AND ACROSS SOCIAL CONTEXTS.*

In matching child and adult language, it is important to compare frequencies of appearance of a particular structure in these two sets of data. A traditional or typological grammar provides information concerning linguistic rules but does not specify the extent to which that rule is applied in actual adult language use. Matching children's frequencies against such a description runs the risk of over-estimating adult behavior (and underestimating children's behavior). For example, while a grammar may specify word-order patterns of verb, subject, and object, it may not reveal the extent to which all three constituents are expressed in adult language use. The examination of transitive utterances in adult Samoan, for instance, indicated that three-constituent utterances were relatively infrequent across several social contexts. The low frequency of three-constituent utterances in Samoan child language must be evaluated in this light, i.e. as reflecting an adult language norm (rather than violating an adult norm). Differences between children's speech and adult speech (with respect to this phenomenon) are quantitative, with the children's speech showing lower frequencies. This in turn leads to another arena of discussion concerning the implications of quantitative differences.

4. IT EVALUATES CAREGIVER SPEECH IN TERMS OF REGISTRAL VARIATION WITHIN THE SPEECH COMMUNITY.

A sociolinguistic knowledge of the language would refine substantially our understanding of what constitutes input in general and caregiver speech register in particular. For example, the results of the ergativity study in Samoan indicate that the way in which adults speak to young children is part of a larger register of speech used among family members. It also indicates that the features of caregiver speech are characteristic of informal women's speech in and out of the family. This means that adults do not speak to a young child in a certain manner because he/she is a child (immature) but because he/she is an intimate or because the speaker is a woman speaking in an informal setting.

5. IT PROVIDES SOCIAL SOURCES FOR ACQUISITION STRATEGIES.

A sociological account of language specifies not only the repertoire of speakers but VALUES attached to particular codes (dialects, registers, etc.) within the repertoire. A good deal of sociolinguistic research has addressed the effects of such values on speech use (see Ferguson, 1959; Blom & Gumperz, 1972; Hymes, 1974; Labov, 1963; for example).

Of particular interest to acquisition research is the fact that social values may lead speakers to overgeneralize (or undergeneralize) particular grammatical rules. Labov's research on hypercorrection (Labov, 1966, 1972), for example, demonstrates that lower-middle-class speakers in New York City will use, in their careful speech, phonological features of the prestige dialect in environments beyond those characteristic of upper-middle-class speech. Similarly, certain speakers of Samoan will overextend the use of the prestigious phonological feature /t/ in their use of "good speech" (*tautala lelei*).

These processes are not limited to adult speech behavior. I have demonstrated that Samoan children are sensitive to the features associated with highly valued *tautala lelei* register such that they use them in phonological contexts not characteristic of standard *tautala lelei*. Like adults, the children are sensitive to the particular importance gven to the feature /t/ as a distinctive marker of *tautala lelei* in that the bulk of their overextensions concerns overuse of /t/. of /t/.

Information concerning the SOCIAL characteristics of linguistic structures needs to be integrated with what we already know about the PHYSICAL characteristics of these structures and their grammatical environment, to assess constraints on acquisition and strategies that children implement over developmental time. Children pay attention to the ends of words and to the order of words. At the same time they acquire language in a social world and will pay attention to the social significance of words and the social conditions for using them.

ACKNOWLEDGMENT

The research on which this study is based has been supported by The National Science Foundation (Grant No. 53-482-2480) and a Senior Fellowship from The Department of Anthropology, Research School of Pacific Studies, The Australian National University.

REFERENCES

Andersen, E. *Learning to speak with syle: A study of the sociolinguistic skills of young children.* Unpublished doctoral dissertation, Stanford University, 1977.

Bever, T. The cognitive basis for linguistic structures. In J. R. Hayes (Ed.), *Cognition and the development of language.* New York: Wiley, 1970.

Blom, J-P., & Gumperz, J. J. Social meaning in linguistic structures: Code-switching in Norway. In J. J. Gumperz & D. Hymes (Eds.), *Directions in sociolinguistics: The ethnography of communication.* New York: Holt, Rinehart & Winston, 1972.

Bloom, L. *Language development: Form and function in emerging grammars.* Cambridge, MA: MIT Press, 1977.

Braine, M. D. S. The ontogeny of English phrase structure: The first phase. *Language,* 1963, *39,* 1–13.

Brown, R. *A first language: The early stages.* Cambridge, MA: Harvard University Press, 1973.

Brown, R., & Gilman, A. The pronouns of power and solidarity. In T. Sebeok (Ed.), *Style in language.* Cambridge, MA: MIT Press, 1960.

Cedergren, H., & Sankoff, D. Variable rules: Performance as a statistical reflection of competence. *Language,* 1974,

Chomsky, N. Deep structure, surface structure and semantic interpretation. In D. Steinberg & L. Jakobovits (Eds.), *Semantics.* Cambridge: Cambridge University Press, 1971.

Chung, S. *Case marking and grammatical relations in Polynesian.* Austin: University of Texas Press, 1978.

Churchward, S. *A new Samoan grammar.* Melbourne: Spectator Press, 1926.

Comrie, B. Ergativity. In W. P. Lehmann (Ed.), *Syntactic typology: Studies in the phenomenology of language.* Austin: University of Texas Press, 1978.

Dixon, R. M. W. Ergativity. *Language,* 1979,

Duranti, A. *Lāuga* and *talanoaga:* Structure and variation in the language of a Samoan speech event. In R. Bauman & J. Scherzer (Eds.), *Working Papers in Sociolinguistics,* No. 7. University of Texas, Austin, 1980.

Duranti, A. *The Samoan fono: A sociolinguistic study. Pacific Linguistics,* Series B, No. 80, Department of Linguistics, The Australian National University, Canberra, Australia, 1981.

Ervin-Tripp, S. On sociolinguistic rules: Alternation and cooccurence.'' In J. J. Gumperz & D. Hymes (Eds.) *Directions in sociolinguistics: The ethnography of communication.* New York: Holt, Rinehart & Winston, 1972.

Ferguson, C. Diglossia. *Word, 1959,*

Givón, T. (Ed.) *Syntax and semantics, Vol. 12: Discourse and syntax.* New York: Academic Press, 1979.

Goldin-Meadow, S. *The representation of semantic relations in a manual language created by deaf children of hearing parents: A language you can't dismiss out of hand.* Technical Report XXVI. University of Pennsylvania, 1975.

Greenberg, J. H. (Ed.). *Universals of language,* 2nd ed. Cambridge, MA: MIT Press, 1966.

Gumperz, J. Sociocultural knowledge in conversational inference. In M. Saville-Troike (Ed.), *Georgetown University 28th Round Table on Languages and Linguistics.* Washington, D.C.: Georgetown University, 1977.

Hymes, D. *Foundations in sociolinguistics: An ethnographic approach.* Philadelphia: University of Pennsylvania Press, 1974.

Irvine, J. Formality and informality in communicative events. *American Anthropologist,* 1979, *81,*

Kernan, K. *The acquisition of language by Samoan children.* Unpublished doctoral dissertation, University of California, Berkeley, 1969.

Kernan, K. The acquisition of formal and colloquial styles of speech by Samoan Children. *Anthropological Linguistics,* 1974.

Labov, W. The social motivation of a sound change, *Word,* 1963.

Labov, W. *The social stratification of English in New York City.* Washington, D.C.: Center for Applied Linguistics, 1966.

Labov, W. *Sociolinguistic patterns.* Philadelphia: University of Pennsylvania Press, 1972.

Li, C. (Ed.). *Subject and topic.* New York: Academic Press, 1976.

Milner, G. B. Active, passive, or perfective in Samoan: A fresh appraisal of the problem. *Journal of Polynesian Soc.,* 1962.

Milner, G. B. *Samoan Dictionary.* London: Oxford University Press, 1966.

Milner, G. B. It is aspect (not voice) which is marked in Samoan. *Oceanic Linguistics,* XII, 1–2, 1973.

Ochs, E. Ergativity and word order in Samoan child language: A sociolinguistic study. *Language,* 1982.

Partridge, E. *Origins: A short etymological dictionary of modern English.* London: Routledge & Kegan Paul, 1966.

Pawley, A. Polynesian languages: A sub-grouping based on shared innovations in morphology.'' *Journal of Polynesian Soc.,* 1966, *75,*

Pawley, A. Samoan phrase structure: The morphology syntax of a western Polynesian language *Anthroplogical Linguistics, 1,* 1–63.

Pawley, A. The relationships of Polynesian outlier languages. *Journal of Polynesian Soc.,* 1967, *76,*

Pratt, G. *Pratt's grammar and dictionary of the Samoan language.* Apia: Malua Printing Press, 1911.

Radulovic, L. *Acquisition of language: Studies of Dubrovnik children.* Unpublished doctoral dissertation. University of California, Berkeley, 1975.

Schegloff, E., Jefferson, G. & Sacks, H. The preference for self-correction in the organization of repair in conversation. *Language,* 1977, *53,*

Schenkein, J. (Ed.). *Studies in the organization of conversational interaction.* New York: Academic Press, 1978.

Schieffelin, B. *How Kaluli children learn what to say, what to do, and how to feel: An ethnographic study of the development of communicative competence.* Unpublished doctoral dissertation, Columbia University, 1979.

Schieffelin, B. B. The acquisition of Kaluli. In D. I. Slobin (Ed.), *The crosslinguistic study of language acquisition* (Vol. 1). Hillsdale, NJ: Lawrence Erlbaum Associates, 1985.

Shore, B. *A Samoan theory of action: Social control and social order in a Polynesian paradox.* Unpublished doctoral dissertation, University of Chicago, 1977.

Shore, B. *Sala'ilua: A Samoan mystery.* New York: Columbia University Press, 1982.

Slobin, D. I. Cognitive prerequisites for the acquisition of grammar. In C. A. Ferguson & D. I. Slobin (Eds.), *Studies of child language development.* New York: Holt, Rinehart & Winston, 1973.

Slobin, D. I. Language change in childhood and in history. In J. Macnamara (Ed.), *Language learning and thought*. New York: Academic Press, 1977.

Slobin, D. I. Universal and particular in the acquisition of language. In E. Wanner & L. R. Gleitman (Eds.), *Language acquisition: The state of the art*. Cambridge: Cambridge University Press, 1982.

Tuitele, M. T., & Kneubuhl, J. *'Upu Samoa/Samoan words*. Pago Pago: Bilingual/Bicultural Education Project of American Samoa, 1978.

9 The Acquisition of Turkish

Ayhan A. Aksu-Koç
Boğaziçi University, Istanbul

Dan I. Slobin
University of California, Berkeley

INTRODUCTION

1. Brief Grammatical Sketch of Turkish

Turkish is an Altaic language, exhibiting in almost pure form the classic features of an object-verb language (Greenberg, 1966; Lehmann, 1978). The most accessible brief grammar in English is Lewis (1953), which can be supplemented by his extensive *Turkish grammar* (1967). A collection of linguistic studies of Turkish can be found in Slobin and Zimmer (in press).

839

The neutral word order is SOV, with concomitant features of suffixed inflections, postpositions, and preposed demonstratives, numerals, possessives, adjectives, and relative clauses. Word order in simple sentences and main clauses exhibits a high degree of variation for pragmatic purposes (Erguvanlı, 1979). Morphology is agglutinating and remarkably regular, with only a handful of exceptions to general principles.

Vowel harmony operates throughout all words of native origin and for all grammatical suffixes, which harmonize with the last vowel of the noun or verb stem. Suffixes follow one of two main alternations: (1) a front-back alteration of unrounded low vowels, *e/a*, represented here by the phonematic unit *E*, and (2) a front-back, rounded-unrounded alternation of high vowels, *i/ı/ü/u/*, represented by *I*. Compare, for example, the locative suffix *-dE*, realized as *İzmir-de* 'in Izmir' and *İstanbul-da* 'in Istanbul', and the genitive *-In*, realized as *İzmir-in, Tahran-ın, İstanbul-un,* and *Atatürk-ün*. Uninterrupted vowel sequences are avoided by the use of buffer consonants for vowel-initial suffixes, each such inflection carrying its own buffer, as, for example, the *-(n)In* of the genitive, resulting in such forms as *Ankara-nın*.

In strings of agglutinated morphemes, each element retains its phonological and semantic identity as well as its relative position in the string. For example, consider the order of noun suffixes: stem + (plural) + (possessive) + (case), as in *el* 'hand', *-ler* 'plural', *-im* 'first person possessive', *-de* 'locative'. The following combinations are possible:

el 'hand'	*el-ler* 'hands'
el-im 'my hand'	*el-ler-im* 'my hands'
el-de 'in hand'	*el-ler-de* 'in hands'
el-im-de 'in my hand'	*el-ler-im-de* 'in my hands'

With very few exceptions, the language avoids homophonous morphs. Each morph is syllabic and stress is fairly evenly distributed across syllables, with typical word-final stress.

Nouns are case-marked for genitive, accusative, dative-directional, locative, ablative, comitative-instrumental, and deprivative ('without'). The same suffixes are also applied to pronouns, demonstratives, question words, and derived nouns. Consider, for example, the ablative forms of nouns (*masa-DAN* 'from (the) table'), pronouns (*sen-DEN* 'from you'), demonstratives (*bun-DAN* 'from this'), question words (*nere-DEN* 'from where', *kim-DEN* 'from whom'), and derived nouns (*yüz-mek-TEN* 'swim-NOML-ABL' = 'from swimming'). There is a variety of denominal and deverbal derivational suffixes, as discussed in regard to typical errors below. There is no grammatical marking of gender.

Verbal affixes mark voice, negation, modality, aspect, tense, person, and number, with person and number affixes bearing much similarity with nominal suffixes for the same functions. For example, consider the plural *-lar* and first singular *-um* in the following verb examples, already familiar from the noun suffixes listed above:

al
take

al *-ıyor*	*al* *-ıyor* *-lar*
take PROG	take PROG PL
'he/she/it is taking'	'they are taking'

al   *-ıyor*   *-um*
take   PROG   1SG

'I am taking'

Even at early ages fairly elaborated strings of verbal affixes are produced by children. Several examples, picked at random, show the character of Turkish verbal morphology (ages in parentheses):

(2;1) *getir*   *-me*   *-di*   *-n*
bring NEG PAST   2SG

'you didn't bring'

(2;4) *ağla* *-dı*   *-lar*
cry   PAST   PL

'they cried'

(3;2) *düz*   *kon*   *-ul*   *-ur*   *-sa*
straight put   PASS   AORIST   COND

'if one puts (it) straight'

Roughly, the verb in Turkish allows for the following series of affixes (within the bounds of semantic plausibility, of course):

stem—reflexive—reciprocal—causative—
passive—potential—negative—necessitative—
tense—conditional—question—person—number

As this scheme shows, the particles affixed to the verb express notions of tense, aspect, mood, and modality and various combinations of such notions. In terms of tense, there is distinct marking of past (*-dI* or *-mIş*), present (*-Iyor* or *-Ir*), and future (*-EcEk*). Within the past, a modal distinction is drawn between statements made on the basis of direct evidence (*-dI*) vs. indirect evidence such as inference or hearsay (*-mIş*) (for detailed discussion of this distinction, see Slobin & Aksu,

1982). In the present there is an aspectual distinction between progressive (*-Iyor*) and habitual (*-Ir*) (frequently referred to as "aorist"). In addition to these tense and aspect markers, there is a conditional suffix (*-sE*), a necessitative suffix (*-mEll*), and a collection of optative-imperative suffixes marked for both person and mood (e.g. 1SG *-EyIm,* 3SG *-sIn*). Each of these suffixes can be used alone with a verb, followed only by person-number marking.

In addition, there is a collection of particles that can only be interposed between the verb and the above suffixes. Four of these "interfixes" modify the verb in the following ways: passive (*-Il-*), causative (*-dIr-*), reciprocal (*-Iş-*), and reflexive (*-In-*). A fifth is the negative (*-mE-*), which follows these operators on the verb, or the verb stem alone, shifting stress back, onto the preceding syllable.

Three of the suffixes can be used to further modify the meanings of verbs already containing particles listed above to express complex temporal, aspectual, and modal notions. These three suffixes are the past of direct evidence (*-dI*), the past of indirect evidence (*-mIş*), and the conditional (*-sE*). Ordering of particles is crucial for resultant meanings. For example, past + conditional expresses 'past conditional' (e.g. *gel-di-yse* 'come-PAST-COND' = 'if he came') while conditional + past expresses counterfactual (e.g. *gel-se-ydi* 'come-COND-PAST' = 'if he had come'). Where only one resultant meaning is possible, ordering is fixed (e.g. *gel-iyor-du* 'come-PROG-PAST' = 'he was coming' but not *gel-di-iyor).

Verbal complexes of any length can be nominalized and treated as embedded clauses, as discussed in examples from child speech below, in regard to nominalization errors and relative clauses. As an example of such forms, which are fairly infrequent in child speech, consider relative clauses formed on underlying objects, as in the Turkish equivalent of 'the man whom Ali saw'. 'Ali', the underlying subject in the relative clause, surfaces in the genitive, symbolically possessing a nominalized form of his action of 'seeing', and this entire possessed nominal is preposed to the head noun 'man':

Ali	*-nin*	*gör*	*-düğ*	*-ü*	*adam*
Ali	GEN	see	PART	POSS:3	man

Neutral word order is SOV, with frequent deletion of subject pronouns, since person and number of subject are marked on the verb (see Enç, in press, for a discussion of pragmatic factors governing pronoun use and deletion; and Slobin and Talay, in press, for a developmental study of these issues.). The preverbal position is one of focus, thus allowing for OVS to focus objects and OSV to focus subjects. Although the language is basically verb-final, subjects and adverbials are frequently placed after the verb in conversation, performing pragmatic functions relating to topic continuity and turn-taking. Question words normally appear in preverbal position.

Sentences are conjoined either by conjunctions or by verbal suffixes, the latter device being more natural to the language. A collection of verbal particles or "converbs" allow for various sorts of verb chaining to indicate temporal and causal relations. In such series, only the last verb is finite, as in the following example from a play monologue of a child of 4;4. The first verb, suffixed by-*ip*, indicates an action that is prior in the series of events:

Deniz	*-e*	*atlay*	*-ıp*	*yüz*	*-eceğ*	*-im.*
sea	DAT	jump	PTL	swim	FUT	1SG

'I'll jump into the sea and swim.'

Numerous postpositions are also available to encode interclausal relations. In the following example, a child of 3;0 uses the postposition *için* 'for, in order to' to explain why she has removed her doll's clothes:

Yıka	*-mak*	*için*	*çıkarttım.*
wash	INF	for	removed + 1SG

'I took off (doll's clothing) in order to wash (it).'

Further aspects of Turkish grammar relevant to acquisition are discussed in more detail at various points below.

2. Sources of Evidence

The first published work on Turkish child language is a report in Turkish by Özbaydar (1970), briefly summarizing a longitudinal observation of one boy and one girl between the ages of 12–24 months. A detailed longitudinal study is presented in Ekmekçi's (1979) dissertation, presenting the results of monthly hour-long recordings of a girl between the ages of 1;3 and 2;4. Ekmekçi (in press) has recently published a detailed discussion of the development of word order in this child. In addition to these published reports, we have had access to diary observations gathered by Belma and Sabri Özbaydar, Doğan Cüceloğlu, Özcan Başkan, and Nail Şahin and his students. To all of those investigators we express our thanks. Our own materials, gathered by Slobin in 1969–70 and 1972–73, and by Aksu in 1977–78, include extensive speech corpora from about a dozen children, ranging in age from 1;10 to 5;11. These corpora consist primarily of child-investigator interactions, though mother-child and sibling interactions are also included.

In 1972–73, as part of the Berkeley Cross-Linguistic Acquisition Project,[1] a

---

[1]The Berkeley Cross-Linguistic Acquisition Project was carried out with support from the William T. Grant Foundation to the Institute of Human Learning and from NIMH to the Language-

cross-sectional and micro-longitudinal sample of 48 children was studied in depth. We worked with groups of six children—three boys and three girls—at each of eight age levels, spaced at 4-month intervals between the ages of 2;0 and 4;4. In addition to this cross-sectional design, each child was retested 4 months later, providing one longitudinal check, and giving an overall age range of 2;0 to 4;8. A large range of linguistic areas was examined, including locatives, causatives, agent-patient relations, temporal expressions, comparatives, relative clauses, question comprehension, and free speech samples. The overall study, comparing Turkish, Serbo-Croatian, Italian, and English, is summarized in Slobin (1982). The locative elicitation study is reported by Johnston and Slobin (1979); the causative study by Ammon and Slobin (1979); the agent-patient (word-order vs. inflection) test by Slobin and Bever (1982), and Slobin (1982). Some aspects of input are summarized in Slobin (1975). Aksu (1975) examines the development of the expression of cause-effect relations. Clancy, Jacobsen, and Silva (1976) compare the acquisition of conjunctions in Turkish, Italian, English, and German. Slobin and Talay (in press) study the development of pragmatic uses of subject pronouns.

Aksu's (1978) dissertation is a detailed examination of aspect and modality in the child's acquisition of the Turkish past tense. The order of emergence of past tense forms for direct and indirect experience is traced longitudinally across three children between the ages of 21 and 30 months, and experimental data from children between 3;0 and 6;4 are analyzed in regard to issues of aspect and modality. Savaşır's (1983) Master's Thesis explores the use of various forms of future expression in three 2-year-olds from the Berkeley sample.

All of the data listed above were consulted in the preparation of this chapter. Crucial gaps exist in several places—especially in regard to very early stages and the emergence of the inflectional system, and the nature of input in natural adult-child and child-child interaction. We also know little about the development of discourse skills. (İskender Savaşır [1983] is beginning to study developmental relations between activity types and verb forms at Berkeley.) There are no

Behavior Research Laboratory, University of California, Berkeley. Computer facilities in the Berkeley Child Language Archive have been provided by the Sloan Foundation and NSF, allowing for continuing analysis of Turkish speech data. Ayhan Aksu, Francesco Antinucci, Thomas G. Bever, Eve V. Clark, Herbert H. Clark, Susan Ervin-Tripp, Judith R. Johnston, and Ljubica Radulović collaborated with Dan I. Slobin in designing the investigation. Ayla Algar and Alev Alatlı served as testers in Istanbul and Ankara. Aksu's dissertation research received partial support from the American Research Institute in Turkey. The Max-Planck-Institut für Psycholinguistik, Nijmegen, The Netherlands, provided support in the summer of 1981 for further analysis of our Turkish child speech data, as well as a collegial setting in which to work on the revised draft of this chapter. We wish to acknowledge the assistance of all of these institutions and individuals in contributing to the data summarized here. We have benefited from discussion with many colleagues and friends, and would like to thank, especially, Mary Sue Ammon, Francesco Antinucci, Judith Johnston, Brian MacWhinney, Ruth Miller, Nail Şahin, İskender Savaşır, Bambi Schieffelin, and Karl Zimmer.

systematic observations of the development of prosody or phonology in Turkish. There are few data on later ages, but Nail Şahin at Middle East Technical University in Ankara is making an inventory of syntactic structures and lexicon of school-age children.

3. Brief Summary of Overall Course of Linguistic Development in Turkish

The inflectional system appears early, and the entire set of noun inflections and much of the verbal paradigm is mastered by 24 months of age or earlier. By this age, Turkish children inflect nouns for case (accusative, dative, ablative, possessive, instrumental) and number (plural), and verbs for tense-aspect (past result, ongoing process, intention), person, negation, and interrogation. Both noun and verb inflections are present in the one-word stage, and there is some evidence for productive use as young as 15 months. Early words typically include inflections, since stems tend to be mono- or bisyllabic, and inflections are stressed suffixes. For example, *bitti* 'all-gone' or 'all done' is made up of the verb stem *bit* 'finish' and the past-tense suffix *-ti;* negative imperatives are composed of the verb stem and the suffix *-mE,* as in *gitme* 'don't go'; and so forth. Such suffixes are quickly used with a wide variety of words. Evidence for productivity appears as early as age 15 months, when children fail to delete a stem-final *-k* before a suffix beginning with a vowel, thus indicating that the suffix is not simply part of a rote-learned amalgam. There are no errors in the order of agglutinated morphemes; however the very few available possibilities for morphological over-generalizations are followed by the child. Overall, morphological errors are remarkably rare, because the extreme regularity of the language precludes them. Morphophonological adjustments for vowel harmony and voicing assimilation are also correct at very early ages.

As a result of precocious acquisition of grammatical morphology and lack of overgeneralizations, Turkish child speech transcripts do not have the familiar "child language" look evidenced in most other languages. Early utterances are not telegraphic, since the stressed, suffixed inflections are present. Child utterances are short and simple, but rarely ungrammatical or incomplete from the point of view of the adult language. Thus Turkish acquisition provides evidence that grammatically relevant notions are accessible to quite young children if the means of expression are sufficiently salient and analyzable.

Word order is used flexibly for pragmatic functions, as in the adult language. For example, children younger than 2 correctly place new information before the verb and presupposed or predictable information after the verb. All six orders of subject, verb, and object are comprehended in a reversible transitive sentence test at 24 months. Fixed word order is adhered to where required in the language (e.g. adjective + noun; noun + attribute; possessor + possessed).

Two- and 3-year-olds are engaged in mastering verb inflections for voice and modality (passive, nonwitnessed past tense, conditional, causative) and syntactic means for temporal and causal linking of clauses.

The tense-aspect system evolves from (1) a distinction between immediately completed changes of state (-dI) and durational events (-Iyor), to (2) generalization of the meaning of the past-tense morpheme -dI from completion to past tense, to (3) a distinction in the past between directly experienced events (-dI) and events inferred from their endstates (-mIş), and finally to (4) a general past-tense distinction between witnessed (-dI) and nonwitnessed (-mIş) events, including hearsay in the latter category.

The passive, which is agentless in Turkish, emerges early to focus on desired changes of state in objects. For example, a child of 2;4, wanting to open a box, said: Böyle aç-ıl-ır 'thus open-PASS-AORIST' (= 'It is opened like this').

The conditional is a simple verb affix, and is used by 2-year-olds to express contingencies. For example, a child of 2;7, covering her doll's eyes, said: Karanlık ol-sa gör-mez-sin 'dark be-COND see-NEG:AOR-2SG' (= 'If it's dark you won't see'). (Counterfactual uses of the conditional are a much later acquisition.)

The causative morpheme is often extended from the meaning of instigation ('make someone do something') to causation generally, with inappropriate affixation to verbs that are already inherently causative. For example, a child of 2;3 intended to use the verb kes 'cut' as a simple transitive, using the causative morpheme, -tir-, to mark transitivity; however, the form kes-tir should mean 'have someone cut'. Thus although the general notion of 'cause' is marked early on, it takes a while for children to sort out different types of causality for grammatical marking.

Locative postpositions, question words, and temporal and causal clause relations emerge in the standard crosslinguistic order, presumably based on conceptual development. Locatives emerge in the order: 'in'/'on'/'under' < 'beside' < 'back with objects having back-front orientation' < 'front with oriented objects' < 'between' < 'back with unoriented objects' < 'front with unoriented objects'. Early clausal conjoining expresses temporal and causal sequences; simultaneity and directed temporal relations ('before', 'after') develop later.

Late acquisitions (after age 4) are seen in a variety of complex constructions requiring the insertion of nominalized verb forms of various sorts into sentences (relative clauses and verb complements). Whereas the grammar of simple sentences and main clauses is quite transparent and easily acquired, the syntax and morphology of subordinate clauses pose considerable difficulty to the Turkish child. Means of combining clauses to express temporal and causal relations develop in the following sequence: (1) Until about 2;6, simple juxtaposition of sentences predominates, without explicit grammatical markers of connection. (2) During the next year children begin to use connectives that don't require nominalizations (conjunctions and converbs). (3) After age 4 children begin to more frequently use nominalizations for various subordinate clauses, but with prolonged confusion between the various forms, and syntactic errors.

Systematic data are not available beyond age 6.

THE DATA

4. Typical Errors

The discussion of typical morphological errors in this section is briefer than comparable chapter sections on the development of other languages, since the remarkable regularity and transparency of Turkish morphology precludes a high rate of error in the early phases of development. Where errors typically occur is in later phases, when the Turkish-speaking child encounters problems of complex syntax, as discussed in regard to nominalization errors and errors in deverbal and denominal derivation, and late acquisition of relative clauses.

4.1. *Morphological Overregularizations*

The few possible morphological overgeneralizations do occur. One source of error is failure to delete a stem-final *k* preceding suffixes beginning with a vowel. For example, the corrective accusative of *tabak* 'plate' is *tabağı*, where *ğ* is not pronounced.

Ekmekçi's child practiced this accusative form at 15 months: *daba, daba, daba, dabagı*. Similarly, at the same age, she rendered the genitive of *bebek* 'baby' as *bebeki* (=*bebeğin*). These are common errors for this class of words, rarely heard after age 28 months. Such analogical errors (compare the correct early accusative, as, for example, *Ahmedi*), so abundant in Indo-European child language, also occur where possible in Turkish. They indicate that the child has carried out a segmentation of root and affix, and suggest that the early correct forms are probably also productive. The common explanation is applicable to the Turkish child—namely that the child is sensitive to patterned regularities in morphological paradigms, and applies a standard inflectional principle to all relevant members of a class.

4.2. *Meaningless Overmarking of Verbs*

At early stages of development (below age 2;6 or so), verbs are sometimes pronounced with extra, meaningless syllables between the stem and the final person-number affixes. Early on, it seems that the child attempts to retain some rhythmic picture of complex verbs, incomprehendingly inserting morphemes that sound like passive and causative particles. Such errors are quite different from the errors considered below, where the added morphemes perform an interpretable semantic function in context. Whereas later errors of overmarking reveal a semantically motivated analysis of the morphological system, the early errors seem to reveal a semantically unmotivated analysis of words into combinable syllables—an obvious prerequisite to the discovery of principles of productive morphology.

4.3. Errors in Causative Marking

The causative morpheme can be inserted in intransitive verbs to make them transitive, as in *öl* 'die' and *öl-dür* 'kill'. When this morpheme occurs with a verb which is already transitive, it renders an instigative meaning as in *kır* 'break' and *kır-dır* 'have (someone) break'. The morpheme can be doubled in verbs of the first type, bringing about an instigative meaning ('have (someone) kill'). Some children apparently abstract a general causative meaning from this morpheme, using it incorrectly with verbs which are already inherently causative-transitive. For example:

Adult: Kim   kes -ti   onu?
        who   cut PAST   it+ACC

'Who cut it?'

Child (2;3): Ben kes -tir   -di   -m.
              I   cut CAUS   PAST   1SG

'Intended meaning: 'I cut (it).'
Literal meaning: 'I had (someone) cut (it).'

Children also have difficulty in determining which verbs have lexical causative forms and which verbs allow for productive causative derivation. (The latter option is much more widely represented in the language.) For example, a girl of 3, pointing to her hurt eye, said:

*Bu -ra -sı   -nı   yan   -dır   -ıyor
this LOC POSS ACC   burn CAUS   PROG

'It's making this point burn (hurt).'

Here, the intransitive verb *yan* 'burn' has been transitivized with the causative particle *-dIr*, whereas it has a lexical causative counterpart *yak* 'cause to burn'. (See Clark & Hecht, 1982, for children's problems in distinguishing between conventional and productive parts of the lexicon.)

The other side of the coin is represented by errors of undermarking the causative, treating an intransitive verb as if it were lexically transitive, as shown in the following interchange, which arose when a child wanted the experimenter to remove a small plastic toy pasted to a cardboard mounting:

Child: *Şu   -nu   kalk.
        that   ACC   get:up

Adult: Efendim?
        Excuse me?

Child: *Şu   -nu   kalk   -sana.
        that   ACC   get:up IMP

The child's intended meaning was 'lift that up' (disconnect it), but he used the intransitive verb *kalk* 'get up'. The grammatical form requires the causative particle: *kal-dır-sana*.

4.4. *Simplification of the Negative System*

Some children younger than 2 have been observed to make various attempts to simplify the system of negation. Verbal predicates are negated by the insertion of the negative particle *-mE-* immediately after the verb root or verb + voice particles, but before the modal, tense, and person suffixes. Stress is shifted to the syllable preceding the negative particle (a clear exception to the usual pattern of word-final stress); for example, *al-dí* 'take-PAST:3SG'—*ál-ma-dı* 'take-NEG-PAST:3SG'. Negation of nonverbal predicates, on the other hand, involves the uses of lexical negatives *yok* 'nonexistent' and *değil* 'is not'. *Değil* is the negative for substantive (adjectival and nominal) predicates, while *yok* negates existential predicates. For example: *su değil* 'water NEG:BE' (= 'it isn't water') vs. *su yok* 'water NEG:EXIS' (= 'there is no water'). The negative existential, *yok*, is also used for negative possessives, contrasting with the affirmative existential, *var*. Compare *adam-ın at-ı var* 'man-GEN horse-POSS EXIS' (= 'the man has a horse') and *adam-ın at-ı yok* 'man-GEN horse-POSS NEG:EXIS' (= 'the man doesn't have a horse'), along with the contrasting substantive negative *adam at değil* 'man horse NEG:BE' (= 'a man is not a horse'). (These examples are only relevant to timeless or nontensed statements. Both types of nonverbal predicates, substantive and existential, appear as the negation of the auxiliary verb *ol* 'be' when they take tense-aspect-modality markers and when they are embedded.)

It appears that some children at first pick only one of these lexical forms, or a phonological variant of *-mE-* (*mı mı*), or *ı-ıh* (the sound accompanying gestural negation in Turkish) as a universal negative marker, applying it to all types of predication after the model for negation of nonverbal predicates. Thus the negation paradigm of nonverbal predicates is overgeneralized to verbal predicates. (Note that thereby the child adheres to a pattern of negation that is more widespread among the languages of the world, as well as being consistent with an early tendency in child speech for sentence external negation.) One child is reported to have used *değil* as a general negative marker until age 2;3, and another to have used *ıh* until about 2;6. Another child was observed to use *mı mı* as a negator until age 2;0. To cite examples from two of these children:

> **Anne   otur,   kalk   değil.*
> mother   sit   get:up   NEG
> 'Mother sit, don't get up' (= *kalk-ma* 'get:up-NEG').

> **Yap   -ıcağ   -ım   ıh.*
> do   FUT   1SG   NEG
> 'I won't do (it)' (= *yap-mı-yacağ-ım* 'do-NEG-FUT-1SG').

The occasional carryover of this early tendency is exemplified below in the speech of one child who did produce inflectional negation.

> **Ay,   koy   -du   -m   yok.*
> oh   put   PAST   1SG   NEG
> Intended meaning: 'I can't put it.' (= *koy-ma-dım*)

> Adult: *Büsküi   ver   -eyim   mi   sana?*
> cookie   give   OPT:1SG   Q   2SG+DAT
> 'Shall I give you a cookie?'
> Child: **Büsküi   yok.*
> cookie   NEG
> 'Intended meaning: 'Don't give me cookies.' (= *Büsküi ver-me*)
> Literal meaning: 'There are no cookies.'

Although systematic longitudinal data from earlier periods are needed to understand the exact course of such developments, it appears that the paradigm for the negation of nonverbal predicates is acquired earlier than that for verbal predicates. The early isolation of lexical negatives is probably facilitated by the fact that these forms are perceptually salient, independent words which occur in sentence final position. In addition, their use avoids problems of interruption of linguistic units called for in the insertion of the inflectional negative *-mE-* within the verb. When the latter form emerges, one often hears laboriously slow and clear syllable-by-syllable enunciation of negated verbs, with unusual stress on the usually unstressed negative particle. Although accomplished fairly early, analysis and composition of inflected negative forms is not carried out without difficulty.

4.5. Nominalization Errors

Errors are made in various participial forms from age 3 on, increasing in frequency for 4- and 5-year-olds, as occasions to use such forms become more common, given increased complexity in the child's communicative intent. The means of deriving such forms are complex, based on principles probably relatively abstract to the child, and often resulting in surface forms in which a clause is conflated in a nominalized verb. For example, statements of fact and statements of potentiality or activity require different nominalizations, using the participle *-dIk* for factive clauses and *-mE* for potential clauses, as shown below:

Ahmed	-in	yüz	-düğ	-ü	-nü	biliyorum.
Ahmet	GEN	swim	FACT	POSS	ACC	know+1SG.

'I know that Ahmet swam/is swimming.'   [fact]

Ahmed	-in	yüz	-me	-si	-ni	bekliyorum.
Ahmet	GEN	swim	POT	POSS	ACC	wait+1SG

'I'm waiting for Ahmet to swim.'   [potentiality]

Children tend to use the latter form for both types of constructions. It may be that the distinction between fact and potentiality is not accessible to children of this age. In addition, the use of a single form for these two closely-related complement constructions may reflect a common tendency of economy of means. But, in either case, why should the latter form, the *-mE* participle, be preferred? The avoidance of the *-dIk* form may be due to morphological complexity. Note that in the above two examples the subject of the embedded clause, *Ahmet,* is in the genitive case, *Ahmedin.* The subject is thus treated as the "symbolic possessor" of the action attributed to him (literally 'Ahmet's fact-of-swimming I know' and 'Ahmet's potentiality-of-swimming I await'). The form is therefore doubly opaque, in that the subject is marked in a nonstandard way, and the verb has lost its characteristic verbal morphology. However, when the subject of the main clause is coreferential with the subject of the embedded clause the genitive is not required, allowing for the syntactically simpler forms:

Ahmet	yüz	-me	-si	-ni	biliyor.
Ahmet	swim	POT	POSS	ACC	know+3SG.

Ahmet	yüz	-me	-yi	biliyor.
Ahmet	swim	POT	ACC	know+3SG.

'Ahmet knows how to swim.'

This simpler nominal complement is acquired earlier than the two more complex forms presented above. When children begin to use the factive nominalization, they often tend to mention the embedded subject in the standard nominative (unmarked) case, as in the coreferential situation, rather than in the required genitive. As a general principle, there is probably a tendency to limit the range of functions carried out by a given case inflection, resulting here in the avoidance of using the genitive—normally the case of the possessor—to mark a subject. The simpler option, thus, is to use the *-mE* participle with embedded nominative subject for both factives and potentials, and, upon emergence of the *-dIk* participle, still to avoid genitive marking of the embedded subject.

4.6. *Errors in Deverbal Derivation*

Other participial errors occur in the formation of deverbal attributions—another set in which similar forms are distinguished by fairly abstract formal criteria. The details are arcane for the general reader, but the general interpretation is that it takes children a while to sort out nuances of verbal aspect and a range of surface forms which all serve to convert actions into states (e.g. forms expressing such notions as 'sleeping cat', 'sliced meat', 'fallen leaf'). The range of forms incorrectly chosen in particular instances all come from a class of verbal affixes which depict an event in a stative or timeless mode, but the particular choice is often incorrect. Several types of examples are given below. In all of these situations semantic motivation seems to take precedence over the acquisition of more formally motivated means of expression.

Aksu (1978) has experimentally studied two such affixes that form deverbal attributives, the present participle suffix *-En* and the past participle suffix *-mIş*. In describing stative representations of actions, 3-year-olds prefer either verbal predications in the present progressive or substantive and existential predications. Attributive descriptions with *-En* and *-mIş* show a significant increase after age 4, with constructions with *-En* reaching a comparable level of production about six months later than *-mIş*. The past participle, *-mIş,* is used to encode resultant states, such as *piş-miş elma* 'cook-mIş apple' (= 'cooked apple'), whereas the present participle, *-En,* stativizes processes, such as *koş-an çocuk* 'run-*En* child' (= 'running child' / 'child who is running'). As discussed in Section 5.3, below, the *-mIş* suffix is acquired earlier as a verbal inflection referring to present states resulting from past processes. At the point of acquiring the syntactic function of forming participial adjectives, the child may begin with *-mIş*, extending this already established form to a new function. Once this syntactic function has been established for past participials, it may be easier for the child to acquire a new form, *-En*, for deriving present participials. Here we may have a realization on the syntactic plane of the principle: "New forms first express old functions, and new functions are first expressed by old forms."

Most common errors up to age 4 are attributives derived with the future participle *-EcEk*, the infinitive suffix *-mEk*, and the nominalizing suffix *-mE*, in contexts where the stative *-mIş* participle would be appropriate. The following examples are ungrammatical although the choice of *-mE* instead of *-mIş* is appropriate on semantic grounds since both suffixes derive adjectives with passive meaning. Typical responses in describing a picture of a cut or bitten apple were:

```
*kes    -il     -me         elma
cut     PASS    NOMINAL     apple
```

```
*ısır   -ıl     -ma         elma
bite    PASS    NOMINAL     apple
```

In both cases the passive notion has been marked twice, i.e., redundantly. The grammatically correct description of a picture of a cut apple would be:

```
kes    -il     -miş         elma
cut    PASS    PAST.PART    apple
```

Using the *-mE* nominal, without the passive particle *-Il-*, results in grammatically correct but frozen forms expressing potentiality:

```
yar     -ma          şeftalı
split   NOMINAL      peach
'peach that can be split'
```

These errors suggest some uncertainty in the range of meanings carried by the *-mE* nominal and the passive in situations where states are to be described with forms based on verbal stems.

Difficulty with such notions is also revealed in another typical error of derivational morphology—in this case, undermarking of the passive. Children often neglect to passivize transitive verbs in forming present participial adjectives. The result is an ungrammatical active participle modifying an inanimate patient noun, as in:

```
*ısır   -an          elma
bite    PRES.PART    apple
'apple that is biting'
```

```
*yi    -yen          elma
eat    PRES.PART     apple
'apple that is eating'
```

Grammatical versions require the passive particle:

```
ısır   -ıl     -an           elma
bite   PASS    PRES.PART     apple
'bitten apple'
```

ye	-nil	-en	elma
eat	PASS	PRES.PART	apple

'eaten apple'

These errors may be due to the taxing operations of morphological derivation. They may also be due to an insufficient analysis of certain predicates in terms of transitivity/intransitivity, as is also suggested by errors of overcausativization discussed above. The facts that errors observed in morphological derivation are the same as those in inflectional derivation strengthens the second interpretation.

4.7. Errors in Denominal Derivation

Occasional errors occur in the formation of denominal attributives with -lI, a highly productive suffix denoting 'the possession of the object or quality indicated by the noun'. The following example is an error because it makes no sense semantically, but on the other hand it reflects the underlying knowledge that -lI derives adjectives from nouns, since the child has correctly nominalized the verb. In attempting to describe a picture of an apple from which a bite has been taken, the child has added -mE to the verb stem, thus nominalizing it, followed by the adjectival derivation -lI:

*ye	-me	-li	elma
eat	NOMINAL	ADJECTIVAL	apple

5. Error-Free Acquisition

5.1. Morphology

With the exception of the marginal early and late errors summarized above, Turkish child speech is almost entirely free of error. This is undoubtedly attributable to the extreme regularity of the morphological systems, resulting in a situation in which the language hardly provides opportunity for error. Most of the agglutinative morphology—nominal and verbal—is used productively at the two-word period, before the age of 2.

There are many interlocking reasons for the ease of acquisition of these systems. We can think of at least 12 factors which play a role in facilitating acquisition, and they cannot all be pulled apart in considering any single language. The morphemes are: (1) postposed, (2) syllabic, and (3) stressed, making them especially salient to perception and immediate memory. They are (4) obligatory, rather than optional. (For example, the optionality of the Japanese object particle delays its acquisition and its use in sentence comprehension, in relation to Turkish [Hakuta, 1977; Slobin, 1982].) (5) The inflections are tied to the content word, noun or verb, and are not conflated with other parts of speech.

(For example, the German case system, conflated with articles, is acquired much more slowly than the corresponding Slavic noun suffixes.) (6) The postposing of inflections is consistent with the verb-final typology of Turkish, and children may be sensitive to such typological consistencies. Semantically, the Turkish particles (7) seem to follow the stem in an order reflecting decreasing relevance (Bybee, 1985) to the inherent meaning of the stem (NOUN-PLURAL-POS-SESSIVE-CASE and VERB-MODALITY-TENSE/ASPECT-PERSON/NUM-BER), and (8) are generally nonsynthetic in their mapping of functions onto form. Clairty of semantic mapping probably facilitates acquisition. (By comparison, the fusional quality of Indo-European inflectional morphemes probably adds to their complexity; e.g. the typical conflation of number, gender, and case.) (9) Functionally, the morphemes express only grammatical roles, while other devices, such as contrastive word orders and focusing particles, are used for pragmatic functions. (By comparison, Japanese particles, which express both pragmatic and syntactic functions, seem to be more difficult to master.) In terms of distribution and diversity, the paradigms are (10) almost entirely regular (i.e. exceptionless), (11) consistently applied to all content words and pro-forms (nouns and pronouns, demonstratives, question words, nominalizations; main verbs and auxiliaries), and (12) relatively distinct (i.e. there are almost no homonymous functors). Whatever the relative strengths of all of these factors, it is clear that at least some of them greatly facilitate the acquisition of inflections in Turkish.

5.2. *Morpheme and Word Order*

Order rules, where they apply, are also acquired free of error. The agglutinated morphemes occur in proper order. This seems remarkable given the range and complexity of possible combinations in both the nominal and verbal systems, as summarized in the grammatical sketch above. It is not uncommon, for example, to find verbs in 3-year-old speech containing particles of negation, voice, modality, tense-aspect, and person-number—all in the proper order. Obligatory word order within clauses is adhered to (e.g. adjective-noun, possessor-possessed, noun-predicative attribute, postposing of postpositions). On the other hand, varying word order within sentences for pragmatic effect is also easily mastered (e.g. using preverbal position for focus, resulting in postposed subjects for object focusing and postposed objects for subject focusing). There appears to be a sensitivity to the role of ordering at different linguistic levels. At the word level, where morphemes are bound by vowel harmony and word intonation, strict ordering is adhered to. Strict ordering is also adhered to within constituent phrases. At the sentence level, however, ordering of main sentence elements is free to vary in appropriate discourse contexts, as discussed in Section 6.1.2, below. General principles like ordering, therefore, do not apply across the board, but interact with definition of linguistic level.

6. Timing of Acquisition

6.1. Early Acquisition

6.1.1. *Inflections.* The agglutinative morphology is acquired strikingly early, parts of it apparently productive as early as 15 months. Explanations come from the consistency of the system, as discussed above.

In sentence comprehension experiments (Slobin & Bever, 1982), children rely on the accusative inflection, rather than word order, to identify agent and patient. From the youngest age group tested—2;0—children correctly acted out reversible transitive sentences in all six orders of subject, verb, and object. Slobin and Bever also presented children with strings of two nouns and a verb, with no case inflection on either noun, in the orders NNV, NVN, and VNN. By and large, response to such strings was random, indicating that Turkish children rely on inflections rather than word order for the identification of grammatical relations.

6.1.2. *Word Order.* Ekmekçi (in press) has documented early use of a variety of word orders in one child during the age range 1;7–2;4. Early control of the functions of word order is reflected in a number of contrastive uses, including the following: (1) Preposed adjectives are used in attributive expressions (e.g. *soğuk su* 'cold water', said at 1;7 when asking for cold water), whereas postposed adjectives are used in predicative expressions (e.g. *çorba sıcak* 'soup hot', said at 2;0 as a complaint). (2) Indefinite or nonreferential direct objects always directly precede the verb (e.g. *kalem getir* 'bring (a) pencil'), whereas definite direct objects (marked by the accusative inflection) can also follow the verb (e.g. both *kalem-i getir* 'pencil-ACC bring'' and *getir kalem-i* 'bring pencil-ACC' = 'bring the pencil') [age 1;10]. (3) Such examples reflect a more general tendency to place new information before the verb and presupposed or predictable information after the verb. Consider, for example, the following narrative sequence, in which 'three sisters' are introduced as a sentence-initial topic in the first sentence, followed by postposing of 'sister' in a following sentence:

Üç   kardeş   var   -mış.
three   sister   EXIS   PAST:REPORT
'There were three sisters.'

Bir   -i   büyüğ   -ümüş   kardeş   -in.
one   POSS   big   PAST:REPORT   sister   GEN
'One of the sisters was big.'

The verb can be highlighted by verb initialization and postposing of all additional material, as in the following (2;0):

Sev	*-mi*	*-eceğ*	*-im*	*onu*	*daha.*
love	NEG	FUT	1SG	3SG:ACC	more

'I won't love her anymore.'

In reading through our own transcripts of Turkish child speech we have been struck by the extreme rarity of contextually inappropriate word orders, reinforcing the impression that pragmatic variation in word order is a precocious acquisition. (Support is given by discourse constraints of adult-child conversation, as pointed out in the discussion of input, below.)

Work by Slobin and Talay (in press) on children between 2;1 and 3;8 shows early control of the pragmatics of first-person pronoun placement. For example, utterances with 'I' in normal preverbal position are used when the subject is at issue, as in responses to 'who'-questions or in drawing a contrast with the subject of a previous utterance, as well as in making a neutral report of past action. By contrast, postverbal 'I' is used when the verb or object is in focus, and the continuing subject is presupposed. Such uses of subject pronouns are standard for adult conversation as well; however, where young children may differ from adults is in overuse of pronouns. This issue is taken up in more detail below, in the discussion of reorganizations in development (Section 11.4).

In the Slobin and Bever (1982) sentence comprehension study reported above, there is suggestive evidence that children are sensitive to the fact that SOV is the standard word order of the language. Although most children responded randomly to strings containing two uninflected nouns and a verb, a small number of children did respond consistently to some of these strings, picking either the first or second noun as agent. Their responses reflected the frequency of occurrence of word order types in Turkish speech: 13 children responded consistently to NNV strings, which parallel the standard SOV order; 7 were consistent on NVN, which is the next most frequent order in speech samples; and only 4 were consistent on VNN, which is the least frequent order. Children's imitations of sentences in the six orders of S, V, and O showed both great tolerance for word order variability and a degree of sensitivity to the standard SOV order. Overall, children tended to imitate sentences correctly, regardless of word order. Although reorderings in imitation were rare, when they did occur they again reflected a sensitivity to the frequency of occurrence of the order types in speech: (1) Verb-final sentences were almost never reordered; (2) verb-medial (NVN) sentences were reordered less frequently than verb-initial (VNN) sentences, and always into verb-final order (NNV); (3) verb initial sentences were reordered most frequently—generally into NNV order, but also into NVN. Younger children reordered most frequently (from 46% at age 3;0 to 11% by 3;8) and made more conversions into verb-final order in their imitations. Thus even though Turkish children vary word order freely in their speech, and are guided by inflectional cues in sentence comprehension, they are also cognizant of the basic verb-final character of their language.

6.1.3. *Passive*.   The passive is an early acquisition in Turkish, where it is always agentless, and is indicated by a simple and regular verbal affix, as are other parts of the verbal system discussed above. The pragmatic function that it serves is one of focusing on the state of the patient, such as the English truncated passive (e.g. *it got broken*). The Turkish child does not have to face the complexities of forms like the full passive of English, since variations in word order, as discussed above, allow for shifts in focus. Savaşır (1983) has examined uses of the passive in three children from the Berkeley sample in the age range 2;3–2;4. He notes a preponderance of early use of passives in the negative, in situations in which the child fails to bring about a desired goal (e.g. *aç-ıl-mı-yor* 'open-PASS-NEG-PROG' (= 'it is not being opened', uttered by a child of 2;4 who has not succeeded in opening a box). Savaşır suggests that the passive is used in third person present negative utterances, such as this one, to attribute a nonoccurrence of an event to an object: "It would seem that the arliest occurrences of the passive in the present tense are used to report those instances in which the child's intentions or plans are inhibited due to a resistance from an object" (p. 39). He suggests that the next developmental advance involves a distinction between focus on the agent and a non-agentive focus on objects, as revealed in alternations between first person active and third person passive utterances, such as *böyle aç-ar-ım* 'thus open-AORIST-ISG (= 'I open (it) like this')and *böyle aç-ıl -ır* 'thus open-PASS-AORIST' (= 'It is open like this'). In Savaşır's terms, children come to "use the passive voice to represent the changes that arise out of the properties of the object" (pp. 39–40). (He notes, as well, that the aorist, in distinction to the present progressive, is used in such situations which are viewed "non-agentively." Thus the combination of aorist and passive allows children to talk about events per se.)

6.2. *Late Acquisition*

Relative clauses, verb complements, and some types of conjoined constructions are strikingly late, not fully mastered until age 5 or later. These are all constructions in which an embedded sentence is treated as a participle, as discussed above. Such clauses are relatively opaque—that is, they do not look like surface sentences, since the verbs appear in various nominal or participial forms and casemarking on nouns is often different than in the corresponding simple clauses. In all of the forms discussed below there is abundant morphological and syntactic complexity. Such constructions, which increase the distance between surface form and underlying meaning, pose special acquisitional problems to children.

6.2.1. *Causal conjunction*.   The order of acquisition of the various syntactic structures for conjoining two clauses in a causal relation presents a control case, since the semantic complexity of the underlying notions can be assumed to be constant across various forms of conjunction. The connectives constituted of a demonstrative pronoun in the ablative case, *on-dan* 'that-ABL' (= 'from that'), or in the genitive case followed by a postposition, *on-un için* 'that-GEN for' (= 'for that reason'), are quite transparent and are acquired first. These forms allow for conjoining of independent clauses, as in the following example from a child of 2;8:

> Oyuncakları   götürdün   de   ONUN   İÇİN   kızdı.
> toys+ACC   you+brought   PTL   got:angry+3SG
> 'You brought the toys, THAT'S WHY she got angry.'

On the other hand, participial or infinitival nominalizations of the verb followed by a postposition, *-dIğ-I için* 'NOML-GEN for' (= 'because of his . . . ing'), and *-mEk için* 'INF for' (= 'in order to'), emerge much later in the expression of the same causal relation. In such constructions there is a clear distinction between main and subordinate clause, and only the main clause has a finite verb, as in the following example from a child of 3;8, representing the earliest appearance of such constructions in a cross-sectional sample from 2;1 to 5;0:

> Oyuncak   ol   -duğ   -u   için   uçmaz.
> toy   be   PART   GEN   for   fly+NEG+AORIST
> 'Because it's a toy it doesn't fly.'

(The order of development of conjunction types is discussed in Section 7.2, below.)

6.2.2. *Relative Clauses.*   Difficulties in dealing with nontransparent embedded clauses are most evident in the acquisition of relative clauses, clearly a very late acquisition for Turkish children. Slobin (in press) has compared the use of relative clauses in 57 matched English and Turkish child speech samples between the ages of 1;0 and 4;8, extracting all of the relative clauses spoken by the children and the adult investigators who interacted with them in standard settings (playing with toys and discussing everyday events). In both languages, relative clauses are quite rare, and none are found before age 2;4; however, they are twice as frequent in English as in Turkish. Overall, there are 96 relative clauses in the English transcripts and only 42 in Turkish (based on over 40 hours of interaction). The same asymmetry is reflected in the investigators' speech to the children, with 40 relative clauses in English and 22 in Turkish. As shown in Fig. 9.1, the development of relative clauses is much faster in English, with a major spurt around age 3;6, while the mastery of relative clauses in Turkish must take place later than 4;8, the oldest age in our sample. (Similar evidence comes from experiments on the comprehension of relative clauses, discussed in Section 12.1.3, below. Turkish children of 4;8 are able to extract only the main clause for acting out.)

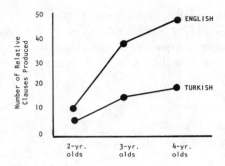

FIG. 9.1.   Growth of Relative Clauses in English and Turkish Child Speech

The difficulty in Turkish relative clauses lies in the deformation of the embedded clause, which loses the finite verb and normal case inflections of a canonical main clause, as pointed out in the grammatical sketch, above. In addition, different participles are required for subject and nonsubject relatives (details in Slobin, in press). Consider, for example, the following Turkish utterances from our sample of adult speech to children, along with their English equivalents in the glosses:

Bizim	ev	-in	önün	-e	gel	-en	kedi	-ye
our	house	GEN	front	DAT	come	SUBJ.REL	cat	DAT

benziyor,
resembles

'It looks like the cat that comes to the front of our house.'

Kazan	-dığ	-ın	para	-yla	ne	yapacan?
earn	OBJ.REL	POSS.2SG	money	with	what	do+FUT+2SG

'What will you do with the money that you earn?'

The Turkish sentences have nonfinite verbs, with different participles for subject and object relatives. In addition, in the first example, normal subject-verb order is reversed: *gelen kedi* 'cat come+SUBJ.REL' (= 'cat that comes') as opposed to canonical *kedi geliyor* 'come+PRES cat' ('cat comes'). The equivalent English form is maximally transparent: *the cat that comes,* corresponding to canoncial *the cat comes.* The second example, an object relative, condenses subject and transitive verb into a single word in Turkish, the possessed nominalization *kazandığın,* in comparison with the full *you earn* in English. Small wonder that relative clauses are a late acquisition in Turkish. They are replaced in discourse by periphrastic circumlocutions which serve to establish common reference. Typically, a referent will be set up in one clause, and then referred back to in the following clause—something like the equivalent of: 'You know, I keep my cars in a box? Well, that's the box.' (where an English-speaking child would say something like: "That's the box I keep my cars in.").

THE SETTING OF LANGUAGE ACQUISITION

7. Cognitive Pacesetting of Language Development

7.1. Locative Development

The course of development of locative notions follows a standard order, presumably based on language-free conceptual development, even though the principles of locative suffixation and postpositions are acquired early. The first locative expressions are simple nominal suffixes: -E 'moving towards', -dE 'located at', -dEn 'moving away from'. These suffixes do not require encoding of specific object and locational features, expressing the simple oppositions between location and movement, and movement towards and away from a referent point. These basic notions are accessible at a fairly early stage of cognitive development.

The locative postpositions are possessed names of locations, with the locative suffixes appended, e.g.:

masa	-nın	üst	-ün	-de
table	GEN	top	POSS	LOC

'on the table'   (literally: 'at the table's top')

masa	-nın	üst	-ün	-den
table	GEN	top	POSS	ABL

'off of the table'   (literally: 'from the table's top')

It can be seen that the nominal suffixes, originally mastered in relation to nouns (e.g. ev-de 'in the house' [literally: 'house-at'], ev-den 'from the house' ['house-from']), can be simply extended to postpositions, which are formally nouns. These locative postpositions are easily analyzable and semantically transparent; that is, each one is the name of a familiar location (e.g. arka 'back', yan 'side', alt 'bottom', etc.). One might predict, then, on formal grounds, that the entire set would be quickly and easily mastered.

However, the underlying spatial-relational notions differ in complexity and have their own developmental history. The order of emergence of locative postpositions in a production test follows a developmental history roughly similar to child speech in Indo-European languages, and matches perfectly an order of acquisition based on cognitive grounds proposed by Johnston and Slobin (1979): 'in'/'on'/'under' < 'beside' < 'back with objects having back-front orientation' < 'front with objects having back-front orientation' < 'between' < 'back with unoriented objects' < 'front with unoriented objects'. Thus early acquisition of a formal expression can only facilitate language development within limits set by cognitive development upon the content which can be encoded by the child.

7.2. Conjunctions

Clancy, Jacobsen, and Silva (1976) studied longitudinal and cross-sectional speech data between the ages of 1;2 and 4;8 in Turkish, English, Italian, and German, tracking the order of acquisition of conjunction types. They found very similar crosslinguistic orders of acquisition, which they summarize in the following terms, appealing to cognitive pacesetting as the underlying explanation (pp. 79–80):

> The very earliest conjoined sentences express notions of symmetric coordination, antithesis, sequence, and causality. Soon after the early causal statements, the first conditional notions emerge, appended to simple directives. At the next stage we find early "when" statements, which are both conditional and temporal. In all cases, the use of "when" expressing sequences of states and events precedes notions of simultaneity, which describe two overlapping actions or states. The last development we find is the use of "before" and "after" in subordinate clauses. The consistency of these findings across the four languages suggests an underlying cognitive basis for the order of emergence we have discussed.

The cognitively-based sequence of development, however, interacts with surface complexity of the corresponding structures. We find the following developmental series in our data: (1) The earliest means for temporal and causal relations between clauses (from about 2;0 to 2;6) is simple juxtaposition of two propositions without the use of any explicit grammatical means of connection. Often one proposition is provided by the adult, the child responding with an addition. Verb inflections indicate tense and modality in each clause. (2) During the next year (about 2;6 to 3;6) we find the use of connectives which do not require nominalization of the verb, either in the form of separate conjunctions between full clauses, such as the equivalents of 'then' and 'so that', or in the form of converbs, in which a suffix on the first, nonfinite verb indicates its temporal relation to the subsequent, finite verb, as in the following examples from children of 3;0 and 3;4:

Ben   gel   -ince   *okuyalım.*
I   come   CONVERB (= 'when')   read+OPT+1PL
'Let's read when I come (back).'

Bunu   ben   gid   −erken   *giyiyorum.*
this+ACC   I   go   CONVERB (= 'while')   wear+PRES+1SG
'I wear this while walking.'

(3) After age 4;0 one finds the use of connectives which involve nominalization of the verb for subordination, such as examples discussed above in regard to causal subordination. At this stage, temporal relations can be expressed by

relative clauses modifying the word *zaman* 'time', as in the following example, in which a child of 4;8 explains when it is that his mother does the housecleaning:

Hizmetçimiz	*gel*	*-me*	*-diğ*	*–i*	*zaman*	*annem*
our+maid	come	NEG	OBJ.REL.PART	POSS	time	my+mother

yapıyor.
do+PRES+3SG

'When our maid doesn't come, my mother does (it).'
(literally, 'at the time of our maid's not coming')

Thus, although there is evidence of cognitive pacesetting of the interclausal relations that can be expressed, development of the various means of expression is clearly tied to psycholinguistic constraints on formal acquisition. Again, we find an early preference for distinctly identifiable separate clauses, and late acquisition of participial forms. It is interesting that the gerund-like converbs seem to be easier than the noun-like participials. The converbs, more clearly maintaining their verbal identity, may form a bridge towards the eventual recognition of more opaque nonfinite and deverbal constructions.

7.3. *Tense-Aspect-Modality*

The adult language provides a three-way split between past, present, and future, with further subdivision of present into progressive and habitual, and of past into witnessed and nonwitnessed. The child, however, begins with a simpler set of distinctions, similar to those formed by children speaking a variety of other types of languages. The course of development goes from a cognitively-based framework of distinguishing between punctual vs. ongoing, dynamic events, to the later marking of states, and eventually to the set of linguistically-based distinctions encoded in the language.

Aksu (1978) has documented a developmental sequence of tense forms in a longitudinal study of three children beginning at 1;9. Two verb inflections were present by 21 months, used to mark aspectual (event characteristics) rather than tense distinctions. The past tense, -*dI*, encoded punctual changes of state resulting in immediately observable end states at the time of speech (completive-resultant aspect); the progressive -*Iyor* marked durational events. The -*dI* suffix evolved into a general past tense, as the child became cognizant of the fact that a current state is the result of a past process. This process is suggestive of Piaget's early observation (1927; transl. 1969, p. 284) that temporal thought for the very small child is characterized by "living purely in the present and assessing the past exclusively by its results."

A further development in the Turkish past tense system is the distinction between witnessed (-*dI*) and nonwitnessed (-*mIş*) modalities (for psycholinguistic details, see Slobin & Aksu, 1982). The -*mIş* inflection is used in the adult language to encode inference from physical evidence of a past state of affairs, as well as hearsay—i.e. to distinguish directly-experienced events (*-dI*) from indirect experience (*-mIş*). In child speech, the *-mIş* inflection emerges later, first being limited to picture descriptions and story-telling (among its standard uses), and for the encoding of states with some stative verbs. For example, a child of 2;3, looking at a picture book, said of a stative condition: *o dur-muş orda* 'it stand-*mIş* (=stood) there', using *-mIş,* followed by a description of a dynamic event with *-dI: adam vur-du eşeği* '(the) man hit-*dI* (the) donkey'. Thus the first use of *-mIş* simply refers to a stative event without carrying any inferential connotation. At this stage there is a distinction between ongoing event (*-Iyor*), past event (*-dI*), and state (*-mIş*). Later, *-mIş* evolves into a past-tense marker of indirect experience. The cognitive link in development is apparently from a current state to inference of the preceding process, just as the *-dI* past tense evolved from immediate changes of state to past processes generally. Thus, at first, the cognitive processes underlying the development of both past-tense forms are similar, with the *-mIş* form emerging about three months later than the *-dI* form. This lag may be due to the added complexity of the act of making an inference about a past process as compared to that of reconstructing the process from memory on the basis of its observable end results. Both forms gradually extend to refer to events of the nonimmediate past, but clear differentiation of the two forms is not stabilized until about 4;0. The nonwitnessed modality clearly requires some advanced cognitive skills, including the abilities: (1) to distinguish between different kinds of knowledge on the basis of their source, i.e. direct versus indirect, (2) the construction of an information-speaker relationship, i.e. the informational perspective of a speaker, and (3) the ability to recognize what constitutes justifiable evidence for the assertion of indirectly acquired information in the language. As suggested in Section 8, below, formal marking of this modality may even play some role in drawing children's attention to the relevant distinctions.

The latest phase in the acquisition of these forms is the emergence of the hearsay function of the *-mIş* form. Marking information for its source seems to be the most complex function cognitively; in that it requires the child to consider different informational perspectives at the same time. The overall sequence of past-tense development, analyzed in detail by Aksu (1978), shows a subtle interaction between cognitive and linguistic abilities in regard to notions of temporality, evidentiality, and communication.

Savaşır (1983) and Savaşır and Gee (1982) have recently developed the notion of "activity type" to situate patterned use of language forms in a framework of intention and interaction as well as cognition. Savaşır has explored the development of future reference in Turkish from this point of view. He finds an early level in which the future tense morpheme *-EcEk* is used to express both the child's own intentions to act, and the consequences or results of her actions. Later, distinctions emerge between these future perspectives. By 2;4 some children distinguish intentions and consequences, using the following forms in different types of activities: (1) The optative is used in joint play, in which child and adult plan out future actions. Savaşir considers the optative to express a confluence of the child's own desires with collective motivation or sanction for carrying out these desires: "The optative seems to identify an action as belonging to a conventionally coded and intersubjectively motivated activity. . . . [She] uses the optative whenever she regards her actions as being dependent upon the approval of her (adult) interlocutor" (1983, p. 49). (2) First-person future tense *-EcEğ-Im* is used to express actions the child intends to carry out on her own. (3) The aorist *-Ir* is used to describe the results of the child's actions, without focusing on the child as actor.

Any discussion of cognitive pacesetting of linguistic development, accordingly, must be embedded in a conception of the communicative and social activities in which particular forms are used. A similar discussion of activity types in regard to the past tense, for example, could add depth to the finding that the hearsay use of *-mIş* is a late development. The form is undoubtedly conceptually complex; however, at the same time, we need to know more about the kinds of discourse situations in which children are called upon to make distinctions in regard to source of information. Looked at most broadly, "cognitive" pacesetting of language acquisition embraces not only the concepts underlying particular grammatical and semantic distinctions, but also the child's conceptualizations of the contexts and goals of talk.

8. Linguistic Pacesetting of Cognitive Development

There is no evidence that aspects of Turkish acquisition influence the cognitive development of Turkish children. The precocious acquisition of inflectional morphology has no obvious effects on other aspects of development, though this may be an interesting topic for future research. An intriguing research task would be to investigate the possibility that marking of the distinction between direct experience and inference/hearsay might make Turkish children more sensitive at an early age to issues of evidence, point of view, and source of information.

It is also worth considering the possible influence that certain distinctions may have on social cognition. Such evidence can be obtained from studies of the acquisition of different social functions of language which require control over an interacting set of social variables and rules (e.g., forms of address, polite requests, honorifics, verbal argumentations). In a developmental study of requests, Aksu (1973, 1974) found the politeness requirements underlying different surface forms and the social factors determining appropriateness in context to be very similar for Turkish and English, supporting the suggestion that the underlying assumptions of this speech act are universal (Lakoff, 1972; Ervin-Tripp, 1977). The order and age of acquisition of the different surface realizations were found to be similar in the two languages. The most polite forms expressed in the interrogative (embedded imperatives) were acquired latest. This is despite the fact that question formation is an early acquisition in Turkish, due to morphosyntactic simplicity. Given that the syntactic means in question is used much earlier for different functions (in this case, asking information questions or making declarative statements with the aorist or optative tense-aspect modality inflections), though not for the pragmatic function, the reason for late emergence of polite forms must be either (a) some underlying cognitive ability, or (b) the underlying knowledge of the relevant social-conventional rules for that function, or both. To the extent that making polite requests rests on the cognitive ability for taking the point of view of the other—recognizing that s/he has an option for noncompliance, and the like—we have another instance of cognitive pacesetting of linguistic development. On the other hand, evidence shows that children acquire the polite forms as a result of overt verbal socialization by adults (as discussed in Section 9.4 below). That is, the linguistic options that the child is trained to utilize in different contexts bring about learning of the critical social differentiations regarding status relationships, and thus influence the acquisition of knowledge of social conventional rules. As such, we have an instance of linguistic pacesetting of cognitive development. Indeed, Halliday (1973) has stressed this dependence, pointing to the reciprocal interaction between the semantic system of a language and the learning of the social system.

In Turkish, there is the additional marking of status relationships with a *sen-siz* 'tu-vous' distinction which children are explicitly taught to observe. The presence of such a distinction in the language might facilitate the discovery of rules of social interaction prevalent in the culture. Comparative studies between languages making such distinctions might reveal interesting facts about the facilitative effects of language on social development.

Similarly, use of the linguistic medium in the teaching of culturally effective modes of negotiation has been observed by Schieffelin (1979, 1985) in a Kaluli-speaking New Guinea tribe, suggesting the value of comparative developmental study of discourse functions of language. Clancy's observations (1985) on the early acquisition of the pragmatics of Japanese sentence-final particles also point to linguistically-mediated learning of norms of social interaction.

9. Input and Adult-Child Interaction

9.1. Word Order

The input is characterized by variable word order, employed in normal pragmatic fashion by adults in speaking to children (see Slobin, 1975, for crosslinguistic comparisons and Turkish examples). Although SOV is the dominant order, it represents only 48% of adult speech in a broad sample of input to preschoolers. In a sample of 500 adult utterances to a child of 3;2, the first noun in the sentence was the subject only 47% of the time. (Consequently, over half the sentences addressed to the child began with a case-inflected noun.) In addition, adults change word order in the face of noncomprehension or non-compliance on the part of a child, often resulting in extensions and elaborations of the child's utterance in a different order than that initially used by the child. Consider, for example, the following interchange between an adult and a girl of 2;4, in which the child's OV utterances are first responded to in OV order (confirming the child's request), and then responded to in VO order (foregrounding the adult's insistence that the act be carried out):

Child: *Ben onu   koyayım   mı?*
             I   it+ACC   put+OPT   Q
             'Should I put it (in)?'

Adult: *Koy! Onu   da   koy   bakalım.*
            put   it+ACC   too   put   let's:see
            'Put it (in)! Let's see you put that one in too.'

Child: *Onu   da   koyayım   mı?*
             it+ACC   too   put+OPT   Q
             'Should I put that one (in) too?'

Adult: *Koy bakalım   onu   da.*
            put   let's:see   it+ACC   too
            'Let's see you put that one in too.'

The input, therefore, provides little basis for the induction of word-order rules to identify basic grammatical relations, while providing ample basis for the induction of pragmatic word-order rules. Indeed, this is consistent with the findings reported above in regard to early and appropriate use of pragmatic variations in word order. Furthermore, as discussed in Section 12.1.2, below, Turkish children do not use word-order strategies in sentence comprehension tests (Slobin & Bever, 1982), relying instead on case inflections as signals of grammatical relations. Data of production and comprehension thus demonstrate that Turkish children have accurately induced the roles of both word order and inflection in the input language.

9.2. *Inflection*

The input does provide ample opportunities for the discovery of inflectional principles. At an early period, as pointed out above, unanalyzed forms (amalgams) picked up from parental speech often contain the equivalents of English function words, since these tend to be suffixed morphemes, usually bearing stress, and therefore part of imitated lexical material. Roots are generally mono- or bisyllabic, so that most words will be imitated along with grammatical morphemes, providing the very young child with a rich data base for the induction of grammatical elements. As a consequence of this sort of morphological structure, the input precludes telegraphic imitation. Even short imitated sentences tend to contain the requisite grammatical morphology.

Question-answer sequences clearly exemplify the grammatical morphology, since the same affixes appear on questions and corresponding answers. The common adult-child interaction routines may thus function to direct attention to suffixes, since they remain constant across question and answer. For example, a parent asks a 2-year-old, *Kimi gördün?* 'Whom did you see?' (with the accusative inflection on the question word, *kim*) and the reply is *Ahmedi* or *Muradı*, providing a name with the same accusative inflection. Similar grammatical parallelism is seen in all question-answer pairs.

In addition, such correspondence between the affixes of question-answer pairs might be functional for the differentiation of the various "wh-words" from one another and the discovery of conjoining or adverbial structures that would be semantically appropriate in their answers. For example, the three forms of the question 'why', *ne-DEN, n-İÇİN,* and *n-İYE,* share the same affixes with three different causal connectives, *on-DAN* 'that-ABL' (= 'from that', i.e. 'because of that'), *o-nun İÇİN* 'that-GEN for' ('for that', i.e. 'for that reason'), and *di-YE* 'say-DAT' (= 'for'), among a set of others. This might be why children up to 3;0 years can produce a response which is semantically empty or irrelevant but contains some kind of causal connective indicating the correct recognition of the question type (Aksu, 1975). Thus, input is significant in leading the child to linguistic structures from surface cues, but the conceptual content of language is dependent on the child's cognitive developmental level.

9.3. *Discourse Scaffolding*

Adult-child discourse provides (a) a skeletal structure or frame which constitutes a base for the construction of the child's utterances, (b) the context in which the child can simultaneously exploit and master the means for establishing cohesive relations in his or her language, and (c) the linguistic content to be acquired. Clear examples of the interactive role of discourse can be seen in the use of anaphoric reference and ellipsis, which allow for the communication of intentions in "grammatically incomplete but contextually appropriate and interpretable sentence fragments" (Lyons, 1977, p. 589). A relevant Turkish example is the acquisition of causal connectives (Aksu, 1975), which were found to emerge first in response to adult questions and only later in spontaneous utterances. Furthermore, forms that were acquired first were those which can make deictic or anaphoric reference within the situational or verbal context (namely, *işte,* a deictic adverb; *ondan* and *onun için,* demonstrative pronouns marked for the ablative and genitive cases, respectively). These forms thus allow the child to build on the prior adult utterance, freeing him/her of the necessity of constructing an entire conjoined cause-effect statement. As discussed above, structures which conjoin two clauses in complex syntactic interdependence emerge later (nominalizers *-dIğI için* and *-mEk için*). The possibility of ellipsis between speakers, however, facilitates the acquisition of both types of connectives, with the parent providing a portion that the child can build on.

9.4. Politeness Norms

Rules that underlie the different social functions of speech are implicitly or explicitly presented to the child in the course of social interaction. Middle-class Turkish children go through an explicit socialization process for polite requests in which they are repeatedly prompted by adults to "talk nicely." Request forms expressing degrees of politeness are acquired in a progressive sequence between the ages of 2 and 4: (1) *ver* 'give' (bare imperative); (2) *ver-sene* 'give' (imperative + "softener"); (3) *ver-ir-mi-sin* 'will you:familiar give' ('give-AORIST-Q-2SG'); (4) *ver-ir-mi-siniz* 'will you:polite give' ('give-AORIST-Q-2PL'). Most explicit adult attention is paid to the use of the more polite forms marked by the second person plural, lexical forms like 'please', and polite vocatives. This is one aspect of language development in which one observes conscious modeling and reinforcement on the part of adults.

10. Individual Differences

Turkish developmental data have not yet been analyzed in terms of individual differences.

CONCLUSIONS

11. Reorganizations in Development

Under this heading we suggest some development periods in the acquisition of Turkish during which the child has to carry out a reorganization of the underlying principles of some domain of the language in order to move on towards a more mature system.

11.1. Simple and Complex Sentences

Inflectional strategies for comprehending simple sentences develop early in Turkish—by 2;0 in the Slobin and Bever (1982) experimental study. Case inflections clearly identify grammatical roles of nouns, and are used consistently and productively in speech well before 2;0. At some point, however, Turkish children must come to terms with the fact that matters are not so direct in embedded clauses of various types, with nonfinite or participial verbs and noncanonical casemarking. As discussed in Section 12.1.3, below, children as old as 4;8 fail to identify relative clauses in an experimental task, acting out only main clauses according to strategies for simple sentences. We have noted numerous problems in mastering relative clauses and complement structures in child speech. A major reorganization for Turkish children must involve recognition that not all verb endings are part of the finite conjugational patterns, followed by a period of protracted sorting out of the functions of the various means of indicating clause type on the verb. As we suggested above, in the discussion of cognitive pacesetting and the development of connectives (Section 7.2), adverbial converbs may provide the child with the first clue to this necessary reorganization in sentence structure. Eventually, the child must realize a clear distinction between simple sentences and main clauses, on the one hand, and all subordinated and embedded clauses on the other.

11.2. *Lexical Reorganization*

The errors of overmarking and undermarking observed with regard to passive and causative particles strongly suggest that a reorganizational process is responsible for the final correct organization of the verbal lexicon. At some point there must be a reanalysis of the underlying semantic structure of certain verbs, such as lexical causatives and inherently passive or reflexive verbs, resulting in the abstraction of a subcategory for which a given rule does not apply (e.g., verbs which cannot be transitivized by addition of the causative particle). In these domains the child must come to realize what Clark and Hecht (1982, p. 6) have called the "principle of conventionality": "For certain meanings, there is a conventional word or word-form device that should be used in the language community." Conventionality must come to override productive word-formation principles for particular verbs.

In addition, the verb lexicon must eventually be organized to take account of the valences required by individual verbs and classes of verbs. It appears that all acquisitions of verbal predicates involve a process of analysis of the underlying semantic configuration inherent in the verb. As part of the Berkeley Cross-Linguistic Acquisition Study, children between the ages of 2;0 and 4;8 were asked why-questions involving four different verbs ('run', 'bite', 'drink', and 'scratch'), such as 'Why do dogs bite?'. Developmental changes in response to these questions suggest that such a process of forming predicate configurations proceeds through the following phases: (1) a global understanding of the predicate only in terms of the general nature of the action involved; (2) analysis of the predicate into its different underlying components, with differential focus or value attached to each, depending on the nature of the verb (e.g. focus on the patient of transitive verbs, on the manner of activity for intransitive verbs, etc.), verbalizing all of the associated arguments (e.g. Agent-Action-Patient).

11.3. *Tense-Aspect Reorganization*

The eventual acquisition of the semantic functions of marking the past of direct experience (*-dI*) versus the past of indirect experience (*-mIş*), also seems to be the result of a reorganization of the underlying semantic domain, as discussed in Section 7.3, above. The child must come to realize the range of notions—temporal, modal, and aspectual—that control the use of verb inflections.

11.4. *Referential and Pragmatic Use of Pronouns*

As discussed in Section 6.1.2, above, Slobin and Talay have found that children appropriately prepose and postpose subject pronouns in response to pragmatic issues of information and focus. However, it seems that, overall, subject pronouns appear more frequently in the child transcripts than they would in adult speech. That is, although the pragmatic functions of pronoun placement appear to have been mastered, children also hold onto pronouns for their strictly referential value, overusing pronouns where adults would more normally delete them. Thus children have to reorganize their rules for language use at some point, realizing that the semantic information carried by a pronoun can be conveyed by the corresponding verb inflection, while overt use of the pronoun itself conveys specifically discourse-marked information. Similar overmarking is noted in regard to the acquisition of other languages in this volume, suggesting a general developmental transition from explicit surface marking of underlying semantic notions to more flexible use of elaborated and condensed expression of a particular notion in relation to broader discourse needs than simply referential communication.

12. Operating Principles

The notion of "Operating Principles" for language acquisition comes from Slobin (1973), and has been elaborated by MacWhinney (1978, 1985) and Peters (1983, 1985). Operating principles are strategies for the perception, production, and analysis of speech. They are part of the initial equipment of language acquisition, and are phrased as "self-instructions" to the language acquisition device. (The phrasing, however, is simply for clarity; equivalent formulations in third-person passives or in invented symbolic notations would not change the status of Operating Principles as initial strategies of processing and structuring language.) The principles suggested in this chapter build on principles suggested in Slobin (1973, 1982), but precede the reformulations presented in Slobin's chapter in this series (1985).

The Operating Principles suggested below are presented in three groups: (1) receptive principles, which guide processes of perceptual segmentation, analysis, and interpretation of speech; (2) speech production principles, which play a role in the child's own speech; and (3) rule formulational principles, which guide the child in the construction of grammatical systems.

12.1. *Receptive Principles*

12.1.1. *Ends of Units.* Slobin's (1973) Operating Principle, "Pay attention to the ends of words," is probably at play in the precocious acquisition of suffixed morphology and postpositions. Virtually all grammatical morphemes are of this sort in Turkish; in addition, they are always syllabic and generally receive stress. These factors make grammatical morphemes perceptually salient and available to immediate memory. Most of these morphemes are joined to the preceding word by vowel harmony. Since roots are generally short, with a high proportion of monosyllables, even very early imitated words will be stored with their associated grammatical markers, thus providing a stock of useful "amalgams" (MacWhinney, 1978) for later grammatical analysis.

12.1.2. *Local Cues.* A number of phenomena, summarized by Slobin (1982), point to the role of surface cues to underlying structure in facilitating children's sentence processing in Turkish (as reflected in the Operating Principle: "Underlying semantic relations should be marked overtly and clearly"). Ammon and Slobin (1979) introduced the notion of "local cue" to explain the facilitatory role of case inflections and verb participles in sentence comprehension tests. On the level of simple sentences (Slobin & Bever, 1982), Turkish children as young as 2;0 correctly interpret all six possible orders of subject, verb, and object when asked to act out reversible transitive sentences with toy animals (e.g. 'the horse kicks the cow'), whereas children acquiring a fixed word-order language like English do not correctly interpret noun-verb-noun sequences until about 2;6. Interpretation of the Turkish sentences can be based simply upon noticing which noun has an accusative inflection, whereas the word-order pattern of the entire English sentence must be taken into account in identifying subject and object. The accusative inflection is a LOCAL cue in that it operates on a localized sentence element. It applies to a particular noun, regardless of its position, and can be processed without taking the entire sentence into account. (Thus word-order languages may impose a greater burden on short-term processing capacity, with a correspondingly later emergence of word-order strategies in sentence comprehension.)

Ammon and Slobin (1979) have made a similar argument in regard to a comprehension test of causative-instigative sentences (e.g. 'the horse makes the camel run'). In Turkish, the instigated animal (the camel) is marked with the accusative inflection, and the verb contains an infixed causative particle, as discussed above. For example, the Turkish version of this particular test item was:

At	deve	-yi	koş	-tur	-sun.
horse	camel	ACC	run	CAUS	OPT

Both of these cues (ACC and CAUS) seem to facilitate comprehension of such sentences in comparison with the Indo-European periphrastic means of expression (*make . . . run*).

Another sort of local cue may play a role in facilitating comprehension of constructions with 'before' (Slobin, 1982). Turkish grammar honors the fact that the consequent clause in a before-construction may encode an event which has not occurred (e.g. 'I caught the glass before it broke'). This notion is reflected in the presence of a negative particle in the subordinate clause (something like, 'the glass not-having-broken first, I caught'). This particle may well function as a local cue, making the meaning of such constructions more accessible to the young child.

12.1.3. *Transfer of Processing Strategies.*   There seems to be a processing principle: "Attempt to apply the strategies for processing simple sentences to complex sentences." We have noted that 2-year-olds use an inflectional strategy to identify the object in reversible transitive sentences, and that slightly older children use the same strategy to identify the object in causative sentences in comprehension tests. The same strategy is used by 4-year-olds in attempting to interpret complex relative clause sentences in tests. In this test (Slobin, 1982; following Sheldon, 1974), children were asked to act out relations between three animals (e.g., 'The donkey that the sheep touches rubs the camel'). The four sentences and the relevant results are presented in Table 9.1. None of the children tested (up to age 4;8) correctly performed a single one of these instructions (although English-speaking children of a comparable age can correctly interpret some of these forms). Generally a single action was carried out, and the nature of such partial responses reveals the use of an inflectional strategy. As one would expect, the children consistently ignored the embedded verb, which is always a nominalized form (perhaps even unrecognizable as a verb) and performed the action of the final verb, which appears in the normal position for Turkish. The patient was always the accusative noun in its normal preverbal position at the end

TABLE 9.1

Schematic Descriptions

of Turkish Relative Clause Constructions[a]

---

(1) *subject embedded, object focus:*
      The donkey that the sheep touches rubs the camel.
      Sheep-GEN   touch-OBJ.REL.PART-POSS   DONKEY   camel-ACC   rubs.
(2) *subject embedded, subject focus:*
      The donkey that touches the sheep rubs the camel.
      Sheep-ACC   touch-SUBJ.REL.PART   DONKEY   camel-ACC   rubs.
(3) *object embedded, object focus:*
      The donkey touches the sheep that the camel rubs.
      DONKEY   camel-GEN   rub-OBJ.REL.PART-POSS   sheep-ACC   touches.
(4) *object embedded, subject focus:*
      The donkey touches the sheep that rubs the camel.
      DONKEY   camel-ACC   rub-SUBJ.REL.PART   sheep-ACC   touches.

---

[a]Animal name in capital letters indicates participant most frequently selected as agent of single action. (Patient was always the third animal, given in the accusative before the final, finite verb.)

of the sentence. Local cues play their role in the choice of agent. Turkish children do not pick the first noun as agent, which one would expect in the case of word-order strategy, just as they do not pick the first noun as agent in the transitive sentence comprehension test (unless it is in the uninflected, subject case). Their procedure seems to be to scan the sentence for the first uninflected noun (i.e. subject noun), as indicated by the animal name in capital letters in Table 9.1. If the initial noun is marked as nonsubject (by the accusative or genitive inflection) it is passed over, as in the transitive task. Thus, several years after the acquisition of simple sentences Turkish children employ the same strategies in encountering complex sentences. In the case of sentences with relative clauses, this strategy results in isolation of the main clause (which may eventually facilitate the comprehension of such constructions, along with the necessary reorganization in comprehension of verbmarking discussed above).

12.2. Speech Production Principles

12.2.1. *Analysis Reflected in Enunciation.* There is some evidence for a speech production interpretation of Slobin's Operating Principle (1973), "Underlying semantic relations should be marked overtly and clearly." Shortly after the emergence of the agglutinated inflectional systems in the second year of life, there seems to be an exaggerated tendency to clearly mark morpheme boundaries in some utterances, especially those containing long strings of agglutinated morphemes. Some children have been observed to put heavy stress on each morpheme, with a slight pause between morphemes. This is especially evident in verbs containing particles such as negative, abilitative, and tense-aspect.

12.2.2. *Reliance on Situational Support.* A speech production principle that would apply at the level of discourse can be suggested. As was discussed above, production of question responses and complex spontaneous utterances appears to be facilitated by the presence of some of the elements of the proposition in the preceding adult or child utterance, which can then be presupposed through anaphoric reference and ellipsis. That is, the context of discourse provides some global cues that trigger the use of cohesive mechanisms that operate either on the whole of a sentence or on an element of it. To the extent that procedures of cohesion allow for economy of expression, their use can be said to facilitate production. Thus, there may be an Operating Principle which states: "Presuppose as much relevant propositional content as possible, either from the situational or the linguistic context; proceed onwards using local cues you may have picked from the presupposed material."

12.3. Rule Formation Principles

12.3.1. *Semantic Transparency.* On the rule-formation side, the Operating Principle to mark semantic relations overtly and clearly plays a role in facilitating the early acquisition of the morphological system. Each morpheme tends to express a single element of meaning, without fusion (e.g. noun + plural + possessive + case), and there are almost no homonymous suffixes. The system is close to a 1:1 mapping of semantic elements and surface forms. Many of the reasons suggested above for error-free acquisition of this system undoubtedly relate to the ease with which rule systems of this sort can be acquired by young children.

Some of the errors discussed above also reveal a tendency to prefer uniform, 1:1 mappings of form and meaning. The insertion of redundant or erroneous causative particles is one example. It can also be argued that one of the reasons for late acquisition of relative clause and verb complement constructions is that they involve embedded sentences which no longer look like sentences, thus posing difficulty for a rule-formational system oriented to clear mapping from underlying to surface form.

12.3.2. *Limited Plurifunctionality.*   There may be an Operating Principle to the effect that: "Grammatical functors should have limited and consistent semantic functions." In regard to the case-inflectional system, diversity of functions of a given surface form should pose difficulties. This may be one reason why children avoid interpreting a noun marked by the genitive case as the subject of a relative clause, in sentence-comprehension experiments. Similarly, we have noted above that children avoid marking the subject with the genitive case in some verb complement constructions.

12.3.3. *Direct Order of Mention.*   Although Turkish word order is quite free within sentences, there is evidence for a preference to order conjoined clauses on semantic grounds. Evidence from free speech and response to *why*-questions (Aksu, 1975) indicates a preference for order of mention to mirror the order of occurrence of referent events, as attested in numerous studies in English (e.g. Clark, 1973). The Turkish child has several options in conjoining causally related clauses. The simplest option, on formal grounds, is the use of the conjunction *çünkü* 'because', which joins two full sentences, as in English. However, this option requires reversed order of mention (e.g., 'I woke up because the clock rang'). In order to maintain direct order of mention, Turkish requires that the cause be expressed as a nominalized participle followed by a postposition indicating causal relationship (something like, 'the clock's ringing therefore, I woke up'). These are the sorts of constructions, as we have pointed out, which children tend to avoid. However, avoidance of morphological and syntactic complexity in this instance would lead the child to the cognitive problems of reversed order of mention. The solution is to attempt the more complex morpho-syntactic forms and fail to be fully grammatical, maintaining direct order of mention. Thus children as old as 4;8 will incorrectly use these forms, making errors in participle formation or replacing the participle with the finite verb, rather than using the formally simpler *because*-construction.

13. Suggestions for Further Study

The set of 12 proposed factors facilitating morphological acquisition in Turkish can be examined by studying the acquisition of other inflectional languages, making it possible to pull apart some of the factors.

Faced with difficulties in forming relative clause and verb complement constructions, the Turkish child is driven to devise various sorts of circumlocutions and periphrastic constructions. It would be valuable to study such forms in order to better understand the range of expressive options available to children. Comparisons with pidgin and creole languages may be instructive in this regard (Slobin, 1977), as well as examination of historical changes in Turkic relative clause constructions, both under internal pressures and in response to language-contact situations with languages using more transparent relative clause constructions (Slobin, in press).

The distinction between witnessed and nonwitnessed modalities in the past tense may have effects on cognitive abilities to attend to sources of evidence and draw inferences. A comparative cognitive study between Turkish children and children in languages lacking this distinction would be informative.

We need to have much more data on a number of issues: earliest stages of productive grammar; adult input; individual differences; coordination of the large set of verbal affixes for modality, aspect, and tense; pragmatic uses of word order and particles; relations between grammar and discourse in various genres; development of prosody and its interaction with semantics and pragmatics.

REFERENCES

Aksu, A. *The development of request forms in Turkish children.* Unpublished paper, Department of Psychology, University of California, Berkeley, 1973.

Aksu, A. *Order of emergence of request forms in terms of semantic complexity.* Unpublished paper, Department of Psychology, University of California, Berkeley, 1974.

Aksu, A. *Development of the expression of cause-effect relations in Turkish.* Unpublished paper, Department of Psychology, University of California, Berkeley, 1975. [Abbreviated version published as Aksu, A. The acquisition of causal connectives in Turkish. *Papers and Reports on Child Language Development* (Department of Linguistics, Stanford University)], 1978, No. 15, 129–139.]

Aksu, A. *Aspect and modality in the child's acquisition of the Turkish past tense.* Unpublished doctoral dissertation, University of California, Berkeley, 1978. (Cambridge University Press, in preparation.)

Ammon, M. S., & Slobin, D. I. A cross-linguistic study of the processing of causative sentences. *Cognition,* 1979, 7, 1–17.

Bybee, J.L. *Morphology: A study of the relation between meaning and form.* Amsterdam: John Benjamins, 1985.

Clancy, P. The acquisition of Japanese. In D. I. Slobin (Ed.), *The crosslinguistic study of language acquisition* (Vol. 1). Hillsdale, NJ: Lawrence Erlbaum Associates, 1985.

Clancy, P., Jacobsen, T., & Silva, M. The acquisition of conjunction: A cross-linguistic study.

Papers and Reports on Child Language Development (Department of Linguistics, Stanford University), 1976, No. 12, 71–80.

Clark, E. V. How children describe time and order. In C. A. Ferguson & D. I. Slobin (Eds.), *Studies of child language development*. New York: Holt, Rinehart & Winston, 1973.

Clark, E. V. Convention and innovation in acquiring the lexicon. *Papers and Reports on Child Language Development* (Department of Linguistics, Stanford University), 1980, No. 19, 1–20.

Clark, E. V., & Hecht, B. F. Learning to coin agent and instrument nouns. *Cognition*, 1982, *12*, 1–24.

Ekmekçi, Ö. F. *Acquisition of Turkish: A longitudinal study on the early language development of a Turkish child*. Unpublished doctoral dissertation, University of Texas, Austin, 1979.

Ekmekçi, Ö. F. Significance of word order in the acquisition of Turkish. In D. I. Slobin & K. Zimmer (Eds.), *Studies in Turkish linguistics*, in press.

Enç, M. Topic switching and pronominal subjects in Turkish. In D. I. Slobin & K. Zimmer (Eds.), *Studies in Turkish linguistics*. Amsterdam: John Benjamins, in press.

Erguvanlı, E. E. *The function of word order in Turkish grammar*. Berkeley: University of California Press, 1984.

Ervin-Tripp, S. Wait for me, roller skate! In S. Ervin-Tripp & C. Mitchell-Kernan (Eds.), *Child discourse*. New York: Academic Press, 1977.

Greenberg, J. H. Some universals of grammar with particular reference to the order of meaningful elements. In J. H. Greenberg (Ed.), *Universals of language*. Cambridge, MA: MIT Press, 1963.

Hakuta, K. Word order and particles in the acquisition of Japanese. *Papers and Reports on Child Language Development* (Department of Linguistics, Stanford University), 1977, No. 13, 110–117.

Halliday, M. A. K. *Explorations in the functions of language*. London: Edward Arnold, 1973.

Johnson, J. R., & Slobin, D. I. The development of locative expressions in English, Italian, Serbo-Croatian and Turkish. *Journal of Child Language*, 1979, *6*, 529–545.

Lakoff, R. Language in context. *Language*, 1972, *48*, 907–927.

Lehmann, W. P. *Syntactic typology: Studies in the phenomenology of language*. Austin: University of Texas Press, 1978.

Lewis, G. L. *Teach yourself Turkish*. London: The English Universities Press, Ltd., 1953.

Lewis, G. L. *Turkish grammar*. Oxford: Oxford University Press, 1967.

Lyons, J. *Semantics*. Cambridge: Cambridge University Press, 1977.

MacWhinney, B. Processing a first language: The acquisition of morphophonology. *Monographs of the Society for Research in Child Development*, 1978, *43*(1–2).

MacWhinney, B. Hungarian language acquisition as an exemplification of a general model of grammatical development. In D. I. Slobin (Ed.), *The crosslinguistic study of language acquisition* (Vol. 2). Hillsdale, NJ: Lawrence Erlbaum Associates, 1985.

Özbaydar, B. 12–24 ay arasında dil gelişmesi. *İstanbul Üniversitesi Tecrübî Psikoloji Çalışmaları*, 1970, *8*, 79–86.

Peters, A. M. *The units of language acquisition*. New York: Cambridge University Press, 1983.

Peters, A. M. Language segmentation: Operating principles for perception and analysis of language. In D. I. Slobin (Ed.), *The crosslinguistic study of language acquisition* (Vol. 2). Hillsdale, NJ: Lawrence Erlbaum Associates, 1985.

Piaget, J. *Le développement de la notion de temps chez l'enfant*. Paris: Presses Universitaires de France, 1927. (Eng. transl. by A. J. Pomerans, *The child's conception of time*. New York: Routledge and Kegan Paul, 1969.)

Savaşır, I. *How many futures? A study of future reference in early child language*. Unpublished M.A. dissertation, University of California, Berkeley, 1983.

Savaşır, I., & Gee, J. The functional equivalents of the middle voice in child language. *Proceedings of the Eighth Annual Meeting of the Berkeley Linguistics Society*, 1982.

Schieffelin, B. S. *How Kaluli children learn what to say, what to do, and how to feel: An eth-*

nographic study of the development of communicative competence. Unpublished doctoral dissertation, Columbia University, 1979. (Cambridge University Press, in preparation.)

Schieffelin, B. S. The acquisition of Kaluli. In D. I. Slobin (Ed.), *The crosslinguistic study of language acquisition* (Vol. 1). Hillsdale, NJ: Lawrence Erlbaum Associates, 1985.

Sheldon, A. The role of parallel function in the acquisition of relative clauses in English. *Journal of Verbal Learning and Verbal Behavior,* 1974, *13,* 272–281.

Slobin, D. I. Cognitive prerequisites for the development of grammar. In C. A. Ferguson & D. I. Slobin (Eds.), *Studies of child language development.* New York: Holt, Rinehart & Winston, 1973.

Slobin, D. I. On the nature of talk to children. In E. H. Lenneberg & E. Lenneberg (Eds.), *Foundations of language development: A multidisciplinary approach* (Vol. 1). New York: Academic Press, 1975.

Slobin, D. I. Language change in childhood and in history. In J. Macnamara (Ed.), *Language learning and thought.* New York: Academic Press, 1977.

Slobin, D. I. The origins of grammatical encoding of events. In W. Deutsch (Ed.), *The child's construction of language.* London: Academic Press, 1981.

Slobin, D. I. Universal and particular in the acquisition of Language. In E. Wanner & L. R. Gleitman (Eds.), *Language acquisition: The state of the art.* Cambridge: Cambridge University Press, 1982.

Slobin D. I. Crosslinguistic evidence for the Language-Making Capacity. In D. I. Slobin (Ed.), *The crosslinguistic study of language acquisition* (Vol. 2). Hillsdale, NJ: Lawrence Erlbaum Associaties, 1985.

Slobin, D. I. The acquisition and use of relative clauses in Turkic and Indo-European languages. In D. I. Slobin & K. Zimmer (Eds.), *Studies in Turkish linguistics,* Amsterdam: John Benjamins, in press.

Slobin, D. I., & Aksu, A. A. Tense, aspect and modality in the use of the Turkish evidential. In P. J. Hopper (Ed.), *Tense-aspect: Between semantics and pragmatics.* Amsterdam: John Benjamins, 1982.

Slobin, D. I., & Bever, T. G. Children use canonical sentence schemas: A crosslinguistic study of word order and inflections. *Cognition,* 1982, *12,* 229–265.

Slobin, D. I., & Talay, A. Development of pragmatic uses of subject pronouns in Turkish child language. In A. Aksu-Koç & E. Taylan, *Proceedings of the Second Conference on Turkish linguistics.* Istanbul: Boğaziçi University Press, in press.

Stephany, U. *The modality constituent—a neglected area in the study of first language acquisition.* Universität Köln—Institut für Sprachwissenschaft: Arbeitspapier Nr. 36, 1978.

SIGNED LANGUAGES

10 The Acquisition of American Sign Language

Elissa L. Newport
Richard P. Meier
University of Illinois

Contents

INTRODUCTION

1. Descriptive Sketch of American Sign Language

American Sign Language (ASL) is a visual-gestural language which has arisen as a natural language within the deaf community of the United States and other parts of North America. In previous times it has been viewed as either a pantomimic (therefore non-linguistic) system, or a representation of English on the hands. Neither of these descriptions is correct, as we detail below. ASL is a fully grammaticized language, not a pantomimic communication system, and it displays the various grammatical characteristics typically found in spoken languages of the world, despite the apparent potential for a different type of organization offered by the visual-gestural modalities. However, it does not partake of these characteristics by representing English or any other spoken language; in fact, as can be seen from the details below, it is quite different typologically from English.

Unlike English, ASL is a morphologically complex language, perhaps most comparable to polysynthetic spoken languages. It differs from typologically similar spoken languages in at least two striking ways: First, because it apparently derives at least in part from nonlinguistic roots in gesture and pantomime, some "iconic" characteristics remain in the language, despite their significant historical modification and grammaticization. Second, apparently because of the character of visual-gestural perception and production, much of ASL phonology and morphology consists of units combined with one another simultaneously rather than sequentially. Thus, for example, although signs occur in sentences in sequence, as in spoken languages, morphemes within a sign often occur simultaneously (e.g. in ASL verbs of motion, the shape of the hand is one morpheme, while its path of movement is another).

For these and other reasons, the study of ASL acquisition may shed unique light on language acquisition processes more generally: comparisons of the acquisition of American Sign Language with the acquisition of spoken languages may help to delineate those aspects of acquisition which are universal over languages of varying types, and those aspects of acquisition which are specific to certain linguistic and modality-related typologies.

Before reviewing the literature on the acquisition of ASL, we briefly describe the structure of the language.

1.1. *Iconicity*

Unlike spoken languages where, as de Saussure (1915) noted, the relationship between form and meaning is arbitrary, that same relationship in ASL is often quite motivated. Many ASL signs are "iconic"; in other words, the visual form of such signs resembles in some way that of their referents. Thus, the sign BIRD[1] looks like the opening and closing of a bird's beak, and the sign TREE suggests a deciduous tree waving in the wind. However, as research has amply demonstrated, this iconicity is only partly present in ASL and is often quite irrelevant to the way the language is organized and processed.

Although signs in sign languages are indeed more highly motivated than most words of spoken languages, signs and words are alike in being highly conven-

---

[1]Following the conventions of the literature on American Sign Language, we use an English word in capital letters to represent a sign (e.g. BOY), and hyphenated English words in capital letters to represent a multi-morphemic sign in terms of its internal morphemes (e.g. HUMAN-MOVE-RANDOMLY).

tionalized. For example, the sign for 'tree' in Chinese Sign Language, unlike the corresponding ASL sign, seems to sketch the trunk, whereas the Danish sign sketches the shape of the crown and the trunk (Klima & Bellugi, 1979a). Thus even though all three signs are in some sense iconic, they are conventionalized in different ways within different (and mutually unintelligible) sign languages. The origin of a particular sign must thus be at least in part an arbitrary choice among the possible icons for a referent. Moreover, much of the vocabularly of ASL and other sign languages is indeed entirely arbitrary, just as in spoken languages. Some of the synchronically arbitrary signs may have iconic origins in early stages of the language but have lost their iconicity through processes of historical change (Frishberg, 1975); others have no apparent iconic source at all.

Perhaps most important, grammatical description of ASL rarely requires the linguist (or, apparently, the language user) to make reference to the iconic properties of signs: the grammatical rules of ASL are much like those of spoken languages, and therefore can be stated in the same terms as are the rules of spoken languages; and the processes of sign perception, memory, and acquisition of ASL show remarkably infrequent effects of iconicity (see for example, Klima & Bellugi, 1979a; Wilbur, 1979; and below).

1.2. *Phonology*

Early dictionaries of ASL typically described signs as global iconic wholes. However, in a groundbreaking study, Stokoe (1965) proposed an "emic" analysis of ASL, in which he described the form of signs in terms of three independent parameters: hand configuration, place of articulation, and movement. He further proposed that each parameter may assume only a limited number of values, or "primes." For example, primes for place of articulation include the nose and the forehead, but not portions of the face between these. Thus signs, like words in spoken languages, form minimal pairs with one another, and only certain values of physically possible articulations are contrastive in the language. Moreover, the inventory of primes and their permissible combinations are not the same in ASL as in other sign languages (Klima, Bellugi, & Siple, 1979). Greek etymology aside, then, the obvious parallels between the formational analysis of signs and the phonological description of speech justify the extension of the term "phonology" to encompass signed and spoken languages.

ASL phonology may differ from that of spoken languages in that, at least in now-traditional descriptions of ASL, the meaningless units of form are arrayed in a largely simultaneous fashion, unlike the sequential organization of phonemes in speech (Klima, Bellugi, Newkirk, & Battison, 1979). In such descriptions, the prime for handshape, place of articulation, and movement are articulated simultaneously. Even this may turn out not to be so, however: recent descriptions of portions of ASL have uncovered sequentiality more similar to that of spoken languages (see, for example, Supalla, 1982).

1.3. *Syntax*

The basic form classes in ASL, as in spoken languages, include nouns and pronouns, verbs, adjectives, and adverbs. ASL does not have prepositions; spatial relations conveyed by prepositions in English are represented by verbs in ASL, while case relations conveyed in prepositions in English are represented by morphological devices in ASL. Pronouns are of two types: Deictic pronouns consist of a point to the real-world location of a nearby referent; for example, the sign YOU is a point to the addressee. However, if the referent of a noun is not physically present within the conversational context, a spatial locus may be established for that noun by pointing to an arbitrary location within the space immediately surrounding the signer. Subsequent reference to this noun may then be made with an anaphoric pronoun, which is a point to this spatial locus.

ASL, like many spoken languages, has a basic or canonical word order (that is, sign order), but considerable word order flexibility. Verbs in ASL differ in whether they are inflected to agree with their noun arguments. Some verbs (particularly those articulated on the body) do not undergo agreement. For these verbs, then, word order is used to mark relations among the nouns. SVO order is the unmarked order; other orders are possible only when one of the constituents is topicalized (that is, fronted and marked with a grammatical facial expression for topic) (Fischer, 1973b; Fischer & Gough, 1978; Friedman, 1976; Liddell, 1980; Padden, 1983). Most verbs, however, are inflected to agree with their noun arguments. (This agreement process is described in Section 1.4. *Morphology*.) In sentences with verbs inflected for agreement, word order is quite flexible.

Grammaticized facial expressions are used as obligatory markers for topics (as described earlier), questions, negation, and subordinate clauses of various types (Liddell, 1980; Coulter, 1979; Padden, 1981).

1.4. *Morphology*

The inflectional and derivational morphology of ASL has received the most sustained attention of any aspect of the grammar of ASL. In the complexity of its morphology, as mentioned above, ASL more closely resembles polysynthetic languages like Navaho than it does English. With the exception of compounding and certain limited aspects of complex verbal stems, ASL morphology is largely simultaneously organized; the sign stem and its attendant morphology are often either totally simultaneous (as when the handshape is one morpheme and its path of movement is another morpheme) or at least heavily fusional (as when the direction of the verb stem is modified to agree with one of its noun arguments).

1.4.1. Verb Agreement: Inflectional Morphology for the Role of Noun Arguments. As mentioned earlier, many verbs in ASL are inflected to agree with their noun arguments. These inflections take the form of modifying the verb's location, orientation, and/or direction of movement to agree with the spatial loci of the relevant nouns (Fischer, 1973b; Fischer & Gough, 1978; Padden, 1983). Some verbs agree with only a single argument; if these verbs involve movement, they will then move toward or away from (depending on the individual verb) the locus of this argument, whereas if they do not involve movement, they will orient toward or be located at the locus of this argument. Other verbs may optionally agree with a second argument as well; in this case, the verb will move from the locus of one argument (typically the agent, source, or subject) to the locus of the other argument (typically the patient, goal, or object).

1.4.2. *Morphology of Verbal Stems.* Newport (1981) and Supalla (1982) have distinguished two classes of signs in ASL: one group which they have called the "frozen lexicon," which comprises unanalyzable, monomorphemic stems, and a second group, primarily verbs of motion and location, in which the stems are composed of a number of component morphemes. (In either case, inflections for aspect, number, etc. may be added to the stem.) Various phonological parameters which are meaningless in frozen signs are each morphemes within verbs of motion and location (Newport, 1981; Supalla, 1982). The handshape is a classifier for the semantic category (e.g. human vs. animate nonhuman vs. vehicle) or size and shape of the moving object; the movement path (one of a small number of discretely different movements, e.g. straight vs. circular vs. arc) is a morpheme representing the path of motion of the moving object; the manner of movement is a morpheme for the manner of motion along the path (e.g. bounce vs. roll vs. random); a second handshape (typically produced on the left hand) is a classifier for a secondary object, with respect to which the primary object moves; and the placement of the second handshape along the path is a morpheme for the spatial relationship of the movement path with respect to this secondary object (e.g. from vs. to vs. past).

1.4.3. *Derivational Morphology.* Just as the lexicon of English contains such pairs as *contrast* (noun) and *contrast* (verb), the ASL lexicon includes many formationally related noun-verb pairs. These pairs typically share the same hand configuration, place of articulation, and movement path; they differ, however, in that the noun has a restrained manner and a repeated movement, while the verb may have either a continuous or hold manner (depending on whether the action has a specified goal) and either a single or repeated movement (depending on whether the action is punctual or durative) (Supalla & Newport, 1978). These distinctions, which constitute derivational morphemes for nominal vs. verbal stems, are highly productive for concrete object-action noun-verb pairs, but (as in spoken languages) are only semiproductive for nominalization-verb pairs.

1.4.4. *Inflectional Morphology for Aspect and Number.* ASL contains numerous inflections for temporal aspect, distributive apect, and number (Fischer, 1973a; Supalla & Newport, 1978; Klima, Bellugi, Newkirk et al., 1979; Klima,

Bellu-gi, & Pedersen, 1979). Temporal inflections, which take the form of a dynamic pattern superimposed upon the verbal or adjectival stem, mark such distinctions as whether the action described by the verb is an iterated punctual action or a prolonged durative action, or whether the state described by the adjective is one to which a given person is highly susceptible. ASL possesses no inflectional markers of tense; rather, tense is marked lexically by such signs as WILL, PAST, and NOW.

Inflections for distributive aspect and number on verbs are marked by the displacement of the verb within the signing space. Thus, the dual inflection is marked on verbs whose actions are performed on two objects or in two locations; its form involves reduplicating the verb stem and performing the two iterations in two different spatial locations.

Related inflections for distribution and number can be applied to nouns, but with somewhat different grammatical restrictions and phonological outcomes (Supalla & Newport, 1978).

1.4.5. *Compounding.* There are several processes in ASL by which new signs may be formed by compounding two or more lexical stems (Klima & Bellugi, 1979b; Newport & Bellugi, 1979). Unlike many of the other processes of sign formation, the morphology of ASL compounding is sequential: the component lexical stems are sequenced in restricted ways, and the phonology of the compound is modified in regular ways from that of the component lexemes produced independently. One large class of lexical compounds, for example, involves phonologically reducing the first component and phonologically assimilating it in various ways to the second component; thus, unlike English, stress within these compounds falls on the second component rather than the first (Klima & Bellugi, 1979b). Other types of compounds involve somewhat different phonological processes (Newport & Bellugi, 1979).

2. Sources of Data

Linguistic work on ASL dates only to the early 1960s (Stokoe, 1960; Stokoe et al., 1965). Not surprisingly, then, the research on ASL acquisition is briefer still. However, in recent years a small explosion of work has deepened and broadened our understanding in this area. Unless stated otherwise, all of the work we will review investigates the acquisition of ASL as a native language, by congenitally deaf children whose parents are also deaf and are users of ASL; these children, like their counterparts in most studies of the acquisition of spoken languages, are acquiring ASL as their first language, from infancy, through everyday exposure to it in the home. From school-age and beyond, deaf signers are typically also exposed to English, either through training in speech and lipreading, through reading, or through exposure to a manual representation of English in school;

however, available statistics on English skills in the congenitally deaf suggest that the children (and their parents) have only limited knowledge of the syntax and morphology of English (for a review, see Wilbur, 1979).

Most of the data on the acquisition of ASL come from videotapes of spontaneous signing, collected and analyzed in ways comparable to studies of spontaneous speech. However, there are also studies of elicited production (Kantor, 1980; Pizzuto & Williams, 1980; Newport, 1981; Supalla, 1982; Launer, 1982b; Petitto, 1983) and elicited imitation (Launer, 1982b; Meier, 1982).

Much of the literature is found in recent doctoral dissertations (Hoffmeister, 1978a; Kantor, 1982a; Launer, 1982b; Meier, 1982; Supalla, 1982; Loew, 1984) or in the work of a small number of ASL laboratories. Because of the small population of deaf native signers and the concentration of ASL research in a few laboratories, the same pseudonymously named children reappear in the work of different investigators. The subject populations overlap considerably, but not completely, in the studies of Lacy (1972), Fischer (1973b), Newport & Ashbrook (1977); Pizzuto and Williams (1980), Maxwell (1977), Loew (1980, 1981), Meier (1981, 1982), Launer (1982b), Newport (1981), Supalla (1982), and Petitto (1983). Likewise, Ellenberger, Moores, & Hoffmeister (1975), Hoffmeister (1977, 1978a,b), and Ellenberger & Steyaert (1978) share the same subject population.

The acquisition of some facets of ASL grammar has been studied in reasonable depth. The acquisition of deictic pronouns (Hoffmeister, 1977; Pizzuto & Williams, 1980; Bellugi & Klima, 1981, 1982; Petitto, 1983), semantic relations (Newport & Ashbrook, 1977), word order (Hoffmeister, 1978b), verb agreement (Fischer, 1973b; Hoffmeister, 1978b; Loew, 1980, 1981; Meier, 1981, 1982; Kantor, 1982a,b), morphology of verbs of motion and location (Newport, 1981; Supalla, 1982), noun-verb derivational morphology (Launer, 1982b), and anaphoric pronouns (Loew, 1980, 1981, 1984) has received considerable attention. Aside from word order, anaphora, and brief description of negation (Lacy, 1972; Ellenberger, Moores, & Hoffmeister, 1975), the acquisition of the syntax of ASL has received scant attention. The acquisition of ASL phonology has likewise received relatively little study (but see Boyes-Braem, 1973, and McIntire, 1977). A few studies of the input to ASL acquisition have appeared (Maestas y Moores, 1980; Kantor, 1982a,b; Launer, 1982a,b; Meier, 1983). In sum, our understanding of the acquisition of ASL, although considerable, is by no means comprehensive.

In addition to these studies of the acquisition of ASL by deaf children of deaf parents, we will also have occasion to cite research on two other subject populations. In comparisons of the timing of the appearance of the first sign with that of the first word, bilingual hearing children of deaf parents are useful subjects, since they can in effect serve as their own controls (Schlesinger & Meadow, 1972; Prinz & Prinz, 1979; Bonvillian, Orlansky, & Novack, 1983). In addition, we will (in Section 11.2) review studies of deaf children of hearing parents, both with regard to their invention of gestural communication systems in the absence of exposure to any conventional sign language in early childhood (Goldin-Meadow & Feldman, 1975; Feldman, Goldin-Meadow, & Gleitman, 1978; Goldin-Meadow & Mylander, 1983, 1984), and with regard to their success in learning ASL when exposed to it later in life (Mayberry, Fischer, & Hatfield, 1983; Newport & Supalla, forthcoming).

3. Overall Course of Development

3.1. Babbling in the Gestural Mode

As in the acquisition of spoken languages, infants acquiring ASL babble prior to the time of producing their first lexical items; that is, they produce sequences of gestures which phonologically resemble signing but which are not recognizable or apparently meaningful (Prinz & Prinz, 1979; Maestas y Moores, 1980). Unfortunately, there are no detailed studies of this behavior, so the precise phonological status of this babbling (e.g. is it phonologically restricted to those forms which are permissible in gestural languages generally, or in ASL in particular?) is unknown.

3.2. The One-Word Stage

Again as in the acquisition of spoken languages, the first recognizable ASL lexical items are produced one at a time in isolation, and this production of one sign at a time continues for several months in the absence of multisign utterances. Further, the items which the young signer produces during this period are the same kinds of units which adult signers readily identify as the lowest level units which can be produced in isolation. (Within the ASL literature, these units are typically referred to as "signs." Yet lower level units are bound forms.) In short, it is appropriate to use the term "word" in ASL as it is used in spoken language descriptions. Moreover, in ASL acquisition as in the acquisition of spoken language, language use begins with one-word utterances and with a one-word stage.

3.2.1. *Timing of the First Signs.*   It is widely reported that the first signs of ASL emerge significantly earlier than the first words found in English (Schlesinger & Meadow, 1972; McIntire, 1977; Prinz & Prinz, 1979; Bonvillian, Orlansky, & Novack, 1983). For example, Schlesinger & Meadow (1972) report that a bilingual hearing child, learning English from its hearing parents and learning sign language from a deaf grandmother, produced its first sign at 5½ months, but its first word at 11½ months. Prinz & Prinz (1979) report that another bilingual hearing child, learning English from one hearing parent and sign language from one deaf parent, produced her first sign at 7 months 6 days. Although they do not report the age at which she produced her first word, they do say that by 12 months the child had produced five signs but only one word.

A more comprehensive study of this phenomenon was conducted by Bonvillian et al. (1983). They studied 11 children with deaf (signing) parents; ten of these children were themselves hearing and one was deaf. Over this group, the mean age for the production of the first sign was 8.5 months, while the mean age for the production of ten signs was 13.2 months. In comparison, Nelson (1973) reports the mean age for the production of ten English words as 15.1 months.

The apparently early occurrence of first signs relative to first words does not seem to be due to the greater iconicity of signs: First, as we discuss extensively in later sections, there is an abundance of evidence that iconicity in general plays a minor role, if any at all, in the course of ASL acquisition (at least in the acquisition of ASL as a native language by infants; see Brown, 1980, and Mandel, 1980, for some suggestion that iconicity does play a role in the acquisition of individual signs by older children and adults). Second, the early signs of infants acquiring ASL as a native language are not particularly iconic; Bonvillian et al. (1983) report that only one-third of the signs in early sign vocabularies could be considered iconic. This is particularly true when one considers what iconicity might be available to the young child. For example, the sign MILK, which derives from the movements made in milking a cow, might be iconic for an adult but is surely not iconic for an infant; yet it is one of the earliest signs of children learning ASL, as it is often one of the earliest words of children learning a variety of spoken languages.

There are, however, a number of more plausible potential explanations for the relative earliness of first signs: (1) earlier maturation of the motor or receptive systems involved in gesture than in speech (Bonvillian et al., 1983); (2) greater perspicuity, to the infant learner, of gestured than of spoken words; and (3) greater recognizability, to the adult observer, of the ill-formed attempts of infants in gesture than in speech. The first two of these potential explanations would suggest that the onset differences are due to genuine differences between modalities; the last of these potential explanations would of course suggest that the onset differences are an artifact of observers' abilities to report accurately when children are beginning language. But any of these potential explanations would suggest that young children, whether deaf or hearing, may be capable of first language use at somewhat earlier ages than has previously been supposed, if they have access to a modality which favors their earliest attempts (Bonvillian et al., 1983). From this perspective, it is spoken language onset which is slightly delayed (rather than signed language onset which is slightly advanced), relative to when the child is cognitively and linguistically capable of controlling the first lexical usages.

It is of some interest, however, that none of the subsequent milestones (e.g. timing of the first two-word utterances) is convincingly earlier in ASL than in speech. Bonvillian et al. (1983) provide some highly tentative evidence of earlier onset of two-sign utterances (mean age 17 months, range 12;5 to 22 months, in sign, compared with the typically quoted range for two-word spoken utterances of 18–21 months); but they (and we) do not consider this a convincing finding, given the roughness of the quoted norms, the very small differences even then, and the lack of a significant correlation between this onset age and vocabulary size. Assuming, then, that the timing of later milestones in the acquisition of ASL corresponds fairly well to that of their counterparts in spoken language acquisition, it appears that there is not a general advantage for visual-gestural, as compared with auditory-vocal, language; the earlier onset of first words in gesture seems to be due to something (e.g. motor development) which affects only the control over the very first linguistic units. This moreover suggests that the timing of later milestones, in both gesture and speech, is constrained by deeper cognitive or linguistic factors (e.g. cognitive/linguistic maturational readiness, or extent of previously accomplished linguistic analysis), and not by more superficial factors related to modality (Bonvillian et al., 1983).

3.2.2. *Structure of the First Signs*.   The first signs are of two kinds: (1) pointing to real-world objects in the immediate environment, including to the self and the addressee; and (2) lexical signs.

As described in Section 1, above, points are linguistic forms (pronouns) within the adult language. However, when they are produced by young children, there is the problem of deciding whether they are linguistic signs, or rather whether they are nonlinguistic gestures similar to those produced by hearing children. (It should be noted that, because of this problem, points are not included in the data of Section 3.2.1 on early first signs.)

Bellugi & Klima (1982) and Petitto (1983) report the occurrence of points to self as well as other objects at 10 months of age in one deaf child learning ASL. In contrast, while hearing children point at objects at comparable ages, they apparently do not point at themselves until 18 months, when first person pronouns also occur (Petitto, 1983). This may suggest that at least these self-points are linguistic forms for the deaf child. However, Pizzuto (unpublished study cited in Petitto, 1983), using the criterion that only points which occurred in combination with lexical signs were linguistic units, found the first occurrences of linguistic pointing to self at 20 months, the first occurrences of linguistic pointing to the addressee at 24 months, and the first occurrences of linguistic pointing to the third persons at 25 months. Fitting in with this later age for the onset of linguistic pointing is Petitto's finding that points to people disappear entirely from the signing of one child from 12 to 18 months, and reappear only after this time. She interprets this discontinuity as evidence for a shift from nonlinguistic pointing to linguistic pronouns. (See Section 3.3.4 for further discussion.)

In conclusion, points are clearly linguistic objects for the deaf child during the two-word period, when, unlike pointing gestures of hearing children, they are combined syntactically with lexical signs; their status in the one-word period is unclear. It is of some interest on this regard that Feldman (1975) and Feldman,

Goldin-Meadow & Gleitman (1978), studying the invented gestural communications of deaf children deprived of a conventional language, note that these early gestural vocabularies appear quite normal when the referents of points are included, but suspiciously lack many common concrete object names when the points are considered nonlinguistic and are therefore excluded.

In contrast to the problematic status of points, the lexical signs used by one-word signers are clearly linguistic objects (more precisely, this is as clear for signers as it is for speakers of comparable sophistication). The lexical signs used in the one-word period are the conventionalized gestures of the adult language, and are only occasionally iconic, as described in Section 3.2.1 above. Semantically, they are similar to words used by one-word speakers in other languages: MILK, MOMMY, DADDY, etc.

Formationally, the early lexical signs are uninflected citation forms (Fischer, 1973b; Hoffmeister, 1977, 1978a; Newport & Ashbrook, 1977; Ellenberger & Steyaert, 1978; Newport, 1981; Meier, 1981, 1982; and others). The lexical items are what Newport & Supalla (1980) have called FROZEN signs: stems with no internal stem morphology and no derivational morphology (Newport & Supalla, 1980; Newport, 1981; Launer, 1982b). By and large these early lexical signs are those stems which, in the adult language, involve no such morphology; but there is in addition, some occasional usage of items which, although morphologically complex forms for the adult, are unanalyzed amalgams for the child (Newport & Supalla, 1980; Newport, 1981; Meier, 1982). Inflections for number, verb agreement, aspect, and the like are then simply omitted, even when the grammatical context requires them in the adult language (Fischer, 1973b; Newport & Ashbrook, 1977; Meier, 1981, 1982; and see Sections 3.3 and 3.4 for further discussion).

3.2.3. *Phonology of the First Signs.* As in the development of spoken languages, there are phonological (that is, formational) errors characteristic of young children. For example, infants are widely reported to sign MOMMY and DADDY by substituting contact with the index finger for contact with the thumb, and to sign BIRD by substituting contact with the index finger and thumb for contact with the back of the hand. In addition, contact with objects and with the body often replaces producing signs in mid-air, without contact; and we have observed that movement with proximal joints often replaces movement with distal joints (e.g. the sign GUM made with movement at the shoulder rather than at the fingers), and that simultaneous movement often replaces alternating movement (e.g. the sign CAR made by moving the two hands up and down in phase rather than in alternation).

As might be expected from the examples above, there are consistent orders of acquisition of various phonological features, with certain forms characteristically being acquired late and being difficult to control. In particular, Boyes-Braem (1973) and McIntire (1977) have hypothesized, and presented evidence for, four stages in the acquisition of handshape in ASL, and have argued that the order of acquisition is at least in part due to maturation of motor control and to motor difficulty. Those forms which are acquired late are also considered linguistically marked within phonological descriptions of the adult language (Woodward, 1976; Friedman, 1977). Moreover, Kantor (1980) and Supalla (1982) have presented evidence suggesting that young children in later stages of acquisition return to the least marked handshapes in contexts where the more phonologically complex forms are morphologically required but where this morphology is just beginning to be acquired.

3.3. The Two-Word Stage: Early Syntax

As in the acquisition of spoken languages, the one-word stage is followed by a period in which one-word utterances co-occur with two-word (that is, two-sign) utterances. As discussed in Section 3.2.1 above, the age at which young signing children begin to produce two-sign utterances is about the same as that for two-word utterances of young speaking children: about the middle of the second year. In overview, the two-sign stage has the following characteristics: The full range of childhood semantic relations occur, with individual semantic relations emerging in the same order as in the acquisition of spoken languages. In ASL, the two-sign utterance typically consists of lexical items which continue to be uninflected citation forms, with stem, derivation, and inflectional morphology absent. Word order is the primary syntactic device for signalling the role of nouns in the sentence. Each of these characteristics is discussed in detail below.

3.3.1. *Semantic Relations.* Numerous investigators have noted that the range of semantic relations expressed in early two-sign utterances is approximately the same as in spoken languages at the comparable time (Schlesinger & Meadow, 1972; Fischer, 1974; Newport & Ashbrook, 1977; Hoffmeister, 1977, 1978a; Schlesinger, 1978; Prinz & Prinz, 1981). That is, the child signs about the existence and nonexistence of objects, actions on objects, possession of objects, locations of objects, and the like. Within this set, the individual semantic relations emerge in about the same order as that described for English (Newport & Ashbrook, 1977, on ASL, compared with Bloom, Lightbown, & Hood, 1975, on English): existence relations appear early, followed by action and state relations, then locative relations, and finally datives, instruments, causes and manners of action.

It is of particular interest that dative relations emerge relatively late in the two-word stage in ASL, since the expression of the dative in ASL is highly iconic: "person 1 gives to person 2" is signed by moving the hand from the location of person 1 to the location of person 2. The late occurrence of this relation in ASL is thus our first indication that iconicity does not play a significant role in the acquisition process (see Section 3.4 for further evidence).

The timing of the emergence of this relation may instead be due to its conceptual/semantic complexity (i.e. the dative involves three arguments) (Newport & Ashbrook, 1977). Alternatively, it may be due to the fact that the formal device for marking the dative in the adult language is relatively complex. Although when viewed in terms of relationships between sign and referent, the dative seems easy, when viewed formally (that is, in terms of the way the form fits into the language more generally) it is complex: the dative in adult ASL involves morphological inflections for verb agreement, and the young signing child appears to have some difficulty acquiring morphological devices. (See Section 3.4 on the acquisition of morphology, and especially Section 3.4.1 on the acquisition of verb agreement, for further discussion.)

3.3.2. *Word Order.* As just mentioned, the early two-word signer does not control the morphology of the adult language. In particular, the roles of noun arguments within a sentence are not marked by the adult inflectional devices during the period of two-sign utterances, as will be described in some detail in Section 3.4.1. Instead, there is a consistent use of word order (that is, sign order) for marking role (Fischer, 1973b; Newport & Ashbrook, 1977; Hoffmeister, 1978b). This is despite the fact that the adult language shows considerable word order flexibilty, with inflections marking role relations and order (along with grammaticized facial expressions) marking topic.

Hoffmeister (1978b) presents extensive data on the use of order as a syntactic device for marking role, both before and after the acquisition of inflections for role. He studied three children longitudinally, altogether covering the period from 2 to 5 years-of-age, and from early two-sign utterances to more complex utterances. Only utterances containing a verb were included in his analysis. All three children showed strong tendencies to use SV, VO, SVO, VL, and SVL orders, both prior to the acquisition of morphological inflections for role and subsequent to the consistent use of inflections as well (in the latter period, order and inflections were redundant). Moreover, even after the inflections were used with some frequency, the order preferences were just as strong for sentences containing inflected verbs as they were for sentences containing uninflected verbs.

The particular orders adopted by these children are the canonical (that is, least marked or pragmatically most neutral) orders of the adult language. Whether they are also the most frequent orders in adult signing to young children is unknown, since word order counts of maternal or paternal signing have not been performed. In any case, it is clear that young signing children are biased to acquire order prior to inflections, despite the fact that their input language uses inflections more consistently than word order (or perhaps equally consistently as word order) for marking role. Moreover, they are biased to maintain consistent ordering for some time even after acquiring inflections to mark the same function.

3.3.3. *Negation*.   Within the adult language, sentence negation is most commonly marked by the lexical item NOT, which occurs prior to the verb, and/or by a negative headshake, which occurs simultaneously with the entire sentence or the particular constituent being negated. Other somewhat common forms of negation include the sign NO, which is typically used as an interjection or as an anaphoric negation (like the word *no*), the sign CAN'T, which in ASL is formationally unrelated to CAN, and a bound negative morpheme, which can occur with only a very few verbs (e.g. DON'T-KNOW, DON'T-WANT).

In the early portion of the two-word stage in ASL, as in the comparable period in the acquisition of English, the young signing child forms negative utterances by placing a negative operator in utterance-initial position, prior to the verb, with the subject noun omitted (Lacy, 1972; Ellenberger, Moores, & Hoffmeister, 1975). In one child, this early negative was NO, a lexical item which cannot be used as a negative operator in adult ASL but rather is used by the adult as an interjection or an anaphoric negation (Lacy, 1972). This form of early negation is therefore analogous to the English-speaking child's use of *no* for sentence negation. In a second child, the negative headshake was used in the same way, that is, as a lexical negative placed before the verb (Ellenberger et al., 1975). Again, this is a negative which cannot be used in this fashion by the adult, but rather can only occur simultanously with either a lexical sign or an entire sentence (depending on the scope of negation) in the adult language.

For both children, it was not until quite a bit later in the two- and three-word utterance stage that NOT and CAN'T were correctly used sentence-internally, and, for the second child, that the negative headshake was correctly used simultaneously with the negated lexical items.

In short, in ASL as in English acquisition, the young child first acquires a single negative form which is used quite differently than in the adult language; only later are a range of more specific negatives acquired and used in their correct sentence-internal positions.

3.3.4. *Deictic Pronouns*.   In ASL, deictic pronouns involve pointing at real-world objects and people in the immediate environment. (In ASL, unlike English, there is no formal distinction between personal pronouns and other deictic pronouns.) As discussed in Section 1 above, the reason these acts of pointing (or, as we will refer to them, "points") are considered deictic pronouns rather than nonlinguistic gestures within the adult language is that they are systematically integrated into the rest of the language in a way quite unlike otherwise similar acts of pointing that may accompany spoken language. For example, points in ASL occur in the place of (i.e. instead of) lexical nouns in a sentence, and not along with lexical nouns as they do when speaking; these linguistic points in ASL thus observe the syntactic restrictions of pronouns.

Pronouns in spoken languages are typically acquired relatively late compared to the onset of lexical nouns, with the rules of their usage mastered over many months. However, given the transparency of their formation in ASL (that is, that they point at their referents), one might think that in ASL they would be acquired easily and without error. Available acquisition data suggest, however, that this is not the case; rather, deictic pronouns in ASL seem to be acquired slowly and with surprising errors. As in other areas of ASL acquisition, the acquisition of deictic pronous occurs on a developmental schedule, and with types of errors, which are similar to those of the acquisition of spoken languages.

For comparison purposes, the acquisition pattern for gestural pointing and spoken pronouns in hearing children acquiring English is as follows (as reviewed in Petitto, 1983): Nonlinguistic pointing first occurs at approximately 10 months of age. According to Petitto (1983), the child of this age points at objects and persons in the environment, but not to himself. Personal pronouns emerge at approximately 18 months, with the first person pronoun (*I* or *me*) produced first. Again according to Petitto (1983), pointing at self begins at the same time that the first person pronoun is produced. Prior to the acquisition of the various personal pronouns, proper names are often used in lieu of pronouns. At approximately 24 months in some children, a reversal error occurs, with *you* used to mean the child himself. By 27 months, all the pronouns are used correctly.

One deaf child learning ASL, studied by Petitto (1983), acquired ASL deictic pronouns with many similarities to this pattern. At 10 months, pointing first began. Apparently unlike the hearing child, however, this child pointed freely, including at herself, during this period. But from 12 to 18 months, points at persons disappeared, while points at inanimate objects continued. Petitto interprets this disappearance of points at persons as indicating a discontinuity between nonlinguistic pointing and linguistic pronoun usage. Unfortunately, no data were reported between 18 and 22 months; however, another child followed in an unpublished study by Pizzuto, reported by Petitto, pointed at herself (ME) at 20 months, at the addressee (YOU) at 24 months, and a third persons at 25 months. In Petitto's data, at 22 to 23 months, as in some hearing children's personal pronoun usage, the child made a reversal error, using YOU to refer to herself. In ASL, this is particularly surprising error, since the pronoun YOU is a point at the addressee. Although only a very small of such errors occurred spontaneously, a large number of elicited production reversals were obtained. At the same time, production of the pronoun ME (a point at herself) was absent. Elicited comprehension of both YOU and ME were basically correct. Again as in hearing children, throughout this time, personal pronouns were often avoided, with proper names used instead. By 27 months, all the deictic pronouns (including those for herself and other persons) were correct. Hoffmeister's (1977) data on another deaf child, beginning at age 29 months, also showed correct usage of the full set of deictic pronouns at this time (although acquisition of plural, possessive, reflexive, and other inflected forms occurred later).

Petitto (1983) and Bellugi & Klima (1981, 1982) have proposed somewhat different, but related, hypotheses for the occurrence of errorful acquisition of deictic pronouns in ASL. In particular, they have noted that deictic pronouns in ASL share many of their formational properties with ASL lexical signs. For example, the same handshape, with the index finger extended and the remaining fingers closed in a fist, occurs in numerous nondeictic signs in ASL (e.g. HOUR, CANDY). But these formationally similar signs, and most other ASL signs, like words in spoken languages, generally take their meaning from an abstract relation between the sign and a concept or class of referents; signs do not typically gain meaning by indexing a particular real-world object. These investigators have hypothesized that the young child initially treats deictic pronouns in ASL as though they were ordinary lexical signs, and thereby overlooks what would seem to be the transparent workings of ASL deictics. As they note, this hypothesis is similar to that proposed by Clark (1978) for the reversal errors in the acquisition of spoken language deictics, namely that the child first interprets the pronoun YOU as a lexical sign equivalent to her name. (Unlike the Clark hypothesis, however, Petitto attributes this error to a generally correct understanding of the linguistic system, and not to a cognitive inability to engage in perspective-shifting). Only later does she acquire the knowledge of the deictics as a separate subsystem.

In sum, Petitto (1983) views the acquisition of deictic pronouns as passing through three stages: first, the use of gestural (nonlinguistic) pointing; second, the (mis)use of certain deictic pronouns as lexical signs; and finally, the correct use of deictic pronouns as a grammatical subsystem.

If this hypothesis for the errorful acquisition of ASL deictic pronouns is correct, it suggests here, as we have argued in other areas of ASL acquisition, that the child seems more readily able to notice certain linguistic properties across the system (in this case, the phonology and semantics of lexical signs) than to notice the transparency of individual form-referent relations. In the present case, there is one crucial prediction worthy of further investigation: namely, that, while pronoun reversals may commonly occur in the acquisition of ASL, pointing reversals should not occur in the nonlinguistic, gestural use of pointing by hearing children. Further research on the developmental course of pointing in hearing children, in comparison to that of pointing in deaf children acquiring ASL, would therefore be of great interest.

3.4. *The Acquisition of Morphology*

Prior to about age 2½, as described above, lexical items are produced in their citation forms, with no inflectional or derivational morphology added, or are produced as amalgams, with a few inflected forms used in an unanalyzed and unproductive fashion. Acquisition of the morphology of ASL begins at roughly 2½ to 3 years-of-age and, for the most complex morphological subsystems, continues well beyond age 5.

The earliest acquired morphological subsystem is that of verb agreement, in which the verb agrees in location with its noun arguments. This morphology is almost perfectly controlled, but only for real-word locations, by 3 to 3½ years-of-age. At approximately the same time (that is, by 3;6), the morphological distinction between nouns and verbs is fairly well controlled, and many (though not all) of the morphemes involved in verbs of motion and inflections for number and aspect are used productively. At this time, however, verb agreement for abstract spatial loci is just beginning. All of these morphological subsystems are used by and large correctly by about age 5½; however, errors on the morphemes of complex verbs of motion continue as late as age 7 or 8.

Across all of the morphological subsystems, a similar pattern of acquisition occurs: In the earliest stages, an uninflected citation form, or a small number of apparently unanalyzed amalgams, occur. Subsequently, morphemes are acquired but not coordinated, so that forms with missing morphemes are highly frequent, and forms with the morphemes produced sequentially (rather than simultaneously, as in the adult model) also occur. Finally, the morphemes are coordinated; for subsystems where only a few morphemes are required, this production of correct forms occurs by 3;6, whereas for subsystems where many morphemes are required, the production of fully correct forms occurs after age 5.

3.4.1. *Verb Agreement: Inflectional Morphology for the Role of Noun Arguments.*   As described in Section 1, there are two grammatical mechanisms in ASL for indicating the relationship between a verb and its noun arguments: word order, and inflections on the verb which we will call "verb agreement." In the adult language, some verbs do not undergo verb agreement; that is, their forms are not modified in dependence on their associated noun arguments. With these verbs, SVO order predominates, and alternative orders are possible only when one of these constituents is topicalized (i.e. fronted and marked by a grammaticized facial expression for topic). For other verbs, however, the form of the verb stem is modified so that the verb agrees in its orientation or direction of movement with the spatial locations of the associated nouns, and word order is quite flexible. There are two ways in which the inflectional agreement process may operate with respect to nouns. If the noun arguments refer to real-word objects in the immediately surrounding environment, the verb agrees with their real world locations (by orienting or moving to and from points in the signing space which are near these real-world locations). If the noun arguments refer to nonpresent objects, abstract locations in the signing space are established for them, and the verb agrees with these abstract locations. In these two cases, then, the devices involved with establishing spatial locations for the nouns are different, but the inflectional agreement system on the verb is the same.

A number of studies have examined the acquisition of ASL verb agreement (Fischer, 1973b; Hoffmeister, 1978a,b; Loew, 1980, 1981; Meier, 1981, 1982; Kantor, 1982a, 1982b). These studies are consistent in indicating the following picture:

Prior to age 2, verbs which should undergo inflectional agreement are absent from child signing (Kantor 1982a;b; Meier, 1982; see also Ellenberger & Steyaert, 1978). (This appears to be due to the semantics of early signing, and to the fact that there are some semantic consistencies in which verbs undergo agreement; see Newport & Ashbrook, 1977, for data on the order in which various semantic relations appear in early signing.)

From 2;0 to 2;6, verbs which require agreement begin to be used, but are most often produced in their uninflected citation forms, with agreement omitted (Fischer, 1973b; Newport & Ashbrook, 1977; Loew, 1980; Meier, 1981, 1982). As described in Section 3.3.2, word order is used during this period to mark the role of noun arguments. Agreement occurs during the first several months of this period only on one or a small number of verbs, and only in one or a small number of the agreement forms; these usages may largely consist of what MacWhinney (1978) has termed amalgams, i.e. unanalyzed rote forms (Meier, 1982). During the last few months of this period, however, agreement is sometimes used productively (Meier, 1982).

By 3;0 to 3;6, agreement with real-world locations is essentially acquired (Meier, 1982), with occasional overgeneralization of agreement to non-agreeing verbs (Fischer, 1973b). (As observed in Section 3.3.2, canonical SVO word order is maintained for some time as a redundant marking of noun role (Hoffmeister, 1978b)). In Meier's (1982), analyses, using Cazden's (1968) criterion of 90% usage in obligatory contexts for three successive language samples, the three subjects acquired verb agreement at ages 3;0, 3;4, and 3;6, respectively.

In contrast, omission of verb agreement for abstract spatial loci continues well past age 3 (Loew, 1981), even in the same subject (and in the same filming session) for whom Meier found a high frequency of real-world agreement at this age. Largely consistent and correct use of abstract verb agreement does not occur for this child until age 4;9. This could indicate that the child acquires abstract agreement as a separate morphological system, failing to realize that the same morphology applies to agreement with nouns in abstract loci as to agreement with nouns in real-world loci; alternatively, it could indicate that verb agreement, for both real-world and abstract loci, is acquired early, but that establishing and maintaining abstract loci (and therefore correctly producing agreement with these loci) is acquired late. In our opinion, the details of Loew's (1981) data support the latter rather than the former view. We therefore discuss these data further in the Section 3.5.1 *Anaphoric pronouns: the establishment and use of spatial loci for nouns,* and we conclude here that the acquisition of verb agreement is complete at 3;0 to 3;6.

One of the issues considered within Meier's (1981, 1982) study of the acquisition of verb agreement concerns the impact of iconicity upon the acquisition of ASL. Many verbs inflected for agreement are among the most iconic signs in the language. For example, the inflected verb I-GIVE-YOU is largely identical to the motor act the child would actually perform were he or she to give a small object to the addressee (Meier calls this type of iconicity a "mime," imitating an action from the perspective of the agent). In other cases, inflected verbs (e.g.

HE-GIVE-HIM, or all of the inflected forms of the verbs CHASE and KICK) are "spatial analogues," mapping the act in signing space that is described by the sign. Meier developed three models of the acquisition of verb agreement, one which should occur if children are guided by the mimetic properties of agreement, a second which should occur if children are guided by the spatial analogies of agreement, and a third which should occur if children acquire verb agreement as a morphological system independently of iconicity. His results (Meier, 1981, 1982) clearly support the third model, in that the earliest signing omits verb agreement uniformly, regardless of the type of iconicity offered by individual agreeing verbs, and the order of acquisition of aspects of verb agreement follows morphological but not iconic principles (that is, agreement forms are acquired according to their morphological complexity, and not according to which are most iconic in either sense).

Indeed, Meier's data are consistent with a morphological model which predicts the timing of the acquisition of ASL verb agreement on the basis of the typological characteristics of the morphology. In spoken languages, precocious acquisition of agreement and case morphology have been demonstrated only in languages such as Turkish (see Slobin, and Aksu-Koç & Slobin, 1985), in which the morphology is sequentially organized and agglutinative. In contrast, the morphology of ASL verb agreement is simultaneously and more fusionally organized: the verb stem and its inflectional markers of agreement are articulated simultaneously, and the inflectional markers sometimes influence aspects of the phonology of the stem. On these grounds, acquisition of ASL verb agreement should not occur precociously, but should occur at approximately the same time as the acquisition of non-agglutinative morphology in spoken languages. This indeed is the case, with ASL verb morphology acquired fully a year later than the case morphology of Turkish, despite the fact that the form-meaning relationships in Turkish are arbitrary but in ASL are often highly motivated. In sum, the acquisition patterns in ASL strongly indicate that children are analyzing verb agreement as a morphological system, not as an iconic one.

3.4.2. *Morphology of Verbal Stems.* Many verb stems in ASL consist of only one morpheme and vary in form only when derivational or inflectional morphemes are added to this stem. However, a large class of verbs of motion and location are highly variable in form, even when uninflected, as a function of the details of the referent path of motion and the type of object which moves. Until recently, these verbs were viewed as "mimetic depictions," which could vary in an indefinite number of ways to depict in an analogue fashion the indefinite number of motions and locations real-world objects undergo (DeMatteo, 1977). However, Newport (1981) and Supalla (1982; Newport & Supalla, 1980) have provided evidence that ASL verbs of motion and location are not structured in this way; rather, like verbs of motion and location in some spoken languages, they are complex verbal stems constructed from the regular combination of a limited number of component morphemes. A brief description of these morphemes is presented in Section 1.4.2.

Even though ASL verbs of motion are not analogue or mimetic representations of real-world motion, many of them do (when viewed holistically) resemble their referent motions. It therefore seemed possible that young children, in early stages of acquiring ASL, might incorrectly view them as analogue representations. If so, they should acquire complex verbs of motion relatively early, as compared with forms they correctly view as multimorphemic; and their early errors should reflect analogue usages. On the other hand, if young children do not (or cannot) make use of this iconicity, but rather view ASL verbs of motion as multi-morphemic, they should acquire only some of their morphemes early, with additional morphemes added as acquisition proceeds; and the full control over complex verbs of motion should not occur until roughly the age at which complex multi-morphemic forms are acquired in spoken languages (Newport, 1981; Supalla, 1982).

Several investigators have presented data on the acquisition of various aspects of ASL verbs of motion. Ellenberger & Steyaert (1978) examined the spontaneous use of ASL verbs of motion in one child from 3;7 to 5;11. Kantor (1980) tested elicited production, comprehension, and imitation of the handshapes of ASL verbs of motion in nine children ranging in age from 3;0 to 11;0. Newport (1981) and Supalla (1982) investigated the above hypotheses in some detail, by longitudinally testing three children, ages 2;4 to 5;11, for their elicited production of ASL verbs of motion in response to a set of 120 animated events of motion designed to test the morphemes described in their linguistic analysis. Newport (1981) reports on the acquisition of various morphemes of motion; Supalla (1982) reports on the acquisition of various morphemes of handshape and its placement; and unpublished data from Newport and Supalla are included in the description below on the acquisition of other morphemes.

These studies provide the following picture of the acquisition of ASL verbs of motion: Until approximately 2;9, verbs of motion are either frozen, single morpheme stems, or a small number of simple movements (e.g. LINEAR, ARC) combined with incorrectly used central object handshapes; morphemes for manner of movement along the path are typically omitted, as are morphemes classifying secondary objects (Newport, 1981, and unpublished). Beginning at 2;11 to 3;6, several central object handshape classifiers are used correctly, in combination with simple movements or manners of movement (e.g. BOUNCE, RANDOM) (Newport, 1981, and unpublished; Kantor, 1980). However, movements and manners of movement (e.g. LINEAR + BOUNCE) are not yet combined with each other. Rather, the verbs at this age typically include either a movement morpheme or a manner morpheme, with the other morpheme omitted. Beginning a few months later, a small proportion of the productions have both a movement and a manner morpheme, but articulate them sequentially rather than simultaneously (Newport, 1981). Similarly, secondary object classifier handshapes begin to appear at 3;4; but they continue to be omitted in a sizeable proportion of the verbs for at least another year, and, when they occur, are frequently produced sequentially to (rather than simultaneously with) the rest of the verb stem (Supalla, 1982). With increasing age, the proportion of correctly combined morphemes increases. But even by age 5, large numbers of complex verbs of motion include some morphemes but omit others. By age 5;6 and beyond, a substantial proportion of complex verbs of motion are produced correctly (Ellenberger & Steyaert, 1978; Supalla, 1982). However, some errors continue to occur until as late as age 8 (Kantor, 1980).

All of these patterns suggest that young children are not acquiring ASL verbs of motion in an analogue or holistic fashion, but rather are acquiring them morpheme by morpheme, just as in the acquisition of morphologically complex spoken languages.

3.4.3. *Derivational Morphology*   As described in Section 1, nouns for concrete objects and verbs for the associated actions performed with these objects frequently share the same stem, but are distinguished by derivational morphemes: nouns of these pairs have a repeated movement and a restrained manner, while verbs have either a single or repeated movement (depending on whether the action is punctual or durative) and either a continuous or hold manner (depending on whether the action has a specified goal or not). Some or all of this morphological distinction is also used for certain nominalization-verb pairs, although here the morphology (as in most spoken languages) is less productive.

Launer (1982b) has studied the acquisition of the derivational morphology for concrete nouns and verbs in analyses of spontaneous signing, as well as in elicited production, comprehension, and imitation tasks. The spontaneous data from three children ranging in age from 1;0 to 6;0 showed the following sequence: Before age 2;0, derivational morphology was essentially absent, with 86% of the noun-verb usages showing no distinction between noun and verb forms. Between the ages of 2;0 and 2;11, distinctions between related nouns and verbs were frequently (41%) those Launer called "noncanonical"; that is, the child signalled some distinction between noun and verb forms (for example, by marking one with a distinctive facial expression, body posture, or speed of movement), but did not use the adult morphological distinctions. However, an equal proportion (42%) included part or all of the adult morphological distinctions, while only 17% showed no distinction between noun and verb forms. By 3;0 to 3;11, 71% of the forms showed partial or full adult morphology; by 4;0 to 5;11 this proportion had risen to 84%, and innovative noun-verb forms which included this morphology were also produced. In sum, then, this acquisition process begins with the appropriate morphology absent; but the morphology is frequently used in the third year, and sometime between 4 and 6 the bulk of the morphology is essentially acquired.

An elicited production task, which used pictures to elicit noun and verb forms, showed relatively higher proportions of noncanonical distinctions which persisted until older ages, and relatively lower proportions of the full or partial morphological distinction. For example, in this task children aged 4–6 produced only 37% of the items with full or partial morphology, while children aged 6–8 produced only 64% full or partial morphology. Nevertheless, the same trends were evident, with noncanonical distinctions frequent in the younger subjects but declining with age, and morphological distinctions increasing with age.

3.4.4. *Inflectional Morphology for Aspect and Number.*   Data on the acquisition of inflectional morphology for aspect and number are not extensive. Contexts for many of these morphemes in spontaneous usage are relatively rare, and no systematic elicitation tasks have been performed. Our description is therefore limited largely to mention of spontaneous occurrences and their grammatical status.

The available data on inflections for temporal aspect (Meier, 1979, 1980; Meier, Loew, Bahan, Fields, Launer, and S. Supalla, 1980) suggest that these inflections appear in child signing after 3;0. Prior to this age, one subject (2;0) produced frequent spontaneous imitations of her mother's signing which typically lacked the aspectual inflections present in the mother's model. By 4;9, another child spontaneously produced a large variety of distinct aspectual inflections. However, Meier et al. (1980) questioned whether the child was using all of these inflections contrastively.

The data on the acquisition of number inflections, in particular the dual inflection, are somewhat richer than those on temporal aspect (Meier, 1979, 1980; Meier et al., 1980). Nevertheless, these data too are fragmentary and cannot be used to infer any details of the acquisition course.

ASL has several closely related dual constructions. A one-handed sign such as GIVE can take the following dual forms: (1) a one-handed dual in which the stem is produced first to one spatial location and then reduplicated to a second location, horizontally displaced from the first; (2) a two-handed dual in which the stem and its reduplication of 1 are produced simultaneously, one with the left hand to one spatial location and the other with the right hand to the second location; and (3) a two-handed dual as in 2, except that the two parts are produced sequentially. These three dual constructions differ in subtle semantic ways.

The one-handed dual verb form was elicited from one subject, Jane, when she was first observed at 3;1. At the same age, she was asked to imitate the simultaneous two-handed dual of GIVE; however, in her copy she substituted the one-handed dual. At 3;1 an attempt was made to elicit from her a two-handed simultaneous reciprocal inflection, which is semantically and morphologically related to the dual. Jane produced a two-handed simultaneous dual to one side, and then another two-handed simultaneous dual to the other side (i.e. a "dual-dual"). When the experimenter produced the appropriate reciprocal, Jane imitated it by producing a normal two-handed simultaneous dual; this sequence was repeated in a second attempt by the experimenter to get her to produce the reciprocal. Although indicating that her command of the dual and reciprocal inflections was certainly imperfect at 3;1, these errors suggest that Jane may already be organizing the dual and reciprocal inflections into a coherent morphological system, in which the reciprocals and duals share a morpheme /DUAL/ which has several allomorphs. At 3;1 and 3;4 Jane frequently produced "dual-dual" verbs (that is, verbs which were ungrammatically marked by two dual allomorphs). At 3;7 Jane overextended the two-handed simultaneous dual to a noun (only the sequential dual is grammatical on nouns). Again, such errors indicate productive usage of the dual morpheme, but continuing confusion about the relationships among the various allomorphs. By 4;9 Jane's signing included frequent spontaneous and correct usages of the dual (although an isolated error of omission occurred at that age as well).

MacWhinney (1978) cites Omar (1970) as finding that the dual noun suffixes in Arabic appear quite late (after age 6), after the the acquisition of the Arabic plural, and suggests that the concept of duality as opposed to plurality is elusive for young children. The ASL data on dual, fragmentary as they are, nevertheless suggest that dual enters soon after age 3 and may be fully acquired under age 5, despite complexities of the allomorphy. They therefore suggest that the concept of duality is not as complex as Omar and MacWhinney have hypothesized.

ASL forms various distributive plurals of verbs through reduplication and spatial displacement of the verb stem; reduplication marks that the action is repeated or of extended duration, while spatial displacement marks that the action is distributed over multiple persons, objects, or locations. From the ages of 3;7 to 4;8 three children rarely produced grammatically correct forms for distributive plurals; rather, they consistently erred by producing the reduplication without spatial displacement (a form which, in the adult language, would refer to repeating the action to one object).

3.5. Later Acquisition

3.5.1. *Anaphoric Pronouns: The Establishment and Use of Spatial Loci for Nouns.* As described in Section 1, while deictic pronouns in ASL involve pointing at nearby real-world objects, anaphoric pronouns are points at spatial loci previously established within the signing space for reference to objects which are not in the immediately surrounding environment. For example, within a discourse concerning two non-present people, the first mention of these people will involve pointing to an abstract location in space for each of them; subsequent reference to either of the people then involves pointing to the appropriate locus for that person. In addition, verb agreement and other inflectional devices requiring spatial agreement with the nouns are performed with respect to these spatial loci.

The acquisition of anaphoric pronouns thus requires the ability to establish such loci, as well as the ability to maintain the identities of these loci and distinguish them from one another over sometimes lengthy spans of discourse.

As might be expected from these cognitive and linguistic requirements, the acquisition of these devices occurs relatively late; as in other domains of ASL, the iconicity of the devices (that is, the resemblance of such abstract loci to setting up a miniature replica of a real-world space in front of the signer) does not promote early acquisition.

Hoffmeister (1977) and Loew (1980, 1981, 1984) have investigated the acquisition of anaphora in two children ranging in age from 2;5 to 4;9. Hoffmeister's analyses are of longitudinal spontaneous conversation; Loew's analyses are of longitudinal spontaneous telling of multi-character stories (e.g., Goldilocks and the Three Bears). Unpublished data have also been presented by Petitto (1980) and Pizzuto (1982).

Hoffmeister's and Loew's subjects show remarkable similarities to one another, and to those more limited data reported by other investigators, in their ages and patterns of acquisition. We therefore describe them together, although only Loew's data provide most of the detail on the use of anaphora for multiple referents.

Both children produced deictic pronouns and verb agreement with real-world objects prior to 3;6 (Meier's, 1982, data on real-world verb agreement, discussed in Section 3.4.1, are partly from the same subject studied by Loew with regard to anaphora). However, at these ages neither child established abstract spatial loci or performed verb agreement with such loci; pronouns referring to non-present people or objects were absent, and verbs referring to the actions of such people or objects were produced in their citation forms, omitting inflectional agreement. As in spoken languages, then, multicharacter stories were often fairly unintelligible, since few devices were used to indicate which character was performing which action (cf. Piaget, 1955, and Karmiloff-Smith, 1979, 1981, for similar problems in hearing children's use of pronouns).

From 3;6 to 3;11, there was still almost no establishment of abstract spatial loci for nonpresent referents. Some verbs were inflected for agreement with such referents; however, particularly in the early months of this period, almost all of these were agreements with a single spatial locus. Since they were not all to the same locus, Loew (1980, 1981, 1984) has argued that the children are not merely producing an unanalyzed amalgam; she suggests they have learned that spatial marking is required for the verb, but have not yet acquired a set of spatial markings which are consistently distinguished from one another.

Toward the latter part of this period, the children sometimes produced verb agreement with multiple loci; however, verbs in different parts of the discourse which referred to actions of a single individual did not consistently agree with the same locus, and verbs which referred to actions of different individuals did not consistently agree with different loci. Loew (1981, 1984) suggests that the child during this period uses abstract verb agreement (and other abstract spatial devices) in a contrastive but not identifying way: that is, she suggests that the child uses these devices to contrast one reference with another just preceding or following it, but does not yet understand that in the adult language distinct loci for individual referents must be maintained throughout the discourse. However, an alternative (related) hypothesis is that the child of this age uses agreement correctly over short spans of discourse, but is unable to maintain correct and complex agreement relations over longer spans; this latter interpretation suggests a performance rather than a competence problem.

By 4;0 to 4;4, the children still typically failed to establish an abstract locus at the beginning of discourse; however, they both occasionally used what Hoffmeister (1977) calls "semi-real world" forms, that is, they used a real-world object present in the environment to establish a locus for an absent object. In addition, they sometimes established an abstract locus by gazing at a point in space while performing the noun for this object. They now produced abstract verb agreement to multiple loci in space; but these distinct loci were still frequently not maintained over the discourse. Loew views the loci as distributed randomly in space, still having only a contrastive but not an identifying function; however, the alternative view suggested above, that the child is simply unable to maintain the locus identities over long discourse spans, is still viable.

Finally, by about 4;6 to 4;9, the children explicitly established loci in space for non-present objects and then produced subsequent verb agreement with these loci; multiple loci were distinguished for several different objects, and the identifies of these loci were maintained over the discourse (although errors and self-corrections did occur).

Hoffmeister (1977) has noted that a variety of ASL grammatical operations are acquired first for real-world objects and are only later controlled for abstract spatial loci. This pattern raises two questions concerning the arguments we have made in previous sections.

First, in Section 3.4.1, we suggested that verb agreement was acquired by 3;6; however, as we noted there, agreement with abstract spatial loci is not used until much later. This might suggest that the child separates real-world verb agreement from abstract verb agreement, acquiring only the former by 3;6 but acquiring the latter not until 4;6. Our interpretation of these data, however, is that verb agreement in general is acquired by 3;6. Omission and other errors of verb agreement with respect to abstract spatial loci clearly continue well past this time; however, we see no reason to implicate the morphology of verb agreement per se as the source of these errors. Rather, the data seem to us to suggest that the errors arise from difficulties inherent in establishing and maintaining abstract spatial loci. In particular, if the child were acquiring abstract verb agreement *de novo,* as a separate system from real-world verb agreement, one would expect to see the establishment of abstract loci occur first, and only later the gradual acquisition of verb agreement with these loci (thus recapitulating the acquisition of real-world verb agreement). In contrast, what one actually finds is the production of abstract verb agreement long prior to the establishment of abstract loci, with verb agreement errors suggesting that the child is able to utilize agreement but has not established or is unable to maintain the loci with which correct agreement must operate. When loci are correctly established and maintained, verb agreement with these loci is immediately correct. In sum, then, the late acquisition seems to be of the establishment and maintenance of abstract spatial loci; other spatial devices are used incorrectly because they must agree with loci which themselves are not well controlled.

Second, we have argued that iconicity has few effects on the acquisition of ASL. The earlier acquisition of spatial devices involving real-world objects as compared with those involving nonpresent objects might be viewed as suggesting such an effect. We would argue, however, that real-world and abstract spatial devices do not differ in their iconicity (both are to some degree iconic, as for example when abstract loci are used to represent real-world loci which happen not to be present in the environment at the time of speaking); rather, they differ in the degree to which the real-world environment offers props which can ease memorial and other performance problems. Similarly earlier acquisition of deictic than anaphoric devices occurs in the acquisition of spoken languages. In short, it does appear that linguistic devices marking present objects and actions appear before those marking nonpresent objects and actions; but this does not seem to suggest an effect of iconicity in the acquisition of ASL.

3.5.2. *Compounding.*   S. Supalla (1980) examined the spontaneous signing of one child, Jane, from 3;1 to 4;10, for the occurrence of compound signs. No compounds appeared until 3;6. At 3;6, Jane produced several compounds which S. Supalla called "lexical compounds," that is, items which are conventional compounds in ASL and whose occurrence do not therefore indicate whether the child has internally analyzed them as compound items. However, all of these at 3;6 were articulated without the required phonological reductions and phrasing of compound items, but rather were articulated as though they were two independent lexical items. (This may suggest that indeed the child has analyzed them, but has not yet acquired the morphological and/or phonological rules that govern compounding.) From 3;9 to 4;4 all compounds were still lexical compounds, but were now produced with the correct compounding phonology. At 4;5, lexical compounds continued to be produced (some with the correct phonology, but some with the phonology of independent lexical items); but in addition several innovative compounds were produced, suggesting that the child had begun to acquire productive compounding rules. As in the lexical compounds, however, some of the innovative compounds were articulated as two independent lexical items rather than with the phonology of a single compound item. In addition, some of the innovative compounds were odd in the sense that they seemed to mean no more than would the second lexical stem alone (e.g. FRIEND-CHUM is produced with the apparent meaning CHUM). All of these patterns continued through 4;10, indicating that the full acquisition of compounding occurs fairly late.

3.5.3. *Later Syntax.* No research currently exists on the acquisition of the ASL devices marking topicalization, relative clauses, complement clauses and the like.

THE DATA

4. Typical Errors

4.1. Omission of Morphology

As described in Section 3 above, one of the typical errors seen in the acquisition of ASL is the early omission of morphological inflections, derivational morphology, and complex stem morphology. Instead, the young signing child uses frozen, citation forms of lexical items, with word order consistently used to signal role. Although this occurs in the acquisition of many spoken languages as well, it is particularly striking in ASL for several reasons.

First, the adult language is morphologically quite rich (and quite flexible in order). As in many spoken languages, then, the signing child is ignoring many of the predominant properties of his input language in the early stages of acquisition, and is instead selecting or devising his own regularities.

Second, in ASL but not in spoken languages, the morphologically complex forms are often highly iconic when viewed as global wholes (that is, they have rather transparent relations to their meanings). In fact, citation forms are typically much LESS iconic than are morphologically marked forms. In producing citation forms and omitting morphologically marked forms, the young signing child demonstrates a surprising disinterest in, or inability to take advantage of, nonarbitrary relations between form and meaning.

Newport (1981) and Supalla (1982; Newport & Supalla, 1980), as described in Section 3.4.2, investigated the acquisition of the morphology of verbs of motion primarily because of the potential iconicity of verbs of motion: complex verbs of motion in ASL are performed by moving the hand through space in paths roughly analogous to the paths taken by the referent object. However, their findings, that the morphology of verbs of motion is acquired relatively late and without apparent use of analogy to referent paths of motion, suggest rather strongly that the child does not take advantage of this potential iconicity. (See also the discussion below of sequentialization errors.) Instead, the child seems to omit the morphological structure in early stages, thereby producing relatively non-iconic lexical forms. Subsequently the child acquires the morphology component by component (that is, morpheme by morpheme). This pattern of acquisition suggests that deaf children view the morphology of ASL similarly to the ways that hearing children view spoken language morphology: as formal, componential systems which require formal distributional analyses, and whose mastery therefore requires lengthy developmental time.

Meier (1981, 1982) has performed perhaps the most direct test of whether the child is able to take advantage of iconicity in acquiring verb agreement in ASL. As described in Section 3.4.1, his study predicts one pattern of acquisition if the child uses the mimetic properties of verb agreement (specifically, that agreement will be acquired early for verbs that are mimetic and that occur with first person subjects and second- or third-person objects, but later for nonmimetic verbs and for verbs with other persons); a second pattern of acquisition if the child uses the spatial analogy properties of verb agreement (specifically, that agreement will be acquired early for verbs involving motion and transference, and that occur with optional double agreement, but later for nontransfer verbs and for verbs with single agreement); and a third pattern of acquisition if the child uses neither mimetic nor spatial properties of verb agreement but rather attends to the linguistic, and particularly formal morphological, properties of verb agreement (specifically, that verb agreement will uniformly be acquired relatively late as compared with the predictions of the other models, and that omission of agreement will predominate in early signing). His results show the third pattern of acquisition.

These studies, taken together and in combination with the other findings of relatively late acquisition of ASL morphology (see Section 3.4), demonstrate convincingly that the potential iconicity of ASL morphology does not assist in its acquisition.

Moreover, the early omission of morphology occurs despite the fact that morphology in ASL is often highly regular (e.g. as in verbs of motion, where the same morphemes of path, manner, and the like occur for a large set of verbs; this degree of regularity does not characterize verb agreement, where individual lexical stems vary in whether they take no agreement, agreement only with objects, or subject and object agreement).

Finally, the early omission of morphology occurs despite the fact that some domains of ASL morphology are agglutinative. For example, in ASL verbs of motion, one set of morphemes involves the shape of the hands; another set involves the path of motion; yet another set involves the manner of motion; etc. These morphemes then combine with one another agglutinatively, in the sense that the form of one set of morphemes is relatively unaffected by the form of the others with which it co-occurs. Nevertheless, the morphemes are controlled relatively late in acquisition.

There are two possible reasons why the morphological systems of ASL are acquired relatively late. First, unlike agglutinative processes in most spoken languages, in ASL the morphemes combine simultaneously rather than sequentially. Note that, by distinguishing "agglutinative" from "sequential vs. simultaneous," we are in essence advocating that a third orthogonal dimension be added to Sapir's (1921) classification. His scheme categorizes morphologies according to, first, whether they are isolating or synthetic and, second, whether they are analytic, agglutinative, or fused. The third dimension which we would add to this taxonomy is whether the lexical stem and its attendant morphology (if any) are arrayed sequentially or whether they are articulated simultaneously. We suspect that this additional dimension can be motivated not only by the facts of ASL but also by data from spoken languages (cf. Hebrew: McCarthy, 1981; tone languages: Goldsmith, 1976). Moreover, we believe that the simultaneity of forms in ASL contributes to their late acquisition and overrides factors which would otherwise make the morphology relatively easier (Meier, 1982; and see Section 4.3 for further evidence on the difficulty of simultaneity).

Second, there may be some general difficulty in morphological analysis for the young child, and a general priority of lexical over morphological forms in the earliest stages of acquisition (Newport, 1981, 1982; and see Section 4.3 for further evidence on this point). In languages where morphological analysis is accomplished very early (e.g. Turkish; see Aksu-Koç & Slobin, 1985), it has been suggested that additional factors (e.g. stress) may make the morphological components more salient, and perhaps somewhat more like independent lexical units (Gleitman & Wanner, 1982).

4.2. Partial Omission of Morphology

A type of error seen in subsequent stages of the acquisition of ASL is the occurrence of some morphemes of an adult complex form, but the omission of other morphemes.

For example, in the acquisition of complex verbs of motion, young children virtually never produce all of the required morphemes (except in an early stage where they produce some signs as frozen amalgams which the adult would produce as morphologically complex signs). The predominant error, produced for as many as 80 to 90% of the complex movement targets in children age 2;6 to 3;1 and declining gradually to 35% in children age 4;7 to 5;1, is one in which some morphemes are produced correctly while others are omitted (Newport & Supalla, 1980; Newport, 1981, 1982). Thus one child, shown a film of a hen jumping from the ground to the roof of a barn, should have produced a sign whose movement included an ARC movement simultaneously combined with an UPWARD direction; instead, however, this child produced only an ARC, omitting the UPWARD component. Similarly, a child shown a dot moving randomly should have produced a sign whose movement included a LINEAR movement simultaneously combined with a RANDOM affix; instead, the child produced only the RANDOM affix (Newport, 1981).

Similar errors occur in the acquisition of handshape classifiers marking central and secondary objects within complex verbs of motion (Supalla, 1982). Classifiers for the central (moving) object virtually always occur, but when they involve multiple morphemes, one of these morphemes may be omitted. For example, one child shown a cylindrical object, which requires a ROUND plus MID-SIZE classifier, instead produced a ROUND classifier which omitted the morpheme for MID-SIZE. Classifiers for secondary objects (e.g. a telephone pole toward which another object moved) were omitted entirely in over 50% of their required contexts for children under 4;0 (Supalla, 1982).

The occurrence of such errors within verbs of motion is particularly striking, since, as in certain other domains of ASL morphology, the complex forms are highly iconic when viewed holistically. The fact that the child omits portions of signs which are proper component morphemes provides supporting evidence for a linguistic analysis of these forms as morphologically complex. Moreover, the child's production of some morphemes but not others (resulting in forms which are holistically much less iconic than the correct adult target) provides evidence of his tendency to treat lexical items as constructed from morphological components, despite the seemingly greater iconicity that could be noticed if these forms were viewed holistically.

4.3. *Sequentialization of Morphology*

One more type of error, which occurs frequently in the acquisition of ASL, provides evidence for the positions stated above. In the adult language, morphemes are often combined with one another simultaneously (rather than sequentially, as is most frequently the case in spoken languages). Thus, for example, in adults' complex verbs of motion, morphemes for the path of motion are articulated simultaneously with morphemes for the manner of motion along this path and the direction of the path in space. However, several months after the time at which children begin to produce some morphemes and omit others, they begin to produce occasional examples of another type of error, in which the required morphemes are all produced but are articulated sequentially instead of simultaneously.

In Newport's (1981) data discussed in the preceding section, errors of partial omission of morphology began at age 2;4. Beginning at 3;4 and continuing through 5;1, children produced errors in which movement, manner, and direction morphemes of complex verbs of motion were all produced, but sequentially rather than simultaneously. Such errors occurred on between 6 and 18% of the complex movement targets. For example, in the previous section we described a film in which a hen jumped from the ground to the roof of a barn, for which the adult form would include simultaneous ARC and UPWARD morphemes, and an early child error in which the ARC was produced without the UPWARD morpheme. A somewhat older child, responding to the same film, produced an ARC (without the UPWARD morpheme), followed by an UPWARD morpheme (without the ARC): that is, he produced the correct morphemes in sequence.

Similarly, in Supalla's (1982) data on the acquisition of handshape classifiers within complex verbs of motion, he found frequent occurrences of the sequential production of handshape morphemes which should have been simultaneous. For example, for verbs which should have had two simultaneous classifiers, one for the central (moving) object and one for the secondary object against which the central object moved, his subjects frequently produced the two classifiers sequentially, in two separate lexical items. His subject of 3;6 produced such forms for 24% of the signs which should have had simultaneous C.O. and S.O. classifiers; this proportion declined gradually to 0% by age 5;9.

The data from Meier et al. (1980) show examples of perhaps the same phenomenon in the acquisition of inflection for number. There, for example, a child of 3;1, asked to imitate a two-handed simultaneous reciprocal form, instead produced two two-handed sequential dual forms. At 3;1 and 3;4 she produced several duals in which the stems were reduplicated both simultaneously and sequentially.

Finally, the data from S. Supalla (1980) show examples of a related phenomenon in the acquisition of compounding, where even the adult forms require sequential morphemes. Compound lexical items in the adult language, as described in Section 1.4.5, involve sequencing two independent lexical stems, but phonologically reducing them so that the combination forms a single lexical item. One child began at 3;6 to produce compounds, but articulated them without the required phonological reductions and phrasing of compound items; rather, they were articulated as though the components were two independent lexical items (S. Supalla, 1980). Even when the target forms involve sequential rather than simultaneous morphemes, then, children sometimes produce forms which are more sequential than the targets.

In sum, in the acquisition of the simultaneous morphology of ASL, there is evidence suggesting, first, a period in which morphology is omitted entirely, second, a subsequent period in which some of the morphemes are produced while others are omitted, and, third, a still subsequent period in which all of the morphemes are produced, but sequentially rather than simultaneously (Newport, 1981, 1982; Supalla, 1982). Similar errors of sequentialization occur as well in other morphological subsystems of ASL.

The sequentialization errors make two important points: First, like omission errors, sequentialization errors are often much less iconic than the correct adult forms. Their occurrence thus supports the claim, made on the basis of partial omission errors, that young children are more biased to find a componential analysis of the language that relates forms to one another than to notice holistic relations between individual forms and their referents.

Second, the occurrence of sequentialization errors prior to the correct production of simultaneous morphemes suggests, as we have argued in Section 4.1, that simultaneity of forms is difficult for the child. This supports our hypothesis that the relatively late acquisition of morphology in ASL may be due to its simultaneity, and the the difficulty of simultaneity may override factors such as agglutination, which might otherwise make the morphology relatively easy to analyze.

Finally, the sequentialization errors often involve producing bound morphemes as independent lexical items. This supports our further hypothesis, discussed in Section 4.1, that there may be some general difficulty in morphological analysis for the child, and a general priority of lexical over morphological forms in early stages of acquisition.

4.4. Errors in Pronouns and the Use of Space

There are two other striking types of errors in the acquisition of ASL. One of these is the occurrence of reversal errors in the acquisition of deictic pronouns: as described in Section 3.3.4, young children sometimes use YOU (a point at the addressee) to mean 'me'. A second, in the acquisition of anaphoric pronouns and abstract verb agreement with these pronouns described in Section 3.5.1, is the absence of anaphoric pronouns and the occurrence of numerous errors in agreement of verbs with these (absent) pronouns. Both of these errors, and their implications for the acquisition of ASL, are discussed in Section 7. *Reorganizations in Development.*

5. Error-Free Acquisition

Only word order is acquired early and without error (if acquiring and consistently using the canonical order of a language with great order flexibility can be considered a nonerror).

As emphasized in Section 4 above, it is important to note the absence of any error-free acquisition of ASL morphology, despite the fact that some of the morphological subsystems are highly iconic (e.g. verb agreement and the complex stem morphology of verbs of motion), highly regular (e.g. verbs of motion), and agglutinative, although simultaneous, in character (e.g. verbs of motion).

6. Precocious and Delayed Acquisition

6.1. First Words

One precocious acquisition is the first lexical items of ASL. As described in Section 3.2.1, first signs are produced several months earlier than first words. Since subsequent milestones occur at the same time in ASL as in the acquisition of spoken languages, and since in general iconicity does not have a noticeable effect on ASL acquisition, the earlier occurrence of first signs must not be due to deeper facts about the languages, but rather must be due to more peripheral facts about the input/output modes. That is, first words occur earlier in the visual/gestural mode than in the aduitory/vocal mode because of earlier maturation of the relevant sensory or motor systems, or because of earlier recognition of linguistic units by either the child learner or the adult observer.

6.2. Word Order

One more precocious acquisition in ASL, as compared with some spoken languages, is the consistent use of word order. As described above, however, the child uses word order much more consistently for signalling role than does the input language. It therefore may be misleading to label this a precocious acquisition; more precisely, it is a precocious use of the available devices of the language, but for purposes other than those for which the adult uses it.

6.3. Morphology

As described in some detail above, complex morphology is acquired with some delay relative to its acquisition in languages like Turkish. Relative to many or most inflected languages, however, morphology is acquired in ASL at the expected time: the acquisition of morphology in ASL begins at about age 2½ or 3, and, as in spoken languages with extensive complex morphology, continues until after age 5.

6.4. Anaphoric Pronouns and Abstract Verb Agreement

Finally, as in the acquisition of spoken languages, the child acquires rather late the ability to explicitly introduce and establish nouns to which subsequent anaphoric reference will occur. In our view, the late acquisition of ASL verb agreement for abstract (as opposed to real-world) loci—that is, the late acquisition of verb agreement with anaphoric pronouns—is due to this late acquisition of establishing nouns, and not to the late acquisition of the morphology of verb agreement *per se*.

7. Reorganizations in Development

There are three notable phenomena suggesting reorganization in the acquisition of ASL. First, patterns in the acquisition of deictic pronouns described in Section 3.3.4 suggest a surprising reorganization, from an initial stage in which deictic pronouns are apparently nonlinguistic pointing gestures, to a second stage in which they are treated as nondeictic lexical items (and thus are produced with reversed meaning, so that a point to the addressee is used to mean 'me'), and finally to a third stage in which they are correctly interpreted as deictic pronouns. These stages strongly resemble the acquisition of deictic pronouns in English. However, they are surprising in ASL because the transparency of ASL deictic pronouns (pointing to the referent object) would lead one to expect errorless acquisition. As discussed in Section 3.3.4, Petitto (1983) and Bellugi & Klima (1981, 1982) have hypothesized that the errors of the second stage occur because the child has correctly learned that signs generally take their meaning from an abstract relation to a concept or class of referents, and not from indexing a real-world object; they therefore overgeneralize this semantic regularity to items which are actually indexics. The occurrence of reorganization in this subsystem, and the parallels between the acquisition of signed and spoken deictics, that suggest that the child is more readily able to notice regularities across the language in general than to notice individual form-referent relations.

Second, there is another reorganizational pattern, perhaps related to the first, across many of the morphological subsystems. In these subsystems, there is an early stage in which children produce correct but frozen (or amalgamated) forms, followed by a second stage in which they make errors of morpheme omission or sequentialization on previously correct forms, followed finally by a third stage in which the correct forms are organized as combinations of independent morphemes. For example, in the domain of complex verbs of motion, young children quite early produce the frozen sign FALL, which for the native adult is composed of a number of independent morphemes, one for the semantic class of the object (HUMAN), one for the path of motion (LINEAR), one for the manner of motion along this path (ROTATE), and one for the direction of motion (DOWN). Subsequently, they no longer correctly produce FALL, but instead produce ROTATE or LINEAR-DOWN alone. Finally, they return to producing FALL, but now modified morphologically depending on the details of the referent event.

Since the first stage involves non-analysis of forms which are analyzed in later stages, one might question whether "reorganization," as opposed to "organization," is the correct descriptive term. However, since such patterns are precisely like those called reorganizations in the spoken language literature (cf. Bowerman, 1985), we follow this terminology.

As in the first type of reorganization, this pattern occurs analogously to that in the acquisition of spoken language morphology, despite the fact that in ASL the child might alternatively have exploited sometimes transparent relations between individual forms and their referents to produce the more complex forms at earlier points in acquisition. In the present case, the occurrence of errors in which individual morphemes are produced and others are omitted, following a period in which the more complex forms were produced correctly, suggests that the children have noticed that portions of complex forms are shared by several of their previously unanalyzed lexical items and are in the process of determining their correct analysis. Again, then, as in the first type of reorganization, it appears that children move toward organizing forms in relation to one another across the language, rather than focusing on the relations individual forms bear to their referents, and thereby discover the internal components of previously unanalyzed units.

Finally, a third type of reorganization shows this pattern carried yet further: In the acquisition of anaphoric devices, the child begins with unanalyzed citation forms, then goes through a stage in which individual verbs are marked for agreement but do not agree with one another or with spatial loci for their nouns over the discourse, and finally establishes loci for nouns and successfully marks agreement on the appropriate verbs over long stretches of discourse. Again, this pattern appears to move from isolated forms to forms organized in relation to one another; while the previous examples of organization were over the child's internal lexicon, this organization occurs over sequential sentences. All of these types of reorganization occur at ages and in stages which parallel the acquisition of spoken languages (see Bowerman, 1985; Karmiloff-Smith, 1979).

THE SETTING OF LANGUAGE ACQUISITION

8. Cognitive Pacesetting of Language Development

There are several areas of ASL acquisition in which we hypothesize that the timing of the acquisition is set, at least in part, by the conceptual relations which the linguistic devices signal.

8.1. *First Words*

As we have argued in Section 3.2.1, the early occurrence of first words (that is, first signs) in ASL suggests that the cognitive abilities underlying first symbol usage are available quite early, in fact several months before they are used in acquiring first words in spoken languages. The additional months required for control over first words in spoken languages are apparently occupied by the maturation of the auditory/vocal input and output systems, or by the development of sufficient output skill for an adult observer to recognize the child's early attempts.

8.2. *Classifiers*

Classifiers in ASL, as in the spoken languages in which they occur, mark the semantic category, or the size and shape, of the relevant noun. Acquisition of the classifier system thus requires that the child have the ability to categorize objects into semantic or size/shape classes: human, animate nonhuman, plant, vehicle, and the like, or straight, round, large, small, and the like. It may in part be for this reason that the acquisition of classifiers in ASL does not begin until approximately age 3 and continues until perhaps age 8.

The details of this acquisition process, including the order in which the classifiers are acquired, should be of interest to cognitive developmentalists for the information they provide about the young child's classification abilities; see Kantor (1980) and Supalla (1982) for these details.

8.3. *Anaphoric Pronouns and Establishing Referents*

In English, the use of anaphoric pronouns and the linking of such pronouns to earlier nouns are usually syntactic or discourse phenomena. In ASL, however, morphological devices are involved as well.

As described in Section 3.5.1 above, ASL nouns whose referents are not present in the real-world environment must be established in abstract loci in the signing space, and subsequent reference to these nouns (in both pronouns and verb agreement) involve these loci. Once a noun is established in a spatial locus, that locus is maintained for the noun until the locus is explicitly moved (e.g. by predicating of it a verb of motion, for example, HE-TRAVEL-FROM-HERE-TO-THERE), or until the discourse topic changes and new nouns are introduced. The acquisition of these devices thus involves explicitly introducing nouns to which subsequent anaphoric reference will be made, and then maintaining consistent distinctions between the referent nouns (in both pronouns and verb agreement) in subsequent anaphoric usages.

In part, then, the acquisition of these devices requires discourse and perspective-taking abilities, as well as memorial abilities, in order to note when the listener has or has not been introduced to the referents of anaphora and to maintain distinctions between various anaphoric usages within a discourse topic. The difficulties of young children in these cognitive domains have been frequently noted (e.g. Piaget, 1955; Karmiloff-Smith, 1979).

These conceptual acquisitions may therefore be partially responsible for the late acquisition of anaphoric devices in ASL. In fact, the age at which such anaphoric devices are controlled in ASL is approximately the same as that for the control of narrative devices performing similar functions in spoken languages (see Clancy, 1985).

8.4. *Iconicity and the Use of Space*

Numerous investigators have suggested that the special features of spatial representation and, in some parts of the language, the somewhat transparent mapping between form and meaning in ASL might influence the acquisition process. There have been two types of suggestions along these lines.

First, as we have discussed repeatedly above, investigators have often considered the possibility that the iconicity of certain forms in ASL might lead to their earlier acquisition. This hypothesis implicitly assumes that the child is cognitively able, at an early age, to notice and exploit relationships between the forms of ASL and their referents. However, the findings have uniformly indicated that the acquisition of ASL proceeds in ways analogous to the acquisition of formally comparable spoken languages, and that iconicity is virtually never a contributor to the acquisition process. We have argued above that this suggests that the child is biased to approach language in certain formal ways, and to analyze relationships among forms within the language as opposed to relationships between form and referent. But it also may be the case that the young child is cognitively unable to exploit the available iconicity, and that the iconicity of mapping between form and referent is accessible only to the older child or adult (for discussion, see Meier, 1982). In the latter case, it may be the cognitive DIFFICULTY of iconicity that forces the child to acquire ASL in ways that are similar to the acquisition of spoken languages.

Second, in view of the relatively extended time over which ASL morphology is acquired, it has sometimes been suggested that spatial representation is conceptually difficult for the child, and therefore is a cognitively complex medium in which to signal linguistic functions. On this view, the acquisition of morphological devices in ASL should occur somewhat later than the acquisition of formally similar devices in spoken languages, where spatial representation is not involved. The evidence, however, suggests to us that spacial representation does not constrain the acquisition process, since the acquisition of morphological devices in ASL occurs on a strikingly similar timetable to the acquisition of formally similar spoken language devices. In ASL, as in spoken languages with any degree of temporal overlap between separate morphemes, the analysis of morphology begins between the ages of 2 and 3; and, as in spoken languages with a comparable degree of complex (even polysynthetic) morphology, the acquisition process continues until well after age 5.

The most extended acquisition processes in ASL occur within the morphological systems of complex verbs of motion and of anaphoric pronominalization and verb agreement. However, within verbs of motion, most of the system is controlled well and productively at age 5½ to 6, with only the most complex combinations of morphemes showing errors after this time (Kantor, 1980; Newport, 1981; Supalla, 1982). Such extended acquisition timespans are also found in spoken language for the acquisition of morphological systems that involve a large number of co-occurring morphemes. Within the morphological marking of anaphora, nouns are appropriately introduced and established at distinct spatial loci, and consistent distinctions are maintained between anaphoric referents over long narratives, shortly before age 5, with only occasional performance difficulties continuing past this time. As described in Section 8.3 above, this timing corresponds well to the acquisition of comparable discourse functions in spoken languages, where the marking of these functions is not morphological.

In sum, the timing of ASL acquisition appears to be governed by morphological and functional complexity, and not by the conceptual ease or difficulty of the medium in which the forms occur.

9. Linguistic Pacesetting of Cognitive Development

9.1. Effects of ASL vs. Other Languages on Cognitive Development

It has sometimes (informally) been suggested that the acquisition of the spatial devices of ASL might result in greater nonlinguistic spatial abilities, or that the acquisition of ASL classifiers might result in greater nonlinguistic categorization abilities. However, appropriate studies have not been done, and there is thus no evidence that aspects of ASL acquisition influence the cognitive development of its speakers, relative to the speakers of other languages. Moreover, for two reasons, we are doubtful that such evidence will be obtained. First, with regard to spatial devices and spatial abilities, the findings on ASL acquisition uniformly suggest that the spatialization of grammar in ASL has no discernable influence on the timing or course of native acquisition. It therefore seems unlikely (though not impossible) that the spatialization, which was ignored in acquisition, should have an effect on cognitive development. Second, it does not generally seem to be the case in spoken language that the particular linguistic devices of a language influence the nonlinguistic cognitive development of its speakers (see Brown, 1976, for a review of this literature). We would therefore not expect it to be the case for sign language.

9.2. Effects of ASL vs. No Early Linguistic Experience on Cognitive Development

There is one area related to ASL acquisition in which there may be evidence of linguistic influences on cognitive development. As will be described in detail in Section 11, the deaf community is quite diverse in the time at which its members are first exposed to ASL. Throughout the present review, we have considered only those deaf children who are acquiring ASL from deaf parents in the home, beginning at birth; these are the native users of the language. However, native learners constitute only 5 to 10% of the deaf population. The remaining 90 to 95% of the deaf community are born to hearing parents and most often are exposed to ASL, if at all, at school age or later. In Section 11 we review evidence that suggests that these non-native learners do not achieve the same levels of fluency in ASL that are achieved by native learners. In addition, these non-native learners of ASL are also typically not fully fluent in English, since profound deafness prohibits early or full access to the spoken medium. Therefore, by comparing deaf children of deaf parents with deaf children of hearing parents, one can ask whether early exposure and native fluency in a language has consequences for cognitive development, as compared with the lack of early exposure and native fluency in a language. However, any conclusions in this area must be highly tentative, since deaf children of deaf parents also differ from deaf children of hearing parents in a number of other ways (e.g. acceptance by and ability to communicate with their families, early socialization experiences, and the like).

Furth (1966b, 1971, 1973) compared deaf children with hearing children in performances on a variety of cognitive tasks, including concept attainment, memory, and tests of concrete and formal operations. His intention was to study the development of thinking in the absence of language, and he chose deaf subjects for the reason that most are not skilled in spoken language. However, it is likely that most, if not all, of his subjects knew American Sign Language at the time of testing. Nevertheless, since (given the overall population statistics) most of his subjects were probably deaf children of hearing parents, one can interpret his findings as evidence about the effects of early and native language knowledge, versus its absence, on thinking. He found that the performances of deaf children were fairly comparable to those of hearing children, despite the reported considerable difficulties in communicating with his deaf subjects (when possible, tests were administered nonverbally). Where differences did occur, they were attributable to a poor intellectual environment, rather than to a poor linguistic environment: hearing subjects from a rural community (but native in English) performed almost identically to deaf subjects (Furth & Youniss, 1965; Furth, 1966b, 1973).

In contrast, numerous studies which explicitly compare deaf children of deaf parents with deaf children of hearing parents show consistent advantages for deaf children of deaf parents in a number of areas (see Furth, 1973, and Wilbur, 1979, for reviews). For example, deaf children of deaf parents reach higher levels of formal education (Stevenson, 1964), show superior reading and writing of English (Stuckless & Birch, 1966; Meadow, 1966, 1968; Vernon & Koh, 1970), larger English vocabularies (Quigley & Frisina, 1961; Vernon & Koh, 1970), and higher academic achievement scores (Meadow, 1966, 1968; Vernon & Koh, 1970). It is of some interest that they do better in English, since English is not their native language, while it is the language in which most of the children of hearing parents have received intensive training. These differences may possibly show effects of early language (ANY language) on subsequent linguistic and metalinguistic, as well as more general academic, skills. On the other hand, as cautioned above, they may instead (or in addition) show more general effects of intellectual environment (for example, the intellectual effects of successful parental communications), or effects of socialization (for example, the effects of greater acceptance and higher self-esteem on subsequent achievement).

The evidence on this question is thus quite unclear, although possibly suggestive of linguistic effects on cognitive skills. More research is needed in this area.

10. Input and Adult–Child Interaction

10.1. General Properties of Input in ASL

Just as high, variable pitch distinguishes English Motherese from the adult-to-adult register (Phillips, 1970; Remick, 1971), enlarged size and frequent repetition of sign movement characterize the parent-to-child register in ASL (Launer, 1982b). However, given the differences between the visual/gestural and auditory/vocal modalities, certain properties of ASL Motherese lack obvious analogues in spoken Motherese. ASL parents of a child under age 2 sometimes sign on the child's body; in such situations, a sign which is normally articulated in contact with the signer's own body is instead articulated in contact with the child's. These parents may also "mold" the child's hands into an approximation of a sign and then lead the child's hands through the sign movement. Finally, in conversation with the child, a signing parent may sometimes sign in contact with a referent object, especially if that object is the referent of a deictic point. For a discussion of these properties of ASL input to children, see Maestas y Moores (1980) and Launer (1982b).

Whether these modality-specific properties of ASL Motherese have any impact upon the acquisition of sign is not known. If they indeed have the apparently intended effect of making either the form or the meaning of individual signs more salient for the young child, they may contribute to the somewhat earlier emergence of first signs in ASL than of first words in speech.

10.2. *Iconic Properties of Input in ASL*

Launer (1982a,b) and Newhoff & Launer (in press) report that, in 8% of the sign tokens addressed to children under age 2, the way the sign was articulated by the adult enhanced the iconic qualities of the sign as compared with what would be apparent in the adult-to-adult register. They also cite some instances in which a mother apparently attempted to explicate the iconicity of a sign to her child. However, the frequent enlargement of sign movement in ASL Motherese, noted above, often "submerged" the image suggested by a sign (Launer, 1982b). Furthermore, in some tokens in which a sign addressed to a child was phonologically simplified or otherwise modified as compared to its citation form, the mother's production was in fact countericonic. We conclude from Launer's results that, although signing mothers do occasionally attend to the iconic properties of signs, enhancement of iconicity is not a general property of ASL Motherese.

10.3. *Morphology in ASL Motherese*

10.3.1. *Verb Agreement in Maternal Input.* In our discussion of the acquisition of ASL verb agreement (Section 3.4.4), we noted that a frequent error type produced by young children in the process of acquiring verb agreement is the production of an uninflected, citation form verb in linguistic contexts requiring the use of agreement.

Kantor (1982a,b), examining the use of verb agreement by deaf native signing mothers to their two children, ages 1;0 to 2;8, has claimed that mothers likewise omit verb agreement in their signing, produce independent lexical points to the relevant noun arguments, and thereby in general analyze the language for the child into its potentially discrete units. If correct, Kantor's claim about ASL Motherese leads to the further hypothesis that the developmental process by which children acquire verb agreement may be driven not so much by their internal learning abilities (the position we have taken in earlier sections), but rather by the changing properties of the signing addressed to them by their mothers.

Kantor's data (1982a,b) consisted primarily of the overall frequency with which verb agreement was used in her corpora, which she found to be low. Unfortunately, however, she quantified use of verb agreement over the total number of signs used by the mothers, and did not distinguish omission of verb agreement in its obligatory contexts from omission of verbs requiring agreement or omission of verbs in general. Her data thus do not provide unambiguous support for her larger claim, or for the alternative hypothesis about the child's acquisition of verb agreement.

Meier (1983) examined input from deaf parents to two children under the age of 2 (that is, prior to the age at which children acquire verb agreement). He found, first, that occurrences of verb agreement indeed appeared, as they did in Kantor's data, and were often quite numerous. Moreover, he found that all of the mothers' utterances were grammatical in terms of adult ASL: verb agreement for an optional second noun argument was frequently omitted (as is true, presumably, in adult-to-adult signing), and verbs which do not undergo agreement sometimes occurred where a verb requiring agreement could have been used instead; but there were no occurrences of omission of verb agreement for verbs which obligatorily undergo agreement in the adult language. In contrast, young children's signing at these ages is characterized by the highly frequent omission of verb agreement in grammatically obligatory contexts (Meier, 1981, 1982).

Moreover, even the overall frequencies of usage of verb agreement reported by Kantor (1982a,b) are well within the range of frequencies of usage for English morphemes which are acquired earliest by hearing children learning English; and, as is well known in literature on the latter, at least within this range frequency of usage is not a predictor of acquisition (Brown, 1973).

In sum, we find little reason to believe that properties of maternal input will explain the available data on the acquisition of ASL verb agreement. Rather, the character of the early stages of this acquisition process, as we have argued earlier, must come from the way the child analyzes the language, and not from the way the mother organizes the input. Nevertheless, mothers may adjust the semantics of their signing to young children so as to provied more of the relevant verbs for this analysis shortly prior to the time the acquisition process begins.

10.3.2. *Derivational Morphology in Maternal Input.*   Contrary to the usual characterization of maternal input as being thoroughly grammatical, Launer (1982b) has found evidence of ungrammaticality in mothers' productions of related noun-verb pairs in ASL, especially in conversation to children under 3;0. Launer suggests that intonational properties of ASL Motherese, e.g., enlargement and repetition of sign movement, often neutralize the movement distinctions (manner, size, and frequency) which are the morphological markers of the noun-verb distinction in these sign pairs. The grammaticality of the mothers' signing in Launer's longitudinal study increased as their children matured, so that, by age 4, the mothers' productions were almost entirely grammatical.

As Launer (1982a) notes, it is not obvious how the mothers' apparent failure to mark the noun-verb distinction in conversation with their 1- and 2-year old children can aid those children in acquiring the distinction. Nevertheless, since this failure seems to arise as the consequence of regular phonological processes (and is therefore predictable), and since its frequency diminishes as the children approach age 3, it may not hinder their acquisition.

If indeed the ungrammatical absence of morphological markers of form class is attributable to the intonation of ASL Motherese, we can make sense of the fact that unlike noun-verb morphology, production of verb agreement in ASL Motherese is consistently grammatical: intonational features of size and frequency of movement will obviously have consequences for grammatical properties signalled by size and movement (in this case, noun-verb morphology), but should not interact with grammatical properties signaled by direction or orientation of movement with respect to spatial loci (in this case, verb agreement).

11. Individual and Group Differences

11.1. Individual Differences in Language Acquisition Strategies

No research has been done on individual differences in the acquisition of American Sign Language.

11.2. Acquisition of Language by Subgroups within the Deaf Population

All of the research on the acquisition of American Sign Language reviewed thus far concerns the acquisition of ASL as a native language, by deaf children of deaf parents for whom ASL is the language of the home from earliest infancy. However, this group is in fact a small minority of the deaf community; only 5 to 10% of deaf people are born to deaf parents (Schein & Delk, 1974). The remaining 90 to 95% of the deaf population are children of hearing parents, and they therefore do not typically grow up in homes where American Sign Language is used. Most of these children will be spoken to by their families in English, and, until very recently, would receive intensive and formal training only in English. Nevertheless, because of the limited access they have to spoken language, they do not typically become highly fluent in English (Bonvillian, Charrow, & Nelson, 1973; Quigley, Wilbur, Power, Montanelli, & Steinkamp, 1976; and see Quigley & Kretchmer, 1982, and Wilbur, 1979, for a review): for example, less than 12% of high school deaf students can read at a fourth-grade reading level or above (Furth, 1966a, 1973; and see Wilbur's 1979 review). In addition, they will first be exposed to American Sign Language at highly variable times, depending on the accidents of when they happen to meet other signers. Several investigators have therefore studied the acquisition of gestural languages by this group, some with an interest in the gestural communication systems which are devised on an ad-hoc basis within the family, and others with an interest in the acquisition of ASL late in life.

11.2.1. *Home Sign: The Acquisition of Gestural Communication in the Absence of a Conventional Linguistic Environment.* It has frequently been observed that deaf children who are not exposed to American Sign Language, or to any other conventional sign language, nevertheless may spontaneously gesture to members of their family or to one another (Tervoort, 1961; Lenneberg, 1964; Fant, 1972; Moores, 1974; Goldin-Meadow & Feldman, 1975, 1977; Mohay, 1982; Volterra, Massoni, & Beronesi, 1983). Within the deaf community, these gestures devised by communicative partners are known as "home signs."

Most of the research on these gesture systems has been conducted by Goldin-Meadow and her colleagues (Goldin-Meadow & Feldman, 1975, 1977; Feldman, Goldin-Meadow & Gleitman, 1978; Goldin-Meadow, 1979, 1982, 1985; Goldin-Meadow & Mylander, 1983, 1984). They have investigated the sources of these gesture systems (that is, whether they are devised by the deaf children themselves, or rather whether they are modelled or shaped by the hearing partners who are already fluent in a spoken language), as well as the structure of the gesture systems (that is, whether they show any consistent syntactic patterns, or rather whether they are random concatenations of gestures).

Their subjects were ten congenitally deaf children born to hearing parents. The children all had severe to profound hearing losses, and were all unable to acquire more than very minimal skills in spoken language (English), even when equipped with hearing aids and provided with intensive formal training in sound sensitivity, speech, and lipreading. Their vocalizations were 1–4% of all of their communications, and even of these, only 1–10% were recognizable words. All of the recognizable words were produced in isolation; none of the children evidenced any ability to combine spoken words, and therefore none evidenced any knowledge of English syntax (Goldin-Meadow & Mylander, 1984).

Neither did these children have any knowledge of any conventional sign language (either American Sign Language or Signed English). Their preschools, which emphasized oral education, avoided the use of any conventional sign language and discouraged their families from learning or using sign language. None of the children's parents or siblings (all of whom were hearing) knew any sign language. In sum, then, to the best of the experimenters' knowledge, none of the children had any effective conventional linguistic environment beyond a few isolated words of English (although their nonlinguistic environments were normal).

Nonetheless, the children were observed to gesture spontaneously and extensively to their family members and to the experimenters. These gestural interactions were videotaped longitudinally, with the videotaped sessions for the ten children altogether covering the period from age 1;4 to 4;6. (Only two children were observed below the age of 2; most of the observations cover the age range from 2 to 4 years.)

Using the methods of the spoken language literature for determining the meanings and structures used by the children, Goldin-Meadow and her colleagues have demonstrated that these children first produce one gesture at a time, and subsequently combine gestures to produce two-gesture and even more complex utterances (upper bounds range from three to nine gestures per utterance across the ten children). Most of the data reported thus far come from the two-gesture utterances. Surprisingly, these two-gesture utterances are in many ways like two-word utterances of children exposed to conventional linguistic environments.

For present purposes, two characteristics are of special interest. First, the gesture utterances express approximately the same range of semantic relations as two-word utterances. Second, they are syntactically patterned, using gesture order in a consistent way to mark the role of noun arguments in the utterance. For most of the subjects the order was PATIENT-ACT-RECIPIENT in transitive utterances (where the actor was typically omitted) and ACTOR-ACT in intransitive utterances, orders which are characteristic of many spoken languages, but not of either English or American Sign Language. (Two subjects, while using order consistently, used particular orders slightly different than these.) In short, two of the most typical characteristics of two-word speech and two-word sign—a restricted range of semantic relations, and a tendency to use the order of lexical items to mark those relations—occur in a communication system developed entirely in the absence of a conventional linguistic environment. Further data show the occurrence of recursion and of differential production probabilities for semantic elements, both of which occur in children acquiring conventional languages.

A major question is whether these characteristics emerge because of structured, although not conventional, features of the communicative environments of these children, or rather whether they emerge solely because of predispositions in the children themselves. The most comprehensive examination of this question is presented in Goldin-Meadow & Mylander (1984). Their data argue, first, that although the mothers of these children do gesture (typically while they speak) to their children, their gestures do not show the same characteristics as those of their children. Mothers tended to produce single gestures, and combined their gestures in two-or-more-gesture utterances much more rarely than did their children. Moreover, their two-gesture (and more complex) utterances did not in general show reliable use of gesture order, and never showed, with any greater than chance frequency, the same gesture orders that their children used. The children's patterned use of gesture is therefore not based on a similarly patterned use of gesture in their environments.

Second, Goldin-Meadow & Mylander have demonstrated that the children are not producing gestures in immediate imitation of their mothers, and that their gesture patterns are not being shaped by their communicative partners. Neither their mothers nor strangers show better comprehension of those gestured utterances which show the typical patterns than of those which violate these patterns. Thus it does not appear that comprehensibility pressures shape the children's gestures. Moreover, their mothers do not give either relevant responses or contingent approval more frequently to utterances which show the typical patterns than to those which do not. Thus there do not appear to be other communicative pressures which shape the children's gestures.

Third, they have demonstrated that the syntactic patterns of the two-gesture utterances are not marking or reflecting new vs. old information, or first and second vs. third person, as have been suggested by pragmatic or communicative interpretations of the data. Rather, as in the utterances of children acquiring conventional languages, the syntactic patterns seem to mark semantic-syntactic categories (e.g. agent or subject vs. patient or object).

In sum, the gestural communication of deaf children who are not exposed to a conventional language has many of the typical properties of early conventional utterances. These properties do not seem to arise from modelling, shaping, or other communicative pressures of the environment, but rather seem to be devised by the children themselves. These results suggest rather strongly, then, as we have argued from data on the acquisition of a conventional sign language, that many of the features of early language arise from biases or predispositions of the child learner.

11.2.2. *The Acquisition of American Sign Language as a Primary Language Beyond Infancy.* Several investigators have recently begun to study deaf off-spring of hearing parents who have been exposed to ASL at varying times of life, in an effort to determine the effects of such acquisition on language organization and processing. In particular, in the spoken language literature, Lenneberg (1967) has hypothesized that there is a critical period within which normal language learning occurs, but outside of which language is acquired only with more effort or in a different fashion. However, the evidence regarding such a critical period, or, in more recent terminology, regarding whether there is a special effect of early experience on the acquisition of language, has largely been indirect, since within spoken language communities children are uniformly exposed to their primary language from birth.

However, within the deaf community there are a number of individuals who, as described in the section above, are not effectively exposed to a conventional language until school-age or even later. At some point, often in residential schools for the deaf or in deaf social groups, they may be exposed to (and immersed in) ASL, which they will then acquire through informal exposure; for many of these individuals, ASL will then become their primary language, although it is a language they have acquired after infancy. There are currently several on-going research projects examining the way in which these ASL users organize and process the language in adulthood, after having acquired it under these unusual circumstances.

Scattered bits of evidence have existed for several years to suggest that native learners of ASL (those who have acquired it from their deaf parents beginning in earliest infancy) differ from non-native learners. For example, Woodward (1973) reported that the use of certain aspects of ASL morphology could be predicted in part by whether the users had deaf parents and had been exposed to the language before or after age 5. Fischer (1978) suggested that the ASL situation bears resemblances to the pidgin-creole situation found in certain spoken language communities, and that differences in structure between native and non-native ASL may reflect the age differences of their learners. Similarly, Newport & Supalla (1980; Newport, 1981, 1982) have suggested that observed differences between native and non-native ASL signers in the use of complex morphology is due to age of exposure to the language.

More recently, experimental evidence has begun to be collected to detail these differences. Mayberry (1979) found differences between adult native signers and non-native signers who had acquired ASL after age 16, in their ability to shadow ASL stories. Hatfield (1980) measured true/false reaction times of deaf adults to ASL sentences and found that the best predictor of performance was the age at which subjects first learned to sign. Mayberry, Fischer, & Hatfield (1983) tested adult signers' abilities to shadow and recall ASL sentences for four groups of signers: those exposed to the language from birth, at age 5, at ages 11 to 13, and at age 18 or later. They found linearly declining performance over these four groups, with those exposed to the language from birth performing at or near ceiling and each of the other groups performing significantly worse. However, as they note, because their subjects were all young adults between the ages of 20 and 35, their results could be the effect of the length of time subjects had been using the language, rather than the age at which they were first exposed to it.

In an on-going series of studies, Newport & Supalla (forthcoming) have tested adult signers for their elicited production and comprehension of various aspects of ASL morphology and syntax. Their subjects fall into three groups in terms of their age of first exposure to ASL (birth vs. ages 4 to 6 vs. after age 12) and two groups in terms of their length of experience with the language (under 30 years of experience vs. over 50 years of experience). Their results so far, on the elicited production and comprehension of the morphology of ASL verbs of motion, show no effects of length of experience with the language, but significant linear effects of age of first exposure to the language on virtually every morpheme tested in both production and comprehension.

In sum, linguistic performance and language organization seem to show size-able effects of early vs. late exposure to ASL as a primary language, even after more than 50 years of everyday use of the language. Ongoing studies (Newport & Supalla, forthcoming) investigate the character of the knowledge these various learners possess; in addition, they investigate the nature of the learning process as it begins in native vs. non-native learners, in an attempt to discover why these learners differ in later years. Presumably, these effects are not special to sign languages, but reflect more general sensitivities of language acquisition to the age or maturational state during which it occurs. They therefore lend support to the claim that native learners are biased or predisposed to analyze their input during language learning in particular ways, since learners acquiring ASL later in life do not achieve the same outcomes.

CONCLUSIONS

12. Suggestions for Further Study

In previous sections we have mentioned issues for which further data would be clarifying. One instance concerns the status of iconicity for young children. The evidence we have reviewed clearly suggests an absence of an effect of iconicity on the acquisition of ASL. However, as discussed in Section 8.4, this could be due either to the child's biases to attend to properties of input other than iconicity, or to her inability to exploit iconicity (Meier, 1982). Further research on whether young children are capable of appreciating the holistic iconicity of forms, apart from whether they use this iconicity in their acquisition of the language, would be informative here.

A second instance in which further data would clarify issues in ASL acquisition concerns the comparison between pointing in deaf children acquiring ASL and pointing in hearing children who use it nonlinguistically. For example, Petitto (1983) cites an observation that hearing children do not point at themselves at 10 months, when deaf children do; further data on this issue would help to determine whether this early pointing by deaf children is already linguistically influenced, or rather whether it is the same as nonlinguistic pointing. Similarly, Petitto reports the disappearance of pointing at people in deaf children ages 12–18 months, and reversal errors in the pointing behavior of deaf children ages 22–23 months. Presumably, neither of these phenomena occur in hearing children, and therefore both are reflections of the linguistic analysis of pointing within ASL. However, documentation of the absence of these phenomena in hearing children would be helpful.

In addition, there are a number of areas in the study of ASL acquisition in which virtually no data exist at all; in particular, any research in the areas mentioned below would be highly desirable:

Most of the available literature on the acquisition of American Sign Language involves the acquisition of morphology. This is not surprising or inappropriate, since ASL is extremely rich morphologically and is, in this sense, probably most comparable in typology to polysynthetic spoken languages (e.g. Navaho). However, virtually no work has been done to date on the acquisition of ASL syntax, and in fact relatively little work has been done on the syntax of the adult language. This is particularly interesting area for future study, since there is little known in general about the acquisition of syntax in polysynthetic languages. For example, it is of some interest to know whether the syntaxes of polysynthetic languages are less complex or differently organized than those of languages with less morphological complexity (e.g. see Hale, 1978, for a suggestion that the syntax of one polysynthetic spoken language is organized fundamentally differently in terms of its constituent structure than are the typical "X bar" languages). If so, it is of additional interest to know whether such a syntax is acquired differently, or on a strikingly different timetable, than in languages where the morphology is simpler or earlier acquired. Moreover, even if the syntax of ASL is similar to that of more well-studied languages, it may be acquired in different ways or on a somewhat different timetable, in view of the fact that its morphology is acquired over such a long developmental period.

A related issue which has received no study to date is the acquisition of grammaticized facial expressions. In ASL, facial expression serves a number of grammatical purposes that it does not serve in spoken languages. For example, some facial expressions are obligatory parts of individual lexical items; others are adverbial in function, modifying the meaning of verbs in regular ways; others mark topicalized noun phrases; and still others mark relative clauses (Liddell, 1980; Coulter, 1979, 1980). In addition, Coulter (1979) has presented evidence that certain grammaticized facial expressions are internally analyzable, being composed of facial components which each have independent grammatical functions and contributions to meaning. On this view, facial expressions are in some ways like grammatical morphemes. It is of some interest to know how and when they are acquired, and to compare their acquisition to the other morphological and syntactic devices of ASL, as well as of spoken languages. In addition, unlike most formal devices in spoken languages, grammaticized facial expressions have a clear nonlinguistic system (that is, nonlinguistic facial expressions) from which they derive, but from which they differ strikingly in organization. The study of their acquisition, in comparison with the acquisition of nonlinguistic facial expressions, may thus allow particularly perspicuous observations of the contrasts between nonlinguistic and linguistic development.

Finally, it is of great interest to know what the acquisition process looks like for natural sign languages other than American Sign Language. With such information, one should be able to determine what are universal principles of the acquisition of sign languages in particular, and what are universal principles of the acquisition of languages in general.

13. Theoretical Implications

Because ASL is in certain ways typologically different from most spoken languages, a comparison of its acquisition with that of spoken languages can help to clarify our notions of the factors influencing acquisition in general. In particular, ASL differs from spoken languages in its more frequent availability of iconicity, and in its more predominant use of simultaneous rather than sequential morphological devices. These differences seem to us to shed important light on issues of form-function mapping, agglutination vs. fusion in morphology, and lexical vs. morphological priority, all of which have been thoughtfully considered (particularly by Slobin) within the spoken language literature.

13.1. *Clarity of Form-Function Mapping*

Slobin (1973), and subsequently others, have hypothesized on the basis of spoken language acquisition that clarity in the mapping between forms and their functions or meanings (sometimes called the one-to-one mapping principle) plays a crucial role in the child's acquisition of these forms. The data from ASL acquisition, however, suggest an important limitation of this principle, and an equally equally important suggestion that form-form mappings rather than form-function mappings may at least sometimes guide the learning (see also Bowerman, 1985, for related suggestions from spoken language acquisition).

In particular, one type of potentially clear form-function mapping, that of iconicity, appears to have virtually no impact on the acquisition of American Sign Language. As we have seen repeatedly, the young child acquiring ASL as a native language either does not, or cannot, take advantage of iconicity to acquire relatively early those devices which are transparently related to their meanings. Rather, the child appears to be more interested in, and more guided by, the relations of forms to one another over the language, than the relations of individual forms to their meanings or referents. Typical ASL acquisition patterns and errors suggest that the child is comparing complex forms to one another and, piece by piece, finding components of form which various lexical items share. He thus acquires ASL lexical items in terms of these components, producing some morphemes but omitting others, and in general learning ASL as though it were an entirely arbitrary formal system.

One might argue that these findings speak only to the issue of iconicity in particular, and not to the issue of form-function mappings more generally. In our opinion, however, they underline the tendency in children acquiring spoken languages as well as signed languages to seek out and analyze relations among forms.

13.2. *Factors Concerning the Ways in which Forms are Arrayed*

Slobin and his colleagues (1982; Aksu-Koç & Slobin, 1985) have determined that the morphology of Turkish is acquired surprisingly early, much of it prior to age 2. Several characteristics of Turkish have been suggested as contributing to this precocious acquisition, for example that the morphology is agglutinating rather than fusional in the way morphemes are combined, and that the morphemes are syllabic, stressed, and highly regular. The typological characteristics of ASL and the patterns of its acquisition contrast with those of Turkish in ways that permit us to comment on some of these characteristics and their role in acquisition.

13.2.1. *Agglutination vs. Temporal Sequencing.*   When one compares ASL with spoken languages, it becomes clear that agglutination in Turkish includes two factors that may influence acquisition in separate ways. As we suggest in Section 4.1, the morphology of Turkish is both agglutinative (that is, the components of form combine with one another in noninteracting ways) and sequential, while at least certain subsystems of the morphology of ASL are agglutinative and simultaneous. However, in ASL, unlike Turkish, this morphology is not acquired precociously; rather, it is acquired at approximately the same time as more fusional morphology in spoken languages. Moreover, errors made in the process of acquiring ASL morphology include sequentialization of morphemes which should be produced simultaneously.

These facts taken together suggest that one crucial factor in the acquisition of these languages may be their temporal characteristics, rather than agglutination or fusion per se. On this view, Turkish morphemes are temporally sequenced, ASL morphemes are temporally simultaneous (although agglutinative), and the morphemes of many other spoken languages are temporally overlapping. The precocious acquisition of Turkish morphology may thus be due, at least in part, to its temporal sequencing: temporally distinct, nonoverlapping components of form may be easier to acquire than either agglutinative or fusional components which overlap in time.

As an aside to those interested particularly in signed languages, we should note that there are sign systems (e.g. SEE) whose morphologies are temporally sequenced. However, none of these (to our knowledge) are natural sign languages; rather, they are systems invented by deaf educators for representing English on the hands. Anecdotal evidence suggests that these systems may not become natural languages, in the sense that children exposed to them often creolize them into systems which are more like American Sign Language or abandon them to acquire American Sign Language instead (S. Supalla & Newport, in progress). Moreover, evidence from the processing of American Sign Language (Bellugi & Fischer, 1972) suggests a possible explanation for these facts: slower articulation with the hands than the tongue may make temporally sequenced morphology unwieldy in the gestural modality. If these suggestions are correct, the simultaneous morphology of ASL (and other natural signed languages) may be required by the nature of processing in the gestural modality, despite the fact that it is less easy to acquire than a morphology like that in Turkish. Interestingly, the simultaneous morphology of ASL is no more difficult to acquire than the somewhat overlapping morphology of fusional spoken languages: the ages of acquisition for these two types of languages are remarkably comparable.

13.2.2. *Priority of the Word vs. the Morpheme*   On the basis of the precocious acquisition of Turkish morphology, Slobin (1982; Aksu-Koç & Slobin, 1985) has also hypothesized that morphological devices may be easier to acquire than lexical devices, since the former offer local cues while the latter distribute their cues over stretches of words. (On this view, morphological devices in fusional languages are not acquired early simply because they are fusional.) However, the data on the acquisition of ASL suggest that there may not be a general priority of morphemes over words in the early stages of acquisition, but, on the contrary, a general priority of words over morphemes.

The evidence for this claim comes from several sources: First, as discussed above, the morphemes of ASL, like those of many spoken languages, are not acquired early. However, we have already suggested a reason for this. More compelling, when ASL morphemes begin to be acquired, they are often articulated as separate lexemes rather than as morphemes within a single sign. For example, within verbs of motion and location, sequentialization errors (see Section 4.3) often involve not just producing morphemes sequentially within a sign, but articulating them as though they were separate signs. This occurs with morphemes for movement and manner of movement (Newport, 1981), as well as for handshape classifiers for central and secondary objects (Supalla, 1982; see also Section 4.3); and it occurs with the sequential morphemes of lexical compounds (S. Supalla, 1980; Section 4.3). Finally, the same phenomenon is reported in early stages of the acquisition of Turkish morphology: Aksu-Koç & Slobin (1985) report an exaggerated tendency to clearly mark morpheme boundaries, sometimes with slight pauses between morphemes.

All of these phenomena may suggest that words are easier units for the child, in early stages of acquisition, than morphemes, and moreover that when morphemes begin to be analyzed, they are processed like separate words. On this view, Turkish and other sequential agglutinative morphologies may be acquired early because their morphemes are prosodically like words (that is, syllabic and stressed). Gleitman & Wanner (1982) have suggested a somewhat different, but related account, of early acquisition in terms of prosodic factors. On the other hand, Aksu-Koç & Slobin have suggested that these phenomena are speech production strategies, rather than strategies of analysis. Further research on this issue is needed.

13.2.3. *Other Factors.*   Finally, the acquisition of ASL makes suggestions with regard to several other important, if somewhat more mundane, factors in language acquisition.

Much of the research on the acquisition of spoken languages has suggested the importance of the degree of regularity of morphological devices in determining the timing of their acquisition. Certainly the data from ASL do not contradict this; however, they do suggest that the notion of regularity might be examined in greater detail. The earliest acquired morphological subsystem in ASL, that of verb agreement, is irregular in the sense that it applies only to some verbs (partly predictable from the phonology of the stem, but partly lexically idiosyncratic; see Fischer & Gough, 1978, and Padden, 1983), and in the sense that it applies differently to verbs whose stems involve movement than to those whose stems do not involve movement. ASL morphological subsystems that are acquired somewhat later, for example, noun-verb derivational morphology and the morphology of verbs of motion, are more regular in the sense that the morphological distinctions appear in more similar ways on the various stems to which they apply; but they are less regular in the sense that their domain of application is more restricted. (That is, verb agreement applies to most verbs, although not all, whereas noun-verb derivational morphology applies primarily to a set of stems referring to concrete objects and their associated actions, and verbs of motion morphology applies primarily to verbs of motion.) The ASL evidence thus suggests that, in addition to regularity within the domain of application, the breadth of this domain of application may be important in determining the timing of acquisition.

Finally, of course, the sheer complexity of the morphology, in terms of the number of morphemes required for an adult form, as well as the complexity of the semantic distinctions it requires, influence the timing of acquisition. Thus the latest morphemes to be acquired within ASL include those of verbs of motion (which involve a very large number of morphemes) and anaphoric pronouns (which involve establishing and maintaining abstract spatial loci for absent objects).

13.2.4. *Final Remarks.* In sum, the comparison of the acquisition of American Sign Language with that of spoken languages may greatly enrich our understanding of the typological distinctions significant in understanding language structure and acquisition. Comparisons of the acquisition of ASL with the acquisition of spoken languages have afforded us the opportunity to contrast the acquisition of language in the visual modality with the acquisition in the more familiar speech modality, to contrast the acquisition of a language with substantial inconicity to the acquisition of spoken languages with their virtually complete arbitrariness, and to contrast the acquisition of simultaneously-organized morphology with the acquisition of differently organized spoken language morphologies. In each case, these comparisons help to reveal the biases and processing strategies which the child, deaf or hearing, signing or speaking, brings to bear on the task of language acquisition. Future research on the acquisition of ASL and other natural signed languages will help to delineate this picture even more.

ACKNOWLEDGMENTS

The preparation of this chapter was supported in part by NIH and NSF Research Grants NS16878 and BNS80-13509 to E. Newport and T. Supalla, by NIH Research Grant HD05951 to J. Campione, and by NIH Training Grant HD07205 to the University of Illinois. We would like to thank Ted Supalla for his helpful comments on an earlier draft of this chapter.

REFERENCES

Aksu-Koç, A. A., & Slobin, D. I. The acquisition of Turkish. In D. I. Slobin (Ed.), *The crosslinguistic study of language acquisition* (Vol. 1). Hillsdale, NJ: Lawrence Erlbaum Associates, 1985.

Bellugi, U., & Fischer, S. A comparison of sign language and spoken language. *Cognition*, 1972, *1*, 173–200.

Bellugi, U., & Klima, E. S. From gesture to sign: Deixis in a visual-gestural language. In R. J. Jarvella & W. Klein (Eds.), In *Speech, place and action: Studies of language in context*. Sussex: Wiley, 1981.

Bellugi, U., & Klima, E. S. The acquisition of three morphological systems in American Sign Language. *Papers and Reports on Child Language Development*, 1982, *21*, 1–34.

Bloom, L., Lightbown, P., & Hood, L. Structure and variation in child language. *Monographs of the Society for Research in Child Development*, 1975, *40* (2), Ser. No. 160.

Bonvillian, J. D., Charrow, V. & Nelson, K. E. Psycholinguistic and educational implications of deafness. *Human Development*, 1973, *16*, 321–345.

Bonvillian, J. D., Orlansky, M. D., & Novack, L. L. Early sign language acquisition and its relation to cognitive and motor development. In J. Kyle & B. Woll (Eds.), *Language in sign: An international perspective on sign language*. London: Groom Helm, 1983.

Bowerman, M. What shapes children's grammars? In D. I. Slobin (Ed.), *The crosslinguistic study of language acquisition* (Vol. 2). Hillsdale, NJ: Lawrence Erlbaum Associates, 1985.

Boyes-Braem, P. *A study of the acquisition of the DEZ in American Sign Language.* Unpublished manuscript, University of California, Berkeley, 1973.

Brown, R. *A first language: The early stages.* Cambridge, MA: Harvard University Press, 1973.

Brown, R. Reference: In memorial tribute to Eric Lenneberg. *Cognition*, 1976, *4*, 125–153.

Brown, R. Why are signed languages easier to learn than spoken language? In W. C. Stokoe (Ed). *Proceedings of the First National Symposium on Sign Language Research and Teaching.* Siver Spring, MD: National Association of the Deaf, 1980.

Cazden, C. B. The acquistion of noun and verb inflections. *Child Development*, 1968, *39*, 433–438.

Clancy, P. M. The acquisition of Japanese. In D. I. Slobin (Ed.), *The crosslinguistic study of language acquisition* (Vol. 1). Hillsdale, NJ: Lawrence Erlbaum Associates, 1985.

Clark, E. V. From gesture to word: On the natural history of deixis in language acquisition. In J. S. Bruner, & A. Garton (Eds.), *Human growth and development: Wolfson College Lectures 1976.* Oxford: Clarendon Press, 1978.

Coulter, G. R. *American Sign Language Typology.* Unpublished doctoral dissertation, University of California, San Diego, 1979.

Coulter, G. R. Continuous representation in American Sign Language. In W. C. Stokoe (Ed.). *Proceedings of the First National Symposium on Sign Language Research and Teaching.* Silver Spring, MD: National Association of the Deaf, 1980.

Coulter, G. R. Raised eyebrows and wrinkled noses: The gramatical function of facial expression in relative clauses and related functions. In F. Caccamise & D. Hicks (Eds.). *Proceedings of the Second National Symposium on Sign Language Research and Teaching.* Silver Spring, MD: National Association of the Deaf, 1980.

DeMatteo, A. Visual imagery and visual analogues in American Sign Language. In L. Friedman (Ed.), *On the other hand.* New York: Academic Press, 1977.

Ellenberger, R. L., Moores, D. F., & Hoffmeister, R. J. Early stages in the acquisition of negation by a deaf child of deaf parents. Research Report #94, *Research, Development and Demonstration Center in the Education of Handicapped Children,* University of Minnesota, 1975.

Ellenberger, R., & Steyaert, M. A child's representation of action in American Sign Language. In P. Siple (Ed.), *Understanding language through sign language research.* New York: Academic Press, 1978.

Fant, L. J. *Ameslan: An introduction to American Sign Language.* Silver Spring, MD: National Association of the Deaf, 1972.

Feldman, H. *The development of a lexicon by deaf children of hearing parents, or there's more to language than meets the ear.* Unpublished doctoral dissertation, University of Pennsylvania, 1975.

Feldman, H., Goldin-Meadow, S., & Gleitman, L. R. Beyond Herodotus: The creation of language by linguistically deprived deaf children. In A. Locke (Ed.), *Action, symbol, and gesture: The emergence of language.* New York: Academic Press, 1978.

Fischer, S. The ontogenetic development of language. In E. W. Straus (Ed.), *Language and language disturbances: Fifth Lexington Conference on pure and applied phenomenology.* Pittsburgh, PA: Duquesne University Press, 1974.

Fischer, S. Two processes of reduplication in the American Sign Language, *Foundations of Language,* 1973, *9,* 469–480. (a)

Fischer, S. Verb inflections in American Sign Language and their acquisition by the deaf child. *Paper presented to the Linguistic Society of America,* 1973. (b)

Fischer, S., & Gough, B. Verbs in American Sign Language. *Sign Language Studies,* 1978, *18,* 14–48.

Friedman, L. The manifestation of subject, object, and topic in American Sign Language. In C. Li (Ed.), *Subject and topic.* New York: Academic Press, 1976.

Friedman, L. A. Formational properties of American Sign Language. In L. Friedman (Ed.), *On the other hand: New perspectives on American Sign Language.* New York: Academic Press, 1977.

Furth, H. B. A comparison of reading test norms of deaf and hearing children. *American Annals Deaf,* 1966, *III,* 461–462. (a)

Furth, H. G. *Thinking without language: Psychological implications of deafness.* New York: Free Press, 1966. (b)

Furth, H. G. Linguistic deficiency and thinking: Research with deaf subjects 1964–69. *Psychology Bulletin,* 1971, *76,* 58–72.

Furth, H. G. *Deafness and learning: A psychosocial approach.* Belmont, CA: Wadworth Publishing Co., 1973.

Furth, H. G., & Youniss, J. The influence of language and experience on discovery and use of logical symbols. *British Journal of Psychology,* 1965, *56,* 381–390.

Gleitman, L. R., & Wanner, E. The state of the state of the art. In E. Wanner & L. R. Gleitman (Eds), *Language acquisition: The state of the art.* New York: Cambridge University Press, 1982.

Goldin-Meadow, S. Structure in a manual communications system developed without a conventional language model: Language without a helping hand. In H. Whitaker & H. A. Whitaker (Eds.), *Studies in neurolinguistics* (Vol. 4). New York: Academic Press, 1979.

Goldin-Meadow, S. The resilience of recursion: A study of a communication system developed without a conventional language model. In E. Wanner & L. R. Gleitman (Eds.), *Language acquisition: The state of the art.* New York: Cambridge University Press, 1982.

Goldin-Meadow, S. Language development under atypical learning conditions: Replication and implications of a study of deaf children of hearing parents. In K. E. Nelson (Ed.), *Children's Language* (Vol. 5). Hillsdale, NJ: Lawrence Erlbaum Association, 1985.

Goldin-Meadow, S., & Feldman, H. The creation of a communication system: A study of deaf children of hearing parents. *Sign Language Studies,* 1975, *8,* 225–234.

Goldin-Meadow, S., & Feldman, H. The development of language-like communication without a language model. *Science,* 1977, *197,* 401–403.

Goldin-Meadow, S., & Mylander, C. Gestural communication in deaf children: The non-effects of parental input on language development. *Science,* 1983, *221,* 372–374.

Goldin-Meadow, S., & Mylander, C. Gestural communication in deaf children: The effects and noneffects of parental input on early language development. *Monographs of the Society for Research in Child Development,* 1984, *49* (3–4), Serial no. 207.

Goldsmith, J. A. *Autosegmental phonology*. Unpublished doctoral dissertation, MIT, 1976.

Hale, K. *On the position of Walbiri in a typology of the base*. Unpublished manuscript, MIT, 1978.

Hatfield, N. *An investigation of bilingualism in two signed languages: American Sign Language and manually coded English*. Unpublished doctoral dissertation, University of Rochester, 1980.

Hoffmeister, R. J. The influential POINT.

Hoffmeister, R. J. *The development of demonstrative pronouns, locatives and personal pronouns in the acquisition of American Sign Language by deaf children of deaf parents*. Unpublished doctoral dissertation, University of Minnestoa, 1978. (a)

Hoffmeister, R. J. Word order in the acquisition of ASL. *Paper presented at the Boston University Conference on Language Development*, 1978. (b)

Kantor, R. The acquistion of classifiers in American Sign Language. *Sign Language Studies*, 1980, *28*, 193–208.

Kantor, R. *Communicative interacation in American Sign Language between deaf mothers and their children: A psycholinguistic analysis*. Unpublished doctoral dissertation, Boston University, 1982. (a)

Kantor, R. Communication interaction: Mother modification and child acquisition of American Sign Language, *Sign Language Studies*, 1982, *36*, 233–282. (b)

Karmiloff-Smith, A. Language as a formal problem space for children. *Paper presented at the Conference "Beyond Description in Child Language Research,"* Nijmegen, 1979.

Karmiloff-Smith, A. The grammatical marking of thematic structure in the development of language production. In W. Deutsch (Ed.), *The child's construction of language*. London: Academic Press, 1981.

Klima, E. S., & Bellugi, U. Iconicity in signs and signing. In E. S. Klima & U. Bellugi, *The signs of language*. Cambridge, MA: Harvard University Press, 1979. (a)

Klima, E. S., & Bellugi, U. On the creation of new lexical items by compounding. In E. S. Klima U. Bellugi, *The signs of language*. Cambridge, MA: Harvard University Press, 1979. (b)

Klima, E. S., & Bellugi, U. *The signs of language*. Cambridge, MA: Harvard University Press, 1979. (c)

Klima, E. S., Bellugi, U., Fischer, S., & Newkirk, D. The rate of speaking and signing. In E. S. Klima & U. Bellugi, *The signs of language*. Cambridge, MA: Harvard University Press, 1979.

Klima, E. S., Bellugi, U., Newkirk, D., & Battison, R. Properties of symbols in a silent language. In E. S. Klima & U. Bellugi, *The signs of language*. Cambridge, MA: Harvard University Press, 1979.

Klima, E. S., Bellugi, U., Newkirk, D., Pedersen, C. C., & Fischer, S. The structured use of space and movement: Morphological processes In E. S. Klima & U. Bellugi, *The signs of language*. Cambridge, MA: Harvard University Press, 1979.

Klima, E. S., Bellugi, U., & Pedersen, C. C. Aspectual modulations on adjectival predicates. In E. S. Klima, & U. Bellugi, *The signs of languages*. Cambridge, MA: Harvard University Press, 1979.

Klima, E. S., Bellugi, U., & Siple, P. A comparison of Chinese and American signs. In E. S. Klima & U. Bellugi, *The signs of language*. Cambridge, MA: Harvard University Press, 1979.

Lacy, R. The development of Pola's negation. *Working Paper, The Salk Institute, 1972*.

Launer, P. B. Early signs of motherhood: Motherese in American Sign Language. *Paper presented to the American Speech-Hearing-Language Association*, Toronto, November 1982. (a)

Launer, P. B. *"A Plane" is not "To Fly": Acquiring the distinction between related nouns and verbs in American Sign Language*. Unpublished doctoral dissertation, City University of New York, 1982. (b)

Lenneberg, E. H. Capacity for language acquisition. In J. A. Fodor & J. J. Katz (Eds.), *The structure of language: Readings in the philosophy of language*. Englewood Cliffs, NJ: Prenctice-Hall, 1964.

Lenneberg, E. H. *Biological foundations of language*. New York: Wiley, 1967.

Liddell, S. *American Sign Language Syntax.* The Hague: Mouton, 1980.

Loew, R. Some observations on the acquisition of indexic incorporation in American Sign Language. *Working paper, The Salk Institute,* 1980.

Loew, R. Learning American Sign Language as a first language: Roles and reference. In F. Caccamise, M. Garreston, & U. Bellugi (Eds.), *Proceedings of the Third National Symposium on Sign Language Research and Teaching.* Silver Spring, MD: National Association of the Deaf, 1981.

Loew, R. *Roles and reference in American Sign Language: A developmental perspective.* Unpublished doctoral dissertation, University of Minnesota, 1984.

Maestas y Moores, J. Early linguistic environment: Interactions of deaf parents with their infants. *Sign Language Studies,* 1980, *26,* 1–13.

MacWhinney, B. The acquisition of morphophonology. *Monographs of the Society for Research in Child Development,* 1978, *43,* (1–2), Serial no. 174.

Mandel, M. Iconicity of signs and their learnability by non-signers. In W. C. Stokoe (Ed.), *Proceedings of the First National Symposium on Sign Language Research and Teaching.* Silver Spring, MD: National Association of the Deaf, 1980.

Maxwell, M. A child's garden of lexical gaps. *Working paper, The Salk Institute and the University of Arizona,* 1977.

Mayberry, R. *Facial expression and redundancy in American Sign Language.* Unpublished doctoral dissertation, McGill University, 1979.

Mayberry, R., Fischer, S., & Hatfield, N. Sentence repetition in American Sign Language. In J. G. Kyle & B. Woll (Eds.), *Language in sign: International perspectives on sign language.* London: Groom Helm, 1983.

McCarthy, J. J. A prosodic theory of nonconcatenative morphology. *Linguistic Inquiry,* 1981, *12,* 373–417.

McIntire, M. L. The acquisition of American Sign Language hand configurations. *Sign Langauge Studies,* 1977, *16,* 247–266.

Meadow, K. P. *The effects of early manual communication and family climate on the deaf child's early development.* Unpublished doctoral dissertation, University of California, Berkeley, 1966.

Meadow, K. P. Early manual communication in relation to the deaf child's intellectual, social, and communicative functioning. *American Annals of the Deaf,* 1968, *113,* 29–41.

Meier, R. P. Towards an analysis of the acquisition of morphology in American Sign Language. *Working paper, The Salk Institute,* 1979.

Meier, R. P. Acquisition of inflections in American Sign Language. *Working paper, The Salk Institute,* 1980.

Meier, R. Icons and morphemes: Models of the acquisition of verb agreement in ASL. *Papers and Reports on Child Language Development,* 1981, *20,* 92–99.

Meier, R. *Icons, analogues, and morphemes: The acquisition of verb agreement in ASL.* Unpublished doctoral dissertation, University of California, San Diego, 1982.

Meier, R. P. *Mother does it right: Verb agreement in American Sign Language Motherese.* Unpublished manuscript, University of Illinois at Urbana-Champaign, 1983.

Meier, R. P., Loew, R., Bahan, B., Fields, J., Launer, P. B., & Supalla, S. An overview of one child's acquisition of American Sign Language. *Working paper, The Salk Institute,* 1980.

Mohay, H. A. A preliminary description of the communicative systems evolved by two deaf children in the absence of a sign language model. *Sign Language Studies,* 1982, *34,* 73–90.

Moores, D. F. Nonvocal systems of verbal behavior. In R. L. Schiefelbusch & L. L. Loyd (Eds.), *Language perspectives: Acquisition, retardation, and intervention.* Baltimore, MD: University Park Press, 1974.

Nelson, K. Structure and strategy in learning to talk. *Monographs of the Society for Research in Child Development,* 1973, *38,* Serial no. 149.

Newhoff, M., & Launer, P. Input as interaction: Shall we dance? In R. Naremore (Ed.), *Recent advances: Language sciences.* College-Hill Press, in press.

Newport, E. L. Constraints on structure: Evidence from American Sign Language and language learning. In W. A. Collins (Ed.), *Aspects of the development of competence. Minnesota symposia on child psychology,* (Vol. 14). Hillsdale, NJ: Lawrence Erlbaum Associates, 1981.

Newport, E. L. Task specificity in language learning? Evidence from speech perception and American Sign Language. In E. Wanner & L. R. Gleitman (Eds.), *Language acquisition: The state of the art.* New York: Cambridge University Press, 1982.

Newport, E. L., & Ashbrook, E. The emergence of semantic relations in American Sign Language. *Papers and Reports on Child Language Development,* 1977, *13,* 16–21.

Newport, E. L., & Bellugi, U. Linguistic expression of category levels. In E. S. Klima & U. Bellugi, *The signs of language.* Cambridge, MA: Harvard University Press, 1979.

Newport, E. L., & Supalla, T. The structuring of language: Clues from the acquisition of signed and spoken language. In U. Bellugi & M. Studdert-Kennedy (Eds.), *Signed and spoken language: Biological constraints on linguistic form.* Dahlem Konferenzen. Weinheim: Verlag Chemie, 1980.

Omar, M. *The acquisition of Egyptian Arabic as a native language.* The Hague: Mouton, 1974.

Padden, C. Some arguments for syntactic patterning in American Sign Language, *Sign Language Studies,* 1981, *32,* 237–259.

Padden, C. *Interaction of morphology and syntax in American Sign Language.* Unpublished doctoral dissertation, University of California, San Diego, 1983.

Petitto, L. A. On the acquisition of anaphoric reference in American Sign Language. Working Paper, The Salk Institute, 1980.

Petitto, L. A. *From gesture to symbol: The acquisition of personal pronouns in American Sign Language.* Unpublished qualifying paper, Harvard University, 1983.

Phillips, J. R. *Formal characteristics of speech which mothers address to their young children.* Unpublished doctoral dissertation, Johns Hopkins University, 1970.

Piaget, J. *The language and thought of the child.* Cleveland, OH: Meridian, 1955.

Pizzuto, E., & Williams, M. The acquisition of the possessive forms of American Sign Language. In B. Frokjaer-Jensen (Ed.), *Recent developments in language and cognition.* Copenhagen: University of Denmark, 1980.

Prinz, P. M., & Prinz, E. A. Simultaneous acquisition of ASL and spoken English (In a hearing child of a deaf mother and hearing father). Phase I: Early lexical development. *Sign Language Studies,* 1979, *25,* 283–296.

Prinz, P. M., & Prinz, E. A. Acquisition of ASL and spoken English by a hearing child of a deaf mother and a hearing father: Phase II. Early combinatorial patterns. *Sign Language Studies,* 1981, *30,* 78–88.

Quigley, S., & Kretschmer, R. E. *The Education of deaf children.* Baltimore, MD: University Park Press, 1982.

Quigley, S. P., & Frisina, R. Institutionalization and psychoeducational development in deaf children. *Council on Exceptional Children,* Washington, D.C., 1961.

Quigley, S. P., Wilbur, R. B., Power, D. J., Montanelli, D. S., & Steinkamp, M. W. *Syntactic structures in the language of deaf children.* Urbana, IL: Institute for Child Behavior and Development, University of Illinois, 1976.

Remick, H. *The maternal environment of linguistic development.* Unpublished doctoral dissertation, University of California, Davis, 1971.

Sapir, E. *Language.* New York: Harvest Books, 1921.

de Saussure, F. *Course in general linguistics.* (1959 reprint of 3rd Edition.) New York: McGraw-Hill, 1915.

Schein, J., & Delk, T. *The deaf population of the United States.* Washington, D.C.: National Association of the Deaf, 1974.

Schlesinger, H. S. The acquisition of bimodal language. In I. M. Schlesinger & L. Namir (Eds.), *Sign language of the deaf: Psychological, linguistic, and sociological perspective.* New York: Academic Press, 1978.

Schlesinger, H. S., & Meadow, K. P. *Sound and sign: Childhood deafness and mental health.* Berkeley: University of California Press, 1972.

Slobin, D. I. Cognitive prerequisites for the development of grammar. In C. A. Ferguson & D. I. Slobin (Eds.), *Studies of child language development.* New York: Holt, Rinehart, & Winston, 1973.

Slobin, D. I. Universal and particular in the acquisition of language. In E. Wanner & L. R. Gleitman (Eds.), *Language acquisition: The state of the art.* New York: Cambridge University Press, 1982.

Stevenson, E. A study of the educational achievement of deaf children of deaf parents. *California News,* 1964, *80,* 143.

Stokoe, W. C. Sign language structure: An outline of the visual communication systems of the American Deaf. *Studies in Linguistics:* Occasional papers, 1960, 8.

Stokoe, W. C., Casterline, D. C., & Croneberg, C. G. *A dictionary of American Sign Language on linguistic principles.* Washington, D.C.: Gallaudet College Press, 1965.

Stuckless, R., & Birch, J. The influence of early manual communication on the linguistic development of deaf children. *American Annals of the Deaf,* 1966, *111,* 452–460.

Supalla, S. The acquisition of compounds in ASL by a deaf child. Working paper, The Salk Institute, 1980.

Supalla, S., & Newport, E. L. *Manually coded English: The modality question in sign language development,* in progress.

Supalla, T. *Structure and acquisition of verbs of motion and location in American Sign Language.* Unpublished doctoral dissertation, University of California, San Diego, 1982.

Supalla, T., & Newport, E. L. How many seats in a chair? The derivation of nouns and verbs in American Sign Language. In P. Siple (Ed.), *Understanding language through sign language research.* New York: Academic Press, 1978.

Tervoort, B. T. Esoteric symbolism in the communicative behavior of young deaf children. *American Annals of the Deaf,* 1961, 106, 436–480.

Thompson, J. S., & Thompson, M. W. *Genetics in medicine.* Philadelphia: W. B. Saunders Co., 1966.

Vernon, M., & Koh, S. Effects of early manual communication on achievement of deaf children. *American Annals of the Deaf,* 1970, *115,* 527–536.

Volterra, V., Massoni, P., & Beronesi, S. Quando la Communicazione diventa linguaggio. In *I Gesti e I Segni.* Rome: Bulzoni, 1983.

Wilbur, R. B. *American Sign Language and sign systems.* Baltimore, MD: University Park Press, 1979.

Woodward, J. C. Inter-rule implication in American Sign Language. *Sign Language Studies,* 1973, *3,* 47–56.

Woodward, J. C. Signs of change: Historical variation in American Sign Language. *Sign Language Studies,* 1976, *10,* 81–94.

Subject Index

The abbreviations given below indicate discussion of an index category with regard to a particular language. Entries without a language code refer to a general discussion of the category in question. Note that the grammatical sketches of individual languages are not included in the index. All references refer to discussions of acquisition or of general linguistic issues in the chapters.

ABBREVIATIONS FOR LANGUAGE CODES

A

Author Index

Numbers in *italics* indicate pages with complete bibliographic information.

A

Abramovitch, R., 97, 98, *135*
Acton, W. R., 335, *368*
Adelson, E., 230, *250*
Aimard, P., 698, 739, 740, 755, 766, *767*
Akiyama, M., 411, *516*
Akmajian, A., 31, *128*
Aksu, A. A., 5, *22*, 646, *681*, 841, 843, 844,
    852, 863, 864, 865, 868, 875, *876*, 878
Aksu-Koç, A. A., 8, 11, *22*, 493, 504, *516*,
    517, 669, *681*, 899, 909, 929, 930, 931,
    932
Alfonso, A., 374, 432, *517*
Altmann, G., 218, *249*
Amir, M., 265, 275, 354, *368*
Ammon, M. S., 16, *23*, 698, *767*, 844, 872,
    876
Anders, K., 236, 238, *249*
Andersen, E. S., 236, *249*, 513, *517*, 833,
    836
Anglin, J. M., 126, *128*
Anisfeld, M., 68, *130*
Annibaldi-Vion, M., 712, *767*
Antinucci, F., 7, 9, 17, *23*, *24*, 60, 84, *128*,
    232, *252*, 269, 294, 353, *364*, 646, *681*,
    698, 718, 723, 736, 746, 750, *767*, 779
Aoki, H., 374, *517*
Arbel, T., 265, 275, 354, *368*
Ardery, G., 105, *128*

Argoff, H. D., 5, *23*
Ariel, S., 265, *364*
Arndt, W. W., 218, *249*
Arrivé, M., 688, *770*
Asano, A., 468, 469, *517*
Asbach-Schnitker, B., 233, *249*
Ashbrook, E., 887, 891, 893, 898, *937*
Atsmon, I., 266, *364*
Augst, G., 220, 221, 227, *249*
Avery, A., 100, *131*
Aviezer, O., 266, 272, 331, *364*
Avineri, I., 264, *364*
Axia, G., 745, *767*
Azuma, H., 380, 490, 491, 499, *517*, *518*,
    519

B

Badry, F., 5, *23*, 334, 347, *365*
Bahan, B., 902, *936*
Baker, C. L., 93, 95, 126, *128*
Baldie, B. J., 97, 98, *128*
Bar-Adon, A., 264, 288, 308, 309, 344, *365*
Barless, A., 264, *365*
Baron, N., 343, *365*
Bartnicka-Dąbkowska, B., 664, *681*
Bartsch, R., 159, *249*
Bates, E., 41, 53, 54, 65, 127, *128*, *129*, *135*,
    230, *249*, 419, 423, 424, 511, *517*, 672,